D0991601

Beyond Our Borders

Management Perspective

Sixth Edition

The Legal Environment Today

Business in Its Ethical, Regulatory, E-Commerce, and Global Setting

Roger LeRoy Miller

Institute for University Studies
Arlington, Texas

Frank B. Cross

Herbert D. Kelleher
Centennial Professor in Business Law
University of Texas at Austin

SOUTH-WESTERN
CENGAGE Learning

Australia • Brazil • Japan • Korea • Mexico • Singapore • Spain • United Kingdom • United States

SOUTH-WESTERN
CENGAGE Learning™

The Legal Environment Today

Business in Its Ethical, Regulatory, E-Commerce, and Global Setting

SIXTH EDITION

Roger LeRoy Miller
Frank B. Cross

Vice President and Editorial Director:
Jack Calhoun

Editor-in-Chief:
Rob Dewey

Acquisition Editor:
Vicky True

Senior Developmental Editor:
Jan Lamar

Executive Marketing Manager:
Lisa L. Lysne

Marketing Manager:
Jennifer Garamy

Marketing Coordinator:
Gretchen Swann

Marketing Communications Manager:
Sarah Greber

Associate Marketing Communications Manager:
Jill Scheibaum

Production Manager:
Bill Stryker

Technology Project Manager:
Kristen Meere

Manufacturing Buyer:
Kevin Kluck

Editorial Assistant:
Krista Kellman

Compositor:
Parkwood Composition Service

Senior Art Director:
Michelle Kunkler

Internal Designer:
Bill Stryker

Cover Designer:
Lisa A. Albonetti

Cover Images: © Chris Collins/ Veer, Inc.; © szefei/Shutterstock; © Comstock Images; © Goodshoot/ Jupiter Images; © Don Carstens/ Brand X Pictures

For product information and technology assistance, contact us at **Cengage Learning Academic Resource Center, 1-800-423-0563**

For permission to use material from this text or product, submit all requests online at **www.cengage.com/permissions** Further permissions questions can be emailed to **permissionrequest@cengage.com**

ExamView® and ExamView Pro® are registered trademarks of FSCreations, Inc. Windows is a registered trademark of the Microsoft Corporation used herein under license. Macintosh and Power Macintosh are registered trademarks of Apple Computer, Inc. used herein under license.

© 2010, 2007 Cengage Learning. All Rights Reserved. Cengage Learning WebTutor™ is a trademark of Cengage Learning.

Library of Congress Control Number: 2008925366

Student's Edition:
ISBN-13: 978-0-324-59925-1
ISBN-10: 0-324-59925-0

Instructor's Edition:
ISBN-13: 978-0-324-78421-3
ISBN-10: 0-324-78421-X

SOUTH-WESTERN CENGAGE LEARNING
5191 Natorp Blvd.
Mason, OH 45040
USA

Cengage Learning products are represented in Canada by Nelson Education, Ltd.

For your course and learning solutions, visit **www.cengage.com** Purchase any of our products at your local college store or at our preferred online store **www.ichapters.com**

Printed in the United States of America
1 2 3 4 5   12 11 10 09 08

Contents in Brief

Unit Four

The Regulatory Environment 639

Contents

The Foundations 1

The Commercial Environment 235

Unit Three

Business and Employment 451

It is no exaggeration to say that today's legal environment is changing at a pace never before experienced. In many instances, technology is both driving and facilitating this change. The expanded use of the Internet for both business and personal transactions has led to new ways of doing business and, consequently, to a changing legal environment for the twenty-first century. In the midst of this evolving environment, however, one thing remains certain: for those entering the business world, an awareness of the legal and regulatory environment of business is critical.

The Sixth Edition of *The Legal Environment Today: Business in Its Ethical, Regulatory, E-Commerce, and Global Setting* is designed to bring this awareness to your students. They will learn not only about the traditional legal environment but also about some of the most significant recent developments in the e-commerce environment. They will also be motivated to learn more through our use of high-interest pedagogical features that explore real-life situations and legal challenges facing businesspersons and consumers. We believe that teaching the legal environment can be enjoyable and so, too, can learning about it.

WHAT'S NEW IN THE SIXTH EDITION

Instructors have come to rely on the coverage, accuracy, and applicability of *The Legal Environment Today.* To make sure that our text engages your students' interest, solidifies their understanding of the legal concepts presented, and provides the best teaching tools available, we now offer the following items either in the text or in conjunction with the text.

New *Preventing Legal Disputes* Provide Practical Information in Every Chapter

For the Sixth Edition of *The Legal Environment Today,* we have added a **special new feature entitled *Preventing Legal Disputes.*** These brief features offer practical guidance on what steps businesspersons can take in their daily transactions to avoid legal disputes and litigation. These features are integrated throughout the text as appropriate to the topics being discussed, with at least one *Preventing* feature in every chapter.

New *Insight into Ethics* Features

For the Sixth Edition, we have created **special new *Insight into Ethics* features.** These features, which appear in selected chapters, provide valuable insights into how the courts and the law are dealing with specific ethical issues. Each of these features also ends with a critical-thinking question that explores some cultural, environmental, political, social, or technological aspect of the issue. Some examples of these features include the following:

- Implications of an increasingly private justice system (Chapter 3).
- Does tort law impose an unfair economic burden on society as a whole? (Chapter 5).

- Is the death penalty cruel and unusual punishment? (Chapter 6).
- Patent law and the seed police (Chapter 8).
- Internet click fraud (Chapter 10).
- Should companies be able to escape liability for defective products that were the subject of government regulation? (Chapter 12).
- Are mortgage lending practices responsible for an epidemic of foreclosures? (Chapter 13).
- Should courts allow employees to sue their employers under RICO based on a pattern of hiring illegal immigrants? (Chapter 17).

Expanded Ethics Coverage and New Questions of Ethics in Every Chapter

For the Sixth Edition of *The Legal Environment Today*, we have significantly revised and updated the chapter on ethics and business decision making (Chapter 2). The chapter now presents a more practical, realistic, case-study approach to business ethics and the dilemmas facing persons in the legal environment today. The emphasis on ethics is reiterated in materials throughout the text, particularly in the new *Insight into Ethics* features, and in the pedagogy that accompanies selected cases and features.

For this edition, we have also added **A *Question of Ethics* based on a 2006 or 2007 case to every chapter of the text.** These problems provide modern-day examples of the kind of ethical issues faced by businesspersons and the way courts typically resolve them.

New Streamlined Organization

For the Sixth Edition of *The Legal Environment Today*, we have rearranged and revamped the chapters to streamline our presentation of topics. In doing so, we have reduced the number of units in the text from six to four. Each unit now includes approximately the same number of chapters, which makes it easier to break down the materials into logical chunks for purposes of improving student comprehension and testing.

The first unit, The Foundations, includes basic topics that students need to know as a foundation for further exploration of the legal environment, including materials on ethics, courts, constitutional law, torts, and crimes. Given the increased importance of the global environment, we have moved our coverage of international law up to this unit. The second unit, The Commercial Environment, deals with topics such as intellectual property, Internet law, contracts, sales, product liability, and the laws pertaining to debtors and creditors.

The third unit, Business and Employment, covers the various types of business entities, as well as issues relating to employment and labor. We have also added coverage of immigration laws, a topic of growing significance today. The final unit, The Regulatory Environment, discusses areas that are the subject of numerous federal regulations, such as antitrust and securities regulations, and laws protecting consumers and the environment.

Two Critical-Thinking Questions at the End of *Every* Case Presented in This Text

In every case in every chapter of the Sixth Edition of *The Legal Environment Today*, we have included two case-ending questions designed to guide students' analysis of the case and help build their legal reasoning skills. In addition to the *What*

If the Facts Were Different? questions and *Impact of This Case on Today's Legal Environment* sections that appeared in the Fifth Edition, we've devised an entirely new set of questions. These new *Dimension* questions focus on meeting aspects of your curriculum requirements, including:

■ *The Ethical Dimension*
■ *The E-Commerce Dimension*
■ *The Global Dimension*
■ *The Legal Environment Dimension*

   Suggested answers to all questions following cases can be found in both the *Instructor's Manual* and the *Answers Manual* that accompany this text. (The full title of this manual is *Answers to Questions and Case Problems and Alternate Problem Sets with Answers.*)

Greater Emphasis on Critical Thinking

Today's business leaders are often required to think "outside the box" when making business decisions. For this reason, **we have added a number of critical-thinking elements for the Sixth Edition** that are designed to challenge students' understanding of the materials beyond simple retention. Your students' critical-thinking and legal reasoning skills will be increased as they work through the numerous pedagogical devices within the book. Almost every feature and every case presented in the text conclude with some type of critical-thinking question. These questions include *For Critical Analysis, What If the Facts Were Different?* and the *Ethical, E-Commerce, Global,* and *Legal Environment Dimension* questions discussed previously. They also include the questions in the *Reviewing* features, which are described next.

Reviewing Features in Every Chapter

For the Sixth Edition of *The Legal Environment Today,* we have included a special feature at the end of every chapter that helps solidify students' understanding of the chapter materials. The feature, which appears just before the *Terms and Concepts,* is entitled *Reviewing [chapter topic].* Each of these features presents a hypothetical scenario and then asks a series of questions that require students to identify the issues and apply the legal concepts discussed in the chapter. The features are designed to help students review the chapter topics in a simple and interesting way and see how the legal principles discussed in the chapter affect the world in which they live. An instructor can use these features as the basis for in-class discussion or encourage students to use them for self-study prior to completing homework assignments. **Suggested answers to the questions posed in the *Reviewing* features can be found in both the *Instructor's Manual* and the *Answers Manual* that accompany this text.**

   The *Reviewing* features are also tied to a set of questions for each chapter in the Web-based CengageNOW system, to be discussed next. Students can read through the scenario in the text and then answer the four Applications and Analysis questions online. **By using the CengageNOW system, students will receive instant feedback on their answers to these questions, and instructors will obtain automatically graded assignments that enable them to assess students' understanding of the materials.**

Improved Content and Features on CengageNOW for *The Legal Environment Today*

For those instructors who want their students to learn how to identify and apply the legal principles they study in this text, we have created new content and improved the features of our Web-based product for this edition. The system provides interactive, automatically graded assignments for every chapter and unit in this text. For each of the twenty-four chapters, we have devised different categories of multiple-choice questions that stress different aspects of learning the chapter materials. By using the optional **CengageNOW** system, students can complete the assignments from any location via the Internet and can receive instant feedback on why their answers to questions were incorrect or correct (if the instructor wishes to allow feedback). Instructors can customize the system to meet their own specifications and can track students' progress.

1. **Chapter Review Questions**—The first set of ten to fifteen questions reviews the basic concepts and principles discussed in the chapter and may include questions based on the cases presented in the text.

2. **Brief Hypotheticals**—The next group of seven to ten questions emphasizes spotting the issue and identifying the rule of law that applies in the context of a short factual scenario.

3. **Legal Reasoning**—The third category includes five questions that require students to analyze the factual situation provided and apply the rules of law discussed in the chapter to arrive at an answer.

4. **IRAC Case Analysis**—The next set of four questions requires students to perform all the basic elements of legal reasoning (identify the *issue,* determine the *rule* of law, *apply* the rule to the facts presented, and arrive at a *conclusion*). These questions are based on one of the case excerpts that appear in each chapter of the text.

5. **Application and Analysis**—The final set of four questions is new and is linked to the *Reviewing* features (discussed previously) that appear in every chapter of the text. The student is required to read through the hypothetical scenario, analyze the facts presented, identify the issues in dispute, and apply the rules discussed in the chapter to answer the questions.

6. **Essay Questions**—In addition to the multiple-choice questions available on CengageNOW, we now also provide essay questions that allow students to compose and submit essays online. Students' essays are automatically recorded to the gradebook, which permits instructors to quickly and easily evaluate the essays and record grades.

7. **Video Questions**—CengageNOW also now includes links to the Digital Video Library for *The Legal Environment Today* so that students can access and view the video clips and answer questions related to the topics in the chapter.

8. **Cumulative Questions for Each Unit**—In addition to the questions relating to each chapter, the CengageNOW system provides a set of cumulative questions, entitled "Synthesizing Legal Concepts," for each of the four units in the text.

9. **Additional Advantages of CengageNOW**—Instructors can utilize the system to upload their course syllabi, create and customize homework assignments, keep track of their students' progress, communicate with their students about assignments and due dates, and create reports summarizing the data for an individual student or for the whole class.

More on the Sarbanes-Oxley Act of 2002

In a number of places in this text, we discuss the Sarbanes-Oxley Act of 2002 and the corporate scandals that led to the passage of that legislation. For example, Chapter 2 contains a section examining the requirements of the Sarbanes-Oxley Act relating to confidential reporting systems. In Chapter 24, we discuss this act in the context of securities law and present an exhibit (Exhibit 24–5) containing some of the key provisions of the act relating to corporate accountability with respect to securities transactions.

Because the act is a topic of significant concern in today's business climate, we also include **excerpts and explanatory comments on the Sarbanes-Oxley Act of 2002 as Appendix H.** Students and instructors alike will find it useful to have the provisions of the act immediately available for reference.

THE LEGAL ENVIRONMENT TODAY ON THE WEB

For the Sixth Edition of *The Legal Environment Today,* we have redesigned and streamlined the text's Web site so that users can easily locate the resources they seek. When you visit our Web site at **www.cengage.com/blaw/let**, you will find a broad array of teaching/learning resources, including the following:

- *Relevant Web sites* for all of the *Landmark in the Legal Environment* features and *Landmark and Classic Cases* that are presented in this text.
- *Sample answers* to the *Case Problem with Sample Answer,* which appears in the *Questions and Case Problems* section at the end of every chapter. This problem/answer set is designed to help your students learn how to answer case problems by acquainting them with model answers to selected problems. In addition, we offer the answers to the hypothetical *Questions with Sample Answers* on the Web site, as well as in the text (Appendix I).
- *Video Questions* appear in selected chapters of the text and are provided on the Web site along with a link to view the specific video for that chapter. Access to our Digital Video Library, which features more than sixty video clips, can be packaged with the text or purchased online, as discussed shortly.
- *Practical Internet exercises* for every chapter in the text (at least two per chapter). These exercises have been refocused to provide more practical information to business law students on topics covered in the chapters and to acquaint students with the legal resources that are available online.
- *Interactive quizzes* for every chapter in this text.
- *Glossary terms* for every chapter in the text.
- *Flashcards* that provide students with an optional study tool to review the key terms in every chapter.
- *PowerPoint slides* that have been revised for this edition.
- *Legal reference materials* including a "Statutes" page that offers links to the full text of selected statutes referenced in the text, a Spanish glossary, and links to other important legal resources that are available for free on the Web.
- *Link to CengageNOW for* **The Legal Environment Today** with different types of questions related to every chapter in the text and one set of cumulative questions for each unit in the text.
- *Online Legal Research Guide* that offers complete yet brief guidance to using the Internet and evaluating information obtained from the Internet. As an online resource, it now includes hyperlinks to the Web sites discussed for click-through convenience.
- *Court case updates,* updated each month, that present summaries of new cases from around the country that specifically relate to the topics covered in chapters of this text.

A DYNAMIC DIGITAL VIDEO LIBRARY

The Legal Environment Today continues to include special *Video Questions* at the end of selected chapters. Each of these questions directs students to the text's Web site (at **www.cengage.com/blaw/let**) to view a video relevant to a topic covered in the chapter. This is followed by a series of questions based on the video. The questions are again repeated on the Web site under the "Video Question" tab, at which the student can access the video. An access code for the videos can be packaged with each new copy of this textbook for no additional charge. If Digital Video Library access did not come packaged with the textbook, students who would like to purchase it can do so online at **www.cengage.com/blaw/dvl**.

These videos can be used for homework assignments, discussion starters, or classroom demonstrations and are useful for generating student interest. Some of the videos are clips from actual movies, such as *The Jerk* and *Bowfinger.* By watching a video and answering the questions, students will gain an understanding of how the legal concepts they have studied in the chapter apply to the real-life situation portrayed in the video. **Suggested answers for all of the *Video Questions* are given in both the *Instructor's Manual* and the *Answers Manual* that accompany this text.** The videos are part of our Digital Video Library, a dynamic library of more than sixty video clips that spark class discussion and clarify core legal principles.

ADDITIONAL SPECIAL FEATURES IN THIS TEXT

We have included in the Sixth Edition of *The Legal Environment Today* a number of pedagogical devices and special features, including those discussed here.

Online Developments

Many chapters in the Sixth Edition contain a special **Online Developments** feature, which explores how traditional legal concepts or laws are being adapted or applied in cyberspace. Here are some examples of these features:

- How the Internet Is Expanding Precedent (Chapter 1).
- E-Discovery and Cost-Shifting (Chapter 3).
- Laptop Searches at the U.S. Border—A New Way to Find Evidence (Chapter 4).
- When Spamming Is a Crime (Chapter 6).
- Legal Issues Facing Bloggers and Podcasters (Chapter 8).
- Are Online Fantasy Sports Gambling? (Chapter 9).
- Online Personals—Fraud and Misrepresentation Issues (Chapter 10).
- The SEC Adopts New E-Proxy Rules (Chapter 15).

Each *Online Developments* feature concludes with a *For Critical Analysis* section that asks the student to think critically about some aspect of the issue discussed in the feature. **Suggested answers to these questions are included in both the *Instructor's Manual* and the *Answers Manual* that accompany this text.**

Management Perspective

Each **Management Perspective** feature begins with a section titled "Management Faces a Legal Issue" that describes a practical issue facing management (such as whether employees have a right to privacy in their e-mail communications). A section titled "What the Courts Say" then follows, in which we discuss what the courts have concluded with respect to this issue. The feature concludes with an "Implications for Managers" section that indicates the importance of the court's decision for business decision making and offers some practical guidance.

Some examples of these features include the following:

- Arbitration Clauses in Employment Contracts (Chapter 3).
- Can a Businessperson Use Deadly Force to Prevent a Crime on the Premises? (Chapter 6).
- Protecting Trade Secrets (Chapter 8).
- Independent Contractor Negligence (Chapter 16).
- Restricting Union Communications via Corporate E-Mail Systems (Chapter 17).
- Interviewing Job Applicants with Disabilities (Chapter 18).

Landmark in the Legal Environment

The **Landmark in the Legal Environment** feature, which appears in selected chapters, discusses a landmark case, statute, or other law that has had a significant effect on business law. Each of these features includes a section titled *Application to Today's Legal Environment,* which indicates how the law discussed in the feature affects the contemporary legal environment of business. In addition, each feature concludes with a *Relevant Web Sites* section that directs students to the book's companion Web site for links to additional information available online.

Preventing Legal Disputes

Every chapter includes at least one **Preventing Legal Disputes** feature, integrated as appropriate with the topics being discussed. As already mentioned, these features provide practical information to future businesspersons on how to avoid legal problems.

Insight into Ethics

As discussed, in addition to a chapter on ethics, chapter-ending ethical questions, and the *Ethical Dimension* questions following selected cases presented in this text, we have included special features called **Insight into Ethics.** These features, which are closely integrated with the text, address an ethical dimension of the topic being discussed.

Reviewing Hypothetical Features

As discussed previously, the **Reviewing** features present a hypothetical scenario and ask a series of questions that require students to identify the issues and apply the legal concepts discussed in the chapter. Each chapter concludes with one of these features, which are intended to help students review the chapter materials in a simple and interesting way.

Beyond Our Borders

Special **Beyond Our Borders** features give students an awareness of the global legal environment by indicating how international laws or the laws of other nations deal with the specific legal topics being discussed in the text. Because business today is conducted in the global context, it is important for students to understand that what happens beyond our borders can have a significant impact on the legal environment. Each of these features concludes with a *For Critical Analysis* question. **Suggested answers to these questions are included in**

both the *Instructor's Manual* and the *Answers Manual* that accompany this text. Below are some examples of *Beyond Our Borders* features:

■ The Role of the United States in Combating Corruption Globally (Chapter 2).
■ The Impact of Foreign Law on the United States Supreme Court (Chapter 4).
■ Cross-Border Spam (Chapter 5).
■ International Use and Regulation of the Internet (Chapter 11).
■ Protecting U.S. Consumers from Cross-Border Telemarketers (Chapter 20).
■ U.S.-Style Antitrust Lawsuits Become More Popular in the United Kingdom (Chapter 23).

Exhibits

When appropriate, we also illustrate important aspects of the law in graphic or summary form in exhibits. For the Sixth Edition of *The Legal Environment Today*, we have added a number of exhibits to facilitate your students' understanding of the materials.

An Effective Case Format

In each chapter, we present cases that illustrate the principles of law discussed in the text. The cases are numbered sequentially for easy referencing in class discussions, homework assignments, and examinations. In selecting the cases to be included in this edition, our goal has been to choose high-interest cases that reflect the most current law or that represent significant precedents in case law.

Each case is presented in a special format, beginning with the case title and citation (including parallel citations). Whenever possible, we also include a URL, just below the case citation, that can be used to access the case online (a footnote to the URL explains how to find the specific case at that Web site). We then briefly outline the background and facts of the dispute, after which the court's reasoning is presented in the words of the court. To enhance student understanding, we paraphrase the court's decision and remedy. We also provide bracketed definitions for any terms in the opinion that might be difficult for students to understand. As stated previously, each case normally concludes with two critical-thinking questions.

We give special emphasis to *Landmark and Classic Cases* by setting them off with a special heading and logo. Each of these cases also includes an *Impact of This Case on Today's Legal Environment* section that stresses the significance of that particular decision for the evolution of the law in that area. For the Sixth Edition, we have included a section titled *Relevant Web Sites* at the conclusion of each landmark and classic case that directs students to additional online resources.

Cases may include one or more of the following sections:

■ ***Company Profiles***—Certain cases include a profile describing the history of the company involved to give students an awareness of the context of the case before the court. Some profiles include the URL for the company's Web site.
■ ***What If the Facts Were Different?***—One case in each chapter concludes with this special section. The student is asked to decide whether a specified change in the facts of the case would alter its outcome. **Suggested answers to these questions are included in both the *Instructor's Manual* and the *Answers Manual* that accompany this text.**
■ ***The Ethical [E-Commerce, Global, or Legal Environment] Dimension***— As discussed previously, these special new questions ask students to explore different aspects of the issues of the case and help instructors meet core

curriculum requirements for business law. **Suggested answers to these questions are included in both the *Instructor's Manual* and the *Answers Manual* that accompany this text.**

■ *Impact of This Case on Today's Legal Environment*—Because many students are unclear about how some of the older cases presented in this text affect today's court rulings, we include a special section at the end of landmark and classic cases that clarifies the relevance of the particular case to modern law.

Questions and Case Problems with Sample Answers

In response to those instructors who would like students to have sample answers available for some of the questions and case problems, we have included two questions with sample answers in each chapter. The **Question with Sample Answer** is a hypothetical question for which students can access a sample answer in Appendix I at the end of the text. Every chapter also has one **Case Problem with Sample Answer** that is based on an actual case and answered on the text's Web site (located at **www.cengage.com/blaw/let**). Students can compare the answers provided with their own answers to determine whether they have done a good job of responding to the question and to learn what should be included when answering the end-of-chapter questions and case problems.

THE MOST COMPLETE SUPPLEMENTS PACKAGE AVAILABLE TODAY

This edition of *The Legal Environment Today* is accompanied by a vast number of teaching and learning supplements, including those listed next. For further information on the items contained in the teaching/learning package, contact your local sales representative or visit the Web site that accompanies this text at **www.cengage.com/blaw/let**.

Each chapter of the *Instructor's Manual* contains teaching suggestions, discussion questions, and additional information on key statutes or other legal sources that you may wish to use in your classroom. These and numerous other supplementary materials (including printed and multimedia supplements) all contribute to the goal of making *The Legal Environment Today* the most flexible teaching/learning package on the market.

Printed Supplements

■ *Instructor's Manual*—Includes additional cases on point with at least one case summary per chapter, answers to all *For Critical Analysis* questions in the features and all case-ending questions, and answers for the *Video Questions* at the end of selected chapters (also available on the Instructor's Resource CD-ROM [IRCD]).
■ *Study Guide.*
■ A comprehensive *Test Bank* (also available on the IRCD).
■ *Answers Manual*—Includes answers to the *Questions and Case Problems,* answers to the *For Critical Analysis* questions in the features and all case-ending questions, answers for the *Video Questions* that conclude selected chapters, and answers to the unit-ending *Cumulative Business Hypotheticals* (also available on the IRCD).

Software, Video, and Multimedia Supplements

- **Instructor's Resource CD-ROM (IRCD)**—The IRCD includes the following supplements: *Instructor's Manual, Answers Manual, Test Bank,* Case-Problem Cases, Case Printouts, PowerPoint slides, ExamView, *Online Legal Research Guide, Handbook of Landmark Cases and Statutes in Business Law and the Legal Environment, Guide to Personal Law, Handbook on Critical Thinking and Writing in Business Law and the Legal Environment,* transparencies, and *Instructor's Manual* for the *Drama of the Law* video series.
- **ExamView Testing Software** (also available on the IRCD).
- **PowerPoint slides** (also available on the IRCD).
- **WebTutor**
- **Case Printouts**—Provides the full opinion of all cases presented in the text and referred to in selected features (available only on the IRCD).
- **Case-Problem Cases** (available only on the IRCD).
- **Transparency Acetates** (available only on the IRCD).
- **Westlaw®**—Ten free hours on Westlaw are available to qualified adopters.
- **Business Law Digital Video Library**—This dynamic video library features more than sixty video clips that spark class discussion and clarify core legal principles. Access is available for free as an optional package item with each new text. If Digital Video Library access did not come packaged with the textbook, your students can purchase it online at **www.cengage.com/blaw/dvl**.

ACKNOWLEDGMENTS

Numerous careful and conscientious users of *The Legal Environment Today* were kind enough to help us revise the book. In addition, Cengage Learning went out of its way to make sure that this edition came out early and in accurate form. In particular, we wish to thank Rob Dewey and Vicky True for their countless new ideas, many of which have been incorporated into the Sixth Edition. Our production manager and designer, Bill Stryker, made sure that we came out with an error-free, visually attractive edition. We will always be in his debt. We also extend special thanks to Jan Lamar, our longtime developmental editor, for her many useful suggestions and for her efforts in coordinating reviews and ensuring the timely and accurate publication of all supplemental materials. We are particularly indebted to Jennifer Garamy, our marketing manager, for her support and excellent marketing advice.

We must especially thank Katherine Marie Silsbee, who provided expert research, editing, and proofing services for this project. We also wish to thank William Eric Hollowell, co-author of the *Instructor's Manual, Study Guide, Test Bank,* and *Online Legal Research Guide,* for his excellent research efforts. The copyediting and proofreading services of Lorretta Palagi, Beverly Peavler, and Kristi Wiswell will not go unnoticed. We also thank Roxanna Lee and Lavina Leed Miller for their proofreading and other assistance, and Suzanne Jasin for her many special efforts on the project. We are also indebted to Parkwood Composition, our compositor. Its ability to generate the pages for this text quickly and accurately made it possible for us to meet our ambitious printing schedule.

Finally, numerous thorough and meticulous users of previous editions have been gracious enough to offer us their comments and suggestions on how to improve this text. We are particularly indebted to these reviewers, whom we list below. With their help, we have been able to make this book even more useful for professors and students alike.

Acknowledgments for Previous Editions

Muhammad Abdullah
Pfeiffer University

Jane Bennett
Orange Coast College

Brent D. Clark
Davenport University

Richard L. Coffinberger
George Mason University

Teri Elkins
University of Houston

Teresa Gillespie
Seattle Pacific University

Gary Greene
Manatee Community College

Penelope L. Herickhoff
Mankato State University

James F. Kelley
Santa Clara University

Susan Key
University of Alabama
at Birmingham

Karrin Klotz
University of Washington

Y. S. Lee
Oakland University

Tom Moore
Georgia College and State University

Michael J. O'Hara
University of Nebraska at Omaha

Mark Phelps
University of Oregon

G. Keith Roberts
University of Redlands

Gary Sambol
Rutgers, the State University of
New Jersey, Camden Campus

Martha Wright Sartoris
North Hennepin Community College

Gwen Seaquist
Ithaca College

Craig Stilwell
Michigan State University

Dawn R. Swink
University of St. Thomas

Daphyne Thomas
James Madison University

Wayne Wells
St. Cloud State University

Acknowledgments for the Sixth Edition

Eloise Hassell
University of North Carolina,
Greensboro

Arlene M. Hibschweiler
University at Buffalo

William J. McDevitt
Saint Joseph's University

Lemoine D. Pierce
Georgia State University

Linda Samuels
George Mason University

Carrie Vaia
North Hennepin Community College

We know that we are not perfect. If you or your students find something you don't like or want us to change, we would like to hear from you. That is how we can make *The Legal Environment Today,* Sixth Edition, an even better book in the future.

Roger LeRoy Miller
Frank B. Cross

Dedication

To Jean-Baptiste Ansaldi,

Thanks for introducing me to the world's greatest sport and encouraging me to do more. My life has never been the same since.

R. L. M.

To my parents and sisters.

F.B.C.

The Foundations

Chapter 1

Business and Its Legal Environment

CHAPTER OBJECTIVES

After reading this chapter, you should be able to answer the following questions:

1. **What are the primary sources of law?**

2. **What is the common law tradition?**

3. **What is a precedent? When might a court depart from precedent?**

4. **What is the difference between remedies at law and remedies in equity?**

5. **What are some important differences between civil law and criminal law?**

CONTENTS

" The law is of as much interest to the layman as it is to the lawyer."

— LORD BALFOUR,
1848–1930 (British prime minister, 1902–1905)

Lord Balfour's assertion in the chapter-opening quotation emphasizes the underlying theme of every page in this book—that law is of interest to all persons, not just to lawyers. Those entering the world of business will find themselves subject to numerous laws and government regulations. A basic knowledge of these laws and regulations is beneficial—if not essential—to anyone contemplating a successful career in today's business world.

In this introductory chapter, we first look at the nature of law and at some concepts that have significantly influenced how jurists (those skilled in the law, including judges, lawyers, and legal scholars) view the nature and function of law. We then look at an important question for any student reading this text: How does the legal environment affect business decision making? We next describe the basic sources of American law, the common law tradition, and the importance of the common law today. We conclude the chapter with a discussion of some general classifications of law.

THE NATURE OF LAW

Law has had and will continue to have different definitions. Although the definitions vary in their particulars, they all are based on the general observation that, at a minimum, **law** consists of *enforceable rules governing relationships among individuals and between individuals and their society.* These "enforceable rules" may consist of unwritten principles of behavior established by a nomadic tribe. They may be set forth in an ancient or a contemporary law code. They may consist of written laws and court decisions created by modern legislative and judicial bodies, as in the United States. Regardless of how such rules are created, they all have

LAW

A body of enforceable rules governing relationships among individuals and between individuals and their society.

one thing in common: they establish rights, duties, and privileges that are consistent with the values and beliefs of their society or its ruling group.

Those who embark on a study of law will find that these broad statements leave unanswered some important questions concerning the nature of law. Part of the study of law, often referred to as **jurisprudence,** involves learning about different schools of legal thought and discovering how each school's approach to law can affect judicial decision making.

You may think that legal philosophy is far removed from the practical study of business law and the legal environment. In fact, it is not. As you will learn in the chapters of this text, how judges apply the law to specific disputes, including disputes relating to the business world, depends in part on their philosophical approaches to law. We look now at some of the significant schools of legal, or jurisprudential, thought that have evolved over time.

The Natural Law Tradition

An age-old question about the nature of law has to do with the finality of a nation's laws, such as the laws of the United States at the present time. For example, what if a substantial number of that nation's citizens consider a particular law to be a "bad" law? Must a citizen obey the law if doing so goes against his or her conscience? Is there a higher or universal law to which individuals can appeal? One who adheres to the natural law tradition would answer this question in the affirmative. **Natural law** denotes a system of moral and ethical principles that are inherent in human nature and thus can be discovered through the use of people's own native intelligence.

The natural law tradition is one of the oldest and most significant schools of jurisprudence. It dates back to the days of the Greek philosopher Aristotle (384–322 B.C.E.), who distinguished between natural law and the laws governing a particular nation. According to Aristotle, natural law applies universally to all humankind.

The notion that people have "natural rights" stems from the natural law tradition. Those who claim that a specific foreign government is depriving certain citizens of their human rights are implicitly appealing to a higher law that has universal applicability. The question of the universality of basic human rights also comes into play in the context of international business operations. For example, U.S. companies that have operations abroad often hire foreign workers as employees. Should the same laws that protect U.S. employees apply to these foreign employees? This question is rooted implicitly in a concept of universal rights that has its origins in the natural law tradition.

Legal Positivism

In contrast, **positive law,** or national law (the written law of a given society at a particular point in time), applies only to the citizens of that nation or society. Those who adhere to **legal positivism** believe that there can be no higher law than a nation's positive law. According to the positivist school, there is no such thing as "natural rights." Rather, human rights exist solely because of laws. If the laws are not enforced, anarchy will result. Thus, whether a law is "bad" or "good" is irrelevant. The law is the law and must be obeyed until it is changed—in an orderly manner through a legitimate lawmaking process. A judge with positivist

Was Aristotle a proponent of the natural or positive law tradition? (Collection of The Louvre/Photo by Eric Gaba/Wikimedia Commons)

JURISPRUDENCE
The science or philosophy of law.

NATURAL LAW
The belief that government and the legal system should reflect universal moral and ethical principles that are inherent in human nature. The natural law school is the oldest and one of the most significant schools of legal thought.

POSITIVE LAW
The body of conventional, or written, law of a particular society at a particular point in time.

LEGAL POSITIVISM
A school of legal thought centered on the assumption that there is no law higher than the laws created by a national government. Laws must be obeyed, even if they are unjust, to prevent anarchy.

leanings probably would be more inclined to defer to an existing law than would a judge who adheres to the natural law tradition.

The Historical School

HISTORICAL SCHOOL
A school of legal thought that emphasizes the evolutionary process of law and looks to the past to discover what the principles of contemporary law should be.

The **historical school** of legal thought emphasizes the evolutionary process of law by concentrating on the origin and history of the legal system. Thus, this school looks to the past to discover what the principles of contemporary law should be. The legal doctrines that have withstood the passage of time—those that have worked in the past—are deemed best suited for shaping present laws. Hence, law derives its legitimacy and authority from adhering to the standards that historical development has shown to be workable. Followers of the historical school are more likely than those of other schools to adhere strictly to decisions made in past cases.

Legal Realism

LEGAL REALISM
A school of legal thought of the 1920s and 1930s that generally advocated a less abstract and more realistic approach to the law, an approach that takes into account customary practices and the circumstances in which transactions take place. This school left a lasting imprint on American jurisprudence.

SOCIOLOGICAL SCHOOL
A school of legal thought that views the law as a tool for promoting justice in society.

In the 1920s and 1930s, a number of jurists and scholars, known as *legal realists,* rebelled against the historical approach to law. **Legal realism** is based on the idea that law is just one of many institutions in society and that it is shaped by social forces and needs. The law is a human enterprise, and judges should take social and economic realities into account when deciding cases. Legal realists also believe that the law can never be applied with total uniformity. Given that judges are human beings with unique personalities, value systems, and intellects, obviously different judges will bring different reasoning processes to the same case.

Legal realism strongly influenced the growth of what is sometimes called the **sociological school** of jurisprudence. This school views law as a tool for promoting justice in society. In the 1960s, for example, the justices of the United States Supreme Court played a leading role in the civil rights movement by upholding long-neglected laws calling for equal treatment for all Americans, including African Americans and other minorities. Generally, jurists who adhere to the sociological school are more likely to depart from past decisions than are those jurists who adhere to the other schools of legal thought.

BUSINESS ACTIVITIES AND THE LEGAL ENVIRONMENT

As those entering the world of business will learn, laws and government regulations affect virtually all business activities—hiring and firing decisions, workplace safety, the manufacturing and marketing of products, and business financing, to name just a few. To make good business decisions, a basic knowledge of the laws and regulations governing these activities is beneficial, if not essential. In today's world, though, a knowledge of "black-letter" law is not enough. Businesspersons are also pressured to make ethical decisions. Thus, the study of business law necessarily involves an ethical dimension.

Many Different Laws May Affect a Single Business Transaction

As you will note, each chapter in this text covers a specific area of the law and shows how the legal rules in that area affect business activities. Although compartmentalizing the law in this fashion facilitates learning, it does not indicate the extent to which many different laws may apply to just one transaction. **EXAMPLE #1** Suppose that you are the president of NetSys, Inc., a company that creates and maintains computer network systems for its clients, including business firms. NetSys also markets software for customers who require an internal computer network. One day, Janet Hernandez, an operations officer for Southwest Distribution Corporation (SDC), contacts you by e-mail about a possible contract involving SDC's computer network. In deciding whether to enter into a contract with SDC, you need to consider, among other things, the legal requirements for an enforceable contract. Are the requirements different for a contract for services and a contract for products? What are your options if SDC **breaches** (breaks, or fails to perform) the contract? The answers to these questions are part of contract law and sales law.

BREACH
The failure to perform a legal obligation.

Other questions might concern payment under the contract. How can you guarantee that NetSys will be paid? For example, if SDC pays with a check that is returned for insufficient funds, what are your options? Answers to these questions can be found in the laws that relate to negotiable instruments (such as checks) and creditors' rights. Also, a dispute may arise over the rights to NetSys's software, or there may be a question of liability if the software is defective. There may be an issue as to whether you and Hernandez had the authority to make the deal in the first place, or an accountant's evaluation of the contract may lead to a dispute. Resolutions of these questions may be found in the laws that relate to intellectual property, e-commerce, torts, product liability, agency, business organizations, or professional liability.

Finally, if any dispute cannot be resolved amicably, then the laws and the rules concerning courts and court procedures spell out the steps of a lawsuit. Exhibit 1–1 on the following page illustrates the various areas of the law that may influence business decision making.

Preventing Legal Disputes

To prevent potential legal disputes, businesspersons need to be aware of the many different laws that may apply to a single business transaction. It is equally important for businesspersons to understand enough about the law to know when to turn to an expert for advice. Obtaining competent legal advice *before* a dispute arises may enable a businessperson to avoid potentially costly mistakes. Also, keep in mind that sometimes higher-priced attorneys from larger firms may be worth the extra expense because they may have more clout in the local legal community to wield on your behalf.

Ethics and Business Decision Making

Merely knowing the areas of law that may affect a business decision is not sufficient in today's business world. Businesspersons must also take ethics into account. As you will learn in Chapter 2, *ethics* is generally defined as the study of what constitutes right or wrong behavior. Today, business decision makers need to consider not just whether a decision is legal, but also whether it is ethical.

Throughout this text, you will learn about the relationship between the law and ethics, as well as about some of the types of ethical questions that often arise in the business context. Not only is Chapter 2 devoted solely to an examination of the importance of ethical considerations in business decision making, but various other elements in every chapter of this text are designed to help you become

EXHIBIT 1–1 AREAS OF THE LAW THAT MAY AFFECT BUSINESS DECISION MAKING

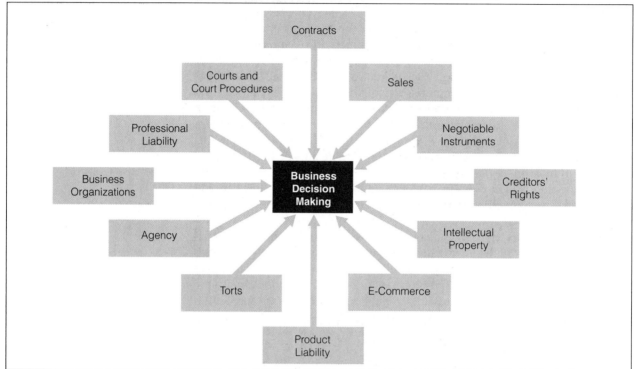

aware of the ethical aspects of questions that businesspersons may face. For example, the *Insight into Ethics* features throughout the text explore the ethical dimensions of the topics being discussed. In addition, the case problems at the end of each chapter include *A Question of Ethics* designed to introduce you to the ethical aspects of a specific case involving a real-life situation.

SOURCES OF AMERICAN LAW

There are numerous sources of American law. **Primary sources of law,** or sources that establish the law, include the following:

- The U.S. Constitution and the constitutions of the various states.

- Statutes, or laws, passed by Congress and by state legislatures.

- Regulations created by administrative agencies, such as the federal Food and Drug Administration.

- Case law (court decisions).

We describe each of these important primary sources of law in the following pages. (See the appendix at the end of this chapter for a discussion of how to find statutes, regulations, and case law.)

Secondary sources of law are books and articles that summarize and clarify the primary sources of law. Legal encyclopedias, compilations (such as *Restatements of the Law,* which organizes and summarizes case law on a particular topic), official comments to statutes, treatises, articles in law reviews published by law schools, and articles in other legal journals are examples of

PRIMARY SOURCE OF LAW
A document that establishes the law on a particular issue, such as a constitution, a statute, an administrative rule, or a court decision.

SECONDARY SOURCE OF LAW
A publication that summarizes or interprets the law, such as a legal encyclopedia, a legal treatise, or an article in a law review.

Citizens wait their turn to view the U.S. Constitution, on display in Washington, D.C. Can a law be in violation of the Constitution and still be enforced? Why or why not?
("Dan_H," Creative Commons)

secondary sources of law. Courts often refer to secondary sources of law for guidance in interpreting and applying the primary sources of law discussed here.

Constitutional Law

The federal government and the states have separate written constitutions that set forth the general organization, powers, and limits of their respective governments. **Constitutional law** is the law as expressed in these constitutions.

The U.S. Constitution is the supreme law of the land. As such, it is the basis of all law in the United States. A law in violation of the Constitution, if challenged, will be declared unconstitutional and will not be enforced no matter what its source. Because of its paramount importance in the American legal system, we discuss the U.S. Constitution at length in Chapter 4 and present the complete text of the Constitution in Appendix B.

The Tenth Amendment to the U.S. Constitution reserves to the states all powers not granted to the federal government. Each state in the union has its own constitution. Unless it conflicts with the U.S. Constitution or a federal law, a state constitution is supreme within the state's borders.

CONSTITUTIONAL LAW
The body of law derived from the U.S. Constitution and the constitutions of the various states.

Statutory Law

Laws enacted by legislative bodies at any level of government, such as the statutes passed by Congress or by state legislatures, make up the body of law generally referred to as **statutory law.** When a legislature passes a statute, that statute ultimately is included in the federal code of laws or the relevant state code of laws. Whenever a particular statute is mentioned in this text, we usually provide a footnote showing its **citation** (a reference to a publication in which a legal authority—such as a statute or a court decision—or other source can be found). In the appendix following this chapter, we explain how you can use these citations to find statutory law.

STATUTORY LAW
The body of law enacted by legislative bodies (as opposed to constitutional law, administrative law, or case law).

CITATION
A reference to a publication in which a legal authority—such as a statute or a court decision—or other source can be found.

ORDINANCE
A regulation enacted by a city or county legislative body to govern matters not covered by state or federal law.

Statutory law also includes local **ordinances**—statutes (laws, rules, or orders) passed by municipal or county governing units to govern matters not covered by federal or state law. Ordinances commonly have to do with city or county land use (zoning ordinances), building and safety codes, and other matters affecting the local governing unit.

A federal statute, of course, applies to all states. A state statute, in contrast, applies only within the state's borders. State laws thus may vary from state to state. No federal statute may violate the U.S. Constitution, and no state statute or local ordinance may violate the U.S. Constitution or the relevant state constitution.

Uniform Laws   During the 1800s, the differences among state laws frequently created difficulties for businesspersons conducting trade and commerce among the states. To counter these problems, a group of legal scholars, judges, and lawyers formed the National Conference of Commissioners on Uniform State Laws (NCCUSL) in 1892 to draft **uniform laws** ("model statutes") for the states to consider adopting. The NCCUSL still exists today and continues to issue uniform laws.

UNIFORM LAW
A model law created by the National Conference of Commissioners on Uniform State Laws and/or the American Law Institute for the states to consider adopting. If a state adopts the law, it becomes statutory law in that state. Each state has the option of adopting or rejecting all or part of a uniform law.

Each state has the option of adopting or rejecting a uniform law. *Only if a state legislature adopts a uniform law does that law become part of the statutory law of that state.* Note that a state legislature may adopt all or part of a uniform law as it is written, or the legislature may rewrite the law however the legislature wishes. Hence, even though many states may have adopted a uniform law, those states' laws may not be entirely "uniform."

The earliest uniform law, the Uniform Negotiable Instruments Law, was completed by 1896 and was adopted in every state by the early 1920s (although not all states used exactly the same wording). Over the following decades, other acts were drawn up in a similar manner. In all, the NCCUSL has issued more than two hundred uniform acts since its inception and also periodically revises these acts. The most ambitious uniform act of all, however, was the Uniform Commercial Code.

The Uniform Commercial Code (UCC)   The Uniform Commercial Code (UCC), which was created through the joint efforts of the NCCUSL and the American Law Institute, was first issued in 1952. The UCC has been adopted in all fifty states,[1] the District of Columbia, and the Virgin Islands. The UCC facilitates commerce among the states by providing a uniform, yet flexible, set of rules governing commercial transactions. The UCC assures businesspersons that their contracts, if validly entered into, normally will be enforced. Because of its importance in the area of commercial law, we cite the UCC frequently in this text and discuss it more fully in Chapter 11. We also present excerpts of the UCC in Appendix C.

Administrative Law

ADMINISTRATIVE LAW
The body of law created by administrative agencies (in the form of rules, regulations, orders, and decisions) in order to carry out their duties and responsibilities.

ADMINISTRATIVE AGENCY
A federal or state government agency established to perform a specific function. Administrative agencies are authorized by legislative acts to make and enforce rules in order to administer and enforce the acts.

An increasingly important source of American law is **administrative law,** which consists of the rules, orders, and decisions of administrative agencies. An **administrative agency** is a federal, state, or local government agency established to perform a specific function. Rules issued by various administrative agencies now affect virtually

---

1. Louisiana has adopted only Articles 1, 3, 4, 5, 7, 8, and 9.

every aspect of a business's operations, including the firm's capital structure and financing, its hiring and firing procedures, its relations with employees and unions, and the way it manufactures and markets its products.

Federal Agencies   At the national level, numerous **executive agencies** exist within the cabinet departments of the executive branch. For example, the Food and Drug Administration is within the U.S. Department of Health and Human Services. Executive agencies are subject to the authority of the president, who has the power to appoint and remove officers of federal agencies. There are also many **independent regulatory agencies** at the federal level, including the Federal Trade Commission, the Securities and Exchange Commission, and the Federal Communications Commission. The president's power is less pronounced in regard to independent agencies, whose officers serve for fixed terms and cannot be removed without just cause.

State and Local Agencies   There are administrative agencies at the state and local levels as well. Commonly, a state agency (such as a state pollution-control agency) is created as a parallel to a federal agency (such as the Environmental Protection Agency). Just as federal statutes take precedence over conflicting state statutes, so do federal agency regulations take precedence over conflicting state regulations. Because the rules of state and local agencies vary widely, we focus here exclusively on federal administrative law.

Agency Creation   Because Congress cannot possibly oversee the actual implementation of all the laws it enacts, it must delegate such tasks to agencies, especially when the legislation involves highly technical matters, such as air and water pollution. Congress creates an administrative agency by enacting **enabling legislation,** which specifies the name, composition, purpose, and powers of the agency being created.

   EXAMPLE #2 The Federal Trade Commission (FTC) was created in 1914 by the Federal Trade Commission Act.[2] This act prohibits unfair and deceptive trade practices. It also describes the procedures the agency must follow to charge persons or organizations with violations of the act, and it provides for judicial review (review by the courts) of agency orders. Other portions of the act grant the agency powers to "make rules and regulations for the purpose of carrying out the Act," to conduct investigations of business practices, to obtain reports from interstate corporations concerning their business practices, to investigate possible violations of the act, to publish findings of its investigations, and to recommend new legislation. The act also empowers the FTC to hold trial-like hearings and to **adjudicate** (resolve judicially) certain kinds of disputes that involve FTC regulations. □

   Note that the powers granted to the FTC incorporate functions associated with the legislative branch of government (rulemaking), the executive branch (investigation and enforcement), and the judicial branch (adjudication). Taken together, these functions constitute **administrative process,** which is the administration of law by administrative agencies.

Rulemaking   One of the major functions of an administrative agency is **rulemaking**—creating or modifying rules, or regulations, pursuant to its enabling

EXECUTIVE AGENCY
An administrative agency within the executive branch of government. At the federal level, executive agencies are those within the cabinet departments.

INDEPENDENT REGULATORY AGENCY
An administrative agency that is not considered part of the government's executive branch and is not subject to the authority of the president. Independent agency officials cannot be removed without cause.

ENABLING LEGISLATION
A statute enacted by Congress that authorizes the creation of an administrative agency and specifies the name, composition, purpose, and powers of the agency being created.

ADJUDICATE
To render a judicial decision. In the administrative process, adjudication is the trial-like proceeding in which an administrative law judge hears and decides issues that arise when an administrative agency charges a person or a firm with violating a law or regulation enforced by the agency.

ADMINISTRATIVE PROCESS
The procedure used by administrative agencies in the administration of law.

RULEMAKING
The process undertaken by an administrative agency when formally adopting a new regulation or amending an old one. Rulemaking involves notifying the public of a proposed rule or change and receiving and considering the public's comments.

---

2. 15 U.S.C. Sections 45–58.

legislation. The Administrative Procedure Act (APA) of 1946[3] imposes strict procedural requirements that agencies must follow in their rulemaking and other functions.

The most common rulemaking procedure involves three steps. First, the agency must give public notice of the proposed rulemaking proceedings, where and when the proceedings will be held, the agency's legal authority for the proceedings, and the terms or subject matter of the proposed rule. The notice must be published in the *Federal Register,* a daily publication of the U.S. government. Second, following this notice, the agency must allow ample time for interested parties to comment in writing on the proposed rule. After the comments have been received and reviewed, the agency takes them into consideration when drafting the final version of the regulation. The third and last step is the drafting of the final rule and its publication in the *Federal Register.* (See the appendix at the end of this chapter for an explanation of how to find agency regulations.)

Note that in addition to *legislative rules,* which are subject to the procedural requirements of the APA, agencies also create *interpretive rules*—rules that specify how the agency will interpret and apply its regulations. The APA does not apply to interpretive rulemaking. Moreover, although a firm that challenges an agency's rule may appeal the agency's decision in the matter to a court, the courts generally defer to agency rules, including interpretive rules, and to agency decisions, as will be discussed in Chapter 19.

Investigation and Enforcement   Agencies have both investigatory and prosecutorial powers. An agency can request that individuals or organizations hand over specified books, papers, electronic records, or other documents. In addition, agencies may conduct on-site inspections, although a search warrant is normally required for such inspections. Sometimes, a search of a home, an office, or a factory is the only means of obtaining evidence needed to prove a regulatory violation. Agencies investigate a wide range of activities, including coal mining, automobile manufacturing, and the industrial discharge of pollutants into the environment.

After conducting its own investigation of a suspected rule violation, an agency may decide to take action against an individual or a business. Most administrative actions are resolved through negotiated settlement at their initial stages without the need for formal adjudication. If a settlement cannot be reached, though, the agency may issue a formal complaint and proceed to adjudication.

ADMINISTRATIVE LAW JUDGE (ALJ)
One who presides over an administrative agency hearing and has the power to administer oaths, take testimony, rule on questions of evidence, and make determinations of fact.

Adjudication   Agency adjudication involves a trial-like hearing before an **administrative law judge (ALJ).** Hearing procedures vary widely from agency to agency. After the hearing, the ALJ renders a decision in the case. The ALJ can compel the charged party to pay a fine or can prohibit the party from carrying on some specified activity. Either side may appeal the ALJ's decision to the commission or board that governs the agency. If the party fails to get relief there, appeal can be made to a federal court. If no party appeals the case, the ALJ's decision becomes final.

Case Law and Common Law Doctrines

The rules of law announced in court decisions constitute another basic source of American law. These rules of law include interpretations of constitutional provisions, of statutes enacted by legislatures, and of regulations created by adminis-

---

3. 5 U.S.C. Sections 551–706.

trative agencies. Today, this body of judge-made law is referred to as **case law.** Case law—the doctrines and principles announced in cases—governs all areas not covered by statutory law or administrative law and is part of our common law tradition. We look at the origins and characteristics of the common law tradition in some detail in the pages that follow.

THE COMMON LAW TRADITION

Because of our colonial heritage, much of American law is based on the English legal system. A knowledge of this tradition is crucial to understanding our legal system today because judges in the United States still apply common law principles when deciding cases.

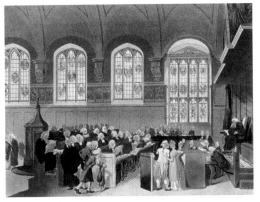

Court of Chancery, London, early nineteenth century. Early English court decisions formed the basis of what type of law?
(The Court of Chancery, as drawn by Augustus Pugin and Thomas Rowlandson for Ackermann's *Microcosm of London,* 1808–1811)

Early English Courts

After the Normans conquered England in 1066, William the Conqueror and his successors began the process of unifying the country under their rule. One of the means they used to do this was the establishment of the king's courts, or *curiae regis.* Before the Norman Conquest, disputes had been settled according to the local legal customs and traditions in various regions of the country. The king's courts sought to establish a uniform set of rules for the country as a whole. What evolved in these courts was the beginning of the **common law**—a body of general rules that applied throughout the entire English realm. Eventually, the common law tradition became part of the heritage of all nations that were once British colonies, including the United States.

Courts developed the common law rules from the principles underlying judges' decisions in actual legal controversies. Judges attempted to be consistent, and whenever possible, they based their decisions on the principles suggested by earlier cases. They sought to decide similar cases in a similar way and considered new cases with care, because they knew that their decisions would make new law. Each interpretation became part of the law on the subject and served as a legal **precedent**—that is, a decision that furnished an example or authority for deciding subsequent cases involving similar legal principles or facts.

In the early years of the common law, there was no single place or publication where court opinions, or written decisions, could be found. Beginning in the late thirteenth and early fourteenth centuries, however, each year portions of significant decisions of that year were gathered together and recorded in *Year Books.* The *Year Books* were useful references for lawyers and judges. In the sixteenth century, the *Year Books* were discontinued, and other reports of cases became available. (See the appendix to this chapter for a discussion of how cases are reported, or published, in the United States today.)

Stare Decisis

The practice of deciding new cases with reference to former decisions, or precedents, eventually became a cornerstone of the English and U.S. judicial systems. The practice forms a doctrine called **stare decisis**[4] ("to stand on decided cases").

CASE LAW
The rules of law announced in court decisions. Case law includes the aggregate of reported cases that interpret judicial precedents, statutes, regulations, and constitutional provisions.

COMMON LAW
The body of law developed from custom or judicial decisions in English and U.S. courts, not attributable to a legislature.

PRECEDENT
A court decision that furnishes an example or authority for deciding subsequent cases involving identical or similar facts.

STARE DECISIS
A common law doctrine under which judges are obligated to follow the precedents established in prior decisions.

---

4. Pronounced *stahr*-ee dih-*si*-sis.

The Importance of Precedents in Judicial Decision Making   Under the doctrine of *stare decisis,* once a court has set forth a principle of law as being applicable to a certain set of facts, that court and courts of lower rank within the jurisdiction must adhere to that principle and apply it in future cases involving similar fact patterns. (The term *jurisdiction* refers to an area in which a court or courts have the power to apply the law—see Chapter 3.) *Stare decisis* has two aspects: first, that decisions made by a higher court are binding on lower courts; and second, that a court should not overturn its own precedents unless there is a strong reason to do so.

Controlling precedents in a jurisdiction are referred to as binding authorities. A **binding authority** is any source of law that a court must follow when deciding a case. Binding authorities include constitutions, statutes, and regulations that govern the issue being decided, as well as court decisions that are controlling precedents within the jurisdiction. United States Supreme Court case decisions, no matter how old, remain controlling until they are overruled by a subsequent decision of the Supreme Court, by a constitutional amendment, or by congressional legislation.

BINDING AUTHORITY
Any source of law that a court must follow when deciding a case. Binding authorities include constitutions, statutes, and regulations that govern the issue being decided, as well as court decisions that are controlling precedents within the jurisdiction.

***Stare Decisis* and Legal Stability**   The doctrine of *stare decisis* helps the courts to be more efficient because if other courts have carefully reasoned through a similar case, their legal reasoning and opinions can serve as guides. *Stare decisis* also makes the law more stable and predictable. If the law on a given subject is well settled, someone bringing a case to court can usually rely on the court to make a decision based on what the law has been.

Departures from Precedent   Sometimes a court will depart from the rule of precedent if it decides that a given precedent should no longer be followed. If a court decides that a precedent is simply incorrect or that technological or social changes have rendered the precedent inapplicable, the court might rule contrary to the precedent. Cases that overturn precedent often receive a great deal of publicity.

PERSUASIVE AUTHORITY
Any legal authority or source of law that a court may look to for guidance but on which it need not rely in making its decision. Persuasive authorities include cases from other jurisdictions and secondary sources of law.

EXAMPLE #3   In *Brown v. Board of Education of Topeka,*[5] the United States Supreme Court expressly overturned precedent when it concluded that separate educational facilities for whites and blacks, which had been upheld as constitutional in numerous previous cases,[6] were inherently unequal. The Supreme Court's departure from precedent in Brown received a tremendous amount of publicity as people began to realize the ramifications of this change in the law. □

When There Is No Precedent   At times, a court hears a case for which there are no precedents within its jurisdiction on which to base its decision. When hearing such cases, called "cases of first impression," courts often look at precedents established in other jurisdictions for guidance. Precedents from other jurisdictions, because they are not binding on the court, are referred to as **persuasive authorities.** A court may also consider various other factors, including legal principles and policies underlying previous court decisions or existing statutes, fairness, social values and customs, public policy, and data and concepts drawn from the social sciences.

Can a court consider unpublished decisions as persuasive precedent? See this chapter's *Online Developments* feature for a discussion of this issue.

In a 1954 photo, Nettie Hunt sits on the steps of the United States Supreme Court building with her daughter after the Court's landmark ruling in Brown v. Board of Education of Topeka. *(Library of Congress, Prints & Photographs Division/U.S. News & World Report Magazine Collection)*

---

5. 347 U.S. 483, 74 S.Ct. 686, 98 L.Ed. 873 (1954). See the appendix at the end of this chapter for an explanation of how to read legal citations.
6. See *Plessy v. Ferguson,* 163 U.S. 537, 16 S.Ct. 1138, 41 L.Ed. 256 (1896).

The notion that courts should rely on precedents to decide the outcome of similar cases has long been a cornerstone of U.S. law. Nevertheless, the availability of "unpublished opinions" over the Internet is changing what the law considers to be precedent. An *unpublished opinion* is a decision made by an appellate court that is not intended for publication in a reporter (the bound books that contain court opinions).[a] Courts traditionally have not considered unpublished opinions to be "precedent," binding or persuasive, and attorneys were often not allowed to refer to these decisions in their arguments.

An Increasing Number of Decisions Are Not Published in Case Reporters but Are Available Online

The number of court decisions not published in printed books has risen dramatically in recent years. By some estimates, nearly 80 percent of the decisions of the federal appellate courts are unpublished. The number is equally high in some state court systems. California's intermediate appellate courts, for example, publish only about 7 percent of their decisions.

Even though certain decisions are not intended for publication, they are posted ("published") almost immediately on online legal databases, such as Westlaw and Lexis. With the proliferation of free legal databases and court Web sites, the general public also has almost instant access to the unpublished decisions of most courts. This situation has caused a substantial amount of debate over whether unpublished opinions should be given the same precedential effect as published opinions.

Should Unpublished Decisions Establish Precedent?

Prior to the Internet, one might have been able to justify not considering unpublished decisions to be precedent on the grounds of fairness. How could courts and lawyers be expected to consider the reasoning in unpublished decisions if they were not printed in the case reporters? Now that opinions are so readily available on the Web, however, this justification is no longer valid. Moreover, it now seems

a. Recently decided cases that are not yet published are also sometimes called *unpublished opinions,* but because these decisions will eventually be printed in reporters, we do not include them here.

unfair not to consider these decisions as precedent to some extent because they are so publicly accessible.

Another argument against allowing unpublished decisions to be precedent concerns the quality of the legal reasoning set forth in these decisions. Staff attorneys and law clerks frequently write unpublished opinions so that judges can spend more time on the opinions intended for publication. Consequently, some claim that allowing unpublished decisions to establish precedent could result in bad precedents because the reasoning may not be up to par. If the decision is regarded merely as persuasive precedent, however, then judges who disagree with the reasoning are free to reject the conclusion.

The United States Supreme Court Changes Federal Rules on Unpublished Opinions after 2007

In spite of objections from several hundred judges and lawyers, the United States Supreme Court made history in 2006 when it announced that it would allow lawyers to refer to (cite) unpublished decisions in all federal courts. The new rule, Rule 32.1 of the Federal Rules of Appellate Procedure, states that federal courts may not prohibit or restrict the citation of federal judicial opinions that have been designated as "not for publication," "non-precedential," or "not precedent." The rule applies only to federal courts and only to unpublished opinions issued after January 1, 2007. It does not specify the effect that a court must give to one of its unpublished opinions or to an unpublished opinion from another court. Basically, the rule simply makes all the federal courts follow a uniform rule that allows attorneys to cite—and judges to consider as persuasive precedent—unpublished decisions beginning in 2007.

The impact of this new rule remains to be seen. At present, the majority of states do not allow their state courts to consider the rulings in unpublished cases as persuasive precedent, and this rule does not affect the states. The Supreme Court's decision, however, provides an example of how technology—the availability of unpublished opinions over the Internet—has affected the law.

FOR CRITICAL ANALYSIS Now that the Supreme Court is allowing unpublished decisions to form persuasive precedent in federal courts, should state courts follow? Why or why not?

Equitable Remedies and Courts of Equity

A **remedy** is the means given to a party to enforce a right or to compensate for the violation of a right. **EXAMPLE #4** Suppose that Shem is injured because of Rowan's wrongdoing. A court may order Rowan to compensate Shem for the harm by paying Shem a certain amount. ▫

REMEDY

The relief given to an innocent party to enforce a right or compensate for the violation of a right.

In the early king's courts of England, the kinds of remedies that could be granted were severely restricted. If one person wronged another, the king's courts could award as compensation either money or property, including land. These courts became known as *courts of law,* and the remedies were called *remedies at law.* Even though this system introduced uniformity in the settling of disputes, when plaintiffs wanted a remedy other than economic compensation, the courts of law could do nothing, so "no remedy, no right."

Remedies in Equity   *Equity* refers to a branch of the law, founded in justice and fair dealing, that seeks to supply a fair and adequate remedy when no remedy is available at law. In medieval England, when individuals could not obtain an adequate remedy in a court of law, they petitioned the king for relief. Most of these petitions were decided by an adviser to the king called the *chancellor.* The chancellor was said to be the "keeper of the king's conscience." When the chancellor thought that the claim was a fair one, new and unique remedies were granted. In this way, a new body of rules and remedies came into being, and eventually formal *chancery courts,* or *courts of equity,* were established. The remedies granted by these courts were called *remedies in equity.* Thus, two distinct court systems were created, each having its own set of judges and its own set of remedies.

PLAINTIFF
One who initiates a lawsuit.

DEFENDANT
One against whom a lawsuit is brought; the accused person in a criminal proceeding.

   Plaintiffs (those bringing lawsuits) had to specify whether they were bringing an "action at law" or an "action in equity," and they chose their courts accordingly. **EXAMPLE #5** A plaintiff might ask a court of equity to order a **defendant** (a person against whom a lawsuit is brought) to perform within the terms of a contract. A court of law could not issue such an order because its remedies were limited to payment of money or property as compensation for damages. A court of equity, however, could issue a decree for *specific performance*—an order to perform what was promised. A court of equity could also issue an *injunction,* directing a party to do or refrain from doing a particular act. In certain cases, a court of equity could allow for the *rescission* (cancellation) of the contract, thereby returning the parties to the positions that they held prior to the contract's formation.□ Equitable remedies will be discussed in greater detail in Chapter 10.

REMEMBER
Even though, in most states, courts of law and equity have merged, the principles of equity still apply.

The Merging of Law and Equity   Today, in most states, the courts of law and equity have merged, and thus the distinction between the two courts has largely disappeared. A plaintiff may now request both legal and equitable remedies in the same action, and the trial court judge may grant either form—or both forms—of relief. The merging of law and equity, however, does not diminish the importance of distinguishing legal remedies from equitable remedies. To request the proper remedy, a businessperson (or her or his attorney) must know what remedies are available for the specific kinds of harms suffered. Today, as a rule, courts will grant an equitable remedy only when the remedy at law (money damages) is inadequate. Exhibit 1–2 summarizes the procedural differences (applicable in most states) between an action at law and an action in equity.

EQUITABLE PRINCIPLES AND MAXIMS
General propositions or principles of law that have to do with fairness (equity).

Equitable Principles and Maxims   Over time, the courts have developed a number of **equitable principles and maxims** that provide guidance in deciding whether plaintiffs should be granted equitable relief. Because of their importance, both historically and in our judicial system today, these principles and maxims are set forth in this chapter's *Landmark in the Legal Environment* feature.

In medieval England, courts of equity had the responsibility of using discretion in supplementing the common law. Even today, when the same court can award both legal and equitable remedies, it must exercise discretion. Courts often invoke equitable principles and maxims when making their decisions. Here are some of the most significant equitable principles and maxims:

1 *Whoever seeks equity must do equity.* (Anyone who wishes to be treated fairly must treat others fairly.)
2 *Where there is equal equity, the law must prevail.* (The law will determine the outcome of a controversy in which the merits of both sides are equal.)
3 *One seeking the aid of an equity court must come to the court with clean hands.* (Plaintiffs must have acted fairly and honestly.)
4 *Equity will not suffer a wrong to be without a remedy.* (Equitable relief will be awarded when there is a right to relief and there is no adequate remedy at law.)
5 *Equity regards substance rather than form.* (Equity is more concerned with fairness and justice than with legal technicalities.)
6 *Equity aids the vigilant, not those who rest on their rights.* (Equity will not help those who neglect their rights for an unreasonable period of time.)

The last maxim has become known as the *equitable doctrine of laches.* The doctrine arose to encourage people to bring lawsuits while the evidence was fresh; if they failed to do so, they would not be allowed to bring a lawsuit. What constitutes a reasonable time, of course, varies according to the circumstances of the case. Time periods for different types of cases are now usually fixed by **statutes of limitations.** After the time allowed under a statute of limitations has expired, no action can be brought, no matter how strong the case was originally.

APPLICATION TO TODAY'S LEGAL ENVIRONMENT

The equitable maxims listed here underlie many of the legal rules and principles that are commonly applied by the courts today—and that you will read about in this book. For example, in Chapter 9 you will read about the doctrine of promissory estoppel. Under this doctrine, a person who has reasonably and substantially relied on the promise of another may be able to obtain some measure of recovery, even though no enforceable contract, or agreement, exists. The court will estop (bar, or impede) the one making the promise from asserting the lack of a valid contract as a defense. The rationale underlying the doctrine of promissory estoppel is similar to that expressed in the fourth and fifth maxims above.

RELEVANT WEB SITES

To locate information on the Web concerning equitable principles and maxims, go to this text's Web site at **www.cengage.com/blaw/let**, select "Chapter 1," and click on "URLs for Landmarks."

CLASSIFICATIONS OF LAW

The huge body of the law may be broken down according to several classification systems. For example, one classification system divides law into **substantive law** (all laws that define, describe, regulate, and create legal rights and obligations) and **procedural law** (all laws that establish the methods of enforcing the rights established by substantive law). Other classification systems divide law into federal law and state law or private law (dealing with relationships between persons) and public law (addressing the relationship between persons and their governments).

STATUTE OF LIMITATIONS
A federal or state statute setting the maximum time period during which a certain action can be brought or certain rights enforced.

SUBSTANTIVE LAW
Law that defines, describes, regulates, and creates legal rights and obligations.

PROCEDURAL LAW
Law that establishes the methods of enforcing the rights established by substantive law.

EXHIBIT 1–2 PROCEDURAL DIFFERENCES BETWEEN AN ACTION AT LAW AND AN ACTION IN EQUITY

PROCEDURE	ACTION AT LAW	ACTION IN EQUITY
Initiation of lawsuit	By filing a complaint	By filing a petition
Decision	By jury or judge	By judge (no jury)
Result	Judgment	Decree
Remedy	Monetary damages	Injunction, specific performance, or rescission

CYBERLAW
An informal term used to refer to all laws governing electronic communications and transactions, particularly those conducted via the Internet.

Frequently, people use the term **cyberlaw** to refer to the emerging body of law that governs transactions conducted via the Internet. Cyberlaw is not really a classification of law, nor is it a new *type* of law. Rather, it is an informal term used to describe traditional legal principles that have been modified and adapted to fit situations that are unique to the online world. Of course, in some areas new statutes have been enacted, at both the federal and state levels, to cover specific types of problems stemming from online communications. Throughout this book, you will read how the law in a given area is evolving to govern specific legal issues that arise in the online context.

Civil Law and Criminal Law

CIVIL LAW
The branch of law dealing with the definition and enforcement of all private or public rights, as opposed to criminal matters.

Civil law spells out the rights and duties that exist between persons and between persons and their governments, and the relief available when a person's rights are violated. Typically, in a civil case, a private party sues another private party (although the government can also sue a party for a civil law violation) to make that other party comply with a duty or pay for the damage caused by the failure to comply with a duty. **EXAMPLE #6** If a seller fails to perform a contract with a buyer, the buyer may bring a lawsuit against the seller. The purpose of the lawsuit will be either to compel the seller to perform as promised or, more commonly, to obtain money damages for the seller's failure to perform. □

Much of the law that we discuss in this text is civil law. Contract law, for example, which we discuss in Chapters 9 through 11, is civil law. The whole body of tort law (see Chapter 5) is civil law. Note that *civil law* is not the same as a *civil law system*. As you will read shortly, a **civil law system** is a legal system based on a written code of laws.

CIVIL LAW SYSTEM
A system of law derived from that of the Roman Empire and based on a code rather than case law; the predominant system of law in the nations of continental Europe and the nations that were once their colonies. In the United States, Louisiana, because of its historical ties to France, has in part a civil law system.

CRIMINAL LAW
Law that defines and governs actions that constitute crimes. Generally, criminal law has to do with wrongful actions committed against society for which society demands redress.

Criminal law has to do with wrongs committed against society for which society demands redress. Criminal acts are proscribed by local, state, or federal government statutes. Thus, criminal defendants are prosecuted by public officials, such as a district attorney (D.A.), on behalf of the state, not by their victims or other private parties. Whereas in a civil case the object is to obtain remedies (such as money damages) to compensate the injured party, in a criminal case the object is to punish the wrongdoer in an attempt to deter others from similar actions. Penalties for violations of criminal statutes consist of fines and/or imprisonment—and, in some cases, death. We will discuss the differences between civil and criminal law in greater detail in Chapter 6.

National and International Law

Although the focus of this book is U.S. business law, increasingly businesspersons in this country engage in transactions that extend beyond our national borders. In these situations, the laws of other nations or the laws governing relationships among nations may come into play. For this reason, those who pursue a career in business today should have an understanding of the global legal environment.

NATIONAL LAW
Law that pertains to a particular nation (as opposed to international law).

National Law   The law of a particular nation, such as the United States or Sweden, is **national law.** National law, of course, varies from country to country because each country's law reflects the interests, customs, activities, and values that are unique to that nation's culture. Even though the laws and legal systems of various countries differ substantially, broad similarities do exist, as discussed in this chapter's *Beyond Our Borders* feature.

Despite their varying cultures and customs, virtually all countries have laws governing torts, contracts, employment, and other areas, just as the United States does. In part, this is because two types of legal systems predominate around the globe today. One is the common law system of England and the United States, which we have discussed elsewhere. The other system is based on Roman civil law, or "code law." The term *civil law,* as used here, refers not to civil as opposed to criminal law but to codified law—an ordered grouping of legal principles enacted into law by a legislature or governing body. In a *civil law system,* the primary source of law is a statutory code, and case precedents are not judicially binding, as they normally are in a common law system. Although judges in a civil law system commonly refer to previous decisions as sources of legal guidance, they are not bound by precedent; in other words, the doctrine of *stare decisis* does not apply.

A third, less prevalent, legal system is common in Islamic countries, where the law is often influenced by *sharia,* the religious law of Islam. *Sharia* is a comprehensive code of principles that governs both the public and private lives of Islamic persons, directing many aspects of day-to-day life, including politics, economics, banking, business law, contract law, and social issues. Although *sharia* affects the legal codes of many Muslim countries, the extent of its impact and its interpretation vary widely. In some Middle Eastern nations, aspects of *sharia* have been codified in modern legal codes and are enforced by national judicial systems.

The accompanying exhibit lists some countries that today follow either the common law system or the civil law system. Generally, those countries that were once colonies of Great Britain retained their English common law heritage after they achieved independence. Similarly, the civil law system, which is followed in most continental European nations, was retained in the Latin American, African, and Asian countries that were once colonies of those nations. Japan and South Africa also have civil law systems. In the United States, the state of Louisiana, because of its historical ties to France, has in part a civil law system. The legal systems of Puerto Rico, Québec, and Scotland are similarly characterized as having elements of the civil law system.

Realize that although national law systems share many commonalities, they also have distinct differences. Even when the basic principles are fundamentally similar (as they are in contract law, for example), significant variations exist in the practical application and effect of these laws across countries. Therefore, those persons who plan to do business in another nation would be wise to become familiar with the laws of that nation.

FOR CRITICAL ANALYSIS Does the civil law system offer any advantages over the common law system, or vice versa? Explain.

THE LEGAL SYSTEMS OF SELECTED NATIONS

CIVIL LAW		COMMON LAW	
Argentina	Indonesia	Australia	Nigeria
Austria	Iran	Bangladesh	Singapore
Brazil	Italy	Canada	United Kingdom
Chile	Japan	Ghana	United States
China	Mexico	India	Zambia
Egypt	Poland	Israel	
Finland	South Korea	Jamaica	
France	Sweden	Kenya	
Germany	Tunisia	Malaysia	
Greece	Venezuela	New Zealand	

International Law In contrast to national law, international law applies to more than one nation. **International law** can be defined as a body of written and unwritten laws observed by independent nations and governing the acts of individuals as well as governments. International law is an intermingling of rules and constraints derived from a variety of sources, including the laws of individual nations, the customs that have evolved among nations in their relations with one another, and treaties and international organizations. In essence, international law is the result of centuries-old attempts to reconcile the traditional need of each nation to be the final authority over its own affairs with the desire of nations to benefit economically from trade and harmonious relations with one another.

INTERNATIONAL LAW
The law that governs relations among nations. National laws, customs, treaties, and international conferences and organizations are generally considered to be the most important sources of international law.

The key difference between national law and international law is that government authorities can enforce national law. If a nation violates an international law, however, the most that other countries or international organizations can do (if persuasive tactics fail) is to resort to coercive actions against the violating nation. Coercive actions range from the severance of diplomatic relations and boycotts to, as a last resort, war. We examine the laws governing international business transactions in later chapters (including Chapter 7 and Chapter 11).

Reviewing . . . Business and Its Legal Environment

Suppose the California legislature passes a law that severely restricts carbon dioxide emissions from automobiles in that state. A group of automobile manufacturers files suit against the state of California to prevent the enforcement of the law. The automakers claim that a federal law already sets fuel economy standards nationwide and that these standards are essentially the same as carbon dioxide emission standards. According to the automobile manufacturers, it is unfair to allow California to impose more stringent regulations than those set by the federal law. Using the information presented in the chapter, answer the following questions.

1. Who are the parties (the plaintiffs and the defendant) in this lawsuit?

2. Are the plaintiffs seeking a legal remedy or an equitable remedy? Why?

3. What is the primary source of the law that is at issue here?

4. Read through the appendix that follows this chapter, and then answer the following question: Where would you look to find the relevant California and federal laws?

Key Terms

adjudicate 9
administrative agency 8
administrative law 8
administrative law judge
    (ALJ) 10
administrative process 9
binding authority 12
breach 5
case law 11
citation 7
civil law 16
civil law system 16
common law 11
constitutional law 7
criminal law 16
cyberlaw 16

defendant 14
enabling legislation 9
equitable principles and
    maxims 14
executive agency 9
historical school 4
independent regulatory
    agency 9
international law 17
jurisprudence 3
law 2
legal positivism 3
legal realism 4
national law 16
natural law 3
ordinance 8

persuasive authority 12
plaintiff 14
positive law 3
precedent 11
primary source of law 6
procedural law 15
remedy 13
rulemaking 9
secondary source of law 6
sociological school 4
stare decisis 11
statute of limitations 15
statutory law 7
substantive law 15
uniform law 8

Chapter Summary

The Nature of Law
(See pages 2–4.)

Law can be defined as a body of enforceable rules governing relationships among individuals and between individuals and their society. Four important schools of legal thought, or legal philosophies, are the following:

1. *Natural law tradition*–One of the oldest and most significant schools of legal thought. Those who believe in natural law hold that there is a universal law applicable to all human beings and that this law is of a higher order than positive, or conventional, law.

2. *Legal positivism*–A school of legal thought centered on the assumption that there is no law higher than the laws created by the government. Laws must be obeyed, even if they are unjust, to prevent anarchy.

3. *Historical school*–A school of legal thought that stresses the evolutionary nature of law and looks to doctrines that have withstood the passage of time for guidance in shaping present laws.

4. *Legal realism*–A school of legal thought, popular during the 1920s and 1930s, that left a lasting imprint on American jurisprudence. Legal realists generally advocated a less abstract and more realistic approach to the law, an approach that would take into account customary practices and the circumstances in which transactions take place.

Sources of American Law
(See pages 6–11.)

1. *Constitutional law*–The law as expressed in the U.S. Constitution and the various state constitutions. The U.S. Constitution is the supreme law of the land. State constitutions are supreme within state borders to the extent that they do not violate the U.S. Constitution or a federal law.

2. *Statutory law*–Laws or ordinances created by federal, state, and local legislatures and governing bodies. None of these laws can violate the U.S. Constitution or the relevant state constitutions. Uniform laws, when adopted by a state legislature, become statutory law in that state.

3. *Administrative law*–The rules, orders, and decisions of federal or state government administrative agencies. Federal administrative agencies are created by enabling legislation enacted by the U.S. Congress. Agency functions include rulemaking, investigation and enforcement, and adjudication.

4. *Case law and common law doctrines*–Judge-made law, including interpretations of constitutional provisions, of statutes enacted by legislatures, and of regulations created by administrative agencies. The common law–the doctrines and principles embodied in case law–governs all areas not covered by statutory law (or agency regulations issued to implement various statutes).

The Common Law Tradition
(See pages 11–15.)

1. *Common law*–Law that originated in medieval England with the creation of the king's courts, or *curlae regis,* and the development of a body of rules that were common to (or applied throughout) the land.

2. *Stare decisis*–A doctrine under which judges "stand on decided cases"–or follow the rule of precedent–in deciding cases. *Stare decisis* is the cornerstone of the common law tradition.

3. *Remedies*–

   a. Remedies at law–Money or something else of value.

   b. Remedies in equity–Remedies that are granted when the remedies at law are unavailable or inadequate. Equitable remedies include specific performance, an injunction, and contract rescission (cancellation).

Classifications of Law
(See pages 15–18.)

The law may be broken down according to several classification systems, such as substantive or procedural law, federal or state law, and private or public law. Two broad classifications are civil and criminal law, and national and international law. Cyberlaw is not really a classification of law but a term that is used for the growing body of case law and statutory law that applies to Internet transactions.

For Review

1. What are the primary sources of law?
2. What is the common law tradition?
3. What is a precedent? When might a court depart from precedent?
4. What is the difference between remedies at law and remedies in equity?
5. What are some important differences between civil law and criminal law?

Questions and Case Problems

1–1. Binding versus Persuasive Authority. A county court in Illinois is deciding a case involving an issue that has never been addressed before in that state's courts. The Iowa Supreme Court, however, recently decided a case involving a very similar fact pattern. Is the Illinois court obligated to follow the Iowa Supreme Court's decision on the issue? If the United States Supreme Court had decided a similar case, would that decision be binding on the Illinois court? Explain.

1–2. Remedies. Arthur Rabe is suing Xavier Sanchez for breaching a contract in which Sanchez promised to sell Rabe a Van Gogh painting for $150,000.

  1. In this lawsuit, who is the plaintiff, and who is the defendant?

  2. If Rabe wants Sanchez to perform the contract as promised, what remedy should Rabe seek?

  3. Suppose that Rabe wants to cancel the contract because Sanchez fraudulently misrepresented the painting as an original Van Gogh when in fact it is a copy. In this situation, what remedy should Rabe seek?

  4. Will the remedy Rabe seeks in either situation be a remedy at law or a remedy in equity?

  5. Suppose that the court finds in Rabe's favor and grants one of these remedies. Sanchez then appeals the decision to a higher court. Read through the subsection entitled "Appellants and Appellees" in the appendix following this chapter. On appeal, which party in the Rabe-Sanchez case will be the appellant (or petitioner), and which party will be the appellee (or respondent)?

1–3. Legal Systems. What are the key differences between a common law system and a civil law system? Why do some countries have common law systems and others have civil law systems?

Question with Sample Answer

1–4. This chapter discussed a number of sources of American law. Which source of law takes priority in each of the following situations, and why?

  1. A federal statute conflicts with the U.S. Constitution.

  2. A federal statute conflicts with a state constitution.

  3. A state statute conflicts with the common law of that state.

  4. A state constitutional amendment conflicts with the U.S. Constitution.

  5. A federal administrative regulation conflicts with a state constitution.

For a sample answer to Question 1–4, go to Appendix I at the end of this text.

1–5. Philosophy of Law. After World War II ended in 1945, an international tribunal of judges convened at Nuremberg, Germany. The judges convicted several Nazi war criminals of "crimes against humanity." Assuming that the Nazis who were convicted had not disobeyed any law of their country and had merely been following their government's (Hitler's) orders, what law had they violated? Explain.

1–6. Reading Citations. Assume that you want to read the court's entire opinion in the case of *Menashe v. V Secret Catalogue, Inc.,* 409 F.Supp.2d 412 (S.D.N.Y. 2006). The case focuses on whether "SEXY LITTLE THINGS" is a suggestive or descriptive trademark and which of the parties to the suit used the mark first in commerce. (Note that this case is presented in Chapter 8 of this text as Case 8.2.) Read the section entitled "Finding Case Law" in the appendix that follows this chapter, and then explain specifically where you would find the court's opinion.

1–7. Stare Decisis. In the text of this chapter, we stated that the doctrine of *stare decisis* "became a cornerstone of the English and U.S. judicial systems." What does *stare decisis* mean, and why has this doctrine been so fundamental to the development of our legal tradition?

1–8. Court Opinions. Read through the subsection entitled "Case Titles and Terminology" in the appendix following this chapter. What is the difference between a concurring opinion and a majority opinion? Between a concurring opinion and a dissenting opinion? Why do judges and justices write concurring and dissenting opinions, given that these opinions will not affect the outcome of the case at hand, which has already been decided by majority vote?

A Question of Ethics

1–9. On July 5, 1884, Dudley, Stephens, and Brooks—"all able-bodied English seamen"—and a teenage English boy were cast adrift in a lifeboat following a storm at sea. They had no water with them in the boat, and all they had for sustenance were two one-pound tins of turnips. On July 24, Dudley proposed that one of the four in the lifeboat be sacrificed to save the others. Stephens agreed with Dudley, but Brooks refused to consent—and the boy was never asked for his opinion. On July 25, Dudley killed the boy, and the three men then fed on the boy's body and blood. Four days later, the men were rescued by a passing vessel. They were taken to England and tried for the murder of the boy. If the men had not fed on the boy's body, they would probably have died of starvation within the four-day period. The boy, who was in a much weaker condition, would likely have died before the rest. [*Regina v. Dudley and Stephens*, 14 Q.B.D. (Queen's Bench Division, England) 273 (1884)]

1. The basic question in this case is whether the survivors should be subject to penalties under English criminal law, given the men's unusual circumstances. You be the judge, and decide the issue. Give the reasons for your decision.

2. Should judges ever have the power to look beyond the written "letter of the law" in making their decisions? Why or why not?

Critical-Thinking Legal Question

1–10. John's company is involved in a lawsuit with a customer, Beth. John argues that for fifty years, in cases involving circumstances similar to this case, judges have ruled in a way that indicates that the judge in this case should rule in favor of John's company. Is this a valid argument? If so, must the judge in this case rule as those other judges have? What argument could Beth use to counter John's reasoning?

Interacting with the Internet

Today, business law professors and students can go online to access information on virtually every topic covered in this text. A good point of departure for online legal research is the Web site for *The Legal Environment Today,* Sixth Edition, at

www.cengage.com/blaw/let

There you will find numerous materials relevant to this text and to the legal environment of business generally, including links to various legal resources on the Web. Additionally, every chapter in this text ends with an *Interacting with the Internet* feature that contains selected Web addresses.

You can access many of the sources of law discussed in Chapter 1, including links to federal and state statutes, at the FindLaw Web site, which is probably the most comprehensive source of free legal information on the Internet. Go to

www.findlaw.com

The Legal Information Institute (LII) at Cornell Law School, which offers extensive information about U.S. law, is also a good starting point for legal research. The URL for this site is

www.law.cornell.edu

The Library of Congress offers numerous links to state and federal government resources at

www.loc.gov

You can find proposed and final rules issued by administrative agencies by accessing the *Federal Register* online at

www.gpoaccess.gov/fr/index.html

PRACTICAL INTERNET EXERCISES

Go to this text's Web site at **www.cengage.com/blaw/let**, select "Chapter 1," and click on "Practical Internet Exercises." There you will find the following Internet research exercises that you can perform to learn more about the topics covered in this chapter.

Practical Internet Exercise 1–1: LEGAL PERSPECTIVE—**Internet Sources of Law**
Practical Internet Exercise 1–2: MANAGEMENT PERSPECTIVE—**Online Assistance from Government Agencies**

BEFORE THE TEST

Go to this text's Web site at **www.cengage.com/blaw/let**, select "Chapter 1," and click on "Interactive Quizzes." You will find a number of interactive questions relating to this chapter.

The statutes, agency regulations, and case law referred to in this text establish the rights and duties of businesspersons engaged in various types of activities. The cases presented in the following chapters provide you with concise, real-life illustrations of how the courts interpret and apply these laws. Because of the importance of knowing how to find statutory, administrative, and case law, this appendix offers a brief introduction to how these laws are published and to the legal "shorthand" employed in referencing these legal sources.

FINDING STATUTORY AND ADMINISTRATIVE LAW

When Congress passes laws, they are collected in a publication titled *United States Statutes at Large*. When state legislatures pass laws, they are collected in similar state publications. Most frequently, however, laws are referred to in their codified form—that is, the form in which they appear in the federal and state codes. In these codes, laws are compiled by subject.

United States Code

The *United States Code* (U.S.C.) arranges all existing federal laws of a public and permanent nature by subject. Each of the fifty subjects into which the U.S.C. arranges the laws is given a title and a title number. For example, laws relating to commerce and trade are collected in "Title 15, Commerce and Trade." Titles are subdivided by sections. A citation to the U.S.C. includes title and section numbers. Thus, a reference to "15 U.S.C. Section 1" means that the statute can be found in Section 1 of Title 15. ("Section" may also be designated by the symbol §, and "Sections" by §§.)

Sometimes a citation includes the abbreviation *et seq.*—as in "15 U.S.C. Sections 1 *et seq.*" The term is an abbreviated form of *et sequitur*, which is Latin for "and the following"; when used in a citation, it refers to sections that concern the same subject as the numbered section and follow it in sequence.

Commercial publications of these laws and regulations are available and are widely used. For example, West Group publishes the *United States Code Annotated* (U.S.C.A.). The U.S.C.A. contains the complete text of laws included in the U.S.C., notes of court decisions that interpret and apply specific sections of the statutes, and the text of presidential proclamations and executive orders. The U.S.C.A. also includes research aids, such as cross-references to related statutes, historical notes, and library references. A citation to the U.S.C.A. is similar to a citation to the U.S.C.: "15 U.S.C.A. Section 1."

State Codes

State codes follow the U.S.C. pattern of arranging law by subject. The state codes may be called codes, revisions, compilations, consolidations, general statutes, or statutes, depending on the preferences of the states. In some codes, subjects are designated by number. In others, they are designated by name. For example, "13 Pennsylvania Consolidated Statutes Section 1101" means that the statute can be found in Title 13, Section 1101, of the Pennsylvania code. "California Commercial Code Section 1101" means the statute can be found in Section 1101 under the subject heading "Commercial Code" of the California code. Abbreviations may be used. For example, "13 Pennsylvania Consolidated Statutes Section 1101" may be abbreviated "13 Pa. C.S. § 1101," and "California Commercial Code Section 1101" may be abbreviated "Cal. Com. Code § 1101."

Administrative Rules

Rules and regulations adopted by federal administrative agencies are compiled in the *Code of Federal Regulations* (C.F.R.). Like the U.S.C., the C.F.R. is divided into fifty titles. Rules within each title are assigned section numbers. A full citation to the C.F.R. includes title and section numbers. For example, a reference to "17 C.F.R. Section 230.504" means that the rule can be found in Section 230.504 of Title 17.

FINDING CASE LAW

Before discussing the case reporting system, we need to look briefly at the court system (which will be discussed more fully in Chapter 3). There are two types of courts in the United States, federal courts and state courts. Both the federal and state court systems consist of several levels, or tiers, of courts. *Trial courts,* in which evidence is presented and testimony given, are on the bottom tier (which also includes lower courts handling specialized issues). Decisions from a trial court can be appealed to a higher court, which commonly would be an interme-diate *court of appeals,* or an *appellate court.* Decisions from these intermediate courts of appeals may be appealed to an even higher court, such as a state supreme court or the United States Supreme Court.

State Court Decisions

Most state trial court decisions are not published. Except in New York and a few other states that publish selected opinions of their trial courts, decisions from state trial courts are merely filed in the office of the clerk of the court, where the deci-sions are available for public inspection. (Sometimes, they can be found online as well.) Written decisions of the appellate, or reviewing, courts, however, are pub-lished and distributed. As you will note, most of the state court cases presented in this book are from state appellate courts. The reported appellate decisions are pub-lished in volumes called *reports* or *reporters,* which are numbered consecutively. State appellate court decisions are found in the state reporters of that particular state.

Additionally, state court opinions appear in regional units of the *National Reporter System,* published by West Group. Most lawyers and libraries have the West reporters because they report cases more quickly and are distributed more widely than the state-published reports. In fact, many states have eliminated their own reporters in favor of West's National Reporter System. The National Reporter System divides the states into the following geographic areas: *Atlantic* (A. or A.2d), *North Eastern* (N.E. or N.E.2d), *North Western* (N.W. or N.W.2d), *Pacific* (P., P.2d, or P.3d), *South Eastern* (S.E. or S.E.2d), *South Western* (S.W., S.W.2d, or S.W.3d), and *Southern* (So. or So.2d). (The *2d* and *3d* in the abbreviations refer to *Second Series* and *Third Series,* respectively.) The states included in each of these regional divisions are indi-cated in Exhibit 1A–1, which illustrates West's National Reporter System.

EXHIBIT 1A-1 WEST'S NATIONAL REPORTER SYSTEM—REGIONAL/FEDERAL

Regional Reporters	Coverage Beginning	Coverage
Atlantic Reporter (A. or A.2d)	1885	Connecticut, Delaware, District of Columbia, Maine, Maryland, New Hampshire, New Jersey, Pennsylvania, Rhode Island, and Vermont.
North Eastern Reporter (N.E. or N.E.2d)	1885	Illinois, Indiana, Massachusetts, New York, and Ohio.
North Western Reporter (N.W. or N.W.2d)	1879	Iowa, Michigan, Minnesota, Nebraska, North Dakota, South Dakota, and Wisconsin.
Pacific Reporter (P., P.2d, or P.3d)	1883	Alaska, Arizona, California, Colorado, Hawaii, Idaho, Kansas, Montana, Nevada, New Mexico, Oklahoma, Oregon, Utah, Washington, and Wyoming.
South Eastern Reporter (S.E. or S.E.2d)	1887	Georgia, North Carolina, South Carolina, Virginia, and West Virginia.
South Western Reporter (S.W., S.W.2d, or S.W.3d)	1886	Arkansas, Kentucky, Missouri, Tennessee, and Texas.
Southern Reporter (So. or So.2d)	1887	Alabama, Florida, Louisiana, and Mississippi.
Federal Reporters		
Federal Reporter (F., F.2d, or F.3d)	1880	U.S. Circuit Courts from 1880 to 1912; U.S. Commerce Court from 1911 to 1913; U.S. District Courts from 1880 to 1932; U.S. Court of Claims (now called U.S. Court of Federal Claims) from 1929 to 1932 and since 1960; U.S. Courts of Appeals since 1891; U.S. Court of Customs and Patent Appeals since 1929; U.S. Emergency Court of Appeals since 1943.
Federal Supplement (F.Supp. or F.Supp.2d)	1932	U.S. Court of Claims from 1932 to 1960; U.S. District Courts since 1932; U.S. Customs Court since 1956.
Federal Rules Decisions (F.R.D.)	1939	U.S. District Courts involving the Federal Rules of Civil Procedure since 1939 and Federal Rules of Criminal Procedure since 1946.
Supreme Court Reporter (S.Ct.)	1882	United States Supreme Court since the October term of 1882.
Bankruptcy Reporter (Bankr.)	1980	Bankruptcy decisions of U.S. Bankruptcy Courts, U.S. District Courts, U.S. Courts of Appeals, and the United States Supreme Court.
Military Justice Reporter (M.J.)	1978	U.S. Court of Military Appeals and Courts of Military Review for the Army, Navy, Air Force, and Coast Guard.

NATIONAL REPORTER SYSTEM MAP

Pacific
North Western
South Western
North Eastern
Atlantic
South Eastern
Southern

After appellate decisions have been published, they are normally referred to (cited) by the name of the case; the volume, name, and page number of the state's official reporter (if different from West's National Reporter System); the volume, name, and page number of the *National Reporter;* and the volume, name, and page number of any other selected reporter. This information is included in the *citation.* (Citing a reporter by volume number, name, and page number, in that order, is common to all citations.) When more than one reporter is cited for the same case, each reference is called a *parallel citation.* For example, consider the following case: *Ramirez v. Health Net of Northeast, Inc.,* 285 Conn. 1, 938 A.2d 576 (2008). We see that the opinion in this case may be found in Volume 285 of the official *Connecticut Reports* (which reports only the decisions of the Supreme Court of Connecticut), on page 1. The parallel citation is to Volume 938 of the *Atlantic Reporter, Second Series,* page 576. In presenting opinions in this text, in addition to the reporter, we give the name of the court hearing the case and the year of the court's decision.

A few states—including those with intermediate appellate courts, such as California, Illinois, and New York—have more than one reporter for opinions issued by their courts. Sample citations from these courts, as well as others, are listed and explained in Exhibit 1A–2 on pages 27–29.

Federal Court Decisions

Federal district court decisions are published unofficially in West's *Federal Supplement* (F. Supp. or F.Supp.2d), and opinions from the circuit courts of appeals (federal reviewing courts) are reported unofficially in West's *Federal Reporter* (F., F.2d, or F.3d). Cases concerning federal bankruptcy law are published unofficially in West's *Bankruptcy Reporter* (Bankr.). The official edition of United States Supreme Court decisions is the *United States Reports* (U.S.), which is published by the federal government. Unofficial editions of Supreme Court cases include West's *Supreme Court Reporter* (S.Ct.) and the *Lawyers' Edition of the Supreme Court Reports* (L.Ed. or L.Ed.2d). Sample citations for federal court decisions are also listed and explained in Exhibit 1A–2.

Unpublished Opinions and Old Cases

Many court opinions that are not yet published or that are not intended for publication can be accessed through Westlaw® (abbreviated in citations as "WL"), an online legal database maintained by West Group. When no citation to a published reporter is available for cases cited in this text, we give the WL citation (see Exhibit 1A–2 for an example).

On a few occasions, this text cites opinions from old, classic cases dating to the nineteenth century or earlier; some of these are from the English courts. The citations to these cases may not conform to the descriptions given above because the reporters in which they were published have since been replaced.

READING AND UNDERSTANDING CASE LAW

The cases in this text have been condensed from the full text of the courts' opinions and paraphrased by the authors. For those wishing to review court cases for future research projects or to gain additional legal information, the following sections will provide useful insights into how to read and understand case law.

EXHIBIT 1A-2 HOW TO READ CITATIONS

STATE COURTS

274 Neb. 796, 743 N.W.2d 632 (2008)[a]

N.W. is the abbreviation for West's publication of state court decisions rendered in the *North Western Reporter* of the National Reporter System. *2d* indicates that this case was included in the *Second Series* of that reporter. The number 743 refers to the volume number of the reporter; the number 632 refers to the page in that volume on which this case begins.

Neb. is an abbreviation for *Nebraska Reports,* Nebraska's official reports of the decisions of its highest court, the Nebraska Supreme Court.

159 Cal.App.4th 1114, 72 Cal.Rptr.3d 81 (2008)

Cal.Rptr. is the abbreviation for West's unofficial reports—titled *California Reporter*—of the decisions of California courts.

8 N.Y.3d 422, 867 N.E.2d 381, 835 N.Y.S.2d 530 (2007)

N.Y.S. is the abbreviation for West's unofficial reports—titled *New York Supplement*—of the decisions of New York courts.

N.Y. is the abbreviation for *New York Reports*, New York's official reports of the decisions of its court of appeals. The New York Court of Appeals is the state's highest court, analogous to other states' supreme courts. In New York, a supreme court is a trial court.

289 Ga.App. 85, 656 S.E.2d 222 (2008)

Ga.App. is the abbreviation for *Georgia Appeals Reports,* Georgia's official reports of the decisions of its court of appeals.

FEDERAL COURTS

___ U.S. ___, 128 S.Ct. 1184, ___ L.Ed.2d ___ (2008)

L.Ed. is an abbreviation for *Lawyers' Edition of the Supreme Court Reports*, an unofficial edition of decisions of the United States Supreme Court.

S.Ct. is the abbreviation for West's unofficial reports—titled *Supreme Court Reporter*—of decisions of the United States Supreme Court.

U.S. is the abbreviation for *United States Reports*, the official edition of the decisions of the United States Supreme Court. The blank lines in this citation (or any other citation) indicate that the appropriate volume of the case reporter has not yet been published and no page number is available.

a. The case names have been deleted from these citations to emphasize the publications. It should be kept in mind, however, that the name of a case is as important as the specific page numbers in the volumes in which it is found. If a citation is incorrect, the correct citation may be found in a publication's index of case names. In addition to providing a check on errors in citations, the date of a case is important because the value of a recent case as an authority is likely to be greater than that of older cases from the same court.

EXHIBIT CONTINUES

EXHIBIT 1A–2 HOW TO READ CITATIONS–Continued

FEDERAL COURTS (Continued)

512 F.3d 582 (9th Cir. 2008)

9th Cir. is an abbreviation denoting that this case was decided in the U.S. Court of Appeals for the Ninth Circuit.

533 F.Supp.2d 740 (W.D.Mich. 2008)

W.D. Mich. is an abbreviation indicating that the U.S. District Court for the Western District of Michigan decided this case.

ENGLISH COURTS

9 Exch. 341, 156 Eng.Rep. 145 (1854)

Eng.Rep. is an abbreviation for *English Reports, Full Reprint,* a series of reports containing selected decisions made in English courts between 1378 and 1865.

Exch. is an abbreviation for *English Exchequer Reports*, which includes the original reports of cases decided in England's Court of Exchequer.

STATUTORY AND OTHER CITATIONS

18 U.S.C. Section 1961(1)(A)

U.S.C. denotes *United States Code*, the codification of *United States Statutes at Large*. The number 18 refers to the statute's U.S.C. title number and 1961 to its section number within that title. The number 1 in parentheses refers to a subsection within the section, and the letter A in parentheses to a subdivision within the subsection.

UCC 2–206(1)(b)

UCC is an abbreviation for *Uniform Commercial Code*. The first number 2 is a reference to an article of the UCC, and 206 to a section within that article. The number 1 in parentheses refers to a subsection within the section, and the letter b in parentheses to a subdivision within the subsection.

Restatement (Second) of Torts, Section 568

Restatement (Second) of Torts refers to the second edition of the American Law Institute's *Restatement of the Law of Torts*. The number 568 refers to a specific section.

17 C.F.R. Section 230.505

C.F.R. is an abbreviation for *Code of Federal Regulations*, a compilation of federal administrative regulations. The number 17 designates the regulation's title number, and 230.505 designates a specific section within that title.

EXHIBIT 1A-2 HOW TO READ CITATIONS–Continued

Westlaw® Citations[b]

2008 WL 427478

WL is an abbreviation for Westlaw. The number 2008 is the year of the document that can be found with this citation in the Westlaw database. The number 427478 is a number assigned to a specific document. A higher number indicates that a document was added to the Westlaw database later in the year.

Uniform Resource Locators (URLs)

http://www.westlaw.com[c]

The suffix *com* is the top level domain (TLD) for this Web site. The TLD *com* is an abbreviation for "commercial," which usually means that a for-profit entity hosts (maintains or supports) this Web site.

westlaw is the host name—the part of the domain name selected by the organization that registered the name. In this case, West Group registered the name. This Internet site is the Westlaw database on the Web.

www is an abbreviation for "World Wide Web." The Web is a system of Internet servers that support documents formatted in *HTML* (hypertext markup language). HTML supports links to text, graphics, and audio and video files.

http://www.uscourts.gov

This is "The Federal Judiciary Home Page." The host is the Administrative Office of the U.S. Courts. The TLD *gov* is an abbreviation for "government." This Web site includes information and links from, and about, the federal courts.

http://www.law.cornell.edu/index.html

This part of a URL points to a Web page or file at a specific location within the host's domain. This page is a menu with links to documents within the domain and to other Internet resources.

This is the host name for a Web site that contains the Internet publications of the Legal Information Institute (LII), which is a part of Cornell Law School. The LII site includes a variety of legal materials and links to other legal resources on the Internet. The TLD *edu* is an abbreviation for "educational institution" (a school or a university).

http://www.ipl.org/div/news

This part of the Web site points to a static *news* page at this Web site, which provides links to online newspapers from around the world.

div is an abbreviation for "division," which is the way that the Internet Public Library tags the content on its Web site as relating to a specific topic.

ipl is an abbreviation for "Internet Public Library," which is an online service that provides reference resources and links to other information services on the Web. The IPL is supported chiefly by the School of Information at the University of Michigan. The TLD *org* is an abbreviation for "organization" (normally nonprofit).

b. Many court decisions that are not yet published or that are not intended for publication can be accessed through Westlaw®, an online legal database.

c. The basic form for a URL is "service://hostname/path." The Internet service for all of the URLs in this text is *http* (hypertext transfer protocol). Because most Web browsers add this prefix automatically when a user enters a host name or a hostname/path, we have omitted the http:// from the URLs listed in this text.

Case Titles and Terminology

The title of a case, such as *Adams v. Jones,* indicates the names of the parties to the lawsuit. The *v.* in the case title stands for *versus,* which means "against." In the trial court, Adams was the plaintiff—the person who filed the suit. Jones was the defendant. If the case is appealed, however, the appellate court will sometimes place the name of the party appealing the decision first, so the case may be called *Jones v. Adams.* Because some reviewing courts retain the trial court order of names, it is often impossible to distinguish the plaintiff from the defendant in the title of a reported appellate court decision. You must carefully read the facts of each case to identify the parties.

The following terms and phrases are frequently encountered in court opinions and legal publications. Because it is important to understand what these terms and phrases mean, we define and discuss them here.

Parties to Lawsuits   As mentioned in Chapter 1, the party initiating a lawsuit is referred to as the *plaintiff* or *petitioner,* depending on the nature of the action, and the party against whom a lawsuit is brought is the *defendant* or *respondent.* Lawsuits frequently involve more than one plaintiff and/or defendant. When a case is appealed from the original court or jurisdiction to another court or jurisdiction, the party appealing the case is called the *appellant.* The *appellee* is the party against whom the appeal is taken. (In some appellate courts, the party appealing a case is referred to as the *petitioner,* and the party against whom the suit is brought or appealed is called the *respondent.*)

Judges and Justices   The terms *judge* and *justice* are usually synonymous and represent two designations given to judges in various courts. All members of the United States Supreme Court, for example, are referred to as justices, and justice is the formal title often given to judges of appellate courts, although this is not always the case. In New York, a justice is a judge of the trial court (which is called the Supreme Court), and a member of the Court of Appeals (the state's highest court) is called a judge. The term *justice* is commonly abbreviated to J., and *justices* to JJ. A Supreme Court case might refer to Justice Alito as Alito, J., or to Chief Justice Roberts as Roberts, C.J.

Decisions and Opinions   Most decisions reached by reviewing, or appellate, courts are explained in written *opinions.* The opinion contains the court's reasons for its decision, the rules of law that apply, and the judgment.

Unanimous, Concurring, and Dissenting Opinions   When all judges or justices unanimously agree on an opinion, the opinion is written for the entire court and can be deemed a *unanimous opinion.* When there is not a unanimous opinion, a *majority opinion* is written; the majority opinion outlines the view supported by the majority of the judges or justices deciding the case. If a judge agrees, or concurs, with the majority's decision, but for different reasons, that judge may write a *concurring opinion.* A *dissenting opinion* presents the views of one or more judges who disagree with the majority's decision. The dissenting opinion is important because it may form the basis of the arguments used years later in overruling the precedential majority opinion.

Other Types of Opinions   Occasionally, a court issues a *per curiam* opinion. *Per curiam* is a Latin phrase meaning "of the court." In *per curiam* opinions, there is no indication as to which judge or justice authored the opinion. This term may also be used for an announcement of a court's disposition of a case that is not accompanied by a written opinion. Some of the cases presented in this text are *en banc* decisions. When an appellate court reviews a case *en banc,* which is a French term (derived from a Latin term) for "in the bench," generally all of the judges "sitting on the bench" of that court review the case.

A Sample Court Case

To illustrate the elements in a court opinion, we present an annotated opinion in Exhibit 1A–3 on pages 33–35. The opinion is from an actual case that the United States Court of Appeals for the Ninth Circuit decided in 2008.

Background of the Case   The Seattle Center is an entertainment "zone" in downtown Seattle, Washington, that attracts almost ten million tourists every year. The center encompasses theaters, arenas, museums, exhibition halls, conference rooms, outdoor stadiums, and restaurants. Street performers add to the festive atmosphere. Under the authority of the city, the center's director issued rules to address safety concerns and other matters. Staff at the Seattle Center cited one of the street performers, a balloon artist, for several rule violations. The artist filed a suit in a federal district court against the city and others, alleging that the rules violated his rights under the U.S. Constitution. The court issued a judgment in the plaintiff's favor. The city appealed to the United States Court of Appeals for the Ninth Circuit.

Editorial Practice   You will note that triple asterisks (* * *) and quadruple asterisks (* * * *) frequently appear in the opinion. The triple asterisks indicate that we have deleted a few words or sentences from the opinion for the sake of readability or brevity. Quadruple asterisks mean that an entire paragraph (or more) has been omitted. Additionally, when the opinion cites another case or legal source, the citation to the case or other source has been omitted to save space and to improve the flow of the text. These editorial practices are continued in the other court opinions presented in this book. In addition, whenever we present a court opinion that includes a term or phrase that may not be readily understandable, a bracketed definition or paraphrase has been added.

Briefing Cases   Knowing how to read and understand court opinions and the legal reasoning used by the courts is an essential step in undertaking accurate legal research. A further step is "briefing," or summarizing, the case. Legal researchers routinely brief cases by reducing the texts of the opinions to their essential elements. Generally, when you brief a case, you first summarize the background and facts of the case. You then indicate the issue (or issues) before the court. An important element in the case brief is, of course, the court's decision on the issue and the legal reasoning used by the court in reaching that decision. (Detailed instructions on how to brief a case are given in Appendix A, which also includes a briefed version of the sample court case presented in Exhibit 1A–3.)

The cases contained within the chapters of this text have already been analyzed and briefed by the authors, and the essential aspects of each case are presented in a convenient format consisting of three basic sections: *Background and Facts, In the Words of the Court* (excerpts of the court's opinion), and *Decision and Remedy.*

In addition to this basic format, we sometimes include a special introductory section entitled *Historical and Social [Economic, Technological, Political,* or other] *Setting.* In some instances, a *Company Profile* is included in place of the introductory setting. These profiles provide background on one of the parties to the lawsuit. Each case is followed by two critical-thinking questions regarding some issue raised by the case. A section entitled *Impact of This Case on Today's Law* concludes the *Landmark and Classic Cases* that appear throughout the text to indicate the significance of the case for today's legal landscape.

The United States Supreme Court building in Washington, D.C. In what reporters are Supreme Court opinions published?
(PhotoDisc)

EXHIBIT 1A–3 A SAMPLE COURT CASE

This section contains the citation—the name of the case, the name of the court that heard the case, the year of the decision, and the reporter in which the court's opinion can be found.

> BERGER v. CITY OF SEATTLE
> United States Court of Appeals,
> Ninth Circuit, 2008.
> 512 F.3d 582.

This line provides the name of the justice (or judge) who authored the court's opinion.

> *O'SCANNLAIN*, Circuit Judge:
>
> We must determine the bounds of a city's authority to restrict expression in a public forum.

The court divides the opinion into several parts, headed by Roman numerals. The first part of the opinion summarizes the factual background of the case.

> **I**
>
> The public forum is the "Seattle Center," an entertainment zone covering roughly 80 acres of land in downtown Seattle, Washington. Each year, the Seattle Center's theaters, arenas, museums, exhibition halls, conference rooms, outdoor stadiums, and restaurants attract nearly ten million visitors. The city wields authority over this large tract of land and has delegated its power

To formally announce or publish; to issue an order making a law or regulation known and enforceable.

> to **promulgate** rules to the Seattle Center Director ("Director"). * * * In 2002, after an open process of public comment, the Director issued a * * * set of provisions in response to specific complaints and safety concerns, which became known as the Seattle Center Campus Rules.
>
> This litigation, originally brought by Michael Berger, a street performer, requires us to consider the validity of [the] Campus Rules.

Relating to the words of the rules in their apparent or obvious meaning, without any explanations, interpretations, modifications, or additions from outside sources.

> * * * Rule F.1 requires a permit for street performances and requires badges to be worn during street performances * * * .

The U.S. Constitution is the supreme law of the land. If a federal, state, or local law violates the Constitution, the law will be struck down.

> Berger mounts a **facial** attack on the **constitutionality** of these * * * restrictions.
>
> Berger has performed in the Seattle Center since the 1980s, making balloon creations and "talk[ing] to his audience about his personal beliefs, especially the importance of reading books."

A document that, when filed with a court, initiates a lawsuit.

A court decree ordering a person to do or refrain from doing a certain act.

A federal trial court in which a lawsuit is initiated.

A judgment that a court enters without beginning or continuing a trial. It can be entered only if no facts are in dispute and the only question is how the law applies.

> When the revised Campus Rules were enacted in 2002, Berger obtained a permit. Yet he * * * face[d] problems with the Seattle Center authorities: members of the public filed numerous complaints alleging that Berger exhibited threatening behavior and Seattle Center staff reported several rule violations. In 2003, Berger filed this **complaint** seeking damages and **injunctive relief** [alleging that the revised rules violated the Constitution]. * * * In 2005,

The First Amendment to the Constitution guarantees, among other freedoms, the right of free speech—to express one's views without governmental restrictions.

> [a federal] **district court** granted **summary judgment** to Berger, concluding that these rules facially violated the **First Amendment**.

EXHIBIT CONTINUES

EXHIBIT 1A-3 A SAMPLE COURT CASE—Continued

| A rejection or overruling of the district court's judgment. |
| The second major section of this opinion sets out the law that applies to the facts of the case. |
| The third major section of the opinion responds to the plaintiff's argument. |

The city timely appeals the district court's order of summary judgment and seeks **reversal** with instructions to enter summary judgment in its favor.

II

The First Amendment states that "Congress shall make no law * * * abridging the freedom of speech, or of the press."

Expression, whether oral or written or symbolized by conduct, is subject to reasonable time, place, or manner restrictions. Such restrictions * * * must be justified without reference to the content of the regulated speech, [and] they must be narrowly tailored to serve a significant governmental interest * * * .

III

* * * *

We begin with Berger's challenge to the permit requirement. Rule F.1 states that any person wishing to conduct a street performance must obtain a $5 annual permit from the Director. This rule dovetails with the badge requirement in Rule F.1, which mandates that a badge "shall be worn or displayed by the performer in plain view at all times during a performance."

* * * *

* * * The principal inquiry in determining content neutrality, in speech cases generally and in time, place, or manner cases in particular, is whether the government has adopted a regulation of speech because of disagreement with the message it conveys. A licensing statute lacks content neutrality if it burdens only certain messages or if it imposes a burden on all messages, but allows officials unchecked discretion to treat messages differently.

* * * *

* * * Contrary to Berger's argument, a rule does not discriminate based on content simply because it restricts a certain "medium" of communication. * * * We are satisfied that the rules meet * * * the test for a valid time, place, or manner restriction [on] speech.

* * * *

* * * A rule is narrowly tailored if it promotes a substantial government interest that would be achieved less effectively absent the regulation. Berger disputes the significance of the

EXHIBIT 1A–3 A SAMPLE COURT CASE–Continued

city's interests, and also contends that the rule does not match the city's asserted aims to reduce territorial disputes among performers, deter patron harassment, and facilitate the identification and apprehension of offending performers.

As a general matter, it is clear that a State's interest in protecting the safety and convenience of persons using a public forum is a valid governmental objective. Here, * * * the Seattle Center authorities enacted the permit requirement after encountering "chronic" territorial disputes between performers and threats to public citizens by street performers. [A city employee stated that]

> Before the performer rules went into effect * * * there were approximately 3 or 4 complaints by performers against other performers per week. If Magic Mike [Berger] was here, we could expect one or more from him. * * * The general complaints by performers against other performers would be 'that is my spot and he can't be there' and/or 'that performer is doing what I am doing and they won't move.' The general complaints by the tenants against performers usually concerned too much noise or blocking access.

These complaints show that street performances posed a threat to the city's interests in maintaining order in the Seattle Center and providing harassment-free facilities. We are satisfied that the city's permit scheme was designed to further valid governmental objectives.

* * * *

| In the final major section of this excerpt of the opinion, the court states its decision and gives its order. |

V

In sum, [the] Rules * * * satisfy the requirements for valid restrictions on expression under the First Amendment. Such content neutral and narrowly tailored rules * * * must be upheld.

The order granting summary judgment to Berger is REVERSED. The case is **REMANDED** to the district court for further proceedings consistent with this opinion.

| Sent back. |

Chapter 2

Ethics and Business Decision Making

CHAPTER OBJECTIVES

After reading this chapter, you should be able to answer the following questions:

1. What is business ethics and why is it important?

2. How can business leaders encourage their companies to act ethically?

3. How do duty-based ethical standards differ from outcome-based ethical standards?

4. What are six guidelines that an employee can use to evaluate whether his or her actions are ethical?

5. What types of ethical issues might arise in the context of international business transactions?

CONTENTS

" New occasions teach new duties. "

— JAMES RUSSELL LOWELL,
1819–1891 (American editor, poet, and diplomat)

All of the following businesspersons have been in the news in the past few years:

- Dennis Kozlowski (former chairman and chief executive officer of Tyco International).

- Mark H. Swartz (former chief financial officer of Tyco International).

- Jeffrey Skilling (former chief executive officer of Enron Corporation).

- Bernard Ebbers (former chief executive officer of WorldCom).

What do these individuals have in common? They are all in prison, and some may stay there until they die. They were all convicted of various crimes ranging from overseeing revenue exaggeration in order to increase stock prices to personal use of millions of dollars of public company funds. Not only did they break the law, but they also clearly violated even the minimum ethical principles that a civil society expects to be followed. Other officers and directors of the companies mentioned in the preceding list cost shareholders billions of dollars. In the case of those companies that had to enter bankruptcy, such as Enron Corporation, tens of thousands of employees lost their jobs.

Acting ethically in a business context is not child's play; it can mean billions of dollars—up or down—for corporations, shareholders, and employees. In the wake of the recent scandals, Congress attempted to prevent similar unethical business behavior in the future by passing stricter legislation in the form of the Sarbanes-Oxley Act of 2002, which will be explained in detail in Chapter 24. This act generally imposed more reporting requirements on corporations in an effort to deter unethical behavior and encourage accountability.

BUSINESS ETHICS

As you might imagine, business ethics is derived from the concept of ethics. **Ethics** can be defined as the study of what constitutes right or wrong behavior. It is a branch of philosophy focusing on morality and the way moral principles are derived. Ethics has to do with the fairness, justness, rightness, or wrongness of an action.

ETHICS
Moral principles and values applied to social behavior.

What Is Business Ethics?

Business ethics focuses on what is right and wrong behavior in the business world. It has to do with how businesses apply moral and ethical principles to situations that arise in the workplace. Because business decision makers must often address more complex ethical issues in the workplace than they face in their personal lives, business ethics is more complicated than personal ethics.

BUSINESS ETHICS
Ethics in a business context; a consensus as to what constitutes right or wrong behavior in the world of business and the application of moral principles to situations that arise in a business setting.

Why Is Business Ethics Important?

For an answer to the question of why business ethics is so important, reread the first paragraph of this chapter. All of the individuals who are sitting behind bars could have avoided these outcomes. Had they engaged in ethical decision making throughout their business careers, these problems would not have arisen. The corporations, shareholders, and employees who suffered because of those individuals' unethical and criminal behavior certainly paid a high price. Thus, an in-depth understanding of business ethics is important to the long-run viability of any corporation today. It is also important to the well-being of individual officers and directors and to the firm's employees. Finally, unethical corporate decision making can negatively affect suppliers, consumers, the community, and society as a whole.

Common Reasons Why Ethical Problems Occur

Not that many years ago, the popular painkiller Vioxx was recalled because its long-term use increased the risk of heart attack and stroke. Little by little, evidence surfaced that the drug's maker, Merck & Company, had known about these dangers yet had allowed Vioxx to remain on the market. Merck's failure to recall the drug earlier could potentially have adversely affected the health of thousands of patients. In addition, Merck has undergone investigations by both Congress and the U.S. Department of Justice. Merck was facing thousands of lawsuits, years of litigation, and millions of dollars in attorneys' fees and settlements when it agreed, in November 2007, to settle all outstanding cases concerning Vioxx for $4.85 billion. How did a major corporation manage to make so many missteps? The answer is simply that certain officers and employees of Merck felt that it was not necessary to reveal the results of studies that might have decreased sales of Vioxx.

In other words, the common thread among the ethical problems that occur in business is the desire to increase sales (or not lose them), thereby increasing profits and, for the corporation, increasing market value. In most situations, though, ethically wrong behavior by a corporation turns out to be costly to everyone concerned. Just ask the shareholders of Merck (and, of course, Enron, WorldCom, and Tyco).

Studies found that patients who took high doses of Vioxx over long periods had significantly more heart attacks and strokes than similar patients who took other medications. Does this finding necessarily mean that the makers of Vioxx behaved unethically by continuing to market the drug? Why or why not?
(Justin Griffith/Creative Commons)

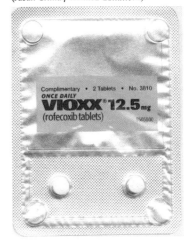

Short-Run Profit Maximization   Some people argue that a corporation's only goal should be profit maximization, which will be reflected in a higher market value. When all firms strictly adhere to the goal of profit maximization, resources tend to flow to where they are most highly valued by society. Ultimately, profit maximization, in theory, leads to the most efficient allocation of scarce resources.

Corporate executives and employees have to distinguish, though, between *short-run* and *long-run* profit maximization. In the short run, the employees of Merck & Company may have increased profits because of the continuing sales of Vioxx. In the long run, however, because of lawsuits, large settlements, and bad publicity, profits have suffered. Thus, business ethics is consistent only with long-run profit maximization.

Determining Society's Rules—The Role of Corporate Influence
Another possible cause of bad business ethics has to do with corporations' role in influencing the law. Corporations may use lobbyists to persuade government agencies not to institute new regulations that would increase the corporations' costs and reduce their profits. Once regulatory rules are promulgated, corporations may undertake actions to reduce their impact. One way to do this is to make it known that members of regulatory agencies will always have jobs waiting for them when they leave the agencies. This revolving door, as it is commonly called, has existed as long as there have been regulatory agencies at the state and federal levels of government.

The Importance of Ethical Leadership

Talking about ethical business decision making is meaningless if management does not set standards. Furthermore, managers must apply the same standards to themselves as they do to the employees of the company.

"What you do speaks so loudly that I cannot hear what you say."
—RALPH WALDO EMERSON, 1803–1882
(American poet and essayist)

Attitude of Top Management   One of the most important ways to create and maintain an ethical workplace is for top management to demonstrate its commitment to ethical decision making. A manager who is not totally committed to an ethical workplace rarely succeeds in creating one. Management's behavior, more than anything else, sets the ethical tone of a firm. Employees take their cues from management. If a firm's managers adhere to obvious ethical norms in their business dealings, employees will likely follow their example. In contrast, if managers act unethically, employees will see no reason not to do so themselves.
EXAMPLE #1 Suppose that Kevin observes his manager cheating on her expense account. Kevin quickly understands that such behavior is acceptable. Later, when Kevin is promoted to a managerial position, he "pads" his expense account as well—knowing that he is unlikely to face sanctions for doing so.■

Managers who set unrealistic production or sales goals increase the probability that employees will act unethically. If a sales quota can be met only through high-pressure, unethical sales tactics, employees will try to act "in the best interest of the company" and will continue to behave unethically.

A manager who looks the other way when she or he knows about an employee's unethical behavior also sets an example—one indicating that ethical transgressions will be accepted. Managers have found that discharging even one employee for ethical reasons has a tremendous impact as a deterrent to unethical behavior in the workplace.

Behavior of Owners and Managers   Business owners and managers sometimes take more active roles in fostering unethical and illegal conduct. This may
indicate to their co-owners, co-managers, employees, and others that unethical
business behavior will be tolerated. The following case illustrates how business
owners' misbehavior can have negative consequences for themselves and their
business. Not only can a court sanction the business owners and managers, but
it can also issue an injunction that prevents them from engaging in similar patterns of conduct in the future.

Case 2.1   **Baum v. Blue Moon Ventures, LLC**

United States Court of Appeals,
Fifth Circuit, 2008.
513 F.3d 181.

BACKGROUND AND FACTS   Douglas Baum runs an asset
recovery business, along with his brother, Brian Baum, and his
father, Sheldon Baum (the Baums). The Baums research
various unclaimed funds, try to locate the rightful owners, and
receive either a finder's fee or the right to some or all of the
funds recovered. In 2002, the Baums became involved in a
federal district court case by recruiting investors—through
misrepresentation—to file a lawsuit against a receiver (a court-
appointed person who oversees a business firm's affairs),
among others. The district court in that case determined that
the Baums' legal allegations were without merit and that their
conduct was a malicious attempt to extort funds. The court
sanctioned the Baums for wrongfully interfering in the case,
wrongfully holding themselves out to be attorneys licensed to
practice in Texas, lying to the parties and the court, and
generally abusing the judicial system. The district court also
issued a permanent injunction against all three Baums to
prohibit them from filing claims related to the same case in
Texas state courts without the express permission of Judge
Lynn Hughes (the district court judge).

In June 2005, the Baums entered an appearance in a
bankruptcy proceeding (bankruptcy will be discussed in
Chapter 13) involving Danny Hilal and Blue Moon Ventures,
LLC. Blue Moon's primary business was purchasing real
property at foreclosure sales and leasing those properties to
residential tenants. Sheldon Baum claimed to be a creditor in
the bankruptcy, but he would not identify his claim. Brian
Baum misled the parties and the court about being a licensed
attorney in Texas. Douglas Baum participated by posting a fake
notice stating that the Internal Revenue Service might
foreclose on some property to collect unpaid taxes. The
bankruptcy court concluded that this was a continuation of a
pattern of malicious conduct and forwarded a memo on the
case to the district court that had imposed the sanctions on
the Baums. The district court, after conducting two hearings
and listening to testimony from all of the Baums, also found
that the Baums had continued in their abusive practices. The
district court therefore modified and expanded its injunction to
include the filing of any claim in any federal or state court or
agency in Texas. Douglas Baum filed an appeal, claiming that
the court had exceeded its power and arguing that the
injunction would impede his business.

IN THE WORDS OF THE COURT . . . *DEMOSS*, Circuit Judge.

*   *   *   *

*   *   * Douglas Baum argues that the district court lacked jurisdiction to *   *   *
modify the pre-filing injunction. We disagree.

A district court has jurisdiction to impose a pre-filing injunction to deter vexatious,
abusive, and harassing litigation.

*   *   *   *

*   *   * *Federal courts have both the inherent power and the constitutional obligation to
protect their jurisdiction from conduct [that] impairs their ability to carry out [their] functions.*
If such power did not exist, or if its exercise were somehow dependent upon the
actions of another branch of government or upon the entitlement of a private party
to injunctive relief, the independence and constitutional role of [the] courts would be
endangered. Because the district court has jurisdiction to *   *   * impose a pre-filing
injunction to deter vexatious filings, it also has jurisdiction to *   *   * modify an existing permanent injunction to accomplish the same goal. [Emphasis added.]

CASE 2.1—CONTINUED

CASE 2.1–CONTINUED

* * * *

* * * Modification of an injunction is appropriate when the legal or factual circumstances justifying the injunction have changed.

Federal courts have the power to enjoin [prevent] plaintiffs from future filings when those plaintiffs consistently abuse the court system and harass their opponents. [Emphasis added.]

* * * *

The district court could consider Baum's conduct in the state court proceedings in determining whether his conduct before the bankruptcy court was undertaken in bad faith or for an improper motive. Limiting the injunction to any particular defendants did not stop Baum from repeating his pattern of abusive litigation practices; therefore, the district court did not abuse its discretion in determining that a broader injunction is necessary to protect both the court and future parties.

* * * *

* * * Baum argues that the district court abused its discretion in extending the injunction to prohibit Baum from filing any claims in state courts or agencies.

* * * *

* * * A district court's pre-filing injunction may extend to filings in lower federal courts within the circuit that the issuing court is located, * * * a district court's pre-filing injunction may not extend to filings in any federal appellate court, and * * * a district court's pre-filing injunction may not extend to filings in any state court. Based on the facts of this case, we find that the district court abused its discretion in extending the pre-filing injunction to filings in state courts, state agencies, and this Court. * * * Those courts or agencies are capable of taking appropriate action on their own. We uphold those provisions of the pre-filing injunction that prevent Douglas Baum from filing claims in federal bankruptcy courts, federal district courts, and federal agencies in the state of Texas without the express written permission of Judge Hughes.

DECISION AND REMEDY   The U.S. Court of Appeals for the Fifth Circuit upheld the modified pre-filing injunction as it applied to all filings in Texas state courts, in lower federal courts located in Texas, and in administrative agencies in Texas. The court struck down those portions of the injunction that attempted to require the Baums to obtain Judge Hughes's permission prior to filing a claim in any court or agency located outside the state of Texas, or prior to filing in any federal appellate court.

THE LEGAL ENVIRONMENT DIMENSION   What might the Baums have done to avoid the sanctions that were imposed on them in this case?

THE ETHICAL DIMENSION   Are there situations in which a business owner's conduct would be more reprehensible than the Baums' behavior in this case? Explain.

Periodic Evaluation   Some companies require their managers to meet individually with employees and to grade them on their ethical (or unethical) behavior. **EXAMPLE #2** Brighton Company asks its employees to fill out ethical checklists each month and return them to their supervisors. This practice serves two purposes: First, it demonstrates to employees that ethics matters. Second, employees have an opportunity to reflect on how well they have measured up in terms of ethical performance.□

APPROACHES TO ETHICAL REASONING

ETHICAL REASONING
A reasoning process in which an individual links his or her moral convictions or ethical standards to the particular situation at hand.

Each individual, when faced with a particular ethical dilemma, engages in **ethical reasoning**—that is, a reasoning process in which the individual examines the situation at hand in light of his or her moral convictions or ethical standards. Businesspersons do likewise when making decisions with ethical implications.

How do business decision makers decide whether a given action is the "right" one for their firms? What ethical standards should be applied? Broadly speaking, ethical reasoning relating to business traditionally has been characterized by two fundamental approaches. One approach defines ethical behavior in terms of duty, which also implies certain rights. The other approach determines what is ethical in terms of the consequences, or outcome, of any given action. We examine each of these approaches here.

In addition to the two basic ethical approaches, a few theories have been developed that specifically address the social responsibility of corporations. Because these theories also influence today's business decision makers, we conclude this section with a short discussion of the different views of corporate social responsibility.

Duty-Based Ethics

Duty-based ethical standards often are derived from revealed truths, such as religious precepts. They can also be derived through philosophical reasoning.

Religious Ethical Standards   In the Judeo-Christian tradition, which is the dominant religious tradition in the United States, the Ten Commandments of the Old Testament establish fundamental rules for moral action. Other religions have their own sources of revealed truth. Religious rules generally are absolute with respect to the behavior of their adherents. **EXAMPLE #3** The commandment "Thou shalt not steal" is an absolute mandate for a person who believes that the Ten Commandments reflect revealed truth. Even a benevolent motive for stealing (such as Robin Hood's) cannot justify the act because the act itself is inherently immoral and thus wrong. □

Kantian Ethics   Duty-based ethical standards may also be derived solely from philosophical reasoning. The German philosopher Immanuel Kant (1724–1804), for example, identified some general guiding principles for moral behavior based on what he believed to be the fundamental nature of human beings. Kant believed that human beings are qualitatively different from other physical objects and are endowed with moral integrity and the capacity to reason and conduct their affairs rationally. Therefore, a person's thoughts and actions should be respected. When human beings are treated merely as a means to an end, they are being treated as the equivalent of objects and are being denied their basic humanity.

A central theme in Kantian ethics is that individuals should evaluate their actions in light of the consequences that would follow if *everyone* in society acted in the same way. This **categorical imperative** can be applied to any action. **EXAMPLE #4** Suppose that you are deciding whether to cheat on an examination. If you have adopted Kant's categorical imperative, you will decide *not* to cheat because if everyone cheated, the examination (and the entire education system) would be meaningless. □

The Principle of Rights   Because a duty cannot exist without a corresponding right, duty-based ethical standards imply that human beings have basic rights. The principle that human beings have certain fundamental rights (to life, freedom, and the pursuit of happiness, for example) is deeply embedded in Western culture. As discussed in Chapter 1, the natural law tradition embraces the concept that certain actions (such as killing another person) are morally

BE CAREFUL
Ethical concepts about what is right and what is wrong can change.

CATEGORICAL IMPERATIVE
A concept developed by the philosopher Immanuel Kant as an ethical guideline for behavior. In deciding whether an action is right or wrong, or desirable or undesirable, a person should evaluate the action in terms of what would happen if everybody else in the same situation, or category, acted the same way.

PRINCIPLE OF RIGHTS
The principle that human beings have certain fundamental rights (to life, freedom, and the pursuit of happiness, for example). Those who adhere to this "rights theory" believe that a key factor in determining whether a business decision is ethical is how that decision affects the rights of various groups. These groups include the firm's owners, its employees, the consumers of its products or services, its suppliers, the community in which it does business, and society as a whole.

wrong because they are contrary to nature (the natural desire to continue living). Those who adhere to this **principle of rights,** or "rights theory," believe that a key factor in determining whether a business decision is ethical is how that decision affects the rights of others. These others include the firm's owners, its employees, the consumers of its products or services, its suppliers, the community in which it does business, and society as a whole.

A potential dilemma for those who support rights theory, however, is that they may disagree on which rights are most important. Management constantly faces ethical conflicts and trade-offs. When considering all those affected by a business decision, for example, how much weight should be given to employees relative to shareholders, customers relative to the community, or employees relative to society as a whole?

In general, rights theorists believe that whichever right is stronger in a particular circumstance takes precedence. **EXAMPLE #5** Suppose that a firm can either keep a plant open, saving the jobs of twelve workers, or shut the plant down and avoid contaminating a river with pollutants that would endanger the health of thousands of people. In this situation, a rights theorist can easily choose which group to favor. (Not all choices are so clear-cut, however.)□

Outcome-Based Ethics: Utilitarianism

UTILITARIANISM
An approach to ethical reasoning that evaluates behavior in light of the consequences of that behavior for those who will be affected by it, rather than on the basis of any absolute ethical or moral values. In utilitarian reasoning, a "good" decision is one that results in the greatest good for the greatest number of people affected by the decision.

"The greatest good for the greatest number" is a paraphrase of the major premise of the utilitarian approach to ethics. **Utilitarianism** is a philosophical theory developed by Jeremy Bentham (1748–1832) and modified by John Stuart Mill (1806–1873)—both British philosophers. In contrast to duty-based ethics, utilitarianism is outcome oriented. It focuses on the consequences of an action, not on the nature of the action itself or on any set of preestablished moral values or religious beliefs.

Under a utilitarian model of ethics, an action is morally correct, or "right," when, among the people it affects, it produces the greatest amount of good for the greatest number. When an action affects the majority adversely, it is morally wrong. Applying the utilitarian theory thus requires (1) a determination of which individuals will be affected by the action in question; (2) a **cost-benefit analysis,** which involves an assessment of the negative and positive effects of alternative actions on these individuals; and (3) a choice among alternative actions that will produce maximum societal utility (the greatest positive net benefits for the greatest number of individuals).

COST-BENEFIT ANALYSIS
A decision-making technique that involves weighing the costs of a given action against the benefits of that action.

Corporate Social Responsibility

CORPORATE SOCIAL RESPONSIBILITY
The idea that corporations can and should act ethically and be accountable to society for their actions.

For many years, groups concerned with civil rights, employee safety and welfare, consumer protection, environmental preservation, and other causes have pressured corporate America to behave in a responsible manner with respect to these causes. Thus was born the concept of **corporate social responsibility**—the idea that those who run corporations can and should act ethically and be accountable to society for their actions. Just what constitutes corporate social responsibility has been debated for some time, however, and there are a number of different theories today.

Stakeholder Approach   One view of corporate social responsibility stresses that corporations have a duty not just to shareholders, but also to other groups affected by corporate decisions ("stakeholders"). Under this approach, a corporation would consider the impact of its decision on the firm's employees, customers, creditors, suppliers, and the community in which the corporation operates. The reasoning behind this "stakeholder view" is that in some circumstances, one or more of these other groups may have a greater stake in company decisions than the shareholders do. Although this may be true, it is often difficult to decide which group's interests should receive greater weight if the interests conflict (see the discussion of the principle of rights on pages 41 and 42).

Corporate Citizenship Another theory of social responsibility argues that corporations should behave as good citizens by promoting goals that society deems worthwhile and taking positive steps toward solving social problems. The idea is that because business controls so much of the wealth and power of this country, business in turn has a responsibility to society to use that wealth and power in socially beneficial ways. Under a corporate citizenship view, companies are judged on how much they donate to social causes, as well as how they conduct their operations with respect to employment discrimination, human rights, environmental concerns, and similar issues.

In the following case, a corporation's board of directors did not seem to doubt the priority of the firm's responsibilities. Focused solely on the profits delivered into the hands of the shareholders, the board failed to check the actions of the firm's chief executive officer (CEO) and, in fact, appeared to condone the CEO's misconduct. If the board had applied a different set of priorities, the shareholders might have been in a better financial position, however. A regulatory agency soon found the situation "troubling" and imposed a restriction on the firm. The board protested. The protest reminded the court of "the old saw about the child who murders his parents and then asks for mercy because he is an orphan."

One of the vice presidents at Sun Microsystems discusses eco-responsibility at a climate protection summit. The electricity used by computers is thought to create 200 million tons of carbon dioxide emissions per year—more than all the cars in China. As part of Sun's commitment to corporate social responsibility, the company is focusing on creating computer servers that use less power. Sun also has a program that allows employees to work from home, which further reduces the amount of carbon dioxide emitted into the air. How might a company's environmentally friendly practices positively affect the ethical culture within the corporation and its standing within the community? (Kevin Krejci/Creative Commons)

Case 2.2 Fog Cutter Capital Group, Inc. v. Securities and Exchange Commission

United States Court of Appeals, District of Columbia Circuit, 2007. 474 F.3d 822.

BACKGROUND AND FACTS The National Association of Securities Dealers (NASD) operates the Nasdaq, an electronic securities exchange, on which Fog Cutter Capital Group was listed.[a] Andrew Wiederhorn had founded Fog Cutter in 1997 to manage a restaurant chain and make other investments. With family members, Wiederhorn controlled more than 50 percent of Fog Cutter's stock. The firm agreed that if Wiederhorn was terminated "for cause," he was entitled only

a. Securities (stocks and bonds) can be bought and sold through national exchanges. Whether a security is listed on an exchange is subject to the discretion of the organization that operates it. The Securities and Exchange Commission oversees the securities exchanges (see Chapter 24).

to his salary through the date of termination. If terminated "without cause," he would be owed three times his $350,000 annual salary, three times his largest annual bonus from the previous three years, and any unpaid salary and bonus. "Cause" included the conviction of a felony. In 2001, Wiederhorn became the target of an investigation into the collapse of Capital Consultants, LLC. Fog Cutter then redefined "cause" in his termination agreement to cover only a felony involving Fog Cutter. In June 2004, Wiederhorn agreed to plead guilty to two felonies, serve eighteen months in prison, pay a $25,000 fine, and pay $2 million to Capital Consultants. The day before he entered his plea, Fog Cutter agreed that while he was in prison, he would keep his title, responsibilities, salary, bonuses, and other benefits. It also agreed to a

CASE 2.2–CONTINUED

$2 million "leave of absence payment." In July, the NASD delisted Fog Cutter from the Nasdaq. Fog Cutter appealed this decision to the Securities and Exchange Commission (SEC), which dismissed the appeal. Fog Cutter petitioned the U.S. Court of Appeals for the District of Columbia Circuit for review.

IN THE WORDS OF THE COURT . . . *RANDOLPH*, Circuit Judge.

*   *   *   *

Fog Cutter's main complaint is that the Commission failed to take into account the company's sound business reasons for acting as it did. The decision to enter into the leave-of-absence agreement was, Fog Cutter argues, in the best interest of its shareholders. The company tells us that Wiederhorn's continuing commitment to the company and his return to an active role in the company after his incarceration were essential to preserving Fog Cutter's core business units.

*   *   *   *

*   *   * Fog Cutter made a deal with Wiederhorn that cost the company $4.75 million in a year in which it reported a $3.93 million net loss. We know as well that Fog Cutter handed Wiederhorn a $2 million bonus right before he went off to prison, a bonus stemming directly from the consequences of Wiederhorn's criminal activity.

*   *   *   *

Here there was ample evidence supporting the NASD's grounds for taking action against Fog Cutter: Wiederhorn's guilty plea, the leave-of-absence deal and its cost to the company, the Board's determination that Wiederhorn should retain his positions with Fog Cutter, and the concern that Wiederhorn would continue to exert influence on company affairs even while he was in prison. *The decision was in accordance with NASD rules giving the organization broad discretion to determine whether the public interest requires delisting securities in light of events at a company. That rule is obviously consistent with the [law], and NASD's decision did not burden competition.* [Emphasis added.]

Fog Cutter claims that it had to pay Wiederhorn and retain him because if it fired him in light of his guilty plea, it would have owed him $6 million. This scarcely speaks well for the company's case. The potential obligation is a result of an amendment the Board granted Wiederhorn in 2003 while he was under investigation. *   *   * Before the amendment to Wiederhorn's employment agreement in 2003, termination "for cause" included the conviction of any felony other than a traffic offense. In the 2003 amendment, the relevant provision allowed the Board to terminate Wiederhorn "for cause" upon conviction of a felony involving Fog Cutter. The Board had known about the investigation of Wiederhorn in connection with Capital Consultants for more than two years when it agreed to this amendment.

Fog Cutter thinks NASD's action was "unfair." But it was the company that bowed to Wiederhorn's demand for an amendment to his employment agreement, knowing full well that it was dramatically increasing the cost of firing him. Now it argues that terminating Wiederhorn would have been too expensive. One is reminded of the old saw about the child who murders his parents and then asks for mercy because he is an orphan. The makeup of Fog Cutter's Board was virtually unchanged between the time it amended the employment agreement and entered into the leave-of-absence agreement. It was, to say the least, not arbitrary or capricious for the Commission to find that Wiederhorn exercised thorough control over the Board, and to find this troubling. We agree that the Board provided little or no check on Wiederhorn's conduct, and that the Board's actions only aggravated the concerns Wiederhorn's conviction and imprisonment raised.

That Fog Cutter did not itself violate the [law] and that it disclosed the relevant events does not demonstrate any error in the delisting decision. The NASD's rules state that it may apply criteria more stringent than the minimum [legal] standards for listing. Fog Cutter's disclosure of its arrangements with Wiederhorn did not change the nature of those arrangements, which is what led the NASD to find that the company's actions were contrary to the public interest and a threat to public confidence in the Nasdaq exchange.

DECISION AND REMEDY The U.S. Court of Appeals for the District of Columbia Circuit denied Fog Cutter's petition for review of the SEC's decision. The NASD was concerned with "the integrity and the public's perception of the Nasdaq exchange" in light of Wiederhorn's legal troubles and the Fog Cutter board's acquiescence to his demands. The SEC "amply supported these concerns and was well within its authority to dismiss Fog Cutter's" appeal.

THE ETHICAL DIMENSION Should more consideration have been given to the fact that Fog Cutter was not convicted of a violation of the law? Why or why not?

THE GLOBAL DIMENSION What does the decision in this case suggest to foreign investors who may be considering investments in securities listed on U.S. exchanges?

Creating Ethical Codes of Conduct

One of the most effective ways to set a tone of ethical behavior within an organization is to create an ethical code of conduct. A well-written code of ethics explicitly states a company's ethical priorities and demonstrates the company's commitment to ethical behavior. This chapter concludes with a foldout exhibit showing the code of ethics of Costco Wholesale Corporation as an example.

Preventing Legal Disputes

Business owners wishing to avoid disputes over ethical violations must focus on creating a written ethical code that is clear and understandable (in plain English). The code should establish specific procedures that employees can follow if they have questions or complaints. It should assure employees that their jobs will be secure and that they will not face reprisals if they do file a complaint. Business owners should also explain to employees why these ethics policies are important to the company. A well-written code might include examples to clarify what the company considers to be acceptable and unacceptable conduct. ■

Providing Ethics Training to Employees For an ethical code to be effective, its provisions must be clearly communicated to employees. Most large companies have implemented ethics training programs in which management discusses with employees on a face-to-face basis the firm's policies and the importance of ethical conduct. Some firms hold periodic ethics seminars during which employees can openly discuss any ethical problems that they may be experiencing and learn how the firm's ethical policies apply to those specific problems. Smaller firms should also offer some form of ethics training to employees, because this is one factor that courts will consider if the firm is later accused of an ethics violation.

The Sarbanes-Oxley Act and Web-Based Reporting Systems The Sarbanes-Oxley Act of 2002[1] requires that companies set up confidential systems

---

1. 15 U.S.C. Section 7201 *et seq.* This act will be discussed in Chapter 24.

President George W. Bush shakes hands with Congressman Mike Oxley (R., Ohio) during the signing ceremony for the Sarbanes-Oxley Act of 2002. The president stated, "This new law sends very clear messages that all concerned must heed. This law says to every dishonest corporate leader: you will be exposed and punished; the era of low standards and false profits is over; no boardroom in America is above or beyond the law." Has the 2002 act deterred unethical business conduct by corporate leaders? (White House Photo)

MORAL MINIMUM
The minimum degree of ethical behavior expected of a business firm, which is usually defined as compliance with the law.

so that employees and others can "raise red flags" about suspected illegal or unethical auditing and accounting practices.

Some companies have created online reporting systems to accomplish this goal. In one such system, employees can click on an icon on their computers that anonymously links them with Ethicspoint, an organization based in Portland, Oregon. Through Ethicspoint, employees can report suspicious accounting practices, sexual harassment, and other possibly unethical behavior. Ethicspoint, in turn, alerts management personnel or the audit committee at the designated company to the potential problem. Those who have used the system say that it is less inhibiting than calling a company's toll-free number.

HOW THE LAW INFLUENCES BUSINESS ETHICS

Although business ethics and the law are closely related, they are not always identical. Here, we examine some situations in which what is legal and what is ethical may not be the same.

The Moral Minimum

Compliance with the law is normally regarded as the **moral minimum**—the minimum acceptable standard for ethical business behavior. In many corporate scandals, had most of the businesspersons involved simply followed the law, they would not have gotten into trouble. Note, though, that in the interest of preserving personal freedom, as well as for practical reasons, the law does not—and cannot—codify all ethical requirements. As they make business decisions, businesspersons must remember that just because an action is legal does not necessarily make it ethical. Look at Exhibit 2–1. Here, you see that there is an intersection between what is ethical and what is legal. Businesspersons should attempt to operate in the area where what is legal and what is ethical intersect.

Excessive Executive Pay   As just mentioned, business behavior that is legal may still be unethical. Consider executive pay. There is no law that specifies what public corporations can pay their officers. Consequently, "executive-pay scandals" do not have to do with executives breaking the law. Rather, such scandals have to do with the ethical underpinnings of executive-pay scales that can exceed millions of dollars. Such high pay for executives may appear unethical when their companies are not making very high profits (or are even suffering losses) and their share prices are falling.

Even this subject, though, does not lend itself to a black-and-white ethical analysis. As with many other things, there is a market for executives that operates according to supply and demand. Sometimes, corporate boards decide to offer executives very large compensation packages in order either to entice them to come to work for the company or to keep them from leaving for another corporation. There is no simple formula for determining the ethical level of compensation for a given executive in a given company. If a law were passed that limited executive compensation to, say, twenty times the salary of the lowest-paid worker in the company, there would be fewer individuals willing to undergo the stress and long hours associated with running major companies.

EXHIBIT 2–1 THE INTERSECTION OF WHAT IS LEGAL AND WHAT IS ETHICAL

Determining the Legality of a Given Action   It may seem that determining the legality of a given action should be simple. Either something is legal or it is not. In fact, one of the major challenges businesspersons face is that the legality of a particular action is not always clear. In part, this is because there are so many laws regulating business that it is increasingly possible to violate one of them without realizing it. The law also contains numerous "gray areas," making it difficult to predict with certainty how a court will apply a given law to a particular action.

Determining whether a planned action is legal thus requires that decision makers keep abreast of the law. Normally, large business firms have attorneys on their staffs to assist them in making key decisions. Small firms must also seek legal advice before making important business decisions because the consequences of just one violation of a regulatory rule may be costly.

Ignorance of the law will not excuse a business owner or manager from liability for violating a statute or regulation. **EXAMPLE #6** In one case, Riverdale Mills Corp. was held liable for its employee's attempt to board a plane with two cans of flammable hazardous material from Riverdale in his luggage. The court found that even though the employer was unaware of the employee's actions—and the employee was ignorant of the illegality of his actions—Riverdale had violated Federal Aviation Administration (FAA) regulations.[2]□

The Law Cannot Control All Business Behavior

Congress, the regulatory agencies, and state and local governments do not have perfect knowledge. Often they only discover the negative impact of corporate activities after the fact. The same can be true of corporate executives. They do not always know the full impact of their actions. **EXAMPLE #7** In the past, asbestos was used for insulation. At that time, the corporations that supplied the asbestos did not know that it was capable of causing a rare type of cancer.□

At other times, though, the law is not ambiguous. Nevertheless, it may still be unable to control business behavior—at least initially.

Breaking the Law—Backdating Stock Options   Sometimes, a practice that is legal, such as granting stock options, is used in an unethical and illegal manner. Stock options are a device that potentially rewards hard work. Publicly held corporations offer stock options to employees at the current price of the company's stock on the day that the options are granted. If at a later time the market price of the stock has gone up, an employee can exercise the stock options and reap the difference between the price of the options and the current market price.

In 2006 and 2007, it was revealed that a number of large corporations had backdated stock options. If stock options are granted and the price of the company's stock subsequently falls or does not rise very much, the value of the stock options is essentially zero. One way around this problem is to go back and change the date on which the stock options were granted to the employee. In other words, the date of the stock options is simply moved back to a day when the stock had a lower price than it has currently, thereby making the options valuable again.

---

2. *Riverdale Mills Corp. v. U.S. F.A.A.,* 417 F. Supp.2d 167 (D.Mass. 2006).

When Is Backdating Illegal?

Backdating stock options can be legal or illegal, depending on whether the company follows proper accounting procedures and Securities and Exchange Commission (SEC) disclosure rules. Generally, **backdating** stock options is legal if all of the following are true:

- No documents have been falsified.
- The shareholders (owners) of the corporation have been notified that stock options were backdated.
- The corporation correctly reported the backdated options as earnings in its financial statements.
- The backdating is properly reflected in taxes.

If a company fails to meet any of these conditions, then backdating is illegal. Those that do not properly account for and disclose backdating risk prosecution by the SEC or the U.S. Department of Justice.

Even when it is legal, backdating may be unethical because shareholders suffer a loss by paying inflated compensation to those persons whose stock options were backdated. A company's shareholders can bring a lawsuit against the company for improper backdating and seek to have the corporation reimbursed for the loss. Many of the companies that the SEC has investigated for backdating (discussed next) have faced civil lawsuits by their shareholders.

The Consequences of Illegal Backdating

During the past few years, the SEC has prosecuted numerous corporate executives involved in backdating scandals. These include individuals at Apple, Inc.; Comverse Technology, Inc.; Engineered Support Systems, Inc.; McAfee, Inc.; Monster Worldwide, Inc.; and Safe-Net, Inc. Many executives have pleaded guilty and agreed to pay back their ill-gotten gains. For example, in 2008, Nancy M. Tullos, former vice president of human resources at Broadcom Corp., agreed to settle the SEC's case against her by repaying more than $1.3 million and paying a $100,000 penalty. As a result of the backdating, Broadcom also had to restate its financial results and report an additional $2.22 billion in compensation expenses.

In December 2007, William W. McGuire, M.D., the former chief executive officer (CEO) of UnitedHealth Group, Inc., agreed to a $468 million settlement, which is the largest to date. Ryan Ashley Brant, former CEO of Take-Two Interactive Software, Inc., the maker of the popular *Grand Theft Auto* video games, was ordered to pay more than $6 million in penalties. Others, such as Gregory L. Reyes, Jr., have been sentenced to serve time in jail as a result of participating in illegal backdating. In 2007, Reyes was sentenced to twenty-one months in prison plus a $15 million fine for "tampering" with records of stock option grants.

The backdating scandal is another example of unethical behavior resulting in long-run profit reduction. As of 2009, at least 252 public companies had disclosed that they had undertaken internal investigations to discover if backdating had occurred without following proper procedures. The companies involved face more than 125 shareholder lawsuits and as many SEC investigations, plus fifty-eight Department of Justice investigations and even six criminal cases.

BACKDATING
The practice of marking a document with a date that precedes the actual date. Persons who backdate stock options are picking a date when the stock was trading at a lower price than the date of the options grant.

Steve Jobs, Chief Executive Officer of Apple, Inc., delivers a speech at a MacWorld conference apologizing for the company's backdating of at least fifteen stock option grants to corporate executives. Jobs claimed that although he knew that some company stock options had been backdated, he personally did not receive any and he was unaware of the accounting implications of backdating. If a company's top executive is aware that the company is backdating stock options, what steps should that person take to ensure that the backdating is legal?
(MarketWatch)

Misleading Regulators—The Case of OxyContin   In 1996, the pharmaceutical company Purdue Pharma, LP, started marketing a "wonder" narcotic painkiller called OxyContin. This powerful, long-lasting drug provides pain relief for twelve hours. Just a few years after its introduction, Purdue Pharma's annual sales of the drug reached $1 billion.

The company's executives initially contended that OxyContin, because of its time-release formulation, posed no risk for serious abuse or addiction. Quickly, though, experienced drug abusers and even teenagers discovered that chewing on an OxyContin tablet or crushing one and snorting the powder produced a powerful high, comparable to that of heroin. By 2000, large parts of the United States were experiencing increases in addiction and crime related to OxyContin.

In reality, the company and three of its executives had fraudulently marketed OxyContin for over six years as a drug unlikely to lead to abuse. Internal company documents showed that even before OxyContin was marketed, executives recognized that if physicians knew that the drug could be abused and become addictive, they would be less likely to prescribe it. Consequently, the company simply kept the information secret.

In 2007, Purdue Pharma and three former executives pleaded guilty to criminal charges that they had misled regulators, patients, and physicians about OxyContin's risks of addiction. Purdue Pharma agreed to pay $600 million in fines and other payments. The three ex-executives agreed to pay $34.5 million in fines. Once again, company executives resorted to unethical reasoning because they wanted to maximize profits in the short run, rather than engaging in behavior that would lead to profit maximization in the long run.

"Gray Areas" in the Law

In many situations, business firms can predict with a fair amount of certainty whether a given action is legal. For instance, firing an employee solely because of that person's race or gender clearly violates federal laws prohibiting employment discrimination. In some situations, though, the legality of a particular action may be less clear.

EXAMPLE #8   Suppose that a firm decides to launch a new advertising campaign. How far can the firm go in making claims for its products or services? Federal and state laws prohibit firms from engaging in "deceptive advertising." At the federal level, the test for deceptive advertising normally used by the Federal Trade Commission is whether an advertising claim would deceive a "reasonable consumer."[3] At what point, though, would a reasonable consumer be deceived by a particular ad?□

In addition, many rules of law require a court to determine what is "foreseeable" or "reasonable" in a particular situation. Because a business has no way of predicting how a specific court will decide these issues, decision makers need to proceed with caution and evaluate an action and its consequences from an ethical perspective. The same problem often occurs in cases involving the Internet because it is often unclear how a court will apply existing laws in the context of cyberspace. Generally, if a company can demonstrate that it acted in good faith and responsibly in the circumstances, it has a better chance of successfully defending its action in court or before an administrative law judge.

---

3. See Chapter 20 for a discussion of the Federal Trade Commission's role in regulating deceptive trade practices, including misleading advertising.

The following case shows that businesses and their customers have different expectations with respect to the standard of care regarding the handling of personal information. The case also illustrates that the legal standards in this area may be inconsistent and vague.

Case 2.3 Guin v. Brazos Higher Education Service Corp.

United States District Court, District of Minnesota, 2006. __ F.Supp.2d __.

BACKGROUND AND FACTS   Brazos Higher Education Service Corporation, which is based in Waco, Texas, makes and services student loans. Brazos issued a laptop computer to its employee John Wright, who worked from an office in his home in Silver Spring, Maryland, analyzing loan information. Wright used the laptop to store borrowers' personal information. In September 2004, Wright's home was burglarized and the laptop was stolen. Based on Federal Trade Commission (FTC) guidelines and California state law (which requires notice to all resident borrowers), Brazos sent a letter to all of its 550,000 customers. The letter stated that "some personal information associated with your student loan, including your name, address, Social Security number and loan balance, may have been inappropriately accessed by [a] third party." The letter urged borrowers to place "a free 90-day security alert" on their credit bureau files and review FTC consumer assistance materials. Brazos set up a call center to answer further questions and track any reports of identity theft. Stacy Guin, a Brazos customer, filed a suit in a federal district court against Brazos, alleging negligence. Brazos filed a motion for summary judgment.

IN THE WORDS OF THE COURT . . . *KYLE*, J. [Judge]

*   *   *   *

*   *   * *Negligence [is] the failure to exercise due or reasonable care. In order to prevail on a claim for negligence, a plaintiff must prove [among other things] the existence of a duty of care [and] a breach of that duty* *   *   * . [Emphasis added.]

*   *   *   *

Guin argues that the Gramm-Leach-Bliley Act (the "GLB Act") establishes a statutory-based duty for Brazos to protect the security and confidentiality of customers' nonpublic personal information. *   *   * Brazos concedes that the GLB Act applies to these circumstances and establishes a duty of care. The GLB Act was created "to protect against unauthorized access to or use of such records which could result in substantial harm or inconvenience to any customer [of a financial institution]." Under the GLB Act, a financial institution must comply with several objectives, including:

> Develop, implement, and maintain a comprehensive written information security program that is written in one or more readily accessible parts and contains administrative, technical, and physical safeguards that are appropriate to your size and complexity, the nature and scope of your activities, and the sensitivity of any customer information at issue *   *   * .

Guin argues that Brazos breached the duty imposed by the GLB Act by (1) "providing Wright with [personal information] that he did not need for the task at hand," (2) "permitting Wright to continue keeping [personal information] in an unattended, insecure personal residence," and (3) "allowing Wright to keep [personal information] on his laptop unencrypted."

The Court concludes that Guin has not presented sufficient evidence from which a fact finder could determine that Brazos failed to comply with the GLB Act. In September 2004, when Wright's home was burglarized and the laptop was stolen, Brazos had written security policies, current risk assessment reports, and proper safeguards for its customers' personal information as required by the GLB Act. Brazos authorized Wright to have access to customers' personal information because Wright needed the information to analyze loan portfolios *   *   * . Thus, his access to the personal information was within "the nature and scope of [Brazos's] activities." Furthermore, the GLB Act does not prohibit someone from working with sensitive data on a laptop computer in a home office. Despite Guin's persistent argument that any nonpublic personal information stored on a laptop computer should be encrypted, the GLB Act does not contain any such requirement. Accordingly, Guin has not presented any evidence showing that Brazos violated the GLB Act requirements.

DECISION AND REMEDY   The court granted the defendant's motion for summary judgment and dismissed the case. Brazos may have owed Guin a duty of care under the GLB Act, but neither Brazos nor Wright breached that duty. Wright had followed Brazos's written security procedures, which was all that the GLB Act required.

WHAT IF THE FACTS WERE DIFFERENT?   Suppose that Wright had not been a financial analyst and his duties for Brazos had not included reviewing confidential loan data. How might the opinion of the court have been different?

THE ETHICAL DIMENSION   Do businesses have an ethical duty to use enhanced security measures to protect confidential customer information? Why or why not? Does the fact that Brazos allowed its employees to store customers' unencrypted personal information on a laptop outside the office violate any ethical duty?

MAKING ETHICAL BUSINESS DECISIONS

As Dean Krehmeyer, executive director of the Business Roundtable's Institute for Corporate Ethics, once said, "Evidence strongly suggests being ethical—doing the right thing—pays." Instilling ethical business decision making into the fabric of a business organization is no small task, even if ethics "pays." The job is to get people to understand that they have to think more broadly about how their decisions will affect employees, shareholders, customers, and even the community. Great companies, such as Enron and the accounting firm Arthur Andersen, were brought down by the unethical behavior of a few. A two-hundred-year-old British investment banking firm, Barings Bank, was destroyed by the actions of one employee and a few of his friends. Clearly, ensuring that all employees get on the ethical business decision-making "bandwagon" is crucial in today's fast-paced world.

The George S. May International Company has provided six basic guidelines to help corporate employees judge their actions. Each employee—no matter what his or her level in the organization—should evaluate his or her actions using the following six guidelines:

1. *The law.* Is the action you are considering legal? If you do not know the laws governing the action, then find out. Ignorance of the law is no excuse.
2. *Rules and procedures.* Are you following the internal rules and procedures that have already been laid out by your company? They have been developed to avoid problems. Is what you are planning to do consistent with your company's policies and procedures? If not, stop.
3. *Values.* Laws and internal company policies reinforce society's values. You might wish to ask yourself whether you are attempting to find a loophole in the law or in your company's policies. Next, you have to ask yourself whether you are following the "spirit" of the law as well as the letter of the law or the internal policy.

4. *Conscience.* If you have any feeling of guilt, let your conscience be your guide. Alternatively, ask yourself whether you would be happy to be interviewed by a national news magazine about the actions you are going to take.

5. *Promises.* Every business organization is based on trust. Your customers believe that your company will do what it is supposed to do. The same is true for your suppliers and employees. Will your actions live up to the commitments you have made to others, both inside the business and outside?

6. *Heroes.* We all have heroes who are role models for us. Is what you are planning on doing an action that your hero would take? If not, how would your hero act? That is how you should be acting.

BUSINESS ETHICS ON A GLOBAL LEVEL

Given the various cultures and religions throughout the world, conflicts in ethics frequently arise between foreign and U.S. businesspersons. **EXAMPLE #9** In certain countries, the consumption of alcohol and specific foods is forbidden for religious reasons. Under such circumstances, it would be thoughtless and imprudent for a U.S. businessperson to invite a local business contact out for a drink. □ Different cultural views about rights that Americans consider to be fundamental, such as free speech, can cause ethical firestorms, as discussed in this chapter's *Insight into Ethics* feature.

The role played by women in other countries may also present some difficult ethical problems for firms doing business internationally. Equal employment opportunity is a fundamental public policy in the United States, and Title VII of the Civil Rights Act of 1964 prohibits discrimination against women in the employment context (see Chapter 18). Some other countries, however, offer little protection for women against gender discrimination in the workplace, including sexual harassment.

We look here at how the employment practices that affect workers in other countries, particularly developing countries, have created some especially difficult ethical problems for U.S. sellers of goods manufactured in foreign nations. We also examine some of the ethical ramifications of laws prohibiting bribery and the expansion of ethics programs in the global community.

Should global companies engage in censorship?

Doing business on a global level can sometimes involve serious ethical challenges, as Google, Inc., discovered when it decided to market "Google China." This version of Google's widely used search engine was especially tailored to the Chinese government's censorship requirements. To date, the Chinese government has maintained strict control over the flow of information in that country. The government's goal is to stop the flow of what it considers to be "harmful information." Web sites that offer pornography, criticism of the government, or information on sensitive topics, such as the Tiananmen Square massacre in 1989, are censored—that is, they cannot be accessed by Web users. Government agencies enforce the censorship and encourage citizens to inform on one another. Thousands of Web sites are shut down each year, and the sites' operators are subject to potential imprisonment.

Google's code of conduct opens with the company's informal motto: "Don't be evil." Yet critics question whether Google is following this motto. Human rights groups have come out strongly against Google's decision, maintaining that the company is seeking profits in a lucrative marketplace at the expense of assisting the Chinese Communist Party in suppressing free speech. In February 2006, Tom Lantos, the only Holocaust survivor serving in Congress, stated that the "sickening collaboration" of Google and three other Web companies (Cisco Systems, Microsoft Corporation, and Yahoo!, Inc.) with the Chinese government was "decapitating the voice of dissidents" in that nation.[4]

Google's Response

Google defends its actions by pointing out that its Chinese search engine at least lets users know which sites are being censored. Google China includes the links to censored sites, but when a user tries to access a link, the program states that it is not accessible. Google claims that its approach is essentially the "lesser of two evils": if U.S. companies did not cooperate with the Chinese government, Chinese residents would have less user-friendly Internet access. Moreover, Google asserts that providing Internet access, even if censored, is a step toward more open access in the future because technology is, in itself, a revolutionary force.

The Chinese Government's Defense

The Chinese government insists that in restricting access to certain Web sites, it is merely following the lead of other national governments, which also impose controls on information access. As an example, it cites France, which bans access to any Web sites selling or portraying Nazi paraphernalia. The United States itself prohibits the dissemination of certain types of materials, such as child pornography, over the Internet. Furthermore, the U.S. government monitors Web sites and e-mail communications to protect against terrorist threats.

Monitoring the Employment Practices of Foreign Suppliers

Many U.S. businesses now contract with companies in developing nations to produce goods, such as shoes and clothing, because the wage rates in those nations are significantly lower than those in the United States. Yet what if a foreign company hires women and children at below-minimum-wage rates, for example, or requires its employees to work long hours in a workplace full of health hazards? What if the company's supervisors routinely engage in workplace conduct that is offensive to women?

Given today's global communications network, few companies can assume that their actions in other nations will go unnoticed by "corporate watch" groups that discover and publicize unethical corporate behavior. As a result, U.S. businesses today usually take steps to avoid such adverse publicity—either by refusing to deal with certain suppliers or by arranging to monitor their suppliers' workplaces to make sure that the employees are not being mistreated.

The Foreign Corrupt Practices Act

Another ethical problem in international business dealings has to do with the legitimacy of certain side payments to government officials. In the United States, the majority of contracts are formed within the private sector. In many foreign

---

4. As quoted in Tom Ziller, Jr., "Web Firms Questioned on Dealings in China," *The New York Times,* February 16, 2006.

countries, however, government officials make the decisions on most major construction and manufacturing contracts because of extensive government regulation and control over trade and industry. Side payments to government officials in exchange for favorable business contracts are not unusual in such countries, nor are they considered to be unethical. In the past, U.S. corporations doing business in these nations largely followed the dictum, "When in Rome, do as the Romans do."

In the 1970s, however, the U.S. press uncovered a number of business scandals involving large side payments by U.S. corporations to foreign representatives for the purpose of securing advantageous international trade contracts. In response to this unethical behavior, in 1977 Congress passed the Foreign Corrupt Practices Act (FCPA), which prohibits U.S. businesspersons from bribing foreign officials to secure beneficial contracts. (For a discussion of how the United States is now applying this law to foreign companies, see this chapter's *Beyond Our Borders* feature.)

Prohibition against the Bribery of Foreign Officials   The first part of the FCPA applies to all U.S. companies and their directors, officers, shareholders, employees, and agents. This part prohibits the bribery of most officials of foreign governments if the purpose of the payment is to get the official to act in his or her official capacity to provide business opportunities.

The FCPA does not prohibit payment of substantial sums to minor officials whose duties are ministerial. These payments are often referred to as "grease," or facilitating payments. They are meant to accelerate the performance of administrative services that might otherwise be carried out at a slow pace. Thus, for example, if a firm makes a payment to a minor official to speed up an import licensing process, the firm has not violated the FCPA. Generally, the act, as amended, permits payments to foreign officials if such payments are lawful within the foreign country. The act also does not prohibit payments to private foreign companies or other third parties unless the U.S. firm knows that the payments will be passed on to a foreign government in violation of the FCPA.

Accounting Requirements   In the past, bribes were often concealed in corporate financial records. Thus, the second part of the FCPA is directed toward accountants. All companies must keep detailed records that "accurately and fairly" reflect their financial activities. In addition, all companies must have accounting systems that provide "reasonable assurance" that all transactions entered into by the companies are accounted for and legal. These requirements assist in detecting illegal bribes. The FCPA further prohibits any person from making false statements to accountants or false entries in any record or account.

Penalties for Violations   In 1988, the FCPA was amended to provide that business firms that violate the act may be fined up to $2 million. Individual officers or directors who violate the FCPA may be fined up to $100,000 (the fine cannot be paid by the company) and may be imprisoned for up to five years.

The Foreign Corrupt Practices Act (FCPA) was enacted in the 1970s, but has only recently been used to prosecute companies in the global business environment for suspected bribery. The problems facing BAE Systems (formerly known as British Aerospace), a company in the United Kingdom, illustrate how the pursuit of commercial interests can clash with ethics. BAE is a multinational company that makes and supplies military planes and weapons systems. It has been selling arms to Saudi Arabia since the 1980s and has been widely accused of engaging in bribery and unethical conduct in its negotiations with the Saudis.

The United Kingdom Drops Its Investigation

BAE first came under investigation by Britain's Serious Fraud Office (SFO) in 2004. The investigation, which focused on alleged improprieties in an arms deal with the Saudis in 1985, was dropped in 2006 at the urging of U.K. prime minister Tony Blair for reasons of national security. Anticorruption groups have challenged that decision in an effort to prevent BAE from winning more lucrative contracts with the Saudis.

Critics claim that the United Kingdom's decision to stop investigating BAE's conduct shows that it has put commercial interests before ethics. They also argue that the United Kingdom has given in to Saudi blackmail—the Saudis had apparently threatened to withdraw cooperation in the fight against terrorism if the SFO continued its investigation.[a] Although it might be in the public interest to suspend investigations of an ally's past unethical conduct during wartime, opponents contend that the United Kingdom should not allow BAE to continue profiting from its unethical practices.

The Allegedly Unethical Conduct

The conduct that has caused so much controversy for BAE is the billions of dollars in secret payments BAE has made to Saudi Arabia during the last twenty years. The questionable payments appear to be connected to the $80 billion in contracts that the company has made with the Saudis to supply fighter jets, advanced weapons systems, and other military goods. BAE made payments to accounts in Switzerland, the Caribbean, and elsewhere—including the United States. It attempted to keep these payments secret and claims that they were reimbursements for travel expenses.

a. "Saudis Buy Eurofighters from UK," BBC News, September 17, 2007; see news.bbc.co.uk/2/hi/business/6998774.stm.

Saudi prince Bandar bin Sultan, who is the son of the crown prince and former ambassador to the United States, is the head of the Saudi National Security Council. In February 2008, Prince Bandar was publicly accused of threatening to hold back information about suicide bombers and terrorists to get the United Kingdom to stop investigating BAE. The prince also faces accusations that he himself took more than $2 billion in secret payments from BAE.[b]

The United States Steps In

BAE generates a substantial amount of revenue in the United States. In 2007, despite controversy over its conduct, BAE bought out Florida-based Armor Holdings, the maker of the armored Humvees used in the Iraq war, for $4.1 billion. BAE seeks to tap into the demand from the American military for vehicles in Iraq and other war zones.

The U.S. Department of Justice (DOJ) became interested in BAE because the company used the U.S. banking system to transfer regular payments to accounts at Riggs Bank in Washington, D.C., that were controlled by Prince Bandar.[c] The DOJ then launched its own investigation into the possibly illegal payments that BAE made to Prince Bandar of Saudi Arabia to secure arms contracts.[d]

The U.S. government's action of asserting jurisdiction (legal authority) over a foreign company—BAE—to enforce the FCPA's antibribery provisions, stands out: BAE is the highest-profile corrupt practices case to date. It marks a shift in policy that indicates the United States is now willing to take on corporate corruption on a global level, even when the United States was not directly involved in the situation or contract.

FOR CRITICAL ANALYSIS   What should the United States do if Saudi Arabia threatens to withdraw its support in the war against terrorism if prosecuted for violating the FCPA?

b. Marlena Telvick, "U.S. Law Is Directed at Global Corruption," *International Herald Tribune*, November 26, 2007. David Leigh and Rob Evans, "BAE: Secret Papers Reveal Threats from Saudi Prince," *The Guardian*, February 15, 2008.
c. "US to probe BAE over Corruption," BBC News, June 26, 2007.
d. "Investigating BAE–Saudi Weapons Deal," *The Boston Globe*, June 17, 2007.

Reviewing . . . Ethics and Business Decision Making

Isabel Arnett was promoted to CEO of Tamik, Inc., a pharmaceutical company that manufactures a vaccine called Kafluk, which supposedly provides some defense against bird flu. The company began marketing Kafluk throughout Asia. After numerous media reports that bird flu could soon become a worldwide epidemic, the demand for Kafluk increased, sales soared, and Tamik earned record profits. Tamik's CEO, Arnett, then began receiving disturbing reports from Southeast Asia that in some patients, Kafluk had caused psychiatric disturbances, including severe hallucinations, and heart and lung problems. Arnett was informed that six children in Japan had committed suicide by jumping out of windows after receiving the vaccine. To cover up the story and prevent negative publicity, Arnett instructed Tamik's partners in Asia to offer cash to the Japanese families whose children had died in exchange for their silence. Arnett also refused to authorize additional research within the company to study the potential side effects of Kafluk. Using the information presented in the chapter, answer the following questions.

1. This scenario illustrates one of the main reasons why ethical problems occur in business. What is that reason?

2. Would a person who adheres to the principle of rights consider it ethical for Arnett not to disclose potential safety concerns and to refuse to perform additional research on Kafluk? Why or why not?

3. If Kafluk prevented fifty Asian people who were infected with bird flu from dying, would Arnett's conduct in this situation be ethical under a utilitarian model of ethics? Why or why not?

4. Did Tamik or Arnett violate the Foreign Corrupt Practices Act in this scenario? Why or why not?

Key Terms

backdating 48	cost-benefit analysis 42	utilitarianism 42
business ethics 37	ethical reasoning 40	
categorical imperative 41	ethics 37	
corporate social	moral minimum 46	
responsibility 42	principle of rights 42	

Chapter Summary

Business Ethics
(See pages 37–40.)

1. Ethics can be defined as the study of what constitutes right or wrong behavior. Business ethics focuses on how moral and ethical principles are applied in the business context.

2. *Reasons for ethical problems*—One of the most pervasive reasons why ethical breaches occur is the desire to increase sales (or not lose them), thereby increasing profits (and for corporations, market value). Some people believe that a corporation's only goal should be profit maximization. Even if this is true, executives should distinguish between short-run and long-run profit goals and focus on maximizing profits over the long run because only long-run profit maximization is consistent with business ethics.

3. *Behavior of owners and managers*—Management's commitment and behavior are essential in creating an ethical workplace. Management's behavior, more than anything else, sets the ethical tone of a firm and influences the behavior of employees.

**Business Ethics—
Continued**

4. *Ethical trade-offs*—Management constantly faces ethical trade-offs because firms have ethical and legal duties to a number of groups, including shareholders and employees.

**Approaches to
Ethical Reasoning**
(See pages 40–46.)

1. *Duty-based ethics*—Ethics based on religious beliefs; philosophical reasoning, such as that of Immanuel Kant; and the basic rights of human beings (the principle of rights). A potential problem for those who support this approach is deciding which rights are more important in a given situation. Management constantly faces ethical conflicts and trade-offs when considering all those affected by a business decision.

2. *Outcome-based ethics (utilitarianism)*—Ethics based on philosophical reasoning, such as that of John Stuart Mill. Applying this theory requires a cost-benefit analysis, weighing the negative effects against the positive and deciding which course of conduct produces the best outcome.

3. *Corporate social responsibility*—A number of theories based on the idea that corporations can and should act ethically and be accountable to society for their actions. These include the stakeholder approach and corporate citizenship.

4. *Ethical codes*—Most large firms have ethical codes or policies and training programs to help employees determine whether certain actions are ethical. In addition, the Sarbanes-Oxley Act requires firms to set up confidential systems so that employees and others can report suspected illegal or unethical auditing or accounting practices.

**How the Law
Influences Business
Ethics**
(See pages 46–51.)

1. *The moral minimum*—Lawful behavior is a moral minimum. The law has its limits, though, and some actions may be legal but not ethical. The law cannot control all business behavior (such as the backdating of stock options).

2. *Legal uncertainties*—It may be difficult to predict with certainty whether particular actions are legal, given the numerous and frequent changes in the laws regulating business and the "gray areas" in the law.

**Making Ethical
Business Decisions**
(See pages 51–52.)

Although it can be difficult for businesspersons to ensure that all employees make ethical business decisions, it is crucial in today's legal environment. Doing the right thing pays off in the long run, both in terms of increasing profits and in terms of avoiding negative publicity and the potential for bankruptcy (such as Enron). Each employee should be taught to evaluate her or his action using guidelines set forth by the company. We provide a set of six guidelines to make ethical business decisions on pages 51–52.

**Business Ethics
on a Global Level**
(See pages 52–55.)

Businesses must take account of the many cultural, religious, and legal differences among nations. Notable differences relate to the role of women in society, employment laws governing workplace conditions, and the practice of giving side payments to foreign officials to secure favorable contracts.

For Review

1. What is business ethics and why is it important?
2. How can business leaders encourage their companies to act ethically?
3. How do duty-based ethical standards differ from outcome-based ethical standards?
4. What are six guidelines that an employee can use to evaluate whether his or her actions are ethical?
5. What types of ethical issues might arise in the context of international business transactions?

2–1. Business Ethics. Some business ethicists maintain that whereas personal ethics has to do with "right" or "wrong" behavior, business ethics is concerned with "appropriate" behavior. In other words, ethical behavior in business has less to do with moral principles than with what society deems to be appropriate behavior in the business context. Do you agree with this distinction? Do personal and business ethics ever overlap? Should personal ethics play any role in business ethical decision making?

Question with Sample Answer

 2–2. If a firm engages in "ethical" behavior solely for the purpose of gaining profits from the goodwill it generates, the "ethical" behavior is essentially a means toward a self-serving end (profits and the accumulation of wealth). In this situation, is the firm acting unethically in any way? Should motive or conduct carry greater weight on the ethical scales in this situation?

For a sample answer to Question 2–2, go to Appendix I at the end of this text.

2–3. Business Ethics and Public Opinion. Assume that you are a high-level manager for a shoe manufacturer. You know that your firm could increase its profit margin by producing shoes in Indonesia, where you could hire women for $40 a month to assemble them. You also know, however, that human rights advocates recently accused a competing shoe manufacturer of engaging in exploitative labor practices because the manufacturer sold shoes made by Indonesian women working for similarly low wages. You personally do not believe that paying $40 a month to Indonesian women is unethical because you know that in their impoverished country, $40 a month is a better-than-average wage rate. Assuming that the decision is yours to make, should you have the shoes manufactured in Indonesia and make higher profits for your company? Or should you avoid the risk of negative publicity and the consequences of that publicity for the firm's reputation and subsequent profits? Are there other alternatives? Discuss fully.

2–4. Ethical Decision Making. Shokun Steel Co. owns many steel plants. One of its plants is much older than the others. Equipment at the old plant is outdated and inefficient, and the costs of production at that plant are now twice as high as at any of Shokun's other plants. Shokun cannot increase the price of its steel because of competition, both domestic and international. The plant employs more than a thousand workers; it is located in Twin Firs, Pennsylvania, which has a population of about forty-five thousand. Shokun is contemplating whether to close the

plant. What factors should the firm consider in making its decision? Will the firm violate any ethical duties if it closes the plant? Analyze these questions from the two basic perspectives on ethical reasoning discussed in this chapter.

Case Problem with Sample Answer

 2–5. Eden Electrical, Ltd., owned twenty-five appliance stores throughout Israel, at least some of which sold refrigerators made by Amana Co. Eden bought the appliances from Amana's Israeli distributor, Pan El A/Yesh Shem, which approached Eden about taking over the distributorship. Eden representatives met with Amana executives. The executives made assurances about Amana's good faith, its hope of having a long-term business relationship with Eden, and its willingness to have Eden become its exclusive distributor in Israel. Eden signed a distributorship agreement and paid Amana $2.4 million. Amana failed to deliver this amount in inventory to Eden, continued selling refrigerators to other entities for the Israeli market, and represented to others that it was still looking for a long-term distributor. Less than three months after signing the agreement with Eden, Amana terminated it, without explanation. Eden filed a suit in a federal district court against Amana, alleging fraud. The court awarded Eden $12.1 million in damages. Is this amount warranted? Why or why not? How does this case illustrate why business ethics is important? [*Eden Electrical, Ltd. v. Amana Co.*, 370 F.3d 824 (8th Cir. 2004)]

After you have answered Problem 2–5, compare your answer with the sample answer given on the Web site that accompanies this text. Go to www.cengage.com/blaw/let, select "Chapter 2," and click on "Case Problem with Sample Answer."

2–6. Ethical Conduct. Richard Fraser was an "exclusive career insurance agent" under a contract with Nationwide Mutual Insurance Co. Fraser leased computer hardware and software from Nationwide for his business. During a dispute between Nationwide and the Nationwide Insurance Independent Contractors Association, an organization representing Fraser and other exclusive career agents, Fraser prepared a letter to Nationwide's competitors asking whether they were interested in acquiring the represented agents' policyholders. Nationwide obtained a copy of the letter and searched its electronic file server for e-mail indicating that the letter had been sent. It found a stored e-mail that Fraser had sent to a co-worker indicating that the letter had been sent to at least one competitor. The e-mail was retrieved from the co-worker's file of already received and discarded messages stored on the server. When Nationwide canceled its contract with Fraser, he filed a suit in a federal district court against the firm, alleging, among other things, violations of various federal laws that prohibit the interception of electronic communications during transmission. In whose favor should the court rule, and why? Did Nationwide act ethically in retrieving the e-mail? Explain. [*Fraser v. Nationwide Mutual Insurance Co.,* 352 F.3d 107 (3d Cir. 2004)]

2–7. Ethical Conduct. Ernest Price suffered from sickle-cell anemia. In 1997, Price asked Dr. Ann Houston, his physician, to prescribe OxyContin, a strong narcotic, for the pain. Over the next several years, Price saw at least ten different physicians at ten different clinics in two cities, and used seven pharmacies in three cities, to obtain and fill simultaneous prescriptions for OxyContin. In March 2001, when Houston learned of these activities, she refused to write more prescriptions for Price. As other physicians became aware of Price's actions, they also stopped writing his prescriptions. Price filed a suit in a Mississippi state court against Purdue Pharma Co. and other producers and distributors of OxyContin, as well as his physicians and the pharmacies that had filled the prescriptions. Price alleged negligence, among other things, claiming that OxyContin's addictive nature caused him injury and that this was the defendants' fault. The defendants argued that Price's claim should be dismissed because it arose from his own wrongdoing. Who should be held *legally* liable? Should any of the parties be considered *ethically* responsible? Why or why not? [*Price v. Purdue Pharma Co.,* 920 So.2d 479 (Miss. 2006)]

2–8. Ethical Leadership. In 1999, Andrew Fastow, chief financial officer of Enron Corp., asked Merrill Lynch, an investment firm, to participate in a bogus sale of three barges so that Enron could record earnings of $12.5 million from the sale. Through a third entity, Fastow bought the barges back within six months and paid Merrill for its participation. Five Merrill employees were convicted of conspiracy to commit wire fraud, in part, on an "honest services" theory. Under this theory, an employee deprives his or her employer of "honest services" when the employee promotes his or her own interests, rather than the interests of the employer. Four of the employees appealed to the U.S. Court of Appeals for the Fifth Circuit, arguing that this charge did not apply to the conduct in which they engaged. The court agreed, reasoning that the barge deal was conducted to benefit Enron, not to enrich the Merrill employees at Enron's expense. Meanwhile, Kevin Howard, chief financial officer of Enron Broadband Services (EBS), engaged in "Project Braveheart," which enabled EBS to show

earnings of $111 million in 2000 and 2001. Braveheart involved the sale of an interest in the future revenue of a video-on-demand venture to nCube, a small technology firm, which was paid for its help when EBS bought the interest back. Howard was convicted of wire fraud, in part, on the "honest services" theory. He filed a motion to vacate his conviction on the same basis that the Merrill employees had argued. Did Howard act unethically? Explain. Should the court grant his motion? Discuss. [*United States v. Howard,* 471 F.Supp.2d 772 (S.D.Tex. 2007)]

A Question of Ethics

2–9. Steven Soderbergh is the Academy Award–winning director of *Traffic, Erin Brockovich,* and many other films. CleanFlicks, LLC, filed a suit in a federal district court against Soderbergh, fifteen other directors, and the Directors Guild of America. The plaintiff asked the court to rule that it had the right to sell DVDs of the defendants' films altered without the defendants' consent to delete scenes of "sex, nudity, profanity and gory violence." CleanFlicks sold or rented the edited DVDs under the slogan "It's About Choice" to consumers, sometimes indirectly through retailers. It would not sell to retailers that made unauthorized copies of the edited films. The defendants, with DreamWorks, LLC, and seven other movie studios that own the copyrights to the films, filed a counterclaim against CleanFlicks and others engaged in the same business, alleging copyright infringement. Those filing the counterclaim asked the court to enjoin (prevent) CleanFlicks and the others from making and marketing altered versions of the films. [*CleanFlicks of Colorado, LLC v. Soderbergh,* 433 F.Supp.2d 1236 (D.Colo. 2006)]

1. Movie studios often edit their films to conform to content and other standards and sell the edited versions to network television and other commercial buyers. In this case, however, the studios objected when CleanFlicks edited the films and sold the altered versions directly to consumers. Similarly, CleanFlicks made unauthorized copies of the studios' DVDs to edit the films, but objected to others' making unauthorized copies of the altered versions. Is there anything unethical about these apparently contradictory positions? Why or why not?

2. CleanFlicks and its competitors asserted, among other things, that they were making "fair use" of the studios' copyrighted works. They argued that by their actions "they are criticizing the objectionable content commonly found in current movies and that they are providing more socially acceptable alternatives to enable families to view the

films together, without exposing children to the presumed harmful effects emanating from the objectionable content." If you were the judge, how would you view this argument? Is a court the appropriate forum for making determinations of public or social policy? Explain.

Video Question

2–10. Go to this text's Web site at **www.cengage.com/blaw/let** and select "Chapter 2." Click on "Video Questions" and view the video titled *Ethics: Business Ethics an Oxymoron?* Then answer the following questions.

1. According to the instructor in the video, what is the primary reason that businesses act ethically?
2. Which of the two approaches to ethical reasoning that were discussed in the chapter seems to have had more influence on the instructor in the discussion of how business activities are related to societies? Explain your answer.
3. The instructor asserts that "[i]n the end, it is the unethical behavior that becomes costly, and conversely, ethical behavior creates its own competitive advantage." Do you agree with this statement? Why or why not?

Interacting with the Internet

For updated links to resources available on the Web, as well as a variety of other materials, visit this text's Web site at

www.cengage.com/blaw/let

You can find articles on issues relating to shareholders and corporate accountability at the Corporate Governance Web site. Go to

www.corpgov.net

For an example of an online group that focuses on corporate activities from the perspective of corporate social responsibility, go to

www.corpwatch.org

Global Exchange offers information on global business activities, including some of the ethical issues stemming from those activities, at

www.globalexchange.org

PRACTICAL INTERNET EXERCISES

Go to this text's Web site at **www.cengage.com/blaw/let**, select "Chapter 2," and click on "Practical Internet Exercises." There you will find the following Internet research exercises that you can perform to learn more about the topics covered in this chapter.

Practical Internet Exercise 2–1: LEGAL PERSPECTIVE—**Ethics in Business**
Practical Internet Exercise 2–2: MANAGEMENT PERSPECTIVE—**Environmental Self-Audits**

BEFORE THE TEST

Go to this text's Web site at **www.cengage.com/blaw/let**, select "Chapter 2," and click on "Interactive Quizzes." You will find a number of interactive questions relating to this chapter.

Chapter 3

Courts and Alternative Dispute Resolution

CHAPTER OBJECTIVES

After reading this chapter, you should be able to answer the following questions:

1. What is judicial review? How and when was the power of judicial review established?

2. Before a court can hear a case, it must have jurisdiction. Over what must it have jurisdiction? How are the courts applying traditional jurisdictional concepts to cases involving Internet transactions?

3. What is the difference between a trial court and an appellate court?

4. In a lawsuit, what are the pleadings? What is discovery, and how does electronic discovery differ from traditional discovery? What is electronic filing?

5. How are online forums being used to resolve disputes?

CONTENTS

" The Judicial Department comes home in its effects to every man's fireside: it passes on his property, his reputation, his life, his all. "

— JOHN MARSHALL,
1755–1835 (Chief Justice of the United States Supreme Court, 1801–1835)

As Chief Justice John Marshall remarked in the chapter-opening quotation, ultimately, we are all affected by what the courts say and do. This is particularly true in the business world—nearly every businessperson will face either a potential or an actual lawsuit at some time or another. For this reason, anyone contemplating a career in business will benefit from an understanding of court systems in the United States, including the mechanics of lawsuits.

In this chapter, after examining the judiciary's overall role in the American governmental scheme, we discuss some basic requirements that must be met before a party may bring a lawsuit before a particular court. We then look at the court systems of the United States in some detail and, to clarify judicial procedures, follow a hypothetical case through a state court system. The chapter concludes with an overview of some alternative methods of settling disputes, including methods for settling disputes in online forums.

THE JUDICIARY'S ROLE IN AMERICAN GOVERNMENT

As you learned in Chapter 1, the body of American law includes the federal and state constitutions, statutes passed by legislative bodies, administrative law, and the case decisions and legal principles that form the common law. These laws would be meaningless, however, without the courts to interpret and apply them. This is the essential role of the judiciary—the courts—in the American governmental system: to interpret and apply the law.

In New York City, the federal courthouse (left) and the New York State Court of Appeals (right). Are the federal courts superior to the state courts?
(Left: Wally Gobetz/ Flickr/Creative Commons; right: Courtesy of New York State Court of Appeals)

Judicial Review

As the branch of government entrusted with interpreting the laws, the judiciary can decide, among other things, whether the laws or actions of the other two branches are constitutional. The process for making such a determination is known as **judicial review.** The power of judicial review enables the judicial branch to act as a check on the other two branches of government, in line with the checks-and-balances system established by the U.S. Constitution. (Judicial review can also be found in other countries—see this chapter's *Beyond Our Borders* feature.)

JUDICIAL REVIEW
The process by which a court decides on the constitutionality of legislative enactments and actions of the executive branch.

The Origins of Judicial Review in the United States

The power of judicial review was not mentioned in the Constitution, but the concept was not new at the time the nation was founded. Indeed, before 1789 state courts had already overturned state legislative acts that conflicted with state constitutions. Additionally, many of the founders expected the United States Supreme Court to assume a similar role with respect to the federal Constitution. Alexander Hamilton and James Madison both emphasized the importance of judicial review in their essays urging the adoption of the new Constitution. When was the doctrine of judicial review established? See this chapter's *Landmark in the Legal Environment* feature on page 64 for the answer.

BASIC JUDICIAL REQUIREMENTS

Before a court can hear a lawsuit, certain requirements must first be met. These requirements relate to jurisdiction, venue, and standing to sue. We examine each of these important concepts here.

Jurisdiction

In Latin, *juris* means "law," and *diction* means "to speak." Thus, "the power to speak the law" is the literal meaning of the term **jurisdiction.** Before any court can hear a case, it must have jurisdiction over the person (or company) against whom the suit is brought (the defendant) or over the property involved in the suit. The court must also have jurisdiction over the subject matter.

JURISDICTION
The authority of a court to hear and decide a specific case.

The concept of judicial review was pioneered by the United States. Some maintain that one of the reasons the doctrine was readily accepted in this country was that it fit well with the checks and balances designed by the founders. Today, all established constitutional democracies have some form of judicial review—the power to rule on the constitutionality of laws—but its form varies from country to country.

For example, Canada's Supreme Court can exercise judicial review but is barred from doing so if a law includes a provision explicitly prohibiting such review. In France, the Constitutional Council rules on the constitutionality of laws *before* the laws take effect. Laws can be referred to the council for prior review by the president, the prime minister, and the heads of the two chambers of parliament. Prior review is also an option in Germany and Italy, if requested by the national or a regional government. In contrast, the United States Supreme Court does not give advisory opinions; the Supreme Court will render a decision only when there is an actual dispute concerning an issue.

Members of the Constitutional Council of France. The Council rules on the constitutionality of laws before the laws take effect. Does the United States have a similar system?
(Photo Courtesy of the Conseil Constitutionnel)

FOR CRITICAL ANALYSIS   In any country in which a constitution sets forth the basic powers and structure of government, some governmental body has to decide whether laws enacted by the government are consistent with that constitution. Why might the courts be best suited to handle this task? What might be a better alternative?

Jurisdiction over Persons   Generally, a court can exercise personal jurisdiction (*in personam* jurisdiction) over any person or business that resides in a certain geographic area. A state trial court, for example, normally has jurisdictional authority over residents (including businesses) in a particular area of the state, such as a county or district. A state's highest court (often called the state supreme court)[1] has jurisdiction over all residents of that state.

Jurisdiction over Nonresident Defendants   In addition, under the authority of a state **long arm statute,** a court can exercise personal jurisdiction over certain out-of-state defendants based on activities that took place within the state. Before exercising long arm jurisdiction over a nonresident, however, the court must be convinced that the defendant had sufficient contacts, or *minimum contacts,* with the state to justify the jurisdiction.[2] Generally, this means that the defendant must have enough of a connection to the state for the judge to conclude that it is fair for the state to exercise power over the defendant. If an out-of-state defendant caused an automobile accident or sold defective goods within the state, for instance, a court will usually find that minimum contacts exist to exercise jurisdiction over that defendant.

LONG ARM STATUTE

A state statute that permits a state to obtain personal jurisdiction over nonresident defendants. A defendant must have certain "minimum contacts" with that state for the statute to apply.

---

1. As will be discussed shortly, a state's highest court is frequently referred to as the state supreme court, but there are exceptions. For example, the court that is labeled the supreme court in New York is actually a trial court.

2. The minimum-contacts standard was established in *International Shoe Co. v. State of Washington,* 326 U.S. 310, 66 S.Ct. 154, 90 L.Ed. 95 (1945).

The *Marbury v. Madison* [a] decision is widely viewed as a cornerstone of constitutional law. When Thomas Jefferson defeated John Adams in the presidential election of 1800, Adams feared the Jeffersonians' antipathy toward business and also toward a strong national government. Adams thus rushed to "pack" the judiciary with loyal Federalists (those who believed in a strong national government) by appointing what came to be called "midnight judges" just before Jefferson took office. All of the fifty-nine judicial appointment letters had to be certified and delivered, but Adams's secretary of state (John Marshall) was only able to deliver forty-two of them by the time Jefferson took over as president. Jefferson refused to order his secretary of state, James Madison, to deliver the remaining commissions.

Marshall's Dilemma

William Marbury and three others to whom the commissions had not been delivered sought a writ of *mandamus* (an order directing a government official to fulfill a duty) from the United States Supreme Court, as authorized by the Judiciary Act of 1789. As fate would have it, John Marshall (Adams's secretary of state) had just been appointed as chief justice of the Supreme Court. Marshall faced a dilemma: If he ordered the commissions delivered, the new secretary of state (Madison) could simply refuse to deliver them—and the Court had no way to compel action. At the same time, if Marshall merely allowed the new administration to do as it wished, the Court's power would be severely eroded.

Marshall's Decision

Marshall masterfully fashioned his decision to enlarge the power of the Supreme Court by affirming the Court's power of judicial review.

a. 5 U.S. (1 Cranch) 137, 2 L.Ed. 60 (1803).

He stated, "It is emphatically the province and duty of the Judicial Department to say what the law is. . . . If two laws conflict with each other, the courts must decide on the operation of each. . . . So if the law be in opposition to the Constitution . . . [t]he Court must determine which of these conflicting rules governs the case."

Marshall's decision did not require anyone to do anything. He concluded that the highest court did not have the power to issue a writ of *mandamus* in this particular case. Although the Judiciary Act of 1789 specified that the Supreme Court could issue writs of *mandamus* as part of its original jurisdiction, Article III of the U.S. Constitution, which spelled out the Court's original jurisdiction, did not mention writs of *mandamus*. Because Congress did not have the right to expand the Supreme Court's jurisdiction, this section of the Judiciary Act was unconstitutional—and thus void. The decision still stands today as a judicial and political masterpiece.

APPLICATION TO TODAY'S LEGAL ENVIRONMENT

Since the *Marbury v. Madison* decision, the power of judicial review has remained unchallenged and today is exercised by both federal and state courts. If the courts did not have the power of judicial review, the constitutionality of Congress's acts could not be challenged in court—a congressional statute would remain law until changed by Congress. The courts of other countries that have adopted a constitutional democracy often cite this decision as a justification for judicial review.

RELEVANT WEB SITES

To locate information on the Web concerning the *Marbury v. Madison* decision, go to this text's Web site at **www.cengage.com/blaw/let**, select "Chapter 3," and click on "URLs for Landmarks."

Similarly, a state may exercise personal jurisdiction over a nonresident defendant who is sued for breaching a contract that was formed within the state, even when that contract was negotiated over the phone or through correspondence. EXAMPLE #1 Nick Mileti, a resident of California, co-produced a movie called *Streamers* and organized a corporation, Streamers International Distributors, Inc., to distribute the film. Joseph Cole, a resident of Ohio, bought two hundred shares of Streamers stock and loaned the firm $475,000, which he borrowed from an Ohio bank. The film was unsuccessful. Mileti agreed to repay Cole's loan in a contract arranged through phone calls and correspondence between California and Ohio. When Mileti did not repay the loan, the bank sued Cole, who in turn filed a suit against Mileti in a federal district court in Ohio. The court held that Mileti—through phone calls and letters—had sufficient contacts with the state of Ohio for the court to exercise jurisdiction over him.[3]

3. *Cole v. Mileti*, 133 F.3d 433 (6th Cir. 1998).

Personal Jurisdiction over Corporations Because corporations are considered legal persons,[4] courts use the same principles to determine whether it is fair to exercise jurisdiction over a corporation. Usually, a corporation has met the minimum-contacts requirement if it does business within the state or has an office or branch within the state. **EXAMPLE #2** Suppose that a Maine corporation has a branch office or a manufacturing plant in Georgia. Does this Maine corporation have sufficient minimum contacts with the state of Georgia to allow a Georgia court to exercise jurisdiction over it? Yes, it does. If the Maine corporation advertises and sells its products in Georgia, those activities will also likely suffice to meet the minimum-contacts requirement, even if the corporate headquarters are located in a different state.□

Some corporations, however, do not sell or advertise products or place any goods in the stream of commerce. Determining what constitutes minimum contacts in these situations can be more difficult, as the following case—involving a resort hotel in Mexico and a hotel guest from New Jersey—illustrates.

---

4. In the eyes of the law, corporations are "legal persons"—entities that can sue and be sued. See Chapter 15.

Case 3.1   Mastondrea v. Occidental Hotels Management S.A.

Superior Court of New Jersey, Appellate Division, 2007.
391 N.J.Super. 261, 918 A.2d 27.
lawlibrary.rutgers.edu/search.shtml[a]

BACKGROUND AND FACTS Libgo Travel, Inc., in Ramsey, New Jersey, with Allegro Resorts Management Corporation (ARMC), a marketing agency in Miami, Florida, placed an ad in the *Newark Star Ledger,* a newspaper in Newark, New Jersey, to tout vacation packages for accommodations at the Royal Hideaway Playacar, an all-inclusive resort hotel in Quintana

a. In the "SEARCH THE N.J. COURTS DECISIONS" section, type "Mastondrea" in the box, and click on "Search!" In the result, click on the case name to access the opinion. Rutgers University Law School in Camden, New Jersey, maintains this Web site.

Roo, Mexico. ARMC is part of Occidental Hotels Management, B.V., a Netherlands corporation that owns the hotel with Occidental Hoteles Management S.A., a Spanish company. In response to the ad, Amanda Mastondrea, a New Jersey resident, bought one of the packages through Liberty Travel, a chain of travel agencies in the eastern United States that Libgo owns and operates. On June 16, 2003, at the resort, Mastondrea slipped and fell on a wet staircase, breaking her ankle. She filed a suit in a New Jersey state court against the hotel, its owners, and others, alleging negligence. The defendants asked the court to dismiss the suit on the ground that it did not have personal jurisdiction over them. The court ruled in part that it had jurisdiction over the hotel. The hotel appealed this ruling to a state intermediate appellate court.

IN THE WORDS OF THE COURT . . . *PAYNE,* J.A.D. [Judge, Appellate Division]

*   *   *   *

It is unquestionably true that the Hotel has no direct presence in New Jersey. *   *   * The Hotel's operations are located in Quintana Roo, Mexico. The Hotel is not registered, licensed or otherwise authorized to do business in New Jersey. It has no registered agent in this state for service of process, and it pays no state taxes. The Hotel maintains no business address here, it has never owned property or maintained any bank accounts in this state, and it has no employees in New Jersey.

However, *   *   * "Tour Operator Agreements" between the Hotel and Libgo *   *   * provide that the Hotel will allot a specific number of rooms at its resort to Libgo at agreed-upon rates. Libgo, as "tour operator," is then authorized by the Hotel to book those rooms on behalf of Libgo's customers. Pursuant to the contract, Libgo is required to provide the Hotel with weekly sales reports listing the number of rooms booked by

CASE 3.1–CONTINUED

CASE 3.1–CONTINUED

Libgo and the rates at which those rooms were booked. It must also confirm all reservations in a writing sent to the Hotel.

Courts have generally sustained the exercise of personal jurisdiction over a defendant who, as a party to a contract, has had some connection with the forum state [the state in which the lawsuit is filed] or who should have anticipated that his conduct would have significant effects in that state. Here, the Hotel entered into a contract with a New Jersey entity, Libgo, which agreed to solicit business for the Hotel and derived a profit from that solicitation through sales of vacation packages. Although Libgo's business extends beyond New Jersey and throughout much of the East Coast, at least part of its customer base resides in this state. Likewise, as a result of this contract, the Hotel purposefully and successfully sought vacationers from New Jersey, and it derived a profit from them. Therefore, the Hotel should have reasonably anticipated that its conduct would have significant effects in New Jersey. [Emphasis added.]

*   *   *   *

*   *   * Additional evidence of purposeful acts in New Jersey [include] *   *   * an ongoing, but undefined, relationship between the Hotel and [ARMC]. ARMC is a marketing organization that solicits business in the United States for the "Occidental Hotels & Resorts," a group of which the defendant Hotel is a part. ARMC *   *   * works closely with Libgo in developing marketing strategies for the Occidental Hotels & Resorts in the New Jersey area pursuant to cooperative marketing agreements between ARMC and Libgo.

*   *   *   *

*   *   * The defendant Hotel was featured, singly, [in 2003] in advertisements in the *Newark Star Ledger* on four occasions, including one in January *   *   * , prior to plaintiff's decision to book a vacation there.

We are satisfied *   *   * that *   *   * ARMC was operating [on behalf] of the Hotel when ARMC entered into cooperative marketing agreements with Libgo, and that ARMC's extensive contacts with Libgo in New Jersey regarding the marketing plan, together with the New Jersey fruits of that plan, can be attributed to the Hotel for jurisdictional purposes.

We are further persuaded that the *targeted advertising conducted pursuant to the cooperative marketing agreement on behalf of the Hotel provided the minimum contacts necessary to support* *   *   * *jurisdiction in this case.* [Emphasis added.]

DECISION AND REMEDY   The state intermediate appellate court affirmed the lower court's ruling. The appellate court concluded that the hotel had contacts with New Jersey, consisting of a tour operator contract and marketing activities through ARMC and Libgo, during the relevant time period and that, in response to the marketing, Mastondrea booked a vacation at the hotel. "This evidence was sufficient to support the assertion of *   *   * personal jurisdiction over the Hotel in this State."

WHAT IF THE FACTS WERE DIFFERENT?   If Mastondrea had not seen Libgo and Allegro's ad, but had bought a Royal Hideaway vacation package on the recommendation of a Liberty Travel agent, is it likely that the result in this case would have been different? Why or why not?

THE GLOBAL DIMENSION   What do the circumstances and the holding in this case suggest to a business firm that actively attempts to attract customers in a variety of jurisdictions?

Jurisdiction over Property   A court can also exercise jurisdiction over property that is located within its boundaries. This kind of jurisdiction is known as *in rem* jurisdiction, or "jurisdiction over the thing." **EXAMPLE #3** Suppose that a dispute arises over the ownership of a boat in dry dock in Fort Lauderdale, Florida. The boat is owned by an Ohio resident, over whom a Florida court normally cannot exercise personal jurisdiction. The other party to the dispute is a resident of Nebraska. In this situation, a lawsuit concerning the boat could be brought in a Florida state court on the basis of the court's *in rem* jurisdiction.□

Jurisdiction over Subject Matter   Jurisdiction over subject matter is a limitation on the types of cases a court can hear. In both the federal and state court systems, there are courts of *general* (unlimited) *jurisdiction* and courts of *limited jurisdiction*. An example of a court of general jurisdiction is a state trial court or a federal district court. An example of a state court of limited jurisdiction is a probate court. **Probate courts** are state courts that handle only matters relating to the transfer of a person's assets and obligations after that person's death, including matters relating to the custody and guardianship of children. An example of a federal court of limited subject-matter jurisdiction is a bankruptcy court. **Bankruptcy courts** handle only bankruptcy proceedings, which are governed by federal bankruptcy law (discussed in Chapter 13). In contrast, a court of general jurisdiction can decide a broad array of cases.

A court's jurisdiction over subject matter is usually defined in the statute or constitution creating the court. In both the federal and state court systems, a court's subject-matter jurisdiction can be limited not only by the subject of the lawsuit but also by the amount in controversy, by whether a case is a felony (a more serious type of crime) or a misdemeanor (a less serious type of crime), or by whether the proceeding is a trial or an appeal.

PROBATE COURT
A state court of limited jurisdiction that conducts proceedings relating to the settlement of a deceased person's estate.

BANKRUPTCY COURT
A federal court of limited jurisdiction that handles only bankruptcy proceedings, which are governed by federal bankruptcy law.

Original and Appellate Jurisdiction   The distinction between courts of original jurisdiction and courts of appellate jurisdiction normally lies in whether the case is being heard for the first time. Courts having original jurisdiction are courts of the first instance, or trial courts—that is, courts in which lawsuits begin, trials take place, and evidence is presented. In the federal court system, the *district courts* are trial courts. In the various state court systems, the trial courts are known by various names, as will be discussed shortly.

The key point here is that any court having original jurisdiction is normally known as a trial court. Courts having appellate jurisdiction act as reviewing courts, or appellate courts. In general, cases can be brought before appellate courts only on appeal from an order or a judgment of a trial court or other lower court.

Jurisdiction of the Federal Courts   Because the federal government is a government of limited powers, the jurisdiction of the federal courts is limited. Article III of the U.S. Constitution establishes the boundaries of federal judicial power. Section 2 of Article III states that "[t]he judicial Power shall extend to all Cases, in Law and Equity, arising under this Constitution, the Laws of the United States, and Treaties made, or which shall be made, under their Authority."

Federal Questions   Whenever a plaintiff's cause of action is based, at least in part, on the U.S. Constitution, a treaty, or a federal law, then a **federal question** arises, and the case comes under the judicial power of the federal courts. Any lawsuit involving a federal question can originate in a federal court. People who claim that their rights under the U.S. Constitution have been violated can begin their suits in a federal court. Note that most cases involving a federal question do not have to be tried in a federal court. The plaintiff can file the action in either a federal court or a state trial court (because the federal and state courts have *concurrent jurisdiction* over many matters, as will be discussed shortly).

FEDERAL QUESTION
A question that pertains to the U.S. Constitution, acts of Congress, or treaties. A federal question provides a basis for federal jurisdiction.

DIVERSITY OF CITIZENSHIP
Under Article III, Section 2, of the U.S. Constitution, a basis for federal district court jurisdiction over a lawsuit between (1) citizens of different states, (2) a foreign country and citizens of a state or of different states, or (3) citizens of a state and citizens or subjects of a foreign country. The amount in controversy must be more than $75,000 before a federal district court can take jurisdiction in such cases.

CONCURRENT JURISDICTION
Jurisdiction that exists when two different courts have the power to hear a case. For example, some cases can be heard in a federal or a state court.

EXCLUSIVE JURISDICTION
Jurisdiction that exists when a case can be heard only in a particular court or type of court.

Diversity of Citizenship   Federal district courts can also exercise original jurisdiction over cases involving **diversity of citizenship.** Such cases may arise between (1) citizens of different states, (2) a foreign country and citizens of a state or of different states, or (3) citizens of a state and citizens or subjects of a foreign country. The amount in controversy must be more than $75,000 before a federal court can take jurisdiction in such cases. For purposes of diversity jurisdiction, a corporation is a citizen of both the state in which it is incorporated and the state in which its principal place of business is located. A case involving diversity of citizenship can be filed in the appropriate federal district court, or, if the case starts in a state court, it can sometimes be transferred to a federal court. A large percentage of the cases filed in federal courts each year are based on diversity of citizenship.

Note that in a case based on a federal question, a federal court will apply federal law. In a case based on diversity of citizenship, however, a federal court will apply the relevant state law (which is often the law of the state in which the court sits).

Exclusive versus Concurrent Jurisdiction   When both federal and state courts have the power to hear a case, as is true in suits involving diversity of citizenship, **concurrent jurisdiction** exists. When cases can be tried only in federal courts or only in state courts, exclusive jurisdiction exists. Federal courts have **exclusive jurisdiction** in cases involving federal crimes, bankruptcy, patents, and copyrights; in suits against the United States; and in some areas of admiralty law (law governing transportation on ocean waters). States also have exclusive jurisdiction over certain subject matter—for example, divorce and adoption. The concepts of exclusive and concurrent jurisdiction are illustrated in Exhibit 3–1.

When concurrent jurisdiction exists, a party has a choice of whether to bring a suit in, for example, a federal or a state court. The party's lawyer will consider several factors in counseling the party as to which choice is preferable. The lawyer may prefer to litigate the case in a state court because he or she is more familiar with the state court's procedures, or perhaps the attorney believes that the state's judge or jury would be more sympathetic to the client and the case.

EXHIBIT 3–1 EXCLUSIVE AND CONCURRENT JURISDICTION

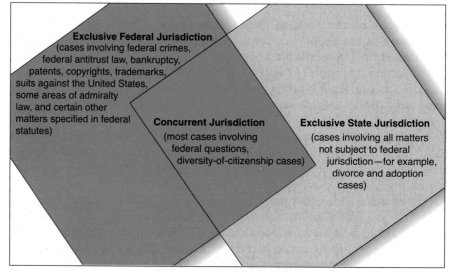

Exclusive Federal Jurisdiction
(cases involving federal crimes, federal antitrust law, bankruptcy, patents, copyrights, trademarks, suits against the United States, some areas of admiralty law, and certain other matters specified in federal statutes)

Concurrent Jurisdiction
(most cases involving federal questions, diversity-of-citizenship cases)

Exclusive State Jurisdiction
(cases involving all matters not subject to federal jurisdiction—for example, divorce and adoption cases)

Alternatively, the lawyer may advise the client to sue in federal court. Perhaps the state court's **docket** (the court's schedule listing the cases to be heard) is crowded, and the case could come to trial sooner in a federal court. Perhaps some feature of federal practice or procedure could offer an advantage in the client's case. Other important considerations include the law in the particular jurisdiction, how that law has been applied in the jurisdiction's courts, and what the results in similar cases have been in that jurisdiction.

DOCKET
The list of cases entered on a court's calendar and thus scheduled to be heard by the court.

Jurisdiction in Cyberspace

The Internet's capacity to bypass political and geographic boundaries undercuts the traditional basic limitations on a court's authority to exercise jurisdiction. These limits include a party's contacts with a court's geographic jurisdiction. As already discussed, for a court to compel a defendant to come before it, there must be at least minimum contacts—the presence of a salesperson within the state, for example. Are there sufficient minimum contacts if the defendant's only connection to a jurisdiction is an ad on the Web originating from a remote location?

The "Sliding-Scale" Standard Gradually, the courts are developing a standard—called a "sliding-scale" standard—for determining when the exercise of jurisdiction over an out-of-state defendant is proper. In developing this standard, the courts have identified three types of Internet business contacts: (1) substantial business conducted over the Internet (with contracts and sales, for example), (2) some interactivity through a Web site, and (3) passive advertising. Jurisdiction is proper for the first category, is improper for the third, and may or may not be appropriate for the second.[5] An Internet communication is typically considered passive if people have to voluntarily access it to read the message and active if it is sent to specific individuals.

In certain situations, even a single contact can satisfy the minimum-contacts requirement. **EXAMPLE #4** A Louisiana man, Daniel Crummey, purchased a used recreational vehicle (RV) from sellers in Texas after viewing numerous photos of the RV on eBay. The sellers' statements on eBay claimed that "everything works great on this RV and will provide comfort and dependability for years to come. This RV will go to Alaska and back without problems!" Crummey picked up the RV in Texas, but on the drive back to Louisiana, the RV quit working. He filed a lawsuit in Louisiana against the sellers alleging that the vehicle was defective. The sellers claimed that the Louisiana court lacked jurisdiction, but the court held that because the sellers had used eBay to market and sell the RV to a Louisiana buyer, jurisdiction was proper.[6]□

Today's entrepreneurs are often eager to establish Web sites to promote their products and solicit orders. Many of these individuals may not be aware that defendants can be sued in states in which they have never been physically present, provided they have had sufficient contacts with that state's residents over the Internet. Businesspersons who contemplate making their Web sites the least bit interactive should consult an attorney to find out whether by doing so they will be

---

5. For a leading case on this issue, see *Zippo Manufacturing Co. v. Zippo Dot Com, Inc.*, 952 F.Supp. 1119 (W.D.Pa. 1997).
6. *Crummey v. Morgan*, 965 So.2d 497 (La.App. 1 Cir. 2007).

subjecting themselves to jurisdiction in every state. Becoming informed about the extent of potential exposure to lawsuits in various locations is an important part of preventing litigation. ■

International Jurisdictional Issues   Because the Internet is global in scope, international jurisdictional issues understandably have come to the fore. What seems to be emerging in the world's courts is a standard that echoes the minimum-contacts requirement applied by the U.S. courts. Most courts are indicating that minimum contacts—doing business within the jurisdiction, for example—are enough to compel a defendant to appear and that a physical presence is not necessary. The effect of this standard is that a business firm has to comply with the laws in any jurisdiction in which it targets customers for its products. This situation is complicated by the fact that many countries' laws on particular issues—free speech, for example—are very different from U.S. laws.

EXAMPLE #5   Yahoo!, Inc., operates an online auction site on which Nazi memorabilia have been offered for sale. In France, the display of any objects representing symbols of Nazi ideology subjects the person or entity displaying such objects to both criminal and civil liability. The International League against Racism and Anti-Semitism filed a lawsuit in Paris against Yahoo for displaying Nazi memorabilia and offering them for sale via its Web site.

The French court asserted jurisdiction over Yahoo on the ground that the materials on the company's U.S.-based servers could be viewed on a Web site accessible in France. The French court ordered Yahoo to eliminate all Internet access in France to the Nazi memorabilia offered for sale through its online auctions. Yahoo then took the case to a federal district court in the United States, claiming that the French court's order violated the First Amendment. Although the federal district court ruled in favor of Yahoo, the U.S. Court of Appeals for the Ninth Circuit reversed. According to the appellate court, U.S. courts lacked personal jurisdiction over the French groups involved. The ruling leaves open the possibility that Yahoo, and anyone else who posts anything on the Internet, could be held answerable to the laws of any country in which the message might be received.[7] ■

Venue

VENUE

The geographic district in which a legal action is tried and from which the jury is selected.

Jurisdiction has to do with whether a court has authority to hear a case involving specific persons, property, or subject matter. **Venue**[8] is concerned with the most appropriate physical location for a trial. Two state courts (or two federal courts) may have the authority to exercise jurisdiction over a case, but it may be more appropriate or convenient to hear the case in one court than in the other.

Basically, the concept of venue reflects the policy that a court trying a suit should be in the geographic neighborhood (usually the county) where the incident leading to the lawsuit occurred or where the parties involved in the lawsuit reside. Venue in a civil case typically is where the defendant resides, whereas venue in a criminal case normally is where the crime occurred. Pretrial publicity or other factors, though, may require a change of venue to another community, especially

---

7. *Yahoo!, Inc. v. La Ligue Contre le Racisme et l'Antisemitisme,* 379 F.3d 1120 (9th Cir. 2004); on rehearing, *Yahoo!, Inc. v. La Ligue Contre le Racisme et l'Antisemitisme,* 433 F.3d 1199 (9th Cir. 2006); *cert.* denied, 126 S.Ct. 2332, 164 L.Ed.2d 841 (2006).

8. Pronounced *ven*-yoo.

in criminal cases when the defendant's right to a fair and impartial jury has been impaired. **EXAMPLE #6** Suppose that a defendant is charged with sexually abusing several teenagers from the local high school. One of the alleged victims is also the daughter of the city's mayor. The local newspaper publishes many reports about the sexual abuse scandal, some of which are not accurate. In this situation, a court will likely grant a defense request to change venue because the defendant's right to a fair and impartial trial in the local court may be impaired.□

Standing to Sue

Before a person can bring a lawsuit before a court, the party must have **standing to sue,** or a sufficient "stake" in the matter to justify seeking relief through the court system. In other words, to have standing, a party must have a legally protected and tangible interest at stake in the litigation. The party bringing the lawsuit must have suffered a harm, or have been threatened by a harm, as a result of the action about which she or he has complained. Standing to sue also requires that the controversy at issue be a **justiciable**[9] **controversy**—a controversy that is real and substantial, as opposed to hypothetical or academic.

EXAMPLE #7 To persuade DaimlerChrysler Corporation to build a $1.2 billion Jeep assembly plant in the area, the city of Toledo, Ohio, gave the company an exemption from local property tax for ten years, as well as a state franchise tax credit. Toledo taxpayers filed a lawsuit in state court claiming that the tax breaks violated the commerce clause in the U.S. Constitution. The taxpayers alleged that the tax exemption and credit injured them because they would have to pay higher taxes to cover the shortfall in tax revenues. The United States Supreme Court ruled that the taxpayers lacked standing to sue over the incentive program because their alleged injury was "conjectural or hypothetical" and, therefore, there was no justiciable controversy.[10] □

Note that in some situations a person may have standing to sue on behalf of another person, such as a minor or a mentally incompetent person. **EXAMPLE #8** Suppose that three-year-old Emma suffers serious injuries as a result of a defectively manufactured toy. Because Emma is a minor, her parent or legal guardian can bring a lawsuit on her behalf.□

The Jeep assembly plant in Toledo, Ohio, which was built after the makers of Jeep, the DaimlerChrysler Corporation, received substantial tax breaks and tax credits from state and city governments. Ohio residents complained that the tax breaks given to DaimlerChrysler would result in a higher tax burden for individuals. What did the United States Supreme Court conclude about whether taxpayers in this situation have standing to sue? (Photo Courtesy of the city of Toledo, Ohio.)

STANDING TO SUE
The requirement that an individual must have a sufficient stake in a controversy before he or she can bring a lawsuit. The plaintiff must demonstrate that he or she has been either injured or threatened with injury.

JUSTICIABLE CONTROVERSY
A controversy that is not hypothetical or academic but real and substantial; a requirement that must be satisfied before a court will hear a case.

THE STATE AND FEDERAL COURT SYSTEMS

As mentioned earlier in this chapter, each state has its own court system. Additionally, there is a system of federal courts. Although state court systems differ, Exhibit 3–2 on page 72 illustrates the basic organizational structure characteristic of the court systems in many states. The exhibit also shows how the federal court system is structured. We turn now to an examination of these court systems, beginning with the state courts. (See this chapter's *Insight into Ethics* feature on pages 72–73 for a discussion of the impact that the use of private judges and out-of-court settlements is having on the nation's court systems and our notions of justice.)

9. Pronounced jus-*tish*-uh-bul.
10. *DaimlerChrysler Corp., v. Cuno,* 547 U.S. 332, 126 S.Ct.1854, 164 L.Ed.2d 589 (2006).

EXHIBIT 3-2 FEDERAL COURTS AND STATE COURT SYSTEMS

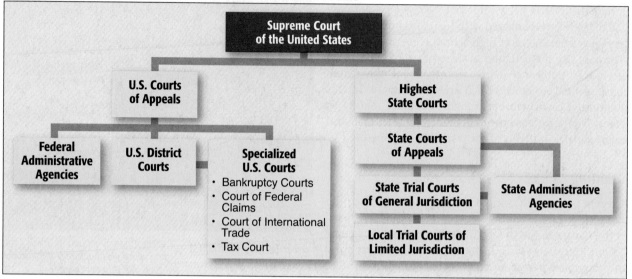

Supreme Court of the United States

U.S. Courts of Appeals

Highest State Courts

Federal Administrative Agencies

U.S. District Courts

Specialized U.S. Courts
- Bankruptcy Courts
- Court of Federal Claims
- Court of International Trade
- Tax Court

State Courts of Appeals

State Trial Courts of General Jurisdiction

State Administrative Agencies

Local Trial Courts of Limited Jurisdiction

Insight into Ethics

Implications of an increasingly private justice system

Downtown Houston boasts a relatively new courthouse with thirty-nine courtrooms, but more and more often, many of those courtrooms stand empty. Has litigation in Texas slowed down? Indeed, it has not—the courtrooms are empty because fewer civil lawsuits are going to trial. A similar situation is occurring in the federal courts. In the northern district of Florida, for example, the four federal judges presided over only a dozen civil trials in 2007. In 1984, more than 12,000 civil trials were heard in our federal courts. Today, only about 3,500 federal civil trials take place annually. University of Wisconsin law professor Mark Galanter has labeled this trend the "vanishing trial." Two developments in particular are contributing to the disappearance of civil trials—arbitration and private judges.

Arbitration Is One Cause

Since the 1980s, corporations have been eschewing the public court system and taking cases to arbitration instead. Every day millions of Americans sign arbitration agreements (discussed later in this chapter), often unknowingly committing themselves to allow private arbitrators to solve their disputes with employers and the corporations with which they do business, such as cell phone service providers.

This trend raises some troublesome ethical issues, however. For one thing, arbitration agreements may force consumers to travel long distances to participate in these private forums. Perhaps more disturbing is that the supposedly neutral arbitrators may actually be captive to the industries they serve. Arbitrators are paid handsomely and typically would like to serve again. Thus, they might be reluctant to rule against a company that is involved in a dispute. After all, the company may well need arbitrators to resolve a subsequent dispute, whereas the other party—a consumer or employee—is unlikely to need the arbitrators again.

Private Judges Are Another Cause

Another reason for the decline in the number of civil trials in our public courts is the growing use of private judges. A private judge, who is usually a retired judge, has the power to conduct trials and grant legal resolutions of disputes. Private judges increasingly are being used to resolve commercial disputes, as well as divorces and custody battles, for two reasons. One reason is that a case can be heard by a private judge much sooner than it would be heard in a public court. The other reason is that proceedings before a private judge can be kept secret.

In Ohio, for example, a state statute allows the parties to any civil action to have their dispute tried by a retired judge of their choosing who will make a decision in the matter.[11] Recently, though, private judging came under criticism in that state because private judges were conducting jury trials in county courtrooms at taxpayers' expense. A public judge, Nancy Margaret Russo, refused to give up jurisdiction over one case on the ground that private judges are not authorized to conduct jury trials. The Ohio Supreme Court agreed. As the state's highest court noted, private judging raises significant public-policy issues that the legislature needs to consider.[12]

One issue is that private judges charge relatively large fees. This means that litigants who are willing and able to pay the extra cost can have their case heard by a private judge long before they would be able to set a trial date in a regular court. Is it fair that those who cannot afford private judges should have to wait longer for justice? Similarly, is it ethical to allow parties to pay extra for secret proceedings before a private judge and thereby avoid the public scrutiny of a regular trial? Some even suggest that the use of private judges is leading to two different systems of justice.

A Threat to the Common Law System?

The decline in the number of civil trials may also be leading to the erosion of this country's common law system. As discussed in Chapter 1, courts are obligated to consider precedents—the decisions rendered in previous cases with similar facts and issues—when deciding the outcome of a dispute. If fewer disputes go to trial because they are arbitrated or heard by a private judge, then they will never become part of the body of cases and appeals that form the case law on that subject. With fewer precedents on which to draw, individuals and businesses will have less information about what constitutes appropriate business behavior in today's world. Furthermore, private dispute resolution does not allow our case law to keep up with new issues related to areas such as biotechnology and the online world. Thus, the long-term effects of the decline of public justice could be a weakening of the common law itself.

State Court Systems

Typically, a state court system will include several levels, or tiers, of courts. As indicated in Exhibit 3–2, state courts may include (1) trial courts of limited jurisdiction, (2) trial courts of general jurisdiction, (3) appellate courts, and (4) the state's highest court (often called the state supreme court). Generally, any person who is a party to a lawsuit has the opportunity to plead the case before a trial court and then, if he or she loses, before at least one level of appellate court. Finally, if the case involves a federal statute or federal constitutional issue, the decision of the state supreme court on that issue may be further appealed to the United States Supreme Court.

---

11. Ohio Revised Code Section 2701.10.

12. *State ex rel. Russo v. McDonnell,* 110 Ohio St.3d 144, 852 N.E.2d 145 (2006). (The term *ex rel.* is Latin for *ex relatione.* This phrase refers to an action brought on behalf of the state, by the attorney general, at the instigation of an individual who has a private interest in the matter.)

The states use various methods to select judges for their courts. Usually, voters elect judges, but sometimes judges are appointed. In Iowa, for example, the governor appoints judges, and then the general population decides whether to confirm their appointment in the next general election. The states usually specify the number of years that the judge will serve. In contrast, as you will read shortly, judges in the federal court system are appointed by the president of the United States and, if they are confirmed by the Senate, hold office for life—unless they engage in blatantly illegal conduct.

Trial Courts   Trial courts are exactly what their name implies—courts in which trials are held and testimony taken. State trial courts have either general or limited jurisdiction. Trial courts that have general jurisdiction as to subject matter may be called county, district, superior, or circuit courts.[13] The jurisdiction of these courts is often determined by the size of the county in which the court sits. State trial courts of general jurisdiction have jurisdiction over a wide variety of subjects, including both civil disputes and criminal prosecutions. (In some states, trial courts of general jurisdiction may hear appeals from courts of limited jurisdiction.)

Some courts of limited jurisdiction are called special inferior trial courts or minor judiciary courts. **Small claims courts** are inferior trial courts that hear only civil cases involving claims of less than a certain amount, such as $5,000 (the amount varies from state to state). Suits brought in small claims courts are generally conducted informally, and lawyers are not required (in a few states, lawyers are not even allowed). Another example of an inferior trial court is a local municipal court that hears mainly traffic cases. Decisions of small claims courts and municipal courts may sometimes be appealed to a state trial court of general jurisdiction. Other courts of limited jurisdiction as to subject matter include domestic relations courts, which handle primarily divorce actions and child-custody disputes, and probate courts, as mentioned earlier.

Appellate, or Reviewing, Courts   Every state has at least one court of appeals (appellate court, or reviewing court), which may be an intermediate appellate court or the state's highest court. About three-fourths of the states have intermediate appellate courts. Generally, courts of appeals do not conduct new trials, in which evidence is submitted to the court and witnesses are examined. Rather, an appellate court panel of three or more judges reviews the record of the case on appeal, which includes a transcript of the trial proceedings, and determines whether the trial court committed an error.

Usually, appellate courts focus on questions of law, not questions of fact. A **question of fact** deals with what really happened in regard to the dispute being tried—such as whether a party actually burned a flag. A **question of law** concerns the application or interpretation of the law—such as whether flag-burning is a form of speech protected by the First Amendment to the Constitution. Only a judge, not a jury, can rule on questions of law. Appellate courts normally defer to a trial court's findings on questions of fact because the trial court judge and jury were in a better position to evaluate testimony by directly observing witnesses' gestures, demeanor, and nonverbal behavior during the trial. At the

SMALL CLAIMS COURT
A special court in which parties may litigate small claims (such as $5,000 or less). Attorneys are not required in small claims courts and, in some states, are not allowed to represent the parties.

QUESTION OF FACT
In a lawsuit, an issue that involves only disputed facts, and not what the law is on a given point. Questions of fact are decided by the jury in a jury trial (by the judge if there is no jury).

QUESTION OF LAW
In a lawsuit, an issue involving the application or interpretation of a law. Only a judge, not a jury, can rule on questions of law.

---

13. The name in Ohio is court of common pleas; the name in New York is supreme court.

Child custody cases sometimes make national news, as this one did in 2007. After the death of Anna Nicole Smith—a former Playboy Playmate and actress—a number of disputes erupted over who would take custody of Smith's infant daughter. In this photo, attorneys ask the court for a DNA sample to be taken from Smith's body to assist the court in determining the identify of the child's father. Are child custody disputes normally heard by courts of general jurisdiction or courts of limited jurisdiction?
(AP Photo/Lou Toman/Pool)

appellate level, the judges review the written transcript of the trial, which does not include these nonverbal elements.

An appellate court will challenge a trial court's finding of fact only when the finding is clearly erroneous (that is, when it is contrary to the evidence presented at trial) or when there is no evidence to support the finding. **EXAMPLE #9** Suppose that a jury concluded that a manufacturer's product harmed the plaintiff but no evidence was submitted to the court to support that conclusion. In that situation, the appellate court would hold that the trial court's decision was erroneous.□ The options exercised by appellate courts will be discussed further later in this chapter.

Highest State Courts The highest appellate court in a state is usually called the supreme court but may be called by some other name. For example, in both New York and Maryland, the highest state court is called the court of appeals. The decisions of each state's highest court are final on all questions of state law. Only when issues of federal law are involved can a decision made by a state's highest court be overruled by the United States Supreme Court.

BE CAREFUL
The decisions of a state's highest court are final on questions of state law.

The Federal Court System

The federal court system is basically a three-tiered model consisting of (1) U.S. district courts (trial courts of general jurisdiction) and various courts of limited jurisdiction, (2) U.S. courts of appeals (intermediate courts of appeals), and (3) the United States Supreme Court. Unlike state court judges, who are usually elected, federal court judges—including the justices of the Supreme Court—are appointed by the president of the United States and confirmed by the U.S. Senate. All federal judges receive lifetime appointments (because under Article III they "hold their offices during Good Behavior").

U.S. District Courts At the federal level, the equivalent of a state trial court of general jurisdiction is the district court. There is at least one federal district court in every state. The number of judicial districts can vary over time, primarily owing to population changes and corresponding caseloads. Currently, there are ninety-four federal judicial districts.

U.S. district courts have original jurisdiction in federal matters. Federal cases typically originate in district courts. There are other courts with original, but special (or limited), jurisdiction, such as the federal bankruptcy courts and others shown in Exhibit 3–2 on page 72.

U.S. Courts of Appeals   In the federal court system, there are thirteen U.S. courts of appeals—also referred to as U.S. circuit courts of appeals. The federal courts of appeals for twelve of the circuits, including the U.S. Court of Appeals for the District of Columbia Circuit, hear appeals from the federal district courts located within their respective judicial circuits. The Court of Appeals for the Thirteenth Circuit, called the Federal Circuit, has national appellate jurisdiction over certain types of cases, such as cases involving patent law and cases in which the U.S. government is a defendant.

The decisions of the circuit courts of appeals are final in most cases, but appeal to the United States Supreme Court is possible. Exhibit 3–3 shows the geographic boundaries of the U.S. circuit courts of appeals and the boundaries of the U.S. district courts within each circuit.

The United States Supreme Court   The highest level of the three-tiered model of the federal court system is the United States Supreme Court. According to the language of Article III of the U.S. Constitution, there is only one national

EXHIBIT 3–3 BOUNDARIES OF THE U.S. COURTS OF APPEALS AND U.S. DISTRICT COURTS

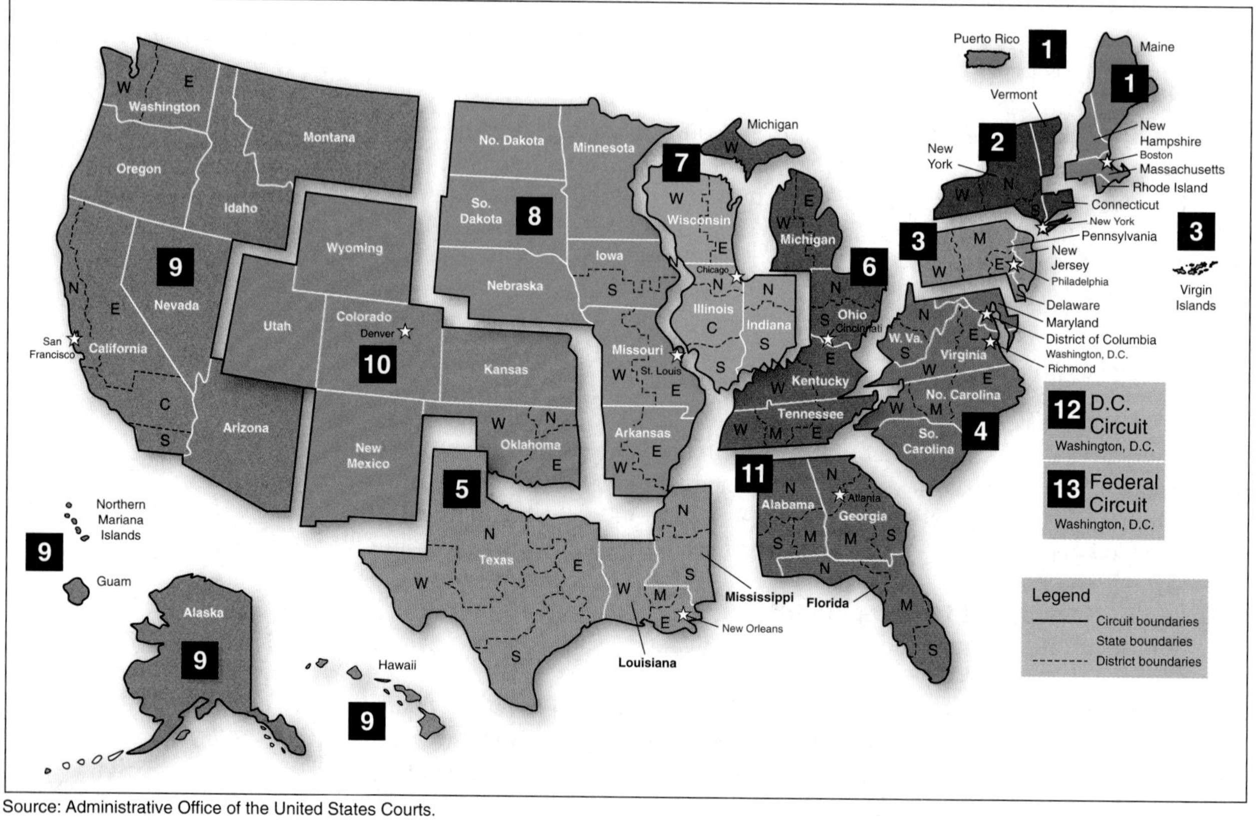

Source: Administrative Office of the United States Courts.

Supreme Court. All other courts in the federal system are considered "inferior." Congress is empowered to create other inferior courts as it deems necessary. The inferior courts that Congress has created include the second tier in our model—the U.S. courts of appeals—as well as the district courts and any other courts of limited, or specialized, jurisdiction.

The United States Supreme Court consists of nine justices. Although the Supreme Court has original, or trial, jurisdiction in rare instances (set forth in Article III, Section 2), most of its work is as an appeals court. The Supreme Court can review any case decided by any of the federal courts of appeals, and it also has appellate authority over some cases decided in the state courts.

Appeals to the Supreme Court   To bring a case before the Supreme Court, a party requests that the Court issue a writ of *certiorari*. A **writ of *certiorari***[14] is an order issued by the Supreme Court to a lower court requiring the latter to send it the record of the case for review. The Court will not issue a writ unless at least four of the nine justices approve of it. This is called the **rule of four.** Whether the Court will issue a writ of *certiorari* is entirely within its discretion. The Court is not required to issue one, and most petitions for writs are denied. (Thousands of cases are filed with the Supreme Court each year; yet it hears, on average, fewer than one hundred of these cases.)[15] A denial is not a decision on the merits of a

WRIT OF *CERTIORARI*
A writ from a higher court asking the lower court for the record of a case.

RULE OF FOUR
A rule of the United States Supreme Court under which the Court will not issue a writ of *certiorari* unless at least four justices approve of the decision to issue the writ.

---

14. Pronounced sur-shee-uh-*rah*-ree.
15. From the mid-1950s through the early 1990s, the United States Supreme Court reviewed more cases per year than it has in the last few years. In the Court's 1982–1983 term, for example, the Court issued opinions in 151 cases. In contrast, in its 2007–2008 term, the Court issued opinions in only 72 cases.

The justices of the United States Supreme Court (as of 2008). Does the fact that these justices are appointed for life have any effect on the decisions they reach in the cases they hear? Why or why not? (Photos from collection of the Supreme Court of the United States)

case, nor does it indicate agreement with the lower court's opinion. Furthermore, a denial of the writ has no value as a precedent.

Petitions Granted by the Court Typically, the Court grants petitions when cases raise important constitutional questions or when the lower courts are issuing conflicting decisions on a significant question. The justices, however, never explain their reasons for hearing certain cases and not others, so it is difficult to predict which type of case the Court might select.

FOLLOWING A STATE COURT CASE

To illustrate the procedures that would be followed in a civil lawsuit brought in a state court, we present a hypothetical case and follow it through the state court system. The case involves an automobile accident in which Kevin Anderson, driving a Mercedes, struck Lisa Marconi, driving a Ford Taurus. The accident occurred at the intersection of Wilshire Boulevard and Rodeo Drive in Beverly Hills, California. Marconi suffered personal injuries, incurring medical and hospital expenses as well as lost wages for four months. Anderson and Marconi are unable to agree on a settlement, and Marconi sues Anderson. Marconi is the plaintiff, and Anderson is the defendant. Both are represented by lawyers.

During each phase of the **litigation** (the process of working a lawsuit through the court system), Marconi and Anderson will have to observe strict procedural requirements. A large body of law—procedural law—establishes the rules and standards for determining disputes in courts. Procedural rules are very complex, and they vary from court to court and from state to state. There is a set of federal rules of procedure as well as various sets of rules for state courts. Additionally, the applicable procedures will depend on whether the case is a civil or criminal proceeding. Generally, the Marconi-Anderson civil lawsuit will involve the procedures discussed in the following subsections. Keep in mind that attempts to settle the case may be ongoing throughout the trial.

The Pleadings

The complaint and answer (and the counterclaim and reply)—all of which are discussed below—taken together are called the **pleadings.** The pleadings inform each party of the other's claims and specify the issues (disputed questions) involved in the case. Because the rules of procedure vary depending on the jurisdiction of the court, the style and form of the pleadings may be quite different in different states.

The Plaintiff's Complaint Marconi's suit against Anderson commences when her lawyer files a **complaint** with the appropriate court. The complaint contains a statement alleging (asserting to the court, in a pleading) the facts necessary for the court to take jurisdiction, a brief summary of the facts necessary to show that the plaintiff is entitled to a remedy, and a statement of the remedy the plaintiff is seeking. Complaints may be lengthy or brief, depending on the complexity of the case and the rules of the jurisdiction.

After the complaint has been filed, the sheriff, a deputy of the county, or another *process server* (one who delivers a complaint and summons) serves a **summons** and a copy of the complaint on defendant Anderson. The summons notifies Anderson that he must file an answer to the complaint with both the

LITIGATION
The process of resolving a dispute through the court system.

PLEADINGS
Statements made by the plaintiff and the defendant in a lawsuit that detail the facts, charges, and defenses involved in the litigation. The complaint and answer are part of the pleadings.

COMPLAINT
The pleading made by a plaintiff alleging wrongdoing on the part of the defendant; the document that, when filed with a court, initiates a lawsuit.

SUMMONS
A document informing a defendant that a legal action has been commenced against him or her and that the defendant must appear in court on a certain date to answer the plaintiff's complaint. The document is delivered by a sheriff or any other person so authorized.

court and the plaintiff's attorney within a specified time period (usually twenty to thirty days). The summons also informs Anderson that failure to answer may result in a **default judgment** for the plaintiff, meaning the plaintiff could be awarded the damages alleged in her complaint.

DEFAULT JUDGMENT
A judgment entered by a court against a defendant who has failed to appear in court to answer or defend against the plaintiff's claim. *Rloger*

The Defendant's Answer The defendant's **answer** either admits the statements or allegations set forth in the complaint or denies them and outlines any defenses that the defendant may have. If Anderson admits to all of Marconi's allegations in his answer, the court will enter a judgment for Marconi. If Anderson denies any of Marconi's allegations, the litigation will go forward.

ANSWER
Procedurally, a defendant's response to the plaintiff's complaint.

Anderson can deny Marconi's allegations and set forth his own claim that Marconi was in fact negligent and therefore owes him compensation for the damage to his Mercedes. This is appropriately called a **counterclaim.** If Anderson files a counterclaim, Marconi will have to answer it with a pleading, normally called a **reply,** which has the same characteristics as an answer.

COUNTERCLAIM
A claim made by a defendant in a civil lawsuit against the plaintiff. In effect, the defendant is suing the plaintiff.

REPLY
Procedurally, a plaintiff's response to a defendant's answer.

Anderson can also admit the truth of Marconi's complaint but raise new facts that may result in dismissal of the action. This is called raising an *affirmative defense.* For example, Anderson could assert as an affirmative defense the expiration of the time period under the relevant *statute of limitations* (a state or federal statute that sets the maximum time period during which a certain action can be brought or rights enforced).

Motion to Dismiss A **motion to dismiss** requests the court to dismiss the case for stated reasons. Grounds for dismissal of a case include improper delivery of the complaint and summons, improper venue, and the plaintiff's failure to state a claim for which a court could grant relief (a remedy). For example, if Marconi had suffered no injuries or losses as a result of Anderson's negligence, Anderson could move to have the case dismissed because Marconi had not stated a claim for which relief could be granted.

beweging (un gesto)
MOTION TO DISMISS
A pleading in which a defendant asserts that the plaintiff's claim fails to state a cause of action (that is, has no basis in law) or that there are other grounds on which a suit should be dismissed. Although the defendant normally is the party requesting a dismissal, either the plaintiff or the court can also make a motion to dismiss the case.

If the judge grants the motion to dismiss, the plaintiff generally is given time to file an amended complaint. If the judge denies the motion, the suit will go forward, and the defendant must then file an answer. Note that if Marconi wishes to discontinue the suit because, for example, an out-of-court settlement has been reached, she can likewise move for dismissal. The court can also dismiss the case on its own motion.

Pretrial Motions

Either party may attempt to get the case dismissed before trial through the use of various pretrial motions. We have already mentioned the motion to dismiss. Two other important pretrial motions are the motion for judgment on the pleadings and the motion for summary judgment.

MOTION FOR JUDGMENT ON THE PLEADINGS
A motion by either party to a lawsuit at the close of the pleadings requesting the court to decide the issue solely on the pleadings without proceeding to trial. The motion will be granted only if no facts are in dispute.

At the close of the pleadings, either party may make a **motion for judgment on the pleadings**, or on the merits of the case. The judge will grant the motion only when there is no dispute over the facts of the case and the sole issue to be resolved is a question of law. In deciding on the motion, the judge may consider only the evidence contained in the pleadings.

In contrast, in a **motion for summary judgment,** the court may consider evidence outside the pleadings, such as sworn statements (affidavits) by parties or

MOTION FOR SUMMARY JUDGMENT
A motion requesting the court to enter a judgment without proceeding to trial. The motion can be based on evidence outside the pleadings and will be granted only if no facts are in dispute.

witnesses, or other documents relating to the case. A motion for summary judgment can be made by either party. As with the motion for judgment on the pleadings, a motion for summary judgment will be granted only if there are no genuine questions of fact and the sole question is a question of law.

Discovery

Before a trial begins, each party can use a number of procedural devices to obtain information and gather evidence about the case from the other party or from third parties. The process of obtaining such information is known as **discovery.** Discovery includes gaining access to witnesses, documents, records, and other types of evidence.

The Federal Rules of Civil Procedure and similar rules in the states set forth the guidelines for discovery activity. The rules governing discovery are designed to make sure that a witness or a party is not unduly harassed, that privileged material (communications that need not be presented in court) is safeguarded, and that only matters relevant to the case at hand are discoverable.

Discovery prevents surprises at trial by giving parties access to evidence that might otherwise be hidden. This allows both parties to learn as much as they can about what to expect at a trial before they reach the courtroom. It also serves to narrow the issues so that trial time is spent on the main questions in the case.

Depositions and Interrogatories   Discovery can involve the use of depositions or interrogatories, or both. A **deposition** is sworn testimony by a party to the lawsuit or any witness. The person being deposed (the deponent) answers questions asked by the attorneys, and the questions and answers are recorded by an authorized court official and sworn to and signed by the deponent. (Occasionally, written depositions are taken when witnesses are unable to appear in person.) The answers given to depositions will, of course, help the attorneys prepare their cases. They can also be used in court to impeach (challenge the credibility of) a party or a witness who changes his or her testimony at the trial. In addition, the answers given in a deposition can be used as testimony if the witness is not available at trial.

Interrogatories are written questions for which written answers are prepared and then signed under oath. The main difference between interrogatories and written depositions is that interrogatories are directed to a party to the lawsuit (the plaintiff or the defendant), not to a witness, and the party can prepare answers with the aid of an attorney. The scope of interrogatories is broader because parties are obligated to answer the questions, even if that means disclosing information from their records and files.

Requests for Other Information   A party can serve a written request on the other party for an admission of the truth of matters relating to the trial. Any matter admitted under such a request is conclusively established for the trial. For example, Marconi can ask Anderson to admit that he was driving at a speed of forty-five miles an hour. A request for admission saves time at trial because the parties will not have to spend time proving facts on which they already agree.

A party can also gain access to documents and other items not in her or his possession in order to inspect and examine them. Likewise, a party can gain "entry upon land" to inspect the premises. Anderson's attorney, for example, normally can gain permission to inspect and photocopy Marconi's car repair bills.

DISCOVERY
A phase in the litigation process during which the opposing parties may obtain information from each other and from third parties prior to trial.

DEPOSITION
The testimony of a party to a lawsuit or a witness taken under oath before a trial.

INTERROGATORIES
A series of written questions for which written answers are prepared by a party to a lawsuit, usually with the assistance of the party's attorney, and then signed under oath.

When the physical or mental condition of one party is in question, the opposing party can ask the court to order a physical or mental examination. If the court is willing to make the order, which it will do only if the need for the information outweighs the right to privacy of the person to be examined, the opposing party can obtain the results of the examination.

Electronic Discovery   Any relevant material, including information stored electronically, can be the object of a discovery request. The federal rules and most state rules (as well as court decisions) now specifically allow individuals to obtain discovery of electronic "data compilations." Electronic evidence, or **e-evidence,** consists of all computer-generated or electronically recorded information, such as e-mail, voice mail, spreadsheets, word-processing documents, and other data. E-evidence can reveal significant facts that are not discoverable by other means. For example, computers automatically record certain information about files— such as who created the file and when, and who accessed, modified, or transmitted it—on their hard drives. This information can only be obtained from the file in its electronic format—not from printed-out versions.

Amendments to the Federal Rules of Civil Procedure (FRCP) that took effect in December 2006 deal specifically with the preservation, retrieval, and production of electronic data. Although traditional means, such as interrogatories and depositions, are still used to find out whether e-evidence exists, a party must usually hire an expert to retrieve the evidence in its electronic format. The expert uses software to reconstruct e-mail exchanges to establish who knew what and when they knew it. The expert can even recover files from a computer that the user thought had been deleted. Reviewing back-up copies of documents and e-mail can provide useful—and often quite damaging—information about how a particular matter progressed over several weeks or months.

Electronic discovery has significant advantages over paper discovery, but it is also time consuming and expensive. For a discussion of how the courts are apportioning the costs associated with electronic discovery, see this chapter's *Online Developments* feature on the following two pages.

E-EVIDENCE
Evidence that consists of computer-generated or electronically recorded information, including e-mail, voice mail, spreadsheets, word-processing documents, and other data.

Pretrial Conference

Either party or the court can request a pretrial conference, or hearing. Usually, the hearing consists of an informal discussion between the judge and the opposing attorneys after discovery has taken place. The purpose of the hearing is to explore the possibility of a settlement without trial and, if this is not possible, to identify the matters that are in dispute and to plan the course of the trial.

Jury Selection

A trial can be held with or without a jury. The Seventh Amendment to the U.S. Constitution guarantees the right to a jury trial for cases in *federal* courts when the amount in controversy exceeds $20, but this guarantee does not apply to state courts. Most states have similar guarantees in their own constitutions (although the threshold dollar amount is higher than $20). The right to a trial by jury does not have to be exercised, and many cases are tried without a jury. In most states and in federal courts, one of the parties must request a jury in a civil case, or the right is presumed to be waived.

Before the computer age, discovery involved searching through paper records—physical evidence. Today, less than 0.5 percent of new information is created on paper. Instead of sending letters and memos, for example, people send e-mails—about 600 billion of them annually in the United States. The all-inclusive nature of electronic information means that electronic discovery (e-discovery) now plays an important role in almost every business lawsuit.

Changes in the Federal Rules of Civil Procedure

As e-discovery has become ubiquitous, the Federal Rules of Civil Procedure (FRCP) have changed to encompass it. Amended Section 26(f) of the FRCP, for example, requires that the parties confer about "preserving discoverable information" and discuss "any issues relating to . . . discovery of electronically stored information, including the electronic forms in which it should be produced."

The most recent amendment to Section 34(a) of the FRCP expressly permits one party to a lawsuit to request that the other produce "electronically stored information—including . . . data compilation stored in any medium from which information can be obtained." The new rule has put in place a two-tiered process for discovery of electronically stored information. Relevant and nonprivileged information that is reasonably accessible is discoverable as a matter of right. Discovery of less accessible—and therefore more costly to obtain—electronic data may or may not be allowed by the court. The problem of the costs of e-discovery is discussed further below.

The *Ameriwood* Three-Step Process

The new federal rules were applied in *Ameriwood Industries, Inc. v. Liberman,* a major case involving e-discovery in which the court developed a three-step procedure for obtaining electronic data.[a] In the first step, *imaging,* mirror images of a party's hard drives, can be required. The second step involves *recovering* available word-processing documents, e-mails, PowerPoint presentations, spreadsheets, and other files. The final step is *full disclosure,* in which a party sends the other party all responsive and nonprivileged documents and information obtained in the previous two steps.

Limitations on E-Discovery and Cost-Shifting

Complying with requests for electronically discoverable information can cost hundreds of thousands, if not millions, of dollars, especially if a party is a large corporation with thousands of employees creating millions of electronic documents. Consequently, there is a trend toward limiting e-discovery. Under the FRCP, a court can limit electronic discovery (1) when it would be unreasonably cumulative or duplicative, (2) when the requesting party has already had ample opportunity during discovery to obtain the

a. 2007 WL 685623 (E.D.Mo. 2007).

VOIR DIRE
Old French phrase meaning "to speak the truth." In legal language, the phrase refers to the process in which the attorneys question prospective jurors to learn about their backgrounds, attitudes, biases, and other characteristics that may affect their ability to serve as impartial jurors.

TAKE NOTE
A prospective juror cannot be excluded solely on the basis of his or her race or gender.

Before a jury trial commences, a jury must be selected. The jury selection process is known as **voir dire.**[16] During *voir dire* in most jurisdictions, attorneys for the plaintiff and the defendant ask prospective jurors oral questions to determine whether a potential jury member is biased or has any connection with a party to the action or with a prospective witness. In some jurisdictions, the judge may do all or part of the questioning based on written questions submitted by counsel for the parties.

During *voir dire,* a party may challenge a certain number of prospective jurors *peremptorily*—that is, ask that an individual not be sworn in as a juror without providing any reason. Alternatively, a party may challenge a prospective juror *for cause*—that is, provide a reason why an individual should not be sworn in as a juror. If the judge grants the challenge, the individual is asked to step down. A prospective juror may not be excluded from the jury by the use of discriminatory challenges, however, such as those based on racial criteria or gender.

At the Trial

At the beginning of the trial, the attorneys present their opening arguments, setting forth the facts that they expect to provide during the trial. Then the plaintiff's case is presented. In our hypothetical case, Marconi's lawyer would

16. Pronounced vwahr *deehr.*

information, or (3) when the burden or expense outweighs the likely benefit.

Many courts are allowing responding parties to object to e-discovery requests on the ground that complying with the request would cause an undue financial burden. In a suit between E*Trade and Deutsche Bank, for example, the court denied E*Trade's request that the defendant produce its hard drives because doing so would create an undue burden.[b]

In addition, sometimes when a court finds that producing the requested information would create an undue financial burden, the court orders the party to comply but shifts the cost to the requesting party (usually the plaintiff). A major case in this area involved Rowe Entertainment and the William Morris Agency. When the e-discovery costs were estimated to be as high as $9 million, the court determined that cost-shifting was warranted.[c] In deciding whether to order cost-shifting, courts increasingly take into account the amount in controversy and each party's ability to pay. Sometimes, a court may require the responding party to restore and produce representative documents from a small sample of the requested medium to verify the relevance of the data before the party incurs significant expenses.[d]

b. *E*Trade Securities, LLC v. Deutsche Bank A.G.,* 230 F.R.D. 582 (D.Minn. 2005). This is a *Federal Rules Decision* not designated for publication in the *Federal Supplement,* citing *Zubulake v. UBS Warburg, LLC,* 2003 WL 21087884 (S.D.N.Y. 2003).
c. *Rowe Entertainment, Inc. v. William Morris Agency, Inc.,* 2002 WL 975713 (S.D.N.Y. 2002).
d. See, for example, *Quinby v. WestLB AG,* 2006 WL 2597900 (S.D.N.Y. 2006).

The Duty to Preserve E-Evidence

Whenever there is a "reasonable anticipation of litigation," all of the relevant documents must be preserved. Preserving e-evidence can be a challenge, particularly for large corporations that have electronic data scattered across multiple networks, servers, desktops, laptops, handheld devices, and even home computers.

The failure to preserve electronic evidence or to comply with electronic discovery requests can lead a court to impose sanctions (such as fines) on one of the parties. This failure can also convince a party to settle the dispute. For instance, Gateway's failure to preserve and produce a single damaging e-mail caused that firm to settle a dispute on the evening before trial.[e]

Businesspersons should also be aware that their computer systems may contain electronic information that they presumed no longer existed. Even though an e-mail is deleted, for example, it is not necessarily eliminated from the hard drive, unless it is completely overwritten by new data. Experts may be able to retrieve this e-mail.

FOR CRITICAL ANALYSIS How might a large corporation protect itself from allegations that it intentionally failed to preserve electronic data? Given the significant and often burdensome costs associated with electronic discovery, should courts consider cost-shifting in every case involving electronic discovery? Why or why not?

e. *Adams v. Gateway, Inc.,* 2006 WL 2563418 (D.Utah 2006).

---

introduce evidence (relevant documents, exhibits, and the testimony of witnesses) to support Marconi's position. The defendant has the opportunity to challenge any evidence introduced and to cross-examine any of the plaintiff's witnesses.

At the end of the plaintiff's case, the defendant's attorney has the opportunity to ask the judge to direct a verdict for the defendant on the ground that the plaintiff has presented no evidence that would justify the granting of the plaintiff's remedy. This is called a **motion for a directed verdict** (known in federal courts as a *motion for judgment as a matter of law*) If the motion is not granted (it seldom is granted), the defendant's attorney then presents the evidence and witnesses for the defendant's case. At the conclusion of the defendant's case, the defendant's attorney has another opportunity to make a motion for a directed verdict. The plaintiff's attorney can challenge any evidence introduced and cross-examine the defendant's witnesses.

After the defense concludes its presentation, the attorneys present their closing arguments, each urging a verdict in favor of her or his client. The judge instructs the jury in the law that applies to the case (these instructions are often called *charges*), and the jury retires to the jury room to deliberate a verdict. In the Marconi-Anderson case, the jury will not only decide for the plaintiff or for the defendant but, if it finds for the plaintiff, will also decide on the amount of the **award** (the compensation to be paid to her).

MOTION FOR A DIRECTED VERDICT
In a jury trial, a motion for the judge to take the decision out of the hands of the jury and to direct a verdict for the party who filed the motion on the ground that the other party has not produced sufficient evidence to support her or his claim.

AWARD
In litigation, the amount of monetary compensation awarded to a plaintiff in a civil lawsuit as damages. In the context of alternative dispute resolution, the decision rendered by an arbitrator.

Posttrial Motions

After the jury has rendered its verdict, either party may make a posttrial motion. If Marconi wins and Anderson's attorney has previously moved for a directed verdict, Anderson's attorney may make a **motion for judgment *n.o.v.*** (from the Latin *non obstante veredicto,* which means "notwithstanding the verdict"—called a *motion for judgment as a matter of law* in the federal courts). Such a motion will be granted only if the jury's verdict was unreasonable and erroneous. If the judge grants the motion, the jury's verdict will be set aside, and a judgment will be entered in favor of the opposite party (Anderson).

Alternatively, Anderson could make a **motion for a new trial,** asking the judge to set aside the adverse verdict and to hold a new trial. The motion will be granted if, after looking at all the evidence, the judge is convinced that the jury was in error but does not feel it is appropriate to grant judgment for the other side. A judge can also grant a new trial on the basis of newly discovered evidence, misconduct by the participants or the jury during the trial, or error by the judge.

The Appeal

Assume here that any posttrial motion is denied and that Anderson appeals the case. (If Marconi wins but receives a smaller monetary award than she sought, she can appeal also.) Keep in mind, though, that a party cannot appeal a trial court's decision simply because he or she is dissatisfied with the outcome of the trial. A party must have legitimate grounds to file an appeal; that is, he or she must be able to claim that the lower court committed an error. If Anderson has grounds to appeal the case, a notice of appeal must be filed with the clerk of the trial court within a prescribed time. Anderson now becomes the appellant, or petitioner, and Marconi becomes the appellee, or respondent.

Filing the Appeal   Anderson's attorney files with the appellate court the record on appeal, which includes the pleadings, the trial transcript, the judge's rulings on motions made by the parties, and other trial-related documents. Anderson's attorney will also provide a condensation of the record, known as an *abstract,* which is filed with the reviewing court along with the brief. The **brief** is a formal legal document outlining the facts and issues of the case, the judge's rulings or jury's findings that should be reversed or modified, the applicable law, and arguments on Anderson's behalf (citing applicable statutes and relevant cases as precedents).

Marconi's attorney will file an answering brief. Anderson's attorney can file a reply to Marconi's brief, although it is not required. The reviewing court then considers the case.

Appellate Review   As mentioned earlier, a court of appeals does not hear evidence. Rather, it reviews the record for errors of law. Its decision concerning a case is based on the record on appeal and the briefs and arguments. The attorneys present oral arguments, after which the case is taken under advisement. The court then issues a written opinion. In general, appellate courts do not reverse findings of fact unless the findings are unsupported or contradicted by the evidence.

An appellate court has the following options after reviewing a case:

1. The court can *affirm* the trial court's decision.
2. The court can *reverse* the trial court's judgment if it concludes that the trial court erred or that the jury did not receive proper instructions.

MOTION FOR JUDGMENT *N.O.V.*
A motion requesting the court to grant judgment in favor of the party making the motion on the ground that the jury's verdict against him or her was unreasonable and erroneous.

MOTION FOR A NEW TRIAL
A motion asserting that the trial was so fundamentally flawed (because of error, newly discovered evidence, prejudice, or another reason) that a new trial is necessary to prevent a miscarriage of justice.

BRIEF
A formal legal document prepared by a party's attorney (in answer to the appellant's brief) and submitted to an appellate court when a case is appealed. The appellant's brief outlines the facts and issues of the case, the judge's rulings or jury's findings that should be reversed or modified, the applicable law, and the arguments on the client's behalf.

3. The appellate court can *remand* (send back) the case to the trial court for further proceedings consistent with its opinion on the matter.

4. The court might also affirm or reverse a decision *in part*. For example, the court might affirm the jury's finding that Anderson was negligent but remand the case for further proceedings on another issue (such as the extent of Marconi's damages).

5. An appellate court can also *modify* a lower court's decision. If the appellate court decides that the jury awarded an excessive amount in damages, for example, the court might reduce the award to a more appropriate, or fairer, amount.

Appellate courts apply different standards of review depending on the type of issue involved and the lower court's rulings. Generally, these standards require the reviewing court to give a certain amount of deference, or weight, to the findings of lower courts on specific issues. The following case illustrates the importance of standards of review as a means of exercising judicial restraint.

Case 3.2 **Evans v. Eaton Corp. Long Term Disability Plan**

United States Court of Appeals,
Fourth Circuit, 2008.
514 F.3d 315.

BACKGROUND AND FACTS Eaton Corporation is a multinational manufacturing company that funds and administers a long-term disability benefits plan for its employees. Brenda Evans was an employee at Eaton. In 1998, due to severe rheumatoid arthritis, Brenda Evans quit her job at Eaton and filed for disability benefits. Eaton paid disability benefits to Evans without controversy prior to 2003, but that year, Evans's disability status became questionable. Her physician had prescribed a new medication that had dramatically improved Evans's arthritis. In addition, Evans had injured her spine in a car accident in 2002 and was claiming to be disabled by continuing back problems as well as arthritis. But diagnostic exams during that period indicated that the injuries to Evans's back were not severe, and she could cook, shop, do laundry, wash dishes, and drive about seven miles a day. By 2004, several physicians that reviewed Evans's file had determined that she could work and was no longer totally disabled, and Eaton terminated Evans's disability benefits. Evans filed a complaint in the U.S. District Court for South Carolina alleging violations of the Employee Retirement Income Security Act of 1974 (ERISA—a federal law regulating pension plans that will be discussed in Chapter 17). The district court examined the evidence in great detail and concluded that Eaton's termination of Evans's benefits was an abuse of discretion because the physicians who testified in Evans's favor were more believable than the reviewing physicians. Eaton appealed to the U.S. Court of Appeals for the Fourth Circuit.

IN THE WORDS OF THE COURT . . . *WILKINSON*, Circuit Judge.

*   *   *   *

This case turns on a faithful application of the abuse of discretion standard of review, and so we begin with what is most crucial: a clear understanding of what that standard is, and what such standards are for.

The purpose of standards of review is to focus reviewing courts upon their proper role when passing on the conduct of other decision-makers. Standards of review are thus an elemental expression of judicial restraint, which, in their deferential varieties, safeguard the superior vantage points of those entrusted with primary decisional responsibility. *   *   * The clear error standard, for example, protects district courts' primacy as triers of fact. *   *   * Rational basis review protects the political choices of our government's elected branches. And trust law, to which ERISA is so intimately linked, uses the abuse of discretion standard to protect a fiduciary's [one whose relationship is based on trust] decisions concerning the trust funds in his care. [Emphasis added.]

CASE 3.2–CONTINUED

The precise definitions of these various standards, the nuances separating them from one another, "cannot be imprisoned within any forms of words" * * *. But what these and other such standards share is the designation of a primary decision-maker other than the reviewing court, and the instrument, deference, with which that primacy is to be maintained.

* * * In [this] case, the Plan's language giving Eaton "discretionary authority to determine eligibility for benefits" and "the power and discretion to determine all questions of fact * * * arising in connection with the administration, interpretation and application of the Plan" is unambiguous, and Evans does not dispute the standard it requires. Thus the district court functions in this context as a deferential reviewing court with respect to the ERISA fiduciary's decision.

* * * *

At its immovable core, the abuse of discretion standard requires a reviewing court to show enough deference to a primary decision-maker's judgment that the court does not reverse merely because it would have come to a different result * * *. The trial judge has discretion in those cases where his ruling will not be reversed simply because an appellate court disagrees. [Emphasis added.]

* * * *

Under no formulation, however, may a court, faced with discretionary language like that in the plan instrument in this case, forget its duty of deference and its secondary rather than primary role in determining a claimant's right to benefits. The abuse of discretion standard in ERISA cases protects important values: the plan administrator's greater experience and familiarity with plan terms and provisions; the enhanced prospects of achieving consistent application of those terms and provisions that results; the desire of those who establish ERISA plans to preserve at least some role in their administration; and the importance of ensuring that funds which are not unlimited go to those who, according to the terms of the plan, are truly deserving.

* * * *

* * * Where an ERISA administrator rejects a claim to benefits on the strength of substantial evidence, careful and coherent reasoning, faithful adherence to the letter of ERISA and the language in the plan, and a fair and searching process, there can be no abuse of discretion—even if another, and arguably a better, decision-maker might have come to a different, and arguably a better, result.

* * * *

So standards of review do matter, for in every context they keep judges within the limits of their role and preserve other decision-makers' functions against judicial intrusion.

DECISION AND REMEDY   The U.S. Court of Appeals for the Fourth Circuit reversed the district court's award of benefits to Evans and remanded the case with instructions that the district court enter a judgment in favor of Eaton. The district court incorrectly applied the abuse of discretion standard when reviewing Eaton's termination of Evans's benefits.

WHAT IF THE FACTS WERE DIFFERENT?   Suppose that the district court had concluded that Eaton Corporation's termination of Evans's benefits was not an abuse of discretion, and Evans had appealed. In that situation, would Evans have had any grounds for appealing the district court's decision? Explain.

THE ETHICAL DIMENSION   The appellate court noted in this case that the district court's decision—which granted benefits to Evans—may arguably have been a better decision under these facts. If the court believes the district court's conclusion was right, then why did it reverse the decision? What does this tell you about the standards for review that appellate judges use?

Appeal to a Higher Appellate Court   If the reviewing court is an interme-diate appellate court, the losing party may decide to appeal to the state supreme court (the highest state court). Such a petition corresponds to a petition for a writ of *certiorari* from the United States Supreme Court. Although the losing party has a right to ask (petition) a higher court to review the case, the party does not have a right to have the case heard by the higher appellate court. Appellate courts nor-mally have discretionary power and can accept or reject an appeal. Like the United States Supreme Court, in general state supreme courts deny most appeals. If the appeal is granted, new briefs must be filed before the state supreme court, and the attorneys may be allowed or requested to present oral arguments. Like the intermediate appellate court, the supreme court may reverse or affirm the appellate court's decision or remand the case. At this point, the case typically has reached its end (unless a federal question is at issue and one of the parties has legitimate grounds to seek review by a federal appellate court).

Enforcing the Judgment

The uncertainties of the litigation process are compounded by the lack of guar-antees that any judgment will be enforceable. Even if a plaintiff wins an award of damages in court, the defendant may not have sufficient assets or insurance to cover that amount. Usually, one of the factors considered before a lawsuit is initiated is whether the defendant has sufficient assets to cover the amount of damages sought, should the plaintiff win the case. Additional considerations are the time involved and the expenses of litigation.

THE COURTS ADAPT TO THE ONLINE WORLD

We have already mentioned that the courts have attempted to adapt traditional jurisdictional concepts to the online world. Not surprisingly, the Internet has also brought about changes in court procedures and practices, including new methods for filing pleadings and other documents and issuing decisions and opinions. Some jurisdictions are exploring the possibility of cyber courts, in which legal proceedings could be conducted totally online.

Electronic Filing

The federal court system first experimented with an electronic filing system in January 1996, and its Case Management/Electronic Case Files (CM/ECF) system has now been implemented in nearly all of the federal appellate courts and bankruptcy courts, as well as a majority of the district courts. The CM/ECF system allows federal courts to accept documents filed electronically in PDF format via the Internet. A few federal bankruptcy courts now require some documents to be filed electronically.

Nearly half of the states have some form of electronic filing. Some of these states, including Arizona, California, Colorado, Delaware, and New York, offer statewide e-filing systems. Generally, when electronic filing is made available, it is optional. Nonetheless, some state courts have now made e-filing mandatory in certain types of disputes, such as complex civil litigation.

Courts Online

Most courts today have sites on the Web. Of course, each court decides what to make available at its site. Some courts display only the names of court personnel and office phone numbers. Others add court rules and forms. Many appellate court sites include judicial decisions, although the decisions may remain online for only a limited time period. In addition, in some states, such as California and Florida, court clerks offer docket information and other searchable databases online.

Appellate court decisions are often posted online immediately after they are rendered. Recent decisions of the U.S. courts of appeals, for example, are available online at their Web sites. The United States Supreme Court also has an official Web site and publishes its opinions there immediately after they are announced to the public. In fact, even decisions that are designated as unpublished opinions by the appellate courts are often published online (as discussed in the *Online Developments* feature in Chapter 1 on page 13).

Cyber Courts and Proceedings

Someday, litigants may be able to use cyber courts, in which judicial proceedings take place only on the Internet. The parties to a case could meet online to make their arguments and present their evidence. This might be done with e-mail submissions, through video cameras, in designated "chat" rooms, at closed sites, or through the use of other Internet facilities. These courtrooms could be efficient and economical. We might also see the use of virtual lawyers, judges, and juries—and possibly the replacement of court personnel with computer software. Already the state of Michigan has passed legislation creating cyber courts that will hear cases involving technology issues and high-tech businesses. Many lawyers predict that other states will follow suit.

The courts may also use the Internet in other ways. **EXAMPLE #10** A court in Florida granted "virtual" visitation rights in a couple's divorce proceeding. Although the court granted custody of the couple's ten-year-old daughter to the father, the court also ordered each parent to buy a computer and a videoconferencing system so that the mother could "visit" with her child via the Internet at any time. □

ALTERNATIVE DISPUTE RESOLUTION

ALTERNATIVE DISPUTE RESOLUTION (ADR)
The resolution of disputes in ways other than those involved in the traditional judicial process. Negotiation, mediation, and arbitration are forms of ADR.

Litigation is expensive. It is also time consuming. Because of the backlog of cases pending in many courts, several years may pass before a case is actually tried. For these and other reasons, more and more businesspersons are turning to **alternative dispute resolution (ADR)** as a means of settling their disputes.

The great advantage of ADR is its flexibility. Methods of ADR range from the parties sitting down together and attempting to work out their differences to multinational corporations agreeing to resolve a dispute through a formal hearing before a panel of experts. Normally, the parties themselves can control how the dispute will be settled, what procedures will be used, whether a neutral third party will be present or make a decision, and whether that decision will be legally binding or nonbinding.

Today, more than 90 percent of cases are settled before trial through some form of ADR. Indeed, most states either require or encourage parties to undertake ADR prior to trial. Many federal courts have instituted ADR programs as well. In the following pages, we examine the basic forms of ADR. Keep in mind, though, that new methods of ADR—and new combinations of existing methods—are constantly being devised and employed.

Negotiation

The simplest form of ADR is **negotiation,** a process in which the parties attempt to settle their dispute informally, with or without attorneys to represent them. Attorneys frequently advise their clients to negotiate a settlement voluntarily before they proceed to trial. Parties may even try to negotiate a settlement during a trial, or after the trial but before an appeal. Negotiation traditionally involves just the parties themselves and (typically) their attorneys. The attorneys, though, are advocates—they are obligated to put their clients' interests first.

Mediation

In **mediation,** a neutral third party acts as a mediator and works with both sides in the dispute to facilitate a resolution. The mediator talks with the parties separately as well as jointly and emphasizes their points of agreement in an attempt to help the parties evaluate their options. Although the mediator may propose a solution (called a mediator's proposal), he or she does not make a decision resolving the matter. States that require parties to undergo ADR before trial often offer mediation as one of the ADR options or (as in Florida) the only option.

One of the biggest advantages of mediation is that it is not as adversarial as litigation. In trials, the parties "do battle" with each other in the courtroom, trying to prove one another wrong, while the judge is usually a passive observer. In mediation, the mediator takes an active role and attempts to bring the parties together so that they can come to a mutually satisfactory resolution. The mediation process tends to reduce the hostility between the disputants, allowing them to resume their former relationship without bad feelings. For this reason, mediation is often the preferred form of ADR for disputes involving business partners, employers and employees, or other parties involved in long-term relationships.

EXAMPLE #11 Suppose that two business partners have a dispute over how the profits of their firm should be distributed. If the dispute is litigated, the parties will be adversaries, and their respective attorneys will emphasize how the parties' positions differ, not what they have in common. In contrast, when a dispute is mediated, the mediator emphasizes the common ground shared by the parties and helps them work toward agreement. The business partners can work out the distribution of profits without damaging their continuing relationship as partners. □

Arbitration

A more formal method of ADR is **arbitration,** in which an arbitrator (a neutral third party or a panel of experts) hears a dispute and imposes a resolution on the parties. Arbitration is unlike other forms of ADR because the third party hearing the dispute makes a decision for the parties. Exhibit 3–4 on the following page outlines the basic differences among the three traditional forms of ADR. Usually, the parties in arbitration agree that the third party's decision will be *legally binding,* although the parties can also agree to *nonbinding* arbitration. (Additionally, arbitration that is mandated by the courts often is not binding on the parties.) In nonbinding arbitration, the parties can go forward with a lawsuit if they do not agree with the arbitrator's decision.

NEGOTIATION
A process in which parties attempt to settle their dispute informally, with or without attorneys to represent them.

MEDIATION
A method of settling disputes outside of court by using the services of a neutral third party, who acts as a communicating agent between the parties and assists them in negotiating a settlement.

ARBITRATION
The settling of a dispute by submitting it to a disinterested third party (other than a court), who renders a decision that is (most often) legally binding.

EXHIBIT 3-4   BASIC DIFFERENCES IN THE TRADITIONAL FORMS OF ADR

TYPE OF ADR	DESCRIPTION	NEUTRAL THIRD PARTY PRESENT	WHO DECIDES THE RESOLUTION
Negotiation	The parties meet informally with or without their attorneys and attempt to agree on a resolution.	No	The parties themselves reach a resolution.
Mediation	A neutral third party meets with the parties and emphasizes points of agreement to help them resolve their dispute.	Yes	The parties, but the mediator may suggest or propose a resolution.
Arbitration	The parties present their arguments and evidence before an arbitrator at a hearing, and the arbitrator renders a decision resolving the parties' dispute.	Yes	The arbitrator imposes a resolution on the parties that may be either binding or nonbinding.

In some respects, formal arbitration resembles a trial, although usually the procedural rules are much less restrictive than those governing litigation. In the typical arbitration, the parties present opening arguments and ask for specific remedies. Evidence is then presented, and witnesses may be called and examined by both sides. The arbitrator then renders a decision, which is called an *award*.

An arbitrator's award is usually the final word on the matter. Although the parties may appeal an arbitrator's decision, a court's review of the decision will be much more restricted in scope than an appellate court's review of a trial court's decision. The general view is that because the parties were free to frame the issues and set the powers of the arbitrator at the outset, they cannot complain about the results. The award will be set aside only if the arbitrator's conduct or "bad faith" substantially prejudiced the rights of one of the parties, if the award violates an established public policy, or if the arbitrator exceeded her or his powers (arbitrated issues that the parties did not agree to submit to arbitration).

Arbitration Clauses and Statutes   Virtually any commercial matter can be submitted to arbitration. Frequently, parties include an **arbitration clause** in a contract (a written agreement—see Chapter 9); the clause provides that any dispute that arises under the contract will be resolved through arbitration rather than through the court system. Parties can also agree to arbitrate a dispute after a dispute arises.

ARBITRATION CLAUSE
A clause in a contract that provides that, in the event of a dispute, the parties will submit the dispute to arbitration rather than litigate the dispute in court.

Most states have statutes (often based in part on the Uniform Arbitration Act of 1955) under which arbitration clauses will be enforced, and some state statutes compel arbitration of certain types of disputes, such as those involving public employees. At the federal level, the Federal Arbitration Act (FAA), enacted in 1925, enforces arbitration clauses in contracts involving maritime activity and interstate commerce (though its applicability to employment contracts has been controversial, as discussed in a later subsection). Because of the breadth of the commerce clause (see Chapter 4), arbitration agreements involving transactions only slightly connected to the flow of interstate commerce may fall under the FAA.

EXAMPLE #12   Buckeye Check Cashing, Inc., cashes personal checks for consumers in Florida. Buckeye had a policy of agreeing to delay submitting a check for payment in exchange for a consumer's payment of a "finance charge." For each transaction, the consumer signed an agreement that included an arbitration clause. John Cardegna and others filed a lawsuit in a Florida court claiming that

Buckeye was charging an illegally high rate of interest in violation of state law. Buckeye filed a motion to compel arbitration, which the trial court denied, and the case was appealed. The plaintiffs argued that the entire contract—including the arbitration clause—was illegal and therefore arbitration was not required. Ultimately, the case reached the United States Supreme Court, which found that the arbitration provision was *severable,* or capable of being separated, from the rest of the contract. The Supreme Court held that when the challenge is to the validity of a contract as a whole, and not specifically to an arbitration clause within the contract, an arbitrator must resolve the dispute. This is true even if the contract later proves to be unenforceable, because the FAA established a national policy favoring arbitration and that policy extends to both federal and state courts.[17]□

The Issue of Arbitrability   When a dispute arises as to whether the parties have agreed in an arbitration clause to submit a particular matter to arbitration, one party may file suit to compel arbitration. The court before which the suit is brought will decide *not* the basic controversy but rather the issue of arbitrability—that is, whether the matter is one that must be resolved through arbitration. If the court finds that the subject matter in controversy is covered by the agreement to arbitrate, then a party may be compelled to arbitrate the dispute. Even when a claim involves a violation of a statute passed to protect a certain class of people, such as employees, a court may determine that the parties must nonetheless abide by their agreement to arbitrate the dispute. Usually, a court will allow the claim to be arbitrated if the court, in interpreting the statute, can find no legislative intent to the contrary.

No party, however, will be ordered to submit a particular dispute to arbitration unless the court is convinced that the party consented to do so. Additionally, the courts will not compel arbitration if it is clear that the prescribed arbitration rules and procedures are inherently unfair to one of the parties.

The terms of an arbitration agreement can limit the types of disputes that the parties agree to arbitrate. When the parties do not specify limits, however, disputes can arise as to whether the particular matter is covered by the arbitration agreement, and it is up to the court to resolve the issue of arbitrability. In the following case, the parties had previously agreed to arbitrate disputes involving their contract to develop software, but the dispute involved claims of copyright infringement (see Chapter 8). The question was whether the copyright infringement claims were beyond the scope of the arbitration clause.

Supporters of a union that represents firefighters and paramedics stage a protest during a contract dispute with the city of Philadelphia. The parties' contract included an arbitration clause. Suppose the city was refusing to participate in arbitration. What can the union do to legally force the city to arbitrate?
(Photo Courtesy of the Philadelphia Fire Fighters' Union–IAFF Local 22. All rights reserved.)

> **KEEP IN MIND**
> Litigation—even of a dispute over whether a particular matter should be submitted to arbitration—can be time consuming and expensive.

---

17. *Buckeye Check Cashing, Inc. v. Cardegna,* 546 U.S. 440, 126 S.Ct. 1204, 163 L.Ed.2d 1038 (2006).

Case 3.3   **NCR Corp. v. Korala Associates, Ltd.**

United States Court of Appeals,
Sixth Circuit, 2008.
512 F.3d 807.
www.ca6.uscourts.gov[a]

COMPANY PROFILE   In 1884, John H. Patterson founded the National Cash Register Company (NCR), maker of the

a. Click on "Opinions Search." Then, in the "Short Title" box, type "NCR" and click on "Submit Query." Next, click on the opinion link in the first column of the row corresponding to the name of this case.

first mechanical cash registers. In 1906, NCR created a cash register run by an electric motor. By 1914, the company had developed one of the first automated credit systems. By the 1950s, NCR had branched out into transistorized business computers and later into liquid crystal displays and data warehousing. Today, NCR is a worldwide provider of automatic teller machines (ATMs), integrated hardware and software systems, and related maintenance and support

CASE 3.3–CONTINUED

CASE 3.3–CONTINUED

services. More than 300,000 of NCR's ATMs are installed throughout the world.

BACKGROUND AND FACTS   In response to a need to upgrade the security of ATMs, NCR Corporation developed a software solution to install in all of its machines. At the same time, Korala Associates, Ltd. (KAL), claimed to have developed a similar security upgrade for NCR's ATMs. Indeed, KAL had entered into a contract with NCR in 1998 (the "1998 Agreement") to develop such software. To enable KAL to do

so, NCR lent to KAL a proprietary ATM that contained copyrighted software called "APTRA XFS." NCR alleged that KAL "obtained access to, made unauthorized use of, and engaged in unauthorized copying of the APTRA XFS software." By so doing, KAL developed its own version of a security upgrade for NCR's ATMs. When NCR brought a suit against KAL, the latter moved to compel arbitration under the terms of the 1998 Agreement between the two companies. At trial, KAL prevailed. NCR appealed the order compelling arbitration to the U.S. Court of Appeals for the Sixth Circuit.

IN THE WORDS OF THE COURT . . . Chief Justice *BATCHELDER* delivered the opinion of the Court.

*   *   *   *

The arbitration clause contained within the 1998 Agreement provides that:

Any controversy or claim arising out of or relating to this contract, or breach thereof, shall be settled by arbitration and judgment upon the award rendered by the arbitrator may be entered in any court having jurisdiction thereof. The arbitrator shall be appointed upon the mutual agreement of both parties failing which both parties will agree to be subject to any arbitrator that shall be chosen by the President of the Law Society.

The parties do not dispute that a valid agreement to arbitrate exists; rather the issue of contention is whether NCR's claims fall within the substantive scope of the agreement.

As a matter of federal law, any doubts concerning the scope of arbitrable issues should be resolved in favor of arbitration. Despite this strong presumption in favor of arbitration, "arbitration is a matter of contract between the parties, and one cannot be required to submit to arbitration a dispute which it has not agreed to submit to arbitration." *When faced with a broad arbitration clause, such as one covering any dispute arising out of an agreement, a court should follow the presumption of arbitration and resolve doubts in favor of arbitration. Indeed, in such a case, only an express provision excluding a specific dispute, or the most forceful evidence of a purpose to exclude the claim from arbitration, will remove the dispute from consideration by the arbitrators.* [Emphasis added.]

*   *   *   *

*   *   * It is sufficient that a court would have to reference the 1998 Agreement for part of NCR's direct [copyright] infringement claim. Under these circumstances, we find that the copyright infringement claim as to APTRA XFS falls within the scope of the arbitration agreement.

DECISION AND REMEDY   The U.S. Court of Appeals for the Sixth Circuit affirmed part of the district court's decision. Specifically, it affirmed the judgment compelling arbitration as to NCR's claims relating to direct copyright infringement of the APTRA XFS software.

THE ETHICAL DIMENSION   Could NCR have a claim that KAL had engaged in unfair competition because KAL had engaged in unethical business practices? (Hint: Unfair competition may occur when one party deceives the public into believing that his or her goods are the goods of another.) Why or why not?

THE LEGAL ENVIRONMENT DIMENSION   Why do you think that NCR did not want its claims decided by arbitration?

Mandatory Arbitration in the Employment Context A significant question in the last several years has concerned mandatory arbitration clauses in employment contracts. Many claim that employees' rights are not sufficiently protected when the workers are forced, as a condition of being hired, to agree to arbitrate all disputes and thus waive their rights under statutes specifically designed to protect employees. The United States Supreme Court, however, has generally held that mandatory arbitration clauses in employment contracts are enforceable.

EXAMPLE #13 In a landmark 1991 decision, *Gilmer v. Interstate/Johnson Lane Corp.,*[18] the Supreme Court held that a claim brought under a federal statute prohibiting age discrimination (see Chapter 18) could be subject to arbitration. The Court concluded that the employee had waived his right to sue when he agreed, as part of a required registration application to be a securities representative with the New York Stock Exchange, to arbitrate "any dispute, claim, or controversy" relating to his employment.□ For more information on when the courts will enforce arbitration clauses in employment contracts, see this chapter's *Management Perspective* feature on the following page.

Other Types of ADR

The three forms of ADR just discussed are the oldest and traditionally the most commonly used. In recent years, a variety of new types of ADR have emerged. Some parties today are using *assisted negotiation,* in which a third party participates in the negotiation process. The third party may be an expert in the subject matter of the dispute. In *early neutral case evaluation,* the parties explain the situation to the expert, and the expert assesses the strengths and weaknesses of each party's claims. Another form of assisted negotiation is the *mini-trial,* in which the parties present arguments before the third party (usually an expert), who renders an advisory opinion on how a court would likely decide the issue. This proceeding is designed to assist the parties in determining whether they should settle or take the dispute to court.

Other types of ADR combine characteristics of mediation with those of arbitration. In *binding mediation,* for example, the parties agree that if they cannot resolve the dispute, the mediator can make a legally binding decision on the issue. In *mediation-arbitration,* or "med-arb," the parties agree to first attempt to settle their dispute through mediation. If no settlement is reached, the dispute will be arbitrated.

Today's courts are also experimenting with a variety of ADR alternatives to speed up (and reduce the cost of) justice. Numerous federal courts now hold **summary jury trials (SJTs),** in which the parties present their arguments and evidence and the jury renders a verdict. The jury's verdict is not binding, but it does act as a guide to both sides in reaching an agreement during the mandatory negotiations that immediately follow the trial. Other alternatives being employed by the courts include summary procedures for commercial litigation and the appointment of special masters to assist judges in deciding complex issues.

SUMMARY JURY TRIAL (SJT)

A method of settling disputes, used in many federal courts, in which a trial is held, but the jury's verdict is not binding. The verdict acts only as a guide to both sides in reaching an agreement during the mandatory negotiations that immediately follow the summary jury trial.

---

18. 500 U.S. 20, 111 S.Ct. 1647, 114 L.Ed.2d 26 (1991).

Management Faces a Legal Issue

Arbitration is normally simpler, speedier, and less costly than litigation. For that reason, business owners and managers today often incorporate arbitration clauses in their contracts, including employment contracts. What happens, though, if a job candidate whom you wish to hire (or an existing employee whose contract is being renewed) objects to one or more of the provisions in an arbitration clause? If you insist that signing the agreement to arbitrate future disputes is a mandatory condition of employment, will such a clause be enforceable? Put another way, in which situations might a court invalidate an arbitration agreement because it is considered *unconscionable* (morally unacceptable—shocking to the conscience)?

What the Courts Say

The United States Supreme Court has consistently taken the position that because the Federal Arbitration Act (FAA) favors the arbitration of disputes, arbitration clauses in employment contracts should generally be enforced. Nonetheless, some courts have held that arbitration clauses in employment contracts should not be enforced if they are too one sided and unfair to the employee. In one case, for example, the U.S. Court of Appeals for the Ninth Circuit refused to enforce an arbitration clause on the ground that the agreement was unconscionable—so one sided and unfair as to be unenforceable under "ordinary principles of state contract law." The agreement was a standard-form contract drafted by the employer (the party with superior bargaining power), and the employee had to sign it without any modification as a prerequisite to employment. Moreover, only the employees were required to arbitrate their disputes, whereas the employer remained free to litigate any claims it had against its employees in court. Among other things, the contract also severely limited the relief that was available to employees. For these reasons, the court held the entire arbitration agreement unenforceable.[a] Other courts have cited

similar reasons for deciding not to enforce one-sided arbitration clauses.[b]

In a more recent case, employees of a large California law firm were given copies of that firm's new dispute-resolution program. The program culminated in final binding arbitration for most employment-related claims by and against the firm's employees. The new program became effective three months after it was distributed. After leaving employment at the law firm, an employee filed a lawsuit alleging failure to pay overtime wages. She also claimed that her former employer's dispute-resolution program was unconscionable. The reviewing court found that the dispute-resolution program was presented to the employees on a take-it-or-leave-it basis and was therefore procedurally unconscionable. The court also found that the program was substantively unconscionable because it required employees to waive claims if those employees failed to give the firm notice and demand for mediation within one year from the time the claim was discovered.[c]

Implications for Managers

Although the United States Supreme Court has made it clear that arbitration clauses in employment contracts are enforceable under the FAA, managers should be careful when drafting such clauses. It is especially important to make sure that the terms of the agreement are not so one sided that a court could declare the entire agreement unconscionable.

Managers should also be aware that the proposed Arbitration Fairness Act might eventually become law. This planned "consumer protection" bill would render unenforceable all predispute mandatory arbitration provisions in consumer, employment, and franchise contracts. It would amend the Federal Arbitration Act and seriously restrict the ability of firms to require arbitration.

a. *Circuit City Stores, Inc. v. Adams,* 279 F.3d 889 (9th Cir. 2002). (This was the Ninth Circuit Court's decision, on remand, after the United States Supreme Court reviewed the case.)

b. See, for example, *Hooters of America, Inc. v. Phillips,* 173 F.3d 933 (4th Cir. 1999); and *Nagrampa v. MailCoups, Inc.,* 469 F.3d 1257 (9th Cir. 2006).

c. *Davis v. O'Melveny & Myers, LLC,* 485 F.3d 1066 (9th Cir. 2007).

Providers of ADR Services

ADR services are provided by both government agencies and private organizations. A major provider of ADR services is the American Arbitration Association (AAA), which was founded in 1926 and now handles more than 200,000 claims a year in its numerous offices worldwide. Most of the largest U.S. law firms are members of this nonprofit association. Cases brought before the AAA are heard by an expert or a panel of experts in the area relating to the dispute and are usually settled quickly. The AAA has a special team devoted to resolving large complex disputes across a wide range of industries.

Hundreds of for-profit firms around the country also provide various forms of dispute-resolution services. Typically, these firms hire retired judges to conduct arbitration hearings or otherwise assist parties in settling their disputes. The judges follow procedures similar to those of the federal courts and use similar rules. Usually, each party to the dispute pays a filing fee and a designated fee for a hearing session or conference.

Online Dispute Resolution

An increasing number of companies and organizations offer dispute-resolution services using the Internet. The settlement of disputes in these online forums is known as **online dispute resolution (ODR).** The disputes resolved in these forums have most commonly involved disagreements over the rights to domain names[19] (Web site addresses—see Chapter 8) or over the quality of goods sold via the Internet, including goods sold through Internet auction sites.

ODR may be best for resolving small- to medium-sized business liability claims, which may not be worth the expense of litigation or traditional ADR. Rules being developed in online forums, however, may ultimately become a code of conduct for everyone who does business in cyberspace. Most online forums do not automatically apply the law of any specific jurisdiction. Instead, results are often based on general, universal legal principles. As with most offline methods of dispute resolution, any party may appeal to a court at any time.

ONLINE DISPUTE RESOLUTION (ODR)
The resolution of disputes with the assistance of organizations that offer dispute-resolution services via the Internet.

---

19. The Internet Corporation for Assigned Names and Numbers (ICANN), a nonprofit corporation that the federal government set up to oversee the distribution of domain names, has issued special rules for the resolution of domain name disputes. ICANN's Rules for Uniform Domain Name Dispute Resolution Policy are online at **www.icann.org/dndr/udrp/uniform-rules.htm**. Domain names will be discussed in more detail in Chapter 8, in the context of trademark law.

 *Reviewing . . .* **Courts and Alternative Dispute Resolution**

Stan Garner resides in Illinois and promotes boxing matches for SuperSports, Inc., an Illinois corporation. Garner created the promotional concept of the "Ages" fights—a series of three boxing matches pitting an older fighter (George Foreman) against a younger fighter, such as John Ruiz or Riddick Bowe. The concept included titles for each of the three fights ("Challenge of the Ages," "Battle of the Ages," and "Fight of the Ages"), as well as promotional epithets to characterize the two fighters ("the Foreman Factor"). Garner contacted George Foreman and his manager, who both reside in Texas, to sell the idea, and they arranged a meeting at Caesar's Palace in Las Vegas, Nevada. At some point in the negotiations, Foreman's manager signed a nondisclosure agreement prohibiting him from disclosing Garner's promotional concepts unless they signed a contract. Nevertheless, after negotiations between Garner and Foreman fell through, Foreman used Garner's "Battle of the Ages" concept to promote a subsequent fight. Garner filed a lawsuit against Foreman and his manager in a federal district court located in Illinois, alleging breach of contract. Using the information presented in the chapter, answer the following questions.

1. On what basis might the federal district court in Illinois exercise jurisdiction in this case?

2. Does the federal district court have original or appellate jurisdiction?

3. Suppose that Garner had filed his action in an Illinois state court. Could an Illinois state court exercise personal jurisdiction over Foreman or his manager? Why or why not?

4. Assume that Garner had filed his action in a Nevada state court. Would that court have personal jurisdiction over Foreman or his manager? Explain.

Key Terms

alternative dispute resolution (ADR) 88	exclusive jurisdiction 68	motion to dismiss 79
answer 79	federal question 67	negotiation 89
arbitration 89	interrogatories 80	online dispute resolution (ODR) 95
arbitration clause 90	judicial review 62	pleadings 78
award 83	jurisdiction 62	probate court 67
bankruptcy court 67	justiciable controversy 71	question of fact 74
brief 84	litigation 77	question of law 74
complaint 78	long arm statute 63	reply 79
concurrent jurisdiction 68	mediation 89	rule of four 77
counterclaim 79	motion for a directed verdict 83	small claims court 74
default judgment 79	motion for a new trial 84	standing to sue 71
deposition 80	motion for judgment n.o.v. 84	summary jury trial (SJT) 93
discovery 80	motion for judgment on the pleadings 79	summons 78
diversity of citizenship 68	motion for summary judgment 79	venue 70
docket 69		voir dire 82
e-evidence 81		writ of certiorari 77

Chapter Summary

The Judiciary's Role in American Government (See pages 61–62.)	The role of the judiciary—the courts—in the American governmental system is to interpret and apply the law. Through the process of judicial review—determining the constitutionality of laws—the judicial branch acts as a check on the executive and legislative branches of government.
Basic Judicial Requirements (See pages 62–71.)	1. *Jurisdiction*—Before a court can hear a case, it must have jurisdiction over the person against whom the suit is brought or the property involved in the suit, as well as jurisdiction over the subject matter.
	a. Limited versus general jurisdiction—Limited jurisdiction exists when a court is limited to a specific subject matter, such as probate or divorce. General jurisdiction exists when a court can hear any kind of case.
	b. Original versus appellate jurisdiction—Original jurisdiction exists when courts have authority to hear a case for the first time (trial courts). Appellate jurisdiction exists with courts of appeals, or reviewing courts; generally, appellate courts do not have original jurisdiction.

Basic Judicial Requirements— Continued

    c. Federal jurisdiction–Arises (1) when a federal question is involved (when the plaintiff's cause of action is based, at least in part, on the U.S. Constitution, a treaty, or a federal law) or (2) when a case involves diversity of citizenship (citizens of different states, for example) and the amount in controversy exceeds $75,000.

    d. Concurrent versus exclusive jurisdiction–Concurrent jurisdiction exists when two different courts have authority to hear the same case. Exclusive jurisdiction exists when only state courts or only federal courts have authority to hear a case.

2. *Jurisdiction in cyberspace*–Because the Internet does not have physical boundaries, traditional jurisdictional concepts have been difficult to apply in cases involving activities conducted via the Web. Gradually, the courts are developing standards to use in determining when jurisdiction over a Web site owner or operator located in another state is proper.

3. *Venue*–Venue has to do with the most appropriate location for a trial, which is usually the geographic area where the event leading to the dispute took place or where the parties reside.

4. *Standing to sue*–A requirement that a party must have a legally protected and tangible interest at stake sufficient to justify seeking relief through the court system. The controversy at issue must also be a justiciable controversy–one that is real and substantial, as opposed to hypothetical or academic.

The State and Federal Court Systems
(See pages 71–78.)

1. *Trial courts*–Courts of original jurisdiction, in which legal actions are initiated.

    a. State–Courts of general jurisdiction can hear any case; courts of limited jurisdiction include domestic relations courts, probate courts, traffic courts, and small claims courts.

    b. Federal–The federal district court is the equivalent of the state trial court. Federal courts of limited jurisdiction include the U.S. Tax Court, the U.S. Bankruptcy Court, and the U.S. Court of Federal Claims.

2. *Intermediate appellate courts*–Courts of appeals, or reviewing courts; generally without original jurisdiction. Many states have an intermediate appellate court; in the federal court system, the U.S. circuit courts of appeals are the intermediate appellate courts.

3. *Supreme (highest) courts*–Each state has a supreme court, although it may be called by some other name; appeal from the state supreme court to the United States Supreme Court is possible only if the case involves a federal question. The United States Supreme Court is the highest court in the federal court system and the final arbiter of the U.S. Constitution and federal law.

Following a State Court Case
(See pages 78–87.)

Rules of procedure prescribe the way in which disputes are handled in the courts. Rules differ from court to court, and separate sets of rules exist for federal and state courts, as well as for criminal and civil cases. A sample civil court case in a state court would involve the following procedures:

1. *The pleadings*–

    a. Complaint–Filed by the plaintiff with the court to initiate the lawsuit; served with a summons on the defendant.

    b. Answer–A response to the complaint in which the defendant admits or denies the allegations made by the plaintiff; may assert a counterclaim or an affirmative defense.

    c. Motion to dismiss–A request to the court to dismiss the case for stated reasons, such as the plaintiff's failure to state a claim for which relief can be granted.

2. *Pretrial motions (in addition to the motion to dismiss)*–

    a. Motion for judgment on the pleadings–May be made by either party; will be granted if the parties agree on the facts and the only question is how the law applies to the facts. The judge bases the decision solely on the pleadings.

CONTINUED

**Following a State
Court Case—Continued**

   b. Motion for summary judgment—May be made by either party; will be granted if the parties agree on the facts. The judge applies the law in rendering a judgment. The judge can consider evidence outside the pleadings when evaluating the motion.

3. *Discovery*—The process of gathering evidence concerning the case. Discovery involves depositions (sworn testimony by parties to the lawsuit or witnesses), interrogatories (written questions and answers to these questions made by parties to the action with the aid of their attorneys), and various requests (for admissions, documents, and medical examinations, for example). Discovery may also involve electronically recorded information, such as e-mail, voice mail, word-processing documents, and other data compilations. Although electronic discovery has significant advantages over paper discovery, it is also more time consuming and expensive and often requires the parties to hire experts.

4. *Pretrial conference*—Either party or the court can request a pretrial conference to identify the matters in dispute after discovery has taken place and to plan the course of the trial.

5. *Trial*—Following jury selection (*voir dire*), the trial begins with opening statements from both parties' attorneys. Following that, the plaintiff introduces evidence (including the testimony of witnesses) supporting the plaintiff's position. The defendant's attorney can challenge evidence and cross-examine witnesses. Then it's the defendant's turn to present evidence and testimony supporting the defendant's position. Once both sides have finished, the attorneys present their closing arguments. Then come the judge's instructions to the jury and the jury's verdict.

6. *Posttrial motions*—

   a. Motion for judgment *n.o.v.* ("notwithstanding the verdict")—Will be granted if the judge is convinced that the jury was in error.

   b. Motion for a new trial—Will be granted if the judge is convinced that the jury was in error; can also be granted on the grounds of newly discovered evidence, misconduct by the participants during the trial, or error by the judge.

7. *Appeal*—Either party can appeal the trial court's judgment to an appropriate court of appeals. After reviewing the record on appeal, the abstracts, and the attorneys' briefs, the appellate court holds a hearing and renders its opinion.

**The Courts Adapt
to the Online World**
(See pages 87–88.)

A number of state and federal courts now allow parties to file litigation-related documents with the courts via the Internet or other electronic means. Nearly all of the federal appellate courts and bankruptcy courts and a majority of the federal district courts have implemented electronic filing systems. Almost every court now has a Web page offering information about the court and its procedures, and increasingly courts are publishing their opinions online. In the future, we may see "cyber courts," in which all trial proceedings are conducted online.

**Alternative
Dispute Resolution**
(See pages 88–95.)

1. *Negotiation*—The parties come together, with or without attorneys to represent them, and try to reach a settlement without the involvement of a third party.

2. *Mediation*—The parties themselves reach an agreement with the help of a neutral third party, called a mediator, who proposes solutions. At the parties' request, a mediator may make a legally binding decision.

3. *Arbitration*—A more formal method of ADR in which the parties submit their dispute to a neutral third party, the arbitrator, who renders a decision. The decision may or may not be legally binding, depending on the circumstances.

**Online
Dispute Resolution**
(See page 95.)

A number of organizations and firms are now offering dispute-resolution services through online forums. To date, these forums have been a practical alternative for the resolution of domain name disputes and e-commerce disputes in which the amount in controversy is relatively small.

For Review

1. What is judicial review? How and when was the power of judicial review established?
2. Before a court can hear a case, it must have jurisdiction. Over what must it have jurisdiction? How are the courts applying traditional jurisdictional concepts to cases involving Internet transactions?
3. What is the difference between a trial court and an appellate court?
4. In a lawsuit, what are the pleadings? What is discovery, and how does electronic discovery differ from traditional discovery? What is electronic filing?
5. How are online forums being used to resolve disputes?

Questions and Case Problems

3–1. Arbitration. In an arbitration proceeding, the arbitrator need not be a judge or even a lawyer. How, then, can the arbitrator's decision have the force of law and be binding on the parties involved?

Question with Sample Answer

3–2. Marya Callais, a citizen of Florida, was walking along a busy street in Tallahassee when a large crate flew off a passing truck and hit her, causing numerous injuries to Callais. She incurred a great deal of pain and suffering plus significant medical expenses, and she could not work for six months. She wishes to sue the trucking firm for $300,000 in damages. The firm's headquarters are in Georgia, although the company does business in Florida. In what court may Callais bring suit—a Florida state court, a Georgia state court, or a federal court? What factors might influence her decision?

For a sample answer to Question 3–2, go to Appendix I at the end of this text.

3–3. Standing to Sue. Lamar Advertising of Penn, LLC, an outdoor advertising business, wanted to erect billboards of varying sizes in a multiphase operation throughout the town of Orchard Park, New York. An Orchard Park ordinance restricted the signs to certain sizes in certain areas, to advertising products and services available for sale only on the premises, and to other limits. Lamar asked Orchard Park for permission to build signs in some areas larger than the ordinance allowed in those locations (but not as large as allowed in other areas). When the town refused, Lamar filed a suit in a federal district court, claiming that the ordinance violated the First Amendment. Did Lamar have standing to challenge the ordinance? If the court could sever the provisions of the ordinance restricting a sign's content from the provisions limiting a sign's size, would your answer be the same? Explain. [*Lamar*

Advertising of Penn, LLC v. Town of Orchard Park, New York, 356 F.3d 365 (2d Cir. 2004)]

3–4. Jurisdiction. Xcentric Ventures, LLC, is an Arizona firm that operates the Web sites RipOffReport.com and BadBusinessBureau.com. Visitors to the sites can buy a copy of a book titled *Do-It-Yourself Guide: How to Get Rip-Off Revenge*. The price ($21.95) includes shipping to anywhere in the United States, including Illinois, to which thirteen copies have been shipped. The sites accept donations and feature postings by individuals who claim to have been "ripped off." Some visitors posted comments about George S. May International Co., a management-consulting firm. The postings alleged fraud, larceny, possession of child pornography, and possession of controlled substances (illegal drugs). May filed a suit against Xcentric and others in a federal district court in Illinois, alleging in part "false descriptions and representations." The defendants filed a motion to dismiss for lack of jurisdiction. What is the standard for exercising jurisdiction over a party whose only connection to a jurisdiction is over the Web? How would that standard apply in this case? Explain. [*George S. May International Co. v. Xcentric Ventures, LLC*, 409 F.Supp.2d 1052 (N.D.Ill. 2006)]

3–5. Appellate Review. BSH Home Appliances Corp. makes appliances under the Bosch, Siemens, Thermador, and Gaggenau brands. To make and market the "Pro 27 Stainless Steel Range," a restaurant-quality range for home use, BSH gave specifications for its burner to Detroit Radiant Products Co. and requested a price for 30,000 units. Detroit quoted $28.25 per unit, offering to absorb all tooling and research and development costs. In 2001 and 2003, BSH sent Detroit two purchase orders, for 15,000 and 16,000 units, respectively. In 2004, after Detroit had shipped 12,886 units, BSH stopped scheduling deliveries. Detroit filed a suit against BSH, alleging breach of contract. BSH argued, in part, that the second purchase order had not added to the first but had replaced it. After a trial, a federal district court issued its "Findings of Fact and Conclusions of Law." The court found that the two purchase orders "required BSH to purchase 31,000 units of the burner at $28.25 per unit." The court ruled that Detroit was entitled to $418,261 for 18,114 unsold burners. BSH appealed to the U.S. Court of Appeals for the Sixth Circuit. Can an appellate court set aside a trial court's findings of fact? Can an appellate court come to its own conclusions of law? What should the court rule in this case? Explain. [*Detroit Radiant Products Co. v. BSH Home Appliances Corp.*, 473 F.3d 623 (6th Cir. 2007)]

Case Problem with Sample Answer

3–6. Kathleen Lowden sued cellular phone company T-Mobile, claiming that its service agreements were not enforceable under Washington state law. Lowden sued to create a class action suit, in which her claims would extend to similarly affected customers. She contended that T-Mobile had improperly charged her fees beyond the advertised price of service and charged her for roaming calls that should not have been classified as roaming. T-Mobile moved to force arbitration in accord with the arbitration provision in the service agreement. The arbitration provision was clearly explained in the service agreement. The agreement also specified that no class action suit could be brought, so T-Mobile requested the court to dismiss the class action request. Was T-Mobile correct that Lowden's only course of action would be to file arbitration personally? [*Lowden v. T-Mobile USA, Inc.*, 512 F.3d 1213 (9th Cir. 2008)]

After you have answered Problem 3–6, compare your answer with the sample answer given on the Web site that accompanies this text. Go to www.cengage.com/blaw/let, select "Chapter 3," and click on "Case Problem with Sample Answer."

3–7. Jurisdiction. In 2001, Raul Leal, the owner and operator of Texas Labor Contractors in East Texas, contacted Poverty Point Produce, Inc., which operates a sweet potato farm in West Carroll Parish, Louisiana, and offered to provide field workers. Poverty Point accepted the offer. Jeffrey Brown, an owner of, and field manager for, the farm, told Leal the number of workers needed and gave him forms for them to fill out and sign. Leal placed an ad in a newspaper in Brownsville, Texas. Job applicants were directed to Leal's car dealership in Weslaco, Texas, where they were told the details of the work. Leal recruited, among others, Elias Moreno, who lives in the Rio Grande Valley in Texas, and transported Moreno and the others to Poverty Point's farm. At the farm, Leal's brother Jesse oversaw the work with instructions from Brown, lived with the workers in the on-site housing, and gave them their paychecks. When the job was done, the workers were returned to Texas. Moreno and others filed a suit in a federal district court against

Poverty Point and others, alleging, in part, violations of Texas state law related to the work. Poverty Point filed a motion to dismiss the suit on the ground that the court did not have personal jurisdiction. All of the meetings between Poverty Point and the Leals occurred in Louisiana. All of the farmwork was done in Louisiana. Poverty Point has no offices, bank accounts, or phone listings in Texas. It does not advertise or solicit business in Texas. Despite these facts, can the court exercise personal jurisdiction? Explain. [*Moreno v. Poverty Point Produce, Inc.*, 243 F.R.D. 275 (S.D.Tex. 2007)]

3–8. Arbitration. Thomas Baker and others who bought new homes from Osborne Development Corp. sued for multiple defects in the houses they purchased. When Osborne sold the homes, it paid for them to be in a new home warranty program administered by Home Buyers Warranty (HBW). When the company enrolled a home with HBW, it paid a fee and filled out a form that stated the following: "By signing below, you acknowledge that you . . . CONSENT TO THE TERMS OF THESE DOCUMENTS INCLUDING THE BINDING ARBITRATION PROVISION contained therein." HBW then issued warranty booklets to the new homeowners that stated: "Any and all claims, disputes and controversies by or between the Homeowner, the Builder, the Warranty Insurer and/or HBW . . . shall be submitted to arbitration." Would the new homeowners be bound by the arbitration agreement or could they sue the builder, Osborne, in court? [*Baker v. Osborne Development Corp.*, 159 Cal.App.4th 884, 71 Cal.Rptr.3d 854 (2008)]

A Question of Ethics

3–9. Narnia Investments, Ltd., filed a suit in a Texas state court against several defendants, including Harvestons Securities, Inc., a securities dealer. (Securities are documents evidencing an ownership interest in a corporation, in the form of stock, or debts owed by it, in the form of bonds.) Harvestons is registered with the state of Texas and thus may be served with a summons and a copy of a complaint delivered to the Texas Securities Commissioner. In this case, the return of service indicated that process was served on the commissioner "by delivering to JoAnn Kocerek, defendant, in person, a true copy of this [summons] together with the accompanying copy(ies) of the [complaint]." Harvestons did not file an answer, and Narnia obtained a default judgment against the defendant for $365,000, plus attorneys' fees and interest. Five months after this judgment, Harvestons filed a motion for a new trial, which the court denied. Harvestons appealed to a state intermediate appellate court, claiming that it had not been served in strict compliance with the rules governing service of process. [*Harvestons Securities, Inc. v. Narnia Investments, Ltd.*, 218 S.W.3d 126 (Tex.App.—Houston [14 Dist.] 2007)]

1. Harvestons asserted that Narnia's service was invalid in part because "the return of service states that process was delivered to 'JoAnn Kocerek'" and did not show that she "had the authority to accept process on behalf of Harvestons or the Texas Securities Commissioner." Should such a detail, if it is required, be strictly construed and applied? Should it apply in this case? Explain.

2. Whose responsibility is it to see that service of process is accomplished properly? Was it accomplished properly in this case? Why or why not?

Video Question

3–10. Go to this text's Web site at **www.cengage.com/blaw/let** and select "Chapter 3." Click on "Video Questions" and view the video titled *Jurisdiction in Cyberspace*. Then answer the following questions.

1. What standard would a court apply to determine whether it has jurisdiction over the out-of-state computer firm in the video?

2. What factors is a court likely to consider in assessing whether sufficient contacts exist when the only connection to the jurisdiction is through a Web site?

3. How do you think a court would resolve the issue in this case?

Interacting with the Internet

For updated links to resources available on the Web, as well as a variety of other materials, visit this text's Web site at

www.cengage.com/blaw/let

For the decisions of the United States Supreme Court, along with information about the Supreme Court and its justices, go to

www.supremecourtus.gov

The Web site for the federal courts offers information on the federal court system and links to all federal courts at

www.uscourts.gov

For information on alternative dispute resolution, go to the American Arbitration Association's Web site at

www.adr.org

PRACTICAL INTERNET EXERCISES

Go to this text's Web site at **www.cengage.com/blaw/let**, select "Chapter 3," and click on "Practical Internet Exercises." There you will find the following Internet research exercises that you can perform to learn more about the topics covered in this chapter.

Practical Internet Exercise 3–1: LEGAL PERSPECTIVE—**The Judiciary's Role in American Government**
Practical Internet Exercise 3–2: MANAGEMENT PERSPECTIVE—**Alternative Dispute Resolution**
Practical Internet Exercise 3–3: SOCIAL PERSPECTIVE—**Resolve a Dispute Online**

BEFORE THE TEST

Go to this text's Web site at **www.cengage.com/blaw/let**, select "Chapter 3," and click on "Interactive Quizzes." You will find a number of interactive questions relating to this chapter.

Chapter 4

Constitutional Authority to Regulate Business

CHAPTER OBJECTIVES

After reading this chapter, you should be able to answer the following questions:

1. What is the basic structure of the U.S. government?

2. What constitutional clause gives the federal government the power to regulate commercial activities among the various states?

3. What constitutional clause allows laws enacted by the federal government to take priority over conflicting state laws?

4. What is the Bill of Rights? What freedoms does the First Amendment guarantee?

5. Where in the Constitution can the due process clause be found?

CONTENTS

- The Constitutional Powers of Government
- Business and the Bill of Rights
- Due Process and Equal Protection
- Privacy Rights

" The United States Constitution has proved itself the most marvelously elastic compilation of rules of government ever written. "

— FRANKLIN D. ROOSEVELT,
1882–1945 (Thirty-second president of the United States, 1933–1945)

The U.S. Constitution is brief.[1] It consists of only about seven thousand words, which is less than one-third of the number of words in the average state constitution. Perhaps its brevity explains why it has proved to be so "marvelously elastic," as Franklin Roosevelt pointed out in the chapter-opening quotation, and why it has survived for more than two hundred years—longer than any other written constitution in the world.

Laws that govern business have their origin in the lawmaking authority granted by this document, which is the supreme law in this country. As mentioned in Chapter 1, neither Congress nor any state can enact a law that is in conflict with the Constitution.

In this chapter, we first look at some basic constitutional concepts and clauses and their significance for business. Then we examine how certain fundamental freedoms guaranteed by the Constitution affect businesspersons and the workplace.

THE CONSTITUTIONAL POWERS OF GOVERNMENT

Following the Revolutionary War, the states created a *confederal* form of government in which the states had the authority to govern themselves and the national government could exercise only limited powers. When problems arose because the nation was facing an economic crisis and state laws interfered with the free flow of commerce, a national convention was called, and the delegates drafted the U.S. Constitution. This document, after its ratification by the states in 1789, became the basis for an entirely new form of government.

---

1. See Appendix B for the full text of the U.S. Constitution.

A Federal Form of Government

The new government created by the Constitution reflected a series of compromises made by the convention delegates on various issues. Some delegates wanted sovereign power to remain with the states; others wanted the national government alone to exercise sovereign power. The end result was a compromise—a **federal form of government** in which the national government and the states *share* sovereign power.

The Constitution sets forth specific powers that can be exercised by the national government and provides that the national government has the implied power to undertake actions necessary to carry out its expressly designated powers. All other powers are "reserved" to the states. The broad language of the Constitution, though, has left much room for debate over the specific nature and scope of these powers. Generally, it has been the task of the courts to determine where the boundary line between state and national powers should lie—and that line changes over time. In the past, for example, the national government met little resistance from the courts when extending its regulatory authority over broad areas of social and economic life. Today, in contrast, the courts, and particularly the United States Supreme Court, are sometimes more willing to interpret the Constitution in such a way as to curb some of the national government's regulatory powers.

FEDERAL FORM OF GOVERNMENT
A system of government in which the states form a union and the sovereign power is divided between the central government and the member states.

The Separation of Powers

To make it difficult for the national government to use its power arbitrarily, the Constitution divided the national government's powers among the three branches of government. The legislative branch makes the laws, the executive branch enforces the laws, and the judicial branch interprets the laws. Each branch performs a separate function, and no branch may exercise the authority of another branch.

Additionally, a system of **checks and balances** allows each branch to limit the actions of the other two branches, thus preventing any one branch from exercising too much power. The following are examples of these checks and balances:

1. The legislative branch (Congress) can enact a law, but the executive branch (the president) has the constitutional authority to veto that law.
2. The executive branch is responsible for foreign affairs, but treaties with foreign governments require the advice and consent of the Senate.
3. Congress determines the jurisdiction of the federal courts, and the president appoints federal judges, with the advice and consent of the Senate, but the judicial branch has the power to hold actions of the other two branches unconstitutional.[2]

CHECKS AND BALANCES
The principle under which the powers of the national government are divided among three separate branches—the executive, legislative, and judicial branches—each of which exercises a check on the actions of the others.

The Commerce Clause

To prevent states from establishing laws and regulations that would interfere with trade and commerce among the states, the Constitution expressly delegated to the national government the power to regulate interstate commerce. Article I,

---

2. As discussed in the *Landmark in the Legal Environment* feature in Chapter 3 on page 64, the power of judicial review was established by the United States Supreme Court in *Marbury v. Madison,* 5 U.S. (1 Cranch) 137, 2 L.Ed. 60 (1803).

COMMERCE CLAUSE
The provision in Article I, Section 8, of the U.S. Constitution that gives Congress the power to regulate interstate commerce.

Section 8, of the U.S. Constitution expressly permits Congress "[t]o regulate Commerce with foreign Nations, and among the several States, and with the Indian Tribes." This clause, referred to as the **commerce clause,** has had a greater impact on business than any other provision in the Constitution.

Initially, the commerce power was interpreted as being limited to interstate commerce (commerce among the states) and not applicable to *intrastate* commerce (commerce within a state). In 1824, however, in *Gibbons v. Ogden* (see this chapter's *Landmark in the Legal Environment* feature on page 106), the United States Supreme Court held that commerce within a state could also be regulated by the national government as long as the commerce substantially affected commerce involving more than one state.

The Expansion of National Powers and the Commerce Clause   In *Gibbons v. Ogden,* the commerce clause was expanded to regulate activities that "substantially affect interstate commerce." As the nation grew and faced new kinds of problems, the commerce clause became a vehicle for the additional expansion of the national government's regulatory powers. Even activities that seemed purely local came under the regulatory reach of the national government if those activities were deemed to substantially affect interstate commerce. **EXAMPLE #1** In 1942, in *Wickard v. Filburn,*[3] the Supreme Court held that wheat production by an individual farmer intended wholly for consumption on his own farm was subject to federal regulation. The Court reasoned that the home consumption of wheat reduced the market demand for wheat and thus could have a substantial effect on interstate commerce.☐

The following landmark case involved a challenge to the scope of the national government's constitutional authority to regulate local activities.

---

3. 317 U.S. 111, 63 S.Ct. 82, 87 L.Ed. 122 (1942).

Landmark and Classic Cases

Case 4.1 | **Heart of Atlanta Motel v. United States**

Supreme Court of the United States, 1964.
379 U.S. 241, 85 S.Ct. 348, 13 L.Ed.2d 258.
<u>supct.law.cornell.edu/supct/cases/name.htm</u>[a]

HISTORICAL AND SOCIAL SETTING   *In the first half of the twentieth century, state governments sanctioned segregation on the basis of race. In 1954, the United States Supreme Court decided that racially segregated school systems violated the Constitution. In the following decade, the Court ordered an end to racial segregation imposed by the states in other public facilities, such as beaches, golf courses, buses, parks, auditoriums, and courtroom seating. Privately owned facilities that excluded or segregated African Americans and*

others on the basis of race were not subject to the same constitutional restrictions, however. Congress passed the Civil Rights Act of 1964 to prohibit racial discrimination in "establishments affecting interstate commerce." These facilities included "places of public accommodation."

BACKGROUND AND FACTS   The owner of the Heart of Atlanta Motel, in violation of the Civil Rights Act of 1964, refused to rent rooms to African Americans. The motel owner brought an action in a federal district court to have the Civil Rights Act declared unconstitutional, alleging that Congress had exceeded its constitutional authority to regulate commerce by enacting the act. The owner argued that his motel was not engaged in interstate commerce but was "of a purely local character." The motel, however, was accessible to state and interstate highways. The owner advertised nationally, maintained billboards throughout the state, and accepted convention trade from outside the state (75 percent of the guests were residents of other states). The court ruled that the

---

a. This is the "Historic Supreme Court Decisions—by Party Name" page within the "Supreme Court" collection that is available at the Web site of the Legal Information Institute. Click on the "H" link, or scroll down the list of cases to the entry for the *Heart of Atlanta* case. Click on the case name and select the format in which you would like to view the case.

CASE 4.1–CONTINUED

act did not violate the Constitution and enjoined (prohibited) the owner from discriminating on the basis of race. The owner

appealed. The case ultimately went to the United States Supreme Court.

IN THE WORDS OF THE COURT . . . MR. JUSTICE *CLARK* delivered the opinion of the Court.

*   *   *   *

While the Act as adopted carried no congressional findings, the record of its passage through each house is replete [abounding] with evidence of the burdens that discrimination by race or color places upon interstate commerce *   *   * . This testimony included the fact that our people have become increasingly mobile with millions of all races traveling from State to State; that Negroes in particular have been the subject of discrimination in transient accommodations, having to travel great distances to secure the same; that often they have been unable to obtain accommodations and have had to call upon friends to put them up overnight. *   *   * These exclusionary practices were found to be nationwide, the Under Secretary of Commerce testifying that there is "no question that this discrimination in the North still exists to a large degree" and in the West and Midwest as well *   *   * . This testimony indicated a qualitative as well as quantitative effect on interstate travel by Negroes. The former was the obvious impairment of the Negro traveler's pleasure and convenience that resulted when he continually was uncertain of finding lodging. As for the latter, there was evidence that this uncertainty stemming from racial discrimination had the effect of discouraging travel on the part of a substantial portion of the Negro community *   *   * . We shall not burden this opinion with further details since the voluminous testimony presents overwhelming evidence that discrimination by hotels and motels impedes interstate travel.

*   *   *   *

It is said that the operation of the motel here is of a purely local character. But, assuming this to be true, "if it is interstate commerce that feels the pinch, it does not matter how local the operation that applies the squeeze." *   *   * Thus *the power of Congress to promote interstate commerce also includes the power to regulate the local incidents thereof, including local activities in both the States of origin and destination, which might have a substantial and harmful effect upon that commerce.* [Emphasis added.]

DECISION AND REMEDY The United States Supreme Court upheld the constitutionality of the Civil Rights Act of 1964. The power of Congress to regulate interstate commerce permitted the enactment of legislation that could halt local discriminatory practices.

IMPACT OF THIS CASE ON TODAY'S LEGAL ENVIRONMENT If the Supreme Court had invalidated the Civil Rights Act of 1964, the legal landscape of the United States would be much different today. The act prohibited discrimination based on race, color, national origin, religion, or gender in all "public accommodations" as well as discrimination in employment based on these criteria. Although state laws now prohibit many of these forms of discrimination as well, the protections available vary from state to state—and it is not certain when (and if) such laws would have been passed had the 1964 federal Civil Rights Act been deemed unconstitutional.

THE LEGAL ENVIRONMENT DIMENSION Can you think of any businesses in today's economy that are "purely local in character"?

RELEVANT WEB SITES To locate information on the Web concerning the *Heart of Atlanta Motel* case, go to this text's Web site at **academic.cengage.com/blaw/let**, select "Chapter 4," and click on "URLs for Landmarks."

The commerce clause, which is found in Article I, Section 8, of the U.S. Constitution, gives Congress the power "[t]o regulate Commerce with foreign Nations, and among the several States, and with the Indian Tribes." What exactly does "to regulate commerce" mean? What does "commerce" entail? These questions came before the United States Supreme Court in 1824 in the case of *Gibbons v. Ogden.*[a]

Background

In 1803, Robert Fulton, the inventor of the steamboat, and Robert Livingston, who was the ambassador to France, secured a monopoly on steam navigation on the waters in the state of New York from the New York legislature. Fulton and Livingston licensed Aaron Ogden, a former governor of New Jersey and a U.S. senator, to operate steam-powered ferryboats between New York and New Jersey. Thomas Gibbons, who had obtained a license from the U.S. government to operate boats in interstate waters, competed with Ogden without New York's permission. Ogden sued Gibbons. The New York state courts granted Ogden's request for an injunction—an order prohibiting Gibbons from operating in New York waters. Gibbons appealed the decision to the United States Supreme Court.

Marshall's Decision

Sitting as chief justice on the Supreme Court was John Marshall, an advocate of a strong national government. In his decision, Marshall defined the word *commerce* as used in the commerce clause to mean all commercial intercourse—that is, all business dealings—

a. 22 U.S. (9 Wheat.) 1, 6 L.Ed. 23 (1824).

affecting more than one state. The Court ruled against Ogden's monopoly, reversing the injunction against Gibbons. Marshall used this opportunity not only to expand the definition of commerce but also to validate and increase the power of the national legislature to regulate commerce. Said Marshall, "What is this power? It is the power . . . to prescribe the rule by which commerce is to be governed." Marshall held that the power to regulate interstate commerce is an exclusive power of the national government and that this power includes the power to regulate any intrastate commerce that substantially affects interstate commerce.

APPLICATION TO TODAY'S LEGAL ENVIRONMENT

Marshall's broad definition of the commerce power established the foundation for the expansion of national powers in the years to come. Today, the national government continues to rely on the commerce clause for its constitutional authority to regulate business activities. Marshall's conclusion that the power to regulate interstate commerce was an exclusive power of the national government has also had significant consequences. By implication, this means that a state cannot regulate activities that extend beyond its borders, such as out-of-state online gambling operations that affect the welfare of in-state citizens. It also means that state regulations over in-state activities normally will be invalidated if the regulations substantially burden interstate commerce.

RELEVANT WEB SITES

To locate information on the Web concerning the *Gibbons v. Ogden* decision, go to this text's Web site at **www.cengage.com/blaw/let**, select "Chapter 4," and click on "URLs for Landmarks."

The Commerce Power Today Today, at least theoretically, the power over commerce authorizes the national government to regulate every commercial enterprise in the United States. Federal (national) legislation governs virtually every major activity conducted by businesses—from hiring and firing decisions to workplace safety, competitive practices, and financing. In the last fifteen years or so, however, the Supreme Court has begun to curb somewhat the national government's regulatory authority under the commerce clause. In 1995, the Court held—for the first time in sixty years—that Congress had exceeded its regulatory authority under the commerce clause. The Court struck down an act that banned the possession of guns within one thousand feet of any school because the act attempted to regulate an area that had "nothing to do with commerce."[4] Subsequently, the Court invalidated key portions of two other federal acts on the ground that they exceeded Congress's commerce clause authority.[5]

4. *United States v. Lopez,* 514 U.S. 549, 115 S.Ct. 1624, 131 L.Ed.2d 626 (1995).
5. *Printz v. United States,* 521 U.S. 898, 117 S.Ct. 2365, 138 L.Ed.2d 914 (1997), involving the Brady Handgun Violence Prevention Act of 1993; and *United States v. Morrison,* 529 U.S. 598, 120 S.Ct. 1740, 146 L.Ed.2d 658 (2000), concerning the federal Violence Against Women Act of 1994.

In one notable case, however, the Supreme Court did allow the federal government to regulate noncommercial activities taking place wholly within a state's borders. **EXAMPLE #2** Eleven states, including California, have adopted "medical marijuana" laws that legalize marijuana for medical purposes. Marijuana possession, however, is illegal under the federal Controlled Substances Act (CSA).[6] After the federal government seized the marijuana that two seriously ill California women were using on the advice of their physicians, the women argued that it was unconstitutional for the federal act to prohibit them from using marijuana for medical purposes that were legal within the state. In 2003, the U.S. Court of Appeals for the Ninth Circuit agreed, deciding the case on commerce clause grounds. In 2005, however, the United States Supreme Court held that Congress has the authority to prohibit the *intra*state possession and noncommercial cultivation of marijuana as part of a larger regulatory scheme (the CSA).[7] In other words, state laws that allow the use of medical marijuana do not insulate the users from federal prosecution. □

Was John Marshall, chief justice of the United States Supreme Court (1801–1835), in favor of more states' rights? If not, of what was he in favor? (Richard A, Creative Commons)

POLICE POWERS

Powers possessed by the states as part of their inherent sovereignty. These powers may be exercised to protect or promote the public order, health, safety, morals, and general welfare.

The Regulatory Powers of the States As part of their inherent sovereignty, state governments have the authority to regulate affairs within their borders. This authority stems in part from the Tenth Amendment to the Constitution, which reserves to the states all powers not delegated to the national government. State regulatory powers are often referred to as **police powers.** The term encompasses not only the enforcement of criminal law but also the right of state governments to regulate private activities to protect or promote the public order, health, safety, morals, and general welfare. Fire and building codes, antidiscrimination laws, parking regulations, zoning restrictions, licensing requirements, and thousands of other state statutes covering virtually every aspect of life have been enacted pursuant to a state's police powers. Local governments, including cities, also exercise police powers.[8] Generally, state laws enacted pursuant to a state's police powers carry a strong presumption of validity.

The "Dormant" Commerce Clause The United States Supreme Court has interpreted the commerce clause to mean that the national government has the *exclusive* authority to regulate commerce that substantially affects trade and commerce among the states. This express grant of authority to the national government, which is often referred to as the "positive" aspect of the commerce clause, implies a negative aspect—that the states do *not* have the authority to regulate interstate commerce. This negative aspect of the commerce clause is often referred to as the "dormant" (implied) commerce clause.

The dormant commerce clause comes into play when state regulations affect interstate commerce. In this situation, the courts normally weigh the state's interest in regulating a certain matter against the burden that the state's regulation places on interstate commerce. Because courts balance the interests involved, it can be extremely difficult to predict the outcome in a particular case.

EXAMPLE #3 At one time, many states regulated the sale of alcoholic beverages, including wine, through a "three-tier" system. This system required separate

---

6. 21 U.S.C. Sections 801 *et seq.*

7. *Gonzales v. Raich,* 545 U.S. 1, 125 S.Ct. 2195, 162 L.Ed.2d 1 (2005).

8. Local governments derive their authority to regulate their communities from the state because they are creatures of the state. In other words, they cannot come into existence unless authorized by the state to do so.

Congress attempted to create gun-free zones around schools. But those who suppport states' rights contend that only states and municipalities should create and use such police powers. Ultimately, the United States Supreme Court ruled that creating gun-free zones around schools had "nothing to do with commerce" and certainly not interstate commerce. Can state and local jurisdictions still create such zones if they wish?
(AP Photo/Matt York)

licenses for producers, wholesalers, and retailers, subject to a complex set of overlapping regulations that effectively banned direct sales to consumers from out-of-state wineries. In-state wineries, in contrast, could obtain a license for direct sales to consumers. In 2005, the United States Supreme Court ruled that these laws violated the dormant commerce clause. The Court reasoned that by mandating different treatment of in-state and out-of-state economic interests, these laws deprived "citizens of their right to have access to the markets of other states on equal terms."[9] □

The Supremacy Clause

SUPREMACY CLAUSE
The clause in Article VI of the Constitution that provides that the Constitution, laws, and treaties of the United States are "the supreme Law of the Land." Under this clause, state and local laws that directly conflict with federal law will be rendered invalid.

PREEMPTION
A doctrine under which certain federal laws preempt, or take precedence over, conflicting state or local laws.

Article VI of the Constitution provides that the Constitution, laws, and treaties of the United States are "the supreme Law of the Land." This article, commonly referred to as the **supremacy clause,** is important in the ordering of state and federal relationships. When there is a direct conflict between a federal law and a state law, the state law is rendered invalid. Because some powers are *concurrent* (shared by the federal government and the states), however, it is necessary to determine which law governs in a particular circumstance.

Preemption occurs when Congress chooses to act exclusively in a concurrent area. In this circumstance, a valid federal statute or regulation will take precedence over a conflicting state or local law or regulation on the same general subject. Often, it is not clear whether Congress, in passing a law, intended to preempt an entire subject area against state regulation. In these situations, it is left to the courts to determine whether Congress intended to exercise exclusive power over a given area. No single factor is decisive as to whether a court will find preemption. Generally, congressional intent to preempt will be found if a federal law regulating an activity is so pervasive, comprehensive, or detailed that the states have little or no room to regulate in that area. Also, when a federal

---

9. *Granholm v. Heald,* 544 U.S. 460, 125 S.Ct. 1885, 161 L.Ed.2d 796 (2005).

statute creates an agency—such as the National Labor Relations Board—to enforce the law, matters that may come within the agency's jurisdiction will likely preempt state laws.

EXAMPLE #4 In 2008, the United States Supreme Court heard a case involving a man who alleged that he had been injured by a faulty medical device (a balloon catheter that had been inserted into his artery following a heart attack). The Court found that the Medical Device Amendments of 1976 had included a preemption provision and that the device had passed the U.S. Food and Drug Administration's rigorous premarket approval process. Therefore, the Court ruled that the federal regulation of medical devices preempted the man's state common law claims for negligence, strict liability, and implied warranty (see Chapters 5 and 12).[10] □

BUSINESS AND THE BILL OF RIGHTS

The importance of having a written declaration of the rights of individuals eventually caused the first Congress of the United States to enact twelve amendments to the Constitution and submit them to the states for approval. The first ten of these amendments, commonly known as the **Bill of Rights,** were adopted in 1791 and embody a series of protections for the individual against various types of interference by the federal government.[11] Some constitutional protections apply to business entities as well. For example, corporations exist as separate legal entities, or legal persons, and enjoy many of the same rights and privileges as natural persons do. Summarized here are the protections guaranteed by these ten amendments (see the Constitution in Appendix B for the complete text of each amendment):

BILL OF RIGHTS
The first ten amendments to the U.S. Constitution.

1. The First Amendment guarantees the freedoms of religion, speech, and the press and the rights to assemble peaceably and to petition the government.
2. The Second Amendment concerns a well-regulated militia and the right of people to keep and bear arms.
3. The Third Amendment prohibits, in peacetime, the lodging of soldiers in any house without the owner's consent.
4. The Fourth Amendment prohibits unreasonable searches and seizures of persons or property.
5. The Fifth Amendment guarantees the rights to *indictment* (pronounced in-*dyte*-ment) by grand jury (see Chapter 6), to due process of law, and to fair payment when private property is taken for public use. The Fifth Amendment also prohibits compulsory self-incrimination and double jeopardy (trial for the same crime twice).
6. The Sixth Amendment guarantees the accused in a criminal case the right to a speedy and public trial by an impartial jury and with counsel. The accused has the right to cross-examine witnesses against him or her and to solicit testimony from witnesses in his or her favor.
7. The Seventh Amendment guarantees the right to a trial by jury in a civil (noncriminal) case involving at least twenty dollars.[12]
8. The Eighth Amendment prohibits excessive bail and fines, as well as cruel and unusual punishment.

BE CAREFUL
Although most of these rights apply to actions of the states, some of them apply only to actions of the federal government.

---

10. *Riegel v. Medtronic, Inc.,* ___ U.S. ___, 128 S.Ct. 999, 169 L.Ed.2d 892 (2008).
11. One of these proposed amendments was ratified more than two hundred years later (in 1992) and became the Twenty-seventh Amendment to the U.S. Constitution. See Appendix B.
12. Twenty dollars was forty days' pay for the average person when the Bill of Rights was written.

9. The Ninth Amendment establishes that the people have rights in addition to those specified in the Constitution.
10. The Tenth Amendment establishes that those powers neither delegated to the federal government nor denied to the states are reserved for the states.

As originally intended, the Bill of Rights limited only the powers of the national government. Over time, however, the Supreme Court "incorporated" most of these rights into the protections against state actions afforded by the Fourteenth Amendment to the Constitution. That amendment, passed in 1868 after the Civil War, provides in part that "[n]o State shall . . . deprive any person of life, liberty, or property, without due process of law." Starting in 1925, the Supreme Court began to define various rights and liberties guaranteed in the national Constitution as constituting "due process of law," which was required of state governments under the Fourteenth Amendment. Today, most of the rights and liberties set forth in the Bill of Rights apply to state governments as well as the national government.

Here we examine two important guarantees of the First Amendment—freedom of speech and freedom of religion. These and other First Amendment freedoms (of the press, assembly, and petition) have all been applied to the states through the due process clause of the Fourteenth Amendment. We also look at the Fourth Amendment right against unreasonable search and seizure, a topic we revisit in Chapter 6, in the context of criminal law and procedures.

As you read through the following pages, keep in mind that none of these (or other) constitutional freedoms confers an absolute right. Ultimately, it is the United States Supreme Court, as the final interpreter of the Constitution, that gives meaning to these rights and determines their boundaries. (For a discussion of how the Supreme Court may consider other nations' laws when determining the appropriate balance of individual rights, see this chapter's *Beyond Our Borders* feature.

Following a traffic violation, police execute a search of a vehicle and the personal property of the occupants in San Diego, California. Should the driver and passengers receive protection from unreasonable searches and seizures under the U.S. Constitution? Why or why not? (D.B. Blas/Creative Commons)

As noted in the text, the United States Supreme Court interprets and gives meaning to the rights provided in the U.S. Constitution. It is the Court's role to determine the appropriate balance of rights and protections stemming from the Constitution. Clearly, this is a difficult task, in part because society's perceptions and needs change over time. The justices on the Supreme Court are noticeably influenced by the opinions and beliefs of U.S. citizens. This is particularly true when the Court decides cases involving issues of freedom of speech or religion, obscenity, or privacy. Changing views on controversial topics, such as privacy in an era of terrorist threats or the rights of gay men and lesbians, may affect the way the Supreme Court decides a case. But should the Court also consider other nations' laws and world opinion when balancing individual rights in the United States?

Over the last several years, justices on the United States Supreme Court have exhibited an increasing tendency to consider foreign law when deciding issues of national importance. For example, in 2003—for the first time ever—foreign law was cited in a majority opinion of the Supreme Court (references to foreign law had appeared in footnotes and dissents on a few occasions in the past). The case was a controversial one in which the Court struck down laws that prohibit oral and anal sex between consenting adults of the same sex. In the majority opinion (an opinion that the majority of justices have signed), Justice Anthony Kennedy

mentioned that the European Court of Human Rights and other foreign courts have consistently acknowledged that homosexuals have a right "to engage in intimate, consensual conduct."[a] This comment sparked debate in legal circles over whether the Supreme Court, or other U.S. courts, should ever consider world opinion or cite foreign law as persuasive authority.

The practice has many critics, including Justice Scalia, who believes that foreign views are irrelevant to rulings on U.S. law. Other Supreme Court justices, however, including Justices Breyer, Ginsburg, and O'Connor (who is now retired), believe that in our increasingly global community we should not ignore the opinions of courts in the rest of the world.

FOR CRITICAL ANALYSIS Should U.S. courts, and particularly the United States Supreme Court, look to other nations' laws for guidance when deciding important issues—including those involving rights granted by the Constitution? If so, what impact might this have on their decisions? Explain.

a. *Lawrence v. Texas,* 539 U.S. 558, 123 S.Ct. 2472, 156 L.Ed.2d 508 (2003). Other cases in which the Supreme Court has referenced foreign law include *Grutter v. Bollinger,* 539 U.S. 306, 123 S.Ct. 2325, 156 L.Ed.2d 304 (2003), in the dissent, and *Atkins v. Virginia,* 536 U.S. 304, 122 S.Ct. 2242, 153 L.Ed.2d 335 (2002), in footnote 21 to the majority opinion.

The First Amendment—Freedom of Speech

Freedom of speech is the most prized freedom that Americans have. Indeed, it is essential to our democratic form of government, which could not exist if people were not allowed to express their political opinions freely and criticize government actions or policies. Because of its importance, the courts traditionally have protected this right to the fullest extent possible.

Speech often includes not only what we say, but also what we do to express our political, social, and religious views. The courts generally protect **symbolic speech**—gestures, movements, articles of clothing, and other forms of nonverbal expressive conduct. **EXAMPLE #5** The burning of the American flag to protest government policies is a constitutionally protected form of expression. Similarly, participating in a hunger strike or wearing a black armband would be protected as symbolic speech.□

Reasonable Restrictions Expression—oral, written, or symbolized by conduct—is subject to reasonable restrictions. A balance must be struck between a government's obligation to protect its citizens and those citizens' exercise of their rights. Reasonableness is analyzed on a case-by-case basis. If a restriction imposed by the government is content neutral, then a court may allow it. To be content neutral, the restriction must be aimed at combating some societal problem, such as crime, and not be aimed at suppressing the expressive conduct or its message. **EXAMPLE #6** Courts have often protected nude dancing as a form of

REMEMBER
The First Amendment guarantee of freedom of speech applies only to *government* restrictions on speech.

SYMBOLIC SPEECH
Nonverbal expressions of beliefs. Symbolic speech, which includes gestures, movements, and articles of clothing, is given substantial protection by the courts.

111

symbolic expression. Nevertheless, the courts have also allowed content-neutral laws that ban all public nudity, not just erotic dancing.[13] □

The United States Supreme Court has also held that schools may restrict students' free speech rights at school events. **EXAMPLE #7** In 2007, the Court heard a case involving a high school student who had held up a banner saying "Bong Hits 4 Jesus" at an off-campus but school-sanctioned event. In a split decision, the majority of the Court ruled that school officials did not violate the student's free speech rights when they confiscated the banner and suspended the student for ten days. Because the banner could reasonably be interpreted as promoting the use of marijuana, and because the school had a written policy against illegal drugs, the majority concluded that the school's actions were justified. Several justices disagreed, however, noting that the majority's holding creates a special exception that will allow schools to censor any student speech that mentions drugs.[14] □

Corporate Political Speech   Political speech by corporations also falls within the protection of the First Amendment. Many years ago, the United States Supreme Court ruled that a Massachusetts statute, which prohibited corporations from making political contributions or expenditures that individuals were permitted to make, was unconstitutional.[15] Similarly, the Court has held that a law forbidding a corporation from including inserts in its billing to express its views on controversial issues violates the First Amendment.[16] Although the Supreme Court has reversed this trend somewhat,[17] corporate political speech continues to be given significant protection under the First Amendment. **EXAMPLE #8** In 2003 and again in 2007, the Supreme Court struck down portions of bipartisan campaign-finance reform laws as unconstitutional. The Court found that these provisions constituted unlawful restraints on corporate political speech.[18] □

Commercial Speech   The courts also give substantial protection to "commercial" speech, which consists of communications—primarily advertising and marketing—made by business firms that involve only their commercial interests. The protection given to commercial speech under the First Amendment is not as extensive as that afforded to noncommercial speech, however. A state may restrict certain kinds of advertising, for example, in the interest of protecting consumers from being misled by the advertising practices. States also have a legitimate interest in the beautification of roadsides, and this interest allows states to place restraints on billboard advertising. **EXAMPLE #9** Café Erotica, a nude-dancing establishment, sued the state after being denied a permit to erect a billboard along an interstate highway in Florida. The state appel-

---

13. See, for example, *Rameses, Inc. v. County of Orange,* 481 F.Supp.2d 1305 (M.D.Fla. 2007); and *City of Erie v. Pap's A.M.,* 529 U.S. 277, 120 S.Ct. 1382, 146 L.Ed.2d 265 (2000).
14. *Morse v. Frederick,* ___ U.S. ___, 127 S.Ct. 2618 , 168 L.Ed.2d 290 (2007).
15. *First National Bank of Boston v. Bellotti,* 435 U.S. 765, 98 S.Ct. 1407, 55 L.Ed.2d 707 (1978).
16. *Consolidated Edison Co. v. Public Service Commission,* 447 U.S. 530, 100 S.Ct. 2326, 65 L.Ed.2d 319 (1980).
17. See *Austin v. Michigan Chamber of Commerce,* 494 U.S. 652, 110 S.Ct. 1391, 108 L.Ed.2d 652 (1990), in which the Supreme Court upheld a state law prohibiting corporations from using general corporate funds for independent expenditures in state political campaigns.
18. *McConnell v. Federal Election Commission,* 540 U.S. 93, 124 S.Ct. 619, 157 L.Ed.2d 491 (2003); and *Federal Election Commission v. Wisconsin Right to Life, Inc.,* ___U.S. ___, 127 S.Ct. 2652, 168 L.Ed.2d 329 (2007).

late court decided that because the law directly advanced a substantial government interest in highway beautification and safety, it was not an unconstitutional restraint on commercial speech.[19] □

Generally, a restriction on commercial speech will be considered valid as long as it meets three criteria: (1) it must seek to implement a substantial government interest, (2) it must directly advance that interest, and (3) it must go no further than necessary to accomplish its objective. At issue in the following case was whether a government agency had unconstitutionally restricted commercial speech when it prohibited the inclusion of a certain illustration on beer labels.

19. *Café Erotica v. Florida Department of Transportation,* 830 So.2d 181 (Fla.App. 1 Dist. 2002); review denied, *Café Erotica/We Dare to Bare v. Florida Department of Transportation,* 845 So.2d 888 (Fla. 2003).

Case 4.2 Bad Frog Brewery, Inc. v. New York State Liquor Authority

United States Court of Appeals,
Second Circuit, 1998.
134 F.3d 87.
www.findlaw.com/casecode/index.html[a]

BACKGROUND AND FACTS Bad Frog Brewery, Inc., makes and sells alcoholic beverages. Some of the beverages feature labels that display a drawing of a frog making the gesture generally known as "giving the finger." Bad Frog's authorized New York distributor, Renaissance Beer Company, applied to the New York State Liquor Authority (NYSLA) for brand label *etiket merk goedkeure*

approval, as required by state law before the beer could be sold in New York. The NYSLA denied the application, in part, because "the label could appear in grocery and convenience stores, with obvious exposure on the shelf to children of tender age." Bad Frog filed a suit in a federal district court against the NYSLA, asking for, among other things, an injunction against the denial of the application. The court granted summary judgment in favor of the NYSLA. Bad Frog appealed to the U.S. Court of Appeals for the Second Circuit.

IN THE WORDS OF THE COURT . . . JON O. NEWMAN, Circuit Judge.

* * * *

* * * To support its asserted power to ban Bad Frog's labels [NYSLA advances] * * * the State's interest in "protecting children from vulgar and profane advertising" * * * .

[This interest is] substantial * * * . *States have a compelling interest in protecting the physical and psychological well-being of minors* * * * . [Emphasis added.]

* * * *

* * * NYSLA endeavors to advance the state interest in preventing exposure of children to vulgar displays by taking only the limited step of barring such displays from the labels of alcoholic beverages. *In view of the wide currency of vulgar displays throughout contemporary society, including comic books targeted directly at children, barring such displays from labels for alcoholic beverages cannot realistically be expected to reduce children's exposure to such displays to any significant degree.* [Emphasis added.]

* * * If New York decides to make a substantial effort to insulate children from vulgar displays in some significant sphere of activity, at least with respect to materials likely to be seen by children, NYSLA's label prohibition might well be found to make a justifiable contribution to the material advancement of such an effort, but its currently isolated response to the perceived problem, applicable only to labels on a product that children cannot purchase, does not suffice. * * * A state must demonstrate that its commercial speech limitation is part of a substantial effort to advance a valid

a. Under the heading "US Court of Appeals," click on "2nd." Enter "Bad Frog Brewery" in the "Party Name Search" box and click on "Search." On the resulting page, click on the case name to access the opinion.

CASE 4.2—CONTINUED

CASE 4.2–CONTINUED state interest, not merely the removal of a few grains of offensive sand from a beach of vulgarity.

* * * *

* * * Even if we were to assume that the state materially advances its asserted interest by shielding children from viewing the Bad Frog labels, it is plainly excessive to prohibit the labels from all use, including placement on bottles displayed in bars and taverns where parental supervision of children is to be expected. Moreover, to whatever extent NYSLA is concerned that children will be harmfully exposed to the Bad Frog labels when wandering without parental supervision around grocery and convenience stores where beer is sold, that concern could be less intrusively dealt with by placing restrictions on the permissible locations where the appellant's products may be displayed within such stores.

DECISION AND REMEDY The U.S. Court of Appeals for the Second Circuit reversed the judgment of the district court and remanded the case for the entry of a judgment in favor of Bad Frog. The NYSLA's ban on the use of the labels lacked a "reasonable fit" with the state's interest in shielding minors from vulgarity, and the NYSLA did not adequately consider alternatives to the ban.

WHAT IF THE FACTS WERE DIFFERENT? If Bad Frog had sought to use the offensive label to market toys instead of beer, would the court's ruling likely have been the same? Why or why not?

THE LEGAL ENVIRONMENT DIMENSION Whose interests are advanced by the banning of certain types of advertising?

Unprotected Speech The United States Supreme Court has made it clear that certain types of speech will not be given any protection under the First Amendment. Speech that harms the good reputation of another, or defamatory speech (see Chapter 5), will not be protected. Speech that violates criminal laws (such as threatening speech) is not constitutionally protected. Other unprotected speech includes "fighting words," or words that are likely to incite others to respond violently.

The Supreme Court has also held that the First Amendment does not protect obscene speech. Establishing an objective definition of obscene speech has proved difficult, however, and the Court has grappled from time to time with this problem. In a 1973 case, *Miller v. California*,[20] the Supreme Court created a test for legal obscenity, including a set of requirements that must be met for material to be legally obscene. Under this test, material is obscene if (1) the average person finds that it violates contemporary community standards; (2) the work taken as a whole appeals to a prurient (arousing or obsessive) interest in sex; (3) the work shows patently offensive sexual conduct; and (4) the work lacks serious redeeming literary, artistic, political, or scientific merit.

Because community standards vary widely, the *Miller* test has had inconsistent applications, and obscenity remains a constitutionally unsettled issue. Numerous state and federal statutes make it a crime to disseminate obscene materials, including laws prohibiting the sale and possession of child pornography.

Online Obscenity A significant problem facing the courts and lawmakers today is how to control the dissemination of obscenity and child pornography

---

20. 413 U.S. 15, 93 S.Ct. 2607, 37 L.Ed.2d 419 (1973).

via the Internet. Congress first attempted to protect minors from pornographic materials on the Internet by passing the Communications Decency Act (CDA) of 1996. The CDA declared it a crime to make available to minors online any "obscene or indecent" message that "depicts or describes, in terms patently offensive as measured by contemporary community standards, sexual or excretory activities or organs."[21] Civil rights groups challenged the act, and ultimately the Supreme Court ruled that portions of the act were unconstitutional. The Court held that the terms *indecent* and *patently offensive* covered large amounts of nonpornographic material with serious educational or other value.[22]

Subsequent Attempts to Regulate Online Obscenity   Congress's second attempt to protect children from online obscenity, the Child Online Protection Act (COPA) of 1998,[23] met with a similar fate. Although the COPA was more narrowly tailored than its predecessor, the CDA, it still used "contemporary community standards" to define which material was obscene and harmful to minors. Ultimately, in 2004 the Supreme Court concluded that it was likely that the COPA did violate the right to free speech and prevented enforcement of the act.[24]

In 2000, Congress enacted the Children's Internet Protection Act (CIPA),[25] which requires public schools and libraries to install **filtering software** to keep children from accessing adult content. Such software is designed to prevent persons from viewing certain Web sites based on a site's Internet address or its **meta tags,** or key words. The CIPA was also challenged on constitutional grounds, but in 2003 the Supreme Court held that the act does not violate the First Amendment. The Court concluded that because libraries can disable the filters for any patrons who ask, the system is reasonably flexible and does not burden free speech to an unconstitutional extent.[26]

Because of the difficulties of policing the Internet as well as the constitutional complexities of prohibiting online obscenity through legislation, it remains a continuing problem in the United States (and worldwide). In 2005, the Federal Bureau of Investigation established an antiporn squad to target and prosecute companies that distribute child pornography in cyberspace. The Federal Communications Commission has also passed new obscenity regulations for television networks.

The First Amendment—Freedom of Religion

The First Amendment states that the government may neither establish any religion nor prohibit the free exercise of religious practices. The first part of this constitutional provision is referred to as the **establishment clause,** and the second part is known as the **free exercise clause.** Government action, both federal and state, must be consistent with this constitutional mandate.

FILTERING SOFTWARE
A computer program that is designed to block access to certain Web sites based on their content. The software blocks the retrieval of a site whose URL or key words are on a list within the program.

META TAG
A key word in a document that can serve as an index reference to the document. On the Web, search engines return results based, in part, on the tags in Web documents.

ESTABLISHMENT CLAUSE
The provision in the First Amendment to the Constitution that prohibits the government from establishing any state-sponsored religion or enacting any law that promotes religion or favors one religion over another.

FREE EXERCISE CLAUSE
The provision in the First Amendment to the Constitution that prohibits the government from interfering with people's religious practices or forms of worship.

---

21. 47 U.S.C. Section 223(a)(1)(B)(ii).

22. *Reno v. American Civil Liberties Union,* 521 U.S. 844, 117 S.Ct. 2329, 138 L.Ed.2d 874 (1997).

23. 47 U.S.C. Section 231.

24. *American Civil Liberties Union v. Ashcroft,* 542 U.S. 646, 124 S.Ct. 2783, 159 L.Ed.2d 690 (2004). See also *Ashcroft v. American Civil Liberties Union,* 535 U.S. 564, 122 S.Ct. 1700, 152 L.Ed.2d 771 (2002); and *American Civil Liberties Union v. Ashcroft,* 322 F.3d 240 (3d Cir. 2003).

25. 17 U.S.C. Sections 1701–1741.

26. *United States v. American Library Association,* 539 U.S. 194, 123 S.Ct. 2297, 156 L.Ed.2d 221 (2003).

The Establishment Clause   The establishment clause prohibits the government from establishing a state-sponsored religion, as well as from passing laws that promote (aid or endorse) religion or that show a preference for one religion over another. The establishment clause does not require a complete separation of church and state, though. On the contrary, it requires the government to accommodate religions.

The establishment clause covers all conflicts about such matters as the legality of state and local government support for a particular religion, government aid to religious organizations and schools, the government's allowing or requiring school prayers, and the teaching of evolution versus fundamentalist theories of creation. For a government law or policy to be constitutional, it must not have the primary effect of advancing or inhibiting religion. Generally, federal or state regulation that does not promote religion or place a significant burden on religion is constitutional even if it has some impact on religion.

Religious displays on public property have often been challenged as violating the establishment clause, and the United States Supreme Court has ruled on a number of such cases. Generally, the Court has focused on the proximity of the religious display to nonreligious symbols, such as reindeer and candy canes, or to symbols from different religions, such as a menorah (a nine-branched candelabrum used in celebrating Hanukkah). **EXAMPLE #10** In 2005, however, the Supreme Court took a slightly different approach. The dispute involved a six-foot-tall monument of the Ten Commandments on the Texas state capitol grounds. The Court held that the monument did not violate the establishment clause because the Ten Commandments had historical as well as religious significance.[27] ∎

The Free Exercise Clause   The free exercise clause guarantees that a person can hold any religious belief that she or he wants or can choose to have no religious belief. When religious practices work against public policy and the public welfare, however, the government can act. For example, regardless of a child's or parent's religious beliefs, the government can require certain types of vaccinations. Similarly, although children of Jehovah's Witnesses are not required to say the Pledge of Allegiance at school, their parents cannot prevent them from accepting medical treatment (such as blood transfusions) if their lives are in danger. Additionally, public school students can be required to study from textbooks chosen by school authorities.

For business firms, an important issue involves the accommodation that businesses must make for the religious beliefs of their employees. As you will read in Chapter 18, federal employment laws require business firms to accommodate employees' religious beliefs. If an employee's religion prohibits him or her from working on a certain day of the week or at a certain type of job, the employer must make a reasonable attempt to accommodate these religious requirements. Employers must reasonably accommodate an employee's religious beliefs even if the beliefs are not based on the tenets or dogma of a particular church, sect, or denomination. The only requirement is that the belief be religious in nature and sincerely held by the employee. (We will look further at this issue in Chapter 18, in the context of employment discrimination.)

According to the United States Supreme Court, the free exercise clause protects the use of a controlled substance in a sincere religious practice. The case involved a

---

27. *Van Orden v. Perry,* 545 U.S. 677, 125 S.Ct. 2854, 162 L.Ed.2d 607 (2005).

religious sect in New Mexico that follows the practices of a Brazil-based church. Its members ingest hoasca tea as part of a ritual to connect with and better understand God. Hoasca tea, which is brewed from plants native to the Amazon rain forest, contains an illegal hallucinogenic drug, dimethyltryptamine (DMT), that is regulated by the Controlled Substances Act. Federal drug agents had confiscated the church's shipment of hoasca tea as it entered the country. The church members filed a lawsuit, claiming that the confiscation violated their right to freely exercise their religion. Ultimately, the Supreme Court agreed, ruling that the government had failed to demonstrate a sufficiently compelling interest in barring the sect's sacramental use of hoasca. Chief Justice Roberts wrote the decision, relying on the Religious Freedom Restoration Act of 1993[28] and on earlier decisions allowing the sacramental use of peyote (a cactus that contains mescaline, another hallucinogenic drug). In short, the Supreme Court will allow the use of illegal hallucinogenic drugs as a religious practice but will not allow the use of marijuana for medical purposes.[29]

The Fourth Amendment—Searches and Seizures

The Fourth Amendment protects the "right of the people to be secure in their persons, houses, papers, and effects." Before searching or seizing private property, law enforcement officers must usually obtain a **search warrant**—an order from a judge or other public official authorizing the search or seizure.

Search Warrants and Probable Cause To obtain a search warrant, law enforcement officers must convince a judge that they have reasonable grounds, or probable cause, to believe a search will reveal evidence of a specific illegality. To establish probable cause, the officers must have trustworthy evidence that would convince a reasonable person that the proposed search or seizure is more likely justified than not. Furthermore, the Fourth Amendment prohibits *general* warrants. It requires a particular description of whatever is to be searched or seized. General searches through a person's belongings are impermissible. The search cannot extend beyond what is described in the warrant.

The requirement for a search warrant has several exceptions. One exception applies when the items sought are likely to be removed before a warrant can be obtained. **EXAMPLE #11** During a routine traffic stop, a police officer sees evidence that the car is being used to transport illegal drugs. If the officer has probable cause to believe that an automobile contains evidence of a crime and that the vehicle will likely be unavailable by the time a warrant is obtained, the officer can search the vehicle without a warrant.□ Another exception to the warrant requirement involving border searches is discussed in this chapter's *Online Developments* feature on the following two pages.

Searches and Seizures in the Business Context Constitutional protection against unreasonable searches and seizures is important to businesses and professionals. Equally important is the government's interest in ensuring compliance with federal and state regulations, especially rules meant to protect the safety of employees and the public.

SEARCH WARRANT
An order granted by a public authority, such as a judge, that authorizes law enforcement personnel to search particular premises or property.

---

28. 42 U.S.C. Sections 2000bb *et seq.*
29. *Gonzales v. O Centro Espirita Beneficente Uniao Do Vegetal,* 546 U.S. 418, 126 S.Ct. 1211, 163 L.Ed.2d 1017 (2006).

The Fourth Amendment to the U.S. Constitution protects citizens against "unreasonable searches and seizures." Traditionally, this has meant that the government must obtain a court-ordered warrant to search through a person's property unless the person consents to be searched. (The warrant requirement will be discussed in more detail in Chapter 6 in the context of criminal law.) In a post–9/11 world, however, the rules on permissible searches are changing, particularly at the nation's borders. The courts have long permitted warrantless border searches as a means of preventing drugs, contraband, and illegal aliens from entering the United States. In general, authorities at the border may search a person who is entering or leaving the country by land or by air, as well as the individual's automobile, baggage, or goods. Only recently, however, have courts started allowing border guards to search through the temporary files stored on laptop computers and to use the history of Web pages viewed as criminal evidence of possession of child pornography.

The Unsavory Traveler

Stuart Romm, a suspended lawyer and former administrative law judge from Massachusetts, had attended a training seminar held by his new employer in Las Vegas, Nevada, in 2004. After the seminar ended, he flew to Kelowna, British Columbia, on business. When Romm checked through customs at the airport, Canada's border guards discovered that he had a criminal history—a 1997 conviction for soliciting

sex over the Internet from an undercover agent posing as a fourteen-year-old. Romm admitted that he was on probation. A border agent then asked to see Romm's laptop computer and briefly examined the Internet cache, or temporary folder showing the Web sites that Romm had visited.

The agent noticed several child pornography Web sites in Romm's Internet history and asked if viewing these sites had violated the terms of his probation, to which Romm answered "yes." The border guards detained Romm and sent his laptop to a forensic computer specialist to analyze the hard drive. Analysis confirmed that Romm had viewed ten images of child pornography from his laptop during the prior week and then deleted (or attempted to delete) the images from his computer. Romm was rejected by Canada and sent back on the next flight to Seattle, where he was prosecuted for possession of child pornography and sentenced to serve ten to fifteen years in prison.

The Appellate Court Upholds the Search

Romm appealed his conviction, arguing that the forensic analysis of his laptop computer exceeded the border search exception to the warrant requirement. The U.S. Court of Appeals for the Ninth Circuit was not persuaded, however, and ultimately upheld the verdict in 2006.[a] According to the Ninth Circuit court, "the border search doctrine is not limited to those cases where searching officers have reason to

a. *United States v. Romm,* 455 F.3d 990 (9th Cir. 2006).

Because of the strong governmental interest in protecting the public, a warrant normally is not required for the seizure of spoiled or contaminated food. In addition, warrants are not required for searches of businesses in such highly regulated industries as liquor, guns, and strip mining. General manufacturing is not considered to be one of these highly regulated industries, however.

Generally, government inspectors do not have the right to search business premises without a warrant, although the standard of probable cause is not the same as that required in nonbusiness contexts. The existence of a general and neutral enforcement plan normally will justify issuance of the warrant. Lawyers and accountants frequently possess the business records of their clients, and inspecting these documents while they are out of the hands of their true owners also requires a warrant.

In the following case, after receiving a report of suspected health-care fraud, state officials entered and searched the office of a licensed physician without obtaining a warrant. The physician claimed that the search was unreasonable and improper.

suspect the entrant may be carrying foreign contraband." The court cited a 2004 decision by the United States Supreme Court that held that the search of a traveler's property at the border will always be deemed "routine" unless the search technique risks damage to the searched property.[b] (That case had involved a border search of the defendant's gas tank that revealed marijuana rather than a search of electronic evidence, however.)

Potential Implications

The *Romm* case also raised another issue: When does a person have possession of electronic images? Interestingly, this is the first case in which a defendant was convicted of intentionally possessing and receiving cache images even though they were not downloaded. According to the Ninth Circuit court, "In the electronic context, a person can receive and possess child pornography without downloading it, if he or she seeks it out and exercises dominion and control over it."

Although this case involved child pornography, the holding could potentially apply to other types of offenses if a person had, for example, unauthorized images of copyrighted materials or confidential business data (see Chapter 8). Any type of material that is left on a laptop computer—even though the owner has attempted to delete it—can lead to liability if a border guard happens to look at the Internet history in the temporary cache of the computer.

b. *United States v. Flores-Montano,* 541 U.S. 149, 124 S.Ct. 1582, 158 L.Ed.2d 311 (2004).

Moreover, if such searches are considered routine, as in this case, border authorities might also look at deleted e-mails and find evidence of other types of objectionable conduct. For example, consider the 2006 scandal involving former Republican Congressman Mark Foley and his inappropriate and allegedly sexually explicit e-mails and instant messages to teenage boys who worked as congressional pages. If someone had looked at his laptop for deleted e-mails, evidence of his unethical conduct might have been discovered long before it came to light in the press.

FOR CRITICAL ANALYSIS   The *Romm* decision has been criticized as being fundamentally unfair because essentially Romm was convicted of possessing images that he had done everything in his power to delete. Would a businessperson's laptop ever contain information that could be incriminating? Should routine border searches include the temporary cache files on a computer? Why or why not?

Case 4.3   **United States v. Moon**

United States Court of Appeals,
Sixth Circuit, 2008.
513 F.3d 527.
www.ca6.uscourts.gov[a]

BACKGROUND AND FACTS   Young Moon was a licensed physician, specializing in oncology and hematology. Moon operated a medical practice in Crossville, Tennessee. As part of her practice, Moon contracted with the state of Tennessee to provide medical treatment to patients pursuant to a state and federally funded health benefit program for the uninsured known as "TennCare." Moon routinely utilized chemotherapy

a. Click on "Opinions Search" and in the "Short Title contains" box, type in "Moon." Click on "Submit Query." Under "Published Opinions," select the link to "082a0031p.06" to access the opinion.

medications in her treatment of cancer patients insured under the program. In March 2001, the Tennessee Bureau of Investigation (TBI) received a complaint from one of Moon's employees alleging that she had administered partial doses of chemotherapy medication while billing the insurance program for full doses. In January 2002, investigating agents conducted an on-site review at Moon's office. The agents identified themselves, informed Moon of a general complaint against her, and requested permission to "scan" particular patient records. Moon agreed. She also provided the agents with a location where they could scan the requested files. Later, Moon attempted to suppress the evidence, arguing that it was obtained without a search warrant. The federal district court

CASE 4.3–CONTINUED

sentenced Moon to 188 months in prison, followed by two years of supervised release. She was also ordered to pay restitution of $432,000. She appealed her conviction and sentence to the U.S. Court of Appeals for the Sixth Circuit.

IN THE WORDS OF THE COURT . . . *CLAY*, Circuit Judge.

* * * *

The Fourth Amendment bars the government from conducting unreasonable searches and seizures. This prohibition extends to both private homes and commercial premises. Additionally, searches pursuant to criminal as well as administrative investigations must comport to the strictures of the Fourth Amendment. Under the Fourth Amendment, searches "conducted without a warrant issued upon probable cause [are] per se unreasonable * * * subject only to a few specifically established and well-delineated exceptions."

*The well-delineated exception at issue here is consent. If an officer obtains consent to search, a warrantless search does not offend the Constitution. * * * Consent is voluntary when it is "unequivocal, specific and intelligently given, uncontaminated by any duress or coercion."* [Emphasis added.]

* * * *

We find that the district court's denial of the motion to suppress was not clearly erroneous inasmuch as Defendant voluntarily consented to the search of her office. The only evidence on the question of verbal consent was provided in the form of testimony by Agent Andy Corbitt of TBI at the suppression hearing. Agent Corbitt testified that three members of the TBI investigative team entered Defendant's office dressed in "business professional" attire, with weapons concealed. Agents identified themselves to Defendant, explained that there was an ongoing investigation and requested access to particular patient files. Defendant inquired about the nature of the investigation but was not informed of the specific nature of the allegations. Following this conversation, Defendant stated it would be "fine" for agents to access requested files and that they "could scan whatever [they] needed to." Further, Defendant provided agents with a space where they could scan the requested files.

Defendant, however, claims that the verbal consent was not voluntary as she merely acquiesced to a claim of lawful authority.

* * * Based on the totality of the circumstances, we find that Defendant voluntarily consented to the search of her office and therefore the motion to suppress was properly denied.

DECISION AND REMEDY   The U.S. Court of Appeals for the Sixth Circuit affirmed the district court's decision. Because Dr. Moon voluntarily allowed the agents to examine her files and to scan them, the resulting evidence did not have to be suppressed. A search warrant was not necessary.

WHAT IF THE FACTS WERE DIFFERENT?   Assume that Dr. Moon had proved that using partial doses of the chemotherapy drugs did not affect the "cure" rate for her cancer patients. Would the court have ruled differently? Why or why not?

THE LEGAL ENVIRONMENT DIMENSION   Does the length of Dr. Moon's prison sentence seem appropriate here? Why or why not?

DUE PROCESS AND EQUAL PROTECTION

Two other constitutional guarantees of great significance to Americans are mandated by the due process clauses of the Fifth and Fourteenth Amendments and the equal protection clause of the Fourteenth Amendment.

Due Process

Both the Fifth and the Fourteenth Amendments provide that no person shall be deprived "of life, liberty, or property, without due process of law." The **due process clause** of each of these constitutional amendments has two aspects—procedural and substantive. Note that the due process clause applies to "legal persons," such as corporations, as well as to individuals.

Procedural Due Process   Procedural due process requires that any government decision to take life, liberty, or property must be made fairly; that is, the government must give a person proper notice and an opportunity to be heard. Fair procedures must be used in determining whether a person will be subjected to punishment or have some burden imposed on him or her. Fair procedure has been interpreted as requiring that the person have at least an opportunity to object to a proposed action before a fair, neutral decision maker (which need not be a judge).   EXAMPLE #12   In most states, a driver's license is construed as a property interest. Therefore, the state must provide some sort of opportunity for the driver to object before suspending or terminating the license.□

DUE PROCESS CLAUSE
The provisions in the Fifth and Fourteenth Amendments to the Constitution that guarantee that no person shall be deprived of life, liberty, or property without due process of law. Similar clauses are found in most state constitutions.

Many of the constitutional protections discussed in this chapter have become part of our culture in the United States. Due process, especially procedural due process, has become synonymous with what Americans consider "fair." For this reason, businesspersons seeking to avoid legal disputes should consider giving due process to anyone who might object to some business decision or action, whether that person is an employee, a partner, an affiliate, or a customer. For instance, giving ample notice of new policies to all affected persons is a prudent move, as is giving them at least an opportunity to express their opinions on the matter. Providing an opportunity to be heard is often the ideal way to make people feel that they are being treated fairly. If people believe that a businessperson or firm is fair and listens to both sides of an issue, they are less likely to sue that businessperson or firm.◼

Substantive Due Process   Substantive due process protects an individual's life, liberty, or property against certain government actions regardless of the fairness of the procedures used to implement them. Substantive due process limits what the government may do in its legislative and executive capacities. Legislation must be fair and reasonable in content and must further a legitimate governmental objective. Only when government conduct is arbitrary, or shocks the conscience, however, will it rise to the level of violating substantive due process.[30]

If a law or other governmental action limits a fundamental right, the state must have a legitimate and compelling interest to justify its action. Fundamental rights include interstate travel, privacy, voting, marriage and family, and all First Amendment rights. Thus, a state must have substantial reason for taking any action that infringes on a person's free speech rights. In situations not involving fundamental rights, a law or action does not violate substantive due process if it rationally relates to any legitimate government purpose. Under this test, virtually any business regulation will be upheld as reasonable. The United States Supreme Court has sustained insurance regulations, price and wage controls,

---

[30]. See, for example, *Breen v. Texas A&M University*, 485 F.3d 325 (5th Cir. 2007); and *Hart v. City of Little Rock*, 432 F.3d 801 (8th Cir. 2005).

banking limitations, and restrictions on unfair competition and trade practices against substantive due process challenges.

EXAMPLE #13 If a state legislature enacted a law imposing a fifteen-year term of imprisonment without a trial on all businesspersons who appeared in their own television commercials, the law would be unconstitutional on both substantive and procedural grounds. Substantive review would invalidate the legislation because it infringes on freedom of speech. Procedurally, the law is unfair because it imposes the penalty without giving the accused a chance to defend her or his actions. □

Equal Protection

Under the Fourteenth Amendment, a state may not "deny to any person within its jurisdiction the equal protection of the laws." The United States Supreme Court has used the due process clause of the Fifth Amendment to make the **equal protection clause** applicable to the federal government as well. Equal protection means that the government must treat similarly situated individuals in a similar manner.

Both substantive due process and equal protection require review of the substance of the law or other governmental action rather than review of the procedures used. When a law or action limits the liberty of all persons to do something, it may violate substantive due process; when a law or action limits the liberty of some persons but not others, it may violate the equal protection clause. **EXAMPLE #14** If a law prohibits all persons from buying contraceptive devices, it raises a substantive due process question. If a law prohibits only unmarried persons from buying the same devices, it raises an equal protection issue. □

In an equal protection inquiry, when a law or action distinguishes between or among individuals, the basis for the distinction—that is, the classification—is examined. Depending on the classification, the courts apply different levels of scrutiny, or "tests," to determine whether the law or action violates the equal protection clause.

Minimal Scrutiny—The "Rational Basis" Test   Generally, laws regulating economic and social matters are presumed to be valid and are subject to only minimal scrutiny. A classification will be considered valid if there is any conceivable *rational basis* on which the classification might relate to a *legitimate government interest*. It is almost impossible for a law or action to fail the rational basis test. **EXAMPLE #15** A city ordinance that in effect prohibits all pushcart vendors except a specific few from operating in a particular area of the city will be upheld if the city offers a rational basis—such as reducing traffic in the particular area—for the ordinance. In contrast, a law that provides unemployment benefits only to people over six feet tall would clearly fail the rational basis test because it could not further any legitimate government interest. □

Intermediate Scrutiny   A harder standard to meet, that of *intermediate scrutiny*, is applied in cases involving discrimination based on gender or legitimacy. Laws using these classifications must be *substantially related to important government objectives*. **EXAMPLE #16** An important government objective is preventing illegitimate teenage pregnancies. Because males and females are not similarly situated in this circumstance—only females can become pregnant—a law that

EQUAL PROTECTION CLAUSE
The provision in the Fourteenth Amendment to the Constitution that guarantees that no state will "deny to any person within its jurisdiction the equal protection of the laws." This clause mandates that the state governments must treat similarly situated individuals in a similar manner.

"When one undertakes to administer justice, . . . what is done for one, must be done for everyone in equal degree."
—THOMAS JEFFERSON, 1743–1826
(Third president of the United States, 1801–1809)

punishes men but not women for statutory rape will be upheld. Suppose, however, that a state law requires illegitimate children to file a paternity action within six years of their birth in order to seek support from their biological fathers. This law will fail if legitimate children can seek support from their fathers at any time because distinguishing between support claims on the basis of legitimacy has no relation to the objective of preventing fraudulent or stale claims. □

Strict Scrutiny The most difficult standard to meet is that of *strict scrutiny*. Under strict scrutiny, the classification must be necessary to promote a *compelling state interest*. Generally, few laws or actions survive strict-scrutiny analysis by the courts.

Strict scrutiny is applied when a law or action prohibits some persons from exercising a fundamental right or classifies individuals based on a *suspect trait*— such as race, national origin, or citizenship status. **EXAMPLE #17** To prevent violence caused by racial gangs in prisons, corrections officials in California segregated prisoners by race for up to sixty days after they entered (or transferred to) a correctional facility. A prisoner challenged that policy. Ultimately, the United States Supreme Court held that all racial classifications, because they are based on a suspect trait, must be analyzed under strict scrutiny.[31] □

PRIVACY RIGHTS

In the past, privacy issues typically related to personal information that government agencies, including the Federal Bureau of Investigation, might obtain and keep about an individual. Later, concerns about what banks and insurance companies might know and transmit to others about individuals became an issue. Since the 1990s, one of the major concerns of individuals has been how to protect privacy rights in cyberspace and to safeguard private information that may be revealed online (including credit-card numbers and financial information). The increasing value of personal information for online marketers—who are willing to pay a high price for such information to those who collect it—has exacerbated the situation.

The USA Patriot Act allows authorities to review library records without any proof that the patron is suspected of having committed a crime. In this photo, Connecticut librarians speak out against the FBI's ability to demand patrons' records without obtaining a warrant from a court. What aspect of privacy rights might be violated in such situations?
(AP Photo/Shiho Fukada)

Today, individuals face additional concerns about government intrusions into their privacy. The USA Patriot Act, which was passed by Congress in the wake of the terrorist attacks of September 11, 2001, has given increased authority to government officials to monitor Internet activities (such as e-mail and Web site visits) and to gain access to personal financial data and student information.[32]

---

31. *Johnson v. California,* 543 U.S. 499, 125 S.Ct. 1141, 160 L.Ed.2d 949 (2005). See also *Parents Involved in Community Schools v. Seattle School District No. 1,* ___ U.S. ___, 127 S.Ct. 2738, 168 L.Ed.2d 508 (2007).

32. Uniting and Strengthening America by Providing Appropriate Tools Required to Intercept and Obstruct Terrorism Act of 2001, also known as the USA Patriot Act, was enacted as Pub. L. No. 107-56 (2001) and extended in early 2006 by Pub. L. No. 109-173 (2006).

"There was, of course, no
way of knowing whether
you were being watched
at any given moment."
—GEORGE ORWELL, 1903–1950
(Author, from his famous novel *1984*)

Using technology, law enforcement officials can track the telephone and e-mail conversations of one party to find out the identity of the other party or parties. The government must certify that the information likely to be obtained is relevant to an ongoing criminal investigation, but it does not need to provide proof of any wrongdoing to gain access to this information. Privacy advocates argue that this law has adversely affected the constitutional rights of all Americans, and it has been widely criticized in the media, fueling the public debate over how to secure privacy rights in an electronic age.

In this section, we look at the protection of privacy rights under the U.S. Constitution and various federal statutes. Note that state constitutions and statutes also protect individuals' privacy rights, often to a significant degree. Privacy rights are also protected under tort law (see Chapter 5). Additionally, the Federal Trade Commission has played an active role in protecting the privacy rights of online consumers (see Chapter 20). The protection of employees' privacy rights, particularly with respect to electronic monitoring practices, is another area of growing concern (see Chapter 17).

Does the threat of terrorism justify the U.S. government's invasion of its citizens' privacy?

Since the USA Patriot Act was enacted, the National Security Agency (NSA) has engaged in domestic surveillance and monitoring activities that have been highly controversial. Critics claim that these activities endanger numerous constitutionally protected freedoms, such as the right to privacy and the right to be free from unreasonable searches (under the Fourth Amendment). In December 2005, government sources revealed that President George W. Bush had authorized the NSA to secretly intercept phone calls between U.S. citizens and suspected terrorists abroad—without first obtaining a warrant as would be required even under the Patriot Act. Although eavesdropping on phone calls and monitoring e-mails are certainly powerful tools for tracking down terrorists, they are also the kind of activities that the framers of the Constitution sought to curtail.

Some claim that the government's intrusion into our private communications is warranted because the government is looking only for those "bad" people who interact with terrorists. If the government can monitor what any person views or searches for on the Internet, however, are anyone's Internet activities really private? To illustrate, consider what happened in August 2006, when America Online (AOL) released randomly selected user search log data from 658,000 subscribers. AOL thought it was doing a good deed by providing this database to researchers at universities and small businesses that normally do not have access to this type of data. To protect subscribers' privacy, the data identified users by numbers rather than by names. As it turned out, though, an individual's identity could be tracked down using various bits of information. All search engines compile this type of user data, which can be valuable for marketing purposes. Such data can also be invaluable to government law enforcement. For example, searches like "how to make homemade bombs" or "torture methods" *might* indicate a propensity for terrorist activities. But what happens if government monitors find that a person has searched for "underground kiddy porn pictures" or "how to make meth"?

Constitutional Protection of Privacy Rights

The U.S. Constitution does not explicitly mention a general right to privacy, and only relatively recently have the courts regarded the right to privacy as a constitutional right. In a 1928 Supreme Court case, *Olmstead v. United States*,[33] Justice Louis Brandeis stated in his dissent that the right to privacy is "the most comprehensive of rights and the right most valued by civilized men." At that time, the majority of the justices did not agree, and it was not until the 1960s that a majority on the Supreme Court endorsed the view that the Constitution protects individual privacy rights.

In a landmark 1965 case, *Griswold v. Connecticut*,[34] the Supreme Court invalidated a Connecticut law that effectively prohibited the use of contraceptives. The Court held that the law violated the right to privacy. Justice William O. Douglas formulated a unique way of reading this right into the Bill of Rights. He claimed that "emanations" from the rights guaranteed by the First, Third, Fourth, Fifth, and Ninth Amendments formed and gave "life and substance" to "penumbras" (partial shadows) around these guaranteed rights. These penumbras included an implied constitutional right to privacy.

When we read these amendments, we can see the foundation for Justice Douglas's reasoning. Consider the Fourth Amendment. By prohibiting unreasonable searches and seizures, the amendment effectively protects individuals' privacy. Consider also the words of the Ninth Amendment: "The enumeration in the Constitution of certain rights, shall not be construed to deny or disparage others retained by the people." In other words, just because the Constitution, including its amendments, does not specifically mention the right to privacy does not mean that this right is denied to the people. Indeed, many people today consider privacy one of the most important rights guaranteed by the U.S. Constitution.

> *"There is nothing new in the realization that the Constitution sometimes insulates the criminality of a few in order to protect the privacy of us all."*
>
> —ANTONIN SCALIA, 1936–present (United States Supreme Court justice, 1986–present)

---

33. 277 U.S. 438, 48 S.Ct. 564, 72 L.Ed. 944 (1928).
34. 381 U.S. 479, 85 S.Ct. 1678, 14 L.Ed.2d 510 (1965).

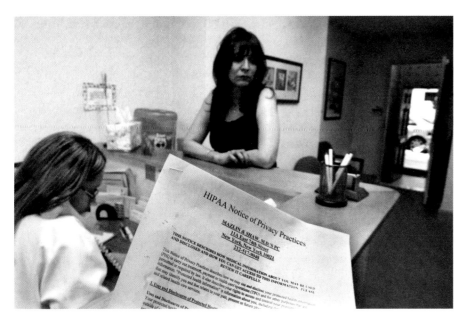

The Health Insurance Portability and Accountability Act (HIPAA) requires that medical records be kept private under most circumstances. This physician's office created higher countertops to prevent others from viewing private records. Under HIPAA, the federal government can levy fines of up to $250,000 for violations of the act. (AP Photo/Bebeto Matthews)

Federal Statutes Protecting Privacy Rights

In the last several decades, Congress has enacted a number of statutes that protect the privacy of individuals in various areas of concern. In the 1960s, Americans were sufficiently alarmed by the accumulation of personal information in government files that they pressured Congress to pass laws permitting individuals to access their files. Congress responded in 1966 with the Freedom of Information Act, which allows any person to request copies of any information on her or him contained in federal government files. In 1974, Congress passed the Privacy Act, which also gives persons the right to access such information. These and other major federal laws protecting privacy rights are listed and described in Exhibit 4–1.

Responding to the growing need to protect the privacy of individuals' health records—particularly computerized records—Congress passed the Health Insurance Portability and Accountability Act (HIPAA) of 1996.[35] This act, which

---

35. The HIPAA was enacted as Pub. L. No. 104-191 (1996) and is codified in 29 U.S.C.A. Sections 1181 *et seq.*

EXHIBIT 4–1 FEDERAL LEGISLATION RELATING TO PRIVACY

TITLE	PROVISIONS CONCERNING PRIVACY
Freedom of Information Act (1966)	Provides that individuals have a right to obtain access to information about them collected in government files.
Family and Educational Rights and Privacy Act (1974)	Limits access to computer-stored records of education-related evaluations and grades in private and public colleges and universities.
Privacy Act (1974)	Protects the privacy of individuals about whom the federal government has information. Under this act, agencies that use or disclose personal information must make sure that the information is reliable and guard against its misuse. Individuals must be able to find out what data concerning them the agency is compiling and how the data will be used. In addition, the agency must give individuals a means to correct inaccurate data and must obtain their consent before using the data for any other purpose.
Tax Reform Act (1976)	Preserves the privacy of personal financial information.
Right to Financial Privacy Act (1978)	Prohibits financial institutions from providing the federal government with access to customers' records unless a customer authorizes the disclosure.
Electronic Communications Privacy Act (1986)	Prohibits the interception of information communicated by electronic means.
Driver's Privacy Protection Act (1994)	Prevents states from disclosing or selling a driver's personal information without the driver's consent.
Health Insurance Portability and Accountability Act (1996)	Prohibits the use of a consumer's medical information for any purpose other than that for which such information was provided, unless the consumer expressly consents to the use. Final rules became effective on April 14, 2003.
Financial Services Modernization Act (Gramm-Leach-Bliley Act) (1999)	Prohibits the disclosure of nonpublic personal information about a consumer to an unaffiliated third party unless strict disclosure and opt-out requirements are met. Final rules became mandatory on July 1, 2001.

took effect on April 14, 2003, defines and limits the circumstances in which an individual's "protected health information" may be used or disclosed.

The HIPAA requires health-care providers and health-care plans, including certain employers that sponsor health plans, to inform patients of their privacy rights and of how their personal medical information may be used. The act also generally states that a person's medical records may not be used for purposes unrelated to health care—such as marketing, for example—or disclosed to others without the individual's permission. Covered entities must formulate written privacy policies, designate privacy officials, limit access to computerized health data, physically secure medical records with lock and key, train employees and volunteers on their privacy policies, and sanction those who violate those policies. These protections are intended to assure individuals that their health information, including genetic information, will be properly protected and not used for purposes that the patient did not know about or authorize.

 **Reviewing . . . Constitutional Authority to Regulate Business**

A state legislature enacted a statute that required any motorcycle operator or passenger on the state's highways to wear a protective helmet. Jim Alderman, a licensed motorcycle operator, sued the state to block enforcement of the law. Alderman asserted that the statute violated the equal protection clause because it placed requirements on motorcyclists that were not imposed on other motorists. Using the information presented in the chapter, answer the following questions.

1. Why does this statute raise equal protection issues instead of substantive due process concerns?

2. What are the three levels of scrutiny that the courts use in determining whether a law violates the equal protection clause?

3. Which standard, or test, of scrutiny would apply to this situation? Why?

4. Applying this standard, or test, is the helmet statute constitutional? Why or why not?

 **Key Terms**

Bill of Rights 109	federal form of	preemption 108
checks and balances 103	government 103	search warrant 117
commerce clause 104	filtering software 115	supremacy clause 108
due process clause 121	free exercise clause 115	symbolic speech 111
equal protection clause 122	meta tag 115	
establishment clause 115	police powers 107	

The Constitutional Powers of Government
(See pages 102–109.)

The U.S. Constitution established a federal form of government, in which government powers are shared by the national government and the state governments. At the national level, government powers are divided among the legislative, executive, and judicial branches.

The Commerce Clause
(See pages 103–108.)

1. *The expansion of national powers*–The commerce clause expressly permits Congress to regulate commerce. Over time, courts expansively interpreted this clause, thereby enabling the national government to wield extensive powers over the economic life of the nation.

2. *The commerce power today*–Today, the commerce power authorizes the national government, at least theoretically, to regulate every commercial enterprise in the United States. In recent years, the Supreme Court has reined in somewhat the national government's regulatory powers under the commerce clause.

3. *The regulatory powers of the states*–The Tenth Amendment reserves to the states all powers not expressly delegated to the national government. Under their police powers, state governments may regulate private activities to protect or promote the public order, health, safety, morals, and general welfare.

4. *The "dormant" commerce clause*–If state regulations substantially interfere with interstate commerce, they will be held to violate the "dormant" commerce clause of the U.S. Constitution. The positive aspect of the commerce clause, which gives the national government the exclusive authority to regulate interstate commerce, implies a "dormant" aspect–that the states do not have this power.

The Supremacy Clause
(See pages 108–109.)

The U.S. Constitution provides that the Constitution, laws, and treaties of the United States are "the supreme Law of the Land." Whenever a state law directly conflicts with a federal law, the state law is rendered invalid.

Business and the Bill of Rights
(See pages 109–120.)

The Bill of Rights, which consists of the first ten amendments to the U.S. Constitution, was adopted in 1791 and embodies a series of protections for individuals–and, in some instances, business entities–against various types of interference by the federal government. Today, most of the protections apply against state governments as well.

1. *Freedom of speech*–Speech, including symbolic speech, is given the fullest possible protection by the courts. Corporate political speech and commercial speech also receive substantial protection under the First Amendment. Certain types of speech, such as defamatory speech and obscene speech, are not protected under the First Amendment. Government attempts to regulate unprotected forms of speech in the online environment have, to date, met with numerous challenges.

2. *Freedom of religion*–Under the First Amendment, the government may neither establish any religion (the establishment clause) nor prohibit the free exercise of religion (the free exercise clause).

3. *Freedom against unreasonable searches and seizures*–The Fourth Amendment protects people from unreasonable searches by government officials of their persons, houses, cars, and other personal effects. Law enforcement officers must normally get a warrant to search a person's home or business premises, but there are exceptions, particularly when a search or seizure is necessary to protect the public's health or safety.

Due Process and Equal Protection
(See pages 120–123.)

1. *Due process*–Both the Fifth and the Fourteenth Amendments provide that no person shall be deprived of "life, liberty, or property, without due process of law." Procedural due process requires that any government decision to take life, liberty, or property must be made fairly, using fair procedures. Substantive due process focuses on the content of legislation. Generally, a law that is not compatible with the Constitution violates substantive due process unless the law promotes a compelling state interest, such as public safety.

Due Process and Equal Protection—Continued	**2.** *Equal protection*—Under the Fourteenth Amendment, a state may not "deny to any person within its jurisdiction the equal protection of the laws." A law or action that limits the liberty of some persons but not others may violate the equal protection clause. Such a law may be deemed valid, however, if there is a rational basis for the discriminatory treatment of a given group or if the law substantially relates to an important government objective.
Privacy Rights (See pages 123–127.)	Americans are increasingly becoming concerned about privacy issues raised by Internet-related technology. The Constitution does not contain a specific guarantee of a right to privacy, but such a right has been derived from guarantees found in several constitutional amendments. A number of federal statutes protect privacy rights. Privacy rights are also protected by many state constitutions and statutes, as well as under tort law.

For Review

1. What is the basic structure of the U.S. government?
2. What constitutional clause gives the federal government the power to regulate commercial activities among the various states?
3. What constitutional clause allows laws enacted by the federal government to take priority over conflicting state laws?
4. What is the Bill of Rights? What freedoms does the First Amendment guarantee?
5. Where in the Constitution can the due process clause be found?

Questions and Case Problems

4–1. Commercial Speech. A mayoral election is about to be held in a large U.S. city. One of the candidates is Luis Delgado, and his campaign supporters wish to post campaign signs on lampposts and utility posts throughout the city. A city ordinance, however, prohibits the posting of any signs on public property. Delgado's supporters contend that the city ordinance is unconstitutional because it violates their rights to free speech. What factors might a court consider in determining the constitutionality of this ordinance?

Question with Sample Answer

4–2. Thomas worked in the nonmilitary operations of a large firm that produced both military and nonmilitary goods. When the company discontinued the production of nonmilitary goods, Thomas was transferred to the plant producing military equipment. Thomas left his job, claiming that it violated his religious principles to participate in the manufacture of goods to be used in destroying life. In effect, he argued, the transfer to the war matériel plant had forced him to quit his job. He was denied unemployment compensation by the state because he had not been effectively "discharged" by the employer but had voluntarily terminated his employment. Did the state's denial of unemployment benefits to Thomas violate the free exercise clause of the First Amendment? Explain.

For a sample answer to Question 4–2, go to Appendix I at the end of this text.

4–3. Commerce Clause. Suppose that Georgia enacts a law requiring the use of contoured rear-fender mudguards on trucks and trailers operating within its state lines. The statute further makes it illegal for trucks and trailers to use straight mudguards. In thirty-five other states, straight mudguards are legal. Moreover, in the neighboring state of Florida, straight mudguards are explicitly required by law. There is some evidence suggesting that contoured mudguards might be a little safer than straight mudguards. Discuss whether this Georgia statute would violate the commerce clause of the U.S. Constitution.

4–4. Freedom of Religion. A business has a backlog of orders, and to meet its deadlines, management decides to run the firm seven days a week, eight hours a day. One of the employees, Marjorie Tollens, refuses to work on Saturday on religious grounds. Her refusal to work means that the firm may not meet its production deadlines and may therefore suffer a loss of future business. The firm fires Tollens and replaces her with an employee who is willing to work seven days a week. Tollens claims that in terminating her employment, her employer violated her constitutional right to the free exercise of her religion. Do you agree? Why or why not?

4–5. Free Speech. Henry Mishkoff is a Web designer whose firm does business as "Webfeats." When Taubman Co. began building a mall called "The Shops at Willow Bend" near Mishkoff's home, Mishkoff registered the domain name "shopsatwillowbend.com" and created a Web site with that address. The site featured information about the mall, a disclaimer indicating that Mishkoff's site was unofficial, and a link to the mall's official site. Taubman discovered Mishkoff's site and filed a suit in a federal district court against him. Mishkoff then registered other names, including "taubmansucks.com," with links to a site documenting his battle with Taubman. (A Web name with a "sucks.com" moniker attached to it is known as a "complaint name," and the process of registering and using such names is known as "cybergriping.") Taubman asked the court to order Mishkoff to stop using all of these names. Should the court grant Taubman's request? On what basis might the court protect Mishkoff's use of the names? [*Taubman Co. v. Webfeats*, 319 F.3d 770 (6th Cir. 2003)]

Case Problem with Sample Answer

4–6. To protect the privacy of individuals identified in information systems maintained by federal agencies, the Privacy Act of 1974 regulates the use of the information. The statute provides for a minimum award of $1,000 for "actual damages sustained" caused by "intentional or willful actions" to the "person entitled to recovery." Buck Doe filed for certain disability benefits with an office of the U.S. Department of Labor (DOL). The application form asked for Doe's Social Security number, which the DOL used to identify his claim on documents sent to groups of claimants, their employers, and the lawyers involved in their cases. This disclosed Doe's Social Security number beyond the limits set by the Privacy Act. Doe filed a suit in a federal district court against the DOL, alleging that he was "torn * * * all to pieces" and "greatly concerned and worried" because of the disclosure of his Social Security number and its potentially "devastating" consequences. He did not offer any proof of actual injury, however. Should damages be awarded in such circumstances solely on the basis of the agency's conduct, or should proof of some actual injury be required? Why? [*Doe v. Chao*, 540 U.S. 614, 124 S.Ct. 1204, 157 L.Ed.2d 1122 (2004)]

After you have answered Problem 4–6, compare your answer with the sample answer given on the Web site that accompanies this text. Go to

www.cengage.com/blaw/let, select "Chapter 4," and click on "Case Problem with Sample Answer."

4–7. Due Process. In 1994, the Board of County Commissioners of Yellowstone County, Montana, created Zoning District 17 in a rural area of the county and a planning and zoning commission for the district. The commission adopted zoning regulations, which provided, among other things, that "dwelling units" could be built only through "on-site construction." Later, county officials could not identify any health or safety concerns that the on-site construction provision addressed, and there was no indication that homes built off-site would affect property values or any other general welfare interest of the community. In December 1999, Francis and Anita Yurczyk bought two forty-acre tracts in District 17. The Yurczyks also bought a modular home and moved it onto the property the following spring. Within days, the county advised the Yurczyks that the home violated the on-site construction regulation and would have to be removed. The Yurczyks filed a suit in a Montana state court against the county, alleging in part that the regulation violated the Yurczyks' due process rights. Should the court rule in the plaintiffs' favor? Explain. [*Yurczyk v. Yellowstone County*, 2004 MT 3, 319 Mont. 169, 83 P.3d 266 (2004)]

4–8. Supremacy Clause. The Federal Communications Act of 1934 grants the right to govern all *interstate* telecommunications to the Federal Communications Commission (FCC) and the right to regulate all *intrastate* telecommunications to the states. The federal Telephone Consumer Protection Act of 1991, the Junk Fax Protection Act of 2005, and FCC rules permit a party to send unsolicited fax ads to recipients with whom they have an "established business relationship" if those ads include an "opt-out" alternative. Section 17538.43 of California's Business and Professions Code (known as "SB 833") was enacted in 2005 to provide the citizens of California with greater protection than that afforded under federal law. SB 833 omits the "established business relationship" exception and requires a sender to obtain a recipient's express consent (or "opt-in") before faxing an ad to that party. The rule applies whether the sender is located in California or outside that state. The Chamber of Commerce of the United States filed a suit against Bill Lockyer, California's state attorney general, seeking to block the enforcement of SB 833. What principles support the plaintiff's position? How should the court resolve the issue? Explain. [*Chamber of Commerce of the United States v. Lockyer*, 463 F.3d 1076 (9th Cir. 2006)]

4–9. Freedom of Speech. For decades, New York City has had to deal with the vandalism and defacement of public property caused by unauthorized graffiti. Among other attempts to stop the damage, in December 2005 the city banned the sale of aerosol spray-paint cans and broad-tipped indelible markers to persons under twenty-one years of age and prohibited them from possessing such items on property other than their own. By May 1, 2006, five people—all under age twenty-one—had been cited for violations of these regulations, while 871 individuals had been arrested for actually making graffiti. Artists who wished to create graffiti on legal surfaces, such as canvas, wood, and clothing, included college student Lindsey Vincenty, who was studying visual arts. Unable to buy her supplies in the city or to carry them in the city if she bought them elsewhere, Vincenty, with others, filed a suit in a federal district court on behalf of themselves and other young artists against Michael Bloomberg, the city's mayor, and others. The plaintiffs claimed that, among other things, the new rules violated their right to freedom of speech. They asked the court to enjoin the enforcement of the rules. Should the court grant this request? Why or why not? [*Vincenty v. Bloomberg*, 476 F.3d 74 (2d Cir. 2007)]

A Question of Ethics

4–10. Aric Toll owns and manages the Balboa Island Village Inn, a restaurant and bar in Newport Beach, California. Anne Lemen owns "Island Cottage," a residence across an alley from the Inn. Lemen often complained to the authorities about excessive noise and the behavior of the Inn's customers, whom she called "drunks" and "whores." Lemen referred to Theresa Toll, Aric's wife, as "Madam Whore." Lemen told the Inn's bartender Ewa Cook that Cook "worked for Satan," was "Satan's wife," and was "going to have Satan's children." She told the Inn's neighbors that it was "a whorehouse" with "prostitution going on inside" and that it sold illegal drugs, sold alcohol to minors, made "sex videos," was involved in child pornography, had "Mafia connections," encouraged "lesbian activity," and stayed open until 6:00 A.M. Lemen also voiced her complaints to potential customers, and the Inn's sales dropped more than 20 percent. The Inn filed a suit in a California state court against Lemen, asserting defamation and other claims. [*Balboa Island Village Inn, Inc. v. Lemen*, 40 Cal.4th 1141, 156 P.3d 339 (2007)]

1. Are Lemen's statements about the Inn's owners, customers, and activities protected by the U.S. Constitution? Should such statements be protected? In whose favor should the court rule? Why?

2. Did Lemen behave unethically in the circumstances of this case? Explain.

Interacting with the Internet

For updated links to resources available on the Web, as well as a variety of other materials, visit this text's Web site at

www.cengage.com/blaw/let

For an online version of the Constitution that provides hypertext links to amendments and other changes, as well as the history of the document, go to

www.constitutioncenter.org

For discussions of current issues involving the rights and liberties contained in the Bill of Rights, go to the Web site of the American Civil Liberties Union at

www.aclu.org

PRACTICAL INTERNET EXERCISES

Go to this text's Web site at **www.cengage.com/blaw/let**, select "Chapter 4," and click on "Practical Internet Exercises." There you will find the following Internet research exercises that you can perform to learn more about the topics covered in this chapter.

Practical Internet Exercise 4–1: LEGAL PERSPECTIVE—**Commercial Speech**
Practical Internet Exercise 4–2: MANAGEMENT PERSPECTIVE—**Privacy Rights in Cyberspace**

BEFORE THE TEST

Go to this text's Web site at **www.cengage.com/blaw/let**, select "Chapter 4," and click on "Interactive Quizzes." You will find a number of interactive questions relating to this chapter.

Chapter 5

Torts and Cyber Torts

Crime

CHAPTER OBJECTIVES

After reading this chapter, you should be able to answer the following questions:

1. **What is a tort?**

2. **What is the purpose of tort law? What are two basic categories of torts?**

3. **What are the four elements of negligence?**

4. **What is a cyber tort, and how are tort theories being applied in cyberspace?**

CONTENTS

" 'Tort' more or less means 'wrong' . . . . One of my friends [in law school] said that Torts is the course which proves that your mother was right."

— SCOTT TUROW,
1949–present (American lawyer and author)

TORT
A civil wrong not arising from a breach of contract; a breach of a legal duty that proximately causes harm or injury to another.

As Scott Turow's statement in the chapter-opening quotation indicates, **torts** are wrongful actions.[1] Through tort law, society compensates those who have suffered injuries as a result of the wrongful conduct of others. Some torts, such as assault and trespass, originated in the English common law. The field of tort law continues to expand. As new ways to commit wrongs are discovered, such as the use of the Internet to commit wrongful acts, the courts are extending tort law to cover these wrongs.

As you will see in later chapters of this book, many of the lawsuits brought by or against business firms are based on the tort theories discussed in this chapter. Some of the torts examined here can occur in any context, including the business environment. Others, traditionally referred to as **business torts,** involve wrongful interference with the business rights of others. Business torts include such vague concepts as *unfair competition* and *wrongfully interfering with the business relations of another.*

BUSINESS TORT
Wrongful interference with another's business rights.

THE BASIS OF TORT LAW

Two notions serve as the basis of all torts: wrongs and compensation. Tort law is designed to compensate those who have suffered a loss or injury due to another person's wrongful act. In a tort action, one person or group brings a personal suit against another person or group to obtain compensation (monetary **damages**) or other relief for the harm suffered.

DAMAGES
The monetary amount awarded by a court in a civil action to compensate a plaintiff for injury or loss.

---

1. The word *tort* is French for "wrong."

The Purpose of Tort Law

Generally, the purpose of tort law is to provide remedies for the invasion of various *protected interests*. Society recognizes an interest in personal physical safety, and tort law provides remedies for acts that cause physical injury or interfere with physical security and freedom of movement. Society recognizes an interest in protecting real and personal property, and tort law provides remedies for acts that cause destruction or damage to property. Society also recognizes an interest in protecting certain intangible interests, such as personal privacy, family relations, reputation, and dignity, and tort law provides remedies for invasion of these protected interests.

Damages Available in Tort Actions

Because the purpose of tort law is to compensate the injured party for the damage suffered, it is important to have a basic understanding of the types of damages that plaintiffs seek in tort actions.

Compensatory Damages   **Compensatory damages** are intended to compensate or reimburse a plaintiff for actual losses—to make the plaintiff whole and put her or him in the same position that she or he would have been in had the tort not occurred. Compensatory damages awards are often broken down into special damages and general damages. *Special damages* compensate the plaintiff for quantifiable monetary losses, such as medical expenses, lost wages and benefits (now and in the future), extra costs, the loss of irreplaceable items, and the costs of repairing or replacing damaged property. *General damages* compensate individuals (not companies) for the nonmonetary aspects of the harm suffered, such as pain and suffering. A court might award general damages for physical or emotional pain and suffering, loss of companionship, loss of consortium (losing the emotional and physical benefits of a spousal relationship), disfigurement, loss of reputation, or loss or impairment of mental or physical capacity.

COMPENSATORY DAMAGES
A monetary award equivalent to the actual value of injuries or damage sustained by the aggrieved party.

Punitive Damages   Occasionally, **punitive damages** may also be awarded in tort cases to punish the wrongdoer and deter others from similar wrongdoing. Punitive damages are appropriate only when the defendant's conduct was particularly egregious (conspicuously bad) or reprehensible (unacceptable). Usually, this means that punitive damages are available mainly in intentional tort actions and only rarely in negligence lawsuits (*intentional torts* and *negligence* are explained later in the chapter). They may be awarded, however, in suits involving *gross negligence,* which can be defined as an intentional failure to perform a manifest duty in reckless disregard of the consequences of such a failure for the life or property of another.

PUNITIVE DAMAGES
Monetary damages that may be awarded to a plaintiff to punish the defendant and deter future similar conduct.

Great judicial restraint is exercised in granting punitive damages to plaintiffs in tort actions, because punitive damages are subject to the limitations imposed by the due process clause of the U.S. Constitution (discussed in Chapter 4). In *State Farm Mutual Automobile Insurance Co. v. Campbell,*[2] the United States Supreme Court held that to the extent an award of punitive damages is grossly excessive, it furthers no legitimate purpose and violates due process requirements. Although this case dealt with intentional torts (fraud and intentional

---

2. 538 U.S. 408, 123 S.Ct. 1513, 155 L.Ed.2d 585 (2003).

infliction of emotional distress), the Court's holding applies equally to punitive damages awards in gross negligence cases (as well as product liability cases, which will be discussed in Chapter 12).

Classifications of Torts

There are two broad classifications of torts: *intentional torts* and *unintentional torts* (torts involving negligence). The classification of a particular tort depends largely on how the tort occurs (intentionally or negligently) and the surrounding circumstances. In the following pages, you will read about these two classifications of torts.

Torts committed via the Internet are sometimes referred to as **cyber torts.** We look at how the courts have applied traditional tort law to wrongful actions in the online environment in the concluding pages of this chapter.

CYBER TORT
A tort committed in cyberspace.

INTENTIONAL TORTS AGAINST PERSONS

An **intentional tort,** as the term implies, requires *intent.* The **tortfeasor** (the one committing the tort) must intend to commit an act, the consequences of which interfere with the personal or business interests of another in a way not permitted by law. An evil or harmful motive is not required—in fact, the actor may even have a benevolent motive for committing what turns out to be a tortious act. In tort law, intent means only that the actor intended the consequences of his or her act or knew with substantial certainty that certain consequences would result from the act. The law generally assumes that individuals intend the *normal* consequences of their actions. Thus, forcefully pushing another—even if done in jest and without any evil motive—is an intentional tort (if injury results), because the object of a strong push can ordinarily be expected to fall down.

This section discusses intentional torts against persons, which include assault and battery, false imprisonment, infliction of emotional distress, defamation, invasion of the right to privacy, appropriation, misrepresentation, abusive or frivolous litigation, and wrongful interference.

INTENTIONAL TORT
A wrongful act knowingly committed.

TORTFEASOR
One who commits a tort.

Assault and Battery

Any intentional, unexcused act that creates in another person a reasonable apprehension of immediate harmful or offensive contact is an **assault.** Apprehension is not the same as fear. If a contact is such that a reasonable person would want to avoid it, and if there is a reasonable basis for believing that the contact will occur, then the plaintiff suffers apprehension whether or not he or she is afraid. The interest protected by tort law concerning assault is the freedom from having to expect harmful or offensive contact. The arousal of apprehension is enough to justify compensation.

The *completion* of the act that caused the apprehension, if it results in harm to the plaintiff, is a **battery,** which is defined as an unexcused and harmful or offensive physical contact *intentionally* performed. Suppose that Ivan threatens Jean with a gun, then shoots her. The pointing of the gun at Jean is an assault; the firing of the gun (if the bullet hits Jean) is a battery. The interest protected by tort law concerning battery is the right to personal security and safety. The contact can be harmful, or it can be merely offensive (such as an unwelcome kiss). Physical injury need not occur. The contact can involve any part of the

ASSAULT
Any word or action intended to make another person fearful of immediate physical harm; a reasonably believable threat.

BATTERY
The unprivileged, intentional touching of another.

body or anything attached to it—for example, a hat or other item of clothing, a purse, or a chair or an automobile in which one is sitting. Whether the contact is offensive or not is determined by the *reasonable person standard*.[3] The contact can be made by the defendant or by some force the defendant sets in motion—for example, a rock thrown, food poisoned, or a stick swung.

Compensation If the plaintiff shows that there was contact, and the jury (or judge, if there is no jury) agrees that the contact was offensive, the plaintiff has a right to compensation. There is no need to show that the defendant acted out of malice; the person could have just been joking or playing around. The underlying motive does not matter, only the intent to bring about the harmful or offensive contact to the plaintiff. In fact, proving a motive is never necessary (but is sometimes relevant). A plaintiff may be compensated for the emotional harm or loss of reputation resulting from a battery, as well as for physical harm.

Defenses to Assault and Battery A defendant who is sued for assault, battery, or both can raise any of the following legally recognized **defenses** (reasons why plaintiffs should not obtain what they are seeking):

1. *Consent.* When a person consents to the act that is allegedly tortious, this may be a complete or partial defense to liability (legal responsibility).
2. *Self-defense.* An individual who is defending her or his life or physical well-being can claim self-defense. In situations of both *real* and *apparent* danger, a person may use whatever force is *reasonably* necessary to prevent harmful contact.
3. *Defense of others.* An individual can act in a reasonable manner to protect others who are in real or apparent danger.
4. *Defense of property.* Reasonable force may be used in attempting to remove intruders from one's home, although force that is likely to cause death or great bodily injury can never be used just to protect property.

> **DEFENSE**
> A reason offered and alleged by a defendant in an action or suit as to why the plaintiff should not recover or establish what she or he seeks.

> **BE AWARE**
> Some of these same four defenses can be raised by a defendant who is sued for other torts.

False Imprisonment

False imprisonment is the intentional confinement or restraint of another person's activities without justification. False imprisonment interferes with the freedom to move without restraint. The confinement can be accomplished through the use of physical barriers, physical restraint, or threats of physical force. Moral pressure or threats of future harm do not constitute false imprisonment. It is essential that the person being restrained not agree to the restraint.

Businesspersons are often confronted with suits for false imprisonment after they have attempted to confine a suspected shoplifter for questioning. Under the "privilege to detain" granted to merchants in some states, a merchant can use the defense of *probable cause* to justify delaying a suspected shoplifter. In this context, probable cause exists when there is sufficient evidence to support the belief that a person is guilty (as you will read in Chapter 6, *probable cause* is defined differently in the context of criminal law). Although laws pertaining to the privilege to detain vary from state to state, generally they require that any detention be conducted in a *reasonable* manner and for only a *reasonable* length of time.

---

3. The reasonable person standard is an "objective" test of how a reasonable person would have acted under the same circumstances, as will be discussed later in this chapter on page 152.

Businesspersons who operate retail establishments need to make sure that their employees are aware of the limitations on the privilege to detain. Even if someone is suspected of shoplifting, businesspersons (and employees) must have probable cause to stop and question the person and must behave reasonably and detain the person for only a sensible amount of time. Undue force or unreasonable detention can lead to liability for the business. ■

Intentional Infliction of Emotional Distress

The tort of *intentional infliction of emotional distress* can be defined as an intentional act that amounts to extreme and outrageous conduct resulting in severe emotional distress to another. To be **actionable** (capable of serving as the ground for a lawsuit), the act must be extreme and outrageous to the point that it exceeds the bounds of decency accepted by society. **EXAMPLE #1** A prankster telephones a pregnant woman and says that her husband and two sons have just been killed in a horrible accident (although they have not). As a result, the woman suffers intense mental pain and has a miscarriage. In that situation, the woman would be able to sue for intentional infliction of emotional distress. □

Courts in most jurisdictions are wary of emotional distress claims and confine them to situations involving truly outrageous behavior. Acts that cause indignity or annoyance alone usually are not sufficient. Many times, however, repeated annoyances (such as those experienced by a person who is being stalked), coupled with threats, are enough.

Note that when the outrageous conduct consists of speech about a public figure, the First Amendment's guarantee of freedom of speech also limits emotional distress claims. For example, *Hustler* magazine once printed a fake advertisement that showed a picture of Reverend Jerry Falwell and described him as having lost his virginity to his mother in an outhouse while he was drunk. Falwell sued the magazine for intentional infliction of emotional distress and won, but the United States Supreme Court overturned the decision. The Court held that creators of parodies of public figures are protected under the First Amendment from intentional infliction of emotional distress claims. (The Court used the same standards that apply to public figures in defamation lawsuits, discussed next.)[4]

Defamation

As discussed in Chapter 4, the freedom of speech guaranteed by the First Amendment to the U.S. Constitution is not absolute. In interpreting the First Amendment, the courts must balance free speech rights against other strong social interests, including society's interest in preventing and redressing attacks on reputation.

Defamation of character involves wrongfully hurting a person's good reputation. The law imposes a general duty on all persons to refrain from making *false*, defamatory *statements of fact* about others. Breaching this duty in writing or other permanent form (such as a digital recording) involves the tort of **libel.** Breaching this duty orally involves the tort of **slander.** As you will read later in

ACTIONABLE
Capable of serving as the basis of a lawsuit. An actionable claim can be pursued in a lawsuit or other court action.

DEFAMATION
Anything published or publicly spoken that causes injury to another's good name, reputation, or character.

LIBEL
Defamation in writing or other form having the quality of permanence (such as a digital recording).

SLANDER
Defamation in oral form.

---

4. *Hustler Magazine, Inc. v. Falwell,* 485 U.S. 46, 108 S.Ct. 876, 99 L.Ed.2d 41 (1988). For another example of how the courts protect parody, see *Busch v. Viacom International, Inc.,* 477 F.Supp.2d 764 (N.D.Tex. 2007), involving a fake endorsement of televangelist Pat Robertson's diet shake.

this chapter, the tort of defamation can also arise when a false statement of fact is made about a person's product, business, or legal ownership rights to property.

Often at issue in defamation lawsuits (including online defamation, discussed later in this chapter) is whether the defendant made a statement of fact or a *statement of opinion*. As you learned in Chapter 4, statements of opinion are normally not actionable because they are protected under the First Amendment. In other words, making a negative statement about another person is not defamation unless the statement is false and represents something as a fact (for example, "Vladik cheats on his taxes") rather than a personal opinion (for example, "Vladik is a jerk").

In the following case, the issue was whether a certain statement was an expression of a person's opinion—and thus protected by the First Amendment— or an unprotected factual assertion.

Case 5.1 Lott v. Levitt

United States District Court,
Northern District of Illinois, Eastern Division, 2007.
469 F.Supp.2d 575.

BACKGROUND AND FACTS In 2005, economist Steven Levitt and journalist Stephen Dubner co-authored the best-selling book *Freakonomics*. Levitt and Dubner discuss in a single paragraph a theory of fellow economist John Lott, Jr., in which Lott claims that violent crime has decreased in areas where law-abiding citizens are allowed to carry concealed weapons. The paragraph states that the idea is intriguing, but questions whether Lott's data were faked and implies that other scholars have not been able to replicate Lott's findings

(that is, to show that right-to-carry gun laws reduce crime). Economist John McCall sent Levitt an e-mail regarding this paragraph. McCall cited an issue of *The Journal of Law and Economics* in which other scholars claimed to "replicate" Lott's research. Levitt responded in an e-mail, "It was not a peer refereed edition of the *Journal*. For $15,000 he was able to buy an issue and put in only work that supported him. My best friend was the editor and was outraged the press let Lott do this." Based in part on this e-mail, Lott filed a suit in a federal district court against Levitt and others, claiming, among other things, defamation. Levitt filed a motion to dismiss, arguing that the First Amendment protects his statements.

IN THE WORDS OF THE COURT . . . *RUBEN CASTILLO*, United States District Court Judge.

* * * *

A statement is considered defamatory if it tends to cause such harm to the reputation of another that it lowers that person in the eyes of the community or deters third persons from associating with that person. [Emphasis added.]

* * * *

* * * Lott contends that the statements about him in * * * the e-mail * * * imply that his results were falsified or that his theories lack merit, and thus impute a lack of ability and integrity in his profession as an economist, academic, and researcher. Indeed, a claim that an academic or economist falsified his results and could only publish his theories by buying an issue of a journal and avoiding peer review would surely impute a lack of ability and prejudice that person in his profession.

* * * *

* * * *The First Amendment protects statements that cannot be reasonably interpreted as stating actual facts.* [Emphasis added.]

The test for whether a statement is a factual assertion is whether the statement is precise, readily understood, and susceptible of being verified as true or false. This test * * * is a reasonableness standard; whether a reasonable reader would understand the defendant to be informing him of a fact or opinion. Language that is loose, figurative, or hyperbolic negates the impression that a statement is asserting actual facts.

CASE 5.1—CONTINUED

CASE 5.1–CONTINUED

Accordingly, *vague, unprovable statements and statements of opinion do not give rise to a defamation claim.* If it is plain that the speaker is expressing a subjective view, an interpretation, a theory, conjecture, or surmise, rather than claiming to be in possession of objectively verifiable facts, the statement is not actionable. [Emphasis added.]

In this case, however, Levitt's e-mail sounds as if he was in possession of objectively verifiable facts. * * * First, it would be unreasonable to interpret Levitt's unqualified statement that the *Journal* edition was not "peer refereed" as Levitt merely giving his opinion on the "peers" chosen to review, or referee, the Special Issue. Indeed, the editor of the *Journal* might be able to verify the truth or falsity of whether the Special Issue was reviewed by peers. Furthermore, while Levitt argues that one person's "'peer' in the academic realm may be another person's 'hack'," this distinction is not reasonable when discussing the review process at a top university's academic journal. Second, a reasonable reader would not interpret Levitt's assertion that "For $15,000 [Lott] was able to buy an issue and put in only work that supported him" as simply a statement of Levitt's opinion. Levitt's e-mail appears to state objectively verifiable facts: that Lott paid $15,000 to control the content of the Special Issue. The editor of the *Journal* again might be the source to verify the truth or falsity of this statement. Third, the same editor could verify whether he was "outraged" by the acts described in the foregoing statements. Therefore, the defamatory statements in Levitt's e-mail to McCall are objectively verifiable * * *.

* * * *

* * * In his e-mail to McCall, * * * Levitt made a string of defamatory assertions about Lott's involvement in the publication of the Special Issue of the *Journal* that—no matter how rash or short-sighted Levitt was when he made them—cannot be reasonably interpreted as innocent or mere opinion.

DECISION AND REMEDY   The federal district court denied the motion to dismiss Lott's complaint. Because Levitt's statements in the e-mail implied that he was in possession of objectively verifiable facts, he could be sued for defamation. The court encouraged the parties to attempt to settle their dispute before proceeding to trial.

THE LEGAL ENVIRONMENT DIMENSION   Did the statements about Lott in *Freakonomics* (rather than in the e-mail) constitute unprotected speech? Why or why not?

THE ETHICAL DIMENSION   Why does the First Amendment protect only expressions of opinion and not all speech?

The Publication Requirement   The basis of the tort of defamation is the publication of a statement or statements that hold an individual up to contempt, ridicule, or hatred. *Publication* here means that the defamatory statements are communicated (either intentionally or accidentally) to persons other than the defamed party. **EXAMPLE #2** If Thompson writes Andrews a private letter accusing him of embezzling funds, the action does not constitute libel. If Peters falsely states that Gordon is dishonest and incompetent when no one else is around, the action does not constitute slander. In neither instance was the message communicated to a third party.□

The courts have generally held that even dictating a letter to a secretary constitutes publication, although the publication may be privileged (privileged communications will be discussed shortly). Moreover, if a third party merely overhears defamatory statements by chance, the courts usually hold that this also constitutes publication. Defamatory statements made via the Internet are also actionable, as you will read later in this chapter. Note further that any individual who republishes or repeats defamatory statements is liable even if that person reveals the source of such statements.

Damages for Libel   Once a defendant's liability for libel is established, *general damages* are presumed as a matter of law. As mentioned earlier, general damages are designed to compensate the plaintiff for nonspecific harms such as disgrace or dishonor in the eyes of the community, humiliation, injured reputation, and emotional distress—harms that are difficult to measure. In other words, to recover damages in a libel case, the plaintiff need not prove that she or he was actually injured in any way as a result of the libelous statement.

Damages for Slander   In contrast to cases alleging libel, in a case alleging slander, the plaintiff must prove *special damages* to establish the defendant's liability. In other words, the plaintiff must show that the slanderous statement caused the plaintiff to suffer actual economic or monetary losses. Unless this initial hurdle of proving special damages is overcome, a plaintiff alleging slander normally cannot go forward with the suit and recover any damages. This requirement is imposed in cases involving slander because slanderous statements have a temporary quality. In contrast, a libelous (written) statement has the quality of permanence, can be circulated widely, and usually results from some degree of deliberation on the part of the author.

Exceptions to the burden of proving special damages in cases alleging slander are made for certain types of slanderous statements. If a false statement constitutes "slander *per se*," no proof of special damages is required for it to be actionable. The following four types of utterances are considered to be slander *per se*:

1. A statement that another has a loathsome disease (historically, leprosy and sexually transmitted diseases, but now also including allegations of mental illness).
2. A statement that another has committed improprieties while engaging in a business, profession, or trade.
3. A statement that another has committed or has been imprisoned for a serious crime.
4. A statement that a person (usually only unmarried persons and sometimes only women) is unchaste or has engaged in serious sexual misconduct.

Defenses against Defamation   Truth is normally an absolute defense against a defamation charge. In other words, if the defendant in a defamation suit can prove that his or her allegedly defamatory statements were true, normally no tort has been committed. Other defenses to defamation may exist if the statement is privileged or concerns a public figure. Note that the majority of defamation actions in the United States are filed in state courts, and the states may differ in how they define both defamation and the particular defenses they allow, such as privilege (discussed next).

PRIVILEGE
A legal right, exemption, or immunity granted to a person or a class of persons. In the context of defamation, an absolute privilege immunizes the person making the statements from a lawsuit, regardless of whether the statements were malicious.

Privileged Communications   In some circumstances, a person will not be liable for defamatory statements because she or he enjoys a **privilege,** or immunity. Privileged communications are of two types: absolute and qualified.[5] Only

5. Note that the term *privileged communication* in this context is not the same as privileged communication between a professional, such as an attorney, and his or her client.

The British edition of the National Enquirer *agreed to pay actress Kate Hudson an undisclosed amount in damages and to print an apology to settle a libel lawsuit she had filed in England. The tabloid had published an article stating that Hudson was "way too thin" and "looked like skin and bones." Would these statements be considered libel under U.S. defamation laws?*

(Katie Kiehn/Creative Commons)

in judicial proceedings and certain government proceedings is an *absolute* privilege granted. For instance, statements made in the courtroom by attorneys and judges during a trial are absolutely privileged. So are statements made by government officials during legislative debate, even if the officials make such statements maliciously—that is, knowing them to be untrue. An absolute privilege is granted in these situations because government personnel deal with matters that are so much in the public interest that the parties involved should be able to speak out fully and freely without restriction.

In other situations, a person will not be liable for defamatory statements because he or she has a *qualified,* or conditional, privilege. An employer's statements in written evaluations of employees are an example of statements protected by qualified privilege. Generally, if the statements are made in good faith and the publication is limited to those who have a legitimate interest in the communication, the statements fall within the area of qualified privilege. **EXAMPLE #3** Jorge applies for membership at the local country club. After the country club's board rejects his application, Jorge sues the club's office manager for making allegedly defamatory statements to the board concerning a conversation she had with Jorge. Assuming that the office manager simply relayed what she thought she was obligated to convey to the club's board, her statements would likely be protected by qualified privilege.▫

The concept of conditional privilege rests on the assumption that in some situations, the right to know or speak takes precedence over the right not to be defamed. Only if the privilege is abused or the statement is knowingly false or malicious will the person be liable for damages.

Public Figures   Public officials who exercise substantial governmental power and any persons in the public limelight are considered *public figures.* In general, public figures are considered fair game, and false and defamatory statements about them that are published in the press will not constitute defamation unless the statements are made with **actual malice.** To be made with actual malice, a statement must be made *with either knowledge of falsity or a reckless disregard of the truth.* Statements made about public figures, especially when the statements are made via a public medium, are usually related to matters of general interest; they are made about people who substantially affect all of us. Furthermore, public figures generally have some access to a public medium for answering disparaging (belittling, discrediting) falsehoods about themselves; private individuals do not. For these reasons, public figures have a greater burden of proof in defamation cases (they must prove actual malice) than do private individuals.

Invasion of the Right to Privacy

A person has a right to solitude and freedom from prying public eyes—in other words, to privacy. As discussed in Chapter 4, the Supreme Court has held that a fundamental right to privacy is also implied by various amendments to the U.S.

ACTUAL MALICE
The deliberate intent to cause harm, which exists when a person makes a statement either knowing that it is false or showing a reckless disregard for whether it is true. In a defamation suit, a statement made about a public figure normally must be made with actual malice for the plaintiff to recover damages.

Constitution. Some state constitutions explicitly provide for privacy rights. In addition, a number of federal and state statutes have been enacted to protect individual rights in specific areas. Tort law also safeguards these rights through the tort *invasion of privacy*. Four acts qualify as an invasion of privacy:

1. *Appropriation of identity.* Under the common law, using a person's name, picture, or other likeness for commercial purposes without permission is a tortious invasion of privacy. Most states today have also enacted statutes prohibiting appropriation (discussed further in the next subsection).
2. *Intrusion into an individual's affairs or seclusion.* For instance, invading someone's home or illegally searching someone's briefcase is an invasion of privacy. The tort has been held to extend to eavesdropping by wiretap, the unauthorized scanning of a bank account, compulsory blood testing, and window peeping.
3. *False light.* Publication of information that places a person in a false light is another category of invasion of privacy. This could be a story attributing to a person ideas not held or actions not taken by the person. (Publishing such a story could involve the tort of defamation as well.)
4. *Public disclosure of private facts.* This type of invasion of privacy occurs when a person publicly discloses private facts about an individual that an ordinary person would find objectionable or embarrassing. A newspaper account of a private citizen's sex life or financial affairs could be an actionable invasion of privacy, even if the information revealed is true, because it is not of public concern.

EXAMPLE #4 After Dick and Karyn Anderson's marriage collapsed and they divorced, Karyn harassed Dick's new wife, Maureen, until Maureen obtained a warrant for Karyn's arrest. Then Karyn's new boyfriend, Paul Mergenhagen, began following Maureen while she was driving or walking with her small children. Paul repeatedly took photographs of Maureen (at least forty times), which frightened and upset her. Maureen called the police, but they would not intervene, so she filed a lawsuit against Paul alleging invasion of privacy. Traditionally, watching a person who is in a public place is not an intrusion into the person's privacy. In this situation, however, the court found that because Paul repeatedly followed Maureen in public in an attempt to frighten her, it could be considered an intrusion into her privacy.[6] □

Appropriation

The use by one person of another person's name, likeness, or other identifying characteristic, without permission and for the benefit of the user, constitutes the tort of **appropriation.** Under the law, an individual's right to privacy normally includes the right to the exclusive use of her or his identity.

EXAMPLE #5 In one early case, Vanna White, the hostess of the popular television game show *Wheel of Fortune,* brought a case against Samsung Electronics America, Inc. Without White's permission, Samsung included in an advertisement a robotic image dressed in a wig, gown, and jewelry, in a setting that resembled the *Wheel of Fortune* set, in a stance for which White is famous. The court ruled in White's favor, holding that the tort of appropriation does not require the use of a celebrity's name or actual likeness. The court stated that

APPROPRIATION
In tort law, the use by one person of another person's name, likeness, or other identifying characteristic without permission and for the benefit of the user.

---

6. *Anderson v. Mergenhagen,* 283 Ga.App. 546, 642 S.E.2d 105 (2007).

Samsung's robot ad left "little doubt" as to the identity of the celebrity that the ad was meant to depict.[7]□

Degree of Likeness   In recent cases, courts have reached different conclusions as to the degree of likeness that is required to impose liability for the tort of appropriation. EXAMPLE #6   A former professional hockey player, Anthony "Tony" Twist, who had a reputation for fighting, sued the publishers of the comic book *Spawn,* which included an evil character named Anthony Tony Twist Twistelli. The Missouri Supreme Court held that the use of Tony Twist's name alone was sufficient proof of likeness to support a misappropriation claim. Ultimately, the hockey player was awarded $15 million in damages.[8]□

 EXAMPLE #7   In California, in contrast, Keirin Kirby, the lead singer in a 1990s funk band called Deee-Lite, lost her appropriation claim against the makers of the video game *Space Channel 5.* Although the video game's character "Ulala" had some of Kirby's distinctive traits—hot pink hair, short skirt, platform shoes, and dance moves—there were not enough similarities, according to the state appellate court, to constitute misappropriation.[9]□

Right of Publicity as a Property Right   The common law tort of appropriation in many states has become known as the right of publicity.[10] Rather than being aimed at protecting a person's right to be left alone (privacy), this right aims to protect an individual's pecuniary (financial) interest in the commercial exploitation of his or her identity. In other words, it gives public figures, celebrities, and entertainers a right to sue anyone who uses their images for commercial benefit without their permission. Cases involving the right of publicity generally turn on whether the use was commercial. For instance, if a television news program reports on a celebrity and shows an image of the person, the use likely would not be classified as commercial; in contrast, including the celebrity's image on a poster without his or her permission would be a commercial use.

Because the right of publicity is similar to a property right, most states have concluded that the right is inheritable and survives the death of the person who held the right. Normally, though, the person must provide for the passage of the right to another in her or his will. EXAMPLE #8   A case involving Marilyn Monroe's right of publicity came before a federal trial court. The court held that because Marilyn Monroe's will did not specifically state a desire to pass the right to publicity to her heirs, the beneficiaries under her will did not have a right to prevent a company from marketing T-shirts and other merchandise using Monroe's name, picture, and likeness.[11]□

Fraudulent Misrepresentation

A misrepresentation leads another to believe in a condition that is different from the condition that actually exists. This is often accomplished through a false or an incorrect statement. Although persons sometimes make misrepresentations

---

7. *White v. Samsung Electronics America, Inc.,* 971 F.2d 1395 (9th Cir. 1992).

8. *Doe v. TCI Cablevision,* 110 S.W.3d 363 (Mo. 2003). The amount of damages was appealed and subsequently affirmed. See *Doe v. McFarlane,* 207 S.W.3d 52 (Mo.App. 2006).

9. *Kirby v. Sega of America, Inc.,* 144 Cal.App.4th 47, 50 Cal.Rptr.3d 607 (2006).

10. See, for example, California Civil Code Sections 3344 and 3344.1.

11. *Shaw Family Archives, Ltd. v. CMG Worldwide, Inc.,* 486 F.Supp.2d 309 (S.D.N.Y. 2007).

accidentally because they are unaware of the existing facts, the tort of **fraudulent misrepresentation,** or *fraud,* involves *intentional* deceit for personal gain. The tort includes several elements:

1. A misrepresentation of material facts or conditions with knowledge that they are false or with reckless disregard for the truth.
2. An intent to induce another party to rely on the misrepresentation.
3. A justifiable reliance on the misrepresentation by the deceived party.
4. Damages suffered as a result of that reliance.
5. A causal connection between the misrepresentation and the injury suffered.

FRAUDULENT MISREPRESENTATION
Any misrepresentation, either by misstatement or by omission of a material fact, knowingly made with the intention of deceiving another and on which a reasonable person would and does rely to his or her detriment.

Fact versus Opinion   For fraud to occur, more than mere **puffery,** or *seller's talk,* must be involved. Fraud exists only when a person represents as a fact something he or she knows is untrue. For example, it is fraud to claim that the roof of a building does not leak when one knows that it does. Facts are objectively ascertainable, whereas seller's talk—such as "I am the best accountant in town"—is not, because the speaker is representing a subjective view.

PUFFERY
A salesperson's often exaggerated claims concerning the quality of property offered for sale. Such claims involve opinions rather than facts and are not considered to be legally binding promises or warranties.

Normally, the tort of fraudulent misrepresentation occurs only when there is reliance on a *statement of fact.* Sometimes, however, reliance on a *statement of opinion* may involve the tort of fraudulent misrepresentation if the individual making the statement of opinion has superior knowledge of the subject matter. For example, when a lawyer makes a statement of opinion about the law in a state in which the lawyer is licensed to practice, a court would construe reliance on such a statement to be equivalent to reliance on a statement of fact.

Negligent Misrepresentation   Sometimes, a tort action can arise from misrepresentations that are made negligently rather than intentionally. The key difference between intentional and negligent misrepresentation is whether the person making the misrepresentation had actual knowledge of its falsity. Negligent misrepresentation only requires that the person making the statement or omission did not have a reasonable basis for believing its truthfulness. Liability for negligent misrepresentation usually arises when the defendant who made the misrepresentation owed a duty of care to the particular plaintiff to supply correct information. Statements or omissions made by attorneys and accountants to their clients, for example, can lead to liability for negligent misrepresentation.

In the following case, a commercial tenant claimed that the landlord made negligent misrepresentations about the size of the leased space.

Case 5.2 **McClain v. Octagon Plaza, LLC**

Court of Appeal of California,
Second District, Division 4, 2008.
159 Cal.App.4th 784, 71 Cal.Rptr.3d 885.
appellatecases.courtinfo.ca.gov[a]

BACKGROUND AND FACTS   Kelly McClain operates a business known as A+ Teaching Supplies. Ted and Wanda Charanian, who are married, are the principals of Octagon Plaza, LLC, which owns and manages a shopping center in

a. Under "Enter the System" select "Second Appellate District," then "Search." Under "Search by Court of Appeal or Trial Court Case Number," enter the Court of Appeal case number: B194037.

Valencia, California. In February 2003, McClain agreed to lease commercial space in the shopping center. The lease described the size of the unit leased by McClain as "approximately 2,624 square feet," and attached to the lease was a diagram of the shopping center that represented the size of the unit as 2,624 square feet. Because the base rent in the shopping center was $1.45 per square foot per month, McClain's total base rent was $3,804 per month. Moreover, because the unit presumably occupied 23 percent of the shopping center, McClain was responsible for this share of the

CASE 5.2–CONTINUED

common expenses. McClain claimed that the Charanians knew that the representations were materially inaccurate. As a result of Octagon's misrepresentations, McClain was induced to enter into a lease that obliged her to pay excess rent. At trial, the Charanians prevailed. McClain appealed.

IN THE WORDS OF THE COURT . . . *MANELLA*, J. [Judge]

* * * *

McClain contends that the [first amended claim at trial] adequately alleges a claim for fraud in the inducement, that is, misrepresentation involving a contract in which "the promisor knows what he or she is signing but consent is induced by fraud." We agree. *Generally, "[t]he elements of fraud, which give rise to the tort action for deceit, are (a) misrepresentation (false representation, concealment, or nondisclosure); (b) knowledge of falsity (or 'scienter'); (c) intent to defraud, i.e., to induce reliance; (d) justifiable reliance; and (e) resulting damage."* Claims for negligent misrepresentation deviate from this set of elements. *"The tort of negligent misrepresentation does not require* scienter *or intent to defraud.* It encompasses '[t]he assertion, as a fact, of that which is not true, by one who has no reasonable ground for believing it to be true', and '[t]he positive assertion, in a manner not warranted by the information of the person making it, of that which is not true, though he believes it to be true.'" [Emphasis added.]

* * * *

It is well established that the kind of disclaimer in Paragraph 2.4 [of the commercial lease], which asserts that McClain had an adequate opportunity to examine the leased unit, does not insulate Octagon from liability for fraud or prevent McClain from demonstrating justified reliance on the Charanians' representations.

* * * *

Here, McClain alleges that the Charanians exaggerated the size of her unit by 186 square feet, or 7.6 percent of its actual size, and increased her share of the common expenses by 4 percent through a calculation that understated the size of the shopping center by 965 square feet, or 8.1 percent of its actual size. [These discrepancies] operated to increase the rental payments incurred by McClain's retail business by more than $90,000 over the term of the lease.

DECISION AND REMEDY   The Court of Appeal of the State of California, Second Appellate District, reversed the trial court's judgment with respect to McClain's claim for misrepresentation.

THE ETHICAL DIMENSION   At what point do the misrepresentations about the size of the leased space become unethical—at 1 percent, 2 percent, or more?

THE LEGAL ENVIRONMENT DIMENSION   What defense could the shopping center owners raise to counter McClain's claim?

Abusive or Frivolous Litigation

Persons or businesses generally have a right to sue when they have been injured. In recent years, however, an increasing number of meritless lawsuits have been filed—sometimes simply to harass the defendant. Defending oneself in any legal proceeding can be costly, time consuming, and emotionally draining. Tort law recognizes that people have a right not to be sued without a legally just and proper reason. It therefore protects individuals from the misuse of litigation. Torts related to abusive litigation include malicious prosecution and abuse of process.

If the party that initiated a lawsuit did so out of malice and without probable cause (a legitimate legal reason), and ended up losing that suit, the party can be sued for *malicious prosecution*. In some states, the plaintiff (who was the defendant in the first proceeding) must also prove injury other than the normal costs of litigation, such as lost profits. *Abuse of process* can apply to any person using a legal process against another in an improper manner or to accomplish a purpose for which the process was not designed. The key difference between the torts of abuse of process and malicious prosecution is the level of proof. Abuse of process does not require the plaintiff to prove malice or show that the defendant (who was previously the plaintiff) lost in a prior legal proceeding.[12] Abuse of process is also not limited to prior litigation. It can be based on the wrongful use of subpoenas, court orders to attach or seize real property, or other types of formal legal process.

Does tort law impose an unfair economic burden on society as a whole?

Critics of the current tort law system contend that it encourages too many frivolous lawsuits, which clog the courts, and is unnecessarily costly. In particular, they say, damages awards are often excessive and bear little relationship to the actual damage suffered. Such large awards encourage plaintiffs to bring frivolous suits, hoping that they will "hit the jackpot." Trial lawyers, in turn, are eager to bring the suits because they are paid on a contingency-fee basis, meaning that they receive a percentage of the damages awarded.

The result, in the critics' view, is a system that disproportionately rewards a few lucky plaintiffs while imposing great costs on business and society as a whole. They refer to the economic burden that the tort system imposes on society as the "tort tax." According to one recent study, more than $300 billion per year is expended on tort litigation, including plaintiffs' and defendants' attorneys' fees, damages awards, and other costs.[13] Furthermore, they say, the tax appears in other ways. Because physicians, hospitals, and pharmaceutical companies are worried about medical malpractice suits, they have changed their behavior. Physicians, for example, engage in defensive medicine by ordering more tests than necessary. PricewaterhouseCoopers has calculated that the practice of defensive medicine increases health-care costs by more than $100 billion per year.

Tort Reform Proposals

To solve the problems they perceive, critics want to reduce both the number of tort cases brought each year and the amount of damages awarded. They advocate the following tort reform measures: (1) limit the amount of punitive damages that can be awarded; (2) limit the amount of general noneconomic damages that can be awarded (for example, for pain and suffering); (3) limit the amount that attorneys can collect in contingency fees; and (4) require the losing party to pay both the plaintiff's and the defendant's expenses to discourage the filing of meritless suits.

---

12. *Bernhard-Thomas Building Systems, LLC v. Duncan,* 918 A.2d 889 (Conn.App. 2007); and *Hewitt v. Rice,* 154 P.3d 408 (Colo. 2007).

13. Lawrence J. McQuillan, Hovannes Abramyan, and Anthony P. Archie, *Jackpot Justice: The True Cost of America's Tort System* (San Francisco: Pacific Research Institute, 2007).

Would Reforming Tort Law Be Unfair?

Others argue that the current system does not need such drastic reform. They say that the prospect of tort lawsuits encourages companies to produce safer products and deters them from putting dangerous products on the market. In the health-care industry, the potential for medical malpractice suits has led to safer and more effective medical practices.

Imposing limits on the amount of punitive and general noneconomic damages would be unfair, say the system's defenders, and would reduce efficiency in our legal and economic system. After all, corporations conduct cost-benefit analyses when they decide how much safety to build into their products. Any limitation on potential damages would mean that corporations would have less incentive to build safer products.

Indeed, Professor Stephen Teret of the Johns Hopkins University School of Public Health says that tort litigation is an important tool for preventing injuries because it forces manufacturers to opt for more safety in their products rather than less.[14] Limiting contingency fees would also be unfair, say those in favor of the current system, because low-income consumers who have been injured could not afford to pay an attorney to take a case on an hourly fee basis—and an attorney would not expend the time needed to pursue a case without the prospect of a large reward in the form of a contingency fee.

Tort Reform Legislation

While the debate continues, the federal government and a number of states have begun to take some steps toward tort reform. At the federal level, the Class Action Fairness Act (CAFA) of 2005[15] shifted jurisdiction over large interstate tort and product liability class-action lawsuits from the state courts to the federal courts. The intent was to prevent plaintiffs' attorneys from shopping around for a state court that might be predisposed to be sympathetic to their clients' cause and to award large damages in class-action suits.

At the state level, more than twenty states have placed caps ranging from $250,000 to $750,000 on noneconomic damages, especially in medical malpractice suits. More than thirty states have limited punitive damages, with some imposing outright bans.

Wrongful Interference

Business torts involving wrongful interference are generally divided into two categories: wrongful interference with a contractual relationship and wrongful interference with a business relationship.

Wrongful Interference with a Contractual Relationship   The body of tort law relating to *wrongful interference with a contractual relationship* has expanded greatly in recent years. **EXAMPLE #9** A landmark case involved an opera singer, Joanna Wagner, who was under contract to sing for a man named Lumley for a specified period of years. A man named Gye, who knew of this contract, nonetheless "enticed" Wagner to refuse to carry out the agreement, and Wagner began to sing for Gye. Gye's action constituted a tort because it wrongfully interfered with the contractual relationship between Wagner and Lumley.[16] (Of course, Wagner's refusal to carry out the agreement also entitled Lumley to sue Wagner for breach of contract.)□

---

14. "Litigation Is an Important Tool for Injury and Gun Violence Prevention," Johns Hopkins University Center for Gun Policy and Research, May 14, 2003.
15. 28 U.S.C.A. Sections 1711–1715, 1453.
16. *Lumley v. Gye,* 118 Eng.Rep. 749 (1853).

Three elements are necessary for wrongful interference with a contractual relationship to occur:

1. A valid, enforceable contract must exist between two parties.
2. A third party must know that this contract exists.
3. The third party must *intentionally* induce a party to breach the contract.

In principle, any lawful contract can be the basis for an action of this type. The contract could be between a firm and its employees or a firm and its customers. Sometimes, a competitor of a firm draws away one of the firm's key employees. Only if the original employer can show that the competitor knew of the contract's existence and intentionally induced the breach can damages be recovered from the competitor.

EXAMPLE #10 Carlin has a contract with Sutter that calls for Sutter to do gardening work on Carlin's large estate every week for fifty-two weeks at a specified price per week. Mellon, who needs gardening services and knows nothing about the Sutter-Carlin contract, contacts Sutter and offers to pay Sutter a wage that is substantially higher than that offered by Carlin. Sutter breaches his contract with Carlin so that he can work for Mellon. Carlin cannot sue Mellon, because Mellon knew nothing of the Sutter-Carlin contract and was totally unaware that the higher wage he offered induced Sutter to breach that contract. □

Wrongful Interference with a Business Relationship Businesspersons devise countless schemes to attract customers, but they are prohibited from unreasonably interfering with another's business in their attempts to gain a share of the market. There is a difference between competitive methods and **predatory behavior**—actions undertaken with the intention of unlawfully driving competitors completely out of the market. The distinction usually depends on whether a business is attempting to attract customers in general or to solicit only those customers who have shown an interest in a similar product or service of a specific competitor.

EXAMPLE #11 A shopping mall contains two athletic shoe stores: Joe's and SneakerSprint. Joe's cannot station an employee at the entrance of SneakerSprint to divert customers to Joe's and tell them that Joe's will beat SneakerSprint's prices. This type of activity constitutes the tort of wrongful interference with a business relationship, which is commonly considered to be an unfair trade practice. If this type of activity were permitted, Joe's would reap the benefits of SneakerSprint's advertising. □

Defenses to Wrongful Interference A person will not be liable for the tort of wrongful interference with a contractual or business relationship if it can be shown that the interference was justified, or permissible. Bona fide competitive behavior is a permissible interference even if it results in the breaking of a contract. **EXAMPLE #12** If Antonio's Meats advertises so effectively that it induces Sam's Restaurant to break its contract with Burke's Meat Company, Burke's Meat Company will be unable to recover against Antonio's Meats on a wrongful interference theory. After all, the public policy that favors free competition through advertising outweighs any possible instability that such competitive activity might cause in contractual relations. □ Although luring customers away from a competitor through aggressive marketing and advertising strategies obviously interferes with the competitor's relationship with its customers, courts typically allow such activities in the spirit of competition.

REMEMBER
It is the intent to do an act that is important in tort law, not the motive behind the intent.

PREDATORY BEHAVIOR
Business behavior that is undertaken with the intention of unlawfully driving competitors out of the market.

REMEMBER
What society and the law consider permissible often depends on the circumstances.

INTENTIONAL TORTS AGAINST PROPERTY

Intentional torts against property include trespass to land, trespass to personal property, conversion, and disparagement of property. These torts are wrongful actions that interfere with individuals' legally recognized rights with regard to their land or personal property. The law distinguishes real property from personal property (see Chapter 22). *Real property* is land and things "permanently" attached to the land. *Personal property* consists of all other items, which are basically movable. Thus, a house and lot are real property, whereas the furniture inside a house is personal property. Cash and stocks and bonds are also personal property.

Trespass to Land

TRESPASS TO LAND
The entry onto, above, or below the surface of land owned by another without the owner's permission or legal authorization.

A **trespass to land** occurs whenever a person, without permission, enters onto, above, or below the surface of land that is owned by another; causes anything to enter onto the land; remains on the land; or permits anything to remain on it. Actual harm to the land is not an essential element of this tort because the tort is designed to protect the right of an owner to exclusive possession of her or his property. Common types of trespass to land include walking or driving on someone else's land, shooting a gun over the land, throwing rocks at a building that belongs to someone else, building a dam across a river and thereby causing water to back up on someone else's land, and constructing a building so that part of it is on an adjoining landowner's property.

Trespass Criteria, Rights, and Duties   Before a person can be a trespasser, the owner of the real property (or other person in actual and exclusive possession of the property) must establish that person as a trespasser. For example, "posted" trespass signs expressly establish as a trespasser a person who ignores these signs and enters onto the property. A guest in your home is not a trespasser—unless she or he has been asked to leave but refuses. Any person who enters onto your property to commit an illegal act (such as a thief entering a lumberyard at night to steal lumber) is established impliedly as a trespasser, without posted signs.

A sign warns trespassers. Should the law allow a trespasser to recover from a landowner for injuries sustained on the premises? Why or why not? (Eugene Peretz/Creative Commons)

At common law, a trespasser is liable for damages caused to the property and generally cannot hold the owner liable for injuries sustained on the premises. This common law rule is being abandoned in many jurisdictions in favor of a *reasonable duty of care* rule that varies depending on the status of the parties; for example, a landowner may have a duty to post a notice that the property is patrolled by guard dogs. Also, under the *attractive nuisance* doctrine, children do not assume the risks of the premises if they are attracted to the property by some object, such as a swimming pool, an abandoned building, or a sand pile. Trespassers normally can be removed from the premises through the use of reasonable force without the owner's being liable for assault, battery, or false imprisonment.

Defenses against Trespass to Land   Trespass to land involves wrongful interference with another person's real property rights. One defense to this claim is to show that the trespass was warranted—for example, that the trespasser entered the property to assist someone in danger. Another defense exists when the trespasser can show that he or she had a license to come onto the land. A *licensee* is one who is invited (or allowed to enter) onto the property of another for the licensee's benefit. A person who enters another's property to read an electric meter, for example, is a licensee. When you purchase a ticket to attend a movie or sporting event, you are licensed to go onto the property of another to view that movie or event. Note that licenses to enter onto another's property are *revocable* by the property owner. If a property owner asks a meter reader to leave and the meter reader refuses to do so, the meter reader at that point becomes a trespasser.

Trespass to Personal Property

Whenever an individual wrongfully takes or harms the personal property of another or otherwise interferes with the lawful owner's possession of personal property, **trespass to personal property** occurs (also called *trespass to chattels* or *trespass to personalty*[17]). In this context, harm means not only destruction of the property, but also anything that diminishes its value, condition, or quality. Trespass to personal property involves intentional meddling with a possessory interest, including barring an owner's access to personal property. **EXAMPLE #13** If Kelly takes Ryan's business law book as a practical joke and hides it so that Ryan is unable to find it for several days prior to the final examination, Kelly has engaged in a trespass to personal property. (Kelly has also committed the tort of *conversion*—to be discussed shortly.)□

If it can be shown that the trespass to personal property was warranted, then a complete defense exists. Most states, for example, allow automobile repair shops to hold a customer's car (under what is called an *artisan's lien,* discussed in Chapter 13) when the customer refuses to pay for repairs already completed.

TRESPASS TO PERSONAL PROPERTY
The unlawful taking or harming of another's personal property; interference with another's right to the exclusive possession of his or her personal property.

Conversion

Whenever a person wrongfully possesses or uses the personal property of another without permission, the tort of **conversion** occurs. Any act that deprives an owner of personal property or the use of that property without that owner's permission and without just cause can be conversion. Even the taking of electronic records and data can form the basis of a conversion claim.[18] Often, when conversion occurs, a trespass to personal property also occurs because the original taking of the personal property from the owner was a trespass, and wrongfully retaining it is conversion. Conversion is the civil side of crimes related to theft, but it is not limited to theft. Even if the rightful owner consented to the initial taking of the property, so there was no theft or trespass, a failure to return the personal property may still be conversion. **EXAMPLE #14** Chen borrows Marik's iPod to use while traveling home from school for the holidays. When Chen returns to school, Marik asks for his iPod back. Chen tells Marik that she gave it to her little brother for Christmas. In this situation, Marik can sue Chen for conversion, and Chen will have to either return the iPod or pay damages equal to its value.□

Even if a person mistakenly believed that she or he was entitled to the goods, the tort of conversion may occur. In other words, good intentions are not a

CONVERSION
Wrongfully taking or retaining possession of an individual's personal property and placing it in the service of another.

KEEP IN MIND
In tort law, the underlying motive for an act does not matter. What matters is the intent to do the act that results in the tort.

---

17. Pronounced *per*-sun-ul-tee.
18. See, for example, *Thyroff v. Nationwide Mutual Insurance Co.,* 8 N.Y.3d 283, 864 N.E.2d 1272, 832 N.Y.S.2d 873 (2007).

defense against conversion; in fact, conversion can be an entirely innocent act. Someone who buys stolen goods, for example, can be liable for conversion even if he or she did not know that the goods were stolen. If the true owner brings a tort action against the buyer, the buyer must either return the property to the owner or pay the owner the full value of the property, despite having already paid the purchase price to the thief.

A successful defense against the charge of conversion is that the purported owner does not, in fact, own the property or does not have a right to possess it that is superior to the right of the holder.

Disparagement of Property

DISPARAGEMENT OF PROPERTY
An economically injurious falsehood made about another's product or property; a general term for torts that are more specifically referred to as *slander of quality* or *slander of title.*

Disparagement of property occurs when economically injurious falsehoods are made about another's product or property, not about another's reputation. Disparagement of property is a general term for torts that can be more specifically referred to as *slander of quality* or *slander of title.*

SLANDER OF QUALITY (TRADE LIBEL)
The publication of false information about another's product, alleging that it is not what its seller claims.

Slander of Quality   Publication of false information about another's product, alleging that it is not what its seller claims, constitutes the tort of **slander of quality**, or **trade libel.** The plaintiff must prove that actual damages proximately resulted from the slander of quality. In other words, the plaintiff must show not only that a third person refrained from dealing with the plaintiff because of the improper publication but also that there were associated damages. The economic calculation of such damages—they are, after all, conjectural—is often extremely difficult.

An improper publication may be both a slander of quality and defamation of character. After all, a statement that disparages the quality of a product may also, by implication, disparage the character of the person who would sell such a product.

SLANDER OF TITLE
The publication of a statement that denies or casts doubt on another's legal ownership of any property, causing financial loss to that property's owner.

Slander of Title   When a publication denies or casts doubt on another's legal ownership of any property, and this results in financial loss to that property's owner, the tort of **slander of title** may exist. Usually, this is an intentional tort in which someone knowingly publishes an untrue statement about property with the intent of discouraging a third person from dealing with the person slandered. For example, it would be difficult for a car dealer to attract customers after competitors published a notice that the dealer's stock consisted of stolen autos.

UNINTENTIONAL TORTS (NEGLIGENCE)

NEGLIGENCE
The failure to exercise the standard of care that a reasonable person would exercise in similar circumstances.

The tort of **negligence** occurs when someone suffers injury because of another's failure to live up to a required *duty of care.* In contrast to intentional torts, in torts involving negligence, the tortfeasor neither wishes to bring about the consequences of the act nor believes that they will occur. The actor's conduct merely creates a *risk* of such consequences. If no risk is created, there is no negligence. Moreover, the risk must be foreseeable—that is, it must be such that a reasonable person engaging in the same activity would anticipate the risk and guard against it. In determining what is reasonable conduct, courts consider the nature of the possible harm.

Many of the actions discussed earlier in the chapter in the section on intentional torts constitute negligence if the element of intent is missing.

Drawing by Maslin; © 1990 The New Yorker Magazine, Inc.

"To answer your question. Yes, if you shoot an arrow into the air and it falls to earth you should know not where, you could be liable for any damage it may cause."

EXAMPLE #15 Suppose that Juarez walks up to Natsuyo and intentionally shoves her. Natsuyo falls and breaks an arm as a result. In this situation, Juarez has committed an intentional tort (assault and battery). If Juarez carelessly bumps into Natsuyo, however, and she falls and breaks an arm as a result, Juarez's action will constitute negligence. In either situation, Juarez has committed a tort. ▫

To succeed in a negligence action, the plaintiff must prove each of the following:

1. That the defendant owed a duty of care to the plaintiff.
2. That the defendant breached that duty.
3. That the plaintiff suffered a legally recognizable injury.
4. That the defendant's breach caused the plaintiff's injury.

We discuss here each of these four elements of negligence.

The Duty of Care and Its Breach

Central to the tort of negligence is the concept of a **duty of care.** The idea is that if we are to live in society with other people, some actions can be tolerated and some cannot; some actions are right and some are wrong; and some actions are reasonable and some are not. The basic principle underlying the duty of care is that people are free to act as they please so long as their actions do not infringe on the interests of others.

DUTY OF CARE
The duty of all persons, as established by tort law, to exercise a reasonable amount of care in their dealings with others. Failure to exercise due care, which is normally determined by the reasonable person standard, constitutes the tort of negligence.

When someone fails to comply with the duty to exercise reasonable care, a potentially tortious act may have been committed. Failure to live up to a standard of care may be an act (setting fire to a building) or an omission (neglecting to put out a campfire). It may be a careless act or a carefully performed but nevertheless dangerous act that results in injury. Courts consider the nature of the act (whether it is outrageous or commonplace), the manner in which the act is performed (cautiously versus heedlessly), and the nature of the injury (whether it is serious or slight) in determining whether the duty of care has been breached.

The Reasonable Person Standard   Tort law measures duty by the **reasonable person standard.** In determining whether a duty of care has been breached, the courts ask how a reasonable person would have acted in the same circumstances. The reasonable person standard is said to be (though in an absolute sense it cannot be) objective. It is not necessarily how a particular person would act. It is society's judgment on how people *should* act. If the so-called reasonable person existed, he or she would be careful, conscientious, even tempered, and honest. The courts frequently use this hypothetical reasonable person in decisions relating to other areas of law as well. That individuals are required to exercise a reasonable standard of care in their activities is a pervasive concept in business law, and many of the issues discussed in subsequent chapters of this text have to do with this duty.

In negligence cases, the degree of care to be exercised varies, depending on the defendant's occupation or profession, her or his relationship with the plaintiff, and other factors. Generally, whether an action constitutes a breach of the duty of care is determined on a case-by-case basis. The outcome depends on how the judge (or jury, if it is a jury trial) decides a reasonable person in the position of the defendant would act in the particular circumstances of the case.

The Duty of Landowners   Landowners are expected to exercise reasonable care to protect persons coming onto their property from harm. As mentioned earlier, in some jurisdictions, landowners are held to owe a duty to protect even trespassers against certain risks. Landowners who rent or lease premises to tenants (see Chapter 22) are expected to exercise reasonable care to ensure that the tenants and their guests are not harmed in common areas, such as stairways, entryways, and laundry rooms.

Duty to Warn Business Invitees of Risks   Retailers and other firms that explicitly or implicitly invite persons to come onto their premises are usually charged with a duty to exercise reasonable care to protect those persons, who are considered **business invitees.** EXAMPLE #16 Suppose that you entered a supermarket, slipped on a wet floor, and sustained injuries as a result. The owner of the supermarket would be liable for damages if, when you slipped, there was no sign warning that the floor was wet. A court would hold that the business owner was negligent because the owner failed to exercise a reasonable degree of care in protecting the store's customers against foreseeable risks about which the owner knew or *should have known*. That a patron might slip on the wet floor and be injured as a result was a foreseeable risk, and the owner should have taken care to avoid this risk or to warn the customer of it (by posting a sign or setting out orange cones, for example). ▫

The landowner also has a duty to discover and remove any hidden dangers that might injure a customer or other invitee. Store owners have a duty to pro-

REASONABLE PERSON STANDARD
The standard of behavior expected of a hypothetical "reasonable person"; the standard against which negligence is measured and that must be observed to avoid liability for negligence.

BUSINESS INVITEE
A person, such as a customer or a client, who is invited onto business premises by the owner of those premises for business purposes.

tect customers from potentially slipping and injuring themselves on merchandise that has fallen off the shelves. Retailers can be held liable when a customer is injured by slipping on shotgun shell pellets or anything else that falls off a display and onto the floor.

Obvious Risks Provide an Exception. Some risks, of course, are so obvious that the owner need not warn of them. For instance, a business owner does not need to warn customers to open a door before attempting to walk through it. Other risks, however, may seem obvious to a business owner but may not be so in the eyes of another, such as a child. EXAMPLE #17 A hardware store owner may think it is unnecessary to warn customers not to climb a stepladder leaning against the back wall of the store. It is possible, though, that a child could climb up and tip the ladder over and be hurt as a result and that the store could be held liable. Similarly, although wet napkins on the floor of a nightclub might seem obvious, the owner still has a duty to its customers to maintain the premises in a safe condition.[19]

A sign in a merchant's window warns business invitees about slippery floors. If a customer subsequently slips on a wet floor and is injured, can the merchant nonetheless be held liable? (Debaird/Creative Commons)

Preventing Legal Disputes

It can sometimes be difficult for business owners to determine whether risks are obvious. Because the law imposes liability on business owners who fail to discover hidden dangers on the premises and protect patrons from being injured, it is advisable to post warnings of any potential risks on the property. Businesspersons should train their employees to be on the lookout for possibly dangerous conditions on the premises at all times and to notify a superior immediately if they notice something. Making the business premises as safe as possible for all persons who might be there, including children, the elderly, and individuals with disabilities, is one of the best ways to prevent potential legal disputes.

The Duty of Professionals If an individual has knowledge, skill, or intelligence superior to that of an ordinary person, the individual's conduct must be consistent with that status. Professionals—including physicians, dentists, architects, engineers, accountants, lawyers, and others—are required to have a standard minimum level of special knowledge and ability. Therefore, in determining whether professionals have exercised reasonable care, their training and expertise are taken into account. In other words, an accountant cannot defend against a lawsuit for negligence by stating, "But I was not familiar with that principle of accounting."

If a professional violates her or his duty of care toward a client, the professional may be sued for **malpractice,** which is essentially professional negligence. For example, a patient might sue a physician for *medical malpractice*. A client might sue an attorney for *legal malpractice.*

The Injury Requirement and Damages

For a tort to have been committed, the plaintiff must have suffered a *legally recognizable* injury. To recover damages (receive compensation), the plaintiff must have suffered some loss, harm, wrong, or invasion of a protected interest.

MALPRACTICE
Professional misconduct or the lack of the requisite degree of skill as a professional. Negligence—the failure to exercise due care—on the part of a professional, such as a physician, is commonly referred to as malpractice.

---

19. *Izquierdo v. Gyroscope, Inc.,* 646 So.2d 115 (Fla.App. 4th Dist. 2007).

Essentially, the purpose of tort law is to compensate for legally recognized injuries resulting from wrongful acts. If no harm or injury results from a given negligent action, there is nothing to compensate—and no tort exists. **EXAMPLE #18** If you carelessly bump into a passerby, who stumbles and falls as a result, you may be liable in tort if the passerby is injured in the fall. If the person is unharmed, however, there normally could be no suit for damages because no injury was suffered. Although the passerby might be angry and suffer emotional distress, few courts recognize negligently inflicted emotional distress as a tort unless it results in some physical disturbance or dysfunction.□

Compensatory damages are the norm in negligence cases. As noted earlier, a court will award punitive damages only if the defendant's conduct was grossly negligent, reflecting an intentional failure to perform a duty with reckless disregard of the consequences to others.

Causation

Another element necessary to a tort is *causation*. If a person fails in a duty of care and someone suffers an injury, the wrongful activity must have caused the harm for the activity to be considered a tort. In deciding whether there is causation, the court must address two questions:

CAUSATION IN FACT

An act or omission without which an event would not have occurred.

1. *Is there causation in fact?* Did the injury occur because of the defendant's act, or would it have occurred anyway? If an injury would not have occurred without the defendant's act, then there is causation in fact. **Causation in fact** can usually be determined by the use of the *but for* test: "but for" the wrongful act, the injury would not have occurred. Theoretically, causation in fact is limitless. One could claim, for example, that "but for" the creation of the world, a particular injury would not have occurred. Thus, as a practical matter, the law has to establish limits, and it does so through the concept of proximate cause.

PROXIMATE CAUSE

Legal cause; exists when the connection between an act and an injury is strong enough to justify imposing liability.

2. *Was the act the proximate cause of the injury?* **Proximate cause,** or legal cause, exists when the connection between an act and an injury is strong enough to justify imposing liability. **EXAMPLE #19** Ackerman carelessly leaves a campfire burning. The fire not only burns down the forest but also sets off an explosion in a nearby chemical plant that spills chemicals into a river, killing all the fish for a hundred miles downstream and ruining the economy of a tourist resort. Should Ackerman be liable to the resort owners? To the tourists whose vacations were ruined? These are questions of proximate cause that a court must decide.□

Both questions must be answered in the affirmative for liability in tort to arise. If a defendant's action constitutes causation in fact but a court decides that the action is not the proximate cause of the plaintiff's injury, the causation requirement has not been met—and the defendant normally will not be liable to the plaintiff.

NOTE

Proximate cause can be thought of as a question of social policy. Should the defendant be made to bear the loss instead of the plaintiff?

Questions of proximate cause are linked to the concept of foreseeability because it would be unfair to impose liability on a defendant unless the defendant's actions created a foreseeable risk of injury. Probably the most cited case on proximate cause is the *Palsgraf* case, discussed in this chapter's *Landmark in the Legal Environment* feature. In determining the issue of proximate cause, the court addressed the following question: Does a defendant's duty of care extend only to those who may be injured as a result of a foreseeable risk, or does it extend also to a person whose injury could not reasonably be foreseen?

In 1928, the New York Court of Appeals (that state's highest court) issued its decision in *Palsgraf v. Long Island Railroad Co.,*[a] a case that has become a landmark in negligence law and proximate cause.

The Facts of the Case

The plaintiff, Helen Palsgraf, was waiting for a train on a station platform. A man carrying a small package wrapped in newspaper was rushing to catch a train that had begun to move away from the platform. As the man attempted to jump aboard the moving train, he seemed unsteady and about to fall. A railroad guard on the train car reached forward to grab him, and another guard on the platform pushed him from behind to help him board the train. In the process, the man's package fell on the railroad tracks and exploded, because it contained fireworks. The repercussions of the explosion caused scales at the other end of the train platform to fall on Palsgraf, who was injured as a result. She sued the railroad company for damages in a New York state court.

The Question of Proximate Cause

At the trial, the jury found that the railroad guards were negligent in their conduct. On appeal, the question before the New York Court of Appeals was whether the conduct of the railroad guards was the proximate cause of Palsgraf's injuries. In other words, did the guards' duty of care extend to Palsgraf, who was outside the zone of danger and whose injury could not reasonably have been foreseen?

a. 248 N.Y. 339, 162 N.E. 99 (1928).

The court stated that the question of whether the guards were negligent *with respect to Palsgraf* depended on whether her injury was *reasonably foreseeable* to the railroad guards. Although the guards may have acted negligently with respect to the man boarding the train, this had no bearing on the question of their negligence with respect to Palsgraf. This was not a situation in which a person commited an act so potentially harmful (for example, firing a gun at a building) that he or she would be held responsible for any harm that resulted. The court stated that here "there was nothing in the situation to suggest to the most cautious mind that the parcel wrapped in newspaper would spread wreckage through the station." The court thus concluded that the railroad guards were not negligent with respect to Palsgraf because her injury was not reasonably foreseeable.

APPLICATION TO TODAY'S LEGAL ENVIRONMENT

The *Palsgraf* case established foreseeability as the test for proximate cause. Today, the courts continue to apply this test in determining proximate cause—and thus tort liability for injuries. Generally, if the victim of a harm or the consequences of a harm done are unforeseeable, there is no proximate cause. Note, though, that in the online environment, distinctions based on physical proximity, such as the "zone of danger" cited by the court in this case, are largely inapplicable.

RELEVANT WEB SITES

To locate information on the Web concerning the *Palsgraf* decision, go to this text's Web site at **www.cengage.com/blaw/let**, select "Chapter 5," and click on "URLs for Landmarks."

Defenses to Negligence

Defendants often defend against negligence claims by asserting that the plaintiffs failed to prove the existence of one or more of the required elements for negligence. Additionally, there are three basic *affirmative* defenses in negligence cases (defenses that a defendant can use to avoid liability even if the facts are as the plaintiff states): (1) assumption of risk, (2) superseding cause, and (3) contributory and comparative negligence.

Assumption of Risk   A plaintiff who voluntarily enters into a risky situation, knowing the risk involved, will not be allowed to recover. This is the defense of **assumption of risk.** The requirements of this defense are (1) knowledge of the risk and (2) voluntary assumption of the risk. This defense is frequently asserted when the plaintiff is injured during recreational activities that involve known risk, such as skiing and parachuting.

The risk can be assumed by express agreement, or the assumption of risk can be implied by the plaintiff's knowledge of the risk and subsequent conduct.

ASSUMPTION OF RISK

A doctrine under which a plaintiff may not recover for injuries or damage suffered from risks he or she knew of and voluntarily assumed.

Two bungee jumpers leap from a platform. If they are injured and sue the operator of the jump for negligence, what defenses might the operator use to avoid liability? (Mark Setchell/Creative Commons)

CONTRIBUTORY NEGLIGENCE
A rule in tort law that completely bars the plaintiff from recovering any damages if the damage suffered is partly the plaintiff's own fault; used in a minority of states.

COMPARATIVE NEGLIGENCE
A rule in tort law that reduces the plaintiff's recovery in proportion to the plaintiff's degree of fault, rather than barring recovery completely; used in the majority of states.

EXAMPLE #20 A driver entering a race knows that there is a risk of being killed or injured in a crash. Of course, a plaintiff does not assume a risk different from or greater than the risk normally carried by the activity. In other words, the race driver does not assume the risk that the banking in the curves of the racetrack will give way during the race because of a construction defect.□ Note, too, that persons attending sporting or recreational events, such as spectators at races, may also have assumed the risks inherent in that activity.

Risks are not deemed to be assumed in situations involving emergencies. Neither are they assumed when a statute protects a class of people from harm and a member of the class is injured by the harm. For example, employees are protected by statute from harmful working conditions and therefore do not assume the risks associated with the workplace. An employee who is injured will generally be compensated regardless of fault under state workers' compensation statutes (discussed in Chapter 17).

Superseding Cause   An unforeseeable intervening event may break the connection between a wrongful act and an injury to another. If so, the event acts as a *superseding cause*—that is, it relieves a defendant of liability for injuries caused by the intervening event. **EXAMPLE #21** Derrick, while riding his bicycle, negligently hits Julie, who is walking on the sidewalk. As a result of the impact, Julie falls and fractures her hip. While she is waiting for help to arrive, a small aircraft crashes nearby and explodes, and some of the fiery debris hits her, causing her to sustain severe burns. Derrick will be liable for the damages caused by Julie's fractured hip because the risk was foreseeable. Normally, Derrick will not be liable for the burns caused by the plane crash—because the risk of a plane's crashing nearby and injuring Julie was not foreseeable.□

Contributory and Comparative Negligence   All individuals are expected to exercise a reasonable degree of care in looking out for themselves. In the past, under the common law doctrine of **contributory negligence,** a plaintiff who was also negligent (failed to exercise a reasonable degree of care) could not recover anything from the defendant. Under this rule, no matter how insignificant the plaintiff's negligence was relative to the defendant's negligence, the plaintiff would be precluded from recovering any damages. Today, only a few jurisdictions still hold to this doctrine.

In the majority of states, the doctrine of contributory negligence has been replaced by a **comparative negligence** standard. Under the comparative negligence standard, both the plaintiff's and the defendant's negligence are computed, and the liability for damages is distributed accordingly. Some jurisdictions have adopted a "pure" form of comparative negligence that allows the plaintiff to recover, even if the extent of his or her fault is greater than that of the defendant. For example, if the plaintiff was 80 percent at fault and the defendant 20 percent at fault, the plaintiff may recover 20 percent of his or her damages. Many states' comparative negligence statutes, however, contain a "50 percent" rule under which the plaintiff recovers nothing if she or he was more than 50 percent at fault. Following this rule, a plaintiff who is 35 percent at fault could recover 65 percent of his or her damages, but a plaintiff who is 65 percent (more than 50 percent) at fault could recover nothing.

Special Negligence Doctrines and Statutes

There are a number of special doctrines and statutes relating to negligence. We examine a few of them here.

Res Ipsa Loquitur Generally, in lawsuits involving negligence, the plaintiff has the burden of proving that the defendant was negligent. In certain situations, however, under the doctrine of **res ipsa loquitur**[20] (meaning "the facts speak for themselves"), the courts may infer that negligence has occurred. Then the burden of proof rests on the defendant to prove she or he was *not* negligent. This doctrine is applied only when the event creating the damage or injury is one that ordinarily would occur only as a result of negligence. **EXAMPLE #22** A person undergoes abdominal surgery and following the surgery has nerve damage in her spine near the area of the operation. In this situation, the person can sue the surgeon under a theory of *res ipsa loquitur,* because the injury would never have occurred in the absence of the surgeon's negligence.[21] □ For the doctrine of *res ipsa loquitur* to apply, the event must have been within the defendant's power to control, and it must not have been due to any voluntary action or contribution on the part of the plaintiff.

Negligence *Per Se* Certain conduct, whether it consists of an action or a failure to act, may be treated as **negligence *per se*** (*per se* means "in or of itself"). Negligence *per se* may occur if an individual violates a statute or ordinance and thereby causes the kind of harm that the statute was intended to prevent. The injured person must prove (1) that the statute clearly sets out what standard of conduct is expected, when and where it is expected, and of whom it is expected; (2) that he or she is in the class intended to be protected by the statute; and (3) that the statute was designed to prevent the type of injury that he or she suffered. The standard of conduct required by the statute is the duty that the defendant owes to the plaintiff, and a violation of the statute is the breach of that duty.

EXAMPLE #23 A statute provides that anyone who operates a motor vehicle on a public highway and fails to give full time and attention to the operation of that vehicle is guilty of inattentive driving. After an accident involving two motor vehicles, one of the drivers is cited for and later found guilty of violating the inattentive driver statute. If the other driver was injured and subsequently files a lawsuit, a court could consider the violation of the statute to constitute negligence *per se*. The statute set forth a standard of attentive driving specifically to protect the safety of the traveling public.[22] □

"Danger Invites Rescue" Doctrine Sometimes, a person who is trying to avoid harm—such as an individual who swerves to avoid a head-on collision with a drunk driver—ends up causing harm to another (such as a cyclist riding in the bike lane) as a result. In those situations, the original wrongdoer (the drunk driver in this scenario) is liable to anyone who is injured, even if the injury actually resulted from another person's attempt to escape harm. The "danger invites rescue" doctrine extends the same protection to a person who is trying to rescue another from harm—the original wrongdoer is liable for injuries to an individual attempting a rescue. The idea is that the rescuer should not be held liable for any damages because he or she did not cause the danger and because danger invites rescue.

EXAMPLE #24 Ludlam, while driving down a street, fails to see a stop sign because he is trying to stop a squabble between his two young children in the car's back seat. Salter, on the curb near the stop sign, realizes that Ludlam is about to hit a pedestrian and runs into the street to push the pedestrian out of the way.

RES IPSA LOQUITUR
A doctrine under which negligence may be inferred simply because an event occurred, if it is the type of event that would not occur in the absence of negligence. Literally, the term means "the facts speak for themselves."

NEGLIGENCE *PER SE*
An action or failure to act in violation of a statutory requirement.

---

20. Pronounced *rehz ihp*-suh *low*-kwuh-tuhr.
21. See, for example, *Gubbins v. Hurson,* 885 A.2d 269 (D.C. 2005).
22. See, for example, *Wright v. Moore,* 931 A.2d 405 (Del.Supr. 2007).

An automobile struck a man who was crossing the street near a shopping mall in Columbus, Ohio. The woman in the photo was a passerby who rushed to his assistance. Suppose that the woman drags the man out of the street so that he will not be hit by another car, and in doing so, she makes his injuries worse. Can she be held liable for damages?
(AP Photo/Jack Kustron)

GOOD SAMARITAN STATUTE
A state statute stipulating that persons who provide emergency services to, or rescue, someone in peril cannot be sued for negligence, unless they act recklessly, thereby causing further harm.

DRAM SHOP ACT
A state statute that imposes liability on the owners of bars and taverns, as well as those who serve alcoholic drinks to the public, for injuries resulting from accidents caused by intoxicated persons when the sellers or servers of alcoholic drinks contributed to the intoxication.

If Ludlam's vehicle hits Salter instead, Ludlam will be liable for Salter's injury, as well as for any injuries the other pedestrian sustains. □ Rescuers may injure themselves, or the person rescued, or even a stranger, but the original wrongdoer will still be liable.

Special Negligence Statutes   A number of states have enacted statutes prescribing duties and responsibilities in certain circumstances. For example, most states now have what are called **Good Samaritan statutes.**[23] Under these statutes, someone who is aided voluntarily by another cannot turn around and sue the "Good Samaritan" for negligence. These laws were passed largely to protect physicians and medical personnel who voluntarily render services in emergency situations to those in need, such as individuals hurt in car accidents.

Many states have also passed **dram shop acts,**[24] under which a tavern owner or bartender may be held liable for injuries caused by a person who became intoxicated while drinking at the bar or who was already intoxicated when served by the bartender. Some states' statutes also impose liability on *social hosts* (persons hosting parties) for injuries caused by guests who became intoxicated at the hosts' homes. Under these statutes, it is unnecessary to prove that the tavern owner, bartender, or social host was negligent.

CYBER TORTS

Torts can also be committed in the online environment. Torts committed via the Internet are often called *cyber torts.* Over the last fifteen years, the courts have had to decide how to apply traditional tort law to torts committed in cyberspace. Consider, for example, issues of proof. How can it be proved that an online defamatory remark was "published" (which requires that a third party see or hear it)? How can the identity of the person who made the remark be discovered? Can an Internet service provider (ISP), such as America Online, Inc. (AOL), be forced to reveal the source of an anonymous comment made by one of its subscribers? We explore some of these questions in this section, as well as some of the legal questions that have arisen with respect to bulk e-mail advertising.

Defamation Online

Recall from the discussion of defamation earlier in this chapter that one who repeats or otherwise republishes a defamatory statement can be subject to liability as if she or he had originally published it. Thus, publishers generally can be held liable for defamatory contents in the books and periodicals that they publish. Now consider online forums. These forums allow anyone—customers, employees, or crackpots—to complain about a firm's personnel, policies, practices, or products. Whatever the truth of the complaint is, it might have an

---

23. These laws derive their name from the Good Samaritan story in the Bible. In that story, a traveler who had been robbed and beaten lay along the roadside, ignored by those passing by.
Eventually, a man from the country of Samaria (the "Good Samaritan") stopped to render assistance to the injured person.
24. Historically, a *dram* was a small unit of liquid, and distilled spirits (strong alcoholic liquor) were sold in drams. Thus, a dram shop was a place where liquor was sold in drams.

impact on the business of the firm. One of the early questions in the online legal arena was whether the providers of such forums could be held liable, as publishers, for defamatory statements made in those forums.

Immunity of Internet Service Providers   Newspapers, magazines, and television and radio stations may be held liable for defamatory remarks that they disseminate, even if those remarks are prepared or created by others. Prior to the passage of the Communications Decency Act (CDA) of 1996, the courts grappled with the question of whether ISPs should be held liable for defamatory messages made by users of their services. The CDA resolved the issue by stating that "[n]o provider or user of an interactive computer service shall be treated as the publisher or speaker of any information provided by another information content provider."[25] The CDA has been invoked to shield ISPs from liability for defamatory postings on their bulletin boards.

    EXAMPLE #25   In a leading case on this issue, America Online, Inc. (AOL, now part of Time Warner, Inc.), was not held liable even though it did not promptly remove defamatory messages of which it had been made aware. A federal appellate court stated that the CDA "plainly immunizes computer service providers like AOL from liability for information that originates with third parties." The court explained that the purpose of the statute is "to maintain the robust nature of Internet communication and, accordingly, to keep government interference in the medium to a minimum."[26]□ The courts have reached similar conclusions in subsequent cases, extending the CDA's immunity to Web message boards, online auction houses, Internet dating services, and any business that provides e-mail and Web browsing services.[27]

    In the following case, the court considered the scope of immunity that could be accorded to an online roommate matching service under the CDA.

---

25. 47 U.S.C. Section 230.

26. *Zeran v. America Online, Inc.,* 129 F.3d 327 (4th Cir. 1997); *cert.* denied, 524 U.S. 937, 118 S.Ct. 2341, 141 L.Ed.2d 712 (1998).

27. See, for example, *Universal Communications Systems, Inc. v. Lycos, Inc.,* 478 F.3d 413 (1st Cir. 2007); and *Barrett v. Rosenthal,* 40 Cal.4th 33, 51 Cal.Rptr.3d 55 (2006).

 Case 5.3   **Fair Housing Council of San Fernando Valley v. Roommate.com, LLC**

United States Court of Appeals,
Ninth Circuit, 2008.
521 F.3d 1157.

BACKGROUND AND FACTS   Roommate.com, LLC (Roommate), operates an online roommate matching Web site at **www.roommates.com**. The site helps individuals find roommates based on their descriptions of themselves and their roommate preferences. Roommate has approximately 150,000 active listings and receives about a million user views per day. To become members of Roommate, users respond to a series of online questions, choosing from answers in drop-down and select-a-box menus. Users disclose information about themselves and their roommate preferences based on

age, gender, and other characteristics, and on whether children will live in the household. Members can create personal profiles, search lists of compatible roommates, and send "roommail" messages to other members. Roommate also e-mails newsletters to members seeking housing, listing compatible members who have places to rent. The Fair Housing Councils of San Fernando Valley and San Diego, California, filed a suit in a federal district court against Roommate, claiming that the defendant violated the Fair Housing Act (FHA). The court held that the Communications Decency Act (CDA) barred this claim and dismissed it. The Councils appealed to the U.S. Court of Appeals for the Ninth Circuit.

CASE 5.3–CONTINUED

IN THE WORDS OF THE COURT . . . *KOZINSKI*, Circuit Judge.

* * * *

Section 230 of the CDA immunizes providers of interactive computer services against liability arising from content created by third parties * * * . This grant of immunity applies only if the interactive computer service provider is not also an "information content provider," which is defined as someone who is "responsible, in whole or in part, for the creation or development of" the offending content.

A Web site operator can be both a service provider and a content provider: If it passively displays content that is created entirely by third parties, then it is only a service provider with respect to that content. *But as to content that it creates itself, or is "responsible, in whole or in part" for creating or developing, the Web site is also a content provider. Thus, a Web site may be immune from liability for some of the content it displays to the public but be subject to liability for other content.* [Emphasis added.]

* * * *

Roommate created the questions and choice of answers, and designed its Web site registration process around them. Therefore, Roommate is undoubtedly the "information content provider" as to the questions and can claim no immunity for posting them on its Web site, or for forcing subscribers to answer them as a condition of using its services.

* * * *

* * * We note that asking questions certainly can violate the Fair Housing Act and analogous laws in the physical world. For example, a real estate broker may not inquire as to the race of a prospective buyer, and an employer may not inquire as to the religion of a prospective employee. *If such questions are unlawful when posed face-to-face or by telephone, they don't magically become lawful when asked electronically online. The Communications Decency Act was not meant to create a lawless no-man's-land on the Internet.* [Emphasis added.]

* * * *

Here, the part of the profile that is alleged to offend the Fair Housing Act and state housing discrimination laws—the information about sex, family status and sexual orientation—is provided by subscribers in response to Roommate's questions, which they cannot refuse to answer if they want to use defendant's services.

* * * By any reasonable use of the English language, Roommate is "responsible" at least "in part" for each subscriber's profile page, because every such page is a collaborative effort between Roommate and the subscriber.

Similarly, Roommate is not entitled to CDA immunity for the operation of its search system, which filters listings, or of its e-mail notification system, which directs e-mails to subscribers according to discriminatory criteria. Roommate designed its search system * * * . If Roommate has no immunity for asking the discriminatory questions, as we concluded above, it can certainly have no immunity for using the answers to the unlawful questions to limit who has access to housing.

DECISION AND REMEDY   The U.S. Court of Appeals for the Ninth Circuit concluded that the CDA does not provide immunity to Roommate for all of the content on its Web site and in its e-mail newsletters. Because Roommate forced subscribers to answer questions that divulged protected characteristics, it was responsible, at least in part, for the development of the content and could be liable for that content. The appellate court reversed and remanded the case to the lower court to determine whether the alleged actions for which Roommate is not immune violated the Fair Housing Act.

THE ETHICAL DIMENSION   Do Internet service providers (ISPs) have an ethical duty to advise their users if the information that the users provide for distribution through the ISPs might violate the law? Explain.

THE E-COMMERCE DIMENSION Should the courts continue to regard the CDA's grant of immunity to ISPs "as vigorously as in the past"? Why or why not?

Piercing the Veil of Anonymity A threshold barrier to anyone who seeks to bring an action for online defamation is discovering the identity of the person who posted the defamatory message online. ISPs can disclose personal information about their customers only when ordered to do so by a court. Consequently, businesses and individuals often resort to filing lawsuits against "John Does" (John Doe is a fictitious name that is used when the name of the particular person is not known). Then, using the authority of the courts, they attempt to obtain from the ISPs the identities of the persons responsible for the messages. This strategy has worked in some cases, but not in others.[28] Courts typically are reluctant to deter those who would potentially post messages on the Internet from exercising their First Amendment right to speak anonymously. After all, speaking anonymously is part of the nature of the Internet and helps to make it a useful forum for public discussion.

Spam

Bulk, unsolicited e-mail ("junk" e-mail) sent to all of the users on a particular e-mailing list is often called **spam.**[29] Typically, spam consists of a product ad sent to all of the users on an e-mailing list or all of the members of a newsgroup. Spam can waste user time and network bandwidth (the amount of data that can be transmitted within a certain time). It also imposes a burden on an ISP's equipment as well as on an e-mail recipient's computer system. Because of the problems associated with spam, a majority of the states now have laws regulating its transmission. In 2003, the U.S. Congress also enacted a law to regulate spam, but the volume of spam has actually increased since the law was enacted. (See this chapter's *Beyond Our Borders* feature on the following page for a discussion of another law passed by Congress in 2006 attempting to address spam originating outside the United States.)

SPAM
Bulk, unsolicited ("junk") e-mail.

State Regulation of Spam In an attempt to combat spam, thirty-six states have enacted laws that prohibit or regulate its use. Many state laws regulating spam require the senders of e-mail ads to instruct the recipients on how they can "opt out" of further e-mail ads from the same sources. For instance, in some states an unsolicited e-mail ad must include a toll-free phone number or return e-mail address through which the recipient can contact the sender to request that no more ads be e-mailed. The most stringent state law is California's antispam law, which went into effect on January 1, 2004. That law follows the "opt-in" model favored by consumer groups and antispam advocates. In other words, the law prohibits any person or business from sending e-mail ads to or from any

---

28. See, for example, *Doe v. Cahill*, 884 A.2d 451 (Del.Supr. 2005); and *Dendrite International, Inc. v. Doe No. 3*, 342 N.J.Super. 134, 775 A.2d 756 (2001).

29. The term *spam* is said to come from a skit by Monty Python, a group of British comedians that was popular in the 1970s and 1980s, in which they sang a song with the lyrics, "Spam spam spam spam, spam spam spam spam, lovely spam, wonderful spam." Like these lyrics, spam online is often considered to be a repetition of worthless text.

Spam is a serious problem in the United States, but enforcing anti-spam laws has been complicated by the fact that many spammers are located outside U.S. borders. After the CAN-SPAM Act of 2003 prohibited false and deceptive e-mails originating in the United States, spamming from other nations increased, and the wrongdoers generally were able to escape detection and legal sanctions.

Prior to 2006, the Federal Trade Commission (FTC) lacked the authority to investigate cross-border spamming activities and to communicate with foreign nations concerning spam and other deceptive practices conducted via the Internet. In 2006, however, Congress passed the U.S. Safe Web Act (also known as the Undertaking Spam, Spyware, and Fraud Enforcement with Enforcers Beyond Borders Act),[a] which increased the FTC's ability to combat spam on a global level.

The act allows the FTC to cooperate and share information with foreign agencies in investigating and prosecuting those involved in Internet fraud and deception, including spamming, spyware, and various Internet scams. Although the FTC and foreign agencies can provide investigative assistance to one another, the act exempts foreign agencies from U.S. public disclosure laws. In other words, the activities undertaken by the foreign agency (even if requested by the FTC) will be kept secret.

FOR CRITICAL ANALYSIS A provision in the U.S. Safe Web Act provides Internet service providers (ISPs) with a "safe harbor" (immunity from liability) for supplying information to the FTC concerning possible unfair or deceptive conduct in foreign jurisdictions. Is this provision fair? Why or why not?

a. Pub. L. No. 109-455, 120 Stat. 3372 (December 22, 2006), which enacted 15 U.S.C.A. Sections 57b-2a, 57b-2b, 57c-1, and 57c-2, and amended various other sections of the *United States Code.*

e-mail address in California unless the recipient has expressly agreed to receive e-mails from the sender. An exemption is made for e-mail sent to consumers with whom the advertiser has a "preexisting or current business relationship."

The Federal CAN-SPAM Act In 2003, Congress enacted the Controlling the Assault of Non-Solicited Pornography and Marketing (CAN-SPAM) Act, which took effect on January 1, 2004. The legislation applies to any "commercial electronic mail messages" that are sent to promote a commercial product or service. Significantly, the statute preempts state antispam laws except for those provisions in state laws that prohibit false and deceptive e-mailing practices.

Generally, the act permits the use of unsolicited commercial e-mail but prohibits certain types of spamming activities, including the use of a false return address and the use of false, misleading, or deceptive information when sending e-mail. The statute also prohibits the use of "dictionary attacks"—sending messages to randomly generated e-mail addresses—and the "harvesting" of e-mail addresses from Web sites through the use of specialized software. Notwithstanding the requirements of the federal act, the reality is that the problem of spam is difficult to address because much of it is funneled through foreign servers.

Reviewing . . . Torts and Cyber Torts

Two sisters, Darla and Irene, are partners in an import business located in a small town in Rhode Island. Irene is also campaigning to be the mayor of their town. Both sisters travel to other countries to purchase the goods they sell at their retail store. Irene buys Indonesian goods, and Darla buys goods from Africa. After a tsunami (tidal wave) destroys many of the cities in Indonesia to which Irene usually travels, she phones one of her contacts there and asks him to procure some items and ship them to her. He informs her that it will be impossible to buy these items now because the townspeople are being evacuated due to a water shortage. Irene is angry and tells the man that if he cannot purchase the goods, he should just take them without paying for them after the town has been evacuated. Darla overhears her sister's instructions and is outraged. They have a falling-out, and Darla decides that she no longer wishes to be in business with her sister. Using the information presented in the chapter, answer the following questions.

1. Suppose that Darla tells several of her friends about Irene's instructing the man to take goods without paying for them from the people of Indonesia after the tsunami disaster. If Irene files a tort action against Darla alleging slander, will her suit be successful? Why or why not?

2. Now suppose that Irene wins the election and becomes the city's mayor. Darla then writes a letter to the editor of the local newspaper disclosing Irene's misconduct. If Irene accuses Darla of committing libel, what defenses could Darla assert?

3. If Irene accepts goods shipped from Indonesia that were wrongfully obtained, has she committed an intentional tort against property? Explain.

4. Suppose now that Darla was in the store one day with an elderly customer, Betty Green, who was looking for a unique gift for her granddaughter's graduation present. When the phone rang, Darla left the customer and walked to the counter to answer the phone. Green wandered around the store and eventually went through an open door into the stockroom area, where she fell over some boxes on the floor and fractured her hip. Green files a negligence action against the store. Did Darla breach her duty of care? Why or why not?

Key Terms

Chapter Summary

Intentional Torts against Persons
(See pages 134–147.)

1. *Assault and battery*–An assault is an unexcused and intentional act that causes another person to be apprehensive of immediate harm. A battery is an assault that results in physical contact.

2. *False imprisonment*–The intentional confinement or restraint of another person's movement without justification.

3. *Intentional infliction of emotional distress*–An intentional act that amounts to extreme and outrageous conduct resulting in severe emotional distress to another.

4. *Defamation (libel or slander)*–A false statement of fact, not made under privilege, that is communicated to a third person and that causes damage to a person's reputation. For public figures, the plaintiff must also prove actual malice.

5. *Invasion of the right to privacy*–The use of a person's name or likeness for commercial purposes without permission, wrongful intrusion into a person's private activities, publication of information that places a person in a false light, or disclosure of private facts that an ordinary person would find objectionable.

6. *Appropriation*–The use of another person's name, likeness, or other identifying characteristic, without permission and for the benefit of the user.

7. *Misrepresentation (fraud)*–A false representation made by one party, through misstatement of facts or through conduct, with the intention of deceiving another and on which the other reasonably relies to his or her detriment.

8. *Frivolous litigation*–When a person initiates a lawsuit out of malice and without a legitimate reason, and then loses that suit, he or she can be sued for the tort of malicious prosecution. Also, a party who uses the legal process in an improper manner or for an unauthorized purpose can be sued for abuse of process, even if there was no malice.

9. *Wrongful interference*–The knowing, intentional interference by a third party with an enforceable contractual relationship or an established business relationship between other parties for the purpose of advancing the economic interests of the third party.

Intentional Torts against Property
(See pages 148–150.)

1. *Trespass to land*–The invasion of another's real property without consent or privilege. Once a person is expressly or impliedly established as a trespasser, the property owner has specific rights, which may include the right to detain or remove the trespasser.

2. *Trespass to personal property*–Unlawfully damaging or interfering with the owner's right to use, possess, or enjoy her or his personal property.

3. *Conversion*–Wrongfully taking personal property from its rightful owner or possessor and placing it in the service of another.

4. *Disparagement of property*–Any economically injurious falsehood that is made about another's product or property; an inclusive term for the torts of slander of quality and slander of title.

Unintentional Torts (Negligence)
(See pages 150–158.)

1. *Negligence*–The careless performance of a legally required duty or the failure to perform a legally required act. Elements that must be proved are that a legal duty of care exists, that the defendant breached that duty, and that the breach caused damage or injury to another.

2. *Defenses to negligence*–The basic affirmative defenses in negligence cases are (a) assumption of risk, (b) superseding cause, and (c) contributory or comparative negligence.

3. *Special negligence doctrines and statutes*–

   a. *Res ipsa loquitur*–A doctrine under which a plaintiff need not prove negligence on the part of the defendant because "the facts speak for themselves."

   b. Negligence *per se*–A type of negligence that may occur if a person violates a statute or an ordinance and the violation causes another to suffer the kind of injury that the statute or ordinance was intended to prevent.

Unintentional Torts (Negligence)— Continued

   c. **Special negligence statutes**—State statutes that prescribe duties and responsibilities in certain circumstances. Dram shop acts and Good Samaritan statutes are examples of special negligence statutes.

Cyber Torts
(See pages 158–162.)

General tort principles are being extended to cover cyber torts, or torts that occur in cyberspace, such as online defamation and spamming. Federal and state statutes may also apply to certain forms of cyber torts. For example, under the federal Communications Decency Act of 1996, Internet service providers are not liable for defamatory messages posted by their subscribers. A majority of the states and the federal government now regulate unwanted e-mail ads (spam).

For Review

1. What is a tort?
2. What is the purpose of tort law? What are two basic categories of torts?
3. What are the four elements of negligence?
4. What is a cyber tort, and how are tort theories being applied in cyberspace?

Questions and Case Problems

[handwritten: should have cleaned it better or more / didn't put up the sign]

5–1. Liability to Business Invitees. Kim went to Ling's Market to pick up a few items for dinner. It was a rainy, windy day, and the wind had blown water through the door of Ling's Market each time the door opened. As Kim entered through the door, she slipped and fell in the approximately one-half inch of rainwater that had accumulated on the floor. The manager knew of the weather conditions but had not posted any sign to warn customers of the water hazard. Kim injured her back as a result of the fall and sued Ling's for damages. Can Ling's be held liable for negligence in this situation? Discuss.

Question with Sample Answer

   5–2. Shannon's physician gives her some pain medication and tells her not to drive after she takes it, because the medication induces drowsiness. In spite of the doctor's warning, Shannon decides to drive to the store while on the medication. Owing to her lack of alertness, she fails to stop at a traffic light and crashes into another vehicle, causing a passenger in that vehicle to be injured. Is Shannon liable for the tort of negligence? Explain fully.

For a sample answer to Question 5–2, go to Appendix I at the end of this text.

5–3. Wrongful Interference. Lothar owns a bakery. He has been trying to obtain a long-term contract with the owner of Martha's Tea Salons for some time. Lothar starts a local advertising campaign on radio and television and in the newspaper. This advertising campaign is so persuasive that Martha decides to break the contract she has had with Harley's Bakery so that she can patronize Lothar's bakery. Is Lothar liable to Harley's Bakery for the tort of wrongful interference with a contractual relationship? Is Martha liable for this tort?

5–4. Defamation. Lydia Hagberg went to her bank, California Federal Bank, FSB, to cash a check made out to her by Smith Barney (SB), an investment services firm. Nolene Showalter, a bank employee, suspected that the check was counterfeit. Showalter called SB and was told that the check was not valid. As she phoned the police, Gary Wood, a bank security officer, contacted SB again and was informed that its earlier statement was "erroneous" and that the check was valid. Meanwhile, a police officer arrived, drew Hagberg away from the teller's window, spread her legs, patted her down, and handcuffed her. The officer searched her purse, asked her whether she had any weapons or stolen property and whether she was driving a stolen vehicle, and arrested her. Hagberg filed a suit in a California state court against the bank and others, alleging, among other things, slander. Should the absolute privilege for communications made in judicial or other official proceedings apply to statements made when a citizen contacts the police to report suspected criminal activity? Why or why not? [*Hagberg v. California Federal Bank, FSB*, 32 Cal.4th 350, 81 P.3d 244, 7 Cal.Rptr.3d 803 (2004)]

5–5. Negligence. In July 2004, Emellie Anderson hired Kenneth Whitten, a licensed building contractor, to construct a two-story addition to her home. The bottom floor was to be a garage and the second floor a home office. In August, the parties signed a second contract under which Whitten agreed to rebuild a deck and railing attached to the house and to further improve the office. A later inspection revealed gaps in the siding on the new garage, nails protruding from incomplete framing, improper support for a stairway to the office, and gaps in its plywood flooring. One post supporting the deck was cracked; another was too short. Concrete had not been poured underneath the old posts. A section of railing was missing, and what was installed was warped, with gaps at the joints. Anderson filed a suit in a Connecticut state court against Whitten, alleging that his work was "substandard, not to code, unsafe and not done in a [workmanlike] manner." Anderson claimed that she would have to pay someone else to repair all of the work. Does Whitten's "work" satisfy the requirements for a claim grounded in negligence? Should Anderson's complaint be dismissed, or should she be awarded damages? Explain. [*Anderson v. Whitten*, 100 Conn.App. 730, 918 A.2d 1056 (2007)]

Case Problem with Sample Answer

5–6. Between 1996 and 1998, Donna Swanson received several anonymous, handwritten letters that, among other things, accused her husband, Alan, of infidelity. In 1998, John Grisham, Jr., the author of *The Firm* and many other best-selling novels, received an anonymous letter that appeared to have been written by the same person. Grisham and the Swansons suspected Katherine Almy, who soon filed a suit in a Virginia state court against them, alleging, among other things, intentional infliction of emotional distress. According to Almy, Grisham intended to have her "really, really, suffer" for writing the letters, and the three devised a scheme to falsely accuse her. They gave David Liebman, a handwriting analyst, samples of Almy's handwriting. These included copies of confidential documents from her children's files at St. Anne's–Belfield School in Charlottesville, Virginia, where Alan taught and Grisham served on the board of directors. In Almy's view, Grisham influenced Liebman to report that Almy might have written the letters and misrepresented this report as conclusive, which led the police to confront Almy. She claimed that she then suffered severe emotional distress and depression, causing "a complete disintegration of virtually every aspect of her life" and requiring her "to undergo extensive therapy." In response, the defendants asked the court to dismiss the complaint for failure to state a claim. Should the court grant this request? Explain. [*Almy v. Grisham*, 273 Va. 68, 639 S.E.2d 182 (2007)]

After you have answered Problem 5–6, compare your answer with the sample answer given on the Web site that accompanies this text. Go to www.cengage.com/blaw/let, select "Chapter 5," and click on "Case Problem with Sample Answer."

5–7. Defenses to Negligence. Neal Peterson's entire family skied, and Peterson started skiing at the age of two. In 2000, at the age of eleven, Peterson was in his fourth year as a member of a ski race team. After a race one morning in February, Peterson continued to practice his skills through the afternoon. Coming down a slope very fast, at a point at which his skis were not touching the ground, Peterson collided with David Donahue. Donahue, a forty-three-year-old advanced skier, was skating (skiing slowly) across the slope toward the parking lot. Peterson and Donahue knew that falls or collisions and accidents and injuries were possible with skiing. Donahue saw Peterson "split seconds" before the impact, which knocked Donahue out of his skis and down the slope ten or twelve feet. When Donahue saw Peterson lying motionless nearby, he immediately sought help. To recover for his injuries, Peterson filed a suit in a Minnesota state court against Donahue, alleging negligence. Based on these facts, which defense to a claim of negligence is Donahue most likely to assert? How is the court likely to apply that defense and rule on Peterson's claim? Why? [*Peterson ex rel. Peterson v. Donahue*, 733 N.W.2d 790 (Minn.App. 2007)]

A Question of Ethics

5–8. White Plains Coat & Apron Co. is a New York–based linen rental business. Cintas Corp. is a nationwide business that rents similar products. White Plains had five-year exclusive contracts with some of its customers. As a result of Cintas's soliciting of business, dozens of White Plains' customers breached their contracts and entered into rental agreements with Cintas. White Plains demanded that Cintas stop its solicitation of White Plains' customers. Cintas refused. White Plains filed a suit in a federal district court against Cintas, alleging wrongful interference with existing contracts. Cintas argued that it had no knowledge of any contracts with White Plains and had not induced any breach. The court dismissed the suit, ruling that Cintas had a legitimate interest as a competitor to solicit business and make a profit. White Plains appealed to the U.S. Court of Appeals for the Second Circuit. [*White Plains Coat & Apron Co. v. Cintas Corp.*, 8 N.Y.3d 422, 867 N.E.2d 381 (2007)]

1. What are the two important policy interests at odds in wrongful interference cases? When

there is an existing contract, which of these interests should be accorded priority?

2. The U.S. Court of Appeals for the Second Circuit asked the New York Court of Appeals to answer a question: Is a general interest in soliciting business for profit a sufficient defense to a claim of wrongful interference with a contractual relationship? What do you think? Why?

Critical-Thinking Managerial Question

5–9. What general principle underlies the common law doctrine that business owners have a duty of care toward their customers? Does the duty of care unfairly burden business owners? Why or why not?

Video Question

5–10. Go to this text's Web site at **www.cengage.com/blaw/let** and select "Chapter 5." Click on "Video Questions" and view the video titled *Jaws*. Then answer the following questions.

1. In the video, the mayor (Murray Hamilton) and a few other men try to persuade Chief Brody (Roy Scheider) not to close the town's beaches. If Chief Brody keeps the beaches open and a swimmer is injured or killed because he failed to warn swimmers about the potential shark danger, has he committed a tort? If so, what kind of tort (intentional tort against persons, intentional tort against property, or negligence)? Explain your answer.

2. Can Chief Brody be held liable for any injuries or deaths to swimmers under any intentional tort theories? Why or why not?

3. Suppose that Chief Brody goes against the mayor's instructions and warns people to stay out of the water. Nevertheless, several swimmers do not heed his warning and are injured as a result. What defense or defenses can Chief Brody raise under these circumstances if he is sued for negligence?

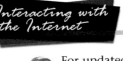

Interacting with the Internet

For updated links to resources available on the Web, as well as a variety of other materials, visit this text's Web site at

www.cengage.com/blaw/let

You can find cases and articles on torts, including business torts, in the tort law library at the Internet Law Library's Web site. Go to

www.lawguru.com/ilawlib

The 'Lectric Law Library's Legal Lexicon includes a useful discussion of the elements of fraud. To access this page, go to

www.lectlaw.com/def/1079.htm

PRACTICAL INTERNET EXERCISES

Go to this text's Web site at **www.cengage.com/blaw/let**, select "Chapter 5," and click on "Practical Internet Exercises." There you will find the following Internet research exercises that you can perform to learn more about the topics covered in this chapter.

Practical Internet Exercise 5–1: LEGAL PERSPECTIVE—**Online Defamation**
Practical Internet Exercise 5–2: SOCIAL PERSPECTIVE—**Legal and Illegal Uses of Spam**
Practical Internet Exercise 5–3: MANAGEMENT PERSPECTIVE—**The Duty to Warn**

BEFORE THE TEST

Go to this text's Web site at **www.cengage.com/blaw/let**, select "Chapter 5," and click on "Interactive Quizzes." You will find a number of interactive questions relating to this chapter.

Chapter 6

Criminal Law and Cyber Crime

CHAPTER OBJECTIVES

After reading this chapter, you should be able to answer the following questions:

1. What two elements must exist before a person can be held liable for a crime? Can a corporation commit crimes?

2. What are five broad categories of crimes? What is white-collar crime?

3. What defenses might be raised by criminal defendants to avoid liability for criminal acts?

4. What constitutional safeguards exist to protect persons accused of crimes? What are the basic steps in the criminal process?

5. What is cyber crime? What laws apply to crimes committed in cyberspace?

CONTENTS

"No state shall . . . deprive any person of life, liberty, or property without due process of law, nor deny to any person within its jurisdiction the equal protection of the laws."

— **FOURTEENTH AMENDMENT TO THE U.S. CONSTITUTION,**
July 28, 1868

The law imposes various sanctions in attempting to ensure that individuals engaging in business in our society can compete and flourish. These sanctions include damages for various types of tortious conduct (as discussed in Chapter 5), damages for breach of contract (to be discussed in Chapter 10), and the equitable remedies discussed in Chapters 1 and 10. Additional sanctions are imposed under criminal law. Many statutes regulating business provide for criminal as well as civil sanctions. Therefore, criminal law joins civil law as an important element in the legal environment of business.

In this chapter, following a brief summary of the major differences between criminal and civil law, we look at how crimes are classified and what elements must be present for criminal liability to exist. We then examine various categories of crimes, the defenses that can be raised to avoid liability for criminal actions, and the rules of criminal procedure. Criminal procedure ensures that a criminal defendant's right to "due process of law" is enforced. This right is guaranteed by the Fourteenth Amendment to the U.S. Constitution, as stated in the chapter-opening quotation. We conclude the chapter with a discussion of crimes that occur in cyberspace, often referred to as **cyber crime.** Generally, cyber crime refers more to the way particular crimes are committed than to a new category of crime.

CYBER CRIME
A crime that occurs online, in the virtual community of the Internet, as opposed to the physical world.

CIVIL LAW AND CRIMINAL LAW

Remember from Chapter 1 that *civil law* spells out the duties that exist between persons or between persons and their governments, excluding the duty not to commit crimes. Contract law, for example, is part of civil law. The whole body of tort law, which deals with the infringement by one person on the legally recognized rights of another, is also an area of civil law.

Criminal law, in contrast, has to do with crime. A **crime** can be defined as a wrong against society proclaimed in a statute and punishable by society through fines and/or imprisonment—or, in some cases, death. As mentioned in Chapter 1, because crimes are *offenses against society as a whole,* they are prosecuted by a public official, such as a district attorney (D.A.) or an attorney general (A.G.), not by victims. The victim often reports the crime to the police, but it is ultimately the D.A.'s office that decides whether to file criminal charges and to what extent to pursue the prosecution or carry out additional investigation.

CRIME
A wrong against society proclaimed in a statute and punishable by society through fines and/or imprisonment—or, in some cases, death.

Key Differences between Civil Law and Criminal Law

Because the state has extensive resources at its disposal when prosecuting criminal cases, numerous procedural safeguards are in place to protect the rights of defendants. We look here at one of these safeguards—the higher burden of proof that applies in a criminal case—as well as the harsher sanctions for criminal acts compared with civil wrongs. Exhibit 6–1 summarizes these and other key differences between civil law and criminal law.

Burden of Proof In a civil case, the plaintiff usually must prove his or her case by a *preponderance of the evidence.* Under this standard, the plaintiff must convince the court that, based on the evidence presented by both parties, it is more likely than not that the plaintiff's allegation is true.

In a criminal case, in contrast, the state must prove its case **beyond a reasonable doubt.** If the jury views the evidence in the case as reasonably permitting either a guilty or a not guilty verdict, then the jury's verdict must be *not* guilty. In other words, the government (prosecutor) must prove beyond a reasonable doubt that the defendant has committed every essential element of the offense with which she or he is charged. If the jurors are not convinced of the defendant's guilt beyond a reasonable doubt, they must find the defendant not guilty. Note also that in a criminal case, the jury's verdict normally must be unanimous—agreed to by all

BEYOND A REASONABLE DOUBT
The standard of proof used in criminal cases. If there is any reasonable doubt that a criminal defendant committed the crime with which she or he has been charged, then the verdict must be "not guilty."

EXHIBIT 6-1 KEY DIFFERENCES BETWEEN CIVIL LAW AND CRIMINAL LAW

ISSUE	CIVIL LAW	CRIMINAL LAW
Party who brings suit	The person who suffered harm	The state
Wrongful act	Causing harm to a person or to a person's property	Violating a statute that prohibits some type of activity
Burden of proof	Preponderance of the evidence	Beyond a reasonable doubt
Verdict	Three-fourths majority (typically)	Unanimous
Remedy	Damages to compensate for the harm or a decree to achieve an equitable result	Punishment (fine, imprisonment, or death)

members of the jury—to convict the defendant. (In a civil trial by jury, in contrast, typically only three-fourths of the jurors need to agree.)

The higher burden of proof in criminal cases reflects a fundamental social value—the belief that it is worse to convict an innocent individual than to let a guilty person go free. We will look at other safeguards later in the chapter, in the context of criminal procedure.

Criminal Sanctions   The sanctions imposed on criminal wrongdoers are also harsher than those that are applied in civil cases. As you read in Chapter 5, the purpose of tort law is to allow persons harmed by the wrongful acts of others to obtain compensation from the wrongdoers rather than to punish the wrongdoers. In contrast, criminal sanctions are designed to punish those who commit crimes and to deter others from committing similar acts in the future. Criminal sanctions include fines as well as the much harsher penalty of the loss of one's liberty by incarceration in a jail or prison. Sanctions may also include probation, community work service, completion of an educational or treatment program, and payment of restitution. The harshest criminal sanction is, of course, the death penalty.

Civil Liability for Criminal Acts

Some torts, such as assault and battery, provide a basis for a criminal prosecution as well as a tort action. **EXAMPLE #1** Joe is walking down the street, minding his own business, when suddenly a person attacks him. In the ensuing struggle, the attacker stabs Joe several times, seriously injuring him. A police officer restrains and arrests the wrongdoer. In this situation, the attacker may be subject both to criminal prosecution by the state and to a tort lawsuit brought by Joe.□ Exhibit 6–2 illustrates how the same act can result in both a tort action and a criminal action against the wrongdoer.

CRIMINAL LIABILITY

Two elements must exist simultaneously for a person to be convicted of a crime: (1) the performance of a prohibited act and (2) a specified state of mind or intent on the part of the actor. Additionally, to establish criminal liability, there must be a *concurrence* between the act and the intent. In other words, these two elements must occur together.

The Criminal Act

Every criminal statute prohibits certain behavior. Most crimes require an act of *commission;* that is, a person must *do* something in order to be accused of a crime. In criminal law, a prohibited act is referred to as the **actus reus,**[1] or guilty act. In some situations, an act of *omission* can be a crime, but only when a person has a legal duty to perform the omitted act. For instance, people in the United States have a legal duty to file tax returns. In 2005, the federal government criminally prosecuted a former winner of the reality TV show *Survivor* for failing to report to the Internal Revenue Service more than $1 million in winnings.

The *guilty act* requirement is based on one of the premises of criminal law— that a person is punished for harm done to society. For a crime to exist, the guilty act must cause some harm to a person or to property. Thinking about killing

ACTUS REUS

A guilty (prohibited) act. The commission of a prohibited act is one of the two essential elements required for criminal liability, the other element being the intent to commit a crime.

---

1. Pronounced *ak*-tuhs *ray*-uhs.

EXHIBIT 6-2 TORT LAWSUIT AND CRIMINAL PROSECUTION FOR THE SAME ACT

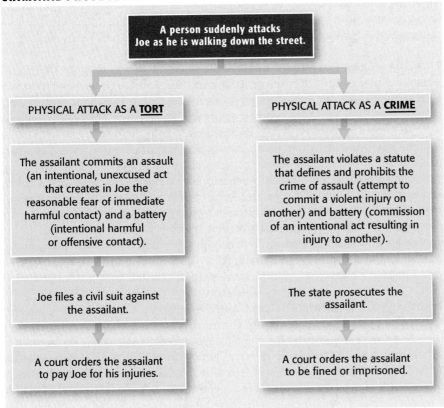

someone or about stealing a car may be wrong, but the thoughts do no harm until they are translated into action. Of course, a person can be punished for attempting murder or robbery, but normally only if he or she took substantial steps toward the criminal objective.

State of Mind

A wrongful mental state (***mens rea***)[2] is generally required to establish criminal liability. What constitutes such a mental state varies according to the wrongful action. For murder, the act is the taking of a life, and the mental state is the intent to take a life. For theft, the guilty act is the taking of another person's property, and the mental state involves both the knowledge that the property belongs to another and the intent to deprive the owner of it.

A guilty mental state can be attributed to acts of negligence or recklessness as well. *Criminal negligence* involves the mental state in which the defendant takes an unjustified, substantial, and foreseeable risk that results in harm. Under the Model Penal Code (on which many states base their criminal laws), a defendant is negligent even if she or he was not actually aware of the risk but *should have been aware* of it.[3] A defendant is criminally reckless if he or she consciously disregards a substantial and unjustifiable risk.

MENS REA
Mental state, or intent. A wrongful mental state is as necessary as a wrongful act to establish criminal liability. What constitutes a mental state varies according to the wrongful action. Thus, for murder, the *mens rea* is the intent to take a life.

---

2. Pronounced *mehns ray*-uh.
3. Model Penal Code Section 2.02(2)(d).

Corporate Criminal Liability

As will be discussed in Chapter 15, a *corporation* is a legal entity created under the laws of a state. Both the corporation as an entity and the individual directors and officers of the corporation are potentially subject to liability for criminal acts.

Liability of the Corporate Entity   At one time, it was thought that a corporation could not incur criminal liability because, although a corporation is a legal person, it can act only through its agents (corporate directors, officers, and employees). Therefore, the corporate entity itself could not "intend" to commit a crime. Under modern criminal law, however, a corporation may be held liable for crimes. Obviously, corporations cannot be imprisoned, but they can be fined or denied certain legal privileges (such as a license).

Today, corporations are normally liable for the crimes committed by their agents and employees within the course and scope of their employment.[4] For such criminal liability to be imposed, the prosecutor normally must show that the corporation could have prevented the act or that there was authorized consent to, or knowledge of, the act by persons in supervisory positions within the corporation. In addition, corporations can be criminally liable for failing to perform specific duties imposed by law (such as duties under environmental laws or securities laws).

Liability of Corporate Officers and Directors   Corporate directors and officers are personally liable for the crimes they commit, regardless of whether the crimes were committed for their personal benefit or on the corporation's behalf. Additionally, corporate directors and officers may be held liable for the actions of employees under their supervision. Under what has become known as the *responsible corporate officer doctrine,* a court may impose criminal liability on a corporate officer regardless of whether she or he participated in, directed, or even knew about a given criminal violation.

EXAMPLE #2 In *United States v. Park,*[5] the chief executive officer of a national supermarket chain was held personally liable for sanitation violations in corporate warehouses in which the food was exposed to contamination by rodents. The United States Supreme Court upheld the imposition of personal liability on the corporate officer not because he intended the crime or even knew about it but because he was in a "responsible relationship" to the corporation and had the power to prevent the violation. ■ Since the *Park* decision, courts have applied the responsible corporate officer doctrine on a number of occasions to hold corporate officers liable for their employees' statutory violations.

Preventing Legal Disputes

Because corporate officers and directors can be held liable for the crimes of their subordinates, the former should always be aware of any criminal statutes relevant to their particular industry or trade. In addition, firms would be wise to train their employees in how to comply with the multitude of applicable laws, particularly environmental laws and health and safety regulations, which frequently involve criminal sanctions. ■

---

4. See Model Penal Code Section 2.07.
5. 421 U.S. 658, 95 S.Ct. 1903, 44 L.Ed.2d 489 (1975).

TYPES OF CRIMES

The number of acts that are defined as criminal is nearly endless. Federal, state, and local laws provide for the classification and punishment of hundreds of thousands of different criminal acts. Traditionally, though, crimes have been grouped into five broad categories, or types: violent crime (crimes against persons), property crime, public order crime, white-collar crime, and organized crime. Within each of these categories, crimes may also be separated into more than one classification. Cyber crime—which consists of crimes committed in cyberspace through the use of computers—is, as mentioned earlier in this chapter, less a category of crime than a new way to commit crime. We will examine cyber crime later in this chapter.

Violent Crime

Crimes against persons, because they cause others to suffer harm or death, are referred to as *violent crimes*. Murder is a violent crime. So is sexual assault, or rape. Assault and battery, which were discussed in Chapter 5 in the context of tort law, are also classified as violent crimes. **Robbery**—defined as the taking of cash, personal property, or any other article of value from a person by means of force or fear—is another violent crime. Typically, states have more severe penalties for *aggravated robbery*—robbery with the use of a deadly weapon.

Each of these violent crimes is further classified by degree, depending on the circumstances surrounding the criminal act. These circumstances include the intent of the person committing the crime, whether a weapon was used, and (in cases other than murder) the level of pain and suffering experienced by the victim.

This is a crime scene in Brockton, Massachusetts. The victim, a fifteen-year-old high school student, was shot and killed on a city street. Violent crime is the type of crime about which the public is most concerned, but is it the most common kind of crime committed?
(AP Photo/Craig Murray/*The Enterprise*)

Property Crime

The most common type of criminal activity is property crime—crimes in which the goal of the offender is to obtain some form of economic gain or to damage property. Robbery is a form of property crime, as well as a violent crime, because the offender seeks to gain the property of another. We look here at a number of other crimes that fall within the general category of property crime.

Burglary Traditionally, **burglary** was defined under the common law as breaking and entering the dwelling of another at night with the intent to commit a felony. Originally, the definition was aimed at protecting an individual's home and its occupants. Most state statutes have eliminated some of the requirements found in the common law definition. The time of day at which the breaking and entering occurs, for example, is usually immaterial. State statutes frequently omit the element of breaking, and some states do not require that the building be a dwelling. When a deadly weapon is used in a burglary, the defendant can be charged with *aggravated burglary* and punished more severely.

Larceny Under the common law, the crime of **larceny** involved the unlawful taking and carrying away of someone else's personal property with the intent to

ROBBERY
The act of forcefully and unlawfully taking cash, personal property, or any other article of value from another. Force or intimidation is usually necessary for an act of theft to be considered robbery.

BURGLARY
The act of unlawfully entering or breaking into a building with the intent to commit a felony. (Some state statutes expand this to include the intent to commit any crime.)

LARCENY
The wrongful taking and carrying away of another person's personal property with the intent to permanently deprive the owner of the property. Some states classify larceny as either grand or petit, depending on the property's value.

A home damaged by Hurricane Katrina and subsequently looted. The sign facetiously thanks the perpetrator for "robbing" the property. Given the circumstances, is the crime committed here robbery, burglary, or some lesser property crime?
(Goatling/Trista B/Creative Commons)

permanently deprive the owner of possession. Put simply, larceny is stealing or theft. Whereas robbery involves force or fear, larceny does not. Therefore, picking pockets is larceny. Similarly, taking company products and supplies home for personal use, if one is not authorized to do so, is larceny. (Note that a person who commits larceny generally can also be sued under tort law because the act of taking possession of another's property involves a trespass to personal property.)

Most states have expanded the definition of property that is subject to larceny statutes. Stealing computer programs may constitute larceny even though the "property" consists of magnetic impulses. Stealing computer time can also constitute larceny. So, too, can the theft of natural gas or Internet and television cable service. Trade secrets can be subject to larceny statutes.

The common law distinguished between grand and petit larceny depending on the value of the property taken. Many states have abolished this distinction, but in those that have not, grand larceny (or theft) is a felony and petit larceny (or theft) is a misdemeanor. (As discussed later in this chapter, a felony is a more serious crime than a misdemeanor.)

Obtaining Goods by False Pretenses   It is a criminal act to obtain goods by means of false pretenses, such as buying groceries with a check knowing that one has insufficient funds to cover it or offering to sell someone a digital camera knowing that one does not actually own the camera. Statutes dealing with such illegal activities vary widely from state to state.

Receiving Stolen Goods   It is a crime to receive (acquire or buy) stolen goods. The recipient of such goods need not know the true identity of the owner or the thief. All that is necessary is that the recipient knows or should have known that the goods are stolen, which implies an intent to deprive the owner of those goods.

ARSON
The intentional burning of a building owned by another. Some statutes have expanded this to include any real property regardless of ownership and the destruction of property by other means—for example, by explosion.

Arson   The willful and malicious burning of a building (and, in some states, personal property) owned by another is the crime of **arson.** At common law, arson traditionally applied only to burning down another person's house. The law was designed to protect human life. Today, arson statutes have been extended to cover the destruction of any building, regardless of ownership, by fire or explosion.

Every state has a special statute that covers the act of burning a building for the purpose of collecting insurance. **EXAMPLE #3** Smith owns an insured apartment building that is falling apart. If he sets fire to it himself or pays someone else to do so, he is guilty not only of arson but also of defrauding the insurer, which is attempted larceny. □ Of course, the insurer need not pay the claim when insurance fraud is proved.

Forgery   The fraudulent making or altering of any writing (including electronic records) in a way that changes the legal rights and liabilities of another is

forgery. EXAMPLE #4 Without authorization, Severson signs Bennett's name to the back of a check made out to Bennett and attempts to cash it. Severson has committed the crime of forgery.□ Forgery also includes changing trademarks, falsifying public records, counterfeiting, and altering a legal document.

FORGERY
The fraudulent making or altering of any writing in a way that changes the legal rights and liabilities of another.

Public Order Crime

Historically, societies have always outlawed activities that are considered to be contrary to public values and morals. Today, the most common public order crimes include public drunkenness, prostitution, pornography, gambling, and illegal drug use. These crimes are sometimes referred to as victimless crimes because they normally harm only the offender. From a broader perspective, however, they are deemed detrimental to society as a whole because they may create an environment that gives rise to property and violent crimes.

White-Collar Crime

Crimes that typically occur only in the business context are popularly referred to as **white-collar crimes.** Although there is no official definition of white-collar crime, the term is commonly used to mean an illegal act or series of acts committed by an individual or business entity using some nonviolent means. Usually, this kind of crime is committed in the course of a legitimate occupation. Corporate crimes fall into this category. In addition, certain property crimes, such as larceny and forgery, may also be white-collar crimes if they occur within the business context.

WHITE-COLLAR CRIME
Nonviolent crime committed by individuals or corporations to obtain a personal or business advantage.

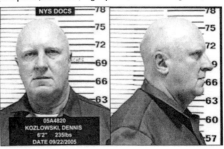

When Dennis Kozlowski was running Tyco International, he often threw lavish parties. On the left, he is shown at one such party for his wife's birthday on the island of Sardinia. Of the $2 million spent on the party, Tyco International—that is, the shareholders—paid for half of it. Eventually, Kozlowski was convicted of twenty-two counts of grand larceny, totaling more than $150 million in unauthorized bonuses. In addition, he was convicted of fraud involving more than $400 million. In 2005, he was sentenced to eight and one-third years in prison, and he could serve up to twenty-five years. What general type of crime did he commit?
(Left photo, AP Photo; Right photo, The Smoking Gun)

Embezzlement   When a person who is entrusted with another person's property or money fraudulently appropriates it, **embezzlement** occurs. Typically, embezzlement is carried out by an employee who steals funds. Banks are particularly prone to this problem, but embezzlement can occur in any firm. In a number of businesses, corporate officers or accountants have fraudulently converted funds for their own benefit and then "fixed" the books to cover up their crime. Embezzlement is not larceny, because the wrongdoer does not physically take the property from the possession of another, and it is not robbery, because force or fear is not used.

Embezzlement Can Take Many Forms   It does not matter whether the accused takes the funds from the victim or from a third person. If the financial officer of a large corporation pockets checks from third parties that were given to her to deposit into the corporate account, she is embezzling. Frequently, an embezzler takes a relatively small amount at one time but does so repeatedly over a long period. This might be done by underreporting income or deposits and embezzling the remaining amount, for example, or by creating fictitious persons or accounts and writing checks to them from the corporate account.

When an employer collects withholding taxes from his or her employees yet fails to remit these funds to the state, does such an action constitute a form of embezzlement? This was the primary issue in the following case.

Case 6.1   **George v. Commonwealth of Virginia**

Court of Appeals of Virginia, 2008.
51 Va.App. 137, 655 S.E.2d 43.
www.courts.state.va.us/wpcap.htm[a]

BACKGROUND AND FACTS   Dr. Francis H. George owned and operated a medical practice in Luray, Virginia. From 2001 to 2004, George employed numerous individuals, including nursing assistants, nurse practitioners, and a pediatrician. George withheld funds from his employees' salaries—funds that represented state income taxes owed to the

commonwealth[b] of Virginia. George placed these funds in the same banking account that he used to pay his personal and business expenses. During this period, George failed to file withholding tax returns as required by state law. Moreover, he did not remit the withheld funds to the state. At trial, a jury convicted George on four counts of embezzlement. George appealed to the state intermediate appellate court, claiming, among other things, that the evidence was insufficient to sustain the convictions because the state had not proved that he was entrusted with the property of another.

IN THE WORDS OF THE COURT . . . *FITZPATRICK*, S.J. [Senior Judge]

*   *   *   *

Appellant [George] *   *   * argues that the Commonwealth's evidence was insufficient to prove him guilty of violating [Virginia] Code Section 18.2-111, which provides:

If any person wrongfully and fraudulently use, dispose of, conceal or embezzle any money, bill, note, check, order, draft, bond, receipt, bill of lading or any other personal property, tangible or intangible, which he shall have received for another or for his

a. Scroll down and click on case "0332064" for January 15, 2008, to access this opinion.
b. In addition to Virginia, three other states designate themselves as commonwealths—Kentucky, Massachusetts, and Pennsylvania. The term *commonwealth* dates to the fifteenth century, when it meant "common well-being."

employer, principal or bailor [someone entrusting another with goods], or by virtue of his office, trust, or employment, or which shall have been entrusted or delivered to him by another or by any court, corporation or company, he shall be guilty of embezzlement.

To sustain a conviction of embezzlement, the Commonwealth must prove that the accused wrongfully appropriated to his or her own benefit property entrusted or delivered to the accused with the intent to deprive the owner thereof. Although the Commonwealth need not establish the existence of a formal fiduciary relationship [one based on trust], it must prove that the defendant was entrusted with the property of another. [Emphasis added.]

Appellant contends the evidence was insufficient to prove embezzlement because the funds he withheld from his employees' paychecks were not owned or entrusted to him by the Commonwealth. The money in appellant's bank account contained fees paid to him and his business for medical services rendered, as well as the withheld funds. Appellant argues that because the withheld funds amounted to nothing more than a debt he owed the Commonwealth, he did not commit embezzlement.

* * * *

However, while appellant at all relevant times remained responsible for paying the Commonwealth the funds he had withheld from his employees' paychecks, the Commonwealth was not merely his creditor. By operation of statute, the funds appellant retained for withholding taxes were maintained in his possession in trust for the Commonwealth. [Virginia] Code Section 58.1-474 provides:

> Every employer who fails to withhold or pay to the Tax Commissioner any sums required by this article to be withheld and paid shall be personally and individually liable therefor. Any sum or sums withheld in accordance with the provisions of this article shall be deemed to be held in trust for the Commonwealth.

* * * *

Despite the obligations of the fiduciary relationship created by [Virginia] Code Section 58.1-474, appellant [George] neither remitted the withheld funds to the Commonwealth nor maintained them for its benefit. In fact, appellant continued to use the money as though it were his own. "A person entrusted with possession of another's personalty [personal property] who converts such property to his own use or benefit is guilty of the statutory offense of embezzlement."

DECISION AND REMEDY   The Court of Appeals of Virginia ruled that the evidence clearly established that Dr. George used for his own benefit funds that he held in trust for the state. Thus, he was guilty of embezzlement, and his appeal to set aside his conviction was denied.

WHAT IF THE FACTS WERE DIFFERENT?   Assume that Dr. George had actually kept a separate account for taxes withheld from his employees' salaries but had simply failed to remit them to the state. Would the court have ruled differently? If so, in what way?

THE ETHICAL DIMENSION   Does an employer ever have a valid reason for failing to remit withholding taxes to the state? Why or why not?

Problems Prosecuting Embezzlement   Practically speaking, an embezzler who returns what has been taken might not be prosecuted. The owner may be unwilling to take the time to make a complaint, cooperate with the state's investigative efforts, and appear in court. Furthermore, the owner may not want the crime to become public knowledge. Nevertheless, the intent to return the embezzled property is not a defense to the crime of embezzlement.

To avoid potential embezzlement by corporate officers and employees, businesspersons should limit access to the firm's financial information and accounts. In addition, because embezzlement often takes place over a prolonged period of time, businesses should regularly conduct audits to discover and account for any discrepancies in the company's financial records. ■

Bribery   The crime of bribery involves offering to give something of value to a person in an attempt to influence that person—who is usually, but not always, a public official—to act in a way that serves a private interest. Three types of bribery are considered crimes: bribery of public officials, commercial bribery, and bribery of foreign officials. As an element of the crime of bribery, intent must be present and proved. The bribe itself can be anything the recipient considers to be valuable. Realize that the *crime of bribery occurs when the bribe is offered*—it is not required that the bribe be accepted. *Accepting a bribe* is a separate crime.

Commercial bribery involves corrupt dealings between private persons or businesses. Typically, people make commercial bribes to obtain proprietary information, cover up an inferior product, or secure new business. Industrial espionage sometimes involves commercial bribes. For example, a person in one firm may offer an employee in a competing firm some type of payoff in exchange for trade secrets or pricing schedules. So-called kickbacks, or payoffs for special favors or services, are a form of commercial bribery in some situations.

Bribing foreign officials to obtain favorable business contracts is a crime. The Foreign Corrupt Practices Act of 1977, which was discussed in detail in Chapter 2, was passed to curb the use of bribery by U.S. businesspersons in securing foreign contracts.

Bankruptcy Fraud   Federal bankruptcy law (see Chapter 13) allows individuals and businesses to be relieved of oppressive debt through bankruptcy proceedings. Numerous white-collar crimes may be committed during the many phases of a bankruptcy action. A creditor, for example, may file a false claim against the debtor, which is a crime. Also, a debtor may fraudulently transfer assets to favored parties before or after the petition for bankruptcy is filed. For instance, a company-owned automobile may be "sold" at a bargain price to a trusted friend or relative. Closely related to the crime of fraudulent transfer of property is the crime of fraudulent concealment of property, such as the hiding of gold coins.

INSIDER TRADING
The purchase or sale of securities on the basis of *inside information* (information that has not been made available to the public).

Insider Trading   An individual who obtains "inside information" about the plans of a publicly listed corporation can often make stock-trading profits by purchasing or selling corporate securities based on this information. **Insider trading** is a violation of securities law and will be considered more fully in Chapter 24. Basically, securities law prohibits a person who possesses inside information and has a duty not to disclose it to outsiders from trading on that information. He or she may not profit from the purchase or sale of securities based on inside information until the information is made available to the public.

The Theft of Trade Secrets   As will be discussed in Chapter 8, trade secrets constitute a form of intellectual property that for many businesses can be extremely valuable. The Economic Espionage Act of 1996[6] makes the theft of

---

6. 18 U.S.C. Sections 1831–1839.

trade secrets a federal crime. The act also makes it a federal crime to buy or possess another person's trade secrets, knowing that the trade secrets were stolen or otherwise acquired without the owner's authorization.

Violations of the act can result in steep penalties. The act provides that an individual who violates the act can be imprisoned for up to ten years and fined up to $500,000. If a corporation or other organization violates the act, it can be fined up to $5 million. Additionally, the law provides that any property acquired as a result of the violation, such as airplanes and automobiles, or used in the commission of the violation, such as computers and other electronic devices, is subject to criminal forfeiture—meaning that the government can take the property. A theft of trade secrets conducted via the Internet, for example, could result in the forfeiture of every computer or other device used to commit or facilitate the violation as well as any assets gained from the stolen trade secrets.

Mail and Wire Fraud   One of the most potent weapons against white-collar criminals is the Mail Fraud Act of 1990.[7] Under this act, it is a federal crime (mail fraud) to use the mails to defraud the public. Illegal use of the mails must involve (1) mailing or causing someone else to mail a writing—something written, printed, or photocopied—for the purpose of executing a scheme to defraud and (2) a contemplated or an organized scheme to defraud by false pretenses. If, for example, Johnson advertises by mail the sale of a cure for cancer that he knows to be fraudulent because it has no medical validity, he can be prosecuted for fraudulent use of the mails.

Federal law also makes it a crime to use wire (for example, the telephone), radio, or television transmissions to defraud.[8] Violators may be fined up to $1,000, imprisoned for up to five years, or both. If the violation affects a financial institution, the violator may be fined up to $1 million, imprisoned for up to thirty years, or both.

The following case involved charges of mail fraud in which funds misrepresented to support charities were acquired through telemarketing. The question was whether the prosecution could offer proof of the telemarketers' commission rate when no one had lied about it.

---

7. 18 U.S.C. Sections 1341–1342.
8. 18 U.S.C. Section 1343.

Case 6.2   **United States v. Lyons**

United States Court of Appeals,
Ninth Circuit, 2007.
472 F.3d 1055.

BACKGROUND AND FACTS   In 1994, in California, Gabriel Sanchez formed the First Church of Life (FCL), which had no congregation, services, or place of worship. Timothy Lyons, Sanchez's friend, formed a fund-raising company called North American Acquisitions (NAA). Through FCL, Sanchez and Lyons set up six charities—AIDS Research Association, Children's Assistance Foundation, Cops and Sheriffs of America, Handicapped Youth Services, U.S. Firefighters, and U.S. Veterans League. NAA hired telemarketers to solicit donations on the charities' behalf. Over time, more than

$6 million was raised, of which less than $5,000 was actually spent on charitable causes. The telemarketers kept 80 percent of the donated funds as commissions, and NAA took 10 percent. Most of the rest of the funds went to Sanchez, who spent it on himself. In 2002, Lyons and Sanchez were charged in a federal district court with mail fraud and other crimes. Throughout the trial, the prosecution referred to the high commissions paid to the telemarketers. The defendants were convicted, and each was sentenced to fifteen years in prison. They asked the U.S. Court of Appeals for the Ninth Circuit to overturn their convictions, asserting that the prosecution had used the high cost of fund-raising as evidence of fraud even though the defendants had not lied about the cost.

CASE 6.2–CONTINUED

CASE 6.2–CONTINUED

IN THE WORDS OF THE COURT . . . *McKEOWN*, Circuit Judge.

* * * *

Rare is the person who relishes getting calls from those great patrons of the telephone, telemarketers. Yet many charities, especially small, obscure or unpopular ones, could not fund their operations without telemarketers. Some professional telemarketers take the lion's share of solicited donations, sometimes requiring and receiving commission rates of up to 80 percent. Most donors would probably be shocked or surprised to learn that most of their contributions were going to for-profit telemarketers instead of charitable activities. *But * * * under the First Amendment, the bare failure to disclose these high costs to donors cannot, by itself, support a fraud conviction. Evidence of high fundraising costs may, nonetheless, support a fraud prosecution when nondisclosure is accompanied by intentionally misleading statements designed to deceive the listener.* [Emphasis added.]

* * * Timothy Lyons and Gabriel Sanchez challenge their convictions for mail fraud and money laundering on the basis that they never lied, and never asked the telemarketers in their employ to lie, about the fact that around 80% of donations to their charities were earmarked for telemarketing commissions.

Lyons and Sanchez did, however, misrepresent to donors how they spent contributions net of telemarketer commissions. Their undoing was not that the commissions were large but that their charitable web was a scam. Donors were told their contributions went to specific charitable activities when, in reality, almost no money did.

* * * *

* * * A rule in criminal prosecutions for fraud involving telemarketing [is that] the bare failure to disclose the high cost of fundraising directly to potential donors does not suffice to establish fraud. That is, the mere fact that a telemarketer keeps 80 percent of contributions it solicits cannot be the basis of a fraud conviction, and neither can the fact that a telemarketer fails to volunteer this information to would-be donors.

* * * [But] when nondisclosure is accompanied by intentionally misleading statements designed to deceive the listener, the high cost of fundraising may be introduced as evidence of fraud in a criminal case. * * * *The State may vigorously enforce its antifraud laws to prohibit professional fundraisers from obtaining money on false pretenses or by making false statements.* [Emphasis added.]

* * * Lyons and Sanchez urge that unless the government could show that they lied to donors about how much the telemarketers would receive, the government was barred from introducing evidence of the high commissions paid to telemarketers.

* * * *

* * * The government both alleged in its indictment and offered evidence at trial of specific misrepresentations and omissions [that Lyons and Sanchez] made regarding the use of donated funds. Specifically, the government's evidence underscored the fact that virtually none of the money that ended up in the bank accounts of the six FCL charities went to any charitable activities at all, let alone the specific charitable activities mentioned in the telemarketers' calls or promotional pamphlets.

* * * Admission of evidence regarding the fundraising costs was essential to understanding the overall scheme and the shell game of the multiple charities. The government did not violate Lyons' or Sanchez's * * * rights by introducing evidence that third-party telemarketers received 80 percent of funds donated to the various FCL charities because the government had also shown that Lyons and Sanchez, through their respective organizations, had made fraudulent misrepresentations regarding disposition of the charitable funds.

DECISION AND REMEDY The U.S. Court of Appeals for the Ninth Circuit upheld the convictions. Evidence of the commissions paid to the telemarketers could be introduced as evidence even though no one lied to the would-be donors about the commissions.

The defendants' "undoing was not that the commissions were large but that their charitable web was a scam."

THE ETHICAL DIMENSION It may have been legal in this case, but was it ethical for the prosecution to repeatedly emphasize the size of the telemarketers' commissions? Why or why not?

THE LEGAL ENVIRONMENT DIMENSION In what circumstance would the prosecution be prevented from introducing evidence of high fund-raising costs? Why?

Organized Crime

White-collar crime takes place within the confines of the legitimate business world. *Organized crime,* in contrast, operates *illegitimately* by, among other things, providing illegal goods and services. For organized crime, the traditional preferred markets are gambling, prostitution, illegal narcotics, and loan sharking (lending at higher-than-legal interest rates), along with more recent ventures into counterfeiting and credit-card scams.

Money Laundering The profits from organized crime and illegal activities amount to billions of dollars a year, particularly the profits from illegal drug transactions and, to a lesser extent, from racketeering, prostitution, and gambling. Under federal law, banks, savings and loan associations, and other financial institutions are required to report currency transactions involving more than $10,000. Consequently, those who engage in illegal activities face difficulties in depositing their cash profits from illegal transactions.

As an alternative to simply storing cash from illegal transactions in a safe-deposit box, wrongdoers and racketeers have invented ways to launder "dirty" money to make it "clean." This **money laundering** is done through legitimate businesses.

EXAMPLE #5 Matt, a successful drug dealer, becomes a partner with a restaurateur. Little by little, the restaurant shows increasing profits. As a partner in the restaurant, Matt is able to report the "profits" of the restaurant as legitimate income on which he pays federal and state taxes. He can then spend those funds without worrying that his lifestyle may exceed the level possible with his reported income.□

MONEY LAUNDERING
Falsely reporting income that has been obtained through criminal activity as income obtained through a legitimate business enterprise—in effect, "laundering" the "dirty money."

The Racketeer Influenced and Corrupt Organizations Act (RICO) In 1970, to curb the apparently increasing entry of organized crime into the legitimate business world, Congress passed the Racketeer Influenced and Corrupt Organizations Act (RICO).[9] The statute, which was part of the Organized Crime Control Act, makes it a federal crime to (1) use income obtained from racketeering activity to purchase any interest in an enterprise, (2) acquire or maintain an interest in an enterprise through racketeering activity, (3) conduct or participate in the affairs of an enterprise through racketeering activity, or (4) conspire to do any of the preceding activities. In addition, RICO creates civil as well as criminal liability.

The broad language of RICO has allowed it to be applied in cases that have little or nothing to do with organized crime. In fact, today the statute is more often used to attack white-collar crimes than organized crime.

---

9. 18 U.S.C. Sections 1961–1968.

The Godfather *series of classic movies depicted the actions of the U.S. Mafia (a secret criminal organization) as well as its Sicilian origins. The Federal Bureau of Investigation (FBI) is responsible for pursuing Mafia members. Since the terrorist attacks of September 11, 2001, however, the FBI has shifted many of its resources to tracking terrorist activity. What do you think has happened to the size of the U.S. Mafia as a result of this switch? Why?*
(Bradley Newman/Creative Commons)

FELONY
A crime—such as arson, murder, rape, or robbery—that carries the most severe sanctions, ranging from one year in a state or federal prison to the death penalty.

MISDEMEANOR
A lesser crime than a felony, punishable by a fine or incarceration in jail for up to one year.

PETTY OFFENSE
In criminal law, the least serious kind of criminal offense, such as a traffic or building-code violation.

Criminal Provisions   RICO incorporates by reference twenty-six separate types of federal crimes and nine types of state felonies—including many business-related crimes, such as bribery, embezzlement, forgery, mail and wire fraud, and securities fraud.[10] For purposes of RICO, a "pattern of racketeering activity" requires a person to commit at least two of these offenses. Any individual who is found guilty is subject to a fine of up to $25,000 per violation, imprisonment for up to twenty years, or both. Additionally, the statute provides that those who violate RICO may be required to forfeit (give up) any assets, in the form of property or cash, that were acquired as a result of the illegal activity or that were "involved in" or an "instrumentality of" the activity.

Civil Liability   In the event of a RICO violation, the government can seek civil penalties, including the divestiture of a defendant's interest in a business (called forfeiture) or the dissolution of the business. Moreover, in some cases, the statute allows private individuals to sue violators and potentially recover three times their actual losses (treble damages), plus attorneys' fees, for business injuries caused by a violation of the statute. This is perhaps the most controversial aspect of RICO and one that continues to cause debate in the nation's federal courts.

The prospect of receiving treble damages in civil RICO lawsuits has given plaintiffs financial incentive to pursue businesses and employers for violations. **EXAMPLE #6** Mohawk Industries, Inc., one of the largest carpeting manufacturers in the United States, was sued by a group of its employees for RICO violations. The employees claimed Mohawk conspired with recruiting agencies to hire and harbor illegal immigrants in an effort to keep labor costs low. The employees argued that Mohawk's pattern of illegal hiring expanded Mohawk's hourly workforce and resulted in lower wages for the plaintiffs. Mohawk filed a motion to dismiss, arguing that its conduct had not violated RICO. In 2006, however, a federal appellate court ruled that the plaintiffs had presented sufficient evidence of racketeering activity and remanded the case for a trial.[11] □

Classification of Crimes

Depending on their degree of seriousness, crimes typically are classified as felonies or misdemeanors. **Felonies** are serious crimes punishable by death or by imprisonment for more than a year. **Misdemeanors** are less serious crimes, punishable by a fine or by confinement for up to a year. In most jurisdictions, **petty offenses** are considered to be a subset of misdemeanors. Petty offenses are minor violations, such as jaywalking or violations of building codes. Even for petty offenses, however, a guilty party can be put in jail for a few days, fined, or both, depending on state or local law.

---

10. See 18 U.S.C. Section 1961(1)(A). The crimes listed in this section include murder, kidnapping, gambling, arson, robbery, bribery, extortion, money laundering, securities fraud, counterfeiting, dealing in obscene matter, dealing in controlled substances (illegal drugs), and a number of others.
11. *Williams v. Mohawk Industries, Inc.,* 465 F.3d 1277 (11th Cir. 2006); *cert.* denied, ___ U.S. ___, 127 S.Ct. 1381, 167 L.Ed.2d 174 (2007). See also *Trollinger v. Tyson Foods, Inc.,* 2007 WL 1574275 (E.D.Tenn. 2007) presented as Case 17.3 on page 588.

Whether a crime is a felony or a misdemeanor can determine in which court the case is tried and, in some states, whether the defendant has a right to a jury trial. Many states also define different degrees of felony offenses (first, second, and third degree murder, for example) and vary the punishment according to the degree. Some states also have different classes (degrees) of misdemeanors.

DEFENSES TO CRIMINAL LIABILITY

In certain circumstances, the law may allow a person to be excused from criminal liability because she or he lacks the required mental state. Criminal defendants may also be relieved of criminal liability if they can show that their criminal actions were justified, given the circumstances. Among the most important defenses to criminal liability are infancy, intoxication, insanity, mistake, consent, duress, justifiable use of force, entrapment, and the statute of limitations. Also, in some cases, defendants are given immunity and thus relieved, at least in part, of criminal liability for crimes they committed. We look at each of these defenses here.

Note that procedural violations, such as obtaining evidence without a valid search warrant, may operate as defenses also. As you will read later in this chapter, evidence obtained in violation of a defendant's constitutional rights normally may not be admitted in court. If the evidence is suppressed, then there may be no basis for prosecuting the defendant.

These two brothers were only thirteen and fourteen years old when they killed their father with a baseball bat and then set their Florida house on fire. In court, they did not deny their wrongdoing. They were sentenced to terms of seven to eight years for third degree murder and arson. Under what circumstances should they not be held responsible for their reprehensible actions?
(The Smoking Gun)

Infancy

The term *infant,* as used in the law, refers to any person who has not yet reached the age of majority. At common law, children under the age of seven could not commit a crime. It was presumed that children between the ages of seven and fourteen were incapable of committing crimes, but this presumption could be disproved by evidence that the child knew that the act was wrong. Today, most state courts no longer presume that children are incapable of criminal conduct, but may evaluate the particular child's state of mind. In all states, certain courts handle cases involving children who allegedly have violated the law. Courts that handle juvenile cases may also have jurisdiction over additional matters. In most states, a child may be treated as an adult and tried in a regular court if she or he is above a certain age (usually fourteen) and is charged with a felony, such as rape or murder.

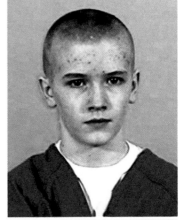

Intoxication

The law recognizes two types of intoxication, whether from drugs or from alcohol: *involuntary* and *voluntary.* Involuntary intoxication occurs when a person either is physically forced to ingest or inject an intoxicating substance or is unaware that a substance contains drugs or alcohol. Involuntary intoxication is a defense to a crime if its effect was to make a person incapable of obeying the law or of understanding that the act committed was wrong. Voluntary intoxication is rarely a defense, but it may be effective in cases in which the defendant was so *extremely* intoxicated as to negate the state of mind that a crime requires.

Insanity

Just as a child is often judged to be incapable of the state of mind required to commit a crime, so also may someone suffering from a mental illness. Thus, insanity may be a defense to a criminal charge. The courts have had difficulty deciding what the test for legal insanity should be, however, and psychiatrists as well as lawyers are critical of the tests used. Almost all federal courts and some states use the relatively liberal standard set forth in the Model Penal Code:

> A person is not responsible for criminal conduct if at the time of such conduct as a result of mental disease or defect he [or she] lacks substantial capacity either to appreciate the wrongfulness of his [or her] conduct or to conform his [or her] conduct to the requirements of the law.

Some states use the *M'Naghten test,*[12] under which a criminal defendant is not responsible if, at the time of the offense, he or she did not know the nature and quality of the act or did not know that the act was wrong. Other states use the irresistible-impulse test. A person operating under an irresistible impulse may know an act is wrong but cannot refrain from doing it. Under any of these tests, proving insanity is extremely difficult. For this reason, the insanity defense is rarely used and usually is not successful.

Mistake

COMPARE
"Ignorance" is a lack of information. "Mistake" is a confusion of information.

Everyone has heard the saying "Ignorance of the law is no excuse." Ordinarily, ignorance of the law or a mistaken idea about what the law requires is not a valid defense. In some states, however, that rule has been modified. Criminal defendants who claim that they honestly did not know that they were breaking a law may have a valid defense if (1) the law was not published or reasonably made known to the public or (2) the defendant relied on an official statement of the law that was erroneous.

A *mistake of fact,* as opposed to a *mistake of law,* operates as a defense if it negates the mental state necessary to commit a crime. **EXAMPLE #7** If Carl Wheaton mistakenly walks off with Julie Tyson's briefcase because he thinks it is his, there is no theft. Theft requires knowledge that the property belongs to another. (If Wheaton's act causes Tyson to incur damages, however, Wheaton may be subject to liability for trespass to personal property or conversion, torts that were discussed in Chapter 5.)◻

Consent

CONSENT
Voluntary agreement to a proposition or an act of another; a concurrence of wills.

What if a victim consents to a crime or even encourages the person intending a criminal act to commit it? **Consent** is not a defense to most crimes. The law forbids murder, prostitution, and drug use whether the victim consents or not. Consent may serve as a defense, however, in certain situations when it negates an element of the alleged criminal offense. Because crimes against property, such as burglary and larceny, usually require that the defendant intended to take someone else's property, the fact that the owner gave the defendant permission to take it will operate as a defense. Consent or forgiveness given after a crime has been committed is never a defense, although it can affect the likelihood of prosecution.

EXAMPLE #8 Barry gives Phong permission to stay in Barry's lakeside cabin and hunt for deer on the adjoining land. After observing Phong carrying a gun into the cabin at night, a neighbor calls the police, and an officer subsequently arrests Phong. If charged with burglary (or aggravated burglary, because he had a weapon), Phong can assert the defense of consent. He had obtained Barry's consent to enter the premises. ◻

---

12. A rule derived from *M'Naghten's Case,* 8 Eng.Rep. 718 (1843).

Duress

Duress exists when the *wrongful threat* of one person induces another person to perform an act that he or she would not otherwise have performed. In such a situation, duress is said to negate the mental state necessary to commit a crime because the perpetrator was forced or compelled to commit the act. Duress can be used as a defense to most crimes except murder.

Duress excuses a crime only when another's unlawful threat of serious bodily injury or death reasonably caused the perpetrator to commit a criminal act. In addition, there must have been no opportunity for the defendant to escape or avoid the threatened danger.[13] Essentially, to successfully assert duress as a defense, a defendant must have believed in the immediate danger, and the jury (or judge) must conclude that the defendant's belief was reasonable.

DURESS
Unlawful pressure brought to bear on a person, causing the person to perform an act that she or he would not otherwise perform.

Justifiable Use of Force

Probably the best-known defense to criminal liability is **self-defense.** Other situations, however, also justify the use of force: the defense of one's dwelling, the defense of other property, and the prevention of a crime. In all of these situations, it is important to distinguish between deadly and nondeadly force. *Deadly force* is likely to result in death or serious bodily harm. *Nondeadly force* is force that reasonably appears necessary to prevent the imminent use of criminal force.

Generally speaking, people can use the amount of nondeadly force that seems necessary to protect themselves, their dwellings, or other property or to prevent the commission of a crime. Deadly force can be used in self-defense if the defender *reasonably believes* that imminent death or grievous bodily harm will otherwise result, if the attacker is using unlawful force (an example of lawful force is that exerted by a police officer), and if the defender has not initiated or provoked the attack. Deadly force normally can be used to defend a dwelling only if the unlawful entry is violent and the person believes deadly force is necessary to prevent imminent death or great bodily harm or—in some jurisdictions—if the person believes deadly force is necessary to prevent the commission of a felony (such as arson) in the dwelling. See this chapter's *Management Perspective* feature on the next page for a discussion of how some states may allow the use of deadly force to prevent the commission of a crime on business premises.

SELF-DEFENSE
The legally recognized privilege to protect oneself or one's property against injury by another. The privilege of self-defense usually applies only to acts that are reasonably necessary to protect oneself, one's property, or another person.

Entrapment

Entrapment is a defense designed to prevent police officers or other government agents from enticing persons to commit crimes in order to later prosecute them for criminal acts. In the typical entrapment case, an undercover agent *suggests* that a crime be committed and somehow pressures or induces an individual to commit it. The agent then arrests the individual for the crime.

For entrapment to be considered a defense, both the suggestion and the inducement must take place. The defense is intended not to prevent law enforcement agents from setting a trap for an unwary criminal but rather to prevent them from pushing the individual into it. The crucial issue is whether the person who committed a crime was predisposed to commit the illegal act or did so because the agent induced it.

ENTRAPMENT
In criminal law, a defense in which the defendant claims that he or she was induced by a public official—usually an undercover agent or police officer—to commit a crime that he or she would otherwise not have committed.

---

13. See, for example, *State v. Heinemann,* 282 Conn. 281, 920 A.2d 278 (2007).

Management Faces a Legal Issue

Traditionally, the justifiable use of force, or self-defense, doctrine required prosecutors to distinguish between deadly and nondeadly force. In general, state laws have allowed individuals to use the amount of *nondeadly force* that is reasonably necessary to protect themselves, or their dwellings, businesses, or other property. Most states have allowed a person to use *deadly force* only when the person reasonably believed that imminent death or bodily harm would otherwise result. Additionally, the attacker had to be using unlawful force, and the defender had to have no other possible response or alternative way out of the life-threatening situation.

What the Courts Say

Today, many states still have "duty-to-retreat" laws. Under these laws, when a person's home is invaded or an assailant approaches, the person is required to retreat and cannot use deadly force unless her or his life is in danger.[a] Other states, however, are taking a very different approach and expanding the occasions when deadly force can be used in self-defense. Because such laws allow or even encourage the defender to stay and use force, they are known as "stand-your-ground" laws.

Florida, for example, enacted a statute in 2005 that allows the use of deadly force to prevent the commission of a "forcible felony," including not only murder but also such crimes as robbery, carjacking, and sexual battery.[b] Under this law, a Florida resident has a right to shoot an intruder in his or her home or a would-be carjacker even if there is no physical threat to the owner's safety. At least fourteen other states have passed similar laws that eliminate the duty to retreat, including Arizona, Georgia, Idaho, Indiana, Kansas, Kentucky, Louisiana, Michigan, Oklahoma, South Carolina, South Dakota, Tennessee, and Texas.

In a number of states, a person may use deadly force to prevent someone from breaking into his or her home, car, or place of business. For example, courts in Louisiana now allow a person to use deadly force to repel an attack while he or she is lawfully in a home, car, or place of business without imposing any duty to retreat.[c] Courts in Connecticut allow the use of deadly force not only to prevent a person from unlawful entry, but also when reasonably necessary to prevent arson or some other violent crime from being committed on the premises.[d]

Implications for Managers

The stand-your-ground laws that many states have enacted often include places of business as well as homes and vehicles. Consequently, businesspersons in those states can be less concerned about the duty-to-retreat doctrine. In addition, business liability insurance often costs less in states without a duty to retreat, because many statutes provide that the business owner is not liable in a civil action for injuries to the attacker. Even in states that impose a duty to retreat, there is no duty to retreat if doing so would increase rather than diminish the danger. Nevertheless, business owners should use deadly force only as a last resort to prevent the commission of crime at their business premises.

a. See, for example, *State v. Sandoval,* 342 Or. 506, 156 P.3d 60 (2007).
b. Florida Statutes Section 776.012.
c. See, for example, *State v. Johnson,* 948 So.2d 1229 (La.App. 3d Cir. 2007); and Lousiana Statutes Ann. Section 14:20.
d. See, for example, *State v. Terwilliger,* 105 Conn.App. 219, 937 A.2d 735 (2008); and Conn. General Statutes Section 53a-20.

Statute of Limitations

With some exceptions, such as for the crime of murder, statutes of limitations apply to crimes just as they do to civil wrongs. In other words, the state must initiate criminal prosecution within a certain number of years. If a criminal action is brought after the statutory time period has expired, the accused person can raise the statute of limitations as a defense.

Immunity

SELF-INCRIMINATION
The giving of testimony that may subject the testifier to criminal prosecution. The Fifth Amendment to the Constitution protects against self-incrimination by providing that no person "shall be compelled in any criminal case to be a witness against himself."

At times, the state may wish to obtain information from a person accused of a crime. Accused persons are understandably reluctant to give information if it will be used to prosecute them, and they cannot be forced to do so. The privilege against **self-incrimination** is granted by the Fifth Amendment to the U.S. Constitution, which reads, in part, "nor shall [any person] be compelled in any criminal case to be a witness against himself." In cases in which the state wishes to obtain information from a person accused of a crime, the state can grant *immunity* from prosecution or agree to prosecute for a less serious offense in exchange for the information. Once immunity is given, the person can no longer refuse to testify on Fifth Amendment grounds because he or she now has an absolute privilege against self-incrimination.

Often, a grant of immunity from prosecution for a serious crime is part of the **plea bargaining** between the defendant and the prosecuting attorney. The defendant may be convicted of a lesser offense, while the state uses the defendant's testimony to prosecute accomplices for serious crimes carrying heavy penalties.

CONSTITUTIONAL SAFEGUARDS AND CRIMINAL PROCEDURES

Criminal law brings the power of the state, with all its resources, to bear against the individual. Criminal procedures are designed to protect the constitutional rights of individuals and to prevent the arbitrary use of power on the part of the government.

The U.S. Constitution provides specific safeguards for those accused of crimes. Most of these safeguards protect individuals against state government actions, as well as federal government actions, by virtue of the due process clause of the Fourteenth Amendment. These protections are set forth in the Fourth, Fifth, Sixth, and Eighth Amendments.

Fourth Amendment Protections

As discussed in Chapter 4, the Fourth Amendment protects the "right of the people to be secure in their persons, houses, papers, and effects." Before searching or seizing private property, law enforcement officers must obtain a **search warrant**— an order from a judge or other public official authorizing the search or seizure. To obtain a search warrant, law enforcement officers must convince a judge that they have reasonable grounds, or **probable cause,** to believe a search will reveal a specific illegality. In addition, the Fourth Amendment prohibits general warrants and requires a particular description of what is to be searched or seized. General searches through a person's belongings are impermissible. The search cannot extend beyond what is described in the warrant. Although search warrants require specificity, if a search warrant is issued for a person's residence, items that are in that residence may be searched even if they do not belong to that individual.

EXAMPLE #9 Paycom Billing Services, Inc., facilitates payments from Internet users to its client Web sites and stores vast amounts of credit-card information in the process. Three partners at Paycom received a letter from an employee, Christopher Adjani, threatening to sell Paycom's confidential client information if the company did not pay him $3 million. Pursuant to an investigation, the Federal Bureau of Investigation (FBI) obtained a search warrant to search Adjani's person, automobile, and residence, including computer equipment. When the FBI agents served the warrant, they discovered evidence of the criminal scheme in the e-mail communications on a computer in the residence. The computer belonged to Adjani's live-in girlfriend. Adjani filed a motion to suppress this evidence, claiming that because he did not own the computer, it was beyond the scope of the warrant. Although the federal trial court granted the defendant's motion and suppressed the incriminating e-mails, in 2006 the U.S. Court of Appeals for the Ninth Circuit reversed. According to the appellate court, despite the novel Fourth Amendment issues raised in the case, the search of the computer was proper given the alleged involvement of computers in the crime.[14]□

PLEA BARGAINING
The process by which a criminal defendant and the prosecutor in a criminal case work out a mutually satisfactory disposition of the case, subject to court approval; usually involves the defendant's pleading guilty to a lesser offense in return for a lighter sentence.

SEARCH WARRANT
An order granted by a public authority, such as a judge, that authorizes law enforcement personnel to search particular premises or property.

PROBABLE CAUSE
Reasonable grounds for believing that a person should be arrested or searched.

---

14. *United States v. Adjani,* 452 F.3d 1140 (9th Cir. 2006); *cert.* denied, ___ U.S. ___, 127 S.Ct. 568, 166 L.Ed.2d 420 (2006).

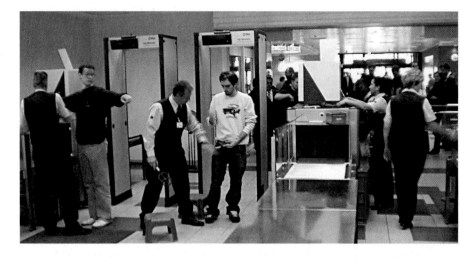

Passengers and their carry-on items are searched at an airport security checkpoint. Do such searches violate passengers' Fourth Amendment rights? (Ralf Roletschek/Wikimedia Commons)

As noted in Chapter 4, the standard of probable cause is not the same in the business context as in nonbusiness contexts. The existence of a general and neutral plan for enforcing government regulations normally will justify the issuance of a search warrant. Moreover, warrants are not required for searches of businesses in highly regulated industries, such as liquor, guns, and strip mining. The standard used for highly regulated industries is sometimes applied in other contexts as well. In the following case, the court considered whether the standard applies to airports and thus permits a suspicionless checkpoint search to be conducted in an airport to screen airline passengers.

Case 6.3 **United States v. Hartwell**

United States Court of Appeals,
Third Circuit, 2006.
436 F.3d 174.

BACKGROUND AND FACTS   Christian Hartwell arrived at the Philadelphia International Airport on Saturday, May 17, 2003, to catch a flight to Phoenix, Arizona. He reached the security checkpoint, placed his hand luggage on a conveyor belt to be x-rayed, and approached the metal detector. Hartwell's luggage was scanned without incident, but he set off the magnetometer when he walked through. He was told to remove all items from his pockets and try again. Hartwell removed several items from his pockets and passed through once more. Carlos Padua, a federal Transportation Security Administration (TSA) agent, took Hartwell aside and scanned him with a handheld magnetometer. The wand revealed a solid object in Hartwell's pants pocket. Padua asked what it was, but Hartwell did not respond. Escorted to a private screening room, Hartwell refused several requests to empty his pocket. By Hartwell's account, Padua then reached into the pocket and removed two packages of crack cocaine. Hartwell was arrested and convicted on charges related to the possession of the drugs. He appealed to the U.S. Court of Appeals for the Third Circuit, arguing that the search violated the Fourth Amendment.

IN THE WORDS OF THE COURT . . . *ALITO*, CIRCUIT JUDGE.

*   *   *   *

Suspicionless checkpoint searches are permissible under the Fourth Amendment when a court finds a favorable balance between the gravity of the public concerns served by the seizure, the degree to which the seizure advances the public interest, and the severity of the interference with individual liberty. [Emphasis added.]

*   *   *   *

In this case, the airport checkpoint passes the *   *   * test. First, there can be no doubt that preventing terrorist attacks on airplanes is of paramount importance.

Second, airport checkpoints also advance the public interest *   *   * . Absent a search, there is no effective means of detecting which airline passengers are reasonably likely to hijack an airplane. Additionally, it is apparent that airport checkpoints have been effective.

Third, the procedures involved in Hartwell's search were minimally intrusive. They were well tailored to protect personal privacy, escalating in invasiveness only after a lower level of screening disclosed a reason to conduct a more probing search. The search began when Hartwell simply passed through a magnetometer and had his bag x-rayed, two screenings that involved no physical touching. Only after Hartwell set off the metal detector was he screened with a wand—yet another less intrusive substitute for a physical pat-down. And only after the wand detected something solid on his person, and after repeated requests that he produce the item, did the TSA agents (according to Hartwell) reach into his pocket.

In addition to being tailored to protect personal privacy, other factors make airport-screening procedures minimally intrusive in comparison to other kinds of searches. Since every air passenger is subjected to a search, there is virtually no stigma attached to being subjected to search at a known, designated airport search point. Moreover, the possibility for abuse is minimized by the public nature of the search. Unlike searches conducted on dark and lonely streets at night where often the officer and the subject are the only witnesses, these searches are made under supervision and not far from the scrutiny of the traveling public. And the airlines themselves have a strong interest in protecting passengers from unnecessary annoyance and harassment.

Lastly, the entire procedure is rendered less offensive—if not less intrusive—because air passengers are on notice that they will be searched. Air passengers choose to fly, and screening procedures of this kind have existed in every airport in the country since at least 1974. The events of September 11, 2001, have only increased their prominence in the public's consciousness. It is inconceivable that Hartwell was unaware that he had to be searched before he could board a plane.

DECISION AND REMEDY The U.S. Court of Appeals for the Third Circuit held that Hartwell's search was permissible under the Fourth Amendment, "even though it was initiated without individualized suspicion and was conducted without a warrant. It is permissible *   *   * because the State has an overwhelming interest in preserving air travel safety, and the procedure is tailored to advance that interest while proving to be only minimally invasive."

WHY IS THIS CASE IMPORTANT? The federal appellate court in this case extended the administrative search doctrine, which typically applies to highly regulated industries, to airport searches. The United States Supreme Court developed this standard for analyzing suspicionless vehicle checkpoints, such as those used to determine the sobriety of randomly selected drivers. The Supreme Court has not yet ruled on the legality of airport screenings. Nevertheless, subsequent federal appellate court rulings in the Second, Sixth, and Ninth Circuits have followed the reasoning of this decision and held that airport searches without consent are constitutionally permissible.

WHAT IF THE FACTS WERE DIFFERENT? Suppose that in his pocket Hartwell had been carrying a flash drive with data on it for his laptop computer, rather than illegal drugs. When the item was discovered, airport security, without Hartwell's permission, took it into another room and plugged it into the airport's computer to search its contents, finding some evidence of illegal activity. Would the suspicionless airport search have been justified in that situation? Why or why not?

Fifth Amendment Protections

The Fifth Amendment offers significant protections for accused persons. One is the guarantee that no one can be deprived of "life, liberty, or property without due process of law." Two other important Fifth Amendment provisions protect persons against double jeopardy and self-incrimination.

Due Process of Law   Remember from Chapter 4 that *due process of law* has both procedural and substantive aspects. Procedural due process requirements underlie criminal procedures. Basically, the law must be carried out in a fair and orderly way. In criminal cases, due process means that defendants should have an opportunity to object to the charges against them before a fair, neutral decision maker, such as a judge. Defendants must also be given the opportunity to confront and cross-examine witnesses and accusers and to present their own witnesses.

Double Jeopardy   The Fifth Amendment also protects persons from **double jeopardy** (being tried twice for the same criminal offense). The prohibition against double jeopardy means that once a criminal defendant is acquitted (found "not guilty") of a particular crime, the government may not retry him or her for the same crime.

> **DOUBLE JEOPARDY**
> A situation occurring when a person is tried twice for the same criminal offense; prohibited by the Fifth Amendment to the Constitution.

The prohibition against double jeopardy does not preclude the crime victim from bringing a civil suit against that same person to recover damages, however. Additionally, a state's prosecution of a crime will not prevent a separate federal prosecution relating to the same activity, and vice versa. **EXAMPLE #10** A person found "not guilty" of assault and battery in a criminal case may be sued by the victim in a civil tort case for damages. A person who is prosecuted for assault and battery in a state court may be prosecuted in a federal court for civil rights violations resulting from the same action.□

Self-Incrimination   As explained earlier, the Fifth Amendment grants a privilege against self-incrimination. Thus, in any criminal proceeding, an accused person cannot be compelled to give testimony that might subject her or him to any criminal prosecution.

The Fifth Amendment's guarantee against self-incrimination extends only to natural persons. Because a corporation is a legal entity and not a natural person, the privilege against self-incrimination does not apply to it. Similarly, the business records of a partnership normally do not receive Fifth Amendment protection. When a partnership is required to produce these records, it must do so even if the information incriminates the persons who constitute the business entity. Sole proprietors and sole practitioners (those who fully own their businesses) who have not incorporated normally cannot be compelled to produce their business records. These individuals have full protection against self-incrimination because they function in only one capacity; there is no separate business entity (see Chapter 14).

> **BE AWARE**
> The Fifth Amendment protection against self-incrimination does not cover partnerships or corporations.

Protections under the Sixth and Eighth Amendments

The Sixth Amendment guarantees several important rights for criminal defendants: the right to a speedy trial, the right to a jury trial, the right to a public trial, the right to confront witnesses, and the right to counsel. **EXAMPLE #11** Law enforcement officers in Nebraska obtained an indictment and arrest warrant for

John Fellers based on his involvement in distributing methamphetamine (meth) with four other individuals. Two police officers went to Fellers's home to arrest him, showed him the warrant, and asked him about the other persons involved. Fellers responded that he knew the individuals and had used meth with them. After that, the officers arrested Fellers and took him to jail, where they informed him of his right to counsel for the first time. He waived his right and repeated what he had told the officers at his home. After a conviction on drug charges, Fellers appealed, claiming that his incriminating statements to the officers should have been excluded because he was not informed of his right to counsel. Ultimately, the United States Supreme Court agreed. Because Fellers was not informed of his right to counsel and had not waived this right when he first made the statements at his home, the statements he repeated after his arrest should have been excluded (see the discussion of the "fruit of the poisonous tree" doctrine on page 193).[15]☐

The Eighth Amendment prohibits excessive bail and fines, as well as cruel and unusual punishment. Under this amendment, prison officials are required to provide humane conditions of confinement, including adequate food, clothing, shelter, and medical care. If a prisoner has a serious medical problem, for instance, and a corrections officer is deliberately indifferent to it, a court could find the prisoner's Eighth Amendment rights have been violated. Critics of the death penalty claim that it constitutes cruel and unusual punishment. For further discussion of this issue, see the *Insight into Ethics* feature that follows.

Insight into Ethics

Is the death penalty cruel and unusual punishment?

One hundred and thirty-five countries worldwide have either abolished the death penalty outright or no longer use it because of the belief that it is unethical and immoral for a government to put individuals to death. The United States, in contrast, continues to impose the death penalty on criminals, with the exception of persons who are mentally retarded (since 2002)[16] and juveniles (since 2005).[17] Nonetheless, there has been a growing uneasiness with the death penalty in our society and in our courts. Moreover, in the global community, it has become increasingly difficult to justify why the United States is one of the few democratic nations in the world that still uses capital punishment. The United Nations—despite opposition from the United States, China, Iran, Pakistan, and Syria—passed a nonbinding resolution in December 2007 calling for a worldwide moratorium on the death penalty.

Death by Lethal Injection Is the Primary Method

Within the United States, each state can decide whether or not to impose capital punishment (the death penalty) and for which offenses. As of 2008, thirty-six states had

15. *Fellers v. United States,* 540 U.S. 519, 124 S.Ct. 1019, 157 L.Ed.2d 1016 (2004).
16. The United States Supreme Court ruled that the execution of capital offenders who are mentally retarded violates the Eighth Amendment in *Atkins v. Virginia,* 536 U.S. 304, 122 S.Ct. 2242, 153 L.Ed.2d 335 (2002).
17. The Supreme Court held that the execution of persons under the age of eighteen at the time they committed a capital crime violates the Eighth and Fourteenth Amendments in *Roper v. Simmons,* 543 U.S. 551, 125 S.Ct. 1183, 161 L.Ed.2d 1 (2005).

the death penalty and fourteen states, plus the District of Columbia, did not. All but one of the states with the death penalty use lethal injection as their primary method. One main reason is that the United States Supreme Court has repeatedly interpreted the Eighth Amendment as containing "an evolving standard of decency" that marks the progress of a maturing society. The application of this evolving standard has meant adopting increasingly less painful methods of execution over time. Lethal injection has become the favored method because most people believe that it is a relatively painless procedure and thus a more humane way to kill.

At least thirty states use a combination of three drugs to sedate, paralyze, and kill the person who was sentenced to death. This three-drug procedure reportedly prolonged a number of executions in Florida and Ohio because prison workers had problems administering the drugs. In those instances, there were strong indications that the prisoners suffered severe pain.[18]

Death Row Inmates Claim the Three-Drug Protocol Is Inhumane

In 2008, the United States Supreme Court heard a case challenging the use of this three-drug protocol in Kentucky as cruel and unusual punishment. Two death row inmates argued that if the first drug—an anesthetic—does not work for any reason, then the combination of the other two drugs might cause excruciating pain. Because one of the drugs is a paralytic (pancuronium bromide), the prisoner would not be able to express his or her discomfort, and the procedure would thus be unusually cruel. The Kentucky inmates argued that the state should be required to administer a single drug, a barbiturate, that causes no pain and can be given in a large enough dose to cause death. The case caused a temporary halt to planned executions for several months while the states awaited the Supreme Court's decision.

The Supreme Court's 2008 Ruling

Ultimately, a majority of justices on the United States Supreme Court concluded that the three-drug procedure did not violate the Eighth Amendment. The majority held that the inmates had failed to show that the risk of pain from incompetent administration of the drug made it cruel and unusual. Chief Justice Roberts, who wrote the majority opinion, ruled that showing that a "slightly or marginally safer alternative" exists is not enough to challenge the state's method of execution. There were five concurring opinions and one dissent, indicating that the justices all applied slightly different reasoning and had their individual views on the matter.

In his concurring opinion, Justice Stevens stated, "Instead of ending the controversy, I am now convinced that this case will generate debate not only about the constitutionality of the three-drug protocol, and specifically about the justification for the use of the paralytic agent, pancuronium bromide, but also about the justification for the death penalty itself." Justice Stevens, for the first time, hinted that he now believes the death penalty may be unconstitutional. Justice Stevens also pointed out that several states, including Kentucky, have banned the use of this particular paralytic agent when euthanizing animals. Stevens found it "unseemly" (improper) that the state of Kentucky would use a drug on these inmates that it would not permit to be used on pets. Although it may be unethical for the state to use a drug to paralyze inmates prior to killing them that it would not use on animals, the Supreme Court held that it is legal.[19] Nevertheless, more legal challenges to the death penalty and to the methods used are expected in coming years.

18. "Supreme Court Ruling Opens Door for States to Resume Executions by Lethal Injection," Fox News.com, April 16, 2008.

19. *Baze v. Rees*, ___ U.S. ___, 128 S.Ct. 1520, 170 L.Ed.2d 420 (2008).

The Exclusionary Rule and the *Miranda* Rule

Two other procedural protections for criminal defendants are the exclusionary rule and the *Miranda* rule.

The Exclusionary Rule   Under what is known as the **exclusionary rule,** all evidence obtained in violation of the constitutional rights spelled out in the Fourth, Fifth, and Sixth Amendments, as well as all evidence derived from illegally obtained evidence, normally must be excluded from the trial. Evidence derived from illegally obtained evidence is known as the "fruit of the poisonous tree." For example, if a confession is obtained after an illegal arrest, the arrest is "the poisonous tree," and the confession, if "tainted" by the arrest, is the "fruit."

> # MIRANDA WARNING
>
> 1. YOU HAVE THE RIGHT TO REMAIN SILENT.
> 2. ANYTHING YOU SAY CAN AND WILL BE USED AGAINST YOU IN A COURT OF LAW.
> 3. YOU HAVE THE RIGHT TO TALK TO A LAWYER AND HAVE HIM PRESENT WITH YOU WHILE YOU ARE BEING QUESTIONED.
> 4. IF YOU CANNOT AFFORD TO HIRE A LAWYER, ONE WILL BE APPOINTED TO REPRESENT YOU BEFORE ANY QUESTIONING IF YOU WISH.
> 5. YOU CAN DECIDE AT ANY TIME TO EXERCISE THESE RIGHTS AND NOT ANSWER ANY QUESTIONS OR MAKE ANY STATEMENTS.
> ### WAIVER
> DO YOU UNDERSTAND EACH OF THESE RIGHTS I HAVE EXPLAINED TO YOU? HAVING THESE RIGHTS IN MIND, DO YOU WISH TO TALK TO US NOW?

The Miranda *warning. Law enforcement officers must deliver this warning to suspects to inform them of their rights under the Fifth and Sixth Amendments.*

The purpose of the exclusionary rule is to deter police from conducting warrantless searches and engaging in other misconduct. The rule is sometimes criticized because it can lead to injustice. Many a defendant has "gotten off on a technicality" because law enforcement personnel failed to observe procedural requirements. Even though a defendant may be obviously guilty, if the evidence of that guilt was obtained improperly (without a valid search warrant, for example), it normally cannot be used against the defendant in court.

EXCLUSIONARY RULE
In criminal procedure, a rule under which any evidence that is obtained in violation of the accused's constitutional rights guaranteed by the Fourth, Fifth, and Sixth Amendments, as well as any evidence derived from illegally obtained evidence, will not be admissible in court.

The *Miranda* Rule   In *Miranda v. Arizona,* a case decided in 1966, the United States Supreme Court established the rule that individuals who are arrested must be informed of certain constitutional rights, including their Fifth Amendment right to remain silent and their Sixth Amendment right to counsel. If the arresting officers fail to inform a criminal suspect of these constitutional rights, any statements the suspect makes normally will not be admissible in court. Although the Supreme Court's *Miranda* decision was controversial, it has survived attempts by Congress to overrule the decision.[20] Because of its importance in criminal procedure, the *Miranda* case is presented as this chapter's *Landmark in the Legal Environment* feature on the following page.

| **REMEMBER** |
Once a suspect has been informed of his or her rights, anything that person says can be used as evidence in a trial.

Over time, as part of a continuing attempt to balance the rights of accused persons against the rights of society, the United States Supreme Court has carved out numerous exceptions to the *Miranda* rule. For example, the "public safety" exception holds that certain statements—such as statements concerning the location of a weapon—are admissible even if the defendant was not given *Miranda* warnings. Additionally, a suspect must unequivocally and assertively request to exercise his or her right to counsel in order to stop police questioning. Saying "Maybe I should talk to a lawyer" during an interrogation after being taken into custody is not enough. Police officers are not required to decipher the suspect's intentions in such situations.

CRIMINAL PROCESS

As mentioned, a criminal prosecution differs significantly from a civil case in several respects. These differences reflect the desire to safeguard the rights of the individual against the state. Exhibit 6–3 on page 195 summarizes the major procedural steps in processing a criminal case. Here we discuss three phases of the criminal process—arrest, indictment or information, and trial—in more detail.

---

20. *Dickerson v. United States,* 530 U.S. 428, 120 S.Ct. 2326, 147 L.Ed.2d 405 (2000).

The United States Supreme Court's decision in *Miranda v. Arizona*[a] has been cited in more court decisions than any other case in the history of American law. Through television shows and other media, the case has also become familiar to most of the adult population in the United States.

The case arose after Ernesto Miranda was arrested in his home, on March 13, 1963, for the kidnapping and rape of an eighteen-year-old woman. Miranda was taken to a police station in Phoenix, Arizona, and questioned by two police officers. Two hours later, the officers emerged from the interrogation room with a written confession signed by Miranda.

Rulings by the Lower Courts

The confession was admitted into evidence at the trial, and Miranda was convicted and sentenced to prison for twenty to thirty years. Miranda appealed the decision, claiming that he had not been informed of his constitutional rights. He did not claim that he was innocent of the crime or that his confession was false or made under duress. He claimed only that he would not have confessed to the crime if he had been advised of his right to remain silent and to have an attorney. The Supreme Court of Arizona held that Miranda's constitutional rights had not been violated and affirmed his conviction. In forming its decision, the court emphasized that Miranda had not specifically requested an attorney.

The Supreme Court's Decision

The *Miranda* case was subsequently consolidated with three other cases involving similar issues and reviewed by the United States

a. 384 U.S. 436, 86 S.Ct. 1602, 16 L.Ed.2d 694 (1966).

Supreme Court. In its decision, the Supreme Court stated that whenever an individual is taken into custody, "the following measures are required: He must be warned prior to any questioning that he has the right to remain silent, that anything he says can be used against him in a court of law, that he has the right to the presence of an attorney, and that if he cannot afford an attorney one will be appointed for him prior to any questioning if he so desires." If the accused waives his or her rights to remain silent and to have counsel present, the government must be able to demonstrate that the waiver was made knowingly, intelligently, and voluntarily.

APPLICATION TO TODAY'S LEGAL ENVIRONMENT

Today, both on television and in the real world, police officers routinely advise suspects of their "*Miranda* rights" on arrest. When Ernesto Miranda himself was later murdered, the suspected murderer was "read his *Miranda* rights." Despite Congress's attempt to overrule the *Miranda* requirements, the Supreme Court has affirmed the decision as constitutional. Interestingly, this decision has also had ramifications for criminal procedure in Great Britain. British police officers are required, when making arrests, to inform suspects, "You do not have to say anything. But if you do not mention now something which you later use in your defense, the court may decide that your failure to mention it now strengthens the case against you. A record will be made of everything you say, and it may be given in evidence if you are brought to trial."

RELEVANT WEB SITES

To locate information on the Web concerning the *Miranda* decision, go to this text's Web site at **www.cengage.com/blaw/let**, select "Chapter 6," and click on "URLs for Landmarks."

Arrest

Before a warrant for arrest can be issued, there must be probable cause for believing that the individual in question has committed a crime. As discussed earlier, *probable cause* can be defined as a substantial likelihood that the person has committed or is about to commit a crime. Note that probable cause involves a likelihood, not just a possibility. An arrest may sometimes be made without a warrant if there is no time to get one, as when a police officer observes a crime taking place, but the action of the arresting officer is still judged by the standard of probable cause.

Indictment or Information

Individuals must be formally charged with having committed specific crimes before they can be brought to trial. If issued by a grand jury, this charge is called an **indictment**.[21] A **grand jury** usually consists of more jurors than the ordinary

INDICTMENT
A charge by a grand jury that a named person has committed a crime.

GRAND JURY
A group of citizens called to decide, after hearing the state's evidence, whether a reasonable basis (probable cause) exists for believing that a crime has been committed and that a trial ought to be held.

21. Pronounced in-*dyte*-ment.

EXHIBIT 6-3 MAJOR PROCEDURAL STEPS IN A CRIMINAL CASE

ARREST
Police officer takes suspect into custody. Most arrests are made without a warrant. After the arrest, the officer searches the suspect, who is then taken to the police station.

BOOKING
At the police station, the suspect is searched again, photographed, fingerprinted, and allowed at least one telephone call. After the booking, charges are reviewed, and if they are not dropped, a complaint is filed and a magistrate (judge) reviews the case for probable cause.

INITIAL APPEARANCE
The defendant appears before the judge, who informs the defendant of the charges and of his or her rights. If the defendant requests a lawyer and cannot afford one, a lawyer is appointed. The judge sets bail (conditions under which a suspect can obtain release pending disposition of the case).

GRAND JURY
A grand jury determines if there is probable cause to believe that the defendant committed the crime. The federal government and about half of the states require grand jury indictments for at least some felonies.

PRELIMINARY HEARING
In a court proceeding, a prosecutor presents evidence, and the judge determines if there is probable cause to hold the defendant over for trial.

INDICTMENT
An *indictment* is a written document issued by the grand jury to formally charge the defendant with a crime.

INFORMATION
An *information* is a formal criminal charge made by the prosecutor.

ARRAIGNMENT
The defendant is brought before the court, informed of the charges, and asked to enter a plea.

PLEA BARGAIN
A plea bargain is a prosecutor's promise to make concessions (or promise to seek concessions) in return for a defendant's guilty plea. Concessions may include a reduced charge or a lesser sentence.

GUILTY PLEA
In many jurisdictions, most cases that reach the arraignment stage do not go to trial but are resolved by a guilty plea, often as a result of a plea bargain. The judge sets the case for sentencing.

TRIAL
Trials can be either jury trials or bench trials. (In a bench trial, there is no jury, and the judge decides questions of fact as well as questions of law.) If the verdict is "guilty," the judge sets a date for the sentencing. Everyone convicted of a crime has the right to an appeal.

trial jury. A grand jury does not determine the guilt or innocence of an accused party. Rather, its function is to hear the state's evidence and determine whether a reasonable basis (probable cause) exists for believing that a crime has been committed and that a trial ought to be held.

Usually, grand juries are used in cases involving serious crimes, such as murder. For lesser crimes, an individual may be formally charged with a crime by what is called an **information,** or criminal complaint. An information will be issued by a government prosecutor if the prosecutor determines that there is sufficient evidence to justify bringing the individual to trial.

INFORMATION
A formal accusation or complaint (without an indictment) issued in certain types of actions (usually criminal actions involving lesser crimes) by a government prosecutor.

Trial

At a criminal trial, the accused person does not have to prove anything; the entire burden of proof is on the prosecutor (the state). As mentioned earlier, the prosecution must show that, based on all the evidence presented, the defendant's guilt is established *beyond a reasonable doubt.* If there is a reasonable doubt as to whether a criminal defendant did, in fact, commit the crime with which she or he has been charged, then the verdict must be "not guilty." Note that giving a verdict of "not guilty" is not the same as stating that the defendant is innocent. Such a verdict merely means that not enough evidence was properly presented to the court to prove guilt beyond a reasonable doubt.

Courts have complex rules about what types of evidence may be presented and how the evidence may be brought out in criminal cases. These rules are designed to ensure that evidence in trials is relevant, reliable, and not prejudicial toward the defendant. For example, under the Sixth Amendment, persons accused of a crime have the right to confront the witnesses against them in open court. If the prosecutor wishes to present a witness's testimony by means of a document obtained in an *ex parte* examination, the prosecutor must show that the witness is unavailable to testify in court and that the defendant had a prior opportunity to cross-examine her or him. (In this context, an *ex parte* examination is a proceeding for the benefit of the prosecution without notice to the defendant.)

Sentencing Guidelines

In 1984, Congress passed the Sentencing Reform Act and created the U.S. Sentencing Commission in an attempt to standardize sentences for federal crimes. The commission's guidelines, which became effective in 1987, established a range of possible penalties for each federal crime and required the judge to select a sentence from within that range. In other words, the guidelines originally established a mandatory system because judges were not allowed to deviate from the specified sentencing range. Some federal judges felt uneasy about imposing long prison sentences on certain criminal defendants, particularly first-time offenders, and in illegal-substances cases involving small quantities of drugs.[22]

In 2005, the Supreme Court held that certain provisions of the federal sentencing guidelines were unconstitutional.[23] The case involved Freddie Booker, who was arrested with 92.5 grams of crack cocaine in his possession. During questioning by police, he signed a written statement in which he admitted to

---

22. See, for example, *United States v. Angelos,* 345 F.Supp.2d 1227 (D. Utah 2004).
23. *United States v. Booker,* 543 U.S. 220, 125 S.Ct. 738, 160 L.Ed.2d 621 (2005).

selling an additional quantity—566 grams of crack cocaine—elsewhere. The additional 566 grams of crack were not brought up at trial. Nevertheless, under the federal sentencing guidelines the judge was required to sentence Booker to twenty-two years in prison. Ultimately, the Supreme Court ruled that this sentence was unconstitutional because a jury did not find beyond a reasonable doubt that Booker had possessed the additional 566 grams of crack.

The Supreme Court's ruling in 2005 essentially changed the federal sentencing guidelines from mandatory to advisory. Depending on the circumstances of the case, a federal trial judge may now depart from the guidelines if he or she believes that it is reasonable to do so. Note, however, that the sentencing guidelines still exist and provide for enhanced punishment for certain types of crimes, including white-collar crimes, violations of the Sarbanes-Oxley Act (see Chapter 2), and violations of securities laws (see Chapter 24).

CYBER CRIME

Some years ago, the American Bar Association defined **computer crime** as any act that is directed against computers and computer parts, that uses computers as instruments of crime, or that involves computers and constitutes abuse. Today, because much of the crime committed with the use of computers occurs in cyberspace, many computer crimes fall under the broad label of cyber crime. Here we look at several types of activity that constitute cyber crimes against persons or property. Other cyber crimes will be discussed in later chapters of this text as they relate to particular topics, such as banking or consumer law. For a discussion of how some states are passing laws making spamming a crime, see this chapter's *Online Developments* feature on the next page.

COMPUTER CRIME
Any act that is directed against computers and computer parts, that uses computers as instruments of crime, or that involves computers and constitutes abuse.

BE AWARE
Technological change is one of the primary factors that lead to new types of crime.

Cyber Theft

In cyberspace, thieves are not subject to the physical limitations of the "real" world. A thief can steal data stored in a networked computer with Internet access from anywhere on the globe. Only the speed of the connection and the thief's computer equipment limit the quantity of data that can be stolen.

Financial Crimes   Computer networks provide opportunities for employees to commit crimes that can involve serious economic losses. For example, employees of a company's accounting department can transfer funds among accounts with little effort and often with less risk than would be involved in transactions evidenced by paperwork.

Generally, the dependence of businesses on computer operations has left firms vulnerable to sabotage, fraud, embezzlement, and the theft of proprietary data, such as trade secrets or other intellectual property. As will be discussed in Chapter 8, the piracy of intellectual property via the Internet is one of the most serious legal challenges facing lawmakers and the courts today.

Identity Theft   A form of cyber theft that has become particularly troublesome in recent years is **identity theft.** Identity theft occurs when the wrongdoer steals a form of identification—such as a name, date of birth, or Social Security number—and uses the information to access the victim's financial resources. This crime existed to a certain extent before the widespread use of the Internet. Thieves would "steal" calling-card numbers by watching people using public

IDENTITY THEFT
The act of stealing another's identifying information—such as a name, date of birth, or Social Security number—and using that information to access the victim's financial resources.

A significant issue today is whether persons who send spam (bulk unsolicited e-mail) over the Internet can be charged with a crime. As discussed in Chapter 5, spamming has become a major problem for businesses. At the time the federal CAN-SPAM Act was passed in 2003, the U.S. Senate found that spam constituted more than half of all e-mail traffic and projected that it would cost corporations more than $113 billion by 2009. By all accounts, though, the amount of spam has actually increased since the federal CAN-SPAM Act was enacted. Given that the CAN-SPAM Act has failed to reduce the amount of spam, some states have taken matters into their own hands and have now passed laws making spamming a crime.

A Few States Have Enacted Criminal Spamming Statutes

A few states, such as Maryland and Virginia, have passed groundbreaking laws that make spamming a crime.[a] Under the Virginia Computer Crimes Act (VCCA), it is a crime against property to use a computer or computer network "with the intent to falsify or forge electronic mail transmission information or other routing information in any manner." The law further provides that attempting to send spam to more than 2,500 recipients in any twenty-four-hour period is a felony. The VCCA also includes provisions allowing authorities to seize the assets or proceeds obtained through an illegal spamming operation.

Maryland's antispamming law similarly prohibits sending commercial e-mail to recipients using false information about the identity of the sender, the origin, transmission path, or subject of the message. Under the Maryland law, however, the number of spam messages required to convict a person of the offense is much lower. Sending ten illegal messages in twenty-four hours violates the statute, and the more spam sent, the more severe the punishment will be, up to a maximum of ten years in prison and a $25,000 fine.

America's First Conviction for Felony Spamming

In the biggest case on criminal spamming to date, the Supreme Court of Virginia in 2008 upheld the conviction of Jeremy Jaynes, a spammer who had sent more than ten thousand junk messages a day. Jaynes, a resident of North Carolina, used sixteen Internet connections, a number of aliases (such as Gaven Stubberfield), and a variety of business names as fronts for his spam. He had sent some of the messages through servers in Virginia.

Prior to his 2004 arrest, Jaynes was widely recognized as the eighth most prolific spammer in the world. He had accumulated a personal fortune of $24 million and was earning $750,000 a month spamming get-rich-quick schemes, pornography, and sham products and services. Jaynes's sister, Jessica DeGroot, was also involved in the criminal scheme, and her name was on the credit card used to purchase domain names for Jaynes's spamming operation. During the search of Jaynes's residence, police found a CD containing at least 176 million full e-mail addresses and more than 1.3 billion user names, as well as zip disks containing 107 million e-mail addresses. Jaynes also had a DVD containing not only e-mail addresses, but also other personal account information for millions of individuals. All of this information had been stolen from America Online (AOL).

State Supreme Court Upholds Conviction

Jaynes was convicted of three counts of felony spamming based on the fact that he had sent more than ten thousand pieces of spam per day on three separate days, using false Internet addresses and aliases. The jury sentenced him to nine years in prison (although prosecutors had asked for a fifteen-year sentence). On appeal, Jaynes argued that Virginia did not have jurisdiction over him and that the state's criminal spamming statute violated his First Amendment rights to free speech. The state appellate court concluded that jurisdiction was proper because Jaynes had utilized servers within the state and concluded that the statute did not violate the First Amendment.[b] Jaynes appealed to the state's highest court, which ultimately upheld Jaynes's conviction, despite some uncertainty as to whether standing requirements differ between state and federal courts.[c] This was the first felony conviction for spamming in the United States.

> **FOR CRITICAL ANALYSIS** How might criminal spamming statutes, which are likely to vary among the states, affect legitimate businesspersons who advertise on the Internet? If a business discovers that a spammer is using the business's name in connection with spam, what recourse does that business have?

---

a. See, for example, Maryland Code, Criminal Law, Section 3-805.1; and Virginia Code Ann. Sections 18.2–152.3:1.

b. *Jaynes v. Commonwealth of Virginia,* 48 Va.App. 673, 634 S.E.2d 357 (2006).
c. *Jaynes v. Commonwealth of Virginia,* 275 Va. 341, 657 S.E.2d 478 (2008); rehearing granted in part and order clarified by 666 S.E.2d 502 (2008).

telephones, or they would rifle through garbage to find bank account or credit-card numbers. The identity thieves would then use the calling-card or credit-card numbers or would withdraw funds from the victims' accounts. The Internet, however, has turned identity theft into perhaps the fastest-growing financial crime in the United States.

Three federal statutes deal specifically with identity theft. The Identity Theft and Assumption Deterrence Act of 1998[24] made identity theft a federal crime and directed the U.S. Sentencing Commission to incorporate the crime into its sentencing guidelines. The Fair and Accurate Credit Transactions Act of 2003[25] gives victims of identity theft certain rights in working with creditors and credit bureaus to remove negative information from their credit reports. This act will be discussed in detail in Chapter 20 in the context of consumer law. The Identity Theft Penalty Enhancement Act of 2004[26] authorized more severe penalties in aggravated cases in which the identity theft was committed in connection with the thief's employment or with other serious crimes (such as terrorism or firearms or immigration offenses).

Preventing Legal Disputes

Businesspersons should take several steps to avoid potential losses from identity theft. First, review what personal information is kept in your computer databases. Wherever possible, eliminate Social Security numbers and other personal information and code all account numbers to limit access to the account holder. Second, limit employee access to databases containing personal account information. Instruct employees in how computers and personal information are to be used and not used. Establish policies on what types of information may be stored on portable sources, such as laptop computers. Consider using passwords to protect data against unauthorized access and use. Also, maintain accurate records of where confidential data are kept and who has access to the data. ■

Hacking and Cyberterrorism

Persons who use one computer to break into another are sometimes referred to as **hackers.** Hackers who break into computers without authorization often commit cyber theft. Sometimes, however, their principal aim is to prove how smart they are by gaining access to others' password-protected computers and causing random data errors or making telephone calls for free. **Cyberterrorists** are hackers who, rather than trying to gain attention, strive to remain undetected so that they can exploit computers for a serious impact. Just as "real" terrorists destroyed the World Trade Center towers and a portion of the Pentagon in September 2001, cyberterrorists might explode "logic bombs" to shut down central computers. Such activities can pose a danger to national security.

Businesses may be targeted by cyberterrorists as well as hackers. The goals of a hacking operation might include a wholesale theft of data, such as a merchant's customer files, or the monitoring of a computer to discover a business firm's plans and transactions. A cyberterrorist might also want to insert false

HACKER
A person who uses one computer to break into another. Professional computer programmers refer to such persons as "crackers."

CYBERTERRORIST
A hacker whose purpose is to exploit a target computer for a serious impact, such as corrupting a program to sabotage a business.

---

24. 18 U.S.C. Section 1028.
25. 15 U.S.C. Sections 1681 *et seq.*
26. 18 U.S.C. Section 1028A.

The brand name SPAM® comes from canned meat that contains pork. In this scene from a Monty Python comedy skit, a small restaurant has a menu that includes only SPAM. Various states have criminalized some online spamming. What arguments are used to justify passing criminal statutes relating to spam on the Internet? (Wikipedia Commons)

codes or data. For example, the processing control system of a food manufacturer could be changed to alter the levels of ingredients so that consumers of the food would become ill.

A cyberterrorist attack on a major financial institution such as the New York Stock Exchange or a large bank could leave securities or money markets in flux and seriously affect the daily lives of millions of citizens. Similarly, any prolonged disruption of computer, cable, satellite, or telecommunications systems due to the actions of expert hackers would have serious repercussions on business operations—and national security—on a global level. Computer viruses are another tool that can be used by cyberterrorists to cripple communications networks.

Prosecuting Cyber Crimes

The "location" of cyber crime (cyberspace) has raised new issues in the investigation of crimes and the prosecution of offenders. A threshold issue is, of course, jurisdiction. A person who commits an act against a business in California, where the act is a cyber crime, might never have set foot in California but might instead reside in New York, or even in Canada, where the act may not be a crime. If the crime was committed via e-mail, the question arises as to whether the e-mail would constitute sufficient "minimum contacts" (see Chapter 3) for the victim's state to exercise jurisdiction over the perpetrator.

Identifying the wrongdoer can also be difficult. Cyber criminals do not leave physical traces, such as fingerprints or DNA samples, as evidence of their crimes. Even electronic "footprints" can be hard to find and follow. For example, e-mail may be sent through a remailer, an online service that guarantees that a message cannot be traced to its source.

For these reasons, laws written to protect physical property are difficult to apply in cyberspace. Nonetheless, governments at both the state and federal levels have taken significant steps toward controlling cyber crime, both by applying existing criminal statutes and by enacting new laws that specifically address wrongs committed in cyberspace.

The Computer Fraud and Abuse Act

Perhaps the most significant federal statute specifically addressing cyber crime is the Counterfeit Access Device and Computer Fraud and Abuse Act of 1984 (commonly known as the Computer Fraud and Abuse Act, or CFAA). This act, as amended by the National Information Infrastructure Protection Act of 1996,[27] provides, among other things, that a person who accesses a computer online, without authority, to obtain classified, restricted, or protected data, or attempts to do so, is subject to criminal prosecution. Such data could include financial and credit records, medical records, legal files, military and national security files, and other confidential information in government or private computers. The crime has two elements: accessing a computer without authority and taking the data.

---

27. 18 U.S.C. Section 1030.

This theft is a felony if it is committed for a commercial purpose or for private financial gain, or if the value of the stolen data (or computer time) exceeds $5,000. Penalties include fines and imprisonment for up to twenty years. A victim of computer theft can also bring a civil suit against the violator to obtain damages, an injunction, and other relief.

Preventing Legal Disputes

Outside hackers are a threat to businesses, but employees, former employees, and other "insiders" are responsible for most computer abuse, including breaches of information security. Therefore, businesspersons need to be cautious about which employees have access to computer data and to give employees access only to information that they need to know. Another important preventive measure is to have employees agree, in a written contract, not to disclose confidential information during or after employment without the employer's consent. Business owners should also make sure that they use the latest methods available to secure their computer systems, including firewalls and encryption techniques, for example. ■

Reviewing . . . Criminal Law and Cyber Crime

Edward Hanousek worked for Pacific & Arctic Railway and Navigation Company (P&A) as a roadmaster of the White Pass & Yukon Railroad in Alaska. As an officer of the corporation, Hanousek was responsible "for every detail of the safe and efficient maintenance and construction of track, structures, and marine facilities of the entire railroad," including special projects. One project was a rock quarry, known as "6-mile," above the Skagway River. Next to the quarry, and just beneath the surface, ran a high-pressure oil pipeline owned by Pacific & Arctic Pipeline, Inc., P&A's sister company. When the quarry's backhoe operator punctured the pipeline, an estimated 1,000 to 5,000 gallons of oil were discharged into the river. Hanousek was charged with negligently discharging a harmful quantity of oil into a navigable water of the United States in violation of the criminal provisions of the Clean Water Act (CWA). Using the information presented in the chapter, answer the following questions.

1. Did Hanousek have the required mental state (*mens rea*) to be convicted of a crime? Why or why not?

2. Which theory discussed in the chapter would enable a court to hold Hanousek criminally liable for violating the statute regardless of whether he participated in, directed, or even knew about the specific violation?

3. Could the backhoe operator who punctured the pipeline also be charged with a crime in this situation? Explain.

4. Suppose that at trial, Hanousek argued that he could not be convicted because he was not aware of the requirements of the CWA. Would this defense be successful? Why or why not?

Key Terms

actus reus   170

arson   174

beyond a reasonable
    doubt   169

burglary   173

computer crime   197

consent   184

crime   169

cyber crime   168

cyberterrorist   199

double jeopardy   190

duress   185

Chapter Summary

Civil Law and Criminal Law
(See pages 169–170.)

1. *Civil law*—Spells out the duties that exist between persons or between citizens and their governments, excluding the duty not to commit crimes.

2. *Criminal law*—Has to do with crimes, which are defined as wrongs against society proclaimed in statutes and punishable by society through fines and/or imprisonment—and, in some cases, death. Because crimes are offenses against society as a whole, they are prosecuted by a public official, not by victims.

3. *Key differences*—An important difference between civil and criminal law is that the standard of proof is higher in criminal cases (see Exhibit 6–1 on page 169 for other differences between civil and criminal law).

4. *Civil liability for criminal acts*—A criminal act may give rise to both criminal liability and tort liability (see Exhibit 6–2 on page 171 for an example of criminal and tort liability for the same act).

Criminal Liability
(See pages 170–172.)

1. *Guilty act*—In general, some form of harmful act must be committed for a crime to exist.

2. *Intent*—An intent to commit a crime, or a wrongful mental state, is generally required for a crime to exist.

Corporate Criminal Liability
(See page 172.)

1. *Liability of corporations*—Corporations normally are liable for the crimes committed by their agents and employees within the course and scope of their employment. Corporations cannot be imprisoned, but they can be fined or denied certain legal privileges.

2. *Liability of corporate officers and directors*—Corporate directors and officers are personally liable for the crimes they commit and may be held liable for the actions of employees under their supervision.

Types of Crimes
(See pages 173–183.)

1. Crimes fall into five general categories: violent crime, property crime, public order crime, white-collar crime, and organized crime.

   a. Violent crimes are those that cause others to suffer harm or death, including murder, assault and battery, sexual assault (rape), and robbery.

   b. Property crimes are the most common form of crime. The offender's goal is to obtain some economic gain or to damage property. This category includes burglary, larceny, obtaining goods by false pretenses, receiving stolen property, arson, and forgery.

   c. Public order crimes are acts such as public drunkenness, prostitution, pornography, gambling, and illegal drug use, that a statute has established are contrary to public values and morals.

   d. White-collar crimes are illegal acts committed by a person or business using nonviolent means to obtain a personal or business advantage. Usually, such crimes are committed in the course of a legitimate occupation. Embezzlement, mail and wire fraud, bribery, bankruptcy fraud, the theft of trade secrets, and insider trading are examples of this category of crime.

Types of Crimes—Continued	e. Organized crime is a form of crime conducted by groups operating illegitimately to satisfy the public's demand for illegal goods and services (such as gambling or illegal narcotics). This category of crime also includes money laundering and racketeering (RICO) violations.
	2. Each type of crime may also be classified according to its degree of seriousness. Felonies are serious crimes punishable by death or by imprisonment for more than one year. Misdemeanors are less serious crimes punishable by fines or by confinement for up to one year.
Defenses to Criminal Liability (See pages 183–187.)	Defenses to criminal liability include infancy, intoxication, insanity, mistake, consent, duress, justifiable use of force, entrapment, and the statute of limitations. Also, in some cases defendants may be relieved of criminal liability, at least in part, if they are given immunity.
Constitutional Safeguards and Criminal Procedures (See pages 187–193.)	1. *Fourth Amendment*—Provides protection against unreasonable searches and seizures and requires that probable cause exist before a warrant for a search or an arrest can be issued.
	2. *Fifth Amendment*—Requires due process of law, prohibits double jeopardy, and protects against self-incrimination.
	3. *Sixth Amendment*—Provides guarantees of a speedy trial, a trial by jury, a public trial, the right to confront witnesses, and the right to counsel.
	4. *Eighth Amendment*—Prohibits excessive bail and fines, and cruel and unusual punishment.
	5. *Exclusionary rule*—A criminal procedural rule that prohibits the introduction at trial of all evidence obtained in violation of constitutional rights, as well as any evidence derived from the illegally obtained evidence.
	6. *Miranda rule*—A rule set forth by the Supreme Court in *Miranda v. Arizona* holding that individuals who are arrested must be informed of certain constitutional rights, including their right to counsel.
Criminal Process (See pages 193–197.)	1. *Arrest, indictment, and trial*—Procedures governing arrest, indictment, and trial for a crime are designed to safeguard the rights of the individual against the state. See Exhibit 6–3 on page 195 for a summary of the procedural steps involved in prosecuting a criminal case.
	2. *Sentencing guidelines*—The federal government has established sentencing laws or guidelines. The federal sentencing guidelines indicate a range of penalties for each federal crime; federal judges consider these guidelines when imposing sentences on those convicted of federal crimes.
Cyber Crime (See pages 197–201.)	Cyber crimes occur in cyberspace. Examples include cyber theft (financial crimes committed with the aid of computers, as well as identity theft), hacking, and cyberterrorism. The Computer Fraud and Abuse Act of 1984, as amended by the National Information Infrastructure Protection Act of 1996, is a significant federal statute that addresses cyber crime.

For Review

1. What two elements must exist before a person can be held liable for a crime? Can a corporation commit crimes?
2. What are five broad categories of crimes? What is white-collar crime?
3. What defenses might be raised by criminal defendants to avoid liability for criminal acts?
4. What constitutional safeguards exist to protect persons accused of crimes? What are the basic steps in the criminal process?
5. What is cyber crime? What laws apply to crimes committed in cyberspace?

Questions and Case Problems

6–1. Types of Crimes. Which, if any, of the following crimes necessarily involve illegal activity on the part of more than one person?

1. Bribery.
2. Forgery.
3. Embezzlement.
4. Larceny.
5. Receiving stolen property.

Question with Sample Answer

6–2. The following situations are similar (all involve the theft of Makoto's laptop computer), yet they represent three different crimes. Identify the three crimes, noting the differences among them.

1. While passing Makoto's house one night, Sarah sees a laptop computer left unattended on Makoto's porch. Sarah takes the computer, carries it home, and tells everyone she owns it.
2. While passing Makoto's house one night, Sarah sees Makoto outside with a laptop computer. Holding Makoto at gunpoint, Sarah forces him to give up the computer. Then Sarah runs away with it.
3. While passing Makoto's house one night, Sarah sees a laptop computer on a desk near a window. Sarah breaks the lock on the front door, enters, and leaves with the computer.

For a sample answer to Question 6–2, go to Appendix I at the end of this text.

6–3. Double Jeopardy. Armington, while robbing a drugstore, shot and seriously injured Jennings, a drugstore clerk. Armington was subsequently convicted of armed robbery and assault and battery in a criminal trial. Jennings later brought a civil tort suit against Armington for damages. Armington contended that he could not be tried again for the same crime, as that would constitute double jeopardy, which is prohibited by the Fifth Amendment to the U.S. Constitution. Is Armington correct? Explain. *charge with the same crime*

6–4. Larceny. In February 2001, a homeowner hired Jimmy Smith, a contractor claiming to employ a crew of thirty workers, to build a garage. The homeowner paid Smith $7,950 and agreed to make additional payments as needed to complete the project, up to $15,900. Smith promised to start the next day and finish within eight weeks. Nearly a month passed with no work, while Smith lied to the homeowner that materials were on "back order." During a second month, footings were created for the foundation, and a subcontractor poured the concrete slab, but Smith did not return the homeowner's phone calls. After eight weeks, the homeowner confronted Smith, who promised to complete the job, worked on the site that day until lunch, and never returned. Three months later, the homeowner again confronted Smith, who promised to "pay [him] off" later that day but did not do so. In March 2002, the state of Georgia filed criminal charges against Smith. While his trial was pending, he promised to pay the homeowner "next week," but again failed to refund any money. The value of the labor performed before Smith abandoned the project was between $800 and $1,000, the value of the materials was $367, and the subcontractor was paid $2,270. Did Smith commit larceny? Explain. [*Smith v. State of Georgia,* 265 Ga.App.57, 592 S.E.2d 871 (2004)]

6–5. Right to Counsel. The Sixth Amendment guarantees to a defendant who faces possible imprisonment the right to counsel at all critical stages of the criminal process, including the arraignment and the trial. In 1996, Felipe Tovar, a twenty-one-year-old college student, was arrested in Ames, Iowa, for operating a motor vehicle while under the influence of alcohol (OWI). Tovar was informed of his right to apply for court-appointed counsel and waived it. At his arraignment, he pleaded guilty. Six weeks later, he appeared for sentencing, again waived his right to counsel, and was sentenced to two days' imprisonment. In 1998, Tovar was convicted of OWI again, and in 2000, he was charged with OWI for a third time. In Iowa, a third OWI offense is a felony. Tovar asked the court not to use his first OWI conviction to enhance the third OWI charge. He argued that his 1996 waiver of counsel was not "intelligent" because the court did not make him aware of "the dangers and disadvantages of self-representation." What determines whether a person's choice in any situation is "intelligent"? What should determine whether a defendant's waiver of counsel is "intelligent" at critical stages of a criminal proceeding? [*Iowa v. Tovar,* 541 U.S. 77, 124 S.Ct. 1379, 158 L.Ed.2d 209 (2004)]

6–6. Trial. Robert Michels met Allison Formal through an online dating Web site in 2002. Michels represented himself as the retired chief executive officer of a large company that he had sold for millions of dollars. In January 2003, Michels proposed that he and Formal create a limited liability company (a special form of business organization discussed in Chapter 14)—Formal Properties Trust, LLC—to "channel their investments in real estate." Formal agreed to contribute $100,000 to the company and wrote two $50,000 checks to "Michels and Associates, LLC." Six months later, Michels told Formal that their LLC had been formed in Delaware. Later,

Formal asked Michels about her investments. He responded evasively, and she demanded that an independent accountant review the firm's records. Michels refused. Formal contacted the police. Michels was charged in a Virginia state court with obtaining money by false pretenses. The Delaware secretary of state verified, in two certified documents, that "Formal Properties Trust, L.L.C." and "Michels and Associates, L.L.C." did not exist in Delaware. Did the admission of the Delaware secretary of state's certified documents at Michels's trial violate his rights under the Sixth Amendment? Why or why not? [*Michels v. Commonwealth of Virginia*, 47 Va.App. 461, 624 S.E.2d 675 (2006)]

Case Problem with Sample Answer

 6–7. Helm Instruction Co. in Maumee, Ohio, makes custom electrical control systems. Helm hired Patrick Walsh in September 1998 to work as comptroller. Walsh soon developed a close relationship with Richard Wilhelm, Helm's president, who granted Walsh's request to hire Shari Price as Walsh's assistant. Wilhelm was not aware that Walsh and Price were engaged in an extramarital affair. Over the next five years, Walsh and Price spent more than $200,000 of Helm's funds on themselves. Among other things, Walsh drew unauthorized checks on Helm's accounts to pay his personal credit cards, and issued to Price and himself unauthorized salary increases, overtime payments, and tuition reimbursement payments, altering Helm's records to hide the payments. After an investigation, Helm officials confronted Walsh. He denied the affair with Price, claimed that his unauthorized use of Helm's funds was an "interest-free loan," and argued that it was less of a burden on the company to pay his credit cards than to give him the salary increases to which he felt he was entitled. Did Walsh commit a crime? If so, what crime did he commit? Discuss. [*State v. Walsh*, 113 Ohio App.3d 1515, 866 N.E.2d 513 (6 Dist. 2007)]

After you have answered Problem 6–7, compare your answer with the sample answer given on the Web site that accompanies this text. Go to www.cengage.com/blaw/let, select "Chapter 6," and click on "Case Problem with Sample Answer."

Question of Ethics

 6–8. A troublesome issue concerning the constitutional privilege against self-incrimination has to do with the extent to which trickery by law enforcement officers during an interrogation may overwhelm a suspect's will to avoid self-incrimination. For example, in one case two officers questioned Charles McFarland, who was incarcerated in a state prison, about his connection to a handgun that had been used to shoot two other officers. McFarland was advised of his rights but was not asked whether he was willing to waive those rights. Instead, to induce McFarland to speak, the officers deceived him into believing that "[n]obody is going to give you charges," and he made incriminating admissions. He was indicted for possessing a handgun as a convicted felon. [*United States v. McFarland*, 424 F.Supp.2d 427 (N.D.N.Y. 2006)]

1. Review the discussion of *Miranda v. Arizona* in this chapter's *Landmark in the Legal Environment* feature on page 194. Should McFarland's statements be suppressed—that is, not be admissible at trial—because he was not asked whether he was willing to waive his rights before he made his self-incriminating statements? Does *Miranda* apply to McFarland's situation?
2. Do you think that it is fair for the police to resort to trickery and deception to bring those who may have committed crimes to justice? Why or why not? What rights or public policies must be balanced in deciding this issue?

Critical-Thinking Legal Question

 6–9. Ray steals a purse from an unattended car at a gas station. Because the purse contains money and a handgun, Ray is convicted of grand theft of property (cash) and grand theft of a firearm. On appeal, Ray claims that he is not guilty of grand theft of a firearm because he did not know that the purse contained a gun. Can Ray be convicted of the crime of grand theft of a firearm even though he did not know that the gun was in the purse?

Video Question

 6–10. Go to this text's Web site at www.cengage.com/blaw/let and select "Chapter 6." Click on "Video Questions" and view the video titled *Casino*. Then answer the following questions.

1. In the video, a casino manager, Ace (Robert De Niro), discusses how politicians "won their 'comp life' when they got elected." "Comps" are the free gifts that casinos give to high-stakes gamblers to keep their business. If an elected official accepts comps, is he or she committing a crime? If so, what type of crime? Explain your answers.
2. Assume that Ace committed a crime by giving politicians comps. Can the casino, Tangiers Corporation, be held liable for that crime?

Why or why not? How could a court punish the corporation?

3. Suppose that the Federal Bureau of Investigation wants to search the premises of Tangiers for evidence of criminal activity. If casino management refuses to consent to the search, what constitutional safeguards and criminal procedures, if any, protect Tangiers?

Interacting with the Internet

For updated links to resources available on the Web, as well as a variety of other materials, visit this text's Web site at

www.cengage.com/blaw/let

The Bureau of Justice Statistics in the U.S. Department of Justice offers an impressive collection of statistics on crime at the following Web site:

ojp.usdoj.gov/bjs

For summaries of famous criminal cases and documents relating to these trials, go to Court TV's Web site at

www.courttv.com/map/index.html

Many state criminal codes are now online. To find your state's code, go to the following home page and select "States" under the link to "Cases & Codes":

www.findlaw.com

You can learn about some of the constitutional questions raised by various criminal laws and procedures by going to the Web site of the American Civil Liberties Union at

www.aclu.org

The following Web site, which is maintained by the U.S. Department of Justice, offers information ranging from the various types of cyber crime to a description of how computers and the Internet are being used to prosecute cyber crime:

www.cybercrime.gov

PRACTICAL INTERNET EXERCISES

Go to this text's Web site at **www.cengage.com/blaw/let**, select "Chapter 6," and click on "Practical Internet Exercises." There you will find the following Internet research exercises that you can perform to learn more about the topics covered in this chapter.

Practical Internet Exercise 6–1: LEGAL PERSPECTIVE—**Revisiting *Miranda***

Practical Internet Exercise 6–2: MANAGEMENT PERSPECTIVE—**Hackers**

Practical Internet Exercise 6–3: INTERNATIONAL PERSPECTIVE—**Fighting Cyber Crime Worldwide**

BEFORE THE TEST

Go to this text's Web site at **www.cengage.com/blaw/let**, select "Chapter 6," and click on "Interactive Quizzes." You will find a number of interactive questions relating to this chapter.

Chapter 7

International Law in a Global Economy

CHAPTER OBJECTIVES

After reading this chapter, you should be able to answer the following questions:

1. What is the principle of comity, and why do courts deciding disputes involving a foreign law or judicial decree apply this principle?

2. What is the act of state doctrine? In what circumstances is this doctrine applied?

3. Under the Foreign Sovereign Immunities Act of 1976, on what bases might a foreign state be considered subject to the jurisdiction of U.S. courts?

4. In what circumstances will U.S. antitrust laws be applied extraterritorially?

5. Do U.S. laws prohibiting employment discrimination apply in all circumstances to U.S. employees working for U.S. employers abroad?

CONTENTS

- International Law–Sources and Principles

- Doing Business Internationally

- Regulation of Specific Business Activities

- Commercial Contracts in an International Setting

- Payment Methods for International Transactions

- U.S. Laws in a Global Context

" *Our interests are those of the open door—a door of friendship and mutual advantage. This is the only door we care to enter.* "

— WOODROW WILSON,
1856–1924 (Twenty-eighth president of the United States, 1913–1921)

International business transactions are not unique to the modern world. Indeed, as suggested by President Woodrow Wilson's statement in the chapter-opening quotation, people have always found that they can benefit from exchanging goods with others. What is new in our day is the dramatic growth in world trade and the emergence of a global business community. Because the exchange of goods, services, and ideas on a worldwide level is now routine, students of business law and the legal environment should be familiar with the laws pertaining to international business transactions.

Laws affecting the international legal environment of business include both international law and national law. **International law** can be defined as a body of law—formed as a result of international customs, treaties, and organizations—that governs relations among or between nations. International law may be public, creating standards for the nations themselves; or it may be private, establishing international standards for private transactions that cross national borders. **National law** is the law of a particular nation, such as Brazil, Germany, Japan, or the United States.

In this chapter, we examine how both international law and national law frame business operations in the international context. We also look at some selected areas relating to business activities in a global context, including international sales contracts, civil dispute resolution, letters of credit, and investment protection. We conclude the chapter with a discussion of the application of certain U.S. laws in a transnational setting.

INTERNATIONAL LAW
The law that governs relations among nations. International customs and treaties are important sources of international law.

NATIONAL LAW
Laws that pertain to a particular nation (as opposed to international law).

INTERNATIONAL LAW—SOURCES AND PRINCIPLES

The major difference between international law and national law is that government authorities can enforce national law. What government, however, can enforce international law? By definition, a *nation* is a sovereign entity—which means that there is no higher authority to which that nation must submit. If a nation violates an international law and persuasive tactics fail, other countries or international organizations have no recourse except to take coercive actions—from severance of diplomatic relations and boycotts to, as a last resort, war—against the violating nation.

In essence, international law is the result of centuries-old attempts to reconcile the traditional need of each country to be the final authority over its own affairs with the desire of nations to benefit economically from trade and harmonious relations with one another. Sovereign nations can, and do, voluntarily agree to be governed in certain respects by international law for the purpose of facilitating international trade and commerce, as well as civilized discourse. As a result, a body of international law has evolved. In this section, we examine the primary sources and characteristics of that body of law, as well as some important legal principles and doctrines that have been developed over time to facilitate dealings among nations.

Sources of International Law

Basically, there are three sources of international law: international customs, treaties and international agreements, and international organizations and conferences. We look at each of these sources here.

International Customs   One important source of international law consists of the international customs that have evolved among nations in their relations with one another. Article 38(1) of the Statute of the International Court of Justice refers to an international custom as "evidence of a general practice accepted as law." The legal principles and doctrines that you will read about shortly are rooted in international customs and traditions that have evolved over time in the international arena.

Treaties and International Agreements   Treaties and other explicit agreements between or among foreign nations provide another important source of international law. A **treaty** is an agreement or contract between two or more nations that must be authorized and ratified by the supreme power of each nation. Under Article II, Section 2, of the U.S. Constitution, the president has the power "by and with the Advice and Consent of the Senate, to make Treaties, provided two-thirds of the Senators present concur."

A *bilateral* agreement, as the term implies, is an agreement formed by two nations to govern their commercial exchanges or other relations with one another. A *multilateral* agreement is formed by several nations. For example, regional trade associations such as the European Union (EU, which is discussed later in this chapter) are the result of multilateral trade agreements. Other regional trade associations that have been created through multilateral agreements include the Association of Southeast Asian Nations (ASEAN) and the Andean Common Market (ANCOM).

TREATY
In international law, a formal written agreement negotiated between two nations or among several nations. In the United States, all treaties must be approved by the Senate.

International Organizations   In international law, the term **international organization** generally refers to an organization composed mainly of officials of member nations and usually established by treaty. The United States is a member of more than one hundred multilateral and bilateral organizations, including at least twenty through the United Nations. These organizations adopt resolutions, declarations, and other types of standards that often require nations to behave in a particular manner. The General Assembly of the United Nations, for example, has adopted numerous nonbinding resolutions and declarations that embody principles of international law. Disputes with respect to these resolutions and declarations may be brought before the International Court of Justice. That court, however, normally has authority to settle legal disputes only when nations voluntarily submit to its jurisdiction.

The United Nations Commission on International Trade Law has made considerable progress in establishing uniformity in international law as it relates to trade and commerce. One of the commission's most significant creations to date is the 1980 Convention on Contracts for the International Sale of Goods (CISG). The CISG is similar to Article 2 of the Uniform Commercial Code in that it is designed to settle disputes between parties to sales contracts (see Chapter 11). It spells out the duties of international buyers and sellers that will apply if the parties have not agreed otherwise in their contracts. The CISG governs only sales contracts between trading partners in nations that have ratified the CISG, however.

INTERNATIONAL ORGANIZATION
Any membership group that operates across national borders. These organizations can be governmental organizations, such as the United Nations, or nongovernmental organizations (NGOs), such as the Red Cross.

Common Law and Civil Law Systems

Companies operating in foreign nations are subject to the laws of those nations. In addition, international disputes often are resolved through the court systems of foreign nations. Therefore, businesspersons should understand that legal systems around the globe generally are divided into *common law* and *civil law* systems. As discussed in Chapter 1, in a common law system, the courts independently develop the rules governing certain areas of law, such as torts and contracts. These common law rules apply to all areas not covered by statutory law. Although the common law doctrine of *stare decisis* obligates judges to follow precedential decisions in their jurisdictions, courts may modify or even overturn precedents when deemed necessary.

In contrast to common law countries, most of the European nations, as well as nations in Latin America, Africa, and Asia, base their legal systems on Roman civil law, or "code law." The term *civil law,* as used here, refers not to civil as opposed to criminal law but to *codified* law—an ordered grouping of legal principles enacted into law by a legislature or other governing body. In a **civil law system,** the only official source of law is a statutory code. Courts interpret the code and apply the rules to individual cases, but courts may not depart from the code and develop their own laws. In theory, the law code sets forth all of the principles needed for the legal system. Trial procedures also differ in civil law systems. Unlike judges in common law systems, judges in civil systems often actively question witnesses. (The *Beyond Our Borders* feature in Chapter 1 on page 17 provided a list of the nations that use civil law systems and those that use common law systems.)

CIVIL LAW SYSTEM
A system of law derived from that of the Roman Empire and based on a code rather than case law; the predominant system of law in the nations of continental Europe and the nations that were once their colonies.

International Principles and Doctrines

Over time, a number of legal principles and doctrines have evolved and have been employed—to a greater or lesser extent—by the courts of various nations to resolve or reduce conflicts that involve a foreign element. The three important legal principles discussed next are based primarily on courtesy and respect, and are applied in the interests of maintaining harmonious relations among nations.

The Principle of Comity   Under what is known as the principle of **comity,** one nation will defer to and give effect to the laws and judicial decrees of another country, as long as those laws and judicial decrees are consistent with the law and public policy of the accommodating nation.

> **EXAMPLE #1**   A Swedish seller and a U.S. buyer have formed a contract, which the buyer breaches. The seller sues the buyer in a Swedish court, which awards damages. The buyer's assets, however, are in the United States and cannot be reached unless the judgment is enforced by a U.S. court of law. In this situation, if a U.S. court determines that the procedures and laws applied in the Swedish court were consistent with U.S. national law and policy, that court will likely defer to (and enforce) the foreign court's judgment.□

One way to understand the principle of comity (and the *act of state doctrine*, which will be discussed next) is to consider the relationships among the states in our federal form of government. Each state honors (gives "full faith and credit" to) the contracts, property deeds, wills, and other legal obligations formed in other states, as well as judicial decisions with respect to such obligations. On a worldwide basis, nations similarly attempt to honor judgments rendered in other countries when it is feasible to do so. Of course, in the United States the states are constitutionally required to honor other states' actions, whereas internationally, nations are not *required* to honor the actions of other nations.

The Act of State Doctrine   The **act of state doctrine** is a judicially created doctrine that provides that the judicial branch of one country will not examine the validity of public acts committed by a recognized foreign government within the latter's territory.

When a Foreign Government Takes Private Property   The act of state doctrine can have important consequences for individuals and firms doing business with, and investing in, other countries. For example, this doctrine is frequently employed in situations involving expropriation or confiscation. **Expropriation** occurs when a government seizes a privately owned business or privately owned goods for a proper public purpose and awards just compensation. When a government seizes private property for an illegal purpose or without just compensation, the taking is referred to as a **confiscation.** The line between these two forms of taking is sometimes blurred because of differing interpretations of what is illegal and what constitutes just compensation.

> **EXAMPLE #2**   Flaherty, Inc., a U.S. company, owns a mine in Brazil. The government of Brazil seizes the mine for public use and claims that the profits that Flaherty realized from the mine in preceding years constitute just compensation. Flaherty disagrees, but the act of state doctrine may prevent the company's recovery in a U.S. court.□ Note that in a case alleging that a foreign government has wrongfully taken the plaintiff's property, the defendant government has the burden of proving that the taking was an expropriation, not a confiscation.

Doctrine May Immunize a Foreign Government's Actions   When applicable, both the act of state doctrine and the doctrine of *sovereign immunity* (to be discussed next) tend to immunize (protect) foreign governments from the jurisdiction of U.S. courts. This means that firms or individuals who own property

COMITY
The principle by which one nation defers to and gives effect to the laws and judicial decrees of another nation. This recognition is based primarily on respect.

ACT OF STATE DOCTRINE
A doctrine providing that the judicial branch of one country will not examine the validity of public acts committed by a recognized foreign government within its own territory.

EXPROPRIATION
The seizure by a government of a privately owned business or personal property for a proper public purpose and with just compensation.

CONFISCATION
A government's taking of a privately owned business or personal property without a proper public purpose or an award of just compensation.

overseas often have diminished legal protection against government actions in the countries in which they operate.

The Doctrine of Sovereign Immunity
When certain conditions are satisfied, the doctrine of **sovereign immunity** immunizes foreign nations from the jurisdiction of U.S. courts. In 1976, Congress codified this rule in the Foreign Sovereign Immunities Act (FSIA).[1] The FSIA exclusively governs the circumstances in which an action may be brought in the United States against a foreign nation, including attempts to attach (legally seize) a foreign nation's property. Because the law is jurisdictional in nature, a plaintiff generally has the burden of showing that a defendant is not entitled to sovereign immunity.

Section 1605 of the FSIA sets forth the major exceptions to the jurisdictional immunity of a foreign state. A foreign state is not immune from the jurisdiction of U.S. courts in the following situations:

1. When the foreign state has waived its immunity either explicitly or by implication.
2. When the foreign state has engaged in commercial activity within the United States or in commercial activity outside the United States that has "a direct effect in the United States."[2]
3. When the foreign state has committed a tort in the United States or has violated certain international laws.

In applying the FSIA, questions frequently arise as to whether an entity is a "foreign state" and what constitutes a "commercial activity." Under Section 1603 of the FSIA, a *foreign state* includes both a political subdivision of a foreign state and an instrumentality (department or agency of any branch of a government) of a foreign state. Section 1603 broadly defines a *commercial activity* as a commercial activity that is carried out by a foreign state within the United States, but it does not describe the particulars of what constitutes a commercial activity. Thus, the courts are left to decide whether a particular activity is governmental or commercial in nature.

On May 1, 2007, Venezuela's president, Hugo Chavez, told an enthusiastic crowd that he had completed the nationalization of all of that country's formerly private oil companies. What long-term effects might such an action have on foreign investments in Venezuela? (AP Photo/Fernando Llano)

SOVEREIGN IMMUNITY
A doctrine that immunizes foreign nations from the jurisdiction of U.S. courts when certain conditions are satisfied.

DOING BUSINESS INTERNATIONALLY

A U.S. domestic firm can engage in international business transactions in a number of ways. The simplest way is to seek out foreign markets for domestically produced products or services. In other words, U.S. firms can **export** their goods and services to markets abroad. Alternatively, a U.S. firm can establish foreign production facilities so as to be closer to the foreign market or markets in which its

EXPORT
To sell goods and services to buyers located in other countries.

1. 28 U.S.C. Section 1602–1611.
2. See, for example, *Keller v. Central Bank of Nigeria,* 277 F.3d 811 (6th Cir. 2002), in which the court held that failure to pay promised funds to a Cleveland account was an action having a direct effect in the United States.

products are sold. The advantages may include lower labor costs, fewer government regulations, and lower taxes and trade barriers. A domestic firm can also obtain revenues by licensing its technology to an existing foreign company or by selling franchises to overseas entities.

Exporting

Exporting can take two forms: direct exporting and indirect exporting. In *direct exporting,* a U.S. company signs a sales contract with a foreign purchaser that provides for the conditions of shipment and payment for the goods. (How payments are made in international transactions is discussed later in this chapter.) If sufficient business develops in a foreign country, a U.S. corporation may set up a specialized marketing organization in that foreign market by appointing a foreign agent or a foreign distributor. This is called *indirect exporting.*

When a U.S. firm desires to limit its involvement in an international market, it will typically establish an *agency relationship* with a foreign firm (*agency* will be discussed in Chapter 16). The foreign firm then acts as the U.S. firm's agent and can enter contracts in the foreign location on behalf of the principal (the U.S. company).

When a foreign country represents a substantial market, a U.S. firm may wish to appoint a distributor located in that country. The U.S. firm and the distributor enter into a **distribution agreement,** which is a contract between the seller and the distributor setting out the terms and conditions of the distributorship. These terms and conditions—for example, price, currency of payment, availability of supplies, and method of payment—primarily involve contract law. Disputes concerning distribution agreements may involve jurisdictional or other issues (discussed later in this chapter). In addition, in some instances an **exclusive distributorship**—in which the distributor agrees to distribute only the seller's goods—has raised antitrust problems (see Chapter 23).

DISTRIBUTION AGREEMENT
A contract between a seller and a distributor of the seller's products setting out the terms and conditions of the distributorship.

EXCLUSIVE DISTRIBUTORSHIP
A distributorship in which the seller and the distributor of the seller's products agree that the distributor will distribute only the seller's products.

Manufacturing Abroad

An alternative to direct or indirect exporting is the establishment of foreign manufacturing facilities. Typically, U.S. firms establish manufacturing plants abroad if they believe that doing so will reduce their costs—particularly for labor, shipping, and raw materials—and enable them to compete more effectively in foreign markets. Foreign firms have done the same in the United States. Sony, Nissan, and other Japanese manufacturers have established U.S. plants to avoid import duties that the U.S. Congress may impose on Japanese products entering this country.

A U.S. firm can manufacture goods in other countries in several ways. Two of these ways are through licensing and franchising.

Licensing   A U.S. firm can obtain business from abroad by licensing a foreign manufacturing company to use its copy-

A woman holds a Barbie doll that was manufactured in Taiwan. Why would a U.S. corporation, such as Mattel, Inc., outsource its manufacturing jobs to a foreign firm? (AP Photo/Wally Santana)

righted, patented, or trademarked intellectual property or trade secrets. Like any other licensing agreement (see Chapters 8 and 11), a licensing agreement with a foreign-based firm calls for a payment of royalties on some basis—such as so many cents per unit produced or a certain percentage of profits from units sold in a particular geographic territory.

In some circumstances, even in the absence of a patent, a firm may be able to license the "know-how" associated with a particular manufacturing process—for example, a plant design or a secret formula. The foreign firm that agrees to sign the licensing agreement further agrees to keep the know-how confidential and to pay royalties. **EXAMPLE #3** The Coca-Cola Bottling Company licenses firms worldwide to use (and keep confidential) its secret formula for the syrup used in its soft drink. In return, the foreign firms licensed to make the syrup pay Coca-Cola a percentage of the income earned from the sale of the soft drink.□

The licensing of intellectual property rights benefits all parties to the transaction. The firm that receives the license can take advantage of an established reputation for quality. The firm that grants the license receives income from the foreign sales of its products and also establishes a global reputation. Additionally, once a firm's trademark is known worldwide, the firm may experience an increased demand for other products it manufactures or sells—obviously an important consideration.

Franchising   Franchising is a well-known form of licensing. As you will read in Chapter 14, in a franchise arrangement the owner of a trademark, trade name, or copyright (the franchisor) licenses another (the franchisee) to use the trademark, trade name, or copyright under certain conditions or limitations in the selling of goods or services. In return, the franchisee pays a fee, which is usually based on a percentage of gross or net sales. Examples of international franchises include Holiday Inn and Hertz.

REGULATION OF SPECIFIC BUSINESS ACTIVITIES

Doing business abroad can affect the economies, foreign policies, domestic politics, and other national interests of the countries involved. For this reason, nations impose laws to restrict or facilitate international business. Controls may also be imposed by international agreements.

Investing

Firms that invest in foreign nations face the risk that the foreign government may expropriate the investment property. Expropriation, as mentioned earlier in this chapter, occurs when property is taken and the owner is paid just compensation for what is taken. This does not violate generally observed principles of international law. Confiscating property without compensation (or without adequate compensation), however, normally violates these principles. Few remedies are available for confiscation of property by a foreign government. Claims are often resolved by lump-sum settlements after negotiations between the United States and the taking nation.

To counter the deterrent effect that the possibility of confiscation may have on potential investors, many countries guarantee compensation to foreign investors if property is taken. A guaranty can take the form of national constitutional or statutory laws or provisions in international treaties. As further protection for foreign investments, some countries provide insurance for their citizens' investments abroad.

Export Controls

The U.S. Constitution provides in Article I, Section 9, that "No Tax or Duty shall be laid on Articles exported from any State." Thus, Congress cannot impose any export taxes. Congress can, however, use a variety of other devices to restrict or encourage exports. Congress may set export quotas on various items, such as grain being sold abroad. Under the Export Administration Act of 1979,[3] the flow of technologically advanced products and technical data can be restricted. In recent years, the U.S. Department of Commerce has made a controversial attempt to restrict the export of encryption software.

While restricting certain exports, the United States (and other nations) also use incentives and subsidies to stimulate other exports and thereby aid domestic businesses. The Revenue Act of 1971,[4] for instance, promoted exports by exempting from taxes the income earned by firms marketing their products overseas through certain foreign sales corporations. Under the Export Trading Company Act of 1982,[5] U.S. banks are encouraged to invest in export trading companies, which are formed when exporting firms join together to export a line of goods.

> **NOTE**
> Most countries restrict exports for the same reasons: to protect national security, to further foreign policy objectives, and to prevent the spread of nuclear weapons.

Import Controls

"The notion dies hard that in some sort of way exports are patriotic but imports are immoral."

—LORD HARLECH
(DAVID ORMSLEY GORE), 1918–1985
(English writer)

All nations have restrictions on imports, and the United States is no exception. Restrictions include strict prohibitions, quotas, and tariffs. Under the Trading with the Enemy Act of 1917,[6] for example, no goods may be imported from nations that have been designated enemies of the United States. Other laws prohibit the importation of illegal drugs, books that urge insurrection against the United States, and agricultural products that pose dangers to domestic crops or animals.

Importing goods that infringe U.S. patents is also prohibited. The International Trade Commission is an independent agency of the U.S. government that, among other duties, investigates allegations that imported goods infringe U.S. patents and imposes penalties if necessary. In the following case, the court considered an appeal from a party fined more than $13.5 million for importing certain disposable cameras.

3. 50 U.S.C. Sections 2401–2420.
4. 26 U.S.C. Sections 991–994.
5. 15 U.S.C. Sections 4001, 4003.
6. 12 U.S.C. Section 95a.

Case 7.1 **Fuji Photo Film Co., v. International Trade Commission**

United States Court of Appeals,
Federal Circuit, 2007.
474 F.3d 1281.

BACKGROUND AND FACTS   Fuji Photo Film Company owns fifteen patents for "lens-fitted film packages" (LFFPs), popularly known as disposable cameras. An LFFP consists of a plastic shell preloaded with film. To develop the film, a consumer gives the LFFP to a film processor and receives back the negatives and prints, but not the shell. Fuji makes

and sells LFFPs. Jazz Photo Corporation collected used LFFP shells in the United States, shipped them abroad to insert new film, and imported refurbished shells back into the United States for sale. Only LFFP shells that were originally sold in the United States could be refurbished and sold again in the United States without violating Fuji's patents. The International Trade Commission (ITC) determined that Jazz's resale of shells originally sold outside the United States infringed Fuji's patents. In 1999, the ITC issued a cease-and-desist order to stop the imports. While the order was being disputed at the ITC and in the courts, between August 2001 and December 2003 Jazz imported and sold 27 million refurbished LFFPs. Fuji complained to the ITC, which fined Jazz more than $13.5 million. Jack Benun, Jazz's chief operating officer, appealed to the U.S. Court of Appeals for the Federal Circuit.

IN THE WORDS OF THE COURT . . . *DYK,* Circuit Judge.

*   *   *   *

*   *   * The Commission concluded that 40% of the LFFPs in issue were first sold abroad *   *   * . This conclusion was supported by substantial evidence. It was based on *   *   * the identifying numbers printed on the LFFPs and Fuji's production and shipping databases to determine where samples of Fuji-type LFFPs with Jazz packaging (i.e., ones that were refurbished by Jazz) were first sold.

Benun urges that the Commission's decision in this respect was not supported by substantial evidence, primarily arguing that Jazz's so-called informed compliance program required a finding in Jazz's favor. Benun asserts that this program tracked shells from collection through the refurbishment process to sale and insured that only shells collected from the United States were refurbished for sale here. The Commission rejected this argument for two reasons. First, it concluded that the program was too disorganized and incomplete to provide credible evidence that Jazz only refurbished shells collected from the United States. Second, the Commission concluded that at most the program could ensure that Jazz only refurbished LFFPs collected from the United States, not LFFPs that were first sold here.

Responding to the second ground, Benun urges that proof that Jazz limited its activities to shells collected in the United States was sufficient *   *   * because Fuji "infected the pool" of camera shells collected in the United States by taking actions that made it difficult for Jazz and Benun to insure that these shells were from LFFPs first sold here. These actions allegedly included allowing [one company] to import cameras with Japanese writing on them for sale in the United States; allowing [that company] to import spent shells into the United States for recycling; and allowing tourists to bring cameras first sold abroad into the United States for personal use. Under these circumstances, Benun argues that a presumption should arise that shells collected in the United States were first sold here. However, the Commission found that the number of shells falling into these categories was insignificant, and that finding was supported by substantial evidence. Moreover, there was evidence that Jazz treated substantial numbers of its own shells collected in the United States *   *   * as having been sold in the United States even though it knew that 90% of these shells were first sold abroad *   *   * .

In any event, the Commission's first ground—that the program was too incomplete and disorganized to be credible—was supported by substantial evidence. Since there was no suggestion that the incomplete and disorganized nature of the program was due to Fuji's actions, this ground alone was sufficient to justify a conclusion that Benun had not carried his burden to prove [the refurbished LFFPs had been sold first in the United States].

DECISION AND REMEDY The U.S. Court of Appeals for the Federal Circuit held that Jazz had violated the cease-and-desist order, affirming this part of the ITC's decision. The court concluded, among other things, that "substantial evidence supports the finding that the majority of the cameras were first sold abroad."

WHAT IF THE FACTS WERE DIFFERENT? Suppose that, after this decision, Jazz fully compensated Fuji for the infringing sales of LFFPs. Would Jazz have acquired the right to refurbish those LFFPs in the future? Explain.

THE GLOBAL DIMENSION How does prohibiting the importing of goods that infringe U.S. patents protect those patents outside the United States?

QUOTA

A set limit on the amount of goods that can be imported.

TARIFF

A tax on imported goods.

Quotas and Tariffs   Limits on the amounts of goods that can be imported are known as **quotas.** At one time, the United States had legal quotas on the number of automobiles that could be imported from Japan. Today, Japan "voluntarily" restricts the number of automobiles exported to the United States. **Tariffs** are taxes on imports. A tariff is usually a percentage of the value of the import, but it can be a flat rate per unit (such as per barrel of oil). Tariffs raise the prices of imported goods, causing some consumers to purchase more domestically manufactured goods.

Antidumping Duties   The United States has specific laws directed at what it sees as unfair international trade practices. **Dumping,** for example, is the sale of imported goods at "less than fair value." *Fair value* is usually determined by the price of those goods in the exporting country. Foreign firms that engage in dumping in the United States hope to undersell U.S. businesses to obtain a larger share of the U.S. market. To prevent this, an extra tariff—known as an *antidumping duty*—may be assessed on the imports.

DUMPING

The selling of goods in a foreign country at a price below the price charged for the same goods in the domestic market.

The procedure for imposing antidumping duties involves two U.S. government agencies: the International Trade Commission (ITC) and the International Trade Administration (ITA). The ITC assesses the effects of dumping on domestic businesses and then makes recommendations to the president concerning temporary import restrictions. The ITA, which is part of the Department of Commerce, decides whether imports were sold at less than fair value. The ITA's determination establishes the amount of antidumping duties, which are set to equal the difference between the price charged in the United States and the price charged in the exporting country. A duty may be retroactive to cover past dumping.

Minimizing Trade Barriers through Trade Agreements

Restrictions on imports are also known as *trade barriers.* The elimination of trade barriers is sometimes seen as essential to the world's economic well-being. Most of the world's leading trading nations are members of the World Trade Organization (WTO), which was established in 1995. To minimize trade barriers among nations, each member country of the WTO is required to grant **normal trade relations (NTR) status** (formerly known as *most-favored-nation status*) to other member countries. This means that each member is obligated to treat other members at least as well as it treats the country that receives its most favorable treatment with regard to imports or exports. Various regional trade agreements and associations also help to minimize trade barriers between nations.

NORMAL TRADE RELATIONS (NTR) STATUS

A status granted in an international treaty by a provision stating that the citizens of the contracting nations may enjoy the privileges accorded by either party to citizens of its NTR nations. Generally, this status is designed to establish equality of international treatment.

The European Union (EU)   The European Union (EU) arose out of the 1957 Treaty of Rome, which created the Common Market, a free trade zone comprising the nations of Belgium, France, Italy, Luxembourg, the Netherlands, and West Germany. Today, the EU is a single integrated trading unit made up of twenty-seven European nations.

The EU has its own governing authorities. These include the Council of Ministers, which coordinates economic policies and includes one representative from each nation; a commission, which proposes regulations to the council; and an elected assembly, which oversees the commission. The EU also has its own court, the European Court of Justice, which can review each nation's judicial decisions and is the ultimate authority on EU law.

The EU has gone a long way toward creating a new body of law to govern all of the member nations—although some of its efforts to create uniform laws have been confounded by nationalism. The council and the commission issue regulations, or directives, that define EU law in various areas, and these requirements normally are binding on all member countries. EU directives govern such issues as environmental law, product liability, anticompetitive practices, and laws governing corporations. The EU directive on product liability, for example, states that a "producer of an article shall be liable for damages caused by a defect in the article, whether or not he [or she] knew or could have known of the defect." Liability extends to anyone who puts a trademark or other identifying feature on an article, and liability may not be excluded, even by contract.

The North American Free Trade Agreement (NAFTA)   The North American Free Trade Agreement (NAFTA), which became effective on January 1, 1994, created a regional trading unit consisting of Canada, Mexico, and the United States. The goal of NAFTA was to eliminate tariffs among these three nations on substantially all goods by reducing the tariffs incrementally over a period of time. NAFTA gives the three countries a competitive advantage by retaining tariffs on goods imported from countries outside the NAFTA trading unit. Additionally, NAFTA provides for the elimination of barriers that traditionally have prevented the cross-border movement of services, such as financial and transportation services. NAFTA also attempts to eliminate citizenship requirements for the licensing of accountants, attorneys, physicians, and other professionals.

The Central America–Dominican Republic–United States Free Trade Agreement (CAFTA-DR)   A more recent trade agreement, the Central America–Dominican Republic–United States Free Trade Agreement (CAFTA-DR), was signed into law by President George W. Bush in 2005. This agreement was formed by Costa Rica, the Dominican Republic, El Salvador, Guatemala, Honduras, Nicaragua, and the United States. Its purpose was to reduce trade tariffs and improve market access among all of the signatory nations, including the United States. As of 2008, legislatures from all seven countries had approved the CAFTA-DR, despite significant opposition in certain nations, including Costa Rica, where nationwide strikes erupted in response to legislation adopting the treaty.

COMMERCIAL CONTRACTS IN AN INTERNATIONAL SETTING

Like all commercial contracts, an international contract should be in writing. For an example of an actual international sales contract, refer to the foldout contract in Chapter 11.

Contract Clauses

Language and legal differences among nations can create special problems for parties to international contracts when disputes arise. It is possible to avoid these problems by including in a contract special provisions designating the official language of the contract, the legal forum (court or place) in which disputes under the contract will be settled, and the substantive law that will be applied in settling any disputes. Parties to international contracts should also indicate in their contracts what acts or events will excuse the parties from performance under the contract and whether disputes under the contract will be arbitrated or litigated.

WARNING
The interpretation of the words in a contract can be a matter of dispute even when both parties communicate in the same language.

Choice of Language   A deal struck between a U.S. company and a company in another country normally involves two languages. Typically, many phrases in one language are not readily translatable into another. Consequently, the complex contractual terms involved may not be understood by one party in the other party's language. To make sure that no disputes arise out of this language problem, an international sales contract should have a **choice-of-language clause** designating the official language by which the contract will be interpreted in the event of disagreement.

CHOICE-OF-LANGUAGE CLAUSE
A clause in a contract designating the official language by which the contract will be interpreted in the event of a future disagreement over the contract's terms.

Preventing Legal Disputes

When entering into international contracts, businesspersons should always determine whether the foreign nation has any applicable language requirements. Some nations have mandatory language requirements. In France, for instance, certain legal documents, such as the prospectuses used in securities offerings, must be written in French. In addition, contracts with any state or local authority in France, instruction manuals, and warranties for goods and services offered for sale in France must be written in French. To avoid disputes, know the law of the jurisdiction before you enter into any agreements in that nation. Remember that certain legal terms or phrases in documents may not easily translate from one language to another. Finding out that a nation has language requirements may influence your decision whether to enter into a contract in that location and will definitely affect your decision whether to include a choice-of-law clause (to be discussed shortly).■

Choice of Forum   When parties from several countries are involved, litigation may be pursued in courts in different nations. There are no universally accepted rules as to which court has jurisdiction over particular subject matter or parties to a dispute. Consequently, parties to an international transaction should always include in the contract a **forum-selection clause** indicating what court, jurisdiction, or tribunal will decide any disputes arising under the contract. It is especially important to indicate the specific court that will have jurisdiction. The forum does not necessarily have to be within the geographic boundaries of the home nation of either party.

FORUM-SELECTION CLAUSE
A provision in a contract designating the court, jurisdiction, or tribunal that will decide any disputes arising under the contract.

EXAMPLE #4   Garware Polyester, Ltd., based in Mumbai, India, develops and makes plastics and high-tech polyester film. Intermax Trading Corporation, based in New York, acted as Garware's North American sales agent and sold its products on a commission basis. Garware and Intermax had executed a series of agency agreements under which the courts of Bombay, India, would have exclusive jurisdiction over any disputes relating to their agreement. When Intermax fell behind in its payments to Garware, Garware filed a lawsuit in a U.S. court to collect the balance due, claiming that the forum-selection clause did not apply to sales of warehoused goods. The court, however, sided with Intermax. Because the forum-selection clause was valid and enforceable, Garware had to bring its complaints against Intermax in a court in India.[7] ▫

CHOICE-OF-LAW CLAUSE
A clause in a contract designating the law (such as the law of a particular state or nation) that will govern the contract.

Choice of Law   A contractual provision designating the applicable law—such as the law of Germany or the United Kingdom or California—is called a **choice-of-law clause.** International contracts typically include a choice-of-law clause. At

---

7. *Garware Polyester, Ltd. v. Intermax Trading Corp.,* ___ F.Supp.2d ___ (S.D.N.Y. 2001).

common law (and in European civil law systems), parties are allowed to choose the law that will govern their contractual relationship, provided that the law chosen is the law of a jurisdiction that has a substantial relationship to the parties and to the international business transaction.

Under Section 1–105 of the Uniform Commercial Code, parties may choose the law that will govern the contract as long as the choice is "reasonable." Article 6 of the United Nations Convention on Contracts for the International Sale of Goods (discussed in Chapter 11), however, imposes no limitation on the parties' choice of what law will govern the contract. The 1986 Hague Convention on the Law Applicable to Contracts for the International Sale of Goods—often referred to as the Choice-of-Law Convention—allows unlimited autonomy in the choice of law. The Hague Convention indicates that whenever a contract does not specify a choice of law, the governing law is that of the country in which the seller's place of business is located.

Workers at a manufacturing plant owned by Ford Motor Company in Chongqing, China. The factory produces 150,000 cars per year. What term is used to describe a contract provision in which these workers in China agree to resolve any dispute they have with their employer, Ford Motor Company, in a U.S. court? (AP Photo/Joachim Ladefoged)

FORCE MAJEURE CLAUSE
A provision in a contract stipulating that certain unforeseen events—such as war, political upheavals, or acts of God—will excuse a party from liability for nonperformance of contractual obligations.

Force Majeure Clause Every contract, particularly those involving international transactions, should have a **force majeure clause.** *Force majeure* is a French term meaning "impossible or irresistible force"—sometimes loosely identified as "an act of God." In international business contracts, *force majeure* clauses commonly stipulate that in addition to acts of God, a number of other eventualities (such as government orders or embargoes, for example) may excuse a party from liability for nonperformance.

Civil Dispute Resolution

International contracts frequently include arbitration clauses, which were discussed in Chapter 3. By means of such clauses, the parties agree in advance to be bound by the decision of a specified third party in the event of a dispute. The third party may be a neutral entity (such as the International Chamber of Commerce), a panel of individuals representing both parties' interests, or some other group or organization. The United Nations Convention on the Recognition and Enforcement of Foreign Arbitral Awards (often referred to as the New York Convention) assists in the enforcement of arbitration clauses, as do provisions in specific treaties among nations. The New York Convention has been implemented in nearly one hundred countries, including the United States.

If a sales contract does not include an arbitration clause, litigation may occur. If the contract contains forum-selection and choice-of-law clauses, the lawsuit will be heard by a court in the specified forum and decided according to that forum's law. If no forum and choice of law have been specified, however, legal proceedings will be more complex and attended by much more uncertainty. For instance, litigation may take place in two or more countries, with each country applying its own choice-of-law rules to determine the substantive law that will be applied to the particular transactions. Even if a plaintiff wins a favorable judgment in a lawsuit litigated in the plaintiff's country, there is no way to predict whether courts in the defendant's country will enforce the judgment. (For a further discussion of this issue, see this chapter's *Beyond Our Borders* feature.)

PAYMENT METHODS FOR INTERNATIONAL TRANSACTIONS

Currency differences between nations and the geographic distance between parties to international sales contracts add a degree of complexity to international sales that does not exist in the domestic market. Because international contracts involve greater financial risks, special care should be taken in drafting these contracts to specify both the currency in which payment is to be made and the method of payment.

Monetary Systems

Although our national currency, the U.S. dollar, is one of the primary forms of international currency, any U.S. firm undertaking business transactions abroad must be prepared to deal with one or more other currencies. After all, just as a U.S. firm wants to be paid in U.S. dollars for goods and services sold abroad, so, too, does a Japanese firm want to be paid in Japanese yen for goods and services sold outside Japan. Both firms therefore must rely on the convertibility of currencies.

FOREIGN EXCHANGE MARKET
A worldwide system in which foreign currencies are bought and sold.

Foreign Exchange Markets   Currencies are convertible when they can be freely exchanged one for the other at some specified market rate in a **foreign exchange market.** Foreign exchange markets make up a worldwide system for the buying and selling of foreign currencies. At any point in time, the foreign exchange rate is set by the forces of supply and demand in unrestricted foreign exchange markets. The foreign exchange rate is simply the price of a unit of one country's currency in terms of another country's currency. For example, if today's exchange rate is one hundred Japanese yen for one dollar, that means that anybody with one hundred yen can obtain one dollar, and vice versa.

CORRESPONDENT BANK
A bank in which another bank has an account (and vice versa) for the purpose of facilitating fund transfers.

Correspondent Banking   Frequently, a U.S. company can rely on its domestic bank to take care of all international transfers of funds. Commercial banks often transfer funds internationally through their **correspondent banks** in other countries.

EXAMPLE #5 A customer of Citibank wishes to pay a bill in euros to a company in Paris. Citibank can draw a bank check payable in euros on its account in Crédit Agricole, a Paris correspondent bank, and then send the check to the French company to which its customer owes the funds. Alternatively, Citibank's customer can request a wire transfer of the funds to the French company. Citibank then instructs Crédit Agricole by wire to pay the necessary amount in euros.□

The Clearinghouse Interbank Payment System (CHIPS) handles about 90 percent of both national and international interbank transfers of U.S. funds. In addition, the Society for Worldwide International Financial Telecommunications

One of the reasons many businesspersons find it advantageous to include arbitration clauses in their international contracts is that arbitration awards are usually easier to enforce than court judgments. As mentioned, the New York Convention provides for the enforcement of arbitration awards in those countries that have signed the convention. In contrast, the enforcement of court judgments normally depends on the principle of comity and bilateral agreements providing for such enforcement.

How the principle of comity is applied varies from one nation to another, though, and many countries have not signed bilateral agreements to enforce judgments rendered in U.S. courts. Furthermore, a U.S. court may not enforce a foreign court's judgment if it conflicts with U.S. laws or policies, especially if the case involves important constitutional rights such as freedom of the press or freedom of religion. For example, a U.S. federal appellate court refused to enforce the judgment of a British court in a libel (defamation) case. The court pointed out that the judgment was contrary to the public policy of the United States, which generally favors a much broader and more protective freedom of the press than has ever been provided by English law.[a]

Similarly, a U.S. federal district court refused to enforce a French default judgment against Viewfinder, Inc., a U.S. firm that operated a Web site. The firm's Web site posted photographs from fashion shows and information about the fashion industry. Several French clothing designers filed an action in a French court alleging that the Web site showed photos of their clothing designs. Because Viewfinder defaulted and did not appear in the French court to contest the allegations, the French court awarded the designers the equivalent of more than $175,000. When the designers came to the United States to enforce the judgment, Viewfinder asserted a number of arguments as to why the U.S. court should not enforce the French judgment. Ultimately, Viewfinder convinced the U.S. court that its conduct on the Web site was protected expression under the First Amendment.[b]

FOR CRITICAL ANALYSIS   What might be some other advantages of arbitrating disputes involving international transactions? Are there any disadvantages?

a. *Matusevitch v. Telnikoff,* 159 F.3d 636 (D.C.Cir. 1998). Note that a U.S. court may be less likely to have public-policy concerns when enforcing a foreign judgment based on a contract. See, for example, *Society of Lloyd's v. Siemon-Netto,* 457 F.3d 94 (C.A.D.C. 2006).

b. *Sarl Louis Feraud International v. Viewfinder, Inc.,* 489 F.3d 474 (2d Cir. 2007) (S.D.N.Y. 2005).

(SWIFT) is a communication system that provides banks with messages concerning international transactions.

Letters of Credit

Because buyers and sellers engaged in international business transactions are frequently separated by thousands of miles, special precautions are often taken to ensure performance under the contract. Sellers want to avoid delivering goods for which they might not be paid. Buyers desire the assurance that sellers will not be paid until there is evidence that the goods have been shipped. Thus, **letters of credit** are frequently used to facilitate international business transactions.

In a simple letter-of-credit transaction, the *issuer* (a bank) agrees to issue a letter of credit and to ascertain whether the *beneficiary* (seller) performs certain acts. In return, the *account party* (buyer) promises to reimburse the issuer for the amount paid to the beneficiary. The transaction may also involve an *advising bank* that transmits information and a *paying bank* that expedites payment under the letter of credit. See Exhibit 7–1 on the following page for an illustration of a letter-of-credit transaction.

Under a letter of credit, the issuer is bound to pay the beneficiary (seller) when the beneficiary has complied with the terms and conditions of the letter of credit. The beneficiary looks to the issuer, not to the account party (buyer), when it presents the documents required by the letter of credit. Typically, the letter of credit will require that the beneficiary deliver a *bill of lading* to the issuing

LETTER OF CREDIT

A written instrument, usually issued by a bank on behalf of a customer or other person, in which the issuer promises to honor drafts or other demands for payment by third persons in accordance with the terms of the instrument.

[handwritten margin notes:] Italia retailer vs America shipper / doesn't want to pay before receiving goods / doesn't want to ship before receiving money → So letter of credit.

221

EXHIBIT 7-1 A LETTER-OF-CREDIT TRANSACTION

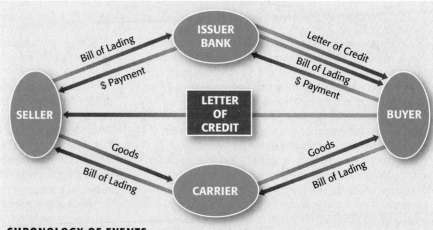

CHRONOLOGY OF EVENTS

1. Buyer contracts with issuer bank to issue a letter of credit; this sets forth the bank's obligation to pay on the letter of credit and buyer's obligation to pay the bank.

2. Letter of credit is sent to seller informing seller that on compliance with the terms of the letter of credit (such as presentment of necessary documents—in this example, a bill of lading), the bank will issue payment for the goods.

3. Seller delivers goods to carrier and receives a bill of lading.

4. Seller delivers the bill of lading to issuer bank and, if the document is proper, receives payment.

5. Issuer bank delivers the bill of lading to buyer.

6. Buyer delivers the bill of lading to carrier.

7. Carrier delivers the goods to buyer.

8. Buyer settles with issuer bank.

bank to prove that shipment has been made. A letter of credit assures the beneficiary (seller) of payment and at the same time assures the account party (buyer) that payment will not be made until the beneficiary has complied with the terms and conditions of the letter of credit.

The Value of a Letter of Credit   The basic principle behind letters of credit is that payment is made against the documents presented by the beneficiary and not against the facts that the documents purport to reflect. Thus, in a letter-of-credit transaction, the issuer does not police the underlying contract; a letter of credit is independent of the underlying contract between the buyer and the seller. Eliminating the need for banks (issuers) to inquire into whether actual contractual conditions have been satisfied greatly reduces the costs of letters of credit. Moreover, the use of letters of credit protects both buyers and sellers.

Compliance with a Letter of Credit   A letter-of-credit transaction generally involves at least three separate and distinct contracts: the contract between the account party (buyer) and the beneficiary (seller); the contract between the issuer (bank) and the account party (buyer); and, finally, the letter of credit itself, which involves the issuer (bank) and the beneficiary (seller). These contracts are separate and distinct, and the issuer's obligations under the letter of credit do

> **DON'T FORGET**
> A letter of credit is independent of the underlying contract between the buyer and the seller.

not concern the underlying contract between the buyer and the seller. Rather, it is the issuer's duty to ascertain whether the documents presented by the beneficiary (seller) comply with the terms of the letter of credit.

If the documents presented by the beneficiary comply with the terms of the letter of credit, the issuer (bank) must honor the letter of credit. If the issuing bank refuses to pay the beneficiary (seller) even though the beneficiary has complied with all the requirements, the beneficiary can bring an action to enforce payment. Sometimes, however, it can be difficult to determine exactly what a letter of credit requires. Traditionally, courts required strict compliance with the terms of a letter of credit, but in recent years, some courts have moved to a standard of *reasonable* compliance.

U.S. LAWS IN A GLOBAL CONTEXT

The internationalization of business raises questions about the extraterritorial application of a nation's laws—that is, the effect of the country's laws outside its boundaries. To what extent do U.S. domestic laws apply to other nations' businesses? To what extent do U.S. domestic laws apply to U.S. firms doing business abroad? Here, we discuss the extraterritorial application of certain U.S. laws, including the Sarbanes-Oxley Act, bribing of foreign officials, antitrust laws, laws prohibiting employment discrimination, and international tort claims.

The Sarbanes-Oxley Act

The Sarbanes-Oxley Act of 2002, which was introduced in Chapter 2, is designed to improve the quality and clarity of financial reporting and auditing of public companies. The act prescribes the issuance of codes of ethics, increases the criminal penalties for securities fraud, and utilizes other means to hold public companies to higher reporting standards.

Three provisions of the act protect whistleblowers. One section requires public companies to adopt procedures that encourage employees to expose "questionable" accounting. Another section imposes criminal sanctions for retaliation against anyone who reports the commission of any federal offense to law enforcement officers.

A third section—18 U.S.C. Section 1514A—creates an administrative complaint procedure and a federal civil cause of action for employees who report violations of the federal laws relating to fraud against the shareholders of public companies. The extraterritorial application of this section was at issue in the following case.

Case 7.2 **Carnero v. Boston Scientific Corp.**

United States Court of Appeals,
First Circuit, 2006.
433 F.3d 1.
www.ca1.uscourts.gov[a]

BACKGROUND AND FACTS Boston Scientific Corporation (BSC) is a Delaware corporation with headquarters in Natick,

a. In the right-hand column, click on "Opinions." When that page opens, in the "Short Title *contains*" box, type "Carnero" and click on "Submit Search." In the result, in the "Click for Opinion" column, click on one of the numbers to access the opinion.

Massachusetts. BSC, which makes medical equipment, operates in many countries throughout the world. BSC's subsidiaries include Boston Scientific Argentina S.A. (BSA) in Argentina and Boston Scientific Do Brasil Ltda. (BSB) in Brazil. In 1997, Ruben Carnero, a citizen of Argentina, began working for BSA in Buenos Aires. Four years later, Carnero accepted a simultaneous assignment with BSB. Soon afterward, he reported to BSC that its Latin American subsidiaries were

CASE 7.2–CONTINUED

CASE 7.2–CONTINUED

improperly inflating sales figures and engaging in other accounting misconduct. His employment with BSA and BSB was terminated. Carnero filed a complaint with the U.S. Department of Labor (DOL) against BSC under the Sarbanes-Oxley Act, seeking reinstatement. The DOL rejected the claim. Carnero filed a suit in a federal district court against BSC on the same basis. The court dismissed the complaint. Carnero appealed to the U.S. Court of Appeals for the First Circuit.

IN THE WORDS OF THE COURT . . . *LEVIN H. CAMPBELL,* Senior Circuit Judge.

* * * *

Carnero argues that [18 U.S.C. Section 1514A] should be given extraterritorial effect, so as to allow him to pursue in federal court his whistleblower claim brought under its provisions. He says his claim not only fits within the literal language of the statute but that to limit the operation of the statute to purely domestic conduct in the United States would improperly insulate the foreign operations of covered companies. This, he says, would frustrate the basic purpose of the Sarbanes-Oxley Act of which the whistleblower protection statute at issue is a part, to protect both the investors in U.S. securities markets and the integrity of those markets.

While Carnero's argument has some force, it faces a high and we think insurmountable hurdle in the well-established presumption against the extraterritorial application of Congressional statutes. Where, as here, a statute is silent as to its territorial reach, and no contrary congressional intent clearly appears, there is generally a presumption against its extraterritorial application.

* * * *

The presumption serves at least two purposes. It protects against unintended clashes between our laws and those of other nations which could result in international discord, and it reflects the notion that when Congress legislates, it is primarily concerned with domestic conditions. [Emphasis added.]

* * * *

* * * Pertinent factors run strongly counter to finding an extraterritorial legislative intent. These contrary *indicia* [signs, or indications] prevent our determining that Congress has evidenced its "clear intent" for extraterritorial application. Not only is the text of 18 U.S.C. Section 1514A silent as to any intent to apply it abroad, the statute's legislative history indicates that Congress gave no consideration to either the possibility or the problems of overseas application. In sharp contrast with this silence, Congress has provided expressly elsewhere in the Sarbanes-Oxley Act for extraterritorial enforcement of a different, criminal, whistleblower statute. By so providing, Congress demonstrated that it was well able to call for extraterritorial application when it so desired. Also in the Act, Congress has provided expressly for the extraterritorial application of certain other unrelated statutes, tailoring these so as to cope with problems of sovereignty and the like—again demonstrating Congress's ability to provide for foreign application when it wished. Here, however, while placing the whistleblower provision's enforcement in the hands of the DOL, a domestic agency, Congress has made no provision for possible problems arising when that agency seeks to regulate employment relationships in foreign nations, nor has Congress provided the DOL with special powers and resources to conduct investigations abroad. Furthermore, judicial venue provisions written into the whistleblower protection statute were made expressly applicable only to whistleblower violations within the United States and to complainants residing here on the date of violation, with no corresponding basis being provided for venue as to foreign complainants claiming violations in foreign countries.

These factors * * * not only fail to imply a clear congressional intent for extraterritorial application, but indicate that Congress never expected such application.

DECISION AND REMEDY   The U.S. Court of Appeals for the First Circuit affirmed the lower court's dismissal of Carnero's complaint under 18 U.S.C. Section 1514A. Congress "made no reference to [the statute's] application abroad and tailored the * * * statute to purely domestic application." This section of the act "does not reflect the necessary clear expression of congressional intent to extend its reach beyond our nation's borders."

WHAT IF THE FACTS WERE DIFFERENT? Suppose that Carnero had been an American working for BSA and BSB. Would the result in this case have been the same? Discuss.

THE LEGAL ENVIRONMENT DIMENSION How might the court's decision in this case frustrate the basic purpose of the Sarbanes-Oxley Act, which is to protect investors in U.S. securities markets and the integrity of those markets?

Bribing Foreign Officials

Giving cash or in-kind benefits to foreign government officials to obtain business contracts and other favors is often considered normal practice. To reduce such bribery by representatives of U.S. corporations, Congress enacted the Foreign Corrupt Practices Act in 1977.[8] This act and its implications for American businesspersons engaged in international business transactions were discussed in Chapter 6.

U.S. Antitrust Laws

U.S. antitrust laws (discussed in Chapter 23) have a wide application. They may *subject* persons in foreign nations to their provisions, as well as *protect* foreign consumers and competitors from violations committed by U.S. citizens. Section 1 of the Sherman Act provides for the extraterritorial effect of the U.S. antitrust laws. The United States is a major proponent of free competition in the global economy. Thus, any conspiracy that has a *substantial effect* on U.S. commerce is within the reach of the Sherman Act. The law applies even if the violation occurs outside the United States, and foreign governments as well as persons can be sued for violations.

Before U.S. courts will exercise jurisdiction and apply antitrust laws, however, it must be shown that the alleged violation had a substantial effect on U.S. commerce. **EXAMPLE #6** A number of companies that manufacture and sell paper on the global market meet in Japan on several occasions and reach a price-fixing agreement (an agreement to set prices—see Chapter 23). Although several of the companies are based in foreign nations, they sell paper in the United States through their wholly owned subsidiaries. Thus, the agreement to sell paper at above-normal prices throughout North America has a *substantial restraining effect* on U.S. commerce. In this situation, a U.S. court has jurisdiction over the defendant companies even though the price-fixing activities took place entirely outside the United States. ☐

Antidiscrimination Laws

As will be explained in Chapter 18, federal laws in the United States prohibit discrimination on the basis of race, color, national origin, religion, gender, age, and disability. These laws, as they affect employment relationships, generally apply extraterritorially. Since 1984, for example, the Age Discrimination in Employment Act of 1967 has covered U.S. employees working abroad for U.S. employers. The Americans with Disabilities Act of 1990, which requires employers

---

8. 15 U.S.C. Sections 78m–78ff.

to accommodate the needs of workers with disabilities, also applies to U.S. nationals working abroad for U.S. firms.

For some time, it was uncertain whether the major U.S. law regulating discriminatory practices in the workplace, Title VII of the Civil Rights Act of 1964, applied extraterritorially. The Civil Rights Act of 1991 addressed this issue. The act provides that Title VII applies extraterritorially to all U.S. employees working for U.S. employers abroad. Generally, U.S. employers must abide by U.S. discrimination laws unless to do so would violate the laws of the country where their workplaces are located. This "foreign laws exception" allows employers to avoid being subjected to conflicting laws.

International Tort Claims

The international application of tort liability is growing in significance and controversy. An increasing number of U.S. plaintiffs are suing foreign (or U.S.) entities for torts that these entities have allegedly committed overseas. Often, these cases involve human rights violations by foreign governments. The Alien Tort Claims Act (ATCA),[9] adopted in 1789, allows even foreign citizens to bring civil suits in U.S. courts for injuries caused by violations of the law of nations or a treaty of the United States.

Since 1980, plaintiffs have increasingly used the ATCA to bring actions against companies operating in other countries. ATCA actions have been brought against companies doing business in nations such as Colombia, Ecuador, Egypt, Guatemala, India, Indonesia, Nigeria, and Saudi Arabia. Some of these cases have involved alleged environmental destruction. In addition, mineral companies in Southeast Asia have been sued for collaborating with oppressive government regimes.

The following case involved claims against "hundreds" of corporations that allegedly "aided and abetted" the government of South Africa in maintaining its apartheid (racially discriminatory) regime.

---

9. 28 U.S.C. Section 1350.

Case 7.3   **Khulumani v. Barclay National Bank, Ltd.**

United States Court of Appeals,
Second Circuit, 2007.
504 F.3d 254.

BACKGROUND AND FACTS   The Khulumani plaintiffs, along with other plaintiff groups, filed class action claims on behalf of victims of apartheid-related atrocities, human rights violations, crimes against humanity, and unfair and discriminatory forced-labor practices. The plaintiffs brought this action under the Alien Tort Claims Act (ATCA) against more than fifty corporate defendants and others. These corporations included Bank of America, Barclay National Bank, Citigroup, Credit Suisse Group, General Electric, and IBM. The plaintiffs filed separate actions in multiple federal district courts. All of the actions were transferred to a federal district court in the Southern District of New York. The defendants filed motions to dismiss. The district court held that the plaintiffs had failed to establish subject-matter jurisdiction under the ATCA. The court dismissed the plaintiffs' complaints in their entirety. The plaintiffs appealed to the U.S. Court of Appeals for the Second Circuit.

***PER CURIAM* [By the whole court].**

* * * *

* * * [This court] vacate[s] the district court's dismissal of the plaintiffs' ATCA claims because the district court erred in holding that aiding and abetting violations of customary international law cannot provide a basis for ATCA jurisdiction. *We hold*

*that * * * a plaintiff may plead a theory of aiding and abetting liability under the ATCA.* * * [The majority of the judges on the panel that heard this case agreed on the result but differed on the reasons, which were presented in two concurring opinions. One judge believed that liability on these facts is "well established in international law," citing such examples as the Rome Statute of the International Criminal Court. Another judge stated that grounds existed in such resources of U.S. law as Section 876(b) of the *Restatement (Second) of Torts,* under which liability could be assessed in part for "facilitating the commission of human rights violations by providing the principal tortfeasor with the tools, instrumentalities, or services to commit those violations."] [Emphasis added.]

 * * * *

* * * We decline to affirm the dismissal of plaintiffs' ATCA claims on the basis of the prudential concerns[a] raised by the defendants. * * * The Supreme Court [has] identified two different respects in which courts should consider prudential concerns [exercise great caution and carefully evaluate international norms and potential adverse foreign policy consequences] in deciding whether to hear claims brought under the ATCA.[b] First, * * * courts should consider prudential concerns in the context of determining whether to recognize a cause of action under the ATCA. Specifically, * * * the determination whether a norm is sufficiently definite to support a cause of action should (and, indeed, inevitably must) involve an element of judgment about the practical consequences of making that cause available to litigants in the federal courts. Second, * * * in certain cases, other prudential principles might operate to limit the availability of relief in the federal courts for violations of customary international law.

 * * * *

One such principle * * * [is] a policy of case-specific deference to the political branches [of the U.S. government]. *This policy of judicial deference to the Executive Branch on questions of foreign policy has long been established under the prudential justiciability [appropriate for a court to resolve] doctrine known as the political question doctrine. Another prudential doctrine that the defendants raise in this case is international comity. This doctrine * * * asks whether adjudication of the case by a United States court would offend amicable working relationships with a foreign country.* [Emphasis added.]

 * * * *

We decline to address these case-specific prudential doctrines now and instead remand to the district court to allow it to engage in the first instance in the careful "case-by-case" analysis that questions of this type require.

DECISION AND REMEDY The U.S. Court of Appeals vacated the district court's dismissal of the plaintiffs' claims and remanded the case for further proceedings. According to the reviewing court, a plaintiff may plead a theory of aiding and abetting liability under the Alien Tort Claims Act.

THE LEGAL ENVIRONMENT DIMENSION What are the ramifications for the defendants of the ruling in this case?

THE ETHICAL DIMENSION Should the companies cited as defendants in this case have refused all business dealings with South Africa while that country's white government placed restrictions on the majority black African population (called apartheid)?

a. The term *prudential concerns* refers to the defendants' arguments that the plaintiffs do not have standing to pursue their case in a U.S. court. Here, *prudential* means that the arguments are based on judicially (or legislatively) created principles rather than on the constitutionally based requirements set forth in Article III of the U.S. Constitution (the case or controversy clause).
b. The court is referring to the decision of the United States Supreme Court in *Sosa v. Alvarez-Machain,* 542 U.S. 692, 124 S.Ct. 2739, 159 L.Ed.2d 718 (2004). In the Sosa case, the Supreme Court outlined the need for caution in deciding actions under the Alien Tort Claims Act and said that the "potential implications for the foreign relations of the United States of recognizing such causes should make courts particularly wary of impinging [encroaching] on the discretion of the Legislative and Executive Branches in managing foreign affairs."

Reviewing . . . International Law in a Global Economy

Robco, Inc., was a Florida arms dealer. The armed forces of Honduras contracted to purchase weapons from Robco over a six-year period. After the government was replaced and a democracy installed, the Honduran government sought to reduce the size of its military, and its relationship with Robco deteriorated. Honduras refused to honor the contract by purchasing the inventory of arms, which Robco could sell only at a much lower price. Robco filed a suit in a federal district court in the United States to recover damages for this breach of contract by the government of Honduras. Using the information provided in the chapter, answer the following questions.

1. Should the Foreign Sovereign Immunities Act (FSIA) preclude this lawsuit? Why or why not?

2. Does the act of state doctrine bar Robco from seeking to enforce the contract? Explain.

3. Suppose that prior to this lawsuit, the new government of Honduras enacted a law making it illegal to purchase weapons from foreign arms dealers. What doctrine might lead a U.S. court to dismiss Robco's case in that situation?

4. Now suppose that the U.S. court hears the case and awards damages to Robco, but the government of Honduras has no assets in the United States that can be used to satisfy the judgment. Under which doctrine might Robco be able to collect the damages by asking another nation's court to enforce the U.S. judgment?

Key Terms

act of state doctrine 210
choice-of-language clause 218
choice-of-law clause 218
civil law system 209
comity 210
confiscation 210
correspondent bank 220
distribution agreement 212
dumping 216

exclusive distributorship 212
export 211
expropriation 210
force majeure clause 219
foreign exchange market 220
forum-selection clause 218
international law 207
international
   organization 209

letter of credit 221
national law 207
normal trade relations (NTR)
   status 216
quota 216
sovereign immunity 211
tariff 216
treaty 208

Chapter Summary

International Law—
Sources and Principles
(See pages 208–211.)

1. *Sources of international law*—The three sources of international law are international customs, treaties and international agreements, and international organizations and conferences.

2. *Common law and civil law systems*—Companies that operate in foreign nations are subject to the laws of those nations. Legal systems around the globe are either common law systems (case law supplements statutory law) or civil law systems (the statutory code governs).

3. *The principle of comity*—Under this principle, nations give effect to the laws and judicial decrees of other nations for reasons of courtesy and international harmony.

4. *The act of state doctrine*—A doctrine under which U.S. courts avoid passing judgment on the validity of public acts committed by a recognized foreign government within its own territory.

International Law—Sources and Principles—Continued	5. *The doctrine of sovereign immunity*—When certain conditions are satisfied, foreign nations are immune from U.S. jurisdiction under the Foreign Sovereign Immunities Act of 1976. Exceptions are made (a) when a foreign state has "waived its immunity either explicitly or by implication" or (b) when the action is taken "in connection with a commercial activity carried on in the United States by the foreign state."
Doing Business Internationally (See pages 211–213.)	Ways in which U.S. domestic firms engage in international business transactions include (a) exporting, which may involve foreign agents or distributors, and (b) manufacturing abroad, which may involve licensing arrangements or franchising operations.
Regulation of Specific Business Activities (See pages 213–217.)	In the interests of their economies, foreign policies, domestic policies, or other national priorities, nations impose laws that restrict or facilitate international business. Such laws regulate foreign investments, exporting, and importing. The World Trade Organization attempts to minimize trade barriers among nations, as do regional trade agreements and associations, including the European Union and the North American Free Trade Agreement.
Commercial Contracts in an International Setting (See pages 217–220.)	International business contracts often include choice-of-language, forum-selection, and choice-of-law clauses to reduce the uncertainties associated with interpreting the language of the agreement and dealing with legal differences. Most domestic and international contracts include *force majeure* clauses. They commonly stipulate that certain events, such as floods, fire, accidents, labor strikes, and government orders, may excuse a party from liability for nonperformance of the contract. Arbitration clauses are also frequently found in international contracts.
Payment Methods for International Transactions (See pages 220–223.)	1. *Currency conversion*—Because nations have different monetary systems, payment on international contracts requires currency conversion at a rate specified in a foreign exchange market.
	2. *Correspondent banking*—Correspondent banks facilitate the transfer of funds from a buyer in one country to a seller in another.
	3. *Letters of credit*—Letters of credit facilitate international transactions by ensuring payment to sellers and assuring buyers that payment will not be made until the sellers have complied with the terms of the letters of credit. Typically, compliance occurs when a bill of lading is delivered to the issuing bank.
U.S. Laws in a Global Context (See pages 223–227.)	1. *Sarbanes-Oxley Act*—Certain provisions of the Sarbanes-Oxley Act of 2002, including those that protect whistleblowers from retaliation for reporting criminal violations, may apply extraterritorially.
	2. *Antitrust laws*—U.S. antitrust laws may be applied beyond the borders of the United States. Any conspiracy that has a substantial effect on commerce within the United States may be subject to the Sherman Act, even if the violation occurs outside the United States.
	3. *Antidiscrimination laws*—The major U.S. laws prohibiting employment discrimination, including Title VII of the Civil Rights Act of 1964, the Age Discrimination in Employment Act of 1967, and the Americans with Disabilities Act of 1990, cover U.S. employees working abroad for U.S. firms—unless to apply the U.S. laws would violate the laws of the host country.
	4. *Alien Tort Claims Act (ATCA)*—This act allows plaintiffs, including foreign citizens, to bring civil lawsuits in the United States for injuries caused by violations of the law of nations or a treaty of the United States. The ATCA has been used to bring actions against companies operating in other nations, as well as against foreign governments for alleged human rights violations.

For Review

1. What is the principle of comity, and why do courts deciding disputes involving a foreign law or judicial decree apply this principle?
2. What is the act of state doctrine? In what circumstances is this doctrine applied?
3. Under the Foreign Sovereign Immunities Act of 1976, on what bases might a foreign state be considered subject to the jurisdiction of U.S. courts?
4. In what circumstances will U.S. antitrust laws be applied extraterritorially?
5. Do U.S. laws prohibiting employment discrimination apply in all circumstances to U.S. employees working for U.S. employers abroad?

Questions and Case Problems

7–1. Letters of Credit. The Swiss Credit Bank issued a letter of credit in favor of Antex Industries to cover the sale of 92,000 electronic integrated circuits manufactured by Electronic Arrays. The letter of credit specified that the chips would be transported to Tokyo by ship. Antex shipped the circuits by air. Payment on the letter of credit was dishonored because the shipment by air did not fulfill the precise terms of the letter of credit. Should a court compel payment? Explain.

Question with Sample Answer

7–2. As China and other formerly Communist nations move toward free enterprise, they must develop a new set of business laws. If you could start from scratch, what kind of business law system would you adopt, a civil law system or a common law system? What kind of business regulations would you impose?

For a sample answer to Question 7–2, go to Appendix I at the end of this text.

7–3. Sovereign Immunity. Tonoga, Ltd., doing business as Taconic Plastics, Ltd., is a manufacturer incorporated in Ireland with its principal place of business in New York. In 1997, Taconic entered into a contract with a German construction company to supply special material for a tent project designed to shelter religious pilgrims visiting holy sites in Saudi Arabia. Most of the material was made in, and shipped from, New York. The company did not pay Taconic and eventually filed for bankruptcy. Another German firm, Werner Voss Architects and Engineers, acting as an agent for the government of Saudi Arabia, guaranteed the payments due Taconic to induce it to complete the project. When it did not receive the final payment, Taconic filed a suit in a U.S. district court against the government of Saudi Arabia, claiming a breach of the guaranty and seeking to collect, in part, about $3 million. The defendant filed a

motion to dismiss based, among other things, on the doctrine of sovereign immunity. Under what circumstances does this doctrine apply? What are its exceptions? Should this suit be dismissed under the "commercial activity" exception? Explain. [*Tonoga, Ltd. v. Ministry of Public Works and Housing of Kingdom of Saudi Arabia,* 135 F.Supp.2d 350 (N.D.N.Y. 2001)]

7–4. Import Controls. DaimlerChrysler Corp. makes and markets motor vehicles. DaimlerChrysler assembled the 1993 and 1994 model years of its trucks at plants in Mexico. Assembly involved sheet metal components sent from the United States. DaimlerChrysler subjected some of the parts to a complicated treatment process, which included applying coats of paint to prevent corrosion, impart color, and protect the finish. Under U.S. law, goods that are assembled abroad using U.S.-made parts can be imported tariff free. A U.S. *statute* provides that painting is "incidental" to assembly and does not affect the status of the goods. A U.S. *regulation,* however, states that "painting primarily intended to enhance the appearance of an article or to impart distinctive features or characteristics" is not incidental. The U.S. Customs Service levied a tariff on the trucks. DaimlerChrysler filed a suit in the U.S. Court of International Trade, challenging the levy. Should the court rule in DaimlerChrysler's favor? Why or why not? [*DaimlerChrysler Corp. v. United States,* 361 F.3d 1378 (Fed.Cir. 2004)]

7–5. Comity. E&L Consulting, Ltd., is a U.S. corporation that sells lumber products in New Jersey, New York, and Pennsylvania. Doman Industries, Ltd., is a Canadian corporation that also sells lumber products, including green hem-fir, a durable product used for homebuilding. Doman supplies more than 95 percent of the green hem-fir for sale in the northeastern United States. In 1990, Doman contracted to sell green hem-fir through E&L, which received monthly payments plus commissions. In 1998, Sherwood Lumber Corp., a New York firm and an

E&L competitor, approached E&L about a merger. The negotiations were unsuccessful. According to E&L, Sherwood and Doman then conspired to monopolize the green hem-fir market in the United States. When Doman terminated its contract with E&L, the latter filed a suit in a federal district court against Doman, alleging violations of U.S. antitrust law. Doman filed for bankruptcy in a Canadian court and asked the U.S. court to dismiss E&L's suit under the principle of comity, among other things. What is the principle of comity? On what basis would it apply in this case? What would be the likely result? Discuss. [*E&L Consulting, Ltd. v. Doman Industries, Ltd.*, 360 F.Supp.2d 465 (E.D.N.Y. 2005)]

7–6. Dumping. A newspaper printing press system is more than one hundred feet long, stands four or five stories tall, and weighs 2 million pounds. Only about ten of the systems are sold each year in the United States. Because of the size and cost, a newspaper may update its system, rather than replace it, by buying "additions." By the 1990s, Goss International Corp. was the only domestic maker of the equipment in the United States and represented the entire U.S. market. Tokyo Kikai Seisakusho (TKSC), a Japanese corporation, makes the systems in Japan. In the 1990s, TKSC began to compete in the U.S. market, forcing Goss to cut its prices below cost. TKSC's tactics included offering its customers "secret" rebates on prices that were ultimately substantially less than the products' actual market value in Japan. According to TKSC office memos, the goal was to "win completely this survival game" against Goss, the "enemy." Goss filed a suit in a federal district court against TKSC and others, alleging illegal dumping. At what point does a foreign firm's attempt to compete with a domestic manufacturer in the United States become illegal dumping? Was that point reached in this case? Discuss. [*Goss International Corp. v. Man Roland Druckmaschinen Aktiengesellschaft*, 434 F.3d 1081 (8th Cir. 2006)]

Case Problem with Sample Answer

7–7. Jan Voda, M.D., a resident of Oklahoma City, Oklahoma, owns three U.S. patents related to guiding catheters for use in interventional cardiology, as well as corresponding foreign patents issued by the European Patent Office, Canada, France, Germany, and Great Britain. Voda filed a suit in a federal district court against Cordis Corp., a U.S. firm, alleging infringement of the U.S. patents under U.S. patent law and of the corresponding foreign patents under the patent law of the various foreign countries. Cordis admitted, "[T]he XB catheters have been sold domestically and internationally since 1994. The XB catheters were manufactured in Miami Lakes, Florida, from 1993 to 2001 and have been manufactured in Juarez, Mexico, since 2001." Cordis argued,

however, that Voda could not assert infringement claims under foreign patent law because the court did not have jurisdiction over such claims. Which of the important international legal principles discussed in this chapter would be most likely to apply in this case? How should the court apply it? Explain. [*Voda v. Cordis Corp.*, 476 F.3d 887 (Fed.Cir. 2007)]

After you have answered Problem 7–7, compare your answer with the sample answer given on the Web site that accompanies this text. Go to www.cengage.com/blaw/let, select "Chapter 7," and click on "Case Problem with Sample Answer."

A Question of Ethics

7–8. On December 21, 1988, Pan Am Flight 103 exploded 31,000 feet in the air over Lockerbie, Scotland, killing all 259 passengers and crew on board and 11 people on the ground. Among those killed was Roger Hurst, a U.S. citizen. An investigation determined that a portable radiocassette player packed in a brown Samsonite suitcase smuggled onto the plane was the source of the explosion. The explosive device was constructed with a digital timer specially made for, and bought by, Libya. Abdel Basset Ali Al-Megrahi, a Libyan government official and an employee of the Libyan Arab Airline (LAA), was convicted by the Scottish High Court of Justiciary on criminal charges that he planned and executed the bombing in association with members of the Jamahiriya Security Organization (JSO) (an agency of the Libyan government that performs security and intelligence functions) or the Libyan military. Members of the victims' families filed a suit in a U.S. federal district court against the JSO, the LAA, Al-Megrahi, and others. The plaintiffs claimed violations of U.S. federal law, including the Anti-Terrorism Act, and state law, including the intentional infliction of emotional distress. [*Hurst v. Socialist People's Libyan Arab Jamahiriya*, 474 F.Supp.2d 19 (D.D.C. 2007)]

1. Under what doctrine, codified in which federal statute, might the defendants claim to be immune from the jurisdiction of a U.S. court? Should this law include an exception for "state-sponsored terrorism"? Why or why not?
2. The defendants agreed to pay $2.7 billion, or $10 million per victim, to settle all claims for "compensatory death damages." The families of eleven victims, including Hurst, were excluded from the settlement because they were "not wrongful death beneficiaries under applicable state law." These plaintiffs continued the suit. The defendants filed a motion to dismiss. Should the motion be granted on the

ground that the settlement bars the plaintiffs' claims? Explain.

Critical-Thinking Legal Question

7–9. Business cartels and monopolies that are legal in some countries may engage in practices that violate U.S. antitrust laws. In view of this fact, what are some of the implications of applying U.S. antitrust laws extraterritorially?

Video Question

7–10. Go to this text's Web site at **www.cengage.com/blaw/let** and select "Chapter 7." Click on "Video Questions" and view the video titled *International: Letter of Credit.* Then answer the following questions.

1. Do banks always require the same documents to be presented in letter-of-credit transactions? If not, who dictates what documents will be required in the letter of credit?
2. At what point does the seller receive payment in a letter-of-credit transaction?
3. What assurances does a letter of credit provide to the buyer and the seller involved in the transaction?

Interacting with the Internet

For updated links to resources available on the Web, as well as a variety of other materials, visit this text's Web site at

www.cengage.com/blaw/let

FindLaw, which is a part of West Group, includes an extensive array of links to international doctrines and treaties, as well as to the laws of other nations, on its Web site. Go to

www.findlaw.com/12international

For information on the legal requirements of doing business internationally, a good source is the Internet Law Library's collection of laws of other countries. You can access this source at

www.lawguru.com/ilawlib/?id=52

PRACTICAL INTERNET EXERCISES

Go to this text's Web site at **www.cengage.com/blaw/let**, select "Chapter 7," and click on "Practical Internet Exercises." There you will find the following Internet research exercises that you can perform to learn more about the topics covered in this chapter.

Practical Internet Exercise 7–1: LEGAL PERSPECTIVE—**The World Trade Organization**

Practical Internet Exercise 7–2: MANAGEMENT PERSPECTIVE—**Overseas Business Opportunities**

BEFORE THE TEST

Go to this text's Web site at **www.cengage.com/blaw/let**, select "Chapter 7," and click on "Interactive Quizzes." You will find a number of interactive questions relating to this chapter.

Unit One — Cumulative Business Hypothetical

CompTac, Inc., which is headquartered in San Francisco, California, is one of the leading software manufacturers in the United States. The company invests millions of dollars in researching and developing new software applications and computer games, which are sold worldwide. It also has a large service department and has taken great pains to offer its customers excellent support services.

1. CompTac routinely purchases some of the materials necessary to produce its computer games from a New York firm, Electrotex, Inc. A dispute arises between the two firms, and CompTac wants to sue Electrotex for breach of contract. Can CompTac bring the suit in a California state court? Can CompTac bring the suit in a federal court? Explain.

2. A customer at one of CompTac's retail stores stumbles over a crate in the parking lot and breaks her leg. The crate had just moments before fallen off a CompTac truck that was delivering goods from a CompTac warehouse to the store. The customer sues CompTac, alleging negligence. Will she succeed in her suit? Why or why not?

3. Roban Electronics, a software manufacturer and one of CompTac's major competitors, has been trying to convince one of CompTac's key employees, Jim Baxter, to come to work for Roban. Roban knows that Baxter has a written employment contract with CompTac, which Baxter would breach if he left CompTac before the contract expired. Baxter goes to work for Roban, and the departure of its key employee causes CompTac to suffer substantial losses due to delays in completing new software. Can CompTac sue Roban to recoup some of these losses? If so, on what ground?

4. One of CompTac's employees in its accounting division, Alan Green, has a gambling problem. To repay a gambling debt of $10,000, Green decides to "borrow" some money from CompTac to cover the debt. Using his "hacking" skills and his knowledge of CompTac account numbers, Green electronically transfers CompTac funds into his personal checking account. A week later, he is luckier at gambling and uses the same electronic procedures to transfer funds from his personal checking account to the relevant CompTac account. Has Green committed any crimes? If so, what are they?

5. One of CompTac's best-selling products is a computer game that includes some extremely violent actions. Groups of parents, educators, and consumer activists have bombarded CompTac with letters and e-mail messages calling on the company to stop selling the product. CompTac executives are concerned about the public outcry, but at the same time they realize that the game is a major source of profits. If it ceased marketing the game, the company could go bankrupt. If you were a CompTac decision maker, what would your decision be in this situation? How would you justify your decision from an ethical perspective?

6. CompTac wants to sell one of its best-selling software programs to An Phat Company, a firm located in Ho Chi Minh City, Vietnam. CompTac is concerned, however, that after an initial purchase, An Phat will duplicate the software without permission (and in violation of U.S. copyright laws) and sell the illegal bootleg software to other firms in Vietnam. How can CompTac protect its software from being pirated by An Phat Company?

The Commercial Environment

Chapter 8

Intellectual Property and Internet Law

CHAPTER OBJECTIVES

After reading this chapter, you should be able to answer the following questions:

1. What is intellectual property?

2. Why are trademarks and patents protected by the law?

3. What laws protect authors' rights in the works they generate?

4. What are trade secrets, and what laws offer protection for this form of intellectual property?

5. What steps have been taken to protect intellectual property rights in today's digital age?

CONTENTS

"The Internet, by virtue of its ability to mesh what will be hundreds of millions of people together, . . . is . . . a profoundly different capability that by and large human beings have not had before."

— TONY RUTKOWSKI,
1943–present (Executive director of the Internet Society, 1994–1996)

INTELLECTUAL PROPERTY
Property resulting from intellectual, creative processes.

Of significant concern to businesspersons today is the need to protect their rights in intellectual property. **Intellectual property** is any property resulting from intellectual, creative processes—the products of an individual's mind. Although it is an abstract term for an abstract concept, intellectual property is nonetheless familiar to almost everyone. The information contained in books and computer files is intellectual property. The software you use, the movies you see, and the music you listen to are all forms of intellectual property. In fact, in today's information age, it should come as no surprise that the value of the world's intellectual property probably now exceeds the value of physical property, such as machines and houses.

The need to protect creative works was recognized by the framers of the U.S. Constitution more than two hundred years ago: Article I, Section 8, of the Constitution authorized Congress "[t]o promote the Progress of Science and useful Arts, by securing for limited Times to Authors and Inventors the exclusive Right to their respective Writings and Discoveries." Laws protecting patents, trademarks, and copyrights are explicitly designed to protect and reward inventive and artistic creativity. Exhibit 8–1 offers a comprehensive summary of these forms of intellectual property, as well as intellectual property that consists of *trade secrets*.

An understanding of intellectual property law is important because intellectual property has taken on increasing significance, not only in the United States but globally as well. Today, the prosperity of many U.S. companies depends more on their ownership rights in intangible intellectual property than on their tangible assets. As you will read in this chapter, protecting these assets in today's online

EXHIBIT 8–1 FORMS OF INTELLECTUAL PROPERTY

	DEFINITION	HOW ACQUIRED	DURATION	REMEDY FOR INFRINGEMENT
Patent	A grant from the government that gives an inventor exclusive rights to an invention.	By filing a patent application with the U.S. Patent and Trademark Office and receiving its approval.	Twenty years from the date of the application; for design patents, fourteen years.	Monetary damages, including royalties and lost profits, *plus* attorneys' fees. Damages may be tripled for intentional infringements.
Copyright	The right of an author or originator of a literary or artistic work, or other production that falls within a specified category, to have the exclusive use of that work for a given period of time.	Automatic (once the work or creation is put in tangible form). Only the *expression* of an idea (and not the idea itself) can be protected by copyright.	For authors: the life of the author plus 70 years. For publishers: 95 years after the date of publication or 120 years after creation.	Actual damages plus profits received by the party who infringed *or* statutory damages under the Copyright Act, *plus* costs and attorneys' fees in either situation.
Trademark (service mark and trade dress)	Any distinctive word, name, symbol, or device (image or appearance), or combination thereof, that an entity uses to distinguish its goods or services from those of others. The owner has the exclusive right to use that mark or trade dress.	1. At common law, ownership created by use of the mark. 2. Registration with the appropriate federal or state office gives notice and is permitted if the mark is currently in use or will be within the next six months.	Unlimited, as long as it is in use. To continue notice by registration, the owner must renew by filing between the fifth and sixth years, and thereafter, every ten years.	1. Injunction prohibiting the future use of the mark. 2. Actual damages plus profits received by the party who infringed (can be increased under the Lanham Act). 3. Destruction of articles that infringed. 4. *Plus* costs and attorneys' fees.
Trade secret	Any information that a business possesses and that gives the business an advantage over competitors (including formulas, lists, patterns, plans, processes, and programs).	Through the originality and development of the information and processes that constitute the business secret and are unknown to others.	Unlimited, so long as not revealed to others. Once revealed to others, it is no longer a trade secret.	Monetary damages for misappropriation (the Uniform Trade Secrets Act also permits punitive damages if willful), *plus* costs and attorneys' fees.

world has proved particularly challenging. This is because, as indicated in the chapter-opening quotation, the Internet's capability is "profoundly different" from anything we have had in the past.

TRADEMARKS AND RELATED PROPERTY

A **trademark** is a distinctive mark, motto, device, or emblem that a manufacturer stamps, prints, or otherwise affixes to the goods it produces so that they may be identified on the market and their origins made known. At common law, the

TRADEMARK
A distinctive mark, motto, device, or emblem that a manufacturer stamps, prints, or otherwise affixes to the goods it produces so that they may be identified on the market and their origins made known. Once a trademark is established (under the common law or through registration), the owner is entitled to its exclusive use.

person who used a symbol or mark to identify a business or product was protected in the use of that trademark. Clearly, by using another's trademark, a business could lead consumers to believe that its goods were made by the other business. The law seeks to avoid this kind of confusion. In the following classic case concerning Coca-Cola, the defendants argued that the Coca-Cola trademark was entitled to no protection under the law because the term did not accurately represent the product.

Landmark and Classic Cases

Case 8.1 | **The Coca-Cola Co. v. Koke Co. of America**

Supreme Court of the United States,
254 U.S. 143, 41 S.Ct. 113, 65 L.Ed. 189 1920.
www.findlaw.com/casecode/supreme.html[a]

COMPANY PROFILE   John Pemberton, an Atlanta pharmacist, invented a caramel-colored, carbonated soft drink in 1886. His bookkeeper, Frank Robinson, named the beverage Coca-Cola after two of the ingredients, coca leaves and kola nuts. Asa Candler bought the Coca-Cola Company in 1891 and, within seven years, had made the soft drink available in all of the United States, as well as in parts of Canada and Mexico. Candler continued to sell Coke aggressively and to open up new markets, reaching Europe

before 1910. In doing so, however, he attracted numerous competitors, some of whom tried to capitalize directly on the Coke name.

BACKGROUND AND FACTS   The Coca-Cola Company sought to enjoin (prevent) the Koke Company of America and other beverage companies from, among other things, using the word Koke for their products. The Koke Company of America and other beverage companies contended that the Coca-Cola trademark was a fraudulent representation and that Coca-Cola was therefore not entitled to any help from the courts. The Koke Company and the other defendants alleged that the Coca-Cola Company, by its use of the Coca-Cola name, represented that the beverage contained cocaine (from coca leaves), which it no longer did. The trial court granted the injunction against the Koke Company, but the appellate court reversed the lower court's ruling. Coca-Cola then appealed to the United States Supreme Court.

a. This is the "U.S. Supreme Court Opinions" page within the Web site of the "FindLaw Internet Legal Resources" database. This page provides several options for accessing an opinion. Because you know the citation for this case, you can click on the "Citation Search" box, type in the appropriate volume and page numbers for the *United States Reports* ("254" and "143," respectively, for the *Coca-Cola* case), and click on "Search."

IN THE WORDS OF THE COURT . . . Mr. Justice *HOLMES* delivered the opinion of the Court.

*   *   *   *

*   *   * Before 1900 the beginning of [Coca-Cola's] good will was more or less helped by the presence of cocaine, a drug that, like alcohol or caffeine or opium, may be described as a deadly poison or as a valuable [pharmaceutical item, depending on the speaker's purposes]. The amount seems to have been very small,[b] but it may have been enough to begin a bad habit and after the Food and Drug Act of June 30, 1906, if not earlier, long before this suit was brought, it was eliminated from the plaintiff's compound.

*   *   * Since 1900 the sales have increased at a very great rate corresponding to a like increase in advertising. The name now characterizes a beverage to be had at almost any soda fountain. It means a single thing coming from a single source, and well known to the community. It hardly would be too much to say that the drink characterizes the name as much as the name the drink. In other words *Coca-Cola probably means to most persons the plaintiff's familiar product to be had everywhere rather than a compound of particular substances.* *   *   * Before this suit was brought the plaintiff had advertised to the public that it must not expect and would not find cocaine, and had eliminated everything tending to suggest cocaine effects except the name and the pic-

b. In reality, until 1903 the amount of active cocaine in each bottle of Coke was equivalent to one "line" of cocaine.

ture of [coca] leaves and nuts, which probably conveyed little or nothing to most who saw it. It appears to us that it would be going too far to deny the plaintiff relief against a palpable [readily evident] fraud because possibly here and there an ignorant person might call for the drink with the hope for incipient cocaine intoxication. The plaintiff's position must be judged by the facts as they were when the suit was begun, not by the facts of a different condition and an earlier time. [Emphasis added.]

DECISION AND REMEDY The district court's injunction was allowed to stand. The competing beverage companies were enjoined from calling their products Koke.

IMPACT OF THIS CASE ON TODAY'S LEGAL ENVIRONMENT In this early case, the United States Supreme Court made it clear that trademarks and trade names (and nicknames for those marks and names, such as the nickname "Coke" for "Coca-Cola") that are in common use receive protection under the common law. This holding is significant historically because it is the predecessor to the federal statute later passed to protect trademark rights—the Lanham Act of 1946, to be discussed next. In many ways, this act represented a codification of common law principles governing trademarks.

WHAT IF THE FACTS WERE DIFFERENT? Suppose that Coca-Cola had been trying to make the public believe that its product contained cocaine. Would the result in this case likely have been different? Why or why not?

RELEVANT WEB SITES To locate information on the Web concerning the *Coca-Cola* decision, go to this text's Web site at **academic.cengage.com/blaw/let**, select "Chapter 8," and click on "URLs for Landmarks."

Statutory Protection of Trademarks

Statutory protection of trademarks and related property is provided at the federal level by the Lanham Act of 1946.[1] The Lanham Act was enacted in part to protect manufacturers from losing business to rival companies that used confusingly similar trademarks. The Lanham Act incorporates the common law of trademarks and provides remedies for owners of trademarks who wish to enforce their claims in federal court. Many states also have trademark statutes.

Trademark Dilution In 1995, Congress amended the Lanham Act by passing the Federal Trademark Dilution Act,[2] which extended the protection available to trademark owners by allowing them to bring a suit in federal court for trademark *dilution*. Until the passage of this amendment, federal trademark law prohibited only the unauthorized use of the same mark on competing—or on noncompeting but "related"—goods or services when such use would likely confuse consumers as to the origin of those goods and services. Trademark dilution laws protect "distinctive" or "famous" trademarks (such as Jergens, McDonald's, Dell, and Apple) from certain unauthorized uses even when the use is on noncompeting goods or is unlikely to confuse. More than half of the states have also enacted trademark dilution laws.

Use of a Similar Mark May Constitute Trademark Dilution A famous mark may be diluted not only by the use of an *identical* mark but also by the use of a *similar* mark provided that it reduces the value of the famous mark. A similar

---

1. 15 U.S.C. Sections 1051–1128.
2. 15 U.S.C. Section 1125.

mark is more likely to lessen the value of a famous mark when the companies using the marks provide related goods or compete against each other in the same market. EXAMPLE #1 A woman was operating a coffee shop under the name "Sambuck's Coffeehouse" in Astoria, Oregon, even though she knew that "Starbucks" was one of the largest coffee chains in the nation. When Starbucks Corporation filed a dilution lawsuit, the federal court ruled that use of the "Sambuck's" mark constituted trademark dilution because it created confusion for consumers. Not only was there a "high degree" of similarity between the marks, but also both companies provided coffee-related services and marketed their services through "stand-alone" retail stores. Therefore, the use of the similar mark (Sambuck's) reduced the value of the famous mark (Starbucks).[3] □

Note that to establish dilution, it is required that the plaintiff show that the similar (and allegedly infringing) mark actually reduces the value of the famous mark. EXAMPLE #2 Well-known lingerie maker Victoria's Secret brought a trademark dilution action against "Victor's Little Secret," a small retail store that sold adult videos, lingerie, and other items. Although the lower courts granted Victoria's Secret an injunction prohibiting the adult store from using a similar mark, the United States Supreme Court reversed the decision. According to the Court, the likelihood of dilution is not enough to establish dilution. The plaintiff must present some evidence that the allegedly infringing user's mark actually reduces the value of the famous mark or lessens its capacity to identify goods and services.[4] □

Trademark Registration

Trademarks may be registered with the state or with the federal government. To register for protection under federal trademark law, a person must file an application with the U.S. Patent and Trademark Office in Washington, D.C. Under present law, a mark can be registered (1) if it is currently in commerce or (2) if the applicant intends to put the mark into commerce within six months.

In special circumstances, the six-month period can be extended by thirty months, giving the applicant a total of three years from the date of notice of trademark approval to make use of the mark and file the required use statement. Registration is postponed until the mark is actually used. Nonetheless, during this waiting period, any applicant can legally protect his or her trademark against a third party who previously has neither used the mark nor filed an application for it. Registration is renewable between the fifth and sixth years after the initial registration and every ten years thereafter (every twenty years for trademarks registered before 1990).

Various billboards and neon signs in New York City's Times Square. Why are trademarks protected by the law? (Rusty Haskell/Creative Commons)

---

3. *Starbucks Corp. v. Lundberg*, 2005 WL 3183858 (D.Or. 2005).
4. *Moseley v. V Secret Catalogue, Inc.*, 537 U.S. 418, 123 S.Ct. 1115, 155 L.Ed.2d 1 (2003). (A different case involving Victoria's Secret's trademark is presented as Case 8.2 on pages 242–243.)

Trademark Infringement

Registration of a trademark with the U.S. Patent and Trademark Office gives notice on a nationwide basis that the trademark belongs exclusively to the registrant. The registrant is also allowed to use the symbol ® to indicate that the mark has been registered. Whenever that trademark is copied to a substantial degree or used in its entirety by another, intentionally or unintentionally, the trademark has been *infringed* (used without authorization). When a trademark has been infringed, the owner has a cause of action against the infringer. To succeed in a trademark infringement action, the owner must show that the defendant's use of the mark created a likelihood of confusion about the origin of the defendant's goods or services. The owner need not prove that the infringer acted intentionally or that the trademark was registered (although registration does provide proof of the date of inception of the trademark's use).

The purple and orange colors displayed on FedEx envelopes, packets, and delivery vehicles, including this airplane, are a distinctive feature of that company. If a start-up company specializing in courier delivery services used those same colors, would the new company be infringing on FedEx's trademark?
(Adrian Pingstone/Wikipedia Commons)

The most commonly granted remedy for trademark infringement is an injunction to prevent further infringement. Under the Lanham Act, a trademark owner that successfully proves infringement can recover actual damages, plus the profits that the infringer wrongfully received from the unauthorized use of the mark. A court can also order the destruction of any goods bearing the unauthorized trademark. In some situations, the trademark owner may also be able to recover attorneys' fees.

A central objective of the Lanham Act is to reduce the likelihood that consumers will be confused by similar marks. For that reason, only those trademarks that are deemed sufficiently distinct from all competing trademarks will be protected.

Distinctiveness of Mark

A trademark must be sufficiently distinctive to enable consumers to identify the manufacturer of the goods easily and to distinguish between those goods and competing products.

Strong Marks Fanciful, arbitrary, or suggestive trademarks are generally considered to be the most distinctive (strongest) trademarks because they are normally taken from outside the context of the particular product and thus provide the best means of distinguishing one product from another.

EXAMPLE #3 Fanciful trademarks include invented words, such as "Xerox" for one manufacturer's copiers and "Kodak" for another company's photographic products. Arbitrary trademarks use common words in a fictitious or arbitrary manner to create a distinctive mark that identifies the source of the product, such as "Dutch Boy" as a name on a can of paint. Suggestive trademarks suggest something about a product without describing the product directly. For instance, "Dairy Queen" suggests an association between its products and milk, but it does not directly describe ice cream.□

Secondary Meaning Descriptive terms, geographic terms, and personal names are not inherently distinctive and do not receive protection under the law *until* they acquire a secondary meaning. A secondary meaning may arise when customers begin to associate a specific term or phrase, such as "London Fog," with specific trademarked items (coats with "London Fog" labels). Whether a secondary meaning becomes attached to a term or name usually depends on how extensively the product is advertised, the market for the product, the number of sales, and other factors. The United States Supreme Court has held that even a color can qualify for trademark protection.[5] Once a secondary meaning is attached to a term or name, a trademark is considered distinctive and is protected. In one recent case, a federal court ruled that trademark law protects the particular color schemes used by four state university sports teams, including Ohio State University and Louisiana State University.[6]

At issue in the following case was whether a certain mark was suggestive or descriptive.

---

5. *Qualitex Co. v. Jacobson Products Co.,* 514 U.S. 159, 115 S.Ct. 1300, 131 L.Ed.2d 248 (1995).
6. *Board of Supervisors of LA State University v. Smack Apparel Co.,* 438 F.Supp.2d 653 (E.D.La. 2006).

Case 8.2   **Menashe v. V Secret Catalogue, Inc.**

United States District Court,
Southern District of New York,
409 F.Supp.2d 412 2006.

BACKGROUND AND FACTS   In autumn 2002, Victoria's Secret Stores, Inc., and its affiliated companies, including V Secret Catalogue, Inc., began to develop a panty collection to be named "SEXY LITTLE THINGS." In spring 2004, Ronit Menashe, a publicist, and Audrey Quock, a fashion model and actress, began to plan a line of women's underwear also called "SEXY LITTLE THINGS." Menashe and Quock designed their line, negotiated for its manufacture, registered the domain name **www.sexylittlethings.com**, and filed an intent-to-use (ITU) application with the U.S. Patent and

Trademark Office (USPTO). Meanwhile, in July 2004, Victoria's Secret's collection appeared in its stores in Ohio, Michigan, and California and, in less than three months, was prominently displayed in all its stores, in its catalogues, and on its Web site. By mid-November, more than 13 million units of the line had been sold, accounting for 4 percent of the company's sales for the year. When the firm applied to register "SEXY LITTLE THINGS" with the USPTO, it learned of Menashe and Quock's ITU application. The firm warned the pair that their use of the phrase constituted trademark infringement. Menashe and Quock filed a suit in a federal district court against V Secret Catalogue and others, asking the court to, among other things, declare "noninfringement of the trademark."

IN THE WORDS OF THE COURT . . . *BAER,* **District Judge.**

*   *   *   *

Plaintiffs claim that Victoria's Secret has no right of priority in the Mark because "SEXY LITTLE THINGS" for lingerie is a descriptive term that had not attained secondary meaning by the time Plaintiffs filed their ITU application. Consequently, Plaintiffs assert that they have priority based on *   *   * their ITU application on September 13, 2004. Victoria's Secret counters that the Mark is suggestive and thus qualifies for trademark protection without proof of secondary meaning. Therefore, Victoria's Secret has priority by virtue of its *bona fide* use of the Mark in commerce beginning July 28, 2004.

*   *   *   *

To merit trademark protection, a mark must be capable of distinguishing the products it marks from those of others. *   *   * A descriptive term *   *   * conveys an immediate idea of the ingredients, qualities or characteristics of the goods. In contrast, a suggestive term requires imagination, thought and perception to reach a conclusion as to the nature of the goods. *Suggestive marks are automatically protected because they are inherently distinctive, i.e., their intrinsic nature serves to identify a particular source of a* *product.* Descriptive marks are not inherently distinctive and may only be protected on a showing of secondary meaning, i.e., that the purchasing public associates the mark with a particular source. [Emphasis added.]

* * * To distinguish suggestive from descriptive marks [a court considers] whether the purchaser must use some imagination to connect the mark to some characteristic of the product * * * and * * * whether the proposed use would deprive competitors of a way to describe their goods.

* * * I find "SEXY LITTLE THINGS" to be suggestive. First, while the term describes the erotically stimulating quality of the trademarked lingerie, it also calls to mind the phrase "sexy little thing" popularly used to refer to attractive lithe young women. Hence, the Mark prompts the purchaser to mentally associate the lingerie with its targeted twenty- to thirty-year-old consumers. *Courts have classified marks that both describe the product and evoke other associations as inherently distinctive.* * * * [Also] it is hard to believe that Victoria's Secret's use of the Mark will deprive competitors of ways to describe their lingerie products. Indeed, Victoria's Secret's own descriptions of its lingerie in its catalogues and Web site illustrate that there are numerous ways to describe provocative underwear. [Emphasis added.]

* * * *

* * * Victoria's Secret used "SEXY LITTLE THINGS" as a trademark in commerce beginning on July 28, 2004. Commencing on that date, the prominent use of the Mark in four stores * * * satisfies the "use in commerce" requirement * * * . Similarly, Victoria's Secret's prominent use of the Mark in its catalogues beginning on September 4, 2004, and on its Web site beginning on or about September 9, 2004, together with pictures and descriptions of the goods meets the * * * test * * * . I find that because Victoria's Secret made *bona fide* trademark use of "SEXY LITTLE THINGS" in commerce before Plaintiffs filed their ITU application, and has continued to use that Mark in commerce, Victoria's Secret has acquired priority in the Mark.

DECISION AND REMEDY   The district court ruled that Menashe and Quock were not entitled to a judgment of noninfringement and dismissed their complaint. The court concluded that "SEXY LITTLE THINGS" was a suggestive mark and that Victoria's Secret had used it in commerce before the plaintiffs filed their ITU application. For this reason, Victoria's Secret had "priority in the Mark."

THE E-COMMERCE DIMENSION   Under the reasoning of the court in this case, would the use of a purported trademark solely on a Web site satisfy the "use in commerce" requirement? Explain.

WHY IS THIS CASE IMPORTANT?   This case is notable for the court's characterization of the plaintiffs' suit as "defensive." ITU applicants may defend against other parties' claims of infringement, but they do not have the right to charge others with infringement. In this case, however, the court allowed Menashe and Quock to preemptively defend themselves against Victoria's Secret's efforts to stop the use of the "SEXY LITTLE THINGS" mark.

Generic Terms   Generic terms are terms that refer to an entire class of products, such as *bicycle* and *computer*. Generic terms receive no protection, even if they acquire secondary meanings. A particularly thorny problem arises when a trademark acquires generic use. For instance, *aspirin* and *thermos* were originally trademarked products, but today the words are used generically. Other examples are *escalator, trampoline, raisin bran, dry ice, lanolin, linoleum, nylon,* and *corn flakes*.

Note that a generic term will not be protected under trademark law even if the term has acquired a secondary meaning. **EXAMPLE #4** In one case, America

Online, Inc. (AOL), sued AT&T Corporation, claiming that AT&T's use of "You Have Mail" on its WorldNet Service infringed AOL's trademark rights in the same phrase. The court ruled, however, that because each of the three words in the phrase was a generic term, the phrase as a whole was generic. Although the phrase had become widely associated with AOL's e-mail notification service, and thus may have acquired a secondary meaning, this issue was of no significance in this case. The court stated that it would not consider whether the mark had acquired any secondary meaning because "generic marks with secondary meaning are still not entitled to protection."[7]□

Service, Certification, and Collective Marks

A **service mark** is essentially a trademark that is used to distinguish the services (rather than the products) of one person or company from those of another. For instance, each airline has a particular mark or symbol associated with its name. Titles and character names used in radio and television are frequently registered as service marks.

Other marks protected by law include certification marks and collective marks. A **certification mark** is used by one or more persons, other than the owner, to certify the region, materials, mode of manufacture, quality, or other characteristic of specific goods or services. **EXAMPLE #5** Certification marks include such marks as "Good Housekeeping Seal of Approval" and "UL Tested."□ When used by members of a cooperative, association, union, or other organization, a certification mark is referred to as a **collective mark.** **EXAMPLE #6** Collective marks appear at the ends of the credits of movies to indicate the various associations and organizations that participated in making the movie. The union marks found on the tags of certain products are also collective marks.□

Trade Dress

The term **trade dress** refers to the image and overall appearance of a product. Trade dress is a broad concept and can include either all or part of the total image or overall impression created by a product or its packaging. **EXAMPLE #7** The distinctive decor, menu, layout, and style of service of a particular restaurant may be regarded as the restaurant's trade dress. Similarly, trade dress can include the layout and appearance of a mail-order catalogue, the use of a lighthouse as part of the design of a golf hole, the fish shape of a cracker, or the G-shaped design of a Gucci watch.□

Basically, trade dress is subject to the same protection as trademarks. In cases involving trade dress infringement, as in trademark infringement cases, a major consideration is whether consumers are likely to be confused by the allegedly infringing use.

Counterfeit Goods

Counterfeit goods copy or otherwise imitate trademarked goods but are not genuine. The importation of goods that bear a counterfeit (fake) trademark poses a growing problem for U.S. businesses, consumers, and law enforcement. In addition to having negative financial effects on legitimate businesses, sales of certain counterfeit goods, such as pharmaceuticals and nutritional supplements, can

---

SERVICE MARK
A mark used in the sale or the advertising of services to distinguish the services of one person or company from those of others. Titles, character names, and other distinctive features of radio and television programs may be registered as service marks.

CERTIFICATION MARK
A mark used by one or more persons, other than the owner, to certify the region, materials, mode of manufacture, quality, or other characteristic of specific goods or services.

COLLECTIVE MARK
A mark used by members of a cooperative, association, union, or other organization to certify the region, materials, mode of manufacture, quality, or other characteristic of specific goods or services.

TRADE DRESS
The image and overall appearance of a product—for example, the distinctive decor, menu, layout, and style of service of a particular restaurant. Basically, trade dress is subject to the same protection as trademarks.

A UL certification mark. How does a certification mark differ from a trademark?

---

7. *America Online, Inc. v. AT&T Corp.,* 243 F.3d 812 (4th Cir. 2001).

present serious public health risks. It is estimated that nearly 7 percent of the goods imported into the United States from abroad are counterfeit.

Stop Counterfeiting in Manufactured Goods Act   In 2006, Congress enacted the Stop Counterfeiting in Manufactured Goods Act[8] (SCMGA) to combat the growing problem of counterfeit goods. The act makes it a crime to intentionally traffic in or attempt to traffic in counterfeit goods or services, or to knowingly use a counterfeit mark on or in connection with goods or services. Prior to this act, the law did not prohibit the creation or shipment of counterfeit labels that were not attached to any product.[9] Therefore, counterfeiters would make labels and packaging bearing another's trademark, ship the labels to another location, and then affix them to an inferior product to deceive buyers. The SCMGA has closed this loophole by making it a crime to knowingly traffic in or attempt to traffic in counterfeit labels, stickers, packaging, and the like, regardless of whether the item is attached to any goods.

Penalties for Counterfeiting   Persons found guilty of violating the SCMGA may be fined up to $2 million or imprisoned for up to ten years (or more if they are repeat offenders). If a court finds that the statute was violated, it must order the defendant to forfeit the counterfeit products (which are then destroyed), as well as any property used in the commission of the crime. The defendant must also pay restitution to the trademark holder or victim in an amount equal to the victim's actual loss. **EXAMPLE #8** In one case, the defendant pleaded guilty to conspiring with others to import cigarette-rolling papers from Mexico that were falsely marked as "Zig-Zags" and sell them in the United States. The court sentenced the defendant to prison and ordered him to pay $566,267 in restitution. On appeal, the court affirmed the prison sentence but reversed the restitution because the amount exceeded the actual loss suffered by the legitimate sellers of Zig-Zag rolling papers.[10] □

Trade Names

Trademarks apply to *products*. The term **trade name** is used to indicate part or all of a business's name, whether the business is a sole proprietorship, a partnership, or a corporation. Generally, a trade name is directly related to a business and its goodwill. Trade names may be protected as trademarks if the trade name is the same as the name of the company's trademarked product—for example, Coca-Cola. Unless also used as a trademark or service mark, a trade name cannot be registered with the federal government. Trade names are protected under the common law, however. As with trademarks, words must be unusual or fancifully used if they are to be protected as trade names. The word *Safeway*, for instance, is sufficiently fanciful to obtain protection as a trade name for a grocery chain.

TRADE NAME
A term that is used to indicate part or all of a business's name and that is directly related to the business's reputation and goodwill. Trade names are protected under the common law (and under trademark law, if the name is the same as that of the firm's trademarked product).

CYBER MARKS

In cyberspace, trademarks are sometimes referred to as **cyber marks.** We turn now to a discussion of trademark-related issues in cyberspace and how new laws and the courts are addressing these issues. One concern relates to the rights of a

CYBER MARK
A trademark in cyberspace.

---

8. Pub. L. No. 109-181 (2006), which amended 18 U.S.C. Sections 2318–2320.

9. See, for example, *United States v. Giles*, 213 F.3d 1247 (10th Cir. 2000).

10. For a case discussing the appropriate measure of restitution, see *United States v. Beydoun*, 469 F.3d 102 (5th Cir. 2006).

trademark's owner to use the mark as part of a domain name (Internet address). Other issues have to do with cybersquatting, meta tags, and trademark dilution on the Web. In some instances, licensing can be a way to avoid liability for infringing on another's intellectual property rights in cyberspace.

Domain Names

Conflicts over rights to domain names first emerged as e-commerce expanded on a worldwide scale and have reemerged in the last ten years. By using the same, or a similar, domain name, parties have attempted to profit from the goodwill of a competitor, sell pornography, offer for sale another party's domain name, and otherwise infringe on others' trademarks. A **domain name** is the core part of an Internet address—for example, "westlaw.com." It includes at least two parts. Every domain name ends with a generic top level domain (TLD), which is the part of the name to the right of the period. The TLD typically indicates the type of entity that operates the site. For example, *com* is an abbreviation for *commercial,* and *edu* is short for *education.* Although originally there were only six possible TLDs, several more generic TLDs are now available, some of which are not restricted to a particular type of entity (see Exhibit 8–2 for a list of generic TLDs and their uses).

    The second level domain (SLD), which is the part of the name to the left of the period, is chosen by the business entity or individual registering the domain name. Competition among firms with similar names and products for SLDs has caused numerous disputes over domain name rights. The Internet Corporation for Assigned Names and Numbers (ICANN), a nonprofit corporation, oversees the distribution of domain names. ICANN also facilitates the settlement of domain name disputes and operates an online arbitration system. Due to the vast number of complaints and disputes over domain names in the recent past, ICANN has completely overhauled the domain name distribution system and started selling domain names under the new system in mid-2009. One of the goals of the new system is to alleviate the problem of *cybersquatting.* **Cybersquatting** occurs when a person registers a domain name that is the same as, or confusingly similar to, the trademark of another and then offers to sell the domain name back to the trademark owner.

Anticybersquatting Legislation

During the 1990s, cybersquatting led to so much litigation that Congress passed the Anticybersquatting Consumer Protection Act of 1999[11] (ACPA), which amended the Lanham Act—the federal law protecting trademarks discussed earlier. The ACPA makes it illegal for a person to "register, traffic in, or use" a domain name (1) if the name is identical or confusingly similar to the trademark of another and (2) if the one registering, trafficking in, or using the domain name has a "bad faith intent" to profit from that trademark.

    The act does not define what constitutes bad faith. Instead, it lists several factors that courts can consider in deciding whether bad faith exists. Typically, courts focus on the trademark rights of the other person and whether the alleged cybersquatter intended to divert consumers in a way that could harm the goodwill represented by the trademark. Courts also consider whether the alleged cybersquatter offered to transfer or sell the domain name to the trademark owner, or intended to use the domain name to offer goods and services.

DOMAIN NAME
The last part of an Internet address, such as "westlaw.com." The top level (the part of the name to the right of the period) indicates the type of entity that operates the site ("com" is an abbreviation for "commercial"). The second level (the part of the name to the left of the period) is chosen by the entity.

CYBERSQUATTING
The act of registering a domain name that is the same as, or confusingly similar to, the trademark of another and then offering to sell that domain name back to the trademark owner.

---

11. 15 U.S.C. Section 1129.

EXHIBIT 8-2 EXISTING GENERIC TOP LEVEL DOMAIN NAMES

.aero	Reserved for members of the air-transportation industry.
.asia	Restricted to the Pan-Asia and Asia Pacific community.
.biz	For businesses.
.cat	Reserved for the Catalan linguistic and cultural community.
.com	Originally intended for commercial organizations, but is now unrestricted in the United States.
.coop	Restricted to cooperative associations.
.edu	For postsecondary educational establishments.
.gov	Reserved for government agencies in the United States.
.info	For informational sites, but is unrestricted.
.int	Reserved for international organizations established by treaty.
.jobs	Reserved for human resource managers.
.mil	For the U.S. military.
.mobi	Reserved for consumers and providers of mobile products and services.
.museum	Reserved for museums.
.name	Reserved for individuals and families.
.net	Originally intended for network infrastructures, but is now unrestricted.
.org	Originally intended for noncommercial organizations, but is now unrestricted.
.pro	Restricted to certain credentialed professionals.
.tel	For business services involving connections between a telephone network and the Internet.
.travel	Reserved for the travel industry.

The Ongoing Problem of Cybersquatting   The ACPA was intended to stamp out cybersquatting, but it continues to present a problem for businesses today, largely because, as mentioned, more TLDs are available and many more companies are registering domain names. Indeed, domain name registrars have proliferated. These companies charge a fee to businesses and individuals to register new names and to renew annual registrations (often through automated software). Many of these companies also buy and sell expired domain names. Although all domain name registrars are supposed to relay information about these transactions to ICANN and the other companies that keep a master list of domain names, this does not always occur. The speed at which domain names change hands and the difficulty in tracking mass automated registrations have created an environment in which cybersquatting can flourish.

Cybersquatters have also developed new tactics, such as typosquatting, or registering a name that is a misspelling of a popular brand, such as hotmai.com or myspac.com. Because many Internet users are not perfect typists, Web pages using these misspelled names get a lot of traffic. More traffic generally means increased profit (advertisers often pay Web sites based on the number of unique visits, or hits), which in turn provides incentive for more cybersquatters. Also, if the misspelling is significant, the trademark owner may have difficulty proving that the name is identical or confusingly similar to the trademark of another, as the ACPA requires.

Cybersquatting is costly for businesses, which must attempt to register all variations of a name to protect their domain name rights from would-be cybersquatters. Large corporations may have to register thousands of domain names across the globe just to protect their basic brands and trademarks.

Applicability of the ACPA and Sanctions under the Act   The ACPA applies to all domain name registrations. Successful plaintiffs in suits brought under the act can collect actual damages and profits, or they can elect to receive statutory damages ranging from $1,000 to $100,000.

Although some companies have been successful suing under the ACPA, there are roadblocks to succeeding in such lawsuits. Some domain name registrars offer privacy services that hide the true owners of Web sites, making it difficult for trademark owners to identify cybersquatters. Thus, before a trademark owner can bring a suit, he or she has to ask the court for a subpoena to discover the identity of the owner of the infringing Web site. Because of the high costs of court proceedings, discovery, and even arbitration, many disputes over cybersquatting are settled out of court. Some companies have found that simply purchasing the domain name from the cybersquatter is the least expensive solution.

Meta Tags

Search engines compile their results by looking through a Web site's key-word field. *Meta tags,* or key words (see Chapter 4 on page 115), may be inserted into this field to increase the likelihood that a site will be included in search engine results, even though the site may have nothing to do with the inserted words. Using this same technique, one site may appropriate the key words of other sites with more frequent hits so that the appropriating site appears in the same search engine results as the more popular sites. Using another's trademark in a meta tag without the owner's permission, however, normally constitutes trademark infringement.

Some uses of another's trademark as a meta tag may be permissible if the use is reasonably necessary and does not suggest that the owner authorized or sponsored the use. **EXAMPLE #9** Terri Welles, a former model who had been "Playmate of the Year" in *Playboy* magazine, established a Web site that used the terms *Playboy* and *Playmate* as meta tags. Playboy Enterprises, Inc., which publishes *Playboy,* filed suit seeking to prevent Welles from using these meta tags. The court determined that Welles's use of Playboy's meta tags to direct users to her Web site was permissible because it did not suggest sponsorship and there were no descriptive substitutes for the terms *Playboy* and *Playmate*.[12] ∎

Dilution in the Online World

As discussed earlier, trademark *dilution* occurs when a trademark is used, without authorization, in a way that diminishes the distinctive quality of the mark. Unlike a claim of trademark infringement, a claim of dilution does not require proof that consumers are likely to be confused by a connection between the unauthorized use and the mark. For this reason, the products involved do not have to be similar. In the first case alleging dilution on the Web, a court precluded the use of "candyland.com" as the URL for an adult site. The suit was brought by the maker of the Candyland children's game and owner of the Candyland mark. Although consumers were not likely to connect candyland.com with the children's game, the court reasoned that the sexually explicit adult site would dilute the value of the Candyland mark.[13]

---

12. *Playboy Enterprises, Inc. v. Welles,* 279 F.3d 796 (9th Cir. 2002).
13. *Hasbro, Inc. v. Internet Entertainment Group, Ltd.,* 1996 WL 84858 (W.D.Wash. 1996).

Licensing

One of the ways to make use of another's trademark or other form of intellectual property, while avoiding litigation, is to obtain a license to do so. A **license** in this context is essentially an agreement permitting the use of a trademark, copyright, patent, or trade secret for certain limited purposes. The party that owns the intellectual property rights and issues the license is the *licensor,* and the party obtaining the license is the *licensee.* A license grants only the rights expressly described in the license agreement. A licensor might, for example, allow the licensee to use the trademark as part of its company name, or as part of its domain name, but not otherwise use the mark on any products or services.

Note, however, that under modern law a licensor of a trademark has a duty to maintain some form of control over the nature and quality of goods or services sold under the mark. If the license does not include any provisions to protect the quality of goods or services provided under the trademark, then the courts may conclude that the licensor has abandoned the trademark and lost her or his trademark rights. To avoid such problems, licensing agreements normally include detailed provisions that protect the trademark owners' rights.

Typically, license agreements are very detailed and should be carefully drafted. Disputes frequently arise over licensing agreements. **EXAMPLE #10** Perry Ellis's products are well known in the apparel industry for their style, quality, and workmanship. Perry Ellis International, Inc. (PEI), owns a family of registered trademarks, including "Perry Ellis America" (the PEA trademark). The PEA trademark is distinctive and known worldwide as a mark of quality goods. In 2006, PEI entered into a license agreement with URI Corporation, which gave URI an exclusive license to manufacture and distribute footwear using the PEA trademark in the territory of Mexico. URI was required to comply with numerous conditions regarding the manufacturing and distribution of the licensed footwear and agreed to sell the shoes only in certain (listed) high-quality stores. URI was not permitted to authorize any other party to use the PEA trademark. Despite this explicit licensing agreement, PEI discovered that footwear bearing its PEA trademark was being sold in discount stores in Mexico. PEI terminated the licensing agreement and filed a lawsuit in a federal district court against URI. Ultimately, PEI was awarded more than $1 million in damages in the case.[14] □

LICENSE
In the context of intellectual property law, an agreement permitting the use of a trademark, copyright, patent, or trade secret for certain limited purposes.

Preventing Legal Disputes

To avoid litigation, anyone signing a licensing contract should consult with an attorney to make sure that the specific wording in the contract is very clear as to what rights are or are not being conveyed. Moreover, to prevent misunderstandings over the scope of the rights being acquired, the licensee should determine whether any other parties hold licenses to use that particular intellectual property and the extent of those rights. ▣

PATENTS

A **patent** is a grant from the government that gives an inventor the exclusive right to make, use, and sell an invention for a period of twenty years from the date of filing the application for a patent. Patents for designs, as opposed to inventions, are given for a fourteen-year period. For either a regular patent or a

PATENT
A government grant that gives an inventor the exclusive right or privilege to make, use, or sell his or her invention for a limited time period.

---

14. *Perry Ellis International, Inc. v. URI Corp.,* 2007 WL 3047143 (S.D.Fla. 2007).

design patent, the applicant must demonstrate to the satisfaction of the U.S. Patent and Trademark Office that the invention, discovery, process, or design is *novel, useful,* and *not obvious* in light of current technology.

In contrast to patent law in many other countries, in the United States the first person to invent a product or process gets the patent rights rather than the first person to file for a patent on that product or process. Because it is difficult to prove who invented an item first, however, the first person to file an application is often deemed the first to invent (unless the inventor has detailed research notes or other evidence showing the date of invention). An inventor can publish the invention or offer it for sale prior to filing a patent application but must apply for a patent within one year of doing so or forfeit the patent rights. The period of patent protection begins on the date the patent application was filed, rather than when it was issued, which can sometimes be years later. After the patent period ends (either fourteen or twenty years later), the product or process enters the public domain, and anyone can make, sell, or use the invention without paying the patent holder.

Searchable Patent Databases

A significant development relating to patents is the availability online of the world's patent databases. The Web site of the U.S. Patent and Trademark Office provides searchable databases covering U.S. patents granted since 1976. The Web site of the European Patent Office provides online access to fifty million patent documents in more than seventy nations through a searchable network of databases. (The URLs for both Web sites are provided in the *Interacting with the Internet* section at the end of this chapter). Businesses use these searchable databases in many ways. Because patents are valuable assets, businesses may need to perform patent searches to list or inventory their assets. Patent searches may also be conducted to study trends and patterns in a specific technology or to gather information about competitors in the industry. In addition, a business might search patent databases to develop a business strategy in a particular market or to evaluate a job applicant's contributions to a technology. Although online databases are accessible to anyone, businesspersons might consider hiring a specialist to perform advanced patent searches.

What Is Patentable?

Under federal law, "[w]hoever invents or discovers any new and useful process, machine, manufacture, or composition of matter, or any new and useful improvement thereof, may obtain a patent therefor, subject to the conditions and requirements of this title."[15] Thus, to be patentable, the item must be novel and not obvious.

Almost anything is patentable, except (1) the laws of nature,[16] (2) natural phenomena, and (3) abstract ideas (including algorithms[17]). Even artistic meth-

---

15. 35 U.S.C. 101.

16. Note that in 2006, several justices of the United States Supreme Court indicated that they believed a process to diagnose vitamin deficiencies should not be patentable, because allowing a patent would improperly give a monopoly over a scientific relationship, or law of nature. Nevertheless, the majority of the Supreme Court allowed the patent to stand. *Laboratory Corporation of America Holdings v. Metabolite Laboratories, Inc.*, 548 U.S. 124, 126 S.Ct. 2921, 165 L.Ed.2d 399 (2006).

17. An *algorithm* is a step-by-step procedure, formula, or set of instructions for accomplishing a specific task—such as the set of rules used by a search engine to rank the listings contained within its index in response to a particular query.

ods, certain works of art, and the structure of storylines are patentable, provided that they are novel and not obvious. Plants that are reproduced asexually (by means other than from seed), such as hybrid or genetically engineered plants, are patentable in the United States, as are genetically engineered (or cloned) microorganisms and animals.

Is it an abuse of patent law for a company to sue farmers whose crops were accidentally contaminated by genetically modified seed? For a discussion of this issue, see the *Insight into Ethics* feature that follows.

Insight into Ethics

Patent law and the seed police

Monsanto, Inc., has been selling genetically modified (GM) seeds to farmers in the United States and throughout the world as a way to achieve higher yields using fewer pesticides. Monsanto requires farmers who buy GM seeds to sign licensing agreements promising to plant the seeds for only one crop and to pay a technology fee for each acre planted. To ensure that the farmers comply with the restrictions, Monsanto has set aside $10 million a year and a staff of seventy-five individuals to investigate and prosecute farmers who use the GM seeds illegally. If the company receives an anonymous tip about a farmer, it sends its "seed police" to investigate, take samples from the farmer's field for testing, interview neighbors, and even conduct surveillance of the farmer's family and operation.

Even Genetically Modified Seeds Reproduce Like Ordinary Seeds

The problem is that the patented GM seeds, like ordinary seeds, reproduce if they are scattered by the wind or transferred on farm equipment. Thus, they can contaminate neighboring fields. Consider, for example, the situation faced by a Canadian canola farmer, Percy Schmeiser. Schmeiser had not purchased any GM seeds or signed any licensing agreement, but on investigation Monsanto found that some of his crop contained evidence of a Monsanto genetic trait. Schmeiser refused to pay royalties to Monsanto because he had not planted any GM seeds. It turned out that Schmeiser's crop had been contaminated with the GM seed, likely by seed escaping from passing trucks. Nevertheless, the Canadian Supreme Court ruled that Schmeiser had committed patent infringement and ordered him to destroy the crops containing evidence of the patented seed.[18]

Schmeiser's plight is not unusual. Monsanto has filed more than ninety lawsuits against nearly 150 farmers in the United States and has been awarded more than $15 million in damages (not including out-of-court settlement amounts).[19] Farmers claim that Monsanto has acted unethically by intimidating them and threatening to pursue them in court for years if they refuse to settle out of court by paying royalties.

Seed Police Use Questionable Tactics

Farmers complain that the seed police secretly videotape and photograph farmers, seed dealers, store owners, and co-ops. Monsanto's agents have reportedly infiltrated community meetings and used informants to obtain information about farming activities. Sometimes, Monsanto agents have pretended to be surveyors. Other times, the agents confront farmers on their land and try to pressure them to sign papers giving Monsanto access to their private records. Farmers use words such as *Gestapo* and *Mafia* to describe the tactics used by Monsanto's seed police.

---

18. *Monsanto Canada, Inc. v. Schmeiser,* 1 S.C.R. 902, 2004 SCC 34 (CanLII). Note that in contrast to most cases in the United States, the Canadian court did not award damages for the infringement and only ordered Schmeiser to stop the infringing activity.

19. See, for example, *Monsanto Co. v. Scruggs,* 459 F.3d 1328 (2006); *Monsanto Co. v. McFarling,* 2005 WL 1490051 (E.D.Mo. 2005); and *Sample v. Monsanto Co.,* 283 F.Supp.2d 1088 (2003).

In the following case, the focus was on the application of the test for proving whether a patent claim is "obvious."

Case 8.3   KSR International Co. v. Teleflex, Inc.

Supreme Court of the United States, 2007.
__ U.S. __, 127 S.Ct. 1727, 167 L.Ed.2d 705.

BACKGROUND AND FACTS   Teleflex, Inc., sued KSR International for patent infringement. Teleflex holds the exclusive license to a patent for a device developed by Steven J. Engelgau. The patent issued is entitled "Adjustable Pedal with Electronic Throttle Control." In brief, the Engelgau patent combines an electronic sensor with an adjustable automobile pedal so that the pedal's position can be transmitted to a computer that controls the throttle in the vehicle's engine. KSR contended that the patent in question could not create a claim because the subject matter was obvious. The district court concluded that the Engelgau patent was invalid because it was obvious—several existing patents (including patents held by Rixon and Smith) already covered all of the important aspects of electronic pedal sensors for computer-controlled throttles. On appeal, the U.S. Court of Appeals for the Federal Circuit reversed the district court ruling. KSR International appealed to the United States Supreme Court.

IN THE WORDS OF THE COURT . . . Justice *KENNEDY* delivered the opinion of the Court.

*   *   *   *

Seeking to resolve the question of obviousness with *   *   * uniformity and consistency, [the courts have] employed an approach referred to by the parties as the "teaching, suggestion, or motivation" test (TSM test), under which a patent claim is only proved obvious if some motivation or suggestion to combine the prior art teachings can be found in the prior art, the nature of the problem, or the knowledge of a person having ordinary skill in the art. KSR challenges that test, or at least its application in this case.

*   *   *   *

*   *   * The District Court [also] held KSR had satisfied the [TSM] test. It reasoned (1) the state of the industry would lead inevitably to combinations of electronic sensors and adjustable pedals, (2) Rixon [a prior patent] provided the basis for these developments, and (3) Smith [another existing patent] taught a solution to the wire chafing problems in Rixon, namely locating the sensor on the fixed structure of the pedal.

*   *   *   *

*   *   * [The U.S.] Court of Appeals [for the Federal Circuit] reversed.

*   *   *   *

We begin by rejecting the rigid approach of the Court of Appeals. Throughout this Court's engagement with the question of obviousness, our cases have set forth an expansive and flexible approach inconsistent with the way the Court of Appeals applied its TSM test here.

*   *   * *For over a half century, the Court has held that a patent for a combination which only unites old elements with no change in their respective functions* *   *   * *obviously withdraws what is already known into the field of its monopoly and diminishes the resources available to skillful [persons].* [Emphasis added.]

*   *   *   *

*   *   * If a technique has been used to improve one device, and a person of ordinary skill in the art would recognize that it would improve similar devices in the same way, using the technique is obvious unless its actual application is beyond his or her skill.

DECISION AND REMEDY   The United States Supreme Court reversed the judgment of the court of appeals and the case was remanded. The Court reasoned that there was little difference between what existed in the "teachings" of previously filed patents and the adjustable electronic pedal disclosed in the Engelgau patent.

THE LEGAL ENVIRONMENT DIMENSION If a person of ordinary skill can implement a predictable variation of another's patented invention, does the Court's opinion indicate that the new variation is likely not to be patentable? Explain.

THE ETHICAL DIMENSION Based on the Court's reasoning, what other factors should be considered when determining the obviousness of a patent?

Patents for Software At one time, it was difficult for developers and manufacturers of software to obtain patent protection because many software products simply automate procedures that can be performed manually. In other words, it was thought that computer programs did not meet the "novel" and "not obvious" requirements previously mentioned. Also, the basis for software is often a mathematical equation or formula, which is not patentable. In 1981, however, the United States Supreme Court held that it is possible to obtain a patent for a *process* that incorporates a computer program—providing, of course, that the process itself is patentable.[18] Subsequently, many patents have been issued for software-related inventions. EXAMPLE #11 Garmin Corporation and TomTom, Inc., are competitors in the manufacturing and selling of global positioning systems (GPSs). Both Garmin and TomTom hold multiple patents on software used in vehicle navigation devices. (In fact, these two companies became involved in litigation over their respective patents on navigation software in 2006).[19] □

Patents for Business Processes In 1998, in a landmark case, *State Street Bank & Trust Co. v. Signature Financial Group, Inc.,*[20] the U.S. Court of Appeals for the Federal Circuit ruled that business processes are patentable. After this decision, numerous technology firms applied for business process patents. Walker Digital applied for a business process patent for its "Dutch auction" system, which allowed consumers to make offers for airline tickets on the Internet and led to the creation of Priceline.com. Amazon.com obtained a business process patent for its "one-click" ordering system, a method of processing credit-card orders securely. Indeed, after the *State Street* decision, the number of Internet-related patents issued by the U.S. Patent and Trademark Office initially increased dramatically.

Patent Infringement

If a firm makes, uses, or sells another's patented design, product, or process without the patent owner's permission, the tort of patent infringement occurs. Patent infringement may arise even though the patent owner has not put the patented product into commerce. Patent infringement may also occur even though not all features or parts of a product are identical to those used in the patented invention, provided that the features are equivalent. (With respect to a patented process, however, all steps or their equivalent must be copied for infringement to exist.)

Note that, as a general rule, under U.S. law no patent infringement occurs when a patented product is made and sold in another country. EXAMPLE #12 In

---

18. *Diamond v. Diehr,* 450 U.S. 175, 101 S.Ct. 1048, 67 L.Ed.2d 155 (1981).
19. *Garmin Ltd. v. TomTom, Inc.,* 468 F.Supp.2d 988 (W.D.Wis. 2006).
20. 149 F.3d 1368 (Fed.Cir. 1998).

2007, this issue came before the United States Supreme Court in a patent infringement case that AT&T Corporation had brought against Microsoft Corporation. AT&T holds a patent on a device used to digitally encode, compress, and process recorded speech. Microsoft's Windows operating system, as Microsoft admitted, incorporated software code that infringed on AT&T's patent. The only question before the Supreme Court was whether Microsoft's liability extended to computers made in another country. The Court held that it did not. Microsoft was liable only for infringement in the United States and not for the Windows-based computers sold in foreign locations. The Court reasoned that Microsoft had not "supplied" the software for the computers but had only electronically transmitted a master copy, which the foreign manufacturers then copied and loaded onto the computers.[21] ◻

Remedies for Patent Infringement

If a patent is infringed, the patent holder may sue for relief in federal court. The patent holder can seek an injunction against the infringer and can also request damages for royalties and lost profits. In some cases, the court may grant the winning party reimbursement for attorneys' fees and costs. If the court determines that the infringement was willful, the court can triple the amount of damages awarded (treble damages).

In the past, permanent injunctions were routinely granted to prevent future infringement. In 2006, however, the United States Supreme Court ruled that patent holders are not automatically entitled to a permanent injunction against future infringing activities—the federal courts have discretion to decide whether equity requires it. According to the Supreme Court, a patent holder must prove that it has suffered irreparable injury and that the public interest would not be disserved by a permanent injunction.[22]

This decision gives courts discretion to decide what is equitable in the circumstances and allows them to consider what is in the public interest rather than just the interests of the parties. For example, in the first case applying this rule, a court found that although Microsoft had infringed on the patent of a small software company, the latter was not entitled to an injunction. According to the court, the small company had not been irreparably harmed and could be adequately compensated by damages. Also, the public might suffer negative effects from an injunction because the infringement involved part of Microsoft's widely used Office suite software.[23]

Preventing Legal Disputes

Litigation over whether a patent has been infringed is typically expensive and often requires a team of experts to investigate and analyze the commercial, technical, and legal aspects of the case. Because of these costs, a businessperson facing patent infringement litigation—either as the patent holder or as the alleged infringer—should carefully evaluate the evidence as well as the various settlement options. If both sides appear to have good arguments as to whether the patent was infringed or whether it was valid, it may be in a firm's best interest to settle the case. This is

---

21. *Microsoft Corp. v. AT&T Corp.,* ___ U.S. ___, 127 S.Ct. 1746, 167 L.Ed.2d 737 (2007).

22. *eBay, Inc. v. MercExchange, LLC,* 547 U.S. 388, 126 S.Ct. 1837, 164 L.Ed.2d 641 (2006).

23. *Z4 Technologies, Inc. v. Microsoft Corp.,* 434 F.Supp.2d 437 (2006). See also *Printguard, Inc. v. Anti-Marking Systems, Inc.,* 535 F.Supp.2d 189 (D.Mass. 2008).

particularly true if the firm is not certain that the court would grant an injunction. Similarly, if the patented technology is not commercially significant to one's business, it might be best to consider a nonexclusive license as a means of resolving the dispute. This option is more important for patent holders now that injunctions may be harder to obtain. Settlement may be as simple as an agreement that one party will stop making, using, or selling the patented product or process, or it may involve monetary compensation for past activities and/or licensing for future activities. ■

COPYRIGHTS

A **copyright** is an intangible property right granted by federal statute to the author or originator of certain literary or artistic productions. Currently, copyrights are governed by the Copyright Act of 1976,[24] as amended. Works created after January 1, 1978, are automatically given statutory copyright protection for the life of the author plus 70 years. For copyrights owned by publishing houses, the copyright expires 95 years from the date of publication or 120 years from the date of creation, whichever is first. For works by more than one author, the copyright expires 70 years after the death of the last surviving author.

These time periods reflect the extensions of the length of copyright protection enacted by Congress in the Copyright Term Extension Act of 1998.[25] Critics challenged this act as overstepping the bounds of Congress's power and violating the constitutional requirement that copyrights endure for only a limited time. In 2003, however, the United States Supreme Court upheld the act in *Eldred v. Ashcroft*.[26] This ruling obviously favored copyright holders by preventing copyrighted works from the 1920s and 1930s from losing protection and falling into the public domain for an additional two decades.

Copyrights can be registered with the U.S. Copyright Office in Washington, D.C. A copyright owner no longer needs to place a © or *Copr.* or *Copyright* on the work, however, to have the work protected against infringement. Chances are that if somebody created it, somebody owns it.

> **COPYRIGHT**
> The exclusive right of an author or originator of a literary or artistic production to publish, print, or sell that production for a statutory period of time. A copyright has the same monopolistic nature as a patent or trademark, but it differs in that it applies exclusively to works of art, literature, and other works of authorship (including computer programs).

What Is Protected Expression?

Works that are copyrightable include books, records, films, artworks, architectural plans, menus, music videos, product packaging, and computer software. To be protected, a work must be "fixed in a durable medium" from which it can be perceived, reproduced, or communicated. Protection is automatic. Registration is not required.

To obtain protection under the Copyright Act, a work must be original and fall into one of the following categories:

1. Literary works (including newspaper and magazine articles, computer and training manuals, catalogues, brochures, and print advertisements).
2. Musical works and accompanying words (including advertising jingles).
3. Dramatic works and accompanying music.
4. Pantomimes and choreographic works (including ballets and other forms of dance).

> **BE CAREFUL**
> If a creative work does not fall into a certain category, it may not be copyrighted, but it may be protected by other intellectual property law.

---

24. 17 U.S.C. Sections 101 *et seq.*
25. 17 U.S.C.A. Section 302.
26. 537 U.S. 186, 123 S.Ct. 769, 154 L.Ed.2d 683 (2003).

A sign in New York City warns audience members about to attend an improvisational theatrical performance. Can a live performance, especially one that is improvisational in nature, be copyrighted?
(Photo Courtesy of Percy Schmeiser)

5. Pictorial, graphic, and sculptural works (including cartoons, maps, posters, statues, and even stuffed animals).
6. Motion pictures and other audiovisual works (including multimedia works).
7. Sound recordings.
8. Architectural works.

Section 102 Exclusions Section 102 of the Copyright Act specifically excludes copyright protection for any "idea, procedure, process, system, method of operation, concept, principle, or discovery, regardless of the form in which it is described, explained, illustrated, or embodied." Note that it is not possible to copyright an *idea*. The underlying ideas embodied in a work may be freely used by others. What is copyrightable is the particular way in which an idea is *expressed*. Whenever an idea and an expression are inseparable, the expression cannot be copyrighted. Generally, anything that is not an original expression will not qualify for copyright protection. Facts widely known to the public are not copyrightable. Page numbers are not copyrightable because they follow a sequence known to everyone. Mathematical calculations are not copyrightable.

Compilations of Facts Unlike ideas, *compilations* of facts are copyrightable. Under Section 103 of the Copyright Act, a compilation is "a work formed by the collection and assembling of preexisting materials or of data that are selected, coordinated, or arranged in such a way that the resulting work as a whole constitutes an original work of authorship." The key requirement for the copyrightability of a compilation is originality. EXAMPLE #13 The white pages of a telephone directory do not qualify for copyright protection when the information that makes up the directory (names, addresses, and telephone numbers) is not selected, coordinated, or arranged in an original way. The Yellow Pages of a telephone directory, in contrast, can qualify for copyright protection. Similarly, a compilation of information about yachts listed for sale may qualify for copyright protection.[27] ▫

Copyright Infringement

Whenever the form or expression of an idea is copied, an infringement of copyright occurs. The reproduction does not have to be exactly the same as the original, nor does it have to reproduce the original in its entirety. If a substantial part of the original is reproduced, there is copyright infringement.

Damages for Copyright Infringement Those who infringe copyrights may be liable for damages or criminal penalties. These range from actual damages or statutory damages, imposed at the court's discretion, to criminal proceedings for willful violations. Actual damages are based on the harm caused to the copyright holder by the infringement, while statutory damages, not to exceed $150,000, are provided for under the Copyright Act. In addition, criminal proceedings may result in fines and/or imprisonment.

The "Fair Use" Exception An exception to liability for copyright infringement is made under the "fair use" doctrine. In certain circumstances, a person or organization can reproduce copyrighted material without paying royalties (fees paid to the copyright holder for the privilege of reproducing the copyrighted material). Section 107 of the Copyright Act provides as follows:

27. *BUC International Corp. v. International Yacht Council, Ltd.*, 489 F.3d 1129 (11th Cir. 2007).

[T]he fair use of a copyrighted work, including such use by reproduction in copies or phonorecords or by any other means specified by [Section 106 of the Copyright Act,] for purposes such as criticism, comment, news reporting, teaching (including multiple copies for classroom use), scholarship, or research, is not an infringement of copyright. In determining whether the use made of a work in any particular case is a fair use, the factors to be considered shall include—

(1) the purpose and character of the use, including whether such use is of a commercial nature or is for nonprofit educational purposes;
(2) the nature of the copyrighted work;
(3) the amount and substantiality of the portion used in relation to the copyrighted work as a whole; and
(4) the effect of the use upon the potential market for or value of the copyrighted work.

Because these guidelines are very broad, the courts determine whether a particular use is fair on a case-by-case basis. Thus, anyone reproducing copyrighted material may be committing a violation. In determining whether a use is fair, courts have often considered the fourth factor to be the most important.

In the following case, the owner of copyrighted music had issued a license to the manufacturer of karaoke devices to reproduce the sound recordings, but had not given its permission to reprint the song lyrics. The issue was whether the manufacturer should pay additional fees to display the lyrics at the same time as the music was playing. The manufacturer claimed, in part, that its use of the lyrics was educational and therefore did not constitute copyright infringement under the fair use exception.

Case 8.4 Leadsinger, Inc. v. BMG Music Publishing

United States Court of Appeals,
Ninth Circuit, 2008.
512 F.3d 522.
www.ca9.uscourts.gov [a]

BACKGROUND AND FACTS Leadsinger, Inc., manufactures and sells karaoke devices. Specifically, it sells a microphone that has a chip inside with embedded songs and lyrics that appear at the bottom of a TV screen. This device is similar to those in which compact discs and DVDs are inserted to display lyrics on a TV monitor. All karaoke devices necessarily involve copyrighted works. BMG Music Publishing owns and administers copyrights for such music. BMG had issued to Leadsinger the appropriate licenses to copyrighted musical compositions under Section 115 of the Copyright Act. Leadsinger sought a declaration that it was entitled to print or display song lyrics in real time with song recordings without paying any additional fees. In contrast, BMG demanded that Leadsinger and other karaoke companies pay a "lyric reprint" fee and a "synchronization" fee. Leadsinger refused to pay, filing for a declaratory judgment to resolve whether it had the right to display song lyrics in real time with sound recordings without paying any additional fees. The district court concluded that a Section 115 license did not grant Leadsinger the right to display visual images and lyrics in real time with music. Leadsinger appealed to the U.S. Court of Appeals for the Ninth Circuit.

a. Click on "Opinions." When that page opens, select "2008" and then "January." Scroll down to "01/02/08." Find the case name and click on it to access the opinion.

IN THE WORDS OF THE COURT . . . *SMITH, M.D.,* C.J. Circuit Judge.

* * * *

In deciding whether the district court properly dismissed Leadsinger's complaint, we are guided by the language of the Copyright Act. Section 102 of the Copyright Act extends copyright protection to, among other original works of authorship, literary works, musical works (including any accompanying words), and sound recordings.

CASE 8.4–CONTINUED

CASE 8.4–CONTINUED Though Section 106 grants copyright owners the exclusive right to reproduce copy-righted works "in copies or phonorecords" and to "distribute copies or phonorecords of the copyrighted work to the public by sale," [Section 115] limits copyright owners' exclusive rights with respect to phonorecords.

* * * *

* * * Though it is not explicit in the Copyright Act, courts have recognized a copyright holder's right to control the synchronization of musical compositions with the content of audiovisual works and have required parties to obtain synchronization licenses from copyright holders.

* * * Song lyrics are copyrightable as a literary work and, therefore, enjoy sepa-rate protection under the Copyright Act.

* * * *

The district court reasoned that Leadsinger's device falls outside of the definition of phonorecord because the device contains more than sounds. * * * While it is true that the microchip in Leadsinger's device stores visual images and visual representa-tions of lyrics in addition to sounds, the plain language of the Copyright Act does not expressly preclude a finding that devices on which sounds *and* visual images are fixed fall within the definition of phonorecords. The definition of phonorecords is explicit, however, that audiovisual works are not phonorecords and are excluded from Section 115's compulsory licensing scheme. We need not settle upon a precise interpretation of Section 101's definition of phonorecords in this case because Leadsinger's karaoke device meets each element of the statutory definition of audiovisual works and, there-fore, cannot be a phonorecord.

* * * *

We hold that Leadsinger's device falls within the definition of an audiovisual work. As a result, in addition to any Section 115 compulsory licenses necessary to make and distribute phonorecords and reprint licenses necessary to reprint song lyrics, Leadsinger is also required to secure synchronization licenses to display images of song lyrics in timed relation with recorded music. [Emphasis added.]

* * * *

The Copyright Act does not grant a copyright holder exclusive rights to reproduce his or her work. Section 107 of the Copyright Act explains that "the fair use of a copy-righted work .   .   . for purposes such as criticism, comment, news reporting, teach-ing .   .   . , scholarship, or research, is not an infringement of copyright."

* * * *

* * * While Leadsinger argued on appeal that karaoke teaches singing, that alle-gation is not set forth in its complaint. Even if the court could infer that a karaoke device has the potential to teach singing because the device allows consumers to sing along with recorded music, it is not reasonable to infer that teaching is actually the purpose of Leadsinger's use of the copyrighted lyrics.

* * * *

* * * Leadsinger's basic purpose remains a commercial one—to sell its karaoke device for profit. And *commercial use of copyrighted material is "presumptively an unfair exploitation of the monopoly privilege that belongs to the owner of the copyright."* [Emphasis added.]

* * * *

We have * * * concluded that Leadsinger's use is intended for commercial gain, and it is well accepted that when "the intended use is for commercial gain," the like-lihood of market harm "may be presumed." We have not hesitated to apply this pre-sumption in the past, and we are not reluctant to apply it here. Moreover, "the importance of [the market effect] factor [varies], not only with the amount of harm, but also with the relative strength of the showing on the other factors." The showing on all other factors under Section 107 is strong: the purpose and character of Leadsinger's use is commercial; song lyrics fall within the core of copyright protection; and Leadsinger uses song lyrics in their entirety. On this basis, we affirm the district court's dismissal of Leadsinger's request for a declaration based on the fair use doctrine.

DECISION AND REMEDY The U.S. Court of Appeals for the Ninth Circuit affirmed the district court's decision to dismiss Leadsinger's complaint without the possibility of amending it.

THE GLOBAL DIMENSION Could Leadsinger have attempted to show that its karaoke programs were used extensively abroad to help others learn English? If successful in this line of reasoning, might Leadsinger have prevailed on appeal? Explain your answer.

THE LEGAL ENVIRONMENT DIMENSION What was the underlying basis of Leadsinger's attempt to avoid paying additional licensing fees to BMG?

Copyright Protection for Software

In 1980, Congress passed the Computer Software Copyright Act, which amended the Copyright Act of 1976 to include computer programs in the list of creative works protected by federal copyright law.[28] The 1980 statute, which classifies computer programs as "literary works," defines a computer program as a "set of statements or instructions to be used directly or indirectly in a computer in order to bring about a certain result."

Because of the unique nature of computer programs, the courts have had many problems applying and interpreting the 1980 act. Generally, though, the courts have held that copyright protection extends not only to those parts of a computer program that can be read by humans, such as the high-level language of a source code, but also to the binary-language object code of a computer program, which is readable only by the computer. Additionally, such elements as the overall structure, sequence, and organization of a program have been deemed copyrightable. The courts have disagreed as to whether the "look and feel"—the general appearance, command structure, video images, menus, windows, and other screen displays—of computer programs should also be protected by copyright. The courts have tended, however, not to extend copyright protection to look-and-feel aspects of computer programs.

Copyrights in Digital Information

Copyright law is the most important form of intellectual property protection on the Internet. This is because much of the material on the Internet consists of works of authorship (including multimedia presentations, software, and database information), which are the traditional focus of copyright law. Copyright law is also important because the nature of the Internet requires that data be "copied" to be transferred online. Copies have traditionally been a significant part of the controversies arising in this area of the law. (See this chapter's *Online Developments* feature on page 260 for a discussion of how blogs and podcasts can expose a company to legal risks, including lawsuits for copyright infringement.)

The Copyright Act of 1976 When Congress drafted the principal U.S. law governing copyrights, the Copyright Act of 1976, cyberspace did not exist for most of us. At that time, the primary threat to copyright owners was from persons making unauthorized *tangible* copies of works. Because of the nature of

---

28. Pub. L. No. 96-517 (1980), amending 17 U.S.C. Sections 101, 117.

Companies increasingly are using blogs (Web logs) and podcasts (essentially audio blogs, sometimes with video clips) internally to encourage communication among employees and externally to communicate with customers. Blogs offer many advantages, not the least of which is that setting up a blog and keeping it current (making "posts") costs next to nothing because so much easy-to-use free software is available. Podcasts, even those including video, require only a little more sophistication. Nonetheless, both blogs and podcasts also carry some legal risks for the companies that sponsor them.

Benefits of Blogs and Podcasts

Internal blogs used by a company's employees can offer a number of benefits. Blogs provide an open communications platform, potentially allowing new ways of coordinating activities among employees. For example, a team of production workers might use a blog to move a new product idea forward: the team starts a blog, one worker posts a proposal, and other team members quickly post comments in response. The blog can be an excellent way to generate new ideas. Internal blogs also allow for team learning and encourage dialogue. When workers are spread out across the country or around the world, blogging provides a cheap means of communication that does not require sophisticated project management software.

Many companies are also creating external blogs, which are available to clients and customers. External blogs can be used to promote products, obtain feedback from customers, and shape the image that the company presents to outsiders. Even some company chief executive officers (CEOs), including the CEOs of McDonald's, Boeing, and Hewlett-Packard, have started blogs.

Potential Legal Risks

Despite their many advantages, blogs and podcasts can also expose a company to a number of legal risks, including the following.

- **Tort Liability** Internal blogs and podcasts can lead to claims of defamation or sexual harassment if an employee posts racist or sexually explicit comments. At the same time, if a company monitors its employees' blogs and podcasts, it may find itself facing claims of invasion of privacy (see Chapter 17 for a discussion of similar issues involving employees' e-mail).
- **Security of Information** Blogs may also be susceptible to security breaches. If an outsider obtains access to an internal blog, a company's trade secrets could be lost.

Outsiders could also potentially gain access to blogs containing financial information.

- **Discovery Issues** As explained in Chapter 3, litigation today frequently involves electronic discovery. This can extend to blog posts and comments as well as to e-mail. Thus, a company should be aware that anything posted on its blogs can be used as evidence during litigation. A company will therefore need to preserve and retain blog postings related to any dispute likely to go to trial.
- **Compliance Issues** Many corporations are regulated by one or more agencies and are required to comply with various statutes. Laws that require compliance may also apply to blog postings. For example, the Securities and Exchange Commission (SEC) has regulations establishing the information a company must disclose to potential investors and the public in connection with its stock (see Chapter 24). A company regulated by the SEC will find that these rules apply to blogs. The same is true for companies regulated under the Sarbanes-Oxley Act (discussed in Chapters 2 and 15).
- **Copyright Infringement** Blogs can also expose a company to charges of copyright infringement. Suppose, for example, that an employee posts a long passage from a magazine article on the company's blog without the author's permission. Neither written material of this kind nor photos taken from other blogs or Web sites can be posted without prior permission. Note that copyright infringement can occur even if the blog was created without any pecuniary (monetary) motivation. Typically, though, a blogger can claim "fair use" if she or he posts a passage from someone else's work along with an electronic link to the complete version.

External blogs carry most of the same risks as internal blogs. Not only can external blogs lead to charges of invasion of privacy, defamation, or copyright infringement related to what the company and its employees post, but they can also expose the company to liability for what visitors post. If a company's blog allows visitors to post comments and a visitor makes a defamatory statement, the company that created the blog could be held liable for publishing it. Thus, any company considering establishing blogs and podcasts, whether internal or external, should be aware of the risks and take steps to guard against them.

FOR CRITICAL ANALYSIS Do individuals who create blogs face the same risks as companies that use blogs? Explain.

cyberspace, however, one of the early controversies was determining at what point an intangible, electronic "copy" of a work has been made. The courts held that loading a file or program into a computer's random access memory, or RAM, constitutes the making of a "copy" for purposes of copyright law. RAM is a portion of a computer's memory into which a file, for instance, is loaded so that it can be accessed (read or written over). Thus, a copyright is infringed when a party downloads software into RAM without owning the software or otherwise having a right to download it.

Today, technology has vastly increased the potential for copyright infringement. **EXAMPLE #14** Bridgeport Music, Inc., and Westbound Records, Inc., own the composition and recording copyrights to "Get Off Your Ass and Jam" by George Clinton, Jr., and the Funkadelics. "Get Off" opens with a three-note solo guitar riff that lasts four seconds. The rap song "100 Miles and Runnin'" contains a two-second sample from the song's guitar solo, at a lower pitch, looped and repeated several times. When a film company distributed a movie that included "100 Miles" in its sound track, Bridgeport brought an action for copyright infringement. A federal appellate court held that digitally sampling a copyrighted sound recording of any length (even as little as two seconds) without permission constitutes copyright infringement.[29] □

Further Developments in Copyright Law Prior to 1997, criminal penalties under copyright law could be imposed only if unauthorized copies were exchanged for financial gain. Yet much piracy of copyrighted materials was "altruistic" in nature; unauthorized copies were made and distributed not for financial gain but simply for reasons of generosity—to share the copies with others.

To combat altruistic piracy and for other reasons, Congress passed the No Electronic Theft (NET) Act of 1997.[30] This act extends criminal liability for the piracy of copyrighted materials to persons who exchange unauthorized copies of copyrighted works, such as software, even though they realize no profit from the exchange. The act also imposes penalties on those who make unauthorized electronic copies of books, magazines, movies, or music for personal use, thus altering the traditional "fair use" doctrine. The criminal penalties for violating the act are steep; they include fines as high as $250,000 and incarceration for up to five years.

In 1998, Congress passed further legislation to protect copyright holders—the Digital Millennium Copyright Act.[31] Because of its significance in protecting against the piracy of copyrighted materials online, this act is presented as this chapter's *Landmark in the Legal Environment* feature on page 262.

MP3 and File-Sharing Technology

Soon after the Internet became popular, a few enterprising programmers created software to compress large data files, particularly those associated with music. The reduced file sizes make transmitting music over the Internet feasible. The most widely known compression and decompression system is MP3, which enables music fans to download songs or entire CDs onto their computers or onto a portable listening device, such as an iPod. The MP3 system also made it

---

29. *Bridgeport Music, Inc. v. Dimension Films*, 410 F.3d 792 (2005).
30. 17 U.S.C. Sections 2311, 2319, 2319A, 2320, and 28 U.S.C. Sections 994 and 1498.
31. 17 U.S.C. Sections 512, 1204–1205, 1301–1332, and 28 U.S.C. Section 4001.

...

The United States leads the world in the production of creative products, including books, films, videos, recordings, and software. In fact, as indicated earlier in this chapter, the creative industries are more important to the U.S. economy than the traditional product industries are. Exports of U.S. creative products, for example, surpass those of every other U.S. industry in value. Creative industries are growing at nearly three times the rate of the economy as a whole.

Steps have been taken, both nationally and internationally, to protect ownership rights in intellectual property, including copyrights. In 1996, to curb unauthorized copying of copyrighted materials, the World Intellectual Property Organization (WIPO) enacted a treaty to upgrade global standards of copyright protection, particularly for the Internet.

Implementing the WIPO Treaty

In 1998, Congress implemented the provisions of the WIPO treaty by updating U.S. copyright law. The law—the Digital Millennium Copyright Act of 1998—is a landmark step in the protection of copyright owners and, because of the leading position of the United States in the creative industries, serves as a model for other nations. Among other things, the act established civil and criminal penalties for anyone who circumvents (bypasses, or gets around—through clever maneuvering, for example) encryption software or other technological antipiracy protection. Also prohibited are the manufacture, import, sale, and distribution of devices or services for circumvention.

The act provides for exceptions to fit the needs of libraries, scientists, universities, and others. In general, the law does not restrict the "fair use" of circumvention methods for educational and other noncommercial purposes. For example, circumvention is allowed to test computer security, conduct encryption research, protect personal privacy, and enable parents to monitor their children's use of the Internet. The exceptions are to be reconsidered every three years.

Limiting the Liability of Internet Service Providers

The 1998 act also limited the liability of Internet service providers (ISPs). Under the act, an ISP is not liable for any copyright infringement by its customer unless the ISP is aware of the subscriber's violation. An ISP may be held liable only if it fails to take action to shut the subscriber down after learning of the violation. A copyright holder has to act promptly, however, by pursuing a claim in court, or the subscriber has the right to be restored to online access.

APPLICATION TO TODAY'S LEGAL ENVIRONMENT

The application of the Digital Millennium Copyright Act of 1998 to today's world is fairly self-evident. If Congress had not enacted this legislation, copyright owners would have a far more difficult time obtaining legal redress against those who, without authorization, decrypt or copy copyrighted materials. Of course, problems remain, particularly because of the global nature of the Internet. From a practical standpoint, the degree of protection afforded to copyright holders depends on the extent to which other nations that have signed the WIPO treaty actually implement its provisions and agree on the interpretation of terms, such as what constitutes an electronic copy.

Critics of the 1998 act claim that it has not been used as Congress originally envisioned and that it has had the unintended consequences of chilling free speech and scientific research. In one case, for example, a Russian scientist was arrested after speaking at a conference in the United States because he had worked on a software program that enabled owners of Adobe e-books to convert the files to PDF format. The scientist, who was not charged with copyright infringement, was ultimately cleared of any wrongdoing, but the incident has prompted a number of foreign scientists to refuse to attend conferences in the United States. The incident also sparked an ongoing debate over whether the Digital Millennium Copyright Act should be repealed.

RELEVANT WEB SITES

To locate information on the Web concerning the Digital Millennium Copyright Act of 1998, go to this text's Web site at **www.cengage.com/blaw/let**, select "Chapter 8," and click on "URLs for Landmarks."

PEER-TO-PEER (P2P) NETWORKING
The sharing of resources (such as files, hard drives, and processing styles) among multiple computers without necessarily requiring a central network server.

DISTRIBUTED NETWORK
A network that can be used by persons located (distributed) around the country or the globe to share computer files.

possible for music fans to access other music fans' files by engaging in file-sharing via the Internet.

File-sharing via the Internet is accomplished through what is called **peer-to-peer (P2P) networking.** The concept is simple. Rather than going through a central Web server, P2P involves numerous personal computers (PCs) that are connected to the Internet. Files stored on one PC can be accessed by other individuals who are members of the same network. Sometimes this is called a **distributed network.** In other words, parts of the network are distributed all over the country or the world. File-sharing offers an unlimited number of uses for distributed networks. For instance, thousands of researchers allow their home computers' computing power to be simultaneously accessed through file-sharing software so that very large mathematical problems can be solved quickly. Additionally, persons scattered throughout the country or the world can work together on the same project by using file-sharing programs.

Sharing Stored Music Files   When file-sharing is used to download others' stored music files, copyright issues arise. Recording artists and their labels stand to lose large amounts of royalties and revenues if relatively few CDs are purchased and then made available on distributed networks, from which anyone can get them for free. The issue of file-sharing infringement has been the subject of an ongoing debate for some time.

EXAMPLE #15 In the highly publicized case of *A&M Records, Inc. v. Napster, Inc.*,[32] several firms in the recording industry sued Napster, Inc., the owner of the then-popular Napster Web site. The Napster site provided registered users with free software that enabled them to transfer exact copies of the contents of MP3 files from one computer to another via the Internet. Napster also maintained centralized search indices so that users could locate specific titles or artists' recordings on the computers of other members. The firms argued that Napster should be liable for contributory and vicarious[33] (indirect) copyright infringement because it assisted others in obtaining copies of copyrighted music without the copyright owners' permission. Both the federal district court and the U.S. Court of Appeals for the Ninth Circuit agreed and held Napster liable for violating copyright laws. The court reasoned that Napster was liable for its users' infringement because the technology that Napster had used was centralized and gave it "the ability to locate infringing material listed on its search indices and the right to terminate users' access to the system."□

After the *Napster* decision, the recording industry filed and won numerous lawsuits against companies that distribute online file-sharing software. The courts held these companies liable based on two theories: contributory infringement, which applies if the company had reason to know about a user's infringement and failed to stop it, and vicarious liability, which exists if the company was able to control the users' activities and stood to benefit financially from their infringement.

The Evolution of File-Sharing Technologies   In the wake of the *Napster* decision, other companies developed technologies that allow P2P network users to share stored music files, without paying a fee, more quickly and efficiently

DON'T GET SUED OR IMPRISONED:

You can't afford the long arm of the RIAA

Forewarned is Forearmed

Recently, the RIAA (Recording Industry Association of America) has been conducting comprehensive audits on university networks. The Information Technology Division warns students that those illegally downloading and/or distributing copyrighted music, videos, or other works are at a high risk of prosecution. You will be held personally liable for such illegal activities.

You will be held personally liable for such illegal activities.

AS A REMINDER:

· *It is illegal to make, use, or pass along unauthorized copies of software, graphics, music or any other creative art or intellectual property for multimedia projects or any other use. This includes the copying of software programs, etc., required in a class.*

· *Illegal file sharing of copyrighted materials over Texas Tech Networks is strictly prohibited.*

· *It is illegal for anyone to upload or download full-length sound recordings or DVDs without permission of the copyright owners.*

For more detailed information concerning copyright and related laws, please visit http://www.ttu.edu/safecomputing/ttu/riaa/ (eRaider username and password required).

Know the law, protect yourself.

TEXAS TECH UNIVERSITY
Information Technology Division

Texas Tech University sent a notice to its students warning them of the legal risks involved in sharing stored music files. What other types of electronic files do college students share? Might any of this other file-sharing violate copyright laws?

(Wesley Fryer/Creative Commons)

---

32. 239 F.3d 1004 (9th Cir. 2001).

33. *Vicarious (indirect) liability* exists when one person is subject to liability for another's actions. A common example occurs in the employment context when a business is held vicariously liable for torts committed by its employees in the course of their employment.

Will holding the companies that make file-sharing software legally responsible for the copyright infringement of their end users stifle innovation and technology, as these demonstrators suggest?
(Beatrice Murch/Creative Commons)

than ever. Software such as Morpheus, KaZaA, and LimeWire, for example, provides users with an interface that is similar to a Web browser.[34] Instead of the company's locating songs for users on other members' computers, the software automatically annotates files with descriptive information so that the music can easily be categorized and cross-referenced (by artist and title, for instance). When a user performs a search, the software is able to locate a list of peers that have the file available for downloading. Also, to expedite the P2P transfer, the software distributes the download task over the entire list of peers simultaneously. By downloading even one file, the user becomes a point of distribution for that file, which is then automatically shared with others on the network.

Because this type of file-sharing software was decentralized and did not use search indices that would enable the companies to locate infringing material, they had no ability to supervise or control which music (or other media files) their users exchanged. In addition, it was difficult for courts to apply the traditional doctrines of contributory and vicarious liability to these new technologies.

The Supreme Court's *Grokster* Decision   In 2005, the United States Supreme Court expanded the liability of file-sharing companies in its decision in *Metro-Goldwyn-Mayer Studios, Inc. v. Grokster, Ltd.*[35] In that case, organizations in the music and film industry (the plaintiffs) sued several companies that distribute file-sharing software used in P2P networks, including Grokster, Ltd., and StreamCast Networks, Inc. (the defendants). The plaintiffs claimed that the companies were contributorily and vicariously liable for the infringement of their end users. The Supreme Court held that "one who distributes a device [software] with the object of promoting its use to infringe the copyright, as shown by clear expression or other affirmative steps taken to foster infringement, is liable for the resulting acts of infringement by third parties."

Although the Supreme Court did not specify what kind of affirmative steps are necessary to establish liability, it did note that there was ample evidence that the defendants had acted with the intent to cause copyright violations. (Grokster later settled this dispute out of court and stopped distributing its software.) Essentially, this means that file-sharing companies that have taken affirmative steps to promote copyright infringement can be held secondarily liable for millions of infringing acts that their users commit daily. Because the Court did not define exactly what is necessary to impose liability, however, a substantial amount of legal uncertainty remains concerning this issue. Although some file-sharing companies have been shut down, illegal file-sharing—and lawsuits against file-sharing companies and the individuals who use them—has continued in the years since this decision.[36]

---

34. Note that in 2005, KaZaA entered a settlement agreement with four major music companies that had alleged copyright infringement. KaZaA agreed to offer only legitimate, fee-based music downloads in the future.

35. 545 U.S. 913, 125 S.Ct. 2764, 162 L.Ed.2d 781 (2005).

36. See, for example, *Sony BMG Music Entertainment v. Villarreal,* ___ F.Supp.2d___ (M.D.Ga. 2007).

TRADE SECRETS

The law of trade secrets protects some business processes and information that are not or cannot be patented, copyrighted, or trademarked against appropriation by a competitor. **Trade secrets** include customer lists, plans, research and development, pricing information, marketing techniques, production methods, and generally anything that makes an individual company unique and that would have value to a competitor.

Unlike copyright and trademark protection, protection of trade secrets extends both to ideas and to their expression. (For this reason, and because a trade secret involves no filing requirements, trade secret protection may be well suited for software.) Of course, the secret formula, method, or other information must be disclosed to some persons, particularly to key employees. Businesses generally attempt to protect their trade secrets by having all employees who use the process or information agree in their contracts, or in confidentiality agreements, never to divulge it. See the *Management Perspective* feature on the following page for more advice on how a business can protect its trade secrets.

TRADE SECRET
Information or a process that gives a business an advantage over competitors that do not know the information or process.

State and Federal Law on Trade Secrets

Under Section 757 of the *Restatement of Torts,* those who disclose or use another's trade secret, without authorization, are liable to that other party if (1) they discovered the secret by improper means or (2) their disclosure or use constitutes a breach of a duty owed to the other party. The theft of confidential business data by industrial espionage, as when a business taps into a competitor's computer, is a theft of trade secrets without any contractual violation and is actionable in itself.

Until nearly thirty years ago, virtually all law with respect to trade secrets was common law. In an effort to reduce the unpredictability of the common law in this area, a model act, the Uniform Trade Secrets Act, was presented to the states for adoption in 1979. Parts of this act have been adopted in more than thirty states. Typically, a state that has adopted parts of the act has adopted only those parts that encompass its own existing common law. Additionally, in 1996 Congress passed the Economic Espionage Act, which made the theft of trade secrets a federal crime (as discussed in Chapter 6 on page 178).

Trade Secrets in Cyberspace

The nature of computer technology undercuts a business firm's ability to protect its confidential information, including trade secrets. For instance, a dishonest employee could e-mail trade secrets in a company's computer to a competitor or a future employer. If e-mail is not an option, the employee might walk out with the information on a portable device, such as a flash drive.

INTERNATIONAL PROTECTION FOR INTELLECTUAL PROPERTY

For many years, the United States has been a party to various international agreements relating to intellectual property rights. For example, the Paris Convention of 1883, to which about 172 countries are signatory, allows parties in one country to file for patent and trademark protection in any of the other member countries. Other international agreements include the Berne Convention and the Trade-Related Aspects of Intellectual Property Rights, or, more simply, TRIPS

Management Faces a Legal Issue

Most successful businesses have trade secrets. The law protects trade secrets indefinitely provided that the information is not generally known, is kept secret, and has commercial value. Sometimes, of course, a business needs to disclose secret information to a party in the course of conducting business. For example, a company may need to engage a consultant to revamp a computer system or hire a marketing firm to implement a sales program. In addition, the company may also wish to expand its operations and will need a foreign agent or distributor. All of these individuals or firms may need access to some of the company's trade secrets. One way to protect against the unauthorized disclosure of such information is through *confidentiality agreements.* In such an agreement, one party promises not to divulge information about the other party's activities to anyone else and not to use the other party's confidential information for his or her own benefit. Most confidentiality agreements are included in licensing and employment contracts. The legal question is whether the courts will uphold such an agreement if a business claims it has been violated.

What the Courts Say

The courts are divided on the validity of confidentiality agreements, particularly in employment contracts. At issue is often whether the trade secrets described in the confidentiality agreement are truly "secrets." If they are generally known outside the employer's business, the courts normally will not enforce the agreement. When a clear argument can be made that such secrets are truly secret, a court normally will enforce a confidentiality agreement. For example, consider an insurance company. An employee signed both a confidentiality agreement and a *noncompete clause* (see Chapter 9). Just before quitting, that employee copied her employer's proprietary sales, marketing, and product information sheets. She then used them while working for her new employer. She also solicited former clients to move their business to her new employer's

firm. An appellate court upheld an injunction preventing this employee from using, divulging, disclosing, or communicating trade secrets and confidential information derived from her former employer.[a]

In the technology sector, confidentiality agreements are widespread for obvious reasons. One case involved a complicated system for testing flash memory cards, like those used in digital cameras and MP3 music players. An employee copied project documents he had authored and transmitted them to a third party for the purpose of using those documents to launch his own independent business. This employee had signed an explicit confidentiality agreement. At trial, one of his defenses was that his former employer had not used reasonable efforts to maintain secrecy because some employees were uncertain how to apply the company's procedures for handling confidential and trade-secret documents. The court was unimpressed. The former employee was prevented from using those trade secrets.[b]

Employers often attempt to protect trade secrets by requiring potential employees to sign noncompete agreements. If the employer would suffer irreparable harm from the former employee's accepting employment with a competitor, the court will often uphold such agreements.[c]

Implications for Managers

Most companies should require their employees to sign a confidentiality agreement to protect trade secrets. That is not enough, though. Written formal procedures should be created that apply to the selection and retention of documents that relate to valuable trade secrets. If these documents exist only on hard drives, encryption systems should be put in place, and access to the files that contain trade secrets should be limited.

a. *Freeman v. Brown Hiller, Inc.,* _____ S.W.3d _____, 2008 WL 868252 (Ark.App. 2008).
b. *Verigy US, Inc. v. Mayder,* _____ F.Supp.2d _____, 2008 WL 564634 (N.D.Cal. 2008).
c. *Gleeson v. Preferred Sourcing, LLC,* 883 N.E.2d 164 (Ind.App. 2008).

---

agreement. For a discussion of a treaty that allows a company to register its trademark in foreign nations with a single application, see this chapter's *Beyond Our Borders* feature.

The Berne Convention

Under the Berne Convention of 1886, an international copyright agreement, if a U.S. citizen writes a book, every country that has signed the convention must recognize the U.S. author's copyright in the book. Also, if a citizen of a country that has not signed the convention first publishes a book in one of the 170 countries that have signed, all other countries that have signed the convention must recognize that author's copyright. Copyright notice is not needed to gain protection under the Berne Convention for works published after March 1, 1989.

In the past, one of the difficulties in protecting U.S. trademarks internationally was the time and expense required to apply for trademark registration in foreign countries. The filing fees and procedures for trademark registration vary significantly among individual countries. The Madrid Protocol, which President George W. Bush signed into law in the fall of 2003, may help to resolve this problem. The Madrid Protocol is an international treaty that has been signed by sixty-eight countries. Under its provisions, a U.S. company wishing to register its trademark abroad can submit a single application and designate other member countries in which it would like to register the mark. The treaty is designed to reduce the costs of obtaining international trademark protection by more than 60 percent, according to proponents.

Although the Madrid Protocol may simplify and reduce the cost of trademark registration in foreign nations, it remains to be seen whether it will provide significant benefits to trademark owners. Even with an easier registration process, the issue of whether member countries will enforce the law and protect the mark still remains.

FOR CRITICAL ANALYSIS What are some of the pros and cons of having an international standard for trademark protection?

This convention and other international agreements have given some protection to intellectual property on a worldwide level. None of them, however, has been as significant and far reaching in scope as the agreement discussed next.

The TRIPS Agreement

Representatives from more than one hundred nations signed the TRIPS agreement in 1994. The agreement established, for the first time, standards for the international protection of intellectual property rights, including patents, trademarks, and copyrights for movies, computer programs, books, and music. The TRIPS agreement provides that each member country must include in its domestic laws broad intellectual property rights and effective remedies (including civil and criminal penalties) for violations of those rights.

Members Cannot Discriminate against Foreign Intellectual Property Owners Generally, the TRIPS agreement forbids member nations from discriminating against foreign owners of intellectual property rights (in the administration, regulation, or adjudication of such rights). In other words, a member nation cannot give its own nationals (citizens) favorable treatment without offering the same treatment to nationals of all member countries. **EXAMPLE #16** A U.S. software manufacturer brings a lawsuit in Germany for the infringement of intellectual property rights under Germany's national laws. Because Germany is a member nation, the U.S. manufacturer is entitled to receive the same treatment as a domestic manufacturer.□ Each member nation must also ensure that legal procedures are available for parties who wish to bring actions for infringement of intellectual property rights. Additionally, a related document established a mechanism for settling disputes among member nations.

Covers All Types of Intellectual Property Particular provisions of the TRIPS agreement

Despite the Chinese government's periodic crackdowns, imitation designer goods are openly sold at the Xiangyang Fashion Market in Shanghai. What agreement has been the most significant in the effort to protect intellectual property rights internationally? (Emily Walker/Creative Commons)

relate to patent, trademark, and copyright protection for intellectual property. The agreement specifically provides copyright protection for computer programs by stating that compilations of data, databases, or other materials are "intellectual creations" and that they are to be protected as copyrightable works. Other provisions relate to trade secrets and the rental of computer programs and cinematographic works.

Reviewing . . . Intellectual Property and Internet Law

Two computer science majors, Trent and Xavier, have an idea for a new video game, which they propose to call "Hallowed." They form a business and begin developing their idea. Several months later, Trent and Xavier run into a problem with their design and consult with a friend, Brad, who is an expert in creating computer source codes. After the software is completed but before Hallowed is marketed, a video game called Halo 2 is released for both the Xbox and Game Cube systems. Halo 2 uses source codes similar to those of Hallowed and imitates Hallowed's overall look and feel, although not all the features are alike. Using the information presented in the chapter, answer the following questions.

1. Would the name "Hallowed" receive protection as a trademark or as trade dress?

2. If Trent and Xavier had obtained a business process patent on Hallowed, would the release of Halo 2 infringe on their patent? Why or why not?

3. Based only on the facts described above, could Trent and Xavier sue the makers of Halo 2 for copyright infringement? Why or why not?

4. Suppose that Trent and Xavier discover that Brad took the idea of Hallowed and sold it to the company that produced Halo 2. Which type of intellectual property issue does this raise?

Key Terms

certification mark 244
collective mark 244
copyright 255
cyber mark 245
cybersquatting 246
distributed network 262

domain name 246
intellectual property 236
license 249
patent 249
peer-to-peer (P2P)
    networking 262

service mark 244
trade dress 244
trade name 245
trade secret 265
trademark 237

Chapter Summary

Trademarks and Related Property
(See pages 237–245.)

1. A *trademark* is a distinctive mark, motto, device, or emblem that a manufacturer stamps, prints, or otherwise affixes to the goods it produces so that they may be identified on the market and their origin vouched for.

2. The major federal statutes protecting trademarks and related property are the Lanham Act of 1946 and the Federal Trademark Dilution Act of 1995. Generally, to be protected, a trademark must be sufficiently distinct from all competing trademarks.

Trademarks and Related Property—Continued	3. *Trademark infringement* occurs when one uses a mark that is the same as, or confusingly similar to, the protected trademark, service mark, trade name, or trade dress of another without permission when marketing goods or services.
Cyber Marks (See pages 245–249.)	A *cyber mark* is a trademark in cyberspace. Trademark infringement in cyberspace occurs when one person uses, in a domain name or in meta tags, a name that is the same as, or confusingly similar to, the protected mark of another.
Patents (See pages 249–255.)	1. A *patent* is a grant from the government that gives an inventor the exclusive right to make, use, and sell an invention for a period of twenty years (fourteen years for a design patent) from the date of filing the application for a patent. To be patentable, an invention (or a discovery, process, or design) must be genuine, novel, useful, and not obvious in light of current technology. Computer software may be patented.
	2. Almost anything is patentable, except (1) the laws of nature, (2) natural phenomena, and (3) abstract ideas (including algorithms).
	3. *Patent infringement* occurs when one uses or sells another's patented design, product, or process without the patent owner's permission. The patent holder can sue the infringer in federal court and request an injunction, but must prove irreparable injury to obtain a permanent injunction against the infringer. The patent holder can also request damages and attorneys' fees; if the infringement was willful, the court can grant treble damages.
Copyrights (See pages 255–264.)	1. A *copyright* is an intangible property right granted by federal statute to the author or originator of certain literary or artistic productions. Computer software may be copyrighted.
	2. *Copyright infringement* occurs whenever the form or expression of an idea is copied without the permission of the copyright holder. An exception applies if the copying is deemed a "fair use."
	3. Copyrights are governed by the Copyright Act of 1976, as amended. To protect copyrights in digital information, Congress passed the No Electronic Theft Act of 1997 and the Digital Millennium Copyright Act of 1998.
	4. Technology that allows users to share files via the Internet on distributed networks often raises copyright infringement issues.
	5. The United States Supreme Court has ruled that companies that provide file-sharing software to users can be held liable for contributory and vicarious copyright liability if they take affirmative steps to promote copyright infringement.
Trade Secrets (See page 265.)	*Trade secrets* include customer lists, plans, research and development, and pricing information, for example. Trade secrets are protected under the common law and, in some states, under statutory law against misappropriation by competitors. The Economic Espionage Act of 1996 made the theft of trade secrets a federal crime (see Chapter 6).
International Protection for Intellectual Property (See pages 265–268.)	Various international agreements provide international protection for intellectual property. A landmark agreement is the 1994 agreement on Trade-Related Aspects of Intellectual Property Rights (TRIPS), which provides for enforcement procedures In all countries signatory to the agreement.

For Review

1 What is intellectual property?
2 Why are trademarks and patents protected by the law?
3 What laws protect authors' rights in the works they generate?
4 What are trade secrets, and what laws offer protection for this form of intellectual property?
5 What steps have been taken to protect intellectual property rights in today's digital age?

Questions and
Case Problems

8–1. Fair Use. Professor Wise is teaching a business torts class at State University. On several occasions, he makes copies of relevant sections from business law texts and distributes them to his students. Wise does not realize that the daughter of one of the textbook authors is in his class. She tells her father about Wise's copying activities, which have taken place without her father's or his publisher's permission. Her father sues Wise for copyright infringement. Wise claims protection under the fair use doctrine. Who will prevail? Explain.

Question with Sample Answer

8–2. In which of the following situations would a court likely hold Maruta liable for copyright infringement?

1. Maruta owns a video store. She purchases one copy of several popular movie DVDs from various distributors. Then, using blank DVDs, she burns copies of the movies to rent or sell to her customers.
2. Maruta teaches Latin American history at a small university. She has a DVR (digital video recorder) and frequently records television programs relating to Latin America. She then copies the programs to a DVD and takes them to her classroom so that her students can watch them.

For a sample answer to Question 8–2, go to Appendix I at the end of this text.

8–3. Domain Name Disputes. In 1999, Steve and Pierce Thumann and their father, Fred, created Spider Webs, Ltd., a partnership, to, according to Steve, "develop Internet address names." Spider Webs registered nearly two thousand Internet domain names at an average cost of $70 each, including the names of cities, the names of buildings, names related to a business or trade (such as air-conditioning or plumbing), and the names of famous companies. It offered many of the names for sale on its Web site and through eBay.com. Spider Webs registered the domain name "ERNESTANDJULIOGALLO.COM" in Spider Webs' name. E. & J. Gallo Winery filed a suit against Spider Webs, alleging, in part, violations of the Anticybersquatting Consumer Protection Act (ACPA). Gallo asked the court for, among other things, statutory damages. Gallo also sought to have the domain name at issue transferred to Gallo. During the suit, Spider Webs published anticorporate articles and negative opinions about Gallo, as well as discussions of the suit and of the risks associated with alcohol use, at the URL ERNESTANDJULIOGALLO.COM. Should the court rule in Gallo's favor? Why or why not? [*E. & J. Gallo Winery v. Spider Webs, Ltd.*, 129 F.Supp.2d 1033 (S.D.Tex. 2001)]

8–4. Patent Infringement. As a cattle rancher in Nebraska, Gerald Gohl used handheld searchlights to find and help calving animals (animals giving birth) in harsh blizzard conditions. Gohl thought that it would be more helpful to have a portable searchlight mounted on the outside of a vehicle and remotely controlled. He and Al Gebhardt developed and patented practical applications of this idea—the Golight and the wireless, remote-controlled Radio Ray, which could rotate 360 degrees—and formed Golight, Inc., to make and market these products. In 1997, Wal-Mart Stores, Inc., began selling a portable, wireless, remote-controlled searchlight that was identical to the Radio Ray except for a stop piece that prevented the light from rotating more than 351 degrees. Golight sent Wal-Mart a letter, claiming that its device infringed Golight's patent. Wal-Mart sold its remaining inventory of the devices and stopped carrying the product. Golight filed a suit in a federal district court against Wal-Mart, alleging patent infringement. How should the court rule? Explain. [*Golight, Inc. v. Wal-Mart Stores, Inc.*, 355 F.3d 1327 (Fed. Cir. 2004)]

8–5. Trade Dress. Gateway, Inc., sells computers, computer products, computer peripherals, and computer accessories throughout the world. By 1988, Gateway had begun its first national advertising campaign using black-and-white cows and black-and-white cow spots. By 1991, black-and-white cows and spots had become Gateway's symbol. The next year, Gateway registered a black-and-white cow-spots design in association with computers and computer peripherals as its trademark. Companion Products, Inc. (CPI), sells stuffed animals trademarked as "Stretch Pets." Stretch Pets have an animal's head and an elastic body that can wrap around the edges of computer monitors, computer cases, or televisions. CPI produces sixteen Stretch Pets, including a polar bear, a moose, several dogs, and a penguin. One of CPI's top-selling products is a black-and-white cow that CPI identifies as "Cody Cow," which was first sold in 1999. Gateway filed a suit in a federal district court against CPI, alleging trade dress infringement and related claims. What is trade dress? What is the major factor in cases involving trade dress infringement? Does that factor exist in this case? Explain. [*Gateway, Inc. v. Companion Products, Inc.*, 384 F.3d 503 (8th Cir. 2004)]

Case Problem with Sample Answer

8–6. Briefing.com offers Internet-based analyses of investment opportunities to investors. Richard Green is the company's president. One of Briefing.com's competitors is StreetAccount, LLC (limited liability company), whose owners include Gregory Jones and Cynthia

Dietzmann. Jones worked for Briefing.com for six years until he quit in March 2003, and he was a member of its board of directors until April 2003. Dietzmann worked for Briefing.com for seven years until she quit in March 2003. As Briefing.com employees, Jones and Dietzmann had access to confidential business data. For instance, Dietzmann developed a list of contacts through which Briefing.com obtained market information to display online. When Dietzmann quit, however, she did not return all of the contact information to the company. Briefing.com and Green filed a suit in a federal district court against Jones, Dietzmann, and StreetAccount, alleging that they appropriated these data and other "trade secrets" to form a competing business. What are trade secrets? Why are they protected? Under what circumstances is a party liable at common law for their appropriation? How should these principles apply in this case? [*Briefing.com v. Jones*, 2006 WY 16, 126 P.3d 928 (2006)]

After you have answered Problem 8–6, compare your answer with the sample answer given on the Web site that accompanies this text. Go to www.cengage.com/blaw/let, select "Chapter 8," and click on "Case Problem with Sample Answer."

8–7. Trademarks. In 1969, Jack Masquelier, a professor of pharmacology, discovered a chemical antioxidant made from the bark of a French pine tree. The substance supposedly assists in nutritional distribution and blood circulation. Horphag Research, Ltd., began to sell the product under the name Pycnogenol, which Horphag registered as a trademark in 1993. Pycnogenol became one of the fifteen best-selling herbal supplements in the United States. In 1999, through the Web site **healthier-life.com**, Larry Garcia began to sell Masquelier's Original OPCs, a supplement derived from grape pits. Claiming that this product was the "true Pycnogenol," Garcia used the mark as a meta tag and a generic term, attributing the results of research on Horphag's product to Masquelier's and altering quotes in scientific literature to substitute the name of Masquelier's product for Horphag's. Customers contacted Horphag, after buying Garcia's product, to learn that it was not Horphag's product. Others called Horphag to ask whether Garcia "was selling . . . real Pycnogenol." Horphag filed a suit in a federal district court against Garcia, alleging in part that he was diluting Horphag's mark. What is trademark dilution? Did it occur here? Explain. [*Horphag Research, Ltd. v. Garcia*, 475 F.3d 1029 (9th Cir. 2007)]

A Question of Ethics

8–8. Custom Copies, Inc., in Gainesville, Florida, is a copy shop, reproducing and distributing, for profit, on request, material published and owned by others. One of the copy shop's primary activities is the preparation and sale of coursepacks, which contain compilations of readings for college courses. For a particular coursepack, a teacher selects the readings and delivers a syllabus to the copy shop, which obtains the materials from a library and copies them, and then binds and sells the copies. Blackwell Publishing, Inc., in Malden, Massachusetts, publishes books and journals in medicine and other fields and owns the copyrights to these publications. Blackwell and others filed a suit in a federal district court against Custom Copies, alleging copyright infringement for its "routine and systematic reproduction of materials from plaintiffs' publications, without seeking permission," to compile coursepacks for classes at the University of Florida. The plaintiffs asked the court to issue an injunction and award them damages, as well as the profit from the infringement. The defendant filed a motion to dismiss the complaint. [*Blackwell Publishing, Inc. v. Custom Copies, Inc.*, __ F.Supp.2d __ (N.D. Fla. 2007)]

1. Custom Copies argued in part that it did not "distribute" the coursepacks. Does a copy shop violate copyright law if it only copies materials for coursepacks? Does the copying fall under the "fair use" exception? Should the court grant the defendants' motion? Why or why not?
2. What is the potential impact if copies of a book or journal are created and sold without the permission of, and the payment of royalties or a fee to, the copyright owner? Explain.

Critical-Thinking Managerial Question

8–9. Delta Computers, Inc., makes computer-related products under the brand name "Delta," which the company registers as a trademark. Without Delta's permission, E-Product Corp. embeds the Delta mark in E-Product's Web site, in black type on a blue background. This tag causes the E-Product site to be returned at the top of the list of results on a search engine query for "Delta." Does E-Product's use of the Delta mark as a meta tag without Delta's permission constitute trademark infringement? Explain.

Video Question

8–10. Go to this text's Web site at **www.cengage.com/blaw/let** and select "Chapter 8." Click on "Video Questions" and view the video titled *The Jerk*. Then answer the following questions.

1. In the video, Navin (Steve Martin) creates a special handle for Fox's (Bill Macy's) glasses. Can Navin obtain a patent or a copyright protecting his invention? Explain your answer.
2. Suppose that after Navin legally protects his idea, Fox steals it and decides to develop it for himself, without Navin's permission. Has Fox

committed infringement? If so, what kind: trademark, patent, or copyright?

3. Suppose that after Navin legally protects his idea, he realizes he doesn't have the funds to mass-produce the special handle. Navin therefore agrees to allow Fox to manufacture the product. Has Navin granted Fox a license? Explain.

4. Assume that Navin is able to manufacture his invention. What might Navin do to ensure that his product is identifiable and can be distinguished from other products on the market?

Interacting with the Internet

For updated links to resources available on the Web, as well as a variety of other materials, visit this text's Web site at

www.cengage.com/blaw/let

An excellent overview of the laws governing various forms of intellectual property is available at FindLaw's Web site. Go to

profs.lp.findlaw.com

You can find answers to frequently asked questions (FAQs) about patents, trademarks, and copyrights—and links to registration forms, statutes, international patent and trademark offices, and numerous other resources—at the Web site of the U.S. Patent and Trademark Office. Go to

www.uspto.gov

To perform patent searches and to access information on the patenting process, go to

www.bustpatents.com

You can also access the European Patent Office's Web site at

www.european-patent-office.org

For information on copyrights, go to the U.S. Copyright Office at

www.copyright.gov

You can find extensive information on copyright law—including United States Supreme Court decisions in this area and the texts of the Berne Convention and other international treaties on copyright issues—at the Web site of the Legal Information Institute at Cornell University's School of Law. Go to

www.law.cornell.edu/wex/index.php/Copyright

PRACTICAL INTERNET EXERCISES

Go to this text's Web site at **www.cengage.com/blaw/let**, select "Chapter 8," and click on "Practical Internet Exercises." There you will find the following Internet research exercises that you can perform to learn more about the topics covered in this chapter.

Practical Internet Exercise 8–1 Legal Perspective—**Unwarranted Legal Threats**
Practical Internet Exercise 8–2 Technological Perspective—**File-Sharing**
Practical Internet Exercise 8–3 Management Perspective—**Protecting Intellectual Property across Borders**

BEFORE THE TEST

Go to this text's Web site at **www.cengage.com/blaw/let**, select "Chapter 8," and click on "Interactive Quizzes." You will find a number of interactive questions relating to this chapter.

CHAPTER OBJECTIVES

After reading this chapter, you should be able to answer the following questions:

1. What are the four basic elements necessary to the formation of a valid contract?

2. What elements are necessary for an effective offer?

3. What is consideration?

4. Does an intoxicated person have the capacity to enter into an enforceable contract?

5. What is a covenant not to compete? When will such a covenant be enforceable?

CONTENTS

" The social order rests upon the stability and predictability of conduct, of which keeping promises is a large item. "

— ROSCOE POUND,
1870–1964 (American jurist)

As Roscoe Pound—an eminent jurist—observed in the chapter-opening quotation, "keeping promises" is important to a stable social order. Contract law deals with, among other things, the formation and keeping of promises. A **promise** is an assertion that something either will or will not happen in the future.

PROMISE
An assertion that something either will or will not happen in the future.

Like other types of law, contract law reflects our social values, interests, and expectations at a given point in time. It shows, for example, to what extent our society allows people to make promises or commitments that are legally binding. It distinguishes between promises that create only *moral* obligations (such as a promise to take a friend to lunch) and promises that are legally binding (such as a promise to pay for merchandise purchased). Contract law also demonstrates what excuses our society accepts for breaking certain types of promises. In addition, it indicates what promises are considered to be contrary to public policy—against the interests of society as a whole—and therefore legally invalid. When the person making a promise is a child or is mentally incompetent, for example, a question will arise as to whether the promise should be enforced. Resolving such questions is the essence of contract law.

AN OVERVIEW OF CONTRACT LAW

Before we look at the numerous rules that courts use to determine whether a particular promise will be enforced, it is necessary to understand some fundamental concepts of contract law. In this section, we describe the sources and general function of contract law. We also provide the definition of a contract and introduce the objective theory of contracts.

Sources of Contract Law

The common law governs all contracts except when it has been modified or replaced by statutory law, such as the Uniform Commercial Code (UCC),[1] or by administrative agency regulations. Contracts relating to services, real estate, employment, and insurance, for example, generally are governed by the common law of contracts.

Contracts for the sale and lease of goods, however, are governed by the UCC—to the extent that the UCC has modified general contract law. The relationship between general contract law and the law governing sales and leases of goods will be explored in detail in Chapter 11. In this chapter and Chapter 10, covering the common law of contracts, we indicate briefly in footnotes the areas in which the UCC has significantly altered common law contract principles.

The Function of Contracts

No aspect of modern life is entirely free of contractual relationships. You acquire rights and obligations, for example, when you purchase an iPod or when you borrow funds to buy a house. Contract law is designed to provide stability and predictability for both buyers and sellers in the marketplace.

Contract law assures the parties to private agreements that the promises they make will be enforceable. Clearly, many promises are kept because the parties involved feel a moral obligation to do so or because keeping a promise is in their mutual self-interest. The **promisor** (the person making the promise) and the **promisee** (the person to whom the promise is made) may decide to honor their agreement for other reasons. Nevertheless, the rules of contract law are often followed in business agreements to avoid potential problems.

By supplying procedures for enforcing private agreements, contract law provides an essential condition for the existence of a market economy. Without a legal framework of reasonably assured expectations within which to plan and venture, businesspersons would be able to rely only on the good faith of others. Duty and good faith are usually sufficient, but when dramatic price changes or adverse economic conditions make it costly to comply with a promise, these elements may not be enough. Contract law is necessary to ensure compliance with a promise or to entitle the innocent party to some form of relief.

Definition of a Contract

A **contract** is an agreement that can be enforced in court. It is formed by two or more parties who agree to perform or to refrain from performing some act now or in the future. Generally, contract disputes arise when there is a promise of future performance. If the contractual promise is not fulfilled, the party who made it is subject to the sanctions of a court (see Chapter 10). That party may be required to pay monetary damages for failing to perform the contractual promise; in limited instances, the party may be required to perform the promised act.

PROMISOR
A person who makes a promise.

PROMISEE
A person to whom a promise is made.

CONTRACT
An agreement that can be enforced in court; formed by two or more competent parties who agree, for consideration, to perform or to refrain from performing some legal act now or in the future.

---

1. See Chapter 1 on page 8 and Chapter 11 for further discussions of the significance and coverage of the Uniform Commercial Code (UCC). Excerpts from the UCC are presented in Appendix C at the end of this book.

The Objective Theory of Contracts

The manager of a Toyota dealership in Glendora, California, displays the same contract written in four different Asian languages (Chinese, Korean, Vietnamese, and Tagalog). A consumer protection law in California says that certain businesses, such as car dealers and apartment owners, that have employees who orally negotiate contracts in these languages must provide written contracts in these same languages. Why might it be important to the enforceability of a written contract that the consumer can actually read its provisions?
(AP Photo/Damian Dovarganes)

In determining whether a contract has been formed, the element of intent is of prime importance. In contract law, intent is determined by what is referred to as the **objective theory of contracts,** not by the personal or subjective intent, or belief, of a party. The theory is that a party's intention to enter into a contract is judged by outward, objective facts as interpreted by a *reasonable person,* rather than by the party's own secret, subjective intentions. Objective facts include (1) what the party said when entering into the contract, (2) how the party acted or appeared, and (3) the circumstances surrounding the transaction. As will be discussed later in this chapter, in the section on express versus implied contracts, intent to form a contract may be manifested by conduct, as well as by words, oral or written.

OBJECTIVE THEORY OF CONTRACTS
A theory under which the intent to form a contract will be judged by outward, objective facts (what the party said when entering into the contract, how the party acted or appeared, and the circumstances surrounding the transaction) as interpreted by a reasonable person, rather than by the party's own secret, subjective intentions.

Freedom of Contract and Freedom from Contract

As a general rule, the law recognizes everyone's ability to enter freely into contractual arrangements. This recognition is called *freedom of contract,* a freedom protected by the U.S. Constitution in Article I, Section 10. Because freedom of contract is a fundamental public policy of the United States, courts rarely interfere with contracts that have been voluntarily made.

Of course, as in other areas of the law, there are many exceptions to the general rule that contracts voluntarily negotiated will be enforced. For example, illegal bargains, agreements that unreasonably restrain trade, and certain unfair contracts made between one party with a great amount of bargaining power and another with little power are generally not enforced. In addition, certain contracts and clauses may not be enforceable if they are contrary to public policy, fairness, and justice. These exceptions provide *freedom from contract* for persons who may have been pressured into making contracts unfavorable to themselves.

ELEMENTS OF A CONTRACT

The many topics that will be discussed in the following chapters on contract law require an understanding of the basic elements of a valid contract and the way in which the contract was created. The topics to be covered in this unit on contracts also require an understanding of the types of circumstances in which even legally valid contracts will not be enforced.

Requirements of a Valid Contract

The following list briefly describes the four requirements that must be met for a valid contract to exist. If any of these elements is lacking, no contract will have been formed. (Each item will be explained more fully later in this chapter.)

Agreement (Propose and agree)
Consideration (something of value)
Capacity
Legality (legal purpose)

Bilateral = promise for promise
Unilateral = promise for act. going on vacation, can you walk my dog? And I'll pay you?

1. *Agreement.* An agreement to form a contract includes an *offer* and an *acceptance*. One party must offer to enter into a legal agreement, and another party must accept the terms of the offer.
2. *Consideration.* Any promises made by parties must be supported by legally sufficient and bargained-for consideration (something of value received or promised to convince a person to make a deal).
3. *Contractual capacity.* Both parties entering into the contract must have the contractual capacity to do so; the law must recognize them as possessing characteristics that qualify them as competent parties.
4. *Legality.* The contract's purpose must be to accomplish some goal that is legal and not against public policy.

Defenses to the Enforceability of a Contract

Even if all of the elements of a valid contract are present, a contract may be unenforceable if the following requirements are not met.

1. *Genuineness of assent, or voluntary consent.* The consent of both parties must be genuine. For example, if a contract was formed as a result of fraud, mistake, or duress, the contract may not be enforceable.
2. *Form.* The contract must be in whatever form the law requires; for example, some contracts must be in writing to be enforceable.

The failure to fulfill either requirement may be raised as a *defense* to the enforceability of an otherwise valid contract. Both requirements will be explained in more detail in Chapter 10.

TYPES OF CONTRACTS

There are numerous types of contracts. They are categorized based on legal distinctions as to their formation, performance, and enforceability.

Contract Formation

As you can see in Exhibit 9–1, three classifications, or categories, of contracts are based on how and when a contract is formed. The best way to explain each type of contract is to compare one type with another, as we do in the following pages.

EXHIBIT 9–1 CLASSIFICATIONS BASED ON CONTRACT FORMATION

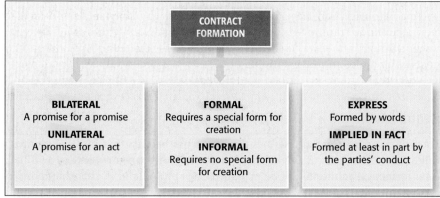

Bilateral versus Unilateral Contracts   Every contract involves at least two parties. The **offeror** is the party making the offer. The **offeree** is the party to whom the offer is made. The offeror always promises to do or not to do something and thus is also a promisor. Whether the contract is classified as *bilateral* or *unilateral* depends on what the offeree must do to accept the offer and bind the offeror to a contract.

OFFEROR
A person who makes an offer.

OFFEREE
A person to whom an offer is made.

Bilateral Contracts   If the offeree can accept the offer simply by promising to perform, the contract is a **bilateral contract.** Hence, a bilateral contract is a "promise for a promise." An example of a bilateral contract is a contract in which one person agrees to buy another person's automobile for a specified price. No performance, such as the payment of funds or delivery of goods, need take place for a bilateral contract to be formed. The contract comes into existence at the moment the promises are exchanged.

BILATERAL CONTRACT
A type of contract that arises when a promise is given in exchange for a return promise.

EXAMPLE #1   Javier offers to buy Ann's digital camera for $200. Javier tells Ann that he will give her the cash for the camera on the following Friday, when he gets paid. Ann accepts Javier's offer and promises to give him the camera when he pays her on Friday. Javier and Ann have formed a bilateral contract.□

Unilateral Contracts   If the offer is phrased so that the offeree can accept only by completing the contract performance, the contract is a **unilateral contract.** Hence, a unilateral contract is a "promise for an act." In other words, the contract is formed not at the moment when promises are exchanged but rather when the contract is *performed*. EXAMPLE #2   Reese says to Celia, "If you drive my car from New York to Los Angeles, I'll give you $1,000." Only on Celia's completion of the act—bringing the car to Los Angeles—does she fully accept Reese's offer to pay $1,000. If she chooses not to accept the offer to drive the car to Los Angeles, there are no legal consequences.□

UNILATERAL CONTRACT
A contract that results when an offer can be accepted only by the offeree's performance.

Contests, lotteries, and other competitions offering prizes are also examples of offers for unilateral contracts. If a person complies with the rules of the contest—such as by submitting the right lottery number at the right place and time—a unilateral contract is formed, binding the organization offering the prize to a contract to perform as promised in the offer.

Revocation of Offers for Unilateral Contracts   A problem arises in unilateral contracts when the promisor attempts to *revoke* (cancel) the offer after the promisee has begun performance but before the act has been completed. EXAMPLE #3   Roberta offers to buy Ed's sailboat, moored in San Francisco, on delivery of the boat to Roberta's dock in Newport Beach, three hundred miles south of San Francisco. Ed rigs the boat and sets sail. Shortly before his arrival at Newport Beach, Ed receives a radio message from Roberta withdrawing her offer. Roberta's offer is to form a unilateral contract, and only Ed's delivery of the sailboat at her dock is an acceptance.□

In contract law, offers are normally *revocable* (capable of being taken back, or canceled) until accepted. Under the traditional view of unilateral contracts, Roberta's revocation would terminate the offer. Because of the harsh effect on the offeree of the revocation of an offer to form a unilateral contract, the modern-day view is that once performance has been *substantially* undertaken, the offeror cannot revoke the offer. Thus, in our example, even though Ed has not yet accepted the offer by complete performance, Roberta is prohibited from revoking it. Ed can deliver the boat and bind Roberta to the contract.

FORMAL CONTRACT
A contract that by law requires a specific form for its validity. Negotiable instruments and letters of credit are examples of formal contracts.

INFORMAL CONTRACT
A contract that does not require a specified form or formality to be valid.

EXPRESS CONTRACT
A contract in which the terms of the agreement are stated in words, oral or written.

IMPLIED-IN-FACT CONTRACT
A contract formed in whole or in part from the conduct of the parties (as opposed to an express contract).

Formal versus Informal Contracts　Another classification system divides contracts into formal contracts and informal contracts. **Formal contracts** are contracts that require a special form or method of creation (formation) to be enforceable. One example is *negotiable instruments,* which include checks, drafts, promissory notes, and certificates of deposit. Negotiable instruments are formal contracts because, under the Uniform Commercial Code (UCC), special forms and language are required to create them. *Letters of credit,* which are frequently used in international sales contracts, are another type of formal contract. As discussed in Chapter 7, letters of credit are agreements to pay contingent on the purchaser's receipt of invoices and bills of lading (documents evidencing receipt of, and title to, goods shipped).

Informal contracts (also called *simple contracts*) include all other contracts. No special form is required (except for certain types of contracts that must be in writing), as the contracts are usually based on their substance rather than their form. Typically, businesspersons put their contracts in writing to ensure that there is some proof of a contract's existence should problems arise.

Express versus Implied Contracts　Contracts may also be formed and categorized as express or implied by the conduct of the parties. In an **express contract,** the terms of the agreement are fully and explicitly stated in words, oral or written. A signed lease for an apartment or a house is an express written contract. If a classmate accepts your offer to sell your textbooks from last semester for $300, an express oral contract has been made.

A contract that is implied from the conduct of the parties is called an **implied-in-fact contract,** or an implied contract. This type of contract differs from an express contract in that the conduct of the parties, rather than their words, creates and defines at least some of the terms of the contract. For an implied-in-fact contract to arise, certain requirements must be met. Normally, if the following conditions exist, a court will hold that an implied contract was formed:

1. The plaintiff furnished some service or property.
2. The plaintiff expected to be paid for that service or property, and the defendant knew or should have known that payment was expected (by using the objective-theory-of-contracts test discussed on page 275).
3. The defendant had a chance to reject the services or property and did not.

What determines whether a contract for accounting, tax preparation, or any other service is an express contract or an implied-in-fact contract? (Getty Images)

EXAMPLE #4 Suppose that you need an accountant to fill out your tax return this year. You look online and find an accounting firm located in your neighborhood. You drop by the firm's office, explain your problem to an accountant, and learn what fees will be charged. The next day you return and give the receptionist all of the necessary information and documents, such as canceled checks and W-2 forms. Then you walk out the door without saying anything expressly to the accountant. In this situation, you have entered into an implied-in-fact contract to pay the accountant the usual and reasonable fees for her accounting services. The contract is implied by your conduct and by hers. She expects to be

paid for completing your tax return. By bringing in the records she will need to do the work, you have implied an intent to pay for her services.☐

Note that a contract can be a mixture of an express contract and an implied-in-fact contract. In other words, a contract may contain some express terms, while others are implied. During the construction of a home, the homeowner often requests that the builder make changes in the original specifications. When do these changes form part of an implied-in-fact contract that makes the homeowner liable to the builder for any extra expenses? That was the issue in the following case.

Case 9.1 Uhrhahn Construction & Design, Inc. v. Hopkins

Court of Appeals of Utah, 2008.
179 P.3d 808.

BACKGROUND AND FACTS   Uhrhahn Construction was hired by Lamar Hopkins (Hopkins) and his wife Joan for several projects in the building of their home. Each project was based on a cost estimate and specifications. Each of the proposals accepted by Hopkins said that any changes in the signed contracts would be done only "upon written orders." When work was in progress, Hopkins made several requests for changes. There was no written record of these changes, but the work was performed and paid for by Hopkins. A dispute arose from Hopkins's request that Uhrhahn use Durisol blocks rather than cinder blocks in some construction. The original proposal specified cinder blocks, but Hopkins told Uhrhahn that the change should be made because Durisol was "easier to install than traditional cinder block and would take half the time." Hopkins said the total cost would be the same. Uhrhahn orally agreed to the change, but discovered that Durisol blocks were more complicated to use than cinder blocks and demanded extra payment. Hopkins refused to pay, claiming the cost should be the same. Uhrhahn sued. The trial court held for Uhrhahn, finding that the Durisol blocks were more costly to install. The homeowners appealed.

IN THE WORDS OF THE COURT . . . *ORME*, Judge.

* * * *

The essential elements of contract formation were present here. The proposal constituted an offer by Uhrhahn to complete certain detailed construction projects for certain prices, and it clearly set forth additional terms regarding the work and the parties' relationship. When Hopkins signed the written proposal multiple times—once for each proposed project under sections titled "Acceptance of Proposal"—he accepted Uhrhahn's offer and promised to pay the amounts delineated for the various projects. Uhrhahn's promise to perform and the homeowners' promise to pay constituted bargained-for consideration. Thus, a valid contract was formed between the parties.

The homeowners challenge the trial court's determination that an implied-in-fact contract existed. They argue that the proposal agreement, which requires any changes to the original estimates and specifications to be put in writing, controls. They therefore assert that they do not owe Uhrhahn for work or monetary amounts that deviated from the original proposal agreement and were not reduced to writing. We disagree. We conclude that the trial court's express and implicit factual findings show that through his conduct Hopkins, and therefore the homeowners, implicitly waived the provision requiring change orders to be put in writing and created a contract implied in fact that permitted changes to the original contract to be made orally.

First, we note that parties to construction contracts frequently make changes to the project as originally agreed upon. Additionally, provisions in construction contracts requiring orders for extra work to be written are generally held to be for the protection of the owner, and the owner can waive such provisions.

To prove that the owner intended to waive such a provision, "the evidence must be of a clear and satisfactory character and clearly show a distinct agreement that the

CASE 9.1—CONTINUED

CASE 9.1—CONTINUED

work be deemed extra work and a definite agreement with the owner to pay extra for such extra work."

* * * *

We also conclude that the trial court correctly determined that an implied-in-fact contract was established through the parties' conduct, which allowed the parties to agree on extra work orally.

A contract implied in fact is the second branch of *quantum meruit* [an equitable remedy that literally means as much as he deserves]. *A contract implied in fact is a "contract" established by conduct. The elements * * * are: (1) the defendant requested the plaintiff to perform work; (2) the plaintiff expected the defendant to compensate him or her for those services; and (3) the defendant knew or should have known that the plaintiff expected compensation.* [Emphasis added.]

In this case, [the] trial court's factual findings show that the parties' conduct established an implied-in-fact contract. The trial court found that Hopkins "made several requests for additional work to the home," and that "Uhrhahn * * * completed a substantial amount of the additional work requested." Additionally, the trial court stated that Hopkins "accepted the benefits of Uhrhahn's hard work." Moreover, Hopkins paid at least three different invoices for the additional work, which invoices itemized the extra (or additional) work performed by Uhrhahn.

The first element is clearly satisfied because Hopkins repeatedly asked Uhrhahn to perform construction work that deviated from the proposal agreement. The second element is also satisfied because Uhrhahn's conduct shows that it expected payment in return for the work it performed at Hopkins's request. Hopkins and Uhrhahn had a business relationship, and Uhrhahn was hired by Hopkins to perform a job. Under these circumstances, Uhrhahn clearly expected to be paid for any work it performed at the homeowners' request, as shown by the regular invoices it sent Hopkins for its completed work, including invoices for the additional work orally requested by Hopkins. Finally, the last element is also satisfied because Hopkins's conduct showed he knew Uhrhahn expected to be paid. Up until the dispute over the Durisol blocks ensued, Hopkins paid or partially paid for the work that deviated from the proposal agreement pursuant to Uhrhahn's invoices that referenced change orders. His payments clearly show that he knew Uhrhahn expected to be paid. Thus, the trial court correctly determined that a contract implied in fact existed, which Hopkins—and therefore the homeowners—breached when they failed to completely pay Uhrhahn for the extra work performed.

* * * *

We affirm the trial court's determination that Hopkins, through his conduct, created an implied-in-fact contract that allowed the parties to orally agree to extras or changes to the original proposal agreement.

DECISION AND REMEDY   The Utah appeals court affirmed the decision of the trial court, finding that there was a valid contract between the parties and that both parties had agreed to oral changes in the contract. The changes created an implied-in-fact contract by which the parties agreed to provide extra work in exchange for extra compensation.

WHAT IF THE FACTS WERE DIFFERENT?   Suppose that Hopkins and Uhrhahn had not agreed to deviate from the contract on previous occasions and that Hopkins had not paid for any additional work performed by Uhrhahn. How might this have changed the court's ruling in this case?

THE E-COMMERCE DIMENSION   Would the outcome of this case have been different if the parties had communicated by e-mail for all details regarding changes in the work performed? Why or why not?

Contract Performance

Contracts are also classified according to their state of performance. A contract that has been fully performed on both sides is called an **executed contract.** A contract that has not been fully performed on either side is called an **executory contract.** If one party has fully performed but the other has not, the contract is said to be executed on the one side and executory on the other, but the contract is still classified as executory.

EXECUTED CONTRACT
A contract that has been completely performed by both parties.

EXECUTORY CONTRACT
A contract that has not yet been fully performed.

  EXAMPLE #5 Assume that you agree to buy ten tons of coal from Western Coal Company. Further assume that Western has delivered the coal to your steel mill, where it is now being burned. At this point, the contract is an executory contract—it is executed on the part of Western and executory on your part. After you pay Western for the coal, the contract will be executed on both sides.□

Contract Enforceability

A **valid contract** has the four elements necessary to entitle at least one of the parties to enforce it in court. Those elements, as mentioned earlier, consist of (1) an agreement (offer and acceptance) (2) supported by legally sufficient consideration (3) made by parties who have the legal capacity to enter into the contract, and (4) made for a legal purpose. As mentioned, we will discuss each of these elements later in this chapter. As you can see in Exhibit 9–2, valid contracts may be enforceable, voidable, or unenforceable. Additionally, a contract may be referred to as a *void contract.* We look next at the meaning of the terms *voidable, unenforceable,* and *void* in relation to contract enforceability.

VALID CONTRACT
A contract that results when the elements necessary for contract formation (agreement, consideration, contractual capacity, and legal purpose) are present.

Voidable Contracts   A **voidable contract** is a *valid* contract but one that can be avoided at the option of one or both of the parties. The party having the option can elect either to avoid any duty to perform or to *ratify* (make valid) the contract. If the contract is avoided, both parties are released from it. If it is ratified, both parties must fully perform their respective legal obligations.

VOIDABLE CONTRACT
A contract that may be legally avoided (canceled, or annulled) at the option of one or both of the parties.

EXHIBIT 9–2 ENFORCEABLE, VOIDABLE, UNENFORCEABLE, AND VOID CONTRACTS

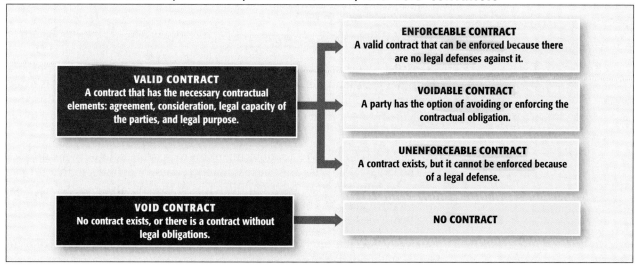

As a general rule, but subject to exceptions, contracts made by minors are voidable at the option of the minor. Contracts entered into under fraudulent conditions are voidable at the option of the defrauded party. In addition, contracts entered into under duress or undue influence are voidable (see Chapter 10).

UNENFORCEABLE CONTRACT
A valid contract rendered unenforceable by some statute or law.

Unenforceable Contracts   An **unenforceable contract** is one that cannot be enforced because of certain legal defenses against it. It is not unenforceable because a party failed to satisfy a legal requirement of the contract; rather, it is a valid contract rendered unenforceable by some statute or law. For example, some contracts must be in writing (see Chapter 10), and if they are not, they will not be enforceable except in certain exceptional circumstances.

VOID CONTRACT
A contract having no legal force or binding effect.

Void Contracts   A **void contract** is no contract at all. The terms *void* and *contract* are contradictory. None of the parties has any legal obligations if a contract is void. A contract can be void because, for example, one of the parties was previously determined by a court to be legally insane (and thus lacked the legal capacity to enter into a contract) or because the purpose of the contract was illegal.

AGREEMENT

AGREEMENT
A meeting of two or more minds in regard to the terms of a contract, usually broken down into two events: an offer and an acceptance.

An essential element for contract formation is **agreement**—that is, the parties must agree on the terms of the contract. Ordinarily, agreement is evidenced by two events: an *offer* and an *acceptance*. One party offers a certain bargain to another party, who then accepts that bargain. The agreement does not necessarily have to be in writing. Both parties, however, must express their agreement to the same bargain. Once an agreement is reached, if the other elements of a contract are present (consideration, capacity, and legality), a valid contract is formed, generally creating enforceable rights and duties between the parties.

Note that not all agreements are contracts. John and Kevin may agree to play golf on a certain day, but a court would not hold that their agreement is an enforceable contract. A *contractual* agreement arises only when the terms of the agreement impose legally enforceable obligations on the parties.

In today's world, contracts are frequently formed via the Internet. Online offers and acceptances will be discussed in Chapter 11, in the context of electronic contracts, or e-contracts.

Requirements of the Offer

The parties to a contract are the *offeror*, the one who makes an offer or proposal to another party, and the *offeree*, the one to whom the offer or proposal is made.

OFFER
A promise or commitment to do or refrain from doing some specified act in the future.

An **offer** is a promise or commitment to do or refrain from doing some specified act in the future. Under the common law, three elements are necessary for an offer to be effective:

1. The offeror must have a serious intention to become bound by the offer.
2. The terms of the offer must be reasonably certain, or definite, so that the parties and the court can ascertain the terms of the contract.
3. The offer must be communicated by the offeror to the offeree, resulting in the offeree's knowledge of the offer.

Once an effective offer has been made, the offeree has the power to accept the offer. If the offeree accepts, an agreement is formed (and thus a contract arises, if other essential elements are present).

Intention The first requirement for an effective offer is a serious intent on the part of the offeror. Serious intent is not determined by the *subjective* intentions, beliefs, and assumptions of the offeror. Rather, it is determined by what a reasonable person in the offeree's position would think the offeror's words and conduct meant. Offers made in obvious anger, jest, or undue excitement do not meet the intent test because a reasonable person would realize that a serious offer was not being made. Because these offers are not effective, an offeree's acceptance does not create an agreement.

EXAMPLE #6 You and three classmates ride to school each day in Dana's new automobile, which has a market value of $20,000. One cold morning, the four of you get into the car, but Dana cannot get the car started. She yells in anger, "I'll sell this car to anyone for $500!" You drop $500 in her lap. Given these facts, a reasonable person, taking into consideration Dana's frustration and the obvious difference in worth between the market value of the car and the proposed purchase price, would declare that her offer was not made with serious intent and that you did not have an agreement.□

The concept of intention can be further clarified through an examination of the types of expressions and statements that are *not* offers. We look at these expressions and statements in the subsections that follow. In the classic case of *Lucy v. Zehmer,* presented next, the court considered whether an offer made "after a few drinks" met the serious-intent requirement.

Landmark and Classic Cases

Case 9.2 Lucy v. Zehmer

Supreme Court of Appeals of Virginia, 1954.
196 Va. 493, 84 S.E.2d 516.

BACKGROUND AND FACTS W. O. Lucy and J. C. Lucy, the plaintiffs, filed a suit against A. H. Zehmer and Ida Zehmer, the defendants, to compel the Zehmers to transfer title of their property, known as the Ferguson Farm, to the Lucys for $50,000, as the Zehmers had allegedly agreed to do. Lucy had known Zehmer for fifteen or twenty years and for the last eight years or so had been anxious to buy the Ferguson Farm from Zehmer. One night, Lucy stopped in to visit the Zehmers in the combination restaurant, filling station, and motor court they operated. While there, Lucy tried to buy the Ferguson

Farm once again. This time he tried a new approach. According to the trial court transcript, Lucy said to Zehmer, "I bet you wouldn't take $50,000 for that place." Zehmer replied, "Yes, I would too; you wouldn't give fifty." Throughout the evening, the conversation returned to the sale of the Ferguson Farm for $50,000. At the same time, the parties continued to drink whiskey and engage in light conversation. Eventually, Lucy enticed Zehmer to write up an agreement to the effect that Zehmer would sell to Lucy the Ferguson Farm for $50,000. Later, Lucy sued Zehmer to compel him to go through with the sale. Zehmer argued that he had been drunk and that the offer had been made in jest and hence was unenforceable. The trial court agreed with Zehmer, and Lucy appealed.

IN THE WORDS OF THE COURT . . . *BUCHANAN, J.* [Justice] delivered the opinion of the court.

* * * *

In his testimony, Zehmer claimed that he "was high as a Georgia pine," and that the transaction "was just a bunch of two doggoned drunks bluffing to see who could talk the biggest and say the most." That claim is inconsistent with his attempt to testify in great detail as to what was said and what was done.

* * * *

The appearance of the contract, the fact that it was under discussion for forty minutes or more before it was signed; Lucy's objection to the first draft because it was written in the singular, and he wanted Mrs. Zehmer to sign it also; the rewriting to meet that objection and the signing by Mrs. Zehmer; the discussion of what was to be

CASE 9.2–CONTINUED

included in the sale, the provision for the examination of the title, the completeness of the instrument that was executed, the taking possession of it by Lucy with no request or suggestion by either of the defendants that he give it back, are facts which furnish persuasive evidence that the execution of the contract was a serious business transaction rather than a casual, jesting matter as defendants now contend.

* * * *

In the field of contracts, as generally elsewhere, *we must look to the outward expression of a person as manifesting his intention rather than to his secret and unexpressed intention.* The law imputes to a person an intention corresponding to the reasonable meaning of his words and acts. [Emphasis added.]

* * * *

Whether the writing signed by the defendants and now sought to be enforced by the complainants was the result of a serious offer by Lucy and a serious acceptance by the defendants, or was a serious offer by Lucy and an acceptance in secret jest by the defendants, in either event it constituted a binding contract of sale between the parties.

DECISION AND REMEDY   The Supreme Court of Virginia determined that the writing was an enforceable contract and reversed the ruling of the lower court. The Zehmers were required by court order to follow through with the sale of the Ferguson Farm to the Lucys.

IMPACT OF THIS CASE ON TODAY'S LEGAL ENVIRONMENT   This is a classic case in contract law because it illustrates so clearly the objective theory of contracts with respect to determining whether a serious offer was intended. Today, the courts continue to apply the objective theory of contracts and routinely cite *Lucy v. Zehmer* as a significant precedent in this area.

WHAT IF THE FACTS WERE DIFFERENT?   Suppose that the day after Lucy signed the purchase agreement for the farm, he decided that he didn't want it after all, and Zehmer sued Lucy to perform the contract. Would this change in the facts alter the court's decision that Lucy and Zehmer had created an enforceable contract? Why or why not?

RELEVANT WEB SITES   To locate information on the Web concerning the *Lucy v. Zehmer* decision, go to this text's Web site at **academic.cengage.com/blaw/let**, select "Chapter 9," and click on "URLs for Landmarks."

Expressions of Opinion   An expression of opinion is not an offer. It does not evidence an intention to enter into a binding agreement. EXAMPLE #7 Hawkins took his son to McGee, a physician, and asked McGee to operate on the son's hand. McGee said that the boy would be in the hospital three or four days and that the hand would *probably* heal a few days later. The son's hand did not heal for a month, but the father did not win a suit for breach of contract. The court held that McGee had not made an offer to heal the son's hand in a few days. He had merely expressed an opinion as to when the hand would heal.[2] □

Statements of Future Intent   A statement of an *intention* to do something in the future is not an offer. EXAMPLE #8 If Arif says, "I *plan* to sell my stock in Novation, Inc., for $150 per share," a contract is not created if John "accepts" and tenders the $150 per share for the stock. Arif has merely expressed his intention to enter into a future contract for the sale of the stock. If John accepts and tenders the $150 per share, no contract is formed because a reasonable person would conclude that Arif was only *thinking about* selling his stock, not *promising* to sell it. □

---

2. *Hawkins v. McGee*, 84 N.H. 114, 146 A. 641 (1929).

Preliminary Negotiations   A request or invitation to negotiate is not an offer. It only expresses a willingness to discuss the possibility of entering into a contract. Included are statements such as "Will you sell Blythe Estate?" or "I wouldn't sell my car for less than $5,000." A reasonable person in the offeree's position would not conclude that these statements evidenced an intention to enter into a binding obligation. Likewise, when the government or private firms require construction work, they invite contractors to submit bids. The *invitation* to submit bids is not an offer, and a contractor does not bind the government or private firm by submitting a bid. (The bids that the contractors submit are offers, however, and the government or private firm can bind the contractor by accepting the bid.)

Agreements to Agree   During preliminary negotiations, the parties may form an agreement to agree to a material term of a contract at some future date. Traditionally, such "agreements to agree" were not considered to be binding contracts. The modern view, however, is that agreements to agree may be enforceable agreements (contracts) if it is clear that the parties intended to be bound by the agreements. In other words, under the modern view the emphasis is on the parties' intent rather than on form.

EXAMPLE #9 After a person was injured and nearly drowned on a water ride at Six Flags Amusement Park, Six Flags, Inc., filed a lawsuit against the manufacturer that had designed the ride. The defendant manufacturer claimed that there was no binding contract between the parties, only preliminary negotiations that were never formalized into a contract to construct the ride. The court, however, held that a faxed document specifying the details of the water ride, along with the parties' subsequent actions (beginning construction and handwriting notes on the fax), was sufficient to show an intent to be bound. Because of the court's finding, the manufacturer was required to provide insurance for the water ride at Six Flags, and its insurer was required to defend Six Flags in the personal-injury lawsuit that arose out of the incident.[3] □

Increasingly, the courts are holding that a preliminary agreement constitutes a binding contract if the parties have agreed on all essential terms and no disputed issues remain to be resolved.[4] In contrast, if the parties agree on certain major terms but leave other terms open for further negotiation, a preliminary agreement is binding only in the sense that the parties have committed themselves to negotiate the undecided terms in good faith in an effort to reach a final agreement.[5]

Preventing Legal Disputes

To avoid potential legal disputes, businesspersons should be cautious when drafting a memorandum outlining a preliminary agreement or understanding with another party. If all the major terms are included, a court might hold that the agreement is binding even though it was intended to be only a tentative agreement. One approach to avoid being bound to the terms of a preliminary agreement is to

---

3. *Six Flags, Inc. v. Steadfast Insurance Co.,* 474 F.Supp.2d 201 (D.Mass. 2007).
4. See, for example, *Tractebel Energy Marketing, Inc. v. AEP Power Marketing, Inc.,* 487 F.3d 89 (2d Cir. 2007); and *Fluorine On Call, Ltd. v. Fluorogas Limited,* No. 01-CV-186 (W.D.Tex. 2002), contract issue affirmed on appeal at 380 F.3d 849 (5th Cir. 2004).
5. See, for example, *MBH, Inc. v. John Otte Oil & Propane, Inc.,* 727 N.W.2d 238 (Neb.App. 2007); and *Barrand v. Whataburger, Inc.,* 214 S.W.2d 122 (Tex.App.—Corpus Christi 2006).

include in the writing not only the points on which the parties agree, but also all of the points of disagreement. Alternatively, a party might add a note or disclaimer to the memorandum stating that, although the parties anticipate entering a contract in the future, neither party intends to be legally bound to the terms discussed in the memorandum. That way, neither party can claim that an agreement on all essential terms has been reached. ■

In the following case, the dispute was over an agreement to settle a case during a trial. One party claimed that the agreement formed via e-mail was binding, and the other party claimed it was merely an agreement to agree or an agreement to work out the terms of a settlement in the future. Can an exchange of e-mails create a complete and unambiguous agreement?

Case 9.3   Basis Technology Corp. v. Amazon.com, Inc.

Appeals Court of Massachusetts, 2008.
71 Mass.App.Ct. 29, 878 N.E.2d 952.
www.malawyersweekly.com/macoa.cfm[a]

BACKGROUND AND FACTS   Basis Technology created software and provided technical services for Amazon's Japanese language Web site. The agreement between the two companies allowed for separately negotiated contracts for additional services that Basis might provide Amazon. At the

a. In the search box on the right, enter "71 Mass.App.Ct. 29," and click on "Search." On the resulting page, click on the case name.

end of 1999, Basis and Amazon entered into stock-purchase agreements. Later, Amazon objected to certain actions related to the securities that Basis sold. Basis sued Amazon for various claims involving these securities and for nonpayment for services performed by Basis that were not included in the original agreement. During the trial, the two parties appeared to reach an agreement to settle out of court via a series of e-mail exchanges outlining the settlement. When Amazon reneged, Basis served a motion to enforce the proposed settlement. The trial judge entered judgment against Amazon, which appealed.

IN THE WORDS OF THE COURT . . . SIKORA, J. [Judge]

*   *   *   *

*   *   * On the evening of March 23, after the third day of evidence and after settlement discussions, Basis counsel sent an e-mail with the following text to Amazon counsel:

> [Amazon counsel]—This e-mail confirms the essential business terms of the settlement between our respective clients *   *   *. Basis and Amazon agree that they promptly will take all reasonable steps to memorialize in a written agreement, to be signed by individuals authorized by each party, the terms set forth below, as well as such other terms that are reasonably necessary to make these terms effective.

> *   *   *   *

> [Amazon counsel], please contact me first thing tomorrow morning if this e-mail does not accurately summarize the settlement terms reached earlier this evening.

> See you tomorrow morning when we report this matter settled to the Court.

At 7:26 A.M. on March 24, Amazon counsel sent an e-mail with a one-word reply: "correct." Later in the morning, in open court and on the record, both counsel reported the result of a settlement without specification of the terms.

On March 25, Amazon's counsel sent a facsimile of the first draft of a settlement agreement to Basis's counsel. The draft comported with all the terms of the e-mail exchange, and added some implementing and boilerplate [standard contract provisions] terms.

* * * *

[Within a few days, though,] the parties were deadlocked. On April 21, Basis served its motion to enforce the settlement agreement. Amazon opposed. * * * The motion and opposition presented the issues whether the e-mail terms were sufficiently complete and definite to form an agreement and whether Amazon had intended to be bound by them.

* * * *

We examine the text of the terms for the incompleteness and indefiniteness charged by Amazon. *Provisions are not ambiguous simply because the parties have developed different interpretations of them.* [Emphasis added.]

* * * *

We must interpret the document as a whole. In the preface to the enumerated terms, Basis counsel stated that the "e-mail confirms the essential business terms of the settlement between our respective clients," and that the parties "agree that they promptly will take all reasonable steps to memorialize" those terms. Amazon counsel concisely responded, "correct." Thus the "essential business terms" were resolved. The parties were proceeding to "memorialize" or record the settlement terms, not to create them.

* * * *

To ascertain intent, a court considers the words used by the parties, the agreement taken as a whole, and surrounding facts and circumstances. The essential circumstance of this disputed agreement is that it concluded a trial.

* * * As the trial judge explained in her memorandum of decision, she "terminated" the trial; she did not suspend it for exploratory negotiations. She did so in reliance upon the parties' report of an accomplished agreement for the settlement of their dispute.

* * * *

In sum, the deliberateness and the gravity attributable to a report of a settlement, especially during the progress of a trial, weigh heavily as circumstantial evidence of the intention of a party such as Amazon to be bound by its communication to the opposing party and to the court.

DECISION AND REMEDY The Appeals Court of Massachusetts affirmed the trial court's finding that Amazon intended to be bound by the terms of the March 23 e-mail. That e-mail constituted a complete and unambiguous statement of the parties' desire to be bound by the settlement terms.

WHAT IF THE FACTS WERE DIFFERENT? Assume that the attorneys for both sides had simply had a phone conversation that included all of the terms they actually agreed on in their e-mail exchanges. Would the court have ruled differently? Why or why not?

THE ETHICAL DIMENSION Under what circumstances could Amazon justify its "about face" after having agreed in an e-mail to the settlement terms?

Advertisements In general, advertisements—including representations made in mail-order catalogues, price lists, and circulars—are treated not as offers to contract but as invitations to negotiate. EXAMPLE #10 Loeser advertises a used paving machine. The ad is mailed to hundreds of firms and reads, "Used Loeser Construction Co. paving machine. Builds curbs and finishes cement work all in one process. Price: $42,350." If Star Paving calls Loeser and says, "We accept your offer," no contract is formed. Any reasonable person would conclude that Loeser was not promising to sell the paving machine but rather was soliciting offers to buy it. If such an ad were held to constitute a legal offer, and fifty people accepted the offer, there would be no way for Loeser to perform all fifty of the resulting contracts. He would have to breach forty-nine contracts. Obviously, the law seeks to avoid such unfairness. □

Price lists are another form of invitation to negotiate or trade. A seller's price list is not an offer to sell at that price; it merely invites the buyer to offer to buy at that price. In fact, the seller usually puts "prices subject to change" on the price list. Only in rare circumstances will a price quotation be construed as an offer.

Although most advertisements and the like are treated as invitations to negotiate, this does not mean that an advertisement can never be an offer. On some occasions, courts have construed advertisements to be offers because the ads contained definite terms that invited acceptance (such as an ad offering a reward for the return of a lost dog).

Definiteness of Terms The second requirement for an effective offer involves the definiteness of its terms. An offer must have terms that are reasonably definite so that, if it is accepted and a contract formed, a court can determine if a breach has occurred and can provide an appropriate remedy. The specific terms required depend, of course, on the type of contract. Generally, a contract must include the following terms, either expressed in the contract or capable of being reasonably inferred from it:

1. The identification of the parties.
2. The identification of the object or subject matter of the contract (also the quantity, when appropriate), including the work to be performed, with specific identification of such items as goods, services, and land.
3. The consideration to be paid.
4. The time of payment, delivery, or performance.

An offer may invite an acceptance to be worded in such specific terms that the contract is made definite. **EXAMPLE #11** Marcus Business Machines contacts your corporation and offers to sell "from one to ten MacCool copying machines for $1,600 each; state number desired in acceptance." Your corporation agrees to buy two copiers. Because the quantity is specified in the acceptance, the terms are definite, and the contract is enforceable. □

Courts sometimes are willing to supply a missing term in a contract when the parties have clearly manifested an intent to form a contract. If, in contrast, the parties have attempted to deal with a particular term of the contract but their expression of intent is too vague or uncertain to be given any precise meaning, the court will not supply a "reasonable" term because to do so might conflict with the intent of the parties. In other words, the court will not rewrite the contract.[6]

Communication A third requirement for an effective offer is communication of the offer to the offeree, resulting in the offeree's knowledge of the offer. Ordinarily, one cannot agree to a bargain without knowing that it exists. **EXAMPLE #12** Estrich advertises a reward for the return of his lost dog. Hoban, not knowing of the reward, finds the dog and returns it to Estrich. Hoban cannot

---

6. See Chapter 11 and UCC 2–204. Article 2 of the UCC specifies different rules relating to the definiteness of terms used in a contract for the sale of goods. In essence, Article 2 modifies general contract law by requiring less specificity.

recover the reward, because she did not know it had been offered. (A few states allow recovery of the reward, but not on contract principles—Hoban would be allowed to recover on the basis that it would be unfair to deny her the reward just because she did not know it had been offered.)□

Termination of the Offer

The communication of an effective offer to an offeree gives the offeree the power to transform the offer into a binding, legal obligation (a contract) by an acceptance. This power of acceptance, however, does not continue forever. It can be terminated either by the *action of the parties* or by *operation of law.* An offer can be terminated by the action of the parties in any of three ways: by revocation by the offeror, by rejection by the offeree, or by counteroffer by the offeree.

Termination by Action of the Offeror The offeror's act of withdrawing (revoking) an offer is known as **revocation.** Unless an offer is irrevocable (irrevocable offers will be discussed shortly), the offeror usually can revoke the offer (even if he or she has promised to keep it open) as long as the revocation is communicated to the offeree before the offeree accepts. Revocation may be accomplished by express repudiation of the offer (for example, with a statement such as "I withdraw my previous offer of October 17") or by performance of acts that are inconsistent with the existence of the offer and are made known to the offeree. EXAMPLE #13 Chakir offers to sell some land to Seda. A month passes and Seda, who has not accepted the offer, learns that Chakir has sold the land to Gomez. Because Chakir's sale of the land to Gomez is inconsistent with the continued existence of the offer to sell the land to Seda, the offer to Seda is revoked.□

REVOCATION
In contract law, the withdrawal of an offer by an offeror; unless the offer is irrevocable, it can be revoked at any time prior to acceptance without liability.

Termination by Action of the Offeree The offer may be rejected by the offeree, in which case the offer is terminated. A rejection is ordinarily accomplished by words or conduct evidencing an intent not to accept the offer. As with revocation, rejection of an offer is effective only when it is actually received by the offeror or the offeror's agent. A **counteroffer** occurs when the offeree rejects the original offer and simultaneously makes a new offer. EXAMPLE #14 Duffy offers to sell her Picasso lithograph to Wong for $4,500. Wong responds, "Your price is too high. I'll offer to purchase your lithograph for $4,000." Wong's response is a counteroffer, because it terminates Duffy's offer to sell at $4,500 and creates a new offer by Wong to purchase at $4,000.□ Merely inquiring about an offer does not constitute rejection, however. If Wong had responded, "Will you accept less?" this would not terminate Duffy's original offer.

COUNTEROFFER
An offeree's response to an offer in which the offeree rejects the original offer and at the same time makes a new offer.

At common law, the **mirror image rule** requires the offeree's acceptance to match the offeror's offer exactly—to mirror the offer. Any material change in, or addition to, the terms of the original offer automatically terminates that offer and substitutes the counteroffer. The counteroffer, of course, need not be accepted; but if the original offeror does accept the terms of the counteroffer, a valid contract is created.[7]

MIRROR IMAGE RULE
A common law rule that requires that the terms of the offeree's acceptance adhere exactly to the terms of the offeror's offer for a valid contract to be formed.

---

7. The mirror image rule has been greatly modified in regard to sales contracts. Section 2–207 of the UCC provides that a contract is formed if the offeree makes a definite expression of acceptance (such as signing the form in the appropriate location), even though the terms of the acceptance modify or add to the terms of the original offer.

Termination by Operation of Law   The power of the offeree to transform the offer into a binding, legal obligation can be terminated by operation of law through the occurrence of any of the following events:

1. Lapse of time.
2. Destruction of the specific subject matter of the offer.
3. Death or incompetence of the offeror or the offeree.
4. Supervening illegality of the proposed contract.

An offer terminates automatically by law when the period of time specified in the offer has passed. **EXAMPLE #15** Alejandro offers to sell his motor home to Kelly if she accepts within twenty days. Kelly must accept within the twenty-day period, or the offer will lapse (terminate).□ The time period specified in an offer normally begins to run when the offer is actually received by the offeree, not when it is sent or drawn up. If the offer does not specify a time for acceptance, the offer terminates at the end of a *reasonable* period of time. What constitutes a reasonable period of time depends on the subject matter of the contract, business and market conditions, and other relevant circumstances. An offer to sell farm produce, for example, will terminate sooner than an offer to sell farm equipment because farm produce is perishable and subject to greater fluctuations in market value.

Irrevocable Offers   Although most offers are revocable, some can be made irrevocable—that is, they cannot be revoked, or canceled. An option contract involves one type of irrevocable offer. An *option contract* is created when an offeror promises to hold an offer open for a specified period of time in return for a payment (consideration) given by the offeree. An option contract takes away the offeror's power to revoke the offer for the period of time specified in the option. If no time is specified, then a reasonable period of time is implied. **EXAMPLE #16** You are in the business of writing movie scripts. Your agent contacts the head of development at New Line Cinema and offers to sell New Line your latest movie script. New Line likes your script and agrees to pay you $25,000 for a six-month option. In this situation, you (through your agent) are the offeror, and New Line is the offeree. You cannot revoke your offer to sell New Line your script for the next six months. If after six months no contract has been formed, however, New Line loses the $25,000, and you are free to sell the script to another movie studio.□

Increasingly, courts also refuse to allow an offeror to revoke an offer when the offeree has changed position because of justifiable reliance on the offer. When the offeree justifiably relies on an offer to her or his detriment, the court may hold that this *detrimental reliance* makes the offer irrevocable. **EXAMPLE #17**   Angela has rented commercial property from Jake for the past thirty-three years under a series of five-year leases. Under business conditions existing as their seventh lease nears its end, the rental property market is more favorable for tenants than for landlords. Angela tells Jake that she is going to look at other, less expensive properties as possible sites for her business. Wanting Angela to remain a tenant, Jake promises to reduce the rent in their next lease. In reliance on the promise, Angela continues to occupy and do business on Jake's property and does not look at other sites. When they sit down to negotiate a new lease, however, Jake says he has changed his mind and will increase the rent. Can he effectively revoke his promise? Normally he cannot, because Angela has been relying on his promise to reduce the rent. Had the promise not been made, she would have relocated her business.□ This is a case of detrimental reliance on a promise, which therefore cannot be revoked. In this situation, the doctrine of **promissory estoppel** comes into play. To **estop** means to bar, impede, or preclude someone from doing something. Thus, promissory estoppel means that the promisor (the offeror) is barred from revoking the offer, in this case because the offeree has already changed her actions in reliance on the offer.

Acceptance

Acceptance is a voluntary act (either words or conduct) by the offeree that shows assent (agreement) to the terms of an offer. The acceptance must be unequivocal and must be communicated to the offeror.

Unequivocal Acceptance To exercise the power of acceptance effectively, the offeree must accept unequivocally. This is the *mirror image rule* previously discussed. If the acceptance is subject to new conditions or if the terms of the acceptance change the original offer, the acceptance may be deemed a counteroffer that implicitly rejects the original offer. An acceptance may be unequivocal even though the offeree expresses dissatisfaction with the contract. For example, "I accept the offer, but I wish I could have gotten a better price" is an effective acceptance. So, too, is "I accept, but can you shave the price?" In contrast, the statement "I accept the offer but only if I can pay on ninety days' credit" is not an unequivocal acceptance and operates as a counteroffer, rejecting the original offer.

Certain terms, when added to an acceptance, will not qualify the acceptance sufficiently to constitute rejection of the offer. **EXAMPLE #18** In response to an offer to sell a piano, the offeree replies, "I accept; please send a written contract." The offeree is requesting a written contract but is not making it a condition for acceptance. Therefore, the acceptance is effective without the written contract. If the offeree replies, "I accept if you send a written contract," however, the acceptance is expressly conditioned on the request for a writing, and the statement is not an acceptance but a counteroffer. (Notice how important each word is!)[8]□

Ordinarily, silence cannot constitute acceptance because an offeree should not be obligated to act affirmatively to reject an offer. Only in rare circumstances will an offeree's silence operate as an acceptance, such as when an offeree takes the benefit of offered services after having had an opportunity to reject them. An offeree might also have a duty to communicate a rejection when he or she has had prior dealings with the offeror that would lead the offeror to believe that silence is acceptance, such as when receiving shipments of goods.

Communication of Acceptance Whether the offeror must be notified of the acceptance depends on the nature of the contract. In a bilateral contract, communication of acceptance is necessary because acceptance is in the form of a promise (not performance) and the contract is formed when the promise is made (rather than when the act is performed). The offeree must communicate the acceptance to the offeror. Communication of acceptance may not be necessary, however, if the offer dispenses with the requirement. Because a unilateral

PROMISSORY ESTOPPEL
A doctrine that applies when a promisor makes a clear and definite promise on which the promisee justifiably relies; such a promise is binding if justice will be better served by the enforcement of the promise.

ESTOP
To bar, impede, or preclude someone from doing something.

ACCEPTANCE
A voluntary act by the offeree that shows assent, or agreement, to the terms of an offer; may consist of words or conduct.

---

8. In regard to sales contracts, the UCC provides that an acceptance may still be valid even if some terms are added. The new terms are simply treated as proposed additions to the contract.

contract calls for the full performance of some act, acceptance is usually evident, and notification is therefore unnecessary unless the offeror requests notice or has no way of knowing whether performance has begun.

Mode and Timeliness of Acceptance   In bilateral contracts, acceptance must be timely. The general rule is that acceptance in a bilateral contract is timely if it is made before the offer is terminated. Problems may arise, though, when the parties involved are not dealing face to face. In such situations, the offeree should use an authorized mode of communication.

Acceptance takes effect, thus completing formation of the contract, at the time the offeree sends or delivers the communication via the mode expressly or impliedly authorized by the offeror. This is the so-called **mailbox rule,** which the majority of courts follow. Under this rule, if the authorized mode of communication is the mail, then an acceptance becomes valid when it is dispatched (placed in the control of the U.S. Postal Service)—*not* when it is received by the offeror.

The mailbox rule was created to prevent the confusion that arises when an offeror sends a letter of revocation but, before it arrives, the offeree sends a letter of acceptance. Thus, whereas a revocation becomes effective only when it is *received* by the offeree, an acceptance becomes effective on *dispatch* (when sent, even if it is never received), provided that an *authorized* means of communication is used.

The mailbox rule does not apply to instantaneous forms of communication, such as when the parties are dealing face to face, by telephone, or by fax. There is still some uncertainty in the courts as to whether e-mail should be considered an instantaneous form of communication to which the mailbox rule does not apply. If the parties have agreed to conduct transactions electronically and if the Uniform Electronic Transactions Act (to be discussed in Chapter 11) applies, then e-mail is considered sent when it either leaves control of the sender or is received by the recipient. This rule takes the place of the mailbox rule when the Uniform Electronic Transactions Act applies but essentially allows an e-mail acceptance to become effective when sent (as it would if sent by U.S. mail).

Authorized Means of Acceptance   A means of communicating acceptance can be expressly authorized by the offeror or impliedly authorized by the surrounding facts and circumstances. If an offer stipulates an authorized mode of acceptance (such as by overnight delivery), then the contract is formed at the moment the offeree accepts the offer using the authorized means. **EXAMPLE #19** Sam Perkins, a dealer in Massachusetts, offers to sell a container of antiques to Leaham's Antiques in Colorado. The offer states that Leaham's must accept the offer via FedEx overnight delivery. The acceptance is effective (and a binding contract is formed) the moment that Leaham's gives the overnight envelope containing the acceptance to the FedEx driver. □

If the offeror does not expressly authorize a certain mode of acceptance, then acceptance can be made by any reasonable means. Courts look at the prevailing business usages and the surrounding circumstances in determining whether the mode of acceptance used was reasonable. Usually, the offeror's choice of a particular means in making the offer implies that the offeree can use the *same or a faster* means for acceptance. Thus, if the offer is made via priority mail, it would be reasonable to accept the offer via priority mail or by a faster method, such as by fax.

If the offeror authorizes a particular method of acceptance, but the offeree accepts by a different means, the acceptance may still be effective if the substi-

MAILBOX RULE

A rule providing that an acceptance of an offer becomes effective on dispatch (on being placed in an official mailbox), if mail is expressly or impliedly an authorized means of communication of acceptance of the offer.

tuted method serves the same purpose as the authorized means. The use of a substitute method of acceptance is not effective on dispatch, though, and no contract will be formed until the acceptance is received by the offeror. Thus, if an offer specifies FedEx overnight delivery but the offeree accepts by overnight delivery from another carrier, such as UPS or DHL, the acceptance will still be effective, but not until the offeror receives it.

Preventing Legal Disputes

An effective way to avoid legal disputes over contracts is to communicate your intentions clearly to the other party and express every detail in writing, even when a written contract is not legally required. If you are the offeror, be explicit in your offer about how long the offer will remain open and stipulate the authorized means of communicating the acceptance. Include a provision requiring the offeree to notify you of acceptance regardless of whether a bilateral or unilateral contract will be formed. If you are the offeree, make sure that the language you use for any counteroffer, negotiation, or acceptance is absolutely clear and unambiguous. A simple "I accept" is best in most situations. The safest approach is to communicate your acceptance by the means authorized by the offeror or, if none, by the same method used to convey the offer. This can lessen the potential for problems arising due to revocation or lost communications. ◼

CONSIDERATION

The fact that a promise has been made does not mean the promise can or will be enforced. Under the common law, a primary basis for the enforcement of promises is consideration. **Consideration** is usually defined as the value (such as cash) given in return for a promise (such as the promise to sell a stamp collection on receipt of payment) or in return for a performance.

Often, consideration is broken down into two parts: (1) something of *legally sufficient value* must be given in exchange for the promise; and (2) usually, there must be a *bargained-for* exchange.

Legal Value

The "something of legally sufficient value" may consist of (1) a promise to do something that one has no prior legal duty to do, (2) the performance of an action that one is otherwise not obligated to undertake, or (3) the refraining from an action that one has a legal right to undertake (called a *forbearance*). Consideration in bilateral contracts normally consists of a promise in return for a promise, as explained earlier. **EXAMPLE #20** In a contract for the sale of goods, the seller promises to ship specific goods to the buyer, and the buyer promises to pay for those goods when they are received. Each of these promises constitutes consideration for the contract. ☐

In contrast, unilateral contracts involve a promise in return for a performance. **EXAMPLE #21** Anita says to her neighbor, "When you finish painting the garage, I will pay you $800." Anita's neighbor paints the garage. The act of painting the garage is the consideration that creates Anita's contractual obligation to pay her neighbor $800. ☐

What if, in return for a promise to pay, a person refrains from pursuing harmful habits (a forbearance), such as the use of tobacco and alcohol? Does such

CONSIDERATION
Generally, the value given in return for a promise. The consideration must be something of legally sufficient value, and there must be a bargained-for exchange.

forbearance constitute legally sufficient consideration? That was the issue before the court in the classic consideration case discussed in this chapter's *Landmark in the Legal Environment* feature.

Bargained-For Exchange

The second element of consideration is that it must provide the basis for the bargain struck between the contracting parties. The promise given by the promisor (offeror) must induce the promisee (offeree) to offer a return promise, a performance, or a forbearance, and the promisee's promise, performance, or forbearance must induce the promisor to make the promise.

This element of bargained-for exchange distinguishes contracts from gifts. **EXAMPLE #22** Arlene says to her son, "In consideration of the fact that you are not as wealthy as your brothers, I will pay you $5,000." The fact that the word *consideration* is used does not, by itself, mean that consideration has been given. Indeed, this is not an enforceable promise because the son need not do anything in order to receive the promised $5,000.[9] The son need not give Arlene something of legal value in return for her promise, and the promised $5,000 does not involve a bargained-for exchange. Rather, Arlene has simply stated her motive for giving her son a gift.□

Adequacy of Consideration

Legal sufficiency of consideration involves the requirement that consideration be something of legally sufficient value in the eyes of the law. Adequacy of consideration involves how much consideration is given. Essentially, adequacy of consideration concerns the fairness of the bargain. On the surface, fairness would appear to be an issue when the items exchanged are of unequal value. In general, however, a court will not question the adequacy of consideration if the consideration is legally sufficient. Under the doctrine of freedom of contract, parties are normally free to bargain as they wish. If people could sue merely because they had entered into an unwise contract, the courts would be overloaded with frivolous suits.

In extreme cases, a court may consider the adequacy of consideration in terms of its amount or worth because inadequate consideration may indicate that fraud, duress, or undue influence was involved or that the element of bargained-for exchange was lacking. It may also reflect a party's incompetence (for instance, an individual might have been too intoxicated or too young to make a contract). **EXAMPLE #23** Dylan has a house worth $180,000 and sells it for $90,000. A $90,000 sale could indicate that the buyer unduly pressured Dylan into selling the house at that price or that Dylan was defrauded into selling the house at far below market value. (Defenses to enforceability will be discussed in Chapter 10.) Of course, it might also indicate that Dylan was simply in a hurry to sell, in which case the amount was legally sufficient.□

Agreements That Lack Consideration

Sometimes, one of the parties (or both parties) to an agreement may think that consideration has been exchanged when in fact it has not. Here, we look at some situations in which the parties' promises or actions do not qualify as contractual consideration.

---

9. See *Fink v. Cox,* 18 Johns. 145, 9 Am.Dec. 191 (N.Y. 1820).

In *Hamer v. Sidway,*[a] the issue before the court arose from a contract created in 1869 between William Story, Sr., and his nephew, William Story II. The uncle promised his nephew that if the nephew refrained from drinking alcohol, using tobacco, and playing billiards and cards for money until he reached the age of twenty-one, the uncle would pay him $5,000 (about $75,000 in today's dollars). The nephew, who indulged occasionally in all of these "vices," agreed to refrain from them and did so for the next six years. (In 1869, it was legal for a teenager to gamble and to use alcohol and tobacco.) Following his twenty-first birthday in 1875, the nephew wrote to his uncle that he had performed his part of the bargain and was thus entitled to the promised $5,000. A few days later, the uncle wrote the nephew a letter stating, "[Y]ou shall have the five thousand dollars, as I promised you." The uncle said that the money was in the bank and that the nephew could "consider this money on interest."

The Issue of Consideration

The nephew left the money in the care of his uncle, who held it for the next twelve years. When the uncle died in 1887, however, the executor of the uncle's estate refused to pay the $5,000 claim brought by Hamer, a third party to whom the promise had been *assigned.* (The law allows parties to assign, or transfer, rights in contracts to third parties; assignments will be discussed further later in this chapter.) The executor, Sidway, contended that the contract was

a. 124 N.Y. 538, 27 N.E. 256 (1891).

invalid because there was insufficient consideration to support it. The uncle had received nothing, and the nephew had actually benefited by fulfilling the uncle's wishes. Therefore, no contract existed.

The Court's Conclusion

Although a lower court upheld Sidway's position, the New York Court of Appeals reversed and ruled in favor of the plaintiff, Hamer. "The promisee used tobacco, occasionally drank liquor, and he had a legal right to do so," the court stated. "That right he abandoned for a period of years upon the strength of the promise of the testator [one who makes a will] that for such forbearance he would give him $5,000. We need not speculate on the effort which may have been required to give up the use of those stimulants. It is sufficient that he restricted his lawful freedom of action within certain prescribed limits upon the faith of his uncle's agreement."

APPLICATION TO TODAY'S LEGAL ENVIRONMENT

Although this case was decided over a century ago, the principles enunciated by the court remain applicable to contracts formed today, including online contracts. For a contract to be valid and binding, consideration must be given, and that consideration must be something of legally sufficient value.

RELEVANT WEB SITES

To locate information on the Web concerning the *Hamer v. Sidway* decision, go to this text's Web site at **www.cengage.com/blaw/let**, select "Chapter 9," and click on "URLs for Landmarks."

Preexisting Duty   Under most circumstances, a promise to do what one already has a legal duty to do does not constitute legally sufficient consideration. The preexisting legal duty may be imposed by law or may arise out of a previous contract. A sheriff, for example, cannot collect a reward for providing information leading to the capture of a criminal if the sheriff already has a legal duty to capture the criminal.

Likewise, if a party is already bound by contract to perform a certain duty, that duty cannot serve as consideration for a second contract. **EXAMPLE #24** Bauman-Bache, Inc., begins construction on a seven-story office building and after three months demands an extra $75,000 on its contract. If the extra $75,000 is not paid, Bauman-Bache will stop working. The owner of the land, finding no one else to complete the construction, agrees to pay the extra $75,000. The agreement is unenforceable because it is not supported by legally sufficient consideration; Bauman-Bache is obligated under a preexisting contract to complete the building.□

Unforeseen Difficulties   The rule regarding preexisting duty is meant to prevent extortion and the so-called holdup game. What happens, though, when an honest contractor who has contracted with a landowner to construct a building runs into extraordinary difficulties that were totally unforeseen at the time the contract was formed? In the interests of fairness and equity, the courts sometimes allow exceptions to the preexisting duty rule. In the example just mentioned, if the landowner agrees to pay extra compensation to the contractor for overcoming unforeseen difficulties, the court may refrain from applying the preexisting duty rule and enforce the agreement. When the "unforeseen difficulties" that give rise to a contract modification involve the types of risks ordinarily assumed in business, however, the courts will usually assert the preexisting duty rule.

Rescission and New Contract The law recognizes that two parties can mutually agree to rescind, or cancel, their contract, at least to the extent that it is executory (still to be carried out). *Rescission* is the unmaking of a contract so as to return the parties to the positions they occupied before the contract was made. When rescission and the making of a new contract take place at the same time, but the duties of both parties remain the same as in their rescinded contract, the courts frequently are given a choice of applying the preexisting duty rule or allowing rescission and letting the new contract stand.

Past Consideration Promises made in return for actions or events that have already taken place are unenforceable. These promises lack consideration in that the element of bargained-for exchange is missing. In short, you can bargain for something to take place now or in the future but not for something that has already taken place. Past consideration is no consideration.

EXAMPLE #25 Blackmon became friends with Iverson when Iverson was a high school student who showed tremendous promise as an athlete. One evening, Blackmon suggested that Iverson use "The Answer" as a nickname in the summer league basketball tournaments. Blackmon said that Iverson would be "The Answer" to all of the National Basketball Association's woes. Later that night, Iverson said that he would give Blackmon 25 percent of any proceeds from the merchandising of products that used "The Answer" as a logo or a slogan. Because Iverson's promise was made in return for past consideration, it is unenforceable; in effect, Iverson stated his intention to give Blackmon a gift.[10] ▪

Promissory Estoppel

As mentioned earlier, under the doctrine of *promissory estoppel* (which is also called *detrimental reliance*), a person who has reasonably and substantially relied on the promise of another may be able to obtain some measure of recovery. This doctrine is applied in a wide variety of contexts in which a promise is otherwise unenforceable, such as when a promise is not supported by consideration. Under this doctrine, a court may enforce an otherwise unenforceable promise to avoid the injustice that would otherwise result. For the doctrine to be applied, the following elements are required:

1. There must be a clear and definite promise.
2. The promisee must justifiably rely on the promise.
3. The reliance normally must be of a substantial and definite character.
4. Justice will be better served by enforcement of the promise.

If these requirements are met, a promise may be enforced even though it is not supported by consideration. In essence, the promisor will be *estopped*

---

10. *Blackmon v. Iverson,* 324 F.Supp.2d 602 (E.D.Pa. 2003).

(prevented) from asserting the lack of consideration as a defense. EXAMPLE #26 Your uncle tells you, "I'll pay you $350 a week so you won't have to work anymore." In reliance on your uncle's promise, you quit your job, but your uncle refuses to pay you. Under the doctrine of promissory estoppel, you may be able to enforce such a promise.[11] □

CAPACITY

In addition to agreement and consideration, for a contract to be deemed valid the parties to the contract must have *contractual capacity*—the legal ability to enter into a contractual relationship. Courts generally presume the existence of contractual capacity, but there are some situations in which capacity is lacking or may be questionable.

Historically, the law has given special protection to those who bargain with the inexperience of youth or those who lack the degree of mental competence required by law. If a court has determined a person to be mentally incompetent, for example, that person cannot form a legally binding contract with another party. In other situations, a party may have the capacity to enter into a valid contract but also have the right to avoid liability under it. For example, minors—or *infants,* as they are commonly referred to in legal terminology—usually are not legally bound by contracts. In this section, we look at the effect of youth, intoxication, and mental incompetence on contractual capacity.

Minors

Today, in virtually all states, the *age of majority* (when a person is no longer a minor) for contractual purposes is eighteen years.[12] In addition, some states provide for the termination of minority on marriage. Minority status may also be terminated by a minor's *emancipation,* which occurs when a child's parent or legal guardian relinquishes the legal right to exercise control over the child. Normally, a minor who leaves home to support himself or herself is considered emancipated. Several jurisdictions permit minors to petition a court for emancipation themselves. For business purposes, a minor may petition a court to be treated as an adult.

The general rule is that a minor can enter into any contract that an adult can, provided that the contract is not one prohibited by law for minors (for example, the sale of tobacco or alcoholic beverages). A contract entered into by a minor, however, is voidable at the option of that minor, subject to certain exceptions. To exercise the option to avoid a contract, a minor need only manifest an intention not to be bound by it. The minor "avoids" the contract by disaffirming it.

Disaffirmance is the legal avoidance, or setting aside, of a contractual obligation. To disaffirm, a minor must express his or her intent, through words or conduct, not to be bound to the contract. The minor must disaffirm the entire contract, not merely a portion of it. For example, the minor cannot decide to keep part of the goods purchased under a contract and return the remaining goods.

---

11. *Ricketts v. Scothorn,* 57 Neb. 51, 77 N.W. 365 (1898).
12. The age of majority may still be twenty-one for other purposes, such as the purchase and consumption of alcohol.

Intoxication

Intoxication is a condition in which a person's normal capacity to act or think is inhibited by alcohol or some other drug. A contract entered into by an intoxicated person can be either voidable or valid (and thus enforceable). If the person was sufficiently intoxicated to lack mental capacity, then the transaction may be voidable at the option of the intoxicated person even if the intoxication was purely voluntary. For the contract to be voidable, the person must prove that the intoxication impaired her or his reason and judgment so severely that she or he did not comprehend the legal consequences of entering into the contract.

Mental Incompetence

If a court has previously determined that a person is mentally incompetent and has appointed a guardian to represent the individual, any contract made by the mentally incompetent person is void—no contract exists. Only the guardian can enter into binding legal obligations on the incompetent person's behalf.

LEGALITY

For a contract to be valid and enforceable, it must be formed for a legal purpose. A contract to do something that is prohibited by federal or state statutory law is illegal and, as such, is void from the outset and thus unenforceable. In addition, a contract to commit a tortious act (see Chapter 5) or to commit an act that is contrary to public policy is illegal and unenforceable. It is important to note that a contract or clause in a contract can be deemed illegal even in the absence of a specific statute prohibiting the action promised in the contract. Here we examine contracts that are contrary to statute or contrary to public policy.

Contracts Contrary to Statute

Any contract to commit a crime is a contract in violation of statute. Thus, a contract to sell an illegal drug in violation of criminal statutes (see Chapter 6) is unenforceable. Similarly, a contract to cover up a corporation's violation of the Sarbanes-Oxley Act (see Chapters 2 and 15) is unenforceable, as is a contract to smuggle undocumented workers from another country into the United States for an employer (see Chapter 17). A contract to provide inside information regarding the sales of stock is illegal and unenforceable because it violates securities laws (see Chapter 24). Another example of a contract that is contrary to statute is a contract to loan funds to a person at an interest rate that is higher than the maximum interest rate allowed by state law.

Gambling   All states have statutes that regulate gambling—defined as any scheme that involves a distribution of property by chance among persons who have paid valuable consideration for the opportunity (chance) to receive the property. Gambling is the creation of risk for the purpose of assuming it. Traditionally, state statutes have deemed gambling contracts to be illegal and thus void. It is sometimes difficult, however, to distinguish a gambling contract from the risk sharing inherent in almost all contracts.

A number of states allow certain forms of gambling, such as horse racing, poker machines, and charity-sponsored bingo, and nearly all states allow state-

As many as 20 million adults in the United States play some form of fantasy sports via the Internet. A fantasy sport is a game in which participants, often called owners, build teams composed of real-life players from different real-life teams. Each fantasy team competes against the fantasy teams belonging to other owners. At the end of each week, the statistical performances of all the real-life players are translated into points, and the points of all the players on an owner's fantasy team are totaled. Although a wide variety of fantasy games are available, most participants play fantasy football. On many fantasy sports sites, participants pay a fee in order to play and use the site's facilities, such as statistical tracking and message boards. At the end of the season, prizes ranging from T-shirts to flat-screen televisions are awarded to the winners.

In other instances, the participants in fantasy sports gamble directly on the outcome. In a fantasy football league, for example, each participant-owner adds a given amount to the pot and then "drafts" his or her fantasy team from actual National Football League players. At the end of the football season, each owner's points are totaled, and the owner with the most points wins the pot.

Congress Weighs In

As online gambling has expanded, Congress has attempted to regulate it. In late 2006, a federal law went into effect that makes it illegal for credit-card companies and banks to engage in transactions with Internet gambling companies.[a] Although the law does not prohibit individuals from placing online bets, in effect it makes it almost impossible for them to do so by preventing them from obtaining financing for online gambling. At first glance, the legislation appears comprehensive, but it specifically exempts Internet wagers on horse racing, state lotteries, and fantasy sports. Hence, one could argue that Congress has determined that fantasy sports do not constitute a prohibited Internet gambling activity.

Testing the Gambling Aspect in Court

Thus far, the courts have had the opportunity to rule only on whether the pay-to-play fantasy sports sites that charge an entrance fee and offer prizes to the winners are running gambling operations. Charles Humphrey brought a lawsuit against Viacom, ESPN, *The Sporting News,* and other hosts of such fantasy sports sites under a New Jersey statute that allows the recovery of gambling losses. Humphrey claimed that the fantasy sports leagues were games of chance, not games of skill, because events beyond the participants' control could determine the outcome—for example, a star quarterback might be injured. He also pointed out that in the offline world, federal law prohibits any games of chance, such as sweepstakes or drawings, that require entrants to submit consideration in order to play. *Consideration* has been defined as the purchase of a product or the payment of money. For these reasons, he argued, the entrance fees constituted gambling losses that could be recovered.

The federal district court that heard the case ruled against Humphrey, mostly on procedural grounds, but the court did conclude that as a matter of law the entrance fees did not constitute "bets" or "wagers" because the fees are paid unconditionally, the prizes offered are for a fixed amount and certain to be awarded, and the defendants do not compete for the prizes.[b] The court also observed that if a combination of entrance fees and prizes constituted gambling, a host of contests ranging from golf tournaments to track meets to spelling bees and beauty contests would be gambling operations—a conclusion that the court deemed "patently absurd."[c] Note, however, that the case involved only pay-to-play sites. The court did not have to address the question of whether fantasy sports sites that enable participants to contibute to a pot in the hopes of winning it at the end of the season constitute gambling sites.

FOR CRITICAL ANALYSIS What arguments can be used to support the idea that playing fantasy sports requires skill?

---

a. Security and Accountability for Every Port Act, Public L. No. 109-347, Sections 5361–5367, 120 Stat. 1884 (2006). (A version of the Unlawful Internet Gambling Enforcement Act of 2006 was incorporated into this statute as Title VIII.)

b. *Humphrey v. Viacom, Inc.,* 2007 WL 1797648 (D.N.J. 2007).

c. In reaching this conclusion, the federal district court cited portions of an Arizona Supreme Court ruling, *State v. American Holiday Association, Inc.,* 151 Ariz. 312, 727 P.2d 807 (1986).

---

operated lotteries and gambling on Indian reservations. Because state laws on gambling differ, Internet gambling has raised some unique issues. Does a person who lives in a state where gambling is illegal violate state law by engaging in online gambling? How can a state enforce its gambling laws on the Internet? Another significant issue is whether entering into contracts that involve gambling on sports teams that do not really exist—fantasy sports—is a form of gambling. For a discussion of this issue, see this chapter's *Online Developments* feature.

Licensing Statutes All states require members of certain professions—including physicians, lawyers, real estate agents, accountants, electricians, and stockbrokers—to have licenses. If the purpose of the licensing statute is to protect the public from unauthorized practitioners, then a contract involving an unlicensed practitioner is generally illegal and unenforceable. If the purpose of the statute is merely to raise government revenues, however, a contract with an unlicensed person may be enforced (and the unlicensed person fined).

Contracts Contrary to Public Policy

Certain contracts are not enforceable because of the negative impact they would have on society. These contracts are said to be *contrary to public policy*. Examples include a contract to commit an immoral act, such as selling a child, and a contract that prohibits marriage. **EXAMPLE #27** Forest offers a young man $10,000 if he refrains from marrying Forest's daughter. If the young man accepts and takes that cash, the contract is void (no contract is formed) because it is contrary to the public policy, which favors marriage. Thus, if the man marries Forest's daughter, Forest cannot sue him for breach of contract.□

Contracts in Restraint of Trade The United States has a strong public policy favoring competition in the economy. Thus, contracts that restrain trade, or anticompetitive agreements, are generally unenforceable because they are contrary to public policy. Typically, anticompetitive agreements also violate one or more federal or state antitrust laws (these laws will be discussed in Chapter 23). An exception is recognized when the restraint is reasonable and it is an ancillary (secondary, or subordinate) part of the contract, such as in a contract for the sale of an ongoing business or an employment contract.

Many contracts involve a type of restraint called a **covenant not to compete,** or *restrictive covenant.* A covenant not to compete may be created when a seller agrees not to open a new store in a certain geographic area surrounding the existing store. Such an agreement enables the seller to sell, and the purchaser to buy, the goodwill and reputation of an ongoing business without having to worry that the seller will open a competing business a block away. Provided the restrictive covenant is reasonable and is an ancillary part of the sale of an ongoing business, it is enforceable.

Agreements not to compete, or *noncompete agreements,* are also often included in employment contracts. People in middle- or upper-level management positions commonly agree not to work for competitors and not to start competing businesses for a specified period of time after termination of employment. Such agreements are legal in most states so long as the specified period of time (of restraint) is not excessive in duration and the geographic restriction is reasonable. What constitutes a reasonable time period may be shorter in the online environment than in conventional employment contracts, as discussed in this chapter's *Management Perspective* feature.

To be reasonable, a restriction on competition must protect a legitimate business interest and must not be any greater than necessary to protect that interest.[13] In the following case, the court had to decide whether it was reasonable for an employer's noncompete agreement to restrict a former employee from competing "in any area of business" in which the employer was engaged.

COVENANT NOT TO COMPETE
A contractual promise of one party to refrain from conducting business similar to that of another party for a certain period of time and within a specified geographic area. Courts commonly enforce such covenants if they are reasonable in terms of time and geographic area and are part of, or supplemental to, a contract for the sale of a business.

---

13. See, for example, *Gould & Lamb, LLC v. D'Alusio,* 949 So.2d 1212 (Fla.App. 2007). See also *Moore v. Midwest Distribution, Inc.,* 76 Ark.App. 397, 65 S.W.3d 490 (2002).

Management Faces a Legal Issue

For some companies today, particularly those in high-tech industries, trade secrets are their most valuable assets. Often, to prevent departing employees from disclosing trade secrets to competing employers, business owners and managers have their key employees sign covenants not to compete. In such a covenant, the employee typically agrees not to set up a competing business or work for a competitor in a specified geographic area for a certain period of time. Generally, the time and geographic restrictions must be reasonable. A serious issue facing management today is whether time and space restrictions that have been deemed reasonable in the past serve as a guide to what might constitute reasonable restrictions in today's changing legal landscape, which includes the Internet environment.

What the Courts Say

There is little case law to guide management on this issue. One case involved Mark Schlack, who worked as a Web site manager for EarthWeb, Inc., in New York. Schlack signed a covenant stating that, on termination of his employment, he would not work for any competing company for one year. When he resigned and accepted an offer from a company in Massachusetts to design a Web site, EarthWeb sued to enforce the covenant not to compete. The court refused to enforce the covenant, in part because there was no evidence that Schlack had misappropriated any of EarthWeb's trade secrets or clients. The court also stated that because the Internet lacks physical borders, a covenant prohibiting an employee from working for a competitor anywhere in the world for one year is excessive in duration.[a]

In a later case, a federal district court enforced a one-year noncompete agreement against the founder of a law-related Web site business even though no geographic restriction was included in the agreement. According to the court, "Although there is no geographic limitation on the provision, this is nonetheless reasonable in light of the national, and indeed international, nature of Internet business."[b]

The sale of an Internet-only business involves literally the full worldwide scope of the Internet itself. In a relatively recent case, a company selling vitamins over the Internet was sold for more than $2 million. The purchase agreement contained a noncompete clause. For four years after the sale, the seller was prohibited from engaging in the sale of nutritional and health products via the Internet. Notwithstanding the noncompete agreement, the seller created at least two other Internet sites from which he sold health products and vitamins. The court held for the buyer of the Internet-only business and enjoined (prevented) the seller from violating the noncompete agreement.[c] The court pointed out that the seller was still able to engage in his former business by other means using non-Internet markets. The seller also remained free to sell other types of products on the Internet.

Implications for Managers

Management in high-tech companies should avoid overreaching in terms of time and geographic restrictions in noncompete agreements. Additionally, when considering the reasonability of time and place restrictions, the courts tend to balance time restrictions against other factors, such as geographic restrictions. Because for Web-based work the geographic restriction can be worldwide in scope, the time restriction should be narrowed considerably to compensate for the extensive geographic restriction.

---

a. *EarthWeb, Inc. v. Schlack,* 71 F.Supp.2d 299 (S.D.N.Y. 1999).

b. *West Publishing Corp. v. Stanley,* 2004 WL 73590 (D.Minn. 2004).

c. *MyVitaNet.com v. Kowalski,* __ F.Supp.2d __ , 2008 WL 203008 (S.D. Ohio 2008).

Case 9.4 — Stultz v. Safety and Compliance Management, Inc.

Court of Appeals of Georgia, 2007.
285 Ga.App. 799, 648 S.E.2d 129.

BACKGROUND AND FACTS Safety and Compliance Management, Inc. (S & C), in Rossville, Georgia, provides alcohol- and drug-testing services in multiple states. In February 2002, S & C hired Angela Burgess. Her job duties included providing customer service, ensuring that specimens were properly retrieved from clients and transported to the testing lab, contacting clients, and managing the office. Burgess signed a covenant not to compete "in any area of business conducted by Safety and Compliance Management . . . for a two-year period . . . beginning at the termination of employment." In May 2004, Burgess quit her job to work at Rossville Medical Center (RMC) as a medical assistant. RMC provides medical services, including occupational medicine, medical physicals, and workers' compensation injury treatment. RMC also offers alcohol- and drug-testing services. Burgess's duties included setting patient appointments, taking patient medical histories, checking vital signs, performing urinalysis testing, administering injections, conducting alcohol breath tests, and collecting specimens for

CASE 9.4–CONTINUED

drug testing. S & C filed a suit in a Georgia state court against Burgess and others (including a defendant named Stultz), alleging, among other things, that she had violated the noncompete agreement. The court issued a summary judgment in S & C's favor. Burgess appealed to a state intermediate appellate court.

IN THE WORDS OF THE COURT . . . *BERNES*, Judge.

*   *   *   *

Restrictive covenants that are ancillary to an employment contract are subject to strict scrutiny and will be voided by Georgia courts if they impose an unreasonable restraint on trade. Whether the restraint imposed by the employment contract is reasonable is a question of law for determination by the court, which considers the nature and extent of the trade or business, the situation of the parties, and all the other circumstances. *A three-element test of duration, territorial coverage, and scope of activity has evolved as a helpful tool in examining the reasonableness of the particular factual setting to which it is applied.* *   *   * [Emphasis added.]

*   *   * Burgess contends that the trial court erred in concluding that the non-competition agreement was reasonable as to the scope of the activity prohibited.

The non-competition agreement provides that Burgess "will not compete *   *   * in any area of business conducted by [S & C]." Although the next sentence of the agreement provides some particularity by referring to the solicitation of existing accounts, the agreement, when read as a whole, plainly is intended to prevent any type of competing activity whatsoever, with the reference to solicitation merely being illustrative of one type of activity that is prohibited. *   *   * Thus, when properly construed, the non-competition agreement prohibits, without qualification, Burgess from competing in any area of business conducted by S & C.

Such a prohibition clearly is unreasonable *   *   * . A non-competition covenant which prohibits an employee from working for a competitor in any capacity, that is, *a covenant which fails to specify with particularity the activities which the employee is prohibited from performing, is too broad and indefinite to be enforceable.* And, Georgia courts have interpreted contractual language similar to that found in the present case as essentially prohibiting an employee from working for a competitor in any capacity whatsoever. *   *   * In light of this case law, we conclude that the non-competition agreement imposes a greater limitation upon Burgess than is necessary for the protection of S & C and therefore is unenforceable. [Emphasis added.]

It is true, as S & C maintains, that there are factual circumstances where an otherwise questionable restrictive covenant that prohibits working for a competitor will be upheld as reasonable. More specifically, a suspect restriction upon the scope of activity may nevertheless be upheld when the underlying facts reflect that the contracting party was the very heart and soul of the business whose departure effectively brought the business to a standstill. Moreover, the "heart and soul" exception is applicable only where the restrictive covenant otherwise applies to a very restricted territory and for a short period of time.

S & C, however, has failed to allege or present evidence showing that Burgess was the heart and soul of its alcohol and drug testing business. Although Burgess was a major player in S & C's business, she was, when all is said and done, an employee. Her departure may have hurt S & C; but it did not bring the business to a halt. It cannot be said, therefore, that Burgess was the heart and soul of the business.

DECISION AND REMEDY   The Court of Appeals of Georgia reversed the judgment of the lower court. The state intermediate appellate court concluded that the covenant not to compete that Burgess signed "is unreasonable as to the scope of the activity prohibited" because "it is overly broad and indefinite." Thus, the covenant was not enforceable.

THE ETHICAL DIMENSION To determine the enforceability of a covenant not to compete, the courts balance the rights of an employer against those of a former employee. What are these rights? How did S & C's covenant not to compete tip the balance in the employer's favor?

THE GLOBAL DIMENSION Should an employer be permitted to restrict a former employee from engaging in a competing business on a global level? Why or why not?

Unconscionable Contracts or Clauses Ordinarily, a court does not look at the fairness or equity of a contract. For example, the courts generally do not inquire into the adequacy of consideration (as discussed earlier). Persons are assumed to be reasonably intelligent, and the courts will not come to their aid just because they have made an unwise or foolish bargain. In certain circumstances, however, bargains are so oppressive that the courts relieve innocent parties of part or all of their duties. Such bargains are deemed **unconscionable** because they are so unscrupulous or grossly unfair as to be "void of conscience."[14] A contract can be unconscionable on either procedural or substantive grounds.

Procedural Unconscionability *Procedural* unconscionability often involves inconspicuous print, unintelligible language ("legalese"), or the lack of an opportunity to read the contract or to ask questions about its meaning. Procedural unconscionability may also occur when there is such disparity in bargaining power between the two parties that the weaker party's consent is not voluntary. These situations often involve an **adhesion contract,** which is a contract written exclusively by one party (the dominant party, usually the seller or creditor) and presented to the other (the adhering party, usually the buyer or borrower) on a take-it-or-leave-it basis. In other words, the adhering party has no opportunity to negotiate the terms of the contract. Standard-form contracts are often adhesion contracts.

Substantive Unconscionability *Substantive* unconscionability characterizes those contracts, or portions of contracts, that are oppressive or overly harsh. Courts generally focus on provisions that deprive one party of the benefits of the agreement or leave that party without a remedy for nonperformance by the other. **EXAMPLE #28** A person with little income and with only a fourth-grade education agrees to purchase a refrigerator for $4,000 and signs a two-year installment contract. The same type of refrigerator usually sells for $900 on the market. Some courts have held this type of contract to be unconscionable because the contract terms are so oppressive as to "shock the conscience" of the court.[15] □

Substantive unconscionability can arise in a wide variety of business contexts. For example, a contract clause that gives the business entity free access to the courts but requires the other party to arbitrate any dispute with the firm may be unconscionable.[16] Similarly, an arbitration clause in a credit-card agreement that prevents credit cardholders from obtaining relief for abusive debt-collection practices under

UNCONSCIONABLE
A term used to describe a contract or clause that is void on the basis of public policy because one party, as a result of disproportionate bargaining power, is forced to accept terms that are unfairly burdensome and that unfairly benefit the dominant party.

ADHESION CONTRACT
A "standard-form" contract, such as that between a large retailer and a consumer, in which the dominant party dictates the terms.

---

14. The Uniform Commercial Code incorporated the concept of unconscionability in Sections 2–302 and 2A–108. These provisions, which apply to contracts for the sale or lease of goods, will be discussed in Chapter 11.
15. See, for example, *Jones v. Star Credit Corp.*, 59 Misc.2d 189, 298 N.Y.S.2d 264 (1969).
16. See, for example, *Wisconsin Auto Title Loans, Inc. v. Jones*, 290 Wis.2d 514, 714 N.W.2d 155 (2006).

consumer law may be unconscionable.[17] Contracts drafted by insurance companies and cell phone providers have been struck down as substantively unconscionable when they included provisions that were overly harsh or one sided.[18]

EXCULPATORY CLAUSE
A provision that releases a contractual party from liability in the event of monetary or physical injury, no matter who is at fault.

Exculpatory Clauses   Closely related to the concept of unconscionability are **exculpatory clauses**—clauses that release a party from liability in the event of monetary or physical injury *no matter who is at fault*. Indeed, courts sometimes refuse to enforce such clauses on the ground that they are unconscionable.

EXAMPLE #29 Speedway SuperAmerica, Inc., hired Sebert Erwin under a contract for five years. The contract contained a clause in which Erwin promised to "hold harmless" Speedway for anything that happened to him while working for the company. One day, Erwin was told to report to a Speedway gas station in another city and help remove a walk-in freezer. When he was helping load it onto a truck, he fell and was injured. Erwin sued Speedway for damages resulting from the injury he suffered. Speedway counterclaimed, seeking to enforce the contract clause. The court held that the clause was unenforceable because it was contrary to public policy: the parties had unequal bargaining power, Erwin had only an eighth-grade education, and he signed a one-sided contract with a large company. Erwin was labeled an independent contractor, and, as such, he had no right to workers' compensation or other benefits that an employee normally would be due (see Chapter 17 for a discussion of state workers' compensation statutes and the differences between an independent contractor and an employee). The clause was the equivalent of an exculpatory clause, releasing the employer from any liability regardless of fault, and the court refused to enforce it.[19] □

Although courts view exculpatory clauses with disfavor, they do enforce such clauses when they do not contravene public policy, are not ambiguous, and do not claim to protect parties from liability for intentional misconduct. Businesses such as health clubs, racetracks, amusement parks, skiing facilities, horse-rental operations, golf-cart concessions, and skydiving organizations frequently use exculpatory clauses to limit their liability for patrons' injuries. Because these services are not essential, the firms offering them are sometimes considered to have no relative advantage in bargaining strength, and anyone contracting for their services is considered to do so voluntarily.

---

17. See, for example, *Coady v. Cross County Bank*, 299 Wis.2d 420, 729 N.W.2d 732 (Wis.App. 2007).
18. See, for example, *Gatton v. T-Mobile USA, Inc.*, 152 Cal.App.4th 571, 61 Cal.Rptr.3d 344 (2007); *Kinkel v. Cingular Wireless, LLC*, 223 Ill.2d 1, 857 N.E.2d 250, 306 Ill.Dec. 157 (2006); and *Aul v. Golden Rule Insurance Co.*, 304 Wis.2d 227, 737 N.W.2d 24 (Wis.App. 2007).
19. *Speedway Superamerica, LLC v. Erwin*, 250 S.W.3d 339 (Ky.App. 2008).

Reviewing . . . **Contract Formation**

Shane Durbin wanted to have a recording studio custom built in his home. He sent invitations to a number of local contractors to submit bids on the project. Rory Amstel submitted the lowest bid, which was $20,000 less than any of the other bids Durbin received. Durbin then called Amstel to ascertain the type and quality of the materials that were included in the bid and to find out if he could substitute a superior brand of acoustic tiles for the same bid price. Amstel said he would have to check into the price difference. The parties also discussed a possible start date for

construction. Two weeks later, Durbin changed his mind and decided not to go forward with his plan to build a recording studio. Amstel filed a suit against Durbin for breach of contract. Using the information presented in the chapter, answer the following questions.

1. Did Amstel's bid meet the requirements of an offer? Explain.

2. Was there an acceptance of the offer? Why or why not?

3. Suppose that the court determines that the parties did not reach an agreement. Further suppose that Amstel, in anticipation of building Durbin's studio, purchased materials and refused other jobs so that he would have time in his schedule for Durbin's project. Under what theory discussed in the chapter might Amstel attempt to recover these costs?

4. Now suppose that Durbin went forward with his plan to build the studio and immediately accepted Amstel's bid without discussing the type or quality of materials. After Amstel began construction, Durbin asked Amstel to substitute a superior brand of acoustic tiles for the tiles that Amstel had intended to use at the time that he bid on the project. Amstel installed the tiles, then asked Durbin to pay the difference in price, but Durbin refused. Can Amstel sue to obtain the price differential from Durbin in this situation? Why or why not?

Key Terms

acceptance 291
adhesion contract 303
agreement 282
bilateral contract 277
consideration 293
contract 274
counteroffer 289
covenant not to compete 300
estop 291
exculpatory clause 304
executed contract 281
executory contract 281

express contract 278
formal contract 278
implied-in-fact contract 278
informal contract 278
mailbox rule 292
mirror image rule 289
objective theory of
  contracts 275
offer 282
offeree 277
offeror 277
promise 273

promisee 274
promisor 274
promissory estoppel 291
revocation 289
unconscionable 303
unenforceable contract 282
unilateral contract 277
valid contract 281
void contract 282
voidable contract 281

Chapter Summary

An Overview of Contract Law
(See pages 273–275.)

1. *Sources of contract law*—The common law governs all contracts except when it has been modified or replaced by statutory law, such as the Uniform Commercial Code (UCC), or by administrative agency regulations. The UCC governs contracts for the sale or lease of goods (see Chapter 11).

2. *The function of contracts*—Contract law establishes what kinds of promises will be legally binding and supplies procedures for enforcing legally binding promises, or agreements.

3. *The definition of a contract*—A contract is an agreement that can be enforced in court. It is formed by two or more competent parties who agree to perform or to refrain from performing some act now or in the future.

CONTINUED

**An Overview
of Contract Law—
Continued**

**Elements
of a Contract**
(See pages 275–276.)

Types of Contracts
(See pages 276–282.)

**Requirements
of the Offer**
(See pages 282–289.)

**Termination
of the Offer**
(See pages 289–291.)

Acceptance
(See pages 291–293.)

Consideration
(See pages 293–297.)

4. *Objective theory of contracts*—In contract law, intent is determined by objective facts, not by the personal or subjective intent, or belief, of a party.

1. *Requirements of a valid contract*—The four requirements of a valid contract are agreement, consideration, contractual capacity, and legality.

2. *Defenses to the enforceability of a contract*—Even if the four requirements of a valid contract are met, a contract may be unenforceable if it lacks genuineness of assent or is not in the required form.

1. *Bilateral*—A promise for a promise.

2. *Unilateral*—A promise for an act (acceptance is the completed—or substantial—performance of the contract by the offeree).

3. *Formal*—Requires a special form for contract formation.

4. *Informal*—Requires no special form for contract formation.

5. *Express*—Formed by words (oral, written, or a combination).

6. *Implied in fact*—Formed at least in part by the conduct of the parties.

7. *Executed*—A fully performed contract.

8. *Executory*—A contract not yet fully performed.

9. *Valid*—A contract that results when the elements necessary for contract formation exist, including an agreement (an offer and an acceptance), consideration, parties with contractual capacity, and a legal purpose.

10. *Voidable*—A contract that may be legally avoided (canceled) at the option of one or both of the parties.

11. *Unenforceable*—A valid contract rendered unenforceable by some statute or legal defense.

12. *Void*—A contract that has no legal force or binding effect and that is treated as if the contract never existed.

1. *Intent*—The offeror must have a serious, objective intention to become bound by the offer. Offers made in anger, jest, or undue excitement do not qualify. Other situations that may lack the required intent include (a) expressions of opinion; (b) statements of future intent; (c) preliminary negotiations; (d) traditionally, agreements to agree in the future; and (e) generally, advertisements, catalogues, price lists, and circulars.

2. *Definiteness*—The terms of the offer must be sufficiently definite to be ascertainable by the parties or by a court.

3. *Communication*—The offer must be communicated to the offeree.

1. *By action of the parties*—An offer can be revoked or withdrawn at any time before acceptance without liability. A counteroffer is a rejection of the original offer and the making of a new offer.

2. *By operation of law*—An offer can terminate by (a) lapse of time, (b) destruction of the subject matter, (c) death or incompetence of the parties, or (d) supervening illegality.

1. Can be made only by the offeree or the offeree's agent.

2. Must be unequivocal. Under the common law (mirror image rule), if new terms or conditions are added to the acceptance, it will be considered a counteroffer.

1. *Elements of consideration*—Consideration is the value given in exchange for a promise. A contract cannot be formed without sufficient consideration. Consideration is often broken down into two parts:

    a. Something of *legally sufficient value* must be given in exchange for the promise. This may consist of a promise, an act, or a forbearance.

Consideration— Continued

b. There must be a *bargained-for exchange.*

2. *Adequacy of consideration*—Adequacy of consideration relates to how much consideration is given and whether a fair bargain was reached. Courts will inquire into the adequacy of consideration (whether the consideration is legally sufficient) only when fraud, undue influence, duress, or unconscionability may be involved.

3. *Agreements that lack consideration*—Consideration is lacking in the following situations:

   a. Preexisting duty—Consideration is not legally sufficient if one is either by law or by contract under a *preexisting duty* to perform the action being offered as consideration for a new contract.

   b. Past consideration—Actions or events that have already taken place do not constitute legally sufficient consideration.

4. *Promissory estoppel*—In some situations, when injustice can be avoided only by enforcing a promise that would otherwise be unenforceable, the doctrine of promissory estoppel might allow a contract to be enforced.

Capacity
(See pages 297–298.)

1. *Minors*—A minor is a person who has not yet reached the age of majority. In virtually all states, the age of majority is eighteen for contract purposes. Contracts with minors are voidable at the option of the minor.

2. *Intoxication*—A contract with an intoxicated person is enforceable if, despite being intoxicated, the person understood the legal consequences of entering into the contract. A contract entered into by an intoxicated person is voidable at the option of the intoxicated person if the person was sufficiently intoxicated to lack mental capacity, even if the intoxication was voluntary.

3. *Mental incompetence*—A contract made by a person whom a court has previously determined to be mentally incompetent is void. Only a guardian can enter into a contract on behalf of an incompetent person.

Legality
(See pages 298–304.)

1. *Contracts contrary to statute*—For a contract to be valid and enforceable, it must be formed for a legal purpose. A contract to do something that is prohibited by federal or state statutory law is illegal and, as such, void from the outset and thus unenforceable. Contracts contrary to statute include contracts to commit crimes as well as contracts that violate other laws, such as state laws setting the maximum interest rate that can be charged by a lender. They also include gambling contracts and some contracts with unlicensed professionals.

   a. Gambling contracts that contravene (go against) state statutes are deemed illegal and thus void.

   b. Contracts entered into with unlicensed persons (when a license is required by statute) are not enforceable *unless* the underlying purpose of the licensing statute is to raise government revenues.

2. *Contracts contrary to public policy*—Contracts that are contrary to public policy are also not enforceable on the grounds of illegality.

   a. Contracts to reduce or restrain free competition are illegal and prohibited by statutes. An exception is a *covenant not to compete,* which is enforceable if the terms are secondary to a contract (such as a contract for the sale of a business or an employment contract) and are reasonable as to time and area of restraint.

   b. When a contract or contract clause is so unfair that it is oppressive to one party, it may be deemed unconscionable; as such, it is illegal and cannot be enforced.

   c. An exculpatory clause is a clause that releases a party from liability in the event of monetary or physical injury, no matter who is at fault. In certain situations, exculpatory clauses may be contrary to public policy and thus unenforceable.

For Review

1. What are the four basic elements necessary to the formation of a valid contract?

2. What elements are necessary for an effective offer?

3. What is consideration?

4. Does an intoxicated person have the capacity to enter into an enforceable contract?

5. What is a covenant not to compete? When will such a covenant be enforceable?

Questions and Case Problems

implied contract – don't talk about it

9–1. Contracts. Suppose that Everett McCleskey, a local businessperson, is a good friend of Al Miller, the owner of a local candy store. Every day on his lunch hour, McCleskey goes into Miller's candy store and spends about five minutes looking at the candy. After examining Miller's candy and talking with Miller, McCleskey usually buys one or two candy bars. One afternoon, McCleskey goes into Miller's candy shop, looks at the candy, and picks up a $1 candy bar. Seeing that Miller is very busy, he catches Miller's eye, waves the candy bar at Miller without saying a word, and walks out. Is there a contract? If so, classify it within the categories presented in this chapter.

implied contract   she was fully aware

Question with Sample Answer

9–2. Janine was hospitalized with severe abdominal pain and placed in an intensive care unit. Her doctor told the hospital personnel to order around-the-clock nursing care for Janine. At the hospital's request, a nursing services firm, Nursing Services Unlimited, provided two weeks of in-hospital care and, after Janine was sent home, an additional two weeks of at-home care. During the at-home period of care, Janine was fully aware that she was receiving the benefit of the nursing services. Nursing Services later billed Janine $4,000 for the nursing care, but Janine refused to pay on the ground that she had never contracted for the services, either orally or in writing. In view of the fact that no express contract was ever formed, can Nursing Services recover the $4,000 from Janine? If so, under what legal theory? Discuss.

For a sample answer to Question 9–2, go to Appendix I at the end of this text.

9–3. Agreement. Ball writes Sullivan and inquires how much Sullivan is asking for a specific forty-acre tract of land Sullivan owns. In a letter received by Ball, Sullivan states, "I will not take less than $60,000 for the forty-acre tract as specified." Ball immediately sends Sullivan a telegram stating, "I accept your offer for $60,000 for the

forty-acre tract as specified." Discuss whether Ball can hold Sullivan to a contract for the sale of the land.

9–4. Requirements of the Offer. The Pittsburgh Board of Public Education in Pittsburgh, Pennsylvania, as required by state law, keeps lists of eligible teachers in order of their rank or standing. According to an "Eligibility List" form made available to applicants, no one may be hired to teach whose name is not within the top 10 percent of the names on the list. In 1996, Anna Reed was in the top 10 percent. She was not hired that year, although four other applicants who placed lower on the list—and not within the top 10 percent—were hired. In 1997 and 1998, Reed was again in the top 10 percent, but she was not hired until 1999. Reed filed a suit in a federal district court against the board and others. She argued in part that the state's requirement that the board keep a list constituted an offer, which she accepted by participating in the process to be placed on that list. She claimed that the board breached this contract by hiring applicants who ranked lower than she did. The case was transferred to a Pennsylvania state court. What are the requirements of an offer? Do the circumstances in this case meet those requirements? Why or why not? [*Reed v. Pittsburgh Board of Public Education,* 862 A.2d 131 (Pa.Cmwlth. 2004)]

9–5. Consideration. As a child, Martha Carr once visited her mother's 108-acre tract of unimproved land in Richland County, South Carolina. In 1968, Betty and Raymond Campbell leased the land. Carr, a resident of New York, was diagnosed as having schizophrenia and depression in 1986, was hospitalized five or six times, and subsequently took prescription drugs for the illnesses. In 1996, Carr inherited the Richland property and, two years later, contacted the Campbells about selling the land to them. Carr asked Betty about the value of the land, and Betty said that the county tax assessor had determined that the land's *agricultural value* was $54,000. The Campbells knew at the time that the county had assessed the total property value at $103,700 for tax purposes. A real estate appraiser found that the *real market value* of the property was $162,000. On August 6, Carr signed a contract to sell the land to the Campbells for $54,000. Believing the price to be unfair, however, Carr did not deliver the deed. The Campbells filed a suit in a South Carolina state court against Carr, seeking specific performance of the contract. At trial, an expert real estate appraiser testified that the real market value of the property was $162,000 at the time of the contract. Under what circumstances will a court examine the adequacy of consideration? Are those circumstances present in this case? Should the court enforce the contract between Carr and the Campbells? Explain. [*Campbell v. Carr*, 361 S.C. 258, 603 S.E.2d 625 (App. 2004)]

Case Problem with Sample Answer

9–6. In 2000, David and Sandra Harless leased 2.3 acres of real property at 2801 River Road S.E. in Winnabow, North Carolina, to Jeanie and Tony Connor (the Harlesses' daughter and son-in-law). The Connors planned to operate a "general store/variety store" on the premises. They agreed to lease the property for sixty months with an option to renew for an additional sixty months. The lease included an option to buy the property for "fair market value at the time of such purchase (based on at least two appraisals)." In March 2003, Tony told David that the Connors wanted to buy the property. In May, Tony gave David an appraisal that estimated the property's value at $140,000. In July, the Connors presented a second appraisal that determined the value to be $160,000. The Connors offered $150,000. The Harlesses replied that "under no circumstances would they ever agree to sell their old store building and approximately 2.5 acres to their daughter . . . and their son-in-law." The Connors filed a suit in a North Carolina state court against the Harlesses, alleging breach of contract. Did these parties have a contract to sell the property? If so, what were its terms? If not, why not? [*Connor v. Harless*, 176 N.C.App. 402, 626 S.E.2d 755 (2006)]

After you have answered Problem 9–6, compare your answer with the sample answer given on the Web site that accompanies this text. Go to www.cengage.com/blaw/let, select "Chapter 9," and click on "Case Problem with Sample Answer."

9–7. Offer. In August 2000, in California, Terry Reigelsperger sought treatment for pain in his lower back from chiropractor James Siller. Reigelsperger felt better after the treatment and did not intend to return for more, although he did not mention this to Siller. Before leaving the office, Reigelsperger signed an "informed consent" form that read, in part, "I intend this consent form to cover the entire course of treatment for my present condition and for any future condition(s) for which

I seek treatment." He also signed an agreement that required the parties to submit to arbitration "any dispute as to medical malpractice. . . . This agreement is intended to bind the patient and the health care provider . . . who now or in the future treat[s] the patient." Two years later, Reigelsperger sought treatment from Siller for a different condition relating to his cervical spine and shoulder. Claiming malpractice with respect to the second treatment, Reigelsperger filed a suit in a California state court against Siller. Siller asked the court to order the dispute to be submitted to arbitration. Did Reigelsperger's lack of intent to return to Siller after his first treatment affect the enforceability of the arbitration agreement and consent form? Why or why not? [*Reigelsperger v. Siller*, 40 Cal.4th 574, 150 P.3d 764, 53 Cal.Rptr.3d 887 (2007)]

A Question of Ethics

9–8. Dow AgroSciences, LLC (DAS), makes and sells agricultural seed products. In 2000, Timothy Glenn, a DAS sales manager, signed a covenant not to compete. He agreed that for two years from the date of his termination, he would not "engage in or contribute my knowledge to any work or activity involving an area of technology or business that is then competitive with a technology or business with respect to which I had access to Confidential Information during the five years immediately prior to such termination." Working with DAS business, operations, and research and development personnel, and being a member of high-level teams, Glenn had access to confidential DAS information, including agreements with DAS's business partners, marketing plans, litigation details, product secrets, new product development, and pricing strategies. In 2006, Glenn resigned to work for Pioneer Hi-Bred International, Inc., a DAS competitor. DAS filed a suit in an Indiana state court against Glenn, asking that he be enjoined from accepting any "position that would call on him to use confidential DAS information." [*Glenn v. Dow AgroSciences, LLC*, 861 N.E.2d 1 (Ind.App. 2007)]

1. Generally, what interests are served by enforcing covenants not to compete? What interests are served by refusing to enforce them?
2. What argument could be made in support of reforming (and then enforcing) illegal covenants not to compete? What argument could be made against this practice?
3. How should the court rule in this case? Why?

Critical-Thinking Legal Question

9–9. Review the list of basic requirements for contract formation given at the beginning of this chapter. In view of those requirements, analyze the relationship entered into when a student enrolls in a college or university. Has a contract been formed? If so, is it a bilateral contract or a unilateral contract? Discuss.

Video Question

9–10. Go to this text's Web site at **www.cengage.com/blaw/let** and select "Chapter 9." Click on "Video Questions" and view the video titled *Bowfinger*. Then answer the following questions.

1. In the video, Renfro (Robert Downey, Jr.) says to Bowfinger (Steve Martin), "You bring me this script and Kit Ramsey and you've got yourself a 'go' picture." Assume for the purposes of this question that their agreement is a contract. Is the contract bilateral or unilateral? Is it express or implied? Is it formal or informal? Explain your answers.

2. Explain whether Renfro's statement that is quoted in the first part of this question meets the three requirements of an effective offer.

3. Recall from the video that the contract between Bowfinger and the producer was oral. Suppose that a statute requires contracts of this type to be in writing. In that situation, would the contract be void, voidable, or unenforceable? Explain.

Interacting with the Internet

For updated links to resources available on the Web, as well as a variety of other materials, visit this text's Web site at

www.cengage.com/blaw/let

The 'Lectric Law Library provides information on contract law, including a definition of a contract, the elements required for a contract, and so on. Go to

www.lectlaw.com/lay.html

A good way to learn more about how the courts decide such issues as whether consideration was lacking for a particular contract is to look at relevant case law. To find recent cases on contract law decided by the United States Supreme Court and the federal appellate courts, access Cornell University's School of Law site at

www.law.cornell.edu/wex/index.php/Contracts

The *New Hampshire Attorney General's Consumer Sourcebook* provides information on contract law, including consideration, from a consumer's perspective. You can access this site at

www.doj.nh.gov/consumer/index.html

To learn what kinds of clauses are included in typical contracts for certain goods and services, you can explore the collection of contract forms made available by FindLaw at

contracts.corporate.findlaw.com/index.html

PRACTICAL INTERNET EXERCISES

Go to this text's Web site at **www.cengage.com/blaw/let**, select "Chapter 9," and click on "Practical Internet Exercises." There you will find the following Internet research exercises that you can perform to learn more about topics covered in this chapter.

Practical Internet Exercise 9–1: LEGAL PERSPECTIVE—Covenants Not to Compete
Practical Internet Exercise 9–2: ETHICAL PERSPECTIVE—Offers and Advertisements
Practical Internet Exercise 9–3: SOCIAL PERSPECTIVE—Online Gambling

BEFORE THE TEST

Go to this text's Web site at **www.cengage.com/blaw/let**, select "Chapter 9," and click on "Interactive Quizzes." You will find a number of interactive questions relating to this chapter.

Chapter 10

Contract Performance, Breach, and Remedies

CHAPTER OBJECTIVES

After reading this chapter, you should be able to answer the following questions:

1. In what types of situations might voluntary consent to a contract's terms be lacking?

2. What are the elements of fraudulent misrepresentation?

3. What is substantial performance?

4. What is the standard measure of compensatory damages when a contract is breached?

5. What equitable remedies can a court grant, and in what circumstances will a court consider granting them?

CONTENTS

- Voluntary Consent
- The Statute of Frauds—Writing Requirement
- Third Party Rights
- Performance and Discharge
- Damages for Breach of Contract
- Equitable Remedies
- Election of Remedies
- Contract Provisions Limiting Remedies

"Men keep their engagements when it is to the advantage of both not to break them."

— SOLON,
sixth century B.C.E. (Athenian legal reformer)

As the Athenian political leader Solon indicated centuries ago, a contract will not be broken so long as "it is to the advantage of both" parties not to break it. In a perfect world, every party who signed a contract would perform his or her duties completely and in a timely fashion, thereby discharging (terminating) the contract. In the real world, however, things frequently become complicated. Certainly, events often occur that may affect our performance or our ability to perform contractual duties. Just as rules are necessary to determine when a legally enforceable contract exists, so also are they required to determine when one of the parties can justifiably say, "I have fully performed, so I am now discharged from my obligations under this contract."

Additionally, the parties to a contract need to know what remedies are available to them if one party decides that he or she does not want to, or cannot, perform as promised. A *remedy* is the relief provided for an innocent party when the other party has breached the contract. It is the means employed to enforce a right or to redress an injury. The most common remedies available to a non-breaching party include damages, rescission and restitution, specific performance, and reformation, all of which will be examined later in this chapter.

VOLUNTARY CONSENT

A contract has been entered into by two parties, each with full legal capacity and for a legal purpose. The contract is also supported by consideration. The contract thus meets the four requirements for a valid contract that were specified in Chapter 9.

VOLUNTARY CONSENT
Knowledge of, and genuine assent to, the terms of a contract. If a contract is formed as a result of a mistake, misrepresentation, undue influence, or duress, voluntary consent is lacking, and the contract will be voidable.

Nonetheless, the contract may be unenforceable if the parties have not genuinely assented to its terms. Lack of **voluntary consent** *(genuineness of assent)* can be used as a defense to the contract's enforceability. Voluntary consent may be lacking because of a mistake, misrepresentation, undue influence, or duress—in other words, because there is no true "meeting of the minds." In this section, we examine problems relating to voluntary consent.

Mistakes

We all make mistakes, and it is therefore not surprising that mistakes are made when contracts are formed. It is important to distinguish between *mistakes of fact* and *mistakes of value or quality.* Only a mistake of fact may allow a contract to be avoided.

If a mistake concerns the future market value or quality of the object of the contract, the mistake is one of *value,* and either party can normally enforce the contract. EXAMPLE #1 Suppose that Chi buys a violin from Bev for $250. Although the violin is very old, neither party believes that it is extremely valuable. An antiques dealer later informs the parties, however, that the violin is rare and worth thousands of dollars. Although both parties were mistaken, the mistake is not a mistake of *fact* that warrants contract rescission.□

Mistakes of fact occur in two forms—*bilateral* and *unilateral.* A bilateral, or mutual, mistake is made by both of the contracting parties. A unilateral mistake is made by only one of the parties. We look next at these two types of mistakes and illustrate them graphically in Exhibit 10–1.

Bilateral (Mutual) Mistakes of Fact   A bilateral, or mutual, mistake occurs when both parties are mistaken as to some *material fact*—that is, a fact important to the subject matter of the contract. When a bilateral mistake occurs, the contract can be rescinded, or canceled, by either party. EXAMPLE #2 Keeley buys a landscape painting from Umberto's art gallery. Both Umberto and Keeley believe that the painting is by the artist Vincent van Gogh. Later, Keeley discovers that the painting is a very clever fake. Because neither Umberto nor Keeley was aware of this material fact when they made their deal, Keeley can rescind the contract and recover the purchase price of the painting.□

A word or term in a contract may be subject to more than one reasonable interpretation. In that situation, if the parties to the contract attach materially different meanings to the term, their mutual mistake of fact may allow the con-

"Mistakes are the inevitable lot of mankind."
—SIR GEORGE JESSEL,1824–1883
(English jurist)

EXHIBIT 10–1 MISTAKES OF FACT

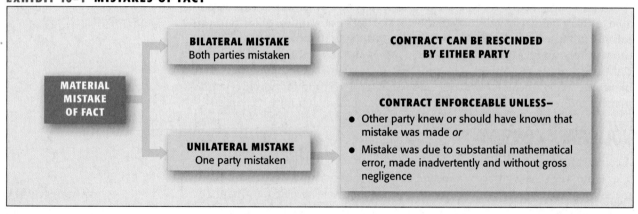

tract to be rescinded because there has been no "meeting of the minds," or true assent, which is required for a contract to arise.

The classic case on bilateral mistake is *Raffles v. Wichelhaus*,[1] which was decided by an English court in 1864. The defendant, Wichelhaus, paid for a shipment of Surat cotton from the plaintiff, Raffles, "to arrive 'Peerless' from Bombay." Wichelhaus expected the goods to be shipped on the *Peerless*, a ship sailing from Bombay, India, in October. Raffles expected to ship the goods on a different *Peerless*, which sailed from Bombay in December. When the goods arrived and Raffles tried to deliver them, Wichelhaus refused to accept them. The court held for Wichelhaus, concluding that no mutual assent existed because the parties had attached materially different meanings to an essential term of the written contract (the ship that was to transport the goods).

In the following case, the court had to grapple with the question of whether a mutual mistake of fact had occurred.

---

1. 159 Eng.Rep. 375 (1864).

Case 10.1 Inkel v. Pride Chevrolet-Pontiac, Inc.

Supreme Court of Vermont, 2008
945 A.2d 855.

BACKGROUND AND FACTS The Inkels, who live in Vermont, called Pride Chevrolet-Pontiac, Inc., in Boston about buying a new Chevy Tahoe sport-utility vehicle. They said they would trade in a high-mileage vehicle that they had leased. The sales representative told them that the high-mileage penalty would probably not apply because the lease was from a bank, not a dealership. When the Inkels took delivery of the new Tahoe and left their old vehicle at Pride, the price on the contract was $41,200. In small print on the back of the agreement was a provision that the buyer was responsible for any problems with the trade-in vehicle. A month after the sale, Pride told the Inkels that they owed another $16,435 because of a misunderstanding with the leasing company about the high-mileage charge. The Inkels refused to pay. Pride demanded the Tahoe back and wanted to cancel the deal; the Inkels refused. The Inkels then sued Pride for breach of contract and other claims. The Vermont trial court held that a mutual mistake had been made in the contract and that the Inkels should have agreed to undo the deal. The court granted summary judgment for Pride, ordering the Inkels to pay damages. They appealed.

IN THE WORDS OF THE COURT . . . *BURGESS*, Justice.

* * * *

The evidence submitted in connection with the parties' cross motions for summary judgment does not establish what happened in the instant case [the case under discussion]. Although the superior court [the trial court] stated in a footnote that it was undisputed that the Chittenden Bank was negligent in giving Pride Chevrolet an incorrect payoff amount, Mr. Inkel testified in his deposition that a bank employee told him that Pride Chevrolet had asked for the wrong payoff amount. Thus, it is not clear whether the Pride Chevrolet employee asked for the wrong information or the bank provided the wrong information. In short, the evidentiary [based on evidence] record does not make it clear how the "mistake" occurred or even whether there was a mistake. Further, the principal facts that the superior court apparently relied on in ruling in favor of Pride Chevrolet—that the Inkels knew they had substantial negative equity [owing more than market value] in their vehicle and that another dealership had recently declined to negotiate with them because of the substantial negative equity in the vehicle—do not necessarily undercut the Inkels' allegation that Pride Chevrolet made, even if good-faith, false and misleading representations * * * by telling them that their lien holder would not seek over-mileage payments on their trade-in.

* * * *

Moreover, we reject Pride Chevrolet's argument that the Inkels "affirmed" the vehicle purchase contract by refusing to accept its offer to "wash the deal" [rescind the contract]

CASE 10.1–CONTINUED

after learning of the parties' mutual mistake. Pride Chevrolet offers no direct legal support for this proposition, and, in any event, the evidence does not conclusively prove mutual mistake. *"A mutual mistake must be a mistake reciprocally involving both parties, a mistake independently made by both parties." "A mistake by one party coupled with ignorance thereof does not constitute mutual mistake."* [Emphasis added.]

Given the current state of the record, whether the Inkels merely accepted Pride Chevrolet's statements as true or took advantage of the dealer's mistaken beliefs, the existence of mutual mistake is questionable at best. Further, even assuming that the parties' mistake was mutual, Pride Chevrolet failed to demonstrate that the offer to "wash the deal" was a legitimate offer to rescind the contract. Pride Chevrolet presented no evidence indicating precisely when the offer was made, who made the offer, or what terms, if any, were offered.

* * * *

Reversed and remanded.

DECISION AND REMEDY   The Vermont high court reversed in favor of the Inkels, holding that it was not clear that a mutual mistake had been made. Evidence would have to be produced at trial to determine if both parties had been mistaken about the same facts for a finding of mutual mistake.

THE ETHICAL DIMENSION   Some car dealerships are notorious for dubious sales practices. If a Pride sales representative led the Inkels to believe the dealership did not care about the excessive miles on the trade-in vehicle, should it be willing to incur the loss? Why or why not?

THE LEGAL ENVIRONMENT DIMENSION   If a dealer wants a quality reputation, how can it avoid the kind of problems that arose in this case?

Unilateral Mistakes of Fact   A unilateral mistake occurs when only one of the contracting parties makes a mistake as to some material fact. The general rule is that a unilateral mistake does not afford the mistaken party any right to relief from the contract. **EXAMPLE #3** DeVinck intends to sell his motor home for $32,500. When he learns that Benson is interested in buying a used motor home, DeVinck faxes Benson an offer to sell the vehicle to him. When typing the fax, however, DeVinck mistakenly keys in the price of $23,500. Benson immediately sends DeVinck a fax accepting DeVinck's offer. Even though DeVinck intended to sell his motor home for $32,500, his unilateral mistake falls on him. He is bound in contract to sell the motor home to Benson for $23,500.□

There are at least two exceptions to this general rule.[2] First, if the *other* party to the contract knows or should have known that a mistake of fact was made, the contract may not be enforceable. **EXAMPLE #4** In the previous example, if Benson knew that DeVinck intended to sell his motor home for $32,500, then DeVinck's unilateral mistake (stating $23,500 in his offer) may render the resulting contract unenforceable.□ The second exception arises when a unilateral mistake of fact was due to a mathematical mistake in addition, subtraction, division, or multiplication and was made inadvertently and without gross (extreme) negligence. If a contractor's bid was significantly low because he or she made a mistake in addition when totaling the estimated costs, any contract resulting from the bid may be rescinded, or canceled. Of course, in both situations, the mistake must still involve some material fact.

---

2. The *Restatement (Second) of Contracts,* Section 153, liberalizes the general rule to take into account the modern trend of allowing avoidance even though only one party has been mistaken.

Fraudulent Misrepresentation

In the context of contract law, fraud affects the genuineness of the innocent party's consent to the contract. Thus, the transaction is not voluntary in the sense of involving "mutual assent." When an innocent party is fraudulently induced to enter into a contract, the contract usually can be avoided because that party has not *voluntarily* consented to its terms. Normally, the innocent party can either rescind (cancel) the contract and be restored to his or her original position or enforce the contract and seek damages for any injuries resulting from the fraud.

The word *fraudulent* means many things in the law. Generally, fraudulent misrepresentation refers only to misrepresentation that is consciously false and is intended to mislead another. The perpetrator of the fraudulent misrepresentation knows or believes that the assertion is false or knows that she or he does not have a basis (stated or implied) for the assertion. Typically, fraudulent misrepresentation consists of the following elements:

1. A misrepresentation of a material fact must occur.
2. There must be an intent to deceive, called **scienter.**[3]
3. The innocent party must justifiably rely on the misrepresentation.

With its anonymity and rapidly changing technology, the online world provides the perfect environment for fraud. This chapter's *Online Developments* feature on page 317 discusses allegations of fraud in connection with online personal ads. Another source of fraudulent misrepresentation on the Web is "click fraud," a topic we discuss in this chapter's *Insight into Ethics* below.

> *"It was beautiful and simple as all truly great swindles are."*
> —O. HENRY, 1862–1910
> (American author)

SCIENTER
Knowledge on the part of the misrepresenting party that material facts have been falsely represented or omitted with an intent to deceive.

Insight into Ethics

Internet click fraud

For many of the Internet's best-known companies, including Google and Yahoo, advertising is the main source of their revenues. Every user of the Internet encounters a multitude of advertisements that invite the user to "click" on the ad to get further information about the product or service. What every user may not know, however, is that the companies selling such ads charge fees based on the number of clicks. Thus, the more clicks, the higher the advertising revenues of the company selling the advertising space. Meanwhile, Web advertisers, who buy space for their ads on sites such as those run by Google and Yahoo, want to pay only for valid clicks—those done by humans with a real interest in the product.

Enter Click Fraud

This system of charging for advertising based on the number of clicks has given rise to many allegations of click fraud, which occurs "when someone clicks on a search advertisement with an ill intent and with no intention of doing business with the advertiser. [Click fraud involves] purposeful clicks on an advertisement for some kind of improper purpose."[4] The exact dimensions of click fraud are unknown, but some

---

3. Pronounced sy-*en*-ter.
4. *Click Defense, Inc. v. Google, Inc.,* No. 5:05-CV-02579-RMW (N.D.Cal. complaint filed June 24, 2005). This case was subsequently settled.

commentators think it could amount to as much as $1 billion per year. Fraud-detection specialist Fair Isaac Corporation claims that 10 to 15 percent of advertising traffic on the Internet is "pathological," indicating a high probability of click fraud.

There are several different types of click fraud. For example, suppose that Company A and Company B are direct competitors. Company A directs its employees to click repeatedly on Company B's online ads in an attempt to run up the advertising fees that Company B will have to pay. In another type of click fraud, the owners of the sites running the ads simply use Internet robots to click on the ads so as to increase the revenues that they receive from running the advertising. Of course, Company A, in the previous example, could also use robots to click on Company B's ads.

Whether it is generated by humans or robots, click fraud is unethical and, at a mimimum, violates the implied covenant of good faith and fair dealing, which requires honesty and the observance of reasonable standards of fair dealing between contracting parties. Additionally, when Web site owners purposefully inflate the number of clicks so that they can charge more for advertising, they can be sued for, among other things, unjust enrichment.

Indeed, in the past few years, both Google and Yahoo have been the defendants in click fraud suits, several of which have been settled for amounts reaching tens of millions of dollars.[5] Google now uses filtering software so that it does not count repetitive clicks that presumably come from Internet robots.

Click Fraud's Close Cousin—Lead Fraud

Closely related to click fraud is lead fraud. "Leads" in this context are simply the names of individuals who have expressed an interest in purchasing a certain product, such as insurance. NetQuote, for example, is a lead-generating site for insurance companies. Users can submit requests on NetQuote's Web page, and NetQuote then sells these "qualified" leads to insurance companies. NetQuote now has brought a fraud claim against MostChoice, a competitor, charging that MostChoice had an employee submit hundreds of fraudulent requests through the NetQuote system.[6] NetQuote maintains that when it submitted these leads to its insurance company clients, the conversion rate—the percentage of leads that actually purchase insurance—dropped dramatically, thereby reducing the value of the leads to the insurance companies.

REMEMBER
An opinion is not a contract offer, nor a contract term, nor fraud.

Reliance on the Misrepresentation   To constitute fraud, the deceived party must have a justifiable reason for relying on the misrepresentation, and the misrepresentation must be an important factor in inducing the party to enter into the contract. Reliance is not justified if the innocent party knows the true facts or relies on obviously extravagant statements.   **EXAMPLE #5** If a used-car dealer tells you, "This old Cadillac will get over sixty miles to the gallon," you normally would not be justified in relying on this statement. Suppose, however, that Merkel, a bank director, induces O'Connell, a co-director, to sign a statement that the bank's assets will satisfy its liabilities by telling O'Connell, "We have plenty of assets to satisfy our creditors." This statement is false. If O'Connell knows the true facts or, as a bank director, should know the true facts, he is not justified in relying on Merkel's statement. If O'Connell does not know

---

5. See, for example, *Checkmate Strategic Group, Inc. v. Yahoo!, Inc.*, No. 2:05-CV-04588-CAS-FMO (C.D.Cal. preliminary settlement approved June 28, 2006); and *Bradley v. Google, Inc.*, 2006 WL3798134 (N.D.Cal. 2006, voluntarily dismissed after a settlement in 2007).

6. *NetQuote, Inc. v. Byrd*, ___ F.Supp.2d ___ (D.Colo. 2008). This case has not yet been fully resolved.

Keying the words *online personals* into the Google search engine will return more than 35 million hits, including Match.com, Chanceforlove.com, Widowsorwidowers.com, Makefriendsonline.com, and Yahoo! Personals. Yahoo! Personals, which calls itself the "top online dating site," offers two options. One is for people looking for casual dates. It allows users to create their own profiles, browse member profiles, and exchange e-mail or instant messages. The second option, called Yahoo! Personals Primer, is for people who want serious relationships. Users must take a relationship test. Then they can use Yahoo's computerized matching system to "zero in on marriage material." With this service, users can chat on the phone, as well as exchange e-mail.

The Thorny Problem of Misrepresentation

When singles (and others) create their profiles for online dating services, they tend to exaggerate their more appealing features and downplay or omit their less attractive attributes. All users of such services are aware that the profiles may not correspond exactly with reality, but they do assume that the profiles are not complete misrepresentations. In 2006, however, Robert Anthony, individually and on behalf of others, brought a suit against Yahoo in federal district court, alleging fraud and negligent misrepresentation, among other things.

In his complaint, Anthony claimed that Yahoo was not just posting fictitious or exaggerated profiles submitted by users but was deliberately and intentionally originating, creating, and perpetuating false profiles. According to Anthony, many profiles used the exact same phrases "with such unique dictation and vernacular [language] that such a random occurrence would not be possible." Anthony also argued that some photo images had multiple identities—that is, the same photo appeared in several different profiles. He also alleged that Yahoo continued to circulate profiles of "actual, legitimate former subscribers whose subscriptions had expired." Finally, Anthony claimed that when a subscription neared its end date, Yahoo would send the subscriber a fake profile, heralding it a "potential 'new match.'"

Did Yahoo Have Immunity?

Yahoo asked the court to dismiss the complaint on the grounds that the lawsuit was barred by the Communications Decency Act (CDA) of 1996.[a] As discussed in Chapter 5, the CDA shields Internet service providers (ISPs) from liability for any information submitted by another information content provider. In other words, an interactive computer service cannot be held liable under state law as a publisher of information that originates from a third party information content provider. The CDA defines an information content provider as "any person or entity that is responsible, in whole or in part, for the creation or development of information provided through the Internet or any other interactive computer service."[b]

The court rejected Yahoo's claim that it had immunity under the CDA and held that Yahoo had become an information content provider itself when it created bogus user profiles. The court observed that "no case of which this court is aware has immunized a defendant from allegations that it created tortious content."[c] Thus, the court denied Yahoo's motion to dismiss and allowed Anthony's claims of fraud and negligent misrepresentation to proceed to trial.[d]

FOR CRITICAL ANALYSIS Assume that Anthony had contacted various users of Yahoo's online dating service only to discover that each user's profile exaggerated the user's physical appearance, intelligence, and occupation. Would Anthony prevail if he brought a lawsuit for fraudulent misrepresentation against Yahoo in that situation? Why or why not?

a. 47 U.S.C. Section 230.
b. 47 U.S.C. Section 230(f)(3).
c. For an example of the types of cases that have been brought against Internet dating services, see *Carafano v. Metrosplash.com, Inc.*, 339 F.3d 1119 (9th Cir. 2003).
d. *Anthony v. Yahoo!, Inc.*, 421 F.Supp.2d 1257 (N.D.Cal. 2006); see also, *Doe v. SexSearch.com*, 502 F.Supp.2d 719 (N.D. Ohio 2007).

the true facts, however, *and has no way of finding them out,* he may be justified in relying on the statement. □

Ordinarily, neither party to a contract has a duty to come forward and disclose facts, and a contract normally will not be set aside because certain pertinent information has not been volunteered. EXAMPLE #6 You are selling a car that has been in an accident and has been repaired. You do not need to volunteer this information to a potential buyer. If, however, the purchaser asks you if the car has had extensive bodywork and you lie, you have committed a fraudulent misrepresentation. □

Employers sometimes run into problems by exaggerating their companies' future prospects or financial health when they are interviewing prospective employees. Obviously, an employer wants to paint the future as bright, but should be careful to avoid making representations that an interviewee may rely on to her or his detriment. **EXAMPLE #7** In one case, an employee accepted a job with a brokerage firm, relying on assurances that the firm was not about to be sold. In fact, as the employee was able to prove in his later lawsuit against the firm for fraud, negotiations to sell the firm were under way at the time he was hired. The trial court awarded the employee over $6 million in damages, a decision that was affirmed on appeal.[7]□ Generally, employers must be truthful during their hiring procedures to avoid possible lawsuits for fraudulent misrepresentation.

Preventing Legal Disputes

To avoid making comments that might later be construed as a misrepresentation of material fact, business owners and managers should be careful what they say to clients and customers. Those in the business of selling products or services should assume that all customers are naïve and are relying on the seller's representations. Instruct each employee to phrase comments so that customers understand that any statements that are not factual are the employee's opinion. If someone asks a question that is beyond the employee's knowledge, it is better to say that he or she does not know than to guess and have the customer rely on a representation that turns out to be false. This can be particularly important when the question concerns a topic such as compatibility or speed of electronic and digital goods, software, or related services.

Businesspersons should also be prudent about what they say when interviewing potential employees. Do not speculate on the financial health of the firm or exaggerate the company's future prospects. Exercising caution in one's statements to others in a business context is one way to avoid potential legal actions for fraudulent misrepresentation. ■

Injury to the Innocent Party   Most courts do not require a showing of injury in an action to *rescind* (cancel) the contract—these courts hold that because rescission returns the parties to the positions they held before the contract was made, a showing of injury to the innocent party is unnecessary.

For a person to recover damages caused by fraud, however, proof of an injury is universally required. The measure of damages is ordinarily equal to the property's value had it been delivered as represented, less the actual price paid for the property. In actions based on fraud, courts often award *punitive damages,* or *exemplary damages,* which are designed to punish the defendant and to deter similar wrongdoing by others.

Innocent Misrepresentation   Misrepresentations can also be innocently made. If a person makes a statement that he or she believes to be true but that actually misrepresents material facts, an *innocent misrepresentation,* not fraud, has occurred. In this situation, the aggrieved party can rescind the contract but usually cannot seek damages. **EXAMPLE #8** Parris tells Roberta that a tract of land contains 250 acres. Parris is mistaken—the tract contains only 215 acres—but Parris

---

7. *McConkey v. AON Corp.,* 354 N.J.Super. 25, 804 A.2d 572 (2002).

does not know that. Roberta is induced by the statement to make a contract to buy the land. Even though the misrepresentation is innocent, Roberta can avoid the contract if the misrepresentation is material.□

Undue Influence

Undue influence arises from special kinds of relationships in which one party can greatly influence another party, thus overcoming that party's free will. A contract entered into under excessive or undue influence lacks voluntary assent and is therefore voidable.

There are various types of relationships in which one party may dominate another party, thus unfairly influencing him or her. Minors and elderly people, for example, are often under the influence of guardians (persons who are legally responsible for others). If a guardian induces a young or elderly ward (the person whom the guardian looks after) to enter into a contract that benefits the guardian, undue influence may have been exerted. Undue influence can arise from a number of confidential or fiduciary relationships: attorney-client, physician-patient, guardian-ward, parent-child, husband-wife, or trustee-beneficiary.

The essential feature of undue influence is that the party being taken advantage of does not, in reality, exercise free will in entering into a contract. It is not enough that a person is elderly or suffers from some mental or physical impairment. There must be clear and convincing evidence that the person did not act out of her or his free will.

Duress

Consent to the terms of a contract is not voluntary if one of the parties is *forced* into the agreement. Forcing a party to do something, including entering into a contract, through fear created by threats is legally defined as *duress*. In addition, blackmail or extortion to induce consent to a contract constitutes duress. Duress is both a defense to the enforcement of a contract and a ground for the rescission of a contract.

Generally, for duress to occur the threatened act must be wrongful or illegal. Threatening to exercise a legal right, such as the right to sue someone, ordinarily is not illegal and usually does not constitute duress. **EXAMPLE #9** Joan injures Olin in an auto accident. The police are not called. Joan has no automobile insurance, but she has substantial assets. Olin wants to settle the potential claim out of court for $3,000, but Joan refuses. After much arguing, Olin loses his patience and says, "If you don't pay me $3,000 right now, I'm going to sue you for $35,000." Joan is frightened and gives Olin a check for $3,000. Later in the day, Joan stops payment on the check, and Olin later sues her for the $3,000. Although Joan argues that she was the victim of duress, the threat of a civil suit normally is not considered duress. Therefore, a court would not allow Joan to use duress as a defense to the enforcement of her settlement agreement with Olin.□

THE STATUTE OF FRAUDS—WRITING REQUIREMENT

A commonly used defense to the enforceability of an oral contract is that it is required to be in writing. Today, almost every state has a statute that stipulates what types of contracts must be in writing. Although the statutes vary slightly from state to state, all states require certain types of contracts to be in writing or evidenced by a written memorandum signed by the party against whom enforcement is sought, unless certain exceptions apply. In this text, we refer to these statutes collectively as the **Statute of Frauds.** The actual name of the Statute of Frauds is misleading because it neither applies to fraud nor invalidates any type of contract. Rather, it denies *enforceability* to certain contracts that do not comply with its requirements.

STATUTE OF FRAUDS
A state statute under which certain types of contracts must be in writing to be enforceable.

Contracts That Must Be in Writing

The following types of contracts are said to fall "within" or "under" the Statute of Frauds and therefore require a writing:

1. Contracts involving interests in land.
2. Contracts that cannot by their terms be performed within one year from the day after the date of formation.
3. Collateral, or secondary, contracts, such as promises to answer for the debt or duty of another and promises by the administrator or executor of an estate to pay a debt of the estate personally—that is, out of his or her own pocket.
4. Promises made in consideration of marriage (including prenuptial agreements, which are made before marriage).
5. Contracts for the sale of goods priced at $500 or more. (It has been proposed that this amount be increased from $500 to $5,000 under the Uniform Commercial Code, or UCC, which will be discussed in Chapter 11.)

Exceptions to the Statute of Frauds

Exceptions to the applicability of the Statute of Frauds are made in certain situations. In some states, an oral contract that would otherwise be unenforceable under the Statute of Frauds may be enforced under the doctrine of promissory estoppel, based on detrimental reliance. Section 139 of the *Restatement (Second) of Contracts* provides that in these circumstances, an oral promise can be enforceable notwithstanding the Statute of Frauds if the reliance was foreseeable to the person making the promise and if injustice can be avoided only by enforcing the promise. A court might also enforce an oral contract if the party against whom enforcement is sought "admits" in pleadings, testimony, or other court proceedings that a contract for sale was made.

THIRD PARTY RIGHTS

Once it has been determined that a valid and legally enforceable contract exists, attention can turn to the rights and duties of the parties to the contract. A contract is a private agreement between the parties who have entered into it, and traditionally these parties alone have rights and liabilities under the contract. This principle is referred to as *privity of contract*. A *third party*—one who is not a direct party to a particular contract—normally does not have rights under that contract.

There are exceptions to the rule of privity of contract. One exception allows a party to a contract to transfer the rights or duties arising from the contract to another person through an *assignment* (of rights) or a *delegation* (of duties). Another exception involves a *third party beneficiary contract*—a contract in which the parties to the contract intend that the contract benefit a third party.

Assignments

In a bilateral contract, the two parties have corresponding rights and duties. One party has a *right* to require the other to perform some task, and the other has a *duty* to perform it. The transfer of contractual *rights* to a third party is known as an **assignment.** When rights under a contract are assigned unconditionally, the rights of the *assignor* (the party making the assignment) are extinguished. The third party (the *assignee,* or party receiving the assignment) has a right to demand performance from the other original party to the contract (the *obligor*). The assignee takes only those rights that the assignor originally had.

ASSIGNMENT
The act of transferring to another all or part of one's rights arising under a contract.

As a general rule, all rights can be assigned. Exceptions are made, however, in some circumstances. If a statute expressly prohibits assignment of a particular right, that right cannot be assigned. When a contract is *personal* in nature, the rights under the contract cannot be assigned unless all that remains is a money payment. A right cannot be assigned if assignment will materially increase or alter the risk or duties of the obligor.[8] If a contract stipulates that a right cannot be assigned, then *ordinarily* the right cannot be assigned.

There are several exceptions to the rule that a contract can, by its terms, prohibit any assignment of the contract. These exceptions are as follows:

1. A contract cannot prevent an assignment of the right to receive money. This exception exists to encourage the free flow of money and credit in modern business settings.
2. The assignment of rights in real estate often cannot be prohibited, because such a prohibition is contrary to public policy. Prohibitions of this kind are called restraints against *alienation* (transfer of land ownership).
3. The assignment of *negotiable instruments* (which include checks and promissory notes) cannot be prohibited.
4. In a contract for the sale of goods, the right to receive damages for breach of contract or for payment of an account owed may be assigned even though the sales contract prohibits such assignment.

Delegations

Just as a party can transfer rights through an assignment, a party can also transfer duties. The transfer of contractual *duties* to a third party is known as a **delegation.** Normally, a delegation of duties does not relieve the party making the delegation (the *delegator*) of the obligation to perform in the event that the party to whom the duty has been delegated (the *delegatee*) fails to perform. No special form is required to create a valid delegation of duties. As long as the delegator expresses an intention to make the delegation, it is effective; the delegator need not even use the word *delegate.*

DELEGATION
The transfer of a contractual duty to a third party. The party delegating the duty (the delegator) to the third party (the delegatee) is still obliged to perform on the contract should the delegatee fail to perform.

As a general rule, any duty can be delegated. Delegation is prohibited, however, in the following circumstances:

1. When special trust has been placed in the obligor (the person contractually obligated to perform).
2. When performance depends on the personal skill or talents of the obligor.
3. When performance by a third party will vary materially from that expected by the *obligee* (the one to whom performance is owed) under the contract.
4. When the contract expressly prohibits delegation.

---

8. UCC 2–210(2).

If a delegation of duties is enforceable, the obligee must accept performance from the delegatee. The obligee can legally refuse performance from the delegatee only if the duty is one that cannot be delegated.

As mentioned, a valid delegation of duties does not relieve the delegator of obligations under the contract. Thus, if the delegatee fails to perform, the delegator is still liable to the obligee.

Third Party Beneficiaries

THIRD PARTY BENEFICIARY
One for whose benefit a promise is made in a contract but who is not a party to the contract.

INTENDED BENEFICIARY
A third party for whose benefit a contract is formed; an intended beneficiary can sue the promisor if such a contract is breached.

INCIDENTAL BENEFICIARY
A third party who incidentally benefits from a contract but whose benefit was not the reason the contract was formed; an incidental beneficiary has no rights in a contract and cannot sue to have the contract enforced.

Another exception to the doctrine of privity of contract exists when the original parties to the contract intend at the time of contracting that the contract performance directly benefit a third person. In this situation, the third person becomes a **third party beneficiary** of the contract. As an **intended beneficiary** of the contract, the third party has legal rights and can sue the promisor directly for breach of the contract.

The benefit that an **incidental beneficiary** receives from a contract between two parties is unintentional. Because the benefit is *unintentional,* an incidental beneficiary cannot sue to enforce the contract. EXAMPLE #10 Spectators at the infamous Mike Tyson boxing match in which Tyson was disqualified for biting his opponent's ear sued Tyson and the fight's promoters for a refund on the basis of breach of contract. The spectators claimed that they were third party beneficiaries of the contract between Tyson and the fight's promoters. The court, however, held that the spectators could not sue because they were not in contractual privity with the defendants. Any benefits they received from the contract were incidental to the contract, and according to the court, the spectators got what they paid for: "the right to view whatever event transpired."[9] ▫

PERFORMANCE AND DISCHARGE

DISCHARGE
The termination of an obligation. In contract law, discharge occurs when the parties have fully performed their contractual obligations or when events, conduct of the parties, or operation of law releases the parties from performance.

PERFORMANCE
In contract law, the fulfillment of one's duties arising under a contract with another; the normal way of discharging one's contractual obligations.

The most common way to **discharge,** or terminate, one's contractual duties is by the **performance** of those duties. For example, a buyer and seller have a contract for the sale of a 2010 Lexus for $39,000. This contract will be discharged on the performance by the parties of their obligations under the contract—the buyer's payment of $39,000 to the seller and the seller's transfer of possession of the Lexus to the buyer.

The duty to perform under a contract may be *conditioned* on the occurrence or nonoccurrence of a certain event, or the duty may be *absolute.* In this section, we look at conditions of performance and the degree of performance required. We then examine some other ways in which a contract can be discharged, including discharge by agreement of the parties and discharge by operation of law.

Conditions of Performance

In most contracts, promises of performance are not expressly conditioned or qualified. Instead, they are *absolute promises.* They must be performed, or the parties promising the acts will be in breach of contract. EXAMPLE #11 JoAnne contracts to sell Alfonso a painting for $10,000. The parties' promises are unconditional: JoAnne's transfer of the painting to Alfonso and Alfonso's payment of $10,000 to JoAnne. The payment does not have to be made if the painting is not transferred. ▫

---

9. *Castillo v. Tyson,* 268 A.D.2d 336, 701 N.Y.S.2d 423 (Sup.Ct.App.Div. 2000).

In some situations, however, contractual promises are conditioned. A **condition** is a possible future event, the occurrence or nonoccurrence of which will trigger the performance of a legal obligation or terminate an existing obligation under a contract. If the condition is not satisfied, the obligations of the parties are discharged. EXAMPLE #12 Alfonso, from the previous example, offers to purchase JoAnne's painting only if an independent appraisal indicates that it is worth at least $10,000. JoAnne accepts Alfonso's offer. Their obligations (promises) are conditioned on the outcome of the appraisal. Should this condition not be satisfied (for example, if the appraiser deems the value of the painting to be only $5,000), their obligations to each other are discharged and cannot be enforced.□

A condition that must be fulfilled before a party's promise becomes absolute is called a **condition precedent.** The condition precedes the absolute duty to perform. For instance, insurance contracts frequently specify that certain conditions, such as passing a physical examination, must be met before the insurance company will be obligated to perform under the contract.

CONDITION
A qualification, provision, or clause in a contractual agreement, the occurrence or nonoccurrence of which creates, suspends, or terminates the obligations of the contracting parties.

CONDITION PRECEDENT
In a contractual agreement, a condition that must be met before a party's promise becomes absolute.

Discharge by Performance

The great majority of contracts are discharged by performance. The contract comes to an end when both parties fulfill their respective duties by performing the acts they have promised. Performance can also be accomplished by tender. **Tender** is an unconditional offer to perform by a person who is ready, willing, and able to do so. Therefore, a seller who places goods at the disposal of a buyer has tendered delivery and can demand payment. A buyer who offers to pay for goods has tendered payment and can demand delivery of the goods. Once performance has been tendered, the party making the tender has done everything possible to carry out the terms of the contract. If the other party then refuses to perform, the party making the tender can sue for breach of contract.

TENDER
An unconditional offer to perform an obligation by a person who is ready, willing, and able to do so.

There are two basic types of performance—*complete performance* and *substantial performance.* A contract may stipulate that performance must meet the personal satisfaction of either the contracting party or a third party. Such a provision must be considered in determining whether the performance rendered satisfies the contract.

Complete Performance When a party performs exactly as agreed, there is no question as to whether the contract has been performed. When a party's performance is perfect, it is said to be complete.

Normally, conditions expressly stated in a contract must be fully satisfied for complete performance to take place. For example, most construction contracts require the builder to meet certain specifications. If the specifications are conditions, complete performance is required to avoid material breach (*material breach* will be discussed shortly). If the conditions are met, the other party to the contract must then fulfill her or his obligation to pay the builder. If the specifications are not conditions and if the builder, without the other party's permission, fails to comply with the specifications, performance is not complete. What effect does such a failure have on the other party's obligation to pay? The answer is part of the doctrine of *substantial performance.*

"There are occasions and causes and why and wherefore in all things."
—WILLIAM SHAKESPEARE,
1564–1616
(English dramatist and poet)

A woman shakes hands with a salesperson after agreeing to purchase a car. Suppose that the agreement is conditioned on the dealer's installing certain optional equipment. When the woman returns to the dealership the following day, she discovers that the optional features that were agreed on have not been added to the car. Is she still obligated to buy the car? Why or why not?
(Brian Teutsch/Creative Commons)

Substantial Performance   A party who in good faith performs substantially all of the terms of a contract can enforce the contract against the other party under the doctrine of substantial performance. Note that good faith is required. Intentionally failing to comply with the terms is a breach of the contract.

To qualify as *substantial performance,* the performance must not vary greatly from the performance promised in the contract, and it must create substantially the same benefits as those promised in the contract. If the omission, variance, or defect in performance is unimportant and can easily be compensated for by awarding damages, a court is likely to hold that the contract has been substantially performed. Courts decide whether the performance was substantial on a case-by-case basis, examining all of the facts of the particular situation. If performance is substantial, the other party's duty to perform remains absolute (except that the party can sue for damages due to the minor deviations).

EXAMPLE #13   A couple contracts with a construction company to build a house. The contract specifies that Brand X plasterboard be used for the walls. The builder cannot obtain Brand X plasterboard, and the buyers are on holiday in the mountains of Peru and unreachable. The builder decides to install Brand Y instead, which he knows is identical in quality and durability to Brand X plasterboard. All other aspects of construction conform to the contract. In this situation, a court will likely hold that the builder has substantially performed his end of the bargain, and therefore the couple will be obligated to pay the builder. The court might award the couple damages for the use of a different brand of plasterboard, but the couple would still have to pay the contractor the contract price, less the amount of damages. ▫

Performance to the Satisfaction of Another   Contracts often state that completed work must personally satisfy one of the parties or a third person. The question is whether this satisfaction becomes a condition precedent, requiring actual personal satisfaction or approval for discharge, or whether the test of satisfaction is performance that would satisfy a *reasonable person* (substantial performance).

When the subject matter of the contract is *personal,* a contract to be performed to the satisfaction of one of the parties is conditioned, and performance must actually satisfy that party. For example, contracts for portraits, works of art, and tailoring are considered personal. Therefore, only the personal satisfaction of the party fulfills the condition—unless a court finds the party is expressing dissatisfaction just to avoid payment or otherwise is not acting in good faith.

Most other contracts need to be performed only to the satisfaction of a reasonable person unless they *expressly state otherwise.* When such contracts require performance to the satisfaction of a third party (for example, "to the satisfaction of Robert Ames, the supervising engineer"), the courts are divided. A majority of courts require the work to be satisfactory to a reasonable person, but some courts hold that the personal satisfaction of the third party designated in the contract (Robert Ames, in this example) must be met. Again, the personal judgment must be made honestly, or the condition will be excused.

BREACH OF CONTRACT
The failure, without legal excuse, of a promisor to perform the obligations of a contract.

Material Breach of Contract   A **breach of contract** is the nonperformance of a contractual duty. The breach is *material* when performance is not at least substantial. If there is a material breach, then the nonbreaching party is excused from the performance of contractual duties and has a cause of action to sue for damages resulting from the breach. If the breach is *minor* (not material), the nonbreaching party's duty to perform can sometimes be suspended until the breach has been remedied, but the duty to perform is not entirely excused. Once the minor breach has been corrected, or cured, the nonbreaching party must resume performance of the contractual obligations undertaken.

Any breach entitles the nonbreaching party to sue for damages, but only a material breach discharges the nonbreaching party from the contract. The policy underlying these rules allows contracts to go forward when only minor problems occur but allows them to be terminated if major difficulties arise.

EXAMPLE #14 Su Yong Kim sold an apartment building in Portland, Oregon, to a group of buyers. At the time of the sale, the building's plumbing violated the city's housing code. The contract therefore included a clause by which the seller (Kim) agreed to correct the plumbing code violations within eight months after signing the contract. A year after the contract was signed, Kim still had not made the necessary repairs, and the new owners were being fined by the city for continuing plumbing code violations. The buyers stopped making payments under the contract, and the dispute ended up in court. The court found that the seller's failure to make the required repairs was a material breach of the contract because it defeated the purpose of the contract. The buyers had purchased the building to lease it out to tenants, but instead were losing tenants and paying fines to the city due to the substandard plumbing. Because Kim's breach was material, the buyers were not obligated to continue to perform their obligation to make payments under the contract.[10] ▫

Different brands of construction supplies displayed at a site. If a contract for the construction of a building or house specifies a particular brand, can a product of a different brand of comparable quality be substituted? Why or why not?
(Tony Freeman/PhotoEdit)

Anticipatory Repudiation of a Contract Before either party to a contract has a duty to perform, one of the parties may refuse to perform her or his contractual obligations. This is called **anticipatory repudiation.**[11] When anticipatory repudiation occurs, it is treated as a material breach of contract, and the nonbreaching party is permitted to bring an action for damages immediately, even though the scheduled time for performance under the contract may still be in the future. Until the nonbreaching party treats this early repudiation as a breach, however, the breaching party can retract the anticipatory repudiation by proper notice and restore the parties to their original obligations.

An anticipatory repudiation is treated as a present, material breach for two reasons. First, the nonbreaching party should not be required to remain ready and willing to perform when the other party has already repudiated the contract. Second, the nonbreaching party should have the opportunity to seek a similar contract elsewhere and may have the duty to do so to minimize his or her loss.

Quite often, an anticipatory repudiation occurs when a sharp fluctuation in market prices creates a situation in which performance of the contract would be extremely unfavorable to one of the parties. **EXAMPLE #15** Shasta Manufacturing Company contracts to manufacture and sell 100,000 personal computers to New Age, Inc., a computer retailer with 100 outlet stores. Delivery is to be made two months from the date of the contract. One month later, three suppliers of computer parts raise their prices to Shasta. Because of these higher prices, Shasta stands to lose $500,000 if it sells the computers to New Age at the contract price.

ANTICIPATORY REPUDIATION
An assertion or action by a party indicating that he or she will not perform an obligation that the party is contractually obligated to perform at a future time.

REMEMBER
The risks that prices will fluctuate and values will change are ordinary business risks for which the law does not normally provide relief.

---

10. *Kim v. Park,* 192 Or.App. 365, 86 P.3d 63 (2004).
11. *Restatement (Second) of Contracts,* Section 253; and UCC 2–610, 2–611.

Shasta writes to New Age, stating that it cannot deliver the 100,000 computers at the agreed-on contract price. Even though you might sympathize with Shasta, its letter is an anticipatory repudiation of the contract, allowing New Age the option of treating the repudiation as a material breach and proceeding immediately to pursue remedies, even though the contract delivery date is still a month away. □

Discharge by Agreement

Any contract can be discharged by agreement of the parties. The agreement can be contained in the original contract, or the parties can form a new contract for the express purpose of discharging the original contract.

Discharge by Rescission   *Rescission* is the process by which a contract is canceled or terminated and the parties are returned to the positions they occupied prior to forming it. For **mutual rescission** to take place, the parties must make another agreement that also satisfies the legal requirements for a contract. There must be an *offer,* an *acceptance,* and *consideration.* Ordinarily, if the parties agree to rescind the original contract, their promises not to perform the acts stipulated in the original contract will be legal consideration for the second contract (the rescission).

Agreements to rescind executory contracts (in which neither party has performed) are generally enforceable, even if the agreement is made orally and even if the original agreement was in writing. An exception applies under the Uniform Commercial Code to agreements rescinding a contract for the sale of goods, regardless of price, when the contract requires a written rescission. Also, agreements to rescind contracts involving transfers of realty must be evidenced by a writing.

When one party has fully performed, an agreement to cancel the original contract normally will not be enforceable. Because the performing party has received no consideration for the promise to call off the original bargain, additional consideration is necessary.

MUTUAL RESCISSION
An agreement between the parties to cancel their contract, releasing the parties from further obligations under the contract. The object of the agreement is to restore the parties to the positions they would have occupied had no contract ever been formed.

Discharge by Novation   A contractual obligation may also be discharged through novation. A **novation** occurs when both of the parties to a contract agree to substitute a third party for one of the original parties. The requirements of a novation are as follows:

1. A previous valid obligation.
2. An agreement by all the parties to a new contract.
3. The extinguishing of the old obligation (discharge of the prior party).
4. A new contract that is valid.

NOVATION
The substitution, by agreement, of a new contract for an old one, with the rights under the old one being terminated. Typically, novation involves the substitution of a new party for one of the original parties to the contract.

EXAMPLE #16 Union Corporation contracts to sell its pharmaceutical division to British Pharmaceuticals, Ltd. Before the transfer is completed, Union, British Pharmaceuticals, and a third company, Otis Chemicals, execute a new agreement to transfer all of British Pharmaceutical's rights and duties in the transaction to Otis Chemicals. As long as the new contract is supported by consideration, the novation will discharge the original contract (between Union and British Pharmaceuticals) and replace it with the new contract (between Union and Otis Chemicals). □

A novation expressly or impliedly revokes and discharges a prior contract. The parties involved may expressly state in the new contract that the old contract is now discharged. If the parties do not expressly discharge the old contract, it will be impliedly discharged if the new contract's terms are inconsistent with the old contract's terms.

Discharge by Substituted Agreement   A *compromise,* or settlement agreement, that arises out of a genuine dispute over the obligations under an existing contract will be recognized at law. Such an agreement will be substituted as a new contract, and it will either expressly or impliedly revoke and discharge the obligations under any prior contract. In contrast to a novation, a substituted agreement does not involve a third party. Rather, the two original parties to the contract form a different agreement to substitute for the original one.

Discharge by Accord and Satisfaction   For a contract to be discharged by accord and satisfaction, the parties must agree to accept performance that is different from the performance originally promised. An *accord* is a contract to perform some act to satisfy an existing contractual duty. The duty has not yet been discharged. A *satisfaction* is the performance of the accord agreement. An accord and its satisfaction discharge the original contractual obligation.

Once the accord has been made, the original obligation is merely suspended. The obligor (the one owing the obligation) can discharge the obligation by performing either the obligation agreed to in the accord or the original obligation. If the obligor refuses to perform the accord, the obligee (the one to whom performance is owed) can bring action on the original obligation or seek a decree compelling specific performance on the accord.

EXAMPLE #17 Frazer obtains a judgment against Ling for $8,000. Later, both parties agree that the judgment can be satisfied by Ling's transfer of his automobile to Frazer. This agreement to accept the auto in lieu of $8,000 in cash is the accord. If Ling transfers the car to Frazer, the accord is fully performed, and the debt is discharged. If Ling refuses to transfer the car, the accord is breached. Because the original obligation is merely suspended, Frazer can sue Ling to enforce the original judgment for $8,000 in cash or bring an action for breach of the accord.☐

Discharge by Operation of Law

Under certain circumstances, contractual duties may be discharged by operation of law. These circumstances include material alteration of the contract, the running of the statute of limitations, bankruptcy, and the impossibility or impracticability of performance.

Alteration of the Contract   To discourage parties from altering written contracts, the law operates to allow an innocent party to be discharged when the other party has materially altered a written contract without consent. For example, contract terms such as quantity or price might be changed without the knowledge or consent of all parties. If so, the party who was not involved in the alteration can treat the contract as discharged or terminated.

Statutes of Limitations   As mentioned earlier in this text, statutes of limitations restrict the period during which a party can sue on a particular cause of action. After the applicable limitations period has passed, a suit can no longer be brought. For example, the limitations period for bringing suits for breach of oral

"Law is a practical matter."
—ROSCOE POUND, 1870–1964
(American jurist)

contracts is usually two to three years; for written contracts, four to five years; and for recovery of amounts awarded in judgments, ten to twenty years, depending on state law. Suits for breach of a contract for the sale of goods generally must be brought within four years after the cause of action has accrued. By their original agreement, the parties can reduce this four-year period to not less than one year, but they cannot agree to extend it.

Bankruptcy   A proceeding in bankruptcy attempts to allocate the assets a debtor owns to creditors in a fair and equitable fashion. Once the assets have been allocated, the debtor receives a *discharge in bankruptcy.* A discharge in bankruptcy will ordinarily bar creditors from enforcing most of their contracts with the debtor. Partial payment of a debt *after* discharge in bankruptcy will not revive the debt. (Bankruptcy will be discussed in detail in Chapter 13.)

Impossibility or Impracticability of Performance   After a contract has been made, performance may become impossible in an objective sense. This is known as **impossibility of performance** and may discharge a contract.

Objective Impossibility of Performance   *Objective impossibility* ("It can't be done") must be distinguished from *subjective impossibility* ("I'm sorry, I simply can't do it"). Examples of subjective impossibility include the situation in which goods cannot be delivered on time because of freight car shortages and the situation in which payment cannot be made on time because the bank is closed. In effect, the party in each of these situations is saying, "It is impossible for me to perform," not "It is impossible for anyone to perform." Accordingly, such excuses do not discharge a contract, and the nonperforming party is normally held in breach of contract. Three basic types of situations, however, generally qualify as grounds for the discharge of contractual obligations based on impossibility of performance:[12]

1. *When one of the parties to a personal contract dies or becomes incapacitated prior to performance.* EXAMPLE #18 Fred, a famous dancer, contracts with Ethereal Dancing Guild to play a leading role in its new ballet. Before the ballet can be performed, Fred becomes ill and dies. His personal performance was essential to the completion of the contract. Thus, his death discharges the contract and his estate's liability for his nonperformance. □

2. *When the specific subject matter of the contract is destroyed.* EXAMPLE #19 A-1 Farm Equipment agrees to sell Gudgel the green tractor on its lot and promises to have it ready for Gudgel to pick up on Saturday. On Friday night, however, a truck veers off the nearby highway and smashes into the tractor, destroying it beyond repair. Because the contract was for this specific tractor, A-1's performance is rendered impossible owing to the accident. □

3. *When a change in law renders performance illegal.* EXAMPLE #20 A contract to build an apartment building becomes impossible to perform when the zoning laws are changed to prohibit the construction of residential rental property at the planned location. A contract to paint a bridge using lead paint becomes impossible when the government passes new regulations forbidding the use of lead paint on bridges.[13] □

IMPOSSIBILITY OF PERFORMANCE
A doctrine under which a party to a contract is relieved of his or her duty to perform when performance becomes objectively impossible or totally impracticable (through no fault of either party).

---

12. *Restatement (Second) of Contracts,* Sections 262–266; and UCC 2–615.
13. *M. J. Paquet, Inc. v. New Jersey Department of Transportation,* 171 N.J. 378, 794 A.2d 141 (2002).

Temporary Impossibility   An occurrence or event that makes performance temporarily impossible operates to suspend performance until the impossibility ceases. Then, ordinarily, the parties must perform the contract as originally planned. If, however, the lapse of time and the change in circumstances surrounding the contract make it substantially more burdensome for the parties to perform the promised acts, the contract is discharged.

The leading case on the subject, *Autry v. Republic Productions,*[14] involved an actor (Gene Autry) who was drafted into the army in 1942. Being drafted rendered the actor's contract temporarily impossible to perform, and it was suspended until the end of the war. When the actor got out of the army, the purchasing power of the dollar had so diminished that performance of the contract would have been substantially burdensome to him. Therefore, the contract was discharged.

EXAMPLE #21 On August 22, 2005, Keefe Hurwitz contracted to sell his home in Madisonville, Louisiana, to Wesley and Gwendolyn Payne for a price of $241,500. On August 26—just four days after the parties signed the contract—Hurricane Katrina made landfall and caused extensive property damage to the house. The cost of repairs was estimated at $60,000 and Hurwitz would have to make the repairs before the *closing date* (see Chapter 22). Hurwitz did not have the funds and refused to pay $60,000 for the repairs only to sell the property to the Paynes for the previously agreed-on price of $241,500. The Paynes filed a lawsuit to enforce the contract. Hurwitz claimed that Hurricane Katrina had made it impossible for him to perform and had discharged his duties under the contract. The court, however, ruled that Hurricane Katrina had only caused a temporary impossibility. Hurwitz was required to pay for the necessary repairs and to perform the contract as written. In other words, he could not obtain a higher purchase price to offset the cost of the repairs.[15] □

Commercial Impracticability   When a supervening event does not render performance objectively impossible, but does make it much more difficult or expensive to perform, the courts may excuse the parties' obligations under the contract. For someone to invoke the doctrine of **commercial impracticability** successfully, however, the anticipated performance must become significantly more difficult or costly than originally contemplated at the time the contract was formed.[16]

The added burden of performing not only must be extreme but also *must not have been known by the parties when the contract was made.* **EXAMPLE #22** In one case, the court allowed a party to rescind a contract for the sale of land because of a potential problem with contaminated groundwater under the land. The court found that "the potential for substantial and unbargained-for" liability made contract performance economically impracticable. Interestingly, the court in that case also noted that the possibility of "environmental degradation with consequences extending well beyond the parties' land sale" was just as important to its decision as the economic considerations.[17] □

The contract dispute in the following case arose out of the cancellation of a wedding reception due to a power failure. Is a power failure sufficient to invoke the doctrine of commercial impracticability?

COMMERCIAL IMPRACTICABILITY
A doctrine under which a court may excuse the parties from performing a contract when the performance becomes much more difficult or costly due to an event that the parties did not foresee or anticipate at the time the contract was made.

14. 30 Cal.2d 144, 180 P.2d 888 (1947).
15. *Payne v. Hurwitz,* 978 So.2d 1000 (La.App. 1st Cir., 2008).
16. *Restatement (Second) of Contracts,* Section 264.
17. *Cape-France Enterprises v. Estate of Peed,* 305 Mont. 513, 29 P.3d 1011 (2001).

Case 10.2 Facto v. Pantagis

Superior Court of New Jersey,
Appellate Division, 2007.
390 N.J.Super. 227, 915 A.2d 59.
lawlibrary.rutgers.edu/search.shtml[a]

BACKGROUND AND FACTS   Leo and Elizabeth Facto contracted with Snuffy Pantagis Enterprises, Inc., for the use of Pantagis Renaissance, a banquet hall in Scotch Plains, New Jersey, for a wedding reception in August 2002. The Factos paid the $10,578 price in advance. The contract excused Pantagis from performance "if it is prevented from doing so by an act of God (for example, flood, power failure, etc.), or other

a. In the "Search by party name" section, select the "Appellate Division," type "Pantagis" in the "First Name:" box, and click on "Submit Form." In the result, click on the "click here to get this case" link to access the opinion. The Rutgers University School of Law in Camden, New Jersey, maintains this Web site.

unforeseen events or circumstances." Soon after the reception began, there was a power failure. The lights and the air-conditioning shut off. The band hired for the reception refused to play without electricity to power their instruments, and the lack of lighting prevented the photographer and videographer from taking pictures. The temperature was in the 90s, the humidity was high, and the guests quickly became uncomfortable. Three hours later, after a fight between a guest and a Pantagis employee, the emergency lights began to fade, and the police evacuated the hall. The Factos filed a suit in a New Jersey state court against Pantagis, alleging breach of contract, among other things. The Factos sought to recover their prepayment, plus amounts paid to the band, the photographer, and the videographer. The court concluded that Pantagis did not breach the contract and dismissed the complaint. The Factos appealed to a state intermediate appellate court.

IN THE WORDS OF THE COURT . . . SKILLMAN, P.J.A.D. [Presiding Judge, Appellate Division]

*   *   *   *

Even if a contract does not expressly provide that a party will be relieved of the duty to perform if an unforeseen condition arises that makes performance impracticable, a court may relieve him of that duty if performance has unexpectedly become impracticable as a result of a supervening event. *In deciding whether a party should be relieved of the duty to perform a contract, a court must determine whether the existence of a specific thing is necessary for the performance of a duty and its *   *   * destruction or *   *   * deterioration *   *   * makes performance impracticable.* *   *   * A power failure is the kind of unexpected occurrence that may relieve a party of the duty to perform if the availability of electricity is essential for satisfactory performance. [Emphasis added.]

*   *   *   *

The *   *   * Pantagis Renaissance contract provided: "Snuffy's will be excused from performance under this contract if it is prevented from doing so by an act of God (e.g., flood, power failure, etc.), or other unforeseen events or circumstances." Thus, the contract specifically identified a "power failure" as one of the circumstances that would excuse the Pantagis Renaissance's performance. We do not attribute any significance to the fact the *   *   * clause refers to a power failure as an example of an "act of God." *This term has been construed to refer not just to natural events such as storms but to comprehend all misfortunes and accidents arising from inevitable necessity which human prudence could not foresee or prevent.* Furthermore, the *   *   * clause in the Pantagis Renaissance contract excuses performance not only for "acts of God" but also "other unforeseen events or circumstances." Consequently, even if a power failure caused by circumstances other than a natural event were not considered to be an "act of God," it still would constitute an unforeseen event or circumstance that would excuse performance. [Emphasis added.]

The fact that a power failure is not absolutely unforeseeable during the hot summer months does not preclude relief from the obligation to perform. *   *   * *Absolute unforeseeability of a condition is not a prerequisite to the defense of impracticability.* The party seeking to be relieved of the duty to perform only needs to show that the destruction, or *   *   * deterioration of a specific thing necessary for the performance of the contract makes performance impracticable. In this case, the Pantagis Renaissance sought to eliminate any possible doubt that the availability of electricity was a specific thing necessary for the wedding reception by specifically referring to a "power failure" as an example of an "act of God" that would excuse performance. [Emphasis added.]

It is also clear that the Pantagis Renaissance was "prevented from" substantial performance of the contract. The power failure began less than forty-five minutes after the start of the reception and continued until after it was scheduled to end. The lack of electricity prevented the band from playing, impeded the taking of pictures by the photographer and videographer and made it difficult for guests to see inside the banquet hall. Most significantly, the shutdown of the air conditioning system made it unbearably hot shortly after the power failure began. It is also undisputed that the power failure was an area-wide event that was beyond the Pantagis Renaissance's control. These are precisely the kind of circumstances under which the parties agreed * * * [in their contract] that the Pantagis Renaissance would be excused from performance.

* * * Where one party to a contract is excused from performance as a result of an unforeseen event that makes performance impracticable, the other party is also generally excused from performance.

* * * Therefore, the power failure that relieved the Pantagis Renaissance of the obligation to furnish plaintiffs with a wedding reception also relieved plaintiffs of the obligation to pay the contract price for the reception.

Nevertheless, since the Pantagis Renaissance partially performed the contract by starting the reception before the power failure, it is entitled * * * to recover the value of the services it provided to plaintiffs.

DECISION AND REMEDY   The state intermediate appellate court agreed that the power failure relieved Pantagis of its contractual obligation, but held that Pantagis's inability to perform also relieved the Factos of their obligation. The court reversed the dismissal and remanded the case for an award to the Factos of the amount of their prepayment less the value of the services they received.

THE ETHICAL DIMENSION   Should Pantagis have offered to reschedule the reception? Would this have absolved Pantagis of the obligation to refund the Factos' prepayment? Explain.

THE LEGAL ENVIRONMENT DIMENSION   Does a power failure always constitute the kind of unexpected occurrence that relieves a party of the duty to perform a contract? In what circumstances might a power failure have no effect on a contract? (Hint: Is electricity always necessary for the performance of a contract?)

Frustration of Purpose   A theory closely allied with the doctrine of commercial impracticability is the doctrine of **frustration of purpose.** In principle, a contract will be discharged if supervening circumstances make it impossible to attain the purpose both parties had in mind when making the contract.

The origins of the doctrine lie in the old English "coronation cases." A coronation procession was planned for Edward VII when he became king of England following the death of his mother, Queen Victoria. Hotel rooms along the coronation route were rented at exorbitant prices for that day. When the king became ill and the procession was canceled, a flurry of lawsuits resulted. Hotel and building owners sought to enforce the room-rent bills against would-be parade observers, and would-be parade observers sought to be reimbursed for rental monies paid in advance on the rooms. Would-be parade observers were excused from their duty of payment because the purpose of the room contracts had been "frustrated."

Exhibit 10–2 on the following page graphically illustrates the ways in which a contract can be discharged.

FRUSTRATION OF PURPOSE
A court-created doctrine under which a party to a contract will be relieved of his or her duty to perform when the objective purpose for performance no longer exists (due to reasons beyond that party's control).

EXHIBIT 10–2 CONTRACT DISCHARGE

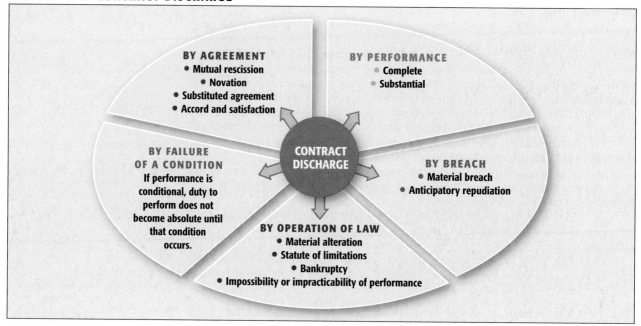

DAMAGES FOR BREACH OF CONTRACT

A breach of contract entitles the nonbreaching party to sue for monetary damages. Damages are designed to compensate a party for harm suffered as a result of another's wrongful act. In the context of contract law, damages compensate the nonbreaching party for the loss of the bargain. Often, courts say that innocent parties are to be placed in the position they would have occupied had the contract been fully performed.

Realize at the outset, though, that to collect damages through a court judgment means litigation, which can be expensive and time consuming. Also keep in mind that court judgments are often difficult to enforce, particularly if the breaching party does not have sufficient assets to pay the damages awarded (as discussed in Chapter 3). For these reasons, the majority of actions for damages (or other remedies) are settled by the parties before trial.

Types of Damages

There are basically four broad categories of damages:

1. Compensatory (to cover direct losses and costs).
2. Consequential (to cover indirect and foreseeable losses).
3. Punitive (to punish and deter wrongdoing).
4. Nominal (to recognize wrongdoing when no monetary loss is shown).

Compensatory and punitive damages were discussed in Chapter 5 in the context of tort law. Here, we look at compensatory and consequential damages in the context of contract law.

Compensatory Damages   Damages compensating the nonbreaching party for the *loss of the bargain* are known as *compensatory damages*. These damages compensate the injured party only for damages actually sustained and proved to have arisen directly from the loss of the bargain caused by the breach of contract. They simply replace what was lost because of the wrong or damage. The standard measure of compensatory damages is the difference between the value of the breaching party's promised performance under the contract and the value of her or his actual performance. This amount is reduced by any loss that the injured party has avoided, however.

EXAMPLE #23 Wilcox contracts to perform certain services exclusively for Hernandez during the month of March for $4,000. Hernandez cancels the contract and is in breach. Wilcox is able to find another job during the month of March but can earn only $3,000. He can sue Hernandez for breach and recover $1,000 as compensatory damages. Wilcox can also recover from Hernandez the amount that he spent to find the other job.□ Expenses that are caused directly by a breach of contract—such as those incurred to obtain performance from another source—are known as *incidental damages*.

The measurement of compensatory damages varies by type of contract. Certain types of contracts deserve special mention. They are contracts for the sale of goods and the sale of land.

Sale of Goods. In a contract for the sale of goods, the usual measure of compensatory damages is an amount equal to the difference between the contract price and the market price. In other words, the amount is the difference between the contract price and the market price at the time and place at which the goods were to be delivered or tendered.[18]

EXAMPLE #24 Chrylon Corporation contracts to buy ten model UTS network servers from an XEXO Corporation dealer for $8,000 each. The dealer, however, fails to deliver the ten servers to Chrylon. The market price of the servers at the time the buyer learns of the breach is $8,150. Chrylon's measure of damages is therefore $1,500 (10 × $150) plus any incidental damages (expenses) caused by the breach.□ In a situation in which the buyer breaches and the seller has not yet produced the goods, compensatory damages normally equal lost profits on the sale, not the difference between the contract price and the market price.

Sale of Land. Ordinarily, because each parcel of land is unique, the remedy for a seller's breach of a contract for a sale of real estate is specific performance—that is, the buyer is awarded the parcel of property for which she or he bargained (specific performance will be discussed more fully later in this chapter). When this remedy is unavailable (for example, when the seller has sold the property to someone else), or when the breach is on the part of the buyer, the measure of damages is ordinarily the same as in contracts for the sale of goods—that is, the difference between the contract price and the market price of the land. The majority of states follow this rule.

Consequential Damages Foreseeable damages that result from a party's breach of contract are referred to as **consequential damages,** or *special damages*. Consequential damages differ from compensatory damages in that they are caused by special circumstances beyond the contract itself. They flow from the consequences, or results, of a breach. When a seller fails to deliver goods, knowing that the buyer is planning to use or resell those goods immediately, consequential damages are awarded for the loss of profits from the planned resale.

"The duty to keep a contract at common law means a prediction that you must pay damages if you do not keep it— and nothing else."

—OLIVER WENDELL HOLMES, JR.,
1841–1935
(Associate justice of the United States Supreme Court, 1902–1932)

CONSEQUENTIAL DAMAGES
Special damages that compensate for a loss that does not directly or immediately result from the breach (for example, lost profits). For the plaintiff to collect consequential damages, they must have been reasonably foreseeable at the time the breach or injury occurred.

---

18. See UCC 2–708 and 2–713.

A seller who does not wish to take on the risk of consequential damages can limit the buyer's remedies via contract.

EXAMPLE #25 Gilmore contracts to have a specific item shipped to her—one that she desperately needs to repair her printing press. In her contract with the shipper, Gilmore states that she must receive the item by Monday or she will not be able to print her paper and will lose $950. If the shipper is late, Gilmore normally can recover the consequential damages caused by the delay (that is, the $950 in losses). □

To recover consequential damages, the breaching party must know (or have reason to know) that special circumstances will cause the nonbreaching party to suffer an additional loss. When was this rule first enunciated? See this chapter's *Landmark in the Legal Environment* feature for a discussion of *Hadley v. Baxendale,* a case decided in England in 1854.

Mitigation of Damages

MITIGATION OF DAMAGES
A rule requiring a plaintiff to do whatever is reasonable to minimize the damages caused by the defendant.

In most situations, when a breach of contract occurs, the innocent injured party is held to a duty to mitigate, or reduce, the damages that he or she suffers. Under this doctrine of **mitigation of damages,** the duty owed depends on the nature of the contract.

EXAMPLE #26 Some states require a landlord to use reasonable means to find a new tenant if a tenant abandons the premises and fails to pay rent. If an acceptable tenant is found, the landlord is required to lease the premises to this tenant to mitigate the damages recoverable from the former tenant. The former tenant is still liable for the difference between the amount of the rent under the original lease and the rent received from the new tenant. If the landlord has not used the reasonable means necessary to find a new tenant, presumably a court can reduce the award made by the amount of rent the landlord could have received had such reasonable means been used. □

In the majority of states, persons whose employment has been wrongfully terminated owe a duty to mitigate damages suffered because of their employers' breach of the employment contract. In other words, wrongfully terminated employees have a duty to take similar jobs if they are available. If the employees fail to do this, the damages they are awarded will be equivalent to their salaries less the incomes they would have received in similar jobs obtained by reasonable means. The employer has the burden of proving that such a job existed and that the employee could have been hired. Normally, the employee is under no duty to take a job of a different type and rank, however.

Liquidated Damages Provisions

LIQUIDATED DAMAGES
An amount, stipulated in the contract, to be paid in the event of a default or breach of contract. The amount must be a reasonable estimate of the damages that would result from a breach in order for the court to enforce it as liquidated damages.

A **liquidated damages** provision in a contract specifies that a certain dollar amount is to be paid in the event of a *future* default or breach of contract. (*Liquidated* means determined, settled, or fixed.) For example, a provision requiring a construction contractor to pay $300 for every day he or she is late in completing the construction is a liquidated damages provision. Liquidated damages provisions are frequently used in construction contracts because it is difficult to estimate the amount of damages that would be caused by a delay in completing construction. These clauses are also common in contracts for the sale of goods, and Section 2–718(1) of the Uniform Commercial Code specifically authorizes the use of liquidated damages clauses.

Liquidated Damages versus Penalties   When a contract specifies a sum to be paid for nonperformance, the issue becomes whether the amount should be

The rule that notice of special ("consequential") circumstances must be given if consequential damages are to be recovered was first enunciated in *Hadley v. Baxendale,*[a] a landmark case decided in 1854.

Case Background

This case involved a broken crankshaft used in a flour mill run by the Hadley family in Gloucester, England. The crankshaft attached to the steam engine in the mill broke, and the shaft had to be sent to a foundry located in Greenwich so that a new shaft could be made to fit the other parts of the engine.

The Hadleys hired Baxendale, a common carrier, to transport the shaft from Gloucester to Greenwich. Baxendale received payment in advance and promised to deliver the shaft the following day. It was not delivered for several days, however. As a consequence, the mill was closed during those days because the Hadleys had no extra crankshaft on hand to use. The Hadleys sued Baxendale to recover the profits they lost during that time. Baxendale contended that the loss of profits was "too remote."

In the mid-1800s, it was common knowledge that large mills, such as that run by the Hadleys, normally had more than one crankshaft in case the main one broke and had to be repaired, as happened in this case. It is against this background that the parties argued their respective positions on whether the damages resulting from loss of profits while the crankshaft was out for repair were "too remote" to be recoverable.

The Issue before the Court and the Court's Ruling

The crucial issue before the court was whether the Hadleys had informed the carrier, Baxendale, of the special circumstances surrounding the crankshaft's repair, particularly that the mill would have to shut down while the crankshaft was being repaired. If Baxendale had been notified of this circumstance at the time the contract was formed, then the remedy for breaching the contract would have been the amount of damages that would reasonably follow from the breach—including the Hadleys' lost profits.

In the court's opinion, however, the only circumstances communicated by the Hadleys to Baxendale at the time the contract was made were that the item to be transported was a broken crankshaft of a mill and that the Hadleys were the owners and operators of that mill. The court concluded that these circumstances did not reasonably indicate that the mill would have to stop operations if the delivery of the crankshaft was delayed.

APPLICATION TO TODAY'S LEGAL ENVIRONMENT

Today, the rule enunciated by the court in this case still applies. When damages are awarded, compensation is given only for those injuries that the defendant could reasonably have foreseen as a probable result of the usual course of events following a breach. If the injury complained of is outside the usual and foreseeable course of events, the plaintiff must show specifically that the defendant had reason to know the facts and foresee the injury. This rule applies to contracts in the online environment as well. For example, suppose that a Web merchant loses business (and profits) due to a computer system's failure. If the failure was caused by malfunctioning software, the merchant normally may recover the lost profits from the software maker if these consequential damages were foreseeable.

RELEVANT WEB SITES

To locate information on the Web concerning *Hadley v. Baxendale,* go to this text's Web site at **www.cengage.com/blaw/let**, select "Chapter 10," and click on "URLs for Landmarks."

a. 9 Exch. 341, 156 Eng.Rep. 145 (1854).

---

treated as liquidated damages or as a penalty. Liquidated damages provisions are enforceable; penalty provisions are not. Generally, if the amount stated is excessive and the clause is designed to *penalize* the breaching party, a court will consider it a **penalty.** If the amount specified is a reasonable estimation of actual damages, a court may enforce it as a liquidated damages provision.

Factors Courts Consider To determine if a particular provision is for liquidated damages or for a penalty, two questions must be answered:

1. When the contract was entered into, was it apparent that damages would be difficult to estimate in the event of a breach?
2. Was the amount set as damages a reasonable estimate and not excessive?[19]

If the answers to both questions are yes, the provision normally will be enforced. If either answer is no, the provision normally will not be enforced. EXAMPLE #27

PENALTY

An amount, stipulated in the contract, to be paid in the event of a default or breach of contract. When the amount is not a reasonable measure of damages, the court will not enforce it but will limit recovery to actual damages.

---

19. *Restatement (Second) of Contracts,* Section 356(1).

In a case involving a sophisticated business contract to lease computer equipment, the court held that a liquidated damages provision that valued computer equipment at more than four times its market value was a reasonable estimate. According to the court, the amount of actual damages was difficult to ascertain at the time the contract was formed because of the "speculative nature of the value of computers at termination of lease schedules."[20] □

EQUITABLE REMEDIES

In some situations, damages are an inadequate remedy for a breach of contract. In these cases, the nonbreaching party may ask the court for an equitable remedy. Equitable remedies include rescission and restitution, specific performance, and reformation. Additionally, a court acting in the interests of equity may sometimes step in and impose contractual obligations in an effort to prevent the unjust enrichment of one party at the expense of another.

Rescission and Restitution

As discussed earlier in this chapter, *rescission* is essentially an action to undo, or cancel, a contract—to return nonbreaching parties to the positions that they occupied prior to the transaction. When fraud, mistake, duress, or failure of consideration is present, rescission is available. The failure of one party to perform under a contract entitles the other party to rescind the contract.[21] The rescinding party must give prompt notice to the breaching party.

RESTITUTION
An equitable remedy under which a person is restored to his or her original position prior to loss or injury, or placed in the position he or she would have been in had the breach not occurred.

Restitution   To rescind a contract, both parties generally must make **restitution** to each other by returning goods, property, or funds previously conveyed. If the physical property or goods can be returned, they must be. If the property or goods have been consumed, restitution must be made in an equivalent dollar amount.

Essentially, restitution involves the recapture of a benefit conferred on the defendant that has unjustly enriched her or him. **EXAMPLE #28** Andrea pays $12,000 to Myles in return for his promise to design a house for her. The next day, Myles calls Andrea and tells her that he has taken a position with a large architectural firm in another state and cannot design the house. Andrea decides to hire another architect that afternoon. Andrea can require restitution of $12,000 because Myles has received an unjust benefit of $12,000. □

CONTRAST
Restitution offers several advantages over traditional damages. First, restitution may be available in situations when damages cannot be proved or are difficult to prove. Second, restitution can be used to recover specific property. Third, restitution sometimes results in a greater overall award.

Restitution Is Not Limited to Rescission Cases   Restitution may be required when a contract is rescinded, but the right to restitution is not limited to rescission cases. Restitution may be sought in actions for breach of contract, tort actions, and other actions at law or in equity. Usually, restitution can be obtained when funds or property has been transferred by mistake or because of fraud. An award in a case may include restitution of cash or property obtained through embezzlement, conversion, theft, copyright infringement, or misconduct by a party in a confidential or other special relationship.

---

20. *Winthrop Resources Corp. v. Eaton Hydraulics, Inc.*, 361 F.3d 465 (8th Cir. 2004).
21. The rescission discussed here refers to *unilateral* rescission, in which only one party wants to undo the contract. In *mutual* rescission, both parties agree to undo the contract. Mutual rescission discharges the contract; unilateral rescission is generally available as a remedy for breach of contract.

Specific Performance

The equitable remedy of **specific performance** calls for the performance of the act promised in the contract. (Interestingly, specific performance is the primary remedy for contract breach in some other nations, as discussed in this chapter's *Beyond Our Borders* feature on page 340.) This remedy is quite attractive to the nonbreaching party for three reasons:

1. The nonbreaching party need not worry about collecting the monetary damages awarded by a court (see the discussion in Chapter 3 of some of the difficulties that may arise when trying to enforce court judgments).
2. The nonbreaching party need not spend time seeking an alternative contract.
3. The performance is more valuable than the monetary damages.

Normally, however, specific performance will not be granted unless the party's legal remedy (monetary damages) is inadequate. For this reason, contracts for the sale of goods rarely qualify for specific performance. The legal remedy—monetary damages—is ordinarily adequate in such situations because substantially identical goods can be bought or sold in the market. Only if the goods are unique will a court grant specific performance. For example, paintings, sculptures, or rare books or coins are unique, so monetary damages will not enable a buyer to obtain substantially identical substitutes in the market.

Sale of Land   Specific performance is granted to a buyer in a contract for the sale of land. The legal remedy for breach of a land sales contract is inadequate because every parcel of land is considered to be unique. Monetary damages will not compensate a buyer adequately because the same land in the same location obviously cannot be obtained elsewhere. Only when specific performance is unavailable (for example, when the seller has sold the property to someone else) will monetary damages be awarded instead.

Is specific performance warranted when one of the parties has substantially—but not *fully*—performed under the contract? That was the question in the following case.

SPECIFIC PERFORMANCE

An equitable remedy requiring exactly the performance that was specified in a contract; usually granted only when money damages would be an inadequate remedy and the subject matter of the contract is unique (for example, real property).

Suppose that a seller contracts to sell some valuable coins to a buyer. If the seller breaches the contract, would specific performance be an appropriate remedy for the buyer to seek? Why or why not?
(Axel Buhrmann, Creative Commons)

Case 10.3 **Stainbrook v. Low**

Court of Appeals of Indiana, 2006.
842 N.E.2d 386.

BACKGROUND AND FACTS   In April 2004, Howard Stainbrook agreed to sell to Trent Low forty acres of land in Jennings County, Indiana, for $45,000. Thirty-two of the acres were wooded and eight were tillable. Under the agreement, Low was to pay for a survey of the property and other costs, including a tax payment due in November. Low gave Stainbrook a check for $1,000 to show his intent to fulfill the contract. They agreed to close the deal on May 11, and Low made financial arrangements to meet his obligations. On May 8, a tractor rolled over on Stainbrook, and he died. Howard's son David became the executor of Stainbrook's estate. David asked Low to withdraw his offer to buy the forty acres. Low refused and filed a suit in an Indiana state court against David, seeking to enforce the contract. The court ordered specific performance. David appealed to a state intermediate appellate court, arguing in part that his father's contract with Low was "ambiguous and inequitable."

CASE 10.3–CONTINUED

IN THE WORDS OF THE COURT . . . *VAIDIK*, Judge.

*   *   *   *

The Estate [David] *   *   * contends that Low failed to preserve the remedy of specific performance here because he failed to perform sufficiently under the Agreement. *   *   * The Estate argues that "in order to be entitled to specific performance, the claimant has the burden to prove *full and complete performance* on their part of the contract." Low *   *   * argues that specific performance was appropriate because he either *substantially performed* his obligations under the Agreement or offered to do so, and this, rather than full and complete performance, is all that is required to preserve a claim for specific performance.

We agree with Low. Because Low offered to perform his obligations under the Agreement, specific performance was a proper remedy. *   *   * The Estate argues that Low is not entitled to the remedy of specific performance because he did not pay the November 2004 property taxes. Low, however, *   *   * offered to make the tax payment and the Estate refused his offer.

The Estate also contends *   *   * that specific performance was inappropriate because Low failed to tender the purchase price listed in the Agreement and arrange for a survey of the land before the closing date. *   *   * The Estate's argument assumes that a party may not be granted specific performance unless that party has fully and completely performed under the terms of the contract. On the contrary, *   *   * *specific performance is an appropriate remedy to a party who has* substantially *performed under the terms of the contract.* Regarding Low's payment of the purchase price, we note that Low *   *   * had obtained financing before the closing date, and there is nothing *   *   * to indicate that he was not prepared to meet his financial obligations at that time. Further, *   *   * shortly after Stainbrook's death, the Executor of the Estate requested that Low withdraw his offer, and Low declined to do so, indicating that he was prepared to go forward. Regarding Low's failure to order a land survey, the Estate presents no evidence to suggest that this matter, particularly in isolation, reaches the level of failure to perform under the Agreement, and we decline to sanction such a rule. [Emphasis added.]

*   *   *   *

The Estate finally argues that the trial court should not have awarded specific performance here because the Agreement between Low and Stainbrook was unfair. *   *   * Since Low was twenty-two years old and Stainbrook was eighty-nine at the time of contract, and because the combined estimates of property and timber values was as high as $121,000.00 and Low and Stainbrook had agreed to a $45,000.00 purchase price, the Estate argues that the trial court should have found the contract to be unfair or unconscionable and to have found that Low would be unjustly enriched by its execution.

*   *   * The Estate stipulated at trial that Stainbrook was competent at the time of contract, and evidence was presented that Stainbrook consulted a lawyer regarding the Agreement and that he insisted upon several handwritten changes to the contract that benefited his own interests. We find no support for the Estate's contention that Stainbrook was anything less than a party entirely capable of entering into this Agreement, nor for its contention that the Agreement was unfair.

DECISION AND REMEDY   The state intermediate appellate court held that specific performance was an appropriate remedy in this case and affirmed the lower court's order. The appellate court explained that a contracting party's substantial performance is sufficient to support a court's order for specific performance. Here, "Low both offered to perform and substantially performed his contractual obligations."

WHY IS THIS CASE IMPORTANT?   The court reaffirmed the principle that "[s]pecific performance is a matter of course when it involves contracts to purchase real estate." The circumstances emphasized that "[a] party seeking specific performance of a real estate contract must prove that he has substantially performed his contract obligations or offered to do so." The court's reasoning underscored the importance of focusing on the elements of a principle to resolve a case fairly.

THE GLOBAL DIMENSION Suppose that Stainbrook and Low had been citizens and residents of other countries. Would the location of the land that was the subject of their contract have been sufficient to support the Indiana state court's jurisdiction and award in this case? Discuss.

Contracts for Personal Services Personal-service contracts require one party to work personally for another party. Courts normally refuse to grant specific performance of contracts for personal services. This is because to order a party to perform personal services against his or her will amounts to a type of involuntary servitude (slavery), which is contrary to the public policy expressed in the Thirteenth Amendment to the Constitution. Moreover, the courts do not want to monitor contracts for personal services.

EXAMPLE #29 If you contract with a brain surgeon to perform brain surgery on you and the surgeon refuses to perform, the court will not compel (and you certainly would not want) the surgeon to perform under these circumstances. There is no way the court can ensure meaningful performance in such a situation. □

Reformation

Reformation is an equitable remedy used when the parties have *imperfectly* expressed their agreement in writing. Reformation enables a court to modify, or rewrite, the contract to reflect the parties' true intentions.

REFORMATION
A court-ordered correction of a written contract so that it reflects the true intentions of the parties.

When Fraud or Mutual Mistake Is Present Reformation occurs most often when fraud or mutual mistake (for example, a clerical error) is present. It is almost always sought so that some other remedy can then be pursued. EXAMPLE #30 If Keshan contracts to buy a certain parcel of land from Malboa but their contract mistakenly refers to a parcel of land different from the one being sold, the contract does not reflect the parties' intentions. Accordingly, a court can reform the contract so that it conforms to the parties' intentions and accurately refers to the parcel of land being sold. Keshan can then, if necessary, show that Malboa has breached the contract as reformed. She can at that time request an order for specific performance. □

Oral Contracts and Covenants Not to Compete There are two other situations in which the courts frequently reform contracts. The first involves two parties who have made a binding oral contract. They further agree to put the oral contract in writing, but in doing so, they make an error in stating the terms. Normally, the courts will allow into evidence the correct terms of the oral contract, thereby reforming the written contract.

The second situation is when the parties have executed a written covenant not to compete (discussed in Chapter 9). If the covenant is for a valid and legitimate purpose (such as the sale of a business) but the area or time restraints of the covenant are unreasonable, some courts will reform the restraints by making them reasonable and will enforce the entire contract as reformed. Other courts, however, will throw out the entire covenant as illegal.

The types of remedies available for breach of contract vary widely throughout the world. In many countries, as in the United States, the normal remedy is damages—money given to the nonbreaching party to compensate that party for the losses incurred owing to the breach. The calculation of damages resulting from a breach of contract, however, may differ from one country to another.

National contract laws also differ as to whether and when equitable remedies, such as specific performance, will be granted. Germany's typical remedy for a breach of contract is specific performance, which means that the party must go forward and perform the contract. Damages are available only after certain procedures have been employed to seek performance. In contrast, in the United States, the equitable remedy of specific performance usually will not be granted unless the remedy at law (monetary damages) is inadequate and the subject matter of the contract is unique.

The effect of unforeseen events on a contract can also vary dramatically depending on the nation. In the United States, when a party alleges that contract performance is impossible or impracticable because of circumstances unforeseen at the time the contract was formed, a court will either discharge the party's contractual obligations or hold the party to the contract. In other words, if a court agrees that the contract is impossible or impracticable to perform, the remedy is to rescind (cancel) the contract. Under German law, however, a court may adjust the terms of (reform) a contract in light of economic developments. If an unforeseen event affects the foundation of the agreement, the court can alter the contract's terms in view of the disruption in expectations, thus making the contract fair to the parties.

FOR CRITICAL ANALYSIS If specific performance were the typical remedy for breaching a contract in the United States, as it is in Germany, would the parties be more likely to perform their obligations and not breach the contract? Discuss.

Exhibit 10–3 graphically summarizes the remedies, including reformation, that are available to the nonbreaching party.

Recovery Based on Quasi Contract

QUASI CONTRACT
A fictional contract imposed on parties by a court in the interests of fairness and justice; usually imposed to avoid the unjust enrichment of one party at the expense of another.

In some situations, when no actual contract exists, a court may step in to prevent one party from being unjustly enriched at the expense of another party. **Quasi contract** is a legal theory under which an obligation is imposed in the absence of an agreement. It allows the courts to act as if a contract exists when there is no actual contract or agreement between the parties. The courts can also use this theory when the parties entered a contract that is unenforceable for some reason.

Quasi-contractual recovery is often granted when one party has partially performed under a contract that is unenforceable. It provides an alternative to suing for damages and allows the party to recover the reasonable value of the partial performance. **EXAMPLE #31** Ericson contracts to build two oil derricks for Petro Industries. The derricks are to be built over a period of three years, but the parties do not create a written contract. Therefore, the Statute of Frauds will bar the enforcement of the contract. After Ericson completes one derrick, Petro Industries informs him that it will not pay for the derrick. Ericson can sue Petro Industries under the theory of quasi contract.□

To recover on quasi contract, the party seeking recovery must show the following:

1. The party conferred a benefit on the other party.
2. The party conferred the benefit with the reasonable expectation of being paid.
3. The party did not act as a volunteer in conferring the benefit.
4. The party receiving the benefit would be unjustly enriched by retaining the benefit without paying for it.

EXHIBIT 10-3 REMEDIES FOR BREACH OF CONTRACT

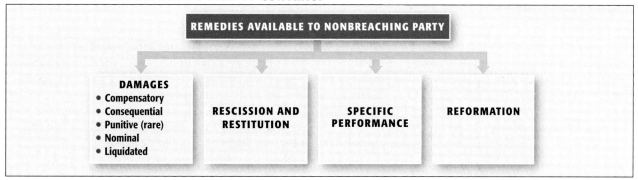

ELECTION OF REMEDIES

In many cases, a nonbreaching party has several remedies available. Because the remedies may be inconsistent with one another, the common law of contracts requires the party to choose which remedy to pursue. This is called *election of remedies*. The purpose of the doctrine of election of remedies is to prevent double recovery. **EXAMPLE #32** Jefferson agrees to sell his land to Adams. Then Jefferson changes his mind and repudiates the contract. Adams can sue for compensatory damages or for specific performance. If Adams receives damages as a result of the breach, she should not also be granted specific performance of the sales contract because that would mean she would unfairly end up with both the land and the damages. The doctrine of election of remedies requires Adams to choose the remedy she wants, and it eliminates any possibility of double recovery.□

In contrast, remedies under the Uniform Commercial Code (UCC) are cumulative. They include all of the remedies available under the UCC for breach of a sales or lease contract.[22] We will discuss the UCC provisions on limited remedies and the remedies available on the breach of a contract for the sale or lease of goods in Chapter 11.

CONTRACT PROVISIONS LIMITING REMEDIES

A contract may include provisions stating that no damages can be recovered for certain types of breaches or that damages must be limited to a maximum amount. The contract may also provide that the only remedy for breach is replacement, repair, or refund of the purchase price. Provisions stating that no damages can be recovered are called *exculpatory clauses*. Provisions that affect the availability of certain remedies are called *limitation-of-liability clauses*.

Whether these contract provisions and clauses will be enforced depends on the type of breach that is excused by the provision. Normally, a provision excluding liability for fraudulent or intentional injury will not be enforced. Likewise, a clause excluding liability for illegal acts or violations of law will not be enforced. A clause excluding liability for negligence may be enforced in certain cases, however. When an exculpatory clause for negligence is contained in a contract made between parties who have roughly equal bargaining positions, the clause usually will be enforced.

---

22. See UCC 2–703 and 2–711.

Reviewing . . . Contract Performance, Breach, and Remedies

Val's Foods signs a contract to buy 1,500 pounds of basil from Sun Farms, a small organic herb grower, as long as an independent organization inspects and certifies that the crop contains no pesticide or herbicide residue. Val's has a number of contracts with different restaurant chains to supply pesto and intends to use Sun Farms' basil in its pesto to fulfill these contracts. While Sun Farms is preparing to harvest the basil, an unexpected hailstorm destroys half the crop. Sun Farms attempts to purchase additional basil from other farms, but it is late in the season and the price is twice the normal market price. Sun Farms is too small to absorb this cost and immediately notifies Val's that it will not fulfill the contract. Using the information presented in the chapter, answer the following questions.

1. Suppose that the basil does not pass the chemical-residue inspection. Which concept discussed in the chapter might allow Val's to refuse to perform the contract in this situation?

2. Under which legal theory or theories might Sun Farms claim that its obligation under the contract has been discharged by operation of law? Discuss fully.

3. Suppose that Sun Farms contacts every basil grower in the country and buys the last remaining chemical-free basil anywhere. Nevertheless, Sun Farms is only able to ship 1,475 pounds to Val's. Would this fulfill Sun Farms' obligations to Val's? Why or why not?

4. Now suppose that Sun Farms sells its operations to Happy Valley Farms. As a part of the sale, all three parties agree that Happy Valley will provide the basil as stated under the original contract. What is this type of agreement called? Does it discharge the obligations of any of the parties? Explain.

Key Terms

Chapter Summary

Voluntary Consent
(See pages 311–319.)

1. *Mistakes–*

   a. Bilateral (mutual) mistakes–When both parties are mistaken about the same material fact, such as identity, either party can avoid the contract. If the mistake concerns value or quality, either party can enforce the contract.

   b. Unilateral mistakes–Generally, the mistaken party is bound by the contract *unless* (a) the other party knows or should have known of the mistake or (b) the mistake is an

Voluntary Consent— Continued	inadvertent mathematical error—such as an error in addition or subtraction—committed without gross negligence.
	2. *Fraudulent misrepresentation*—When fraud occurs, usually the innocent party can enforce or avoid the contract. For damages, the innocent party must suffer an injury. When innocent misrepresentation occurs, the contract may be rescinded (canceled), but damages are not available.
	3. *Undue influence*—Undue influence arises from special relationships in which one party can greatly influence another party, thus overcoming that party's free will. Usually, the contract is voidable.
	4. *Duress*—Duress is the tactic of forcing a party to enter a contract under the fear of a threat—for example, the threat of violence or serious economic loss. The party forced to enter the contract can rescind the contract.
The Statute of Frauds—Writing Requirement (See pages 319–320.)	The following types of contracts fall under the Statute of Frauds and must be in writing to be enforceable:
	1. Contracts involving interests in land.
	2. Contracts that cannot by their terms be performed within one year from the day after the date of formation.
	3. Collateral, or secondary, contracts, such as promises to answer for the debt or duty of another.
	4. Promises made in consideration of marriage.
	5. Under the UCC, contracts for the sale of goods priced at $500 or more.
Third Party Rights (See pages 320–322.)	1. *Assignments*—An assignment is the transfer of rights under a contract to a third party. The third party to whom the rights are assigned has a right to demand performance from the other original party to the contract. Generally, all rights can be assigned, but there are a few exceptions, such as when a statute prohibits assignment or when the contract calls for personal services.
	2. *Delegations*—A delegation is the transfer of duties under a contract to a third party, who then assumes the obligation of performing the contractual duties previously held by the one making the delegation. As a general rule, any duty can be delegated, except in a few situations, such as when the contract expressly prohibits delegation or when performance depends on the personal skills of the original party.
	3. *Third party beneficiaries*—A third party beneficiary is one who benefits from a contract between two other parties. If the party was an intended beneficiary, then the third party has legal rights and can sue the promisor directly to enforce the contract. If the contract benefits the third party unintentionally, then the third party cannot sue to enforce the contract.
Performance and Discharge (See pages 322–332.)	1. *Conditions of performance*—Contract obligations are sometimes subject to conditions. A condition is a possible future event, the occurrence or nonoccurrence of which will trigger the performance of a contract obligation or terminate an existing obligation. A condition that must be fulfilled before a party's promise becomes absolute is called a *condition precedent*.
	2. *Discharge by performance*—A contract may be discharged by complete (strict) performance or by substantial performance. In some cases, performance must be to the satisfaction of another. Totally inadequate performance constitutes a material breach of contract. An anticipatory repudiation of a contract allows the other party to sue immediately for breach of contract.
	3. *Discharge by agreement*—Parties may agree to discharge their contractual obligations in several ways:
	a. *By rescission*—The parties mutually agree to rescind (cancel) the contract.
	b. *By novation*—A new party is substituted for one of the primary parties to a contract.

CONTINUED

**Performance
and Discharge—
Continued**

   c. *By substituted agreement*—The parties agree to a new contract that replaces the old contract as a means of settling a dispute.

   d. *By accord and satisfaction*—The parties agree to render and accept performance different from that on which they originally agreed.

4. *Discharge by operation of law*—Parties' obligations under contracts may be discharged by operation of law owing to one of the following:

   a. Contract alteration.

   b. Statutes of limitations.

   c. Bankruptcy.

   d. Impossibility or impracticability of performance.

**Damages for
Breach of Contract**
(See pages 332–336.)

The legal remedy designed to compensate the nonbreaching party for the loss of the bargain. By awarding monetary damages, the court tries to place the parties in the positions that they would have occupied had the contract been fully performed.

1. *Compensatory damages*—Damages that compensate the nonbreaching party for injuries actually sustained and proved to have arisen directly from the loss of the bargain resulting from the breach of contract.

   a. In breached contracts for the sale of goods, the usual measure of compensatory damages is the difference between the contract price and the market price.

   b. In breached contracts for the sale of land, the measure of damages is ordinarily the same as in contracts for the sale of goods.

2. *Consequential damages*—Damages resulting from special circumstances beyond the contract itself; the damages flow only from the consequences of a breach. For a party to recover consequential damages, the damages must be the foreseeable result of a breach of contract, and the breaching party must have known at the time the contract was formed that special circumstances existed that would cause the nonbreaching party to incur additional loss on breach of the contract. Also called *special damages.*

3. *Mitigation of damages*—The nonbreaching party frequently has a duty to *mitigate* (lessen or reduce) the damages incurred as a result of the contract's breach.

4. *Liquidated damages*—Damages that may be specified in a contract as the amount to be paid to the nonbreaching party in the event the contract is breached in the future. Clauses providing for liquidated damages are enforced if the damages were difficult to estimate at the time the contract was formed and if the amount stipulated is reasonable. If the amount is construed to be a penalty, the clause will not be enforced.

Equitable Remedies
(See pages 336–340.)

1. *Rescission*—A remedy whereby a contract is canceled and the parties are restored to the original positions that they occupied prior to the transaction. Available when fraud, a mistake, duress, or failure of consideration is present. The rescinding party must give prompt notice of the rescission to the breaching party.

2. *Restitution*—When a contract is rescinded, both parties must make restitution to each other by returning the goods, property, or funds previously conveyed. Restitution prevents the unjust enrichment of the parties.

3. *Specific performance*—An equitable remedy calling for the performance of the act promised in the contract. This remedy is available only in special situations—such as those involving contracts for the sale of unique goods or land—in which monetary damages would be an inadequate remedy. Specific performance is not available as a remedy in breached contracts for personal services.

4. *Reformation*—An equitable remedy allowing a contract to be "reformed," or rewritten, to reflect the parties' true intentions. Available when an agreement is imperfectly expressed in writing.

Recovery Based on Quasi Contract (See page 340.)	An equitable theory imposed by the courts to obtain justice and prevent unjust enrichment in a situation in which no enforceable contract exists. The party seeking recovery must show the following:
	1. A benefit was conferred on the other party.
	2. The party conferring the benefit did so with the expectation of being paid.
	3. The benefit was not volunteered.
	4. Retaining the benefit without paying for it would result in the unjust enrichment of the party receiving the benefit.
Election of Remedies (See page 341.)	A common law doctrine under which a nonbreaching party must choose one remedy from those available. This doctrine prevents double recovery. Under the UCC, remedies are cumulative for the breach of a contract for the sale of goods.
Contract Provisions Limiting Remedies (See page 341.)	A contract may provide that no damages (or only a limited amount of damages) can be recovered in the event the contract is breached. Clauses excluding liability for fraudulent or intentional injury or for illegal acts cannot be enforced. Clauses excluding liability for negligence may be enforced if both parties hold roughly equal bargaining power.

For Review

1. In what types of situations might voluntary consent to a contract's terms be lacking?
2. What are the elements of fraudulent misrepresentation?
3. What is substantial performance?
4. What is the standard measure of compensatory damages when a contract is breached?
5. What equitable remedies can a court grant, and in what circumstances will a court consider granting them?

Questions and Case Problems

10–1. Substantial Performance. The Caplans own a real estate lot, and they contract with Faithful Construction, Inc., to build a house on it for $360,000. The specifications list "all plumbing bowls and fixtures . . . to be Crane brand." The Caplans leave on vacation, and during their absence Faithful is unable to buy and install Crane plumbing fixtures. Instead, Faithful installs Kohler brand fixtures, an equivalent in the industry. On completion of the building contract, the Caplans inspect the work, discover the substitution, and refuse to accept the house, claiming Faithful has breached the conditions set forth in the specifications. Discuss fully the Caplans' claim.

Question with Sample Answer

10–2. Junior owes creditor Iba $1,000, which is due and payable on June 1. Junior has been in a car accident, has missed a great deal of work, and consequently will not have the funds on June 1. Junior's father, Fred, offers

to pay Iba $1,100 in four equal installments if Iba will discharge Junior from any further liability on the debt. Iba accepts. Is this transaction a novation or an accord and satisfaction? Explain.

For a sample answer to Question 10–2, go to Appendix I at the end of this text.

10–3. Impossibility of Performance. In the following situations, certain events take place after the formation of contracts. Discuss which of these contracts are discharged because the events render the contracts impossible to perform.

1. Jimenez, a famous singer, contracts to perform in your nightclub. He dies prior to performance.
2. Raglione contracts to sell you her land. Just before title is to be transferred, she dies.
3. Oppenheim contracts to sell you one thousand bushels of apples from her orchard in the state of Washington. Because of a severe frost, she is unable to deliver the apples.

4. Maxwell contracts to lease a service station for ten years. His principal income is from the sale of gasoline. Because of an oil embargo by foreign oil-producing nations, gasoline is rationed, cutting sharply into Maxwell's gasoline sales. He cannot make his lease payments.

10–4. Measure of Damages. Ken owns and operates a famous candy store and makes most of the candy sold in the store. Business is particularly heavy during the Christmas season. Ken contracts with Sweet, Inc., to purchase ten thousand pounds of sugar to be delivered on or before November 15. Ken has informed Sweet that this particular order is to be used for the Christmas season business. Because of problems at the refinery, the sugar is not tendered to Ken until December 10, at which time Ken refuses it as being too late. Ken has been unable to purchase the quantity of sugar needed to meet his Christmas orders and has had to turn down numerous regular customers, some of whom have indicated that they will purchase candy elsewhere in the future. What sugar Ken has been able to purchase has cost him 10 cents per pound above the price contracted for with Sweet. Ken sues Sweet for breach of contract, claiming as damages the higher price paid for sugar from others, lost profits from this year's lost Christmas sales, future lost profits from customers who have indicated that they will discontinue doing business with him, and punitive damages for failure to meet the contracted delivery date. Sweet claims Ken is limited to compensatory damages only. Discuss who is correct, and why.

10–5. Fraudulent Misrepresentation. According to the student handbook at Cleveland Chiropractic College (CCC) in Missouri, *academic misconduct* includes "selling . . . any copy of any material intended to be used as an instrument of academic evaluation in advance of its initial administration." Leonard Verni was enrolled at CCC in Dr. Aleksandr Makarov's dermatology class. Before the first examination, Verni was reported to be selling copies of the test. CCC investigated and concluded that Verni had committed academic misconduct. He was dismissed from CCC, which informed him of his right to an appeal. According to the handbook, at the hearing on appeal a student could have an attorney or other adviser, present witnesses' testimony and other evidence, and "question any testimony . . . against him/her." At his hearing, however, Verni did not bring his attorney, present evidence on his behalf, or question any adverse witnesses. When the dismissal was upheld, Verni filed a suit in a Missouri state court against CCC and others, claiming, in part, fraudulent misrepresentation. Verni argued that because he "relied" on the handbook's "representation" that CCC would follow its appeal procedure, he was unable to properly refute the charges against him. Can Verni succeed with this argument? Explain. [*Verni v. Cleveland Chiropractic College,* 212 S.W.3d 150 (Mo. 2007)]

Case Problem with Sample Answer

10–6. On July 7, 2000, Frances Morelli agreed to sell to Judith Bucklin a house at 126 Lakedell Drive in Warwick, Rhode Island, for $77,000. Bucklin made a deposit on the house. The closing at which the parties would exchange the deed for the price was scheduled for September 1. The agreement did not state that "time is of the essence," but it did provide, in "Paragraph 10," that "[i]f Seller is unable to [convey good, clear, insurable, and marketable title], Buyer shall have the option to: (a) accept such title as Seller is able to convey without abatement or reduction of the Purchase Price, or (b) cancel this Agreement and receive a return of all Deposits." An examination of the public records revealed that the house did not have marketable title. Wishing to be flexible, Bucklin offered Morelli time to resolve the problem, and the closing did not occur as scheduled. Morelli decided "the deal is over" and offered to return the deposit. Bucklin refused and, in mid-October, decided to exercise her option under Paragraph 10(a). She notified Morelli, who did not respond. Bucklin filed a suit in a Rhode Island state court against Morelli. In whose favor should the court rule? Should damages be awarded? If not, what is the appropriate remedy? Why? [*Bucklin v. Morelli,* 912 A.2d 931 (R.I. 2007)]

After you have answered Problem 10–6, compare your answer with the sample answer given on the Web site that accompanies this text. Go to www.cengage.com/blaw/let, select "Chapter 10," and click on "Case Problem with Sample Answer."

10–7. Material Breach. Kermit Johnson formed FB&I Building Products, Inc., in Watertown, South Dakota, to sell building materials. In December 1998, FB&I contracted with Superior Truss & Components in Minneota, Minnesota, "to exclusively sell Superior's open-faced wall panels, floor panels, roof trusses and other miscellaneous products." In March 2000, FB&I agreed to exclusively sell Component Manufacturing Co.'s building products in Colorado. Two months later, Superior learned of FB&I's deal with Component and terminated its contract with FB&I. That contract provided that on cancellation, "FB&I will be entitled to retain the customers that they continue to sell and service with Superior products." Superior refused to honor this provision. Between the cancellation of FB&I's contract and 2004, Superior made $2,327,528 in sales to FB&I customers without paying a commission. FB&I filed a suit in a South Dakota state court against Superior, alleging, in part, breach of contract and seeking the unpaid commissions. Superior insisted that FB&I had materially breached their contract, excusing Superior from performing. In whose favor should the court rule and why? [*FB&I Building Products, Inc. v.*

Superior Truss & Components, a Division of Banks Lumber, Inc., 2007 SD 13, 727 N.W.2d 474 (2007)]

A Question of Ethics

 10–8. King County, Washington, hired Frank Coluccio Construction Co. (FCCC) to act as general contractor for a public works project involving the construction of a small utility tunnel under the Duwamish Waterway. FCCC hired Donald B. Murphy Contractors, Inc. (DBM), as a subcontractor. DBM was responsible for constructing an access shaft at the eastern end of the tunnel. Problems arose during construction, including a "blow-in" of the access shaft that caused it to fill with water, soil, and debris. FCCC and DBM incurred substantial expenses from the repairs and delays. Under the project contract, King County was supposed to buy an insurance policy to "insure against physical loss or damage by perils included under an 'All-Risk' Builder's Risk policy." Any claim under this policy was to be filed through the insured. King County, which had general property damage insurance, did not obtain an all-risk builder's risk policy. For the losses attributable to the blow-in, FCCC and DBM submitted builder's risk claims, which the county denied. FCCC filed a suit in a Washington state court against King County, alleging, among other claims, breach of contract. [*Frank Coluccio Construction Co. v. King County*, 136 Wash.App. 751, 150 P.3d 1147 (Div. 1 2007)]

1. King County's property damage policy specifically excluded, at the county's request, coverage of tunnels. The county drafted its contract with FCCC to require the all-risk builder's risk policy and authorize itself to "sponsor" claims. When FCCC and DBM filed their claims, the county secretly colluded with its property damage insurer to deny payment. What do these facts indicate about the county's ethics and legal liability in this situation?

2. Could DBM, as a third party to the contract between King County and FCCC, maintain an action on the contract against King County? Discuss.

3. All-risk insurance is a promise to pay on the "fortuitous" happening of a loss or damage from any cause except those that are specifically excluded. Payment usually is not made on a loss that, at the time the insurance was obtained, the claimant subjectively knew would occur. If a loss results from faulty workmanship on the part of a contractor, should the obligation to pay under an all-risk policy be discharged? Explain.

Critical-Thinking Social Question

 10–9. The concept of substantial performance permits a party to be discharged from a contract even though the party has not fully performed his or her obligations according to the contract's terms. Is this fair? What policy interests are at issue here?

Video Question

 10–10. Go to this text's Web site at **www.cengage.com/blaw/let** and select "Chapter 10." Click on "Video Questions" and view the video titled *Midnight Run.* Then answer the following questions.

1. In the video, Eddie (Joe Pantoliano) and Jack (Robert DeNiro) negotiate a contract for Jack to find the Duke, a mob accountant who embezzled funds, and bring him back for trial. Assume that the contract is valid. If Jack breaches the contract by failing to bring in the Duke, what kinds of remedies, if any, can Eddie seek? Explain your answer.

2. Would the equitable remedy of specific performance be available to either Jack or Eddie in the event of a breach? Why or why not?

3. Now assume that the contract between Eddie and Jack is unenforceable. Nevertheless, Jack performs his side of the bargain (brings in the Duke). Does Jack have any legal recourse in this situation? Why or why not?

Interacting with the Internet

For updated links to resources available on the Web, as well as a variety of other materials, visit this text's Web site at

www.cengage.com/blaw/let

For a summary of how contracts may be discharged and other principles of contract law, go to

www.rnoon.com/law_for_laymen/contracts/performance.html

For a collection of leading cases involving topics covered in this chapter, go to

www.lectlaw.com/files/lws49.htm

The Contracting and Organizations Research Institute (CORI) at the University of Missouri posts a variety of information and articles pertaining to contract law on its Web site at

cori.missouri.edu

PRACTICAL INTERNET EXERCISES

Go to this text's Web site at **www.cengage.com/blaw/let**, select "Chapter 10," and click on "Practical Internet Exercises." There you will find the following Internet research exercises that you can perform to learn more about the topics covered in this chapter.

Practical Internet Exercise 10–1: LEGAL PERSPECTIVE—**Anticipatory Repudiation**
Practical Internet Exercise 10–2: MANAGEMENT PERSPECTIVE—**Commercial Impracticability**
Practical Internet Exercise 10–3: MANAGEMENT PERSPECTIVE—**The Duty to Mitigate**

BEFORE THE TEST

Go to this text's Web site at **www.cengage.com/blaw/let**, select "Chapter 10," and click on "Interactive Quizzes." You will find a number of interactive questions relating to this chapter.

Chapter 11

Sales, Leases, and E-Contracts

CHAPTER OBJECTIVES

After reading this chapter, you should be able to answer the following questions:

1. How do Article 2 and Article 2A of the UCC differ? What types of transactions does each article cover?

2. In a sales contract, if an offeree includes additional or different terms in an acceptance, will a contract result? If so, what happens to these terms?

3. What remedies are available to a seller or lessor when the buyer or lessee breaches the contract? What remedies are available to a buyer or lessee if the seller or lessor breaches the contract?

4. What implied warranties arise under the UCC?

5. What are some important clauses to include when making offers to form electronic contracts, or e-contracts?

CONTENTS

" *The great object of the law is to encourage commerce.* "

— J. CHAMBRE,
1739–1823 (British jurist)

The chapter-opening quotation states that the object of the law is to encourage commerce. This is particularly true with respect to the Uniform Commercial Code (UCC). The UCC facilitates commercial transactions by making the laws governing sales and lease contracts uniform, clearer, simpler, and more readily applicable to the numerous difficulties that can arise during such transactions. Recall from Chapter 1 that the UCC is one of many uniform (model) acts drafted by the National Conference of Commissioners on Uniform State Laws and submitted to the states for adoption.[1] Once a state legislature has adopted a uniform act, the act becomes statutory law in that state. Thus, when we turn to sales and lease contracts, we move away from common law principles and into the area of statutory law. Relevant sections of the UCC are noted in the discussion of sales and lease contracts, and Article 2 is included in Appendix C at the back of this book.

We open this chapter with a look at the scope of Article 2 and Article 2A. Article 2 of the UCC sets out the requirements of sales contracts and how they are formed. Article 2 regulates performance and obligations required under sales contracts. It also delineates when a breach by either the buyer or the seller occurs and what remedies normally may be sought. A sale of goods usually carries with

---

1. The UCC has been adopted in whole or in part by all of the states. Louisiana, however, has not adopted Articles 2 and 2A.

it at least one type of warranty; sales warranties, express and implied, likewise are governed by the UCC. Article 2A covers similar issues for lease contracts.

In the final section of this chapter, we look at how traditional laws are being applied to contracts formed online. We also examine some relatively new laws that have been created to apply in situations in which traditional laws governing contracts have sometimes been thought inadequate. For example, traditional laws governing signature and writing requirements are not easily adapted to contracts formed in the online environment. Thus, new laws have been created to address these issues.

THE SCOPE OF ARTICLE 2–THE SALE OF GOODS

SALES CONTRACT
A contract for the sale of goods under which the ownership of goods is transferred from a seller to a buyer for a price.

Article 2 of the UCC governs **sales contracts,** or contracts for the sale of goods. To facilitate commercial transactions, Article 2 modifies some of the common law contract requirements that were discussed in the previous chapters. To the extent that it has not been modified by the UCC, however, the common law of contracts also applies to sales contracts. For example, the common law requirements for a valid contract—agreement (offer and acceptance), consideration, capacity, and legality—that were discussed in Chapter 9 are also applicable to sales contracts. Thus, you should reexamine these common law principles when studying the law of sales.

In general, the rule is that whenever there is a conflict between a common law contract rule and the UCC, the UCC controls. In other words, when a UCC provision addresses a certain issue, the UCC governs; when the UCC is silent, the common law governs.

In regard to Article 2, you should keep in mind two things. First, Article 2 deals with the sale of *goods;* it does not deal with real property (real estate), services, or intangible property such as stocks and bonds. Thus, if the subject matter of a dispute is goods, the UCC governs. If it is real estate or services, the common law applies. The relationship between general contract law and the law governing sales of goods is illustrated in Exhibit 11–1. Second, in some cases, the rules may vary quite a bit, depending on whether the buyer or the seller is a *merchant.* We look now at how the UCC defines a *sale, goods,* and *merchant status.*

What Is a Sale?

SALE
The passing of title to property from the seller to the buyer for a price.

Section 2–102 of the UCC states that Article 2 "applies to transactions in goods." This implies a broad scope—covering gifts, bailments (temporary deliveries of personal property), and purchases of goods. In this chapter, however, we treat Article 2 as being applicable only to an actual sale (as would most authorities and courts). The UCC defines a **sale** as "the passing of title from the seller to the buyer for a price," where title refers to the formal right of ownership of property [UCC 2–106(1)]. The price may be payable in money or in goods, services, or real estate.

What Are Goods?

TANGIBLE PROPERTY
Property that has physical existence and can be distinguished by the senses of touch, sight, and so on. A car is tangible property; a patent right is intangible property.

To be characterized as a *good,* an item of property must be *tangible,* and it must be *movable.* **Tangible property** has physical existence—it can be touched or seen. Intangible property—such as corporate stocks and bonds, patents and copyrights, and ordinary contract rights—has only conceptual existence and thus

EXHIBIT 11–1 LAW GOVERNING CONTRACTS

This exhibit graphically illustrates the relationship between general contract law and the law governing contracts for the sale of goods. Contracts for the sale of goods are not governed exclusively by Article 2 of the UCC but are also governed by general contract law whenever it is relevant and has not been modified by the UCC.

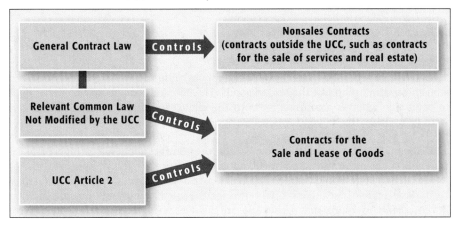

does not come under Article 2. A *movable* item can be carried from place to place. Hence, real estate is excluded from Article 2.

Sometimes, a transaction involves a combination of goods and services, which can make it difficult to characterize the contract as for the sale of goods. For instance, is furnishing blood to a patient during an operation a "sale of goods" or the "performance of a medical service"? Some courts say it is a good; others say it is a service. Because the UCC does not provide the answers, courts generally use the *predominant-factor test* to determine whether a contract is primarily for the sale of goods or for the sale of services. Whether the transaction in question involves the sale of goods or services is important because the majority of courts treat services as being excluded by the UCC. If the transaction is not covered by the UCC, then UCC provisions, including those relating to contract formation and implied warranties, will not apply.

If an entire business, including a truck and equipment, is sold, but the contract does not specify what part of the sale price relates to the goods, does Article 2 of the UCC still apply to the transaction? That was the main issue in the following case.

Case 11.1 Jannusch v. Naffziger

Appellate Court of Illinois,
Fourth District, 2008.
379 Ill.App. 3d 381, 883 N.E.2d 711.

BACKGROUND AND FACTS Gene and Martha Jannusch ran Festival Foods, which provided concessions at events around Illinois and Indiana. They owned a truck, trailer, freezers, roasters, chairs, tables, fountain service, signs, and lighting. Lindsey and Louann Naffziger were interested in buying the concession business. They met with the Jannusches and orally agreed to a price of $150,000. The Naffzigers paid $10,000 down with the balance to come from a bank loan. They took possession of the equipment and began to use it immediately in Festival Foods operations at various events, although Jannusch kept titles to the truck and trailer in his name. Gene Jannusch was paid to attend two events with the Naffzigers to provide advice about running the operation. After six events, and at the end of the outdoor season, the Naffzigers returned the truck and all equipment to its storage location and wanted

CASE 11.1–CONTINUED

out of the deal. They said the business did not generate as much income as they expected. The Jannusches sued the Naffzigers for the balance due on the purchase price. The trial court held that the Uniform Commercial Code (UCC)

governed the case but that there was not enough evidence to show that the parties had a sufficient meeting of the minds to form a contract. The Jannusches appealed.

IN THE WORDS OF THE COURT . . . *CHARLES J. REYNARD,* Judge Presiding.

* * * *

Defendants argue the UCC should not apply because this case involves the sale of a business rather than just the sale of goods. The "predominant purpose" test is used to determine whether a contract for both the sale of goods and the rendition of services falls within the scope of Article 2 of the UCC.

* * * *

Defendants argue that nothing was said in the contract about allocating a price for goodwill, a covenant not to compete, allocating a price for the equipment, how to release liens, what would happen if there was no loan approval, and other issues. Defendants argue these are essential terms for the sale of a business and the Internal Revenue Service requires that parties allocate the sales price. "None of these items were even discussed much less agreed to. There is not an enforceable agreement when there are so many essential terms missing."

"A contract may be enforced even though some contract terms may be missing or left to be agreed upon, but if the essential terms are so uncertain that there is no basis for deciding whether the agreement has been kept or broken, there is no contract."

The essential terms were agreed upon in this case. The purchase price was $150,000, and the items to be transferred were specified. No essential terms remained to be agreed upon; the only action remaining was the performance of the contract. Defendants took possession of the items to be transferred and used them as their own. *"Rejection of goods must be within a reasonable time after their delivery or tender. It is ineffective unless the buyer seasonably [timely] notifies the seller."* [UCC 2-602(1)] Defendants paid $10,000 of the purchase price. The fact that defendants were disappointed in the income from the events they operated is not inconsistent with the existence of a contract. [Emphasis added.]

The trial court noted that "the parties have very different views about what transpired in the course of the contract-formation discussions." It is not necessary that the parties share a subjective understanding as to the terms of the contract; the parties' conduct may indicate an agreement to the terms. The conduct in this case is clear. Parties discussing the sale of goods do not transfer those goods and allow them to be retained for a substantial period before reaching agreement. Defendants replaced equipment, reported income, paid taxes, and paid Gene for his time and expenses, all of which is inconsistent with the idea that defendants were only "pursuing buying the business." An agreement to make an agreement is not an agreement, but there was clearly more than that here.

* * * The parties' agreement could have been fleshed out with additional terms, but the essential terms were agreed upon. [Naffziger] admitted there was an agreement to purchase Festival Foods for $150,000 but could not recall specifically making an oral agreement on any particular date. "An agreement sufficient to constitute a contract for sale may be found even though the moment of its making is undetermined."[UCC 2-204(2)] *Returning the goods at the end of the season was not a rejection of plaintiffs' offer to sell; it was a breach of contract.* [Emphasis added.]

We conclude there was an agreement to sell Festival Foods for the price of $150,000 and that defendants breached that agreement. We reverse the circuit court's judgment and remand for the entry of an order consistent with this opinion.

DECISION AND REMEDY The appeals court reversed the decision of the trial court, finding that a contract had been formed under the UCC and that the Naffzigers had breached it. The primary value of the contract was in the goods, not the value of the business; the parties agreed on a price; and the Naffzigers took possession of the business. They had no right to return it.

WHAT IF THE FACTS WERE DIFFERENT? Suppose the contract had stated that the truck and other equipment were worth $50,000 and the goodwill value of the business was $100,000. Would that change the outcome?

THE ETHICAL DIMENSION Given that the business was not what the Naffzigers expected it to be, and that they returned everything, was it fair for the Jannusches to demand full payment?

Who Is a Merchant?

Article 2 governs the sale of goods in general. It applies to sales transactions between all buyers and sellers. In a limited number of instances, however, the UCC presumes that in certain phases of sales transactions involving merchants, special business standards ought to be imposed because of the merchants' relatively high degree of commercial expertise.[2] Such standards do not apply to the casual or inexperienced seller or buyer ("consumer").

In general, a person is a **merchant** when he or she, acting in a mercantile capacity, possesses or uses an expertise specifically related to the goods being sold. This basic distinction is not always clear-cut. For example, courts in some states have determined that farmers may be merchants, while courts in other states have determined that the drafters of the UCC did not intend to include farmers as merchants.

MERCHANT
A person engaged in the purchase and sale of goods. Under the UCC, a person who deals in goods of the kind involved in the sales contract, or who holds himself or herself out as having skill and knowledge peculiar to the practices or goods involved in the transaction, or who employs a merchant as an intermediary. For definitions, see UCC 2–104.

THE SCOPE OF ARTICLE 2A–LEASES

In the past few decades, leases of personal property (goods) have become increasingly common. Consumers and business firms lease automobiles, industrial equipment, items for use in the home (such as floor polishers), and many other types of goods. Until Article 2A was added to the UCC, no specific body of law addressed the legal problems that arose when goods were leased, rather than sold. In cases involving leased goods, the courts generally applied a combination of common law rules, real estate law, and principles expressed in Article 2 of the UCC.

Article 2A of the UCC was created to fill the need for uniform guidelines in this area. Article 2A covers any transaction that creates a **lease** of goods, as well as subleases of goods [UCC 2A–102, 2A–103(k)]. Article 2A is essentially a repetition of Article 2, except that it applies to leases of goods, rather than sales of goods, and thus varies to reflect differences between sales and lease transactions.

LEASE
Under the UCC, a transfer of the right to possess and use goods for a period in exchange for payment.

---

2. The provisions that apply only to merchants deal principally with the Statute of Frauds, firm offers, confirmatory memoranda, warranties, and contract modification. These special rules reflect expedient business practices commonly known to merchants in the commercial setting. They will be discussed later in this chapter.

Article 2A defines a *lease agreement* as the bargain of the lessor and lessee, as found in their language and as implied by other circumstances [UCC 2A–103(k)]. A **lessor** is one who sells the right to the possession and use of goods under a lease [UCC 2A–103(p)]. A **lessee** is one who acquires the right to the possession and use of goods under a lease [UCC 2A–103(o)]. Article 2A applies to all types of leases of goods, including commercial leases and consumer leases.

THE FORMATION OF SALES AND LEASE CONTRACTS

In regard to the formation of sales and lease contracts, the UCC modifies the common law of contracts in several ways. We look here at how Article 2 and Article 2A of the UCC modify common law contract rules. Remember that parties to sales contracts are free to establish whatever terms they wish. The UCC comes into play when the parties have not, in their contract, provided for a contingency that later gives rise to a dispute. The UCC makes this very clear time and again by its use of such phrases as "unless the parties otherwise agree" and "absent a contrary agreement by the parties."

The foldout exhibit that follows this chapter shows an actual sales contract used by Starbucks Coffee Company. The contract illustrates many of the terms and clauses that are typically contained in contracts for the sale of goods.

Offer

In general contract law, the moment a definite offer is met by an unqualified acceptance, a binding contract is formed. In commercial sales transactions, the verbal exchanges, the correspondence, and the actions of the parties may not reveal exactly when a binding contractual obligation arises. The UCC states that an agreement sufficient to constitute a contract can exist even if the moment of its making is undetermined [UCC 2–204(2), 2A–204(2)].

Open Terms   According to contract law, an offer must be definite enough for the parties (and the courts) to ascertain its essential terms when it is accepted. Section 2–204 of the UCC provides that a sales or lease contract will not fail for indefiniteness even if one or more terms are left open as long as (1) the parties intended to make a contract and (2) there is a reasonably certain basis for the court to grant an appropriate remedy. A seller and buyer of goods can thus create an enforceable contract even if several terms, including terms relating to price, payment, and delivery, are left unspecified. For example, if the price term is left open, Article 2 provides that the price will be "a reasonable price at the time of delivery" [UCC 2–305(1)]. If the payment term is left open, Article 2 states that "payment is due at the time and place at which the buyer is to receive the goods" [UCC 2–310(a)]. Under Article 2, the only term that normally must be specified is the quantity term; otherwise, the court will have no basis for determining a remedy.

LESSOR

In a lease of personal property, a person who transfers his or her right to possess and use certain goods for a period to another in exchange for payment (rent).

LESSEE

In a lease of personal property, a person who acquires the right to possess and use another's goods for a period in exchange for paying rent.

NOTE

Under the UCC, it is the actions of the parties that determine whether they intended to form a contract.

Preventing Legal Disputes

Businesspersons should be aware that if they leave certain terms of a sales or lease contract open, the UCC allows a court to supply the missing terms. Although this can sometimes be advantageous (to establish that a contract existed, for example), it can also be a major disadvantage. If a business engaged in selling goods fails to state a price in its contract offer, for example, a court will impose a reasonable price by looking at the market price of similar goods *at the time of delivery.* In other words, instead of receiving its standard price for the goods, the business will receive what a court considers a reasonable price when the goods are delivered. Allowing the court to supply a price term can thus reduce one of the potential benefits of contracting—profit realized by the sale of goods at the contract price, despite a subsequent decline in the market price of the goods being sold. Therefore, when drafting contracts for the sale or lease of goods, make sure that the contract clearly states any terms that are essential to the bargain, particularly price. Remember that it is often better to establish the terms of your own contracts rather than to leave it up to a court to determine what terms are reasonable after a dispute has arisen.■

Merchant's Firm Offer   Under common law contract principles (discussed in Chapter 9), an offer can be revoked at any time before acceptance. The UCC has an exception that applies only to **firm offers** for the sale or lease of goods made by a merchant (regardless of whether or not the offeree is a merchant). A firm offer arises when a merchant gives assurances *in a signed writing* that the offer will remain open. A firm offer is irrevocable without the necessity of consideration for the stated period or, if no definite period is stated, a reasonable period (neither to exceed three months) [UCC 2–205, 2A–205]. EXAMPLE #1 Osaka, a used-car dealer, writes a letter to Saucedo on January 1 stating, "I have a 2005 Suzuki on the lot that I'll sell you for $8,500 any time between now and January 31." This writing creates a firm offer, and Osaka will be liable for breach if he sells the Suzuki to someone other than Saucedo before January 31.□

FIRM OFFER
An offer (by a merchant) that is irrevocable without consideration for a stated period of time or, if no definite period is stated, for a reasonable time (neither period to exceed three months). A firm offer by a merchant must be in writing and must be signed by the offeror.

Acceptance

Acceptance of an offer to buy, sell, or lease goods generally may be made in any reasonable manner and by any reasonable means. The UCC permits acceptance of an offer to buy goods "either by a prompt promise to ship or by the prompt or current shipment of conforming or nonconforming goods" [UCC 2–206(1)(b)]. *Conforming* goods accord with the contract's terms; *nonconforming* goods do not. The prompt shipment of *nonconforming goods* constitutes both an *acceptance,* which creates a contract, and a *breach* of that contract. This rule does not apply if the seller seasonably (within a reasonable amount of time) notifies the buyer that the nonconforming shipment is offered only as an *accommodation,* or as a favor. The notice of accommodation must clearly indicate to the buyer that the shipment does not constitute an acceptance and that, therefore, no contract has been formed.

EXAMPLE #2 McFarrell Pharmacy orders five cases of Johnson & Johnson 3-by-5-inch gauze pads from Halderson Medical Supply, Inc. If Halderson ships five cases of Xeroform 3-by-5-inch gauze pads instead, the shipment acts as both an acceptance of McFarrell's offer and a *breach* of the resulting contract. McFarrell may sue Halderson for any appropriate damages. If, however, Halderson notifies McFarrell that the Xeroform gauze pads are being shipped *as an accommodation*— because Halderson has only Xeroform pads in stock—the shipment will constitute a counteroffer, not an acceptance. A contract will be formed only if McFarrell accepts the Xeroform gauze pads.□

Communication of Acceptance   Under the common law, because a unilateral offer invites acceptance by a performance, the offeree need not notify the offeror of performance unless the offeror would not otherwise know about it.

The UCC is more stringent than the common law in this regard. Under the UCC, if an offeror is not notified within a reasonable time that the offeree has impliedly accepted the contract by beginning performance, then the offeror can treat the offer as having lapsed before acceptance [UCC 2–206(2), 2A–206(2)].

Additional Terms If the acceptance includes terms additional to, or different from, those contained in the offer and one (or both) of the parties is a *nonmerchant,* the contract is formed according to the terms of the original offer submitted by the original offeror and not according to the additional terms of the acceptance [UCC 2–207(2)]. The drafters of the UCC created a special rule for merchants that is designed to avoid the "battle of the forms," which occurs when two merchants exchange standard forms containing different contract terms. Under UCC 2–207(2), in contracts *between merchants,* the additional terms *automatically* become part of the contract *unless* one of the following conditions exists:

1. The original offer expressly limited acceptance to its terms.
2. The new or changed terms materially alter the contract.
3. The offeror objects to the new or changed terms within a reasonable period of time.

Generally, if the modification involves no unreasonable element of surprise or hardship for the offeror, a court is likely to hold that the modification did not materially alter the contract. Of course, any contract modification must be made in good faith [UCC 1–203]. Courts also consider the parties' prior dealings and course of performance when determining whether the alteration is material. **EXAMPLE #3** Woolf has ordered meat from Tupman sixty-four times over a two-year period. Each time, Woolf placed the order over the phone, and Tupman mailed a confirmation form, and then an invoice, to Woolf. Tupman's confirmation form and invoice have always included an arbitration clause. If Woolf places another order and fails to pay for the meat, the court will likely hold that the additional term—the arbitration provision—did not materially alter the contract because Woolf should not have been surprised by the term. The result might be different, however, if the parties had only dealt with each other on two prior occasions and the arbitration clause was only received later on the back of a faxed invoice rather than being mentioned in the confirmation forms.□

In the following case, the court explains the "revolutionary change in contract law" caused by the UCC's principles on additional terms.

 Sun Coast Merchandise Corp. v. Myron Corp.

Superior Court of New Jersey,
Appellate Division, 2007.
393 N.J.Super. 55, 922 A.2d 782.
lawlibrary.rutgers.edu/search.shtml[a]

BACKGROUND AND FACTS Sun Coast Merchandise Corporation, a California firm, designs and sells products that businesses distribute as promotional items. Myron Corporation, a New Jersey firm, asked Sun about a flip-top calculator on which Myron could engrave the names of its

a. In the "SEARCH THE N.J. COURTS DECISIONS" section, type "Sun Coast" in the box, and click on "Search!" In the result, click on the case name to access the opinion.

customers. In December 2000, Myron began to submit purchase orders for about 400,000 of what the parties referred to as "Version I" calculators. In April 2001, Sun redesigned the flip-top. Over the next few weeks, the parties discussed terms for the making and shipping of 4 million of the "Version II" calculators before the Christmas season. By May 27, Myron had faxed four orders with specific delivery dates. Two days later, Sun announced a delayed schedule and asked Myron to submit revised orders. Unwilling to agree to the new dates, Myron did not honor this request. The parties attempted to negotiate the issue but were unsuccessful. Finally, Sun filed a suit in a New Jersey state court against Myron, claiming, among other things, breach of contract. The court entered a judgment in Sun's favor. On appeal to a state intermediate appellate court, Myron argued, among other things, that the judge's instruction to the jury regarding Sun's claim was inadequate.

IN THE WORDS OF THE COURT . . . *FISHER*, J.A.D. [Judge, Appellate Division]

* * * *

The era when a valid, binding contract could only come into existence when a party's acceptance mirrored the other party's offer ended with the adoption of the Uniform Commercial Code (UCC). The UCC altered the common law approach, finding it to be inconsistent with the modern realities of commerce. * * * Article 2 of the UCC radically altered sales law and expanded our conception of a contract. The heart of this revolutionary change in contract law can be found in [New Jersey Statutes Annotated (N.J.S.A.)] 12A:2-207(1) [New Jersey's version of UCC 2–207(1)], which declares that "[a] definite and seasonable expression of acceptance or a written confirmation which is sent within a reasonable time operates as an acceptance even though it states terms additional to or different from those offered or agreed upon, unless acceptance is expressly made conditional on assent to the additional or different terms." *No longer are communicating parties left to debate whether an acceptance perfectly meets the terms of an offer, but instead the existence of a binding contract may be based on words or conduct, which need not mirror an offer, so long as they reveal the parties' intention to be bound.* [Emphasis added.]

Considering that the UCC permits the formation of a contract by way of conduct that reveals the parties' understanding that a contract exists, and notwithstanding the suggestion of additional or even non-conforming terms, the complex of communications between [Sun and Myron] demonstrates that neither can the formation of a contract be confirmed or foreclosed without a resolution of the existing factual disputes and the weighing of the significance of the parties' convoluted communications.

* * * *

In short, it is conceivable—and the jury could find—that the parties' inability to agree on certain terms reveals the lack of an intent to be bound; in other words, that their communications constituted mere negotiations that never ripened into a contract. By the same token, the jury could find that a contract was formed despite a failure or an inability to agree on all terms. N.J.S.A. 12A:2-207(2) provides that an acceptance coupled with the proposal of new or different terms does not necessarily preclude the formation of a contract. *In such a circumstance,* * * * *the new or different terms proposed by the offeree [could] become part of the contract* * * * . [Emphasis added.]

All these questions required that the factfinder analyze the meaning and significance of the parties' communications based upon the legal framework provided by the UCC.

* * * *

* * * The trial judge correctly determined that the [contentions about] contract formation * * * raised fact questions to be decided by the jury * * * .

* * * *

In describing for the jury what it takes for the parties to form a binding contract, the judge stated:

> A proposal to accept an offer on any different terms is not an acceptance of the original offer. If any new or different terms are proposed in response to the offer, the response is not an acceptance, but rather a counteroffer. A counteroffer is a new offer by the party making that proposal. The new offer must in turn be agreed to by the party who made the original offer for there to be an acceptance.

As we have already explained, the UCC does not require that a party's response mirror an offer to result in a binding contract. The offeree may propose additional or

CASE 11.2–CONTINUED

CASE 11.2—CONTINUED   different terms without necessarily having the response viewed as a non-binding counteroffer. Instead, an offeree's proposal of additional or conflicting terms may be found to constitute an acceptance, and the other or different terms viewed as mere proposals to modify the contract thus formed.

The judge's misstatement in this regard was hardly harmless * * * . In describing when the law recognizes that a contract was formed, the judge provided the jury with erroneous instructions that struck directly at the heart of the case.

DECISION AND REMEDY   The state intermediate appellate court concluded that the judge's instruction to the jury with respect to the question of whether Sun and Myron had formed a contract was "fundamentally flawed" and "provided insufficient guidance for the jury's resolution of the issues." On this basis, the court reversed the lower court's judgment and remanded the case for a new trial.

WHAT IF THE FACTS WERE DIFFERENT?   How would the outcome of this case differ if the contract had been between a merchant and an ordinary consumer rather than between two merchants?

THE LEGAL ENVIRONMENT DIMENSION   Applying the correct principles to the facts in this case, how would you have decided the issue? Explain.

Consideration

The common law rule that a contract requires consideration also applies to sales and lease contracts. Unlike the common law, however, the UCC does not require a contract modification to be supported by new consideration. The UCC states that an agreement modifying a contract for the sale or lease of goods "needs no consideration to be binding" [UCC 2–209(1), 2A–208(1)].

THE STATUTE OF FRAUDS

As discussed in Chapter 10, the Statute of Frauds requires that certain types of contracts, to be enforceable, must be in writing or evidenced by a writing. The UCC contains Statute of Frauds provisions covering sales and lease contracts. Under these provisions, sales contracts for goods priced at $500 or more and lease contracts requiring total payments of $1,000 or more must be in writing to be enforceable [UCC 2–201(1), 2A–201(1)]. (Note that these low threshold amounts may eventually be raised.)

Sufficiency of the Writing

A writing or a memorandum will be sufficient as long as it indicates that the parties intended to form a contract and as long as it is signed by the party (or agent of the party) against whom enforcement is sought. A sales contract normally will not be enforceable beyond the quantity of goods shown in the writing, however. All other terms can be proved in court by oral testimony. For leases, the writing must reasonably identify and describe the goods leased and the lease term.

Special Rules for Contracts between Merchants

Once again, the UCC provides a special rule for merchants engaged in sales transactions (there is no corresponding rule that applies to leases under Article 2A). Merchants can satisfy the requirements of a writing for the Statute of Frauds if, after the parties have agreed orally, one of the merchants sends a signed written confirmation to the other merchant. The communication must indicate the terms of the agreement, and the merchant receiving the confirmation must have reason to know of its contents. Unless the merchant who receives the confirmation gives written notice of objection to its contents within ten days after receipt, the writing is sufficient against the receiving merchant, even though he or she has not signed anything [UCC 2–201(2)]. What happens if a merchant sends an e-mail confirmation? For a discussion of this issue, see this chapter's *Online Developments* feature on the following page.

Exceptions

The UCC defines three exceptions to the writing requirements of the Statute of Frauds. An oral contract for the sale of goods priced at $500 or more or the lease of goods involving total payments of $1,000 or more will be enforceable despite the absence of a writing in the circumstances described in the following subsections [UCC 2–201(3), 2A–201(4)]. These exceptions and other ways in which sales law differs from general contract law are summarized in Exhibit 11–2.

Specially Manufactured Goods An oral contract is enforceable if (1) it is for goods that are specially manufactured for a particular buyer or specially manufactured or obtained for a particular lessee, (2) these goods are not suitable for resale or lease to others in the ordinary course of the seller's or lessor's business, and (3) the seller or lessor has substantially started to manufacture the goods or has made commitments for the manufacture or procurement of the goods. In this situation, once the seller or lessor has taken action, the buyer or lessee cannot repudiate the agreement claiming the Statute of Frauds as a defense. Note that the

An artisan creates a specially designed "bowl within a bowl" out of one piece of clay. If a restaurant orally contracted with the artisan to create twenty of the specially designed bowls for use in its business, at a price of $800, would the contract have to be in writing to be enforceable? Why or why not? (AP/Wide World Photos)

EXHIBIT 11–2 MAJOR DIFFERENCES BETWEEN CONTRACT LAW AND SALES LAW

	CONTRACT LAW	SALES LAW
Contract Terms	Contract must contain all material terms.	Open terms are acceptable if parties intended to form a contract, but contract is not enforceable beyond quantity term.
Acceptance	*Mirror* image rule applies. If additional terms are added in acceptance, counteroffer is created.	Additional terms will not negate acceptance unless acceptance is expressly conditioned on assent to the additional terms.
Contract Modification	Modification requires consideration.	Modification does not require consideration.
Statute of Frauds Requirements	All material terms must be included in the writing.	Writing is required for sale of goods priced at $500 or more, but contract is not enforceable beyond quantity specified. Merchants can satisfy the writing requirement by a confirmatory memorandum evidencing their agreement. *Exceptions:* 1. Specially manufactured goods. 2. Admissions by party against whom enforcement is sought. 3. Partial performance.

Many contracts require a writing to satisfy the Statute of Frauds. As more and more contracts are negotiated orally or through e-mail, the question arises as to whether e-mail communications can fulfill the writing requirement. This issue was at the heart of a case involving a textile merchandising company and its supplier.

Was There an Enforceable Contract?

Bazak International Corporation contracted to buy numerous pairs of jeans from Tarrant Apparel Group. The total price for the transaction was around $2 million. After a series of disputes between the companies, Tarrant sold the jeans to a third party at a higher price. Bazak sued for breach of contract. Tarrant claimed that the contract was not enforceable because there was no signed writing.

Although the parties never drew up a written contract, they did engage in a series of e-mail transmissions. In one, Bazak provided details of the purchase and attached a letter on its own company stationery. Bazak claimed that this e-mail constituted a written confirmation that satisfied the Statute of Frauds. Tarrant disagreed, arguing that because an e-mail transmission is electronic, it cannot qualify as a written confirmation of the agreement. Tarrant also contended that the e-mail was not a written memorandum between merchants because it was not signed. Finally, Tarrant argued that using e-mail transmissions between the two companies was not an appropriate means of communication in the apparel industry.

The Court Rules in Favor of E-Mail Communications

The court ruled against all three of Tarrant's arguments (and against several others as well). Even though the e-mails were "intangible messages," they still qualified as writings. After all, the court pointed out, faxes, telexes, and telegrams are all intangible forms of communication while they are being transmitted. Whether an e-mail is printed on paper or saved on a server, it remains "an objectively observable and tangible record that such a confirmation exists."

In today's online world, said the court, a signed writing does not necessarily mean a piece of paper to which a signature is physically applied. In this case, the e-mail attachment, consisting of a letter on company letterhead on which the president of the company typed in his "signature," was sufficient.

Finally, merely stating that e-mail transmissions between the two parties were an inappropriate method of communication meant very little. Tarrant would have to prove that trade usage and the parties' prior course of dealing in the textile and apparel industry rarely involved e-mails. The court found that there was evidence to the contrary.[a]

Indeed, a court in a subsequent case in the apparel industry applied the same reasoning to allow a breach of contract claim to go forward based on an e-mail confirmation. In that case, Great White Bear, LLC, a clothing maker, alleged that Mervyns, LLC, had agreed to purchase $11.7 million in clothing from Great White Bear over an eighteen-month period. In January 2006, after placing only $2.3 million in orders, Mervyns informed Great White that it would not be placing any more orders. Great White filed a lawsuit, claiming that an e-mail confirmation between the two merchants was sufficient to satisfy the Statute of Frauds. The court agreed, noting that "there are no rigid requirements as to the form or content of a confirmatory writing" and quoting the opinion in the *Bazak* case that e-mail suffices as much as a letter.[b]

FOR CRITICAL ANALYSIS   Are there any trades or industries in today's environment for which e-mail confirmation would be inappropriate? Explain.

---

a. *Bazak International Corp. v. Tarrant Apparel Group*, 378 F.Supp.2d 377 (S.D.N.Y. 2005).
b. *Great White Bear, LLC v. Mervyns, LLC*, 2007 WL 1295747 (S.D.N.Y. 2007).

---

seller must have made a substantial beginning in manufacturing the specialized item prior to the buyer's repudiation.

Admissions   An oral contract for the sale or lease of goods is enforceable if the party against whom enforcement is sought admits in pleadings, testimony, or other court proceedings that a sales or lease contract was made. In this situation, the contract will be enforceable even though it was oral, but enforceability will be limited to the quantity of goods admitted.

EXAMPLE #4   Lane and Byron negotiate an agreement over the telephone. During the negotiations, Lane requests a delivery price for five hundred gallons of gasoline and a separate price for seven hundred gallons of gasoline. Byron replies that the price would be the same, $2.50 per gallon. Lane orally orders five hundred gallons. Byron honestly believes that Lane ordered seven hundred gallons and tenders that amount. Lane refuses the shipment of seven hundred gallons, and Byron sues for breach. In his pleadings and testimony, Lane admits that an oral contract was made, but only for five hundred gallons. Because Lane admits the existence of the oral contract, Lane cannot plead the Statute of Frauds as a defense. The contract is enforceable, however, only to the extent of the quantity admitted (five hundred gallons). □

Partial Performance An oral contract for the sale or lease of goods is enforceable if payment has been made and accepted or goods have been received and accepted. This is the "partial performance" exception. The oral contract will be enforced at least to the extent that performance *actually* took place.

EXAMPLE #5 Allan orally contracts to lease to Opus Enterprises a thousand chairs at $2 each to be used during a one-day concert. Before delivery, Opus sends Allan a check for $1,000, which Allan cashes. Later, when Allan attempts to deliver the chairs, Opus refuses delivery, claiming the Statute of Frauds as a defense, and demands the return of its $1,000. Under the UCC's partial performance rule, Allan can enforce the oral contract by tender of delivery of five hundred chairs for the $1,000 accepted. Similarly, if Opus had made no payment but had accepted the delivery of five hundred chairs from Allan, the oral contract would have been enforceable against Opus for $1,000, the lease payment due for the five hundred chairs delivered. □

PERFORMANCE OF SALES AND LEASE CONTRACTS

To understand the obligations of the parties under a sales or lease contract, it is necessary to know the duties and obligations each party has assumed under the terms of the contract. Keep in mind that "duties and obligations" under the contract terms include those specified by the agreement, by custom, and by the UCC.

In the performance of a sales or lease contract, the basic obligation of the seller or lessor is to *transfer and deliver conforming goods*. The basic obligation of the buyer or lessee is to *accept and pay for conforming goods* in accordance with the contract [UCC 2–301, 2A–516(1)]. Overall performance of a sales or lease contract is controlled by the agreement between the parties. When the contract is unclear and disputes arise, the courts look to the UCC.

The Good Faith Requirement

The obligations of good faith and commercial reasonableness underlie every sales and lease contract within the UCC. These obligations can form the basis for a suit for breach of contract later on. The UCC's good faith provision, which can never be disclaimed, reads as follows: "Every contract or duty within this Act imposes an obligation of good faith in its performance or enforcement" [UCC 1–203]. Good faith means honesty in fact. In the case of a merchant, it means honesty in fact and the observance of reasonable commercial standards of fair dealing in the trade [UCC 2–103(1)(b)]. In other words, merchants are held to a higher standard of performance or duty than nonmerchants. For a discussion of the importance of good faith in contract performance, see this chapter's *Management Perspective* feature on the next page.

Management Faces a Legal Issue

All contracts governed by the Uniform Commercial Code (UCC) must meet the requirements of good faith and fair dealing. Yet do these requirements supersede the written terms of a contract? In other words, if a party adheres strictly to the express, written terms of a contract, can that party nonetheless face liability for breaching the UCC's good faith requirements?

What the Courts Say

Generally, the courts take the good faith provisions of the UCC very seriously. Some courts have held that good faith can be breached even when the parties have equal bargaining power. In one case, for example, the court held that, although the plaintiffs were sophisticated businesspersons who had the assistance of highly competent counsel, they could still maintain an action for breach of good faith and fair dealing. The court reasoned that "the presence of bad faith is to be found in the eye of the beholder or, more to the point, in the eye of the trier of fact," indicating that it was up to a jury to determine whether the parties had performed in good faith.[a]

Courts even apply the implied covenant of good faith and fair dealing with respect to individuals who form partnerships. In one

case, two individuals who had jointly bought properties for development over a ten-year period had a "falling out." One of them filed a complaint alleging breach of the implied good faith covenant. The reviewing court in this case stated that the "implied covenant of good faith and fair dealing is present in every contract." Further, "the duty imposed by this covenant prohibits either party from doing anything that would have the effect of injuring the other party's right to receive the fruits of the contract." That is why juries are entitled to afford great weight to the conduct of the parties when they determine the meaning of the contract.[b]

Implications for Managers

The message for business owners and managers involved in sales contracts (and even other contracts) is clear: compliance with the literal terms of a contract is not enough—the standards of good faith and fair dealing must also be met. Although the specific standards of good faith performance are still evolving, the overriding principle is that the parties to a contract should do nothing to injure or destroy the rights of the other party to receive the fruits of the contract.

a. *Seidenberg v. Summit Bank,* 348 N.J.Super. 243, 791 A.2d 1068 (2002).

b. *Stankovits v. Schrager,* __ A.2d__ , 2007 WL 4410247 (N.J.Super.A.D. 2007).

Obligations of the Seller or Lessor

TENDER OF DELIVERY
Under the Uniform Commercial Code, a seller's or lessor's act of placing conforming goods at the disposal of the buyer or lessee and giving the buyer or lessee whatever notification is reasonably necessary to enable the buyer or lessee to take delivery.

CONFORMING GOODS
Goods that conform to contract specifications.

The major obligation of the seller or lessor under a sales or lease contract is to tender conforming goods to the buyer or lessee. **Tender of delivery** requires that the seller or lessor have and hold *conforming goods* at the disposal of the buyer or lessee and give the buyer or lessee whatever notification is reasonably necessary to enable the buyer or lessee to take delivery [UCC 2–503(1), 2A–508(1)]. **Conforming goods** are goods that conform exactly to the description of the goods in the contract.

Tender must occur at a *reasonable hour* and in a *reasonable manner.* For example, a seller cannot call the buyer at 2:00 A.M. and say, "The goods are ready. I'll give you twenty minutes to get them." Unless the parties have agreed otherwise, the goods must be tendered for delivery at a reasonable hour and kept available for a reasonable period of time to enable the buyer to take possession of them [UCC 2–503(1)(a)].

All goods called for by a contract must be tendered in a single delivery unless the parties agree otherwise [UCC 2–612, 2A–510] or the circumstances are such that either party can rightfully request delivery in lots [UCC 2–307].

Place of Delivery   If the contract does not designate the place of delivery for the goods, and the buyer is expected to pick them up, the place of delivery is the *seller's place of business* or, if the seller has none, the *seller's residence* [UCC 2–308]. If the contract involves the sale of *identified goods*—that is, the specific goods provided for in the contract—and the parties know when they enter into the contract that these goods are located somewhere other than at the seller's place of business (such as at a warehouse), then the *location of the goods* is the place for their delivery [UCC 2–308].

The Perfect Tender Rule   Under the **perfect tender rule,** the seller or lessor is required to deliver goods that conform to the terms of the contract in every detail. If the goods or tender of delivery fail *in any respect* to conform to the contract, the buyer or lessee has the right to accept the goods, reject the entire shipment, or accept part and reject part [UCC 2–601, 2A–509].

PERFECT TENDER RULE
A rule under which a seller or lessor is required to deliver goods that conform perfectly to the requirements of the contract. A tender of nonconforming goods automatically constitutes a breach of contract.

Exceptions to the Perfect Tender Rule   Because of the rigidity of the perfect tender rule, several exceptions to the rule have been created, some of which we discuss here.

Agreement of the Parties   Exceptions to the perfect tender rule may be established by agreement. If the parties have agreed, for example, that defective goods or parts will not be rejected if the seller or lessor is able to repair or replace them within a reasonable period of time, the perfect tender rule does not apply.

Cure   The UCC does not specifically define the term **cure,** but it refers to the right of the seller or lessor to repair, adjust, or replace defective or nonconforming goods [UCC 2–508, 2A–513]. When any tender of delivery is rejected because of nonconforming goods and the time for performance has not yet expired, the seller or lessor can promptly notify the buyer or lessee of the intention to cure and can then do so *within the contract time for performance* [UCC 2–508(1), 2A–513(1)]. Once the time for performance under the contract has expired, the seller or lessor can still exercise the right to cure if he or she has *reasonable grounds to believe that the nonconforming tender will be acceptable to the buyer or lessee* [UCC 2–508(2), 2A–513(2)].

CURE
The right of a party who tenders nonconforming performance to correct that performance within the contract period [UCC 2–508(1)].

The right to cure substantially restricts the right of the buyer or lessee to reject goods. For example, if a lessee refuses a tender of goods as nonconforming but does not disclose the nature of the defect to the lessor, the lessee cannot later assert the defect as a defense if the defect is one that the lessor could have cured. Generally, buyers and lessees must act in good faith and state specific reasons for refusing to accept goods [UCC 2–605, 2A–514].

Substitution of Carriers   When an agreed-on manner of delivery (such as the use of a particular carrier to transport the goods) becomes impracticable or unavailable through no fault of either party, but a commercially reasonable substitute is available, the seller must perform using this substitute [UCC 2–614(1)].

Commercial Impracticability   Occurrences unforeseen by either party when a contract was made may make performance commercially impracticable. When this occurs, the rule of perfect tender no longer holds. According to UCC 2–615(a) and 2A–405(a), delay in delivery or nondelivery in whole or in part is not a breach when performance has been made impracticable "by the occurrence of a

Competitors' trucks travel the same route. When is it acceptable to substitute one carrier for the one that was specified in the contract?
(Keith Tyler/Creative Commons)

contingency the nonoccurrence of which was a basic assumption on which the contract was made." The seller or lessor must, however, notify the buyer or lessee as soon as practicable that there will be a delay or nondelivery.

Destruction of Identified Goods   Sometimes, an unexpected event, such as a fire, totally destroys goods through no fault of either party and before risk passes to the buyer or lessee. In such a situation, if the *goods were identified at the time the contract was formed*, the parties are excused from performance [UCC 2–613, 2A–221]. If the goods are only partially destroyed, however, the buyer or lessee can inspect them and either treat the contract as void or accept the damaged goods with a reduction of the contract price.

EXAMPLE #6 Atlas Sporting Equipment agrees to lease to River Bicycles sixty bicycles of a particular model that has been discontinued. No other bicycles of that model are available. River specifies that it needs the bicycles to rent to tourists. Before Atlas can deliver the bicycles, they are destroyed by a fire. In this situation, Atlas is not liable to River for failing to deliver the bicycles. The goods were destroyed through no fault of either party, before the risk of loss passed to the lessee. The loss was total, so the contract is avoided. Clearly, Atlas has no obligation to tender the bicycles, and River has no obligation to pay for them.□

Cooperation and Assurance   The performance of one party sometimes depends on the cooperation of the other. The UCC provides that when such cooperation is not forthcoming, the other party can either suspend his or her own performance without liability and hold the uncooperative party in breach or proceed to perform the contract in any reasonable manner [see UCC 2–311(3)(b)].

In addition, if one of the parties to a contract has "reasonable grounds" to believe that the other party will not perform as contracted, he or she may *in writing* "demand adequate assurance of due performance" from the other party. Until such assurance is received, he or she may "suspend" further performance without liability. What constitutes "reasonable grounds" is determined by commercial standards. If such assurances are not forthcoming within a reasonable time (not to exceed thirty days), the failure to respond may be treated as a *repudiation* of the contract [UCC 2–609, 2A–401].

Obligations of the Buyer or Lessee

Once the seller or lessor has adequately tendered delivery, the buyer or lessee is obligated to accept the goods and pay for them according to the terms of the contract.

Payment   In the absence of any specific agreements, the buyer or lessee must make payment at the time and place the buyer or lessee *receives* the goods [UCC 2–310(a), 2A–516(1)]. When a sale is made on credit, the buyer is obliged to pay according to the specified credit terms (for example, 60, 90, or 120 days), not when the goods are received. The credit period usually begins on the *date of shipment* [UCC 2–310(d)]. Under a lease contract, a lessee must make the lease payment specified in the contract [UCC 2A–516(1)].

Payment can be made by any means agreed on between the parties—cash or any other method generally acceptable in the commercial world. If the seller demands cash when the buyer

A fire destroys a building holding warehoused goods in Bloomington, Illinois. Suppose that there were goods inside that had been identified to a sales contract but for which the risk of loss had not yet passed to the buyer. If the buyer sues the seller for breaching the contract by not delivering the goods, will the seller be held liable? Why or why not? ("Syslfrog"/Creative Commons)

offers a check, credit card, or the like, the seller must permit the buyer reasonable time to obtain legal tender [UCC 2–511].

Acceptance   A buyer or lessee can manifest acceptance of the delivered goods in any of the following ways:

1. There is an acceptance if the buyer or lessee, after having had a reasonable opportunity to inspect the goods, signifies agreement to the seller or lessor that the goods are either conforming or are acceptable in spite of their nonconformity [UCC 2–606(1)(a), 2A–515(1)(a)].

2. Acceptance is presumed if the buyer or lessee has had a reasonable opportunity to inspect the goods and has failed to reject them within a reasonable period of time [UCC 2–602(1), 2–606(1)(b), 2A–515(1)(b)].

3. In sales contracts, the buyer will be deemed to have accepted the goods if he or she performs any act inconsistent with the seller's ownership. For example, any use or resale of the goods generally constitutes an acceptance. Limited use for the sole purpose of testing or inspecting the goods is not an acceptance, however [UCC 2–606(1)(c)].

If some of the goods delivered do not conform to the contract and the seller or lessor has failed to cure, the buyer or lessee can make a *partial* acceptance [UCC 2–601(c), 2A–509(1)]. The same is true if the nonconformity was not reasonably discoverable before acceptance. A buyer or lessee cannot accept less than a single commercial unit, however. A *commercial unit* is defined by the UCC as a unit of goods that, by commercial usage, is viewed as a "single whole" for purposes of sale, division of which would materially impair the character of the unit, its market value, or its use [UCC 2–105(6), 2A–103(c)]. A commercial unit can be a single article (such as a machine), a set of articles (such as a suite of furniture or an assortment of sizes), a quantity (such as a bale, a gross, or a carload), or any other unit treated in the trade as a single whole.

Anticipatory Repudiation

What if, before the time for contract performance, one party clearly communicates to the other the intention not to perform? Such an action is a breach of the contract by *anticipatory repudiation*. When anticipatory repudiation occurs, the nonbreaching party has a choice of two responses. One option is to treat the repudiation as a final breach by pursuing a remedy; the other is to wait and hope that the repudiating party will decide to honor the obligations required by the contract despite the avowed intention to renege [UCC 2–610, 2A–402]. In either situation, the nonbreaching party may suspend performance.

Should the second option be pursued, the UCC permits the breaching party (subject to some limitations) to "retract" his or her repudiation. This can be done by any method that clearly indicates an intent to perform. Once retraction is made, the rights of the repudiating party under the contract are reinstated [UCC 2–611, 2A–403].

REMEDIES FOR BREACH OF SALES AND LEASE CONTRACTS

Sometimes, circumstances make it difficult for a person to carry out the performance promised in a contract, in which case the contract may be breached. When breach occurs, the aggrieved party looks for remedies. These remedies range from retaining the goods to requiring the breaching party's performance under the contract. The general purpose of these remedies is to put the aggrieved party "in as good a position as if the other party had fully performed." Remedies under the UCC are *cumulative* in nature. In other words, an innocent party to a breached sales or lease contract is not limited to one, exclusive remedy. (Of course, a party still may not recover twice for the same harm.)

Remedies of the Seller or Lessor

A buyer or lessee breaches a sales or lease contract by any of the following actions: (1) wrongfully rejecting tender of the goods, (2) wrongfully revoking acceptance of the goods, (3) failing to make payment on or before delivery of the goods, or (4) repudiating the contract. On the buyer's or lessee's breach, the seller or lessor is afforded several distinct remedies under the UCC, including those discussed here.

The Right to Withhold Delivery   In general, sellers and lessors can withhold or discontinue performance of their obligations under sales or lease contracts when the buyers or lessees are in breach. If a buyer or lessee has wrongfully rejected or revoked acceptance of contract goods (rejection and revocation of acceptance will be discussed shortly), failed to make proper and timely payment, or repudiated a part of the contract, the seller or lessor can withhold delivery of the goods in question [UCC 2–703(a), 2A–523(1)(c)]. If the breach results from the buyer's or lessee's insolvency (inability to pay debts as they become due), the seller or lessor can refuse to deliver the goods unless the buyer or lessee pays in cash [UCC 2–702(1), 2A–525(1)].

The Right to Resell or Dispose of the Goods   When a buyer or lessee breaches or repudiates the contract while the seller or lessor is still in possession of the goods, the seller or lessor can resell or dispose of the goods, holding the buyer or lessee liable for any loss [UCC 2–703(d), 2–706(1), 2A–523(1)(e), 2A–527(1)].

The Right to Recover the Purchase Price or the Lease Payments Due
Under the UCC, an unpaid seller or lessor can bring an action to recover the purchase price or payments due under the lease contract, plus incidental damages, if the seller or lessor is unable to resell or dispose of the goods [UCC 2–709(1), 2A–529(1)].

   EXAMPLE #7 Southern Realty contracts with Gem Point, Inc., to purchase one thousand pens with Southern Realty's name inscribed on them. Gem Point delivers the pens, but Southern Realty wrongfully refuses to accept them. Gem Point has tendered delivery of conforming goods, and Southern Realty, by failing to accept the goods, is in breach. Because Gem Point obviously cannot sell to anyone else the pens inscribed with the buyer's business name, this situation falls under UCC 2–709, and Gem Point can bring an action for the purchase price.▫

   If a seller or lessor is unable to resell or dispose of goods and sues for the contract price or lease payments due, the goods must be held for the buyer or lessee. The seller or lessor can resell or dispose of the goods at any time prior to collection (of the judgment) from the buyer or lessee but must credit the net proceeds from the sale to the buyer or lessee. This is an example of the duty to mitigate damages.

The Right to Recover Damages   If a buyer or lessee repudiates a contract or wrongfully refuses to accept the goods, a seller or lessor can maintain an action to recover the damages that were sustained. Ordinarily, the amount of damages equals the difference between the contract price or lease payments and the market price or lease payments (at the time and place of tender of the goods), plus incidental damages [UCC 2–708(1), 2A–528(1)].

Remedies of the Buyer or Lessee

A seller or lessor breaches a sales or lease contract by failing to deliver conforming goods or repudiating the contract prior to delivery. On the breach, the buyer or lessee has a choice of several remedies under the UCC, including those discussed here.

The Right of Cover In certain situations, buyers and lessees can protect themselves by obtaining **cover**—that is, by buying or leasing goods to substitute for those that were due under the contract. This option is available when the seller or lessor repudiates the contract or fails to deliver the goods. It is also available to a buyer or lessee who has rightfully rejected goods or revoked acceptance. Rejection and revocation of acceptance will be discussed shortly.

In obtaining cover, the buyer or lessee must act in good faith and without unreasonable delay [UCC 2–712, 2A–518]. After purchasing or leasing substitute goods, the buyer or lessee can recover from the seller or lessor the difference between the cost of cover and the contract price (or lease payments), plus incidental and consequential damages, less the expenses (such as delivery costs) that were saved as a result of the breach [UCC 2–712, 2–715, 2A–518]. Consequential damages include any loss suffered by the buyer or lessee that the seller or lessor could have foreseen (had reason to know about) at the time of contract formation.

COVER
A buyer's or lessee's purchase on the open market of goods to substitute for those promised but never delivered by the seller. Under the UCC, if the cost of cover exceeds the cost of the contract goods, the buyer or lessee can recover the difference, plus incidental and consequential damages.

The Right to Obtain Specific Performance A buyer or lessee can obtain specific performance when the goods are unique or when the remedy at law is inadequate [UCC 2–716(1), 2A–521(1)]. Ordinarily, an award of money damages is sufficient to place a buyer or lessee in the position he or she would have occupied if the seller or lessor had fully performed. When the contract is for the purchase of a particular work of art or a similarly unique item, however, money damages may not be sufficient. Under these circumstances, equity will require that the seller or lessor perform by delivering exactly the particular goods identified to the contract (a remedy of specific performance).

The Right to Recover Damages If a seller or lessor repudiates the sales contract or fails to deliver the goods, or the buyer or lessee has rightfully rejected or revoked acceptance of the goods, the buyer or lessee can sue for damages. The measure of recovery is the difference between the contract price (or lease payments) and the market price of (or lease payments that could be obtained for) the goods at the time the buyer (or lessee) *learned* of the breach. The market price or market lease payments are determined at the place where the seller or lessor was supposed to deliver the goods. The buyer or lessee can also recover incidental and consequential damages, less the expenses that were saved as a result of the breach [UCC 2–713, 2A–519].

EXAMPLE #8 Schilling orders ten thousand bushels of wheat from Valdone for $5 a bushel, with delivery due on June 14 and payment due on June 20. Valdone does not deliver on June 14. On June 14, the market price of wheat is $5.50 per bushel. Schilling chooses to do without the wheat. He sues Valdone for damages for nondelivery. Schilling can recover $0.50 × 10,000, or $5,000, plus any expenses the breach may have caused him. The measure of damages is the market price less the contract price on the day Schilling was to have received delivery. Any expenses Schilling saved by the breach would be deducted from the damages.□

The Right to Reject the Goods   If either the goods or the tender of the goods by the seller or lessor fails to conform to the contract *in any respect,* the buyer or lessee can reject the goods. If some of the goods conform to the contract, the buyer or lessee can keep the conforming goods and reject the rest [UCC 2–601, 2A–509]. The buyer or lessee must reject the goods within a reasonable amount of time after delivery or tender of delivery, and the seller or lessor must be notified *seasonably—* that is, in a timely fashion or at the proper time [UCC 2–602(1), 2A–509(2)].

If a *merchant buyer* or *lessee* rightfully rejects goods, he or she is required to follow any reasonable instructions received from the seller or lessor with respect to the goods controlled by the buyer or lessee. For instance, the seller might ask the buyer to store the goods in the buyer's warehouse until the next day when the seller can retrieve them. The buyer or lessee is entitled to reimbursement for the care and cost entailed in following the instructions [UCC 2–603, 2A–511]. If no instructions are forthcoming, the buyer or lessee may store the goods or reship them to the seller or lessor [UCC 2–604, 2A–512].

The Right to Recover Damages for Accepted Goods   A buyer or lessee who has accepted nonconforming goods may also keep the goods and recover for any loss "resulting in the ordinary course of events . . . as determined in any manner which is reasonable" [UCC 2–714(1), 2A–519(3)]. The buyer or lessee, however, must notify the seller or lessor of the breach within a reasonable time after the defect was or should have been discovered.

When the goods delivered and accepted are not as warranted, the measure of damages equals the difference between the value of the goods as accepted and their value if they had been delivered as warranted, plus incidental and consequential damages if appropriate [UCC 2–714, 2A–519].

Revocation of Acceptance   Acceptance of the goods precludes the buyer or lessee from exercising the right of rejection, but it does not necessarily prevent the buyer or lessee from pursuing other remedies. Additionally, in certain circumstances, a buyer or lessee is permitted to *revoke* his or her acceptance of the goods. Acceptance of a lot or a commercial unit can be revoked if the nonconformity *substantially* impairs the value of the lot or unit and if one of the following factors is present:

1. Acceptance was predicated on the reasonable assumption that the nonconformity would be cured, and it has not been cured within a reasonable period of time [UCC 2–608(1)(a), 2A–517(1)(a)].
2. The buyer or lessee did not discover the nonconformity before acceptance, either because it was difficult to discover before acceptance or because the seller's or lessor's assurance that the goods were conforming kept the buyer or lessee from inspecting the goods [UCC 2–608(1)(b), 2A–517(1)(b)].

Revocation of acceptance is not effective until notice is given to the seller or lessor. Notice must occur within a reasonable time after the buyer or lessee either discovers or *should have discovered* the grounds for revocation. Once acceptance is revoked, the buyer or lessee can pursue remedies, just as if the goods had been rejected.

Is two years after a sale of goods a reasonable time period in which to discover a defect in those goods and notify the seller or lessor of a breach? That was the question in the following case.

Case 11.3 **Fitl v. Strek**

Supreme Court of Nebraska, 2005.
269 Neb. 51, 690 N.W.2d 605.
www.findlaw.com/11stategov/ne/neca.html[a]

BACKGROUND AND FACTS Over the Labor Day weekend in 1995, James Fitl attended a sports-card show in San Francisco, California, where he met Mark Strek (doing business as Star Cards of San Francisco), an exhibitor at the show. Later, on Strek's representation that a certain 1952 Mickey Mantle Topps baseball card was in near-mint condition, Fitl bought the card from Strek for $17,750. Strek delivered it to Fitl in Omaha,

a. In the "Supreme Court Opinions" section, in the "2005" row, click on "January." In the result, click on the appropriate link next to the name of the case to access the opinion.

Nebraska, where Fitl placed it in a safe-deposit box. In May 1997, Fitl sent the card to Professional Sports Authenticators (PSA), a sports-card grading service. PSA told Fitl that the card was ungradable because it had been discolored and doctored. Fitl complained to Strek, who replied that Fitl should have initiated a return of the card within "a typical grace period for the unconditional return of a card, . . . 7 days to 1 month" of its receipt. In August, Fitl sent the card to ASA Accugrade, Inc. (ASA), another grading service, for a second opinion on its value. ASA also concluded that the card had been refinished and trimmed. Fitl filed a suit in a Nebraska state court against Strek, seeking damages. The court awarded Fitl $17,750, plus his court costs. Strek appealed to the Nebraska Supreme Court.

IN THE WORDS OF THE COURT . . . *WRIGHT*, J. [Justice]

* * * *

Strek claims that the [trial] court erred in determining that notification of the defective condition of the baseball card 2 years after the date of purchase was timely pursuant to [UCC] 2–607(3)(a).

* * * The [trial] court found that Fitl had notified Strek within a reasonable time after discovery of the breach. Therefore, our review is whether the [trial] court's finding as to the reasonableness of the notice was clearly erroneous.

Section 2–607(3)(a) states: "Where a tender has been accepted * * * the buyer must within a reasonable time after he discovers or should have discovered any breach notify the seller of breach or be barred from any remedy." [Under UCC 1–204(2)] *"what is a reasonable time for taking any action depends on the nature, purpose, and circumstances of such action."* [Emphasis added.]

The notice requirement set forth in Section 2–607(3)(a) serves three purposes. * * *

* * * The most important one is to enable the seller to make efforts to cure the breach by making adjustments or replacements in order to minimize the buyer's damages and the seller's liability. A second policy is to provide the seller a reasonable opportunity to learn the facts so that he may adequately prepare for negotiation and defend himself in a suit. A third policy * * * is the same as the policy behind statutes of limitation: to provide a seller with a terminal point in time for liability.

* * * *A party is justified in relying upon a representation made to the party as a positive statement of fact when an investigation would be required to ascertain its falsity.* In order for Fitl to have determined that the baseball card had been altered, he would have been required to conduct an investigation. We find that he was not required to do so. Once Fitl learned that the baseball card had been altered, he gave notice to Strek. [Emphasis added.]

* * * One of the most important policies behind the notice requirement * * * is to allow the seller to cure the breach by making adjustments or replacements to minimize the buyer's damages and the seller's liability. However, even if Fitl had learned immediately upon taking possession of the baseball card that it was not authentic and had notified Strek at that time, there is no evidence that Strek could have made any adjustment or taken any action that would have minimized his liability. In its altered condition, the baseball card was worthless.

* * * Earlier notification would not have helped Strek prepare for negotiation or defend himself in a suit because the damage to Fitl could not be repaired. Thus, the policies behind the notice requirement, to allow the seller to correct a defect, to prepare for negotiation and litigation, and to protect against stale claims at a time beyond which an

CASE 11.3–CONTINUED

investigation can be completed, were not unfairly prejudiced by the lack of an earlier notice to Strek. Any problem Strek may have had with the party from whom he obtained the baseball card was a separate matter from his transaction with Fitl, and an investigation into the source of the altered card would not have minimized Fitl's damages.

DECISION AND REMEDY   The state supreme court affirmed the decision of the lower court. In the circumstances of this case, notice of a defect in the goods two years after their purchase was reasonable. The buyer had reasonably relied on the seller's representation that the goods were "authentic" (which they were not), and when their defects were discovered, the buyer had given a timely notice.

WHAT IF THE FACTS WERE DIFFERENT?   Suppose that Fitl and Strek had included in their agreement a clause requiring Fitl to give notice of any defect in the card within "7 days to 1 month" of its receipt. Would the result have been different? Why or why not?

THE LEGAL ENVIRONMENT DIMENSION   What might a buyer who prevails in a dispute such as the one in this case be awarded?

Contractual Provisions Affecting Remedies

The parties to a sales or lease contract can vary their respective rights and obligations by contractual agreement. For example, a seller and buyer can expressly provide for remedies in addition to those provided in the UCC. They can also specifiy remedies in lieu of those provided in the UCC, or they can change the measure of damages. The seller can stipulate that the buyer's only remedy on the seller's breach be repair or replacement of the item, or the seller can limit the buyer's remedy to return of the goods and refund of the purchase price. In sales and lease contracts, an agreed-on remedy is in addition to those provided in the UCC unless the parties expressly agree that the remedy is exclusive of all others [UCC 2–719(1), 2A–503(1)].

If the parties state that a remedy is exclusive, then it is the sole remedy. When circumstances cause an exclusive remedy to fail in its essential purpose, however, it is no longer exclusive [UCC 2–719(2), 2A–503(2)].   **EXAMPLE #9**   A sales contract limits the buyer's remedy to repair or replacement. If the goods cannot be repaired and no replacements are available, the remedy fails in its essential purpose. In this situation, the buyer normally will be entitled to seek other remedies available under the UCC. ◻

Containers sit on a ship as they wait to be unloaded at a port in San Francisco, California. If the buyer discovers that some of the goods are defective, what remedies under the UCC are available to the buyer?
(Darin Marshall/Creative Commons)

SALES AND LEASE WARRANTIES

Warranty is an age-old concept. In sales and lease law, a warranty is an assurance by one party of the existence of a fact on which the other party can rely. Article 2 and Article 2A of the UCC designate several types of warranties that can arise in a sales or lease contract. These warranties include warranties of title, express warranties, and implied warranties.

Because a warranty imposes a duty on the seller or lessor, a breach of warranty is a breach of the seller's or lessor's promise. If the parties have not agreed to limit or modify the remedies available to the buyer or lessee and if the seller or lessor breaches a warranty, the buyer or lessee can sue to recover damages from the seller or lessor. Under some circumstances, a breach can allow the buyer or lessee to rescind (cancel) the agreement.[3]

Warranty of Title

Title warranty arises automatically in most sales contracts under Section 2–312 of the UCC. In most situations, sellers warrant that they have good and valid title to the goods sold and that transfer of the title is rightful [UCC 2–312(1)(a)]. A second warranty of title provided by the UCC protects buyers who are *unaware* of any encumbrances (claims, charges, or liabilities—usually called *liens*[4]) against goods at the time the contract is made [UCC 2–312(1)(b)]. This warranty protects buyers who unknowingly purchase goods that are subject to a creditor's security interest (see Chapter 13). If a creditor legally repossesses the goods from a buyer *who had no actual knowledge of the security interest,* the buyer can recover from the seller for breach of warranty. (The buyer who has *actual knowledge of a security interest* has no recourse against a seller.) Article 2A affords similar protection for lessees [UCC 2A–211(1)]. A merchant seller is also deemed to warrant that the goods delivered are free from any copyright, trademark, or patent claims of a third person [UCC 2–312(3), 2A–211(2)].

In an ordinary sales transaction, the title warranty can be disclaimed or modified only by *specific language* in a contract. For example, sellers may assert that they are transferring only such rights, title, and interest as they have in the goods. In a lease transaction, the disclaimer must "be specific, be by a writing, and be conspicuous" [UCC 2A–214(4)].

Express Warranties

A seller or lessor can create an **express warranty** by making representations concerning the quality, condition, description, or performance potential of the goods. Under UCC 2–313 and 2A–210, express warranties arise when a seller or lessor indicates any of the following:

1. That the goods conform to any *affirmation* (declaration that something is true) *or promise of fact* that the seller or lessor makes to the buyer or lessee about the goods. Such affirmations or promises are usually made during the bargaining process. Statements such as "these drill bits will penetrate stainless steel and without dulling" are express warranties.
2. That the goods conform to any *description* of them. For example, a label that reads "Crate contains one 150-horsepower diesel engine" or a contract that calls for the delivery of a "wool coat" creates an express warranty.
3. That the goods conform to any *sample or model* of the goods shown to the buyer or lessee.

Express warranties can be found in a seller's or lessor's advertisement, brochure, or promotional materials, in addition to being made orally or in an express warranty provision in a sales or lease contract. To create an express warranty, a seller or lessor does not have to use formal words such as *warrant* or *guarantee.* It is only necessary that a reasonable buyer or lessee would regard the representation as part of the basis of the bargain [UCC 2–313(2), 2A–210(2)].

EXPRESS WARRANTY
A seller's or lessor's oral or written promise or affirmation of fact, ancillary to an underlying sales or lease agreement, as to the quality, description, or performance of the goods being sold or leased.

---

3. *Rescission* restores the parties to the positions they were in before the contract was made.
4. Pronounced *leens.* Liens will be discussed in more detail in Chapter 13.

A woman tries on a garment at a New York fur company. If the salesperson represents that the fur is mink, is that enough to create an express warranty? Why or why not?
(AP Photo/Joe Appell/*Pittsburgh Tribune-Review*)

Basis of the Bargain   The UCC requires that for an express warranty to be created, the affirmation, promise, description, or sample must become part of the "basis of the bargain" [UCC 2–313(1), 2A–210(1)]. Just what constitutes the basis of the bargain is difficult to say. The UCC does not define the concept, and it is a question of fact in each case whether a representation was made at such a time and in such a way that it induced the buyer or lessee to enter into the contract. Therefore, if an express warranty is not intended, the marketing agent or salesperson should not promise too much.

Preventing Legal Disputes

Businesspersons engaged in selling or leasing goods should be careful about the words they use with customers, in writing and orally. Express warranties can be found in a seller's or lessor's advertisement, brochure, or promotional materials, in addition to being made orally or in an express warranty provision in a contract. Avoiding unintended warranties is crucial in preventing legal disputes, and all employees should be instructed on how the promises they make to buyers during a sale can create warranties. ■

Statements of Opinion and Value   If the seller or lessor merely makes a statement that relates to the value or worth of the goods, or makes a statement of opinion or recommendation about the goods, the seller or lessor is not creating an express warranty [UCC 2–313(2), 2A–210(2)].

EXAMPLE #10   A seller claims that "this is the best used car to come along in years; it has four new tires and a 150-horsepower engine just rebuilt this year." The seller has made several *affirmations of fact* that can create a warranty: the automobile has an engine; it has a 150-horsepower engine; the engine was rebuilt this year; there are four tires on the automobile; and the tires are new. The seller's *opinion* that the vehicle is "the best used car to come along in years," however, is known as *puffery* and creates no warranty. (**Puffery** is an expression of opinion by a seller or lessor that is not made as a representation of fact.)▢ A statement relating to the value of the goods, such as "it's worth a fortune" or "anywhere else you'd pay $10,000 for it," usually does not create a warranty.

PUFFERY
A salesperson's exaggerated claims concerning the quality of property offered for sale. Such claims involve opinions rather than facts and are not considered to be legally binding promises or warranties.

It is not always easy to determine what constitutes an express warranty and what constitutes puffery. The reasonableness of the buyer's or lessee's reliance appears to be the controlling criterion in many cases. For example, a salesperson's statements that a ladder will "never break" and will "last a lifetime" are so clearly improbable that no reasonable buyer should rely on them.

Implied Warranties

An **implied warranty** is one that *the law derives* by inference from the nature of the transaction or the relative situations or circumstances of the parties. Under the UCC, merchants impliedly warrant that the goods they sell or lease are merchantable and, in certain circumstances, fit for a particular purpose. In addition, an implied warranty may arise from a course of dealing or usage of trade. We examine these three types of implied warranties in the following subsections.

Marlboro cigarettes sit on a shelf in a retail store. Suppose that the store clerk tells a customer that these cigarettes "are the best," and the customer buys three cartons. The customer later develops lung cancer from smoking and sues the seller. In this situation, would the seller's statements be enough to create an express warranty? Why or why not? ("Ladyphoenixx"/Creative Commons)

Implied Warranty of Merchantability An **implied warranty of merchantability** automatically arises in every sale or lease of goods made *by a merchant* who deals in goods of the kind sold or leased [UCC 2–314, 2A–212]. Thus, a merchant who is in the business of selling ski equipment makes an implied warranty of merchantability every time the merchant sells a pair of skis, but a neighbor selling his or her skis at a garage sale does not.

This warranty imposes on the merchant liability for the safe performance of the product. It makes no difference whether the merchant knew of, or could have discovered, that a product was defective (not merchantable).

Goods that are *merchantable* are "reasonably fit for the ordinary purposes for which such goods are used." They must be of at least average, fair, or medium-grade quality. The quality must be comparable to quality that will pass without objection in the trade or market for goods of the same description. The goods must also be adequately packaged and labeled, and they must conform to the promises or affirmations of fact made on the container or label, if any.

Implied Warranty of Fitness for a Particular Purpose The **implied warranty of fitness for a particular purpose** arises when any *seller or lessor* (merchant or nonmerchant) knows the particular purpose for which a buyer or lessee will use the goods *and* knows that the buyer or lessee is relying on the skill and judgment of the seller or lessor to select suitable goods [UCC 2–315, 2A–213]. A "particular purpose" of the buyer or lessee differs from the "ordinary purpose for which goods are used" (merchantability). Goods can be merchantable but unfit for a particular purpose.

A seller or lessor does not need to have actual knowledge of the buyer's or lessee's particular purpose. It is sufficient if a seller or lessor "has reason to know" the purpose. The buyer or lessee, however, must have *relied* on the skill or judgment of the seller or lessor in selecting or furnishing suitable goods for an implied warranty to be created.

EXAMPLE #11 Bloomberg leases a computer from Future Tech, a lessor of technical business equipment. Bloomberg tells the clerk that she wants a computer that will run a complicated new engineering graphics program at a reasonable speed. Future Tech leases Bloomberg an Architex One computer with a CPU speed of only

IMPLIED WARRANTY
A warranty that the law derives by inference from the nature of the transaction or the relative situations or circumstances of the parties.

IMPLIED WARRANTY OF MERCHANTABILITY
A warranty that goods being sold or leased are reasonably fit for the ordinary purpose for which they are sold or leased, are properly packaged and labeled, and are of fair quality. The warranty automatically arises in every sale or lease of goods made by a merchant who deals in goods of the kind sold or leased.

IMPLIED WARRANTY OF FITNESS FOR A PARTICULAR PURPOSE
A warranty that goods sold or leased are fit for a particular purpose. The warranty arises when any seller or lessor knows the particular purpose for which a buyer or lessee will use the goods and knows that the buyer or lessee is relying on the skill and judgment of the seller or lessor to select suitable goods.

2.4 gigahertz, even though a speed of at least 3.8 gigahertz would be required to run Bloomberg's graphics program at a reasonable speed. Bloomberg, after realizing that it takes her forever to run her program, wants her money back. Here, because Future Tech has breached the implied warranty of fitness for a particular purpose, Bloomberg normally will be able to recover. The clerk knew specifically that Bloomberg wanted a computer with enough speed to run certain software. Furthermore, Bloomberg relied on the clerk to furnish a computer that would fulfill this purpose. Because Future Tech did not do so, the warranty was breached.□

Implied Warranty Arising from Course of Dealing or Trade Usage Implied warranties can also arise (or be excluded or modified) as a result of the parties' prior course of dealing or the general usage of trade [UCC 2–314(3), 2A–212(3)]. In the absence of evidence to the contrary, when both parties to a sales or lease contract have knowledge of a well-recognized trade custom, the courts will infer that both parties intended for that custom to apply to their contract. For example, if it is an industry-wide custom to lubricate a new car before it is delivered and a dealer fails to do so, the dealer can be held liable to a buyer for damages resulting from the breach of an implied warranty. (This, of course, would also be negligence on the part of the dealer.)

Warranty Disclaimers

Express warranties can be excluded or limited by specific and unambiguous language, provided that this is done in a manner that protects the buyer or lessee from surprise. Therefore, a written disclaimer in language that is clear and conspicuous, and called to a buyer's or lessee's attention, can negate all oral express warranties not included in the written sales or lease contract [UCC 2–316(1), 2A–214(1)].

Generally speaking, unless circumstances indicate otherwise, the implied warranties of merchantability and fitness are disclaimed by the expressions "as is," "with all faults," and other similar expressions that in common understanding for *both* parties call the buyer's or lessee's attention to the fact that there are no implied warranties [UCC 2–316(3)(a), 2A–214(3)(a)].

The UCC also permits a seller or lessor to specifically disclaim an implied warranty either of fitness or of merchantability [UCC 2–316(2), 2A–214(2)]. To disclaim an implied warranty of fitness for a particular purpose, the disclaimer must be in writing and be conspicuous. The word *fitness* does not have to be mentioned in the writing; it is sufficient if, for example, the disclaimer states, "THERE ARE NO WARRANTIES THAT EXTEND BEYOND THE DESCRIPTION ON THE FACE HEREOF." A merchantability disclaimer must be more specific; it must mention *merchantability*. It need not be written; but if it is, the writing must be conspicuous [UCC 2–316(2), 2A–214(4)].

E-CONTRACTS

E-CONTRACT
A contract that is formed electronically.

The basic principles of contract law evolved over a long period of time. Certainly, they were formed long before cyberspace and electronic contracting became realities. Therefore, new legal theories, new adaptations of existing laws, and new laws are needed to govern **e-contracts,** or contracts entered into electronically. To date, however, most courts have adapted traditional contract law principles and, when applicable, provisions of the UCC to cases involving e-contract disputes.

Forming Contracts Online

Numerous contracts are formed online. Although the medium through which these contracts are generated has changed, the age-old problems attending contract formation have not. Disputes concerning contracts formed online continue to center around contract terms and whether the parties voluntarily assented to those terms.

Note that online contracts may be formed not only for the sale of goods and services but also for the purpose of *licensing*. The "sale" of software, for instance, generally involves a license, or a right to use the software, rather than the passage of title (ownership rights) from the seller to the buyer. **EXAMPLE #12** Galynn wants to obtain software that will allow her to work on spreadsheets on her BlackBerry. She goes online and purchases GridMagic. During the transaction, she has to click on several on-screen "I agree" boxes to indicate that she understands that she is purchasing only the right to use the software and will not obtain any ownership rights. After she agrees to these terms (the licensing agreement), she can download the software to her computer.□ As you read through the following pages, keep in mind that although we typically refer to the offeror and offeree as a *seller* and a *buyer,* in many transactions these parties would be more accurately described as a *licensor* and a *licensee.*

Online Offers　　Sellers doing business via the Internet can protect themselves against contract disputes and legal liability by creating offers that clearly spell out the terms that will govern their transactions if the offers are accepted. All important terms should be conspicuous and easily viewed by potential buyers.

Displaying the Offer　　The seller's Web site should include a hypertext link to a page containing the full contract so that potential buyers are made aware of the terms to which they are assenting. The contract generally must be displayed online in a readable format, such as a twelve-point typeface. **EXAMPLE #13** Netquip sells a variety of heavy equipment, such as trucks and trailers, online at its Web site. Netquip must include its full pricing schedule on the Web site with explanations of all complex provisions. In addition, the terms of the sale (such as any warranties and Netquip's refund policy) must be fully disclosed.□

Is an online contract enforceable if the offeror requires an offeree to scroll down or print the contract to read its terms, which are otherwise readily accessible and clear? That was the question in the following case.

Case 11.4 **Feldman v. Google, Inc.**

United States District Court,
Eastern District of Pennsylvania, 2007.
513 F.Supp.2d 229.

COMPANY PROFILE　　In the mid-1990s, Larry Page and Sergey Brin, Stanford University graduate students in computer science, began work on an Internet search engine called "BackRub." Renamed "Google" after the mathematical term for a 1 followed by 100 zeros, the engine was made available in 1998. In less than a year, the service began acquiring major

clients, receiving achievement awards, being included on many "Top Web Site" lists, and handling millions of queries per day. By 2000, Google had become the world's largest search engine. According to Google, Inc.'s Web site at **www.google.com**, its mission is to organize the world's information and make it universally accessible and useful. The company's revenue derives from keyword-targeted advertising.

BACKGROUND AND FACTS　　In Google, Inc.'s AdWords program, when an Internet user searches on

CASE 11.4—CONTINUED

www.google.com using key words that an advertiser has identified, an ad appears. If the user clicks on it, Google charges the advertiser. Google requires an advertiser to agree to certain terms before placing an ad. These terms—set out in a preamble and seven paragraphs—are displayed online in a window with a scroll bar. A link to a printer-friendly version of the terms is at the top of the window. At the bottom of the page, viewable without scrolling, are the words, "Yes, I agree to the above terms and conditions," and a box on which an advertiser must click to proceed. Among the terms, a forum-selection clause provides that any dispute over the program is to be "adjudicated in Santa Clara County, California." Lawrence Feldman, a lawyer, participated in the program by selecting key words, including "Vioxx," "Bextra," and "Celebrex," to trigger a showing of his ad to potential clients. In a subsequent suit between Feldman and Google in a federal district court in Pennsylvania, Feldman claimed that at least 20 percent of the clicks for which he was charged $100,000 between January 2003 and January 2006 were fraudulent.[a] Feldman filed a motion for summary judgment. Google asked the court to transfer the case to a court in Santa Clara County, California.

IN THE WORDS OF THE COURT . . . *GILES*, J. [Judge]

*   *   *   *

The type of contract at issue here is commonly referred to as a "clickwrap" agreement. A clickwrap agreement appears on an Internet web page and requires that a user consent to any terms or conditions by clicking on a dialog box on the screen in order to proceed with the Internet transaction. *Even though they are electronic, clickwrap agreements are considered to be writings because they are printable and storable.* [Emphasis added.]

To determine whether a clickwrap agreement is enforceable, courts presented with the issue apply traditional principles of contract law and focus on whether the plaintiffs had reasonable notice of and manifested assent to the clickwrap agreement. *Absent a showing of fraud, failure to read an enforceable clickwrap agreement, as with any binding contract, will not excuse compliance with its terms.* [Emphasis added.]

*   *   *   *

Plaintiff [Feldman] claims he did not have notice or knowledge of the forum selection clause, and therefore that there was no "meeting of the minds" required for contract formation.

*   *   *   *

*   *   * In order to activate an AdWords account, the user had to visit a Web page which displayed the Agreement in a scrollable text box. *   *   * The user did not have to scroll down to a submerged screen or click on a series of hyperlinks to view the Agreement. Instead, text of the AdWords Agreement was immediately visible to the user, as was a prominent admonition in boldface to read the terms and conditions carefully, and with instruction to indicate assent if the user agreed to the terms.

That the user would have to scroll through the text box of the Agreement to read it in its entirety does not defeat notice because there was sufficient notice of the Agreement itself and clicking "Yes" constituted assent to all of the terms. The preamble, which was immediately visible, also made clear that assent to the terms was binding. The Agreement was presented in readable 12-point font. It was only seven paragraphs long—not so long so as to render scrolling down to view all of the terms inconvenient or impossible. A printer-friendly, full-screen version was made readily available. The user had ample time to review the document.

*   *   * The user *   *   * had to take affirmative action and click the "Yes, I agree to the above terms and conditions" button in order to proceed to the next step. Clicking "Continue" without clicking the "Yes" button would have returned the user to the same Web page. If the user did not agree to all of the terms, he could not have activated his account, placed ads, or incurred charges.

*   *   *   *

a. Feldman was alleging that *click fraud* had taken place. Click fraud occurs when someone, such as a competitor or a prankster with no interest in an advertiser's goods or services, clicks repeatedly on an ad, driving up the ad's cost to the advertiser without generating a sale.

A reasonably prudent Internet user would have known of the existence of terms in the AdWords Agreement. Plaintiff had to have had reasonable notice of the terms. By clicking on "Yes, I agree to the above terms and conditions" button, Plaintiff indicated assent to the terms.

DECISION AND REMEDY The court held that "the requirements of an express contract for reasonable notice of terms and mutual assent are satisfied." Feldman and Google were bound to the terms. The court denied Feldman's motion for summary judgment and granted Google's motion to transfer the case.

THE ETHICAL DIMENSION With respect to click fraud, which was the heart of Feldman's claim in this case, what circumstances might suggest unethical behavior by Google?

THE E-COMMERCE DIMENSION Under what different facts might the court have held that the plaintiff did not have reasonable notice of the terms of the agreement and thus did not assent to them?

Provisions to Include An important rule to keep in mind is that the offeror controls the offer and thus the resulting contract. Therefore, the seller should anticipate the terms that he or she wants to include in a contract and provide for them in the offer. At a minimum, an online offer should include the following provisions:

1. A clause that clearly indicates what constitutes the buyer's agreement to the terms of the offer, such as a box containing the words "I accept" that the buyer can click on to indicate acceptance. (Mechanisms for accepting online offers are discussed in detail later in the chapter.)
2. A provision specifying how payment for the goods and of any applicable taxes must be made.
3. A statement of the seller's refund and return policies.
4. Disclaimers of liability for certain uses of the goods. For example, an online seller of business forms may add a disclaimer that the seller does not accept responsibility for the buyer's reliance on the forms rather than on an attorney's advice.
5. A provision specifying the remedies available to the buyer if the goods are found to be defective or if the contract is otherwise breached. Any limitation of remedies should be clearly spelled out.
6. A statement indicating how the seller will use the information gathered about the buyer.
7. Provisions relating to dispute settlement, such as an arbitration clause, a choice-of-law clause (see Chapter 7), or a *forum-selection clause* (discussed next).

Dispute-Settlement Provisions Online offers frequently include provisions relating to dispute settlement. An arbitration clause might be included, indicating that any dispute arising under the contract will be arbitrated in a specified forum. Many online contracts also contain a **forum-selection clause,** which indicates the forum, or place (such as the court or jurisdiction), for the resolution of any dispute arising under the contract. These clauses can help online sellers avoid having to appear in court in many distant jurisdictions when customers are dissatisfied with their purchases.

FORUM-SELECTION CLAUSE
A provision in a contract designating the court, jurisdiction, or tribunal that will decide any disputes arising under the contract.

Online Acceptances   Section 2–204 of the UCC provides that any contract for the sale of goods "may be made in any manner sufficient to show agreement, including conduct by both parties which recognizes the existence of such a contract." The *Restatement (Second) of Contracts,* a compilation of common law contract principles, has a similar provision. It states that parties may agree to a contract "by written or spoken words or by other action or by failure to act."[5]

Click-On Agreements   The courts have used the provisions just discussed to conclude that a binding contract can be created by conduct, including conduct accepting an online offer by clicking on a box indicating "I agree" or "I accept." The agreement resulting from such an acceptance is often called a **click-on agreement.** Generally, the law does not require that all of the terms in a contract must actually have been read by all of the parties to be effective. Therefore, clicking on a button or box that states "I agree" to certain terms can be enough.[6]

Browse-Wrap Terms   Like the terms of a click-on agreement, **browse-wrap terms** can occur in a transaction conducted over the Internet. Unlike a click-on agreement, however, browse-wrap terms do not require an Internet user to agree to the terms before, say, downloading or using certain software. In other words, a person can install the software without clicking "I agree" to the terms of a license. Offerors of browse-wrap terms generally assert that the terms are binding without the user's active consent. Critics contend that browse-wrap terms are not enforceable because they do not satisfy the basic elements of contract formation—voluntary consent. Courts are much more likely to enforce the terms of a click-on agreement than browse-wrap terms because of this lack of an express indication that the user consents to browse-wrap terms.

E-Signatures

In many instances, a contract cannot be enforced unless it is signed by the party against whom enforcement is sought. A significant issue in the context of e-commerce has to do with how electronic signatures, or **e-signatures,** can be created and verified on e-contracts.

E-Signature Technologies   Today, numerous technologies allow electronic documents to be signed. These technologies generally fall into one of two categories, *digitized handwritten signatures* and *public-key infrastructure–based digital signatures*. A digitized signature is a graphical image of a handwritten signature, which is often created using a digital pen and pad, such as an ePad, and special software. For security reasons, the strokes of a person's signature can be measured by software to authenticate the identity of the person signing (this is referred to as *signature dynamics*). In a public-key infrastructure (such as an *asymmetric cryptosystem*), two mathematically linked but different keys are generated—a private signing key and a public validation key. A digital signature is created when the signer uses the private key to create a unique mark on an electronic document. The appropriate software enables the recipient of the document to use the public key to verify the identity of the signer. A *cybernotary,* or legally recognized

---

CLICK-ON AGREEMENT
An agreement that arises when a buyer, engaging in a transaction on a computer, indicates his or her assent to be bound by the terms of an offer by clicking on a button that says, for example, "I agree"; sometimes referred to as a *click-on license* or a *click-wrap agreement.*

BROWSE-WRAP TERMS
Terms and conditions of use that are presented to an Internet user at the time certain products, such as software, are being downloaded but to which the user need not agree (by clicking "I agree," for example) before being able to install or use the product.

E-SIGNATURE
Under the Uniform Electronic Transactions Act, any electronic sound, symbol, or process attached to electronically stored information and intended to function as a signature. This definition is intentionally broad in order to give legal effect to acts that people intend to be the equivalent of their written signatures.

---

5. *Restatement (Second) of Contracts,* Section 19.
6. See, for example, *i.LAN Systems, Inc. v. Netscout Service Level Corp.,* 183 F.Supp.2d 328 (D.Mass. 2002).

certification authority, issues the key pair, identifies the owner of the keys, and certifies the validity of the public key. The cybernotary also serves as a repository for public keys.

State Laws Governing E-Signatures   Most states have laws governing e-signatures. The problem is that state e-signature laws are not uniform. Some states—California is a notable example—prohibit many types of documents from being signed with e-signatures, whereas other states are more permissive.

In an attempt to create more uniformity among the states, in 1999 the National Conference of Commissioners on Uniform State Laws and the American Law Institute promulgated the Uniform Electronic Transactions Act (UETA). To date, the UETA has been adopted, at least in part, by forty-eight states. (We will look more closely at the UETA shortly.) Among other things, the UETA states that a signature may not be denied legal effect or enforceability solely because it is in electronic form. Most states have also included a similar provision in their version of the UCC.

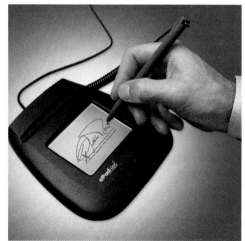

The ePad-Ink is an electronic signature pad that can be used to insert handwritten signatures into electronic documents. What type of e-signature technology does this device utilize? What procedure is used to verify the authenticity of a signature created using this ePad?
(Photo Courtesy of Interlink Electronics)

Federal Law Governing E-Signatures and E-Documents   In 2000, Congress enacted the Electronic Signatures in Global and National Commerce Act (E-SIGN Act),[7] which provides that no contract, record, or signature may be "denied legal effect" solely because it is in an electronic form. In other words, under this law, an e-signature is as valid as a signature on paper, and an e-document can be as enforceable as a paper one.

For an e-signature to be enforceable, the contracting parties must have agreed to use electronic signatures. For an electronic document to be valid, it must be in a form that can be retained and accurately reproduced.

The E-SIGN Act does not apply to all types of documents, however. Contracts and documents that are exempt include court papers, divorce decrees, evictions, foreclosures, health-insurance terminations, prenuptial agreements, and wills. Also, the only agreements governed by the UCC that fall under this law are those covered by Articles 2 and 2A and UCC 1–107 and 1–206. Despite these limitations, the E-SIGN Act significantly expanded the possibilities for contracting online. For a discussion of e-signature laws and e-commerce issues worldwide, see this chapter's *Beyond Our Borders* feature on the following page.

The E-SIGN Act refers explicitly to the UETA and provides that if a state has enacted the uniform version of the UETA, that law is not preempted by the E-SIGN Act. In other words, if the state has enacted the UETA without modification, state law will govern. The problem is that many states have enacted nonuniform (modified) versions of the UETA, largely for the purpose of excluding other areas of state law from the UETA's terms. The E-SIGN Act specifies that those exclusions will be preempted to the extent that they are inconsistent with the E-SIGN Act's provisions.

The Uniform Electronic Transactions Act

As noted, the UETA represents one of the first comprehensive efforts to create uniformity and introduce certainty in state laws pertaining to e-commerce. The primary purpose of the UETA is to remove barriers to e-commerce by giving the

---

7. 15 U.S.C. Sections 7001 *et seq.*

Today, most e-commerce conducted on a worldwide basis involves buyers, sellers, and enablers from the United States. Not surprisingly, then, U.S. law is often used to resolve legal issues related to global e-commerce. The preeminence of U.S. law in this area is likely to be challenged in the future, however, as Internet use continues to expand around the globe. Already, several international organizations have created their own codes of conduct, rules, and regulations for global Internet transactions. We examine a few of them here.

A United Nations Convention

An important step toward creating international rules for Internet transactions was taken in 2005, when the United Nations Convention on the Use of Electronic Communications in International Contracts was completed. This convention will go into effect as soon as enough countries ratify it, which may have happened by the time you read this. A major goal of the convention is to improve commercial certainty by determining an Internet user's location for legal purposes. The convention also establishes standards for creating functional equivalence between electronic communciations and paper documents. Like the E-SIGN Act discussed in the text, the convention provides that e-signatures should be treated as the equivalent of signatures on paper documents. The drafters also attempted to codify the proper use of automated message systems for contract formation.

Choice of Court

Another recent treaty that will help to foster international trade is the Convention on the Choice of Court Agreements, completed by the Hague Conference on Private International Law on June 30, 2005. Although this convention does not specifically address e-commerce and applies only to business-to-business transactions, not business-to-consumer transactions, it will provide more certainty regarding jurisdiction and recognition of judgments by other nations' courts. Such matters are important to both offline and online transactions, so the convention should enhance e-commerce as well.

The Choice of Court Convention was designed to promote international trade and investment by providing more certainty in resolving international contract disputes. It governs business agreements that designate a single court, or the courts of a single country, to be the forum for resolving disputes. One of its goals is to offer parties entering into international trade contracts a balanced choice between litigation and arbitration when selecting a method of settling disputes. In this sense, the convention is similar to the United Nations Convention on the Recognition and Enforcement of Foreign Arbitral Awards of 1958, commonly referred to as the New York Arbitration Convention (see Chapter 3 for further discussion of this convention).

Fighting International Cyber Crime

Unfortunately, cyber crime (see Chapter 6) has expanded along with the Internet, but steps are beginning to be taken to combat cyber crime on an international basis. At the beginning of this decade, the Council of Europe created the Cyber-Crime Convention, which has been signed by thirty nations including the United States. This treaty provides mechanisms for international cooperation in the battle against Internet-related crime. It prohibits unauthorized access to an Internet computer system, unauthorized interception of Internet data, Internet fraud and forgery, and copyright infringement through the use of the Internet.

FOR CRITICAL ANALYSIS   There are about two hundred sovereign nations in the world today, but only seventeen have signed the Electronic Communications Convention, and thirty have signed the Cyber-Crime Convention. Why do you think so many nations' governments are reluctant to be bound by international conventions?

same legal effect to electronic records and signatures as is currently given to paper documents and signatures. The UETA broadly defines an *e-signature* as "an electronic sound, symbol, or process attached to or logically associated with a record and executed or adopted by a person with the intent to sign the record."[8] A *record* is defined as "information that is inscribed on a tangible medium or that is stored in an electronic or other medium and is retrievable in perceivable [visual] form."[9]

The UETA does not apply to all writings and signatures but only to electronic records and electronic signatures *relating to a transaction.* A transaction is defined as an interaction between two or more people relating to business, commercial, or governmental activities.[10] The act specifically does not apply to laws govern-

---

8. UETA 102(8).
9. UETA 102(15).
10. UETA 2(12) and 3.

ing wills or testamentary trusts or the UCC (other than Articles 2 and 2A).[11] In addition, the provisions of the UETA allow the states to exclude its application to other areas of law.

---

11. UETA 3(b).

Reviewing . . . Sales, Leases, and E-Contracts

GFI, Inc., a Hong Kong company, makes audio decoder chips, one of the essential components used in the manufacture of MP3 players. Egan Electronics contracts with GFI to buy a total of 10,000 chips, with 2,500 chips to be shipped every three months via Air Express. At the time for the first delivery, GFI delivers only 2,400 chips but explains to Egan that while the shipment is less than 5 percent short, the chips are of a higher quality than those specified in the contract and are worth 5 percent more than the contract price. Egan accepts the shipment and pays GFI the contract price. At the time for the second shipment, GFI makes a shipment identical to the first. Egan again accepts and pays for the chips. At the time for the third shipment, GFI ships 2,400 of the same chips, but this time GFI sends them via Hong Kong Air instead of Air Express. While in transit, the chips are destroyed. Shortly after the third shipment is made, GFI's manufacturing plant burns down and its entire inventory of chips is destroyed. GFI is financially ruined by the fire and unable to continue making decoder chips or to purchase them elsewhere. Using the information presented in the chapter, answer the following questions.

1. Suppose that Egan accepted but refused to pay for the first shipment, and instead sued GFI for breach of contract. If a court found that GFI had breached the contract, what would be the measure of damages?

2. Does the substitution of carriers for the third shipment constitute a breach of the contract by GFI? Why or why not?

3. Suppose that the silicon used for the chips becomes unavailable for a period of time and that GFI cannot manufacture enough chips to fulfill the contract, but does ship as many as it can to Egan. Under what doctrine might a court release GFI from further performance of the contract?

4. Suppose that three years after the fire, GFI notifies Egan that it is back in business, has rebuilt its plant, and is now accepting orders via its Web site. The owner of Egan goes to the Web site and places an order for 3,000 chips from GFI, clicking on the "I agree" button without reading the specific terms. What is this type of online contract called? Will a court be likely to enforce the agreement even if one party did not read it?

Key Terms

browse-wrap terms 378	forum-selection clause 377	lessor 354
click-on agreement 378	implied warranty 373	merchant 353
conforming goods 362	implied warranty of	perfect tender rule 363
cover 367	fitness for a particular	puffery 372
cure 363	purpose 373	sale 350
e-contract 374	implied warranty of	sales contract 350
e-signature 378	merchantability 373	tangible property 350
express warranty 371	lease 353	tender of delivery 362
firm offer 355	lessee 354	

Chapter Summary

The Scope of Article 2—Sales
(See pages 350–353.)

Article 2 governs contracts for the sale of goods (tangible, movable personal property). The common law of contracts also applies to sales contracts to the extent that the common law has not been modified by the UCC. If there is a conflict between a common law rule and the UCC, the UCC controls.

The Scope of Article 2A—Leases
(See pages 353–354.)

Article 2A governs contracts for the lease of goods. Except that it applies to leases, instead of sales, of goods, Article 2A is essentially a repetition of Article 2 and varies only to reflect differences between sales and lease transactions.

Offer and Acceptance
(See pages 354–358.)

1. *Offer—*

   a. Not all terms have to be included for a contract to be formed (only the subject matter and quantity term must be specified). The price does not have to be included for a contract to be formed.

   b. A written and signed offer by a *merchant,* covering a period of three months or less, is irrevocable without payment of consideration.

2. *Acceptance—*

   a. Acceptance may be made by any reasonable means of communication; it is effective when dispatched.

   b. The acceptance of a unilateral offer can be made by a promise to ship or by prompt shipment of conforming goods, or by prompt shipment of nonconforming goods if not accompanied by a notice of accommodation.

   c. Acceptance by performance requires notice within a reasonable time; otherwise, the offer can be treated as lapsed.

   d. A definite expression of acceptance creates a contract even if the terms of the acceptance vary from those of the offer unless the additional terms in the acceptance are expressly conditioned on the offeror's assent to the additional terms.

3. *Consideration—*A modification of a contract for the sale of goods does not require consideration.

The Statute of Frauds
(See pages 358–361.)

1. All contracts for the sale of goods priced at $500 or more must be in writing. A writing is sufficient as long as it indicates a contract between the parties and is signed by the party against whom enforcement is sought. A contract is not enforceable beyond the quantity shown in the writing.

2. When written confirmation of an oral contract *between merchants* is not objected to in writing by the receiver within ten days, the contract is enforceable.

3. Exceptions to the requirement of a writing exist in the following situations:

   a. When the oral contract is for specially manufactured goods not suitable for resale to others, and the seller has substantially started to manufacture the goods.

   b. When the defendant admits in pleadings, testimony, or other court proceedings that an oral contract for the sale of goods was made. In this case, the contract will be enforceable to the extent of the quantity of goods admitted.

   c. The oral agreement will be enforceable to the extent that payment has been received and accepted by the seller or to the extent that the goods have been received and accepted by the buyer.

Performance of Sales and Lease Contracts
(See pages 361–365.)

1. The seller or lessor must tender *conforming goods* to the buyer. Tender must take place at a *reasonable hour* and in a *reasonable manner.* Under the perfect tender doctrine, the seller or lessor must tender goods that conform exactly to the terms of the contract [UCC 2–503(1), 2A–508(1)].

Chapter Summary

Performance of Sales and Lease Contracts—Continued	**2.** If the seller or lessor tenders nonconforming goods prior to the performance date and the buyer or lessee rejects them, the seller or lessor may cure (repair or replace the goods) within the contract time for performance [UCC 2–508(1), 2A–513(1)]. If the seller or lessor has reasonable grounds to believe the buyer or lessee would accept the tendered goods, on the buyer's or lessee's rejection the seller or lessor has a reasonable time to substitute conforming goods without liability [UCC 2–508(2), 2A–513(2)].
	3. If the agreed-on means of delivery becomes impracticable or unavailable, the seller must substitute an alternative means (such as a different carrier) if one is available [UCC 2–614(1)].
	4. When performance becomes commercially impracticable owing to circumstances that were not foreseeable when the contract was formed, the perfect tender rule no longer holds [UCC 2–615, 2A–405].
	5. On tender of delivery by the seller or lessor, the buyer or lessee must pay for the goods at the time and place the buyer or lessee receives the goods, even if the place of shipment is the place of delivery, unless the sale is made on credit.
	6. The buyer or lessee can manifest acceptance of delivered goods expressly in words or by conduct or by failing to reject the goods after a reasonable period of time following inspection or after having had a reasonable opportunity to inspect them [UCC 2–606(1), 2A–515(1)]. A buyer will be deemed to have accepted goods if he or she performs any act inconsistent with the seller's ownership [UCC 2–606(1)(c)].
	7. If, before the time for performance, either party clearly indicates to the other an intention not to perform, this is called anticipatory repudiation. Under UCC 2–610 and 2A–402, the nonbreaching party may choose whether to treat the breach as final by pursuing a remedy or wait and hope that the other party will perform. In either situation, the nonbreaching party may suspend performance.
Remedies for Breach of Sales and Lease Contracts (See pages 365–370.)	**1.** *Remedies of the seller or lessor*—When a buyer or lessee breaches the contract, a seller or lessor can withhold or discontinue performance. If the seller or lessor is still in possession of the goods, the seller or lessor can resell or dispose of the goods and hold the buyer or lessee liable for any loss [UCC 2–703(d), 2–706(1), 2A–523(1)(e), 2A–527(1)]. If the goods cannot be resold or disposed of, an unpaid seller or lessor can bring an action to recover the purchase price or payments due under the contract, plus incidental damages [UCC 2–709(1), 2A–529(1)]. If the buyer or lessee repudiates the contract or wrongfully refuses to accept goods, the seller or lessor can recover the damages that were sustained.
	2. *Remedies of the buyer or lessee*—When the seller or lessor breaches, the buyer or lessee can choose from a number of remedies, including the following:
	a. Obtain cover (in certain situations) [UCC 2–712, 2A–518].
	b. Obtain specific performance (when the goods are unique and when the remedy at law is inadequate) [UCC 2–716(1), 2A–521(1)].
	c. Sue to recover damages [UCC 2–713, 2A–519].
	d. Reject the goods [UCC 2–601, 2A–509].
	e. Accept the goods and recover damages [UCC 2–607, 2–714, 2–717, 2A–519].
	f. Revoke acceptance (in certain circumstances) [UCC 2–608, 2A–517].
	3. The parties can agree to vary their respective rights and remedies in their agreement. If the contract states that a remedy is exclusive, then that is the sole remedy—unless the remedy fails in its essential purpose.

CONTINUED

Sales and Lease Warranties (See pages 370–374.)	1. *Title warranties*—The seller or lessor automatically warrants that he or she has good title, and that there are no liens or infringements on the property being sold or leased.
	2. *Express warranties*—An express warranty arises under the UCC when a seller or lessor indicates, as part of the basis of the bargain, that the goods conform to any of the following:
	a. An affirmation or promise of fact.
	b. A description of the goods.
	c. A sample shown to the buyer or lessee [UCC 2–313, 2A–210].
	3. *Implied warranties*—
	a. The implied warranty of merchantability automatically arises when the seller or lessor is a merchant who deals in the kind of goods sold or leased. The seller or lessor warrants that the goods sold or leased are of proper quality, are properly labeled, and are reasonably fit for the ordinary purposes for which such goods are used [UCC 2–314, 2A–212].
	b. The implied warranty of fitness for a particular purpose arises when the buyer's or lessee's purpose or use is expressly or impliedly known by the seller or lessor and the buyer or lessee purchases or leases the goods in reliance on the seller's or lessor's selection [UCC 2–315, 2A–213].
	4. Warranties, both express and implied, can be disclaimed or qualified by a seller or lessor, but disclaimers generally must be specific and unambiguous, and often must be in writing.
E-Contracts (See pages 374–381.)	1. The terms of an online offer should be just as inclusive as the terms of an offer made in a written (paper) document, including dispute-settlement provisions such as a forum-selection clause. The offer should be displayed in an easily readable and clear format.
	2. An online offer should also include some mechanism, such as an "I agree" or "I accept" box, by which the customer can accept the offer.
	3. A click-on agreement is created when a buyer, completing a transaction on a computer, is required to indicate her or his assent to be bound by the terms of an offer by clicking on a button that says, for example, "I agree." The courts generally enforce click-on agreements because the offeree has indicated acceptance by conduct.
	4. Browse-wrap terms, which are terms in a license that an Internet user does not have to read or agree to prior to downloading the product (such as software), may not be enforced on the ground that the user is not made aware that he or she is entering into a contract.
	5. The Uniform Electronic Transactions Act (UETA) defines the term *e-signature* as "an electronic sound, symbol, or process attached to or logically associated with a record and executed or adopted by a person with the intent to sign the record."
	6. Although most states have laws governing e-signatures, these laws are not uniform. The UETA provides for the validity of e-signatures and encourages uniformity among the states.
	7. Federal law on e-signatures and e-documents, such as the Electronic Signatures in Global and National Commerce Act (E-SIGN Act) of 2000, gave validity to e-signatures by providing that no contract, record, or signature may be "denied legal effect" solely because it is in an electronic form.
	8. Under the Uniform Electronic Transactions Act (UETA), contracts entered into online, as well as other electronic records relating to a transaction, are presumed to be valid. The UETA does not apply to transactions governed by the UCC or to wills or testamentary trusts.

For Review

1. How do Article 2 and Article 2A of the UCC differ? What types of transactions does each article cover?
2. In a sales contract, if an offeree includes additional or different terms in an acceptance, will a contract result? If so, what happens to these terms?
3. What remedies are available to a seller or lessor when the buyer or lessee breaches the contract? What remedies are available to a buyer or lessee if the seller or lessor breaches the contract?
4. What implied warranties arise under the UCC?
5. What are some important clauses to include when making offers to form electronic contracts, or e-contracts?

Questions and Case Problems

11–1. Offer and Acceptance. A. B. Zook, Inc., is a manufacturer of washing machines. Over the telephone, Zook offers to sell Radar Appliances one hundred model Z washers at a price of $150 per unit. Zook orally agrees to keep this offer open for ninety days. Radar tells Zook that the offer appears to be a good one and that it will let Zook know of its acceptance within the next two to three weeks. One week later, Zook sends, and Radar receives, notice that Zook has withdrawn its offer. Radar immediately thereafter telephones Zook and accepts the $150-per-unit offer. Zook claims, first, that no sales contract was ever formed between it and Radar and, second, that if there is a contract, the contract is unenforceable. Discuss Zook's contentions.

Question with Sample Answer

11–2. Anne is a reporter for *Daily Business Journal,* a print publication consulted by investors and other businesspersons. She often uses the Internet to conduct research for the articles that she writes for the publication. While visiting the Web site of Cyberspace Investments Corp., Anne reads a pop-up window that states, "Our business newsletter, *E-Commerce Weekly,* is available at a one-year subscription rate of $5 per issue. To subscribe, enter your e-mail address below and click 'SUBSCRIBE.' By subscribing, you agree to the terms of the subscriber's agreement. To read this agreement, click 'AGREEMENT.' " Anne enters her e-mail address, but does not click on "AGREEMENT" to read the terms. Has Anne entered into an enforceable contract to pay for *E-Commerce Weekly?* Explain.

For a sample answer to Question 11–2, go to Appendix I at the end of this text.

11–3. Remedies. McDonald has contracted to purchase five hundred pairs of shoes from Vetter. Vetter manufactures the shoes and tenders delivery to McDonald. McDonald accepts the shipment. Later, on inspection, McDonald discovers that ten pairs of the shoes are poorly made and will have to be sold to customers as seconds. If McDonald decides to keep all five hundred pairs of shoes, what remedies are available to her? Discuss.

11–4. Warranty Disclaimers. Roger's Fence, Inc., bought a wheel loader made by Hyundai Construction Equipment, U.S.A., Inc., from Abele Tractor and Equipment Co. in Syracuse, New York. Abele faxed the purchase agreement to the vice president of Roger's. The agreement stated, in capital letters directly above the signature line, that the warranty terms were on the reverse side. On the reverse side, Abele disclaimed all implied warranties and limited damages to the repair or replacement of defective parts for two years or 3,000 hours of operation, whichever came first. The reverse side, however, was not faxed to Roger's, whose vice president nevertheless signed a delivery report indicating that he had reviewed and understood the warranty coverage. Certain repairs were made during the warranty period, and after 3,000 hours, the wheel loader was still operating properly. Later, when it broke down, Roger's filed a suit in a New York state court against Abele and Hyundai, alleging, in part, that the warranty disclaimers were invalid. What are the arguments for and against the position of Roger's? In whose favor should the court rule? Why? [*Roger's Fence, Inc. v. Abele Tractor and Equipment Co.,* 26 A.D.3d 788, 809 N.Y.S.2d 712 (4 Dept. 2006)]

Case Problem with Sample Answer

11–5. In 1998, Johnson Controls, Inc. (JCI), began buying auto parts from Q.C. Onics Ventures, LP. For each part, JCI would inform Onics of its need and ask the price. Onics would analyze the specifications, contact its suppliers, and respond with a formal quotation. A quote listed a part's number and description, the price per unit, and an estimate of units available for a given year. A quote did not state payment terms, an acceptance date, timing of performance, warranties, or quantities. JCI would select a supplier and issue a purchase order for a part. The purchase order required the seller to supply all of JCI's requirements for the part but gave the buyer the right to end the deal at any time. Using this procedure, JCI issued hundreds of purchase orders. In July 2001, JCI terminated its relationship with Onics and began buying parts through another supplier. Onics filed a suit in a federal district court against Johnson, alleging breach of contract. Which documents—the price quotations or the purchase orders—constituted offers? Which were acceptances? What effect would the answers to these questions have on the result in this case? Explain. [*Q.C. Onics Ventures, LP v. Johnson Controls, Inc.*, __ F.Supp.2d __ (N.D.Ind. 2006)]

After you have answered Problem 11–5, compare your answer with the sample answer given on the Web site that accompanies this text. Go to www.cengage.com/blaw/let, select "Chapter 11," and click on "Case Problem with Sample Answer."

11–6. Online Acceptances. Internet Archive (IA) is devoted to preserving a record of resources on the Internet for future generations. IA uses the "Wayback Machine" to automatically browse Web sites and reproduce their contents in an archive. IA does not ask the owners' permission before copying their material but will remove it on request. Suzanne Shell, a resident of Colorado, owns **www.profane-justice.org**, which is dedicated to providing information to individuals accused of child abuse or neglect. The site warns, "IF YOU COPY OR DISTRIBUTE ANYTHING ON THIS SITE YOU ARE ENTERING INTO A CONTRACT." The terms, which can be accessed only by clicking on a link, include, among other charges, a fee of $5,000 for each page copied "in advance of printing." Neither the warning nor the terms require a user to indicate assent. When Shell discovered that the Wayback Machine had copied the contents of her site—approximately eighty-seven times between May 1999 and October 2004—she asked IA to remove the copies from its archive and pay her $100,000. IA removed the copies and filed a suit in a federal district court against Shell, who responded, in part, with a counterclaim for breach of contract. IA filed a motion to dismiss this claim. Did IA contract with Shell? Explain. [*Internet Archive v. Shell*, 505 F.Supp.2d 755 (D.Colo. 2007)]

11–7. Contractual Provisions Affecting Remedies. Nomo Agroindustrial Sa De CV is a farm company based in Mexico that grows tomatoes, cucumbers, and other vegetables to sell in the United States. In the early 2000s, Nomo had problems when its tomato plants contracted a disease: tomato spotted wilt virus (TSWV). To obtain a crop that was resistant to TSWV, Nomo contacted Enza Zaden North America, Inc., an international corporation

that manufactures seeds. Enza's brochures advertised—and Enza told Nomo—that its Caiman variety was resistant to TSWV. Based on these assurances, Nomo bought Caiman seeds. The invoice, which Nomo's representative signed, limited any damages to the purchase price of the seeds. The plants germinated from the Caiman seeds contracted TSWV, destroying Nomo's entire tomato crop. Nomo filed a suit in a federal district court against Enza, seeking to recover for the loss. Enza argued, in part, that any damages were limited to the price of the seeds. Can parties agree to limit their remedies under the UCC? If so, what are Nomo's best arguments against the enforcement of the limitations clause in Enza's invoice? What should the court rule on this issue? Why? [*Nomo Agroindustrial Sa De CV v. Enza Zaden North America, Inc.*, 492 F.Supp.2d 1175 (D.Ariz. 2007)]

A Question of Ethics

11–8. Scotwood Industries, Inc., sells calcium chloride flake for use in ice-melt products. Between July and September 2004, Scotwood delivered thirty-seven shipments of flake to Frank Miller & Sons, Inc. After each delivery, Scotwood billed Miller, which paid thirty-five of the invoices and processed 30 to 50 percent of the flake. In August, Miller began complaining about the quality. Scotwood assured Miller that it would remedy the situation. Finally, in October, Miller told Scotwood, "This is totally unacceptable. We are willing to discuss Scotwood picking up the material." Miller claimed that the flake was substantially defective because it was chunked. Calcium chloride maintains its purity for up to five years but chunks if it is exposed to and absorbs moisture, making it unusable. In response to Scotwood's suit to collect payment on the unpaid invoices, Miller filed a counterclaim in a federal district court for breach of contract, seeking to recover based on revocation of acceptance, among other things. [*Scotwood Industries, Inc. v. Frank Miller & Sons, Inc.*, 435 F.Supp.2d 1160 (D.Kan. 2006)]

1. What is revocation of acceptance? How does a buyer effectively exercise this option? Do the facts in this case support this theory as a ground for Miller to recover damages? Why or why not?
2. Is there an ethical basis for allowing a buyer to revoke acceptance of goods and recover damages? If so, is there an ethical limit to this right? Discuss.

Video Question

11–9. Go to this text's Web site at **www.cengage.com/blaw/let** and select "Chapter 11." Click on "Video Questions" and view the video titled *E-Contracts: Agreeing Online*. Then answer the following questions.

1. According to the instructor in the video, what is the key factor in determining whether a particular term in an online agreement is enforceable?

2. Suppose that you click on "I accept" in order to download software from the Internet. You do not read the terms of the agreement before accepting it, even though you know that such agreements often contain forum-selection and arbitration clauses. The software later causes irreparable harm to your computer system, and you want to sue. When you go to the Web site and view the agreement, however, you discover that a choice-of-law clause in the contract specifies that the law of Nigeria controls. Is this term enforceable? Is it a term that should be reasonably expected in an online contract?

3. Does it matter what the term actually says if it is a type of term that one could reasonably expect to be in a contract? What arguments can be made for and against enforcing a choice-of-law clause in an online contract?

Critical-Thinking Technological Question

11–10. Delta Co. buys accounting software from Omega Corp. On the outside of the software box, on the inside cover of the instruction manual, and on the first screen that appears each time the program is accessed is a license that claims to cover the use of the product. The license also includes a limitation on Omega's liability arising from the use of the software. One year later, Delta discovers that the software has a bug that has imposed on Delta a financial loss. Delta files a suit against Omega. Is the limitation-of-liability clause on the software box enforceable?

Interacting with the Internet

For updated links to resources available on the Web, as well as a variety of other materials, visit this text's Web site at

www.cengage.com/blaw/let

For information about the National Conference of Commissioners on Uniform State Laws (NCCUSL) and links to online uniform acts, go to

www.nccusl.org

Cornell University's Legal Information Institute offers online access to the UCC, as well as to UCC articles as enacted by particular states and proposed revisions to articles, at

www.law.cornell.edu/ucc/index.html

PRACTICAL INTERNET EXERCISES

Go to this text's Web site at **www.cengage.com/blaw/let**, select "Chapter 11," and click on "Practical Internet Exercises." There you will find the following Internet research exercises that you can perform to learn more about topics covered in this chapter.

Practical Internet Exercise 11–1: LEGAL PERSPECTIVE—E-Contract Formation
Practical Internet Exercise 11–2: MANAGEMENT PERSPECTIVE—A Checklist for Sales Contracts

BEFORE THE TEST

Go to this text's Web site at **www.cengage.com/blaw/let**, select "Chapter 11," and click on "Interactive Quizzes." You will find a number of interactive questions relating to this chapter.

Chapter 12

Strict Liability and Product Liability

CHAPTER OBJECTIVES

After reading this chapter, you should be able to answer the following questions:

1. What is meant by strict liability?

2. How can negligence and misrepresentation provide a basis for a product liability action?

3. Can a manufacturer be held liable to any person who suffers an injury proximately caused by the manufacturer's negligently made product?

4. What are the elements of a cause of action in strict product liability?

5. What defenses to liability can be raised in a product liability lawsuit?

CONTENTS

" *If the nature of a thing is such that it is reasonably certain to place life and limb in peril when negligently made, it is then a thing of danger.* "

— BENJAMIN N. CARDOZO,
1870–1938 (Associate Justice of the United States Supreme Court, 1932–1938)

STRICT LIABILITY

Liability regardless of fault. Strict liability may be imposed in cases involving abnormally dangerous activities, dangerous animals, or defective products.

PRODUCT LIABILITY

The legal liability of manufacturers, sellers, and lessors of goods to consumers, users, and bystanders for injuries or damages that are caused by the goods.

The intentional torts and torts of negligence discussed in Chapter 5 involve acts that depart from a reasonable standard of care, and cause injuries. In this chapter, we look at another category of tort—**strict liability,** or liability without fault. Under the doctrine of strict liability, a person who engages in certain activities can be held responsible for harm that results to others even if the person used the utmost care. We open this chapter with an examination of the doctrine of strict liability.

We then look at an area of tort law of particular importance to businesspersons—product liability. **Product liability** refers to the liability incurred by manufacturers and sellers of products when defects in the products cause injury or property damage to consumers, users, or bystanders (people in the vicinity of the product).

As indicated in the chapter-opening quotation, a court can hold that a product is unreasonably dangerous because of a manufacturer's negligence when making it. The injured party can bring a lawsuit against the manufacturer based on the tort theory of negligence, discussed in Chapter 5. Product liability cases may also involve intentional tort theories and contract law claims, including fraudulent misrepresentation and breach of warranty. Frequently, product liability lawsuits allege strict product liability, and the injured party claims that the product was unreasonably dangerous due to a manufacturing defect, a design defect, or an inadequate warning. We discuss various theories of product liability in this chapter.

STRICT LIABILITY

Under the doctrine of strict liability, liability for injury is imposed for reasons other than fault. **EXAMPLE #1** The modern concept of strict liability traces its origins, in part, to the 1868 English case of *Rylands v. Fletcher.*[1] In the coal-mining

---

1. 3 L.R.–E & I App. [Law Reports, English & Irish Appeal Cases] (H.L. [House of Lords] 1868).

area of Lancashire, England, the Rylands, who were mill owners, had constructed a reservoir on their land. Water from the reservoir broke through a filled-in shaft of an abandoned coal mine nearby and flooded the connecting passageways in an active coal mine owned by Fletcher. Fletcher sued the Rylands, and the court held that the defendants (the Rylands) were liable, even though the circumstances did not fit within existing tort liability theories. The court held that a "person who for his own purposes brings on his land and collects and keeps there anything likely to do mischief if it escapes . . . is *prima facie* [on initial examination] answerable for all the damage which is the natural consequence of its escape." □

British courts liberally applied the doctrine that emerged from the *Rylands v. Fletcher* case. At first, few U.S. courts accepted this doctrine, presumably because the courts were worried about its effect on the expansion of American business. Today, however, the doctrine of strict liability is the norm rather than the exception.

Abnormally Dangerous Activities

Strict liability for damages proximately caused by an abnormally dangerous, or ultrahazardous, activity is one application of strict liability. Courts apply the doctrine of strict liability in these situations because of the extreme risk of the activity. Abnormally dangerous activities are those that involve a high risk of serious harm to persons or property that cannot be completely guarded against by the exercise of reasonable care—activities such as blasting or storing explosives. **EXAMPLE #2** Even if blasting with dynamite is performed with all reasonable care, there is still a risk of injury. Balancing that risk against the potential for harm, it seems reasonable to ask the person engaged in the activity to pay for injuries caused by that activity. Although there is no fault, there is still responsibility because of the dangerous nature of the undertaking. □

Other Applications of Strict Liability

Persons who keep wild animals are strictly liable for any harm inflicted by the animals. The basis for applying strict liability is that wild animals, should they escape from confinement, pose a serious risk of harm to persons in the vicinity. An owner of domestic animals (such as dogs, cats, cows, or sheep) may be strictly liable for harm caused by those animals if the owner knew, or should have known, that the animals were dangerous or had a propensity to harm others.

A significant application of strict liability is in the area of product liability—liability of manufacturers and sellers for harmful or defective products. Liability here is a matter of social policy and is based on two factors: (1) the manufacturing company can better bear the cost of injury because it can spread the cost throughout society by increasing prices of goods, and (2) the manufacturing company is making a profit from its activities and therefore should bear the cost of injury as an operating expense. We discuss product liability in greater detail throughout the remainder of this chapter.

PRODUCT LIABILITY

Those who make, sell, or lease goods can be held liable for physical harm or property damage caused by those goods to a consumer, user, or bystander. This is called product liability. Product liability claims may be based on the warranty theories discussed in Chapter 11, as well as on the theories of negligence, misrepresentation, and strict liability. We look here at product liability based on negligence and misrepresentation.

Negligence

Chapter 5 defined *negligence* as the failure to exercise the degree of care that a reasonable, prudent person would have exercised under the circumstances. If a manufacturer fails to exercise "due care" to make a product safe, a person who is injured by the product may sue the manufacturer for negligence.

Due Care Must Be Exercised   The manufacturer must exercise due care in designing the product, selecting the materials, using the appropriate production process, assembling the product, and placing adequate warnings on the label informing the user of dangers of which an ordinary person might not be aware. The duty of care also extends to the inspection and testing of any purchased products that are used in the final product sold by the manufacturer.

Privity of Contract Not Required   A product liability action based on neg-ligence does not require *privity of contract* between the injured plaintiff and the defendant manufacturer. As mentioned in Chapter 10, *privity of contract* refers to the relationship that exists between the promisor and the promisee of a contract; privity is the reason that only the parties to a contract can enforce that contract. In the context of product liability law, privity is not required. This means that a person who was injured by a product need not be the one who actually pur-chased the product—that is, need not be in privity—to maintain a negligence suit against the manufacturer or seller of a defective product. A manufacturer is liable for its failure to exercise due care to *any* person who sustains an injury proximately caused by a negligently made (defective) product.

Relative to the long history of the common law, this exception to the privity requirement is a fairly recent development, dating to the early part of the twen-tieth century. A leading case in this respect is *MacPherson v. Buick Motor Co.*, which we present as this chapter's *Landmark in the Legal Environment* feature.

Misrepresentation

When a fraudulent misrepresentation has been made to a user or consumer, and that misrepresentation ultimately results in an injury, the basis of liability may be the tort of fraud. For example, the intentional mislabeling of packaged cos-metics or the intentional concealment of a product's defects would constitute fraudulent misrepresentation. The misrepresentation must be of a material fact, and the seller must have had the intent to induce the buyer's reliance on the misrepresentation. Misrepresentation on a label or advertisement is enough to show an intent to induce the reliance of anyone who may use the product. In addition, the buyer must have relied on the misrepresentation.

STRICT PRODUCT LIABILITY

Under the doctrine of strict liability, parties may be liable for the results of their acts regardless of their intentions or their exercise of reasonable care. In addition, liability does not depend on privity of contract. The injured party does not have to be the buyer or a third party beneficiary, as required under contract warranty

MacPherson v. Buick Motor Co. (1916)

In the landmark case of *MacPherson v. Buick Motor Co.,*[a] the New York Court of Appeals—New York's highest court—dealt with the liability of a manufacturer that failed to exercise reasonable care in manufacturing a finished product.

Case Background

The case was brought by Donald MacPherson, who suffered injuries while riding in a Buick automobile that suddenly collapsed because one of the wheels was made of defective wood. The spokes crumbled into fragments, throwing MacPherson out of the vehicle and injuring him.

MacPherson had purchased the car from a Buick dealer, but he brought a lawsuit against the manufacturer, Buick Motor Company. Buick itself had not made the wheel but had bought it from another manufacturer. There was evidence, though, that the defects could have been discovered by a reasonable inspection by Buick and that no such inspection had taken place. MacPherson charged Buick with negligence for putting a human life in imminent danger.

The Issue before the Court and the Court's Ruling

The major issue before the court was whether Buick owed a duty of care to anyone except the immediate purchaser of the car—that is, the Buick dealer. In deciding the issue, Justice Benjamin Cardozo stated that "[i]f the nature of a thing is such that it is reasonably certain to place life and limb in peril when negligently made, it is then a thing of danger. . . . If to the element of danger there is added knowledge that the thing will be used by persons other than the purchaser, and used without new tests, then, irrespective of contract, the manufacturer of this thing of danger is under a duty to make it carefully."

a. 217 N.Y. 382, 111 N.E. 1050 (1916).

The court concluded that "[b]eyond all question, the nature of an automobile gives warning of probable danger if its construction is defective. This automobile was designed to go 50 miles an hour. Unless its wheels were sound and strong, injury was almost certain." Although Buick had not manufactured the wheel itself, the court held that Buick had a duty to inspect the wheels and that Buick "was responsible for the finished product." Therefore, Buick was liable to MacPherson for the injuries he sustained when he was thrown from the car.

APPLICATION TO TODAY'S LEGAL ENVIRONMENT

This landmark decision was a significant step in creating the legal environment of the modern world. Today, it is common for an automobile manufacturer to be held liable when its negligence causes a product user to be injured. As is often the situation, technological developments necessitated changes in the law. Had the courts continued to require privity of contract in product liability cases, today's legal landscape would be quite different indeed. Certainly, fewer cases would be pending before the courts; and just as certainly, many purchasers of products, including automobiles, would have little recourse for obtaining legal redress for injuries caused by those products.

RELEVANT WEB SITES

To locate information on the Web concerning the *MacPherson* decision, go to this text's Web site at **www.cengage.com/blaw/let**, select "Chapter 12," and click on "URLs for Landmarks."

theory. In the 1960s, courts applied the doctrine of strict liability in several land-mark cases involving manufactured goods, and it has since become a common method of holding manufacturers liable.

Strict Product Liability and Public Policy

The law imposes strict product liability as a matter of public policy. This public policy rests on the threefold assumption that (1) consumers should be protected against unsafe products; (2) manufacturers and distributors should not escape liability for faulty products simply because they are not in privity of contract with the ultimate user of those products; and (3) manufacturers, sellers, and lessors of products are generally in a better position than consumers to bear the costs associated with injuries caused by their products—costs that they can ulti-mately pass on to all consumers in the form of higher prices.

California was the first state to impose strict product liability in tort on manufacturers. In a landmark 1963 decision, *Greenman v. Yuba Power Products, Inc.,*[2] the California Supreme Court set out the reason for applying tort law rather than contract law in cases involving consumers injured by defective products. According to the court, the "purpose of such liability is to [e]nsure that the costs of injuries resulting from defective products are borne by the manufacturers . . . rather than by the injured persons who are powerless to protect themselves."

Damages Available in Strict Product Liability Actions

Suppose that Ford Motor Company installs Firestone tires on all new Ford Explorers. The tires are defective and cause numerous accidents involving people driving new Explorers. Who should bear the costs of the resulting injuries (Ford, Firestone, or the drivers' insurance companies) and why? (AP Photo/Eric Gay)

Today, a majority of states allow strict product liability actions, but a few states award damages only for personal injuries (rather than property damage). In addition, some states now have laws that limit the amount of noneconomic damages that can be awarded for such items as pain and suffering, emotional distress, disfigurement, and loss of consortium (losing the emotional and physical benefits of a spousal relationship).

Punitive damages may also be available when the defendant's conduct in putting an unsafe product on the market was intentional or reprehensible (highly unacceptable and deserving of strong censure). If the injured person can show that the manufacturer or seller had a reckless disregard for safety, for example, he or she may be entitled to punitive damages. The amount of punitive damages awarded cannot be grossly excessive, however, or it will violate the due process standards of the U.S. Constitution (as discussed in Chapters 4 and 5).

RECALL

Recall from Chapter 5 that punitive damages are designed to punish the defendant and deter others from engaging in similar conduct in the future.

In the following case, the court had to decide whether the punitive damages that were awarded in a product liability case were excessive.

---

2. 59 Cal.2d 57, 377 P.2d 897, 27 Cal.Rptr. 697 (1963).

Case 12.1 **Buell-Wilson v. Ford Motor Co.**

Court of Appeal, Fourth District, Division 1, California, 2008. 160 Cal.App.4th 1107, 73 Cal.Rptr.3d 277.

COMPANY PROFILE Henry Ford founded the Ford Motor Company (**www.ford.com**) in Dearborn, Michigan, in 1903 to design and make a mass-produced automobile. Five years later, Ford introduced the Model T, which was made affordable by the company's efficient use of assembly lines. By 1920, 60 percent of all of the vehicles on the road were made by Ford. Today, Ford is the world's largest maker of pickup trucks and

the second-largest producer of cars. Ford brand names include Aston Martin, Jaguar, Lincoln, Mercury, and Volvo. Its most popular models are Ford Taurus cars and F-Series pickup trucks. Ford also makes the Ford Explorer.

BACKGROUND AND FACTS Benetta Buell-Wilson was driving her 1997 Ford Explorer when a piece of metal came off another vehicle and headed for her windshield. She swerved to avoid being hit and lost control, and her car rolled four and a half times. During the rollover, the roof collapsed almost a foot. The force from the collapsing roof severed her spine, leaving her with no control of her body from the waist down. She had many surgeries and suffers constant pain likely to worsen over time. She requires extensive care. Evidence showed the Ford had two major defects: (1) a design that made it unstable and prone to rollover and (2) an inadequately supported roof likely to collapse on rollover. Records showed that Ford had long been aware of these problems. The jury found the defects were substantial factors in causing the injuries. Buell-Wilson was awarded $4.6 million for economic loss, $105 million for noneconomic losses, and

$246 million in punitive damages. Her husband was awarded $13 million for loss of consortium damages. The trial judge reduced the noneconomic damages to $65 million and reduced punitive damages to $75 million. Ford appealed, but the California Supreme Court refused to review the decision. The United States Supreme Court vacated the judgment and remanded the case for reconsideration in light of other recent decisions by the Court concerning excessive damages awards.

IN THE WORDS OF THE COURT . . . *NARES*, J. [Judge]

* * * *

Ford characterizes the jury's award to the Wilsons of $118 million in noneconomic damages ($105 million to Mrs. Wilson + $13 million to Mr. Wilson) and the court-reduced award of approximately $70 million (approximately $65 million to Mrs. Wilson + $5 million to Mr. Wilson) as "irrational, punitive, and the clear product of passion and prejudice" and asserts that the evidence "does not come close to supporting this unprecedented award." Although Mrs. Wilson's injuries were catastrophic, analyzing all appropriate factors, reviewing the trial court record, and using our collective experience, we conclude we must reduce the noneconomic damage award as excessive and the product of passion and prejudice.

In discussing noneconomic damages in his closing argument, counsel for the Wilsons described some of the matters that could be included in such an award. This included past and future physical pain, mental suffering, and loss of enjoyment of life. Counsel then suggested a method for calculating these numbers, taking into account the past injury, as well as future injuries over her 33-year life expectancy. * * * Thus, counsel was requesting the jury award noneconomic damages to Mrs. Wilson in an amount three to four times the amount they awarded in economic damages, or $13.8 to $18.4 million.

We conclude the award of noneconomic damages to Mrs. Wilson * * * was excessive, and the facts of this case instead support an award of $18 million, within the ratio/range requested by the Wilsons' counsel. * * * [There] is compelling evidence the jury acted out of "passion and prejudice" in awarding noneconomic damages.

Ford argues that the amount of the punitive damages awarded to the Wilsons is excessive under the federal due process clause of the 14th Amendment to the United States Constitution. We conclude that, after reducing the noneconomic damages award to Mrs. Wilson to $18 million, the award of punitive damages is excessive and is, therefore, reduced to $55 million, an approximate two-to-one ratio to the total compensatory damages award ($4.6 million in economic damages + $18 million in noneconomic damages + $5 million in loss of consortium damages = $27.6 million × 2 = $55.2 million).

The United States Supreme Court and the California Supreme Court have stated there are three factors to consider in determining whether the amount of a punitive damages award comports with the federal due process clause: "(1) the degree of reprehensibility of the defendant's misconduct; (2) the disparity between the * * * harm suffered by the plaintiff and the punitive damages award; and (3) the difference between the punitive damages [and comparable civil penalties where available]." [Emphasis added.]

Based on our *de novo* review [looking at everything anew] of the record, we conclude that the reprehensibility of Ford's conduct was high, given the catastrophic nature of Mrs. Wilson's injuries, Ford's reckless disregard for the safety of others, the repeated nature of Ford's conduct, and the fact that Ford's acts were intentional.

Based on the foregoing factors, and using our combined experience and judgment, we conclude that a two-to-one ratio of punitive damages to compensatory damages is sufficient to punish Ford and deter it from similar conduct in the future. This ratio is

CASE 12.1—CONTINUED

proportionate to the degree of harm suffered and the substantial award of compensatory damages. An award exceeding a two-to-one ratio would exceed the constitutional maximum that could be awarded under the facts of this case. Accordingly, we reduce the punitive damage award to $55 million, approximately two times the total compensatory damage award to the Wilsons.

DECISION AND REMEDY   The state court of appeal concluded that the jury had acted with passion and prejudice when it imposed noneconomic damages far above those requested by the plaintiff, so those damages were reduced. The court determined that Ford acted intentionally in placing consumers at risk, so punitive damages were justified. Those damages were calculated to be double the other damages as suggested by the Supreme Court in recent rulings on the limits of punitive damages.[a]

THE ETHICAL DIMENSION   The court stated that punitive damages are designed to punish the defendant for reprehensible behavior. If so, should the punitive damages go to one plaintiff or be shared by all buyers of Ford products or by the general public?

THE LEGAL ENVIRONMENT DIMENSION   The appellate court also indicated that the plaintiff had been "healthy prior to the accident." Why did the court include this statement in its opinion?

a. The Supreme Court of California granted review of this case and had not yet issued a decision at the time this book went to press [187 P.3d 887, 80 Cal.Rptr.3d 27 (2008)].

Requirements for Strict Product Liability

The courts often look to the *Restatements of the Law* for guidance, even though the *Restatements* are not binding authorities (see Chapter 1). Section 402A of the *Restatement (Second) of Torts,* which was originally issued in 1964, has become a widely accepted statement of the liabilities of sellers of goods (including manufacturers, processors, assemblers, packagers, bottlers, wholesalers, distributors, retailers, and lessors).

The bases for an action in strict liability as set forth in Section 402A of the *Restatement (Second) of Torts,* and as commonly applied, can be summarized as a series of six requirements, which are listed here. Depending on the jurisdiction, if these requirements are met, a manufacturer's liability to an injured party can be virtually unlimited.

1. The product must be in a *defective condition* when the defendant sells it.
2. The defendant must normally be engaged in the *business of selling* (or otherwise distributing) that product.
3. The product must be *unreasonably dangerous* to the user or consumer because of its defective condition (in most states).
4. The plaintiff must incur *physical harm* to self or property by use or consumption of the product.
5. The defective condition must be the *proximate cause* of the injury or damage.
6. The *goods must not have been substantially changed* from the time the product was sold to the time the injury was sustained.

Proving a Defective Condition   Under these requirements, in any action against a manufacturer, seller, or lessor, the plaintiff does not have to show why or in what manner the product became defective. The plaintiff does, however, have to prove that the product was defective at the time it left the hands of the seller or lessor and that this defective condition made it "unreasonably dangerous" to the user or consumer. Unless evidence can be presented that will support the conclusion that the product was defective when it was sold or leased, the plaintiff normally will not succeed. If the product was delivered in a safe condition and subsequent mishandling made it harmful to the user, the seller or lessor is not strictly liable.

Unreasonably Dangerous Products   The *Restatement* recognizes that many products cannot possibly be made entirely safe for all consumption, and thus holds sellers or lessors liable only for products that are *unreasonably* dangerous. A court may consider a product so defective as to be an **unreasonably dangerous product** in either of the following situations:

1. The product is dangerous beyond the expectation of the ordinary consumer.
2. A less dangerous alternative was economically feasible for the manufacturer, but the manufacturer failed to produce it.

As will be discussed next, a product may be unreasonably dangerous due to a flaw in the manufacturing process, a design defect, or an inadequate warning.

Product Defects—Restatement (Third) of Torts

Because Section 402A of the *Restatement (Second) of Torts* did not clearly define such terms as "defective" and "unreasonably dangerous," they were interpreted differently by different courts. In 1997, to address these concerns, the American Law Institute issued the *Restatement (Third) of Torts: Products Liability.* This *Restatement* defines the three types of product defects that have traditionally been recognized in product liability law—manufacturing defects, design defects, and inadequate warnings.

Manufacturing Defects   According to Section 2(a) of the *Restatement (Third) of Torts: Products Liability,* a product "contains a manufacturing defect when the product departs from its intended design even though all possible care was exercised in the preparation and marketing of the product." Basically, a manufacturing defect is a departure from a product's design specifications that results in products that are physically flawed, damaged, or incorrectly assembled. A glass bottle that is made too thin and explodes in a consumer's face is an example of a product with a manufacturing defect. Liability is imposed on the manufacturer (and on the wholesaler and retailer) regardless of whether the manufacturer's quality control efforts were "reasonable." The idea behind holding defendants strictly liable for manufacturing defects is to encourage greater investment in product safety and stringent quality control standards.

EXAMPLE #3   Kevin Schmude had just purchased an eight-foot stepladder that he was using to install radio-frequency shielding in a hospital room. While Schmude was standing on the ladder, it collapsed, and he was seriously injured. He filed a lawsuit against the ladder's maker, Tricam Industries, Inc., based on a manufacturing defect. Experts testified that when the ladder was assembled, the preexisting holes in the top cap did not properly line up with the holes in the rear right rail and backing plate. As a result of the misalignment, the rivet at the rear legs of the ladder was more likely to fail. A jury concluded that this manufacturing defect made the ladder unreasonably dangerous and awarded Schmude more than $677,000 in damages.[3] □

UNREASONABLY DANGEROUS PRODUCT

In product liability law, a product that is defective to the point of threatening a consumer's health and safety. A product will be considered unreasonably dangerous if it is dangerous beyond the expectation of the ordinary consumer or if a less dangerous alternative was economically feasible for the manufacturer, but the manufacturer failed to produce it.

Sony manufactured defective lithium-ion cell batteries, some of which caught on fire. Dell and other computer companies bought these Sony batteries for use in their laptop computers. To what extent is Sony liable? To what extent are Dell and other laptop makers who purchased these batteries liable?
(Photo Courtesy of theinquirer.net)

---

3. *Schmude v. Tricam Industries, Inc.,* 550 F.Supp.2d 846 (E.D.Wis. 2008).

Design Defects   Unlike a product with a manufacturing defect, a product with a design defect is made in conformity with the manufacturer's design specifications but nevertheless results in injury to the user because the design itself was improper. The product's design creates an unreasonable risk to the user. A product "is defective in design when the foreseeable risks of harm posed by the product could have been reduced or avoided by the adoption of a reasonable alternative design by the seller or other distributor, or a predecessor in the commercial chain of distribution, and the omission of the alternative design renders the product not reasonably safe."[4]

Test for Design Defects   To successfully assert a design defect, a plaintiff has to show that a reasonable alternative design was available and that the defendant's failure to adopt the alternative design rendered the product not reasonably safe. In other words, a manufacturer or other defendant is liable only when the harm was reasonably preventable. **EXAMPLE #4** Gillespie, who cut off several of his fingers while operating a table saw, alleged that the blade guards on the saw were defectively designed. At the trial, however, an expert testified that the alternative design for blade guards used for table saws could not have been used for the particular cut that Gillespie was performing at the time he was injured. The court found that Gillespie's claim that the blade guards were defective failed because there was no proof that a guard with a "better" design would have prevented his injury.[5] □

Factors to Be Considered   According to the *Restatement,* a court can consider a broad range of factors, including the magnitude and probability of the foreseeable risks, as well as the relative advantages and disadvantages of the product as it was designed and as it could have been designed. Basically, most courts engage in a risk-utility analysis, determining whether the risk of harm from the product as designed outweighs its utility to the user and to the public.

EXAMPLE #5 A nine-year-old child finds rat poison in a cupboard at the local boys' club and eats it, thinking that it is candy. The child dies, and his parents file a suit against the manufacturer alleging that the rat poison was defectively designed because it looked like candy and was supposed to be placed in cupboards. In this situation, a court would probably consider factors such as the foreseeability that a child would think the rat poison was candy, the gravity of the potential harm from consumption, the availability of an alternative design, and the usefulness of the product. If the parents could offer sufficient evidence for a reasonable person to conclude that the harm was reasonably preventable, then the manufacturer could be held liable. □

Can videos, video games, and Internet transmissions that contain violence be deemed "defective products"? For a discussion of this question, see this chapter's *Online Developments* feature.

Segway, Inc., manufacturer of the Segway® Personal Transporter, voluntarily recalled all of its transporters to fix a software problem that could have led to users falling and injuring themselves. If a person was injured by such a malfunction, what would the victim have to prove to establish that the device had a design defect?

(Nelson Pavlosky/Creative Commons)

---

4. *Restatement (Third) of Torts: Products Liability,* Section 2(b).
5. *Gillespie v. Sears, Roebuck & Co.,* 386 F.3d 21 (1st Cir. 2004).

During the past decade, school shootings have led to lawsuits that pose a novel question for the courts: Can the producers and distributors of violence-laden media, such as video games and Internet transmissions, be held liable for the shootings? In one case, for example, the plaintiffs were the parents of several students who were killed by their classmate Michael Carneal in a 1997 high school shooting in Kentucky. The plaintiffs sued Meow Media, Inc., and other companies (the defendants), alleging that the defendants should be held liable for the shootings. The plaintiffs contended that the defendants' products—including videos, video games, and Internet transmissions—"desensitized" Carneal to violence. Carneal's indifference to violence, in turn, "caused" the shootings.

The Negligence Claim

One of the plaintiffs' claims was that the defendants had breached a duty of care by distributing such violent products and were thus negligent. The court, however, did not agree with the plaintiffs that the defendants owed a duty of care to the victims. Recall from Chapter 5 that a defendant's duty of care extends only to those who are injured as a result of a foreseeable risk. In the court's eyes, a school shooting was not a foreseeable risk for the defendants. Thus, the court dismissed the negligence claim.

Were the "Products" Defective?

The plaintiffs also alleged that the defendants should be held liable in strict product liability because the violence contained in their products rendered those products "defective." The court never reached the issue of whether the products were defective, however, because it concluded that the violence communicated by the videos, video games, and Internet transmissions was not a "product."

Although agreeing that videos and video games may be considered products for some purposes, the court found that the communications within those videos and games were not products for purposes of strict liability. The argument that an Internet transmission could constitute a product also failed. The plaintiffs had asserted that if electricity could be labeled a product, as it has been in some cases, then Internet transmissions, which can be characterized as a series of electrical impulses, should also be considered a product. The court pointed out, though, that the relevant state law defined the term *product* as something tangible—something that can be touched, felt, or otherwise perceived by the senses. The communicative element (ideas and images) of an Internet transmission was not a tangible object.

Furthermore, stated the court, even assuming that the videos, video games, and Internet transmissions were products, the plaintiffs could not succeed in a strict product liability action. For strict product liability to apply, the injuries complained of must have been caused by the products themselves. In this case, the injuries were caused not by the products but by Carneal's *reaction* to the products.[a]

> **FOR CRITICAL ANALYSIS** Another defense raised by the defendants in this case was that the expression in their videos, video games, and Internet transmissions was a protected form of speech under the First Amendment. Should such speech ever be restrained in the interests of protecting society against violence? Why or why not?

a. *James v. Meow Media, Inc.,* 300 F.3d 683 (6th Cir. 2002). For another case on this issue in which the court reached similar conclusions, see *Sanders v. Acclaim Entertainment, Inc.,* 188 F.Supp.2d 1264 (D.Colo. 2002).

In the following case, a smoker who developed lung cancer sued a cigarette manufacturer claiming, among other things, that there was a defect in the design of its cigarettes. The jury instruction given by the trial court and quoted by the appellate court shows the numerous factors that judges and juries consider in determining design defects.

Case 12.2 **Bullock v. Philip Morris USA, Inc.**

Court of Appeal of California,
Second District, Division 3, 2008.
159 Cal.App.4th 655, 71 Cal.Rptr.3d 775.

COMPANY PROFILE Philip Morris started as a tobacco products shop in London in 1847. Philip Morris & Co., Ltd.,

was incorporated in New York in 1902. It introduced the famous Marlboro cigarette in 1924. From 1954 on, it established itself on a worldwide basis. It is the largest seller of cigarettes in the United States. The company, along with other cigarette makers, has been the object of numerous lawsuits.

CASE 12.2–CONTINUED

CASE 12.2–CONTINUED

BACKGROUND AND FACTS   Jodie Bullock smoked cigarettes manufactured by Philip Morris for forty-five years, from 1956, when she was seventeen years old, until she was diagnosed with lung cancer in 2001. By the late 1950s, scientific professionals in the United States had proved that cigarette smoking caused lung cancer. Nonetheless, Philip Morris issued full-page announcements stating that there was no proof that cigarette smoking caused cancer and that "numerous scientists" questioned "the validity of the statistics themselves." Philip Morris's chief executive officer, Joseph Cullman III, stated on the television news program *Face the*

Nation (CBS, January 3, 1971), "We do not believe that cigarettes are hazardous; we don't accept that." Jodie Bullock sued Philip Morris in April 2001 seeking to recover damages for personal injuries based on product liability, among other claims. At trial, the jury found that there was a defect in the design of the cigarettes and that they had been negligently designed. It awarded Bullock $850,000 in compensatory damages, including $100,000 in noneconomic damages for pain and suffering, and later awarded her $28 million in punitive damages. Philip Morris appealed.

IN THE WORDS OF THE COURT . . . *CROSKEY*, J. [Judge]

*   *   *   *

Philip Morris heavily advertised its cigarettes on television in the 1950's and 1960's, until the federal government banned cigarette advertising on television in 1970. Television advertising had a particularly strong influence on youths under the age of 18, for whom there was a positive correlation between television viewing time and the incidence of smoking. Philip Morris's print advertisements for Marlboro and other cigarette brands in 1956, when Bullock began smoking at the age of 17, and generally in the years from 1954 to 1969, depicted handsome men and glamorous young women. Some advertisements featured slogans such as "Loved for Gentleness" and "'The <u>gentlest</u> cigarette you can smoke.'"

*   *   *   *

Philip Morris contends (1) the evidence failed to establish a design defect under the risk-benefit test because there is no substantial evidence that a safer alternative cigarette design was available, that the failure to use a safer design was a cause of Bullock's lung cancer, or that Bullock would have smoked a safer cigarette if it were available; (2) the evidence failed to establish a design defect under the consumer expectations test or liability based on a failure to warn because there is no substantial evidence that the ordinary consumer was unaware of the dangers of cigarette smoking.

*   *   *   *

A product is defective in design for purposes of tort liability if the benefits of the design do not outweigh the risk of danger inherent in the design, or if the product, used in an intended or reasonably foreseeable manner, has failed to perform as safely as an ordinary consumer would expect. [Emphasis added.]

Philip Morris challenges the finding of liability for design defect based on a risk-benefit theory by challenging the sufficiency of the evidence that a safer alternative design existed and the sufficiency of the evidence that its failure to use a safer alternative design caused Bullock's injuries. Philip Morris's argument is based on the premise that a plaintiff alleging a design defect based on a risk-benefit theory must prove that the defendant could have used a safer alternative design. The jury, however, was not so instructed. The court instructed the jury to determine whether the benefits of the design outweighed the risks by considering several factors, but did not instruct that any single factor was essential:

"In determining whether the benefits of the design outweigh its risks, you should consider, among other things, the gravity of the danger posed by the design, the likelihood that the danger would cause damage, the existence or nonexistence of warnings, the time of the manufacture, the financial cost of an improved design, and the adverse consequences to the product and the consumer that would result from an alternate design."

* * * We review the sufficiency of the evidence to support a verdict under the law stated in the instructions given, rather than under some other law on which the jury was not instructed. * * * Accordingly, we conclude that Philip Morris has shown no error with respect to the finding of liability for a design defect based on the risk-benefit test.

DECISION AND REMEDY   The Court of Appeal of California for the Second District affirmed the trial court's judgment as to the finding of liability. Philip Morris failed to show any error with respect to its liability based on a design defect.

WHAT IF THE FACTS WERE DIFFERENT?   Assume that Philip Morris had never publicly denied the scientific link between smoking and lung cancer. In other words, the company simply sold cigarettes without saying anything about the medical consequences of smoking. Do you think the jury award would have been the same? Explain your answer.

THE ETHICAL DIMENSION   Under what circumstances, if any, could Philip Morris have justified its continuing campaign to discredit the scientific arguments that linked smoking with lung cancer?

Inadequate Warnings   A product may also be deemed defective because of inadequate instructions or warnings. A product will be considered defective "when the foreseeable risks of harm posed by the product could have been reduced or avoided by the provision of reasonable instructions or warnings by the seller or other distributor, or a predecessor in the commercial chain of distribution, and the omission of the instructions or warnings renders the product not reasonably safe."[6]

Important factors for a court to consider include the risks of a product, the "content and comprehensibility" and "intensity of expression" of warnings and instructions, and the "characteristics of expected user groups."[7] A "reasonableness" test applies to determine if the warnings adequately alert consumers to the product's risks. For example, children would likely respond readily to bright, bold, simple warning labels, whereas educated adults might need more detailed information.

If a warning is provided with a product, can its manufacturer or seller assume that the warning will be read and obeyed? That was a question in the following case.

---

6. *Restatement (Third) of Torts: Products Liability,* Section 2(c).
7. *Restatement (Third) of Torts: Products Liability,* Section 2, Comment h.

Case 12.3 Crosswhite v. Jumpking, Inc.

United States District Court,
District of Oregon, 2006.
411 F.Supp.2d 1228.

BACKGROUND AND FACTS   Jumpking, Inc., makes "backyard" trampolines for consumer use. The trampolines are produced with nine warning labels affixed to various components. With each trampoline, Jumpking provides a large,

laminated warning placard that is designed for the consumer to attach to the metal frame near the ladder on which jumpers mount the trampoline. Jumpking also includes a *User Manual* and a videotape that explains and illustrates "safe and responsible" trampoline use. In 1999, Jack and Misty Urbach bought a round, fourteen-foot Jumpking trampoline from Costco, Inc., in Oregon. On May 11, 2002, sixteen-year-old

CASE 12.3–CONTINUED

Gary Crosswhite, who had six years' experience with trampolines, was jumping on the Urbachs' trampoline with another boy. Crosswhite attempted to perform a back flip. He fell and landed on his head and neck, fracturing his cervical spine, which resulted in paraplegia. Crosswhite filed a suit in a federal district court against Jumpking, grounded in strict liability and other product liability claims, alleging that his injuries were caused by inadequate warnings, among other things. Jumpking filed a motion for summary judgment.

IN THE WORDS OF THE COURT . . . *AIKEN*, J. [Judge]

* * * *

Uniform trampoline safety standards are published by the American Society for Testing and Materials (ASTM). The ASTM standards set forth specific warning language to accompany trampolines. The record supports defendant's [Jumpking's] allegation that the trampoline at issue, including the warning that accompanied it, complied with all ASTM standards relevant at the time. Moreover, the ASTM standards at that time did not require warnings against users performing somersaults (flips) and/or jumping with multiple people to appear on the trampoline itself[;] however, defendant did affix those warnings to the trampoline as well as on a large warning placard attached to the trampoline at the point of entry or mounting. Specifically, one warning attached to the trampoline frame leg stated:

> **! WARNING**
> **Do not land on head or neck.**
> **Paralysis or death can result, even if you land in the middle of the trampoline mat (bed).**
> **To reduce the chance of landing on your head or neck, do not do flips.**

Accompanying these warning labels is a "stick-figure" drawing of an individual landing on his head. The drawing is located above the warning language and is enclosed in a circular "x-ed" or "crossed-out" notation, commonly understood to mean that the conduct described should be avoided.

Another pair of warning labels affixed to the trampoline legs read:

> **! WARNING**
> **Only one person at a time on the trampoline. Multiple jumpers increase the chances of loss of control, collision, and falling off. This can result in broken head, neck, back, or leg.**

Accompanying these warnings and placed above the warning language is a drawing of two individuals jumping on a single trampoline, which is also enclosed in a "crossed out" or "x-ed" notation. These same warning labels warning users against performing flips or somersaults and against jumping with multiple people were also on the trampoline frame pad, the large 8″ × 11″ warning placard framed by the colors orange and yellow and attached to the trampoline frame at the point of entry, and in various places throughout the *User Manual*. The court notes that these warnings went beyond what was required by the ASTM safety standards.

Further, Jack Urbach testified that the warning placard, which specifically warns against both multiple jumping and performing flips or somersaults and the risk of paralysis, was included in the trampoline he purchased, and that he attached the placard to the trampoline upon its initial assembly. Urbach further testified that he had his entire family watch the safety video provided by defendant prior to assembling and using the trampoline.

* * * Defendant is entitled to assume that its many warnings will be read, watched, and heeded.

DECISION AND REMEDY The court issued a summary judgment in Jumpking's favor, holding that its warnings were "adequate as a matter of law." To prevent a product from being unreasonably dangerous, its seller may be required to include a warning about its use. When a warning is provided, the seller may reasonably assume that it will be read and followed, and a product with an adequate warning is not defective or unreasonably dangerous.

WHAT IF THE FACTS WERE DIFFERENT? If Crosswhite had proved that he had not seen, before his accident, the warnings that Jumpking provided, might the court have considered the trampoline defective or unreasonably dangerous?

THE ETHICAL DIMENSION Is the danger from jumping on a trampoline so obvious that the manufacturer should not be held liable for a user's injuries even if its product lacks warnings? Explain.

Obvious Risks There is no duty to warn about risks that are obvious or commonly known. Warnings about such risks do not add to the safety of a product and could even detract from it by making other warnings seem less significant. As will be discussed later in the chapter, the obviousness of a risk and a user's decision to proceed in the face of that risk may be a defense in a product liability suit based on an inadequate warning. Nevertheless, risks that may seem obvious to some users will not be obvious to all users, especially when the users are likely to be children. EXAMPLE #6 An eleven-year-old child dives into a shallow, above-ground pool, hits the bottom, and is paralyzed as a result. She later sues the pool maker. The manufacturer cannot escape liability for failing to warn about the hazards of diving into a pool simply by claiming that the risk was obvious.[8]□

Foreseeable Misuses Generally, a seller must warn those who purchase its product of the harm that can result from the foreseeable misuse of the product as well. The key is the foreseeability of the misuse. Sellers are not required to take precautions against every conceivable misuse of a product, just those that are foreseeable.

Market-Share Liability

Ordinarily, a plaintiff must prove that the defective product that caused his or her injury was the product of a specific defendant. In a few situations, however, courts have dropped this requirement when plaintiffs could not prove which of many distributors of a harmful product supplied the particular product that caused the injuries. EXAMPLE #7 A plaintiff who was a hemophiliac received injections of a blood protein known as antihemophiliac factor (AHF) concentrate. The plaintiff later tested positive for the AIDS (acquired immune deficiency syndrome) virus. Because it was not known which manufacturer was responsible for the particular AHF received by the plaintiff, the court held that all of the manufacturers of AHF could be held liable in proportion to each firm's respective share of the market under the theory of **market-share liability.**[9]□

MARKET-SHARE LIABILITY
Liability shared among all firms that manufactured and distributed a particular product during a certain period of time in proportion to the firms' respective shares of the market. Only some jurisdictions apply this theory and only when the true source of the harmful product is unidentifiable.

---

8. *Bunch v. Hoffinger Industries, Inc.,* 123 Cal.App.4th 1278, 20 Cal.Rptr.3d 780 (2004).
9. *Smith v. Cutter Biological, Inc.,* 72 Haw. 416, 823 P.2d 717 (1991); *Sutowski v. Eli Lilly & Co.,* 82 Ohio St.3d 347, 696 N.E.2d 187 (1998); and *In re Methyl Tertiary Butyl Ether ("MTBE") Products Liability Litigation,* 447 F.Supp.2d 289 (S.D.N.Y. 2006).

Courts in many jurisdictions do not recognize this theory of liability, believing that it deviates too significantly from traditional legal principles.[10] In jurisdictions that do recognize market-share liability, it is usually applied in cases involving drugs or chemicals, when it is difficult or impossible to determine which company made a particular product.

Other Applications of Strict Product Liability

Virtually all courts extend the strict liability of manufacturers and other sellers to injured bystanders. Thus, if a defective forklift that will not go into reverse injures a passerby, that individual can sue the manufacturer for product liability (and possibly bring a negligence action against the forklift operator as well).

Strict product liability also applies to suppliers of component parts. **EXAMPLE #8** General Motors buys brake pads from a subcontractor and puts them in Chevrolets without changing their composition. If those pads are defective, both the supplier of the brake pads and General Motors will be held strictly liable for the damages caused by the defects. □

DEFENSES TO PRODUCT LIABILITY

Defendants in product liability suits can raise a number of defenses. One defense, of course, is to show that there is no basis for the plaintiff's claim. For example, in a product liability case based on negligence, if a defendant can show that the plaintiff has *not* met the requirements (such as causation) for an action in negligence, generally the defendant will not be liable. In regard to strict product liability, a defendant can claim that the plaintiff failed to meet one of the requirements for an action in strict liability. For instance, if the defendant establishes that the goods have been altered, normally the defendant will not be held liable.[11] Another contention that defendants are now raising as a defense in product liability actions is preemption—that government regulations preempt claims for product liability. We discuss the ethical implications of such a defense in the *Insight into Ethics* feature that follows. Defendants may also assert the defenses discussed next.

Should companies be able to escape liability for defective products that were the subject of government regulation?

In today's world, the federal government has numerous regulations that attempt to ensure the safety of products distributed to the public (consumer protection legislation will be discussed in Chapter 20). Prior to 2008, a person who was injured by a product could assert a product liability claim regardless of whether the product was subject to

---

10. For the Illinois Supreme Court's position on market-share liability, see *Smith v. Eli Lilly & Co.,* 137 Ill.2d 222, 560 N.E.2d 324 (1990). Pennsylvania law also does not recognize market-share liability. See *Bortell v. Eli Lilly & Co.,* 406 F.Supp.2d 1 (D.D.C. 2005).
11. See, for example, *Edmondson v. Macclesfield L-P Gas Co.,* 642 S.E.2d 265 (N.C.App. 2007); and *Pichardo v. C. S. Brown Co.,* 35 A.D.3d 303, 827 N.Y.S.2d 131 (N.Y.App. 2006).

government regulations. Today, however, under the United States Supreme Court decision in *Riegel v. Medtronic, Inc.,*[12] the injured party may *not* be able to sue the manufacturer of defective products that are subject to federal regulatory schemes. Is it fair to deny an injured party relief from the company that made a defective product simply because the federal government was supposed to ensure the product's safety?

Medical Devices and Preemption

In the *Medtronic* case, the United States Supreme Court observed that the Medical Device Amendments of 1976 (MDA) created a comprehensive scheme of federal safety oversight for medical devices. The MDA requires the Food and Drug Administration (FDA) to review the design, labeling, and manufacturing of these devices to make sure that they are safe and effective before they are marketed. The Court reasoned that because premarket approval is a "rigorous process," it preempts all common law claims challenging the safety or effectiveness of a medical device that has been approved. Therefore, a man who was injured by an approved medical device (in this case, a balloon catheter) could not sue its maker for negligence or strict product liability or claim that the device was defectively designed.

   The fact that the plaintiff (Riegel) could not maintain a lawsuit, of course, does not mean that the product was truly safe or did not cause his injuries. Nor does it mean that the FDA process clearly establishes the safety of medical devices. The majority of medical devices submitted to the FDA for approval each year are variants of products that are already on the market—items like pacemakers, defibrillators, and artificial hips. The FDA does not require extensive safety and effectiveness testing on variants before they are marketed and relies largely on documentation provided by manufacturers.

Preemption May Bar Product Liability Claims Based on Warning Defects and Design Defects

Courts are already extending the preemption defense in *Medtronic* to other product liability actions. For example, surviving family members of consumers who had committed suicide after taking the prescription antidepressants Paxil and Zoloft brought product liability actions against the drug makers for failing to warn of an increased tendency to commit suicide. Because the FDA has detailed regulations regarding drug labels and the labels for these products had been approved, a federal appellate court concluded that the families' failure-to-warn claims were preempted by the FDA's regulatory actions.[13]

   In another case, six-year-old Brittany Carter was severely burned when her five-year-old brother, Jonas, accidentally set fire to her dress with a J-26 model BIC lighter. Janace Carter filed a lawsuit on Brittany's behalf against BIC Pen Corporation in a Texas court, claiming Brittany's injuries resulted from manufacturing and design defects in the J-26 lighter. A jury found for Carter and awarded her $3 million dollars in actual damages and $2 million dollars in exemplary damages. BIC appealed to the highest court in Texas, which held that the federal standards for childproof lighters preempted Brittany's design defect claim (but not her manufacturing defect claim) and reversed the decision.[14]

Assumption of Risk

Assumption of risk can sometimes be used as a defense in a product liability action. To establish such a defense, the defendant must show that (1) the plaintiff knew and appreciated the risk created by the product defect and (2) the

---

12. ___ U.S. ___, 128 S.Ct. 999, 169 L.Ed.2d 892 (2008). This case was mentioned in Example #4 in Chapter 4.

13. *Colacicco v. Apotex Inc.,* 521 F.3d 253 (3d Cir. 2008).

14. *BIC Pen Corp. v. Carter,* 251 S.W.3d 500 (Tex. 2008).

plaintiff voluntarily assumed the risk, even though it was unreasonable to do so. For instance, if a buyer failed to heed a seller's product recall, the buyer may be deemed to have assumed the risk of the product defect that the seller offered to cure. (See Chapter 5 for a more detailed discussion of assumption of risk.)

Product Misuse

Similar to the defense of voluntary assumption of risk is that of *product misuse,* which occurs when a product is used for a purpose for which it was not intended. Here, in contrast to assumption of risk, the injured party *does not know that the product is dangerous for a particular use.* The courts have severely limited this defense, however. Even if the injured party does not know about the inherent danger of using the product in a wrong way, if the misuse is reasonably foreseeable, the seller must take measures to guard against it.

Comparative Negligence (Fault)

Developments in the area of comparative negligence, or fault (discussed in Chapter 5), have also affected the doctrine of strict liability. In the past, the plaintiff's conduct was never a defense to liability for a defective product. Today, courts in many jurisdictions will consider the negligent or intentional actions of both the plaintiff and the defendant when apportioning liability and damages.[15] This means that a defendant may be able to limit at least some of its liability if it can show that the plaintiff's misuse of the product contributed to his or her injuries. When proved, comparative negligence does not completely absolve the defendant of liability (as do other defenses), but it can reduce the total amount of damages that will be awarded to the plaintiff.

Note that some jurisdictions allow only intentional conduct to affect a plaintiff's recovery, whereas other states allow ordinary negligence to be used as a defense to product liability. **EXAMPLE #9** Dan Smith, a mechanic in Alaska, was not wearing a hard hat at work when he was asked to start the diesel engine of an air compressor. Because the compressor was an older model, he had to prop open a door to start it. When he got the engine started, the door fell from its position and hit Smith's head. The injury caused him to suffer from seizures and epilepsy. Smith sued the manufacturer, claiming that the engine was defectively designed. The manufacturer contended that Smith had been negligent by failing to wear a hard hat and propping open the door in an unsafe manner. Smith's attorney argued that ordinary negligence could not be used as a defense in product liability cases. The Alaska Supreme Court ruled that defendants in product liability actions can raise the plaintiff's ordinary negligence to reduce their liability proportionately.[16]

Commonly Known Dangers

The dangers associated with certain products (such as matches and sharp knives) are so commonly known that, as already mentioned, manufacturers need not warn users of those dangers. If a defendant succeeds in convincing the court that

---

15. See, for example, *State Farm Insurance Companies v. Premier Manufactured Systems, Inc.,* 213 Ariz. 419, 142 P.3d 1232 (2006); and *Ready v. United/Goedecke Services, Inc.,* 367 Ill.App.3d 272, 854 N.E.2d 758 (2006).
16. *Smith v. Ingersoll-Rand Co.,* 14 P.3d 990 (Alaska 2000).

a plaintiff's injury resulted from a *commonly known danger,* the defendant will not be liable.

EXAMPLE #10 A classic case on this issue involved a plaintiff who was injured when an elastic exercise rope she had purchased slipped off her foot and struck her in the eye, causing a detachment of the retina. The plaintiff claimed that the manufacturer should be liable because it had failed to warn users that the exerciser might slip off a foot in such a manner. The court stated that to hold the manufacturer liable in these circumstances "would go beyond the reasonable dictates of justice in fixing the liabilities of manufacturers." After all, stated the court, "[a]lmost every physical object can be inherently dangerous or potentially dangerous in a sense. . . . A manufacturer cannot manufacture a knife that will not cut or a hammer that will not mash a thumb or a stove that will not burn a finger. The law does not require [manufacturers] to warn of such common dangers."[17] □

Knowledgeable User

A related defense is the *knowledgeable user* defense. If a particular danger (such as electrical shock) is or should be commonly known by particular users of a product (such as electricians), the manufacturer need not warn these users of the danger.

EXAMPLE #11 In one case, the parents of a group of teenagers who had become overweight and developed health problems filed a product liability suit against McDonald's. The teenagers claimed that the well-known fast-food chain should be held liable for failing to warn customers of the adverse health effects of eating its food products. The court rejected this claim, however, based on the *knowledgeable user defense.* The court found that it is well known that the food at McDonald's

---

17. *Jamieson v. Woodward & Lothrop,* 247 F.2d 23 (D.C. Cir.1957).

Is becoming overweight a commonly known danger of eating fast food on a regular basis? Why or why not?
(AP Photo/Shakh Aivazov)

contains high levels of cholesterol, fat, salt, and sugar and is therefore unhealth-ful. The court's opinion, which thwarted future lawsuits against fast-food restau-rants, stated: "If consumers know (or reasonably should know) the potential ill health effects of eating at McDonald's, they cannot blame McDonald's if they, nonetheless, choose to satiate their appetite with a surfeit [excess] of supersized McDonald's products."[18]□

Statutes of Limitations and Repose

As previously discussed, statutes of limitations restrict the time within which an action may be brought. The statute of limitations for product liability cases varies according to state law, and unlike warranty claims, product liability claims are not subject to the UCC's limitation period. Usually, the injured party must bring a product liability claim within two to four years. Often, the running of the prescribed period is *tolled* (that is, suspended) until the party suffering an injury has discovered it or should have discovered it. To ensure that sellers and manufacturers will not be left vulnerable to lawsuits indefinitely, many states have passed laws, called **statutes of repose,** that place *outer* time limits on prod-uct liability actions. For instance, a statute of repose may require that claims be brought within twelve years from the date of sale or manufacture of the defec-tive product. If the plaintiff does not bring an action before the prescribed period expires, the seller cannot be held liable.

STATUTE OF REPOSE
Basically, a statute of limitations that is not dependent on the happening of a cause of action. Statutes of repose generally begin to run at an earlier date and run for a longer period of time than statutes of limitations.

---

18. *Pelman v. McDonald's Corp.,* 237 F.Supp.2d 512 (S.D.N.Y. 2003).

 *Reviewing . . .* **Strict Liability and Product Liability**

Shalene Kolchek bought a Great Lakes spa from Val Porter, a dealer who was selling spas at the state fair. Kolchek signed an installment contract; then Porter and Kolchek arranged for the spa to be delivered and installed for her the next day. Three months later, Kolchek left her six-year-old daughter, Litisha, alone in the spa. While exploring the spa's hydromassage jets, Litisha stuck her index finger into one of the jet holes and was unable to remove her finger from the jet. Litisha yanked hard, injuring her finger, then panicked and screamed for help. Kolchek was unable to remove Litisha's finger, and the local police and rescue team were called to assist. After a three-hour operation that included draining the spa, sawing out a section of the spa's plastic molding, and slicing the jet casing, Litisha's finger was freed. Following this procedure, the spa was no longer functional. Litisha was taken to the local emergency room, where she was told that a bone in her finger was broken in two places. Using the information presented in the chapter, answer the following questions.

1. Under which theory or theories of product liability can Kolchek sue to recover for Litisha's injuries? Could Kolchek sue Porter or Great Lakes?

2. Would privity of contract be required for Kolchek to succeed in a product liability action against Great Lakes?

3. For an action in strict product liability against Great Lakes, what six requirements must Kolchek meet?

4. What defenses to product liability might Porter or Great Lakes be able to assert?

Key Terms

Chapter Summary

Product Liability Based on Negligence (See page 390.)	1. The manufacturer must use due care in designing the product, selecting materials, using the appropriate production process, assembling and testing the product, and placing adequate warnings on the label or product.
	2. Privity of contract is not required. A manufacturer is liable for failure to exercise due care to any person who sustains an injury proximately caused by a negligently made (defective) product.
Product Liability Based on Misrepresentation (See page 390.)	Fraudulent misrepresentation of a product may result in product liability based on the tort of fraud.
Strict Product Liability—Requirements (See pages 394–395.)	1. The defendant must sell the product in a defective condition.
	2. The defendant must normally be engaged in the business of selling that product.
	3. The product must be unreasonably dangerous to the user or consumer because of its defective condition (in most states).
	4. The plaintiff must incur physical harm to self or property by use or consumption of the product. (Courts will also extend strict liability to include injured bystanders.)
	5. The defective condition must be the proximate cause of the injury or damage.
	6. The goods must not have been substantially changed from the time the product was sold to the time the injury was sustained.
Strict Product Liability—Product Defects (See pages 395–401.)	A product may be defective in three basic ways:
	1. In its manufacture.
	2. In its design.
	3. By including inadequate warnings or instructions.
Market-Share Liability (See pages 401–402.)	When plaintiffs cannot prove which of many distributors of a defective product supplied the particular product that caused the plaintiffs' injuries, some courts apply market-share liability and hold all firms that manufactured and distributed the harmful product during the period in question liable.
Other Applications of Strict Product Liability (See page 402.)	1. Manufacturers and other sellers are liable for harms suffered by bystanders as a result of defective products.
	2. Suppliers of component parts are strictly liable for defective parts that, when incorporated into a product, cause injuries to users.
Defenses to Product Liability (See pages 402–406.)	1. *Assumption of risk*—The user or consumer knew of the risk of harm and voluntarily assumed it. *Product misuse* is a similar defense in which the manufacturer claims that the user or consumer misused the product in an unintended way, but the courts have severely limited this defense.
	2. *Comparative negligence and liability*—Liability may be distributed between the plaintiff and the defendant under the doctrine of comparative negligence if the plaintiff's misuse of the product contributed to the risk of injury.

CONTINUED

Defenses to Product Liability— Continued

3. *Commonly known dangers*—If a defendant succeeds in convincing the court that a plaintiff's injury resulted from a commonly known danger, such as the danger associated with using a sharp knife, the defendant will not be liable.

4. *Knowledgeable user*—When a particular danger is commonly known by a certain group of users of a product, the manufacturer need not warn these users of the danger.

5. *Other defenses*—A defendant can also defend against a product liability claim by showing that there is no basis for the plaintiff's claim (that the plaintiff has not met the requirements for an action in negligence or strict liability, for example) or that the claim is barred by a statute of limitation or repose.

For Review

1. What is meant by strict liability?
2. How can negligence and misrepresentation provide a basis for a product liability action?
3. Can a manufacturer be held liable to any person who suffers an injury proximately caused by the manufacturer's negligently made product?
4. What are the elements of a cause of action in strict product liability?
5. What defenses to liability can be raised in a product liability lawsuit?

Questions and Case Problems

12–1. Product Liability. Chen buys a television set manufactured by Quality TV Appliance, Inc. She is going on vacation, so she takes the set to her mother's house for her mother to use. Because the set is defective, it explodes, causing her mother to be seriously injured. Chen's mother sues Quality to obtain compensation for her injury and for the damage to her house. Under what theory or theories discussed in this chapter might Chen's mother recover damages from Quality?

Question with Sample Answer

12–2. Colt manufactures a new pistol. The firing of the pistol depends on an enclosed high-pressure device. The pistol has been thoroughly tested in two laboratories in the Midwest, and its design and manufacture are in accord with current technology. Wayne purchases one of the new pistols from Hardy's Gun and Rifle Emporium. When he uses the pistol in the high altitude of the Rockies, the difference in pressure causes the pistol to misfire, resulting in serious injury to Wayne. Colt can prove that all due care was used in the manufacturing process, and it refuses to pay for Wayne's injuries. Discuss Colt's liability in tort.

For a sample answer to Question 12–2, go to Appendix I at the end of this text.

12–3. Defenses to Liability. A water pipe burst, flooding a company's switchboard and tripping the switchboard circuit breakers. Company employees assigned to reactivate the switchboard included an electrical technician with twelve years of on-the-job training, a licensed electrician, and an electrical engineer who had studied power engineering in college and had twenty years of experience. The employees attempted to switch one of the circuit breakers back on without testing for short circuits, which they later admitted they knew how to do and should have done. The circuit breaker failed to engage but ignited an explosive fire. The company sued the supplier of the circuit breakers for damages, alleging that the supplier had failed to give adequate warnings and instructions regarding the circuit breakers. How might the supplier defend against this claim? Discuss.

12–4. Strict Product Liability. Gina is standing on a street corner waiting for a ride to work. Gomez has just purchased a new car manufactured by Optimal Motors. He is driving down the street when suddenly the steering mechanism breaks, causing him to run over Gina. Gina suffers permanent injuries. Gomez's total income per year has never exceeded $15,000. Thus, instead of suing Gomez, Gina files suit against Optimal under the theory of strict liability in tort. Optimal claims that it is not liable because (1) due care was used in the manufacture of the car, (2) Optimal is not the manufacturer of the steering mechanism (Smith is), and (3) strict product liability applies only to users or consumers, and Gina is neither. Discuss the validity of the defenses claimed by Optimal.

12–5. Liability to Third Parties. Lee Stegemoller was a union member who insulated large machinery between 1947 and 1988. During his career, he worked for a number of different companies. Stegemoller primarily worked with asbestos insulation, which was used on industrial boilers, engines, furnaces, and turbines. After he left a work site, some of the asbestos dust always remained on his clothing. His wife, Ramona, who laundered his work clothes, was also exposed to the dust on a daily basis. Allegedly as a result of this contact, she was diagnosed with colon cancer, pulmonary fibrosis, and pleural thickening in April 1998. The Stegemollers filed a suit in an Indiana state court against ACandS, Inc., and thirty-three others, contending among other things that the asbestos originated from products attributable to some of the defendants and from the premises of other defendants. Several defendants filed a motion to dismiss the complaint, asserting that Ramona was not a "user or consumer" of asbestos because she was not in the vicinity of the product when it was used. Should the court dismiss the suit on this basis? Explain. [*Stegemoller v. ACandS, Inc.*, 767 N.E.2d 974 (Ind. 2002)]

12–6. Product Liability. In January 1999, John Clark of Clarksdale, Mississippi, bought a paintball gun. Clark practiced with the gun and knew how to screw in the carbon dioxide cartridge, pump the gun, and use its safety and trigger. He hunted and had taken a course in hunter safety education. He knew that protective eyewear was available for purchase, but he chose not to buy it. Clark also understood that it was "common sense" not to shoot anyone in the face. Chris Rico, another Clarksdale resident, owned a paintball gun made by Brass Eagle, Inc. Rico was similarly familiar with the gun's use and its risks. At that time and place, Clark, Rico, and their friends played a game that involved shooting paintballs at cars whose occupants also had the guns. One night, while Clark and Rico were cruising with their guns, Rico shot at Clark's car but hit Clark in the eye. Clark filed a suit in a Mississippi state court against Brass Eagle to recover for the injury, alleging, among other things, that its gun was defectively designed. During the trial, Rico testified that his gun "never malfunctioned." In whose favor should the court rule? Why? [*Clark v. Brass Eagle, Inc.*, 866 So.2d 456 (Miss. 2004)]

than other cigarettes and lacked effective filters, which would have reduced the amount of tar inhaled into the lungs. In 1996, Mary Jane developed lung cancer. She and her husband, Henry Boerner, filed a suit in a federal district court against Brown & Williamson Tobacco Co., the maker of Pall Malls. The Boerners claimed, among other things, that Pall Malls contained a design defect. Mary Jane died in 1999. According to Dr. Peter Marvin, her treating physician, she died from the effects of cigarette smoke. Henry continued the suit, offering evidence that Pall Malls featured a filter that actually increased the amount of tar taken into the body. When is a product defective in design? Does this product meet the requirements? Why or why not? [*Boerner v. Brown & Williamson Tobacco Co.*, 394 F.3d 594 (8th Cir. 2005)]

After you have answered Problem 12–7, compare your answer with the sample answer given on the Web site that accompanies this text. Go to www.cengage.com/blaw/let, select "Chapter 12," and click on "Case Problem with Sample Answer."

12–8. Product Liability. Bret D'Auguste was an experienced skier when he rented equipment to ski at Hunter Mountain Ski Bowl, Inc., owned by Shanty Hollow Corp., in New York. The adjustable retention/release value for the bindings on the rented equipment was set at a level that, according to skiing industry standards, was too low—meaning that the skis would be released too easily—given D'Auguste's height, weight, and ability. When D'Auguste entered a "double black diamond," or extremely difficult, trail, he noticed immediately that the surface consisted of ice and virtually no snow. He tried to exit the steeply declining trail by making a sharp right turn, but in the attempt, his left ski snapped off. D'Auguste lost his balance, fell, and slid down the mountain, striking his face and head against a fence along the trail. According to a report by a rental shop employee, one of the bindings on D'Auguste's skis had a "cracked heel housing." D'Auguste filed a suit in a New York state court against Shanty Hollow and others, including the bindings' manufacturer, on a theory of strict product liability. The manufacturer filed a motion for summary judgment. On what basis might the court *grant* the motion? On what basis might the court *deny* the motion? How should the court rule? Explain. [*D'Auguste v. Shanty Hollow Corp.*, 26 A.D.3d 403, 809 N.Y.S.2d 555 (2 Dept. 2006)]

Case Problem with Sample Answer

12–7. Mary Jane Boerner began smoking in 1945 at the age of fifteen. For a short time, she smoked Lucky Strikes (a brand of cigarettes) before switching to the Pall Mall brand, which she smoked until she quit altogether in 1981. Pall Malls had higher levels of carcinogenic tar

A Question of Ethics

12–9. Susan Calles lived with her four daughters, Amanda, age 11; Victoria, age 5; and Jenna and Jillian, age 3. In March 1998, Calles bought an Aim N Flame utility lighter, which she stored on the top shelf of her kitchen cabinet. A trigger can ignite the Aim N Flame after an

"ON/OFF" switch is slid to the "on" position. On the night of March 31, Calles and Victoria left to get videos. Jenna and Jillian were in bed, and Amanda was watching television. Calles returned to find fire trucks and emergency vehicles around her home. Robert Finn, a fire investigator, determined that Jenna had started a fire using the lighter. Jillian suffered smoke inhalation, was hospitalized, and died on April 21. Calles filed a suit in an Illinois state court against Scripto-Tokai Corp., which distributed the Aim N Flame, and others. In her suit, which was grounded, in part, in strict liability claims, Calles alleged that the lighter was an "unreasonably dangerous product." Scripto filed a motion for summary judgment. [*Calles v. Scripto-Tokai Corp.*, 224 Ill.2d 247, 864 N.E.2d 249, 309 Ill.Dec. 383 (2007)]

1. A product is "unreasonably dangerous" when it is dangerous beyond the expectation of the ordinary consumer. Whose expectation—Calles's or Jenna's—applies here? Why? Does the lighter pass this test? Explain.
2. A product is also "unreasonably dangerous" when a less dangerous alternative was economically feasible for its maker, who failed to produce it. Scripto contended that because its

product was "simple" and the danger was "obvious," it should be excepted from this test. Do you agree? Why or why not?
3. Calles presented evidence as to the likelihood and seriousness of injury from lighters that do not have child-safety devices. Scripto argued that the Aim N Flame is a useful, inexpensive, alternative source of fire and is safer than a match. Calles admitted that she was aware of the dangers presented by lighters in the hands of children. Scripto admitted that it had been a defendant in at least twenty-five suits for injuries that occurred under similar circumstances. With these factors in mind, how should the court rule? Why?

Critical-Thinking Legal Question

12–10. The United States has the strictest product liability laws in the world today. Why do you think many other countries, particularly developing countries, are more lax with respect to holding manufacturers liable for product defects?

For updated links to resources available on the Web, as well as a variety of other materials, visit this text's Web site at

www.cengage.com/blaw/let

The Federal Trade Commission posts *A Businessperson's Guide to Federal Warranty Law* at

www.ftc.gov/bcp/conline/pubs/buspubs/warranty.htm

For information on product liability suits against tobacco companies, go to the Web site of the Library & Center for Knowledge Management, which is maintained by the University of California–San Francisco, at

library.ucsf.edu/tobacco/litigation

PRACTICAL INTERNET EXERCISES

Go to this text's Web site at **www.cengage.com/blaw/let**, select "Chapter 12," and click on "Practical Internet Exercises." There you will find the following Internet research exercises that you can perform to learn more about the topics covered in this chapter.

Practical Internet Exercise 12–1: LEGAL PERSPECTIVE—Product Liability Legislation
Practical Internet Exercise 12–2: MANAGEMENT PERSPECTIVE—The Duty to Warn

BEFORE THE TEST

Go to this text's Web site at **www.cengage.com/blaw/let**, select "Chapter 12," and click on "Interactive Quizzes." You will find a number of interactive questions relating to this chapter.

Chapter 13

Creditor-Debtor Relations and Bankruptcy

CHAPTER OBJECTIVES

After reading this chapter, you should be able to answer the following questions:

1. What is a prejudgment attachment? What is a writ of execution? How does a creditor use these remedies?

2. What is garnishment? When might a creditor undertake a garnishment proceeding?

3. In a bankruptcy proceeding, what constitutes the debtor's estate in property? What property is exempt from the estate under federal bankruptcy law?

4. What is the difference between an exception to discharge and an objection to discharge?

5. In a Chapter 11 reorganization, what is the role of the debtor in possession?

CONTENTS

- Laws Assisting Creditors
- Laws Assisting Debtors
- Bankruptcy Proceedings
- Chapter 7—Liquidation
- Chapter 11—Reorganization
- Bankruptcy Relief under Chapter 13 and Chapter 12

" *Creditors are . . . great observers of set days and times.* "

— **BENJAMIN FRANKLIN,**
1706–1790 (American diplomat, author, and scientist)

In the chapter-opening quotation, America's font of practical wisdom, Benjamin Franklin, observed a truth known to all debtors—that creditors do observe "set days and times" and will expect to recover their loaned funds by the agreed-on dates. Historically, debtors and their families have been subjected to punishment, including involuntary servitude and imprisonment, for their inability to pay debts. The modern legal system, however, has moved away from a punishment philosophy in dealing with debtors. In fact, until reforms were passed in 2005, many observers argued that it had moved too far in the other direction, to the detriment of creditors.

Normally, creditors have no problem collecting the debts owed to them. When disputes arise over the amount owed, however, or when the debtor simply cannot or will not pay, what happens? What remedies are available to creditors when debtors **default** (fail to pay as promised)? In this chapter, we first focus on some basic laws that assist debtors and creditors in resolving disputes. We then examine the process of bankruptcy as a last resort in resolving creditor-debtor problems. We specifically include changes resulting from the 2005 Bankruptcy Reform Act.

DEFAULT
The failure to observe a promise or to dischage an obligation. The term is commonly used to mean the failure to pay a debt when it is due.

LAWS ASSISTING CREDITORS

Both the common law and statutory laws other than Article 9 of the Uniform Commercial Code (UCC) create various rights and remedies for creditors. Here we discuss some of these rights and remedies.

Liens

A **lien** is an encumbrance on (claim against) property to satisfy a debt or protect a claim for the payment of a debt. Creditors' liens may arise under the common law or under statutory law. Statutory liens include *mechanic's liens*. Liens created at common law include *artisan's liens*. *Judicial liens* include those that represent a creditor's efforts to collect on a debt before or after a judgment is entered by a court.

Generally, a lien creditor has priority over most other creditors—except those creditors with a "perfected" security interest in the property. *Perfection,* which is usually accomplished by filing a financing statement with a state official, is the legal process by which a lender protects its security interest in property from the claims of others. If a person becomes a lien creditor *before* another party perfects a security interest in the same property, the lienholder has priority. If a lien is obtained *after* another's security interest in the property is perfected, the lienholder does not have priority. This is true for all liens except mechanic's and artisan's liens, which normally have priority over perfected security interests—unless a statute provides otherwise.

Mechanic's Lien   When a person contracts for labor, services, or materials to be furnished for the purpose of making improvements on real property (land and things attached to the land, such as buildings and trees—see Chapter 22) but does not immediately pay for the improvements, the creditor can file a **mechanic's lien** on the property. This creates a special type of debtor-creditor relationship in which the real estate itself becomes security for the debt.

EXAMPLE #1 A painter agrees to paint a house for a homeowner for an agreed-on price to cover labor and materials. If the homeowner refuses to pay for the work or pays only a portion of the charges, a mechanic's lien against the property can be created. The painter is the lienholder, and the real property is encumbered (burdened) with a mechanic's lien for the amount owed. If the homeowner does not pay the lien, the property can be sold to satisfy the debt. Notice of the foreclosure (the process by which the creditor deprives the debtor of his or her property) and sale must be given to the debtor in advance, however.□

Note that state law governs the procedures that must be followed to create a mechanic's lien. Generally, the lienholder must file a written notice of lien against the particular property involved. The notice of lien must be filed within a specific time period, normally measured from the last date on which materials or labor were provided (usually within 60 to 120 days). If the property owner fails to pay the debt, the lienholder is entitled to foreclose on the real estate on which the work or materials were provided and to sell it to satisfy the amount of the debt.

Artisan's Lien   An **artisan's lien** is a security device created at common law through which a creditor can recover payment from a debtor for labor and materials furnished for the repair or improvement of personal property. In contrast to a mechanic's lien, an artisan's lien is *possessory*. The lienholder ordinarily must have retained possession of the property and have expressly or impliedly agreed to provide the services on a cash, not a credit, basis. The lien remains in existence as long as the lienholder main-

---

LIEN
An encumbrance on (claim against) property to satisfy a debt or protect a claim for the payment of a debt.

MECHANIC'S LIEN
A statutory lien on the real property of another, created to ensure payment for work performed and materials furnished in the repair or improvement of real property, such as a building.

ARTISAN'S LIEN
A possessory lien given to a person who has made improvements and added value to another person's personal property as security for payment for services performed.

Painters finish the trim on a house. If the homeowner does not pay for the work, what can the painters do to collect what they are owed?
(Joshin Yamada/Creative Commons)

tains possession, and the lien is terminated once possession is voluntarily surrendered—unless the surrender is only temporary.

EXAMPLE #2 Tenetia leaves her diamond ring at the jeweler's to be repaired and to have her initials engraved on the band. In the absence of an agreement, the jeweler can keep the ring until Tenetia pays for the services. Should Tenetia fail to pay, the jeweler has a lien on Tenetia's ring for the amount of the bill and normally can sell the ring in satisfaction of the lien.□

Modern statutes permit the holder of an artisan's lien to foreclose and sell the property subject to the lien to satisfy payment of the debt. As with a mechanic's lien, the holder of an artisan's lien is required to give notice to the owner of the property prior to foreclosure and sale. The sale proceeds are used to pay the debt and the costs of the legal proceedings, and the surplus, if any, is paid to the former owner.

Judicial Liens   When a debt is past due, a creditor can bring a legal action against the debtor to collect the debt. If the creditor is successful in the action, the court awards the creditor a judgment against the debtor (usually for the amount of the debt plus any interest and legal costs incurred in obtaining the judgment). Frequently, however, the creditor is unable to collect the awarded amount.

To ensure that a judgment in the creditor's favor will be collectible, the creditor is permitted to request that certain nonexempt property of the debtor be seized to satisfy the debt. (As will be discussed later in this chapter, under state or federal statutes, certain property is exempt from attachment by creditors.) If the court orders the debtor's property to be seized prior to a judgment in the creditor's favor, the court's order is referred to as a *writ of attachment*. If the court orders the debtor's property to be seized following a judgment in the creditor's favor, the court's order is referred to as a *writ of execution.*

Writ of Attachment   In the context of judicial liens, **attachment** is a court-ordered seizure and taking into custody of property prior to the securing of a judgment for a past-due debt. Attachment rights are created by state statutes. Normally, attachment is a *prejudgment* remedy occurring either at the time a lawsuit is filed or immediately afterward. To attach before judgment, a creditor must comply with the specific state's statutory restrictions and requirements. The due process clause of the Fourteenth Amendment to the U.S. Constitution also applies and requires that the debtor be given notice and an opportunity to be heard (see Chapter 4).

The creditor must have an enforceable right to payment of the debt under law and must follow certain procedures. Otherwise, the creditor can be liable for damages for wrongful attachment. She or he must file with the court an *affidavit* (a written or printed statement, made under oath or sworn to) stating that the debtor is in default and indicating the statutory grounds under which attachment is sought. The creditor must also post a bond to cover at least the court costs, the value of the loss of use of the property suffered by the debtor, and the value of the property attached. When the court is satisfied that all the requirements have been met, it issues a **writ of attachment,** which directs the sheriff or other public officer to seize nonexempt property. If the creditor prevails at trial, the seized property can be sold to satisfy the judgment.

Writ of Execution   If the creditor wins and the debtor will not or cannot pay the judgment, the creditor is entitled to go back to the court and request a **writ of execution.** This writ is a court order directing the sheriff to seize (levy) and sell any of the debtor's nonexempt real or personal property that is within the

ATTACHMENT
In the context of judicial liens, a court-ordered seizure and taking into custody of property prior to the securing of a judgment for a past-due debt.

WRIT OF ATTACHMENT
A court's order, issued prior to a trial to collect a debt, directing the sheriff or other public officer to seize nonexempt property of the debtor. If the creditor prevails at trial, the seized property can be sold to satisfy the judgment.

WRIT OF EXECUTION
A court's order, issued after a judgment has been entered against a debtor, directing the sheriff to seize (levy) and sell any of the debtor's nonexempt real or personal property. The proceeds of the sale are used to pay off the judgment, accrued interest, and costs of the sale; any surplus is paid to the debtor.

court's geographic jurisdiction (usually the county in which the courthouse is located). The proceeds of the sale are used to pay off the judgment, accrued interest, and the costs of the sale. Any excess is paid to the debtor. The debtor can pay the judgment and redeem the nonexempt property any time before the sale takes place. (Because of exemption laws and bankruptcy laws, however, many judgments are virtually uncollectible.)

Garnishment

GARNISHMENT
A legal process used by a creditor to collect a debt by seizing property of the debtor (such as wages) that is being held by a third party (such as the debtor's employer).

An order for **garnishment** permits a creditor to collect a debt by seizing property of the debtor that is being held by a third party. In a garnishment proceeding, the third party—the person or entity that the court is ordering to garnish an individual's property—is called the *garnishee*. Frequently, a garnishee is the debtor's employer. A creditor may seek a garnishment judgment against the debtor's employer so that part of the debtor's usual paycheck will be paid to the creditor. In some situations, however, the garnishee is a third party that holds funds belonging to the debtor (such as a bank) or has possession of, or exercises control over, other types of property belonging to the debtor. Almost all types of property can be garnished, including tax refunds, pensions, and trust funds—as long as the property is not exempt from garnishment and is in the possession of a third party.

Garnishment Proceedings   The legal proceeding for a garnishment action is governed by state law, and garnishment operates differently from state to state. As a result of a garnishment proceeding, as noted, the court orders a third party (such as the debtor's employer) to turn over property owned by the debtor (such as wages) to pay the debt. Garnishment can be a prejudgment remedy, requiring a hearing before a court, but is most often a postjudgment remedy. According to the laws in some states, the creditor needs to obtain only one order of garnishment, which will then apply continuously to the debtor's wages until the entire debt is paid. In other states, the judgment creditor must go back to court for a separate order of garnishment for each pay period.

Laws Limiting the Amount of Wages Subject to Garnishment   Both federal and state laws limit the amount that can be taken from a debtor's weekly take-home pay through garnishment proceedings.[1] Federal law provides a framework to protect debtors from suffering unduly when paying judgment debts.[2] State laws also provide dollar exemptions, and these amounts are often larger than those provided by federal law. Under federal law, an employer cannot dismiss an employee because his or her wages are being garnished.

Creditors' Composition Agreements

**CREDITORS'
COMPOSITION AGREEMENT**
An agreement formed between a debtor and his or her creditors in which the creditors agree to accept a lesser sum than that owed by the debtor in full satisfaction of the debt.

Creditors may contract with the debtor for discharge of the debtor's liquidated debts (debts that are definite, or fixed, in amount) on payment of a sum less than that owed. These agreements are called **creditors' composition agreements,** or simply *composition agreements,* and are usually held to be enforceable.

---

1. Some states (for example, Texas) do not permit garnishment of wages by private parties except under a child-support order.
2. For example, the federal Consumer Credit Protection Act of 1968, 15 U.S.C. Sections 1601–1693r, provides that a debtor can retain either 75 percent of the disposable earnings per week or a sum equivalent to thirty hours of work paid at federal minimum-wage rates, whichever is greater.

Mortgage Foreclosure

A **mortgage** is a written instrument giving a creditor an interest in (lien on) the debtor's real property as security for the payment of a debt. Financial institutions grant mortgage loans for the purchase of property—usually a dwelling and the land on which it sits (*real property* will be discussed in Chapter 22). Given the relatively large sums that many individuals borrow to purchase a home, defaults are not uncommon. See the *Insight into Ethics* feature below for a discussion of the subprime mortgage crisis that has developed in recent years.

MORTGAGE
A written instrument giving a creditor an interest in (lien on) the debtor's real property as security for payment of a debt.

Insight into Ethics

Are mortgage lending practices responsible for an epidemic of foreclosures?

Mortgage lenders usually extend credit to high-risk borrowers using higher-than-normal interest rates (called subprime mortgages) and adjustable-rate mortgages (ARMs). The widespread use of subprime and ARM mortgages in recent years has resulted in many borrowers being overextended and unable to pay their loan payments as they come due. In addition, housing prices in the United States have dropped, which means that some borrowers are not able to sell their homes for the amount they owe on the mortgage. As a consequence, there was a sharp increase in the number of home foreclosures in 2007 and 2008, prompting debate about whether the government should step in to rescue debtors from foreclosure.

New Legislation

In July 2008, Congress passed historic and controversial legislation designed to help borrowers facing foreclosure and to bolster the housing market.[3] The law raised the national debt ceiling to $10.6 trillion (an increase of $800 billion) and authorized the Treasury to rescue the two mortgage company giants, Fannie Mae and Freddie Mac, which took place in September 2008. (These two companies own or guarantee half of the nation's $12 trillion in mortgages, and were experiencing declining stock prices.)

One important provision expanded the Federal Housing Administration (FHA) loan guarantee programs to $300 billion. This was intended to help troubled borrowers refinance, but the FHA can only guarantee new fixed-rate loans if the existing lenders agree to write down loan balances to 90 percent of the homes' current appraised value. There are other eligibility rules as well, which limit the number of homeowners that benefit from the new law and make implementing its provisions more difficult. Even optimistic forecasts suggest that the law will help only about 400,000 of the estimated 3 million homeowners who will likely lose their homes by the end of 2009.[4]

The Blame Factor

The big question underlying the controversy about what the government should do to fix the mortgage foreclosure epidemic is who was responsible for the crisis? Is it the mortgage lenders, who sometimes encouraged persons to borrow more and buy more than they could "afford," and may have occasionally misrepresented the terms of the loans or omitted pertinent details? Or is it the debtors, who knew or should have known the terms they were agreeing to and should have figured out that they would be unable

---

3. House Resolution 3221, a bill to provide needed housing reform and for other purposes, also known as the Foreclosure Prevention Act of 2008.
4. Ron Scherer, "Big housing bill: no rescues soon," *The Christian Science Monitor,* August 1, 2008. David M. Herszenhorn, "Bush Signs Sweeping Housing Bill," *The New York Times,* July 31, 2008; Jeanne Sahadi, "Senate passes landmark housing bill," *CNNMoney.com,* July 26, 2008.

to repay the mortgage according to its terms? After all, freedom of contract means people are free to enter into bad bargains, and contracts are generally binding regardless of whether one of the parties signed without taking the time to read or understand the terms. Anyone borrowing funds to purchase a home should look closely at the terms of the mortgage loan. Finally, many borrowers knew that they would not make the mortgage payments for very long. They believed, though, they could quickly resell their homes at a profit, but then the housing market stalled before they could do so.

Mortgage holders have the right to foreclose on mortgaged property in the event of a debtor's default. The usual method of foreclosure is by judicial sale of the property, although the statutory methods of foreclosure vary from state to state. If the proceeds of the foreclosure sale are sufficient to cover both the costs of the foreclosure and the mortgaged debt, the debtor receives any surplus. If the sale proceeds are insufficient to cover the foreclosure costs and the mortgaged debt, however, the **mortgagee** (the creditor-lender) can seek to recover the difference from the **mortgagor** (the debtor) by obtaining a deficiency judgment representing the difference between the mortgaged debt and the amount actually received from the proceeds of the foreclosure sale.

The mortgagee obtains a deficiency judgment in a separate legal action pursued subsequent to the foreclosure action. The deficiency judgment entitles the mortgagee to recover the amount of the deficiency from other property owned by the debtor.

MORTGAGEE
Under a mortgage agreement, the creditor who takes a security interest in the debtor's property.

MORTGAGOR
Under a mortgage agreement, the debtor who gives the creditor a security interest in the debtor's property in return for a mortgage loan.

Suretyship and Guaranty

When a third person promises to pay a debt owed by another in the event the debtor does not pay, either a *suretyship* or a *guaranty* relationship is created. Suretyship and guaranty provide creditors with the right to seek payment from the third party if the primary debtor defaults on her or his obligations. Exhibit 13–1

EXHIBIT 13–1 SURETYSHIP AND GUARANTY PARTIES

In a suretyship or guaranty arrangement, a third party promises to be responsible for a debtor's obligations. A third party who agrees to be responsible for the debt even if the primary debtor does not default is known as a surety; a third party who agrees to be *secondarily* responsible for the debt—that is, responsible only if the primary debtor defaults—is known as a guarantor. Normally, a promise of guaranty (a collateral, or secondary, promise) must be in writing to be enforceable.

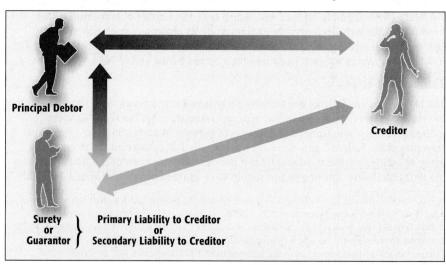

Principal Debtor

Creditor

Surety or Guarantor } Primary Liability to Creditor or Secondary Liability to Creditor illustrates the relationship between a suretyship or guaranty party and the creditor. At common law, there were significant differences in the liability of a *surety* and a *guarantor,* as will be discussed in the following subsections. Today, however, the distinctions outlined here have been abolished in some states.

Surety   A contract of strict **suretyship** is a promise made by a third person to be responsible for the debtor's obligation. It is an express contract between the **surety** (the third party) and the creditor. The surety in the strictest sense is primarily liable for the debt of the principal. The creditor need not exhaust all legal remedies against the principal debtor before holding the surety responsible for payment. The creditor can demand payment from the surety from the moment the debt is due.

SURETYSHIP
An express contract in which a third party to a debtor-creditor relationship (the surety) promises to be primarily responsible for the debtor's obligation.

SURETY
A person, such as a cosigner on a note, who agrees to be primarily responsible for the debt of another.

EXAMPLE #3 Roberto Delmar wants to borrow from the bank to buy a used car. Because Roberto is still in college, the bank will not lend him the funds unless his father, José Delmar, who has dealt with the bank before, will cosign the note (add his signature to the note, thereby becoming a surety and thus jointly liable for payment of the debt). When José Delmar cosigns the note, he becomes primarily liable to the bank. On the note's due date, the bank can seek payment from either Roberto or José Delmar, or both jointly.☐

Guaranty   With a suretyship arrangement, the surety is *primarily* liable for the debtor's obligation. With a guaranty arrangement, the **guarantor**—the third person making the guaranty—is *secondarily* liable. The guarantor can be required to pay the obligation *only after the principal debtor defaults,* and default usually takes place only after the creditor has made an attempt to collect from the debtor.

GUARANTOR
A person who agrees to satisfy the debt of another (the debtor) only after the principal debtor defaults. Thus, a guarantor's liability is secondary.

EXAMPLE #4 A small corporation, BX Enterprises, needs to borrow funds to meet its payroll. The bank is skeptical about the creditworthiness of BX and requires Dawson, its president, who is a wealthy businessperson and the owner of 70 percent of BX Enterprises, to sign an agreement making himself personally liable for payment if BX does not pay off the loan. As a guarantor of the loan, Dawson cannot be held liable until BX Enterprises is in default.☐

The Statute of Frauds requires that a guaranty contract between the guarantor and the creditor must be in writing to be enforceable unless the *main purpose* exception applies. Under this exception, if the main purpose of the guaranty agreement is to benefit the guarantor, then the contract need not be in writing to be enforceable. A suretyship agreement, by contrast, need not be in writing to be enforceable. In other words, surety agreements can be oral, whereas guaranty contracts must be written.

In the following case, the issue was whether a guaranty form for the debt of a partnership was actually made out in the guarantors' names and whether the guarantors signed this form.

Case 13.1   **Capital Color Printing, Inc. v. Ahern**

Court of Appeals of Georgia, 2008.
291 Ga.App. 101, 661 S.E.2d 578.

BACKGROUND AND FACTS   Quality Printing is a printing broker that sells printing services to customers, but

subcontracts the printing work to third parties. It contacted Capital Color Printing (CCP) about doing some work. The credit manager at CCP said that Jason Ahern and Todd Heflin, the owners of Quality, would have to execute personal guaranties before CCP would do any work. Quality sent CCP a

CASE 13.1—CONTINUED

credit application, which contained a guaranty. The names "Ahern" and "Heflin" appeared on the "Your Name" line. Quality's name, address, tax number, and other information were provided in the "Customer" box on the form. Ahern and Heflin stated that they were partners who owned Quality. Below the signature line was the following statement: "The undersigned guarantees payment of any and all invoices for services rendered to customer." Ahern and Heflin did not sign on the signature line, but their names were signed where printed names were requested. The back of the form stated that the guarantors agreed to be liable for any unpaid bills.

When Quality did not pay CCP $76,000 for work it had done, CCP sued Ahern, Heflin, and Quality. Ahern and Heflin moved for summary judgment as to CCP's claims against them, contending that the guaranty failed to specifically identify the principal debtor (Quality) and thus was unenforceable as a matter of law because it violated the Statute of Frauds (see Chapter 11). Ahern claimed that he was not liable because he had stopped working with Heflin and Heflin had put his name on the guaranty without his permission. The trial court agreed with the defendants and dismissed the claim. CCP appealed.

IN THE WORDS OF THE COURT . . . *MILLER,* Judge.

* * * *

The Statute of Frauds requires that, to be enforceable, a promise to answer for another's debt "must be in writing and signed by the party to be charged therewith. This requirement has been interpreted to mandate further that a guaranty identify the debt, the principal debtor, the promisor, and the promisee." [Emphasis added.]

Here, the trial court found that the Guaranty failed to satisfy the Statute of Frauds because it "omitted the name" of the principal debtor.

* * * *

As the Supreme Court of Georgia has explained, the Statute of Frauds does not mandate "that [a written guaranty] must be of a certain type or form." Rather, to satisfy the Statute of Frauds, the document must sufficiently identify the party whose debts are being guaranteed. Here, that party was identified as the "customer" to whom CCP was extending credit. The question, therefore, is whether the credit application identifies that "customer" as Quality Printing.

* * * *

As Ahern and Heflin acknowledge, the customer whose debts are being guaranteed can only be either Quality Printing or Ahern and Heflin individually, based on the appearance of their names in the box captioned "CUSTOMER." Logically, it would be unnecessary for Ahern and Heflin to personally guarantee their own debt. The only reasonable interpretation of the Guaranty, therefore, is that the term "customer" refers to Quality Printing, thereby identifying that entity as the principal debtor.

This conclusion is reinforced by the fact that Quality Printing's corporate address, telephone and fax numbers, and Federal Employer Identification Number are listed in response to the questions contained in the "customer" box found on the front side of the credit application. The credit application also required the "customer" to identify itself as either a corporation, partnership, sole proprietorship, or an LLC, and to list the names of its "officers or owners." In response, the "customer" identified itself as a partnership and listed Ahern and Heflin as the sole owners thereof.

* * * *

In light of the foregoing, we find that the Guaranty adequately identifies the principal debtor and satisfies the Statute of Frauds, and that the trial court erred in holding otherwise.

The trial court also found that Ahern's signature on the credit application was a forgery, thereby making the Guaranty unenforceable against him, even if it was otherwise valid and that Ahern had not authorized anyone to sign his name. This holding, however, ignores evidence which demonstrates the existence of a jury question as to: (1) whether it was Heflin who signed Ahern's name on the credit application; and, if so (2) whether Ahern, by his conduct, clothed Heflin with the apparent authority to do so. We therefore reverse the trial court's grant of summary judgment in favor of Ahern.

DECISION AND REMEDY   The appeals court reversed the lower court's ruling, holding that CCP was entitled to summary judgment against Heflin as a guarantor for services performed for Quality. At trial it would be determined if Ahern was liable on the debt or if Heflin had forged his name on the guaranty.

THE GLOBAL DIMENSION   If a firm was attempting to obtain a guaranty from third parties to a contract with a company in another country, what steps might be taken?

THE ETHICAL DIMENSION   At the time that Ahern and Heflin were partners, was it improper for Heflin to insert Ahern's name as a guarantor on the contract with CCP, or was that an acceptable business practice? Explain.

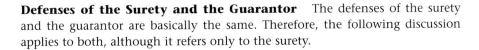

Preventing Legal Disputes

Businesspersons should be careful when signing guaranty contracts and should explicitly indicate if they are signing on behalf of a company rather than personally. If a corporate officer or director, for example, signs her or his name on a guaranty for a third party without indicating that she or he is signing as a representative of the corporation, that individual might be held personally liable as the guarantor. A guaranty contract may be preferable to a suretyship contract in many situations because it creates secondary rather than primary liability. Nevertheless, substantial risk is involved. Moreover, depending on the wording used in a guaranty contract, the extent of the guarantor's liability may be unlimited or may continue over a series of transactions. Be absolutely clear about the potential liability before agreeing to serve as a guarantor, and contact an attorney for guidance. ∎

Defenses of the Surety and the Guarantor   The defenses of the surety and the guarantor are basically the same. Therefore, the following discussion applies to both, although it refers only to the surety.

Actions Releasing the Surety   Certain actions will release the surety from the obligation. For example, making any material modification in the terms of the original contract between the principal debtor and the creditor—including a binding extension of time for payment—without first obtaining the consent of the surety will discharge a gratuitous surety completely. (A *gratuitous surety* is one who receives no consideration in return for acting as a surety, such as a father who agrees to assume responsibility for his daughter's obligation.) A surety who is compensated (such as a venture capitalist who will profit from a loan made to the principal debtor) will be discharged to the extent that the surety suffers a loss. Naturally, if the principal obligation is paid by the debtor or by another person on behalf of the debtor, the surety is discharged from the obligation. Similarly, if valid tender of payment is made, and the creditor rejects it with knowledge of the surety's existence, the surety is released from any obligation on the debt.

In addition, if a creditor surrenders the collateral to the debtor or impairs the collateral while knowing of the surety and without the surety's consent, the surety is released to the extent of any loss suffered as a result of the creditor's actions. The primary reason for this requirement is to protect a surety who agreed to become obligated only because the debtor's collateral was in the possession of the creditor.

Defenses of the Principal Debtor   Generally, the surety can use any defenses available to a principal debtor to avoid liability on the obligation to the creditor. The ability of the surety to assert any defenses the debtor may have against the creditor is the most important concept in suretyship. A few exceptions do exist, however. The surety cannot assert the principal debtor's incapacity or bankruptcy as a defense, nor can the surety assert the statute of limitations as a defense.

Obviously, a surety may also have his or her own defenses—for instance, his or her own incapacity or bankruptcy. If the creditor fraudulently induced the surety to guarantee the debt of the debtor, the surety can assert fraud as a defense. In most states, the creditor has a legal duty to inform the surety, prior to the formation of the suretyship contract, of material facts known by the creditor that would substantially increase the surety's risk. Failure to so inform may constitute fraud and makes the suretyship obligation voidable.

Rights of the Surety and the Guarantor   Generally, when the surety or guarantor pays the debt owed to the creditor, the surety or guarantor is entitled to certain rights. Because the rights of the surety and guarantor are basically the same, the following discussion applies to both.

RIGHT OF SUBROGATION
The right of a person to stand in the place of (be substituted for) another, giving the substituted party the same legal rights that the original party had.

The Right of Subrogation   The surety has the legal **right of subrogation.** Simply stated, this means that any right the creditor had against the debtor now becomes the right of the surety. Included are creditor rights in bankruptcy, rights to collateral possessed by the creditor, and rights to judgments secured by the creditor. In short, the surety now stands in the shoes of the creditor and may pursue any remedies that were available to the creditor against the debtor.

RIGHT OF REIMBURSEMENT
The legal right of a person to be restored, repaid, or indemnified for costs, expenses, or losses incurred or expended on behalf of another.

The Right of Reimbursement   The surety has a **right of reimbursement** from the debtor. Basically, the surety is entitled to receive from the debtor all outlays made on behalf of the suretyship arrangement. Such outlays can include expenses incurred as well as the actual amount of the debt paid to the creditor.

CO-SURETY
A joint surety; a person who assumes liability jointly with another surety for the payment of an obligation.

RIGHT OF CONTRIBUTION
The right of a co-surety who pays more than her or his proportionate share on a debtor's default to recover the excess paid from other co-sureties.

The Right of Contribution   In a situation involving **co-sureties** (two or more sureties on the same obligation owed by the debtor), a surety who pays more than her or his proportionate share on a debtor's default is entitled to recover from the co-sureties the amount paid above the surety's obligation. This is the **right of contribution.** Generally, a co-surety's liability either is determined by agreement between the co-sureties or, in the absence of an agreement, can be specified in the suretyship contract itself.

EXAMPLE #5 Two co-sureties are obligated under a suretyship contract to guarantee the debt of a debtor. Together, the sureties' maximum liability is $25,000. As specified in the suretyship contract, surety A's maximum liability is $15,000, and surety B's is $10,000. The debtor owes $10,000 and is in default. Surety A pays the creditor the entire $10,000. In the absence of any agreement between the two co-sureties, surety A can recover $4,000 from surety B ($10,000/$25,000 × $10,000 = $4,000). ◻

LAWS ASSISTING DEBTORS

The law protects debtors as well as creditors. Certain property of the debtor, for example, is exempt from creditors' actions. Consumer protection statutes (see Chapter 20) and bankruptcy laws (which will be discussed shortly) also protect debtors' rights.

In most states, certain types of property are exempt from execution or attachment. State exemption statutes usually include both real and personal property.

Exempted Real Property

Probably the most familiar exemption is the **homestead exemption.** Each state permits the debtor to retain the family home, either in its entirety or up to a specified dollar amount, free from the claims of unsecured creditors or trustees in bankruptcy (a *bankruptcy trustee* is appointed by the court to hold and protect the debtor's property, as will be discussed later in this chapter). The purpose of the homestead exemption is to ensure that the debtor will retain some form of shelter.

EXAMPLE #6 Van Cleave owes Acosta $40,000. The debt is the subject of a lawsuit, and the court awards Acosta a judgment of $40,000 against Van Cleave. Van Cleave's home is valued at $50,000, and the state exemption on homesteads is $25,000. There are no outstanding mortgages or other liens. To satisfy the judgment debt, Van Cleave's family home is sold at public auction for $45,000. The proceeds of the sale are distributed as follows:

1. Van Cleave is given $25,000 as his homestead exemption.
2. Acosta is paid $20,000 toward the judgment debt, leaving a $20,000 deficiency judgment (that is, "left-over debt") that can be satisfied from any other nonexempt property (personal or real) that Van Cleave may have, if allowed by state law.□

Exempted Personal Property

Various types of personal property may also be exempt from satisfaction of judgment debts. Personal property that is most often exempt includes the following:

1. Household furniture up to a specified dollar amount.
2. Clothing and certain personal possessions, such as family pictures or a Bible or other religious text.
3. A vehicle (or vehicles) for transportation (at least up to a specified dollar amount).
4. Certain classified animals, usually livestock but including pets.
5. Equipment that the debtor uses in a business or trade, such as tools or professional instruments, up to a specified dollar amount.

BANKRUPTCY PROCEEDINGS

Bankruptcy law in the United States has two goals—to protect a debtor by giving him or her a fresh start, free from creditors' claims, and to ensure equitable treatment to creditors who are competing for a debtor's assets. Bankruptcy law is federal law, but state laws on secured transactions, liens, judgments, and exemptions also play a role in federal bankruptcy proceedings.

Bankruptcy law prior to 2005 was based on the Bankruptcy Reform Act of 1978, as amended (called the Bankruptcy Code). In 2005, Congress enacted bankruptcy reform legislation that significantly overhauled certain provisions of the Bankruptcy Code for the first time in twenty-five years.[5] Because of its significance for creditors and debtors alike, we present the Bankruptcy Reform Act of 2005 as this chapter's *Landmark in the Legal Environment* feature on page 422.

---

5. The full title of the act is the Bankruptcy Abuse Prevention and Consumer Protection Act of 2005, Pub. L. No. 109-8, 119 Stat. 23 (April 20, 2005).

HOMESTEAD EXEMPTION
A law permitting a debtor to retain the family home, either in its entirety or up to a specified dollar amount, free from the claims of unsecured creditors or trustees in bankruptcy.

Livestock, such as the cattle shown here, is usually considered exempt property under laws that assist debtors. Why is this?
(PhotoDisc)

When Congress enacted the Bankruptcy Reform Act of 1978, many claimed that the act made it too easy for debtors to file for bankruptcy protection. The Bankruptcy Reform Act of 2005 was passed, in part, in response to businesses' concerns about the rise in personal bankruptcy filings. Certainly, the facts cannot be denied: from 1978 to 2005, personal bankruptcy filings increased ninefold, reaching a peak of 1,613,097 in the year ending June 30, 2003. By the early 2000s, various business groups—including credit-card companies, banks, and firms providing loans for automobile purchases—were claiming that the bankruptcy process was being abused and that reform was necessary. As Mallory Duncan of the National Retail Federation put it, bankruptcy had gone from being a "stigma" to being a "financial planning tool" for many debtors.[a]

More Repayment Plans, Fewer Liquidation Bankruptcies

One of the major goals of the Bankruptcy Reform Act of 2005 was to require consumers to pay as many of their debts as they possibly can instead of having those debts fully discharged in bankruptcy. Prior to the reforms, the vast majority of bankruptcies were filed under Chapter 7 of the Bankruptcy Code, which permitted debtors, with some exceptions, to have *all* of their debts discharged in bankruptcy. Only about 20 percent of personal bankruptcies were filed under Chapter 13 of the Bankruptcy Code. As you will read later in this chapter, this part of the Bankruptcy Code requires the debtor to establish a repayment plan and pay off as many of his or her debts as possible over a maximum period of five years. Under the 2005 legislation, more debtors now must file for bankruptcy under Chapter 13.

---

a. As cited in Nedra Pickler, "Bush Signs Big Rewrite of Bankruptcy Law," *The Los Angeles Times*, April 20, 2005.

Other Significant Provisions of the Act

Another important provision of the Bankruptcy Reform Act of 2005 involved the homestead exemption. Prior to the passage of the act, some states allowed debtors petitioning for bankruptcy to exempt all of the equity (the market value minus the outstanding mortgage owed) in their homes during bankruptcy proceedings. The 2005 act left these exemptions in place but put some limits on their use. The 2005 act also included a number of other changes. For example, one provision gave child-support obligations priority over other debts and allowed enforcement agencies to continue efforts to collect child-support payments.

APPLICATION TO TODAY'S LEGAL ENVIRONMENT

The Bankruptcy Reform Act of 2005 subjected a large class of individuals in the United States to increased financial risk. Supporters of the law hope that it will curb abuse by deterring financially troubled debtors from viewing bankruptcy as a mere "planning tool" instead of as a last resort. Certainly, fewer debtors are allowed to have their debts discharged in Chapter 7 liquidation proceedings. At the same time, the 2005 act made it more difficult for debtors to obtain a "fresh start" financially—one of the major goals of bankruptcy law in the United States. Under the 2005 act, more debtors are forced to file under Chapter 13. Additionally, the act made the bankruptcy process more time consuming and costly because it requires more extensive documentation and certification.

RELEVANT WEB SITES

To locate information on the Web concerning the 2005 bankruptcy reform legislation, go to this text's Web site at **www.cengage.com/blaw/let**, select "Chapter 13," and click on "URLs for Landmarks."

Bankruptcy Courts

RECALL
Congress regulates the jurisdiction of the federal courts, within the limits set by the U.S. Constitution. Congress can expand or reduce the number of federal courts at any time.

Bankruptcy proceedings are held in federal bankruptcy courts, which are under the authority of U.S. district courts, and rulings by bankruptcy courts can be appealed to the district courts. Essentially, a bankruptcy court fulfills the role of an administrative court for the district court concerning matters in bankruptcy. The bankruptcy court holds proceedings dealing with the procedures required to administer the debtor's estate in bankruptcy (the debtor's assets, as will be discussed shortly). A bankruptcy court can conduct a jury trial if the appropriate district court has authorized it and if the parties to the bankruptcy consent to a jury trial.

Types of Bankruptcy Relief

The Bankruptcy Code is contained in Title 11 of the *United States Code* (U.S.C.) and has eight "chapters." Chapters 1, 3, and 5 of the Code include general definitional provisions and provisions governing case administration and procedures, creditors, the debtor, and the estate. These three chapters of the Code normally apply to all types of bankrupties. There are five other chapters that set forth the different types of relief that debtors may seek. Chapter 7 provides for **liquidation** proceedings (the selling of all nonexempt assets and the distribution of the proceeds to the debtor's creditors). Chapter 9 governs the adjustment of the debts of municipalities. Chapter 11 governs reorganizations. Chapter 12 (for family farmers) and Chapter 13 (for individuals) provide for adjustment of the debts of parties with regular income.[6] A debtor (except for a municipality) need not be insolvent[7] to file for bankruptcy relief under the Bankruptcy Code. Anyone obligated to a creditor can declare bankruptcy.

Special Treatment of Consumer-Debtors

A **consumer-debtor** is a debtor whose debts result primarily from the purchase of goods for personal, family, or household use. To fully inform a consumer-debtor of the various types of relief available, the Code requires that the clerk of the court provide certain information to all consumer-debtors prior to the commencement of a bankruptcy filing. First, the clerk must give consumer-debtors written notice of the general purpose, benefits, and costs of each chapter of bankruptcy under which they may proceed. Second, the clerk must provide consumer-debtors with informational materials on the types of services available from credit counseling agencies.

In the following pages, we deal first with liquidation proceedings under Chapter 7 of the Code. We then examine the procedures required for Chapter 11 reorganizations and for Chapter 12 and Chapter 13 plans.

CHAPTER 7–LIQUIDATION

Liquidation is the most familiar type of bankruptcy proceeding and is often referred to as an *ordinary,* or *straight, bankruptcy.* Put simply, a debtor in a liquidation bankruptcy turns all assets over to a trustee. The trustee sells the nonexempt assets and distributes the proceeds to creditors. With certain exceptions, the remaining debts are then **discharged** (extinguished), and the debtor is relieved of the obligation to pay the debts.

Any "person"—defined as including individuals, partnerships, and corporations[8]—may be a debtor under Chapter 7. Railroads, insurance companies, banks, savings and loan associations, investment companies licensed by the Small Business Administration, and credit unions *cannot* be Chapter 7 debtors, however. Other chapters of the Code or other federal or state statutes apply to them. A husband and wife may file jointly for bankruptcy under a single petition.

LIQUIDATION
The sale of all of the nonexempt assets of a debtor and the distribution of the proceeds to the debtor's creditors. Chapter 7 of the Bankruptcy Code provides for liquidation bankruptcy proceedings.

CONSUMER-DEBTOR
An individual whose debts are primarily consumer debts (debts for purchases made primarily for personal, family, or household use).

DISCHARGE
In bankruptcy proceedings, the extinction of the debtor's dischargeable debts, which relieves the debtor of the obligation to pay the debts.

---

6. There are no Chapters 2, 4, 6, 8, or 10 in Title 11. Such "gaps" are not uncommon in the *United States Code.* They occur because, when a statute is enacted, chapter numbers (or other subdivisional unit numbers) are sometimes reserved for future use. (A gap may also appear if a law has been repealed.)

7. The inability to pay debts as they become due is known as *equitable* insolvency. A *balance-sheet* insolvency, which exists when a debtor's liabilities exceed assets, is not the test. Thus, it is possible for debtors to petition voluntarily for bankruptcy even though their assets far exceed their liabilities. This situation may occur when a debtor's cash-flow problems become severe.

8. The definition of *corporation* includes unincorporated companies and associations. It also covers labor unions.

A straight bankruptcy may be commenced by the filing of either a voluntary or an involuntary **petition in bankruptcy**—the document that is filed with a bankruptcy court to initiate bankruptcy proceedings. If a debtor files the petition, then it is a *voluntary bankruptcy.* If one or more creditors file a petition to force the debtor into bankruptcy, then it is called an *involuntary bankruptcy.* We discuss both voluntary and involuntary bankruptcy proceedings under Chapter 7 in the following subsections.

Voluntary Bankruptcy

To bring a voluntary petition in bankruptcy, the debtor files official forms designated for that purpose in the bankruptcy court. The Bankruptcy Reform Act of 2005 specifies that *before* debtors can file a petition, they must receive credit counseling from an approved nonprofit agency within the 180-day period preceding the date of filing. The act provides detailed criteria for the **U.S. trustee** (a government official who performs appointment and other administrative tasks that a bankruptcy judge would otherwise have to perform) to approve nonprofit budget and counseling agencies and requires a list of approved agencies to be made publicly available. A debtor filing a Chapter 7 petition must include a certificate proving that he or she attended an individual or group briefing from an approved counseling agency within the last 180 days (roughly six months).

The Code requires a consumer-debtor who has opted for liquidation bankruptcy proceedings to confirm the accuracy of the petition's contents. The debtor must also state in the petition, at the time of filing, that he or she understands the relief available under other chapters of the Code and has chosen to proceed under Chapter 7. If an attorney is representing the consumer-debtor, the attorney must file an affidavit stating that she or he has informed the debtor of the relief available under each chapter of bankruptcy. In addition, the 2005 act requires the attorney to reasonably attempt to verify the accuracy of the consumer-debtor's petition and schedules (described below). Failure to do so is considered perjury.

Chapter 7 Schedules   The voluntary petition contains the following schedules:

1. A list of both secured and unsecured creditors, their addresses, and the amount of debt owed to each.
2. A statement of the financial affairs of the debtor.
3. A list of all property owned by the debtor, including property claimed by the debtor to be exempt.
4. A listing of current income and expenses.
5. A certificate of credit counseling (as discussed previously).
6. Proof of payments received from employers within sixty days prior to the filing of the petition.
7. A statement of the amount of monthly income, itemized to show how the amount is calculated.
8. A copy of the debtor's federal income tax return for the most recent year ending immediately before the filing of the petition.

As previously noted, the official forms must be completed accurately, sworn to under oath, and signed by the debtor. To conceal assets or knowingly supply false information on these schedules is a crime under the bankruptcy laws.

Those seeking relief in a U.S. bankruptcy court wait in line in order to file their petitions. What type of information must a petitioner (or his or her attorney) provide in the petition for voluntary Chapter 7 bankruptcy? (AP Photo/Richard Drew)

Additional Information May Be Required   At the request of the court, the U.S. trustee, or any party of interest, the debtor must file tax returns at the end of each tax year while the case is pending and provide copies to the court. This requirement also applies to Chapter 11 and 13 bankruptcies (discussed later in this chapter). Also, if requested by the U.S. trustee or bankruptcy trustee, the debtor must provide a photo document establishing his or her identity (such as a driver's license or passport) or other such personal identifying information.

With the exception of tax returns, failure to file the required schedules within forty-five days after the filing of the petition (unless an extension of up to forty-five days is granted) will result in an automatic dismissal of the petition. The debtor has up to seven days before the date of the first creditors' meeting to provide a copy of the most current tax returns to the trustee.

When Substantial Abuse Will Be Presumed   Prior to 2005, a bankruptcy court could dismiss a Chapter 7 petition if it found that the debtor's use of Chapter 7 would constitute a "sustantial abuse" of that chapter. The 2005 act established a new system of "means testing"—based on the debtor's income—to determine whether a debtor's petition is presumed to be a "substantial abuse" of Chapter 7. If the debtor's family income is greater than the median family income in the state in which the petition is filed, the trustee or any party in interest (such as a creditor) can bring a motion to dismiss the Chapter 7 petition. State median incomes vary from state to state and are calculated and reported by the U.S. Bureau of the Census.

The debtor's current monthly income is calculated using the last six months' average income, less certain "allowed expenses" reflecting the basic needs of the debtor. The monthly amount is then multiplied by twelve. If the resulting income exceeds the state median income by $6,000 or more,[9] abuse is presumed, and the trustee or any creditor can file a motion to dismiss the petition. A debtor can rebut

---

9. This amount ($6,000) is the equivalent of $100 per month for five years, indicating that the debtor could pay at least $100 per month under a Chapter 13 five-year repayment plan.

(refute) the presumption of abuse "by demonstrating special circumstances that justify additional expenses or adjustments of current monthly income for which there is no reasonable alternative." (An example might be anticipated medical costs not covered by health insurance.) These additional expenses or adjustments must be itemized and their accuracy attested to under oath by the debtor.

When Substantial Abuse Will Not Be Presumed   If the debtor's income is below the state median (or if the debtor has successfully rebutted the means-test presumption), abuse will not be presumed. In these situations, the court may still find substantial abuse, but the creditors will not have standing (see Chapter 3) to file a motion to dismiss. Basically, this leaves intact the prior law on substantial abuse, allowing the court to consider such factors as the debtor's bad faith or circumstances indicating substantial abuse.

Can a debtor seeking relief under Chapter 7 exclude voluntary contributions to a retirement plan as a reasonably necessary expense in calculating her income? The Code does not disallow the contributions, but whether their exclusion constitutes substantial abuse requires a review of the debtor's circumstances, as in the following case.

Case 13.2 **Hebbring v. U.S. Trustee**

United States Court of Appeals,
Ninth Circuit, 2006.
463 F.3d 902.

BACKGROUND AND FACTS   In 2003, Lisa Hebbring owned a single-family home in Reno, Nevada, valued at $160,000, on which she owed $154,103. She also owned a 2001 Volkswagen Beetle valued at $14,000, on which she owed $18,839, and other personal property valued at $1,775. She earned $49,000 per year as a customer service representative for SBC Nevada. In June, Hebbring filed a Chapter 7 petition in a federal bankruptcy court, seeking relief from $11,124 in credit-card debt. Her petition listed monthly net income of $2,813 and expenditures of $2,897, for a deficit of $84. In calculating her income, Hebbring excluded a $232 monthly

pretax deduction for a contribution to a retirement plan maintained by her employer and an $81 monthly after-tax deduction for a contribution to her own retirement savings. At the time, Hebbring was thirty-three years old. The U.S. trustee assigned to oversee her case filed a motion to dismiss her petition for substantial abuse, arguing in part that the retirement savings contributions should be disallowed. According to the trustee, these and other adjustments would leave Hebbring $615 per month in disposable income, which would be enough to repay 100 percent of her credit-card debt over three years. The court dismissed her petition. She appealed to a federal district court, which affirmed the dismissal. Hebbring appealed to the U.S. Court of Appeals for the Ninth Circuit.

IN THE WORDS OF THE COURT . . . *WARDLAW*, Circuit Judge.

*   *   * In determining whether a petition constitutes a substantial abuse of Chapter 7, we examine the totality of the circumstances, focusing principally on whether the debtor will have sufficient future disposable income to fund a Chapter 13 plan that would pay a substantial portion of his unsecured debt. To calculate a debtor's disposable income, we begin with current monthly income and subtract amounts reasonably necessary to be expended *   *   * for the maintenance or support of the debtor or a dependent of the debtor.

*   *   * [Some] courts *   *   * have adopted a case-by-case approach, under which contributions to a retirement plan may be found reasonably necessary depending on the debtor's circumstances.

We believe this *   *   * approach better comports [is consistent] with Congress's intent, as expressed in the language, purpose, and structure of the Bankruptcy Code. By not defining the phrase "reasonably necessary" or providing any examples of expenses that categorically are or are not reasonably necessary, the Code suggests courts should examine each debtor's specific circumstances to determine whether a claimed expense is reasonably necessary for that debtor's maintenance or support. We find no evidence that Congress intended courts to employ a *per se* rule against retirement contributions, which may be crucial for debtors' support upon retirement, particularly for older debtors who have little or no savings. Where Congress intended courts to use a *per se* rule rather than a case-by-case approach in classifying financial interests or obligations under the Bankruptcy Code, it has explicitly communicated its intent. *Congress's decision not to categorically exclude any specific expense, including retirement contributions, from being considered reasonably necessary is probative* [an indication] *of its intent.* [Emphasis added.]

  *   *   *   *

In light of these considerations, and in the absence of any indication that Congress sought to prohibit debtors from voluntarily contributing to retirement plans *per se,* we conclude that bankruptcy courts have discretion to determine whether retirement contributions are a reasonably necessary expense for a particular debtor based on the facts of each individual case. In making this fact-intensive determination, courts should consider a number of factors, including but not limited to: the debtor's age, income, overall budget, expected date of retirement, existing retirement savings, and amount of contributions; the likelihood that stopping contributions will jeopardize the debtor's fresh start by forcing the debtor to make up lost contributions after emerging from bankruptcy; and the needs of the debtor's dependents. *Courts must allow debtors to seek bankruptcy protection while voluntarily saving for retirement if such savings appear reasonably necessary for the maintenance or support of the debtor or the debtor's dependents.* [Emphasis added.]

  *   *   *   *

Here, the bankruptcy court * * * found * * * that Hebbring's retirement contributions are not a reasonably necessary expense based on her age and specific financial circumstances. * * * When she filed her bankruptcy petition, Hebbring was only thirty-three years old and was contributing approximately 8% of her gross income toward her retirement. Although Hebbring had accumulated only $6,289 in retirement savings, she was earning $49,000 per year and making mortgage payments on a house. In light of these circumstances, the bankruptcy court's conclusion that Hebbring's retirement contributions are not a reasonably necessary expense is not clearly erroneous.

  *   *   *   *

For the foregoing reasons, the district court's order affirming the bankruptcy court's order dismissing this case is AFFIRMED.

DECISION AND REMEDY The U.S. Court of Appeals for the Ninth Circuit affirmed the lower court's decision, finding that Hebbring's retirement contributions were not reasonably necessary based on her age and financial circumstances.

THE ETHICAL DIMENSION Is it fair for the court to treat retirement contributions differently depending on a person's age?

WHAT IF THE FACTS WERE DIFFERENT? Would it likely have made a difference to the result in this case if the debtor's retirement contributions had been automatically and electronically deducted from her pay? Explain.

Additional Grounds for Dismissal As noted, a debtor's voluntary petition for Chapter 7 relief may be dismissed for substantial abuse or for failure to provide the necessary documents (such as schedules and tax returns) within the specified time. In addition, a motion to dismiss a Chapter 7 filing might be granted in two other situations under the Bankruptcy Reform Act of 2005. First, if the debtor has been convicted of a violent crime or a drug-trafficking offense, the victim can file a motion to dismiss the voluntary petition.[10] Second, if the debtor fails to pay postpetition domestic-support obligations (which include child and spousal support), the court may dismiss the debtor's Chapter 7 petition.

Order for Relief   If the voluntary petition for bankruptcy is found to be proper, the filing of the petition will itself constitute an order for relief. (An **order for relief** is the court's grant of assistance to a debtor.) Once a consumer-debtor's voluntary petition has been filed, the clerk of the court (or other appointee) must give the trustee and creditors notice of the order for relief by mail not more than twenty days after the entry of the order.

Involuntary Bankruptcy

An involuntary bankruptcy occurs when the debtor's creditors force the debtor into bankruptcy proceedings. An involuntary case cannot be commenced against a farmer[11] or a charitable institution. For an involuntary action to be filed against other debtors, the following requirements must be met: If the debtor has twelve or more creditors, three or more of those creditors having unsecured claims totaling at least $13,475 must join in the petition. If a debtor has fewer than twelve creditors, one or more creditors having a claim of $13,475 or more may file.

If the debtor challenges the involuntary petition, a hearing will be held, and the debtor's challenge will fail if the bankruptcy court finds either of the following:

1. That the debtor is generally not paying debts as they become due.
2. That a general receiver, custodian, or assignee took possession of, or was appointed to take charge of, substantially all of the debtor's property within 120 days before the filing of the involuntary petition.

If the court allows the bankruptcy to proceed, the debtor will be required to supply the same information in the bankruptcy schedules as in a voluntary bankruptcy.

An involuntary petition should not be used as an everyday debt-collection device, and the Code provides penalties for the filing of frivolous (unjustified) petitions against debtors. Judgment may be granted against the petitioning creditors for the costs and attorneys' fees incurred by the debtor in defending against an involuntary petition that is dismissed by the court. If the petition was filed in bad faith, damages can be awarded for injury to the debtor's reputation. Punitive damages may also be awarded.

Automatic Stay

The moment a petition, either voluntary or involuntary, is filed, an **automatic stay,** or suspension, of virtually all actions by creditors against the debtor or the debtor's property normally goes into effect. In other words, once a petition has been filed, creditors cannot contact the debtor by phone or mail or start any legal proceedings to recover debts or to repossess property. A secured creditor or other party in

---

10. Note that the court may not dismiss a case on this ground if the debtor's bankruptcy is necessary to satisfy a claim for a domestic-support obligation.

11. The definition of *farmer* includes persons who receive more than 50 percent of their gross income from farming operations, such as tilling the soil; dairy farming; ranching; or the production or raising of crops, poultry, or livestock. Corporations and partnerships, as well as individuals, can be farmers.

interest, however, may petition the bankruptcy court for relief from the automatic stay. If a creditor knowingly violates the automatic stay (a willful violation), any injured party, including the debtor, is entitled to recover actual damages, costs, and attorneys' fees and may be entitled to recover punitive damages as well.

Underlying the Code's automatic-stay provision for a secured creditor is a concept known as *adequate protection*. The adequate protection doctrine, among other things, protects secured creditors from losing their security as a result of the automatic stay. The bankruptcy court can provide adequate protection by requiring the debtor or trustee to make periodic cash payments or a one-time cash payment (or to provide additional collateral or replacement liens) to the extent that the stay may actually cause the value of the property to decrease.

Exceptions to the Automatic Stay   The 2005 Bankruptcy Reform Act created several exceptions to the automatic stay. It provided an exception for domestic-support obligations, which include any debt owed to or recoverable by a spouse, former spouse, or child of the debtor; a child's parent or guardian; or a governmental unit. In addition, proceedings against the debtor related to divorce, child custody or visitation, domestic violence, or support enforcement are not stayed. Also excepted are investigations by a securities regulatory agency (see Chapter 24) and certain statutory liens for property taxes.

Limitations on the Automatic Stay   If a creditor or other party in interest requests relief from the stay, the stay will automatically terminate sixty days after the request, unless the court grants an extension or the parties agree otherwise. Also, the automatic stay on secured debts normally will terminate thirty days after the petition is filed if the debtor had filed a bankruptcy petition that was dismissed within the prior year. Any party in interest can request the court to extend the stay by showing that the filing was made in good faith.

If the debtor had two or more bankruptcy petitions dismissed during the prior year, the Code presumes bad faith, and the automatic stay does not go into effect until the court determines that the filing was made in good faith. In addition, if the petition is subsequently dismissed (because the debtor failed to file the required documents within thirty days of filing, for example), the stay is terminated. Finally, the automatic stay on secured property terminates forty-five days after the creditors' meeting (to be discussed shortly) unless the debtor redeems or reaffirms certain debts (*reaffirmation* is discussed later in this chapter). In other words, the debtor cannot keep the secured property (such as a financed automobile), even if she or he continues to make payments on it, without reinstating the rights of the secured party to collect on the debt.

Property of the Estate

On the commencement of a liquidation proceeding under Chapter 7, an **estate in property** is created. The estate consists of all the debtor's interests in property currently held, wherever located, together with community property (property jointly owned by a husband and wife in certain states—see Chapter 22), property transferred in a transaction voidable by the trustee, proceeds and profits from the property of the estate, and certain after-acquired property. Interests in certain property—such as gifts, inheritances, property settlements (from divorce), and life insurance death proceeds—to which the debtor becomes entitled *within 180 days after filing* may also become part of the estate. Withholdings

ESTATE IN PROPERTY
In bankruptcy proceedings, all of the debtor's interests in property currently held, wherever located, together with certain jointly owned property, property transferred in transactions voidable by the trustee, proceeds and profits from the property of the estate, and certain property interests to which the debtor becomes entitled within 180 days after filing for bankruptcy.

for employee benefit plan contributions are excluded from the estate. Generally, though, the filing of a bankruptcy petition fixes a dividing line: property acquired prior to the filing of the petition becomes property of the estate, and property acquired after the filing of the petition, except as just noted, remains the debtor's.

Creditors' Meeting and Claims

Within a reasonable time after the order of relief has been granted (not less than ten days or more than thirty days), the trustee must call a meeting of the creditors listed in the schedules filed by the debtor. The bankruptcy judge does not attend this meeting, but the debtor is required to attend and to submit to an examination under oath. At the meeting, the trustee ensures that the debtor is aware of the potential consequences of bankruptcy and of his or her ability to file under a different chapter of the Bankruptcy Code.

To be entitled to receive a portion of the debtor's estate, each creditor normally files a *proof of claim* with the bankruptcy court clerk within ninety days of the creditors' meeting.[12] The proof of claim lists the creditor's name and address, as well as the amount that the creditor asserts is owed to the creditor by the debtor. A proof of claim is necessary if there is any dispute concerning the claim. If a creditor fails to file a proof of claim, the bankruptcy court or trustee may file the proof of claim on the creditor's behalf but is not obligated to do so.

Exemptions

The trustee takes control over the debtor's property, but an individual debtor is entitled to exempt certain property from the bankruptcy. The Bankruptcy Code exempts the following property:[13]

1. Up to $20,200 in equity in the debtor's residence and burial plot (the homestead exemption).
2. Interest in a motor vehicle up to $3,225.
3. Interest, up to $525 for a particular item, in household goods and furnishings, wearing apparel, appliances, books, animals, crops, and musical instruments (the aggregate total of all items is limited, however, to $10,775).
4. Interest in jewelry up to $1,350.
5. Interest in any other property up to $1,075, plus any unused part of the $20,200 homestead exemption up to $10,125.
6. Interest in any tools of the debtor's trade up to $2,025.
7. Any unmatured life insurance contracts owned by the debtor.
8. Certain interests in accrued dividends and interest under life insurance contracts owned by the debtor, not to exceed $10,775.
9. Professionally prescribed health aids.

Because of Florida's unlimited homestead exemption law, the state has been a haven for wealthy individuals looking to shield equity from creditors. This house in Boca Raton, Florida, shown while still under construction, belonged to Scott Sullivan, former CFO of WorldCom. WorldCom, now known as MCI, filed the largest bankruptcy in U.S. history about the same time this picture was taken in 2002. In 2005, Sullivan settled the WorldCom Securities Class Action Litigation by, among other things, surrendering the proceeds from the sale of the Florida house. The ten-bedroom, twelve-bath mansion with a boathouse, dock, and wine cellar went for $9.7 million, although the asking price was once $22.5 million. Under the 2005 Code, would Sullivan have thought he could take advantage of Florida's unlimited homestead exemption? Why or why not?
(Joe Raedle/Getty Images)

---

12. This ninety-day rule applies in Chapter 12 and Chapter 13 bankruptcies as well.

13. The dollar amounts stated in the Bankruptcy Code are adjusted automatically every three years on April 1 based on changes in the Consumer Price Index. The adjusted amounts are rounded to the nearest $25. The amounts stated in this chapter are in accordance with those computed on April 1, 2007.

10. The right to receive Social Security and certain welfare benefits, alimony and support, certain retirement funds and pensions, and education savings accounts held for specific periods of time.
11. The right to receive certain personal-injury and other awards up to $20,200.

Individual states have the power to pass legislation precluding debtors from using the federal exemptions within the state; a majority of the states have done this. In those states, debtors may use only state, not federal, exemptions. In the rest of the states, an individual debtor (or a husband and wife filing jointly) may choose either the exemptions provided under state law or the federal exemptions.

The Homestead Exemption

The 2005 Bankruptcy Reform Act significantly changed the law for those debtors seeking to use state homestead exemption statutes. In six states, including Florida and Texas, homestead exemptions allowed debtors petitioning for bankruptcy to shield *unlimited* amounts of equity in their homes from creditors. The Code now places limits on the amount that can be claimed as exempt in bankruptcy. Also, a debtor must have lived in a state for two years prior to filing the petition to be able to use the state homestead exemption (prior law required only six months).

In general, if the homestead was acquired within three and one-half years preceding the date of filing, the maximum equity exempted is $136,875, even if the state law would permit a higher amount. Also, if the debtor owes a debt arising from a violation of securities law or if the debtor committed certain criminal or tortious acts in the previous five years that indicate the filing was substantial abuse, the debtor may not exempt any amount of equity.

The Trustee

Promptly after the order for relief in the liquidation proceeding has been entered, a trustee is appointed. The basic duty of the trustee is to collect the debtor's available estate and reduce it to cash for distribution, preserving the interests of both the debtor and unsecured creditors. The trustee is required to promptly review all materials filed by the debtor to determine if there is substantial abuse. Within ten days after the first meeting of the creditors, the trustee must file a statement indicating whether the case is presumed to be an abuse under the means test and provide a copy to all creditors. When there is a presumption of abuse, the trustee must either file a motion to dismiss the petition (or convert it to a Chapter 13 case) or file a statement setting forth the reasons why a motion would not be appropriate. If the debtor owes a domestic-support obligation (such as child support), the trustee is required to provide written notice of the bankruptcy to the claim holder (a former spouse, for instance). (Note that these provisions are not limited to Chapter 7 bankruptcies.)

The Code gives the trustee certain powers, which must be exercised within two years of the order for relief. The trustee occupies a position *equivalent* in rights to that of certain other parties. For example, the trustee has the same rights as a creditor who could have obtained a judicial lien or levy execution on the debtor's property. This means that a trustee has priority over certain secured parties to the debtor's property. This right of a trustee, equivalent to that of a lien creditor, is known as the *strong-arm power*. A trustee also has power equivalent to that of a *bona fide purchaser* of real property from the debtor.

The Right to Possession of the Debtor's Property   The trustee has the power to require persons holding the debtor's property at the time the petition is filed to deliver the property to the trustee. Usually, a trustee does not take actual physical possession of a debtor's property but instead takes constructive possession by exercising control over the property. EXAMPLE #7 A trustee needs to obtain possession of a debtor's business inventory. To effectively take (constructive) possession, the trustee could notify the debtor, change the locks on the business's doors, and hire a security guard.□

Avoidance Powers   The trustee also has specific powers of *avoidance*—that is, the trustee can set aside a sale or other transfer of the debtor's property, taking it back as a part of the debtor's estate. These powers include any voidable rights available to the debtor, preferences, certain statutory liens, and fraudulent transfers by the debtor. Each of these powers is discussed in more detail below. Note that under the 2005 act, the trustee no longer has the power to avoid any transfer that was a bona fide payment of a domestic-support debt.

The debtor shares most of the trustee's avoidance powers. Thus, if the trustee does not take action to enforce one of the rights mentioned above, the debtor in a liquidation bankruptcy can still enforce that right.[14]

Voidable Rights   A trustee steps into the shoes of the debtor. Thus, any reason that a debtor can use to obtain the return of his or her property can be used by the trustee as well. These grounds for recovery include fraud, duress, incapacity, and mutual mistake.

EXAMPLE #8 Blane sells his boat to Inga. Inga gives Blane a check, knowing that she has insufficient funds in her bank account to cover the check. Inga has committed fraud. Blane has the right to avoid that transfer and recover the boat from Inga. Once an order for relief under Chapter 7 of the Code has been entered for Blane, the trustee can exercise the same right to recover the boat from Inga, and the boat becomes part of the debtor's estate.□

Preferences   A debtor is not permitted to make a property transfer or a payment that favors—or gives a **preference** to—one creditor over others. The trustee is allowed to recover payments made both voluntarily and involuntarily to one creditor in preference over another. If a **preferred creditor** (one who has received a preferential transfer from the debtor) has sold the property to an innocent third party, the trustee cannot recover the property from the innocent party. The preferred creditor, however, generally can be held accountable for the value of the property.

To have made a preferential payment that can be recovered, an *insolvent* debtor generally must have transferred property, for a *preexisting* debt, during the *ninety days* prior to the filing of the petition in bankruptcy. The transfer must have given the creditor more than the creditor would have received as a result of the bankruptcy proceedings. The trustee does not have to prove insolvency, as the Code provides that the debtor is presumed to be insolvent during this ninety-day period.

PREFERENCE
In bankruptcy proceedings, property transfers or payments made by the debtor that favor (give preference to) one creditor over others. The bankruptcy trustee is allowed to recover payments made both voluntarily and involuntarily to one creditor in preference over another.

PREFERRED CREDITOR
In the context of bankruptcy, a creditor who has received a preferential transfer from a debtor.

---

14. Under a Chapter 11 bankruptcy (to be discussed later), for which no trustee other than the debtor generally exists, the debtor has the same avoidance powers as a trustee under Chapter 7. Under Chapters 12 and 13 (also to be discussed later), a trustee must be appointed.

Preferences to Insiders Sometimes, the creditor receiving the preference is an *insider*—an individual, a partner, a partnership, or an officer or a director of a corporation (or a relative of one of these) who has a close relationship with the debtor. In this situation, the avoidance power of the trustee is extended to transfers made within *one year* before filing; the *presumption* of insolvency is still confined to the ninety-day period, though. Therefore, the trustee must prove that the debtor was insolvent at the time of an earlier transfer.

Transfers That Do Not Constitute Preferences Not all transfers are preferences. To be a preference, the transfer must be made in exchange for something other than current consideration. Therefore, most courts do not consider a debtor's payment for services rendered within fifteen days prior to the payment to be a preference. If a creditor receives payment in the ordinary course of business, such as payment of last month's telephone bill, the trustee in bankruptcy cannot recover the payment. To be recoverable, a preference must be a transfer for an antecedent (preexisting) debt, such as a year-old printing bill. In addition, the Code permits a consumer-debtor to transfer any property to a creditor up to a total value of $5,475, without the transfer's constituting a preference (this amount was increased from $600 to $5,000 by the 2005 act and is increased periodically under the law). Payment of domestic-support debts do not constitute a preference. Also, transfers that were made as part of an alternative repayment schedule negotiated by an approved credit counseling agency are not preferences.

Liens on Debtor's Property The trustee has the power to avoid certain statutory liens against the debtor's property, such as a landlord's lien for unpaid rent. The trustee can avoid statutory liens that first became effective at the time the bankruptcy petition was filed or when the debtor became insolvent. The trustee can also avoid any lien against a good faith purchaser that was not perfected or enforceable on the date of the bankruptcy filing.

Fraudulent Transfers The trustee may avoid fraudulent transfers or obligations if they were made within two years of the filing of the petition or if they were made with actual intent to hinder, delay, or defraud a creditor. Transfers made for less than reasonably equivalent consideration are also vulnerable if the debtor thereby became insolvent, was left engaged in business with an unreasonably small amount of capital, or intended to incur debts that would be beyond his or her ability to pay. When a fraudulent transfer is made outside the Code's two-year limit, creditors may seek alternative relief under state laws. State laws often allow creditors to recover for transfers made up to three years prior to the filing of a petition.

> **NOTE**
> Usually, when property is recovered as a preference, the trustee sells it and distributes the proceeds to the debtor's creditors.

Distribution of Property

The Code provides specific rules for the distribution of the debtor's property to secured and unsecured creditors (to be discussed shortly). If any amount remains after the priority classes of creditors have been satisfied, it is turned over to the debtor. Exhibit 13–2 on the following page illustrates graphically the collection and distribution of property in most voluntary bankruptcies.

In a bankruptcy case in which the debtor has no assets (called a "no-asset" case), creditors are notified of the debtor's petition for bankruptcy but are instructed not to file a claim. In such a case, the unsecured creditors will receive no payment, and most, if not all, of these debts will be discharged.

EXHIBIT 13–2 COLLECTION AND DISTRIBUTION OF PROPERTY IN MOST VOLUNTARY BANKRUPTCIES
This exhibit illustrates the property that might be collected in a debtor's voluntary bankruptcy and how it might be distributed to creditors. Involuntary bankruptcies and some voluntary bankruptcies could include additional types of property and other creditors.

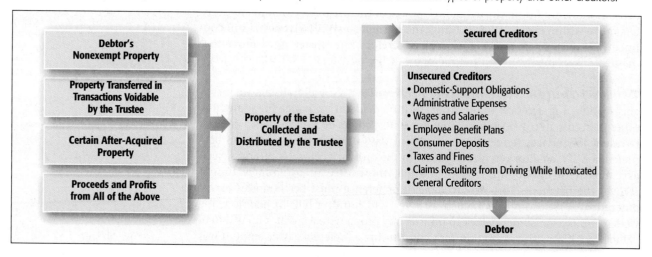

Distribution to Secured Creditors   The Code provides that a consumer-debtor, either within thirty days of filing a liquidation petition or before the date of the first meeting of the creditors (whichever is first), must file with the clerk a statement of intention with respect to the secured collateral. The statement must indicate whether the debtor will redeem the collateral (make a single payment equal to the current value of the property), reaffirm the debt (continue making payments on the debt), or surrender the property to the secured party.[15] The trustee is obligated to enforce the debtor's statement within forty-five days after the meeting of the creditors. As noted previously, failure of the debtor to redeem or reaffirm within forty-five days terminates the automatic stay.

Distribution to Unsecured Creditors   Bankruptcy law establishes an order of priority for classes of debts owed to *unsecured* creditors, and they are paid in the order of their priority. Each class must be fully paid before the next class is entitled to any of the remaining proceeds. If there are insufficient proceeds to pay fully all the creditors in a class, the proceeds are distributed *proportionately* to the creditors in that class, and classes lower in priority receive nothing. If there is any balance remaining after all the creditors are paid, it is returned to the debtor.

The reform act elevated domestic-support (mainly child-support) obligations to the highest priority of unsecured claims—so these are the first debts to be paid. After that, administrative expenses related to the bankruptcy (such as court costs, trustee fees, and attorneys' fees) are paid; next come any expenses that a debtor in an involuntary bankruptcy incurs in the ordinary course of business. Unpaid wages, salaries, and commissions earned within ninety days prior to the petition are paid next, followed by certain claims for contributions to employee benefit plans, claims by farmers and fishermen, consumer deposits, and certain taxes. Claims of general creditors rank last in the order of priority, which is why these unsecured creditors often receive little, if anything, in a Chapter 7 bankruptcy.

---

15. Also, if applicable, the debtor must specify whether the collateral will be claimed as exempt property.

Discharge

From the debtor's point of view, the purpose of a liquidation proceeding is to obtain a fresh start through the discharge of debts.[16] As mentioned earlier, once the debtor's assets have been distributed to creditors as permitted by the Code, the debtor's remaining debts are then discharged, meaning that the debtor is not obligated to pay them. Certain debts, however, are not dischargeable in bankruptcy. Also, certain debtors may not qualify to have all debts discharged in bankruptcy. These situations are discussed below.

Exceptions to Discharge Discharge of a debt may be denied because of the nature of the claim or the conduct of the debtor. A court will not discharge claims that are based on a debtor's willful or malicious conduct or fraud, or claims related to property or funds that the debtor obtained by false pretenses, embezzlement, or larceny. Any monetary judgment against the debtor for driving while intoxicated cannot be discharged in bankruptcy. When a debtor fails to list a creditor on the bankruptcy schedules (and thus the creditor is not notified of the bankruptcy), that creditor's claims are not dischargeable.

Claims that are not dischargeable in a liquidation bankruptcy include amounts due to the government for taxes, fines, or penalties.[17] Additionally, amounts borrowed by the debtor to pay these taxes will not be discharged. Domestic-support obligations and property settlements arising from a divorce or separation cannot be discharged. Certain student loans and educational debts are not dischargeable (unless payment of the loans imposes an undue hardship on the debtor and the debtor's dependents), nor are amounts due on a retirement account loan. Consumer debts for purchasing luxury items worth more than $550 and cash advances totaling more than $825 are generally not dischargeable.

In the following case, the court considered whether to order the discharge of a debtor's student loan obligations. What does a debtor have to prove to show "undue hardship"?

> **BE AWARE**
> Often, a discharge in bankruptcy—even under Chapter 7—does not free a debtor of *all* of her or his debts.

---

16. Discharges are granted under Chapter 7 only to *individuals,* not to corporations or partnerships. The latter may use Chapter 11, or they may terminate their existence under state law.

17. Taxes accruing within three years prior to bankruptcy are nondischargeable, including federal and state income taxes, employment taxes, taxes on gross receipts, property taxes, excise taxes, customs duties, and any other taxes for which the government claims the debtor is liable in some capacity. See 11 U.S.C. Sections 507(a)(8), 523(a)(1).

 **Case 13.3** **In re Mosley**

United States Court of Appeals,
Eleventh Circuit, 2007.
494 F.3d 1320.

BACKGROUND AND FACTS Keldric Mosley incurred student loans while attending Georgia's Alcorn State University between 1989 and 1994. At Alcorn, Mosley joined the U.S. Army Reserve Officers' Training Corps. During training in 1993, Mosley fell from a tank and injured his hip and back. Medical problems from his injuries led him to resign his commission. He left Alcorn to live with his mother in Atlanta from 1994 to

1999. He worked briefly for several employers, but depressed and physically limited by his injury, he was unable to keep any of the jobs. He tried to return to school but could not obtain financial aid because of the debt he had incurred at Alcorn. In 1999, a federal bankruptcy court granted him a discharge under Chapter 7, but it did not include the student loans. In 2000, after a week at the Georgia Regional Hospital, a state-supported mental-health facility, Mosley was prescribed medication through the U.S. Department of Veterans Affairs for depression, back pain, and other problems. By 2004, his

CASE 13.3—CONTINUED

CASE 13.3–CONTINUED

monthly income consisted primarily of $210 in disability benefits from the Veterans Administration. Homeless and in debt for $45,000 to Educational Credit Management Corporation, Mosley asked the bankruptcy court to reopen his case. The court granted him a discharge of his student loans on the basis of undue hardship. Educational Credit appealed to the U.S. Court of Appeals for the Eleventh Circuit.

IN THE WORDS OF THE COURT . . . *JOHN R. GIBSON*, Circuit Judge.

* * * *

* * * To establish undue hardship [the courts require:]

(1) that the debtor cannot maintain, based on current income and expenses, a "minimal" standard of living * * * if forced to repay the loans; (2) that additional circumstances exist indicating that this state of affairs is likely to persist for a significant portion of the repayment period of the student loans; and (3) that the debtor has made good faith efforts to repay the loans.

Educational Credit * * * contends that the bankruptcy court improperly relaxed Mosley's evidentiary burden [duty to produce enough evidence to prove an assertion] on the second and third requirements * * * . The bankruptcy court concluded that Mosley established undue hardship with his credible testimony that he has tried to obtain work but, for ten years, his "substantial physical and emotional ailments" have prevented him from holding a steady job. * * * Educational Credit argues that corroborating medical evidence independent from the debtor's testimony is required * * * where medical disabilities are the "additional circumstances" * * * .

* * * *

We * * * decline to adopt a rule requiring Mosley to submit independent medical evidence to corroborate his testimony that his depression and back problems were additional circumstances likely to render him unable to repay his student loans. We see no inconsistency between * * * holding that the debtor's detailed testimony was sufficient evidence of undue hardship and the * * * cases cited by Educational Credit where debtors' less detailed testimony was held to be insufficient.

Educational Credit also argues that Mosley's medical prognosis [prediction about how a situation will develop in the future] is a subject requiring specialized medical knowledge * * * and that Mosley was not competent to give his opinion on this matter. Mosley, however, did not purport to give an opinion on his medical prognosis, but rather testified from personal knowledge about how his struggles with depression, back pain, and the side effects of his medication have made it difficult for him to obtain work.

We now turn to Educational Credit's argument that the record does not support a conclusion of undue hardship because Mosley's testimony did not establish * * * that he likely will be unable to repay his student loans in the future and that he has made good faith efforts to repay the loans.

* * * In showing that "additional circumstances" make it unlikely that he will be able to repay his loans for a significant period of time, Mosley testified that his depression and chronic back pain have frustrated his efforts to work, and thus his ability to repay his loans, as well as to provide himself with shelter, food, and transportation, for several years. * * * Mosley's testimony * * * is * * * unrefuted and is corroborated by his Social Security earnings statements. He testified that his back problems preclude him from heavy lifting, which rules out most of the jobs available [through the Georgia Department of Labor where] he seeks work. Exacerbating [aggravating] the problem, his medications make it difficult for him to function. He did not finish college and has been unable to complete the training necessary to learn a trade. Mosley relies on public assistance programs for health care and food, and * * * there is no reason to believe that Mosley's condition will improve in the future.

The bankruptcy court also correctly concluded that Mosley's testimony established the * * * requirement that he has made good faith efforts to repay his student loans. * * * *Good faith is measured by the debtor's efforts to obtain employment, maximize income, and minimize expenses; his default should result, not from his choices, but from factors beyond his reasonable control.* Mosley has attempted to find work, as demonstrated by the series of jobs he held while living with his mother from 1994 to 1999 and his participation in the [state] labor pool since 2000. Because of his medical conditions, Mosley has been largely unsuccessful, and thus has not had the means even to attempt to make payments. * * * His income has been below the poverty line for years. He lives without a home and car and cannot further minimize his expenses. [Emphasis added.]

DECISION AND REMEDY   The U.S. Court of Appeals for the Eleventh Circuit affirmed the lower court's discharge of the debtor's student loans. The debtor's medical problems, lack of skills, and "dire living conditions" made it unlikely that he would be able to hold a job and repay the loans. Furthermore, the debtor "has made good faith efforts to repay his student loans and would suffer undue hardship if they were excepted from discharge."

THE ETHICAL DIMENSION   Should a debtor be required to attempt to negotiate a repayment plan with a creditor to demonstrate good faith? Why or why not?

THE GLOBAL DIMENSION   If this debtor were to relocate to a country with a lower cost of living than the United States, should his change in circumstances be a ground for revoking the discharge? Explain your answer.

Objections to Discharge   In addition to the exceptions to discharge previously listed, a bankruptcy court may deny the discharge of the *debtor* (as opposed to the debt). Grounds for the denial of discharge of the debtor include the following:

1. The debtor's concealment or destruction of property with the intent to hinder, delay, or defraud a creditor.
2. The debtor's fraudulent concealment or destruction of financial records.
3. The granting of a discharge to the debtor within eight years prior to the filing of the petition.
4. The debtor's failure to complete the required consumer education course (unless such a course is unavailable).
5. Proceedings in which the debtor could be found guilty of a felony (basically, a court may not discharge any debt until the completion of felony proceedings against the debtor).

The purpose of denying a discharge on these or other grounds is to prevent a debtor from avoiding, through bankruptcy, the consequences of his or her wrongful conduct. When a discharge is denied under these circumstances, the debtor's assets are still distributed to the creditors, but the debtor remains liable for the unpaid portions of all claims.

Revocation of Discharge   On petition by the trustee or a creditor, the bankruptcy court may, within one year, revoke the discharge decree if it is discovered that the debtor was fraudulent or dishonest during the bankruptcy proceedings. The revocation renders the discharge void, allowing creditors not satisfied by the distribution of the debtor's estate to proceed with their claims against the debtor.

Reaffirmation of Debt   An agreement to pay a debt dischargeable in bankruptcy is called a **reaffirmation agreement.** A debtor may wish to pay a debt—for

REAFFIRMATION AGREEMENT
An agreement between a debtor and a creditor in which the debtor voluntarily agrees to pay, or reaffirm, a debt dischargeable in bankruptcy. To be enforceable, the agreement must be made before the debtor is granted a discharge.

example, a debt owed to a family member, physician, bank, or some other cred-itor—even though the debt could be discharged in bankruptcy. Also, a debtor cannot retain secured property while continuing to pay without entering into a reaffirmation agreement.

To be enforceable, reaffirmation agreements must be made before the debtor is granted a discharge. The agreement must be signed and filed with the court (along with the original disclosure documents, as you will read shortly). Court approval is required unless the debtor is represented by an attorney during the negotiation of the reaffirmation and submits the proper documents and certifi-cations. Even when the debtor is represented by an attorney, court approval may be required if it appears that the reaffirmation will result in undue hardship to the debtor. When court approval is required, a separate hearing will take place. The court will approve the reaffirmation only if it finds that the agreement will not result in undue hardship on the debtor and that the reaffirmation is consis-tent with the debtor's best interests.

Reaffirmation Disclosures   To discourage creditors from engaging in abu-sive reaffirmation practices, the Code provides the specific language for several pages of disclosures that must be given to debtors entering reaffirmation agree-ments. Among other things, these disclosures explain that the debtor is not required to reaffirm any debt, but that liens on secured property, such as mort-gages and cars, will remain in effect even if the debt is not reaffirmed. The reaf-firmation agreement must disclose the amount of the debt reaffirmed, the rate of interest, the date payments begin, and the right to rescind.

The disclosures also caution the debtor: "Only agree to reaffirm a debt if it is in your best interest. Be sure you can afford the payments you agree to make." The original disclosure documents must be signed by the debtor, certified by the debtor's attorney, and filed with the court at the same time as the reaffirmation agreement. A reaffirmation agreement that is not accompanied by the original signed disclosures will not be effective.

CHAPTER 11–REORGANIZATION

The type of bankruptcy proceeding used most commonly by corporate debtors is the Chapter 11 *reorganization*. In a reorganization, the creditors and the debtor formulate a plan under which the debtor pays a portion of its debts and the rest of the debts are discharged. The debtor is allowed to continue in business. Although this type of bankruptcy is generally a corporate reorganization, any debtors (including individuals but excluding stockbrokers and commodities bro-kers) who are eligible for Chapter 7 relief are eligible for relief under Chapter 11. In 1994, Congress established a "fast-track" Chapter 11 procedure for small-business debtors whose liabilities do not exceed $2.19 million and who do not own or manage real estate. This allows bankruptcy proceedings without the appointment of committees and can save time and costs.

The same principles that govern the filing of a liquidation (Chapter 7) peti-tion apply to reorganization (Chapter 11) proceedings. The case may be brought either voluntarily or involuntarily. The same guidelines govern the entry of the order for relief. The automatic-stay provision applies in reorganizations as well. The 2005 Bankruptcy Reform Act's exceptions to the automatic stay also apply to Chapter 11 proceedings, as do the provisions regarding substantial abuse and additional grounds for dismissal (or conversion) of bankruptcy petitions. Also, the 2005 act contains specific rules and limitations for *individual* debtors who file a Chapter 11 petition. For example, an individual debtor's postpetition acquisitions and earnings become the property of the bankruptcy estate.

Must Be in the Best Interests of the Creditors

Under Section 305(a) of the Bankruptcy Code, a court, after notice and a hearing, may dismiss or suspend all proceedings in a case at any time if dismissal or suspension would better serve the interests of the creditors. Section 1112 also allows a court, after notice and a hearing, to dismiss a case under reorganization "for cause." Cause includes the absence of a reasonable likelihood of rehabilitation, the inability to effect a plan, and an unreasonable delay by the debtor that is prejudicial to (may harm the interests of) creditors.

One of the nation's most well-known "record" stores closed its doors after CD sales kept declining. When Tower Records started to get into financial trouble, what were its bankruptcy options?
(Eric Chan/Creative Commons)

Workouts

In some instances, creditors may prefer private, negotiated adjustments of creditor-debtor relations, also known as **workouts,** to bankruptcy proceedings. Often, these out-of-court workouts are much more flexible and thus more conducive to a speedy settlement. Speed is critical because delay is one of the most costly elements in any bankruptcy proceeding. Another advantage of workouts is that they avoid the various administrative costs of bankruptcy proceedings.

WORKOUT
An out-of-court agreement between a debtor and creditors in which the parties work out a payment plan or schedule under which the debtor's debts can be discharged.

Debtor in Possession

On entry of the order for relief, the debtor in Chapter 11 generally continues to operate the business as a **debtor in possession (DIP).** The court, however, may appoint a trustee (often referred to as a *receiver*) to operate the debtor's business if gross mismanagement of the business is shown or if appointing a trustee is in the best interests of the estate.

The DIP's role is similar to that of a trustee in a liquidation. The DIP is entitled to avoid preferential payments made to creditors and fraudulent transfers of assets. The DIP has the power to decide whether to cancel or assume prepetition executory contracts (those that are not yet performed) or unexpired leases

DEBTOR IN POSSESSION (DIP)
In Chapter 11 bankruptcy proceedings, a debtor who is allowed to continue in possession of the estate in property (the business) and to continue business operations.

Creditors' Committees

As soon as practicable after the entry of the order for relief, a committee of unsecured creditors is appointed. If the debtor has filed a plan accepted by the creditors, however, the trustee may decide not to call a meeting of the creditors. The committee may consult with the trustee or the DIP concerning the administration of the case or the formulation of the plan. Additional creditors' committees may be appointed to represent special interest creditors. A court may order the trustee to change the membership of a committee or to increase the number of committee members to include a small-business concern if the court deems it necessary to ensure adequate representation of the creditors.

Orders affecting the estate generally will be entered only with the consent of the committee or after a hearing in which the judge is informed of the position of the committee. As mentioned on page 438, businesses with debts of less than $2.19 million that do not own or manage real estate can avoid creditors' committees. In these cases, orders can be entered without a committee's consent.

The Reorganization Plan

A reorganization plan to rehabilitate the debtor is a plan to conserve and administer the debtor's assets in the hope of an eventual return to successful operation and solvency.

Filing the Plan   Only the debtor may file a plan within the first 120 days after the date of the order for relief. The 120-day period may be extended, but not beyond 18 months from the date of the order for relief. For a small-business debtor, the time for the debtor's filing is 180 days.

The plan must be fair and equitable and must do the following:

1. Designate classes of claims and interests.
2. Specify the treatment to be afforded the classes. (The plan must provide the same treatment for all claims in a particular class.)
3. Provide an adequate means for execution. (Individual debtors must utilize postpetition assets as necessary to execute the plan.)
4. Provide for payment of tax claims over a five-year period.

Acceptance and Confirmation of the Plan   Once the plan has been developed, it is submitted to each class of creditors for acceptance. A class has accepted the plan when a majority of the creditors, representing two-thirds of the amount of the total claim, vote to approve it. Confirmation is conditioned on the debtor's certifying that all postpetition domestic-support obligations have been paid in full. For small-business debtors, if the plan meets the listed requirements, the court must confirm the plan within forty-five days (unless this period is extended).

Even when all classes of creditors accept the plan, the court may refuse to confirm it if it is not "in the best interests of the creditors."[18] A former spouse or child of the debtor can block the plan if it does not provide for payment of her or his claims in cash. Under the 2005 act, if an unsecured creditor objects to the plan, specific rules apply to the value of property to be distributed under the plan. The plan can also be modified upon the request of the debtor, trustee, U.S. trustee, or holder of the unsecured claim. Tax claims must be paid over a five-year period.

Even if only one class of creditors has accepted the plan, the court may still confirm the plan under the Code's so-called **cram-down provision.** In other words, the court may confirm the plan over the objections of a class of creditors. Before the court can exercise this right of cram-down confirmation, it must be demonstrated that the plan is fair and equitable, and does not discriminate unfairly against any creditors.

Discharge   The plan is binding on confirmation; however, confirmation of a plan does not discharge an individual debtor. Individual debtors must complete the plan prior to discharge, unless the court orders otherwise. For all other debtors,

CRAM-DOWN PROVISION
A provision of the Bankruptcy Code that allows a court to confirm a debtor's Chapter 11 reorganization plan even though only one class of creditors has accepted it. To exercise the court's right under this provision, the court must demonstrate that the plan does not discriminate unfairly against any creditors and is fair and equitable.

---

18. The plan need not provide for full repayment to unsecured creditors. Instead, creditors receive a percentage of each dollar owed to them by the debtor.

the court may order discharge from all claims not protected under the plan at any time after the plan is confirmed. This discharge does not apply to any claims that would be denied discharge under liquidation.

BANKRUPTCY RELIEF UNDER CHAPTER 13 AND CHAPTER 12

In addition to bankruptcy relief through liquidation (Chapter 7) and reorganization (Chapter 11), the Code also provides for individuals' repayment plans (Chapter 13) and family-farmer and family-fisherman debt adjustments (Chapter 12), as discussed next.

Individuals' Repayment Plan—Chapter 13

Chapter 13 of the Bankruptcy Code provides for the "Adjustment of Debts of an Individual with Regular Income." Individuals (not partnerships or corporations) with regular income who owe fixed unsecured debts of less than $336,900 or fixed secured debts of less than $1,010,650 may take advantage of bankruptcy repayment plans. Among those eligible are salaried employees; sole proprietors; and individuals who live on welfare, Social Security, fixed pensions, or investment income. Many small-business debtors have a choice of filing under either Chapter 11 or Chapter 13. Repayment plans offer several advantages, however. One advantage is that they are less expensive and less complicated than reorganization proceedings or, for that matter, even liquidation proceedings.

Filing the Petition   A Chapter 13 repayment plan case can be initiated only by the filing of a voluntary petition by the debtor or by the conversion of a Chapter 7 petition (because of a finding of substantial abuse under the means test, for example).[19] A trustee, who will make payments under the plan, must be appointed. On the filing of a repayment plan petition, the automatic stay previously discussed takes effect. Although the stay applies to all or part of the debtor's consumer debt, it does not apply to any business debt incurred by the debtor. The automatic stay also does not apply to domestic-support obligations.

The Bankruptcy Code imposes the requirement of good faith on a debtor at both the time of the filing of the petition and the time of the filing of the plan. The Code does not define good faith—it is determined in each case through a consideration of "the totality of the circumstances." Bad faith can be cause for the dismissal of a Chapter 13 petition. **EXAMPLE #9** Roger and Pauline Buis bought an air show business, including a helicopter, a trailer, and props, from Robert and Annette Hosking. The Buises formed Otto Airshows and decorated the helicopter as "Otto the Clown." They performed in air shows and took passengers on flights for a fee. A few years later, the Buises began accusing a competitor of safety lapses, and the competitor filed and won a defamation lawsuit against the Buises and Otto Airshows. The Buises then stopped doing business as Otto Airshows and formed a new firm, Prop and Rotor Aviation, Inc., to which they leased the Otto equipment. Within a month, they filed a bankruptcy petition under Chapter 13. The plan and the schedules did not mention the lawsuit, the equipment lease, a settlement that the Buises received in an unrelated suit, and other items. The court therefore dismissed the Buises' petition due to bad faith. The debtors had

---

19. A Chapter 13 repayment plan may sometimes be converted to a Chapter 7 liquidation either at the request of the debtor or, under certain circumstances, "for cause" by a creditor. A Chapter 13 case may be converted to a Chapter 11 case after a hearing.

not included all of their assets and liabilities on their initial petition, and had timed its filing to avoid payment on the defamation judgment.◻[20]

The Repayment Plan   The debtor's repayment plan may provide either for payment of all obligations in full or for payment of a lesser amount. The plan must provide for the following:

1. The turning over to the trustee of such future earnings or income of the debtor as is necessary for execution of the plan.
2. Full payment through deferred cash payments of all claims entitled to priority, such as taxes.[21]
3. Identical treatment of all claims within a particular class. (The Code permits the debtor to list co-debtors, such as guarantors or sureties, as a separate class.)

Time Allowed for Repayment   Prior to the 2005 act, the time for repayment was usually three years unless the court approved an extension for up to five years. Now, the length of the payment plan (three or five years) is determined by the debtor's family income. If the debtor's family income is greater than the state median family income under the means test (previously discussed), the proposed plan must be for five years. The term may not exceed five years, however.

The Code requires the debtor to make "timely" payments from her or his disposable income, and the trustee must ensure that the debtor commences these payments. The debtor must begin making payments under the proposed plan within thirty days after the plan has been *filed.* Failure of the debtor to make timely payments or to begin making required payments will allow the court to convert the case to a liquidation bankruptcy or to dismiss the petition.

Confirmation of the Plan   After the plan is filed, the court holds a confirmation hearing, at which interested parties (such as creditors) may object to the plan. The hearing must be held at least twenty days, but no more than forty-five days, after the meeting of the creditors. Confirmation of the plan is dependent on the debtor's certification that postpetition domestic-support obligations have been paid in full and that all prepetition tax returns have been filed. The court will confirm a plan with respect to each claim of a secured creditor under any of the following circumstances:

1. If the secured creditors have accepted the plan.
2. If the plan provides that secured creditors retain their liens until there is payment in full or until the debtor receives a discharge.
3. If the debtor surrenders the property securing the claims to the creditors.

BE CAREFUL
Courts, trustees, and creditors carefully monitor Chapter 13 debtors. If payments are not made, a court can require the debtor to explain why and may allow a creditor to take the property that was used as collateral for the loan from the debtor.

Discharge   After the completion of all payments, the court grants a discharge of all debts provided for by the repayment plan. Except for allowed claims not provided for by the plan, certain long-term debts provided for by the plan, certain tax claims, payments on retirement accounts, and claims for domestic-support obligations, all other debts are dischargeable. Under prior law, a discharge of debts under a Chapter 13 repayment plan was sometimes referred to as a "superdischarge" because it allowed the discharge of fraudulently incurred debt and claims resulting from malicious or willful injury.

---

20. *In re Buis,* 337 Bankr. 243 (N.D. Fla. 2006).
21. As with a Chapter 11 reorganization plan, full repayment of all claims is not always required.

The 2005 Bankruptcy Reform Act, however, deleted most of the "superdischarge" provisions, especially for debts based on fraud. Today, debts for trust fund taxes, taxes for which returns were never filed or filed late (within two years of filing), domestic-support payments, student loans, and debts related to injury or property damage caused while driving under the influence of alcohol or drugs are nondischargeable.

Family Farmers and Fishermen

In 1986, to help relieve economic pressure on small farmers, Congress created Chapter 12 of the Bankruptcy Code. In 2005, Congress extended this protection to family fishermen,[22] modified its provisions somewhat, and made it a permanent chapter in the Bankruptcy Code (previously, the statutes authorizing Chapter 12 had to be periodically renewed by Congress).

For purposes of Chapter 12, a *family farmer* is one whose gross income is at least 50 percent farm dependent and whose debts are at least 80 percent farm related.[23] The total debt must not exceed $3,544,525. A partnership or a closely held corporation (see Chapter 15) that is at least 50 percent owned by the farm family can also qualify as a family farmer.

A *family fisherman* is defined as one whose gross income is at least 50 percent dependent on commercial fishing operations and whose debts are at least 80 percent related to commercial fishing. The total debt for a family fisherman must not exceed $1,642,500. As with family farmers, a partnership or closely held corporation can also qualify.

Filing the Petition The procedure for filing a family-farmer or family-fisherman bankruptcy plan is very similar to the procedure for filing a repayment plan under Chapter 13. The debtor must file a plan not later than ninety days after the order for relief. The filing of the petition acts as an automatic stay against creditors' and co-obligors' actions against the estate.

A farmer or fisherman who has already filed a reorganization or repayment plan may convert the plan to a Chapter 12 plan. The debtor may also convert a Chapter 12 plan to a liquidation plan.

Content and Confirmation of the Plan The content of a plan under Chapter 12 is basically the same as that of a Chapter 13 repayment plan. The plan can be modified by the debtor but, except for cause, must be confirmed or denied within forty-five days of the filing of the plan.

Court confirmation of the plan is the same as for a repayment plan. In summary, the plan must provide for payment of secured debts at the value of the collateral. If the secured debt exceeds the value of the collateral, the remaining debt is unsecured. For unsecured debtors, the plan must be confirmed if either the value of the property to be distributed under the plan equals the amount of the claim or the plan provides that all of the debtor's disposable income to be received in a three-year period (or longer, by court approval) will be applied to making payments. Completion of payments under the plan discharges all debts provided for by the plan.

---

22. Although the Code uses the terms *fishermen* and *fisherman,* Chapter 12 provisions apply equally to men and women.

23. Note that the Bankruptcy Code defines a *family farmer* and a *farmer* differently. To be a farmer, a person or business must receive 50 percent of gross income from a farming operation that the person or business owns or operates—see footnote 11.

Reviewing . . . Creditor-Debtor Relations and Bankruptcy

Three months ago, Janet Hart's husband of twenty years died of cancer. Although he had medical insurance, he left Janet with outstanding medical bills of more than $50,000. Janet has worked at the local library for the past ten years, earning $1,500 per month. Since her husband's death, Janet also has received $1,500 in Social Security benefits and $1,100 in life insurance proceeds every month, giving her a monthly income of $4,100. After she pays the mortgage payment of $1,500 and the amounts due on other debts each month, Janet barely has enough left over to buy groceries for her family (she has two teenage daughters at home). She decides to file for Chapter 7 bankruptcy, hoping for a fresh start. Using the information provided in the chapter, answer the following questions.

1. Under the Bankruptcy Code after the 2005 act, what must Janet do prior to filing a petition for relief under Chapter 7?

2. How much time does Janet have after filing the bankruptcy petition to submit the required schedules? What happens if Janet does not meet the deadline?

3. Assume that Janet files a petition under Chapter 7. Further assume that the median family income in the state in which Janet lives is $49,300. What steps would a court take to determine whether Janet's petition is presumed to be "substantial abuse" under the means test?

4. Suppose that the court determines that no presumption of substantial abuse applies in Janet's case. Nevertheless, the court finds that Janet does have the ability to pay at least a portion of the medical bills out of her disposable income. What would the court likely order in that situation?

Key Terms

Chapter Summary

LAWS ASSISTING CREDITORS

Liens
(See pages 412–414.)

1. *Mechanic's lien*–A nonpossessory, filed lien on an owner's real estate for labor, services, or materials furnished to or made on the realty.

2. *Artisan's lien*–A possessory lien on an owner's personal property for labor performed or value added.

Liens—Continued	3. *Judicial liens—*
	a. Attachment—A court-ordered seizure of property prior to a court's final determination of the creditor's rights to the property. Attachment is available only on the creditor's posting of a bond and strict compliance with the applicable state statutes.
	b. Writ of execution—A court order directing the sheriff to seize (levy) and sell a debtor's nonexempt real or personal property to satisfy a court's judgment in the creditor's favor.
Garnishment (See page 414.)	A collection remedy that allows the creditor to attach a debtor's funds (such as wages owed or bank accounts) and property that are held by a third person.
Creditors' Composition Agreements (See page 414.)	A contract between a debtor and his or her creditors by which the debtor's debts are discharged by payment of a sum less than the amount that is actually owed.
Mortgage Foreclosure (See pages 415–416.)	On the debtor's default, the entire mortgage debt is due and payable, allowing the creditor to foreclose on the realty by selling it to satisfy the debt.
Suretyship and Guaranty (See pages 416–420.)	Under contract, a third person agrees to be primarily or secondarily liable for the debt owed by the principal debtor. A creditor can turn to this third person for satisfaction of the debt.

LAWS ASSISTING DEBTORS

Exemptions (See page 421.)	Numerous laws, including consumer protection statutes, assist debtors. Additionally, state laws exempt certain types of real and personal property.
	1. *Exempted real property*—Each state permits a debtor to retain the family home, either in its entirety or up to a specified dollar amount, free from the claims of unsecured creditors or trustees in bankruptcy (homestead exemption).
	2. *Exempted personal property*—Personal property that is most often exempt from satisfaction of judgment debts includes the following:
	a. Household furniture up to a specified dollar amount.
	b. Clothing and certain personal possessions.
	c. Transportation vehicles up to a specified dollar amount.
	d. Certain classified animals, such as livestock and pets.
	e. Equipment used in a business or trade up to a specified dollar amount.

BANKRUPTCY—A COMPARISON OF CHAPTERS 7, 11, 12, AND 13

Issue	Chapter 7	Chapter 11	Chapters 12 and 13
Purpose	Liquidation.	Reorganization.	Adjustment.
Who Can Petition	Debtor (voluntary) or creditors (involuntary).	Debtor (voluntary) or creditors (involuntary).	Debtor (voluntary) only.
Who Can Be a Debtor	Any "person" (including partnerships and corporations) except railroads, insurance companies, banks, savings and loan institutions, investment companies licensed by the U.S. Small Business Administration, and credit unions. Farmers and charitable institutions cannot be involuntarily petitioned.	Any debtor eligible for Chapter 7 relief; railroads are also eligible.	*Chapter 12*—Any family farmer (one whose gross income is at least 50 percent farm dependent and whose debts are at least 80 percent farm related) or family fisherman (one whose gross income is at least 50 percent dependent on commercial fishing) or any partnership or closely held corporation at least 50 percent owned by a family farmer or fisherman, when total debt does not exceed $3,544,525 for farmers and $1,642,500 for fishermen.

CONTINUED

Issue	Chapter 7	Chapter 11	Chapters 12 and 13
Who Can Be a Debtor— Continued			*Chapter 13*–Any individual (not partnerships or corporations) with regular income who owes fixed unsecured debts of less than $336,900 or fixed secured debts of less than $1,010,650.
Procedure Leading to Discharge	Nonexempt property is sold with proceeds to be distributed (in order) to priority groups. Dischargeable debts are terminated.	Plan is submitted; if it is approved and followed, debts are discharged.	Plan is submitted and must be approved if the value of the property to be distributed equals the amount of the claims or if the debtor turns over disposable income for a three-year or five-year period; if the plan is followed, debts are discharged.
Advantages	On liquidation and distribution, most debts are discharged, and the debtor has an opportunity for a fresh start.	Debtor continues in business. Creditors can either accept the plan, or it can be "crammed down" on them. The plan allows for the reorganization and liquidation of debts over the plan period.	Debtor continues in business or possession of assets. If the plan is approved, most debts are discharged after a three-year period.

For Review

1. What is a prejudgment attachment? What is a writ of execution? How does a creditor use these remedies?
2. What is garnishment? When might a creditor undertake a garnishment proceeding?
3. In a bankruptcy proceeding, what constitutes the debtor's estate in property? What property is exempt from the estate under federal bankruptcy law?
4. What is the difference between an exception to discharge and an objection to discharge?
5. In a Chapter 11 reorganization, what is the role of the debtor in possession?

Questions and Case Problems

13–1. Artisan's Lien. Air Ruidoso, Ltd., operated a commuter airline and air charter service between Ruidoso, New Mexico, and airports in Albuquerque and El Paso. Executive Aviation Center, Inc., provided services for airlines at the Albuquerque International Airport. When Air Ruidoso failed to pay more than $10,000 that it owed for fuel, oil, and oxygen, Executive Aviation took possession of Air Ruidoso's plane. Executive Aviation claimed that it had a lien on the plane and filed a suit in a New Mexico state court to foreclose. Do supplies such as fuel, oil, and oxygen qualify as "materials" for the purpose of creating an artisan's lien? Why or why not?

Question with Sample Answer

13–2. Peaslee is not known for his business sense. He started a greenhouse and nursery business two years ago, and because of his lack of experience, he soon was in debt to a number of creditors. On February 1, Peaslee borrowed $5,000 from his father to pay some of these creditors. On

May 1, Peaslee paid back the $5,000, depleting his entire working capital. One creditor, the Cool Springs Nursery Supply Corp., extended credit to Peaslee on numerous purchases. Cool Springs pressured Peaslee for payment, and on July 1, Peaslee paid Cool Springs half the amount owed. On September 1, Peaslee voluntarily petitioned himself into bankruptcy. The trustee in bankruptcy claims that both Peaslee's father and Cool Springs must turn over to the debtor's estate the amounts Peaslee paid to them. Discuss fully the trustee's claims.

For a sample answer to Question 13–2, go to Appendix I at the end of this text.

13–3. Rights of the Surety. Meredith, a farmer, borrowed $5,000 from Farmer's Bank and gave the bank $4,000 in bearer bonds to hold as collateral for the loan. Meredith's neighbor, Peterson, who had known Meredith for years, signed as a surety on the note. Because of a drought, Meredith's harvest that year was only a fraction of what it normally was, and he was forced to default on his payments to Farmer's Bank. The bank did not immediately sell the bonds but instead requested $5,000 from Peterson. Peterson paid the $5,000 and then demanded that the bank give him the $4,000 in securities. Can Peterson enforce this demand? Explain.

13–4. Discharge in Bankruptcy. Between 1980 and 1987, Craig Hanson borrowed funds from Great Lakes Higher Education Corp. to finance his education at the University of Wisconsin. Hanson defaulted on the debt in 1989, and Great Lakes obtained a judgment against him for $31,583.77. Three years later, Hanson filed a bankruptcy petition under Chapter 13. Great Lakes timely filed a proof of claim in the amount of $35,531.08. Hanson's repayment plan proposed to pay $135 monthly to Great Lakes over sixty months, which in total was only 19 percent of the claim, but said nothing about discharging the remaining balance. The plan was confirmed without objection. After Hanson completed the payments under the plan, without any additional proof or argument being offered, the court granted a discharge of his student loans. In 2003, Educational Credit Management Corp. (ECMC), which had taken over Great Lakes' interest in the loans, filed a motion for relief from the discharge. What is the requirement for the discharge of a student loan obligation in bankruptcy? Did Hanson meet this requirement? Should the court grant ECMC's motion? Discuss. [*In re Hanson*, 397 F.3d 482 (7th Cir. 2005)]

13–5. Exceptions to Discharge. Between 1988 and 1992, Lorna Nys took out thirteen student loans, totaling about $30,000, to finance an associate of arts degree in drafting from the College of the Redwoods and a bachelor of arts degree from Humboldt State University (HSU) in California. In 1996, Nys began working at HSU

as a drafting technician. As a "Drafter II," the highest-paying drafting position at HSU, Nys's gross income in 2002 was $40,244. She was fifty-one years old, Her net monthly income was $2,299.33, and she had $2,295.05 in monthly expenses, including saving $140 for her retirement, which she planned for age sixty-five. When Educational Credit Management Corp. (ECMC) began to collect payments on Nys's student loans, she filed a Chapter 7 petition in a federal bankruptcy court, seeking a discharge of the loans. ECMC argued that Nys did not show any "additional circumstances" that would impede her ability to repay. What is the standard for the discharge of student loans under Chapter 7? Does Nys meet that standard? Why or why not? [*In re Nys*, 446 F.3d 938 (9th Cir. 2006)]

Case Problem with Sample Answer

13–6. James Stout, a professor of economics and business at Cornell College in Mount Vernon, Iowa, filed a petition in bankruptcy under Chapter 7, seeking to discharge about $95,000 in credit-card debts. At the time, Stout had been divorced for ten years and had custody of his children: Z. S., who attended college, and G. S., who was twelve years old. Stout's ex-wife did not contribute child support. According to Stout, G. S. was an "elite" ice-skater who practiced twenty hours a week and had placed between first and third at more than forty competitive events. He had decided to home-school G. S., whose achievements were average for her grade level despite her frequent absences from public school. His petition showed monthly income of $4,227 and expenses of $4,806. The expenses included annual home-school costs of $8,400 and annual skating expenses of $6,000. They did not include Z. S.'s college costs, such as airfare for his upcoming studies in Europe, and other items. The trustee allowed monthly expenses of $3,227—with nothing for skating—and asked the court to dismiss the petition. Can the court grant this request? Should it? If so, what might it encourage Stout to do? Explain. [*In re Stout*, 336 Bankr. 138 (N.D. Iowa 2006)]

After you have answered Problem 13–6, compare your answer with the sample answer given on the Web site that accompanies this text. Go to www.cengage.com/blaw/let, select "Chapter 13," and click on "Case Problem with Sample Answer."

13–7. Attachment. In 2004 and 2005, Kent Avery, on behalf of his law firm—the Law Office of Kent Avery, LLC—contracted with Marlin Broadcasting, LLC, to air commercials on WCCC-FM, 106.9 "The Rock." Avery, who was the sole member of his firm, helped to create the ads, which solicited direct contact with "defense attorney Kent Avery," featured his voice, and repeated his name and experience to make potential clients familiar with him. When WCCC was not paid for the broadcasts, Marlin filed a suit in a Connecticut state court against Avery and his firm, alleging an outstanding balance of $35,250. Pending the court's hearing of the suit, Marlin filed a request for a writ of attachment. Marlin offered in evidence the parties' contracts, the ads' transcripts, and WCCC's invoices. Avery contended that he could not be held personally liable for the cost of the ads. Marlin countered that the ads unjustly enriched Avery by conferring a personal benefit on him to Marlin's detriment. What is the purpose of attachment? What must a creditor prove to obtain a writ of attachment? Did Marlin meet this test? Explain. [*Marlin Broadcasting, LLC v. Law Office of Kent Avery, LLC*, 101 Conn.App. 638, 922 A.2d 1131 (2007)]

13–8. Discharge in Bankruptcy. Rhonda Schroeder married Gennady Shvartsshteyn (Gene) in 1997. Gene worked at Royal Courier and Air Domestic Connect in Illinois, where Melissa Winyard also worked in 1999 and 2000. During this time, Gene and Winyard had an affair. A year after leaving Royal, Winyard filed a petition in a federal bankruptcy court under Chapter 7 and was granted a discharge of her debts. Sometime later, in a letter to Schroeder, who had learned of the affair, Winyard wrote, "I never intentionally wanted any of this to happen. I never wanted to disrupt your marriage." Schroeder obtained a divorce and, in 2005, filed a suit in an Illinois state court against Winyard, alleging "alienation of affection." Schroeder claimed that there had been "mutual love and affection" in her marriage until Winyard engaged in conduct intended to alienate her husband's affection. Schroeder charged that Winyard "caused him to have sexual intercourse with her," resulting in "the destruction of the marital relationship." Winyard filed a motion for summary judgment on the ground that any liability on her part had been discharged in her bankruptcy. Is there an exception to discharge for "willful and malicious conduct"? If so, does Schroeder's claim qualify? Discuss. [*Schroeder v. Winyard*, 375 Ill.App.3d 358, 873 N.E.2d 35, 313 Ill.Dec. 740 (2 Dist. 2007)]

A Question of Ethics

 13–9. In January 2003, Gary Ryder and Washington Mutual Bank, F.A., executed a note in which Ryder promised to pay $2,450,000, plus interest at a rate that could vary from month to month. The amount of the first payment was $10,933. The note was to be paid in full by February 1, 2033. A mortgage on Ryder's real property at 345 Round Hill Road in Greenwich, Connecticut, in favor of the bank secured his obligations under the note. The note and mortgage required that he pay the taxes on the property, which he did not do in 2004 and 2005. The bank notified him that he was in default and, when he

failed to act, paid $50,095.92 in taxes, penalties, interest, and fees. Other disputes arose between the parties, and Ryder filed a suit in a federal district court against the bank, alleging, in part, breach of contract. He charged, among other things, that some of his timely payments were not processed and were subjected to incorrect late fees, forcing him to make excessive payments and ultimately resulting in "non-payment by Ryder." [*Ryder v. Washington Mutual Bank, F.A.*, 501 F.Supp.2d 311 (D.Conn. 2007)]

1. The bank filed a counterclaim, seeking to foreclose on the mortgage. What should a creditor be required to prove to foreclose on mortgaged property? What would be a debtor's most effective defense? Which party in this case is likely to prevail on the bank's counterclaim? Why?

2. The parties agreed to a settlement that released the bank from Ryder's claims and required him to pay the note by January 31, 2007. The court dismissed the suit, but when Ryder did not make the payment, the bank asked the court to reopen the case. The bank then asked for a judgment in its favor on Ryder's complaint, arguing that the settlement had "immediately" released the bank from his claims. Does this seem fair? Why or why not?

Video Question

 13–10. Go to this text's Web site at **www.cengage.com/blaw/let** and select "Chapter 13." Click on "Video Questions" and view the video titled *The River*. Then answer the following questions.

1. In the video, a crowd (including Mel Gibson) is gathered at a farm auction in which a neighbor's (Jim Antonio's) farming goods are being sold. The people in the crowd, who are upset because they believe that the bank is selling out the farmer, begin chanting "no sale, no sale." In an effort to calm the situation, the farmer tells the crowd that "they've already foreclosed" on his farm. What does he mean?

2. Assume that the auction is a result of Chapter 7 bankruptcy proceedings. Was the farmer's petition for bankruptcy voluntary or involuntary? Explain.

3. Suppose that the farmer purchased the homestead three years prior to filing a petition in bankruptcy and that the current market value of the farm is $215,000. What is the maximum amount of equity that the farmer could claim as exempt under the 2005 Bankruptcy Reform Act?

4. Compare the results of a Chapter 12 bankruptcy as opposed to a Chapter 7 bankruptcy for the farmer in the video.

Interacting with the Internet

For updated links to resources available on the Web, as well as a variety of other materials, visit this text's Web site at

www.cengage.com/blaw/let

The U.S. Department of Labor's Web site contains a page on garnishment at

www.dol.gov/dol/topic/wages/garnishments.htm

The U.S. Bankruptcy Code is online at

www.law.cornell.edu/80/uscode/11

Another good resource for bankruptcy information is the American Bankruptcy Institute (ABI) at

www.abiworld.org

PRACTICAL INTERNET EXERCISES

Go to this text's Web site at **www.cengage.com/blaw/let**, select "Chapter 13," and click on "Practical Internet Exercises." There you will find the following Internet research exercises that you can perform to learn more about the topics covered in this chapter.

Practical Internet Exercise 13–1: LEGAL PERSPECTIVE—Debtor-Creditor Relations
Practical Internet Exercise 13–2: MANAGEMENT PERSPECTIVE—Bankruptcy Alternatives

BEFORE THE TEST

Go to this text's Web site at **www.cengage.com/blaw/let**, select "Chapter 13," and click on "Interactive Quizzes." You will find a number of interactive questions relating to this chapter.

Unit Two

Cumulative Business Hypothetical

Samuel Polson has an idea for a new software application. Polson hires an assistant and invests a considerable amount of his own time and funds developing the application. To develop other software, and to manufacture and market his applications, Polson needs financial capital.

1. Polson borrows $5,000 from his friend Michael Brant. Polson promises to repay Brant the $5,000 in three weeks. Brant, in urgent need of money, borrows $5,000 from his friend Mary Viva and assigns his rights to the $5,000 Polson owes him to Viva in return for the loan. Viva notifies Polson of the assignment. Polson pays Brant the $5,000 on the date stipulated in their contract. Brant refuses to give the money to Viva, and Viva sues Polson. Is Polson obligated to pay Viva $5,000 also? Discuss.

2. Polson learns that a competitor, Trivan, Inc., has already filed for a patent on a nearly identical program and has manufactured and sold the software to some customers. Polson learns from a reliable source that Trivan paid Polson's assistant a substantial sum of money to obtain a copy of the program. What legal recourse does Polson have against Trivan? Discuss fully.

3. While Polson is developing his idea and founding his business, he has no income. To meet expenses, Polson and his wife begin a home-based baking business for which he orders and has installed a new model X23 McIntyre oven from a local company, Western Heating Appliances. One day, Polson is baking croissants. When he opens the oven, part of the door becomes detached. As he struggles with the door, his hands are badly burned, and he is unable to work for several months. Polson later learns that the hinge mechanism on the door was improperly installed. He wants to sue the oven's manufacturer to recover damages, including consequential damages for lost profits. In a product liability suit against the manufacturer, under what legal principles and doctrines might Polson recover damages? Discuss fully.

4. During the course of the events described in the preceding questions, the payments on Polson's mortgage, his various credit-card debts, and some loans that he took out to pay for his son's college tuition continue to come due. As his software business begins to make money, Polson files for Chapter 7 liquidation. Polson hopes to be rid of his personal debts entirely, even though he believes he could probably pay his creditors off over a four-year period if he scrimped and used every cent available. Are all of Polson's personal debts dischargeable under Chapter 7, including the debts incurred for his son's education? Given the fact that Polson could foreseeably pay off his debts over a four-year period, will the court allow Polson to obtain relief under Chapter 7? Why or why not?

Business and Employment

CHAPTER OBJECTIVES

After reading this chapter, you should be able to answer the following questions:

1. What advantages and disadvantages are associated with the sole proprietorship?

2. What is meant by joint and several liability? Why is this often considered to be a disadvantage of doing business as a general partnership?

3. What advantages do limited liability partnerships offer to entrepreneurs that are not offered by general partnerships?

4. What are the key differences between the rights and liabilities of general partners and those of limited partners?

5. How are limited liability companies formed, and who decides how they will be managed and operated?

CONTENTS

" [E]veryone thirsteth after gaine."

— SIR EDWARD COKE,
1552–1634 (English jurist and politician)

Many Americans would agree with Sir Edward Coke's comment in the chapter-opening quotation that most people, at least, "thirsteth after gaine." Certainly, an entrepreneur's primary motive for undertaking a business enterprise is to make profits. An **entrepreneur** is by definition one who initiates and assumes the financial risks of a new enterprise and undertakes to provide or control its management.

One of the questions faced by anyone who wishes to start up a business is what form of business organization should be chosen for the business endeavor. In making this determination, the entrepreneur needs to consider a number of factors. Four important factors are (1) ease of creation, (2) the liability of the owners, (3) tax considerations, and (4) the need for capital. In studying this unit on business organizations, keep these factors in mind as you read about the various business organizational forms available to entrepreneurs.

Traditionally, entrepreneurs have used three major forms to structure their business enterprises: the sole proprietorship, the partnership, and the corporation. In this chapter, we examine the forms of business most often used by small business enterprises, including two of these traditional forms—sole proprietorships and partnerships—as well as variations on partnerships, limited liability companies, and franchises. In Chapter 15, we will discuss the third major traditional form of business—the corporation—and summarize and compare aspects of all the business organizations that have been discussed.

ENTREPRENEUR
One who initiates and assumes the financial risk of a new business enterprise and undertakes to provide or control its management.

Sometimes, individuals want to run their own businesses. They can do this as sole proprietors or as partners in a partnership. They can also get a head start on a business by buying a franchise for a well-known product, such as Domino's Pizza.
("The Consumerist"/Creative Commons)

SOLE PROPRIETORSHIPS

The simplest form of business organization is a **sole proprietorship.** In this form, the owner is the business; thus, anyone who does business without creating a separate business organization has a sole proprietorship. More than two-thirds of all U.S. businesses are sole proprietorships. They are usually small enterprises— about 99 percent of the sole proprietorships in the United States have revenues of less than $1 million per year. Sole proprietors can own and manage any type of business, ranging from an informal, home-office undertaking to a large restaurant or construction firm. Today, a number of online businesses that sell goods and services on a nationwide basis are organized as sole proprietorships.

SOLE PROPRIETORSHIP
The simplest form of business organization, in which the owner is the business. The owner reports business income on his or her personal income tax return and is legally responsible for all debts and obligations incurred by the business.

Advantages of the Sole Proprietorship

A major advantage of the sole proprietorship is that the proprietor owns the entire business and has a right to receive all of the profits (because he or she assumes all of the risk). In addition, it is often easier and less costly to start a sole proprietorship than to start any other kind of business, as few legal formalities are involved.[1] One does not need to file any documents with the government to start a sole proprietorship (though a state business license may be required to operate certain businesses).

This type of business organization also entails more flexibility than does a partnership or a corporation. The sole proprietor is free to make any decision she or he wishes concerning the business—including whom to hire, when to take a vacation, and what kind of business to pursue, for example. In addition, the proprietor can sell or transfer all or part of the business to another party at any time and does not need approval from anyone else (as would be required from partners in a partnership or, normally, from shareholders in a corporation).

---

1. Although starting up a sole proprietorship involves relatively few legal formalities compared with other business organizational forms, even small sole proprietorships may need to comply with certain zoning requirements, obtain appropriate licenses, and the like.

This woman creates floral arrangements. She owns the business by herself. What are the advantages of doing business as a sole proprietorship?
(Salim Fadhley/Creative Commons)

A sole proprietor pays only personal income taxes (including Social Security, or self-employment, tax) on the business's profits, which are reported as personal income on the proprietor's personal income tax return. Sole proprietors are also allowed to establish certain rertirement accounts that are tax-exempt until the funds are withdrawn.

Disadvantages of the Sole Proprietorship

The major disadvantage of the sole proprietorship is that the proprietor alone bears the burden of any losses or liabilities incurred by the business enterprise. In other words, the sole proprietor has unlimited liability, or legal responsibility, for all obligations incurred in doing business. Any lawsuit against the business or its employees can lead to unlimited personal liability for the owner of a sole proprietorship. Creditors can go after the owner's personal assets to satisfy any business debts. This unlimited liability is a major factor to be considered in choosing a business form.

EXAMPLE #1 Sheila Fowler operates a golf shop business as a sole proprietorship. The shop is located near one of the best golf courses in the country. A professional golfer, Dean Maheesh, is seriously injured when a display of golf clubs, which one of Fowler's employees has failed to secure, falls on him. If Maheesh sues Fowler's shop (a sole proprietorship) and wins, Fowler's personal liability could easily exceed the limits of her insurance policy. In this situation, not only might Fowler lose her business, but she could also lose her house, her car, and any other personal assets that can be attached to pay the judgment.□

The sole proprietorship also has the disadvantage of lacking continuity on the death of the proprietor. When the owner dies, so does the business—it is automatically dissolved. Another disadvantage is that the proprietor's opportunity to raise capital is limited to personal funds and the funds of those who are willing to make loans.

The personal liability of the owner of a sole proprietorship was at issue in the following case. The case involved the federal Cable Communications Act, which prohibits a commercial establishment from broadcasting television programs to its patrons without authorization. The court had to decide whether the owner of a sole proprietorship that installed a satellite television system was personally liable for violating this act by identifying a restaurant as a "residence" for billing purposes.

Case 14.1 **Garden City Boxing Club, Inc. v. Dominguez**

United States District Court,
Northern District of Illinois,
Eastern Division, 2006. ___ F.Supp.2d ___.

BACKGROUND AND FACTS   Garden City Boxing Club, Inc. (GCB), which is based in San Jose, California, owned the exclusive right to broadcast via closed-circuit television several

prizefights, including the match between Oscar De La Hoya and Fernando Vargas on September 14, 2002. GCB sold the right to receive the broadcasts to bars and other commercial venues. The fee was $20 multiplied by an establishment's maximum fire code occupancy. Antenas Enterprises in Chicago, Illinois, sells and installs satellite television systems under a contract with DISH Network. After installing a system,

Antenas sends the buyer's address and other identifying information to DISH. In January 2002, Luis Garcia, an Antenas employee, identified a new customer as Jose Melendez at 220 Hawthorn Commons in Vernon Hills. The address was a restaurant—Mundelein Burrito—but Garcia designated the account as residential. Mundelein's patrons watched the De La Hoya–Vargas match on September 14, as well as three other fights on other dates, for which the restaurant paid only the residential rate to DISH and nothing to GCB. GCB filed a suit in a federal district court against Luis Dominguez, the sole proprietor of Antenas, to collect the fee.

IN THE WORDS OF THE COURT . . . *LEINENWEBER*, J. [Judge]

* * * *

Section 605(a) [of the Cable Communications Act] states "an authorized intermediary of a communication violates the Act when it divulges communication through an electronic channel to one other than the addressee." Mundelein Burrito was clearly a commercial establishment. The structure of the building, an exterior identification sign, and its location in a strip mall made this obvious. Mundelein Burrito paid only the residential fee for the four fights it broadcast to its patrons. It was not an authorized addressee of any of the four fights. By improperly listing Mundelein Burrito as a residence, Antenas Enterprises allowed the unauthorized broadcast of the Event, and three additional fights, to Mundelein Burrito. Antenas Enterprises is liable under [Section] 605 of the Act.

* * * *

The unauthorized broadcast of the four separate events deprived GCB of the full value of its business investment. * * * [Under the Cable Communications Act] an aggrieved party * * * may recover an award of damages "for each violation of [Section 605(a)] involved in the action in a sum of not less than $1,000 or more than $10,000, as the court considers just." If the violation was willful and for purposes of commercial advantage or private financial gain, the court in its discretion may increase the award of damages—by an amount not more than $100,000. The court must award attorneys' fees to the prevailing party.

GCB argues that the Antenas Enterprises failure to properly list Mundelein Burrito resulted in four separate violations. According to the license fee charged for each of the four fights that were illegally broadcast by Mundelein Burrito, the proper amount would have been $20.00 times the maximum fire code occupancy (46) or $3,680.00. Instead, due to the improper identification of the account as residential, Mundelein Burrito paid only $184.40 to broadcast the four events. GCB did not receive any of the $184.40.

* * * [Considering] the willfulness of the defendant's conduct and the deterrent value of the sanction imposed * * * twice the amount of actual damages is reasonable for this case. Therefore, Antenas Enterprises is liable to GCB for the sum of $7,360.00. Pursuant to the Act, GCB is also entitled to reasonable attorneys' fees.

* * * *

GCB argues Luis Dominguez is personally liable for Antenas Enterprises' violation of [Section] 605 of the Act. The term "person" in the Act means an "individual, partnership, association, joint stock company, trust, corporation or governmental entity."

Antenas Enterprises is a sole proprietorship, owned by Dominguez. *A sole proprietor is personally responsible for actions committed by his employees within the scope of their employment.* Accordingly, Dominguez is personally liable for the damages caused by the violation of [Section] 605 of the Act. [Emphasis added.]

DECISION AND REMEDY   The court issued a summary judgment in GCB's favor, holding that the plaintiff was entitled to the amount of Mundelein's fee, for which Dominguez was personally liable, plus damages and attorneys' fees.

WHAT IF THE FACTS WERE DIFFERENT?   If Mundelein had identified itself as a residence when ordering the satellite system, how might the result in this case have been different?

CASE 14.1–CONTINUED

THE GLOBAL DIMENSION   Because the Internet has made it possible for sole proprietorships to do business worldwide without greatly increasing their costs, should they be considered, for some purposes, the equivalent of other business forms? Why or why not?

PARTNERSHIPS

A *partnership* arises from an agreement, express or implied, between two or more persons to carry on a business for profit. Partners are co-owners of a business and have joint control over its operation and the right to share in its profits.

Partnerships are governed both by common law concepts—in particular, those relating to agency (discussed in Chapter 16)—and by statutory law. The National Conference of Commissioners on Uniform State Laws has drafted the Uniform Partnership Act (UPA), which governs the operation of partnerships *in the absence of express agreement* and has done much to reduce controversies in the law relating to partnerships. In other words, the partners are free to establish rules for their partnership that differ from those stated in the UPA. The UPA was originally set forth by the National Conference of Commissioners on Uniform State Laws in 1914 and has undergone several major revisions. Except for Louisiana, every state has adopted the UPA. The majority of states have adopted the most recent version of the UPA, which was issued in 1994 and amended in 1997 to provide limited liability for partners in a limited liability partnership. We therefore base our discussion of the UPA in this chapter on the 1997 version of the act and include excerpts of the UPA in Appendix E.

Agency Concepts and Partnership Law

When two or more persons agree to do business as partners, they enter into a special relationship with one another. To an extent, their relationship is similar to an agency relationship because each partner is deemed to be the agent of the other partners and of the partnership. The common law agency concepts you will read about in Chapter 16 thus apply—specifically, the imputation of knowledge of, and responsibility for, acts done within the scope of the partnership relationship. In their relations with one another, partners, like agents, are bound by fiduciary ties.

In one important way, however, partnership law is distinct from agency law. A partnership is based on a voluntary contract between two or more competent persons who agree to place financial capital, labor, and skill in a business with the understanding that profits and losses will be shared. In a nonpartnership agency relationship, the agent usually does not have an ownership interest in the business, nor is he or she obliged to bear a portion of the ordinary business losses.

When Does a Partnership Exist?

PARTNERSHIP
An agreement by two or more persons to carry on, as co-owners, a business for profit.

Conflicts commonly arise over whether a business enterprise is legally a partnership, especially in the absence of a formal, written partnership agreement. The UPA defines a **partnership** as "an association of two or more persons to carry on as co-owners a business for profit" [UPA 101(6)]. Note that under the UPA a corporation is a "person" [UPA 101(10)]. The *intent* to associate is a key element of a partnership, and a person cannot join a partnership unless all of the other partners consent [UPA 401(i)].

Partnerships create benefits, but they have costs—the main one being the unlimited personal liability of all partners. Some large accounting firms have therefore gone to great lengths to reduce potential partner liability problems. Shown here is an annual meeting of Ernst & Young, a firm with more than 140,000 employees in 140 countries. This accounting services business has created separate legal entities to provide services to clients, thereby reducing liability exposure to those working in other countries for other clients.
(Rob Lee/Creative Commons)

In resolving disputes over whether partnership status exists, courts will usually look for the following three essential elements, which are implicit in the UPA's definition of a partnership:

1. A sharing of profits and losses.
2. A joint ownership of the business.
3. An equal right to be involved in the management of the business.

KEEP IN MIND
Forming a partnership requires two or more persons. Other forms of business can be organized by a single individual.

Joint ownership of property, obviously, does not in and of itself create a partnership. In fact, the sharing of gross revenues and even profits from such ownership is usually not enough to create a partnership [UPA 202(c)(1), (2)]. **EXAMPLE #2** Chiang and Burke jointly own a piece of rural property. They lease the land to a farmer, with the understanding that—in lieu of set rental payments—they will receive a share of the profits from the farming operation conducted by the farmer. This arrangement normally would not make Chiang, Burke, and the farmer partners.□

Note, though, that although the sharing of profits from ownership of property does not prove the existence of a partnership, sharing *both profits and losses* usually does. **EXAMPLE #3** Two sisters, Zoe and Cienna, buy a restaurant together, open a joint bank account from which they pay for expenses and supplies, and share the net profits that the restaurant generates. Zoe manages the restaurant and Cienna handles the bookkeeping. After eight years, Cienna stops doing the bookkeeping and does no other work for the restaurant. Zoe, who is now operating the restaurant by herself, no longer wants to share the profits with Cienna. She offers to buy her sister out, but the two cannot agree on a fair price. When Cienna files a lawsuit, a question arises as to whether the two sisters were partners in the restaurant. In this situation, a court would find that a partnership existed because the sisters shared management responsibilities, had joint accounts, and shared the profits and the losses of the restaurant equally.□

Entity versus Aggregate Theory of Partnerships

At common law, a partnership was treated only as an aggregate of individuals and never as a separate legal entity. Thus, at common law a suit could never be brought by or against the firm in its own name; each individual partner had to sue or be sued.

Today, in contrast, a majority of the states follow the UPA and treat a partnership as an entity for most purposes. For example, a partnership usually can sue or be sued, collect judgments, and have all accounting procedures in the name of the partnership entity [UPA 201, 307(a)]. As an entity, a partnership may hold the title to real or personal property in its name rather than in the names of the individual partners. Additionally, federal procedural laws permit the partnership to be treated as an entity in suits in federal courts and bankruptcy proceedings.

For federal income tax purposes, however, the partnership is treated as an aggregate of the individual partners rather than a separate legal entity. The partnership is a pass-through entity and not a taxpaying entity. A **pass-through entity** is a business entity that has no tax liability; the entity's income is passed through to the owners of the entity, who pay taxes on it. Thus, the income or losses the partnership incurs are "passed through" the entity framework and attributed to the partners on their individual tax returns. The partnership itself has no tax liability and is responsible only for filing an **information return** with the Internal Revenue Service. In other words, the firm itself pays no taxes. A partner's profit from the partnership (whether distributed or not) is taxed as individual income to the individual partner.

Partnership Formation

As a general rule, agreements to form a partnership can be *oral, written,* or *implied by conduct.* Some partnership agreements, however, must be in writing to be legally enforceable under the Statute of Frauds (see Chapter 10 for details). A written partnership agreement, called **articles of partnership,** can include virtually any terms that the parties wish, unless they are illegal or contrary to public policy or statute [UPA 103]. The agreement usually specifies the name and location of the business, the duration of the partnership, the purpose of the business, each partner's share of the profits, how the partnership will be managed, how assets will be distributed on dissolution, and other provisions.

The partnership agreement can specify the duration of the partnership by stating that it will continue until a certain date or the completion of a particular project. A partnership that is specifically limited in duration is called a *partnership for a term.* Generally, withdrawing from a partnership for a term prematurely (prior to the expiration date) constitutes a breach of the agreement, and the responsible partner can be held liable for any resulting losses [UPA 602(b)(2)]. If no fixed duration is specified, the partnership is a *partnership at will.*

Occasionally, persons who are not partners may nevertheless hold themselves out as partners and make representations that third parties rely on in dealing with them. In such a situation, a court may conclude that a *partnership by estoppel* exists. The law does not confer any partnership rights on these persons, but it may impose liability on them. This is also true when a partner represents, expressly or impliedly, that a nonpartner is a member of the firm [UPA 308]. EXAMPLE #4 Sorento owns a small shop. Knowing that Midland Bank will not make a loan on his credit alone, Sorento represents that Lukas, a financially secure businessperson, is a partner in Sorento's business. Lukas knows of Sorento's misrepresentation but fails to correct it. Midland Bank, relying on the strength of Lukas's reputation and credit, extends a loan to Sorento. Sorento will be liable to the bank for repaying the loan. Lukas could also be held liable to the bank in many states. Because Lukas has implicitly consented to the misrepresentation, she will normally be estopped (prevented) from denying that she is

PASS-THROUGH ENTITY
A business entity that has no tax liability. The entity's income is passed through to the owners, and the owners pay taxes on the income.

INFORMATION RETURN
A tax return submitted by a partnership that only reports the income and losses earned by the business. The partnership as an entity does not pay taxes on the income received by the partnership. A partner's profit from the partnership (whether distributed or not) is taxed as individual income to the individual partner.

ARTICLES OF PARTNERSHIP
A written agreement that sets forth each partner's rights and obligations with respect to the partnership.

Sorento's partner. A court normally will treat Lukas as if she were in fact a partner in Sorento's business insofar as this loan is concerned.□

Rights of Partners

The rights of partners in a partnership relate to the following areas: management, interest in the partnership, compensation, inspection of books, accounting, and property. In the absence of provisions to the contrary in the partnership agreement, the law imposes the rights discussed here.

Management Rights In a general partnership, all partners have equal rights in managing the partnership [UPA 401(f)]. Unless the partners agree otherwise, each partner has one vote in management matters *regardless of the proportional size of his or her interest in the firm*. Often, in a large partnership, partners will agree to delegate daily management responsibilities to a management committee made up of one or more of the partners.

The majority rule controls decisions in ordinary matters connected with partnership business, unless otherwise specified in the agreement. Decisions that significantly affect the nature of the partnership or that are not apparently for carrying on the ordinary course of the partnership business, or business of the kind, however, require the *unanimous* consent of the partners [UPA 301(2), 401(i), (j)]. Unanimous consent is likely to be required for a decision to undertake any of the following actions:

1. To alter the essential nature of the firm's business as expressed in the partnership agreement or to alter the capital structure of the partnership.
2. To admit new partners or to enter a wholly new business.
3. To assign partnership property to a trust for the benefit of creditors.
4. To dispose of the partnership's goodwill.
5. To confess judgment against the partnership or to submit partnership claims to arbitration. (A **confession of judgment** is the act of a debtor in permitting a judgment to be entered against her or him by a creditor, for an agreed sum, without the institution of legal proceedings.)
6. To undertake any act that would make further conduct of partnership business impossible.
7. To amend the articles of the partnership agreement.

CONFESSION OF JUDGMENT
The act or agreement of a debtor in permitting a judgment to be entered against him or her by a creditor, for an agreed sum, without the institution of legal proceedings.

Interest in the Partnership Each partner is entitled to the proportion of business profits and losses that is designated in the partnership agreement. If the agreement does not apportion profits (indicate how the profits will be shared), the UPA provides that profits will be shared equally. If the agreement does not apportion losses, losses will be shared in the same ratio as profits [UPA 401(b)].

EXAMPLE #5 The partnership agreement for Rico and Brent provides for capital contributions of $60,000 from Rico and $40,000 from Brent, but it is silent as to how Rico and Brent will share profits or losses. In this situation, Rico and Brent will share both profits and losses equally. If their partnership agreement provided for profits to be shared in the same ratio as capital contributions, however, 60 percent of the profits would go to Rico, and 40 percent of the profits would go to Brent. If their partnership agreement was silent as to losses, losses would be shared in the same ratio as profits (60 percent and 40 percent, respectively).□

Compensation   Devoting time, skill, and energy to partnership business is a partner's duty and generally is not a compensable service. Rather, as mentioned, a partner's income from the partnership takes the form of a distribution of profits according to the partner's share in the business. Partners can, of course, agree otherwise. For instance, the managing partner of a law firm often receives a salary in addition to her or his share of profits for performing special administrative duties, such as managing the office or personnel.

Inspection of Books   Partnership books and records must be kept at the firm's principal business office and be accessible to all partners. Each partner has the right to receive (and the corresponding duty to produce) full and complete information concerning the conduct of all aspects of partnership business [UPA 403]. Every partner is entitled to inspect all books and records on demand and to make copies of the materials.

Accounting of Partnership Assets or Profits   An accounting of partnership assets or profits is required to determine the value of each partner's share in the partnership. An accounting can be performed voluntarily, or it can be compelled by court order. Under UPA 405(b), a partner has the right to bring an action for an accounting during the term of the partnership, as well as on the firm's dissolution and winding up (discussed later in this chapter).

Property Rights   Property acquired by a partnership is the property of the partnership and not of the partners individually [UPA 203]. Partnership property includes all property that was originally contributed to the partnership and anything later purchased by the partnership or in the partnership's name (except in rare circumstances) [UPA 204]. A partner may use or possess partnership property only on behalf of the partnership [UPA 401(g)]. A partner is *not* a co-owner of partnership property and has no right to sell, mortgage, or transfer partnership property to another. (A partner can assign her or his right to a share of the partnership profits to another to satisfy a debt, however.)

Duties and Liabilities of Partners

Partners examine accounting records. Are there any restrictions on the right of a partner to inspect his or her firm's books and records? Why or why not? (PhotoDisc)

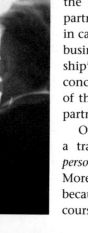

The duties and liabilities of partners are basically derived from agency law (discussed in Chapter 16). Each partner is an agent of every other partner and acts as both a principal and an agent in any business transaction within the scope of the partnership agreement. Each partner is also a general agent of the partnership in carrying out the usual business of the firm "or business of the kind carried on by the partnership" [UPA 301(1)]. Thus, every act of a partner concerning partnership business and "business of the kind," and every contract signed by that partner in the partnership's name, bind the firm.

One significant disadvantage associated with a traditional partnership is that partners are *personally* liable for the debts of the partnership. Moreover, the liability is essentially unlimited because the acts of one partner in the ordinary course of business subject the other partners to personal liability [UPA 305]. We examine here the fiduciary duties of partners, the authority of partners, the liability of partners, and the limitations imposed on the liability of incoming partners for preexisting partnership debts.

Fiduciary Duties   The fiduciary duties a partner owes to the partnership and the other partners are the duty of loyalty and the duty of care [UPA 404(a)]. The duty of loyalty requires a partner to account to the partnership for "any property, profit, or benefit" derived by the partner from the partnership's business or the use of its property [UPA 404(b)]. A partner must also refrain from competing with the partnership in business or dealing with the firm as an adverse party. A partner's duty of care involves refraining from "grossly negligent or reckless conduct, intentional misconduct, or a knowing violation of law" [UPA 404(c)].

These duties may not be waived or eliminated in the partnership agreement, and in fulfilling them each partner must act consistently with the obligation of good faith and fair dealing, which applies to all contracts, including partnership agreements [UPA 103(b), 404(d)]. The agreement can specify acts that the partners agree will violate a fiduciary duty.

Note that a partner may pursue his or her own interests without automatically violating these duties [UPA 404(e)]. The key is whether the partner has disclosed the interest to the other partners. For instance, a partner who owns a shopping mall may vote against a partnership proposal to open a competing mall, provided that the partner has fully disclosed her interest in the shopping mall to the other partners at the firm. A partner cannot make secret profits or put self-interest before his or her duty to the interest of the partnership, however.

Authority of Partners   Under the UPA and agency law, a partner has the authority to bind a partnership in contract. A partner may also subject the partnership to tort liability under the agency principles. When a partner is carrying on partnership business or business of the kind with third parties in the usual way, both the partner and the firm share liability.

Partners have the implied authority to perform acts that are reasonably necessary and customary to carry on the partnership's business. Their implied powers thus depend on the type of business the partnership operates. Partners in a trading partnership (a firm that has inventory and profits from buying and selling goods), for instance, have the implied authority to advertise products, hire employees, and make warranties.

Provisions of the UPA allow a partnership to attempt to limit a partner's implied powers by filing a statement of partnership authority with a state official [UPA 105, 303]. Such statements are only effective against third parties who know about the limitations.

If a partner acts within the scope of her or his authority, the partnership is legally bound to honor the partner's commitments to third parties. The partnership will not be liable, however, if the third parties know that the partner had no authority to commit the partnership. Agency concepts that we explore in Chapter 16 relating to actual (express and implied) authority, apparent authority, and ratification also apply to partnerships.

Joint Liability of Partners   Each partner in a partnership is jointly liable for the partnership's obligations. **Joint liability** means that a third party must sue all of the partners as a group, but each partner can be held liable for the full amount. Under the prior version of the UPA, which is still in effect in a few states, partners were subject to joint liability on partnership debts and contracts,

JOINT LIABILITY
Shared liability. In partnership law, partners share liability for partnership obligations and debts. Thus, if a third party sues a partner on a partnership debt, the partner has the right to insist that the other partners be sued with him or her.

but not on partnership debts arising from torts.[2] If, for instance, a third party sues a partner on a partnership contract, the partner has the right to demand that the other partners be sued with her or him. In fact, if the third party does not sue all of the partners, the assets of the partnership cannot be used to satisfy the judgment. Under the theory of joint liability, the partnership's assets must be exhausted before creditors can reach the partners' individual assets.[3]

Joint and Several Liability of Partners   In the majority of states, under UPA 306(a), partners are jointly and severally (separately or individually) liable for all partnership obligations, including contracts, torts, and breaches of trust. **Joint and several liability** means that a third party may sue all of the partners together (jointly) or one or more of the partners separately (severally) at his or her option. All partners in a partnership can be held liable regardless of whether the partner participated in, knew about, or ratified the conduct that gave rise to the lawsuit. Generally, under UPA 307(d), however, a creditor cannot bring an action to collect a partnership debt from the partner of a nonbankrupt partnership without first attempting to collect from the partnership or convincing a court that the attempt would be unsuccessful.

A judgment against one partner severally (separately) does not extinguish the others' liability. (Similarly, a release of one partner does not discharge the partners' several liability.) Thus, those partners not sued in the first action may be sued subsequently, unless the first action was conclusive for the partnership on the question of liability. In other words, if an action is brought against one partner and the court holds that the partnership was in no way liable, the third party cannot bring an action against another partner and succeed on the issue of the partnership's liability.

If a third party is successful in a suit against a partner or partners, she or he may collect on the judgment only against the assets of those partners named as defendants. A partner who commits a tort is required to indemnify (reimburse) the partnership for any damages it pays.

Liability of Incoming Partner   A newly admitted partner to an existing partnership normally has limited liability for whatever debts and obligations the partnership incurred prior to the new partner's admission. The new partner's liability can be satisfied only from partnership assets [UPA 306(b)]. This means that the new partner usually has no personal liability for these debts and obligations, but any capital contribution that he or she made to the partnership is subject to these debts. **EXAMPLE #6** Smartclub is a partnership with four members. Alex Jaff, a newly admitted partner, contributes $100,000 to the partnership. Smartclub has about $600,000 in debt at the time Jaff joins the firm. Although Jaff's capital contribution of $100,000 can be used to satisfy Smartclub's obligations, Jaff is not personally liable for partnership debts that were incurred before he became a partner. Thus, his personal assets cannot be used to satisfy the partnership's antecedent debt. If, however, the managing partner at Smartclub borrows funds after Jaff becomes a partner, Jaff will be personally liable for those amounts. □

JOINT AND SEVERAL LIABILITY
In partnership law, a plaintiff can file a lawsuit against all of the partners together (jointly) or one or more of the partners separately (severally, or individually). All partners in a partnership can be held liable regardless of whether the partner participated in, knew about, or ratified the conduct that gave rise to the lawsuit.

---

2. Under the previous version of the UPA, the partners were subject to *joint and several liability*, which is discussed next, on debts arising from torts. States that still follow this rule include Connecticut, West Virginia, and Wyoming.

3. For a case applying joint liability to partnerships, see *Shar's Cars, LLC v. Elder,* 97 P.3d 724 (Utah App. 2004).

Partner's Dissociation

Dissociation occurs when a partner ceases to be associated in the carrying on of the partnership business. Although a partner always has the *power* to dissociate from the firm, he or she may not have the *right* to dissociate. Dissociation normally entitles the partner to have his or her interest purchased by the partnership and terminates his or her actual authority to act for the partnership and to participate with the partners in running the business. Otherwise, the partnership continues to do business without the dissociating partner.[4]

DISSOCIATION
The severance of the relationship between a partner and a partnership when the partner ceases to be associated with the carrying on of the partnership business.

Events Causing Dissociation   Under UPA 601, a partner can be dissociated from a partnership in any of the following ways:

1. By the partner's voluntarily giving notice of an "express will to withdraw."
2. By the occurrence of an event agreed to in the partnership agreement.
3. By a unanimous vote of the other partners under certain circumstances, such as when a partner transfers substantially all of her or his interest in the partnership, or when it becomes unlawful to carry on partnership business with that partner.
4. By order of a court or arbitrator if the partner has engaged in wrongful conduct that affects the partnership business, breached the partnership agreement or violated a duty owed to the partnership or the other partners, or engaged in conduct that makes it "not reasonably practicable to carry on the business in partnership with the partner" [UPA 601(5)].
5. By the partner's declaring bankruptcy, assigning his or her interest in the partnership for the benefit of creditors, or becoming physically or mentally incapacitated, or by the partner's death. Note that although the bankruptcy or death of a partner represents that partner's "dissociation" from the partnership, it is not an *automatic* ground for the partnership's dissolution (*dissolution* will be discussed shortly).

Wrongful Dissociation   As mentioned, a partner has the power to dissociate from a partnership at any time, but if she or he lacks the right to dissociate, then the dissociation is considered wrongful under the law [UPA 602]. When a partner's dissociation is in breach of the partnership agreement, for instance, it is wrongful. **EXAMPLE #7** Suppose that a partnership agreement states that it is a breach of the partnership agreement for any partner to assign partnership property to a creditor without the consent of the others. If a partner, Janis, makes such an assignment, she has not only breached the agreement but has also wrongfully dissociated from the partnership.□ Similarly, if a partner refuses to perform duties required by the partnership agreement—such as accounting for profits earned from the use of partnership property—this breach can be treated as wrongful dissociation. A partner who wrongfully dissociates is liable to the partnership and to the other partners for damages caused by the dissociation.

Effects of Dissociation   Dissociation (rightful or wrongful) terminates some of the rights of the dissociated partner, requires that the partnership purchase his

---

4. Under the previous version of the UPA, when a partner dissociated from a partnership, the partnership was considered dissolved, its business had to be wound up, and the proceeds had to be distributed to creditors and among partners. The amendments to the UPA recognize that a partnership may not want to break up just because one partner has left the firm.

or her interest, and alters the liability of both parties to third parties. On a partner's dissociation, his or her right to participate in the management and conduct of the partnership business terminates [UPA 603]. The partner's duty of loyalty also ends. A partner's other fiduciary duties, including the duty of care, continue only with respect to events that occurred before dissociation, unless the partner participates in winding up the partnership's business (to be discussed shortly). **EXAMPLE #8** Debbie Pearson, a partner who leaves an accounting firm, Bubb & Pearson, can immediately compete with the firm for new clients. She must exercise care in completing ongoing client transactions, however, and must account to the firm for any fees received from the old clients based on those transactions.□

After a partner's dissociation, his or her interest in the partnership must be purchased according to the rules in UPA 701. The **buyout price** is based on the amount that would have been distributed to the partner if the partnership were wound up on the date of dissociation. Offset against the price are amounts owed by the partner to the partnership, including any damages for the partner's wrongful dissociation.

For two years after a partner dissociates from a continuing partnership, the partnership may be bound by the acts of the dissociated partner based on apparent authority [UPA 702]. In other words, the partnership may be liable to a third party with whom a dissociated partner enters into a transaction if the third party reasonably believed that the dissociated partner was still a partner. Similarly, a dissociated partner may be liable for partnership obligations entered into during a two-year period following dissociation [UPA 703].

Partnership Termination

The same events that cause dissociation can result in the end of the partnership if the remaining partners no longer wish to (or are unable to) continue the partnership business. The termination of a partnership is referred to as **dissolution,** which essentially means the commencement of the winding up process. **Winding up** is the actual process of collecting, liquidating, and distributing the partnership assets.[5] We discuss here the dissolution and winding up of partnership business.

Dissolution   Dissolution of a partnership generally can be brought about by the acts of the partners, by the operation of law, and by judicial decree [UPA 801]. Any partnership (including one for a fixed term) can be dissolved by the partners' agreement. Similarly, if the partnership agreement states that it will dissolve on a certain event, such as a partner's death or bankruptcy, then the occurrence of that event will dissolve the partnership. A partnership for a fixed term or a particular undertaking is dissolved by operation of law at the expiration of the term or on the completion of the undertaking. Under the UPA, a court may order dissolution when it becomes obviously impractical for the firm to continue—for example, if the business can only be operated at a loss [UPA 801(5)].

Winding Up   After dissolution, the partnership continues for the limited purpose of the winding up process. The partners cannot create new obligations on

---

BUYOUT PRICE
The amount payable to a partner on his or her dissociation from a partnership, based on the amount distributable to that partner if the firm were wound up on that date, and offset by any damages for wrongful dissociation.

DISSOLUTION
The formal disbanding of a partnership or a corporation. It can take place by (1) acts of the partners or, in a corporation, acts of the shareholders and board of directors; (2) the subsequent illegality of the firm's business; (3) the expiration of a time period stated in a partnership agreement or a certificate of incorporation; or (4) judicial decree.

WINDING UP
The second of two stages in the termination of a partnership or corporation. Once the firm is dissolved, it continues to exist legally until the process of winding up all business affairs (collecting and distributing the firm's assets) is complete.

DON'T FORGET
Secured creditors have priority over unsecured creditors to any assets that serve as collateral for a partnership's debts.

---

5. Although "winding down" would seem to describe more accurately the process of settling accounts and liquidating the assets of a partnership, "winding up" has been traditionally used in English and U.S. statutory and case law to denote this final stage of a partnership's existence.

behalf of the partnership. They have authority only to complete transactions begun but not finished at the time of dissolution and to wind up the business of the partnership [UPA 803, 804(1)]. *Winding up* includes collecting and preserving partnership assets, discharging liabilities (paying debts), and accounting to each partner for the value of her or his interest in the partnership. Partners continue to have fiduciary duties to one another and to the firm during this process. UPA 401(h) provides that a partner is entitled to compensation for services in winding up partnership affairs (and reimbursement for expenses incurred in the process) above and apart from his or her share in the partnership profits.

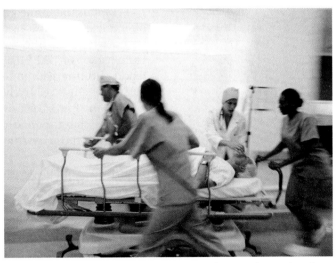

Both creditors of the partnership and creditors of the individual partners can make claims on the partnership's assets. In general, partnership creditors share proportionately with the partners' individual creditors in the assets of the partners' estates, which include their interests in the partnership. A partnership's assets are distributed according to the following priorities [UPA 807]:

If a partner becomes incapacitated or dies, how does this affect the existence of the partnership? (PhotoDisc)

1. Payment of debts, including those owed to partner and nonpartner creditors.
2. Return of capital contributions and distribution of profits to partners.

If the partnership's liabilities are greater than its assets, the partners bear the losses—in the absence of a contrary agreement—in the same proportion in which they shared the profits (rather than, for example, in proportion to their contributions to the partnership's capital).

Preventing Legal Disputes

Usually, when people enter into partnerships, they are getting along with one another. Obviously, the situation can change, and partners often become unable to work together amicably. To prepare for this possibility, businesspersons entering a partnership should agree on how their assets will be valued and divided in the event the partnership dissolves. The parties should make express arrangements during the formation of the partnership to provide for its smooth dissolution. Partners can enter a buy-sell, or buyout, agreement, which provides that one or more partners will buy out the other or others, should the relationship deteriorate. Agreeing beforehand on who buys what, under what circumstances, and, if possible, at what price may eliminate costly negotiations or litigation later. Alternatively, the agreement may specify that one or more partners will determine the value of the interest being sold and that the other or others will decide whether to buy or sell. ■

LIMITED LIABILITY PARTNERSHIPS

The **limited liability partnership (LLP)** is a hybrid form of business designed mostly for professionals, such as attorneys and accountants, who normally do business as partners in a partnership. In fact, nearly all the big accounting firms are LLPs. The major advantage of the LLP is that it allows a partnership to continue as a *pass-through entity* for tax purposes, but limits the personal liability of the partners.

LIMITED LIABILITY PARTNERSHIP (LLP)
A hybrid form of business organization that is used mainly by professionals who normally do business in a partnership. Like a partnership, an LLP is a pass-through entity for tax purposes, but the personal liability of the partners is limited.

LLPs must be formed and operated in compliance with state statutes, which often include provisions of the UPA. The appropriate form must be filed with a state agency, and the business's name must include either "Limited Liability Partnership" or "LLP" [UPA 1001, 1002]. In addition, an LLP must file an annual report with the state to remain qualified as an LLP in that state [UPA 1003]. In most states, it is relatively easy to convert a traditional partnership into an LLP because the firm's basic organizational structure remains the same. Additionally, all of the statutory and common law rules governing partnerships still apply (apart from those modified by the state's LLP statute).

Liability in an LLP

Many professionals work together using the partnership business form. Family members often do business together as partners also. As discussed previously, a major disadvantage of the general partnership is the unlimited personal liability of its owner-partners. Partners in a general partnership are also subject to joint and several (individual) liability for partnership obligations, which exposes each partner to potential liability for the malpractice of another partner.

The LLP allows professionals to avoid personal liability for the malpractice of other partners. A partner in an LLP is still liable for her or his own wrongful acts, such as negligence, however. Also liable is the partner who supervised the party who committed a wrongful act. This is generally true for all types of partners and partnerships, not just LLPs.

Although LLP statutes vary from state to state, generally each state statute limits the liability of partners in some way. For example, Delaware law protects each innocent partner from the "debts and obligations of the partnership arising from negligence, wrongful acts, or misconduct." The UPA more broadly exempts partners from personal liability for any partnership obligation, "whether arising in contract, tort, or otherwise" [UPA 306(c)].

Family Limited Liability Partnerships

FAMILY LIMITED LIABILITY PARTNERSHIP (FLLP)
A type of limited liability partnership owned by family members or fiduciaries of family members.

A **family limited liability partnership (FLLP)** is a limited liability partnership in which the majority of the partners are persons related to each other, essentially as spouses, parents, grandparents, siblings, cousins, nephews, or nieces. A person acting in a fiduciary capacity for persons so related can also be a partner. All of the partners must be natural persons or persons acting in a fiduciary capacity for the benefit of natural persons.

Probably the most significant use of the FLLP form of business organization is in agriculture. Family-owned farms sometimes find this form to their benefit. The FLLP offers the same advantages as other LLPs with some additional advantages, such as, in Iowa, an exemption from real estate transfer taxes when partnership real estate is transferred among partners.[6]

LIMITED PARTNERSHIPS

LIMITED PARTNERSHIP
A partnership consisting of one or more general partners (who manage the business and are liable to the full extent of their personal assets for debts of the partnership) and one or more limited partners (who contribute only assets and are liable only up to the extent of their contributions).

We now look at a business organizational form that limits the liability of *some* of its owners—the **limited partnership.** Limited partnerships originated in medieval Europe and have been in existence in the United States since the early 1800s. In many ways, limited partnerships are like the general partnerships discussed ear-

---

6. Iowa Statutes Section 428A.2.

lier in this chapter, but they differ from general partnerships in several ways. Because of this, they are sometimes referred to as *special partnerships*.

A limited partnership consists of at least one **general partner** and one or more **limited partners.** A general partner assumes management responsibility for the partnership and so has full responsibility for the partnership and for all debts of the partnership. A limited partner contributes cash or other property and owns an interest in the firm but does not undertake any management responsibilities and is not personally liable for partnership debts beyond the amount of his or her investment. A limited partner can forfeit limited liability by taking part in the management of the business.

Until 1976, the law governing limited partnerships in all states except Louisiana was the Uniform Limited Partnership Act (ULPA). Since 1976, most states and the District of Columbia have adopted the revised version of the ULPA, known as the Revised Uniform Limited Partnership Act (RULPA). Because the RULPA is the dominant law governing limited partnerships in the United States, we will refer to the RULPA in the following discussion of limited partnerships (excerpts of this law are included as Appendix F).

Formation of the Limited Partnership

In contrast to the informal, private, and voluntary agreement that usually suffices for a general partnership, the formation of a limited partnership is formal and public. The parties must follow specific statutory requirements and file a certificate with the state. A limited partnership must have at least one general partner and one limited partner, as mentioned previously. Additionally, the partners must sign a **certificate of limited partnership,** which requires information similar to that found in articles of incorporation (see Chapter 15), such as the name, mailing address, and capital contribution of each general and limited partner. The certificate is usually open to public inspection.

Liabilities of Partners in a Limited Partnership

General partners, unlike limited partners, are personally liable to the partnership's creditors; thus, at least one general partner is necessary in a limited partnership so that someone has personal liability. This policy can be circumvented in states that allow a corporation to be the general partner in a partnership. Because the corporation has limited liability by virtue of corporate laws, if a corporation is the general partner, no one in the limited partnership has personal liability.

In contrast to the personal liability of general partners, the liability of a limited partner is limited to the capital that she or he contributes or agrees to contribute to the partnership [RULPA 502]. Limited partners enjoy limited liability so long as they do not participate in management [RULPA 303]. A limited partner who participates in management will be just as liable as a general partner to any creditor who transacts business with the limited partnership and believes, based on a limited partner's conduct, that the limited partner is a general partner [RULPA 303]. How much actual review and advisement a limited partner can engage in before being exposed to liability is an unsettled question.

Dissociation and Dissolution

A general partner has the power to voluntarily dissociate, or withdraw, from a limited partnership unless the partnership agreement specifies otherwise. A limited partner theoretically can withdraw from the partnership by giving six

GENERAL PARTNER
In a limited partnership, a partner who assumes responsibility for the management of the partnership and liability for all partnership debts.

LIMITED PARTNER
In a limited partnership, a partner who contributes capital to the partnership but has no right to participate in the management and operation of the business. The limited partner assumes no liability for partnership debts beyond the capital contributed.

CERTIFICATE OF LIMITED PARTNERSHIP
The basic document filed with a designated state official by which a limited partnership is formed.

NOTE
A limited partner is liable to the extent of any contribution that she or he made to the partnership.

months' notice unless the partnership agreement specifies a term, which most do. Also, some states have passed laws prohibiting the withdrawal of limited partners.

In a limited partnership, a general partner's voluntary dissociation from the firm normally will lead to dissolution *unless* all partners agree to continue the business. Similarly, the bankruptcy, retirement, death, or mental incompetence of a general partner will cause the dissociation of that partner and the dissolution of the limited partnership unless the other members agree to continue the firm [RULPA 801]. Bankruptcy of a limited partner, however, does not dissolve the partnership unless it causes the bankruptcy of the firm. Death or an assignment of the interest of a limited partner does not dissolve a limited partnership [RULPA 702, 704, 705]. A limited partnership can be dissolved by court decree [RULPA 802].

On dissolution, creditors' claims, including those of partners who are creditors, take first priority. After that, partners and former partners receive unpaid distributions of partnership assets and, except as otherwise agreed, amounts representing returns on their contributions and amounts proportionate to their shares of the distributions [RULPA 804].

In the following case, two limited partners wanted the business of the partnership to be sold on its dissolution, while another limited partner—actor Kevin Costner—and the general partner wanted it to continue.

Case 14.2 **In re Dissolution of Midnight Star Enterprises, L.P.**

Supreme Court of South Dakota, 2006.
2006 SD 98, 724 N.W.2d 334.

BACKGROUND AND FACTS   Midnight Star Enterprises, Limited Partnership, consists of a casino, bar, and restaurant in Deadwood, South Dakota. The owners are Midnight Star Enterprises, Limited (MSEL), the general partner, which owns 22 partnership units; actor Kevin Costner, a limited partner, who owns 71.50 partnership units; and Carla and Francis Caneva, limited partners, who own 3.25 partnership units each. Costner also owns MSEL and thus controls 93.5 partnership units. The Canevas were the business's managers,

for which they received salaries and bonuses. When MSEL voiced concerns about the management, communication among the partners broke down. MSEL filed a petition in a South Dakota state court to dissolve the partnership. MSEL hired Paul Thorstenson, an accountant, to determine the firm's fair market value, which he calculated to be $3.1 million. The Canevas solicited a competitor's offer to buy the business for $6.2 million, which the court ruled was the appropriate amount. At the Canevas' request, the court ordered MSEL and Costner to buy the business for that price within ten days or sell it on the open market to the highest bidder. MSEL appealed to the South Dakota Supreme Court.

IN THE WORDS OF THE COURT . . . *SABERS*, Justice.

*   *   *   *

MSEL *   *   * brought a Petition for Dissolution [in a South Dakota state court]. In order to dissolve, the fair market value of Midnight Star had to be assessed. MSEL hired Paul Thorstenson, an accountant, to determine the fair market value. *   *   * The Canevas solicited an "offer" from Ken Kellar, a Deadwood casino, restaurant, and hotel owner *   *   * .

*   *   * Thorstenson determined the fair market value was $3.1 million based on the hypothetical transaction standard of valuation. *   *   * The *   *   * court *   *   * found Kellar's offer of $6.2 million to be the fair market value *   *   * [and] ordered the majority owners to buy the business for $6.2 million within 10 days or the court would order the business to be sold on the open market. [MSEL appealed to the South Dakota Supreme Court.]

* * * *

[The] Canevas claim the partnership agreement does not allow the general partner to buy out their interest in Midnight Star. Instead, the Canevas argue, the agreement mandates the partnership be sold on the open market upon dissolution. * * * Article 10.4 provides:

> After all of the debts of the Partnership have been paid, the General Partner * * * may distribute in kind any Partnership property provided that a good faith effort is first made to sell * * * such property * * * at its estimated fair value to one or more third parties * * * .

* * * *

* * * This provision clearly states the General Partner "may distribute in kind any partnership property" if the property is first offered to a third party for a fair value. While the General Partner may offer the property on the open market, Article 10.4 does not require it.

This interpretation is reinforced when read together with Article 10.3.1 * * * [which] instructs that "no assets * * * shall be sold or otherwise transferred to [any partner] unless the assets are valued at their then fair market value * * * ." *If Article 10.4 requires a forced sale, then there would be no need to have the fair market value provision of Article 10.3.1.* [Emphasis added.]

* * * Read as a whole, the partnership agreement does not require a mandatory sale upon dissolution. Instead, the general partner can opt to liquidate using either a sale or transfer under Article 10.3.1. * * * Because MSEL decided to pursue dissolution under Article 10.3.1, we decide the correct standard for determining the fair market value of the partnership.

* * * *

MSEL claims the correct standard * * * is the hypothetical transaction analysis * * * . [The] Canevas argue that * * * the offer from Kellar represented the fair market value * * * .

* * * *

* * * *[There are] sound policy reasons why an offer cannot be the fair market value.* * * * What if a businessman, for personal reasons, offers 10 times the real value of the business? What if the partnership, for personal reasons, such as sentimental value, refuses to sell for that absurdly high offer? *These arbitrary, emotional offers and rejections cannot provide a rational and reasonable basis for determining the fair market value.* [Emphasis added.]

Conversely, the hypothetical transaction standard does provide a rational and reasonable basis for determining the fair market value * * * by removing the irrationalities, strategies, and emotions * * * .

* * * *

Since it was error for the [lower] court to value Midnight Star at $6.2 million, it was also error to force the general partners to buy the business for $6.2 million or sell the business.

* * * *

* * * Instead of ordering the majority partners to purchase the whole partnership for the appraised value, the majority partners should only be required to pay any interests the withdrawing partner is due. * * * The majority partners should only be required to pay the Canevas the value of their 6.5 partnership units * * * .

DECISION AND REMEDY The South Dakota Supreme Court reversed the judgment of the lower court and remanded the case to allow MSEL and Costner to pay the Canevas the value of their 6.5 partnership units after a revaluation of the partnership. The court concluded that under the partnership agreement, during liquidation, the firm's property could be distributed in kind among the partners if it was first offered for sale to a third party. The court also concluded that the correct value of the business was the

CASE 14.2–CONTINUED

CASE 14.2–CONTINUED accountant's figure, which was based on a fair market value analysis using a hypothetical buyer.

THE LEGAL ENVIRONMENT DIMENSION   Why did the court hold that a forced sale of the property of the limited partnership was not appropriate in this case?

THE ETHICAL DIMENSION   Under what circumstances might a forced sale of the property of a limited partnership on its dissolution be appropriate?

Limited Liability Limited Partnerships

LIMITED LIABILITY LIMITED PARTNERSHIP (LLLP)
A type of limited liability partnership in which the liability of all of the partners, including general partners, is limited to the amount of their investments.

A **limited liability limited partnership (LLLP)** is a type of limited partnership. An LLLP differs from a limited partnership in that a general partner in an LLLP has the same liability as a limited partner in a limited partnership. In other words, the liability of all partners is limited to the amount of their investments in the firm.

A few states provide expressly for LLLPs. In states that do not provide for LLLPs but do allow for limited partnerships and limited liability partnerships, a limited partnership should probably still be able to register with the state as an LLLP.

LIMITED LIABILITY COMPANIES

For many entrepreneurs and investors, the ideal business form would combine the tax advantages of the partnership form of business with the limited liability of the corporate enterprise. Although the limited partnership partially addresses these needs, the limited liability of limited partners is conditional: limited liability exists only so long as the limited partner does *not* participate in management.

LIMITED LIABILITY COMPANY (LLC)
A hybrid form of business enterprise that offers the limited liability of the corporation but the tax advantages of a partnership.

This is one reason that every state has adopted legislation authorizing a form of business organization called the **limited liability company (LLC).** The LLC is a hybrid form of business enterprise that offers the limited liability of the corporation but the tax advantages of a partnership. The origins and characteristics of this increasingly significant form of business organization are discussed in this chapter's *Landmark in the Legal Environment* feature.

Formation of an LLC

Like an LLP or LP, an LLC must be formed and operated in compliance with state law. About one-fourth of the states specifically require LLCs to have at least two owners, called **members.** In the rest of the states, although some LLC statutes are silent on this issue, one-member LLCs are usually permitted.

MEMBER
A person who has an ownership interest in a limited liability company.

ARTICLES OF ORGANIZATION
The document filed with a designated state official by which a limited liability company is formed.

To form an LLC, **articles of organization** must be filed with a state agency—usually the secretary of state's office. Typically, the articles are required to set forth such information as the name of the business, its principal address, the name and address of a registered agent, the names of the owners, and information on how the LLC will be managed. The business's name must include the words "Limited Liability Company" or the initials "LLC." In addition to filing the articles of organization, a few states require that a notice of the intention to form an LLC be published in a local newspaper.

Businesspersons sometimes enter into contracts on behalf of a business organization that is not yet formed. For example, as you will read in Chapter 15, persons forming a corporation may enter into contracts during the process of

In 1977, Wyoming became the first state to pass legislation authorizing the creation of a limited liability company (LLC). Although LLCs emerged in the United States only in 1977, they have been in existence for over a century in other areas, including several European and South American nations. The South American *limitada*, for example, is a form of business organization that operates more or less as a partnership but provides limited liability for the owners.

Taxation of LLCs

In the United States, after Wyoming's adoption of an LLC statute, it still was not known how the Internal Revenue Service (IRS) would treat the LLC for tax purposes. In 1988, however, the IRS ruled that Wyoming LLCs would be taxed as partnerships instead of as corporations, providing that certain requirements were met. Prior to this ruling, only one other state—Florida, in 1982—had authorized LLCs. The 1988 ruling encouraged other states to enact LLC statutes, and in less than a decade, all states had done so.

IRS rules that went into effect on January 1, 1997, also encouraged widespread use of LLCs in the business world. These rules provide that any unincorporated business will automatically be taxed as a partnership unless it indicates otherwise on the tax form. The exceptions involve publicly traded companies, companies formed under a state incorporation statute, and certain foreign-owned companies. If a business chooses to be taxed as a corporation, it can indicate this choice by checking a box on the IRS form.

Foreign Entities May Be LLC Members

Part of the impetus behind the creation of LLCs in this country is that foreign investors are allowed to become LLC members. Generally, in an era increasingly characterized by global business efforts and investments, the LLC offers U.S. firms and potential investors from other countries flexibility and opportunities greater than those available through partnerships or corporations.

APPLICATION TO TODAY'S LEGAL ENVIRONMENT

Once it became clear that LLCs could be taxed as partnerships, the LLC form of business organization was widely adopted. Members could avoid the personal liability associated with the partnership form of business as well as the double taxation of the corporate form of business. Today, LLCs, which not long ago were largely unknown in this country, are a widely used form of business organization.

RELEVANT WEB SITES

To locate information on the Web concerning limited liability company statutes, go to this text's Web site at **www.cengage.com/blaw/let**, select "Chapter 14," and click on "URLs for Landmarks."

---

incorporation but before the corporation becomes a legal entity. These contracts are referred to as preincorporation contracts. Once the corporation is formed and adopts the preincorporation contract (by means of a *novation,* discussed in Chapter 10), it can then enforce the contract terms.

In the following case, the question was whether the same principle extends to LLCs. A person in the process of forming an LLC entered into a preorganization contract under which it would be obligated to purchase the Park Plaza Hotel in Hollywood, California. Once the LLC legally existed, the owners of the hotel refused to sell the property to the LLC, claiming that the contract was unenforceable.

Case 14.3 **O2 Development, LLC v. 607 South Park, LLC**

Court of Appeal,
Second District, Division 1, California, 2008.
159 Cal.App.4th 609, 71 Cal.Rptr.3d 608.

BACKGROUND AND FACTS In March 2004, 607 South Park, LLC, entered into a written agreement to sell Park Plaza Hotel to 607 Park View Associates, Ltd., for $8.7 million. The general partner of 607 Park View Associates was Creative Environments of Hollywood, Inc. In February 2005, Creative Environments assigned the rights to the hotel purchase to another company, O2 Development, LLC. At the time, O2 Development did not yet exist; it was legally created several months later. O2 Development sued 607 South Park for breach of the hotel purchase agreement. 607 South Park moved for summary judgment, arguing that no enforceable contract existed because at the time of the assignment, O2

CASE 14.3–CONTINUED

Development did not yet legally exist. Furthermore, 607 South Park argued that 02 Development suffered no damages because it was "not ready, willing, and able to fund the purchase of the hotel." The trial court granted the motion and entered judgment in favor of 607 South Park. 02 Development appealed.

IN THE WORDS OF THE COURT . . . *ROTHSCHILD,* J. [Judge]

DISCUSSION

*   *   *   *

I. Enforceability of Pre-Organization Contracts

It is hornbook law [black letter law] that a corporation can enforce preincorporation contracts made in its behalf, as long as the corporation "has adopted the contract or otherwise succeeded to it." *   *   * California law does not deviate from that well-established norm. *607 South Park does not argue that limited liability companies should be treated differently from corporations in this respect, and we are aware of no authority that would support such a position.* 607 South Park's first ground for its summary judgment motion—that there is no enforceable contract between 607 South Park and 02 Development because 02 Development did not exist when the assignment agreement was executed—therefore fails as a matter of law. [Emphasis added.]

607 South Park's principal contention to the contrary is that a nonexistent business entity cannot be a party to a contract. The contention is true but irrelevant. *When the assignment agreement was executed, 02 Development did not exist, so it was not then a party to the agreement. But once 02 Development came into existence, it could enforce any pre-organization contract made in its behalf, such as the assignment agreement, if it adopted or ratified it.* [Emphasis added.]

*   *   *   *

II. Causation

In the trial court, 607 South Park contended that in order to prove causation, 02 Development would have to prove either that it had the $8.7 million necessary to fund the transaction or that it had legally binding commitments from third parties to provide the necessary funding. *   *   * 607 South Park disavows [this contention] on appeal.

Instead, 607 South Park now argues that its motion was based on the proposition that 02 Development "must present admissible evidence that it would have been financially able to close the transaction." But 607 South Park's evidence in support of its motion showed only that 02 Development had neither the $8.7 million to fund the transaction nor legally binding commitments from third parties to provide the funding. *607 South Park presented no evidence that 02 Development would have been unable to arrange for the necessary funding to close the transaction on time if 607 South Park had given it the opportunity instead of repudiating the contract in advance.* Because 607 South Park introduced no evidence to support an argument based on the proposition of law that 607 South Park is now advocating, the burden of production never shifted to 02 Development to present contrary evidence. For all of these reasons, the trial court erred when it granted 607 South Park's motion for summary judgment. [Emphasis added.]

DECISION AND REMEDY   The California intermediate appellate court reversed the judgment and directed the trial court to enter an order denying 607 South Park's motion for summary judgment. According to the appellate court, limited liability companies should be treated the same as corporations with respect to preorganization contracts.

THE LEGAL ENVIRONMENT DIMENSION   Why was it unimportant to the appellate court that 02 Development did not have to prove that it had funding commitments for $8.7 million?

THE ETHICAL DIMENSION Presumably, 607 South Park repudiated the real estate purchase agreement because it either had, or believed it could obtain, a better offer for the property. Are there any circumstances under which this reason could justify 607 South Park's behavior?

Jurisdictional Requirements

One of the significant differences between LLCs and corporations has to do with federal jurisdictional requirements. Under the federal jurisdiction statute, a corporation is deemed to be a citizen of the state where it is incorporated and maintains its principal place of business. The statute does not mention the state citizenship of partnerships, LLCs, and other unincorporated associations, but the courts have tended to regard these entities as citizens of every state in which their members are citizens.

The state citizenship of an LLC may come into play when a party sues the LLC based on diversity of citizenship. Remember from Chapter 3 that when parties to a lawsuit are from different states and the amount in controversy exceeds $75,000, a federal court can exercise diversity jurisdiction. *Total* diversity of citizenship must exist, however. **EXAMPLE #9** Fong, a citizen of New York, wishes to bring a suit against Skycel, an LLC formed under the laws of Connecticut. One of Skycel's members also lives in New York. Fong will not be able to bring a suit against Skycel in federal court on the basis of diversity jurisdiction because the defendant LLC is also a citizen of New York. The same would be true if Fong was bringing a suit against multiple defendants and one of the defendants lived in New York. □

Advantages and Disadvantages of the LLC

Although the LLC offers many advantages to businesspersons, this form of business organization also has some disadvantages. We look now at some of the advantages and disadvantages of the LLC. For a discussion of business organizations in other nations that are similar to the LLC, see this chapter's *Beyond Our Borders* feature on the next page.

Advantages of the LLC A key advantage of the LLC is that the liability of members is limited to the amount of their investments. Another advantage is the flexibility of the LLC in regard to both taxation and management.

An LLC that has *two or more members* can choose to be taxed either as a partnership or as a corporation. As you will read in Chapter 15, a corporate entity must pay income taxes on its profits, and the shareholders pay personal income taxes on profits distributed as dividends. An LLC that wants to distribute profits to the members may prefer to be taxed as a partnership to avoid the "double-taxation" characteristic of the corporate entity. Unless an LLC indicates that it wishes to be taxed as a corporation, the IRS automatically taxes it as a partnership. This means that the LLC as an entity pays no taxes; rather, as in a partnership, profits are "passed through" the LLC to the members who then personally pay taxes on the profits. If an LLC's members want to reinvest the profits in the business, however, rather than distribute the profits to members, they may prefer that the LLC be taxed as a corporation. Corporate income tax rates may be

Stan Ovshinsky, founder of Ovonic Hydrogen Systems, LLC, a developer of alternative energy technologies. What are some of the advantages of doing business as an LLC instead of a corporation? Are there any disadvantages?
(Photo Courtesy of ECD Ovonics)

Limited liability companies are not unique to the United States. Many nations have business forms that provide limited liability, although these organizations may differ significantly from domestic LLCs. In Germany, for example, the *GmbH*, or *Gesellschaft mit beschränkter Haftung* (which means "company with limited liability"), is a type of business entity that has been available since 1892. The GmbH is now the most widely used business form in Germany. A GmbH, however, is owned by shareholders and thus resembles a U.S. corporation in certain respects. German laws also impose numerous restrictions on the operations and business transactions of GmbHs, whereas LLCs in the United States are not even required to have an operating agreement.

Variants of the LLC form of business that limit the liability of owners are available today to businesspersons around the globe. Limited liability companies known as *limitadas* are common in many Latin American nations. In France, *a société à responsabilité limitée* (meaning "society with limited liability") is an entity that provides business owners with limited liability. In 2002, the United Kingdom and Ireland passed laws that allow limited liability. Although these laws use the term *limited liability partnership,* the entities are similar to our domestic LLCs. In 2006, Japan enacted legislation that created a new type of business organization, called the *godo kaisha (GK)*, which is also quite similar to a U.S. LLC. In most nations, some type of document that is similar to the LLC's articles of organization must be filed with the government to form the business. Many countries limit the number of owners that such businesses may have, and some also require the member-owners to choose one or more persons who will manage the business affairs.

FOR CRITICAL ANALYSIS Clearly, limited liability is an important aspect of doing business globally. Why might a nation limit the number of member-owners in a limited liability company?

---

lower than personal tax rates. Part of the attractiveness of the LLC is this flexibility with respect to taxation.

For federal income tax purposes, one-member LLCs are automatically taxed as sole proprietorships unless they indicate that they wish to be taxed as corporations. With respect to state taxes, most states follow the IRS rules. Still another advantage of the LLC for businesspersons is the flexibility it offers in terms of business operations and management—as will be discussed shortly. Finally, because foreign investors can participate in an LLC, the LLC form of business is attractive as a way to encourage investment.

Disadvantages of the LLC The disadvantages of the LLC are relatively few. Although initially there was uncertainty over how LLCs would be taxed, that disadvantage no longer exists. One remaining disadvantage is that state LLC statutes are not yet uniform. Until all of the states have uniform LLC laws, an LLC in one state will have to check the rules in the other states in which the firm does business to ensure that it retains its limited liability. Generally, though, most—if not all—states apply to a foreign LLC (an LLC formed in another state) the law of the state where the LLC was formed.

Still another disadvantage is the lack of case law dealing with LLCs. How the courts interpret statutes provides important guidelines for businesses. Given the relative newness of the LLC as a business form in the United States, there is not, as yet, a substantial body of case law to provide this kind of guidance.

REMEMBER
A uniform law is a "model" law. It does not become the law of any state until the state legislature adopts it, either in part or in its entirety.

OPERATING AGREEMENT
In a limited liability company, an agreement in which the members set forth the details of how the business will be managed and operated. State statutes typically give the members wide latitude in deciding for themselves the rules that will govern their organization.

The LLC Operating Agreement

The members of an LLC can decide how to operate the various aspects of the business by forming an **operating agreement** [ULLCA 103(a)]. Operating agreements typically contain provisions relating to management, how profits will be divided, the transfer of membership interests, whether the LLC will be dissolved on the death or departure of a member, and other important issues.

An operating agreement need not be in writing and indeed need not even be formed for an LLC to exist. Generally, though, LLC members should protect their interests by forming a written operating agreement. As with any business arrangement, disputes may arise over any number of issues. If there is no agreement covering the topic under dispute, such as how profits will be divided, the state LLC statute will govern the outcome. For example, most LLC statutes provide that if the members have not specified how profits will be divided, they will be divided equally among the members. Generally, when an issue is not covered by an operating agreement or by an LLC statute, the courts apply the principles of partnership law.

Management of an LLC

Basically, there are two options for managing an LLC. The members may decide in their operating agreement to be either a "member-managed" LLC or a "manager-managed" LLC. Most LLC statutes and the Uniform Limited Liability Company Act (ULLCA) provide that unless the articles of organization specify otherwise, an LLC is assumed to be member managed [ULLCA 203(a)(6)].

In a *member-managed* LLC, all of the members participate in management, and decisions are made by majority vote [ULLCA 404(a)]. In a *manager-managed* LLC, the members designate a group of persons to manage the firm. The management group may consist of only members, both members and nonmembers, or only nonmembers. Managers in a manager-managed LLC owe fiduciary duties to the LLC and its members, including the duty of loyalty and the duty of care [ULLCA 409(a), (h)], just as corporate directors and officers owe fiduciary duties to the corporation and its shareholders (see Chapter 15).

The members of an LLC can also set forth in their operating agreement provisions governing decision-making procedures. For instance, the agreement can include procedures for choosing or removing managers. Although most LLC statutes are silent on this issue, the ULLCA provides that members may choose and remove managers by majority vote [ULLCA 404(b)(3)].

Members may also specify in their agreement how voting rights will be apportioned. If they do not, LLC statutes in most states provide that voting rights are apportioned according to each member's capital contributions. Some states provide that, in the absence of an agreement to the contrary, each member has one vote.

Dissociation and Dissolution of an LLC

Recall that in the context of partnerships, *dissociation* occurs when a partner ceases to be associated in the carrying on of the business. The same concept applies to limited liability companies. A member of an LLC has the *power* to dissociate from the LLC at any time, but he or she may not have the *right* to dissociate. Under the ULLCA, the events that trigger a member's dissociation in an LLC are similar to the events causing a partner to be dissociated under the Uniform Partnership Act (UPA). These include voluntary withdrawal, expulsion by other members or by court order, bankruptcy, incompetence, and death.

Members of a manager-managed LLC hold a formal members' meeting. What is the difference between a member-managed LLC and a manager-managed LLC? How are managers typically chosen?
(PhotoDisc)

Generally, even if a member dies or otherwise dissociates from an LLC, the other members may continue to carry on LLC business, unless the operating agreement has contrary provisions.

The Effect of Dissociation   When a member dissociates from an LLC, he or she loses the right to participate in management and the right to act as an agent for the LLC. His or her duty of loyalty to the LLC also terminates, and the duty of care continues only with respect to events that occurred before dissociation. Generally, the dissociated member also has a right to have his or her interest in the LLC bought out by the other members of the LLC. The LLC's operating agreement may contain provisions establishing a buyout price, but if it does not, the member's interest is usually purchased at a fair value. In states that have adopted the ULLCA, the LLC must purchase the interest at "fair" value within 120 days after the dissociation.

If the member's dissociation violates the LLC's operating agreement, it is considered legally wrongful, and the dissociated member can be held liable for damages caused by the dissociation. **EXAMPLE #10** Chadwick and Barrel are members in an LLC. Chadwick manages the accounts, and Barrel, who has many connections in the community and is a skilled investor, brings in the business. If Barrel wrongfully dissociates from the LLC, the LLC's business will suffer, and Chadwick can hold Barrel liable for the loss of business resulting from her withdrawal.▫

Dissolution   Regardless of whether a member's dissociation was wrongful or rightful, normally the dissociated member has no right to force the LLC to dissolve. The remaining members can opt to either continue or dissolve the business. Members can also stipulate in their operating agreement that certain events will cause dissolution, or they can agree that they have the power to dissolve the LLC by vote. As with partnerships, a court can order an LLC to be dissolved in certain circumstances, such as when the members have engaged in illegal or oppressive conduct, or when it is no longer feasible to carry on the business.

When an LLC is dissolved, any members who did not wrongfully dissociate may participate in the winding up process. To wind up the business, members must collect, liquidate, and distribute the LLC's assets. Members may preserve the assets for a reasonable time to optimize their return, and they continue to have the authority to perform reasonable acts in conjunction with winding up. In other words, the LLC will be bound by the reasonable acts of its members during the winding up process. Once all the LLC's assets have been sold, the proceeds are distributed to pay off debts to creditors first (including debts owed to members who are creditors of the LLC). The member's capital contributions are returned next, and any remaining amounts are then distributed to members in equal shares or according to their operating agreement.

Preventing Legal Disputes

Because disputes often arise among members of an LLC during dissociation and dissolution, businesspersons forming an LLC should carefully draft their operating agreement. Stipulate what events will cause dissociation and how the fair-value buyout price will be calculated. Set a time limit by which the LLC must pay the dissociated member (or her or his estate) in the event that she or he withdraws, becomes disabled, or dies. Include provisions that clearly limit the authority of dissociated members to act on behalf of the LLC, and provide a right to seek damages from members who exceed the agreed-on parameters. Also, remember to notify third parties when any member dissociates and file a notice of dissociation with the state to limit the extent of the former member's apparent authority to act on behalf of the LLC. It is also advisable to set forth in the operating agreement any events that will automatically cause a dissolution, as well as which members will have a right to participate in—or make decisions about—the winding up. ■

FRANCHISES

Instead of setting up a business through which to market their own products or services, many entrepreneurs opt to purchase a franchise. A **franchise** is defined as any arrangement in which the owner of a trademark, a trade name, or a copyright licenses others to use the trademark, trade name, or copyright in the selling of goods or services. A **franchisee** (a purchaser of a franchise) is generally legally independent of the **franchisor** (the seller of the franchise). At the same time, the franchisee is economically dependent on the franchisor's integrated business system. In other words, a franchisee can operate as an independent businessperson but still obtain the advantages of a regional or national organization.

Today, franchising companies and their franchisees account for a significant portion of all retail sales in this country. Well-known franchises include 7-Eleven, Holiday Inn, and McDonald's.

FRANCHISE
Any arrangement in which the owner of a trademark, trade name, or copyright licenses another to use that trademark, trade name, or copyright in the selling of goods or services.

FRANCHISEE
One receiving a license to use another's (the franchisor's) trademark, trade name, or copyright in the sale of goods and services.

FRANCHISOR
One licensing another (the franchisee) to use the owner's trademark, trade name, or copyright in the selling of goods or services.

Types of Franchises

Because the franchising industry is so extensive and so many different types of businesses sell franchises, it is difficult to summarize the many types of franchises that now exist. Generally, though, the majority of franchises fall into one of three classifications: distributorships, chain-style business operations, or manufacturing or processing-plant arrangements. We briefly describe these types of franchises here.

KEEP IN MIND
Because a franchise involves the licensing of a trademark, a trade name, or a copyright, the law governing intellectual property may apply in some cases.

Distributorship A *distributorship* arises when a manufacturing concern (franchisor) licenses a dealer (franchisee) to sell its product. Often, a distributorship covers an exclusive territory. An example is an automobile dealership or beer distributorship.

EXAMPLE #11 Anheuser-Busch distributes its brands of beer through a network of authorized wholesale distributors, each with an assigned territory. Marik signs a distributorship contract for the area from Gainesville to Ocala, Florida. If the contract states that Marik is the exclusive distributor in that area, then no other franchisee may distribute Anheuser-Busch beer in that region. □

Chain-Style Business Operation In a *chain-style business operation,* a franchise operates under a franchisor's trade name and is identified as a member of a select group of dealers that engage in the franchisor's business. The franchisee is generally required to follow standardized or prescribed methods of operation. Often, the franchisor requires that the franchisee maintain certain standards of operation. In addition, sometimes the franchisee is obligated to obtain materials and supplies exclusively from the franchisor. Examples of this type of franchise are McDonald's and most other fast-food chains. Chain-style franchises are also common in service-related businesses, including real estate brokerage firms, such as Century 21, and tax-preparing services, such as H & R Block, Inc.

Manufacturing or Processing-Plant Arrangement   In a *manufacturing or processing-plant arrangement,* the franchisor transmits to the franchisee the essential ingredients or formula to make a particular product. The franchisee then markets the product either at wholesale or at retail in accordance with the franchisor's standards. Examples of this type of franchise are Coca-Cola and other soft-drink bottling companies.

Laws Governing Franchising

Because a franchise relationship is primarily a contractual relationship, it is governed by contract law. If the franchise exists primarily for the sale of products manufactured by the franchisor, the law governing sales contracts as expressed in Article 2 of the Uniform Commercial Code applies (see Chapter 11). Additionally, the federal government and most states have enacted laws governing certain aspects of franchising. Generally, these laws are designed to protect prospective franchisees from dishonest franchisors and to prohibit franchisors from terminating franchises without good cause.

Preventing Legal Disputes

Businesspersons should realize that federal and state laws control the franchising relationship. Ultimately, it falls to the courts to interpret the laws and determine whether a franchise relationship exists. In some cases, courts have held that even though the parties signed a franchising agreement, the franchisees are in fact employees because of the degree of control exercised over them by the franchisors. In other cases, courts have held that a franchising relationship exists even in the absence of a franchising contract. Because of the myriad of federal laws that apply, and because state laws on franchising vary dramatically, businesspersons should seek the advice of counsel within the state prior to entering a franchising relationship. ■

Federal Regulation of Franchising   The federal government has enacted laws that protect franchisees in certain industries, such as automobile dealerships and service stations. These laws protect the franchisee from unreasonable demands and bad faith terminations of the franchise by the franchisor. If an automobile manufacturer-franchisor terminates a franchise because of a dealer-franchisee's failure to comply with unreasonable demands (for example, failure to attain an unrealistically high sales quota), the manufacturer may be liable for damages.[7] Similarly, federal law prescribes the conditions under which a franchisor of service stations can terminate the franchise.[8] Federal antitrust laws (to be discussed in Chapter 23) also apply in certain circumstances to prohibit certain types of anticompetitive agreements.

Additionally, the Franchise Rule of the Federal Trade Commission (FTC) requires franchisors to disclose material facts that a prospective franchisee needs

---

7. Automobile Dealers' Franchise Act of 1965, also known as the Automobile Dealers' Day in Court Act, 15 U.S.C. Sections 1221 *et seq.*

8. Petroleum Marketing Practices Act (PMPA) of 1979, 15 U.S.C. Sections 2801 *et seq.*

to make an informed decision concerning the purchase of a franchise.[9] The rule was designed to enable potential franchisees to weigh the risks and benefits of an investment. The rule requires the franchisor to make numerous written disclosures to prospective franchisees. For example, a franchisor is required to disclose whether projected earnings figures are based on actual data or hypothetical examples. If a franchisor makes sales or earnings projections based on actual data for a specific franchise location, the franchisor must disclose the number and percentage of its actual franchises that have achieved this result. All representations made to a prospective franchisee must have a reasonable basis. Franchisors are also required to explain termination, cancellation, and renewal provisions of the franchise contract to potential franchisees before the agreement is signed. Those who violate the Franchise Rule are subject to substantial civil penalties, and the FTC can sue on behalf of injured parties to recover damages.

Can a franchisor satisfy the Franchise Rule by providing disclosures via the Internet? See this chapter's *Online Developments* feature on the following page for a discussion of this topic.

State Regulation of Franchising   State legislation varies but often is aimed at protecting franchisees from unfair practices and bad faith terminations by franchisors. Approximately fifteen states have laws similar to the federal rules requiring franchisors to provide presale disclosures to prospective franchisees.[10] Some states also require a disclosure document (known as a *Uniform Franchise Offering Circular,* or UFOC) to be filed with a state official. To protect franchisees, a state law might require the disclosure of information such as the actual costs of operation, recurring expenses, and profits earned, along with data substantiating these figures. To protect franchisees against arbitrary or bad faith terminations, the law might also require that certain procedures be followed in terminating a franchising relationship. State deceptive trade practices acts (see Chapter 20) may also apply and prohibit certain types of actions on the part of franchisors.

EXAMPLE #12 The Illinois Franchise Disclosure Act prohibits any untrue statement of a material fact in connection with the offer or sale of any franchise. Miyamoto, a franchisor of bagel restaurants, understates the start-up costs and exaggerates the anticipated yearly profits from operating a bagel shop when meeting with prospective buyers. After the sale, the buyers discover that Miyamoto's statements were not true. Because these statements were false and materially influenced the franchisees' decisions to buy, Miyamoto has violated state law.[11] □

The Franchise Contract

The franchise relationship is defined by a contract between the franchisor and the franchisee. The franchise contract specifies the terms and conditions of the franchise and spells out the rights and duties of the franchisor and the franchisee. If either party fails to perform the contractual duties, that party may be subject to a lawsuit for breach of contract. Generally, statutes and case law

---

9. 16 C.F.R. Part 436.
10. These states include California, Hawaii, Illinois, Indiana, Maryland, Michigan, Minnesota, New York, North Dakota, Oregon, Rhode Island, South Dakota, Virginia, Washington, and Wisconsin.
11. *Bixby's Food Systems, Inc. v. McKay,* 193 F.Supp.2d 1053 (N.D.Ill. 2002).

The Federal Trade Commission (FTC) issued its Franchise Rule in 1978, when the normal medium for transmission of information in a permanent form was on paper. When the Internet became a reality for a large number of people in the 1990s, the FTC was faced with the possibility that franchisors might use Web sites to provide downloadable information to prospective franchisees. Is such online information the equivalent of an offer that requires compliance with the FTC's Franchise Rule? The FTC said yes.

The FTC Began Allowing Electronic Disclosures Years Ago

The FTC has issued advisory opinions since the 1990s that allowed electronic disclosures via CD-ROM and DVD as long as the prospective franchisee was given the option of receiving paper disclosures and chose electronic. Also, the CD-ROM or DVD must have a label indicating that it contains the disclosures required by the FTC and the date when it was issued.

In 1999, the FTC began its formal rulemaking process (see Chapter 19) to create new regulations that would apply to online disclosures.[a] The time period for public comment closed in 2000.[b]

Franchise.com Gets the Green Light

In 2001, Franchise.com, a marketer of existing franchises, became the first Web-based franchise operation to win the FTC's approval of its plan to provide electronic disclosure services for all of its franchisor advertisers. Franchise.com requires any franchisor that wishes to advertise on its Web site to provide a disclosure document containing the FTC's proposed cover-page statement regarding electronic disclosures. When a prospective franchisee comes to the

Franchise.com Web site, he or she must agree to receive disclosures electronically by clicking on the appropriate button. The prospect can then obtain information on a particular franchise through the Web site. Whenever prospective franchisees access their accounts at the Web site, there are hyperlinks to written summary documents. Each time a prospective franchisee clicks on the hyperlinks, she or he is advised to download or print the disclosure document for future reference.

The FTC determined that Franchise.com's system was consistent with the Franchise Rule and issued an informal staff advisory opinion to that effect. In 2003, McGarry Internet, Ltd., of Dublin, Ireland, received similar approval. This company sends each prospective franchisee a Uniform Franchise Offering Circular via e-mail. In 2005, the FTC approved the request of VaultraNet, which had developed an Internet-based file delivery and signature system that it uses to provide disclosure documents to prospective franchisees.

Amendments to the Franchise Rule Became Effective in 2007

In July 2007, amendments to the Franchise Rule went into effect allowing franchisors to provide disclosure documents via the Internet as long as they meet certain requirements. For instance, prospective franchisees must be able to download or save all electronic disclosure documents. Additional disclosures are required about lawsuits that the franchisor has filed and settlement agreements that it has reached with franchisees in the past. These amendments bring the federal rule into closer alignment with state franchise disclosure laws.

FOR CRITICAL ANALYSIS   Why do you think it took so long for the FTC to amend its rules about franchisors using the Internet?

a. 16 C.F.R. Part 436, 64 Fed.Reg. 57,294 (October 22, 1999).
b. 65 Fed.Reg. 44,484 (July 18, 2000).

governing franchising tend to emphasize the importance of good faith and fair dealing in franchise relationships.

Because each type of franchise relationship has its own characteristics, it is difficult to describe the broad range of details a franchising contract may include. Here, we look at some of the major issues that typically are addressed in a franchise contract.

Payment for the Franchise   The franchisee ordinarily pays an initial fee or lump-sum price for the franchise license (the privilege of being granted a franchise). This fee is separate from the various products that the franchisee purchases from or through the franchisor. In some industries, the franchisor relies heavily on the initial sale of the franchise for realizing a profit. In other industries, the continued dealing between the parties brings profit to both. In most situations, the franchisor will receive a stated percentage of the annual sales or annual volume of business done by the franchisee. The franchise agreement may also require the franchisee to pay a percentage of advertising costs and certain administrative expenses.

Business Premises and Organization The franchise agreement may specify whether the premises for the business must be leased or purchased outright. In some cases, a building must be constructed or remodeled to meet the terms of the agreement. The agreement usually will specify whether the franchisor supplies equipment and furnishings for the premises or whether this is the responsibility of the franchisee.

The business organization of the franchisee is of great concern to the franchisor. Depending on the terms of the franchise agreement, the franchisor may specify particular requirements for the form and capital structure of the business. The franchise agreement may also require that the franchisee adhere to certain standards of operation in such aspects of the business as sales quotas, quality, and record keeping. Furthermore, a franchisor may wish to retain stringent control over the training of personnel involved in the operation and over administrative aspects of the business.

Location of the Franchise Typically, the franchisor will determine the territory to be served. Some franchise contracts give the franchisee exclusive rights, or "territorial rights," to a certain geographic area. Other franchise contracts, though they define the territory allotted to a particular franchise, either specifically state that the franchise is nonexclusive or are silent on the issue of territorial rights.

Many franchise cases involve disputes over territorial rights, and the implied covenant of good faith and fair dealing often comes into play in this area of franchising. For example, suppose that the franchise contract either does not give a franchisee exclusive territorial rights or is silent on the issue. If the franchisor allows a competing franchise to be established nearby, the franchisee may suffer a significant loss in profits. In this situation, a court may hold that the franchisor's actions breached an implied covenant of good faith and fair dealing.

Quality Control by the Franchisor Although the day-to-day operation of the franchise business is normally left to the franchisee, the franchise agreement may provide for the amount of supervision and control agreed on by the parties. When the franchisee prepares a product, such as food, or provides a service, such as a motel, the contract often provides that the franchisor will establish certain standards for the facility. Typically, the contract will state that the franchisor is permitted to make periodic inspections to ensure that the standards are being maintained so as to protect the franchise's name and reputation.

As a general rule, the validity of a provision permitting the franchisor to establish and enforce certain quality standards is unquestioned. Because the franchisor has a legitimate interest in maintaining the quality of the product or

Franchises can extend to foreign countries, even for very American brands such as Disney. In 2006, the RJ Corporation of India signed a franchise agreement with Disney Consumer Products. What do you think some of the elements of that agreement were?
(AP Photo/Saurabh Das)

service to protect its name and reputation, it can exercise greater control in this area than would otherwise be tolerated. Increasingly, however, franchisors are finding that if they exercise too much control over the operations of their franchisees, they may incur vicarious (indirect) liability under agency theory (see Chapter 16) for the acts of their franchisees' employees. The actual exercise of control, or at least the right to control, is the key consideration.

Termination of the Franchise

The duration of the franchise is a matter to be determined between the parties. Sometimes, a franchise will start out for a short period, such as a year, so that the franchisor can determine whether it wants to stay in business with the franchisee. Other times, the duration of the franchise contract correlates with the term of the lease for the business premises, and both are renewable at the end of that period. Usually, the franchise agreement will specify that termination must be "for cause," such as death or disability of the franchisee, insolvency of the franchisee, breach of the franchise agreement, or failure to meet specified sales quotas. Most franchise contracts provide that notice of termination must be given. If no set time for termination is specified, then a reasonable time, with notice, will be implied. A franchisee must be given reasonable time to wind up the business—that is, to do the accounting and return the copyright or trademark or any other property of the franchisor.

Wrongful Termination   Because a franchisor's termination of a franchise often has adverse consequences for the franchisee, much franchise litigation involves claims of wrongful termination. Generally, the termination provisions of contracts are more favorable to the franchisor. This means that the franchisee, who normally invests a substantial amount of time and funds to make the franchise operation successful, may receive little or nothing for the business on termination. The franchisor owns the trademark and hence the business.

It is in this area that statutory and case law become important. The federal and state laws discussed earlier attempt, among other things, to protect franchisees from the arbitrary or unfair termination of their franchises by the franchisors. Generally, both statutory and case law emphasize the importance of good faith and fair dealing in terminating a franchise relationship.

Preventing Legal Disputes

To avoid potential disputes regarding franchise termination, a prospective franchisee should always do preliminary research on a franchisor before agreeing to enter into a franchise contract. Find out whether the franchisor has terminated franchises in the past, how many times, and for what reasons. Contact five to ten franchisees of the same franchisor and ask questions about their relationships and any problems. Learning whether the franchisor has been honest, reliable, and reasonable with its franchisees in the past can be invaluable in preventing disputes over termination and bad faith actions of a franchisor. ■

The Importance of Good Faith and Fair Dealing   In determining whether a franchisor has acted in good faith when terminating a franchise agreement, the courts generally try to balance the rights of both parties. If a court perceives that a franchisor has arbitrarily or unfairly terminated a franchise, the franchisee will be provided with a remedy for wrongful termination. If a franchisor's decision to terminate a franchise was made in the normal course of the franchisor's business operations, however, and reasonable notice of termination was given to the franchisee, generally a court will not consider the termination wrongful.

Reviewing . . . Small Business Organizations

A bridge on a prominent public roadway in the city of Papagos, Arizona, was deteriorating and in need of repair. The city posted notices seeking proposals for an artistic bridge design and reconstruction. Davidson Masonry, LLC, which was owned and managed by Carl Davidson and his wife, Marilyn Rowe, submitted a bid for a decorative concrete project that incorporated artistic metalwork. They contacted Shana Lafayette, a local sculptor who specialized in large-scale metal forms, to help them design the bridge. The city selected their bridge design and awarded them the contract for a commission of $184,000. Davidson Masonry and Lafayette then entered into an agreement to work together on the bridge project. Davidson Masonry agreed to install and pay for concrete and structural work, and Lafayette agreed to install the metalwork at her expense. They agreed that overall profits would be split, with 25 percent going to Lafayette and 75 percent going to Davidson Masonry. Lafayette designed numerous metal sculptures of salmon that were incorporated into colorful decorative concrete forms designed by Rowe, while Davidson performed the structural engineering. Using the information presented in the chapter, answer the following questions.

1. Would Davidson Masonry automatically be taxed as a partnership or a corporation?

2. Is Davidson Masonry a member-managed or manager-managed LLC?

3. Suppose that during construction, Lafayette had entered into an agreement to rent space in a warehouse that was close to the bridge so that she could work on her sculptures near the site where they would eventually be installed. She entered into the contract without the knowledge or consent of Davidson Masonry. In this situation, would a court be likely to hold that Davidson Masonry was bound by the contract that Lafayette entered? Why or why not?

4. Now suppose that Rowe has an argument with her husband and wants to withdraw from being a member of Davidson Masonry. What is the term for such a withdrawal, and what effect does it have on the LLC?

Key Terms

articles of organization 470
articles of partnership 458
buyout price 464
certificate of limited
    partnership 467
confession of judgment 459
dissociation 463
dissolution 464
entrepreneur 452
family limited liability
    partnership (FLLP) 466
franchise 477

franchisee 477
franchisor 477
general partner 467
information return 458
joint and several liability 462
joint liability 461
limited liability company
    (LLC) 470
limited liability limited
    partnership (LLLP) 470
limited liability partnership
    (LLP) 465

limited partner 467
limited partnership 466
member 470
operating agreement 474
partnership 456
pass-through entity 458
sole proprietorship 453
winding up 464

Chapter Summary

Sole Proprietorships
(See pages 453–456.)

The simplest form of business organization; used by anyone who does business without creating a separate organization. The owner is the business. The owner pays personal income taxes on all profits and is personally liable for all business debts.

Partnerships
(See pages 456–465.)

1. A partnership is created by agreement of the parties.

2. A partnership is treated as an entity except for limited purposes.

3. Each partner pays a proportionate share of income taxes on the net profits of the partnership, whether or not they are distributed; the partnership files only an information return with the Internal Revenue Service.

4. Each partner has an equal voice in management unless the partnership agreement provides otherwise.

5. In the absence of an agreement, partners share profits equally and share losses in the same ratio as they share profits.

6. The capital contribution of each partner is determined by agreement.

7. Partners have unlimited liability for partnership debts.

8. A partnership can be terminated by agreement or can be dissolved by action of the partners, operation of law (subsequent illegality), or court decree.

Limited Liability Partnerships (LLPs)
(See pages 465–466.)

1. *Formation*–LLPs must be formed in compliance with state statutes. Typically, an LLP is formed by professionals who normally work together as partners in a partnership. Under most state LLP statutes, it is relatively easy to convert a traditional partnership into an LLP.

2. *Liability of partners*–LLP statutes vary, but under the UPA, professionals generally can avoid personal liability for acts committed by other partners. The extent to which partners' limited liability will be recognized when the partnership does business in another state depends on the other state's laws. Partners in an LLP continue to be liable for their own wrongful acts and for the wrongful acts of those whom they supervise.

3. *Family limited liability partnership (FLLP)*–A form of LLP in which all of the partners are family members or fiduciaries of family members; the most significant use of the FLLP is by families engaged in agricultural enterprises.

Limited Partnerships
(See pages 466–470.)

1. *Formation*–A certificate of limited partnership must be filed with the secretary of state's office or other designated state official. The certificate must include information about the business, similar to the information included in a corporate charter. The partnership consists of one or more general partners and one or more limited partners.

2. *Rights and liabilities of partners*–With some exceptions, the rights of partners are the same as the rights of partners in a general partnership. General partners have unlimited liability for partnership obligations; limited partners are liable only to the extent of their contributions.

3. *Limited partners and management*–Only general partners can participate in management. Limited partners have no voice in management; if they do participate in management activities, they risk having general-partner liability.

4. *Dissociation and Dissolution*–Generally, a limited partnership can be dissolved in much the same way as an ordinary partnership. A general partner has the power to voluntarily dissociate unless the parties' agreement specifies otherwise. Some states limit the power of limited partners to voluntarily withdraw from the firm. The death or assignment of interest of a limited partner does not dissolve the partnership; bankruptcy of a limited partner also will not dissolve the partnership unless it causes the bankruptcy of the firm.

Limited Partnerships—Continued	5. *Limited liability limited partnerships (LLLPs)*—A special type of limited partnership in which the liability of all partners, including general partners, is limited to the amount of their investments.
Limited Liability Companies (LLCs) (See pages 470–477.)	1. *Formation*—Articles of organization must be filed with the appropriate state office—usually the office of the secretary of state—setting forth the name of the business, its principal address, the names of the owners (called *members*), and other relevant information.
	2. *Advantages and disadvantages of the LLC*—Advantages of the LLC include limited liability, the option to be taxed as a partnership or as a corporation, and flexibility in deciding how the business will be managed and operated. Disadvantages relate mainly to the absence of uniformity in state LLC statutes and the lack of case law dealing with LLCs.
	3. *Operating agreement*—When an LLC is formed, the members decide, in an operating agreement, how the business will be managed and what rules will apply to the organization.
	4. *Management*—An LLC may be managed by members only, by some members and some nonmembers, or by nonmembers only.
	5. *Dissociation and dissolution*—Members of an LLC have the power to dissociate from the LLC at any time, but they may not have the right to dissociate. Dissociation does not always result in the dissolution of an LLC; the remaining members can choose to continue the business. Dissociated members have a right to have their interest purchased by the other members. If the LLC is dissolved, the business must be wound up and the assets sold. Creditors are paid first; then members' capital investments are returned. Any remaining proceeds are distributed to members.
Franchises (See pages 477–483.)	1. *Types of franchises*— a. Distributorship (for example, automobile dealerships). b. Chain-style operation (for example, fast-food chains). c. Manufacturing or processing-plant arrangement (for example, soft-drink bottling companies, such as Coca-Cola).
	2. *Laws governing franchising*— a. Franchises are governed by contract law. b. Franchises are also governed by federal and state statutory and regulatory laws, as well as agency law.
The Franchise Contract (See pages 479–482.)	The franchise relationship is defined by a contract between the franchisor and the franchisee. The contract normally spells out the following terms: 1. *Payment for the franchise*—Ordinarily, the contract requires the franchisee (purchaser) to pay an initial fee or lump-sum price for the franchise license. 2. *Business premises and organization*—Specifies whether the business premises will be leased or purchased by the franchisee. The franchisor may specify particular requirements for the form and capital structure of the business. 3. *Location of the franchise*—Specifies the territory to be served by the franchisee. 4. *Quality control*—The franchisor may require the franchisee to abide by certain standards of quality relating to the product or service offered.
Termination of the Franchise (See pages 482–483.)	Usually, the contract provides for the date and/or conditions of termination of the franchise arrangement. Both federal and state statutes attempt to protect franchisees from franchisors who unfairly or arbitrarily terminate franchises.

For Review

1. What advantages and disadvantages are associated with the sole proprietorship?
2. What is meant by joint and several liability? Why is this often considered to be a disadvantage of doing business as a general partnership?
3. What advantages do limited liability partnerships offer to entrepreneurs that are not offered by general partnerships?
4. What are the key differences between the rights and liabilities of general partners and those of limited partners?
5. How are limited liability companies formed, and who decides how they will be managed and operated?

Questions and Case Problems

14–1. Limited Liability Companies. John, Lesa, and Tabir form a limited liability company. John contributes 60 percent of the capital, and Lesa and Tabir each contribute 20 percent. Nothing is decided about how profits will be divided. John assumes that he will be entitled to 60 percent of the profits, in accordance with his contribution. Lesa and Tabir, however, assume that the profits will be divided equally. A dispute over the question arises, and ultimately a court has to decide the issue. What law will the court apply? In most states, what will result? How could this dispute have been avoided in the first place? Discuss fully.

Question with Sample Answer

14–2. Dorinda, Luis, and Elizabeth form a limited partnership. Dorinda is a general partner, and Luis and Elizabeth are limited partners. Consider each of the separate events below, and discuss fully which would constitute a dissolution of the limited partnership.

1. Luis assigns his partnership interest to Ashley.
2. Elizabeth is petitioned into involuntary bankruptcy.
3. Dorinda dies.

For a sample answer to Question 14–2, go to Appendix I at the end of this text.

14–3. Partnership Formation. Daniel is the owner of a chain of shoe stores. He hires Rubya to be the manager of a new store, which is to open in Grand Rapids, Michigan. Daniel, by written contract, agrees to pay Rubya a monthly salary and 20 percent of the profits. Without Daniel's knowledge, Rubya represents himself to Classen as Daniel's partner, showing Classen the agreement to share profits. Classen extends credit to Rubya. Rubya defaults. Discuss whether Classen can hold Daniel liable as a partner.

14–4. Indications of Partnership. At least six months before the 1996 Summer Olympic Games in Atlanta, Georgia, Stafford Fontenot, Steve Turner, Mike Montelaro, Joe Sokol, and Doug Brinsmade agreed to sell Cajun food at the games and began making preparations. Calling themselves "Prairie Cajun Seafood Catering of Louisiana," on May 19 the group applied for a license with the Fulton County, Georgia, Department of Public Health–Environmental Health Services. Later, Ted Norris sold a mobile kitchen for an $8,000 check drawn on the "Prairie Cajun Seafood Catering of Louisiana" account and two promissory notes, one for $12,000 and the other for $20,000. The notes, which were dated June 12, listed only Fontenot "d/b/a Prairie Cajun Seafood" as the maker (*d/b/a* is an abbreviation for "doing business as"). On July 31, Fontenot and his friends signed a partnership agreement, which listed specific percentages of profits and losses. They drove the mobile kitchen to Atlanta, but business was "disastrous." When the notes were not paid, Norris filed a suit in a Louisiana state court against Fontenot, seeking payment. What are the elements of a partnership? Was there a partnership among Fontenot and the others? Who is liable on the notes? Explain. [*Norris v. Fontenot,* 867 So.2d 179 (La.App. 3 Cir. 2004)]

14–5. Sole Proprietorship. James Ferguson operates "Jim's 11-E Auto Sales" in Jonesborough, Tennessee, as a sole proprietorship. In 1999, Consumers Insurance Co. issued a policy to "Jim Ferguson, Jim's 11E Auto Sales" covering "Owned 'Autos' Only." *Auto* was defined to include "a land motor vehicle," which was not further explained in the policy. Coverage extended to damages caused by the owner or driver of an underinsured motor vehicle. In 2000, Ferguson bought and titled in his own name a 1976 Harley-Davidson motorcycle, intending to repair and sell the cycle through his dealership. In October 2001, while driving the motorcycle, Ferguson was struck by an auto driven by John Jenkins. Ferguson filed a suit in a Tennessee state court against Jenkins—who was underinsured with respect to Ferguson's medical bills—and Consumers. The insurer argued, among other things, that because the motorcycle was bought and titled in Ferguson's own name, and he was driving it at the time of the accident, it was his personal vehicle and thus was not covered under the dealership's policy. What is the relationship between a sole proprietor and a sole proprietorship? How might this status affect the court's decision in this case? [*Ferguson v. Jenkins*, 204 S.W.3d 779 (Tenn.App. 2006)]

Case Problem with Sample Answer

14–6. In August 2003, Tammy Duncan began working as a waitress at Bynum's Diner, which was owned by her mother, Hazel Bynum, and her stepfather, Eddie Bynum, in Valdosta, Georgia. Less than a month later, the three signed an agreement under which Eddie was to relinquish his management responsibilities, allowing Tammy to be co-manager. At the end of this six-month period, Eddie would revisit this agreement and could then extend it for another six-month period. The diner's bank account was to remain in Eddie's name. There was no provision with regard to the diner's profit, if any, and the parties did not change the business's tax information. Tammy began doing the bookkeeping, as well as waiting tables and performing other duties. On October 30, she slipped off a ladder and injured her knees. At the end of the six-month term, Tammy quit working at the diner. The Georgia State Board of Workers' Compensation determined that she had been the diner's employee and awarded her benefits under the diner's workers' compensation policy with Cypress Insurance Co. Cypress filed a suit in a Georgia state court against Tammy, arguing that she was not an employee, but a co-owner. What are the essential elements of a partnership? Was Tammy a partner in the business of the diner? Explain. [*Cypress Insurance Co. v. Duncan*, 281 Ga.App. 469, 636 S.E.2d 159 (2006)]

After you have answered Problem 14–6, compare your answer with the sample answer given on the Web site that accompanies this text. Go to www.cengage.com/blaw/let, select "Chapter 14," and click on "Case Problem with Sample Answer."

14–7. Limited Liability Companies. A "Certificate of Formation" (CF) for Grupo Dos Chiles, LLC, was filed with the Delaware secretary of state in February 2000. The CF named Jamie Rivera as the "initial member." The next month, Jamie's mother, Yolanda Martinez, and Alfred Shriver, who had a personal relationship with Martinez at the time, signed an "LLC Agreement" for Grupo, naming themselves "managing partners."

Grupo's business was the operation of Dancing Peppers Cantina, a restaurant in Alexandria, Virginia. Identifying themselves as Grupo's owners, Shriver and Martinez borrowed funds from Advanceme, Inc., a restaurant lender. In June 2003, Grupo lost its LLC status in Delaware for failing to pay state taxes, and by the end of July, Martinez and Shriver had ended their relationship. Shriver filed a suit in a Virginia state court against Martinez to wind up Grupo's affairs. Meanwhile, without consulting Shriver, Martinez paid Grupo's back taxes. Shriver filed a suit in a Delaware state court against Martinez, asking the court to dissolve the firm. What effect did the LLC agreement have on the CF? Did Martinez's unilateral act reestablish Grupo's LLC status? Should the Delaware court grant Shriver's request? Why or why not? [*In re Grupo Dos Chiles, LLC*, __ A.2d __ (Del.Ch. 2006)]

14–8. Franchise Termination. Walid Elkhatib, a Palestinian Arab, emigrated to the United States in 1971 and became a U.S. citizen. Eight years later, Elkhatib bought a Dunkin' Donuts, Inc., franchise in Bellwood, Illinois. Dunkin' Donuts began offering breakfast sandwiches with bacon, ham, or sausage through its franchises in 1984, but Elkhatib refused to sell these items at his store on the ground that his religion forbade the handling of pork. In 1995, Elkhatib opened a second franchise in Berkeley, Illinois, at which he also refused to sell pork products. The next year, at both locations, Elkhatib began selling meatless sandwiches. In 1998, Elkhatib opened a third franchise in Westchester, Illinois. When he proposed to relocate this franchise, Dunkin' Donuts refused to approve the new location and added that it would not renew any of his franchise agreements because he did not carry the full sandwich line. Elkhatib filed a suit in a federal district court against Dunkin' Donuts and others. The defendants filed a motion for summary judgment. Did Dunkin' Donuts act in good faith in its relationship with Elkhatib? Explain. [*Elkhatib v. Dunkin' Donuts, Inc.*, 493 F.3d 827 (7th Cir. 2007)]

A Question of Ethics

14–9. Blushing Brides, L.L.C., a publisher of wedding planning magazines in Columbus, Ohio, opened an account with Gray Printing Co. in July 2000. On behalf of Blushing Brides, Louis Zacks, the firm's member-manager, signed a credit agreement that identified the firm as the "purchaser" and required payment within thirty days. Despite the agreement, Blushing Brides typically took up to six months to pay the full amount for its orders. Gray printed and shipped 10,000 copies of a fall/winter 2001 issue for Blushing Brides but had not been paid when the firm ordered 15,000 copies of a spring/summer 2002 issue. Gray refused to print the new order without an assurance of payment. On May 22,

Zacks signed a promissory note payable to Gray within thirty days for $14,778, plus interest at 6 percent per year. Gray printed the new order but by October had been paid only $7,500. Gray filed a suit in an Ohio state court against Blushing Brides and Zacks to collect the balance. [*Gray Printing Co. v. Blushing Brides, L.L.C.,* __ N.E.2d __ (Ohio App. 10 Dist. 2006)]

1. Under what circumstances is a member of an LLC liable for the firm's debts? In this case, is Zacks personally liable under the credit agreement for the unpaid amount on Blushing Brides' account? Did Zacks's promissory note affect the parties' liability on the account? Explain.
2. Should a member of an LLC assume an ethical responsibility to meet the obligations of the firm? Discuss.
3. Gray shipped only 10,000 copies of the spring/summer 2002 issue of Blushing Brides' magazine, waiting for the publisher to identify a destination for the other 5,000 copies. The magazine had a retail price of $4.50 per copy. Did

Gray have a legal or ethical duty to "mitigate the damages" by attempting to sell or otherwise distribute these copies itself? Why or why not?

Critical-Thinking Legal Question

14–10. Jordan Mendelson is interested in starting a kitchen franchise business. Customers will come to the business to assemble gourmet dinners and then take the prepared meals to their homes for cooking. The franchisor requires each store to use a specific layout and provides the recipes for various dinners, but the franchisee is not required to purchase the food products from the franchisor. What general factors should Mendelson consider before entering a contract to start such a franchise? Is location important? Are there any laws that Mendelson should consider due to the fact that this franchise involves food preparation and sales? If the franchisor does not insist on a specific type of business entity, should Mendelson operate this business as a sole proprietorship? Why or why not?

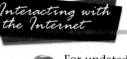

Interacting with the Internet

For updated links to resources available on the Web, as well as a variety of other materials, visit this text's Web site at

www.cengage.com/blaw/let

To learn how the U.S. Small Business Administration assists in forming, financing, and operating businesses, go to

www.sbaonline.sba.gov

LLRX.com, a Web site for legal professionals, provides information on LLCs in its Web journal. Go to

www.llrx.com/features/llc.htm

You can find information on filing fees for LLCs at

www.bizcorp.com

For information on the FTC regulations on franchising, as well as state laws regulating franchising, go to

www.ftc.gov/bcp/franchise/netfran.htm

PRACTICAL INTERNET EXERCISES

Go to this text's Web site at **www.cengage.com/blaw/let**, select "Chapter 14," and click on "Practical Internet Exercises." There you will find the following Internet research exercises that you can perform to learn more about the topics covered in this chapter.

Practical Internet Exercise 14–1: LEGAL PERSPECTIVE—**Starting a Business**
Practical Internet Exercise 14–2: MANAGEMENT PERSPECTIVE—**Limited Liability Companies**

BEFORE THE TEST

Go to this text's Web site at **www.cengage.com/blaw/let**, select "Chapter 14," and click on "Interactive Quizzes." You will find a number of interactive questions relating to this chapter.

Chapter 15

Corporations

CHAPTER OBJECTIVES

After reading this chapter, you should be able to answer the following questions:

1. What steps are involved in bringing a corporation into existence? Who is liable for preincorporation contracts?

2. What is the difference between a *de jure* corporation and a *de facto* corporation?

3. In what circumstances might a court disregard the corporate entity ("pierce the corporate veil") and hold the shareholders personally liable?

4. What are the duties of corporate directors and officers?

5. What is a voting proxy? What is cumulative voting?

CONTENTS

- The Nature and Classification of Corporations

- Corporate Formation

- Piercing the Corporate Veil

- Directors and Officers

- Shareholders

- Major Business Forms Compared

" *A corporation is an artificial being, invisible, intangible, and existing only in contemplation of law.*"

— John Marshall,
1755–1835 (Chief justice of the United States Supreme Court, 1801–1835)

In the previous chapter, we examined the kinds of business forms commonly used by small business entities. Now we turn to the business organization of choice for most larger enterprises—the corporation. The corporation is a creature of statute. As John Marshall indicated in the chapter-opening quotation, a corporation is an artificial being, existing only in law and neither tangible nor visible. Its existence generally depends on state law, although some corporations, especially public organizations, can be created under state or federal law.

Each state has its own body of corporate law, and these laws are not entirely uniform. The Model Business Corporation Act (MBCA) is a codification of modern corporation law that has been influential in the drafting and revision of state corporation statutes. Today, the majority of state statutes are guided by the revised version of the MBCA, which is often referred to as the Revised Model Business Corporation Act (RMBCA—excerpts of this act are presented in Appendix G). You should keep in mind, however, that there is considerable variation among the statutes of the states that have used the MBCA or the RMBCA as a basis for their statutes, and several states do not follow either act. Consequently, individual state corporation laws should be relied on rather than the MBCA or the RMBCA.

In this chapter, we examine the corporate form of business enterprise. We also discuss the rights and duties of directors, officers, and shareholders and the ways in which conflicts among them are resolved. The last part of the chapter compares the various forms of business discussed in the previous chapter and in this chapter.

THE NATURE AND CLASSIFICATION OF CORPORATIONS

CORPORATION
A legal entity formed in compliance with statutory requirements that is distinct from its shareholder-owners.

A **corporation** is a legal entity created and recognized by state law. It can consist of one or more *natural persons* (as opposed to the artificial *legal person* of the corporation) identified under a common name. A corporation can be owned by a single person, or it can have hundreds, thousands, or even millions of owners (shareholders). The corporation substitutes itself for its shareholders in conducting corporate business and in incurring liability, yet its authority to act and the liability for its actions are separate and apart from the individuals who own it.

Corporate Personnel

Responsibility for the overall management of the corporation is entrusted to a *board of directors,* whose members are elected by the shareholders. The board of directors hires *corporate officers* and other employees to run the daily business operations of the corporation.

When an individual purchases a share of stock in a corporation, that person becomes a shareholder and thus an owner of the corporation. Unlike the members of a partnership, the body of shareholders can change constantly without affecting the continued existence of the corporation. A shareholder can sue the corporation, and the corporation can sue a shareholder. Also, under certain circumstances, a shareholder can sue on behalf of a corporation.

CONTRAST
The death of a sole proprietor or a partner can result in the dissolution of a business. The death of a corporate shareholder, however, rarely, if ever, causes the dissolution of a corporation.

The Constitutional Rights of Corporations

A corporation is recognized as a "person" under state and federal law, and it enjoys many of the same rights and privileges that U.S. citizens enjoy. The Bill of Rights guarantees persons certain protections, and corporations are considered persons in most instances. Accordingly, a corporation as an entity has the same right of access to the courts as a natural person and can sue or be sued. It also has a right to due process before denial of life, liberty, or property, as well as freedom from unreasonable searches and seizures (see Chapter 6 for a discussion of searches and seizures in the business context) and from double jeopardy.

Under the First Amendment, corporations are entitled to freedom of speech. As we pointed out in Chapter 4, however, commercial speech (such as advertising) and political speech (such as contributions to political causes or candidates) receive significantly less protection than noncommercial speech.

Generally, a corporation is not entitled to claim the Fifth Amendment privilege against self-incrimination. Agents or officers of the corporation therefore cannot refuse to produce corporate records on the ground that it might incriminate them. Additionally, the privileges and immunities clause of the U.S. Constitution (Article IV, Section 2) does not protect corporations, nor does it protect an unincorporated association. This clause requires each state to treat citizens of other states equally with respect to certain rights, such as access to the courts and travel rights. This constitutional clause does not apply to corporations because corporations are legal persons only, not natural citizens.

The Limited Liability of Shareholders

One of the key advantages of the corporate form is the limited liability of its owners (shareholders). Corporate shareholders normally are not personally liable for the obligations of the corporation beyond the extent of their investments. In certain limited situations, however, the "corporate veil" can be pierced and liability for the corporation's obligations extended to shareholders—a concept that will be explained later in this chapter. Additionally, to enable the firm to obtain credit, shareholders in small companies sometimes voluntarily assume personal liability, as guarantors, for corporate obligations.

Corporate Taxation

Corporate profits are taxed by various levels of government. Corporations can do one of two things with corporate profits—retain them or pass them on to shareholders in the form of **dividends.** The corporation normally receives no tax deduction for dividends distributed to shareholders. Dividends are again taxable as income to the shareholder receiving them (except when they represent distributions of capital). This double-taxation feature of the corporation is one of its major disadvantages.[1] For a discussion of one method that corporations have used to reduce their tax burden, which some people consider ethically questionable, see this chapter's *Insight into Ethics* feature below.

Profits that are not distributed are retained by the corporation. These **retained earnings,** if invested properly, will yield higher corporate profits in the future and thus cause the price of the company's stock to rise. Individual shareholders can then reap the benefits of these retained earnings in the capital gains they receive when they sell their shares.

As you will read later in this chapter, the consequences of a corporation's failure to pay taxes can be severe. The state can suspend corporate status until the taxes are paid, or it can dissolve a corporation for failing to pay taxes.[2]

DIVIDEND
A distribution to corporate shareholders of corporate profits or income, disbursed in proportion to the number of shares held.

RETAINED EARNINGS
The portion of a corporation's profits that has not been paid out as dividends to shareholders.

Insight into Ethics

Is it ethical for a corporation to establish an offshore holding company to reduce U.S. taxes?

In recent years, some U.S. corporations have been using holding companies to reduce or defer their U.S. income taxes. At its simplest, a **holding company** (sometimes referred to as a *parent company*) is a company whose business activity consists of holding shares in another company. Typically, the holding company is established in a low-tax or no-tax offshore jurisdiction, such as those shown in Exhibit 15–1 on page 492. Among the best known are the Cayman Islands, Dubai, Hong Kong, Luxembourg, Monaco, and Panama.

Sometimes, a major U.S. corporation sets up an investment holding company in a low-tax offshore environment. The corporation then transfers its cash, bonds, stocks, and other investments to the holding company. In general, any profits received by the holding company on these investments are taxed at the rate of the offshore jurisdiction in which the company is registered, not the rates applicable to the parent company or its shareholders in their country of residence. Thus, deposits of cash, for example, may earn interest that is taxed at only a minimal rate. Once the profits are brought "onshore," though, they are taxed at the federal corporate income tax rate, and any payments received by the shareholders are also taxable at the full U.S. rates.

HOLDING COMPANY
A company whose business activity is holding shares in another company.

---

1. Congress enacted a law in 2003 that mitigated this double-taxation feature to some extent by providing a reduced federal tax rate on qualifying dividends. See the Jobs Growth Tax Relief Reconciliation Act of 2003, Pub. L. No. 108-27, May 28, 2003, codified at 26 U.S.C. Section 6429.
2. See, for example, *Bullington v. Palangio*, 345 Ark. 320, 45 S.W.3d 834 (2001).

EXHIBIT 15-1 OFFSHORE LOW-TAX JURISDICTIONS

Occasionally, a member of Congress or the media learns that a large U.S. corporation has used an offshore holding company to reduce its U.S. tax liability. Critics then decry the company's actions as both unethical and unpatriotic. Others are not so sure. They point out that those who run corporations have a duty to minimize (legally, of course) taxes owed by the corporation and by its shareholders.

Do Tax Havens Violate Ethical Principles?

Is it illegal or unethical to avoid taxes? Definitely not; most people try to minimize the amount of taxes they pay. Nevertheless, overly aggressive tax avoidance may lead to allegations that a corporation is unethical in failing to pay its "fair" share of taxes. This is particularly true under the corporate social responsibility theory of ethics (see Chapter 2), which asserts that corporations have ethical duties to others beyond shareholders and should behave as good citizens.

Some claim that whether placing funds in an offshore company is ethical depends on whether that offshore location qualifies as a "tax haven." The Organization for Economic Co-operation and Development (OECD) is an international organization of thirty countries that accept the principles of representative democracy and free market economy. According to the OECD, a country is a tax haven, if (1) it has no or nominal taxes, (2) it lacks transparency, and (3) it lacks effective information exchange. Thus, a nation that has secretive tax or financial systems in addition to low taxes for nonresidents qualifies as a tax haven, and it would be unethical for a corporation to invest there. These are places that allow companies to operate under fictitious names and have no regulatory mechanisms to prevent illegal activities. The OECD puts out a list of uncooperative tax havens every year. In contrast, a nation that offers special tax incentives to companies that invest in a particular region is not generally seen as a tax haven, and these arrangements are not necessarily deemed unethical.

Torts and Criminal Acts

A corporation is liable for the torts committed by its agents or officers within the course and scope of their employment. This principle applies to a corporation exactly as it applies to the ordinary agency relationships. Agency relationships will be discussed in Chapter 16.

Under modern criminal law, a corporation may be held liable for the criminal acts of its agents and employees, provided the punishment is one that can be applied to the corporation. Although corporations cannot be imprisoned, they can be fined. (Of course, corporate directors and officers can be imprisoned, and in recent years, many have faced criminal penalties for their own actions or for the actions of employees under their supervision.)

Recall from Chapter 6 that the U.S. Sentencing Commission created standardized sentencing guidelines for federal crimes. The commission created specific sentencing guidelines for crimes committed by corporate employees (white-collar crimes) that became effective in 2004.[3] The net effect of the guidelines has been a significant increase in criminal penalties for crimes committed by corporate personnel. Penalties depend on such factors as the seriousness of the offense, the amount involved, and the extent to which top company executives are implicated. Corporate lawbreakers can face fines amounting to hundreds of millions of dollars, though the guidelines allow judges to impose less severe penalties in certain circumstances.

The question in the following case was whether a corporation could be convicted for its employee's criminal negligence.

> "Did you expect a corporation to have a conscience, when it has no soul to be damned and no body to be kicked?"
>
> —EDWARD THURLOW, 1731–1806
> (English jurist)

---

3. Note that the Sarbanes-Oxley Act of 2002, discussed in Chapter 2, stiffened the penalties for certain types of corporate crime and ordered the U.S. Sentencing Commission to revise the sentencing guidelines accordingly.

Case 15.1 Commonwealth v. Angelo Todesca Corp.

Supreme Judicial Court of Massachusetts, 2006.
446 Mass. 128, 842 N.E.2d 930.
www.findlaw.com/11stategov/ma/maca.html[a]

BACKGROUND AND FACTS   Brian Gauthier worked as a truck driver for Angelo Todesca Corporation, a trucking and paving company. During 2000, Gauthier drove a ten-wheel tri-axle dump truck, which was designated AT-56. Angelo's safety manual required its trucks to be equipped with back-up alarms, which were to sound automatically whenever the vehicles were

a. In the "Supreme Court Opinions" section, in the "2006" row, click on "March." When that page opens, scroll to the name of the case and click on its docket number to access the opinion.

in reverse gear. In November, Gauthier discovered that AT-56's alarm was missing. Angelo ordered a new alarm. Meanwhile, Gauthier continued to drive AT-56. On December 1, Angelo assigned Gauthier to haul asphalt to a work site in Centerville, Massachusetts. At the site, as Gauthier backed up AT-56 to dump its load, he struck a police officer who was directing traffic through the site and facing away from the truck. The officer died of his injuries. The Commonwealth of Massachusetts charged Gauthier and Angelo in a Massachusetts state court with, among other wrongful acts, motor vehicle homicide. Angelo was convicted and fined $2,500. Angelo appealed, and a state intermediate appellate court reversed the conviction. The state appealed to the Massachusetts Supreme Judicial Court, the state's highest court.

IN THE WORDS OF THE COURT . . . *SPINA*, J. [Justice]

* * * *

* * * To prove that a corporation is guilty of a criminal offense, the Commonwealth must prove the following three elements beyond a reasonable doubt: (1) that an individual committed a criminal offense; (2) that at the time of committing the offense, the individual was engaged in some particular corporate business or project; and (3) that the individual had been vested by the corporation with the

CASE 15.1–CONTINUED

authority to act for it, and on its behalf, in carrying out that particular corporate business or project when the offense occurred.

* * * [On this appeal] the essence of the defendant's arguments deals with the first element of corporate criminal liability: namely, the requirement that an employee committed a criminal offense. The defendant maintains that a corporation never can be criminally liable for motor vehicle homicide * * * because * * * a "corporation" cannot "operate" a vehicle. *The Commonwealth, however, argues that corporate liability is necessarily vicarious, and that a corporation can be held accountable for criminal acts committed by its agents, including negligent operation of a motor vehicle causing the death of another* * * * . [Emphasis added.]

We agree with the Commonwealth. Because a corporation is not a living person, it can act only through its agents. By the defendant's reasoning, a corporation never could be liable for any crime. A "corporation" can no more serve alcohol to minors, or bribe government officials, or falsify data on loan applications, than operate a vehicle negligently: only human agents, acting for the corporation, are capable of these actions. *Nevertheless, * * * a corporation may be criminally liable for such acts when performed by corporate employees, acting within the scope of their employment and on behalf of the corporation.* * * * [Emphasis added.]

The defendant further contends that it cannot be found vicariously [indirectly] liable for the victim's death because corporate criminal liability requires criminal conduct by the agent, which is lacking in this case. Operating a truck without a back-up alarm, the defendant notes, is not a criminal act: no State or Federal statute requires that a vehicle be equipped with such a device. Although the defendant is correct that criminal conduct of an agent is necessary before criminal liability may be imputed to the corporation, it mischaracterizes the agent's conduct in this case. Gauthier's criminal act, and the conduct imputed to the defendant, was not simply backing up without an alarm, as the defendant contends; rather, the criminal conduct was Gauthier's negligent operation of the defendant's truck, resulting in the victim's death * * * . Clearly, a corporation cannot be criminally liable for acts of employee negligence that are not criminal; however, [a Massachusetts state statute] criminalizes negligence in a very specific context (the operation of a motor vehicle on a public way) and with a specific outcome (resulting in death). Furthermore, nothing in that statute requires that the negligence be based on a statutory violation; the fact that a back-up alarm is not required by statute, then, is irrelevant to the issue whether vehicular homicide committed by an employee can be imputed to the corporation. If a corporate employee violates [this statute] while engaged in corporate business that the employee has been authorized to conduct, we can see no reason why the corporation cannot be vicariously liable for the crime.

DECISION AND REMEDY   The Massachusetts Supreme Judicial Court affirmed Angelo's conviction. The court recognized that a corporation is not a "living person" and "can act only through its agents," which may include its employees. The court reasoned that if an employee commits a crime "while engaged in corporate business that the employee has been authorized to conduct," a corporation can be held liable for the crime.

WHY IS THIS CASE IMPORTANT?   Other states' courts that have considered the question at issue in this case have concluded that a corporation may be criminally liable for vehicular homicide under those states' statutes. This was the first case in which Massachusetts state courts determined the question under a Massachusetts statute.

THE LEGAL ENVIRONMENT DIMENSION   Under what circumstances might an employee's supervisor, or even a corporate officer or director, be held liable for the employee's crime?

Classification of Corporations

Corporations can be classified in several ways. The classification of a corporation normally depends on its location, purpose, and ownership characteristics, as described in the following subsections.

Domestic, Foreign, and Alien Corporations   A corporation is referred to as a **domestic corporation** by its home state (the state in which it incorporates). A corporation formed in one state but doing business in another is referred to in the second state as a **foreign corporation.** A corporation formed in another country (say, Mexico) but doing business in the United States is referred to in the United States as an **alien corporation.** (For a discussion of when a U.S. court can exercise jurisdiction over an alien corporation, see this chapter's *Beyond Our Borders* feature on the following page.)

A corporation does not have an automatic right to do business in a state other than its state of incorporation. In some instances, it must obtain a *certificate of authority* in any state in which it plans to do business. Once the certificate has been issued, the corporation generally can exercise in that state all of the powers conferred on it by its home state. If a foreign corporation does business in a state without obtaining a certificate of authority, the state can impose substantial fines and sanctions on the corporation, and sometimes even on its officers, directors, or agents.[4]

Public and Private Corporations   A public corporation is one formed by the government to meet some political or governmental purpose. Cities and towns that incorporate are common examples. In addition, many federal government organizations, such as the U.S. Postal Service, the Tennessee Valley Authority, and AMTRAK, are public corporations. Note that a public corporation is not the same as a *publicly held* corporation (often called a *public company*). A publicly held corporation is any corporation whose shares are publicly traded in securities markets, such as the New York Stock Exchange or the over-the-counter market.

---

4. Note that most state statutes specify certain activities, such as soliciting orders via the Internet, that are not considered doing business within the state. Thus, a foreign corporation normally does not need a certificate of authority to sell goods or services via the Internet or by mail.

DOMESTIC CORPORATION
In a given state, a corporation that does business in, and is organized under the law of, that state.

FOREIGN CORPORATION
In a given state, a corporation that does business in the state without being incorporated therein.

ALIEN CORPORATION
A designation in the United States for a corporation formed in another country but doing business in the United States.

BMW automobiles are inspected at the Spartanburg, South Carolina, plant BMW is classified as an alien corporation. What is the difference between an alien corporation and a foreign corporation?
(Courtesy of BMW Manufacturing, Inc.)

If a U.S. consumer is injured by a product manufactured by a corporation based in another country, can the consumer sue that corporation in a U.S. state court? Normally, the answer depends on whether the defendant corporation has sufficient "contacts" with the state in which the lawsuit is filed. As we pointed out in Chapter 3, this requirement is satisfied if a corporation does business in the state, advertises or sells its product in the state, or places its goods within the "stream of commerce" with the intent that the goods be sold in the state.

The jurisdiction issue arose in a case involving Weida, a Chinese corporation that is the world's largest manufacturer of drill chucks. Weida sells its drill chucks to Techtronic Industries, a Hong Kong corporation. Techtronic then uses the drill chucks in manufacturing drills under the RIDGID brand. Home Depot has an exclusive contract to sell RIDGID drills in the United States.

A Delaware corporation, Jacobs, also makes drill chucks. It filed suit against Weida in a Texas state court for patent infringement. Weida argued that the court lacked jurisdiction. The Texas state court disagreed, however, stating that it had jurisdiction over alien corporations in such situations. The court concluded that it was reasonably inferable that Weida knew and expected its chucks would be used as components in RIDGID brand drills manufactured and distributed by Techtronic to Home Depot stores in the United States, including Texas.[a]

Sometimes, alien corporations argue that the cost of transporting witnesses, documents, and other evidence would be so great that U.S. courts should not have jurisdiction over them. In response to such arguments, U.S. courts generally hold that alien corporations marketing their goods in the United States should expect to be "haled into court" in this country.[b]

FOR CRITICAL ANALYSIS

How might a foreign manufacturer selling products in the United States avoid being "haled into court" in this country to defend against a product liability action?

a. *Jacobs Chuck Manufacturing Co. v. Shandong Weida Machinery Co., Ltd.,* ___ F.Supp.2d ___, 2005 WL 3299718 (E.D.Tex. 2005).
b. *Donnelly Corp. v. Reitter & Schefenacker, GmbH & Co. KG,* 189 F.Supp.2d 696 (W.D.Mich. 2002).

NOTE
A private corporation is a voluntary association, but a public corporation is not.

In contrast to public corporations (*not* public companies), private corporations are created either wholly or in part for private benefit. Most corporations are private. Although they may serve a public purpose, as a public electric or gas utility does, they are owned by private persons rather than by the government.[5]

Nonprofit Corporations   Corporations formed for purposes other than making a profit are called *nonprofit* or *not-for-profit* corporations. Private hospitals, educational institutions, charities, and religious organizations, for example, are frequently organized as nonprofit corporations. The nonprofit corporation is a convenient form of organization that allows various groups to own property and to form contracts without exposing the individual members to personal liability.

CLOSE CORPORATION
A corporation whose shareholders are limited to a small group of persons, often including only family members. In a close corporation, the shareholders' rights to transfer shares to others are usually restricted.

Close Corporations   Most corporate enterprises in the United States fall into the category of close corporations. A **close corporation** is one whose shares are held by members of a family or by relatively few persons. Close corporations are also referred to as *closely held, family,* or *privately held* corporations. Usually, the members of the small group constituting a close corporation are personally known to one another. Because the number of shareholders is so small, there is no trading market for the shares.

In practice, a close corporation is often operated like a partnership. Some states have enacted special statutory provisions that apply to close corporations.

---

5. The United States Supreme Court first recognized the property rights of private corporations and clarified the distinction between public and private corporations in the landmark case *Trustees of Dartmouth College v. Woodward,* 17 U.S. (4 Wheaton) 518, 4 L.Ed. 629 (1819).

These provisions expressly permit close corporations to depart significantly from certain formalities required by traditional corporation law.

Additionally, a provision added to the RMBCA in 1991 gives close corporations a substantial amount of flexibility in determining the rules by which they will operate [RMBCA 7.32]. If all of the shareholders of a corporation agree in writing, the corporation can operate without directors, bylaws, annual or special shareholders' or directors' meetings, stock certificates, or formal records of shareholders' or directors' decisions.[6]

Management of Close Corporations

A close corporation has a single shareholder or a closely knit group of shareholders, who usually hold the positions of directors and officers. Management of a close corporation resembles that of a sole proprietorship or a partnership. As a corporation, however, the firm must meet all specific legal requirements set forth in state statutes.

To prevent a majority shareholder from dominating a close corporation, the corporation may require that more than a simple majority of the directors approve any action taken by the board. Typically, this would apply only to extraordinary actions, such as changing the amount of dividends or dismissing an employee-shareholder, and not to ordinary business decisions.

Transfer of Shares in Close Corporations

By definition, a close corporation has a small number of shareholders. Thus, the transfer of one shareholder's shares to someone else can cause serious management problems. The other shareholders may find themselves required to share control with someone they do not know or like.

EXAMPLE #1 Three brothers, Terry, Damon, and Henry Johnson, are the only shareholders of Johnson's Car Wash, Inc. Terry and Damon do not want Henry to sell his shares to an unknown third person. To avoid this situation, the corporation could restrict the transferability of shares to outside persons. Shareholders could be required to offer their shares to the corporation or the other shareholders before selling them to an outside purchaser. In fact, a few states have statutes that prohibit the transfer of close corporation shares unless certain persons—including shareholders, family members, and the corporation—are first given the opportunity to purchase the shares for the same price.□

Control of a close corporation can also be stabilized through the use of a *shareholder agreement*. A shareholder agreement can provide that when one of the original shareholders dies, her or his shares of stock in the corporation will be divided in such a way that the proportionate holdings of the survivors, and thus their proportionate control, will be maintained. Courts are generally reluctant to interfere with private agreements, including shareholder agreements.

S Corporations

A close corporation that meets the qualifying requirements specified in Subchapter S of the Internal Revenue Code can operate as an **S corporation.** If a corporation has S corporation status, it can avoid the imposition of income taxes at the corporate level while retaining many of the advantages of a corporation, particularly limited liability.

S CORPORATION
A close business corporation that has met certain requirements set out in the Internal Revenue Code and thus qualifies for special income tax treatment. Essentially, an S corporation is taxed the same as a partnership, but its owners enjoy the privilege of limited liability.

A drummer plays a set of drums with Zildjian cymbals. Zildjian, founded in 1623, is perhaps the world's longest-running family-owned business. What steps might a small, family-owned corporation take to ensure that ownership of the company stays within the family?
(Photo Courtesy of Drummerworld)

---

6. Shareholders cannot agree, however, to eliminate certain rights of shareholders, such as the right to inspect corporate books and records or the right to bring *derivative actions* (lawsuits on behalf of the corporation, discussed later in this chapter).

Qualification Requirements for S Corporations   Among the numerous requirements for S corporation status, the following are the most important:

1. The corporation must be a domestic corporation.
2. The corporation must not be a member of an affiliated group of corporations.
3. The shareholders of the corporation must be individuals, estates, or certain trusts. Partnerships and nonqualifying trusts cannot be shareholders. Corporations can be shareholders under certain circumstances.
4. The corporation must have no more than one hundred shareholders.
5. The corporation must have only one class of stock, although all shareholders do not have to have the same voting rights.
6. No shareholder of the corporation may be a nonresident alien.

Benefits of S Corporations   At times, it is beneficial for a regular corporation to elect S corporation status. Benefits include the following:

1. When the corporation has losses, the S election allows the shareholders to use the losses to offset other taxable income.
2. When the shareholder's tax bracket is lower than the corporation's tax bracket, the S election causes the corporation's pass-through net income to be taxed in the shareholder's bracket (because it is taxed as personal income). This is particularly attractive when the corporation wants to accumulate earnings for some future business purpose.

Because of these tax benefits, many close corporations have opted for S corporation status. Today, however, two forms of business that we discussed in Chapter 14—the limited liability company and the limited liability partnership—offer similar advantages plus additional benefits, including more flexibility in forming and operating the business. Hence, the S corporation is losing some of its appeal.

Professional Corporations   Professionals such as physicians, lawyers, dentists, and accountants can incorporate. Professional corporations are typically identified by the letters *S.C.* (service corporation), *P.C.* (professional corporation), or *P.A.* (professional association). In general, the laws governing professional corporations are similar to those governing ordinary business corporations, but three basic areas of liability deserve special attention.

First, some courts may, for liability purposes, regard the professional corporation as a partnership in which each partner can be held liable for any malpractice liability incurred by the others within the scope of the business. The reason for this rule is that professionals, in contrast to shareholders in other types of corporations, should not be allowed to avoid liability for their wrongful acts simply by virtue of incorporating. Second, in many states, professional persons are liable not only for their own negligent acts, but also for the misconduct of any person under their direct supervision who is rendering services on behalf of the corporation. Third, a shareholder in a professional corporation is generally protected from contractual liability and cannot be held liable for the torts—other than malpractice or a breach of duty to clients or patients—that are committed by other professionals at the firm.

CONTRAST
Unlike the shareholders of most other corporations, the shareholders of professional corporations must generally be licensed professionals.

CORPORATE FORMATION

Up to this point, we have discussed some of the general characteristics of corporations. We now examine the process by which corporations come into existence. Incorporating a business is much simpler today than it was twenty years ago, and many states allow businesses to incorporate online via the Internet.

Note that one of the most common reasons for creating a corporation is the need for additional capital to finance expansion. Many Fortune 500 companies were originally sole proprietorships or partnerships before converting to corporate entities. A sole proprietor in need of funds can seek partners who will bring capital with them. Although a partnership may be able to secure more funds from potential lenders than the sole proprietor could, the amount is still limited. When a firm wants significant growth, simply increasing the number of partners can result in so many partners that the firm can no longer operate effectively. Therefore, incorporation may be the best choice for an expanding business organization because a corporation can obtain more capital by issuing shares of stock.

Promotional Activities

In the past, preliminary steps were taken to organize and promote the business prior to incorporating. Contracts were made with investors and others on behalf of the future corporation. Today, however, due to the relative ease of forming a corporation in most states, persons incorporating their business rarely, if ever, engage in preliminary promotional activities. Nevertheless, it is important for businesspersons to understand that they are personally liable for all preincorporation contracts made with investors, accountants, or others on behalf of the future corporation. This personal liability continues until the corporation assumes the preincorporation contracts by *novation* (discussed in Chapter 10).

EXAMPLE #2 Jade Sorrel contracts with an accountant, Ray Cooper, to provide tax advice for a proposed corporation, Blackstone, Inc. Cooper provides the services to Sorrel, knowing that the corporation has not yet been formed. Once Blackstone, Inc., is formed, Cooper sends an invoice to the corporation and to Sorrel personally, but the bill is not paid. Because Sorrel is personally liable for the preincorporation contract, Cooper can file a lawsuit against Sorrel for breaching the contract for accounting services. Cooper cannot seek to hold Blackstone, Inc., liable unless he has entered into a novation contract with the corporation. □

Incorporation Procedures

Exact procedures for incorporation differ among states, but the basic steps are as follows: (1) select a state of incorporation, (2) secure the corporate name by confirming its availability, (3) prepare the articles of incorporation, and (4) file the articles of incorporation with the secretary of state accompanied by payment of the specified fees. If the articles contain all of the information required by statute, the secretary of state stamps the articles "Filed," and the corporation comes into existence. These steps are discussed in more detail in the following subsections.

Selecting the State of Incorporation   The first step in the incorporation process is to select a state in which to incorporate. Because state incorporation laws differ, individuals may look for the states that offer the most advantageous tax or incorporation provisions. Another consideration is the fee that a particular state charges to incorporate, as well as the annual fees and the fees for specific transactions (such as stock transfers).

Delaware has historically had the least restrictive laws as well as provisions that favor corporate management. Consequently, many corporations, including a

> *"A man to carry on a successful business must have imagination. He must see things as in a vision, a dream of the whole thing."*
> —CHARLES M. SCHWAB, 1862–1939
> (American industrialist)

number of the largest, have incorporated there. Delaware's statutes permit firms to incorporate in that state and conduct business and locate their operating head-quarters elsewhere. Most other states now permit this as well. Note, though, that closely held corporations, particularly those of a professional nature, generally incorporate in the state where their principal shareholders live and work. For reasons of convenience and cost, a business often chooses to incorporate in the state in which the corporation's business will primarily be conducted.

Securing the Corporate Name   The choice of a corporate name is subject to state approval to ensure against duplication or deception. State statutes usually require that the secretary of state run a check on the proposed name in the state of incorporation. Some states require that the persons incorporating a firm, at their own expense, run a check on the proposed name, which can often be accomplished via Internet-based services. Once cleared, a name can be reserved for a short time, for a fee, pending the completion of the articles of incorporation. All corporate statutes require the corporation name to include the word *Corporation, Incorporated, Company,* or *Limited,* or abbreviations of these terms.

A new corporation's name cannot be the same as (or deceptively similar to) the name of an existing corporation doing business within the state (see Chapter 8). The name should also be one that can be used as the business's Internet domain name. EXAMPLE #3 If an existing corporation is named Digital Synergy, Inc., you cannot choose the name Digital Synergy Company because that name is deceptively similar to the first. The state will be unlikely to allow the corporate name because it could impliedly transfer a part of the goodwill established by the first corporate user to the second corporation. In addition, you would not want to choose the name Digital Synergy Company because you would be unable to acquire an Internet domain name using the name of the business. ■

If those incorporating a firm contemplate doing business in other states—or over the Internet—they need to check on existing corporate names in those states as well. Otherwise, if the firm does business under a name that is the same as or deceptively similar to an existing company's name, it may be liable for trade name infringement.

Preventing Legal Disputes

Businesspersons should be cautious when choosing a corporate name. Recognize that even if a particular state does not require the incorporator to run a name check, doing so is always advisable and can help prevent future disputes. Many states provide online search capabilities, but these searches are usually limited and will only compare the proposed name with the names of active corporations within that state. Trade name disputes, however, are not limited to corporations. Thus, using a business name that is deceptively similar to the name of a partnership or limited liability company can also lead to a dispute. Disputes are even more likely to arise among firms that do business over the Internet. Always check on the availability of a particular domain name before selecting a corporate name. This is an area in which it pays to be very cautious and incur some additional cost to hire an attorney or specialized firm to conduct a name search. If you learn that another business is using a similar name, you can contact that business and ask for its consent to your proposed name. ■

ARTICLES OF INCORPORATION
The document filed with the appropriate governmental agency, usually the secretary of state, when a business is incorporated. State statutes usually prescribe what kind of information must be contained in the articles of incorporation.

Preparing the Articles of Incorporation   The primary document needed to incorporate a business is the **articles of incorporation.** The articles include basic information about the corporation and serve as an important source of authority for its future organization and business functions. The person or persons who execute (sign) the articles are called *incorporators*. Generally, the articles of incorporation *must* include the following information [RMBCA 2.02]:

1. The name of the corporation.
2. The number of shares the corporation is authorized to issue.
3. The name and address of the corporation's initial registered agent.
4. The name and address of each incorporator.

In addition, the articles *may* set forth other information, such as the names and addresses of the initial board of directors, the duration and purpose of the corporation, a par value of shares of the corporation, and any other information pertinent to the rights and duties of the corporation's shareholders and directors. Articles of incorporation vary widely depending on the size and type of corporation and the jurisdiction. Frequently, the articles do not provide much detail about the firm's operations, which are spelled out in the company's **bylaws** (internal rules of management adopted by the corporation at its first organizational meeting).

BYLAWS
Internal rules of management adopted by a corporation or other organization.

Shares of the Corporation   The articles must specify the number of shares of stock authorized for issuance. For instance, a company might state that the aggregate number of shares that the corporation has the authority to issue is five thousand. Sometimes, the articles set forth the capital structure of the corporation and other relevant information concerning equity, shares, and credit.

Registered Office and Agent   The corporation must indicate the location and address of its registered office within the state. Usually, the registered office is also the principal office of the corporation. The corporation must also give the name and address of a specific person who has been designated as an *agent* and who can receive legal documents (such as orders to appear in court) on behalf of the corporation.

Incorporators   Each incorporator must be listed by name and must indicate an address. The incorporators need not have any interest at all in the corporation, and sometimes signing the articles is their only duty. Many states do not have residency or age requirements for incorporators. States vary on the required number of incorporators; it can be as few as one or as many as three. Incorporators frequently participate in the first organizational meeting of the corporation.

Duration and Purpose   A corporation has perpetual existence unless stated otherwise in the articles. The owners may want to prescribe a maximum duration, however, after which the corporation must formally renew its existence.

The RMBCA does not require a specific statement of purpose to be included in the articles. A corporation can be formed for any lawful purpose. Some incorporators choose to include a general statement of purpose "to engage in any lawful act or activity," while others opt to specify the intended business activities ("to engage in the production and sale of agricultural products," for example). It is increasingly common for the articles to state that the corporation is organized for "any legal business," with no mention of specifics, to avoid the need for future amendments to the corporate articles.

Internal Organization   The articles can describe the internal management structure of the corporation, although this is usually included in the bylaws adopted after the corporation is formed. The articles of incorporation commence the corporation; the bylaws are formed after commencement by the board of directors. Bylaws cannot conflict with the incorporation statute or the articles of incorporation [RMBCA 2.06].

Under the RMBCA, shareholders may amend or repeal the bylaws. The board of directors may also amend or repeal the bylaws unless the articles of incorporation or provisions of the incorporation statute reserve this power to the shareholders exclusively [RMBCA 10.20]. Typical bylaw provisions describe such matters as voting requirements for shareholders, the election of the board of directors, the methods of replacing directors, and the manner and time of holding shareholders' and board meetings (these corporate activities are discussed later in this chapter).

KEEP IN MIND
Unlike the articles of incorporation, bylaws do not need to be filed with a state official.

Filing the Articles with the State   Once the articles of incorporation have been prepared, signed, and authenticated by the incorporators, they are sent to the appropriate state official, usually the secretary of state, along with the required filing fee. In most states, as noted previously, the secretary of state then stamps the articles as "Filed" and returns a copy of the articles to the incorporators. Once this occurs, the corporation officially exists. (Note that some states issue a *certificate of incorporation,* or *corporate charter,* which is similar to articles of incorporation, representing the state's authorization for the corporation to conduct business. This procedure was typical under the unrevised MBCA.)

First Organizational Meeting to Adopt Bylaws

After incorporation, the first organizational meeting must be held. If the articles of incorporation named the initial board of directors, then the directors, by majority vote, call for the meeting to adopt the bylaws and complete the company's organization. If the articles did not name the directors (as is typical), then the incorporators hold the meeting to elect the directors, adopt bylaws, and complete the routine business of incorporation (authorizing the issuance of shares and hiring employees, for example). The business transacted depends on the requirements of the state's incorporation statute, the nature of the corporation, the provisions made in the articles, and the desires of the incorporators. Adoption of bylaws—the internal rules of management for the corporation—is usually the most important function of this meeting.

Defects in Formation and Corporate Status

The procedures for incorporation are very specific. If they are not followed precisely, others may be able to challenge the existence of the corporation. Errors in the incorporation procedures might become important when, for instance, a third party who is attempting to enforce a contract or bring suit for a tort injury learns of them. On the basis of improper incorporation, the plaintiff could attempt to hold the would-be shareholders personally liable. Additionally, when the corporation seeks to enforce a contract against a defaulting party, that party may be able to avoid liability on the ground of a defect in the incorporation procedure.

To prevent injustice, courts will sometimes attribute corporate status to an improperly formed corporation by holding it to be a *de jure* corporation or a *de facto* corporation. Occasionally, a corporation may be held to exist by estoppel. Additionally, in certain circumstances involving abuse of the corporate form, a court may disregard the corporate entity ("pierce the corporate veil") and hold the shareholders personally liable, as will be discussed shortly.

***De Jure* and *De Facto* Corporations**   If a corporation has substantially complied with all conditions precedent to incorporation, the corporation is said to have *de jure* (rightful and lawful) existence. In most states and under the RMBCA, the secretary of state's filing of the articles of incorporation is conclusive proof that all mandatory statutory provisions have been met [RMBCA 2.03(b)]. Because a *de jure* corporation is one that is properly formed, neither the state nor a third party can attack its existence.[7]

Sometimes, there is a defect in complying with statutory mandates—for example, the corporation failed to hold an organizational meeting. Under these circumstances, the corporation may have *de facto* (actual) status, meaning that it will be treated as a legal corporation despite the defect in its formation. A corporation with *de facto* status cannot be challenged by third persons (only by the state). In other words, the shareholders of a *de facto* corporation are still protected by limited liability (provided they are unaware of the defect). The following elements are required for *de facto* status:

1. There must be a state statute under which the corporation can be validly incorporated.
2. The parties must have made a good faith attempt to comply with the statute.
3. The enterprise must already have undertaken to do business as a corporation.

Corporation by Estoppel   If a business association holds itself out to others as being a corporation but has made no attempt to incorporate, the firm normally will be estopped (prevented) from denying corporate status in a lawsuit by a third party. This usually occurs when a third party contracts with an entity that claims to be a corporation but has not filed articles of incorporation—or contracts with a person claiming to be an agent of a corporation that does not in fact exist. When the third party brings a suit naming the so-called corporation as the defendant, the association may not escape liability on the ground that no corporation exists. When justice requires, the courts treat an alleged corporation as if it were an actual corporation for the purpose of determining the rights and liabilities of its officers and directors involved in a particular situation. A corporation by estoppel is thus determined by the situation. Recognition of its corporate status does not extend beyond the resolution of the problem at hand.

Corporate Powers

When a corporation is created, the express and implied powers necessary to achieve its purpose also come into existence. The express powers of a corporation are found in its articles of incorporation, in the law of the state of incorporation, and in the state and federal constitutions. Corporate bylaws and the resolutions of the corporation's board of directors also grant or restrict certain powers.

---

7. There is an exception: a few states allow state authorities, in a *quo warranto* proceeding, to bring an action against the corporation for noncompliance with a condition subsequent to incorporation. This might occur if the corporation fails to file annual reports, for example.

The following order of priority is used if a conflict arises among the various documents involving a corporation:

1. U.S. Constitution.
2. Constitution of the state of incorporation.
3. State statutes.
4. Articles of incorporation.
5. Bylaws.
6. Resolutions of the board of directors.

Certain implied powers arise when a corporation is created. Barring express constitutional, statutory, or charter prohibitions, the corporation has the implied power to perform all acts reasonably appropriate and necessary to accomplish its corporate purposes. For this reason, a corporation has the implied power to borrow funds within certain limits, to lend funds, and to extend credit to those with whom it has a legal or contractual relationship.

To borrow funds, the corporation acts through its board of directors to authorize the loan. Most often, the president or chief executive officer of the corporation will execute the necessary papers on behalf of the corporation. Corporate officers such as these have the implied power to bind the corporation in matters directly connected with the *ordinary* business affairs of the enterprise. A corporate officer does not have the authority to bind the corporation to an action that will greatly affect the corporate purpose or undertaking, such as the sale of substantial corporate assets, however.

Ultra Vires Doctrine

ULTRA VIRES
A Latin term meaning "beyond the power." In corporate law, it refers to acts of a corporation that are beyond its express and implied powers to undertake.

The term **ultra vires** means "beyond the power." In corporate law, acts of a corporation that are beyond its express or implied powers are *ultra vires* acts. Most cases dealing with *ultra vires* acts have involved contracts made for unauthorized purposes. **EXAMPLE #4** Suarez is the chief executive officer of SOS Plumbing, Inc. He enters into a contract with Carlini for the purchase of twenty cases of brandy. It is difficult to see how this contract is reasonably related to the conduct and furtherance of the corporation's stated purpose of providing plumbing installation and services. Hence, a court would probably find the contract to be *ultra vires.*□

In some states, when a contract is entirely executory (not yet performed by either party), either party can use a defense of *ultra vires* to prevent enforcement of the contract. Under Section 3.04 of the RMBCA, the shareholders can seek an injunction from a court to prevent the corporation from engaging in *ultra vires* acts. The attorney general in the state of incorporation can also bring an action to obtain an injunction against the *ultra vires* transactions or to institute dissolution proceedings against the corporation on the basis of *ultra vires* acts. The corporation or its shareholders (on behalf of the corporation) can seek damages from the officers and directors who were responsible for the *ultra vires* acts.

PIERCING THE CORPORATE VEIL

PIERCE THE CORPORATE VEIL
An action in which a court disregards the corporate entity and holds the shareholders personally liable for corporate debts and obligations.

Occasionally, the owners use a corporate entity to perpetrate a fraud, circumvent the law, or in some other way accomplish an illegitimate objective. In these situations, the court will ignore the corporate structure and **pierce the corporate veil,** exposing the shareholders to personal liability [RMBCA 2.04]. Generally, when the corporate privilege is abused for personal benefit or when the corporate business is treated so carelessly that the corporation and the controlling shareholder are no longer separate entities, the court will require the owner to assume personal liability to creditors for the corporation's debts.

In short, when the facts show that great injustice would result from the use of a corporation to avoid individual responsibility, a court will look behind the corporate structure to the individual shareholder. The following are some of the factors that frequently cause the courts to pierce the corporate veil:

1. A party is tricked or misled into dealing with the corporation rather than the individual.
2. The corporation is set up never to make a profit or always to be insolvent, or it is too "thinly" capitalized—that is, it has insufficient capital at the time it is formed to meet its prospective debts or potential liabilities.
3. Statutory corporate formalities, such as holding required corporation meetings, are not followed.
4. Personal and corporate interests are mixed together, or **commingled,** to the extent that the corporation has no separate identity.

COMMINGLE
To mix funds or goods together in one mass so that they no longer have separate identities. In corporate law, if personal and corporate interests are commingled to the extent that the corporation has no separate identity, a court may "pierce the corporate veil" and expose the shareholders to personal liability.

In the following case, when a corporation's creditors sought payment of its debts, the owners took for themselves the small value in the business, filed a bankruptcy petition for the firm, and incorporated under a new name to continue the business. Could the court recover the business assets from the new corporation for distribution to the original firm's creditors?

Case 15.2 In re Aqua Clear Technologies, Inc.

United States Bankruptcy Court,
Southern District of Florida, 2007.
361 Bankr. 567.

BACKGROUND AND FACTS Harvey and Barbara Jacobson owned Aqua Clear Technologies, Inc., a small Florida business that installed and serviced home water softening systems. Barbara was Aqua's president, and Sharon, the Jacobsons' daughter, was an officer, but neither participated in the business. Although Harvey controlled the day-to-day operations, he was not an Aqua officer, director, or employee, but an independent contractor in service to the company. Aqua had no compensation agreement with the Jacobsons. Instead, whenever Harvey decided that there were sufficient funds, they took funds out of the business for their personal

expenses, including the maintenance of their home and payments for their cars, health-insurance premiums, and charges on their credit cards. In December 2004, Aqua filed a bankruptcy petition in a federal bankruptcy court. Three weeks later, Harvey incorporated Discount Water Services, Inc., and continued to service water softening systems for Aqua's customers. Discount appropriated Aqua's equipment and inventory without a formal transfer and advertised Aqua's phone number as Discount's own. Kenneth Welt, Aqua's trustee, initiated a proceeding against Discount, seeking, among other things, to recover Aqua's assets. The trustee contended that Discount was Aqua's "alter ego." (An alter ego is the double of something—in this case, the original company.)

IN THE WORDS OF THE COURT . . . JOHN K. OLSON, Bankruptcy Judge.

* * * *

* * * To disregard the corporate entity form and find that one entity is the alter ego of another, three elements must be established under Florida law:

a. Domination and control of the corporation to such an extent that it has no independent existence;
b. That the corporate form was used fraudulently or for an improper purpose; and

CASE 15.2–CONTINUED

CASE 15.2–CONTINUED

c. That the fraudulent or improper use of the form proximately caused the creditor's injury.

* * * *

The Debtor and Defendant Discount Water were in substantially the same business. They used the same telephone number. They operated from the same business address. They serviced the same geographic area and many of the same customers. Until April 27, 2005, when Barbara Jacobson resigned as President of Discount Water, she was the only President either the Debtor or Discount Water had and a director of both. The Debtor and Discount Water had identical officers and directors. *The Court may presume fraud when a transfer occurs between two corporations controlled by the same officers and directors.* There is no credible evidence before the Court that suggests that Discount Water is anything other than a continuation of the Debtor's business under a new name. [Emphasis added.]

Perhaps the clearest piece of evidence demonstrating the identity of the Debtor and Discount Water is in the following letter sent to Aqua Clear's health insurance carrier:

* * * *

We are changing the name of Aqua Clear Technologies Inc., * * * to DISCOUNT WATER SERVICES INC. Please change your records as soon as possible.
* * * *

Clearly, the author of the letter is declaring that Discount Water Services and the Debtor are one and the same.

* * * The evidence makes clear that the Jacobsons created Discount Water simply to continue the business of the Debtor using the Debtor's assets. The Jacobsons divested the Debtor of such assets as it retained at the time of its bankruptcy filing, motivated in large part by a desire to thwart the collection efforts of * * * judgment creditor[s] * * * . The Jacobsons thus delivered an empty shell of the Debtor to the bankruptcy court in contravention of their duty to their creditors.

When conducting an analysis concerning a fraud to avoid the liabilities of a predecessor, * * * *the bottom line question is whether each entity has run its own race, or whether there has been a relay-style passing of the baton from one to the other.* Here, the assets transferred from the Debtor to Discount Water were in exchange for no bona fide consideration, let alone for reasonably equivalent value. * * * Discount Water took the baton passed by the Debtor and has run with it and in the process has become the Debtor's alter ego. Discount Water is therefore liable to the Debtor's creditors for all of the Debtor's liabilities * * * . [Emphasis added.]

DECISION AND REMEDY   The court issued a judgment against Discount, and in the trustee's favor, for $108,732.64, which represented the amount of the claims listed in Aqua's bankruptcy schedules. The court also agreed to add the administrative expenses and all other claims allowed against Aqua once those amounts were determined.

THE ETHICAL DIMENSION   Was the Jacobsons' disregard for corporate formalities unethical? Why or why not?

THE GLOBAL DIMENSION   If the scope of the Jacobsons' business had been global, should the court have issued a different judgment? Explain.

The Commingling of Personal and Corporate Assets

The potential for corporate assets to be used for personal benefit is especially great in a close corporation, in which the shares are held by a single person or by only a few individuals, usually family members. In such a situation, the separate status of the corporate entity and the sole shareholder (or family-member shareholders) must be carefully preserved. Certain practices invite trouble for the one-person or family-owned corporation: the commingling of corporate and personal funds; the failure to remit taxes, including payroll and sales taxes; and the shareholders' continuous personal use of corporate property (for example, vehicles).

EXAMPLE #5 Donald Park incorporated three sports companies—SSP, SSI, and SSII. His mother was the president of SSP and SSII but did not participate in their operations. Park handled most of the corporations' activities out of his apartment and drew funds from their accounts as needed to pay his personal expenses. None of the three corporations had any employees, issued stock or paid dividends, maintained corporate records, or followed other corporate formalities. Park—misrepresenting himself as the president of SSP and the vice president of SSII—obtained loans on behalf of SSP from Dimmitt & Owens Financial, Inc. When the loans were not paid, Dimmitt filed a suit in a federal district court, seeking, among other things, to impose personal liability on Park. Because Park had commingled corporate funds with his personal funds and failed to follow corporate formalities, the court "pierced the corporate veil" and held him personally responsible for the debt.[8] □

Loans to the Corporation

Corporation laws usually do not specifically prohibit a shareholder from lending funds to her or his corporation. When an officer, director, or majority shareholder lends the corporation funds and takes back security in the form of corporate assets, however, the courts will scrutinize the transaction closely. Any such transaction must be made in good faith and for fair value.

DIRECTORS AND OFFICERS

Corporate directors, officers, and shareholders all play different roles within the corporate entity. Sometimes, actions that may benefit the corporation as a whole do not coincide with the separate interests of the individuals making up the corporation. In such situations, it is important to know the rights and duties of all participants in the corporate enterprise, and the ways in which conflicts among corporate participants are resolved.

Role of Directors

The board of directors is the ultimate authority in every corporation. Directors have responsibility for all policymaking decisions necessary to the management of all corporate affairs. Just as shareholders cannot act individually to bind the corporation, the directors must act as a body in carrying out routine corporate business. The board selects and removes the corporate officers, determines the capital structure of the corporation, and declares dividends. Each director has one vote, and customarily the majority rules. The general areas of responsibility of the board of directors are shown in Exhibit 15–2 on the following page.

Directors are sometimes inappropriately characterized as *agents* because they act on behalf of the corporation. No individual director, however, can act as an agent to bind the corporation; and as a group, directors collectively control the

---

8. *Dimmitt & Owens Financial, Inc. v. Superior Sports Products, Inc.,* 196 F.Supp.2d 731 (N.D.Ill. 2002).

EXHIBIT 15–2 DIRECTORS' MANAGEMENT RESPONSIBILITIES

AUTHORIZE MAJOR CORPORATE POLICY DECISIONS	SELECT AND REMOVE CORPORATE OFFICERS AND OTHER MANAGERIAL EMPLOYEES, AND DETERMINE THEIR COMPENSATION	MAKE FINANCIAL DECISIONS
Examples: —Oversee major contract negotiations and management-labor negotiations. —Initiate negotiations on sale or lease of corporate assets outside the regular course of business. —Decide whether to pursue new product lines or business opportunities.	*Examples:* —Search for and hire corporate executives and determine the elements of their compensation packages, including stock options. —Supervise managerial employees and make decisions regarding their termination.	*Examples:* —Make decisions regarding the issuance of authorized shares and bonds. —Decide when to declare dividends to be paid to shareholders.

corporation in a way that no agent is able to control a principal. In addition, although directors occupy positions of trust and control over the corporation, they are not *trustees* because they do not hold title to property for the use and benefit of others.

Few qualifications are required for directors. Only a handful of states impose minimum age and residency requirements. A director may be a shareholder, but that is not necessary (unless the articles of incorporation or bylaws require ownership).

Election of Directors   Subject to statutory limitations, the number of directors is set forth in the corporation's articles or bylaws. Historically, the minimum number of directors has been three, but today many states permit fewer. Normally, the incorporators appoint the first board of directors at the time the corporation is created, or the corporation itself names the directors in the articles. The initial board serves until the first annual shareholders' meeting. Subsequent directors are elected by a majority vote of the shareholders.

A director usually serves for a term of one year—from annual meeting to annual meeting. Longer and staggered terms are permissible under most state statutes. A common practice is to elect one-third of the board members each year for a three-year term. In this way, there is greater management continuity.

Compensation of Directors   In the past, corporate directors rarely were compensated, but today they are often paid at least nominal sums and may receive more substantial compensation in large corporations because of the time, work, effort, and especially risk involved. Most states permit the corporate articles or bylaws to authorize compensation for directors. In fact, the Revised Model Business Corporation Act (RMBCA) states that unless the articles or bylaws provide otherwise, the board of directors may set their own compensation [RMBCA 8.11]. Directors also gain through indirect benefits, such as business contacts and prestige, and other rewards, such as stock options.

In many corporations, directors are also chief corporate officers (president or chief executive officer, for example) and receive compensation in their managerial positions. A director who is also an officer of the corporation is referred to as an **inside director,** whereas a director who does not hold a management position is an **outside director.** Typically, a corporation's board of directors includes both inside and outside directors.

Board of Directors' Meetings The board of directors conducts business by holding formal meetings with recorded minutes. The dates of regular meetings are usually established in the articles or bylaws or by board resolution, and no further notice is customarily required. Special meetings can be called, with notice sent to all directors. Today, most states allow directors to participate in board of directors' meetings from remote locations via telephone or Web conferencing, provided that all the directors can simultaneously hear each other during the meeting [RMBCA 8.20].

Unless the articles of incorporation or bylaws specify a greater number, a majority of the board of directors normally constitutes a quorum [RMBCA 8.24]. (A **quorum** is the minimum number of members of a body of officials or other group that must be present for business to be validly transacted.) Once a quorum is present, the directors transact business and vote on issues affecting the corporation. Each director present at the meeting has one vote.[9] Ordinary matters generally require a simple majority vote; certain extraordinary issues may require a greater-than-majority vote. In other words, the affirmative vote of a majority of the directors present at a meeting binds the board of directors with regard to most decisions.

Rights of Directors

A corporate director must have certain rights to function properly in that position. The *right to participation* means that directors are entitled to participate in all board of directors' meetings and have a right to be notified of these meetings. As mentioned earlier, the dates of regular board meetings are usually preestablished and no notice of these meetings is required. If special meetings are called, however, notice is required unless waived by the director [RMBCA 8.23].

A director also has a *right of inspection,* which means that each director can access the corporation's books and records, facilities, and premises. Inspection rights are essential for directors to make informed decisions and to exercise the necessary supervision over corporate officers and employees. This right of inspection is virtually absolute and cannot be restricted (by the articles, bylaws, or any act of the board of directors).

When a director becomes involved in litigation by virtue of her or his position or actions, the director may also have a *right to indemnification* (reimbursement) for the legal costs, fees, and damages incurred. Most states allow corporations to indemnify and purchase liability insurance for corporate directors [RMBCA 8.51].

INSIDE DIRECTOR
A person on the board of directors who is also an officer of the corporation.

OUTSIDE DIRECTOR
A person on the board of directors who does not hold a management position in the corporation.

QUORUM
The number of members of a decision-making body that must be present before business may be transacted.

Preventing Legal Disputes

Whenever businesspersons serve as corporate directors or officers, they should be aware that they may at some point become involved in litigation as a result of their positions. To protect against personal liability, a director or officer should take several steps. First, make sure that the corporate bylaws explicitly give directors

---

9. Except in Louisiana, which allows a director to vote by proxy under certain circumstances.

and officers a right to indemnification (reimbursement) for any costs incurred as a result of litigation, as well as any judgments or settlements stemming from a lawsuit. Second, have the corporation purchase directors' and officers' liability insurance (D & O insurance). Having D & O insurance policies enables the corporation to avoid paying the substantial costs involved in defending a particular director or officer. The D & O policies offered by most private insurance companies have maximum coverage limits, so make sure that the corporation is required to indemnify directors and officers in the event that the costs exceed the policy limits. ■

Committees of the Board of Directors

When a board of directors has a large number of members and must deal with a myriad of complex business issues, meetings can become unwieldy. Therefore, the boards of large, publicly held corporations typically create committees, appoint directors to serve on individual committees, and delegate certain tasks to these committees. Committees focus on individual subjects and increase the efficiency of the board. The most common types of committees include the following:

CONTRAST
Shareholders own a corporation and directors make policy decisions, but officers who run the daily business of the corporation often have significant decision-making power.

1. *Executive committee.* The board members often elect an executive committee of directors to handle the interim management decisions between board of directors' meetings. The executive committee is limited to making management decisions about ordinary business matters and conducting preliminary investigations into proposals. It cannot declare dividends, authorize the issuance of shares, amend the bylaws, or initiate any actions that require shareholder approval.

2. *Audit committee.* The audit committee is responsible for the selection, compensation, and oversight of the independent public accountants who audit the corporation's financial records. The Sarbanes-Oxley Act of 2002 requires all publicly held corporations to have an audit committee.

3. *Nominating committee.* This committee chooses the candidates for the board of directors that management wishes to submit to the shareholders in the next election. The committee cannot select directors to fill vacancies on the board, however [RMBCA 8.25].

4. *Compensation committee.* The compensation committee reviews and decides the salaries, bonuses, stock options, and other benefits that are given to the corporation's top executives. The committee may also determine the compensation of directors.

5. *Litigation committee.* This committee decides whether the corporation should pursue requests by shareholders to file a lawsuit against some party that has allegedly harmed the corporation. The committee members investigate the allegations and weigh the costs and benefits of litigation.

Corporate executives discuss the business of their firm. Can the same person be both a director and an officer of a corporation?
(John Terence Turner/Getty Images)

In addition to appointing committees, the board of directors can also delegate some of its functions to corporate officers. In doing so, the board is not relieved of its overall responsibility for directing the affairs of the corporation. Instead, corporate officers and managerial personnel are empowered to make decisions relating to ordinary, daily corporate activities within well-defined guidelines.

Corporate Officers and Executives

Officers and other executive employees are hired by the board of directors. At a minimum, most corporations have a president, one or more vice presidents, a secretary, and a treasurer. In most states, an individual can hold more than one office, such as president and secretary, and can be both an officer and a director of the corporation. In addition to carrying out the duties articulated in the bylaws, corporate and managerial officers act as agents of the corporation, and the ordinary rules of agency (discussed in Chapter 16) normally apply to their employment.

Corporate officers and other high-level managers are employees of the company, so their rights are defined by employment contracts. Regardless of the terms of an employment contract, however, the board of directors normally can remove a corporate officer at any time with or without cause—although the officer may then seek damages from the corporation for breach of contract.

The duties of corporate officers are the same as those of directors because both groups are involved in decision making and are in similar positions of control. Hence, officers and directors are viewed as having the same fiduciary duties of care and loyalty in their conduct of corporate affairs, a subject to which we now turn.

Duties and Liabilities of Directors and Officers

Directors and officers are deemed to be fiduciaries of the corporation because their relationship with the corporation and its shareholders is one of trust and confidence. As fiduciaries, directors and officers owe ethical—and legal—duties to the corporation and the shareholders as a whole. These fiduciary duties include the duty of care and the duty of loyalty.

Duty of Care Directors and officers must exercise due care in performing their duties. The standard of *due care* has been variously described in judicial decisions and codified in many state corporation codes. Generally, directors and officers are required to act in good faith, to exercise the care that an ordinarily prudent person would exercise in similar circumstances, and to do what they believe is in the best interests of the corporation [RMBCA 8.30(a), 8.42(a)]. Directors and officers whose failure to exercise due care results in harm to the corporation or its shareholders can be held liable for negligence (unless the business judgment rule applies).

Duty to Make Informed and Reasonable Decisions Directors and officers are expected to be informed on corporate matters and to conduct a reasonable investigation of the situation before making a decision. This means that they must do what is necessary to keep adequately informed: attend meetings and presentations, ask for information from those who have it, read reports, and review other written materials. In other words, directors and officers must investigate, study, and discuss matters and evaluate alternatives before making a decision. They cannot decide on the spur of the moment without adequate research.

Although directors and officers are expected to act in accordance with their own knowledge and training, they are also normally entitled to rely on information given to them by certain other persons. Most states and Section 8.30(b) of the RMBCA allow a director to make decisions in reliance on information furnished by competent officers or employees, professionals such as attorneys and accountants, and committees of the board of directors (on which the director does not serve). The reliance must be in good faith, of course, to insulate a director from liability if the information later proves to be inaccurate or unreliable.

Duty to Exercise Reasonable Supervision   Directors are also expected to exercise a reasonable amount of supervision when they delegate work to corporate officers and employees. **EXAMPLE #6** Morgan, a corporate director at a mortgage company, fails to attend any board of directors' meetings for four years. In addition, Morgan never inspects any of the corporate books or records and generally fails to supervise the efforts of the company's president and mortgage loan managers. Meanwhile, Brennan, who is a corporate officer and loan manager, makes various improper loans and permits large overdrafts. In this situation, Morgan (the corporate director) can be held liable to the corporation for losses resulting from the unsupervised actions of Brennan, the mortgage loan officer.□

Dissenting Directors   Directors are expected to attend board of directors' meetings, and their votes should be entered into the minutes. Sometimes, an individual director disagrees with the majority's vote (which becomes an act of the board of directors). Unless a dissent is entered in the minutes, the director is presumed to have assented. If a decision later leads to the directors being held liable for mismanagement, dissenting directors are rarely held individually liable to the corporation. For this reason, a director who is absent from a given meeting sometimes registers with the secretary of the board a dissent to actions taken at the meeting.

The Business Judgment Rule   Directors and officers are expected to exercise due care and to use their best judgment in guiding corporate management, but they are not insurers of business success. Under the **business judgment rule,** a corporate director or officer will not be liable to the corporation or to its shareholders for honest mistakes of judgment and bad business decisions. Courts give significant deference to the decisions of corporate directors and officers, and consider the reasonableness of a decision at the time it was made, without the benefit of hindsight. Thus, corporate decision makers are not subjected to second-guessing by shareholders or others in the corporation.

The business judgment rule will apply as long as the director or officer (1) took reasonable steps to become informed about the matter, (2) had a rational basis for his or her decision, and (3) did not have a conflict of interest between his or her personal interest and that of the corporation. In fact, unless there is evidence of bad faith, fraud, or a clear breach of fiduciary duties, most courts will apply the rule and protect directors and officers who make bad business decisions from liability for those choices. Consequently, if there is a reasonable basis for a business decision, a court is unlikely to interfere with that decision, even if the corporation suffers as a result.

Duty of Loyalty   *Loyalty* can be defined as faithfulness to one's obligations and duties. In the corporate context, the duty of loyalty requires directors and officers to subordinate their personal interests to the welfare of the corporation.

For instance, directors may not use corporate funds or confidential corporate information for personal advantage. Similarly, they must refrain from putting their personal interests above those of the corporation. For instance, a director

BUSINESS JUDGMENT RULE
A rule that immunizes corporate management from liability for actions that result in corporate losses or damages if the actions are undertaken in good faith and are within both the power of the corporation and the authority of management to make.

should not oppose a transaction that is in the corporation's best interest simply because pursuing it may cost the director her or his position. Cases dealing with the duty of loyalty typically involve one or more of the following:

1. Competing with the corporation.
2. Usurping (taking personal advantage of) a corporate opportunity.
3. Having an interest that conflicts with the interest of the corporation.
4. Engaging in *insider trading* (using information that is not public to make a profit trading securities, as discussed in Chapter 24).
5. Authorizing a corporate transaction that is detrimental to minority shareholders.
6. Selling control over the corporation.

Conflicts of Interest

The duty of loyalty also requires officers and directors to *fully disclose* to the board of directors any potential conflict of interest that might arise in any corporate transaction. State statutes contain different standards, but a contract between a corporation and one of its officers or directors generally will *not* be voidable if all of the following are true: if the contract was fair and reasonable to the corporation at the time it was made, if there was a full disclosure of the interest of the officers or directors involved in the transaction, and if the contract was approved by a majority of the disinterested directors or shareholders.

EXAMPLE #7 Southwood Corporation needs office space. Lambert Alden, one of its five directors, owns the building adjoining the corporation's main office building. He negotiates a lease with Southwood for the space, making a full disclosure to Southwood and the other four board directors. The lease arrangement is fair and reasonable, and it is unanimously approved by the corporation's board of directors. In this situation, Alden has not breached his duty of loyalty to the corporation, and thus the contract is valid. If it were otherwise, directors would be prevented from ever transacting business with the corporations they serve.□

SHAREHOLDERS

The acquisition of a share of stock makes a person an owner and shareholder in a corporation. Shareholders thus own the corporation. Although they have no legal title to corporate property, such as buildings and equipment, they do have an *equitable* (ownership) interest in the firm.

As a general rule, shareholders have no responsibility for the daily management of the corporation, although they are ultimately responsible for choosing the board of directors, which does have such control. Ordinarily, corporate officers and other employees owe no direct duty to individual shareholders. Their duty is to the corporation as a whole. A director, however, is in a fiduciary relationship to the corporation and therefore serves the interests of the shareholders. Generally, there is no legal relationship between shareholders and creditors of the corporation. Shareholders can, in fact, be creditors of the corporation and thus have the same rights of recovery against the corporation as any other creditor.

In this section, we look at the powers and voting rights of shareholders, which are generally established in the articles of incorporation and under the state's general incorporation law.

BE AWARE
Shareholders normally are not agents of their corporations.

Shareholders' Powers

Shareholders must approve fundamental corporate changes before the changes can be effected. Hence, shareholders are empowered to amend the articles of incorporation and bylaws, approve a merger or the dissolution of the corporation, and approve the sale of all or substantially all of the corporation's assets. Some of these powers are subject to prior board approval. Shareholder approval may also be requested (though it is not required) for certain other actions, such as to approve an independent auditor.

Directors are elected to (and removed from) the board of directors by a vote of the shareholders. The first board of directors is either named in the articles of incorporation or chosen by the incorporators to serve until the first shareholders' meeting. From that time on, the selection and retention of directors are exclusively shareholder functions.

Directors usually serve their full terms; if the directors are unsatisfactory, they are simply not reelected. Shareholders have the inherent power, however, to remove a director from office *for cause* (breach of duty or misconduct) by a majority vote.[10] Some state statutes (and some corporate charters) even permit removal of directors *without cause* by the vote of a majority of the holders of outstanding shares entitled to vote.

Shareholders' Meetings

Shareholders' meetings must occur at least annually, and additional, special meetings can be called as needed to take care of urgent matters. Because it is usually not practical for owners of only a few shares of stock of publicly traded corporations to attend shareholders' meetings, such stockholders normally give third parties written authorization to vote their shares at the meeting. This authorization is called a **proxy** (from the Latin *procurare,* "to manage, take care of"). Proxies are often solicited by management, but any person can solicit proxies to concentrate voting power.

PROXY

In corporation law, a written agreement between a stockholder and another under which the stockholder authorizes the other to vote the stockholder's shares in a certain manner.

Proxy Materials and Shareholder Proposals   When shareholders want to change a company policy, they can put their idea up for a shareholder vote. They can do this by submitting a shareholder proposal to the board of directors and asking the board to include the proposal in the proxy materials that are sent to all shareholders before meetings.

The Securities and Exchange Commission (SEC), which regulates the purchase and sale of securities (see Chapter 24), has special provisions relating to proxies and shareholder proposals. SEC Rule 14a-8 provides that all shareholders who own stock worth at least $1,000 are eligible to submit proposals for inclusion in corporate proxy materials. The corporation is required to include information on whatever proposals will be considered at the shareholders' meeting along with proxy materials. Only those proposals that relate to significant policy considerations rather than ordinary business operations must be included. For a discussion of how the SEC is adapting its rules regarding proxy solicitation to take advantage of today's communications technology, see this chapter's *Online Developments* feature.

---

10. A director can often demand court review of removal for cause.

In the past, anyone wishing to solicit proxies from shareholders had to mail each shareholder numerous paper documents relating to the proxy. Required materials often include notice of the meeting, proxy statements and consent solicitation statements, proxy cards, information statements, annual reports, additional soliciting materials, and any amendments made to these materials. Providing all of these documents in paper form can be very costly.

The Securities and Exchange Commission (SEC) adopted voluntary e-proxy rules that went into effect on July 1, 2007.[a] Essentially, the new rules allow companies to furnish proxy materials to shareholders by posting them on a Web site and providing shareholders with notice of the availability of the proxy materials online. This is a significant development that will reduce the printing and mailing costs associated with furnishing proxy materials to shareholders. Because the rules are voluntary, a company may still provide paper proxy documents if it so chooses.

The Notice and Access Model

Under the SEC's new rules, a company may now furnish proxy materials to shareholders using the notice and access model, which includes the following steps:

- The company posts the proxy materials on a publicly accessible Web site.
- The company then sends a (paper) notice to each shareholder at least forty calendar days prior to the date of the shareholders' meeting for which the proxy is being solicited.
- No other materials (such as a proxy card) can be sent along with the initial notice (unless the proxy is being combined with a meeting notice required by state law).
- The notice must be written in plain English and include a prominent statement of the following: the date, time, and location of the shareholders' meeting; the specific Web site at which the shareholders can access the proxy materials; an explanation of how they can obtain paper copies of the proxy materials at no cost (by calling a toll-free phone number, for instance); and a clear and

impartial description of each matter to be considered at the shareholders' meeting.

- After sending the initial notice, the company must wait at least ten days before sending (paper) proxy cards to the shareholders. This ten-day waiting period is designed to provide shareholders with sufficient time to access the proxy materials online or request paper copies.
- If a shareholder requests paper proxy materials, the company must send them to the shareholder within three business days.
- After receiving the initial paper notice, a shareholder can permanently elect to receive all future proxy materials on paper or by e-mail.

Shareholders and other parties conducting their own proxy solicitations can also use the notice and access model with slight modifications. The notice must still be sent forty days before the meeting date and include substantially the same information, but the notice need not be provided to all shareholders. In contrast to company solicitations, other parties can selectively choose the shareholders from whom they wish to solicit proxies without sending information to all other shareholders.

Should E-Proxy Rules Be Mandatory?

The SEC has also proposed making the new e-proxy rules mandatory for all proxy solicitations in the future. The mandatory notice and access model would operate substantially as just outlined, except that the initial notice could be accompanied by a paper or e-mail copy of the proxy statement, annual report, and proxy card. The main difference between the mandatory and voluntary models is that under the voluntary rule, the company (or other party seeking proxies) can choose whether to use electronic or paper means, whereas under a mandatory rule, the SEC would require the use of electronic means. Under either rule, the shareholder can always choose to receive paper documents rather than accessing the materials online.

FOR CRITICAL ANALYSIS Why might a company or other party choose to solicit proxies the old-fashioned way, by providing paper documents instead of Internet access, despite the added costs?

a. 17 C.F.R. Parts 240, 249, and 274.

Shareholder Voting For shareholders to act during a meeting, a quorum must be present. (As already discussed, a quorum is the minimum number of members of a body of officials or other group that must be present in order for business to be validly transacted.) Generally, a quorum exists when shareholders holding more than 50 percent of the outstanding shares are present. Corporate business matters are presented in the form of *resolutions,* which shareholders vote to approve or

BE CAREFUL

Once a quorum is present, a vote can be taken even if some shareholders leave without casting their votes.

disapprove. Some state statutes have set forth specific voting requirements, and corporations' articles or bylaws must abide by these statutory requirements. Some states provide that the unanimous written consent of shareholders is a permissible alternative to holding a shareholders' meeting.

Once a quorum is present, voting can proceed. A majority vote of the shares represented at the meeting is usually required to pass resolutions. At times, more than a simple majority vote will be required either by a statute or by the corporate charter. Extraordinary corporate matters, such as a merger, consolidation, or dissolution of the corporation, require a higher percentage of the representatives of all corporate shares entitled to vote, not just a majority of those present at that particular meeting.

Cumulative Voting   Most states permit or even require shareholders to elect directors by *cumulative voting,* a method of voting designed to allow minority shareholders representation on the board of directors. When cumulative voting is allowed or required, the number of members of the board to be elected is multiplied by the total number of voting shares. The result equals the number of votes a shareholder has, and this total can be cast for one or more nominees for director. All nominees stand for election at the same time. When cumulative voting is not required either by statute or under the articles, the entire board can be elected by a simple majority of shares at a shareholders' meeting.

EXAMPLE #8 A corporation has 10,000 shares issued and outstanding. One group of shareholders (the minority shareholders) holds only 3,000 shares, and the other group of shareholders (the majority shareholders) holds the other 7,000 shares. Three members of the board are to be elected. The majority shareholders' nominees are Acevedo, Barkley, and Craycik. The minority shareholders' nominee is Drake. Can Drake be elected by the minority shareholders?

If cumulative voting is allowed, the answer is yes. The minority shareholders have 9,000 votes among them (the number of directors to be elected times the number of shares held by the minority shareholders equals 3 times 3,000, which equals 9,000 votes). All of these votes can be cast to elect Drake. The majority shareholders have 21,000 votes (3 times 7,000 equals 21,000 votes), but these votes have to be distributed among their three nominees. The principle of cumulative voting is that no matter how the majority shareholders cast their 21,000 votes, they will not be able to elect all three directors if the minority shareholders cast all of their 9,000 votes for Drake, as illustrated in Exhibit 15–3. □

EXHIBIT 15–3   RESULTS OF CUMULATIVE VOTING

This exhibit illustrates how cumulative voting gives minority shareholders a greater chance of electing a director of their choice. By casting all of their 9,000 votes for one candidate (Drake), the minority shareholders will succeed in electing Drake to the board of directors.

BALLOT	MAJORITY SHAREHOLDERS' VOTES			MINORITY SHAREHOLDERS' VOTES	DIRECTORS ELECTED
	Acevedo	Barkley	Craycik	Drake	
1	10,000	10,000	1,000	9,000	Acevedo/Barkley/Drake
2	9,001	9,000	2,999	9,000	Acevedo/Barkley/Drake
3	6,000	7,000	8,000	9,000	Barkley/Craycik/Drake

Other Voting Techniques Before a shareholders' meeting, a group of shareholders can agree in writing to vote their shares together in a specified manner. Such agreements, called *shareholder voting agreements,* are usually held to be valid and enforceable. A shareholder can also appoint a voting agent and vote by proxy. As mentioned previously, a proxy is a written authorization to cast the shareholder's vote, and a person can solicit proxies from a number of shareholders in an attempt to concentrate voting power.

Another technique is for shareholders to enter into a **voting trust,** which is an agreement (a trust contract) under which legal title (record ownership on the corporate books) is transferred to a trustee who is responsible for voting the shares. The agreement can specify how the trustee is to vote, or it can allow the trustee to use his or her discretion. The trustee takes physical possession of the stock certificate and in return gives the shareholder a *voting trust certificate.* The shareholder retains other rights of ownership (for example, the right to receive dividend payments) except the power to vote the shares [RMBCA 7.30].

In the following case, corporate management was concerned about the possibility of losing a proxy contest. The corporation's chief executive officer (CEO) then entered into an agreement with a shareholder who would support management's candidates in return for a seat on the board of directors. A shareholder who opposed the deal filed a lawsuit claiming that this agreement was illegal and a breach of the officer's fiduciary duty.

VOTING TRUST
An agreement (trust contract) under which legal title to shares of corporate stock is transferred to a trustee who is authorized by the shareholders to vote the shares on their behalf.

Case 15.3 **Portnoy v. Cryo-Cell International, Inc.**

Court of Chancery of Delaware, 2008.
940 A.2d 43.

BACKGROUND AND FACTS Cryo-Cell International, Inc., a small public company, was struggling to succeed. Several of its stockholders considered mounting a proxy contest to replace the board of directors. One of those shareholders, Andrew Filipowski, apparently used management's fear of being replaced to create a deal for himself—that is, he would be included in the management's slate of directors at an upcoming stockholders' annual meeting. Another shareholder, David Portnoy, filed an opposing slate of directors. The company's chief executive officer (CEO), Mercedes Walton, created a plan that would allow management and Filipowski to win the proxy contest. This plan involved Walton as a "matchmaker" who would find stockholders willing to sell their shares to Filipowski. Walton promised Filipowski that if

management's slate of directors won, Cryo-Cell's board of directors would then add another board seat that a Filipowski designee would fill. This side deal created by Walton, however, was not made public to the shareholders when they voted. In other words, they did not know that they were in fact electing an additional member to the board of directors when the management slate won. After the election, Walton prepared to add Filipowski's designee to the board of directors. At this time, the dissenting shareholder group led by Portnoy filed a lawsuit claiming that the election results should be overturned. Portnoy argued that the side agreement with Filipowski was not created in the best interests of the company or its shareholders. Portnoy claimed that all of the dealings between the company and Filipowski were tainted by fiduciary misconduct. Indeed, Portnoy claimed that the agreement to add Filipowski to the management slate in exchange for his support in the proxy fight constituted an "illegal vote-buying arrangement."

IN THE WORDS OF THE COURT . . . *STRINE,* V.C. [Vice Chancellor]

* * * *

* * * Portnoy contends that the deal struck between Walton and the other incumbents, on the one hand, and Filipowski, on the other, to add Filipowski to the Management Slate in exchange for his support in the proxy fight constituted an illegal vote-buying arrangement.

CASE 15.3–CONTINUED

On this claim, * * * I find in favor of the defendants. My conclusion rests on several grounds. Initially, I note that an arrangement of this kind fits comfortably, as a linguistic matter, within the traditional definition of so-called "vote buying" used in our jurisprudence. * * * I have no doubt that the voting agreement between the Filipowski Group and the incumbents was only assented to by Filipowski after he was offered a candidacy on the Management Slate.

* * * *

The notion that judges should chew over the complicated calculus made by incumbent boards considering whether to add to the management slate candidates proposed by a large blockholder whose velvety suggestions were cloaking an unmistakably clenched fist seems to run against many of the sound reasons for the business judgment rule. There is, thankfully, a practical and civic dynamic in much of our nation's human relations, including in commerce, by which clashes of viewpoint are addressed peaceably through give and take. *When stockholders can decide for themselves whether to seat a candidate who obtained a place on a management slate by way of such bargaining, it seems unwise to formulate a standard that involves the potential for excessive and imprecise judicial involvement.* [Emphasis added.]

* * * *

In my view, a mere offer of a position on a management slate should not be considered a vote-buying arrangement subject to a test of entire fairness, and for that reason, I see no reason to condemn the addition of Filipowski to the Management Slate. As an alternative matter, the defendants have convinced me that there was nothing unfair about joining forces with Filipowski in this manner. In this regard, I note that there is not a hint that Filipowski sought to receive financial payments from Cryo-Cell in the form of contracts or consulting fees or other such arrangements. What he sought was influence on the board of a company in which he owned a large number of shares, an ownership interest that gave him an incentive to increase the company's value. Stockholders knew he sought a seat and he had to obtain their votes to get on the board.

* * * *

I reach a different conclusion, however, about the later arrangement that was reached with Filipowski shortly before the annual meeting. * * * Walton * * * promised Filipowski that if the Management Slate won, the incumbent board majority would use its powers under the Company's bylaws to expand the Cryo-Cell board from six members to seven and to fill the new seat with Filipowski's designee.

* * * *

I believe that this arrangement differed in materially important respects from the prior agreement to place Filipowski on the Management Slate. For starters, Walton did not merely promise someone a shot at getting elected by the stockholders by running in the advantaged posture of being a member of a management slate. She promised that she and her incumbent colleagues would use their powers as directors of Cryo-Cell to increase the size of the board and seat [Filipowski's designee]. This was therefore a promise that would not be, for the duration of the term, subject to prior approval by the electorate.

* * * *

* * * There is a very clear and important, but narrow, reason why this later arrangement with Filipowski was improper and inequitably tainted the election process: it was a very material event that was not disclosed to the Cryo-Cell stockholders.

* * * *

* * * I think the remedy that best vindicates the interests of Cryo-Cell stockholders as a class is to order a prompt special meeting at which a new election will be held and presided over by a special master.

DECISION AND REMEDY   The court ruled that the incumbent board's actions and the side agreement with the company's CEO (Walton) did constitute serious breaches of fiduciary duty and tainted the election. The court therefore ordered a special meeting of the shareholders at which a new election would be held. The court did not, however, find the addition of Filipowski to the management slate of directors improper.

THE LEGAL ENVIRONMENT DIMENSION   Why was it acceptable to add Filipowski to the management slate of proposed directors but not to agree to increase the board membership by one director, with that director being Filipowski's designee?

THE ETHICAL DIMENSION   If Filipowski had promised to bring additional funding to keep Cryo-Cell from failing due to lack of capital, would the actions described in this case have been considered ethical? Explain your answer.

Rights of Shareholders

Shareholders possess numerous rights. A significant right—the right to vote their shares—has already been discussed. We now look at some additional rights of shareholders.

Stock Certificates   A **stock certificate** is a certificate issued by a corporation that evidences ownership of a specified number of shares in the corporation. In jurisdictions that require the issuance of stock certificates, shareholders have the right to demand that the corporation issue certificates. In most states and under RMBCA 6.26, boards of directors may provide that shares of stock will be uncertificated—that is, no actual, physical stock certificates will be issued. When shares are uncertificated, the corporation may be required to send each shareholder a letter or some other form of notice that contains the same information that would normally appear on the face of stock certificates.

Stock is intangible personal property, and the ownership right exists independently of the certificate itself. If a stock certificate is lost or destroyed, ownership is not destroyed with it. A new certificate can be issued to replace one that has been lost or destroyed.[11] Notice of shareholders' meetings, dividends, and operational and financial reports are all distributed according to the recorded ownership listed in the corporation's books, not on the basis of possession of the certificate.

Preemptive Rights   With **preemptive rights,** which are based on a common law concept, a shareholder receives a preference over all other purchasers to subscribe to or purchase a prorated share of a new issue of stock. In other words, a shareholder who is given preemptive rights can purchase the same percentage of the new shares being issued as she or he already holds in the company. This allows each shareholder to maintain her or his proportionate control, voting power, and financial interest in the corporation. Most statutes either

> **STOCK CERTIFICATE**
> A certificate issued by a corporation evidencing the ownership of a specified number of shares in the corporation.

> **PREEMPTIVE RIGHTS**
> Rights held by shareholders that entitle them to purchase newly issued shares of a corporation's stock, equal in percentage to shares already held, before the stock is offered to any outside buyers. Preemptive rights enable shareholders to maintain their proportionate ownership and voice in the corporation.

Stock certificates are displayed. To be a shareholder, is it necessary to have physical possession of a certificate? Why or why not?
(PhotoDisc)

11. The Uniform Commercial Code (UCC) provides that for a lost or destroyed certificate to be reissued, a shareholder normally must furnish an *indemnity bond*. An indemnity bond is a written promise to reimburse the holder for any actual or claimed loss caused by the issuer's or some other person's conduct. The bond protects the corporation against potential loss should the original certificate reappear at some future time in the hands of a bona fide purchaser [UCC 8–302, 8–405(2)].

(1) grant preemptive rights but allow them to be negated in the corporation's articles or (2) deny preemptive rights except to the extent that they are granted in the articles. The result is that the articles of incorporation determine the existence and scope of preemptive rights. Generally, preemptive rights apply only to additional, newly issued stock sold for cash, and the preemptive rights must be exercised within a specified time period, which is usually thirty days.

EXAMPLE #9 Tran Corporation authorizes and issues 1,000 shares of stock. Lebow purchases 100 shares, making her the owner of 10 percent of the company's stock. Subsequently, Tran, by vote of its shareholders, authorizes the issuance of another 1,000 shares (by amending the articles of incorporation). This increases its capital stock to a total of 2,000 shares. If preemptive rights have been provided, Lebow can purchase one additional share of the new stock being issued for each share she already owns—or 100 additional shares. Thus, she can own 200 of the 2,000 shares outstanding, and she will maintain her relative position as a shareholder. If preemptive rights are not allowed, her proportionate control and voting power may be diluted from that of a 10 percent shareholder to that of a 5 percent shareholder because of the issuance of the additional 1,000 shares.□

Preemptive rights are most important in close corporations because each shareholder owns a relatively small number of shares but controls a substantial interest in the corporation. Without preemptive rights, it would be possible for a shareholder to lose his or her proportionate control over the firm.

Stock Warrants   Usually, when preemptive rights exist and a corporation is issuing additional shares, each shareholder is given **stock warrants,** which are transferable options to acquire a given number of shares from the corporation at a stated price. Warrants are often publicly traded on securities exchanges. When the option to purchase is in effect for a short period of time, the stock warrants are usually referred to as *rights*.

Dividends   As mentioned previously, a *dividend* is a distribution of corporate profits or income *ordered by the directors* and paid to the shareholders in proportion to their respective shares in the corporation. Dividends can be paid in cash, property, stock of the corporation that is paying the dividends, or stock of other corporations.[12]

State laws vary, but each state determines the general circumstances and legal requirements under which dividends are paid. State laws also control the sources of revenue to be used; only certain funds are legally available for paying dividends. All states allow dividends to be paid from *retained earnings,* or the undistributed net profits earned by the corporation, including capital gains from the sale of fixed assets. A few states allow dividends to be issued from current *net profits* without regard to deficits in prior years. A number of states allow dividends to be paid out of any kind of *surplus*.

Illegal Dividends   Sometimes, dividends are improperly paid from an unauthorized account, or their payment causes the corporation to become insolvent. Generally, in such situations, shareholders must return illegal dividends only if they knew that the dividends were illegal when the payment was received. A dividend paid while the corporation is insolvent is automatically an illegal dividend,

STOCK WARRANT
A certificate that grants the owner the option to buy a given number of shares of stock, usually within a set time period.

---

12. Technically, dividends paid in stock are not dividends. They maintain each shareholder's proportionate interest in the corporation. On one occasion, a distillery declared and paid a "dividend" in bonded whiskey.

and shareholders may be required to return the payment to the corporation or its creditors. Whenever dividends are illegal or improper, the board of directors can be held personally liable for the amount of the payment. When directors can show that a shareholder knew that a dividend was illegal when it was received, however, the directors are entitled to reimbursement from the shareholder.

Directors' Failure to Declare a Dividend   When directors fail to declare a dividend, shareholders can ask a court to compel the directors to meet and to declare a dividend. To succeed, the shareholders must show that the directors have acted so unreasonably in withholding the dividend that their conduct is an abuse of their discretion.

Often, a corporation accumulates large cash reserves for a bona fide purpose, such as expansion, research, or other legitimate corporate goals. The mere fact that the firm has sufficient earnings or surplus available to pay a dividend is not enough to compel directors to distribute funds that, in the board's opinion, should not be distributed. The courts are reluctant to interfere with corporate operations and will not compel directors to declare dividends unless abuse of discretion is clearly shown.

Inspection Rights   Shareholders in a corporation enjoy both common law and statutory inspection rights. The shareholder's right of inspection is limited, however, to the inspection and copying of corporate books and records for a *proper purpose*. In addition, the request must be made in advance. The shareholder can inspect in person, or an attorney, accountant, or other type of assistant can do so as the shareholder's agent. The RMBCA requires the corporation to maintain an alphabetical voting list of shareholders with addresses and number of shares owned; this list must be kept open at the annual meeting for inspection by any shareholder of record [RMBCA 7.20].

The power of inspection is fraught with potential abuses, and the corporation is allowed to protect itself from them. For example, a shareholder can properly be denied access to corporate records to prevent harassment or to protect trade secrets or other confidential corporate information. A shareholder who is denied the right of inspection can seek a court order to compel the inspection.

A General Motors shareholder asks a question at the company's annual stockholders' meeting. Shareholders have a limited right to inspect and copy corporate books and records, provided the request is made in advance rather than impromptu in an open forum like a shareholders' meeting. What other limitations are placed on shareholders' inspection rights?
(AP Photo/Chris Gardner)

Transfer of Shares   Corporate stock represents an ownership right in intangible personal property. The law generally recognizes the right to transfer stock to another person unless there are valid restrictions on its transferability. Although stock certificates are negotiable and freely transferable by indorsement and delivery, transfer of stock in closely held corporations usually is restricted. These restrictions must be reasonable and may be set out in the bylaws or in a shareholder agreement. The existence of any restrictions on transferability must always be indicated on the face of the stock certificate.

Sometimes, corporations or their shareholders restrict transferability by reserving the option to purchase any shares offered for resale by a shareholder. This **right of first refusal** remains with the corporation or the shareholders for only a specified time or a reasonable period. Variations on the purchase option are possible. For example, a shareholder might be required to offer the shares to other shareholders first or to the corporation first.

When shares are transferred, a new entry is made in the corporate stock book to indicate the new owner. Until the corporation is notified and the entry is complete, all rights—including voting rights, the right to notice of shareholders' meetings, and the right to dividend distributions—remain with the current record owner.

RIGHT OF FIRST REFUSAL
The right to purchase personal or real property—such as corporate shares or real estate—before the property is offered for sale to others.

Rights on Dissolution   When a corporation is dissolved and its outstanding debts and the claims of its creditors have been satisfied, the remaining assets are distributed to the shareholders in proportion to the percentage of shares owned by each shareholder. Certain classes of stock can be given priority. If no class of stock has been given preferences in the distribution of assets on liquidation, then all of the stockholders share the remaining assets.

In some circumstances, shareholders may petition a court to have the corporation dissolved. If, for example, the minority shareholders know that the board of directors is mishandling corporate assets, those shareholders can petition a court to appoint a *receiver* who will wind up corporate affairs and liquidate the business assets of the corporation.

The Shareholder's Derivative Suit   When those in control of a corporation—the corporate directors—fail to sue in the corporate name to redress a wrong suffered by the corporation, shareholders are permitted to do so "derivatively" in what is known as a **shareholder's derivative suit.** Before a derivative suit can be brought, some wrong must have been done to the corporation, and the shareholders must have presented their complaint to the board of directors. Only if the directors fail to solve the problem or to take appropriate action can the derivative suit go forward.

The right of shareholders to bring a derivative action is especially important when the wrong suffered by the corporation results from the actions of corporate directors or officers. This is because the directors and officers would probably want to prevent any action against themselves.

The shareholder's derivative suit is unusual in that those suing are not pursuing rights or benefits for themselves personally but are acting as guardians of the corporate entity. Therefore, any damages recovered by the suit normally go into the corporation's treasury, not to the shareholders personally. This is even if the company is a small, closely held corporation. **EXAMPLE #10** Zeon Corporation is owned by two shareholders, each holding 50 percent of the corporate shares. Suppose that one of the shareholders wants to sue the other for misusing corporate assets or usurping corporate opportunities. The plaintiff-shareholder will have

SHAREHOLDER'S DERIVATIVE SUIT
A suit brought by a shareholder to enforce a corporate cause of action against a third person.

to bring a shareholder's derivative suit (not a suit in his or her own name) because the alleged harm was suffered by Zeon, not by the plaintiff personally. Any damages awarded will go to the corporation, not to the plaintiff-shareholder. □

Duties and Liabilities of Shareholders

One of the hallmarks of the corporate organization is that shareholders are not personally liable for the debts of the corporation. If the corporation fails, shareholders can lose their investments, but that is generally the limit of their liability. As previously discussed, in certain instances of fraud, undercapitalization, or careless observance of corporate formalities, a court will pierce the corporate veil and hold the shareholders individually liable. These situations are the exception, however, not the rule.

A shareholder can also be personally liable in certain other rare instances. One relates to *watered stock*. When a corporation issues shares for less than their fair market value, the shares are referred to as **watered stock**.[13] Usually, the shareholder who receives watered stock must pay the difference to the corporation (the shareholder is personally liable). In some states, the shareholder who receives watered stock may be liable to creditors of the corporation for unpaid corporate debts.

WATERED STOCK
Shares of stock issued by a corporation for which the corporation receives, as payment, less than the stated value of the shares.

EXAMPLE #11 During the formation of a corporation, Gomez, one of the incorporators, transfers his property, Sunset Beach, to the corporation for 10,000 shares of stock. The stock has a specific face value (*par value*) of $100 per share, and thus the total price of the 10,000 shares is $1 million. After the property is transferred and the shares are issued, Sunset Beach is carried on the corporate books at a value of $1 million. On appraisal, it is discovered that the market value of the property at the time of transfer was only $500,000. The shares issued to Gomez are therefore watered stock, and he is liable to the corporation for the difference. □

In some instances, a majority shareholder is regarded as having a fiduciary duty to the corporation and to the minority shareholders. This occurs when a single shareholder (or a few shareholders acting in concert) owns a sufficient number of shares to exercise *de facto* (actual) control over the corporation. In these situations, majority shareholders owe a fiduciary duty to the minority shareholders. If they breach that duty, the majority shareholders can be held personally liable for damages.[14]

MAJOR BUSINESS FORMS COMPARED

As mentioned in Chapter 14, when deciding which form of business organization would be most appropriate, businesspersons normally take into account several factors, including ease of creation, the liability of the owners, tax considerations, and the need for capital. Each major form of business organization offers advantages and disadvantages with respect to these and other factors. Exhibit 15–4 on the next page summarizes the essential advantages and disadvantages of each form of business organization discussed in Chapter 14, as well as in this chapter.

---

13. The phrase *watered stock* was originally used to describe cattle that were kept thirsty during a long drive and then were allowed to drink large quantities of water just prior to their sale. The increased weight of the "watered stock" allowed the seller to reap a higher profit.

14. See for example, *Robbins v. Sanders*, 890 So.2d 998 (Ala. Sup.Ct. 2004).

EXHIBIT 15–4   MAJOR FORMS OF BUSINESS COMPARED

CHARACTERISTIC	SOLE PROPRIETORSHIP	PARTNERSHIP	CORPORATION
Method of creation	Created at will by owner.	Created by agreement of the parties.	Authorized by the state under the state's corporation law.
Legal position	Not a separate entity; owner is the business.	A traditional partnership is a separate legal entity in most states.	Always a legal entity separate and distinct from its owners—a legal fiction for the purposes of owning property and being a party to litigation.
Liability	Unlimited liability.	Unlimited liability.	Limited liability of shareholders—shareholders are not liable for the debts of the corporation.
Duration	Determined by owner; automatically dissolved on owner's death.	Terminated by agreement of the partners, but can continue to do business even when a partner dissociates from the partnership.	Can have perpetual existence.
Transferability of interest	Interest can be transferred, but individual's proprietorship then ends.	Although partnership interest can be assigned, assignee does not have full rights of a partner.	Shares of stock can be transferred.
Management	Completely at owner's discretion.	Each partner has a direct and equal voice in management unless expressly agreed otherwise in the partnership agreement.	Shareholders elect directors, who set policy and appoint officers.
Taxation	Owner pays personal taxes on business income.	Each partner pays pro rata share of income taxes on net profits, whether or not they are distributed.	Double taxation—corporation pays income tax on net profits, with no deduction for dividends, and shareholders pay income tax on disbursed dividends they receive.
Organizational fees, annual license fees, and annual reports	None or minimal.	None or minimal.	All required.
Transaction of business in other states	Generally no limitation.	Generally no limitation.[a]	Normally must qualify to do business and obtain certificate of authority.

a. A few states have enacted statutes requiring that foreign partnerships qualify to do business there.

EXHIBIT 15–4 MAJOR FORMS OF BUSINESS COMPARED–CONTINUED

CHARACTERISTIC	LIMITED PARTNERSHIP	LIMITED LIABILITY COMPANY	LIMITED LIABILITY PARTNERSHIP
Method of creation	Created by agreement to carry on a business for a profit. At least one party must be a general partner and the other(s) limited partner(s). Certificate of limited partnership is filed. Charter must be issued by the state.	Created by an agreement of the member-owners of the company. Articles of organization are filed. Charter must be issued by the state.	Created by agreement of the partners. A statement of qualification for the limited liability partnership is filed.
Legal position	Treated as a legal entity.	Treated as a legal entity.	Generally, treated same as a traditional partnership.
Liability	Unlimited liability of all general partners; limited partners are liable only to the extent of capital contributions.	Member-owners' liability is limited to the amount of capital contributions or investments.	Varies, but under the Uniform Partnership Act, liability of a partner for acts committed by other partners is limited.
Duration	By agreement in certificate, or by termination of the last general partner (retirement, death, and the like) or last limited partner.	Unless a single-member LLC, can have perpetual existence (same as a corporation).	Remains in existence until cancellation or revocation.
Transferability of interest	Interest can be assigned (same as in a traditional partnership), but if assignee becomes a member with consent of other partners, certificate must be amended.	Member interests are freely transferable.	Interest can be assigned same as in a traditional partnership.
Management	General partners have equal voice or by agreement. Limited partners may not retain limited liability if they actively participate in management.	Member-owners can fully participate in management, or can designate a group of persons to manage on behalf of the members.	Same as a traditional partnership.
Taxation	Generally taxed as a partnership.	LLC is not taxed, and members are taxed personally on profits "passed through" the LLC.	Same as a traditional partnership.
Organizational fees, annual license fees, and annual reports	Organizational fee required; usually not others.	Organizational fee required; others vary with states.	Fees are set by each state for filing statements of qualification, foreign qualification, and annual reports.
Transaction of business in other states	Generally no limitations.	Generally no limitation, but may vary depending on state.	Must file a statement of foreign qualification before doing business in another state.

Reviewing . . . Corporations

David Brock is on the board of directors of Firm Body Fitness, Inc., which owns a string of fitness clubs in New Mexico. Brock owns 15 percent of the Firm Body stock, and he is also employed as a tanning technician at one of the fitness clubs. After the January financial report showed that Firm Body's tanning division was operating at a substantial net loss, the board of directors, led by Marty Levinson, discussed terminating the tanning operations. Brock successfully convinced a majority of the board that the tanning division was necessary to market the club's overall fitness package. By April, the tanning division's financial losses had risen. The board hired a business analyst who conducted surveys and determined that the tanning operations did not significantly increase membership. A shareholder, Diego Peñada, discovered that Brock owned stock in Sunglow, Inc., the company from which Firm Body purchased its tanning equipment. Peñada notified Levinson, who privately reprimanded Brock. Shortly afterwards, Brock and Mandy Vail, who owned 37 percent of Firm Body stock and also held shares of Sunglow, voted to replace Levinson on the board of directors. Using the information presented in the chapter, answer the following questions.

1. What duties did Brock, as a director, owe to Firm Body?

2. Does the fact that Brock owned shares in Sunglow establish a conflict of interest? Why or why not?

3. Suppose that Firm Body brought an action against Brock claiming that he had breached the duty of loyalty by not disclosing his interest in Sunglow to the other directors. What theory might Brock use in his defense?

4. Now suppose that Firm Body did not bring an action against Brock. What type of lawsuit might Peñada be able to bring based on these facts?

Key Terms

alien corporation 495	foreign corporation 495	right of first refusal 522
articles of incorporation 500	holding company 491	S corporation 497
business judgment rule 512	inside director 509	shareholder's derivative
bylaws 501	outside director 509	suit 522
close corporation 496	pierce the corporate veil 504	stock certificate 519
commingle 505	preemptive rights 519	stock warrant 520
corporation 490	proxy 514	*ultra vires* 504
dividend 491	quorum 509	voting trust 517
domestic corporation 495	retained earnings 491	watered stock 523

Chapter Summary

The Nature and Classification of Corporations
(See pages 490–498.)

A corporation is a legal entity distinct from its owners. Formal statutory requirements, which vary somewhat from state to state, must be followed in forming a corporation.

1. *Corporate personnel*—The shareholders own the corporation. They elect a board of directors to govern the corporation. The board of directors hires corporate officers and other employees to run the daily business of the firm.

2. *Corporate taxation*—The corporation pays income tax on net profits; shareholders pay income tax on the disbursed dividends that they receive from the corporation (double-taxation feature).

The Nature and Classification of Corporations—Continued

3. *Torts and criminal acts*—The corporation is liable for the torts committed by its agents or officers within the course and scope of their employment (under the doctrine of *respondeat superior*). In some circumstances, a corporation can be held liable (and be fined) for the criminal acts of its agents and employees. In certain situations, corporate officers may be held personally liable for corporate crimes.

4. *Domestic, foreign, and alien corporations*—A corporation is referred to as a *domestic corporation* within its home state (the state in which it incorporates). A corporation is referred to as a *foreign corporation* by any state that is not its home state. A corporation is referred to as an *alien corporation* if it originates in another country but does business in the United States.

5. *Public and private corporations*—A public corporation is one formed by a government (for example, a city or town that incorporates). A private corporation is one formed wholly or in part for private benefit. Most corporations are private corporations.

6. *Nonprofit corporations*—Corporations formed without a profit-making purpose (for example, charitable, educational, and religious organizations and hospitals).

7. *Close corporations*—Corporations owned by a family or a relatively small number of individuals. Transfer of shares is usually restricted, and the corporation cannot make a public offering of its securities.

8. *S corporations*—Small domestic corporations (must have no more than one hundred shareholders) that, under Subchapter S of the Internal Revenue Code, are given special tax treatment. These corporations allow shareholders to enjoy the limited legal liability of the corporate form but avoid its double-taxation feature (shareholders pay taxes on the income at personal income tax rates, and the S corporation is not taxed separately).

9. *Professional corporations*—Corporations formed by professionals (for example, physicians or lawyers) to obtain the benefits of incorporation (such as tax benefits and limited liability).

Corporate Formation
(See pages 498–504.)

1. *Promotional activities*—Preliminary promotional activities are rarely if ever undertaken today. A person who enters contracts with investors and others on behalf of the future corporation is personally liable on all preincorporation contracts. Liability remains until the corporation is formed and assumes the contract by novation.

2. *Incorporation procedures*—Exact procedures for incorporation differ among states, but the basic steps are as follows: (a) select a state of incorporation, (b) secure the corporate name by confirming its availability, (c) prepare the articles of incorporation, and (d) file the articles of incorporation with the secretary of state accompanied by payment of the specified fees.

   a. The articles of incorporation must include the corporate name, the number of shares of stock the corporation is authorized to issue, the registered office and agent, and the names and addresses of the incorporators. The articles may (but are not required to) include additional information about the corporation's nature and purpose, a statement limiting its duration (a corporation has perpetual existence unless the articles state otherwise), and specifics on its internal organization.

   b. The state's filing of the articles of incorporation (corporate charter) authorizes the corporation to conduct business.

   c. The first organizational meeting is held after incorporation. The board of directors is elected, and other business is completed (for example, adopting bylaws and authorizing the issuance of shares).

3. De jure *or* de facto *corporation*—If a corporation has been improperly incorporated, the courts will sometimes impute corporate status to the firm by holding that it is a *de jure* corporation (cannot be challenged by the state or third persons) or a *de facto* corporation (can be challenged by the state but not by third persons).

CONTINUED

Corporate Formation—Continued	4. *Corporation by estoppel*—If a firm is neither a *de jure* nor a *de facto* corporation but represents itself to be a corporation and is sued as such by a third party, it may be held to be a corporation by estoppel.
	5. *Corporate powers*—The express powers of a corporation are granted by the federal constitution, state constitutions, state statutes, articles of incorporation, bylaws, and resolutions of the board of directors. Barring express constitutional, statutory, or other prohibitions, the corporation has the implied power to do all acts reasonably appropriate and necessary to accomplish its corporate purposes.
	6. *Ultra vires doctrine*—Any act of a corporation that is beyond its express or implied powers to undertake is an *ultra vires* act and may lead to liability for damages.
Piercing the Corporate Veil (See pages 504–507.)	To avoid injustice, courts may "pierce the corporate veil" and hold a shareholder or shareholders personally liable for a judgment against the corporation. This usually occurs only when the corporation was established to circumvent the law, when the corporate form is used for an illegitimate or fraudulent purpose, or when the controlling shareholder commingles his or her own interests with those of the corporation to such an extent that the corporation no longer has a separate identity.
Directors and Officers (See pages 507–513.)	1. *Role of directors*—The board of directors is the ultimate authority in every corporation and makes all policy decisions. Directors are responsible for declaring and paying corporate dividends to shareholders; authorizing major corporate decisions; appointing, supervising, and removing corporate officers and other managerial employees; determining employees' compensation; and making financial decisions, such as the decision to issue authorized shares and bonds. Directors may delegate some of their responsibilities to executive committees and corporate officers and executives. The board of directors conducts business by holding formal meetings with recorded minutes.
	2. *Rights of directors*—Directors' rights include the rights of participation, inspection, compensation, and indemnification. Compensation is usually specified in the corporate articles or bylaws.
	3. *Corporate officers and executives*—Corporate officers and other executive employees are normally hired by the board of directors. As employees, corporate officers and executives have the rights defined by their employment contracts. The duties of corporate officers are the same as those of directors.
	4. *Duty of care*—Directors and officers are obligated to act in good faith, to use prudent business judgment in the conduct of corporate affairs, and to act in the corporation's best interests. If a director fails to exercise this duty of care, she or he can be answerable to the corporation and to the shareholders for breaching the duty.
	5. *Duty of loyalty*—Directors and officers have a fiduciary duty to subordinate their own interests to those of the corporation in matters relating to the corporation.
	6. *Conflicts of interest*—To fulfill their duty of loyalty, directors and officers must make a full disclosure of any potential conflicts between their personal interests and those of the corporation.
	7. *The business judgment rule*—This rule immunizes directors and officers from liability when they acted in good faith, acted in the best interests of the corporation, and exercised due care. For the rule to apply, the directors and officers must have made an informed, reasonable, and loyal decision.
Shareholders (See pages 513–523.)	1. *Shareholders' powers*—Shareholders' powers include the approval of all fundamental changes affecting the corporation and the election of the board of directors.
	2. *Shareholders' meetings*—Shareholders' meetings must occur at least annually; special meetings can be called when necessary. Notice of the date, time, and place of the meeting (and its purpose, if it is specially called) must be sent to shareholders. Shareholders may

Shareholders— Continued

vote by proxy (authorizing someone else to vote their shares) and may submit proposals to be included in the company's proxy materials sent to shareholders before meetings.

3. *Shareholder voting*—A minimum number of shareholders (a quorum—generally, more than 50 percent of shares held) must be present at a meeting for business to be conducted; resolutions are passed (usually) by simple majority vote. Cumulative voting may or may not be required or permitted. Cumulative voting gives minority shareholders a better chance to be represented on the board of directors. A shareholder may appoint a proxy (substitute) to vote her or his shares.

4. *Rights of shareholders*—Shareholders have numerous rights, which may include the following:

   a. The right to a stock certificate, preemptive rights, and the right to stock warrants (depending on the articles of incorporation).

   b. The right to obtain a dividend (at the discretion of the directors).

   c. Voting rights.

   d. The right to inspect the corporate records.

   e. The right to transfer shares (this right may be restricted in close corporations).

   f. The right to a share of corporate assets when the corporation is dissolved.

   g. The right to sue on behalf of the corporation (bring a shareholder's derivative suit) when the directors fail to do so.

5. *Duties and liabilities of shareholders*—Shareholders may be liable for the retention of illegal dividends and for the value of watered stock.

For Review

1. What steps are involved in bringing a corporation into existence? Who is liable for preincorporation contracts?
2. What is the difference between a *de jure* corporation and a *de facto* corporation?
3. In what circumstances might a court disregard the corporate entity ("pierce the corporate veil") and hold the shareholders personally liable?
4. What are the duties of corporate directors and officers?
5. What is a voting proxy? What is cumulative voting?

Questions and Case Problems

15-1. Nature of the Corporation. Jonathan, Gary, and Ricardo are active members of a partnership called Swim City. The partnership manufactures, sells, and installs outdoor swimming pools in the states of Arkansas and Texas. The partners want to continue to be active in management and to expand the business into other states as well. They are also concerned about rather large recent judgments entered against swimming pool companies throughout the United States. Based on these facts only, discuss whether the partnership should incorporate.

Question with Sample Answer

15-2. AstroStar, Inc., has a board of directors consisting of three members (Eckhart, Dolan, and Macero) and has approximately five hundred shareholders. At a regular board meeting, the board selects Galiard as president of the corporation by a two-to-one vote, with Eckhart dissenting. The minutes of the meeting do not register Eckhart's dissenting vote. Later, an audit discovers that

Galiard is a former convict and has embezzled $500,000 from the corporation that is not covered by insurance. Can the corporation hold directors Eckhart, Dolan, and Macero personally liable? Discuss.

For a sample answer to Question 15–2, go to Appendix I at the end of this text.

15–3. Fiduciary Duties and Liabilities. In 1978, David Brandt and Dean Somerville incorporated Posilock Puller, Inc. (PPI), to make and market bearing pullers. Each received half of the stock. Initially operating out of McHenry, North Dakota, PPI moved to Cooperstown, North Dakota, in 1984 into a building owned by Somerville. After the move, Brandt's participation in PPI diminished, and Somerville's increased. In 1998, Somerville formed PL MFG as his own business to make components for the bearing pullers and sell the parts to PPI. The start-up costs included a $450,000 loan from Sheyenne Valley Electric Cooperative. PPI executed the loan documents and indorsed the check. The proceeds were deposited into an account for PL MFG, which did not sign a promissory note payable to PPI until 2000. When Brandt learned of PL MFG and the loan, he filed a suit in a North Dakota state court against Somerville, alleging, in part, a breach of fiduciary duty. What fiduciary duty does a director owe to his or her corporation? What does this duty require? Should the court hold Somerville liable? Why or why not? [*Brandt v. Somerville,* 2005 ND 35, 692 N.W.2d 144 (2005)]

Case Problem with Sample Answer

15–4. Thomas Persson and Jon Nokes founded Smart Inventions, Inc., in 1991 to market household consumer products. The success of their first product, the Smart Mop, continued with later products, which were sold through infomercials and other means. Persson and Nokes were the firm's officers and equal shareholders, with Persson responsible for product development and Nokes in charge of day-to-day operations. By 1998, they had become dissatisfied with each other's efforts. Nokes represented the firm as financially "dying," "in a grim state, . . . worse than ever," and offered to buy all of Persson's shares for $1.6 million. Persson accepted. On the day that they signed the agreement to transfer the shares, Smart Inventions began marketing a new product—the Tap Light—which was an instant success, generating millions of dollars in revenues. In negotiating with Persson, Nokes had intentionally kept the Tap Light a secret. Persson filed a suit in a California state court against Smart Inventions and others, asserting fraud and other claims. Under what principle might Smart Inventions be liable for Nokes's fraud? Is Smart Inventions liable in this case? Explain.

[*Persson v. Smart Inventions, Inc.,* 125 Cal.App.4th 1141, 23 Cal.Rptr.3d 335 (2 Dist. 2005)]

After you have answered Problem 15–4, compare your answer with the sample answer given on the Web site that accompanies this text. Go to www.cengage.com/blaw/let, select "Chapter 15," and click on "Case Problem with Sample Answer."

15–5. Duties of Majority Shareholders. Steve and Marie Venturini were involved in the operation of Steve's Sizzling Steakhouse in Carlstadt, New Jersey, from the day their parents opened it in the 1930s. By the 1980s, Steve, Marie, and her husband Joe were running it. The business was a corporation with Steve and Marie each owning half of the stock. Steve died in 2001, leaving his stock in equal shares to his sons Steve and Gregg. Son Steve had never worked there. Gregg did occasional maintenance work until his father's death. Despite their lack of participation, the sons were paid more than $750 per week each. In 2002, Marie's son Blaise, who had obtained a college degree in restaurant management while working part-time at the steakhouse, took over its management. When his cousins became threatening, he denied them access to the business and its books. Marie refused Gregg and Steve's offer of about $1.4 million for her stock in the restaurant, and they refused her offer of about $800,000 for theirs. They filed a suit in a New Jersey state court against her, claiming, among other things, a breach of fiduciary duty. Should the court order the aunt to buy out the nephews or the nephews to buy out the aunt, or neither? Why? [*Venturini v. Steve's Steakhouse, Inc.,* __ N.J.Super. __, __ A.2d __ (Ch.Div. 2006)]

15–6. Fiduciary Duties and Liabilities. Harry Hoaas and Larry Griffiths were shareholders in Grand Casino, Inc., which owned and operated a casino in Watertown, South Dakota. Griffiths owned 51 percent of the stock and Hoaas 49 percent. Hoaas managed the casino, which Griffiths typically visited once a week. At the end of 1997, an accounting showed that the cash on hand was less than the amount posted in the casino's books. Later, more shortfalls were discovered. In October 1999, Griffiths did a complete audit. Hoaas was unable to account for $135,500 in missing cash. Griffiths then kept all of the casino's most recent profits, including Hoaas's $9,447.20 share, and, without telling Hoaas, sold the casino for $100,000 and kept all of the proceeds. Hoaas filed a suit in a South Dakota state court against Griffiths, asserting, among other things, a breach of fiduciary duty. Griffiths countered with evidence of Hoaas's misappropriation of corporate cash. What duties did these parties owe each other? Did either Griffiths or Hoaas, or both of them, breach those duties? How should their dispute be resolved? How should their finances be reconciled? Explain. [*Hoaas v. Griffiths,* 2006 SD 27, 714 N.W.2d 61 (2006)]

15–7. Improper Incorporation. Denise Rubenstein and Christopher Mayor agreed to form Bayshore Sunrise Corp. (BSC) in New York to rent certain premises and operate a laundromat. BSC entered into a twenty-year commercial lease with Bay Shore Property Trust on April 15, 1999. Mayor signed the lease as the president of BSC. The next day—April 16—BSC's certificate of incorporation was filed with New York's secretary of state. Three years later, BSC defaulted on the lease, which resulted in its termination. Rubenstein and BSC filed a suit in a New York state court against Mayor, his brother-in-law Thomas Castellano, and Planet Laundry, Inc., claiming wrongful interference with a contractual relationship. The plaintiffs alleged that Mayor and Castellano conspired to squeeze Rubenstein out of BSC and arranged the default on the lease so that Mayor and Castellano could form and operate their own business, Planet Laundry, at the same address. The defendants argued that they could not be liable on the plaintiffs' claim because there had never been an enforceable lease—BSC lacked the capacity to enter into contracts on April 15. What theory might Rubenstein and BSC assert to refute this argument? Discuss. [*Rubenstein v. Mayor,* 41 A.D.3d 826, 839 N.Y.S.2d 170 (2 Dept. 2007)]

A Question of Ethics

15–8. New Orleans Paddlewheels, Inc. (NOP), is a Louisiana corporation formed in 1982, when James Smith, Sr., and Warren Reuther were its only shareholders, with each holding 50 percent of the stock. NOP is part of a sprawling enterprise of tourism and hospitality companies in New Orleans. The positions on the board of each company were split equally between the Smith and Reuther families. At Smith's request, his son James Smith, Jr. (JES), became involved in the businesses. In 1999, NOP's board elected JES as president, to be in charge of day-to-day operations, and Reuther as chief executive officer (CEO), to be in charge of marketing and development. Over the next few years, animosity developed between Reuther and JES. In October 2001, JES terminated Reuther as CEO and denied him access to the offices and books of NOP and the other companies, literally changing the locks on the doors. At the next meetings of the boards of NOP and the overall enterprise, deadlock ensued, with the directors voting along family lines on every issue. Complaining that the meetings were a "waste of time," JES began to run the entire enterprise by taking advantage of an unequal balance of power on the companies' executive committees.

In NOP's subsequent bankruptcy proceeding, Reuther filed a motion for the appointment of a trustee to formulate a plan for the firm's reorganization, alleging, among other things, misconduct by NOP's management. [*In re New Orleans Paddlewheels, Inc.,* 350 Bankr. 667 (E.D.La. 2006)]

1. Was Reuther legally entitled to have access to the books and records of NOP and the other companies? JES maintained, among other things, that NOP's books were "a mess." Was JES's denial of that access unethical? Explain.
2. How would you describe JES's attempt to gain control of NOP and the other companies? Were his actions deceptive and self-serving in the pursuit of personal gain or legitimate and reasonable in the pursuit of a business goal? Discuss.

Critical-Thinking Managerial Question

15–9. Tim Rodale, one of the directors of First National Bank, fails to attend any board of directors' meetings in five and a half years, never inspects any of the bank's books or records, and generally neglects to supervise the efforts of the bank president and the loan committee. Meanwhile, the bank president makes various improper loans and permits large overdrafts. Can Rodale be held liable to the bank for losses resulting from the unsupervised actions of the bank president and the loan committee? Explain.

Video Question

15–10. Go to this text's Web site at **www.cengage.com/blaw/let** and select "Chapter 15." Click on "Video Questions" and view the video titled *Corporation or LLC: Which Is Better?* Then answer the following questions.

1. Compare the liability that Anna and Caleb would be exposed to as shareholders/owners of a corporation versus as members of a limited liability company (LLC).
2. How does the taxation of corporations and LLCs differ?
3. Given that Anna and Caleb conduct their business (Wizard Internet) over the Internet, can you think of any drawbacks to forming an LLC?
4. If you were in the position of Anna and Caleb, would you choose to create a corporation or an LLC? Why?

Interacting with the Internet

For updated links to resources available on the Web, as well as a variety of other materials, visit this text's Web site at

www.cengage.com/blaw/let

One of the best sources on the Web for information on corporations, including their directors, is the EDGAR database of the Securities and Exchange Commission (SEC) at

www.sec.gov/edgar.shtml

Cornell University's Legal Information Institute has links to state corporation statutes at

topics.law.cornell.edu/wex/state_statutes.html

PRACTICAL INTERNET EXERCISES

Go to this text's Web site at **www.cengage.com/blaw/let**, select "Chapter 15," and click on "Practical Internet Exercises." There you will find the following Internet research exercises that you can perform to learn more about the topics covered in this chapter.

Practical Internet Exercise 15–1: LEGAL PERSPECTIVE—**Liability of Directors and Officers**
Practical Internet Exercise 15–2: MANAGEMENT PERSPECTIVE—**D & O Insurance**
Practical Internet Exercise 15–3: TECHNOLOGICAL PERSPECTIVE—**Online Incorporation**

BEFORE THE TEST

Go to this text's Web site at **www.cengage.com/blaw/let**, select "Chapter 15," and click on "Interactive Quizzes." You will find a number of interactive questions relating to this chapter.

Chapter 16

Agency

CONTENTS

"[It] is a universal principle in the law of agency, that the powers of the agent are to be exercised for the benefit of the principal only, and not of the agent or of third parties."

— JOSEPH STORY,
1779–1845 (Associate justice of the United States Supreme Court, 1811–1844)

One of the most common, important, and pervasive legal relationships is that of **agency.** In an agency relationship between two parties, one of the parties, called the *agent,* agrees to represent or act for the other, called the *principal.* The principal has the right to control the agent's conduct in matters entrusted to the agent, and the agent must exercise his or her powers "for the benefit of the principal only," as Justice Joseph Story indicated in the chapter-opening quotation. By using agents, a principal can conduct multiple business operations simultaneously in various locations. Thus, for example, contracts that bind the principal can be made at different places with different persons at the same time.

Agency relationships permeate the business world. Indeed, agency law is essential to the existence and operation of a corporate entity, because only through its agents can a corporation function and enter into contracts. A familiar example of an agent is a corporate officer who serves in a representative capacity for the owners of the corporation. In this capacity, the officer has the authority to bind the principal (the corporation) to a contract.

AGENCY
A relationship between two parties in which one party (the agent) agrees to represent or act for the other (the principal).

AGENCY RELATIONSHIPS

Section 1(1) of the *Restatement (Second) of Agency*[1] defines agency as "the fiduciary relation which results from the manifestation of consent by one person to another that the other shall act in his [or her] behalf and subject to his [or her]

---

1. The *Restatement (Second) of Agency* is an authoritative summary of the law of agency and is often referred to by judges and other legal professionals.

control, and consent by the other so to act." In other words, in a principal-agent relationship, the parties have agreed that the agent will act *on behalf and instead of* the principal in negotiating and transacting business with third parties.

The term **fiduciary** is at the heart of agency law. The term can be used both as a noun and as an adjective. When used as a noun, it refers to a person having a duty created by her or his undertaking to act primarily for another's benefit in matters connected with the undertaking. When used as an adjective, as in "fiduciary relationship," it means that the relationship involves trust and confidence.

Agency relationships commonly exist between employers and employees. Agency relationships may sometimes also exist between employers and independent contractors who are hired to perform special tasks or services.

Employer-Employee Relationships

Normally, all employees who deal with third parties are deemed to be agents. A salesperson in a department store, for instance, is an agent of the store's owner (the principal) and acts on the owner's behalf. Any sale of goods made by the salesperson to a customer is binding on the principal. Similarly, most representations of fact made by the salesperson with respect to the goods sold are binding on the principal.

Because employees who deal with third parties are normally deemed to be agents of their employers, agency law and employment law overlap considerably. Agency relationships, though, as will become apparent, can exist outside an employer-employee relationship and thus have a broader reach than employment laws do. Additionally, bear in mind that agency law is based on the common law. In the employment realm, many common law doctrines have been displaced by statutory law and government regulations relating to employment relationships.

Employment laws (state and federal) apply only to the employer-employee relationship. Statutes governing Social Security, withholding taxes, workers' compensation, unemployment compensation, workplace safety, employment discrimination, and the like (see Chapters 17 and 18) are applicable only if employer-employee status exists. *These laws do not apply to an independent contractor.*

Employer–Independent Contractor Relationships

Independent contractors are not employees because, by definition, those who hire them have no control over the details of their physical performance. Section 2 of the *Restatement (Second) of Agency* defines an **independent contractor** as follows:

> [An independent contractor is] a person who contracts with another to do something for him [or her] but who is not controlled by the other nor subject to the other's right to control with respect to his [or her] physical conduct in the performance of the undertaking. *He [or she] may or may not be an agent.* [Emphasis added.]

Building contractors and subcontractors are independent contractors; a property owner does not control the acts of either of these professionals. Truck drivers who own their equipment and hire themselves out on a per-job basis are independent contractors, but truck drivers who drive company trucks on a regular basis are usually employees.

The relationship between a person or firm and an independent contractor may or may not involve an agency relationship. To illustrate: An owner of real estate who hires a real estate broker to negotiate a sale of his or her property not only has contracted with an independent contractor (the real estate broker) but also has

FIDUCIARY
As a noun, a person having a duty created by his or her undertaking to act primarily for another's benefit in matters connected with the undertaking. As an adjective, a relationship founded on trust and confidence.

INDEPENDENT CONTRACTOR
One who works for, and receives payment from, an employer but whose working conditions and methods are not controlled by the employer. An independent contractor is not an employee but may be an agent.

established an agency relationship for the specific purpose of assisting in the sale of the property. Another example is an insurance agent, who is both an independent contractor and an agent of the insurance company for which she or he sells policies. (Note that an insurance *broker,* in contrast, normally is an agent of the person obtaining insurance and not of the insurance company.)

Determining Employee Status

The courts are frequently asked to determine whether a particular worker is an employee or an independent contractor. How a court decides this issue can have an effect on the rights and liabilities of the parties. Employers are required to pay certain taxes, such as Social Security and unemployment taxes, for employees but not for independent contractors. Those who hire independent contractors may also do so in an effort to avoid liability for negligence, as discussed in this chapter's *Management Perspective* feature on page 536.

An independent contractor communicates from a building site. What are some significant differences between employees and independent contractors?
(Greg Younger/Creative Commons)

Criteria Used by the Courts   In determining whether a worker has the status of an employee or an independent contractor, the courts often consider the following questions:

1. How much control can the employer exercise over the details of the work? (If an employer can exercise considerable control over the details of the work, this would indicate employee status. This is perhaps the most important factor weighed by the courts in determining employee status.)
2. Is the worker engaged in an occupation or business distinct from that of the employer? (If so, this points to independent-contractor status, not employee status.)
3. Is the work usually done under the employer's direction or by a specialist without supervision? (If the work is usually done under the employer's direction, this would indicate employee status.)
4. Does the employer supply the tools at the place of work? (If so, this would indicate employee status.)
5. For how long is the person employed? (If the person is employed for a long period of time, this would indicate employee status.)
6. What is the method of payment—by time period or at the completion of the job? (Payment by time period, such as once every two weeks or once a month, would indicate employee status.)
7. What degree of skill is required of the worker? (If little skill is required, this may indicate employee status.)

Sometimes, workers may benefit from having employee status—for tax purposes and to be protected under certain employment laws, for example. As mentioned earlier, federal statutes governing employment discrimination apply only when an employer-employee relationship exists. Protection under employment discrimination statutes provides significant incentive for workers to claim that they are employees rather than independent contractors. EXAMPLE #1 A Puerto Rican television station, WIPR, contracted with a woman to co-host a television show profiling cities in Puerto Rico. The woman signed a new contract for each episode, each of which required her to work a certain number of days. She was under no other commitment to work for WIPR and was free to pursue other

Management Faces a Legal Issue

It is common for managers to hire independent contractors. They do so for a variety of reasons, including reducing paperwork and taxes that have to be paid for employees. More important, managers wish to avoid negligence lawsuits. As a general rule, employers are not liable for torts that an independent contractor commits against third parties. Nevertheless, there are exceptions. If an employer exercises significant control over the activity of the independent contractor, the contractor may be considered an employee. Consequently, the employer can be liable for the contractor's torts.

What the Courts Say

In a case involving a trucking company, the company hired independent contractors to make deliveries. A motorist was killed in a collision with one such independent contractor. At trial, the defendant trucking company prevailed. The plaintiff argued that the trucking company failed to investigate the background, qualifications, or experience of the driver. The appellate court pointed out that an employer of an independent contractor has no control over the manner in which the work is done. The plaintiff failed to offer any proof as to why the trucking company should have investigated the truck driver.[a]

In another case, a tenant whose hand was injured sued the building's owner. The owner had hired an independent contractor to perform repair work on the outside of the building. When the contractor attempted to close the tenant's balcony door, the tenant injured her hand. The appellate court ultimately held that the building's owner and its managing agent could not be held liable for the independent contractor's alleged negligence. As in the previous case, the court pointed out that the employer (the building's owner) had no right to control the manner in which the work was done by the independent contractor. The tenant suffered harm because of the actions of the independent contractor, not because the premises were in disrepair.[b]

Finally, a similar outcome occurred in a case in which two employees of an independent subcontractor suffered electrical burns while working on a construction project. They sued the owner of the project as well as the electric utility. The defendants prevailed at trial and, on appeal, the court agreed.[c]

Implications for Managers

It is best to require in any contract with an independent contractor that the contractor assume liability for harm to a third person caused by the contractor's negligence. Require that the contractor carry liability insurance. Make sure that the policy is current. Do not do anything that would lead a third party to believe that an independent contractor is your employee. And, of course, do not maintain control over the actions of the independent contractor.

a. *Standar v. Dispoz-O-Products, Inc.,* 973 So.2d 603 (Fla.App. 2008).

b. *Stagno v. 143-50 Hoover Owners Corp.,* 48 A.D.3d 548, 853 N.Y.S.2d 85 (2008).

c. *Dalton v. 933 Peachtree, LP,* 291 Ga.App. 123, 661 S.E.2d 156 (2008).

opportunities during the weeks between filming. WIPR did not withhold any taxes from the lump-sum amount it paid her for each contract. When the woman became pregnant, WIPR stopped contracting with her. She filed a lawsuit claiming that WIPR was discriminating against her in violation of federal laws on employment discrimination, but the court found in favor of WIPR. Because the parties had structured their relationship through the use of repeated set-length contracts and had described the woman as an independent contractor on tax documents, she could not maintain an employment discrimination suit.[2]

Criteria Used by the IRS Businesspersons should be aware that the Internal Revenue Service (IRS) has established its own criteria for determining whether a worker is an independent contractor or an employee. Although the IRS once considered twenty factors in determining a worker's status, guidelines that took effect in 1997 encourage IRS examiners to focus on just one of those factors—the degree of control the business exercises over the worker.

The IRS tends to closely scrutinize a firm's classification of its workers because, as mentioned, employers can avoid certain tax liabilities by hiring independent contractors instead of employees. Even when a firm classifies a worker as an independent contractor, if the IRS decides that the worker is actually an employee, the employer will be responsible for paying any applicable Social Security, withholding, and unemployment taxes.

2. *Alberty-Vélez v. Corporación de Puerto Rico para la Difusión Pública,* 361 F.3d 1 (1st Cir. 2004).

EXAMPLE #2 Microsoft Corporation had required a number of workers to become associated with employment agencies so that they could work for Microsoft as temporary workers. The workers sued, alleging that they were actually employees of Microsoft (rather than independent contractors) and thus entitled to participate in the company's stock option plan. The IRS determined that the workers were employees because Microsoft had exercised significant control over their work performance. A court affirmed this decision on appeal. Ultimately, Microsoft was required to pay back payroll taxes for hundreds of workers who had contractually agreed to work for Microsoft as independent contractors.[3]□

Businesspersons should be aware that the mere designation of a person as an independent contractor does not necessarily mean the employer can avoid tax liability. The courts and the IRS look behind the label to ascertain the true relationship between the worker and the business entity. Control is the most significant factor. Because of the potentially significant tax liability if the IRS determines that independent contractors are actually employees, businesspersons should seek the advice of an attorney when classifying workers as independent contractors. ■

Employee Status and "Works for Hire" Under the Copyright Act of 1976, any copyrighted work created by an employee within the scope of her or his employment at the request of the employer is a "work for hire," and the employer owns the copyright to the work. When an employer hires an independent contractor—a freelance artist, writer, or computer programmer, for example—the independent contractor owns the copyright *unless* the parties agree in writing that the work is a "work for hire" and the work falls into one of nine specific categories, including audiovisual and other works.

EXAMPLE #3 Graham marketed CD-ROM discs containing compilations of software programs that are available free to the public. Graham hired James to create a file-retrieval program that allowed users to access the software on the CDs. James built into the final version of the program a notice stating that he was the author of the program and owned the copyright. Graham removed the notice. When James sold the program to another CD-ROM publisher, Graham filed a suit claiming that James's file-retrieval program was a "work for hire" and that Graham owned the copyright to the program. The court, however, decided that James—a skilled computer programmer who controlled the manner and method of his work—was an independent contractor and not an employee for hire. Thus, James owned the copyright to the file-retrieval program.[4]□

HOW AGENCY RELATIONSHIPS ARE FORMED

Agency relationships normally are consensual; that is, they come about by voluntary consent and agreement between the parties. Generally, the agreement need not be in writing,[5] and consideration is not required. A person must have

---

3. *Vizcaino v. U.S. District Court for the Western District of Washington,* 173 F.3d 713 (9th Cir. 1999).
4. *Graham v. James,* 144 F.3d 229 (2d Cir. 1998); also see *Pittsburg State University/Kansas National Education Association v. Kansas Board of Regents/Pittsburg State University,* 280 Kansas 408, 122 P.3d 336 (2005).
5. There are two main exceptions to the statement that agency agreements need not be in writing: (1) Whenever agency authority empowers the agent to enter into a contract that the Statute of Frauds requires to be in writing, the agent's authority from the principal must likewise be in writing (this is called the *equal dignity rule,* to be discussed later in this chapter). (2) A power of attorney, which confers authority to an agent, must be in writing.

contractual capacity to be a principal. Those who cannot legally enter into contracts directly should not be allowed to do so indirectly through an agent. Any person can be an agent, though, regardless of whether he or she has the capacity to enter a contract.

An agency relationship can be created for any legal purpose. An agency relationship that is created for an illegal purpose or that is contrary to public policy is unenforceable. **EXAMPLE #4** Sharp (as principal) contracts with Blesh (as agent) to sell illegal narcotics. This agency relationship is unenforceable because selling illegal narcotics is a felony and is contrary to public policy.□ It is also illegal for physicians and other licensed professionals to employ unlicensed agents to perform professional actions.

Generally, an agency relationship can arise in four ways: by agreement of the parties, by ratification, by estoppel, and by operation of law. Here we look at each of these possibilities.

Agency by Agreement

Most agency relationships are based on an express or implied agreement that the agent will act for the principal and that the principal agrees to have the agent so act. An express agency agreement can take the form of a written contract or be created by an oral agreement. **EXAMPLE #5** Reese asks Cary, a gardener, to contract with others for the care of his lawn on a regular basis. Cary agrees. In this situation, an agency relationship exists between Reese and Cary for the lawn care.□

An agency agreement can also be implied by conduct. **EXAMPLE #6** A hotel expressly allows only Boris Koontz to park cars, but Boris has no employment contract there. The hotel's manager tells Boris when to work, as well as where and how to park the cars. The hotel's conduct amounts to a manifestation of its willingness to have Boris park its customers' cars, and Boris can infer from the hotel's conduct that he has authority to act as a parking valet. It can be inferred that Boris is an agent-employee for the hotel, his purpose being to provide valet parking services for hotel guests.□

RATIFICATION
The act of accepting and giving legal force to an obligation that previously was not enforceable.

A restaurant offers valet parking services. Can it be inferred that the parking attendant shown here is an agent of the restaurant? Why or why not?
(Valerie Everett/Creative Commons)

Agency by Ratification

On occasion, a person who is in fact not an agent (or who is an agent acting outside the scope of her or his authority) may make a contract on behalf of another (a principal). If the principal approves or affirms that contract by word or by action, an agency relationship is created by **ratification.** Ratification involves a question of intent, and intent can be expressed by either words or conduct. The basic requirements for ratification are discussed later in this chapter.

Agency by Estoppel

When a principal causes a third person to believe that another person is his or her agent, and the third person deals with the supposed agent, the principal is "estopped to deny" the agency relationship. In such a situation, the principal's actions create the *appearance* of an agency that does not in fact exist. The third person must prove that she or he *reasonably* believed that an agency relationship existed, though.[6] Facts and circumstances must show that an ordinary, prudent

---

6. These concepts also apply when a person who is in fact an agent undertakes an action that is beyond the scope of her or his authority, as will be discussed later in this chapter.

person familiar with business practice and custom would have been justified in concluding that the agent had authority.

EXAMPLE #7 Andrew accompanies Grant, a seed sales representative, to call on a customer, Steve, the proprietor of the General Seed Store. Andrew has done independent sales work but has never signed an employment agreement with Grant. Grant boasts to Steve that he wishes he had three more assistants "just like Andrew." By making this representation, Grant creates the impression that Andrew is his agent and has authority to solicit orders. Steve has reason to believe from Grant's statements that Andrew is an agent for Grant. Steve then places seed orders with Andrew. If Grant does not correct the impression that Andrew is an agent, Grant will be bound to fill the orders just as if Andrew were really his agent. Grant's representation to Steve created the impression that Andrew was Grant's agent and had authority to solicit orders.□

Note that the acts or declarations of a purported *agent* in and of themselves do not create an agency by estoppel. Rather, it is the deeds or statements *of the principal* that create an agency by estoppel. **EXAMPLE #8** If Andrew walks into Steve's store and claims to be Grant's agent, when in fact he is not, and Grant has no knowledge of Andrew's representations, Grant will not be bound to any deal struck by Andrew and Steve. Andrew's acts and declarations alone do not create an agency by estoppel.□

Under what other circumstances might a third party reasonably believe that an agent has the authority to act for a principal when the agent actually does not have this authority? The following case provides an illustration.

Case 16.1 Motorsport Marketing, Inc. v. Wiedmaier, Inc.

Missouri Court of Appeals, Western District, 2006.
195 S.W.3d 492.
www.courts.mo.gov[a]

BACKGROUND AND FACTS Wiedmaier, Inc., owns and operates Wiedmaier Truck Stop in St. Joseph, Missouri. The owners are Marsha Wiedmaier and her husband, Jerry. Their son Michael does not own an interest in the firm, but in 2002 and 2003, he worked for it as a fuel truck operator. Motorsport Marketing, Inc., sells racing collectibles and memorabilia to retail outlets. In April 2003, Michael faxed a

a. In the "Quick Links" box, click on "Opinion & Minutes." When that page opens, click on the "Missouri Court of Appeals, Western District opinions" link. On the next page, click on the "Search Opinions" link. In that page's "Search for" box, type "Wiedmaier" and click on "Search." In the result, click on the name of the case to access the opinion. The Missouri state courts maintain this Web site.

credit application to Motorsport's sales manager, Lesa James. Michael's mother, Marsha, signed the form as "Secretary-Owner" of Wiedmaier; after she signed, Michael added himself to the list of owners. A credit line was approved. Michael formed Extreme Diecast, LLC, and told Motorsport that it was part of Wiedmaier. He then began ordering Motorsport merchandise. By early 2004, however, Michael had stopped making payments on the account, quit his job, and moved to Columbus, Ohio. Patrick Rainey, the president of Motorsport, contacted Marsha about the account, but she refused to pay. Motorsport filed a suit in a Missouri state court against Wiedmaier and others to collect the unpaid amount. The court entered a judgment in favor of Motorsport, assessing liability against the defendants for the outstanding balance of $93,388.58, plus $13,406.38 in interest and $25,165.93 in attorneys' fees. The defendants appealed to a state intermediate appellate court.

IN THE WORDS OF THE COURT . . . *VICTOR C. HOWARD*, Presiding Judge.

* * * *

To establish the apparent authority of a purported agent, Motorsport must show that

(1) the principal manifested his consent to the exercise of such authority or knowingly permitted the agent to assume the exercise of such authority; (2) the person relying on this exercise of authority knew of the facts and, acting in good faith, had reason to believe, and actually

CASE 16.1–CONTINUED

CASE 16.1–CONTINUED

*believed, the agent possessed such authority; and (3) the person relying on the appearance of authority changed his position and will be injured or suffer loss if the transaction executed by the agent does not bind the principal. *   *   * [Emphasis added.]*

We find that Motorsport has shown that each of the criteria for establishing Michael's apparent agency has been satisfied. First, *   *   * the credit application constituted a direct communication from Wiedmaier, Inc. (through Marsha) to Motorsport causing Motorsport to reasonably believe that Michael had authority to act for Wiedmaier, Inc.

Second, Motorsport, relying on Michael's exercise of authority and acting in good faith, had reason to believe, and actually believed, that Michael possessed such authority. Motorsport received a credit application from Wiedmaier, Inc. signed by owner Marsha Wiedmaier, listing Michael as an owner. Motorsport had no reason to believe that Michael was not an owner of Wiedmaier or was otherwise unauthorized to act on Wiedmaier, Inc.'s behalf.

Wiedmaier, Inc. argues that even if Motorsport's reliance on Michael's apparent authority was reasonably prudent on April 10, 2003, when Michael submitted the credit application, such reliance could not have been and was not reasonably prudent from and after June 23, 2003. At that time, Michael personally made the first payment on the account with a check drawn on the account of Extreme Diecast. *   *   * At the very least, Wiedmaier, Inc. argues, Motorsport had "red flags waving all around it suggesting that Michael was something other than the agent of Wiedmaier, Inc."

We find that this argument is without merit. *   *   * It is a common practice for a truck stop to have a separate division with a separate name to handle its diecast and other related merchandise, and *   *   * Michael represented that this is exactly what Extreme Diecast was. *   *   * This evidence explains what Wiedmaier, Inc. characterizes as "red flags" concerning Michael's authority to act on behalf of Wiedmaier, Inc., and negates any alleged duty on Motorsport's part to investigate Michael's authority.

Third, Motorsport changed its position and will be injured or suffer loss if the transaction executed by Michael does not bind Wiedmaier, Inc. Motorsport extended credit to Wiedmaier, Inc. based on its interaction with Michael and based on its belief that it was dealing with Wiedmaier, Inc. Marsha Wiedmaier has refused to pay the account balance. If the transaction executed by Michael does not bind Wiedmaier, Inc., Motorsport will suffer the loss of the balance due on the account.

DECISION AND REMEDY   The state intermediate appellate court affirmed the judgment of the lower court, echoing the conclusion that "Michael acted as an apparent agent of Wiedmaier, Inc., in its dealings with Motorsport." In other words, Motorsport reasonably believed that Michael acted as Wiedmaier's agent in ordering merchandise.

WHAT IF THE FACTS WERE DIFFERENT?   Suppose that Motorsport's sales manager had telephoned Marsha Wiedmaier. Further suppose that Marsha had vouched for Michael's creditworthiness but informed Motorsport that she and her husband owned Wiedmaier and that Michael worked for them. How might the outcome of this case have been different in that situation?

THE E-COMMERCE DIMENSION   Should the court have applied the law differently in this case if Michael had done business with Motorsport entirely online? Explain.

Agency by Operation of Law

The courts may find an agency relationship in the absence of a formal agreement in other situations as well. This can occur in family relationships. For instance, suppose that one spouse purchases certain basic necessaries (such as food and clothing) and charges them to the other spouse's charge account. The courts will often rule that the latter is liable to pay for the necessaries, either because of a social policy of promoting the general welfare of the spouse or because of a legal duty to supply necessaries to family members.

Agency by operation of law may also occur in emergency situations, when the agent's failure to act outside the scope of his or her authority would cause the principal substantial loss. If the agent is unable to contact the principal, the courts will often grant this emergency power. For instance, a railroad engineer may contract on behalf of her or his employer for medical care for an injured motorist hit by the train. The *Concept Summary* reviews the various ways that agencies are formed.

DUTIES OF AGENTS AND PRINCIPALS

Once the principal-agent relationship has been created, both parties have duties that govern their conduct. As discussed previously, an agency relationship is *fiduciary*—one of trust. In a fiduciary relationship, each party owes the other the duty to act with the utmost good faith. We now examine the various duties of agents and principals.

In general, for every duty of the principal, the agent has a corresponding right, and vice versa. When one party to the agency relationship violates his or her duty to the other party, the remedies available to the nonbreaching party arise out of contract and tort law. These remedies include monetary damages, termination of the agency relationship, an injunction, and required accountings.

Agent's Duties to the Principal

Generally, the agent owes the principal five duties—performance, notification, loyalty, obedience, and accounting.

Performance   An implied condition in every agency contract is the agent's agreement to use reasonable diligence and skill in performing the work. When an agent fails entirely to perform her or his duties, liability for breach of contract normally will result. The degree of skill or care required of an agent is usually that expected of a reasonable person under similar circumstances. Generally, this is

CONCEPT SUMMARY	How Agency Relationships Are Formed
METHOD OF FORMATION	**DESCRIPTION**
By Agreement	The agency relationship is formed through express consent (oral or written) or implied by conduct.
By Ratification	The principal either by act or by agreement ratifies the conduct of a person who is not in fact an agent.
By Estoppel	The principal causes a third person to believe that another person is the principal's agent, and the third person acts to his or her detriment in reasonable reliance on that belief.
By Operation of Law	The agency relationship is based on a social duty (such as the need to support family members) or formed in emergency situations when the agent is unable to contact the principal and failure to act outside the scope of the agent's authority would cause the principal substantial loss.

interpreted to mean ordinary care. If an agent has represented himself or herself as possessing special skills, however, the agent is expected to exercise the degree of skill or skills claimed. Failure to do so constitutes a breach of the agent's duty.

Not all agency relationships are based on contract. In some situations, an agent acts gratuitously—that is, not for monetary compensation. A gratuitous agent cannot be liable for breach of contract, as there is no contract; he or she is subject only to tort liability. Once a gratuitous agent has begun to act in an agency capacity, he or she has the duty to continue to perform in that capacity in an acceptable manner and is subject to the same standards of care and duty to perform as other agents.

Notification   An agent is required to notify the principal of all matters that come to her or his attention concerning the subject matter of the agency. This is the *duty of notification,* or the duty to inform. **EXAMPLE #9** Lang, an artist, is about to negotiate a contract to sell a series of paintings to Barber's Art Gallery for $25,000. Lang's agent learns that Barber is insolvent and will be unable to pay for the paintings. Lang's agent has a duty to inform Lang of this fact because it is relevant to the subject matter of the agency—the sale of Lang's paintings.□ Generally, the law assumes that the principal knows of any information acquired by the agent that is relevant to the agency—regardless of whether the agent actually passes on this information to the principal. It is a basic tenet of agency law that notice to the agent is notice to the principal.

Loyalty   Loyalty is one of the most fundamental duties in a fiduciary relationship. Basically, the agent has the duty to act *solely for the benefit of his or her principal* and not in the interest of the agent or a third party. For example, an agent cannot represent two principals in the same transaction unless both know of the dual capacity and consent to it. The duty of loyalty also means that any information or knowledge acquired through the agency relationship is considered confidential. It would be a breach of loyalty to disclose such information either during the agency relationship or after its termination. Typical examples of confidential information are trade secrets and customer lists compiled by the principal.

In short, the agent's loyalty must be undivided. The agent's actions must be strictly for the benefit of the principal and must not result in any secret profit for the agent. **EXAMPLE #10** Don Cousins contracts with Leo Hodgins, a real estate agent, to negotiate the purchase of an office building as an investment. While working for Cousins, Hodgins discovers that the property owner will sell the building only as a package deal with another parcel. If Hodgins then forms a limited partnership with his brother to buy the two properties and resell the building to Cousins, has he breached his fiduciary duties? The answer is yes, because as a real estate agent, Hodgins has a duty to communicate all offers to his principal and not to secretly purchase the property and then resell it to his principal. Hodgins is

An agent's disclosure of confidential information could constitute the business tort of misappropriation of trade secrets.

A real estate agent meets with clients in her office. Suppose that the agent knows a buyer who is willing to pay more than the asking price for a property. What duty would the agent breach if she bought the property from the seller and sold it at a profit to that buyer?
(Yoon Hernandez/Creative Commons)

required to act in Cousins's best interests and can become the purchaser in this situation only with Cousins's knowledge and approval.[7] □

Obedience   When acting on behalf of a principal, an agent has a duty to follow all lawful and clearly stated instructions of the principal. Any deviation from such instructions is a violation of this duty. During emergency situations, however, when the principal cannot be consulted, the agent may deviate from the instructions without violating this duty. Whenever instructions are not clearly stated, the agent can fulfill the duty of obedience by acting in good faith and in a manner reasonable under the circumstances.

Accounting   Unless an agent and a principal agree otherwise, the agent has the duty to keep and make available to the principal an account of all property and funds received and paid out on behalf of the principal. This includes gifts from third parties in connection with the agency. For instance, a gift from a customer to a salesperson for prompt deliveries made by the salesperson's firm, in the absence of a company policy to the contrary, belongs to the firm. The agent has a duty to maintain separate accounts for the principal's funds and for the agent's personal funds, and the agent must not intermingle these accounts.

Principal's Duties to the Agent

The principal also owes certain duties to the agent. These duties relate to compensation, reimbursement and indemnification, cooperation, and safe working conditions.

Compensation   In general, when a principal requests certain services from an agent, the agent reasonably expects payment. The principal therefore has a duty to pay the agent for services rendered. For example, when an accountant or an attorney is asked to act as an agent, an agreement to compensate the agent for such service is implied. The principal also has a duty to pay that compensation in a timely manner. Except in a gratuitous agency relationship, in which an agent does not act in return for payment, the principal must pay the agreed-on value for an agent's services. If no amount has been expressly agreed on, the principal owes the agent the customary compensation for such services.

Preventing Legal Disputes

Many disputes arise because the principal and agent did not specify how much the agent would be paid. To avoid such disputes, businesspersons should always state in advance, and in writing, the amount or rate of compensation that they will pay their agents. Even when dealing with salespersons, such as real estate agents, who customarily are paid a percentage of the value of the sale, it is best to explicitly state the rate of compensation. When the parties are clear up front about the terms of their agency relationship, a dispute is less likely to surface. ■

Reimbursement and Indemnification   Whenever an agent disburses funds to fulfill the request of the principal or to pay for necessary expenses in the course of a reasonable performance of his or her agency duties, the principal

---

7. *Cousins v. Realty Ventures, Inc.*, 844 So.2d 860 (La.App. 5th Cir. 2003).

has the duty to reimburse the agent for these payments. Agents cannot recover for expenses incurred through their own misconduct or negligence, though.

Subject to the terms of the agency agreement, the principal has the duty to compensate, or *indemnify,* an agent for liabilities incurred because of authorized and lawful acts and transactions. For instance, if the principal fails to perform a contract formed by the agent with a third party and the third party then sues the agent, the principal is obligated to compensate the agent for any costs incurred in defending against the lawsuit.

Additionally, the principal must indemnify (pay) the agent for the value of benefits that the agent confers on the principal. The amount of indemnification is usually specified in the agency contract. If it is not, the courts will look to the nature of the business and the type of loss to determine the amount. Note that this rule applies to acts by gratuitous agents as well. If the finder of a dog that becomes sick takes the dog to a veterinarian and pays the required fees for the veterinarian's services, the agent is entitled to be reimbursed by the owner of the dog for those fees.

Cooperation   A principal has a duty to cooperate with the agent and to assist the agent in performing her or his duties. The principal must do nothing to prevent such performance.

When a principal grants an agent an exclusive territory, for example, the principal creates an *exclusive agency* and cannot compete with the agent or appoint or allow another agent to so compete. If the principal does so, she or he will be exposed to liability for the agent's lost sales or profits. **EXAMPLE #11** Akers (the principal) creates an exclusive agency by granting Johnson (the agent) an exclusive territory within which Johnson may sell Akers's products. In this situation, Akers cannot compete with Johnson within that territory—or appoint or allow another agent to so compete—because this would violate the exclusive agency. If Akers does so, he can be held liable for Johnson's lost sales or profits.□

Safe Working Conditions   Under the common law, a principal is required to provide safe working premises, equipment, and conditions for all agents and employees. The principal has a duty to inspect the working conditions and to warn agents and employees about any unsafe areas. When the agent is an employee, the employer's liability is frequently covered by state workers' compensation insurance, and federal and state statutes often require the employer to meet certain safety standards (to be discussed in Chapter 17).

AGENT'S AUTHORITY

An agent's authority to act can be either *actual* (express or implied) or *apparent.* If an agent contracts outside the scope of his or her authority, the principal may still become liable by ratifying the contract.

Actual Authority

As indicated, an agent's actual authority can be express or implied. We look here at both of these forms of actual authority.

Express Authority   *Express authority* is authority declared in clear, direct, and definite terms. Express authority can be given orally or in writing. In most states,

the **equal dignity rule** requires that if the contract being executed is or must be in writing, then the agent's authority must also be in writing. Failure to comply with the equal dignity rule can make a contract voidable *at the option of the principal.* The law regards the contract at that point as a mere offer. If the principal decides to accept the offer, acceptance must be ratified, or affirmed, in writing.

EXAMPLE #12 Klee (the principal) orally asks Parkinson (the agent) to sell a ranch that Klee owns. Parkinson finds a buyer and signs a sales contract (a contract for an interest in realty must be in writing) on behalf of Klee to sell the ranch. The buyer cannot enforce the contract unless Klee subsequently ratifies Parkinson's agency status *in writing.* Once Parkinson's agency status is ratified, either party can enforce rights under the contract.□

Modern business practice allows an exception to the equal dignity rule. An executive officer of a corporation normally is not required to obtain written authority from the corporation to conduct *ordinary* business transactions. In addition, the equal dignity rule does not apply when an agent acts in the presence of a principal or when the agent's act of signing is merely perfunctory. Thus, if Dickens (the principal) negotiates a contract but is called out of town the day it is to be signed and orally authorizes Santini to sign the contract, the oral authorization is sufficient.

Power of Attorney   Giving an agent a **power of attorney** confers express authority. The power of attorney normally is a written document and is usually notarized. (A document is notarized when a **notary public**—a public official authorized to attest to the authenticity of signatures—signs and dates the document and imprints it with his or her seal of authority.) Most states have statutory provisions for creating a power of attorney. A power of attorney can be special (permitting the agent to do specified acts only), or it can be general (permitting the agent to transact all business for the principal). Because a general power of attorney grants extensive authority to an agent to act on behalf of the principal in many ways, it should be used with great caution. Ordinarily, a power of attorney terminates on the incapacity or death of the person giving the power.[8]

Implied Authority   An agent has the *implied authority* to do what is reasonably necessary to carry out express authority and accomplish the objectives of the agency. Authority can also be implied by custom or inferred from the position the agent occupies. **EXAMPLE #13** Mueller is employed by Al's Supermarket to manage one of its stores. Al's has not expressly stated that Mueller has authority to contract with third persons. In this situation, though, authority to manage a business implies authority to do what is reasonably required (as is customary or can be inferred from a manager's position) to operate the business. This includes forming contracts to hire employees, to buy merchandise and equipment, and to advertise the products sold in the store.□ A difficult question in today's legal environment is whether an agent's implied authority terminates in the event of a breach. For a discussion of that issue, see this chapter's *Insight into Ethics* feature on the following page.

EQUAL DIGNITY RULE
In most states, a rule stating that express authority given to an agent must be in writing if the contract to be made on behalf of the principal is required to be in writing.

POWER OF ATTORNEY
A written document, which is usually notarized, authorizing another to act as one's agent; can be special (permitting the agent to do specified acts only) or general (permitting the agent to transact all business for the principal).

NOTARY PUBLIC
A public official authorized to attest to the authenticity of signatures.

---

8. A *durable* power of attorney, however, continues to be effective despite the principal's incapacity. An elderly person, for example, might grant a durable power of attorney to provide for the handling of property and investments or specific health-care needs should she or he become incompetent.

Does an agent's breach of loyalty terminate the agent's authority?

Suppose that an employee-agent who is authorized to access company trade secrets contained in computer files takes those secrets to a competitor for whom the employee is about to begin working. Clearly, in this situation the agent has violated the ethical—and legal—duty of loyalty to the principal. Does this breach of loyalty mean that the employee's act of accessing the trade secrets was unauthorized? The question has significant implications because if the act was unauthorized, the employee will be subject to state and federal laws prohibiting unauthorized access to computer information and data. If the act was authorized, the employee will not be subject to such laws.

Agent's Authority and the Computer Fraud and Abuse Act

Although a few courts have found that an employee's authority as an agent terminates the moment the employee accesses trade secrets for the purpose of divulging them to a competitor,[9] most courts hold that an agent's authority continues. In one case, for example, Jeff Gast signed a confidentiality agreement promising not to disclose trade secrets when he started as an employee at Shamrock Foods Company. Gast later became Shamrock's regional sales manager for southern Arizona. In January 2008, Gast e-mailed numerous documents containing Shamrock's confidential proprietary information to himself at his personal e-mail account. That same month, Gast quit his job at Shamrock and went to work for Sysco, a competitor.

Shamrock filed a lawsuit in a federal court in Arizona against Gast for violating the Computer Fraud and Abuse Act (CFAA, discussed in Chapter 6). Although the CFAA is primarily a criminal statute, it also provides a civil cause of action to any person who suffers damage or loss by reason of a violation of the act. To succeed, Shamrock had to show that Gast accessed a protected computer without authorization or exceeded authorized access. Gast claimed that he was authorized to access the computer and the information at issue. Shamrock argued that although Gast may previously have had the authority to access its confidential information, he lost that authority once he acquired the improper purpose of using this information to benefit himself and Sysco.

After considering both sides' arguments, the federal district court was persuaded that "without authorization" under the CFAA was meant to refer to outsiders rather than to agents who had a principal's authority to access the computer information. Gast was authorized initially to access the computer he used at Shamrock and to view the specific files containing the information. Therefore, the court concluded that Gast did not access the information at issue "without authorization" or in a manner that "exceeded authorized access" and dismissed the lawsuit.[10] Although the agent's act of stealing confidential data was unethical, the court found that it was not actionable under the CFAA.

> *"The law is not a series of calculating machines where definitions and answers come tumbling out when the right levers are pushed."*
> —WILLIAM O. DOUGLAS, 1898–1980
> (Associate justice of the United States Supreme Court, 1939–1975)

Apparent Authority

Actual authority (express or implied) arises from what the principal manifests *to the agent.* An agent has **apparent authority** when the principal, by either words or actions, causes a *third party* reasonably to believe that an agent has authority to

APPARENT AUTHORITY
Authority that is only apparent, not real. In agency law, a person may be deemed to have had the power to act as an agent for another party if the other party's manifestations to a third party led the third party to believe that an agency existed when, in fact, it did not.

9. See, for example, *International Airport Centers, LLC v. Citrin,* 440 F.3d 418 (7th Cir. 2006); and *ViChip Corp. v. Lee,* 438 F.Supp.2d 1087 (N.D.Cal. 2006).
10. *Shamrock Foods Co. v. Gast,* 535 F.Supp.2d 962 (D.Ariz. 2008). For another case example involving three employee-agents who stole confidential data from their employer-principal, see *Lockheed Martin Corp. v. Speed,* 2006 WL 2683058 (M.D.Fla. 2006).

act, even though the agent has no express or implied authority. If the third party changes her or his position in reliance on the principal's representations, the principal may be *estopped* (prevented) from denying that the agent had authority.

Apparent authority usually comes into existence through a principal's pattern of conduct over time.   **EXAMPLE #14**   Bain is a traveling salesperson with the authority to solicit orders for a principal's goods. Because she does not carry any goods with her, she normally would not have the implied authority to collect payments from customers on behalf of the principal. Suppose that she does accept payments from Corgley Enterprises, however, and submits them to the principal's accounting department for processing. If the principal does nothing to stop Bain from continuing this practice, a pattern develops over time, and the principal confers apparent authority on Bain to accept payments from Corgley. □

At issue in the following case was a question of apparent authority or, as the court referred to it, "ostensible agency."

Case 16.2 Ermoian v. Desert Hospital

Court of Appeal of California,
Fourth District, Division 2, 2007.
152 Cal.App.4th 475, 61 Cal.Rptr.3d 754.

BACKGROUND AND FACTS   In 1990, Desert Hospital in California established a comprehensive perinatal services program (CPSP) to provide obstetrical care to women who were uninsured (*perinatal* is often defined as relating to the period from about the twenty-eighth week of pregnancy to around one month after birth). The CPSP was set up in an office suite across from the hospital and named "Desert Hospital Outpatient Maternity Services Clinic." The hospital contracted with a corporation controlled by Dr. Morton Gubin, which employed Dr. Masami Ogata, to provide obstetrical services. In January 1994, Jackie Shahan went to the hospital's emergency room because of cramping and other symptoms. The emergency room physician told Shahan that she was pregnant and referred her to the clinic. Shahan visited the clinic throughout her pregnancy. On May 15, Shahan's baby, named Amanda, was born with brain abnormalities that left her severely mentally retarded and unable to care for herself. Her conditions could not have been prevented, treated, or cured *in utero*. Amanda, through her parents and a court-appointed guardian, filed a suit in a California state court against the hospital and others, alleging "wrongful life." She claimed that the defendants negligently failed to inform her mother of her abnormalities before her birth, depriving her mother of the opportunity to make an informed choice to terminate the pregnancy. The court ruled in the defendants' favor, holding, among other things, that the hospital was not liable because Drs. Gubin and Ogata were not its employees. Amanda appealed to a state intermediate appellate court, contending in part that the physicians were the hospital's "ostensible agents."

IN THE WORDS OF THE COURT . . . *KING*, J. [Judge]

*   *   *   *

Agency may be either actual or ostensible [apparent]. Actual agency exists when the agent is really employed by the principal. Here, there was evidence that the physicians were not employees of the Hospital, but were physicians with a private practice who contracted with the Hospital to perform obstetric services at the clinic. The written contract between the Hospital and Dr. Gubin's corporation (which employed Dr. Ogata) describes Dr. Gubin and his corporation as "independent contractors with, and not as employees of, [the] Hospital." [Maria Sterling, a registered nurse at the clinic and Shahan's CPSP case coordinator,] testified that Drs. Gubin and Ogata, not the Hospital, provided the obstetric services to the clinic's patients. Donna McCloudy, a director of nursing [who set up the CPSP] at the Hospital, testified that while the Hospital provided some aspects of the CPSP services, "independent physicians *   *   * provided the obstetrical care *   *   * ." Based upon such evidence, the [trial] court reasonably concluded that the physicians were not the employees or actual agents of the Hospital for purposes of vicarious [indirect] liability.

CASE 16.2–CONTINUED

CASE 16.2—CONTINUED

Ostensible [apparent] agency on the other hand, may be implied from the facts of a particular case, and if a principal by his acts has led others to believe that he has conferred authority upon an agent, he cannot be heard to assert, as against third parties who have relied thereon in good faith, that he did not intend to confer such power * * * . The doctrine establishing the principles of liability for the acts of an ostensible agent rests on the doctrine of estoppel. *The essential elements are representations by the principal, justifiable reliance thereon by a third party, and change of position or injury resulting from such reliance.* Before recovery can be had against the principal for the acts of an ostensible agent, the person dealing with an agent must do so with belief in the agent's authority and this belief must be a reasonable one. Such belief must be generated by some act or neglect by the principal sought to be charged and the person relying on the agent's apparent authority must not be guilty of neglect. [Emphasis added.]

* * * *

Here, the Hospital held out the clinic and the personnel in the clinic as part of the Hospital. Furthermore, it was objectively reasonable for Shahan to believe that Drs. Gubin and Ogata were employees of the Hospital. The clinic was located across the street from the Hospital. It used the same name as the Hospital and labeled itself as an outpatient clinic. Numerous professionals at the clinic were employees of the Hospital. [Carol Cribbs, a comprehensive perinatal health worker at the clinic] and Sterling indicated to Shahan that they were employees of the Hospital and that the program was run by the Hospital. Sterling personally set up all of Shahan's appointments at the main Hospital rather than giving Shahan a referral for the various tests. Shahan was referred by individuals in the emergency room specifically to Dr. Gubin. When she called for an appointment she was told by the receptionist that she was calling the Hospital outpatient clinic which was the clinic of Dr. Gubin. On days when Shahan would see either Dr. Gubin or Dr. Ogata at the clinic, she would also see either Cribbs or Sterling, whom she knew were employed by the Hospital.

* * * At her first appointment she signed a document titled "patient rights and responsibilities," which would unambiguously lead a patient to the conclusion that the clinic "was a one-stop shop for the patient," and that all individuals at the clinic were connected with the Hospital. All of Shahan's contacts with the physicians were at the Hospital-run clinic. Most, if not all, of the physician contacts occurred in conjunction with the provision of other services by either Sterling or Cribbs. The entire appearance created by the Hospital, and those associated with it, was that the Hospital was the provider of the obstetrical care to Shahan.

DECISION AND REMEDY   The state intermediate appellate court decided that, contrary to the lower court's finding, Drs. Gubin and Ogata were "ostensible agents of the Hospital." The appellate court affirmed the lower court's ruling, however, on Amanda's "wrongful life" claim, concluding that the physicians were not negligent in failing to advise Shahan to have an elective abortion.

THE ETHICAL DIMENSION   Does a principal have an ethical responsibility to inform an unaware third party that an apparent (ostensible) agent does not in fact have authority to act on the principal's behalf?

THE E-COMMERCE DIMENSION   Could Amanda have established Drs. Gubin and Ogata's apparent authority if Desert Hospital had maintained a Web site that advertised the services of the CPSP clinic and stated clearly that the physicians were not its employees? Explain.

Emergency Powers

When an unforeseen emergency demands action by the agent to protect or preserve the property and rights of the principal, but the agent is unable to communicate with the principal, the agent has emergency power. **EXAMPLE #15** Fulsom is an engineer for Pacific Drilling Company. While Fulsom is acting within the scope of his employment, he is severely injured in an accident at an oil rig many miles from home. Dudley, the rig supervisor, directs Thompson, a physician, to give medical aid to Fulsom and to charge Pacific for the medical services. Dudley, an agent, has no express or implied authority to bind the principal, Pacific Drilling, for Thompson's medical services. Because of the emergency situation, however, the law recognizes Dudley as having authority to act appropriately under the circumstances. □

Ratification

As already mentioned, ratification occurs when the principal affirms an agent's *unauthorized* act. When ratification occurs, the principal is bound to the agent's act, and the act is treated as if it had been authorized by the principal *from the outset.* Ratification can be either express or implied.

If the principal does not ratify the contract, the principal is not bound, and the third party's agreement with the agent is viewed as merely an unaccepted offer. Because the third party's agreement is an unaccepted offer, the third party can revoke the offer at any time, without liability, before the principal ratifies the contract.

The requirements for ratification can be summarized as follows:

1. The agent must have acted on behalf of an identified principal who subsequently ratifies the action.
2. The principal must know of all material facts involved in the transaction. If a principal ratifies a contract without knowing all of the facts, the principal can rescind (cancel) the contract.
3. The principal must affirm the agent's act in its entirety.
4. The principal must have the legal capacity to authorize the transaction at the time the agent engages in the act and at the time the principal ratifies. The third party must also have the legal capacity to engage in the transaction.
5. The principal's affirmation must occur before the third party withdraws from the transaction.
6. The principal must observe the same formalities when approving the act done by the agent as would have been required to authorize it initially.

> **BE AWARE**
> An agent who exceeds his or her authority and enters into a contract that the principal does not ratify may be liable to the third party on the ground of misrepresentation.

LIABILITY IN AGENCY RELATIONSHIPS

Frequently, a question arises as to which party, the principal or the agent, should be held liable for contracts formed by the agent or for torts or crimes committed by the agent. We look here at these aspects of agency law.

Liability for Contracts

Liability for contracts formed by an agent depends on how the principal is classified and on whether the actions of the agent were authorized or unauthorized. Principals are classified as disclosed, partially disclosed, or undisclosed.[11]

A **disclosed principal** is a principal whose identity is known by the third party at the time the contract is made by the agent. A **partially disclosed principal** is a principal whose identity is not known by the third party, but the third party

> **DISCLOSED PRINCIPAL**
> A principal whose identity is known to a third party at the time the agent makes a contract with the third party.
>
> **PARTIALLY DISCLOSED PRINCIPAL**
> A principal whose identity is unknown by a third party, but the third party knows that the agent is or may be acting for a principal at the time the agent and the third party form a contract.

---

11. *Restatement (Second) of Agency,* Section 4.

knows that the agent is or may be acting for a principal at the time the contract is made. **EXAMPLE #16** Sarah has contracted with a real estate agent to sell certain property. She wishes to keep her identity a secret, but the agent makes it perfectly clear to potential buyers of the property that the agent is acting in an agency capacity. In this situation, Sarah is a partially disclosed principal.□ An **undisclosed principal** is a principal whose identity is totally unknown by the third party, and the third party has no knowledge that the agent is acting in an agency capacity at the time the contract is made.

UNDISCLOSED PRINCIPAL
A principal whose identity is unknown by a third person, and the third person has no knowledge that the agent is acting for a principal at the time the agent and the third person form a contract.

Authorized Acts If an agent acts within the scope of her or his authority, normally the principal is obligated to perform the contract regardless of whether the principal was disclosed, partially disclosed, or undisclosed. Whether the agent may also be held liable under the contract, however, depends on the disclosed, partially disclosed, or undisclosed status of the principal.

Disclosed or Partially Disclosed Principal A disclosed or partially disclosed principal is liable to a third party for a contract made by an agent who is acting within the scope of her or his authority. If the principal is disclosed, an agent has no contractual liability for the nonperformance of the principal or the third party. If the principal is partially disclosed, in most states the agent is also treated as a party to the contract, and the third party can hold the agent liable for contractual nonperformance.[12]

EXAMPLE #17 Walgreens leased commercial property to operate a drugstore at a mall owned by Kedzie Plaza Associates. A property management company, Taxman Corporation, signed the lease on behalf of the principal, Kedzie. The lease required the landlord to keep the sidewalks free of snow and ice, so Taxman, on behalf of Kedzie, contracted with another company to remove ice and snow from the sidewalks surrounding the Walgreens store. When a Walgreens employee slipped on ice outside the store and was injured, she sued Taxman for negligence. Because the principal's identity (Kedzie) was fully disclosed in the snow-removal contract, however, the Illinois court ruled that the agent, Taxman, could not be held liable. Taxman did not assume a contractual obligation to remove the snow but merely retained a contractor to do so on behalf of the owner.[13]□

Undisclosed Principal When neither the fact of agency nor the identity of the principal is disclosed, the undisclosed principal is bound to perform just as if the principal had been fully disclosed at the time the contract was made. The agent is also liable as a party to the contract.

When a principal's identity is undisclosed and the agent is forced to pay the third party, the agent is entitled to be indemnified (compensated) by the principal. The principal had a duty to perform, even though his or her identity was undisclosed, and failure to do so will make the principal ultimately liable. Once the undisclosed principal's identity is revealed, the third party generally can elect to hold either the principal or the agent liable on the contract. Conversely, the undisclosed principal can require the third party to fulfill the contract, *unless* (1) the undisclosed principal was expressly excluded as a party in the contract; (2) the contract is a negotiable instrument signed by the agent with no indication of signing

---

12. *Restatement (Second) of Agency,* Section 321.
13. *McBride v. Taxman Corp.,* 327 Ill.App.3d 992, 765 N.E.2d 51 (2002).

in a representative capacity; or (3) the performance of the agent is personal to the contract, allowing the third party to refuse the principal's performance.

Unauthorized Acts   If an agent has no authority but nevertheless contracts with a third party, the principal cannot be held liable on the contract. It does not matter whether the principal was disclosed, partially disclosed, or undisclosed. The *agent* is liable, however. EXAMPLE #18 Scranton signs a contract for the purchase of a truck, purportedly acting as an agent under authority granted by Johnson. In fact, Johnson has not given Scranton any such authority. Johnson refuses to pay for the truck, claiming that Scranton had no authority to purchase it. The seller of the truck is entitled to hold Scranton liable for payment. □

If the principal is disclosed or partially disclosed, the agent is liable to the third party as long as the third party relied on the agency status. The agent's liability here is based on the breach of an *implied warranty of authority* (an agent impliedly warrants that he or she has the authority to enter a contract on behalf of the principal), not on breach of the contract itself.[14] If the third party knows at the time the contract is made that the agent does not have authority—or if the agent expresses to the third party *uncertainty* as to the extent of her or his authority—then the agent is not personally liable.

Liability for E-Agents   Although standard agency principles once applied only to *human* agents, today these same principles are being applied to electronic agents. An electronic agent, or **e-agent,** is a semiautonomous computer program that is capable of executing specific tasks. E-agents used in e-commerce include software that can search through many databases and retrieve only information that is relevant for the user.

The Uniform Electronic Transactions Act (UETA), which was discussed in detail in Chapter 11 and has been adopted by the majority of the states, contains several provisions relating to the principal's liability for the actions of e-agents. Section 15 of the UETA states that e-agents may enter into binding agreements on behalf of their principals. Presumably, then—at least in those states that have adopted the act—the principal will be bound by the terms in a contract entered into by an e-agent. Thus, if you place an order over the Internet, the company (principal) whose system took the order via an e-agent cannot claim that it did not receive your order.

The UETA also stipulates that if an e-agent does not provide an opportunity to prevent errors at the time of the transaction, the other party to the transaction can avoid the transaction. For instance, if an e-agent fails to provide an on-screen confirmation of a purchase or sale, the other party can avoid the effect of any errors.

E-AGENT

A computer program that by electronic or other automated means can independently initiate an action or respond to electronic messages or data without review by an individual.

Today, one can buy an array of products, including groceries, online. What act has taken steps to apply traditional agency principles to online transactions?
(Photo by Bill Stryker)

---

14. The agent is not liable on the contract because the agent was never intended personally to be a party to the contract.

Liability for Torts and Crimes

Obviously, any person, including an agent, is liable for her or his own torts and crimes. Whether a principal can also be held liable for an agent's torts and crimes depends on several factors, which we examine here. In some situations, a principal may be held liable not only for the torts of an agent but also for the torts committed by an independent contractor.

Principal's Tortious Conduct   A principal conducting an activity through an agent may be liable for harm resulting from the principal's own negligence or recklessness. Thus, a principal may be liable for giving improper instructions, authorizing the use of improper materials or tools, or establishing improper rules that resulted in the agent's committing a tort.   **EXAMPLE #19** Jack knows that Suki cannot drive but nevertheless tells her to use the company truck to deliver some equipment to a customer. In this situation, Jack (the principal) will be liable for his own negligence to anyone injured by Suki's negligent driving.□

Principal's Authorization of Agent's Tortious Conduct   A principal who authorizes an agent to commit a tort may be liable to persons or property injured thereby, because the act is considered to be the principal's.   **EXAMPLE #20** Selkow directs his agent, Warren, to cut the corn on specific acreage, which neither of them has the right to do. The harvest is therefore a trespass (a tort), and Selkow is liable to the owner of the corn.□

Note also that an agent acting at the principal's direction can be liable as a *tortfeasor* (one who commits a wrong, or tort), along with the principal, for committing the tortious act even if the agent was unaware of the wrongfulness of the act. Assume in the above example that Warren, the agent, did not know that Selkow had no right to harvest the corn. Warren can nevertheless be held liable to the owner of the field for damages, along with Selkow, the principal.

Liability for Agent's Misrepresentation   A principal is exposed to tort liability whenever a third person sustains a loss due to the agent's misrepresenta-

A serious ski accident occurs under the supervised instruction of a ski resort employee. Are there any circumstances under which the principal (the resort) will not be liable?
(Rob Lee/Creative Commons)

The idea that a master (employer) must respond to third persons for losses negligently caused by the master's servant (employee) first appeared in Lord Holt's opinion in *Jones v. Hart* (1698).[a] By the early nineteenth century, this maxim had been adopted by most courts and was referred to as the doctrine of *respondeat superior.*

Theories of Liability

The vicarious (indirect) liability of the master for the acts of the servant has been supported primarily by two theories. The first theory rests on the issue of *control,* or *fault:* the master has control over the acts of the servant and is thus responsible for injuries arising out of such service. The second theory is economic in nature: because the master takes the benefits or profits of the servant's service, he or she should also suffer the losses; moreover, the master is better able than the servant to absorb such losses.

The *control theory* is clearly recognized in the *Restatement (Second) of Agency,* which defines a master as "a principal who employs an agent to perform service in his [or her] affairs and who controls, or has the right to control, the physical conduct of the other in the performance of the service." Accordingly, a servant is defined as "an agent employed by a master to perform service in his [or her] affairs whose physical conduct in his [or her] performance of the service is controlled, or is subject to control, by the master."

a. K.B. 642, 90 Eng. Reprint 1255 (1698).

Limitations on the Employer's Liability

There are limitations on the master's liability for the acts of the servant, however. An employer (master) is responsible only for the wrongful conduct of an employee (servant) that occurs in "the scope of employment." The criteria used by the courts in determining whether an employee is acting within the scope of employment are set forth in the *Restatement (Second) of Agency* and discussed in the text. Generally, the act must be of a kind the servant was employed to do; must have occurred within "authorized time and space limits"; and must have been "activated, at least in part, by a purpose to serve the master."

APPLICATION TO TODAY'S LEGAL ENVIRONMENT

The courts have accepted the doctrine of *respondeat superior* for nearly two centuries. This theory of vicarious liability is laden with practical implications in all situations in which a principal-agent (master-servant, employer-employee) relationship exists. Today, the small-town grocer with one clerk and the multinational corporation with thousands of employees are equally subject to the doctrinal demand of "let the master respond." (For a further discussion of employers' liability for wrongs committed by their employees, including wrongs committed in the online employment environment, see Chapter 17.)

RELEVANT WEB SITES

To locate information on the Web concerning the doctrine of *respondeat superior,* go to this text's Web site at **www.cengage.com/blaw/let**, select "Chapter 16," and click on "URLs for Landmarks."

---

tion. The principal's liability depends on whether the agent was actually or apparently authorized to make representations and whether such representations were made within the scope of the agency. The principal is always directly responsible for an agent's misrepresentation made within the scope of the agent's authority. **EXAMPLE #21** Bassett is a demonstrator for Moore's products. Moore sends Bassett to a home show to demonstrate the products and to answer questions from consumers. Moore has given Bassett authority to make statements about the products. If Bassett makes only true representations, all is fine; but if he makes false claims, Moore will be liable for any injuries or damages sustained by third parties in reliance on Bassett's false representations. □

Liability for Agent's Negligence   As mentioned, an agent is liable for his or her own torts. A principal may also be liable for harm an agent caused to a third party under the doctrine of **respondeat superior,**[15] a Latin term meaning "let the master respond." This doctrine, discussed in the *Landmark in the Legal Environment* feature, is similar to the theory of strict liability discussed in Chapter 12. The doctrine imposes **vicarious liability,** or indirect liability, on the employer—that is,

RESPONDEAT SUPERIOR
Latin for "let the master respond." A doctrine under which a principal or an employer is held liable for the wrongful acts committed by agents or employees while acting within the course and scope of their agency or employment.

VICARIOUS LIABILITY
Legal responsibility placed on one person for the acts of another; indirect liability imposed on a supervisory party (such as an employer) for the actions of a subordinate (such as an employee) because of the relationship between the two parties.

---

15. Pronounced ree-*spahn*-dee-uht soo-*peer*-ee-your.

liability without regard to the personal fault of the employer for torts committed by an employee in the course or scope of employment.

When an agent commits a negligent act, can the agent also be held liable? That was the issue in the following case.

Case 16.3   Warner v. Southwest Desert Images, LLC

Court of Appeals of Arizona,
Division 2, Department A, 2008.
218 Ariz. 121, 180 P.3d 986.

BACKGROUND AND FACTS   Aegis Communications hired Southwest Desert Images (SDI) to provide landscaping services for its property. SDI employee David Hoggatt was spraying an herbicide to control weeds around the Aegis building one day when he was told that the spray was being sucked into the building by the air-conditioning system and making people sick. The building was evacuated, and employees were treated for breathing problems and itchy eyes. Aegis employee Catherine Warner, who had suffered two heart attacks previously, was taken to the hospital. It was determined that she had suffered a heart attack. She continued experiencing health complications that she blamed on exposure to the spray. Warner sued SDI and Hoggatt for negligence. The trial judge dismissed the suit against Hoggatt. The jury found SDI alone to be liable for Warner's injuries. She was awarded $3,825 in damages. She appealed the decision.

IN THE WORDS OF THE COURT . . . *J. WILLIAM BRAMMER, JR.*, Judge.

*   *   *   *

We agree with Warner that "there was no legal basis for the court's decision to dismiss Hoggatt from the action." *It is well-established law that an agent will not be excused from responsibility for tortious conduct merely because he is acting for his principal.* [Also, as stated in the Restatement (Third) of Agency], "An agent is subject to liability to a third party harmed by the agent's tortious conduct. Unless an applicable statute provides otherwise, an actor remains subject to liability although the actor acts *   *   * within the scope of employment." [Emphasis added.]

Hoggatt cites no authority suggesting this rule should not apply in this case. He does, however, argue the error was harmless. *   *   * Hoggatt asserts Warner was not prejudiced because "the jury apportioned one hundred percent of the fault to SDI. Adding other possible parties to the jury verdict form would not have changed the outcome of this case." We agree that including Hoggatt as a defendant throughout the trial could not have changed Warner's damage award, and Warner does not argue otherwise. Nor is there a need for the jury to apportion fault between Hoggatt and SDI—the liability of those parties is joint and several.

That the error does not warrant a new trial, however, does not mean it was not prejudicial to Warner. She has a right to recover her damages from Hoggatt, and his improper dismissal has deprived her of that right. Accordingly, we reverse the trial court's grant of a directed verdict in Hoggatt's favor and amend the judgment in Warner's favor to show it is against Hoggatt as well.

*   *   *   *

DECISION AND REMEDY   The appeals court held that Hoggatt should have been held jointly and severally liable for the injury suffered by Warner. The fact that Hoggatt was an agent of SDI, and that SDI was liable, did not mean Hoggatt would not be held responsible for his negligent act that caused an injury.

THE ETHICAL DIMENSION   Assume that Hoggatt was following the instructions of his employer, SDI, in applying the spray. Should Hoggatt become personally liable in such a situation, given that the employer is better able financially to pay the judgment and may have insurance that covers the matter?

THE LEGAL ENVIRONMENT DIMENSION   How could SDI reduce the likelihood of similar lawsuits occurring in the future?

Determining the Scope of Employment   The key to determining whether a principal may be liable for the torts of an agent under the doctrine of *respondeat superior* is whether the torts are committed within the scope of the agency or employment. The *Restatement (Second) of Agency,* Section 229, indicates the factors that today's courts will consider in determining whether a particular act occurred within the course and scope of employment. These factors are as follows:

1. Whether the employee's act was authorized by the employer.
2. The time, place, and purpose of the act.
3. Whether the act was one commonly performed by employees on behalf of their employers.
4. The extent to which the employer's interest was advanced by the act.
5. The extent to which the private interests of the employee were involved.
6. Whether the employer furnished the means or instrumentality (for example, a truck or a machine) by which the injury was inflicted.
7. Whether the employer had reason to know that the employee would do the act in question and whether the employee had ever done it before.
8. Whether the act involved the commission of a serious crime.

The Distinction between a "Detour" and a "Frolic"   A useful insight into the "scope of employment" concept may be gained from the judge's classic distinction between a "detour" and a "frolic" in the case of *Joel v. Morison* (1834).[16] In this case, the English court held that if a servant merely took a detour from his master's business, the master will be responsible. If, however, the servant was on a "frolic of his own" and not in any way "on his master's business," the master will not be liable.

Suppose that the driver of the overturned truck in this photo caused a traffic accident that resulted in property damages and personal injuries. If the driver's employer (the principal) learns that the driver had been drinking alcohol during a break right before the incident, can the principal avoid liability? Why or why not? (Sister72/Creative Commons)

   EXAMPLE #22   Mandel, a traveling salesperson, while driving his employer's vehicle to call on a customer, decides to stop at the post office—which is one block off his route—to mail a personal letter. As Mandel approaches the post office, he negligently runs into a parked vehicle owned by Chan. In this situation, because Mandel's detour from the employer's business is not substantial, he is still acting within the scope of employment, and the employer is liable. The result would be different, though, if Mandel had decided to pick up a few friends for cocktails in another city and in the process had negligently run into Chan's vehicle. In that circumstance, the departure from the employer's business would be substantial, and the employer normally would not be liable to Chan for damages. Mandel would be considered to have been on a "frolic" of his own. ▫

16. 6 Car. & P. 501, 172 Eng. Reprint 1338 (1834).

Employee Travel Time   An employee going to and from work or to and from meals is usually considered outside the scope of employment. If travel is part of a person's position, however, such as a traveling salesperson or a regional representative of a company, then travel time is normally considered within the scope of employment. Thus, the duration of the business trip, including the return trip home, is within the scope of employment unless there is a significant departure from the employer's business.

Notice of Dangerous Conditions   The employer is charged with knowledge of any dangerous conditions discovered by an employee and pertinent to the employment situation. **EXAMPLE #23** Chad, a maintenance employee in Martin's apartment building, notices a lead pipe protruding from the ground in the building's courtyard. The employee neglects either to fix the pipe or to inform the employer of the danger. John falls on the pipe and is injured. The employer is charged with knowledge of the dangerous condition regardless of whether or not Chad actually informed the employer. That knowledge is imputed to the employer by virtue of the employment relationship.□

Liability for Agent's Intentional Torts   Most intentional torts that employees commit have no relation to their employment; thus, their employers will not be held liable. Nevertheless, under the doctrine of *respondeat superior,* the employer can be liable for intentional torts of the employee that are committed within the course and scope of employment, just as the employer is liable for negligence. For instance, an employer is liable when an employee (such as a "bouncer" at a nightclub or a security guard at a department store) commits the tort of assault and battery or false imprisonment while acting within the scope of employment.

In addition, an employer who knows or should know that an employee has a propensity for committing tortious acts is liable for the employee's acts even if they would not ordinarily be considered within the scope of employment. For example, if the employer hires a bouncer knowing that he has a history of arrests for assault and battery, the employer may be liable if the employee viciously attacks a patron in the parking lot after hours.

An employer may also be liable for permitting an employee to engage in reckless actions that can injure others. **EXAMPLE #24** An employer observes an employee smoking while filling containerized trucks with highly flammable liquids. Failure to stop the employee will cause the employer to be liable for any injuries that result if a truck explodes.□ (See this chapter's *Beyond Our Borders* feature for a discussion of another approach to an employer's liability for an employee's acts.)

Liability for Independent Contractor's Torts   Generally, an employer is not liable for physical harm caused to a third person by the negligent act of an independent contractor in the performance of the contract. This is because the employer does not have *the right to control* the details of an independent contractor's performance. Exceptions to this rule are made in certain situations, though, such as when unusually hazardous activities are involved. Typical examples of such activities include blasting operations, the transportation of highly volatile chemicals, or the use of poisonous gases. In these situations, an employer cannot be shielded from liability merely by using an independent contractor. Strict liability is imposed on the employer-principal as a matter of law. Also, in some states, strict liability may be imposed by statute.

The doctrine of *respondeat superior* is well established in the legal systems of the United States and most Western countries. As you have already read, under this doctrine employers can be held liable for the acts of their agents, including employees. The doctrine of *respondeat superior* is not universal, however. Middle Eastern countries, for example, do not follow this doctrine. Islamic law, as codified in the *sharia,* holds to a strict belief that responsibility for human actions lies with the individual and cannot be vicariously extended to others. This belief and other concepts of Islamic law are based on the writings of Muhammad, a seventh-century prophet whose revelations formed the basis of the Islamic religion and, by extension, the *sharia.* Muhammad's prophecies are documented in the Qur'an (Koran), which is the principal source of the *sharia.*

FOR CRITICAL ANALYSIS   How would U.S. society be affected if employers could not be held vicariously liable for their employees' torts?

Liability for Agent's Crimes   An agent is liable for his or her own crimes. A principal or employer is not liable for an agent's crime even if the crime was committed within the scope of authority or employment—unless the principal participated by conspiracy or other action. In some jurisdictions, under specific statutes, a principal may be liable for an agent's violation, in the course and scope of employment, of regulations, such as those governing sanitation, prices, weights, and the sale of liquor.

HOW AGENCY RELATIONSHIPS ARE TERMINATED

Agency law is similar to contract law in that both an agency and a contract can be terminated by an act of the parties or by operation of law. Once the relationship between the principal and the agent has ended, the agent no longer has the right (*actual* authority) to bind the principal. For an agent's *apparent* authority to be terminated, though, third persons may also need to be notified that the agency has been terminated.

Termination by Act of the Parties

An agency may be terminated by act of the parties in several ways, including those discussed here.

Lapse of Time   An agency agreement may specify the time period during which the agency relationship will exist. If so, the agency ends when that time period expires. For instance, if the parties agree that the agency will begin on January 1, 2009, and end on December 31, 2011, the agency is automatically terminated on December 31, 2011. If no definite time is stated, then the agency continues for a reasonable time and can be terminated at will by either party. What constitutes a "reasonable time" depends, of course, on the circumstances and the nature of the agency relationship.

Purpose Achieved   An agent can be employed to accomplish a particular objective, such as the purchase of stock for a cattle rancher. In that situation, the agency automatically ends after the cattle have been purchased. If more than one agent is employed to accomplish the same purpose, such as the sale of real estate, the first agent to complete the sale automatically terminates the agency relationship for all the others.

Occurrence of a Specific Event   An agency can be created to terminate on the happening of a certain event. If Posner appoints Rubik to handle her business affairs while she is away, the agency automatically terminates when Posner returns.

Mutual Agreement   Recall from the chapters on contract law that parties can cancel (rescind) a contract by mutually agreeing to terminate the contractual relationship. The same holds true in agency law regardless of whether the agency contract is in writing or whether it is for a specific duration.

Termination by One Party   As a general rule, either party can terminate the agency relationship (the act of termination is called *revocation* if done by the principal and *renunciation* if done by the agent). Although both parties have the *power* to terminate the agency, they may not possess the *right*. Wrongful termination can subject the canceling party to a suit for breach of contract. **EXAMPLE #25** Rawlins has a one-year employment contract with Munro to act as an agent in return for $65,000. Munro has the *power* to discharge Rawlins before the contract period expires. If Munro discharges Rawlins, however, Munro can be sued for breaching the contract and will be liable to Rawlins for damages because he had no *right* to terminate the agency.□

A special rule applies in an *agency coupled with an interest*. This type of agency is not an agency in the usual sense because it is created for the agent's benefit instead of the principal's benefit. **EXAMPLE #26** Julie borrows $5,000 from Rob, giving Rob some of her jewelry and signing a letter giving Rob the power to sell the jewelry as her agent if she fails to repay the loan. After receiving the $5,000 from Rob, Julie attempts to revoke Rob's authority to sell the jewelry as her agent. Julie will not succeed in this attempt because a principal cannot revoke an agency created for the agent's benefit.□

Notice of Termination   When an agency has been terminated by act of the parties, it is the principal's duty to inform any third parties who know of the existence of the agency that it has been terminated (although notice of the termination may be given by others). Although an agent's actual authority ends when the agency is terminated, an agent's *apparent authority* continues until the third party receives notice (from any source) that such authority has been terminated. If the principal knows that a third party has dealt with the agent, the principal is expected to notify that person *directly*. For third parties who have heard about the agency but have not yet dealt with the agent, *constructive notice* is sufficient.[17]

No particular form is required for notice of agency termination to be effective. The principal can personally notify the agent, or the agent can learn of the termination through some other means. **EXAMPLE #27** Manning bids on a shipment of steel and hires Stone as an agent to arrange transportation of the shipment. When Stone learns that Manning has lost the bid, Stone's authority to make the transportation arrangement terminates.□ If the agent's authority is written, however, it normally must be revoked in writing.

---

17. *Constructive notice* is information or knowledge of a fact imputed by law to a person if he or she could have discovered the fact by proper diligence. Constructive notice is often accomplished by newspaper publication.

Termination by Operation of Law

Termination of an agency by operation of law occurs in the circumstances discussed here. Note that when an agency terminates by operation of law, there is no duty to notify third persons.

Death or Insanity   The general rule is that the death or mental incompetence of either the principal or the agent automatically and immediately terminates the ordinary agency relationship. Knowledge of the death is not required. **EXAMPLE #28** Geer sends Pyron to China to purchase a rare painting. Before Pyron makes the purchase, Geer dies. Pyron's agent status is terminated at the moment of Geer's death, even though Pyron does not know that Geer has died.□ Some states, however, have enacted statutes changing this common law rule to make knowledge of the principal's death a requirement for agency termination.

An agent's transactions that occur after the death of the principal are not binding on the principal's estate.[18] **EXAMPLE #29** Carson is hired by Perry to collect a debt from Thomas (a third party). Perry dies, but Carson, not knowing of Perry's death, still collects the funds from Thomas. Thomas's payment to Carson is no longer legally sufficient to discharge the debt to Perry because Carson's authority to collect ended on Perry's death. If Carson absconds with the funds, Thomas is still liable for the debt to Perry's estate.□

Impossibility   When the specific subject matter of an agency is destroyed or lost, the agency terminates. **EXAMPLE #30** Bullard employs Gonzalez to sell Bullard's house. Prior to any sale, the house is destroyed by fire. In this situation, Gonzalez's agency and authority to sell Bullard's house terminate.□ Similarly, when it is impossible for the agent to perform the agency lawfully because of a change in the law, the agency terminates.

Changed Circumstances   When an event occurs that has such an unusual effect on the subject matter of the agency that the agent can reasonably infer that the principal will not want the agency to continue, the agency terminates. **EXAMPLE #31** Roberts hires Mullen to sell a tract of land for $20,000. Subsequently, Mullen learns that there is oil under the land and that the land is worth $1 million. The agency and Mullen's authority to sell the land for $20,000 are terminated.□

Bankruptcy   If either the principal or the agent petitions for bankruptcy, the agency is *usually* terminated. In certain circumstances, as when the agent's financial status is irrelevant to the purpose of the agency, the agency relationship may continue. Insolvency (defined as the inability to pay debts when they become due or the situation in which liabilities exceed assets), as distinguished from bankruptcy, does not necessarily terminate the relationship.

War   When the principal's country and the agent's country are at war with each other, the agency is terminated. In this situation, the agency is automatically suspended or terminated because there is no way to enforce the legal rights and obligations of the parties.

---

18. Note that special rules apply when the agent is a bank. Banks can continue to exercise specific types of authority even after a customer has died or become mentally incompetent unless they have knowledge of the death or incompetence [Section 4–405 of the Uniform Commercial Code]. Even with knowledge of the customer's death, the bank has authority to honor checks for ten days following the customer's death in the absence of a stop-payment order.

Reviewing . . . Agency

Lynne Meyer, on her way to a business meeting and in a hurry, stopped by a Buy-Mart store for a new pair of nylons to wear to the meeting. There was a long line at one of the checkout counters, but a cashier, Valerie Watts, opened another counter and began loading the cash drawer. Meyer told Watts that she was in a hurry and asked Watts to work faster. Watts, however, only slowed her pace. At this point, Meyer hit Watts. It is not clear from the record whether Meyer hit Watts intentionally or, in an attempt to retrieve the nylons, hit her inadvertently. In response, Watts grabbed Meyer by the hair and hit her repeatedly in the back of the head, while Meyer screamed for help. Management personnel separated the two women and questioned them about the incident. Watts was immediately fired for violating the store's no-fighting policy. Meyer subsequently sued Buy-Mart, alleging that the store was liable for the tort (assault and battery) committed by its employee. Using the information presented in the chapter, answer the following questions.

1. Under what doctrine discussed in this chapter might Buy-Mart be held liable for the tort committed by Watts?

2. What is the key factor in determining whether Buy-Mart is liable under this doctrine?

3. How is Buy-Mart's potential liability affected by whether Watts's behavior constituted an intentional tort or a tort of negligence?

4. Suppose that when Watts applied for the job at Buy-Mart, she disclosed in her application that she had previously been convicted of felony assault and battery. Nevertheless, Buy-Mart hired Watts as a cashier. How might this fact affect Buy-Mart's liability for Watts's actions?

Key Terms

agency 533	fiduciary 534	power of attorney 545
apparent authority 546	independent contractor 534	ratification 538
disclosed principal 549	notary public 545	*respondeat superior* 553
e-agent 551	partially disclosed	undisclosed principal 550
equal dignity rule 545	principal 549	vicarious liability 553

Chapter Summary

Agency Relationships (See pages 533–537.)	In a *principal-agent* relationship, an agent acts on behalf of and instead of the principal in dealing with third parties. An employee who deals with third parties is normally an agent. An independent contractor is not an employee, and the employer has no control over the details of physical performance. An independent contractor may or may not be an agent.
How Agency Relationships Are Formed (See pages 537–541.)	Agency relationships may be formed by agreement, by ratification, by estoppel, and by operation of law—see the *Concept Summary* on page 541.
Duties of Agents and Principals (See pages 541–544.)	1. *Duties of the agent—* a. *Performance*—The agent must use reasonable diligence and skill in performing her or his duties or use the special skills that the agent has represented to the principal that the agent possesses.

Duties of Agents and Principals—Continued	b. *Notification*—The agent is required to notify the principal of all matters that come to his or her attention concerning the subject matter of the agency.

c. *Loyalty*—The agent has a duty to act solely for the benefit of the principal and not in the interest of the agent or a third party.

d. *Obedience*—The agent must follow all lawful and clearly stated instructions of the principal.

e. *Accounting*—The agent has a duty to make available to the principal records of all property and funds received and paid out on behalf of the principal.

2. *Duties of the principal*—

a. *Compensation*—Except in a gratuitous agency relationship, the principal must pay the agreed-on value (or reasonable value) for an agent's services.

b. *Reimbursement and indemnification*—The principal must reimburse the agent for all funds disbursed at the request of the principal and for all funds the agent disburses for necessary expenses in the course of reasonable performance of his or her agency duties.

c. *Cooperation*—A principal must cooperate with and assist an agent in performing her or his duties.

d. *Safe working conditions*—A principal must provide safe working conditions for the agent-employee.

Agent's Authority
(See pages 544–549.)

1. *Express authority*—Can be oral or in writing. Authorization must be in writing if the agent is to execute a contract that must be in writing. Express authority can also be granted by executing a power of attorney.

2. *Implied authority*—Authority customarily associated with the position of the agent or authority that is deemed necessary for the agent to carry out expressly authorized tasks.

3. *Apparent authority*—Exists when the principal, by word or action, causes a third party reasonably to believe that an agent has authority to act, even though the agent has no express or implied authority.

4. *Ratification*—The affirmation by the principal of an agent's unauthorized action or promise. For the ratification to be effective, the principal must be aware of all material facts.

Liability in Agency Relationships
(See pages 549–557.)

1. *Liability for contracts*—If the principal's identity is disclosed or partially disclosed at the time the agent forms a contract with a third party, the principal is liable to the third party under the contract if the agent acted within the scope of his or her authority. If the principal's identity is undisclosed at the time of contract formation, the agent is personally liable to the third party, but if the agent acted within the scope of his or her authority, the principal is also bound by the contract.

2. *Liability for agent's negligence*—Under the doctrine of *respondeat superior,* the principal is liable for any harm caused to another through the agent's torts if the agent was acting within the scope of her or his employment at the time the harmful act occurred.

3. *Liability for agent's intentional torts*—Usually, employers are not liable for the intentional torts that their agents commit, *unless:*

a. The acts are committed within the scope of employment, and thus the doctrine of *respondeat superior* applies.

b. The employer allows an employee to engage in reckless acts that cause injury to another.

c. The agent's misrepresentation causes a third party to sustain damage, and the agent had either actual or apparent authority to act.

CONTINUED

Liability in Agency Relationships—Continued

4. *Liability for independent contractor's torts*—A principal is not liable for harm caused by an independent contractor's negligence, unless hazardous activities are involved (in this situation, the principal is strictly liable for any resulting harm) or other exceptions apply.

5. *Liability for agent's crimes*—An agent is responsible for his or her own crimes, even if the crimes were committed while the agent was acting within the scope of authority or employment. A principal will be liable for an agent's crime only if the principal participated by conspiracy or other action or (in some jurisdictions) if the agent violated certain government regulations in the course of employment.

How Agency Relationships Are Terminated
(See pages 557–559.)

1. *By act of the parties*—
   a. Lapse of time (if the parties specified a definite time for the duration of the agency when the agency was established).
   b. Purpose achieved.
   c. Occurrence of a specific event.
   d. Mutual rescission (requires mutual consent of principal and agent).
   e. Termination by act of either the principal (revocation) or the agent (renunciation). (A principal cannot revoke an agency coupled with an interest.)
   f. Notice to third parties is required when an agency is terminated by act of the parties. Direct notice is required for those who have previously dealt with the agency; constructive notice will suffice for all other third parties.

2. *By operation of law*—
   a. Death or mental incompetence of either the principal or the agent.
   b. Impossibility (when the purpose of the agency cannot be achieved because of an event beyond the parties' control).
   c. Changed circumstances (in which it would be inequitable to require that the agency be continued).
   d. Bankruptcy of the principal or the agent, or war between the principal's and agent's countries.
   e. Notice to third parties is not required when an agency is terminated by operation of law.

For Review

1. What is the difference between an employee and an independent contractor?
2. How do agency relationships arise?
3. What duties do agents and principals owe to each other?
4. When is a principal liable for the agent's actions with respect to third parties? When is the agent liable?
5. What are some of the ways in which an agency relationship can be terminated?

Questions and Case Problems

16–1. Ratification by Principal. Springer was a political candidate running for Congress. He was operating on a tight budget and instructed his campaign staff not to purchase any campaign materials without his explicit authorization. In spite of these instructions, one of his campaign workers ordered Dubychek Printing Co. to print some promotional materials for Springer's campaign. When the printed materials arrived, Springer did not return them but instead used them during his campaign. When Springer failed to pay for the materials, Dubychek sued for recovery of the price. Springer contended that he was not liable on the sales contract because he had not authorized his agent to purchase the printing services. Dubychek argued that the campaign worker was Springer's agent and that the worker had authority to make the printing contract. Additionally, Dubychek claimed that even if the purchase was unauthorized, Springer's use of the materials constituted ratification of his agent's unauthorized purchase. Is Dubychek correct? Explain.

Question with Sample Answer

16–2. Paul Gett is a well-known, wealthy financial expert living in the city of Torris. Adam Wade, Gett's friend, tells Timothy Brown that he is Gett's agent for the purchase of rare coins. Wade even shows Brown a local newspaper clipping mentioning Gett's interest in coin collecting. Brown, knowing of Wade's friendship with Gett, contracts with Wade to sell a rare coin valued at $25,000 to Gett. Wade takes the coin and disappears with it. On the payment due date, Brown seeks to collect from Gett, claiming that Wade's agency made Gett liable. Gett does not deny that Wade was a friend, but he claims that Wade was never his agent. Discuss fully whether an agency was in existence at the time the contract for the rare coin was made.

For a sample answer to Question 16–2, go to Appendix I at the end of this text.

16–3. Employee versus Independent Contractor. Stephen Hemmerling was a driver for the Happy Cab Co. Hemmerling paid certain fixed expenses and abided by a variety of rules relating to the use of the cab, the hours that could be worked, and the solicitation of fares, among other things. Rates were set by the state. Happy Cab did not withhold taxes from Hemmerling's pay. While driving the cab, Hemmerling was injured in an accident and filed a claim against Happy Cab in a Nebraska state court for workers' compensation benefits. Such benefits are not available to independent contractors. On what basis might the court hold that Hemmerling is an employee? Explain.

16–4. Agent's Duties to the Principal. Sam and Theresa Daigle decided to build a home in Cameron Parish, Louisiana. To obtain financing, they contacted Trinity United Mortgage Co. In a meeting with Joe Diez, who was acting on Trinity's behalf, on July 18, 2001, the Daigles signed a temporary loan agreement with Union Planters Bank. Diez assured them that they did not need to make payments on this loan until their house was

built and that permanent financing had been secured. Because the Daigles did not make payments on the Union loan, Trinity declined to make the permanent loan. Meanwhile, Diez left Trinity's employ. On November 1, the Daigles moved into their new house. They tried to contact Diez at Trinity but were told that he was unavailable and would get back to them. Three weeks later, Diez came to the Daigles' home and had them sign documents that they believed were to secure a permanent loan but that were actually an application with Diez's new employer. Union filed a suit in a Louisiana state court against the Daigles for failing to pay on its loan. The Daigles paid Union, obtained permanent financing through another source, and filed a suit against Trinity to recover the cost. Who should have told the Daigles that Diez was no longer Trinity's agent? Could Trinity be liable to the Daigles on this basis? Explain. [*Daigle v. Trinity United Mortgage, L.L.C.*, 890 So.2d 583 (La.App. 3 Cir. 2004)]

16–5. Principal's Duties to the Agent. Josef Boehm was an officer and the majority shareholder of Alaska Industrial Hardware, Inc. (AIH), in Anchorage, Alaska. In August 2001, Lincolnshire Management, Inc., in New York, created AIH Acquisition Corp. to buy AIH. The three firms signed a "commitment letter" to negotiate "a definitive stock purchase agreement" (SPA). In September, Harold Snow and Ronald Braley began to work, on Boehm's behalf, with Vincent Coyle, an agent for AIH Acquisition, to produce an SPA. They exchanged many drafts and dozens of e-mails. Finally, in February 2002, Braley told Coyle that Boehm would sign the SPA "early next week." That did not occur, however, and at the end of March, after more negotiations and drafts, Boehm demanded a higher price. AIH Acquisition agreed, and following more work by the agents, another SPA was drafted. In April, the parties met in Anchorage. Boehm still refused to sign. AIH Acquisition and others filed a suit in a federal district court against AIH. Did Boehm violate any of the duties that principals owe to their agents? If so, which duty, and how was it violated? Explain. [*AIH Acquisition Corp. v. Alaska Industrial Hardware, Inc.*, __ F.Supp.2d __ (S.D.N.Y. 2004)]

Case Problem with Sample Answer

16–6. In July 2001, John Warren viewed a condominium in Woodland Hills, California, as a potential buyer. Hildegard Merrill was the agent for the seller. Because Warren's credit rating was poor, Merrill told him he needed a co-borrower to obtain a mortgage at a reasonable rate. Merrill said that her daughter Charmaine would "go on title" until the loan and sale were complete if Warren would pay her $10,000. Merrill also offered to defer her commission on the sale as a loan to Warren so that he could make a 20 percent down payment on the property. He agreed to both plans. Merrill applied for and secured the mortgage in Charmaine's name alone by misrepresenting her daughter's address, business, and income. To close the sale, Merrill had Warren remove his name from the title to the property. In October, Warren moved into the condominium, repaid Merrill the amount of her deferred commission, and began paying the mortgage. Within a few months, Merrill had Warren evicted. Warren filed a suit in a California state court against Merrill and Charmaine. Who among these parties was in an agency relationship? What is the basic duty that an agent owes a principal? Was the duty breached here? Explain. [*Warren v. Merrill*, 143 Cal.App.4th 96, 49 Cal.Rptr.3d 122 (2 Dist. 2006)]

After you have answered Problem 16–6, compare your answer with the sample answer given on the Web site that accompanies this text. Go to www.cengage.com/blaw/let, select "Chapter 16," and click on "Case Problem with Sample Answer."

16–7. Apparent Authority. Lee Dennegar and Mark Knutson lived in Dennegar's house in Raritan, New Jersey. Dennegar paid the mortgage and other household expenses. With Dennegar's consent, Knutson managed their household's financial affairs and the "general office functions concerned with maintaining the house." Dennegar allowed Knutson to handle the mail and "to do with it as he chose." Knutson wrote checks for Dennegar to sign, although Knutson signed Dennegar's name to many of the checks with Dennegar's consent. AT&T Universal issued a credit card in Dennegar's name in February 2001. Monthly statements were mailed to Dennegar's house, and payments were sometimes made on those statements. Knutson died in June 2003. The unpaid charges on the card of $14,752.93 were assigned to New Century Financial Services, Inc. New Century filed a suit in a New Jersey state court against Dennegar to collect the unpaid amount. Dennegar claimed that he never applied for or used the card and knew nothing about it. Under what theory could Dennegar be liable for the charges? Explain. [*New Century Financial Services, Inc. v. Dennegar*, 394 N.J.Super. 595, 928 A.2d 48 (A.D. 2007)]

16–8. Agent's Duties to the Principal. Su Ru Chen owned the Lucky Duck Fortune Cookie Factory in Everett, Massachusetts, which made Chinese-style fortune cookies for restaurants. In November 2001, Chen listed the business for sale with Bob Sun, a real estate broker, for $35,000. Sun's daughter Frances and her fiancé, Chiu Chung Chan, decided that Chan would buy the business. Acting as a broker on Chen's (the seller's) behalf, Frances asked about the Lucky Duck's finances. Chen said that each month the business sold at least 1,000 boxes of cookies at a $2,000 profit. Frances negotiated a price of $23,000, which Chan (her fiancé) paid. When Chan began to operate the Lucky Duck, it became clear that the demand for the cookies was actually about 500 boxes per month—a rate at which the business would suffer losses. Less than two months later, the factory closed. Chan filed a suit in a Massachusetts state court against Chen, alleging fraud, among other things. Chan's proof included Frances's testimony as to what Chen had said to her. Chen objected to the admission of this testimony. What is the basis for this objection? Should the court admit the testimony? Why or why not? [*Chan v. Chen*, 70 Mass.App.Ct. 79, 872 N.E.2d 1153 (2007)]

A Question of Ethics

16–9. Emergency One, Inc. (EO), makes fire and rescue vehicles. Western Fire Truck, Inc., contracted with EO to be its exclusive dealer in Colorado and Wyoming through December 2003. James Costello, a Western salesperson, was authorized to order EO vehicles for his customers. Without informing Western, Costello e-mailed EO about Western's difficulties in obtaining cash to fund its operations. He asked about the viability of Western's contract and his possible employment with EO. On EO's request, and in disregard of Western's instructions, Costello sent some payments for EO vehicles directly to EO. In addition, Costello, with EO's help, sent a competing bid to a potential Western customer. EO's representative e-mailed Costello, "You have my permission to kick [Western's] ass." In April 2002, EO terminated its contract with Western, which, after reviewing Costello's e-mail, fired Costello. Western filed a suit in a Colorado state court against Costello and EO, alleging, among other things, that Costello breached his duty as an agent and that EO aided and abetted the breach. [*Western Fire Truck, Inc. v. Emergency One, Inc.*, 134 P.3d 570 (Colo.App. 2006)]

1. Was there an agency relationship between Western and Costello? Western required monthly reports from its sales staff, but Costello did not report regularly. Does this indicate that Costello was *not* Western's agent? In determining whether an agency relationship exists, is the *right* to control or the *fact* of control more important? Explain.

2. Did Costello owe Western a duty? If so, what was the duty? Did Costello breach it? How?

3. A Colorado state statute allows a court to award punitive damages in "circumstances of fraud, malice, or willful and wanton conduct." Did any of these circumstances exist in this case? Should punitive damages be assessed against either defendant? Why or why not?

Video Question

16–10. Go to this text's Web site at **www.cengage.com/blaw/let** and select "Chapter 16." Click on "Video Questions" and view the video titled *Fast Times at Ridgemont High*. Then answer the following questions.

1. Recall from the video that Brad (Judge Reinhold) is told to deliver an order of Captain Hook Fish and Chips to IBM. Is Brad an employee or an independent contractor? Why?
2. Assume that Brad is an employee and agent of Captain Hook Fish and Chips. What duties does he owe Captain Hook Fish and Chips? What duties does Captain Hook Fish and Chips, as principal, owe to Brad?
3. In the video, Brad throws part of his uniform and several bags of the food that he is supposed to deliver out of his car window while driving. If Brad is an agent-employee and his actions cause injury to a person or property, can Captain Hook Fish and Chips be held liable? Why or why not? What should Captain Hook argue to avoid liability for Brad's actions?

Interacting with the Internet

For updated links to resources available on the Web, as well as a variety of other materials, visit this text's Web site at

www.cengage.com/blaw/let

The Legal Information Institute (LII) at Cornell University provides a great deal of information on agency law, including cases involving agency concepts. You can access the LII Web page on this topic at

www.law.cornell.edu/wex/index.php/Agency

PRACTICAL INTERNET EXERCISES

Go to this text's Web site at **www.cengage.com/blaw/let**, select "Chapter 16," and click on "Practical Internet Exercises." There you will find the following Internet research exercises that you can perform to learn more about the topics covered in this chapter.

Practical Internet Exercise 16–1: LEGAL PERSPECTIVE—Employees or Independent Contractors?
Practical Internet Exercise 16–2: MANAGEMENT PERSPECTIVE—Liability in Agency Relationships

BEFORE THE TEST

Go to this text's Web site at **www.cengage.com/blaw/let**, select "Chapter 16," and click on "Interactive Quizzes." You will find a number of interactive questions relating to this chapter.

Chapter 17

Employment, Immigration, and Labor Law

CHAPTER OBJECTIVES

After reading this chapter, you should be able to answer the following questions:

1. What is the employment-at-will doctrine? When and why are exceptions to this doctrine made?

2. What federal statute governs working hours and wages?

3. What federal law was enacted to protect the health and safety of employees? What are workers' compensation laws?

4. Under the Family and Medical Leave Act of 1993, under what circumstances may an employee take family or medical leave?

5. What federal statute gave employees the right to organize unions and engage in collective bargaining?

CONTENTS

"Show me the country in which there are no strikes, and I'll show you the country in which there is no liberty."

— SAMUEL GOMPERS,
1850–1924 (American labor leader)

Until the early 1900s, most employer-employee relationships were governed by the common law. Today, the workplace is regulated extensively by statutes and administrative agency regulations. Recall from Chapter 1 that common law doctrines apply only to areas not covered by statutory law. Common law doctrines have thus been displaced to a large extent by statutory law.

In the 1930s, during the Great Depression, both state and federal governments began to regulate employment relationships. Legislation during the 1930s and subsequent decades established the right of employees to form labor unions. At the heart of labor rights is the right to unionize and bargain with management for improved working conditions, salaries, and benefits. The ultimate weapon of labor is, of course, the strike. As noted in the chapter-opening quotation, the labor leader Samuel Gompers concluded that without the right to strike, there could be no liberty. A succession of other laws during and since the 1930s provided further protection for employees. Today's employers must comply with a myriad of laws and regulations to ensure that employee rights are protected.

In this chapter, we look at the most significant laws regulating employment relationships. We deal with other important laws regulating the workplace—those that prohibit employment discrimination—in the next chapter.

EMPLOYMENT AT WILL

Traditionally, employment relationships have generally been governed by the common law doctrine of **employment at will.** Other common law rules governing employment relationships—including rules under contract, tort, and agency law—have already been discussed at length in previous chapters of this text.

Given that many employees (those who deal with third parties) are normally deemed agents of an employer, agency concepts are especially relevant in the employment context. The distinction under agency law between employee status and independent-contractor status is also relevant to employment relationships. Generally, the laws discussed in this chapter and in Chapter 18 apply only to the employer-employee relationship; they do not apply to independent contractors.

EMPLOYMENT AT WILL
A common law doctrine under which either party may terminate an employment relationship at any time for any reason, unless a contract specifies otherwise.

Application of the Employment-at-Will Doctrine

Under the employment-at-will doctrine, either party may terminate the employment relationship at any time and for any reason, unless doing so would violate the provisions of an employment contract. The majority of U.S. workers continue to have the legal status of "employees at will." In other words, this common law doctrine is still in widespread use, and only one state (Montana) does not apply the doctrine. Nonetheless, as mentioned in the chapter introduction, federal and state statutes governing employment relationships prevent the doctrine from being applied in a number of circumstances. Today, an employer is not permitted to fire an employee if doing so would violate a federal or state employment statute, such as one prohibiting employment termination for discriminatory reasons (see Chapter 18).

Exceptions to the Employment-at-Will Doctrine

Under the employment-at-will doctrine, as mentioned, an employer may hire and fire employees at will (regardless of the employees' performance) without liability, unless doing so violates the terms of an employment contract or statutory law. Because of the harsh effects of the employment-at-will doctrine for employees, the courts have carved out various exceptions to the doctrine. These exceptions are based on contract theory, tort theory, and public policy.

Exceptions Based on Contract Theory Some courts have held that an *implied* employment contract exists between an employer and an employee. If an employee is fired outside the terms of the implied contract, he or she may succeed in an action for breach of contract even though no written employment contract exists. EXAMPLE #1 An employer's manual or personnel bulletin clearly states that, as a matter of policy, workers will be dismissed only for good cause. If an employee is aware of this policy and continues to work for the employer, a court may find that there is an implied contract based on the terms stated in the manual or bulletin.[1] Generally, the key consideration in determining whether an employment manual creates an implied contractual obligation is the employee's reasonable expectations.

REMEMBER
An implied contract may exist if a party furnishes a service expecting to be paid, and the other party, who knows (or should know) of this expectation, has a chance to reject the service and does not.

---

1. See, for example, *Ross v. May Co.*, 377 Ill.App.3d 387, 880 N.E.2d 210 (1 Dist. 2007).

An employer's oral promises to employees regarding discharge policy may also be considered part of an implied contract. If the employer fires a worker in a manner contrary to what was promised, a court may hold that the employer has violated the implied contract and is liable for damages. Most state courts will judge a claim of breach of an implied employment contract by traditional contract standards.

Courts in a few states have gone further and held that all employment contracts contain an implied covenant of good faith. This means that both sides promise to abide by the contract in good faith. If an employer fires an employee for an arbitrary or unjustified reason, the employee can claim that the covenant of good faith was breached and the contract violated.

Exceptions Based on Tort Theory   In a few situations, the discharge of an employee may give rise to an action for wrongful discharge under tort theories. Abusive discharge procedures may result in a suit for intentional infliction of emotional distress or defamation. In addition, some courts have permitted workers to sue their employers under the tort theory of fraud.   **EXAMPLE #2** An employer induces a prospective employee to leave a lucrative job and move to another state by offering "a long-term job with a thriving business." In fact, the employer is not only having significant financial problems but is also planning a merger that will result in the elimination of the position offered to the prospective employee. If the employee takes the job in reliance on the employer's representations and is fired shortly thereafter, the employee may be able to bring an action against the employer for fraud.[2] □

Exceptions Based on Public Policy   The most widespread common law exception to the employment-at-will doctrine is made on the basis of public policy. Courts may apply this exception when an employer fires a worker for reasons that violate a fundamental public policy of the jurisdiction. Generally, the courts require that the public policy involved be expressed clearly in the statutory law governing the jurisdiction.   **EXAMPLE #3** As you will read later in this chapter, employers with fifty or more employees are required by the Family and Medical Leave Act (FMLA) to give employees up to twelve weeks of unpaid family or medical leave per year. Mila's employer, however, has only forty employees and thus is not covered by the federal law. Nonetheless, if Mila is fired from her job because she takes three weeks of unpaid family leave to help her son through a difficult surgery, a court may deem that the employer's actions violated the public policy expressed in the FMLA. □

Sometimes, an employer will direct employees to perform an illegal act and fire them if they refuse to do so. At other times, an employer will fire or discipline employees who "blow the whistle" on the employer's wrongdoing. **Whistleblowing** occurs when an employee tells government authorities, upper-level managers, or the press that her or his employer is engaged in some unsafe or illegal activity. Whistleblowers on occasion have been protected from wrongful discharge for reasons of public policy.[3] Normally, however, whistleblowers seek protection under statutory law. Most states have enacted so-called whistleblower statutes that protect a whistleblower from subsequent retaliation by the

WHISTLEBLOWING
An employee's disclosure to government authorities, upper-level managers, or the press that the employer is engaged in unsafe or illegal activities.

2. See, for example, *Lazar v. Superior Court of Los Angeles County,* 12 Cal.4th 631, 909 P.2d 981, 49 Cal.Rptr.2d 377 (1996); and *McConkey v. AON Corp.,* 354 N.J.Super. 25, 804 A.2d 572 (A.D. 2002).
3. See, for example, *Wendeln v. The Beatrice Manor, Inc.,* 271 Neb. 373, 712 N.W.2d 226 (2006).

employer. On the federal level, the Whistleblower Protection Act of 1989[4] protects federal employees who blow the whistle on their employers from retaliatory actions. Whistleblower statutes sometimes also offer an incentive to disclose information by providing the whistleblower with a monetary reward. For instance, for disclosing information relating to a fraud perpetrated against the U.S. government, a whistleblower might receive between 15 and 25 percent of the proceeds of a suit against the wrongdoer.[5]

Wrongful Discharge

Whenever an employer discharges an employee in violation of an employment contract or a statute protecting employees, the employee may bring an action for **wrongful discharge.** Even if an employer's actions do not violate any provisions in an employment contract or a statute, the employer may still be subject to liability under a common law doctrine, such as a tort theory or agency. EXAMPLE #4 An employer discharges a female employee and publicly discloses private facts about her sex life to her co-workers. In that situation, the fired employee could bring a wrongful discharge claim against the employer based on the tort of invasion of privacy (see Chapter 5). □

WAGE AND HOUR LAWS

In the 1930s, Congress enacted several laws regulating the wages and working hours of employees. In 1931, Congress passed the Davis-Bacon Act,[6] which requires contractors and subcontractors working on government construction projects to pay "prevailing wages" to their employees. In 1936, the Walsh-Healey Act[7] was passed. This act requires that a minimum wage, as well as overtime pay at 1.5 times regular pay rates, be paid to employees of manufacturers or suppliers entering into contracts with agencies of the federal government.

In 1938, Congress passed the Fair Labor Standards Act[8] (FLSA). This act extended wage and hour requirements to cover all employers engaged in interstate commerce or in the production of goods for interstate commerce, plus selected types of other businesses. We examine here the FLSA's provisions in regard to child labor, maximum hours, and minimum wages.

Child Labor

The FLSA prohibits oppressive child labor. Children under fourteen years of age are allowed to do certain types of work, such as deliver newspapers, work for their parents, and work in the entertainment and (with some exceptions) agricultural areas. Children who are fourteen or fifteen years of age are allowed to work, but not in hazardous occupations. There are also numerous restrictions on how many hours per day and per week they can work. Children under the age of sixteen cannot work during school hours, for more than three hours on a school day (or eight hours on a nonschool day), for more than eighteen hours

This photo, taken in 1938, the same year the FLSA was passed by Congress, shows children working in a cranberry bog in Burlington County, New Jersey. Would work involving harvesting and carrying crates of fruit be allowed under the statute as agricultural work? (Arthur Rothstein/Library of Congress)

WRONGFUL DISCHARGE
An employer's termination of an employee's employment in violation of the law.

---

4. 5 U.S.C. Section 1201.
5. The False Claims Reform Act of 1986, which amended the False Claims Act of 1863, 31 U.S.C. Sections 3729–3733.
6. 40 U.S.C. Sections 276a–276a-5.
7. 41 U.S.C. Sections 35–45.
8. 29 U.S.C. Sections 201–260.

during a school week (or forty hours during a nonschool week), or before 7 A.M. or after 7 P.M. (9 P.M. during the summer). Many states require persons under sixteen years of age to obtain work permits.

Working times and hours are not restricted for persons between the ages of sixteen and eighteen, but they cannot be employed in hazardous jobs or in jobs detrimental to their health and well-being. None of these restrictions apply to persons over the age of eighteen.

Wages and Hours

MINIMUM WAGE
The lowest wage, either by government regulation or union contract, that an employer may pay an hourly worker.

The FLSA provides that a **minimum wage** of a specified amount ($7.25 per hour in 2009) must be paid to employees in covered industries. Congress periodically revises this minimum wage.[9] Under the FLSA, the term *wages* includes the reasonable cost of the employer in furnishing employees with board, lodging, and other facilities if they are customarily furnished by that employer.

Under the FLSA, employees who work more than forty hours per week normally must be paid 1.5 times their regular pay for all hours over forty. Note that the FLSA overtime provisions apply only after an employee has worked more than forty hours per *week*. Thus, employees who work for ten hours a day, four days per week, are not entitled to overtime pay because they do not work more than forty hours per week.

Overtime Exemptions

Certain employees—usually executive, administrative, and professional employees; outside salespersons; and computer programmers—are exempt from the overtime provisions of the FLSA. Employers are not required to pay overtime wages to exempt employees. In order for an exemption to apply, an employee's specific job duties and salary must meet all the requirements of the U.S. Department of Labor (DOL) regulations. In the past, because the salary limits were low and the duties tests were complex and confusing, some employers were able to avoid paying overtime wages to their employees. This prompted the DOL to substantially revise the overtime regulations in 2004 for the first time in more than fifty years. The revisions effectively expanded the number of workers eligible for overtime by nearly tripling the salary threshold.[10]

Employers can continue to pay overtime to ineligible employees if they want to do so, but they cannot waive or reduce the overtime requirements of the FLSA. The exemptions to the overtime-pay requirement do not apply to manual laborers or other workers who perform tasks involving repetitive operations with their hands (such as nonmanagement production-line employees, for example). The exemptions also do not apply to police, firefighters, licensed nurses, and other public-safety workers. White-collar workers who earn more than $100,000 per year, computer programmers, dental hygienists, and insurance adjusters are typically exempt—though they must also meet certain other criteria. An employer cannot deny overtime wages to an employee based solely on the employee's job title.[11] (Does the FLSA require employers to pay overtime wages

---

9. Note that many state and local governments also have minimum-wage laws; these laws sometimes provide for higher minimum-wage rates than required by the federal government.
10. 29 C.F.R. Section 541.
11. See, for example, *In re Wal-Mart Stores, Inc.,* 395 F.3d 1177 (10th Cir. 2005); and *Martin v. Indiana Michigan Power Co.,* 381 F.3d 574 (6th Cir. 2004).

to workers who telecommute? See this chapter's *Online Developments* feature on page 573 for a discussion of this issue.)

Under the overtime-pay regulations, an employee qualifies for the executive exemption if, among other requirements, his or her "primary duty" is management. This requirement was the focus of the dispute in the following case.

Case 17.1   Mims v. Starbucks Corp.

United States District Court,
Southern District of Texas, 2007.
__ F.Supp.2d __.

COMPANY PROFILE   Starbucks Corporation (**www.starbucks.com**) is the largest and best-known purveyor of specialty coffees and coffee products in North America. Named after the first mate in Herman Melville's Moby Dick, Starbucks does business in more than ten thousand retail locations in the United States and forty-one foreign countries and territories. Starbucks also supplies premium, fresh-roasted coffee to bookstores, grocery stores, restaurants, airlines, sports and entertainment venues, movie theaters, hotels, and cruise ship lines throughout the world. Starbucks' success is predicated on the consistently high quality of its coffees and the other products and services it provides. Starbucks has a reputation for excellence and is recognized for its knowledgeable staff and service.

BACKGROUND AND FACTS   In Starbucks Corporation's stores, baristas wait on customers, make drinks for customers,

serve customers, operate the cash register, clean the store, and maintain its equipment. In each store, a manager supervises and motivates six to thirty employees, including baristas, shift supervisors, and assistant managers. The manager oversees customer service and processes employee records, payrolls, and inventory counts. He or she also develops strategies to increase revenues, control costs, and comply with corporate policies. Kevin Keevican was hired as a barista in March 2000. Keevican was subsequently promoted to shift supervisor, assistant manager, and, in November 2001, manager. During his tenure, Keevican doubled pastry sales at one store, nearly tripled revenues at another, and won sales awards at both. As a manager, Keevican worked seventy hours a week for $650 to $800, a 10 to 20 percent bonus, and fringe benefits that were not available to baristas, such as paid sick leave. Keevican resigned in 2004. He and other former managers, including Kathleen Mims, filed a suit in a federal district court against Starbucks, seeking unpaid overtime and other amounts. The plaintiffs admitted that they performed many managerial tasks, but argued that they spent 70 to 80 percent of their time on barista chores. Starbucks filed a motion for summary judgment.

IN THE WORDS OF THE COURT . . . *EWING WERLEIN, JR.*, United States District Judge.

* * * *

* * * An employee's primary duty is usually what the employee does that is of principal value to the employer, not the collateral tasks that she may also perform, even if they consume more than half her time.

* * * *

Where an employee spends less than 50 percent of his time on management, as both Plaintiffs claim they did, management may still be the employee's primary duty if certain pertinent factors support such a conclusion. *The four factors ordinarily considered are: (1) the relative importance of managerial duties compared to other duties; (2) the frequency with which the employee makes discretionary decisions; (3) the employee's relative freedom from supervision; and (4) the relationship between the employee's salary and the wages paid to employees who perform relevant non-exempt work.* * * * [Emphasis added.]

* * * *

The uncontroverted [not put into question] * * * record establishes that Plaintiffs' significant managerial functions—such as ordering and controlling inventory; deciding whom to interview and hire for barista positions; training and scheduling employees; special marketing promotions; and monitoring labor costs—were critical to the successes of their respective stores. If Plaintiffs while each managing a store with annual sales exceeding $1 million were able to spend 70 or 80 percent of their time pouring coffee and performing other barista chores that six to 30 subordinates also

CASE 17.1—CONTINUED

CASE 17.1–CONTINUED

performed, those activities of the manager quite obviously were of minor importance to Defendant when compared to the significant management responsibilities performed during the other 20 to 30 percent of their time, management responsibilities that directly influenced the ultimate commercial and financial success or failure of the store.

* * * *

It is uncontroverted that Plaintiffs, as the highest-ranking employees in their stores, made decisions on matters such as deciding whom to interview and hire as a barista, whom to assign to train new hires, when to discipline employees, whom to deploy in certain positions, what promotions to run, and the amount of product to order for efficient inventory control. Plaintiffs argue, however, that they infrequently exercised discretion because they worked under the "ultimate managing authority" of their district managers, who had authority to hire more senior employees, approve changes to Plaintiffs' work schedules, set rates of pay for newly-hired employees if the pay exceeded Starbucks's guidelines, and establish guidelines for Plaintiffs when completing performance reviews. *However, the manager of a local store in a modern multi-store organization has management as his or her primary duty even though the discretion usually associated with management may be limited by the company's desire for standardization and uniformity.* * * * [Emphasis added.]

Plaintiffs also contend that they were not relatively free from supervision because their district managers spent "substantial amounts of time" in Plaintiffs' stores. * * * On the other hand, it is uncontroverted that each Plaintiff as store manager was the single highest-ranking employee in his particular store and was responsible on site for that store's day-to-day overall operations. Indeed, department and assistant managers have been held exempt under the executive exemption even when their superiors worked in close proximity to them at the same location. Viewing the evidence in the light most favorable to Plaintiffs, Plaintiffs still were vested with enough discretionary power and freedom from supervision to qualify for the executive exemption.

* * * *

The final factor is the relationship between Plaintiffs' salary and the wages paid to non-exempt employees. Plaintiffs argue, with no supporting evidence, that their compensation "approximated that received by some assistant store managers." It is undisputed, however, that Plaintiffs received nearly twice the total annual compensation received by their highest-paid shift supervisors, and Plaintiffs received bonuses and benefits not available to other employees (including assistant managers). This marked disparity in pay and benefits between Plaintiffs and the non-exempt employees is a hallmark of exempt status.

DECISION AND REMEDY   The court issued a summary judgment in Starbucks' favor and dismissed the claims of the plaintiffs, who were exempt from the FLSA's overtime provisions as executive employees. The court concluded that during their employment the plaintiffs' "primary duty" was management.

WHAT IF THE FACTS WERE DIFFERENT?   Suppose that Keevican's job title had been "glorified barista" instead of "manager." Would the result have been different? Explain.

THE LEGAL ENVIRONMENT DIMENSION   What might the court have concluded if the store could have operated successfully without the plaintiffs' performing their "managerial" functions?

WORKER HEALTH AND SAFETY

Under the common law, employees injured on the job had to rely on tort law or contract law theories in suits they brought against their employers. Additionally, workers had some recourse under the common law governing agency relation-

According to WorldatWork, a research organization for human resources professionals, nearly 46 million U.S. workers perform at least part of their job at home, and close to 13 million of them are full-time *telecommuters,* meaning that they work at home or off-site by means of an electronic linkup to the central workplace. The fact that employees work at a remote location does not mean that they are automatically exempt from overtime-pay requirements (or minimum-wage laws). Federal (and sometimes state and local) wage and hour laws often apply to the virtual workforce, as many businesses are finding out the unfortunate way—through litigation.

Telecommuters and Overtime-Pay Requirements
As described in the text, the U.S. Department of Labor revised its regulations in 2004 to clarify how overtime exemptions apply to employees in various occupations. The new regulations established a primary duty test to be used in classifying workers.[a] In general, workers whose primary duty involves the exercise of discretion and independent judgment are more likely to be exempt from the overtime-pay requirements. So are those whose positions require advanced knowledge or specialized instructions, such as computer systems analysts and software engineers.

Although the regulations appear detailed, they do not specifically address how these exemptions apply to telecommuters. Since the new rules went into effect in 2004, telecommuters have filed a barrage of lawsuits claiming that their employers violated the Fair Labor Standards Act by failing to pay them for overtime work and to compensate them for work-related tasks.

a. See 29 C.F.R. Sections 541.203 and 541.400.

An Increasing Number of Cases and Settlements
To date, more cases have been filed in California than in any other state—mostly by telecommuting information technology workers, pharmaceutical sales representatives, and insurance company employees. Suits are also pending in Colorado, the District of Columbia, Illinois, Missouri, New Jersey, New York, and Ohio.

Some defendants with large numbers of employees have decided to settle before their cases go to trial. Computer Sciences Corporation in El Segundo, California, for example, paid $24 million to settle a case brought by telecommuters and call-center employees,[b] and International Business Machines Corporation (IBM) settled a similar suit for $65 million.[c] Other defendants have refused to settle. Farmers Insurance Exchange went to trial but lost and faced a significant jury verdict. On appeal to the U.S. Court of Appeals for the Ninth Circuit, however, the company prevailed.[d] In contrast, Advanced Business Integrators, Inc., had to pay nearly $50,000 in overtime compensation to a computer consultant who had spent the majority of his work time at customers' sites training their employees in the use of his employer's software.[e]

FOR CRITICAL ANALYSIS Why might telecommuting employees sometimes accept being wrongly classified as "executives" or "professionals" under the overtime-pay requirements and thus be exempt from overtime pay?

b. *Computer Sciences Corp.,* No. 03-08201 (C.D.Cal., settled in 2005).
c. *International Business Machines Corp.,* No. 06-00430 (N.D.Cal., settled in 2006).
d. *In re Farmers Insurance Exchange, Claims Representatives' Overtime Pay Litigation,* 481 F.3d 1119 (9th Cir. 2007).
e. *Eicher v. Advanced Business Integrators, Inc.,* 151 Cal.App.4th 1363, 61 Cal.Rptr.3d 114 (2007).

ships (discussed in Chapter 16), which imposes a duty on a principal-employer to provide a safe workplace for an agent-employee. Today, numerous state and federal statutes protect employees and their families from the risk of accidental injury, death, or disease resulting from their employment. This section discusses the primary federal statute governing health and safety in the workplace, along with state workers' compensation laws.

The Occupational Safety and Health Act

At the federal level, the primary legislation protecting employees' health and safety is the Occupational Safety and Health Act of 1970.[12] Congress passed this act in an attempt to ensure safe and healthful working conditions for practically every employee in the country. The act requires employers to meet specific standards in addition to their general duty to keep workplaces safe.

12. 29 U.S.C. Sections 553, 651–678.

Enforcement Agencies   Three federal agencies develop and enforce the standards set by the Occupational Safety and Health Act. The Occupational Safety and Health Administration (OSHA) is part of the U.S. Department of Labor and has the authority to promulgate standards, make inspections, and enforce the act. OSHA has developed safety standards governing many workplace details, such as the structural stability of ladders and the requirements for railings. OSHA also establishes standards that protect employees against exposure to substances that may be harmful to their health.

The National Institute for Occupational Safety and Health is part of the U.S. Department of Health and Human Services. Its main duty is to conduct research on safety and health problems and to recommend standards for OSHA to adopt. Finally, the Occupational Safety and Health Review Commission is an independent agency set up to handle appeals from actions taken by OSHA administrators.

BE AWARE
To check for compliance with safety standards without being cited for violations, an employer can often obtain advice from an insurer, a trade association, or a state agency.

Procedures and Violations   OSHA compliance officers may enter and inspect facilities of any establishment covered by the Occupational Safety and Health Act.[13] Employees may also file complaints of violations. Under the act, an employer cannot discharge an employee who files a complaint or who, in good faith, refuses to work in a high-risk area if bodily harm or death might reasonably result.

Employers with eleven or more employees are required to keep occupational injury and illness records for each employee. Each record must be made available for inspection when requested by an OSHA inspector. Whenever a work-related injury or disease occurs, employers must make reports directly to OSHA. Whenever an employee is killed in a work-related accident or when five or more employees are hospitalized as a result of one accident, the employer must notify the Department of Labor within forty-eight hours. If the company fails to do so, it will be fined. Following the accident, a complete inspection of the premises is mandatory.

Criminal penalties for willful violation of the Occupational Safety and Health Act are limited. Employers may also be prosecuted under state laws, however. In other words, the act does not preempt state and local criminal laws.[14]

State Workers' Compensation Laws

WORKERS' COMPENSATION LAWS
State statutes establishing an administrative procedure for compensating workers for injuries that arise out of—or in the course of—their employment, regardless of fault.

State **workers' compensation laws** establish an administrative procedure for compensating workers injured on the job. Instead of suing, an injured worker files a claim with the administrative agency or board that administers local workers' compensation claims.

Employees Covered by Workers' Compensation   Most workers' compensation statutes are similar. No state covers all employees. Typically, domestic workers, agricultural workers, temporary employees, and employees of common carriers (companies that provide transportation services to the public) are

---

13. In 1978, the United States Supreme Court held that warrantless inspections violated the warrant clause of the Fourth Amendment to the U.S. Constitution. *Marshall v. Barlow's, Inc.*, 436 U.S. 307, 98 S.Ct. 1816, 56 L.Ed.2d 305 (1978). In 1981, the Court held that statutory inspection programs can provide a constitutionally adequate substitute for a warrant. *Donovan v. Dewey*, 452 U.S. 594, 101 S.Ct. 2534, 69 L.Ed.2d 262 (1981).
14. *Pedraza v. Shell Oil Co.*, 942 F.2d 48 (1st Cir. 1991); *cert.* denied, *Shell Oil Co. v. Pedraza*, 502 U.S. 1082, 112 S.Ct. 993, 117 L.Ed.2d 154 (1992).

excluded, but minors are covered. Usually, the statutes allow employers to purchase insurance from a private insurer or a state fund to pay workers' compensation benefits in the event of a claim. Most states also allow employers to be self-insured—that is, employers that show an ability to pay claims do not need to buy insurance.

Requirements for Receiving Workers' Compensation   In general, the right to recover benefits is predicated wholly on the existence of an employment relationship and the fact that the injury was *accidental* and *occurred on the job or in the course of employment,* regardless of fault. Intentionally inflicted self-injury, for example, would not be considered accidental and hence would not be covered. If an injury occurs while an employee is commuting to or from work, it usually will not be considered to have occurred on the job or in the course of employment and hence will not be covered.

An employee must notify her or his employer promptly (usually within thirty days) of an injury. Generally, an employee must also file a workers' compensation claim with the appropriate state agency or board within a certain period (sixty days to two years) from the time the injury is first noticed, rather than from the time of the accident.

Workers' Compensation versus Litigation   An employee's acceptance of workers' compensation benefits bars the employee from suing for injuries caused by the employer's negligence. By barring lawsuits for negligence, workers' compensation laws also prevent employers from raising common law defenses to negligence, such as contributory negligence, assumption of risk, or injury caused by a "fellow servant" (another employee). A worker may sue an employer who *intentionally* injures the worker, however.

INCOME SECURITY

Federal and state governments participate in insurance programs designed to protect employees and their families by covering the financial impact of retirement, disability, death, hospitalization, and unemployment. The key federal law on this subject is the Social Security Act of 1935.[15]

Social Security

The Social Security Act provides for old-age (retirement), survivors, and disability insurance. The act is therefore often referred to as OASDI. Both employers and employees must "contribute" under the Federal Insurance Contributions Act (FICA)[16] to help pay for benefits that will partially make up for the employees' loss of income on retirement.

The basis for the employee's and the employer's contributions is the employee's annual wage base—the maximum amount of the employee's wages that are subject to the tax. The employer withholds the employee's FICA contribution from the employee's wages and then matches this contribution. (In 2008, employers were required to withhold 6.2 percent of each employee's wages, up to a maximum wage base of $102,000, and to match this contribution.)

---

15. 42 U.S.C. Sections 301–1397e.
16. 26 U.S.C. Sections 3101–3125.

NOTE

Social Security covers almost all jobs in the United States. Nine out of ten workers "contribute" to this protection for themselves and their families.

Retired workers are then eligible to receive monthly payments from the Social Security Administration, which administers the Social Security Act. Social Security benefits are fixed by statute but increase automatically with increases in the cost of living.

Medicare

Medicare, a federal government health-insurance program, is administered by the Social Security Administration for people sixty-five years of age and older and for some under the age of sixty-five who are disabled. It originally had two parts, one pertaining to hospital costs and the other to nonhospital medical costs, such as visits to physicians' offices. Medicare now offers additional coverage options and a prescription drug plan. People who have Medicare hospital insurance can also obtain additional federal medical insurance if they pay small monthly premiums, which increase as the cost of medical care increases.

As with Social Security contributions, both the employer and the employee "contribute" to Medicare, but unlike Social Security, Medicare places no cap on the amount of wages subject to the tax. In 2008, both the employer and the employee were required to pay 1.45 percent of *all* wages and salaries to finance Medicare. Thus, for Social Security and Medicare together, in 2008 the employer and employee each paid 7.65 percent of the first $102,000 of income (6.2 percent for Social Security + 1.45 percent for Medicare) for a combined total of 15.3 percent. In addition, all wages and salaries above $102,000 were taxed at a combined (employer and employee) rate of 2.9 percent for Medicare. Self-employed persons pay both the employer and the employee portions of the Social Security and Medicare taxes (15.3 percent of income up to $102,000 and 2.9 percent of income above that amount in 2008).

Private Pension Plans

The Employee Retirement Income Security Act (ERISA) of 1974[17] is the major federal act regulating employee retirement plans set up by employers to supplement Social Security benefits. This act empowers a branch of the U.S. Department of Labor to enforce its provisions governing employers who have private pension funds for their employees. ERISA created the Pension Benefit Guaranty Corporation (PBGC), an independent federal agency, to provide timely and uninterrupted payment of voluntary private pension benefits. The PBGC operates two pension insurance programs, one for single and one for multiple employers (usually in a single industry via collective bargaining agreements). The pension plans pay annual insurance premiums (at set rates indexed for inflation) to the PBGC, and then the PBGC pays benefits to participants. Under the Pension Protection Act of 2006,[18] the director of the PBGC is appointed by the president and confirmed by the Senate.

ERISA does not require an employer to establish a pension plan. When a plan exists, however, ERISA establishes standards for its management. A key provision of ERISA concerns vesting. **Vesting** gives an employee a legal right to receive pension benefits at some future date when he or she stops working. Before ERISA was enacted, some employees who had worked for companies for as long as thirty

VESTING

The creation of an absolute or unconditional right or power.

---

17. 29 U.S.C. Sections 1001 *et seq.*
18. Pub.L.No. 109-280, 120 Stat. 780, which was signed into law by President George W. Bush on August 16, 2006.

years received no pension benefits when their employment terminated, because those benefits had not vested. ERISA establishes complex vesting rules. Generally, however, all employee contributions to pension plans vest immediately, and employee rights to employer contributions to a plan vest after five years of employment.

In an attempt to prevent mismanagement of pension funds, ERISA has established rules on how they must be invested. Pension managers must be cautious in choosing investments and must diversify the plan's investments to minimize the risk of large losses. ERISA also contains detailed record-keeping and reporting requirements.

Unemployment Insurance

To ease the financial impact of unemployment, the United States has a system of unemployment insurance. The Federal Unemployment Tax Act (FUTA) of 1935[19] created a state-administered system that provides unemployment compensation to eligible individuals. Under this system, employers pay into a fund, and the proceeds are paid out to qualified unemployed workers. The FUTA and state laws require employers that fall under the provisions of the act to pay unemployment taxes at regular intervals.

To be eligible for unemployment compensation, a worker must be willing and able to work and be actively seeking employment. Workers who have been fired for misconduct or who have voluntarily left their jobs are not eligible for benefits. To leave a job voluntarily is to leave it without good cause.

| WATCH OUT |
If an employer does not pay unemployment taxes, a state government can place a lien (claim) on the employer's property to secure the debt. Liens were discussed in Chapter 13.

COBRA

Federal legislation also addresses the issue of health insurance for workers whose jobs have been terminated—and who are thus no longer eligible for group health-insurance plans. The Consolidated Omnibus Budget Reconciliation Act (COBRA) of 1985[20] prohibits an employer from eliminating a worker's medical, optical, or dental insurance on the voluntary or involuntary termination of the worker's employment. The act applies to most workers who have either lost their jobs or had their hours decreased so that they are no longer eligible for coverage under the employer's health plan. Only workers fired for gross misconduct are excluded from protection.

Application of COBRA The worker has sixty days (beginning with the date that the group coverage would stop) to decide whether to continue with the employer's group insurance plan. If the worker chooses to discontinue the coverage, the employer has no further obligation. If the worker chooses to continue coverage, though, the employer is obligated to keep the policy active for up to eighteen months. If the worker is disabled, the employer must extend coverage up to twenty-nine months. The coverage provided must be the same as that enjoyed by the worker prior to the termination or reduction of work. If family members were originally included, for example, COBRA prohibits their exclusion. The worker does not receive the insurance coverage for free, however. To receive continued benefits, she or he may be required to pay all of the premiums, as well as a 2 percent administrative charge.

19. 26 U.S.C. Sections 3301–3310.
20. 29 U.S.C. Sections 1161–1169.

Employers' Obligations under COBRA Employers, with some exceptions, must comply with COBRA if they employ twenty or more workers and provide a benefit plan to those workers. An employer must inform an employee of COBRA's provisions when that worker faces termination or a reduction of hours that would affect his or her eligibility for coverage under the plan.

The employer is relieved of the responsibility to provide benefit coverage if the employer completely eliminates its group benefit plan. An employer is also relieved of responsibility if the worker fails to pay the premium or becomes eligible for Medicare, is covered under a spouse's health plan, or is insured under a different plan (with a new employer, for example). An employer that does not comply with COBRA risks substantial penalties, such as a tax of up to 10 percent of the annual cost of the group plan or $500,000, whichever is less.

Employer-Sponsored Group Health Plans

The Health Insurance Portability and Accountability Act (HIPAA),[21] which was discussed in Chapter 4 in the context of privacy protections, contains provisions that affect employer-sponsored group health plans. HIPAA does not require employers to provide health insurance, but it does establish requirements for those that do provide such coverage. For example, under HIPAA, an employer's ability to exclude persons from coverage for "preexisting conditions" is strictly limited. The act defines *preexisting conditions* as those for which medical advice, diagnosis, care, or treatment was recommended or received within the previous six months (excluding pregnancy).

In addition, employers that sponsor plans have significant responsibilities regarding the manner in which they collect, use, and disclose the health information of employees and their families. Essentially, the act requires employers to comply with a number of administrative, technical, and procedural safeguards (such as training employees, designating privacy officials, and distributing privacy notices) to ensure that employees' health information is not disclosed to unauthorized parties. Failure to comply with HIPAA regulations can result in civil penalties of up to $100 per person per violation (with a cap of $25,000 per year). The employer is also subject to criminal prosecution for certain types of HIPAA violations and can face up to $250,000 in criminal fines and imprisonment for up to ten years if convicted.

FAMILY AND MEDICAL LEAVE

In 1993, Congress passed the Family and Medical Leave Act (FMLA)[22] to allow employees to take time off from work for family or medical reasons. A majority of the states also have legislation allowing for a leave from employment for family or medical reasons, and many employers maintain private family-leave plans for their workers.

Coverage and Applicability of the FMLA

The FMLA requires employers that have fifty or more employees to provide employees with up to twelve weeks of unpaid family or medical leave during any twelve-month period. The FMLA expressly covers private and public (govern-

"It is the job of the legislature to follow the spirit of the nation, provided it is not contrary to the principles of government."
—CHARLES-LOUIS DE SECONDAT, BARON DE MONTESQUIEU, 1689–1755 (French philosopher and jurist)

---

21. 29 U.S.C.A. Sections 1181 *et seq.*
22. 29 U.S.C. Sections 2601, 2611–2619, 2651–2654.

ment) employees.[23] Generally, an employee may take family leave after the birth, adoption, or foster-care placement of a child and take medical leave when the employee or the employee's spouse, child, or parent has a "serious health condition" requiring care.[24] The employer must continue the worker's health-care coverage and guarantee employment in the same position or a comparable position when the employee returns to work. An important exception to the FMLA, however, allows the employer to avoid reinstating a *key employee*—defined as an employee whose pay falls within the top 10 percent of the firm's workforce. Also, the act does not apply to part-time or newly hired employees (those who have worked for less than one year).

Employees suffering from certain chronic health conditions—such as asthma and diabetes—and employees who are pregnant, may take FMLA leave for their own incapacities that require absences of less than three days. **EXAMPLE #5** Estel, an employee who has asthma, suffers from periodic episodes of illness. According to regulations issued by the U.S. Department of Labor, employees with such conditions are covered by the FMLA. Thus, Estel may take a medical leave.□

Employees suffering from addiction to drugs and alcohol pose a special problem under the FMLA. Under what circumstances do days off resulting from the addiction, as opposed to days off for medical treatment in a medical facility, count as part of protected leave? That issue is addressed in the following case.

23. The United States Supreme Court affirmed that government employers could be sued for violating the FMLA in *Nevada Department of Human Resources v. Hibbs,* 538 U.S. 721, 123 S.Ct. 1972, 152 L.Ed.2d 953 (2003).
24. The foster care must be state sanctioned for such an arrangement to fall within the coverage of the FMLA.

Case 17.2 **Darst v. Interstate Brands Corp.**

United States Court of Appeals,
Seventh Circuit, 2008.
512 F.3d 903

BACKGROUND AND FACTS Chalimoniuk worked for Interstate Brands Corporation (IBC) for fifteen years before he was fired for excessive absenteeism. Chalimoniuk was an alcoholic who sought treatment for his condition. He requested leave under the Family and Medical Leave Act (FMLA) from July 29 to August 14, 2000, to deal with the problem. From August 4 to August 11, he was hospitalized for treatment of alcohol dependence and withdrawal. When he failed to return

to work on August 15, he was fired for being absent. IBC noted that he was also absent July 29 to August 3, when he was not hospitalized, and those days were counted as improper absences because he was already over the limit for the number of days he could miss under the company's leave policy. Chalimoniuk sued, contending IBC violated his FMLA rights. During the course of litigation, Chalimoniuk filed for bankruptcy and his claim against IBC became part of the bankruptcy estate. Darst, as trustee for the estate, continued to prosecute the claim. The district court granted summary judgment in favor of IBC. Darst appealed.

IN THE WORDS OF THE COURT . . . *ROEVNER,* Circuit Judge.

* * * *

The substantive law at issue is the FMLA. Under the FMLA, eligible employees are entitled to up to twelve weeks of unpaid leave per year for absence due to, among other things, a "Serious Health Condition" that renders the employee unable to perform the functions of his or her job. To ensure the entitlement, the FMLA makes it "unlawful for any employer to interfere with, restrain, or deny the exercise of or the attempt to exercise, any right provided." When an employee alleges a deprivation of the substantive guarantees of the FMLA, the employee must establish, by a preponderance of the evidence, an entitlement to the disputed leave. Because the district court resolved the case

CASE 17.2–CONTINUED

CASE 17.2—CONTINUED on a motion for summary judgment, Chalimoniuk need only raise a genuine issue of material fact regarding his entitlement to FMLA leave on the relevant dates.

A Serious Health Condition is defined as an illness, injury, impairment, or physical or mental condition that involves either (1) inpatient care in a hospital, hospice, or residential medical facility; or (2) continuing treatment by a healthcare provider. Although the statute itself does not specifically address whether alcoholism [and] substance abuse constitute serious health conditions, Department of Labor regulations that implement the statute provide the answer. *As we noted above, substance abuse may be a Serious Health Condition under certain conditions but FMLA leave may be taken only for treatment for substance abuse. On the other hand, absence because of the employee's use of the substance, rather than for treatment, does not qualify for FMLA leave. Under this regulation, Chalimoniuk was entitled to FMLA leave only for treatment for substance abuse.* Because of the final sentence in the regulation, the parties argue over whether Chalimoniuk was intoxicated on July 31, August 2 or August 3, but we will assume for the purposes of summary judgment that he was not intoxicated on those days. Even if he was sober on those days, however, he has provided no explanation for his absence that would excuse the absence under IBC's point system except that he was in treatment for alcoholism. [Emphasis added.]

*   *   *   *

Dr. Pfeifer [Chalimoniuk's physician] confirmed that Chalimoniuk received inpatient treatment at [the hospital] from August 4 until August 11. He produced no records and had no recollection of treating Chalimoniuk prior to that time. Chalimoniuk provided an affidavit from Dr. Pfeifer stating the doctor's belief that "treatment" for alcoholism begins when the patient takes the first step towards seeking professional help. According to Dr. Pfeifer, this includes the first phone call to the health care provider seeking evaluation, treatment or referral. Based on his training and experience as a medical doctor, Dr. Pfeifer averred [asserted] that Chalimoniuk's treatment therefore began on July 29, when he first contacted his physician's office. *Under the FMLA, however, "treatment" is a defined term that does not include actions such as calling to make an appointment. Treatment would include examinations to determine if a serious health condition exists and evaluation of the condition.* But Chalimoniuk has produced no evidence that he was being examined or evaluated on July 29, August 2 or August 3. Treatment does not include "any activities that can be initiated without a visit to a health care provider." Chalimoniuk complains that memories have faded since the time of his termination, that his doctors could have testified regarding his treatment on those days if he had known closer to the time that the company was challenging the fact of treatment on the days in question. But Chalimoniuk knew as of August 15, days after his treatment ended, that the company was denying him FMLA leave for all of the days he was absent except the period of his hospitalization. He had ample opportunities to preserve any relevant evidence. Thus, because Chalimoniuk has produced no evidence that he received any treatment as that term is defined by the FMLA on the days in question, he was not entitled to FMLA leave on those dates. Because he had exceeded the number of points allowable under IBC's absenteeism policy, the defendants were free to terminate his employment without running afoul of the FMLA. [Emphasis added.]

DECISION AND REMEDY   The appeals court affirmed that Chalimoniuk's employer did not violate his FMLA leave by dismissing him for excessive absences. FMLA leave covered the days he was receiving medical treatment, not the days he missed work prior to or after the treatment.

THE ETHICAL DIMENSION   Did IBC take unfair advantage of the "letter of the law" by not granting Chalimoniuk a little more leave time because he was, in fact, dealing with his problem? Explain your answer.

THE LEGAL ENVIRONMENT DIMENSION   Although IBC won this suit, defending the case was costly. How can employers avoid such litigation?

Violations of the FMLA

An employer that violates the FMLA may be held liable for damages to compensate an employee for unpaid wages (or salary), lost benefits, denied compensation, and actual monetary losses (such as the cost of providing for care of the family member) up to an amount equivalent to the employee's wages for twelve weeks. Supervisors may also be subject to personal liability, as employers, for violations of the act. A court may require the employer to reinstate the employee in her or his job or to grant a promotion that was denied. A successful plaintiff is entitled to court costs; attorneys' fees; and, in cases involving bad faith on the part of the employer, two times the amount of damages awarded by a judge or jury.

Employers generally are required to notify employees when an absence will be counted against leave authorized under the act. If an employer fails to provide such notice, and the employee consequently suffers an injury because he or she did not receive notice, the employer may be sanctioned.[25] **EXAMPLE #6** An employee, Isha Hartung, was absent from work for thirty weeks while undergoing treatment for cancer. Her employer did not inform Isha that this time off would count as FMLA leave. At the end of twelve weeks, the employer sent Isha a notice stating that she must return to work the following Monday, but she had not completed her chemotherapy and did not go back to work. In this situation, because the employer did not notify Isha that her absence would be considered FMLA leave, a court might allow her to take additional protected time off. □

A boy leans against his pregnant mother's belly. The mother hopes to take time off from her full-time corporate job when the baby is born. What is required for the Family and Medical Leave Act (FMLA) to apply to her employer? If the employer is covered by the FMLA, how much family leave will the mother be authorized to take?
(PhotoDisc Red)

EMPLOYEE PRIVACY RIGHTS

In the last twenty-five years, concerns about the privacy rights of employees have arisen in response to the sometimes invasive tactics used by employers to monitor and screen workers. Perhaps the greatest privacy concern in today's employment arena has to do with electronic performance monitoring. Clearly, employers need to protect themselves from liability for their employees' online activities. They also have a legitimate interest in monitoring the productivity of their workers. At the same time, employees expect to have a certain zone of privacy in the workplace. Indeed, many lawsuits have involved allegations that employers' intrusive monitoring practices violate employees' privacy rights.

Electronic Monitoring in the Workplace

According to the American Management Association, more than two-thirds of employers engage in some form of surveillance of their employees. Types of monitoring include reviewing employees' e-mail and computer files, video-recording their job performance, and recording and reviewing their telephone conversations and voice mail.

Various specially designed software products have made it easier for an employer to track employees' Internet use. Software now allows an employer to track almost every move made by an employee using the Internet, including the specific Web sites visited and the time spent surfing the Web. Filtering software,

"We are rapidly entering the age of no privacy, where everyone is open to surveillance at all times; where there are no secrets."
—WILLIAM O. DOUGLAS, 1898–1980
(Associate justice of the United States Supreme Court, 1939–1975)

---

25. *Ragsdale v. Wolverine World Wide, Inc.*, 535 U.S. 81, 122 S.Ct. 1155, 152 L.Ed.2d 167 (2002).

Employers are increasingly using sophisticated surveillance systems to monitor their employees' conduct in the workplace. What legitimate interests might employers have for using surveillance cameras? ("Redjar"/Creative Commons)

which was discussed in Chapter 4, can also be used to prevent employees from accessing certain Web sites, such as sites containing pornographic or sexually explicit images. Other filtering software may be used to screen incoming e-mail for viruses and to block junk e-mail (spam).

Although the use of filtering software by public employers (government agencies) has led to charges that blocking access to Web sites violates employees' rights to free speech, this issue does not arise in private businesses. This is because the First Amendment's protection of free speech applies only to *government* restraints on speech, and normally not to restraints imposed in the private sector.

Employee Privacy under Constitutional and Tort Law Recall from Chapter 4 that the U.S. Constitution does not contain a provision that explicitly guarantees a right to privacy. A personal right to privacy, however, has been inferred from other constitutional guarantees provided by the First, Third, Fourth, Fifth, and Ninth Amendments to the Constitution. Tort law (see Chapter 5), state constitutions, and a number of state and federal statutes also provide for privacy rights.

When determining whether an employer should be held liable for violating an employee's privacy rights, the courts generally weigh the employer's interests against the employee's reasonable expectation of privacy. Normally, if employees are informed that their communications are being monitored, they cannot reasonably expect those communications to be private. If employees are not informed that certain communications are being monitored, however, the employer may be held liable for invading their privacy. For this reason, today most employers that engage in electronic monitoring notify their employees about the monitoring.

For the most part, courts have held that an employer's monitoring of electronic communications in the workplace does not violate employees' privacy rights. Even if employees are not informed that their e-mail will be monitored, courts have generally concluded that employees have no expectation of privacy if the employer provided the e-mail system.[26] **EXAMPLE #7** Courts have even found that employers have a right to monitor the e-mail of an independent contractor (such as an insurance agent) when the employer provides the e-mail service and is authorized to access stored messages.[27] ◻

The Electronic Communications Privacy Act The major statute with which employers must comply is the Electronic Communications Privacy Act (ECPA) of 1986.[28] This act amended existing federal wiretapping law to cover electronic forms of communications, such as communications via cellular telephones or e-mail. The ECPA prohibits the intentional interception of any wire or electronic communication and the intentional disclosure or use of the informa-

---

26. For a leading case on this issue, see *Smyth v. Pillsbury Co.,* 914 F.Supp. 97 (E.D.Pa. 1996).
27. See *Fraser v. Nationwide Mutual Insurance Co.,* 352 F.3d 107 (3d Cir. 2004).
28. 18 U.S.C. Sections 2510–2521.

tion obtained by the interception. Excluded from coverage, however, are any electronic communications through devices that are "furnished to the subscriber or user by a provider of wire or electronic communication service" and that are being used by the subscriber or user, or by the provider of the service, "in the ordinary course of its business."

This "business-extension exception" to the ECPA permits employers to monitor employees' electronic communications made in the ordinary course of business. It does not permit employers to monitor employees' personal communications. Under another exception to the ECPA, however, an employer may avoid liability under the act if the employees consent to having their electronic communications intercepted by the employer. Thus, an employer may be able to avoid liability under the ECPA by simply requiring employees to sign forms indicating that they consent to such monitoring.

Preventing Legal Disputes

Although courts have generally sided with employers in monitoring cases, employers do not have *carte blanche* to monitor all employee activities and conversations. Courts have penalized some employers who have gone too far in recording personal conversations among employees or have videotaped employees in bathrooms, locker rooms, or dressing rooms. In fact, a few courts have allowed videotaping of employees only when no audio recording is involved.

To avoid legal disputes, exercise caution when monitoring employees and make sure that any monitoring is conducted in a reasonable place and manner. Establish written policies, and notify employees of how and when they may be monitored. Consider informing employees of the reasons for the monitoring. Explain what the concern is, what job repercussions could result, and what recourse employees have in the event that a negative action is taken against them. By providing more privacy protection to employees than is legally required, a businessperson can both avoid potential privacy complaints and give employees a sense that they retain some degree of privacy in their workplace. An enhanced sense of privacy can lead to greater job satisfaction, and improved employee morale can have financial benefits for employers (such as less turnover, fewer absences, and higher productivity).

Other Types of Monitoring

In addition to monitoring their employees' online activities, employers also engage in other types of employee screening and monitoring practices. These practices, which have included lie-detector tests, drug tests, genetic testing, and employment screening, have often been challenged as violations of employee privacy rights.

Lie-Detector Tests   At one time, many employers required employees or job applicants to take polygraph examinations (lie-detector tests) in connection with their employment. To protect the privacy interests of employees and job applicants, in 1988 Congress passed the Employee Polygraph Protection Act.[29] The act prohibits employers from (1) requiring or causing employees or job applicants to take lie-detector tests or suggesting or requesting that they do so; (2) using, accepting, referring to, or asking about the results of lie-detector tests

---

29. 29 U.S.C. Sections 2001 *et seq.*

taken by employees or applicants; and (3) taking or threatening negative employment-related action against employees or applicants based on results of lie-detector tests or on their refusal to take the tests.

Employers excepted from these prohibitions include federal, state, and local government employers; certain security service firms; and companies manufacturing and distributing controlled substances. Other employers may use polygraph tests when investigating losses attributable to theft, including embezzlement and the theft of trade secrets.

Drug Testing   In the interests of public safety, many employers, including the government, require their employees to submit to drug testing. Government (public) employers, of course, are constrained in drug testing by the Fourth Amendment to the U.S. Constitution, which prohibits unreasonable searches and seizures (see Chapter 4). Drug testing of public employees is allowed by statute for transportation workers and is normally upheld by the courts when drug use in a particular job may threaten public safety.[30] The Federal Aviation Administration also requires drug and alcohol testing of all employees and contractors (including employees of foreign air carriers) who perform safety-related functions.[31] When there is a reasonable basis for suspecting public employees of drug use, courts often find that drug testing does not violate the Fourth Amendment.

The Fourth Amendment does not apply to drug testing conducted by private employers. Hence, the privacy rights and drug testing of private-sector employees are governed by state law, which varies from state to state. Many states have statutes that allow drug testing by private employers but put restrictions on when and how the testing may be performed. A collective bargaining agreement (discussed later in this chapter) may also provide protection against drug testing (or authorize drug testing under certain conditions). The permissibility of a private employee's drug test often hinges on whether the employer's testing was reasonable. Random

---

30. Omnibus Transportation Employee Testing Act of 1991, Pub. L. No. 102-143, Title V, 105 Stat. 917 (1991).

31. Antidrug and Alcohol Misuse Prevention Program for Personnel Engaged in Specified Aviation Activities, 71 *Federal Register* 1666 (January 10, 2006), enacted pursuant to 49 U.S.C. Section 45102(a)(1).

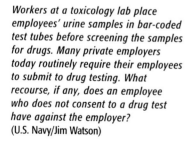

Workers at a toxicology lab place employees' urine samples in bar-coded test tubes before screening the samples for drugs. Many private employers today routinely require their employees to submit to drug testing. What recourse, if any, does an employee who does not consent to a drug test have against the employer?
(U.S. Navy/Jim Watson)

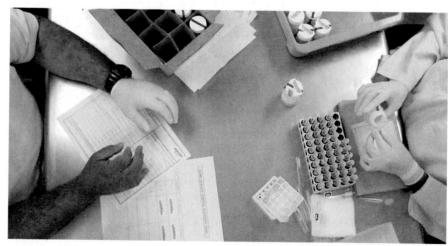

drug tests and even "zero-tolerance" policies (that deny a "second chance" to employees who test positive for drugs) have been held to be reasonable.[32]

Genetic Testing   A serious privacy issue arose when some employers began conducting genetic testing of employees or prospective employees in an effort to identify individuals who might develop significant health problems in the future. **EXAMPLE #8** In one case, the Lawrence Berkeley Laboratory screened prospective employees for the gene that causes sickle-cell anemia, although the applicants were not informed of this. In a lawsuit subsequently brought by the prospective employees, a federal appellate court held that they had a cause of action for violation of their privacy rights.[33] The case was later settled for $2.2 million. □

To prevent the improper use of genetic information in employment and health insurance, in 2008, Congress passed the Genetic Information Nondiscrimination Act (GINA).[34] Under the GINA, employers cannot make decisions about hiring, firing, job placement, or promotion based on the results of genetic testing. The GINA also prohibits group health plans and insurers from denying coverage or charging higher premiums based solely on a genetic predisposition to developing a disease in the future.

Screening Procedures   Preemployment screening procedures are another area of concern to potential employees. What kinds of questions are permissible on an employment application or a preemployment test? What kinds of questions go too far in invading the applicant's privacy? Is it an invasion of privacy, for example, to ask questions about the prospective employee's sexual orientation or religious convictions? Although an employer may believe that such information is relevant to the job for which the individual has applied, the applicant may feel differently about the matter. Generally, questions on an employment application must have a reasonable nexus, or connection, with the job for which the person is applying.

> **KEEP IN MIND**
> An employer may act on the basis of any professionally developed test, provided the test relates to the employment and does not violate the law.

IMMIGRATION LAW

The United States is known as a nation of immigrants and had no laws restricting immigration until the late nineteenth century. The most important laws governing immigration and employment today are the Immigration Reform and Control Act of 1986 (IRCA)[35] and the Immigration Act of 1990.[36] The IRCA provided amnesty to certain groups of illegal aliens then living in the United States and also established a system of sanctions against employers for hiring illegal immigrants lacking work authorization. Both legal and illegal immigration have been surging in recent decades, as illustrated in Exhibit 17–1 on the next page. The expansion of immigration has made an understanding of related legal requirements for business increasingly important. Employers must take steps to avoid hiring illegal immigrants or face serious penalties.

---

32. See *CITGO Asphalt Refining Co. v. Paper, Allied-Industrial, Chemical, and Energy Workers International Union Local No. 2-991,* 385 F.3d 809 (3d Cir. 2004).

33. *Norman-Bloodsaw v. Lawrence Berkeley Laboratory,* 135 F.3d 1260 (9th Cir. 1998).

34. Pub. L. No. 110-283, on May 21, 2008, codified at 42 U.S.C. Sections 300gg–53, 1320–9, 2000ff *et seq.*

35. 29 U.S.C. Section 1802.

36. This act amended various provisions of the Immigration and Nationality Act of 1952, 8 U.S.C. Sections 1101 *et seq.*

EXHIBIT 17–1 FOREIGN-BORN POPULATION AND ILLEGAL ALIENS, 1960–2010 (IN MILLIONS)

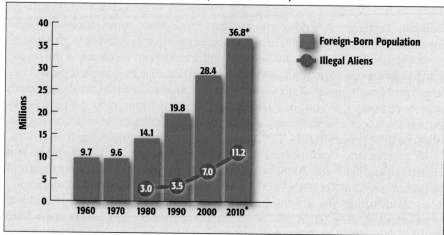

*Authors' estimates.
Source: U.S. Census Bureau, Center for Immigration Studies.

Immigration Reform and Control Act

Today, there are an estimated 11 to 12 million illegal immigrants living in the United States. The overwhelming majority of these immigrants hold jobs, and they are the subject of considerable political controversy. Many contend that the immigrants take jobs from American citizens or hold down wages for such jobs. The IRCA was intended to prevent this and made it illegal to hire, recruit, or refer for a fee someone not authorized to work in the country. The federal government—through Immigration and Customs Enforcement officers—conducts random compliance audits, and the federal government has further engaged in enforcement actions against employers who hire illegal immigrants. This section sets out the compliance requirements for companies.

I-9 Employment Verification To comply with current law (based on the 1986 act), employers must perform **I-9 verifications** for new hires, and this includes even those hired as "contractors" or "day workers" if they work under an employer's direct supervision. Form I-9, Employment Eligibility Verification, available from the U.S. Citizenship and Immigration Services,[37] must be completed within three days of the worker's commencement of employment. The three-day period is to allow the employer to verify the documents and the form's accuracy. The I-9 form requires employers to review and verify documents establishing the prospective worker's identity and eligibility for employment in the United States. Acceptable documents include a U.S. passport establishing a person's citizenship, as well as a document, such as a Permanent Resident Card or Alien Registration Receipt Card, that authorizes a foreign citizen to work in the country.

The employer must attest, under penalty of perjury, that an employee produced documents establishing his or her identity and legal employability. The employee must state that he or she is a U.S. citizen or otherwise authorized to

I-9 VERIFICATION
All employers in the United States must verify the employment eligibility and identity of newly hired workers by completing an I-9 Employment Eligibility Verification form within three business days.

---

37. The U.S. Citizenship and Immigration Services is a federal agency that is part of the U.S. Department of Homeland Security.

work in the United States. The employer is the party legally responsible for any problems with the I-9 verification process. Companies need to establish compliance procedures and keep completed I-9 forms on file for at least three years for potential future government inspection.

The IRCA prohibits "knowing" violations, which include situations in which an employer "should have known" that the worker was unauthorized. Good faith is a defense under the statute, and employers are legally entitled to rely on documentation of authorization to work that reasonably appears on its face to be genuine, even if it is later established to be counterfeit. Good faith is not a defense, however, to the failure to possess the proper paperwork. Moreover, if an employer subsequently learns that an employee is not authorized to work in this country, it must promptly discharge that employee or be in violation of the law.

Enforcement U.S. Immigration and Customs Enforcement (ICE) was established in 2003 as the largest investigative arm of the U.S. Department of Homeland Security. ICE has a general inspection program that conducts random compliance audits. Other audits may occur after the agency receives a written complaint alleging an employer's violations. Government inspections involve a review of an employer's file of I-9 forms. The government need not obtain a subpoena or a warrant to conduct such an inspection.

Administrative Actions After investigation and discovery of a possible violation, ICE will bring an administrative action and issue a Notice of Intent to Fine, which sets out the charges against the employer. The employer has a right to a hearing on the enforcement action, if it files a request within thirty days. This hearing is conducted before an *administrative law judge* (see Chapter 19), and the employer has a right to counsel and to *discovery* (see Chapter 3). The typical defense in such actions is good faith or substantial compliance with the documentation provisions. In past years, the threat of enforcement was regarded as minimal, but the federal government has substantially increased its enforcement activities. This is demonstrated by ICE data presented in Exhibit 17–2 on the following page. In 2007, ICE raided and identified hundreds of illegal workers at plants owned by companies including Koch Foods, Fresh Del Monte Produce, Tarrasco Steel, and Jones Industrial Network.

Criminal Actions ICE has increasingly sought criminal punishment for acts such as harboring an alien or illegally inducing illegal immigration. EXAMPLE #9 In January 2008, an employee of George's Processing, Inc., was convicted by a Missouri federal jury after an ICE raid resulted in the arrest of 136 illegal aliens at the plant. The convicted management employee was in the human resources department of the company and was involved in the hiring process. Evidence suggested that she helped applicants complete their I-9 forms, with knowledge that they had fraudulently obtained identity documents. The potential penalty for this crime is ten years in prison without parole. □

A company may present a defense demonstrating that the employee alleged to be in violation was truly an independent contractor rather than an employee and therefore not subject to the I-9 requirements. Even for independent contractors, though, a party's actual knowledge that a worker was unauthorized is illegal. Ultimately, the administrative law judge reviewing the case makes a ruling and assesses penalties if he or she finds a violation. This hearing may be appealed administratively or to a federal court.

EXHIBIT 17–2 WORKSITE ENFORCEMENT ARRESTS BY THE U.S. IMMIGRATION AND CUSTOMS ENFORCEMENT

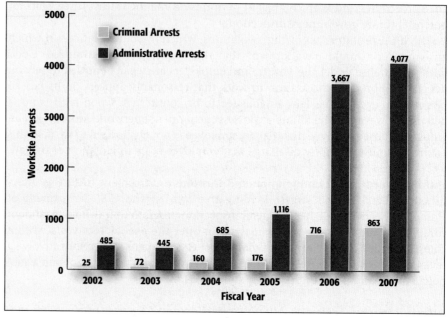

Source: U.S. Immigration and Customs Enforcement, 2008.

Individuals who believe they have suffered as a result of illegal hiring have no direct cause of action to sue an employer under immigration law. They may, however, sue under the Racketeer Influenced and Corrupt Organizations Act (RICO, which was discussed in Chapter 6). (For a discussion of the ethical implications of such lawsuits, see this chapter's *Insight into Ethics* feature.) The following case illustrates such an action.

Case 17.3 Trollinger v. Tyson Foods, Inc.

United States District Court,
Eastern District of Tennessee, 2007.
____ F.Supp.2d ____.

BACKGROUND AND FACTS Tyson Foods, Inc., is one of the nation's largest poultry processors, with more than 100,000 employees. One of its plants was located in Shelbyville, Tennessee. In December 2001, Tyson was indicted for conspiring to smuggle illegal aliens into the country and employ them. Soon after the indictment was filed, four former workers at the Shelbyville facility filed this action against Tyson under the Racketeer Influenced and Corrupt Organizations Act (RICO), alleging that Tyson engaged in an illegal scheme to depress wages by hiring illegal immigrants. Tyson moved to dismiss the complaint.

IN THE WORDS OF THE COURT . . . COLLIER, J. [Judge]

*   *   *   *

*   *   * The Complaint alleges Defendants engaged in a long-term pattern and practice of violating [the Immigration Reform and Control Act]. * * * The Complaint states Tyson signs Employment Eligibility Verification Forms (I-9 forms) in mass quantities before any documents are inspected, more than three days after new hires have been employed, and based on a review of copies of documents rather than reviewing the original documents. The Complaint further alleges Tyson prohibits its employees from taking into account obvious facts which indicate that documents do not relate to the people tendering them; rehires persons whom it previously hired under different names, usually after a short absence; hires workers who appear decades younger than the pictures on their stolen identity documents; uses temporary employment placement services to hire illegal immigrants and then "loan" them to Tyson for a fee; and gives employees leave to "get good documents" after Tyson learns the initial documents submitted by the illegal alien actually belong to someone else.

* * * *

In the context of the present illegal immigration problem in the United States, it is widely, if not universally, known that illegal immigration from Mexico is done in substantial part through smuggling. It is also of note that Tyson's processing plants are all located in areas where the predominant illegal alien population is from Mexico. *This knowledge along with the above allegations satisfies the requirement that the Complaint alleges Defendants had a subjective belief that large numbers of its illegal alien employees had been brought into the United States illegally.* [Emphasis added.]

DECISION AND REMEDY   The court denied Tyson's motion to dismiss the complaint.

WHAT IF THE FACTS WERE DIFFERENT?   Assume that Tyson's human resource managers were acting on their own, in clear violation of that company's written employment policy. Would the judge have ruled differently? Why or why not?

THE GLOBAL DIMENSION   Many businesses in U.S. communities near the border with Mexico rely on the purchasing power of immigrants, both legal and illegal. What incentives, if any, do these businesses have in helping enforce U.S. immigration laws?

Insight into Ethics

Should courts allow employees to sue their employers under RICO based on a pattern of hiring illegal immigrants?

The civil sanctions set forth in the Racketeer Influenced and Corrupt Organizations Act (RICO), which authorize treble (triple) damages, have given plaintiffs a tremendous financial incentive to pursue businesses and employers for RICO violations. RICO was not originally intended to prevent employers from hiring illegal immigrants. Nevertheless, it is increasingly being used by groups of employees who allege that their salaries would have been higher had their employer not been taking advantage of illegal aliens. Employers that have had a history of hiring illegal immigrants, bringing them into the United States, or helping to find them lodging risk being sued by their legal employees under RICO. In addition, legal workers potentially could win three times the amount of damages they actually suffered.

The Case of Mohawk Industries, Inc.

In one case, a group of employees sued their employer, Mohawk Industries, Inc. The employees claimed that Mohawk had engaged in a pattern of hiring illegal immigrants willing to work for lower wages in an effort to drive down the wages of legal employees. Mohawk—the second-largest carpet manufacturer in the United States, with more than 30,000 employees—allegedly conspired with recruiting agencies to hire undocumented workers and even provided illegal aliens with transportation from the border. The plaintiffs claimed that this pattern of illegal hiring expanded Mohawk's hourly workforce and resulted in lower wages for the plaintiffs (and other legal employees). Mohawk filed a motion to dismiss for lack of evidence of racketeering activity, which the federal court denied, and the case was appealed.

The United States Supreme Court initially granted a writ of *certiorari* but later dismissed the writ as "improvidently granted" and remanded the case to the U.S. Court of Appeals for the Eleventh Circuit. Ultimately, in September 2006, the federal appellate court ruled that the plaintiffs had presented sufficient evidence of racketeering activity to go forward with the RICO suit.[38] The potential treble damages award against Mohawk could be substantial. A number of other courts have allowed similar lawsuits against employers who knowingly hired or harbored illegal immigrants.[39]

Penalties   In general, the federal government (through ICE) enforces the current immigration laws. An employer who violates the law by hiring an unauthorized alien is subject to substantial penalties. A first offense can result in a civil fine of up to $2,200 for each unauthorized employee. Fines rise to $5,000 per employee for a second offense and up to $11,000 for subsequent offenses by the same employer. Criminal penalties apply to employers who have engaged in a "pattern or practice of violations," and these penalties include additional fines and imprisonment. A company may also be barred from future government contracts for violations.

ICE regulations provide a list of circumstances that may warrant the mitigation or aggravation of penalties. Considerations include whether the company is a small business and how much the employer cooperated in the investigation. In determining the amount of the penalty, ICE also considers the seriousness of the violation (such as intentional falsification of documents) and the employer's past compliance.

Anti-Discrimination Provisions   The IRCA provides that it is an unfair immigration-related practice for an employer to discriminate against any individual (other than an unauthorized alien) with respect to hiring or discharging the individual from employment.[40] Companies must exercise reasonable care to evaluate the required I-9 documents in a fair and consistent manner. They may not require greater proof from some prospective employees or reject apparently sufficient documentation of work authorization or citizenship. The standards and procedures for evaluating the merits of an employee's discrimination claim parallel those of Title VII of the Civil Rights Act, which will be discussed in Chapter 18.

The Immigration Act

The immigration laws of this country are very elaborate, and individuals can seek authorization to enter the country under numerous different authorities. U.S. businesses can benefit from hiring immigrants who have abilities surpassing

---

38. *Williams v. Mohawk Industries, Inc.*, 465 F.3d 1277 (11th Cir. 2006); *cert.* granted, 546 U.S. 1075, 126 S.Ct. 830, 163 L.Ed.2d 705 (2005); and *cert.* dismissed, 547 U.S. 516, 126 S.Ct. 2016, 164 L.Ed.2d 776 (2006).

39. See, for example, *Mendoza v. Zirkle Fruit Co.*, 301 F.3d 1163 (9th Cir. 2002); and *Hernandez v. Balakian*, 480 F.Supp.2d 1198 (E.D. Cal. 2007).

40. 8 U.S.C. Section 1324b.

those of available domestic workers. Our immigration laws have long made provisions for businesses to hire especially qualified foreign workers. The Immigration Act of 1990 placed caps on the number of visas (entry permits) that can be issued to immigrants each year.

Most temporary visas are set aside for workers who can be characterized as "persons of extraordinary ability," members of the professions holding advanced degrees, or other skilled workers and professionals. To hire these individuals, employers must submit a petition with the Citizenship and Immigration Services, which determines whether the job candidate meets the legal standards. Each visa is for a specific job, and there are legal limits on the employee's ability to switch jobs once in the United States.

I-551 Alien Registration Receipts   A company seeking to hire a noncitizen worker may do so if the worker is self-authorized. This means that the worker either is a lawful permanent resident or has a valid temporary Employment Authorization Document (EAD). A lawful permanent resident can prove his or her status to an employer by presenting an **I-551 Alien Registration Receipt,** known as a "green card," or a properly stamped foreign passport.

Many immigrant workers are not already self-authorized, and employers may obtain labor certification, or green cards, for those immigrants whom they wish to hire. Approximately fifty thousand new green cards are issued each year. The job must be for a permanent, full-time position. (A separate authorization system provides for the temporary entry and hiring of nonimmigrant visa workers.)

To gain such authorization for hiring a foreign worker, the employer must show that no U.S. worker is qualified, willing, and able to take the job. The employer must advertise the job opening in suitable newspapers or professional journals within six months of the hiring action. The government has detailed regulations governing the certification process.[41] Any U.S. applicants who meet the stated job qualifications must be interviewed for the position. The qualifications are also evaluated for their business necessity. A group of administrative law judges rejected one company's notice for hiring kitchen supervisors because the company required that the applicants speak Spanish.[42]

The employer must also determine from a state agency what the "prevailing wage" for the position is in the location and must offer the immigrating worker at least 100 percent of that prevailing wage. The prevailing wage rate is defined as the average wage paid to similarly employed workers in the requested occupation in the area of intended employment. Fringe benefits are also considered in this calculation.

The H-1B Visa Program   The most common and controversial visa program today involves the H-1B visa system. Individuals with H-1B visas can stay and work in the country for three to six years and work only for the sponsoring employer. The recipients of these visas include many high-tech workers. Sixty-five thousand slots for new immigrants were set aside for H-1B visas; the number was temporarily increased to 195,000, but that law expired, and the cap

I-551 ALIEN REGISTRATION RECEIPT
The I-551 Alien Registration Receipt, commonly known as a "green card," is proof that a foreign-born individual is lawfully admitted for permanent residency in the United States. Persons seeking employment can prove to prospective employers that they are legally within the U.S. by showing this receipt.

---

41. The most relevant regulations can be found at 20 C.F.R. 655 (for temporary employment) and 20 C.F.R. 656 (for permanent employment).

42. *In the matter of Malnati Organization, Inc.,* 2007-INA-00035 (Bd. Alien Lab. Cert. App. 2007).

returned to 65,000 in 2004. The available slots go quickly, and many businesses, such as Microsoft, have lobbied Congress to expand the number of H1-B visas offered to immigrants. In recent years, the total allotment of H1-B visas has been filled within the first few weeks of the year, leaving no slots available for the remaining eleven months.

The criteria for such a visa include the potential employee's "specialty occupation," which is defined as involving highly specialized knowledge and the attainment of a bachelor's or higher degree or its equivalent. Qualifying jobs may include computer programmers, electronics specialists, managers in complex businesses, engineers, professionals, and others. In one 2006 ruling, ICE found that the position of "accountant" did not qualify as a specialty occupation because the American Council for Accountancy and Taxation did not require a degree for an individual to be credentialed as such.

Labor Certification   Before an employer can submit an H-1B application, it must obtain a Labor Certification application filed on a form known as ETA 9035. The employer must agree to provide a wage level at least equal to those offered to other individuals with similar experience and qualifications and attest that the hiring will not adversely affect other workers similarly employed. The employer must inform U.S. workers of the intent to hire a foreign worker by posting the form. The U.S. Department of Labor reviews the applications and may reject them for incompleteness or inaccuracies.

EXAMPLE #10 In 2002, a former employee of Sun Microsystems complained to the Justice Department that the company was discriminating against American workers in favor of H-1B visa holders. Sun had laid off nearly four thousand domestic workers while applying for thousands of temporary visa employees. The court ultimately found that Sun had violated only minor technical requirements and ordered it only to change its posting practices for applicants for open positions. □

H-2, O, L, and E Visas   Other specialty temporary visas are available for other categories of employees. H-2 visas provide for workers performing agricultural labor of a seasonal nature. O visas provide entry for persons who have "extraordinary ability in the sciences, arts, education, business or athletics which has been demonstrated by sustained national or international acclaim." L visas allow companies to bring some of their foreign managers or executives to work inside the country. E visas permit the entry of certain foreign investors or entrepreneurs.

Immigration Reform on the Horizon

For many years, the president, members of Congress, business owners, and citizens have debated proposals for immigration reform. Some of the proposals would have allowed illegal immigrants to remain legally in this country and would have allowed many of them to eventually become citizens. At the other extreme, anti-immigration proposals would have required all illegal immigrants to leave this country and go through the full procedures for obtaining a legal way to return in order to work. At the writing of this edition, too many factors were at play to predict what immigration reform would look like in the years to come. One thing is certain: problems with immigration will remain. The average wage differential between Mexico and the United States is more than 400 percent. This wage differential is larger than between any other two countries in the world that share a contiguous border. Thus, the incentives facing those south of the border will remain the same until economic growth in Mexico (and other Latin American countries) boosts average wage rates to be closer to those in the United States.

LABOR UNIONS

In the 1930s, in addition to wage-hour laws, the government also enacted the first of several labor laws. These laws protect employees' rights to join labor unions, to bargain with management over the terms and conditions of employment, and to conduct strikes.

Federal Labor Laws

Federal labor laws governing union-employer relations have developed considerably since the first law was enacted in 1932. Initially, the laws were concerned with protecting the rights and interests of workers. Subsequent legislation placed some restraints on unions and granted rights to employers. We look here at four major federal statutes regulating union-employer relations.

Norris-LaGuardia Act   Congress protected peaceful strikes, picketing, and boycotts in 1932 in the Norris-LaGuardia Act.[43] The statute restricted the power of federal courts to issue injunctions against unions engaged in peaceful strikes. In effect, this act established a national policy permitting employees to organize.

National Labor Relations Act   One of the foremost statutes regulating labor is the National Labor Relations Act (NLRA) of 1935.[44] This act established the rights of employees to engage in collective bargaining and to strike. The act also specifically defined a number of employer practices as unfair to labor:

1. Interference with the efforts of employees to form, join, or assist labor organizations or with the efforts of employees to engage in concerted activities for their mutual aid or protection.
2. An employer's domination of a labor organization or contribution of financial or other support to it.
3. Discrimination in the hiring or awarding of tenure to employees based on union affiliation.
4. Discrimination against employees for filing charges under the act or giving testimony under the act.
5. Refusal to bargain collectively with the duly designated representative of the employees.

To ensure that employees' rights would be protected, the NLRA established the National Labor Relations Board (NLRB). The NLRB has the authority to investigate employees' charges of unfair labor practices and to file complaints against employers in response to these charges. When violations are

Union workers cast their votes in a special election held to determine whether they would accept or reject a third contract offer from their employer during collective bargaining negotiations. Suppose that the employer had threatened to fire any worker who did not vote to accept the contract offer. In that situation, which act would the employer be violating? (Larry W. Smith/Getty Images)

43. 29 U.S.C. Sections 101–110, 113–115.
44. 20 U.S.C. Section 151–169.

CEASE-AND-DESIST ORDER

An administrative or judicial order prohibiting a person or business firm from conducting activities than an agency or court has deemed illegal.

found, the NLRB may also issue **cease-and-desist orders**—orders compelling employers to stop engaging in the unfair practices. Cease-and-desist orders can be enforced by a federal appellate court if necessary. Disputes over alleged unfair labor practices are first decided by the NLRB and may then be appealed to a federal court.

To be protected under the NLRA, an individual must be an employee or a job applicant (otherwise, the NLRA's ban on discrimination in regard to hiring would mean little). Additionally, the United States Supreme Court has held that individuals who are hired by a union to organize a company (union organizers) are to be considered employees of the company for NLRA purposes.[45]

Under the NLRA, employers and unions have a duty to bargain in good faith. Bargaining over certain subjects is mandatory, and a party's refusal to bargain over these subjects is an unfair labor practice that can be reported to the NLRB. **EXAMPLE #11** In one case, an employer was required to bargain with the union over the use of hidden video surveillance cameras.[46] □

Preventing Legal Disputes

Employers should be aware that courts may require collective bargaining over any working conditions that could significantly affect the employees' daily work environment and job security. Therefore, to prevent legal disputes, employers should be straightforward with the union about any policy changes that will affect the employees' workplace. ■

CLOSED SHOP

A firm that requires union membership as a condition of employment. The closed shop was made illegal by the Labor-Management Relations Act of 1947.

UNION SHOP

A firm that requires all workers, once employed, to become union members within a specified period of time as a condition of their continued employment.

RIGHT-TO-WORK LAW

A state law providing that employees may not be required to join a union as a condition of retaining employment.

Labor-Management Relations Act   The Labor-Management Relations Act (LMRA) of 1947[47] was passed to proscribe certain unfair union practices, such as the *closed shop*. A **closed shop** requires union membership as a condition of employment. Although the act made the closed shop illegal, it preserved the legality of the union shop. A **union shop** does not require membership as a prerequisite for employment but can, and usually does, require that workers join the union after a specified amount of time on the job.

The LMRA also prohibited unions from refusing to bargain with employers, engaging in certain types of picketing, and *featherbedding*—causing employers to hire more employees than necessary. The act also allowed individual states to pass their own **right-to-work laws,** which make it illegal for union membership to be required for *continued* employment in any establishment. Thus, union shops are technically illegal in the twenty-three states that have right-to-work laws.

Labor-Management Reporting and Disclosure Act   In 1959, Congress enacted the Labor-Management Reporting and Disclosure Act (LMRDA).[48] The act established an employee bill of rights and reporting requirements for union activities. The act strictly regulates unions' internal business procedures, including union elections. For example, the LMRDA requires a union to hold regularly scheduled elections of officers using secret ballots. Ex-convicts are prohibited from holding union office. Moreover, union officials are accountable for union property and funds. Members have the right to attend and to participate in union meetings, to nominate officers, and to vote in most union proceedings.

---

45. *NLRB v. Town & Country Electric, Inc.,* 516 U.S. 85, 116 S.Ct. 450, 133 L.Ed.2d 371 (1995).
46. *National Steel Corp. v. NLRB,* 324 F.3d 928 (7th Cir. 2003).
47. 29 U.S.C. Sections 141 *et seq.*
48. 29 U.S.C. Sections 401 *et seq.*

The act also outlawed **hot-cargo agreements,** in which employers voluntarily agree with unions not to handle, use, or deal in goods produced by nonunion employees working for other employers. The act made all such boycotts (called **secondary boycotts**) illegal.

Union Organization

Typically, the first step in organizing a union at a particular firm is to have the workers sign authorization cards. An **authorization card** usually states that the worker desires to have a certain union, such as the United Auto Workers, represent the workforce. If a majority of the workers sign authorization cards, the union organizers (unionizers) present the cards to the employer and ask for formal recognition of the union. The employer is not required to recognize the union at this point in the process, but it may do so voluntarily on a showing of majority support. (Under legislation that was proposed in 2007, the employer would have been required to recognize the union as soon as a majority of the workers had signed authorization cards—without holding an election, as described next.)[49]

Union Elections   If the employer refuses to voluntarily recognize the union after a majority of the workers sign authorization cards—or if fewer than 50 percent of the workers sign authorization cards—the union organizers can present the cards to the NLRB with a petition for an election. For an election to be held, the unionizers must demonstrate that at least 30 percent of the workers to be represented support a union or an election on unionization. The NLRB supervises the election and ensures secret voting and voter eligibility. If the proposed union receives majority support in a fair election, the NLRB certifies the union as the bargaining representative for the employees.

The NLRB considers the employees' petition as a basis for calling an election. In addition to a sufficient showing of interest in unionization, the proposed union must represent an *appropriate bargaining unit.* Not every group of workers can form a single union. One key requirement of an appropriate bargaining unit is a *mutuality of interest* among all the workers to be represented. Groups of workers with significantly conflicting interests may not be represented in a single union. One factor in determining the mutuality of interest is the *similarity of the jobs* of all the workers to be unionized. A second factor is geographical, involving the physical location of the employees.

Union Election Campaigns   Many disputes between labor and management arise during union election campaigns. Generally, the employer has control over unionizing activities that take place on company property during working hours. An employer may thus limit the campaign activities of union supporters as long as the employer has a legitimate business reason for doing so. The employer may also reasonably limit the places and times that union solicitation occurs so long as the employer is not discriminating against the union. Can an employer restrict union solicitation via the company's e-mail system? The *Management Perspective* feature on the next page discusses this topic.

HOT-CARGO AGREEMENT
An agreement in which employers voluntarily agree with unions not to handle, use, or deal in other employers' goods that were not produced by union employees; a type of secondary boycott explicitly prohibited by the Labor-Management Reporting and Disclosure Act of 1959.

SECONDARY BOYCOTT
A union's refusal to work for, purchase from, or handle the products of a secondary employer, with whom the union has no dispute, in order to force that employer to stop doing business with the primary employer, with whom the union has a labor dispute.

AUTHORIZATION CARD
A card signed by an employee that gives a union permission to act on his or her behalf in negotiations with management.

---

49. The U.S. House of Representatives passed the Employee Free Choice Act, also known as the Card Check Bill (H.R. 800), in March 2007, but the bill (S 1041) was defeated in the U.S. Senate in June 2007. Because this pro-labor measure enjoyed wide support, similar legislation is likely to be proposed in the future. Thus, some of the law stated here may change dramatically.

Management Faces a Legal Issue

Most companies have e-mail policies for their employees. Some prohibit any personal use of the company's e-mail system. Others are specific about what types of personal e-mails may be sent, such as requests for charitable contributions from other employees. Most companies prohibit solicitations by outside organizations or groups that wish to use the company's e-mail system to sell products or to induce group action. The legal issue that has faced managers is how to avoid discrimination in deciding which communications using the company's e-mail system are allowed and which are not. In particular, some employers have attempted to restrict any union-related communications using corporate e-mail systems. Routinely, the National Labor Relations Board (NLRB) has prevented these employers from enforcing restrictions on union-related communications using the company's e-mail system. As long as the company officially or unofficially allowed non-work-related e-mail communications—invitations to bridal showers or recruiting for fantasy sports leagues—that company was precluded from restricting union-related e-mail communication.

What the Courts Say

In its most recent ruling, the NLRB established a precedent that allows companies to restrict union communications that utilize company e-mail systems. The Eugene (Oregon) Newspaper Guild sued the Guard Publishing Company (doing business as *The Register-Guard*). *The Register-Guard* has a policy that prohibits employees from using the newspaper's e-mail system for "non-job-related-solicitations." The newspaper's policy applied to commercial ventures, outside organizations, and religious and political causes. When the president of the newspaper union sent out several e-mails

to employees using the corporate e-mail system, the *Register-Guard* sent her two written warnings. The union claimed discriminatory restriction. The newspaper argued that it was not discriminatory because it did not permit any outside groups or organizations to use its e-mail system to distribute propaganda or induce group action.

The NLRB reversed a determination against the newspaper by an administrative law judge because the NLRB reasoned that the newspaper's policy did not regulate traditional face-to-face solicitation, which the Supreme Court held was protected in 1945.[a] The board further reasoned that when an employee is rightfully on an employer's premises, that employee does not automatically have an additional right to use the employer's equipment.[b]

Implications for Managers

The latest NLRB ruling most likely does *not* require that *current* corporate e-mail policies be changed. Those companies that do revise their e-mail policies (or prepare such policies for the first time) can impose broad prohibitions, such as allowing e-mail only for work-related purposes. Any new or revised e-mail policy should be based, nonetheless, on a real justification. A real justification might be preventing loss of productivity or protecting against computer viruses. Finally, companies can discipline their employees who use the corporate e-mail systems to send union-related communications if such communications violate the companies' general e-mail policies. Such discipline must be meted out evenly for all violations of company policy with respect to e-mails, however.

a. *Republic Aviation Corp. v. NLRB,* 324 U.S. 793 65 S.Ct. 982, 89 L.Ed. 1372 (1945).
b. *The Guard Publishing Company d/b/a/ The Register-Guard and Eugene Newspaper Guild, CWA Local 37194.*

EXAMPLE #12 A union is seeking to organize clerks at a department store owned by Amanti Enterprises. Amanti can prohibit all union solicitation in areas of the store open to the public because that activity could seriously interfere with the store's business. It can also restrict union-related activities to coffee breaks and lunch hours. If Amanti allows solicitation for charitable causes in the workplace, however, it may not prohibit union solicitation. ▫

An employer may campaign among its workers against the union, but the NLRB carefully monitors and regulates the tactics used by management, and tries to create "laboratory conditions" for a fair election. Otherwise, management might use its economic power to coerce the workers into voting against unionization. If the employer issued threats ("If the union wins, you'll all be fired") or engaged in other unfair labor practices, the NLRB may certify the union even though it lost the election. Alternatively, the NLRB may ask a court to order a new election.

COLLECTIVE BARGAINING
The process by which labor and management negotiate the terms and conditions of employment, including working hours and workplace conditions.

Collective Bargaining

If the NLRB certifies the union, the union becomes the *exclusive bargaining representative* of the workers. The central legal right of a union is to engage in collective bargaining on the members' behalf. **Collective bargaining** is the process by which labor and management negotiate the terms and conditions of employment, including wages, benefits, working conditions, and other matters. Collective bargaining allows union representatives elected by union members to speak on behalf of the members at the bargaining table.

When a union is officially recognized, it may demand to bargain with the employer and negotiate new terms or conditions of employment. In collective bargaining, as in most other business negotiations, each side uses its economic power to pressure or persuade the other side to grant concessions.

Bargaining does not mean that one side must give in to the other or that compromises must be made. It does mean that a demand to bargain with the employer must be taken seriously and that both sides must bargain in "good faith." Good faith bargaining means that management, for instance, must be willing to meet with union representatives and consider the union's wishes when negotiating a contract. Examples of bad faith bargaining on the part of management include engaging in a campaign to undermine the union among workers, constantly shifting positions on disputed contract terms, and sending bargainers who lack authority to commit the company to a contract. If an employer (or a union) refuses to bargain in good faith without justification, it has committed an unfair labor practice, and the other party may petition the NLRB for an order requiring good faith bargaining.

Strikes

Even when labor and management have bargained in good faith, they may be unable to reach a final agreement. When extensive collective bargaining has been conducted and an impasse results, the union may call a strike against the employer to pressure it into making concessions. In a **strike,** the unionized workers leave their jobs and refuse to work. The workers also typically picket the workplace, standing outside the facility with signs stating their complaints.

A strike is an extreme action. Striking workers lose their rights to be paid, and management loses production and may lose customers when orders cannot be filled. Labor law regulates the circumstances and conduct of strikes. A union may strike when the employer has engaged in unfair labor practices, but most strikes take the form of "economic strikes," which are initiated because the union wants a better contract. **EXAMPLE #13** In 2007, the United Auto Workers engaged in an economic strike when General Motors (GM) proposed that its workers accept wage cuts and pay much higher monthly premiums for health care. Approximately 73,000 GM employees walked off the job, shutting down several plants in the United States and Canada. Although the strike was settled quickly, it nevertheless resulted in lost production and profits for the company, its suppliers, and its contractors, as well as lost wages for the strikers.□

The Right to Strike The right to strike is guaranteed by the NLRA, within limits, and strike activities, such as picketing, are protected by the free speech guarantee of the First Amendment to the U.S. Constitution. Nonworkers have a right to participate in picketing an employer. The NLRA also gives workers the right to refuse to cross a picket line of fellow workers who are engaged in a lawful strike. Employers are permitted to hire replacement workers to substitute for the workers who are on strike.

STRIKE

An action undertaken by unionized workers when collective bargaining fails. The workers leave their jobs, refuse to work, and (typically) picket the employer's workplace.

Striking workers picket to publicize their labor dispute. Why is the right to strike important to unions? ("Anandsebastin"/Creative Commons)

The Rights of Strikers after a Strike Ends   An important issue concerns the rights of strikers after the strike ends. In a typical economic strike over working conditions, the employer has a right to hire permanent replacements during the strike and need not terminate the replacement workers when the economic strikers seek to return to work. In other words, striking workers are not guaranteed the right to return to their jobs after the strike if satisfactory replacement workers have been found.

If the employer has not hired replacement workers to fill the strikers' positions, however, then the employer must rehire the economic strikers to fill any vacancies. Employers may not discriminate against former economic strikers, and those who are rehired retain their seniority rights. Different rules apply when a union strikes because the employer has engaged in unfair labor practices. In this situation, the employer may still hire replacements but must give the strikers back their jobs once the strike is over.

Reviewing . . . Employment, Immigration, and Labor Law

Rick Saldona began working as a traveling salesperson for Aimer Winery in 1977. Sales constituted 90 percent of Saldona's work time. Saldona worked an average of fifty hours per week but received no overtime pay. In June 2009, Saldona's new supervisor, Caesar Braxton, claimed that Saldona had been inflating his reported sales calls and required Saldona to submit to a polygraph test. Saldona reported Braxton to the U.S. Department of Labor, which prohibited Aimer from requiring Saldona to take a polygraph test for this purpose. In August 2009, Saldona's wife, Venita, fell from a ladder and sustained a head injury while employed as a full-time agricultural harvester. Saldona delivered to Aimer's human resources department a letter from his wife's physician indicating that she would need daily care for several months, and Saldona took leave until December 2009. Aimer had sixty-three employees at that time. When Saldona returned to Aimer, he was informed that his position had been eliminated because his sales territory had been combined with an adjacent territory. Using the information presented in the chapter, answer the following questions.

1. Would Saldona have been legally entitled to receive overtime pay at a higher rate? Why or why not?

2. What is the maximum length of time Saldona would have been allowed to take leave to care for his injured spouse?

3. Under what circumstances would Aimer have been allowed to require an employee to take a polygraph test?

4. Would Aimer likely be able to avoid reinstating Saldona under the *key employee* exception? Why or why not?

Key Terms

authorization card 595	I-9 verification 586	workers' compensation
cease and desist order 594	minimum wage 570	laws 574
closed shop 594	right-to-work law 594	wrongful discharge 569
collective bargaining 596	secondary boycott 595	
employment at will 567	strike 597	
hot-cargo agreement 595	union shop 594	
I-551 Alien Registration	vesting 576	
Receipt 591	whistleblowing 568	

Chapter Summary

Employment at Will (See pages 567–569.)	1. *Employment-at-will doctrine*–Under this common law doctrine, either party may terminate the employment relationship at any time and for any reason ("at will"). This doctrine is still in widespread use throughout the United States, although federal and state statutes prevent it from being applied in certain circumstances.
	2. *Exceptions to the employment-at-will doctrine*–To protect employees from some of the harsh results of the employment-at-will doctrine, courts have made exceptions to the doctrine on the basis of contract theory, tort theory, and public policy. Whistleblowers have occasionally received protection under the common law for reasons of public policy.
	3. *Wrongful discharge*–Whenever an employer discharges an employee in violation of an employment contract or statutory law protecting employees, the employee may bring a suit for wrongful discharge.
Wage and Hour Laws (See pages 569–572.)	1. *Davis-Bacon Act (1931)*–Requires contractors and subcontractors working on federal government construction projects to pay their employees "prevailing wages."
	2. *Walsh-Healey Act (1936)*–Requires firms that contract with federal agencies to pay their employees a minimum wage and overtime pay.
	3. *Fair Labor Standards Act (1938)*–Extended wage and hour requirements to cover all employers whose activities affect interstate commerce plus certain other businesses. The act has specific requirements in regard to child labor, maximum hours, and minimum wages. The act also requires an employer to pay overtime wages to an employee who has worked more than forty hours a week unless that employee falls into one of the specified exemptions.
Worker Health and Safety (See pages 572–575.)	1. *Occupational Safety and Health Act (1970)*–Requires employers to meet specific safety and health standards that are established and enforced by the Occupational Safety and Health Administration (OSHA).
	2. *State workers' compensation laws*–Establish an administrative procedure for compensating workers who are injured in accidents that occur on the job, regardless of fault.
Income Security (See pages 575–578.)	1. *Social Security and Medicare*–The Social Security Act of 1935 provides for old-age (retirement), survivors, and disability insurance. Both employers and employees must make contributions under the Federal Insurance Contributions Act (FICA) to help pay for benefits that will partially make up for the employees' loss of income on retirement. The Social Security Administration also administers Medicare, a health-insurance program for older or disabled persons.
	2. *Private pension plans*–The federal Employee Retirement Income Security Act (ERISA) of 1974 establishes standards for the management of employer-provided pension plans.
	3. *Unemployment insurance*–The Federal Unemployment Tax Act of 1935 created a system that provides unemployment compensation to eligible individuals. Covered employers are taxed to help defray the costs of unemployment compensation.
	4. *COBRA*–The Consolidated Omnibus Budget Reconciliation Act (COBRA) of 1985 requires employers to give employees, on termination of employment, the option of continuing their medical, optical, or dental insurance coverage for a certain period.
	5. *HIPAA*–The Health Insurance Portability and Accountability Act (HIPAA) does not require employers to provide health insurance, but it does establish certain requirements for employer-sponsored health insurance. Employers must comply with a number of administrative, technical, and procedural safeguards to ensure the privacy of employees' health information.

CONTINUED

**Family and
Medical Leave**
(See pages 578–581.)

NO

The Family and Medical Leave Act (FMLA) of 1993 requires employers with fifty or more employees to provide their employees (except for key employees) with up to twelve weeks of unpaid family or medical leave during any twelve-month period for the following reasons:

1. *Family leave*–May be taken after birth, adoption, or foster-care placement of a child.

2. *Medical leave*–May be taken when the employee or the employee's spouse, child, or parent has a serious health condition requiring care.

**Employee
Privacy Rights**
(See pages 581–585.)

A right to privacy has been inferred from guarantees provided by the First, Third, Fourth, Fifth, and Ninth Amendments to the U.S. Constitution. State laws may also provide for privacy rights. Employer practices that are often challenged by employees as invasive of their privacy rights include electronic performance monitoring, lie-detector tests, drug testing, genetic testing, and screening procedures.

Immigration Law
(See pages 585–593.)

1. *Immigration Reform and Control Act (1986)*–Prohibits employers from hiring illegal immigrants; administered by the U.S. Citizenship and Immigration Services.

2. *Immigration Act (1990)*–Limits the number of legal immigrants entering the United States by capping the number of visas (entry permits) that are issued each year.

Labor Unions
(See pages 593–598.)

NO

1. *Federal labor laws–*

   a. Norris-LaGuardia Act (1932)–Protects peaceful strikes, picketing, and boycotts.

   b. National Labor Relations Act (1935)–Established the rights of employees to engage in collective bargaining and to strike; also defined specific employer practices as unfair to labor. The National Labor Relations Board (NLRB) was created to administer and enforce the act.

   c. Labor-Management Relations Act (1947)–Proscribes certain unfair union practices, such as the closed shop.

   d. Labor-Management Reporting and Disclosure Act (1959)–Established an employee bill of rights and reporting requirements for union activities.

2. *Union organization*–Union campaign activities and elections must comply with the requirements established by federal labor laws and the NLRB.

3. *Collective bargaining*–The process by which labor and management negotiate the terms and conditions of employment (such as wages, benefits, and working conditions). The central legal right of a labor union is to engage in collective bargaining on the members' behalf.

4. *Strikes*–When collective bargaining reaches an impasse, union members may use their ultimate weapon in labor-management struggles–the strike. A strike occurs when unionized workers leave their jobs and refuse to work.

For Review

1. What is the employment-at-will doctrine? When and why are exceptions to this doctrine made?
2. What federal statute governs working hours and wages?
3. What federal law was enacted to protect the health and safety of employees? What are workers' compensation laws?
4. Under the Family and Medical Leave Act of 1993, under what circumstances may an employee take family or medical leave?
5. What federal statute gave employees the right to organize unions and engage in collective bargaining?

Questions and Case Problems

17–1. Wage and Hour. Calzoni Boating Co. is an interstate business engaged in manufacturing and selling boats. The company has five hundred nonunion employees. Representatives of these employees are requesting a four-day, ten-hours-per-day workweek, and management is concerned that this would require paying time and a half after eight hours per day. Which federal act is management thinking of that might require this? Will the act in fact require paying time and a half for all hours worked over eight hours per day if the employees' proposal is accepted? Explain.

Question with Sample Answer

 17–2. Denton and Carlo were employed at an appliance plant. Their job required them to do occasional maintenance work while standing on a wire mesh twenty feet above the plant floor. Other employees had fallen through the mesh; one was killed by the fall. When Denton and Carlo were asked by their supervisor to do work that would likely require them to walk on the mesh, they refused due to their fear of bodily harm or death. Because of their refusal to do the requested work, the two employees were fired from their jobs. Was their discharge wrongful? If so, under what federal employment law? To what federal agency or department should they turn for assistance?

For a sample answer to Question 17–2, go to Appendix I at the end of this text.

17–3. Unfair Labor Practice. The New York Department of Education's e-mail policy prohibits the use of the e-mail system for unofficial purposes, except that officials of the New York Public Employees Federation (PEF), the union representing state employees, can use the system for some limited communications, including the scheduling of union meetings and activities. In 1998, Michael Darcy, an elected PEF official, began sending mass, union-related e-mails to employees, including a summary of a union delegates' convention, a union newsletter, a criticism of proposed state legislation, and a criticism of the state governor and the Governor's Office of Employee Relations. Richard Cate, the department's chief operating officer, met with Darcy and reiterated the department's e-mail policy. When Darcy refused to stop his use of the e-mail system, Cate terminated his access to it. Darcy filed a complaint with the New York Public Employment Relations Board, alleging an unfair labor practice. Do the circumstances support Cate's action? Why or why not? [*Benson v. Cuevas,* 293 A.D.2d 927, 741 N.Y.S.2d 310 (3 Dept. 2002)]

17–4. Collective Bargaining. Verizon New York, Inc. (VNY), provides telecommunications services. VNY and the Communications Workers of America (CWA) are parties to collective bargaining agreements covering installation and maintenance employees. At one time, VNY supported annual blood drives. VNY, CWA, and charitable organizations jointly set dates, arranged appointments, and adjusted work schedules for the drives. For each drive, about a thousand employees, including managers, spent up to four hours traveling to a donor site, giving blood, recovering, and returning to their jobs. Employees received full pay for the time. In 2001, VNY told CWA that it would no longer allow employees to participate "on Company time," claiming that it experienced problems meeting customer requests for service during the drives. CWA filed a complaint with the National Labor Relations Board (NLRB), asking that VNY be ordered to bargain over the decision. Did VNY commit an unfair labor practice? Should the NLRB grant CWA's request? Why or why not? [*Verizon New York, Inc. v. National Labor Relations Board,* 360 F.3d 206 (D.C.Cir. 2004)]

17–5. Workers' Compensation. The Touch of Class Lounge is in a suburban shopping plaza, or strip mall, in Omaha, Nebraska. Patricia Bauer, the Lounge's owner, does not own the parking lot, which is provided for the common use of all of the businesses in the plaza. Stephanie Zoucha was a bartender at the Lounge. Her duties ended when she locked the door after closing. On June 4, 2001, at 1:15 A.M., Zoucha closed the bar and locked the door. An hour later, she walked to her car in the parking lot, where she was struck with "[l]ike a tire iron on the back of my head." Zoucha sustained a skull fracture and other injuries, including significant cognitive impairment (speech and thought formation). Her purse, containing her tip money, was stolen. She identified her attacker as William Nunez, who had been in the Lounge earlier that night. Zoucha filed a petition in a Nebraska state court to obtain workers' compensation. What are the requirements for receiving workers' compensation? Should Zoucha's request be granted or denied? Why? [*Zoucha v. Touch of Class Lounge,* 269 Neb. 89, 690 N.W.2d 610 (2005)]

17–6. Collective Bargaining. Ceridian Corp. provides employment services to other companies. One of its divisions offers counseling to its customers' employees through a call-in center in Eagan, Minnesota. Under Ceridian's "Personal Days Off" (PDO) policy, employees can use a certain amount of paid time off each year for whatever purpose they wish, but unpaid leave is not available. Employees who take time off in excess of their

PDO are subject to discipline, including discharge. In June 2003, the National Labor Relations Board (NLRB) certified Service Employees International Union 113 as the exclusive collective bargaining representative for 130 employees at the call-in center. The union assembled a six-employee team to negotiate a collective bargaining agreement. Ceridian refused to meet with the team during nonworking hours or to grant the members unpaid leave to attend bargaining sessions during working hours, but required them to use their PDO instead. The union filed an unfair-labor-practice charge with the NLRB against Ceridian, alleging that the employer impermissibly interfered with its employees' choice of bargaining representatives. Did Ceridian commit an unfair labor practice? Explain. [*Ceridian Corp. v. National Labor Relations Board,* 435 F.3d 352 (D.C.Cir. 2006)]

Case Problem with Sample Answer

17–7. Jennifer Willis worked for Coca Cola Enterprises, Inc. (CCE), in Louisiana as a senior account manager. On a Monday in May 2003, Willis called her supervisor to tell him that she was sick and would not be able to work that day. She also said that she was pregnant, but she did not say she was sick *because* of the pregnancy. On Tuesday, she called to ask where to report to work and was told that she could not return without a doctor's release. She said that she had a doctor's appointment on "Wednesday," which her supervisor understood to be the next day. Willis meant the *following* Wednesday. More than a week later, during which time Willis did not contact CCE, she was told that she had violated CCE's "No Call/No Show" policy. Under this policy "an employee absent from work for three consecutive days without notifying the supervisor during that period will be considered to have voluntarily resigned." She was fired. Willis filed a suit in a federal district court against CCE under the Family and Medical Leave Act (FMLA). To be eligible for FMLA leave, an employee must inform an employer of the reason for the leave. Did Willis meet this requirement? Did CCE's response to Willis's absence violate the FMLA? Explain. [*Willis v. Coca Cola Enterprises, Inc.,* 445 F.3d 413 (5th Cir. 2006)]

After you have answered Problem 17–7, compare your answer with the sample answer given on the Web site that accompanies this text. Go to www.cengage.com/blaw/let, select "Chapter 17," and click on "Case Problem with Sample Answer."

17–8. Unemployment Insurance. Mary Garas, a chemist, sought work in Missouri through Kelly Services, Inc. Kelly is a staffing agency that places individuals in jobs of varying duration with other companies. Through Kelly, Garas worked at Merial Co. from April 2005 to February 2006. After the assignment ended, Garas asked Kelly for more work. Meanwhile, she filed a claim for unemployment benefits with the Missouri Division of Employment Security (DES). In March, Kelly recruiter Rebecca Cockrum told Garas about a temporary assignment with Celsis Laboratory. Garas said that she would prefer a "more stable position," but later asked Cockrum to submit her résumé to Celsis. Before the employer responded, Kelly told the DES that Garas had refused suitable work. Under a Missouri state statute, a claim for unemployment benefits must be denied if "the claimant failed without good cause . . . to accept suitable work when offered the claimant . . . by an employer by whom the individual was formerly employed." The DES denied Garas's claim for benefits. She filed an appeal with a state court. Was the DES's denial right or wrong? Why? [*Garas v. Kelly Services, Inc.,* 211 S.W.3d 149 (Mo.App. E.D. 2007)]

A Question of Ethics

17–9. Beverly Tull had worked for Atchison Leather Products, Inc., in Kansas for ten years when, in 1999, she began to complain of hand, wrist, and shoulder pain. Atchison recommended that she contact a certain physician, who in April 2000 diagnosed the condition as carpal tunnel syndrome "severe enough" for surgery. In August, Tull filed a claim with the state workers' compensation board. Because Atchison changed workers' compensation insurance companies every year, a dispute arose as to which company should pay Tull's claim. Fearing liability, no insurer would authorize treatment, and Tull was forced to delay surgery until December. The board granted her temporary total disability benefits for the subsequent six weeks that she missed work. On April 23, 2002, Berger Co. bought Atchison. The new employer adjusted Tull's work to be less demanding and stressful, but she continued to suffer pain. In July, a physician diagnosed her condition as permanent. The board granted her permanent partial disability benefits. By May 2005, the bickering over the financial responsibility for Tull's claim involved five insurers—four of which had each covered Atchison for a single year and one of which covered Berger. [*Tull v. Atchison Leather Products, Inc.,* 37 Kan.App.2d 87, 150 P.3d 316 (2007)]

1. When an injured employee files a claim for workers' compensation, there is a proceeding to assess the injury and determine the amount of compensation. Should a dispute between insurers over the payment of the claim be resolved in the same proceeding? Why or why not?

2. The board designated April 23, 2002, as the date of Tull's injury. What is the reason for determining the date of a worker's injury? Should the board in

this case have selected this date or a different date? Why?

3. How should the board assess liability for the payment of Tull's medical expenses and disability benefits? Would it be appropriate to impose joint and several liability on the insurers, or should the individual liability of each of them be determined? Explain.

Video Question

17-10. Go to this text's Web site at **www.cengage.com/blaw/let** and select "Chapter 17." Click on "Video Questions" and view the video titled *Employment at Will*. Then answer the following questions.

1. In the video, Laura asserts that she can fire Ray "For any reason. For no reason." Is this true? Explain your answer.

2. What exceptions to the employment-at-will doctrine are discussed in the chapter? Does Ray's situation fit into any of these exceptions?

3. Would Ray be protected from wrongful discharge under whistleblowing statutes? Why or why not?

4. Assume that you are the employer in this scenario. What arguments can you make that Ray should not be able to sue for wrongful discharge in this situation?

For updated links to resources available on the Web, as well as a variety of other materials, visit this text's Web site at

www.cengage.com/blaw/let

The American Federation of Labor–Congress of Industrial Organizations (AFL-CIO) provides links to labor-related resources at

www.aflcio.org

The Bureau of Labor Statistics provides a wide variety of data on employment. Go to

www.bls.gov

PRACTICAL INTERNET EXERCISES

Go to this text's Web site at **www.cengage.com/blaw/let**, select "Chapter 17," and click on "Practical Internet Exercises." There you will find the following Internet research exercises that you can perform to learn more about the topics covered in this chapter.

Practical Internet Exercise 17–1: LEGAL PERSPECTIVE—**Workers' Compensation**
Practical Internet Exercise 17–2: MANAGEMENT PERSPECTIVE—**Workplace Monitoring and Surveillance**
Practical Internet Exercise 17–3: HISTORICAL PERSPECTIVE—**Labor Unions and Labor Law**

BEFORE THE TEST

Go to this text's Web site at **www.cengage.com/blaw/let**, select "Chapter 17," and click on "Interactive Quizzes." You will find a number of interactive questions relating to this chapter.

Chapter 18

Employment Discrimination

CHAPTER OBJECTIVES

After reading this chapter, you should be able to answer the following questions:

1. Generally, what kind of conduct is prohibited by Title VII of the Civil Rights Act of 1964, as amended?

2. What is the difference between disparate-treatment discrimination and disparate-impact discrimination?

3. What remedies are available under Title VII of the 1964 Civil Rights Act, as amended?

4. What federal acts prohibit discrimination based on age and discrimination based on disability?

5. What are three defenses to claims of employment discrimination?

CONTENTS

" Nor shall any State . . . deny to any person within its jurisdiction the equal protection of the laws. "

— THE FOURTEENTH AMENDMENT TO THE U.S. CONSTITUTION

PROTECTED CLASS

A group of persons protected by specific laws because of the group's defining characteristics. Under laws prohibiting employment discrimination, these characteristics include race, color, religion, national origin, gender, age, and disability.

EMPLOYMENT DISCRIMINATION

Treating employees or job applicants unequally on the basis of race, color, national origin, religion, gender, age, or disability; prohibited by federal statutes.

Out of the 1960s civil rights movement to end racial and other forms of discrimination grew a body of law protecting employees against discrimination in the workplace. This protective legislation further eroded the employment-at-will doctrine, which was discussed in the previous chapter. In the past several decades, judicial decisions, administrative agency actions, and legislation have restricted the ability of employers, as well as unions, to discriminate against workers on the basis of race, color, religion, national origin, gender, age, or disability. A class of persons defined by one or more of these criteria is known as a **protected class.**

Several federal statutes prohibit **employment discrimination** against members of protected classes. The most important statute is Title VII of the Civil Rights Act of 1964.[1] Title VII prohibits discrimination on the basis of race, color, religion, national origin, or gender at any stage of employment. The Age Discrimination in Employment Act of 1967[2] and the Americans with Disabilities Act of 1990[3] prohibit discrimination on the basis of age and disability, respectively.

This chapter focuses on the kinds of discrimination prohibited by these federal statutes. Note, though, that discrimination against employees on the basis of any of these criteria may also violate state human rights statutes or other state laws or public policies prohibiting discrimination.

---

1. 42 U.S.C. Sections 2000e–2000e-17.
2. 29 U.S.C. Sections 621–634.
3. 42 U.S.C. Sections 12102–12118.

TITLE VII OF THE CIVIL RIGHTS ACT OF 1964

Title VII of the Civil Rights Act of 1964 and its amendments prohibit job discrimination against employees, applicants, and union members on the basis of race, color, national origin, religion, or gender at any stage of employment. Title VII applies to employers with fifteen or more employees, labor unions with fifteen or more members, labor unions that operate hiring halls (to which members go regularly to be rationed jobs as they become available), employment agencies, and state and local governing units or agencies. A special section of the act prohibits discrimination in most federal government employment. When Title VII applies to the employer, any employee—including an undocumented (alien) worker—can bring an action for employment discrimination. Moreover, an employer with fewer than fifteen employees is not automatically shielded from a lawsuit filed under Title VII.[4]

The Equal Employment Opportunity Commission

Compliance with Title VII is monitored by the Equal Employment Opportunity Commission (EEOC). A victim of alleged discrimination, before bringing a suit against the employer, must first file a claim with the EEOC. The EEOC may investigate the dispute and attempt to obtain the parties' voluntary consent to an out-of-court settlement. If a voluntary agreement cannot be reached, the EEOC may then file a suit against the employer on the employee's behalf. If the EEOC decides not to investigate the claim, the victim may bring her or his own lawsuit against the employer.

The EEOC does not investigate every claim of employment discrimination, regardless of the merits of the claim. Generally, it investigates only "priority cases," such as cases involving retaliatory discharge (firing an employee in retaliation for submitting a claim to the EEOC) and cases involving types of discrimination that are of particular concern to the EEOC. In recent years, the EEOC has been receiving and investigating an increasing number of claims of religious discrimination in the workplace.[5]

Intentional and Unintentional Discrimination

Title VII prohibits both intentional and unintentional discrimination.

Intentional Discrimination Intentional discrimination by an employer against an employee is known as **disparate-treatment discrimination.** Because intent may sometimes be difficult to prove, courts have established certain procedures for resolving disparate-treatment cases. EXAMPLE #1 A woman applies for employment with a construction firm and is rejected. If she sues on the basis of disparate-treatment discrimination in hiring, she must show that (1) she is a member of a protected class, (2) she applied and was qualified for the job in question, (3) she was rejected by the employer, and (4) the employer continued

DISPARATE-TREATMENT DISCRIMINATION
A form of employment discrimination that results when an employer intentionally discriminates against employees who are members of protected classes.

---

4. The United States Supreme Court has held that even if an employer has fewer than fifteen employees, courts still have jurisdiction to hear an employee's Title VII claim. See *Arbaugh v. Y&H Corp.,* 546 U.S. 500, 126 S.Ct. 1235, 163 L.Ed.2d 1097 (2006).
5. Dick Dahl, "EEOC Reports 10 Percent Increase in Charges," *Lawyers USA,* February 26, 2007.

to seek applicants for the position or filled the position with a person not in a protected class.▫

If the woman can meet these relatively easy requirements, she has made out a **prima facie case** of illegal discrimination. Making out a *prima facie* case of discrimination means that the plaintiff has met her initial burden of proof and will win in the absence of a legally acceptable employer defense. (Defenses to claims of employment discrimination will be discussed later in this chapter.) The burden then shifts to the employer-defendant, who must articulate a legal reason for not hiring the plaintiff. For instance, the employer might say that the plaintiff was not hired because she lacked sufficient experience or training. To prevail, the plaintiff must then show that the employer's reason is a *pretext* (not the true reason) and that discriminatory intent actually motivated the employer's decision.

Unintentional Discrimination   Employers often use interviews and testing procedures to choose from among a large number of applicants for job openings. Minimum educational requirements are also common. These practices and procedures may have an unintended discriminatory impact on a protected class. **Disparate-impact discrimination** occurs when a protected group of people is adversely affected by an employer's practices, procedures, or tests, even though they do not appear to be discriminatory. In a disparate-impact discrimination case, the complaining party must first show statistically that the employer's practices, procedures, or tests are discriminatory in effect. The plaintiff must show a causal link between the practice and the discriminatory effect. Once the plaintiff has made out a *prima facie* case, the burden of proof shifts to the employer to show that the practices or procedures in question were justified. There are two ways of proving that disparate-impact discrimination exists, as discussed next.

Pool of Applicants   A plaintiff can prove a disparate impact by comparing the employer's workforce with the pool of qualified individuals available in the local labor market. The plaintiff must show that as a result of educational or other job requirements or hiring procedures, the percentage of nonwhites, women, or members of other protected classes in the employer's workforce does not reflect the percentage of that group in the pool of qualified applicants. If a person challenging an employment practice can show a connection between the practice and the disparity, he or she has made out a *prima facie* case and need not provide evidence of discriminatory intent.

Rate of Hiring   Disparate-impact discrimination can also occur when an educational or other job requirement or hiring procedure excludes members of a protected class from an employer's workforce at a substantially higher rate than nonmembers, regardless of the racial balance in the employer's workforce. This "rates analysis" compares the selection rate for whites with that for nonwhites (or other members of a protected class). The plaintiff does not have to prove that the workforce does not reflect the percentage of qualified nonwhite persons available in the local labor market.

The EEOC has devised a test, called the "four-fifths rule," to determine whether an employment examination is discriminatory on its face. Under this rule, a selection rate for protected classes that is less than four-fifths, or 80 percent, of the rate for the group with the highest rate will generally be regarded as evidence of disparate impact. **EXAMPLE #2** One hundred white applicants take an

PRIMA FACIE **CASE**
A case in which the plaintiff has produced sufficient evidence of his or her claim that the case can go to a jury; a case in which the evidence compels a decision for the plaintiff if the defendant produces no affirmative defense or evidence to disprove the plaintiff's assertion. (*Prima facie* means "on initial examination of consideration"; it also means "legally sufficient.")

DISPARATE-IMPACT DISCRIMINATION
A form of employment discrimination that results from certain employer practices or procedures that, although not discriminatory on their face, have a discriminatory effect.

employment test, and fifty pass the test and are hired. One hundred minority applicants take the test, and twenty pass the test and are hired. Because twenty is less than four-fifths (80 percent) of fifty, the test would be considered discriminatory under the EEOC guidelines. □

Discrimination Based on Race, Color, and National Origin

If a company's standards or policies for selecting or promoting employees have the effect of discriminating against employees or job applicants on the basis of race, color, or national origin, they are presumed to be illegal. Employers can avoid liability for the discriminatory effect of certain policies (except those that discriminate on the basis of race) by showing a substantial, demonstrable relationship to realistic qualifications for the job in question. Discrimination against these protected classes in regard to employment conditions and benefits is also illegal.

EXAMPLE #3 Cynthia McCullough, an African American woman with a college degree, had worked at a deli in a grocery store for more than a year, but the owner of the store promoted a white woman to the position of "deli manager." The white woman had worked in the deli for only three months, had only a sixth-grade education, and could not calculate prices or read recipes. Although the owner gave various reasons for promoting the white woman instead of McCullough, a court would be likely to hold that these reasons were just excuses and that the real reason was discriminatory intent. □

Reverse Discrimination   Note that discrimination based on race can also take the form of *reverse discrimination,* or discrimination against "majority" individuals, such as white males. **EXAMPLE #4** In one Pennsylvania case, an African American woman fired four white men from their management positions at a school district. The men filed a lawsuit for racial discrimination, alleging that the woman was trying to eliminate white males from the department. The woman claimed that the terminations were part of a reorganization plan to cut costs in the department. The jury sided with the men and awarded them nearly $3 million in damages. The verdict was upheld on appeal (though the damages award was reduced slightly).[6] □

Potential "Section 1981" Claims   Victims of racial or ethnic discrimination may also have a cause of action under 42 U.S.C. Section 1981. This section, which was enacted as part of the Civil Rights Act of 1866 to protect the rights of freed slaves, prohibits discrimination on the basis of race or ethnicity in the formation or enforcement of contracts. Because employment is often a contractual relationship, Section 1981 can provide an alternative (and potentially advantageous) basis for a plaintiff's action.[7] Unlike Title VII, Section 1981 does not place a cap on damages (see the discussion of Title VII remedies later in this chapter). Thus, if an employee can prove that he or she was discriminated against in the formation or enforcement of a contract, the employee may be able to obtain a larger damages award under Section 1981 than would be available under Title VII.

---

6. *Johnston v. School District of Philadelphia,* 2006 WL 999966 (E.D.Pa. 2006).

7. See, for example, *E.E.O.C. v. Sephora USA, LLC,* 419 F.Supp.2d 408 (S.D.N.Y. 2005).

Discrimination Based on Religion

Title VII of the Civil Rights Act of 1964 also prohibits government employers, private employers, and unions from discriminating against persons because of their religion. An employer must "reasonably accommodate" the religious practices of its employees, unless to do so would cause undue hardship to the employer's business. For instance, if an employee's religion prohibits him or her from working on a certain day of the week or at a certain type of job, the employer must make a reasonable attempt to accommodate these religious requirements. Employers must reasonably accommodate an employee's religious belief even if the belief is not based on the tenets or dogma of a particular church, sect, or denomination. The only requirement is that the belief be sincerely held by the employee.

Discrimination Based on Gender

Under Title VII, as well as other federal acts (including the Equal Pay Act of 1963, which we also discuss here), employers are forbidden from discriminating against employees on the basis of gender. Employers are prohibited from classifying jobs as male or female and from advertising in help-wanted columns that are designated male or female unless the employer can prove that the gender of the applicant is essential to the job. Furthermore, employers cannot have separate male and female seniority lists. Generally, to succeed in a suit for gender discrimination, a plaintiff must demonstrate that gender was a determining factor in the employer's decision to hire, fire, or promote her or him. Typically, this involves looking at all of the surrounding circumstances.

The Equal Pay Act of 1963,[8] which amended the Fair Labor Standards Act of 1938 (discussed in Chapter 17), prohibits employers from gender-based wage discrimination. For the act's equal pay requirements to apply, the male and female

---

8. 29 U.S.C. Section 206(d).

Two Muslims, originally from Somalia, perform religious acts in the evening in Nashville, Tennessee. Under Title VII of the Civil Rights Act, do employers have to accommodate the religious practices of their employees?
(AP Photo/Eric Parsons/*The Tennessean*)

employees must work at the same establishment doing similar work (a barber and a beautician, for example). To determine whether the Equal Pay Act has been violated, a court will look to the primary duties of the two jobs. It is the job content rather than the job description that controls in all cases. If a court finds that the wage differential is due to any factor other than gender, such as a seniority or merit system, then it does not violate the Equal Pay Act.

The Pregnancy Discrimination Act of 1978,[9] which amended Title VII, expanded the definition of gender discrimination to include discrimination based on pregnancy. Women affected by pregnancy, childbirth, or related medical conditions must be treated—for all employment-related purposes, including the receipt of benefits under employee benefit programs—the same as other persons not so affected but similar in ability to work.

Constructive Discharge

The majority of Title VII complaints involve unlawful discrimination in decisions to hire or fire employees. In some situations, however, employees who leave their jobs voluntarily can claim that they were "constructively discharged" by the employer. **Constructive discharge** occurs when the employer causes the employee's working conditions to be so intolerable that a reasonable person in the employee's position would feel compelled to quit.

CONSTRUCTIVE DISCHARGE
A termination of employment brought about by making the employee's working conditions so intolerable that the employee reasonably feels compelled to leave.

Proving Constructive Discharge The plaintiff must present objective proof of intolerable working conditions, which the employer knew or had reason to know about yet failed to correct within a reasonable time period. Courts generally also require the employee to show causation—that the employer's unlawful discrimination caused the working conditions to be intolerable. Put a different way, the employee's resignation must be a foreseeable result of the employer's discriminatory action.

EXAMPLE #5 Khalil's employer humiliates him by informing him in front of his co-workers that he is being demoted to an inferior position. Khalil, who was born in Iraq, is then subjected to continued insults, harassment, and derogatory remarks about his national origin by his co-workers. The employer is aware of this discriminatory treatment but does nothing to remedy the situation, despite repeated complaints from Khalil. After several months, Khalil quits his job and files a Title VII claim. In this situation, Khalil would likely have sufficient evidence to maintain an action for constructive discharge in violation of Title VII.□ Although courts weigh the facts on a case-by-case basis, employee demotion is one of the most frequently cited reasons for a finding of constructive discharge, particularly when the employee was subjected to humiliation.

Applies to All Title VII Discrimination Note that constructive discharge is a theory that plaintiffs can use to establish any type of discrimination claims under Title VII, including race, color, national origin, religion, gender, pregnancy, and sexual harassment. Constructive discharge has also been successfully used in situations that involve discrimination based on age or disability (both of which will be discussed later in this chapter). Constructive discharge is most commonly asserted in cases involving sexual harassment, however.

---

9. 42 U.S.C. Section 2000e(k).

When constructive discharge is claimed, the employee can pursue damages for loss of income, including back pay. These damages ordinarily would not be available to an employee who left a job voluntarily.

Sexual Harassment

SEXUAL HARASSMENT
In the employment context, demands for sexual favors in return for job promotions or other benefits, or language or conduct that is so sexually offensive that it creates a hostile working environment.

Title VII also protects employees against **sexual harassment** in the workplace. Sexual harassment can take two forms: *quid pro quo* harassment and hostile-environment harassment. *Quid pro quo* is a Latin phrase that is often translated to mean "something in exchange for something else." *Quid pro quo* harassment occurs when sexual favors are demanded in return for job opportunities, promotions, salary increases, and the like. According to the United States Supreme Court, hostile-environment harassment occurs when "the workplace is permeated with discriminatory intimidation, ridicule, and insult, that is sufficiently severe or pervasive to alter the conditions of the victim's employment and create an abusive working environment."[10]

The courts determine on a case-by-case basis whether the sexually offensive conduct was sufficiently severe or pervasive to create a hostile environment. Typically, a single incident of sexually offensive conduct is not enough to permeate the work environment (although there have been exceptions when the conduct was particularly severe). **EXAMPLE #6** If a male supervisor makes suggestive gestures and tells a female employee on one occasion that he would like to have sexual relations with her, that may not be enough to make the work environment hostile.[11] If a supervisor repeatedly makes sexually offensive comments, however, or asks for specific details about the sexual conduct of a co-worker on several occasions, this may be enough to create a hostile environment.[12]□

Preventing Legal Disputes

It is essential for business owners and managers to be familiar with the laws pertaining to sexual harassment and gender discrimination, and to understand what constitutes a hostile environment. Remember that harassment in the workplace can take many forms and be based on many characteristics (gender, race, national origin, religion, age, and disability) but that sexual harassment is always based on an employee's gender. Establish written policies and review them annually. Any complaint should be taken seriously and investigated. Some employment specialists even suggest that employers assume that hostile-environment harassment has occurred if an employee claims that it has. Prompt remedial action is key, but it must not include any immediate adverse action against the complainant (such as termination). Most importantly, immediately seek the advice of counsel when a complaint arises. ■

Harassment by Supervisors   For an employer to be held liable for a supervisor's sexual harassment, the supervisor must have taken a tangible employment action against the employee. A **tangible employment action** is a significant change

TANGIBLE EMPLOYMENT ACTION
A significant change in employment status, such as a change brought about by firing or failing to promote an employee; reassigning the employee to a position with significantly different responsibilities; or effecting a significant change in employment benefits.

---

10. *Harris v. Forklift Systems*, 510 U.S. 17, 114 S.Ct. 367, 126 L.Ed.2d 295 (1993).
11. *Pomales v. Celulares Telefonica, Inc.*, 447 F.3d 79 (1st Cir. 2006); and *Fontanez-Nunez v. Janssen Ortho, LLC*, 447 F.3d 50 (1st Cir. 2006).
12. See, for example, *Fye v. Oklahoma Corp. Commission*, 2006 WL 895237 (10th Cir. 2006).

in employment status, such as a change brought about by firing or failing to promote an employee, reassigning the employee to a position with significantly different responsibilities, or effecting a significant change in employment benefits.

Only a supervisor, or another person acting with the authority of the employer, can cause this sort of injury. A co-worker can sexually harass another employee, and anyone who has regular contact with an employee can inflict psychological injuries by offensive conduct. A co-worker cannot dock another's pay, demote her or him, or set conditions for continued employment, though.

EXAMPLE #7 Jin was a sales agent at Metropolitan Life Insurance Company (MetLife). Morabito was Jin's supervisor. Morabito made sexual remarks to Jin, offensively touched her, and forced her to engage in sexual acts by threatening to fire her and physically harm her if she did not submit to his demands. When Jin sued MetLife for sexual harassment, the jury found that she had not been subjected to a tangible employment action. A federal appellate court reversed, however. The court reasoned that Morabito had used his authority as a supervisor to impose on Jin the added job requirement that she submit to sexual abuse to keep her job.[13] □

Supreme Court Guidelines In 1998, in two separate cases, the United States Supreme Court issued some significant guidelines relating to the liability of employers for their supervisors' harassment of employees in the workplace. In *Faragher v. City of Boca Raton*,[14] the Court held that an employer (a city) could be held liable for a supervisor's harassment of employees even though the employer was unaware of the behavior. The Court reached this conclusion primarily because, although the city had a written policy against sexual harassment, the policy had not been distributed to city employees. Additionally, the city had not established any procedures that could be followed by employees who felt that they were victims of sexual harassment. In *Burlington Industries, Inc. v. Ellerth*,[15] the Court ruled that a company could be held liable for the harassment of an employee by one of its vice presidents even though the employee suffered no adverse job consequences.

In these two cases, the Court set forth some guidelines on workplace harassment that are helpful to employers and employees alike. On the one hand, employees benefit from the ruling that employers may be held liable for their supervisors' harassment even though the employers were unaware of the actions and even though the employees suffered no adverse job consequences. On the other hand, the Court made it clear in both decisions that employers have an affirmative defense against liability for their supervisors' harassment of employees if the employers can show the following:

1. That they have taken "reasonable care to prevent and correct promptly any sexually harassing behavior" (by establishing effective harassment policies and complaint procedures, for example).
2. That the employees suing for harassment failed to follow these policies and procedures.

> *"Justice is better than chivalry if we cannot have both."*
>
> —ALICE STONE BLACKWELL,
> 1857–1950
> (American suffragist and editor)

---

13. *Jin v. Metropolitan Life Insurance Co.,* 295 F.3d 335 (2d Cir. 2002); republished at 310 F.3d 84 (2d Cir. 2002).
14. 524 U.S. 775, 118 S.Ct. 2275, 141 L.Ed.2d 662 (1998).
15. 524 U.S. 742, 118 S.Ct. 2257, 141 L.Ed.2d 633 (1998).

In 2004, the Supreme Court further clarified the tangible employment action requirement as it applies in constructive discharge cases. The Court held that "[t]o establish constructive discharge, a plaintiff alleging sexual harassment must show that the work environment became so intolerable that resignation was a fitting response. An employer may then assert the *Ellerth/Faragher* affirmative defense unless the plaintiff quit in reasonable response to a tangible employment action."[16]

Retaliation by Employer   Charges of sexual harassment by supervisors—and other claims under Title VII as well—have sometimes resulted in attempts by the employer to retaliate against the employee bringing the claim by demoting him or her or by making some other change in his or her employment status. Title VII includes an antiretaliation provision that makes it unlawful for an employer to "discriminate against" an employee or applicant who has "opposed" a practice that Title VII prohibits. In a *retaliation claim,* the individual asserts that she or he has suffered a harm as a result of making a charge, testifying, or participating in a Title VII investigation or proceeding.

The courts disagreed, however, on what the plaintiff had to show to prove retaliation. Some courts required a plaintiff to show that the challenged action resulted in an adverse effect on the terms or conditions of *employment.* Other courts required a plaintiff to show only that the challenged action would have been material to a reasonable employee. In the following case, the United States Supreme Court considered whether Title VII's ban on retaliation covers acts that are not job related.

---

16. *Pennsylvania State Police v. Suders,* 542 U.S. 129, 124 S.Ct. 2342, 159 L.Ed.2d 204 (2004).

Case 18.1 Burlington Northern and Santa Fe Railway Co. v. White

Supreme Court of the United States, 2006.
548 U.S. 53, 126 S.Ct. 2405, 165 L.Ed.2d 345.

BACKGROUND AND FACTS   Sheila White worked in the maintenance department of the Burlington Northern and Santa Fe Railway Company's Tennessee yard. She was the only female worker in that department. She complained to Burlington officials that her supervisor, Bill Joiner, had repeatedly said that women should not be working in the maintenance department. White was reassigned from forklift duty to "track laborer" duties. Joiner was disciplined for his

remarks. In her new job, White's supervisor complained to Burlington officials that White had been insubordinate. She was suspended without pay but was later reinstated after an investigation. She was awarded back pay for the period of the suspension. Among other actions, White then filed a Title VII suit in federal district court claiming that Burlington's actions in changing her job responsibilities and suspending her without pay amounted to unlawful retaliation. The jury found in White's favor and awarded her $43,500 in damages. On appeal to the U.S. Court of Appeals for the Sixth Circuit, the district court's judgment was affirmed. Burlington then appealed to the United States Supreme Court.

IN THE WORDS OF THE COURT . . . Justice *BREYER* delivered the opinion of the court.

*   *   *   *

*   *   * The language of the [antidiscrimination] provision differs from that of the anti-retaliation provision in important ways.

The *   *   * words in the [antidiscrimination] provision—"hire," "discharge," "compensation, terms, conditions, or privileges of employment," "employment opportunities," and "status as an employee"—explicitly limit the scope of that provision to actions that affect employment or alter the conditions of the workplace. No such limiting words appear in the antiretaliation provision.

* * * The two provisions differ not only in language but in purpose as well. The anti-discrimination provision seeks a workplace where individuals are not discriminated against because of their racial, ethnic, religious, or gender-based status. *The anti-retaliation provision seeks to secure that primary objective by preventing an employer from interfering (through retaliation) with an employee's efforts to secure or advance enforcement of the Act's basic guarantees.* The [antidiscrimination] provision seeks to prevent injury to individuals based on who they are, i.e., their status. *The anti-retaliation provision seeks to prevent harm to individuals based on what they do, i.e., their conduct.* [Emphasis added.]

To secure the first objective, Congress did not need to prohibit anything other than employment-related discrimination.

But one cannot secure the second objective by focusing only upon employer actions and harm that concern employment and the workplace. * * * *An employer can effectively retaliate against an employee by taking actions not directly related to his employment or by causing him harm outside the workplace.* [Emphasis added.]

* * * *

* * * We conclude that * * * the anti-retaliation provision extends beyond workplace-related or employment-related retaliatory acts * * * .

* * * *

* * * A plaintiff must show that a reasonable employee would have found the challenged action materially adverse, which in this context means it well might have dissuaded a reasonable worker from making or supporting a charge of discrimination.

* * * *

* * * [In this case] the track labor duties were by all accounts more arduous [difficult] and dirtier; * * * the forklift operator position required more qualifications, which is an indication of prestige; and * * * the forklift operator position was objectively considered a better job and the male employees resented White for occupying it. Based on this record, a jury could reasonably conclude that the reassignment of responsibilities would have been materially adverse to a reasonable employee.

* * * *

For these reasons, the judgment of the Court of Appeals is affirmed.

DECISION AND REMEDY   The United States Supreme Court affirmed the appellate court's ruling and upheld the damages awarded. The Court found that a reasonable employee could have found the challenged action materially adverse, regardless of whether it was job related.

WHAT IF THE FACTS WERE DIFFERENT?   Assume that White had been reassigned to another job within Burlington that was considered to be of equal "prestige" and was no "dirtier" than her previous job as a forklift operator. Would the outcome of this case have been the same? Why or why not?

THE ETHICAL DIMENSION   How might Burlington have avoided the initial problem of male employees' overtly expressing resentment against White because she was the only female working in the maintenance department?

Harassment by Co-Workers and Nonemployees   Often, employees alleging harassment complain that the actions of co-workers, not supervisors, are responsible for creating a hostile working environment. In such cases, the employee may still have a cause of action against the employer. Normally, though, the employer will be held liable only if the employer knew, or should have known, about the harassment and failed to take immediate remedial action.

Employers may also be liable for harassment by *nonemployees* in certain circumstances. EXAMPLE #8 A restaurant owner or manager knows that a certain customer repeatedly harasses a waitress and permits the harassment to continue. The restaurant owner may be liable under Title VII even though the customer is not an employee of the restaurant. The issue turns on the control that the employer exerts over a nonemployee. In one case, an owner of a Pizza Hut franchise was held liable for the harassment of a waitress by two male customers because no steps were taken to prevent the harassment.[17] ▫

Same-Gender Harassment   The courts have also had to address the issue of whether men who are harassed by other men, or women who are harassed by other women, are protected by laws that prohibit gender-based discrimination in the workplace. For example, what if the male president of a firm demands sexual favors from a male employee? Does this action qualify as sexual harassment? For some time, the courts were widely split on this issue. In 1998, in *Oncale v. Sundowner Offshore Services, Inc.,*[18] the United States Supreme Court resolved the issue by holding that Title VII protection extends to situations in which individuals are harassed by members of the same gender.

Nevertheless, it can be difficult to prove that the harassment in same-gender harassment cases is "based on sex." EXAMPLE #9 Suppose that a gay man is harassed by another man at the workplace. The harasser is not a homosexual and does not treat all men with hostility—just this one man. Does the victim in this situation have a cause of action under Title VII? A court may find that the harasser's conduct does not qualify as sexual harassment under Title VII because it was based on the employee's sexual orientation, not on his "sex."[19] ▫ Note that although Title VII does not prohibit discrimination or harassment based on a person's sexual orientation, a growing number of companies are voluntarily establishing nondiscrimination policies that include sexual orientation. In addition, an increasing number of states have passed laws prohibiting sexual orientation discrimination in the workplace.[20] (Workers in the United States often have more protection against sexual harassment in the workplace than workers in other countries, as this chapter's *Beyond Our Borders* feature explains.)

Online Harassment

Employees' online activities can create a hostile working environment in many ways. Racial jokes, ethnic slurs, or other comments contained in e-mail may become the basis for a claim of hostile-environment harassment or some other form of discrimination. A worker who sees sexually explicit images on a co-worker's computer screen may find the images offensive and claim that they create a hostile working environment.

Nevertheless, employers may be able to avoid liability for online harassment if they take prompt remedial action. EXAMPLE #10 Angela Daniels, an employee

---

17. *Lockard v. Pizza Hut, Inc.,* 162 F.3d 1062 (10th Cir. 1998).
18. 523 U.S. 75, 118 S.Ct. 998, 140 L.Ed.2d 201 (1998).
19. See, for example, *McCown v. St. John's Health System,* 349 F.3d 540 (8th Cir. 2003); and *Rene v. MGM Grand Hotel, Inc.,* 305 F.3d 1061 (9th Cir. 2002).
20. See, for example, 775 Illinois Compiled Statutes 5/1–103.

The problem of sexual harassment in the workplace is not confined to the United States. Indeed, it is a worldwide problem for female workers. In Argentina, Brazil, Egypt, Turkey, and many other countries, there is no legal protection against any form of employment discrimination. Even in those countries that do have laws prohibiting discriminatory employment practices, including gender-based discrimination, those laws often do not specifically include sexual harassment as a discriminatory practice. Several countries have attempted to remedy this omission by passing new laws or amending others to specifically prohibit sexual harassment in the workplace. Japan, for example, has amended its Equal Employment Opportunity Law to include a provision making sexual harassment illegal. Thailand has also passed its first sexual-harassment law. In 2002, the European Union, which some years ago outlawed gender-based discrimination, adopted a directive that specifically identifies sexual harassment as a form of discrimination. Nevertheless, women's groups throughout Europe contend that corporations in European countries tend to view sexual harassment with "quiet tolerance." They contrast this attitude with that of most U.S. corporations, which have implemented specific procedures to deal with harassment claims.

FOR CRITICAL ANALYSIS Why do you think U.S. corporations are more aggressive than European companies in taking steps to prevent sexual harassment in the workplace?

of Robert Half International under contract to WorldCom, Inc., received racially harassing e-mailed jokes from another employee. After receiving the jokes, Daniels complained to WorldCom managers. Shortly afterward, the company issued a warning to the offending employee about the proper use of the e-mail system and held two meetings to discuss company policy on the use of the system. In Daniels's suit against WorldCom for racial discrimination, a federal district court concluded that the employer was not liable for its employee's racially harassing e-mails because the employer took prompt remedial action.[21] □ This chapter's *Online Developments* feature on the following two pages discusses some new issues related to employees' computer use.

Remedies under Title VII

Employer liability under Title VII may be extensive. If the plaintiff successfully proves that unlawful discrimination occurred, he or she may be awarded reinstatement, back pay, retroactive promotions, and damages. Compensatory damages are available only in cases of intentional discrimination. Punitive damages may be recovered against a private employer only if the employer acted with malice or reckless indifference to an individual's rights. The statute limits the total amount of compensatory and punitive damages that the plaintiff can recover from specific employers—ranging from $50,000 against employers with one hundred or fewer employees to $300,000 against employers with more than five hundred employees.

DISCRIMINATION BASED ON AGE

Age discrimination is potentially the most widespread form of discrimination, because anyone—regardless of race, color, national origin, or gender—could be a victim at some point in life. The Age Discrimination in Employment Act (ADEA) of 1967, as amended, prohibits employment discrimination on the basis of age

---

21. *Daniels v. WorldCom, Corp.*, 1998 WL 91261 (N.D.Tex. 1998). See also *Musgrove v. Mobil Oil Corp.*, 2003 WL 21653125 (N.D.Tex. 2003).

As computers come to be used for more and more aspects of both personal and professional life, the line between personal use and work-related use is becoming blurred. As this chapter has explained, employers are legally required to prevent discrimination in the workplace, including a hostile environment created by workers' online activities. That employers have a right—or even an obligation—to monitor their employees' computer use to this end is generally established. Indeed, as discussed in Chapter 17, courts have generally held that employees have no expectation of privacy in their workplace computers when a private employer supplies the equipment. The limits of this privacy exception are still being tested, however, as a number of issues related to computers, privacy, and employment discrimination remain unresolved. A new issue that is just emerging is whether employers can obtain information about job applicants by conducting online searches when asking for the same information on a job application or in an interview might be illegal.

Searches of Workplace Computers

An employee who uses his or her workplace computer to view sexually explicit photographs may create a hostile environment if the photographs can be seen by other employees. Furthermore, if the photographs involve children, the employee's activities may be illegal. Courts have generally held that employers can search a workplace computer for evidence of employee misconduct[a] and that

they can also consent to a search by government officials. If the computer is in a locked office, however, does the employee have a greater expectation of privacy? In 2007, in *United States v. Ziegler,*[b] the court had to answer this question.

The Internet service provider for Frontline Processing Corporation informed the Federal Bureau of Investigation (FBI) that one of Frontline's computers had been used to access child-pornography Web sites in violation of federal criminal law. The FBI investigated and determined that Jeffrey Ziegler, Frontline's director of operations, had used the computer in his office to search for and view online photos of "very young girls in various states of undress." Frontline agreed to cooperate with the FBI, and at some point corporate employees entered Ziegler's locked office and made a backup copy of the hard drive on his computer without his consent.

Ziegler appealed his subsequent conviction for possessing child pornography on the ground that the search of his computer violated his Fourth Amendment rights against unreasonable search and seizure. The U.S. Court of Appeals for the Ninth Circuit first held that Ziegler had no reasonable expectation of privacy, but on rehearing, the court changed its ruling and held that Ziegler did have a reasonable expectation of privacy in the contents of the computer in his locked office. Because the employer (Frontline) owned the computer, however, the court held that Frontline's consent validated the search. According to the court, a "computer is the type of workplace property that remains within control

a. See, for example, *Twymon v. Wells Fargo & Co.*, 462 F.3d 925 (8th Cir. 2006).

b. 474 F.3d 1184 (9th Cir. 2007).

against individuals forty years of age or older. The act also prohibits mandatory retirement for nonmanagerial workers. For the act to apply, an employer must have twenty or more employees, and the employer's business activities must affect interstate commerce. The EEOC administers the ADEA, but the act also permits private causes of action against employers for age discrimination.

The ADEA includes a provision that extends protections against age discrimination to federal government employees.[22] In 2008, the United States Supreme Court ruled that this provision includes not only claims of age discrimination—which its language expressly provides—but also claims of retaliation for complaining about age discrimination—which its language does not mention. The case involved a forty-five-year-old postal worker, Myrna Gómez-Pérez, who asked for and received a transfer to a particular post office in Puerto Rico to be close to her ailing mother. Gómez-Pérez allegedly suffered various forms of retaliation after the transfer, such as being told to "go back" to where she came from, being

22. See 29 U.S.C. Section 623a(a) (2000 ed., Supp. V).

of the employer 'even if the employee has placed personal items in it.'"

Unresolved Issues

Certainly, the trend is toward limiting employees' expectations of privacy in employer-owned computers in the workplace, but several questions remain open. What expectations of privacy does an employee have in a laptop computer that is provided by the company but is used by the employee at home or on the road? Similarly, if the employee works at home on an employer-owned computer, to what degree can the employer justify monitoring the employee's online activities? Although computers in remote locations could be used to send harassing e-mail, other employees are unlikely to view offensive material on such computers, so that justification for monitoring Internet use seems less valid.

Other issues have to do with whether employers must tell employees that their computer use will be monitored and the degree to which employers should monitor employees' online activities that are mostly personal. To date, only two states (Connecticut and Delaware) have passed laws specifically requiring private employers to inform employees that their workplace Internet activities will be monitored. Personal blogs raise an even more complex issue: Does an employer have the right to monitor its employees' personal blogs? If an employee's personal blog contains racially or sexually offensive comments about co-workers, what should the employer do? Thus far, in most of the cases involving employees dismissed for computer misuse, the employer had a written Internet policy and presented evidence that the employee knew about and disregarded the policy. According to recent surveys, however, most organizations do not have policies on employees' blogs.

Even more problematic is another issue that is just emerging. Today, many college students and recent graduates belong to social networking sites, such as Facebook.com and MySpace.com, where they can post photographs, comments, blogs, and even videos about themselves. Some of this material is suggestive, to say the least. A number of employers have begun to use search engines to seek out information on job applicants. A search may turn up not just photos that the applicant intended to be viewed only by close friends but also information about the applicant's marital status, sexual orientation, or political or religious views that the employer could not ask for on a job application or discuss in a job interview. Nevertheless, this information is now readily available to employers. Some colleges and employment counselors are beginning to advise job seekers to make sure that they remove any information they do not want a prospective employer to see, but the issue of whether employers have a right to search for this information is likely to persist.

FOR CRITICAL ANALYSIS   Suppose that an employee writes a message to like-minded persons concerning religious beliefs or political views. Can the employee be fired in that situation? Who decides what is acceptable Internet activity when there is no written policy?

---

falsely accused of sexual harassment and other misconduct, and having her hours drastically reduced. The Supreme Court ruled that the ADEA protects federal workers from retaliation based on age-related complaints, just as it protects private-sector employees from retaliation.[23]

Procedures under the ADEA

The burden-shifting procedure under the ADEA is similar to that under Title VII. If a plaintiff can establish that she or he (1) was a member of the protected age group, (2) was qualified for the position from which she or he was discharged, and (3) was discharged under circumstances that give rise to an inference of discrimination, the plaintiff has established a *prima facie* case of unlawful age discrimination. The burden then shifts to the employer, who must articulate a legitimate reason for the discrimination. If the plaintiff can prove that the

REMEMBER
The Fourteenth Amendment prohibits any state from denying any person "the equal protection of the laws." This prohibition applies to the federal government through the due process clause of the Fifth Amendment.

---

23. *Gómez-Pérez v. Potter, Postmaster General*, ___ U.S. ___, 128 S.Ct. 1931, ___ L.Ed.2d ___ (2008).

employer's reason is only a pretext (excuse) and that the plaintiff's age was a determining factor in the employer's decision, the employer will be held liable under the ADEA.

Replacing Older Workers with Younger Workers

Numerous age discrimination cases have been brought against employers who, to cut costs, replaced older, higher-salaried employees with younger, lower-salaried workers. Whether a firing is discriminatory or simply part of a rational business decision to prune the company's ranks is not always clear. Companies often defend a decision to discharge a worker by asserting that the worker could no longer perform his or her duties or that the worker's skills were no longer needed.

The employee must prove that the discharge was motivated, at least in part, by age bias. Proof that qualified older employees are generally discharged before younger employees or that co-workers continually made unflattering age-related comments about the discharged worker may be enough. The plaintiff need not prove that he or she was replaced by a person outside the protected class (under the age of forty years) as long as the person is younger than the plaintiff. The issue in all ADEA cases is whether age discrimination has, in fact, occurred, regardless of the age of the replacement worker. Nevertheless, the bigger the age gap, the more likely the individual is to succeed in showing age discrimination.

Sometimes large companies go through what they call a restructuring, during which they reduce the size of their overall work force by a large number of employees. Oftentimes when this occurs, older workers are laid off, while younger (lower-salaried) workers are retained. When a laid-off worker subsequently files suit against the company for age discrimination, a court must decide what testimony concerning the company's attitudes toward workers' ages will be allowed as evidence at trial. This issue was at the heart of the following United States Supreme Court case.

Case 18.2 **Sprint/United Management Co. v. Mendelsohn**

Supreme Court of the United States, 2008.
___ U.S. ___, 128 S.Ct. 1140, 170 L.Ed.2d 1.

BACKGROUND AND FACTS   Ellen Mendelsohn worked for Sprint/United Management (Sprint) from 1989 to 2002, when Sprint fired her during a company-wide reduction in force. She sued under the ADEA, alleging disparate treatment based on her age, fifty-one. Five other former Sprint employees testified that they had also suffered discrimination based on age. Three said that they heard managers make remarks belittling older

workers and that age was a factor in planning who was to be fired during the reduction in force. None of the five witnesses worked in the same part of the company as Mendelsohn, however, and none could testify about her supervisors. The district court excluded their testimony as to the impact on Mendelsohn because the witnesses were not "similarly situated" in the company. The district court, nonetheless, held that these witnesses could testify about their contention that the reduction in force was a pretext for age discrimination in general by the employer. The appeals court held that the testimony was *per se* not relevant and had to be excluded. Mendelsohn appealed.

IN THE WORDS OF THE COURT . . . JUSTICE *THOMAS* delivered the opinion of the Court.

* * * *

In deference to a district court's familiarity with the details of the case and its greater experience in evidentiary [based on evidence] matters, courts of appeals afford broad discretion to a district court's evidentiary rulings. This Court has acknowledged:

A district court is accorded a wide discretion in determining the admissibility of evidence under the Federal Rules. Assessing the probative value of [the proffered evidence], and weighing any factors counseling against admissibility is a matter first for the district court's sound judgment under [Federal Evidence] Rules 401 and 403 * * *.

This is particularly true with respect to Rule 403 since it requires an "on-the-spot balancing of probative [supplying proof] value and prejudice, potentially to exclude as unduly prejudicial some evidence that already has been found to be factually relevant." Under this deferential standard, courts of appeals uphold Rule 403 rulings unless the district court has abused its discretion.

* * * *

In the Court of Appeals' view, the District Court excluded the evidence as *per se* irrelevant, and so had no occasion to reach the question whether such evidence, if relevant, should be excluded under Rule 403. The Court of Appeals, upon concluding that such evidence was not *per se* irrelevant, decided that it was relevant in the circumstances of this case and undertook its own balancing under Rule 403. *But questions of relevance and prejudice are for the District Court to determine in the first instance. Rather than assess the relevance of the evidence itself and conduct its own balancing of its probative value and potential prejudicial effect, the Court of Appeals should have allowed the District Court to make these determinations in the first instance, explicitly and on the record.* [Emphasis added.]

* * * *

The question whether evidence of discrimination by other supervisors is relevant in an individual ADEA case is fact based and depends on many factors, including how closely related the evidence is to the plaintiff's circumstances and theory of the case. Applying Rule 403 to determine if evidence is prejudicial also requires a fact-intensive, context-specific inquiry. Because Rules 401 and 403 do not make such evidence *per se* admissible or *per se* inadmissible, and because the inquiry required by those Rules is within the province of the District Court in the first instance, we vacate the judgment of the Court of Appeals and remand the case with instructions to have the District Court clarify the basis for its evidentiary ruling under the applicable Rules.

DECISION AND REMEDY The Supreme Court vacated the appellate court's decision and remanded the case to the district court. The Court found that the district court should have allowed testimony from employees who could comment about the company's attitudes concerning age discrimination. Their testimony is relevant to the plaintiff's claims even if they could not comment specifically on the attitudes of the plaintiff's immediate supervisors.

WHAT IF THE FACTS WERE DIFFERENT? The negative comments made by supervisors about older workers reportedly came from managers in other parts of the company. What if a witness testified that one of Mendelsohn's supervisors had made such negative comments? What might have transpired during the trial?

THE LEGAL ENVIRONMENT DIMENSION What steps should employers take within an organization to reduce the likelihood that supervisors will make negative comments concerning workers' ages?

State Employees Not Covered by the ADEA

Generally, the states are immune from lawsuits brought by private individuals in federal court—unless a state consents to the suit. This immunity stems from the United States Supreme Court's interpretation of the Eleventh Amendment (the text of this amendment is included in Appendix B). EXAMPLE #11 In two Florida cases, professors and librarians contended that their employers—two Florida state universities—denied them salary increases and other benefits because they were getting old and their successors could be hired at lower cost. The universities claimed that as agencies of a sovereign state, they could not be sued in federal court without the state's consent. The cases ultimately reached the United States Supreme Court, which held that the Eleventh Amendment bars private parties from suing state employers for violations of the ADEA.[24]□

State immunity under the Eleventh Amendment is not absolute, however, as the Supreme Court explained in 2004. In some situations, such as when fundamental rights are at stake, Congress has the power to abrogate (abolish) state immunity to private suits through legislation that unequivocally shows Congress's intent to subject states to private suits.[25] As a general rule, though, the Court has found that state employers are immune from private suits brought by employees under the ADEA (for age discrimination, as noted above), the Americans with Disabilities Act[26] (for disability discrimination), and the Fair Labor Standards Act[27] (which relates to wages and hours—see Chapter 17). In contrast, states are not immune from the requirements of the Family and Medical Leave Act[28] (see Chapter 17).

DISCRIMINATION BASED ON DISABILITY

The Americans with Disabilities Act (ADA) of 1990 is designed to eliminate discriminatory employment practices that prevent otherwise qualified workers with disabilities from fully participating in the national labor force. Prior to 1990, the major federal law providing protection to those with disabilities was the Rehabilitation Act of 1973. That act covered only federal government employees and those employed under federally funded programs. The ADA extends federal protection against disability-based discrimination to all workplaces with fifteen or more workers (with the exception of state government employers, who are generally immune under the Eleventh Amendment, as was just discussed). Basically, the ADA requires that employers "reasonably accommodate" the needs of persons with disabilities unless to do so would cause the employer to suffer an "undue hardship."

Procedures under the ADA

To prevail on a claim under the ADA, a plaintiff must show that he or she (1) has a disability, (2) is otherwise qualified for the employment in question, and (3) was excluded from the employment solely because of the disability. As in Title VII cases, a claim alleging a violation of the ADA may be commenced only after the plaintiff has pursued the claim through the EEOC. Plaintiffs may sue for many of the same remedies available under Title VII. The EEOC may decide to investigate and perhaps even sue the employer on behalf of the employee. If the EEOC decides not to sue, then the employee is entitled to sue.

---

24. *Kimel v. Florida Board of Regents,* 528 U.S. 62, 120 S.Ct. 631, 145 L.Ed.2d 522 (2000).
25. *Tennessee v. Lane,* 541 U.S. 509, 124 S.Ct. 1978, 158 L.Ed.2d 820 (2004).
26. *Board of Trustees of the University of Alabama v. Garrett,* 531 U.S. 356, 121 S.Ct. 955, 148 L.Ed.2d 866 (2001).
27. *Alden v. Maine,* 527 U.S. 706, 119 S.Ct. 2240, 144 L.Ed.2d 636 (1999).
28. *Nevada Department of Human Resources v. Hibbs,* 538 U.S. 721, 123 S.Ct. 1972, 155 L.Ed.2d 953 (2003).

Significantly, the United States Supreme Court held in 2002 that the EEOC could bring a suit against an employer for disability-based discrimination even though the employee had agreed to submit any job-related disputes to arbitration (see Chapter 3). The Court reasoned that because the EEOC was not a party to the arbitration agreement, the agreement was not binding on the EEOC.[29]

As mentioned, plaintiffs in lawsuits brought under the ADA may seek many of the same remedies available under Title VII. These include reinstatement, back pay, a limited amount of compensatory and punitive damages (for intentional discrimination), and certain other forms of relief. Repeat violators may be ordered to pay fines of up to $100,000.

What Is a Disability?

The ADA is broadly drafted to cover persons with a wide range of disabilities. Specifically, the ADA defines *disability* as "(1) a physical or mental impairment that substantially limits one or more of the major life activities of such individuals; (2) a record of such impairment; or (3) being regarded as having such an impairment."

Health conditions that have been considered disabilities under the federal law include blindness, alcoholism, heart disease, cancer, muscular dystrophy, cerebral palsy, paraplegia, diabetes, acquired immune deficiency syndrome (AIDS), testing positive for the human immunodeficiency virus (HIV, the virus that causes AIDS), and morbid obesity (which exists when an individual's weight is two times that of a normal person's weight). The ADA excludes from coverage certain conditions, such as kleptomania (the obsessive desire to steal).

Co-workers discuss business matters. What is a disability under the Americans with Disabilities Act? (Johnny Stockshooter/Image State)

Although the ADA's definition of disability is broad, the United States Supreme Court has issued a series of decisions narrowing the definition of what constitutes a disability under the act.

Correctable Conditions In 1999, the Supreme Court reviewed a case raising the issue of whether severe myopia, or nearsightedness, which can be corrected with lenses, qualifies as a disability under the ADA.[30] The Supreme Court ruled that it does not. The determination of whether a person is substantially limited in a major life activity is based on how the person functions when taking medication or using corrective devices, not on how the person functions without these measures.

In a similar case in 2002, a federal appellate court held that a pharmacist suffering from diabetes, which could be corrected by insulin, did not have a cause of action against his employer under the ADA.[31] In other cases decided in the early 2000s, the courts have held that plaintiffs with bipolar disorder, epilepsy, and other such conditions do *not* fall under the ADA's protections if the conditions can be corrected.

---

29. *EEOC v. Waffle House, Inc.*, 534 U.S. 279, 122 S.Ct. 754, 151 L.Ed.2d 755 (2002).
30. *Sutton v. United Airlines, Inc.*, 527 U.S. 471, 119 S.Ct. 2139, 144 L.Ed.2d 450 (1999).
31. *Orr v. Wal-Mart Stores, Inc.*, 297 F.3d 720 (8th Cir. 2002).

Repetitive-Stress Injuries   For some time, the courts were divided on the issue of whether carpal tunnel syndrome (or other repetitive-stress injury) constitutes a disability under the ADA. Carpal tunnel syndrome is a condition of pain and weakness in the hand caused by repetitive compression of a nerve in the wrist. In 2002, in a case involving this issue, the Supreme Court unanimously held that it does not. The Court stated that although the employee could not perform the manual tasks associated with her job, the condition did not constitute a disability under the ADA because it did not "substantially limit" the major life activity of performing manual tasks.[32]

Reasonable Accommodation

The ADA does not require that employers accommodate the needs of job applicants or employees with disabilities who are not otherwise qualified for the work. If a job applicant or an employee with a disability, with reasonable accommodation, can perform essential job functions, however, the employer must make the accommodation. Required modifications may include installing ramps for a wheelchair, establishing more flexible working hours, creating or modifying job assignments, and creating or improving training materials and procedures. Generally, employers should give primary consideration to employees' preferences in deciding what accommodations should be made. If an employee who becomes disabled on the job asks to be reassigned as a reasonable accommodation, does the employer have to reassign the employee as requested? See the *Insight into Ethics* feature below for a discussion of this issue.

Insight into Ethics

Reasonable accommodation, fairness, and preferences

The ADA does not specify what is required for accommodation to be reasonable; it only states that reasonable accommodation *may* include:

> [J]ob restructuring, part-time or modified work schedules, *reassignment to a vacant position,* acquisition or modification of equipment or devices, appropriate adjustment or modifications of examinations, training materials or policies, the provision of qualified readers or interpreters, and other similar accommodations for individuals with disabilities.[33] [Emphasis added.]

Determining what is reasonable depends on the situation, but often involves issues of fairness. As noted in the text, employers should consider a disabled employee's preferences or requests when determining what reasonable accommodation to make. But obviously, an employer's interests in getting the work done quickly or efficiently may sometimes clash with an employee's interests in doing a particular job or earning a certain amount of compensation.

Is an employer required under the ADA to reassign a disabled worker to a vacant position that the employee requests? Is it fair to reassign a disabled worker to a position at which the employee earns half of what she or he previously earned? If the worker was disabled by an

---

32. *Toyota Motor Manufacturing, Kentucky, Inc. v. Williams,* 534 U.S. 184, 122 S.Ct. 681, 151 L.Ed.2d 615 (2002).
33. 42 U.S.C. Section 12111(9)(B).

on-the-job injury, does this affect the employer's obligation? These issues came before the U.S. Court of Appeals for the Eighth Circuit in *Huber v. Wal-Mart Stores, Inc.*[34]

Wal-Mart Refuses to Give Preference to Disabled Employee

Pam Huber worked for Wal-Mart as an order filler, earning $13.00 an hour (plus a $0.50 shift differential). While working at this job, she suffered a permanent injury to her right arm and hand and became disabled. Because Huber could no longer perform the essential functions of an order filler, she asked to be reassigned to a vacant position as a router. Wal-Mart, however, refused to automatically reassign Huber to the vacant router position and instead required her to compete with the entire pool of applicants for that job.

Although Huber was qualified for the router position, Wal-Mart had a policy of hiring the most qualified applicant and ended up hiring a "more qualified" individual. Wal-Mart did reassign Huber, however, to a janitorial position at another facility for which she earned $6.20 per hour (less than half of her former salary). Is this fair? Probably not, but the court in this case did find that it was legal.

The Jurisdictions Are Split on Reassignment Obligations

The ADA left it up to the courts to determine the specifics of reasonable accommodation, and the federal circuit courts have been split on reassignment obligations. Courts in the Tenth Circuit and the District of Columbia have reasoned that "the reassignment obligation must mean something more than merely allowing a disabled person to compete equally with the rest of the world for a vacant position."[35] In those jurisdictions, reassignment means *automatically* awarding a position to a qualified disabled employee regardless of whether better-qualified applicants are available.

Courts in the Seventh and Eighth Circuits, in contrast, hold that an employer is not automatically required to reassign a disabled worker to a vacant position provided the employer is following its stated policy.[36] These courts reason that a policy of giving the job to the best applicant is legitimate and nondiscriminatory, even if it means that the disabled worker is not hired. An employer does not need to provide the accommodation that the worker requested or preferred, and need only do what is reasonable by way of accommodation.

In the *Huber* case, the court basically ruled that disabled workers should not receive a preference in reassignment and can be required to compete against all other applicants for the position. Therefore, Wal-Mart's reassignment of Huber to a janitorial position was reasonable, regardless of the substantial cut in salary that she took as a result of the reassignment. Huber appealed the federal appellate court's ruling, and the United States Supreme Court granted *certiorari*. Although the Supreme Court was scheduled to hear this case in 2008, the parties ultimately reached a settlement, and the case was taken off the Court's calendar.

Undue Hardship   Employers who do not accommodate the needs of persons with disabilities must demonstrate that the accommodations would cause "undue hardship." Generally, the law offers no uniform standards for identifying what is an undue hardship other than the imposition of a "significant difficulty or expense" on the employer. In other words, the focus is on the resources and circumstances of the particular employer in relation to the cost or difficulty of providing a specific accommodation.

---

34. *Huber v. Wal-Mart Stores, Inc.*, 486 F.3d 480 (8th Cir. 2007); *cert. granted*, __ U.S. __,128 S.Ct. 742, 169 L.Ed.2d 579; *cert. dismissed*, __ U.S. __,128 S.Ct. 1116, 169 L.Ed.2d 801 (2008).

35. *Smith v. Midland Brake, Inc.*, 180 F.3d 1154 (10th Cir. 1999).

36. *EEOC v. Humiston-Keeling, Inc.*, 227 F.3d 1024 (7th Cir. 2000).

Usually, the courts decide whether an accommodation constitutes an undue hardship on a case-by-case basis. **EXAMPLE #12** Bryan Lockhart, who uses a wheelchair, works for a cell phone company that provides parking to its employees. Lockhart informs the company supervisors that the parking spaces are so narrow that he is unable to extend the ramp that allows him to get in and out of his van. Lockhart therefore requests that the company reasonably accommodate his needs by paying a monthly fee for him to use a larger parking space in an adjacent lot. In this situation, a court would likely find that it would not be an undue hardship for the employer to pay for additional parking for Lockhart. ◻

Job Applications and Preemployment Physical Exams Employers must modify their job-application process so that those with disabilities can compete for jobs with those who do not have disabilities. **EXAMPLE #13** A job announcement that includes only a phone number would discriminate against potential job applicants with hearing impairments. Thus, the job announcement must also provide an address. ◻

Employers are also restricted in the kinds of questions they may ask on job-application forms and during preemployment interviews. (See the *Management Perspective* feature on interviewing job applicants with disabilities.) Furthermore, they cannot require persons with disabilities to submit to preemployment physicals unless such exams are required of all other applicants. Employers can condition an offer of employment on the applicant's successfully passing a medical examination, but can disqualify the applicant only if the medical problems they discover would render the applicant unable to perform the job. **EXAMPLE #14** When filling the position of delivery truck driver, a company cannot screen out all applicants who are unable to meet the U.S. Department of Transportation's hearing standard. To do so, the company would first have to prove that drivers who are deaf are not qualified to perform the essential job function of driving safely and pose a higher risk of accidents than drivers who are not deaf. ◻[37]

Substance Abusers Drug addiction is considered a disability under the ADA because it is a substantially limiting impairment. Note that the ADA only protects persons with *former* drug addictions—those who have completed a supervised drug-rehabilitation program or who are currently participating in a supervised rehabilitation program. Those who are currently using illegal drugs are not protected by the act, nor are persons who have used drugs casually in the past. The latter are not considered addicts and therefore do not have a disability (addiction).

People suffering from alcoholism are protected by the ADA. Employers cannot legally discriminate against employees simply because they suffer from alcoholism and must treat them the same way other employees are treated. For example, an employee with alcoholism who comes to work late because she or he was drinking excessively the night before cannot be disciplined any differently than an employee who comes to work late for another reason. Of course, employers have the right to prohibit the use of alcohol in the workplace and can require that employees not be under the influence of alcohol while working.

---

37. *Bates v. United Parcel Service, Inc.*, 465 F.3d 1069 (9th Cir. 2006).

Management Faces a Legal Issue

Many employers have been held liable under the Americans with Disabilities Act (ADA) because they have asked the wrong questions when interviewing job applicants with disabilities. The Equal Employment Opportunity Commission (EEOC) has issued guidelines about which questions employers may or may not ask job applicants with disabilities. If you are an interviewer, you may ask a job applicant whether he or she can meet your attendance requirements. You may not, in contrast, ask how many days that person was sick last year. You may ask an applicant whether she or he can do the job. You may not, however, ask how that person would do the job *unless* (1) the disability is obvious, (2) the applicant brings up the subject during the interview, or (3) you ask the question of all applicants for that particular job.

After you have made a job offer, you are allowed to ask the applicant questions concerning her or his disability, including questions about previous workers' compensation claims or about the extent of, say, a drinking or drug problem.

What the Courts Say

In one case, the job applicant suffered from a hearing disability. He alleged that the potential employer discriminated against him because of his deafness when he applied for a position as an information technology specialist. At trial, one of the key issues was how the interview was performed. The interviewer claimed that he had no concerns about the applicant's deafness. But, at one point during the interview, the interviewer passed a handwritten note asking the applicant, "How do you communicate in offices where no one can sign?" The applicant responded, "I have no problem with writing as my basic communication." The court pointed out that the interviewer did not ask this question of any other applicant.

Although the applicant ultimately did not prevail at trial, the court made clear that the interviewer should not have asked any special questions of him.[a]

In another case, an applicant sued the federal government after applying for the position of bank examiner. He claimed that during an interview, there was an improper inquiry about his perceived disability. In fact, the applicant had previously suffered a stroke and slurred his words when he spoke. During the interview, he was asked what was wrong with his arm and whether his disability affected his mental coherence. Ultimately the applicant lost his case because he had lied on his résumé. Nonetheless, the defendants would have had an easier time at trial had the interviewer followed the EEOC guidelines.[b]

Implications for Managers

Most managers should consult with an attorney specializing in employment regulation. The manager should point out the kinds of questions typically asked of job applicants during interviews or following employment offers. Any questions that increase the risk of a lawsuit from an applicant with a disability must be altered. As a general rule, you should never ask questions of a disabled applicant that you would not ask of other applicants. All questions should be consistent with EEOC guidelines. Anyone who interviews job applicants in your company should be made aware of what questions can and cannot be asked of candidates with disabilities. You are allowed to ask a candidate to whom you have offered a job for his or her medical documents to verify the nature of the applicant's disability.

a. *Adeyemi v. District of Columbia D.D.C.*, 2007 WL 1020754 (D.D.C. 2007).
b. *Strong v. Paulson*, __ F.3d __, 2007 WL 2859789 (7th Cir. 2007). See also *Lorah v. Tetra Tech Inc.*, 541 F.Supp.2d 629 (D.Del. 2008).

Employers can also fire or refuse to hire a person with alcoholism if he or she poses a substantial risk of harm either to himself or herself or to others and the risk cannot be reduced by reasonable accommodation.

Health-Insurance Plans Workers with disabilities must be given equal access to any health insurance provided to other employees. Nevertheless, employers can exclude from coverage preexisting health conditions and certain types of diagnostic or surgical procedures. An employer can also put a limit, or cap, on health-care payments under its particular group health policy as long as the cap is applied equally to all insured employees and does not discriminate on the basis of disability. Whenever a group health-care plan makes a disability-based distinction in its benefits, the plan violates the ADA (unless the employer can justify its actions under the business necessity defense, as discussed later in this chapter).

Association Discrimination

The ADA contains an "association provision" that protects qualified individuals from employment discrimination based on an identified disability of a person with whom the qualified individual is known to have a relationship or an association.[38] The purpose of this provision is to prevent employers from taking adverse employment actions based on stereotypes or assumptions about individuals who associate with people who have disabilities. An employer cannot, for instance, refuse to hire the parent of a child with a disability based on the assumption that the person will miss work too often or be unreliable.

To establish a *prima facie* case of association discrimination under the ADA, the plaintiff must show that she or he (1) was qualified for the job, (2) was subjected to adverse employment action, and (3) was known by her or his employer to have a relative or an associate with a disability. In addition, the plaintiff must show that the adverse employment action occurred under circumstances raising a reasonable inference that the disability of the relative or associate was a determining factor in the employer's decision.

In the following case, a man claimed that his employer unlawfully discriminated against him based on his wife's disability. Although the case involved a state law that offers slightly more protection than the ADA, the opinion shows how courts analyze association discrimination claims.

---

38. 42 U.S.C. Section 12112(b)(4).

Case 18.3 Francin v. Mosby, Inc.

Missouri Court of Appeals,
Eastern District, Division Three, 2008.
248 S.W.3d 619.
www.courts.mo.gov[a]

BACKGROUND AND FACTS Randall Francin began working at Mosby, Inc. (doing business as Elsevier), in 1991. He worked as a production assistant until March 2002, when his position was eliminated due to organizational restructuring. Francin was rehired a few months later as an associate database publishing editor. In his new position, Francin updated drug information and proofread information contained in drug inserts. In 2003, Francin's wife was

diagnosed with amyotrophic lateral sclerosis (ALS). He discussed his potential rights for leave under the Family Medical Leave Act (discussed in Chapter 17) with a representative from the human resources department at Elsevier. Francin received a "merit award increase" in salary in January 2004. Later in 2004, Francin's supervisor resigned. During an interview with a new boss, Francin informed him of his wife's illness. On September 21, 2004, Francin was fired. Francin filed a suit under the Missouri Human Rights Act (MHRA), alleging that Elsevier discriminated against him because of his association with a person with a disability. Elsevier filed a motion for summary judgment, which was granted by the trial court. On appeal, Francin claimed that the trial court erred in granting summary judgment because there was a genuine issue of material fact concerning whether his wife's disability was a contributing factor in the decision to terminate his employment.

---

a. Click on "Opinions & Minutes" under the "Quick Links" menu. Select the link for opinions from the Missouri Court of Appeals, Eastern District, and using the "Search Opinions" function, enter "Randall Francin." Click on the opinion (the line ends with the case number ED89814). This is the official Web site of the Missouri courts.

IN THE WORDS OF THE COURT . . . AHRENS, Judge.

* * * *

* * * Summary judgment is appropriate only where the record shows there are no genuine disputes of material fact and the moving party is entitled to judgment as a matter of law. * * * *If there is a dispute over facts that might affect the outcome of the action, summary judgment is not proper because the determination of such facts is for the fact finder at trial.* [Emphasis added.]

As a threshold matter, in its brief Elsevier asserts Francin's claim of discrimination is not a cognizable [recognizable] claim because he only asserted his termination was due to a stated intention to be absent, rather than a real absence. Elsevier's claim is based largely on cases interpreting the federal Americans with Disabilities Act ("ADA") in Federal courts. Elsevier argues that the MHRA is "patterned under and consistent with" the protections afforded by the ADA.

Here, Section 213.070(4) of the Missouri Human Rights Act provides that it is unlawful to "discriminate in any manner against any other person because of such person's association with any person protected by this chapter." [This section] does not qualify this discrimination with any requirement that an employee actually take leave under the Family and Medical Leave Act, as Elsevier attempts to argue. Instead, the statute merely provides a cause of action where an employee is discriminated against for his association with a person protected by the MHRA. Francin claims Elsevier discriminated against him by terminating him because of his association with his wife, who suffered from ALS. Francin presented a cognizable claim for discrimination under [this section], and Elsevier's argument is without merit.

Turning to the merits of Francin's appeal, Francin argues there was a genuine issue of material fact concerning whether his wife's disability was a contributing factor to Maheswaran's [Francin's new boss's] decision to terminate him. According to Francin, this genuine issue of material fact is based upon the evidence of Francin's satisfactory performance coupled with the close timing of the decision to his notification to Maheswaran of his wife's condition.

* * * *

The contradictory evidence regarding Francin's job performance and the memos from [his boss's] meetings with Francin noting [his wife's] illness and [its] effect on Francin, coupled with the close timing of Francin's termination is sufficient to create a genuine issue of material fact concerning whether Francin's wife's illness was a contributing factor to Elsevier's decision to terminate him. Therefore, Elsevier was not entitled to judgment as a matter of law, and the trial court erred in granting summary judgment in favor of Elsevier.

DECISION AND REMEDY The Missouri Court of Appeals, Eastern District, reversed the trial court's decision and remanded the case for further proceedings.

WHAT IF THE FACTS WERE DIFFERENT? Assume that Francin had only discussed his wife's illness with a human resources officer in the company and never mentioned it to his new boss. Would the outcome of the appeal have been different? Explain.

THE ETHICAL DIMENSION Did Elsevier have any ethical duty to keep Francin employed, even if he did indicate he might take time off under the Family Medical Leave Act?

Hostile-Environment Claims under the ADA

As discussed earlier in this chapter, under Title VII of the Civil Rights Act of 1964, an employee may base certain types of employment-discrimination causes of action on a hostile-environment theory. Using this theory, a worker may successfully sue her or his employer, even if the worker was not fired or otherwise discriminated against.

Although the ADA does not expressly provide for hostile-environment claims, a number of courts have allowed such actions. Only a few plaintiffs have been successful, however.[39] For a claim to succeed, the conduct complained of must

---

39. See, for example, *Shaver v. Independent Stave Co.*, 350 F.3d 716 (8th Cir. 2003); *Johnson v. North Carolina Department of Health and Human Services*, 454 F.Supp.2d 467 (M.D.N.C. 2006); and *Lucenti v. Potter*, 432 F.Supp.2d 347 (S.D.N.Y. 2006).

be sufficiently severe or pervasive to permeate the workplace and alter the conditions of employment such that a reasonable person would find the environment hostile or abusive. **EXAMPLE #15** Lester Wenigar was a fifty-seven-year-old man with a low IQ and limited mental capacity who worked at a farm doing manual labor and serving as a night watchman. His employer frequently shouted at him and called him names, did not allow him to take breaks, and provided him with substandard living quarters (a storeroom over a garage without any heat or windows). In this situation, because the employer's conduct was severe and offensive, a court would likely find that the working conditions constituted a hostile environment under the ADA.[40]◻

DEFENSES TO EMPLOYMENT DISCRIMINATION

The first line of defense for an employer charged with employment discrimination is, of course, to assert that the plaintiff has failed to meet his or her initial burden of proving that discrimination occurred. As noted, plaintiffs bringing cases under the ADA sometimes find it difficult to meet this initial burden because they must prove that their alleged disabilities are disabilities covered by the ADA. Furthermore, plaintiffs in ADA cases must prove that they were otherwise qualified for the job and that their disabilities were the sole reason they were not hired or were fired.

Once a plaintiff succeeds in proving that discrimination occurred, the burden shifts to the employer to justify the discriminatory practice. Often, employers attempt to justify the discrimination by claiming that it was the result of a business necessity, a bona fide occupational qualification, or a seniority system. In some situations, as noted earlier, an effective antiharassment policy and prompt remedial action when harassment occurs may shield employers from liability for sexual harassment under Title VII.

Business Necessity

BUSINESS NECESSITY
A defense to allegations of employment discrimination in which the employer demonstrates that an employment practice that discriminates against members of a protected class is related to job performance.

An employer may defend against a claim of disparate-impact (unintentional) discrimination by asserting that a practice that has a discriminatory effect is a **business necessity.** **EXAMPLE #16** If requiring a high school diploma is shown to have a discriminatory effect, an employer might argue that a high school education is necessary for workers to perform the job at a required level of competence. If the employer can demonstrate to the court's satisfaction that a definite connection exists between a high school education and job performance, the employer will normally succeed in this business necessity defense.◻

Bona Fide Occupational Qualification

BONA FIDE OCCUPATIONAL QUALIFICATION (BFOQ)
An identifiable characteristic reasonably necessary to the normal operation of a particular business. These characteristics can include gender, national origin, and religion, but not race.

Another defense applies when discrimination against a protected class is essential to a job—that is, when a particular trait is a **bona fide occupational qualification (BFOQ).** Race, however, can never be a BFOQ. Generally, courts have restricted the BFOQ defense to instances in which the employee's gender is essential to the job. **EXAMPLE #17** A women's clothing store might legitimately hire only female sales

---

40. *Wenigar v. Johnson,* 712 N.W.2d 190 (Minn.App. 2006). This case involved a hostile-environment claim under the Minnesota disability statute rather than the ADA, but the court relied on another court's decision under the ADA.

attendants if part of an attendant's job involves assisting clients in the store's dressing rooms. Similarly, the Federal Aviation Administration can legitimately impose age limits for airline pilots—but an airline cannot impose weight limits only on female flight attendants. □

Seniority Systems

An employer with a history of discrimination might have no members of protected classes in upper-level positions. Even if the employer now seeks to be unbiased, it may face a lawsuit in which the plaintiff asks a court to order that minorities be promoted ahead of schedule to compensate for past discrimination. If no present intent to discriminate is shown, however, and if promotions or other job benefits are distributed according to a fair **seniority system** (in which workers with more years of service are promoted first or laid off last), the employer has a good defense against the suit.

According to the United States Supreme Court, this defense may also apply to alleged discrimination under the ADA. If an employee with a disability requests an accommodation (such as an assignment to a particular position) that conflicts with an employer's seniority system, the accommodation will generally not be considered "reasonable" under the act.[41]

SENIORITY SYSTEM
In regard to employment relationships, a system in which those who have worked longest for the employer are first in line for promotions, salary increases, and other benefits. They are also the last to be laid off if the workforce must be reduced.

After-Acquired Evidence of Employee Misconduct

In some situations, employers have attempted to avoid liability for employment discrimination on the basis of "after-acquired evidence"—that is, evidence that the employer discovers after a lawsuit is filed—of an employee's misconduct. **EXAMPLE #18** Suppose that an employer fires a worker, who then sues the employer for employment discrimination. During pretrial investigation, the employer learns that the employee made material misrepresentations on his or her employment application—misrepresentations that, had the employer known about them, would have served as a ground to fire the individual. □

According to the United States Supreme Court, after-acquired evidence of wrongdoing cannot be used to shield an employer entirely from liability for employment discrimination. It may, however, be used to limit the amount of damages for which the employer is liable.[42]

AFFIRMATIVE ACTION

Federal statutes and regulations providing for equal opportunity in the workplace were designed to reduce or eliminate discriminatory practices with respect to hiring, retaining, and promoting employees. **Affirmative action** programs go a step further and attempt to "make up" for past patterns of discrimination by giving members of protected classes preferential treatment in hiring or promotion. During the 1960s, all federal and state government agencies, private companies that contract to do business with the federal government, and institutions that receive federal funding were required to implement affirmative action policies.

AFFIRMATIVE ACTION
Job-hiring policies that give special consideration to members of protected classes in an effort to overcome present effects of past discrimination.

---

41. *U.S. Airways, Inc. v. Barnett*, 535 U.S. 391, 122 S.Ct. 1516, 152 L.Ed.2d 589 (2002).
42. *McKennon v. Nashville Banner Publishing Co.*, 513 U.S. 352, 115 S.Ct. 879, 130 L.Ed.2d 852 (1995). See also *EEOC v. Dial Corp.*, 469 F.3d 735 (8th Cir. 2006).

Title VII of the Civil Rights Act of 1964 neither requires nor prohibits affirmative action. Thus, most private firms have not been required to implement affirmative action policies, though many have chosen to do so.

Affirmative action programs have aroused much controversy over the last forty years, particularly when they have resulted in what is frequently called "reverse discrimination"—discrimination against "majority" individuals, such as white males. At issue is whether affirmative action programs, because of their inherently discriminatory nature, violate the equal protection clause of the Fourteenth Amendment to the U.S. Constitution.

The *Bakke* Case

An early case addressing this issue, *Regents of the University of California v. Bakke*,[43] involved an affirmative action program implemented by the University of California at Davis. Allan Bakke, who had been turned down for medical school at the Davis campus, sued the university for reverse discrimination after he discovered that his academic record was better than those of some of the minority applicants who had been admitted to the program.

The United States Supreme Court held that affirmative action programs were subject to "intermediate scrutiny." Recall from the discussion of the equal protection clause in Chapter 4 that any law or action evaluated under a standard of intermediate scrutiny, to be constitutionally valid, must be substantially related to important government objectives. Applying this standard, the Court held that the university could give favorable weight to minority applicants as part of a plan to increase minority enrollment so as to achieve a more culturally diverse student body. The Court stated, however, that the use of a quota system, which explicitly reserved a certain number of places for minority applicants, violated the equal protection clause of the Fourteenth Amendment.

---

43. 438 U.S. 265, 98 S.Ct. 2733, 57 L.Ed.2d 750 (1978).

Students at the University of Michigan show their support for affirmative action that allowed race to be considered as a "plus factor" in university admissions.
(AP Photo/Paul Sancya)

The *Adarand* Case

In 1995, in its landmark decision in *Adarand Constructors, Inc. v. Peña*,[44] the United States Supreme Court held that any federal, state, or local affirmative action program that uses racial or ethnic classifications as the basis for making decisions is subject to strict scrutiny by the courts. In effect, the Court's opinion in the *Adarand* case means that an affirmative action program is constitutional only if it attempts to remedy past discrimination and does not make use of quotas or preferences. Furthermore, once such a program has succeeded in the goal of remedying past discrimination, it must be changed or dropped. After this case, other federal courts began to declare affirmative action programs invalid unless they attempt to remedy specific practices of past or current discrimination.

The *Hopwood* Case

In 1996, the U.S. Court of Appeals for the Fifth Circuit, in *Hopwood v. State of Texas*,[45] held that an affirmative action program at the University of Texas School of Law in Austin violated the equal protection clause. In that case, two white law school applicants sued the university when they were denied admission. The court decided that the affirmative action policy unlawfully discriminated in favor of minority applicants. In its opinion, the court directly challenged the *Bakke* decision by stating that the use of race even as a means of achieving diversity on college campuses "undercuts the Fourteenth Amendment." The United States Supreme Court declined to hear the case, thus letting the lower court's decision stand. Over the next years, federal appellate courts were divided over the constitutionality of such programs.

Subsequent Court Decisions

In 2003, the United States Supreme Court reviewed two cases involving issues similar to that in the *Hopwood* case. Both cases involved admissions programs at the University of Michigan. In *Gratz v. Bollinger*,[46] two white applicants who were denied undergraduate admission to the university alleged reverse discrimination. The school's policy gave each applicant a score based on a number of factors, including grade point average, standardized test scores, and personal achievements. The system *automatically* awarded every "underrepresented" minority (African American, Hispanic, and Native American) applicant twenty points—one-fifth of the points needed to guarantee admission. The Court held that this policy violated the equal protection clause.

In contrast, in *Grutter v. Bollinger*,[47] the Court held that the University of Michigan Law School's admissions policy was constitutional. In that case, the Court concluded that "[u]niversities can, however, consider race or ethnicity more flexibly as a 'plus' factor in the context of individualized consideration of each and every applicant." The significant difference between the two admissions policies, in the Court's view, was that the law school's approach did not apply a mechanical formula giving "diversity bonuses" based on race or ethnicity.

---

44. 515 U.S. 200, 115 S.Ct. 2097, 132 L.Ed.2d 158 (1995).
45. 84 F.3d 720 (5th Cir. 1996).
46. 539 U.S. 244, 123 S.Ct. 2411, 156 L.Ed.2d 257 (2003).
47. 539 U.S. 306, 123 S.Ct. 2325, 156 L.Ed.2d 304 (2003).

In 2007, the United States Supreme Court ruled on two more cases involving racial classifications used in assigning students to schools in Seattle, Washington, and Jefferson County, Kentucky. Both school districts had adopted student assignment plans that relied on race to determine which schools certain children attended. The Seattle school district plan classified children as white or nonwhite and used the racial classifications as a "tiebreaker" to determine the particular high school students attended. The school district in Jefferson County classified students as black or other to assign children to elementary schools. A group of parents from the relevant public schools filed lawsuits claiming that the school districts' racial preferences violated the equal protection clause. The Supreme Court applied strict scrutiny and held that the school districts had failed to show that use of racial classifications in their student assignment plans was necessary to achieve their stated goal of racial diversity.[48]

STATE STATUTES

Although the focus of this chapter has been on federal legislation, most states also have statutes that prohibit employment discrimination. Generally, the same kinds of discrimination are prohibited under federal and state legislation. In addition, state statutes often provide protection for certain individuals who are not protected under federal laws. For instance, anyone over the age of eighteen is entitled to sue for age discrimination under New Jersey state law, which specifies no threshold age limit.

Furthermore, as mentioned in Chapter 17, state laws prohibiting discrimination may apply to firms with fewer employees than the threshold number required under federal statutes, thus offering protection to more workers. State laws may also allow for additional damages, such as damages for emotional distress, that are not available under federal statutes.[49] Finally, some states, including California and Washington, have passed laws that end affirmative action programs in those states or modify admissions policies at state-sponsored universities.

---

48. The court consolidated the two cases and issued only one opinion to address the issues presented by both cases. *Parents Involved in Community Schools v. Seattle School Dist. No. 1,* ___ U.S. ___, 127 S.Ct. 2738, 168 L.Ed.2d 508 (2007).

49. For a reverse discrimination case in which a former police officer was awarded nearly $80,000 in emotional distress damages based on a violation of New Jersey's law against discrimination, see *Klawitter v. City of Trenton,* 395 N.J.Super. 302, 928 A.2d 900 (2007).

Reviewing . . . **Employment Discrimination**

Amaani Lyle, an African American woman, took a job as a scriptwriters' assistant at Warner Brothers Television Productions working for the writers of *Friends*, a popular, adult-oriented television series. One of her essential job duties was to type detailed notes for the scriptwriters during brainstorming sessions in which they discussed jokes, dialogue, and story lines. The writers then combed through Lyle's notes after the meetings for script material. During these meetings, the three male scriptwriters told lewd and vulgar jokes and made sexually explicit comments and gestures. They often talked about their personal sexual experiences and fantasies, and some of these conversations were then used in episodes of *Friends*.

During the meetings, Lyle never complained that she found the writers' conduct offensive. After four months, she was fired because she could not type fast enough to keep up with the writers' conversations during the meetings. She filed a suit against Warner Brothers alleging sexual harassment and claiming that her termination was based on racial discrimination. Using the information presented in the chapter, answer the following questions.

1. Would Lyle's claim of racial discrimination be for intentional (disparate-treatment) or unintentional (disparate-impact) discrimination? Explain.

2. Can Lyle establish a *prima facie* case of racial discrimination? Why or why not?

3. Lyle was told when she was hired that typing speed was extremely important to her position. At the time, she maintained that she could type eighty words per minute, so she was not given a typing test. It later turned out that Lyle could type only fifty words per minute. What impact might typing speed have on Lyle's lawsuit?

4. Lyle's sexual harassment claim is based on the hostile work environment created by the writers' sexually offensive conduct at meetings that she was required to attend. The writers, however, argue that their behavior was essential to the "creative process" of writing *Friends*, a show that routinely contained sexual innuendos and adult humor. Which defense discussed in the chapter might Warner Brothers assert using this argument?

Key Terms

affirmative action 629
bona fide occupational
    qualification (BFOQ) 628
business necessity 628
constructive discharge 609
disparate-impact
    discrimination 606

disparate-treatment
    discrimination 605
employment
    discrimination 604
prima facie case 606
protected class 604
seniority system 629

sexual harassment 610
tangible employment
    action 610

Chapter Summary

Title VII of the Civil Rights Act of 1964 (See pages 605–615.)	Title VII prohibits employment discrimination based on race, color, national origin, religion, or gender. 1. *Procedures*—Employees must file a claim with the Equal Employment Opportunity Commission (EEOC). The EEOC may sue the employer on the employee's behalf; if it does not, the employee may sue the employer directly. 2. *Types of discrimination*—Title VII prohibits both intentional (disparate-treatment) and unintentional (disparate-impact) discrimination. Disparate-impact discrimination occurs when an employer's practice, such as hiring only persons with a certain level of education, has the effect of discriminating against a class of persons protected by Title VII. Title VII also extends to discriminatory practices, such as various forms of harassment, in the online environment. 3. *Remedies for discrimination under Title VII*—If a plaintiff proves that unlawful discrimination occurred, he or she may be awarded reinstatement, back pay, and retroactive promotions. Damages (both compensatory and punitive) may be awarded for intentional discrimination.
Discrimination Based on Age (See pages 615–620.)	The Age Discrimination in Employment Act (ADEA) of 1967 prohibits employment discrimination on the basis of age against individuals forty years of age or older. Procedures for bringing a case under the ADEA are similar to those for bringing a case under Title VII.

CONTINUED

Discrimination Based on Disability
(See pages 620–628.)

The Americans with Disabilities Act (ADA) of 1990 prohibits employment discrimination against persons with disabilities who are otherwise qualified to perform the essential functions of the jobs for which they apply.

1. *Procedures and remedies*–To prevail on a claim under the ADA, the plaintiff must show that she or he has a disability, is otherwise qualified for the employment in question, and was excluded from the employment solely because of the disability. Procedures under the ADA are similar to those required in Title VII cases; remedies are also similar to those under Title VII.

2. *Definition of disability*–The ADA defines the term *disability* as a physical or mental impairment that substantially limits one or more major life activities, a record of such impairment, or being regarded as having such an impairment.

3. *Reasonable accommodation*–Employers are required to reasonably accommodate the needs of persons with disabilities. Reasonable accommodations may include altering job-application procedures, modifying the physical work environment, and permitting more flexible work schedules. Employers are not required to accommodate the needs of all workers with disabilities. For example, employers need not accommodate workers who pose a definite threat to health and safety in the workplace or those who are not otherwise qualified for their jobs.

Defenses to Employment Discrimination
(See pages 628–629.)

If a plaintiff proves that employment discrimination occurred, employers may avoid liability by successfully asserting certain defenses. Employers may assert that the discrimination was required for reasons of business necessity, to meet a bona fide occupational qualification, or to maintain a legitimate seniority system. Evidence of prior employee misconduct acquired after the employee has been fired is not a defense to discrimination.

Affirmative Action
(See pages 629–632.)

Affirmative action programs attempt to "make up" for past patterns of discrimination by giving members of protected classes preferential treatment in hiring or promotion. Increasingly, such programs are being strictly scrutinized by the courts and struck down as violating the Fourteenth Amendment.

State Statutes
(See page 632.)

Generally, state laws also prohibit the kinds of discrimination prohibited by federal statutes. State laws may provide for more extensive protection and remedies than federal laws. Also, some states, such as California and Washington, have banned state-sponsored affirmative action programs.

For Review

1. Generally, what kind of conduct is prohibited by Title VII of the Civil Rights Act of 1964, as amended?
2. What is the difference between disparate-treatment discrimination and disparate-impact discrimination?
3. What remedies are available under Title VII of the 1964 Civil Rights Act, as amended?
4. What federal acts prohibit discrimination based on age and discrimination based on disability?
5. What are three defenses to claims of employment discrimination?

Questions and Case Problems

18–1. Title VII Violations. Discuss fully whether any of the following actions would constitute a violation of Title VII of the 1964 Civil Rights Act, as amended.

1. Tennington, Inc., is a consulting firm and has ten employees. These employees travel on consulting jobs in seven states. Tennington has an employment record of hiring only white males.

2. Novo Films, Inc., is making a film about Africa and needs to employ approximately one hundred extras for this picture. To hire these extras, Novo

advertises in all major newspapers in Southern California. The ad states that only African Americans need apply.

Question with Sample Answer

18–2. Chinawa, a major processor of cheese sold throughout the United States, employs one hundred workers at its principal processing plant. The plant is located in Heartland Corners, which has a population that is 50 percent white and 25 percent African American, with the balance Hispanic American, Asian American, and others. Chinawa requires a high school diploma as a condition of employment for its cleaning crew. Three-fourths of the white population complete high school, compared with only one-fourth of those in the minority groups. Chinawa has an all-white cleaning crew. Has Chinawa violated Title VII of the Civil Rights Act of 1964? Explain.

For a sample answer to Question 18–2, go to Appendix I at the end of this text.

18–3. Discrimination Based on Disability. PGA Tour, Inc., sponsors professional golf tournaments. A player may enter in several ways, but the most common method is to successfully compete in a three-stage qualifying tournament known as the "Q-School." Anyone may enter the Q-School by submitting two letters of recommendation and paying $3,000 to cover greens fees and the cost of a golf cart, which is permitted during the first two stages but is prohibited during the third stage. The rules governing the events include the "Rules of Golf," which apply at all levels of amateur and professional golf and do not prohibit the use of golf carts, and the "hard card," which applies specifically to the PGA tour and requires the players to walk the course during most of a tournament. Casey Martin is a talented golfer with a degenerative circulatory disorder that prevents him from walking golf courses. Martin entered the Q-School and asked for permission to use a cart during the third stage. PGA refused. Martin filed a suit in a federal district court against PGA, alleging a violation of the Americans with Disabilities Act (ADA). Is a golf cart in these circumstances a "reasonable accommodation" under the ADA? Why or why not? [*PGA Tour, Inc. v. Martin,* 532 U.S. 661, 121 S.Ct. 1879, 149 L.Ed.2d 904 (2001)]

18–4. Discrimination Based on Age. The United Auto Workers (UAW) is the union that represents the employees of General Dynamics Land Systems, Inc. In 1997, a collective bargaining agreement between UAW and General Dynamics eliminated the company's obligation to provide health insurance to employees who retired after the date of the agreement, except for current workers at least fifty years old. Dennis Cline and 194 other employees, who were over forty years old but under fifty, objected to this term. They complained to the Equal Employment Opportunity Commission, claiming that the agreement violated the Age Discrimination in Employment Act (ADEA) of 1967. The ADEA forbids discriminatory preference for the "young" over the "old." Does the ADEA also prohibit favoring the old over the young? How should the court rule? Explain. [*General Dynamics Land Systems, Inc. v. Cline,* 540 U.S. 581, 124 S.Ct. 1236, 157 L.Ed.2d 1094 (2004)]

18–5. Religious Discrimination. Kimberly Cloutier began working at the Costco store in West Springfield, Massachusetts, in July 1997. Cloutier had multiple earrings and four tattoos, but no facial piercings. In June 1998, Costco promoted Cloutier to cashier. Over the next two years, she engaged in various forms of body modification, including facial piercing and cutting. In March 2001, Costco revised its dress code to prohibit all facial jewelry except earrings. Cloutier was told that she would have to remove her facial jewelry. She asked for a complete exemption from the code, asserting that she was a member of the Church of Body Modification and that eyebrow piercing was part of her religion. She was told to remove the jewelry, cover it, or go home. She went home and was later discharged for her absence. Cloutier filed a suit in a federal district court against Costco, alleging religious discrimination in violation of Title VII. Does an employer have an obligation to accommodate its employees' religious practices? If so, to what extent? How should the court rule in this case? Discuss. [*Cloutier v. Costco Wholesale Corp.,* 390 F.3d 126 (1st Cir. 2004)]

Case Problem with Sample Answer

18–6. For twenty years, Darlene Jespersen worked as a bartender at Harrah's Casino in Reno, Nevada. In 2000, Harrah's implemented a "Personal Best" program that included new grooming standards. Among other requirements, women were told to wear makeup "applied neatly in complimentary colors." Jespersen, who never wore makeup off the job, felt so uncomfortable wearing it on the job that it interfered with her ability to perform. Unwilling to wear makeup and not qualifying for another position at Harrah's with similar compensation, Jespersen quit the casino. She filed a suit in a federal district court against Harrah's Operating Co., the casino's owner, alleging that the makeup policy discriminated against women in violation of Title VII of the Civil Rights Act of 1964. Harrah's argued that any burdens under the new program fell equally on both genders, citing the "Personal Best" short-hair standard that applied only to men. Jespersen responded by describing her personal reaction to the makeup policy and emphasizing her exemplary record during her tenure at Harrah's. In whose favor should the court rule? Why?

[*Jespersen v. Harrah's Operating Co.,* 444 F.3d 1104 (9th Cir. 2006)]

After you have answered Problem 18–6, compare your answer with the sample answer given on the Web site that accompanies this text. Go to www.cengage.com/blaw/let, select "Chapter 18," and click on "Case Problem with Sample Answer."

18–7 Discrimination Based on Disability. Cerebral palsy limits Steven Bradley's use of his legs. He uses forearm crutches for short-distance walks and a wheelchair for longer distances. Standing for more than ten or fifteen minutes is difficult. With support, however, Bradley can climb stairs and get on and off a stool. His condition also restricts the use of his fourth finger to, for example, type, but it does not limit his ability to write—he completed two years of college. His grip strength is normal, and he can lift heavy objects. In 2001, Bradley applied for a "greeter" or "cashier" position at a Wal-Mart Stores, Inc., Supercenter in Richmond, Missouri. The job descriptions stated, "No experience or qualification is required." Bradley indicated that he was available for full- or part-time work from 4:00 P.M. to 10:00 p.m. any evening. His employment history showed that he currently worked as a proofreader and that he had previously worked as an administrator. His application was rejected, according to Janet Daugherty, the personnel manager, based on his "work history" and the "direct threat" that he posed to the safety of himself and others. Bradley claimed, however, that the store refused to hire him due to his disability. What steps must Bradley follow to pursue his claim? What does he need to show to prevail? Is he likely to meet these requirements? Discuss. [*EEOC v. Wal-Mart Stores, Inc.,* 477 F.3d 561 (8th Cir. 2007)]

A Question of Ethics

18–8. Titan Distribution, Inc., employed Quintak, Inc., to run its tire mounting and distribution operation in Des Moines, Iowa. Robert Chalfant worked for Quintak as a second-shift supervisor at Titan. He suffered a heart attack in 1992 and underwent heart bypass surgery in 1997. He also had arthritis. In July 2002, Titan decided to terminate Quintak. Chalfant applied to work at Titan. On his application, he described himself as disabled. After a physical exam, Titan's doctor concluded that Chalfant could work in his current capacity, and he was notified that he would be hired. Despite the notice, Nadis Barucic, a Titan employee, wrote "not pass px" at the top of his application, and he was not hired. He took a job with AMPCO Systems, a parking ramp management company. This work involved walking up to five miles a day and lifting more weight than he had at Titan.

In September, Titan eliminated its second shift. Chalfant filed a suit in a federal district court against Titan, in part under the Americans with Disabilities Act (ADA). Titan argued that the reason it had not hired Chalfant was not because he did not pass the physical, but no one—including Barucic—could explain why she had written "not pass px" on his application. Later, Titan claimed that Chalfant was not hired because the entire second shift was going to be eliminated. [*Chalfant v. Titan Distribution, Inc.,* 475 F.3d 982 (8th Cir. 2007)]

1. What must Chalfant establish to make his case under the ADA? Can he meet these requirements? Explain.
2. In employment discrimination cases, punitive damages can be appropriate when an employer acts with malice or reckless indifference in regard to an employee's protected rights. Would an award of punitive damages to Chalfant be appropriate in this case? Discuss.

Critical-Thinking Legal Question

18–9. Why has the federal government limited the application of the statutes discussed in this chapter to firms with a specified number of employees, such as fifteen or twenty? Should these laws apply to all employers, regardless of size? Why or why not?

Video Question

18–10. Go to this text's Web site at www.cengage.com/blaw/let and select "Chapter 18." Click on "Video Questions" and view the video titled *Parenthood.* Then answer the following questions.

1. In the video, Gil (Steve Martin) threatens to leave his job when he discovers that his boss is promoting another person to partner instead of him. His boss (Dennis Dugan) laughs and tells him that the threat is not realistic because if Gil leaves, he will be competing for positions with workers who are younger than he is and willing to accept lower salaries. If Gil takes his employer's advice and stays in his current position, can he sue his boss for age discrimination based on the boss's statements? Why or why not?
2. Suppose that Gil leaves his current position and applies for a job at another firm. The prospective employer refuses to hire him based on his age. What would Gil have to prove to establish a *prima facie* case of age discrimination? Explain your answer.
3. What defenses might Gil's current employer raise if Gil sues for age discrimination?

Interacting with the Internet

For updated links to resources available on the Web, as well as a variety of other materials, visit this text's Web site at

www.cengage.com/blaw/let

The Employment Law Information Network provides access to many articles on age discrimination and other employment issues at

www.elinfonet.com/fedindex/2

The New York State Governor's Office of Employee Relations maintains an interactive site on sexual harassment and how to prevent sexual harassment in the workplace. Go to

www.goer.state.ny.us/Train/onlinelearning/SH/intro.html

You can find the complete text of Title VII and information about the activities of the EEOC at the agency's Web site. Go to

www.eeoc.gov

PRACTICAL INTERNET EXERCISES

Go to this text's Web site at **www.cengage.com/blaw/let**, select "Chapter 18," and click on "Practical Internet Exercises." There you will find the following Internet research exercises that you can perform to learn more about the topics covered in this chapter.

Practical Internet Exercise 18–1: LEGAL PERSPECTIVE—**Americans with Disabilities**
Practical Internet Exercise 18–2: MANAGEMENT PERSPECTIVE—**Equal Employment Opportunity**
Practical Internet Exercise 18–3: SOCIAL PERSPECTIVE—**Religious and National-Origin Discrimination**

BEFORE THE TEST

Go to this text's Web site at **www.cengage.com/blaw/let**, select "Chapter 18," and click on "Interactive Quizzes." You will find a number of interactive questions relating to this chapter.

Unit Three

Cumulative Business Hypothetical

Two brothers, Ray and Paul Ashford, start a business manufacturing a new type of battery system for hybrid automobiles. They hit the market at the perfect time, and the batteries are in great demand.

1. When Ray and Paul started off, each brother contributed equal amounts of capital to the business, but they signed no formal agreement. What type of business entity would they be presumed to have formed, and how would any profits be divided? If they want to limit their liability but still remain a small business enterprise, what are their options? Which type of limited liability organization would you recommend, and why?

2. As their business becomes more successful, Ray and Paul seek to raise significant capital to build a manufacturing plant. They decide to form a corporation called Ashford Motors, Inc. Outline the steps that Ray and Paul need to follow to incorporate their business.

3. Loren, one of Ashford's salespersons, anxious to make a sale, intentionally quotes a price to a customer that is $500 lower than Ashford has authorized for that particular product. The customer purchases the product at the quoted price. When Ashford learns of the deal, it claims that it is not legally bound to the sales contract because it did not authorize Loren to sell the product at that price. Is Ashford bound by the contract? Discuss fully.

4. One day Gina, an Ashford employee, suffered a serious burn when she accidentally spilled some acid on her hand. The accident occurred because another employee, who was suspected of using illegal drugs, carelessly bumped into her. The hand required a series of skin-grafting operations before it healed sufficiently to allow Gina to return to work.

Gina wants to obtain compensation for her lost wages and medical expenses. Can she do so? If so, how?

5. After Gina's injury, Ashford decides to conduct random drug tests on all of its employees. Several employees claim that the testing violates their privacy rights. If the dispute is litigated, what factors will the court consider in deciding whether the random drug testing is legally permissible?

6. Ashford provides health insurance for its two hundred employees, including Dan. For personal medical reasons, Dan takes twelve weeks of leave. During this period, can Dan continue his coverage under Ashford's health-insurance plan? After Dan returns to work, Ashford closes Dan's division and terminates the employees, including Dan. Can Dan continue his coverage under Ashford's health-insurance plan? If so, at whose expense?

7. Aretha, another employee at Ashford, is disgusted by the sexually offensive behavior of several male employees. She has complained to her supervisor on several occasions about the offensive behavior, but the supervisor merely laughs at her concerns. Aretha decides to bring a legal action against the company for sexual harassment. Does Aretha's complaint concern *quid pro quo* harassment or hostile-environment harassment? What federal statute protects employees from sexual harassment? What remedies are available under that statute? What procedures must Aretha follow in pursuing her legal action?

The Regulatory Environment

Chapter 19

Powers and Functions of Administrative Agencies

CHAPTER OBJECTIVES

After reading this chapter, you should be able to answer the following questions:

1. How are federal administrative agencies created?

2. What are the three basic functions of most administrative agencies?

3. What sequence of events must normally occur before an agency rule becomes law?

4. How do administrative agencies enforce their rules?

5. How do the three branches of government limit the power of administrative agencies?

CONTENTS

"[P]erhaps more values today are affected by [administrative] decisions than by those of all the courts."

— **ROBERT H. JACKSON,**
1892–1954 (Associate justice of the United States Supreme Court, 1941–1954)

As the chapter-opening quotation suggests, government agencies established to administer the law have a significant impact on the day-to-day operation of the government and the economy. In its early years, the United States had a relatively simple, nonindustrial economy with little regulation. Because administrative agencies often exist to create and enforce such regulations, there were relatively few such agencies. Today, however, there are rules covering virtually every aspect of a business's operation. Consequently, agencies have multiplied. At the federal level, the Securities and Exchange Commission regulates a firm's capital structure and financing, as well as its financial reporting. The National Labor Relations Board oversees relations between a firm and any unions with which it may deal. The Equal Employment Opportunity Commission also regulates employment relationships. The Environmental Protection Agency and the Occupational Safety and Health Administration affect the way a firm manufactures its products. The Federal Trade Commission affects the way the firm markets these products.

Added to this layer of federal regulation is a second layer of state regulation that, when not preempted by federal legislation, may cover many of the same activities or regulate independently those activities not covered by federal regulation. Finally, agency regulations at the county and municipal levels also affect certain types of business activities.

Administrative agencies issue rules, orders, and decisions. These regulations make up the body of *administrative law.* You were introduced briefly to some of the main principles of administrative law in Chapter 1. In the following pages, these principles are presented in much greater detail.

THE PRACTICAL SIGNIFICANCE OF ADMINISTRATIVE LAW

Unlike statutory law, administrative law is created by administrative agencies, not by legislatures, but it is nevertheless of overriding significance for businesses. When Congress—or a state legislature—enacts legislation, it typically adopts a rather general statute and leaves the statute's implementation to an administrative agency, which then creates the detailed rules and regulations necessary to carry out the statute. The administrative agency, with its specialized personnel, has the time, resources, and expertise to make the detailed decisions required for regulation. For example, when Congress enacted the Clean Air Act (see Chapter 21), it provided only general directions for the prevention of air pollution. The specific pollution-control requirements imposed on business are almost entirely the product of decisions made by the Environmental Protection Agency (EPA).

Legislation and regulations have great benefits—in the example of the Clean Air Act, a much cleaner environment than existed in decades past. At the same time, these benefits entail costs for business. The EPA has estimated the costs of compliance with the Clean Air Act at tens of billions of dollars yearly. Although the agency has calculated that the overall benefits of its regulations often exceed their costs, the burden on business is substantial. In 2005, the Small Business Administration estimated the costs of regulation to business, by size of business, and produced the figures shown in Exhibit 19–1.[1] These costs are averages and vary considerably by type of business (for example, retail or manufacturing). The costs are proportionately higher for small businesses because they cannot take advantage of the economies of scale available to larger operations. Clearly, the costs of regulation to business are considerable—and are significantly higher today than they were in 2005.

Given the costs that regulation entails, business has a strong incentive to try to influence the regulatory environment. Whenever new regulations are proposed, as happens constantly, companies may lobby the agency to try to persuade it not to adopt a particular regulation or to adopt one that is more cost-effective. These lobbying efforts consist mainly of providing information to regulators about the costs and problems that the rule may pose for business. At the same time, public-interest groups may be lobbying in favor of more stringent regulation. The rulemaking process, including these lobbying efforts, is governed by administrative law. If

---

1. W. Mark Crain, "The Impact of Regulatory Costs on Small Firms," Small Business Research Summary No. 264, September 2005.

EXHIBIT 19–1 COSTS OF REGULATION TO BUSINESSES (Per Year)

TYPE OF REGULATION	COST PER EMPLOYEE (<20 EMPLOYEES)	COST PER EMPLOYEE (500+ EMPLOYEES)
All federal regulations	$7,647	$5,282
Environmental	$3,296	$ 710
Economic	$2,127	$2,952
Workplace	$ 920	$ 841
Tax compliance	$1,304	$ 780

persuasion fails, administrative law also provides a tool by which businesses or other groups may challenge the legality of the new regulation.

AGENCY CREATION AND POWERS

Congress creates federal administrative agencies. By delegating some of its authority to make and implement laws, Congress can monitor indirectly a particular area in which it has passed legislation without becoming bogged down in the details relating to enforcement—details that are often best left to specialists.

ENABLING LEGISLATION
Statutes enacted by Congress that authorize the creation of an administrative agency and specify the name, composition, and powers of the agency being created.

As mentioned in Chapter 1, to create an administrative agency, Congress passes **enabling legislation,** which specifies the name, purposes, functions, and powers of the agency being created. Federal administrative agencies can exercise only those powers that Congress has delegated to them in enabling legislation. Through similar enabling acts, state legislatures create state administrative agencies.

Enabling Legislation—An Example

Congress created the Federal Trade Commission (FTC) with the Federal Trade Commission Act of 1914.[2] The act prohibits unfair and deceptive trade practices. It also describes the procedures that the agency must follow to charge persons or organizations with violations of the act, and it provides for judicial review of agency orders. The act grants the FTC the power to

1. Create "rules and regulations for the purpose of carrying out the Act."
2. Conduct investigations of business practices.
3. Obtain reports from interstate corporations concerning their business practices.
4. Investigate possible violations of federal antitrust statutes. (The FTC shares this task with the Antitrust Division of the U.S. Department of Justice.)
5. Publish findings of its investigations.
6. Recommend new legislation.
7. Hold trial-like hearings to resolve certain kinds of trade disputes that involve FTC regulations or federal antitrust laws.

The commission that heads the FTC is composed of five members, each of whom the president appoints, with the advice and consent of the Senate, for a term of seven years. The president designates one of the commissioners to be chairperson. Various offices and bureaus of the FTC undertake different administrative activities for the agency. The organization of the FTC is illustrated in Exhibit 19–2.

Types of Agencies

There are two basic types of administrative agencies: executive agencies and independent regulatory agencies. Federal *executive agencies* include the cabinet departments of the executive branch, which were formed to assist the president in carrying out executive functions, and the subagencies within the cabinet departments. The Occupational Safety and Health Administration, for example, is a subagency within the Department of Labor. Exhibit 19–3 on page 644 lists the cabinet departments and their most important subagencies.

---

2. 15 U.S.C. Sections 41–58.

EXHIBIT 19-2 ORGANIZATION OF THE FEDERAL TRADE COMMISSION

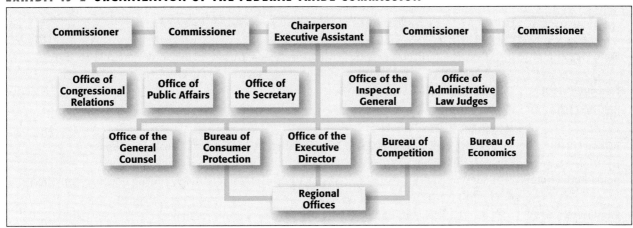

All administrative agencies are part of the executive branch of government, but *independent regulatory agencies* are outside the major executive departments. The Federal Trade Commission and the Securities and Exchange Commission are examples of independent regulatory agencies. These and other selected independent regulatory agencies, as well as their principal functions, are listed in Exhibit 19-4 on page 645.

The significant difference between the two types of agencies lies in the accountability of the regulators. Agencies that are considered part of the executive branch are subject to the authority of the president, who has the power to appoint and remove federal officers. The president can give orders to the head of an executive agency and fire him or her for failing to carry them out. In theory, this power is less pronounced in regard to independent agencies, whose officers serve for fixed terms and cannot be removed without just cause. In practice, however, the president's ability to exert influence over independent agencies is often considerable because the president has the authority to appoint the members of the agencies.

Agency Powers and the Constitution

Administrative agencies occupy an unusual niche in the American legal scheme, because they exercise powers that are normally divided among the three branches of government. The constitutional principle of *checks and balances* allows each branch of government to act as a check on the actions of the other two branches. Furthermore, the Constitution authorizes only the legislative branch to create laws. Yet administrative agencies, to which the Constitution does not specifically refer, make **legislative rules,** or *substantive rules,* that are as legally binding as laws that Congress passes.

Courts generally hold that Article I of the U.S. Constitution authorizes delegating such powers to administrative agencies. In fact, courts generally hold that Article I is the basis for all administrative law. Section 1 of that article grants all legislative powers to Congress and requires Congress to oversee the implementation of all laws. Article I, Section 8, gives Congress the power to make all laws necessary for executing its specified powers. The courts interpret these passages, under what is known as the **delegation doctrine,** as granting Congress the power to establish administrative agencies that can create rules for implementing those laws.

LEGISLATIVE RULE
An administrative agency rule that carries the same weight as a congressionally enacted statute.

DELEGATION DOCTRINE
A doctrine based on Article I, Section 8, of the U.S. Constitution, which has been construed to allow Congress to delegate some of its power to make and implement laws to administrative agencies.

EXHIBIT 19–3 EXECUTIVE DEPARTMENTS AND IMPORTANT SUBAGENCIES

DEPARTMENT AND DATE FORMED	SELECTED SUBAGENCIES
State (1789)	Passport Office; Bureau of Diplomatic Security; Foreign Service; Bureau of Human Rights and Humanitarian Affairs; Bureau of Consular Affairs; Bureau of Intelligence and Research
Treasury (1789)	Internal Revenue Service; U.S. Mint
Interior (1849)	U.S. Fish and Wildlife Service; National Park Service; Bureau of Indian Affairs; Bureau of Land Management
Justice (1870)[a]	Federal Bureau of Investigation; Drug Enforcement Administration; Bureau of Prisons; U.S. Marshals Service
Agriculture (1889)	Soil Conservation Service; Agricultural Research Service; Food Safety and Inspection Service; Forest Service
Commerce (1913)[b]	Bureau of the Census; Bureau of Economic Analysis; Minority Business Development Agency; U.S. Patent and Trademark Office; National Oceanic and Atmospheric Administration
Labor (1913)[b]	Occupational Safety and Health Administration; Bureau of Labor Statistics; Employment Standards Administration; Office of Labor-Management Standards; Employment and Training Administration
Defense (1949)[c]	National Security Agency; Joint Chiefs of Staff; Departments of the Air Force, Navy, Army; service academies
Housing and Urban Development (1965)	Office of Community Planning and Development; Government National Mortgage Association; Office of Fair Housing and Equal Opportunity
Transportation (1967)	Federal Aviation Administration; Federal Highway Administration; National Highway Traffic Safety Administration; Federal Transit Administration
Energy (1977)	Office of Civilian Radioactive Waste Management; Office of Nuclear Energy; Energy Information Administration
Health and Human Services (1980)[d]	Food and Drug Administration; Centers for Medicare and Medicaid Services; Centers for Disease Control and Prevention; National Institutes of Health
Education (1980)[d]	Office of Special Education and Rehabilitation Services; Office of Elementary and Secondary Education; Office of Postsecondary Education; Office of Vocational and Adult Education
Veterans Affairs (1989)	Veterans Health Administration; Veterans Benefits Administration; National Cemetery System
Homeland Security (2002)	U.S. Citizenship and Immigration Services; Directorate of Border and Transportation Services; U.S. Coast Guard; Federal Emergency Management Agency

a. Formed from the Office of the Attorney General (created in 1789).
b. Formed from the Department of Commerce and Labor (created in 1903).
c. Formed from the Department of War (created in 1789) and the Department of the Navy (created in 1798).
d. Formed from the Department of Health, Education, and Welfare (created in 1953).

BUREAUCRACY

The organizational structure, consisting of government bureaus and agencies, through which the government implements and enforces the laws.

The three branches of government exercise certain controls over agency powers and functions, as is discussed later in this chapter, but in many ways administrative agencies function independently. For this reason, administrative agencies, which constitute the **bureaucracy,** are sometimes referred to as the "fourth branch" of the American government.

THE ADMINISTRATIVE PROCEDURE ACT

All federal agencies must follow specific procedural requirements as they go about fulfilling their three basic functions: rulemaking, enforcement, and adjudication. In this section, we focus on agency *rulemaking* (enforcement and adjudication are

EXHIBIT 19-4 SELECTED INDEPENDENT REGULATORY AGENCIES

NAME AND DATE FORMED	PRINCIPAL DUTIES
Federal Reserve System Board of Governors (Fed) (1913)	Determines policy with respect to interest rates, credit availability, and the money supply.
Federal Trade Commission (FTC) (1914)	Prevents businesses from engaging in unfair trade practices; stops the formation of monopolies in the business sector; protects consumer rights.
Securities and Exchange Commission (SEC) (1934)	Regulates the nation's stock exchanges, in which shares of stock are bought and sold; enforces the securities laws, which require full disclosure of the financial profiles of companies that wish to sell stock and bonds to the public.
Federal Communications Commission (FCC) (1934)	Regulates all communications by telegraph, cable, telephone, radio, satellite, and television.
National Labor Relations Board (NLRB) (1935)	Protects employees' rights to join unions and bargain collectively with employers; attempts to prevent unfair labor practices by both employers and unions.
Equal Employment Opportunity Commission (EEOC) (1964)	Works to eliminate discrimination in employment based on religion, gender, race, color, disability, national origin, or age; investigates claims of discrimination.
Environmental Protection Agency (EPA) (1970)	Undertakes programs aimed at reducing air and water pollution; works with state and local agencies to help fight environmental hazards. (It has been suggested recently that its status be elevated to that of a department.)
Nuclear Regulatory Commission (NRC) (1975)	Ensures that electricity-generating nuclear reactors in the United States are built and operated safely; regularly inspects operations of such reactors.

discussed in a later section of this chapter). Sometimes, Congress specifies certain procedural requirements in an agency's enabling legislation. In the absence of any directives from Congress concerning a particular agency procedure, the Administrative Procedure Act (APA) of 1946[3] applies.

The Arbitrary and Capricious Test

One of Congress's goals in enacting the APA was to provide for more judicial control over administrative agencies, which had assumed greater powers during the expansion of government that took place as a result of the Great Depression of the 1930s and World War II (1939–1945). To that end, the APA provides that courts should "hold unlawful and set aside" agency actions found to be "arbitrary, capricious, an abuse of discretion, or otherwise not in accordance with law."[4] Under this standard, parties can challenge regulations as contrary to law or so irrational as to be arbitrary and capricious.

---

3. 5 U.S.C. Sections 551–706.
4. 5 U.S.C. Section 706(2)(A).

The definition of what makes a rule arbitrary and capricious is a vague one, but it includes factors such as whether the agency has done any of the following:

1. Failed to provide a rational explanation for its decision.
2. Changed its prior policy without justification.
3. Considered legally inappropriate factors.
4. Entirely failed to consider a relevant factor.
5. Rendered a decision plainly contrary to the evidence.

The following case considers the application of the arbitrary and capricious standard.

Case 19.1   Fox Television Stations, Inc. v. Federal Communications Commission

United States Court of Appeals, Second Circuit, 2007.
489 F.3d 444.

BACKGROUND AND FACTS   In 1975, the Federal Communications Commission (FCC) started exercising its statutory authority to sanction indecent (but nonobscene) speech. The FCC defines such speech as "language that describes, in terms patently offensive as measured by contemporary community standards for the broadcast medium, sexual or excretory activities and organs." In 2003, the FCC held that any variant of "the F-Word has inherent sexual connotation" and therefore falls within the scope of the indecency definition, even if used "fleetingly" on television or radio. On February 21, 2006, the FCC determined that several Billboard Music Awards shows broadcast by Fox Television Stations, Inc., were "indecent and profane." Fox filed a petition for review of the FCC's order to the U.S. Court of Appeals for the Second Circuit.

IN THE WORDS OF THE COURT . . . *POOLER*, **Circuit Judge.**

*   *   *   *

Agencies are of course free to revise their rules and policies. Such a change, however, must provide a reasoned analysis for departing from prior precedent. *When an agency reverses its course, a court must satisfy itself that the agency knows it is changing course, has given sound reasons for the change, and has shown that the rule is consistent with the law that gives the agency its authority to act.* In addition, the agency must consider reasonably obvious alternatives and, if it rejects those alternatives, it must give reasons for the rejection *   *   * . *The agency must explain why the original reasons for adopting the rule or policy are no longer dispositive* [a deciding factor]. *   *   * [Emphasis added.]

*   *   * The primary reason for the crackdown on fleeting expletives advanced by the FCC is the so-called "first blow" theory *   *   * . Indecent material on the airwaves enters into the privacy of the home uninvited and without warning. *   *   * To say that one may avoid further offense by turning off the [television or] radio when he hears indecent language is like saying that the remedy for an assault is to run away after the first blow.

We cannot accept this argument as a reasoned basis justifying the Commission's new rule. First, the Commission provides no reasonable explanation for why it has changed its perception that a fleeting expletive was not a harmful "first blow" for the nearly thirty years between [the decisions in two earlier cases]. More problematic, however, is that the "first blow" theory bears no rational connection to the Commission's actual policy regarding fleeting expletives. *   *   * A re-broadcast of precisely the same offending clips from the two Billboard Music Award[s] programs for the purpose of providing background information on this case would not result in any action by the FCC *   *   * .

The *   *   * Order makes passing reference to other reasons that purportedly support its change in policy, none of which we find sufficient. For instance, the Commission states that even non-literal uses of expletives fall within its indecency definition because it is "difficult (if not impossible) to distinguish whether a word is being used as an expletive or as a literal description of sexual or excretory functions." This defies any commonsense understanding of these words, which, as the general public well knows, are often used in everyday conversation without any "sexual or excretory" meaning. *   *   * Even the top leaders of our government have used variants of these expletives in a manner that no reasonable person would believe referenced "sexual or excretory organs or activities." [The court proceeded to recount examples of when President [George W.] Bush and Vice President [Dick] Cheney had used the questionable words in public.]

*   *   *   *

Accordingly, we find that the FCC's new policy regarding "fleeting expletives" fails to provide a reasoned analysis justifying its departure from the agency's established practice. For this reason, Fox's petition for review is granted, the *   *   * Order is vacated, and the matter is remanded to the FCC for further proceedings consistent with this opinion.

DECISION AND REMEDY   The federal appellate court granted Fox's petition for review. It vacated the FCC's order and remanded the matter to the FCC for further proceedings.

THE LEGAL ENVIRONMENT DIMENSION   According to the court's opinion in this case, is an administrative agency locked into its first interpretation of a statute?

THE ETHICAL DIMENSION   Were the agency's reasons for its actions rejected in this case because the court disagreed with those reasons? Explain.

Rulemaking

Today, the major function of an administrative agency is **rulemaking**—the formulation of new regulations, or rules, as they are often called. The APA defines a rule as "an agency statement of general or particular applicability and future effect designed to implement, interpret, or prescribe law and policy."[5] Regulations are sometimes said to be *legislative* because, like statutes, they have a binding effect. Like those who violate statutes, violators of agency rules may be punished. Because agency rules have such great legal force, the APA established procedures for agencies to follow in creating rules. Many rules must be adopted using the APA's *notice-and-comment rulemaking* procedure.

Notice-and-comment rulemaking involves three basic steps: notice of the proposed rulemaking, a comment period, and the final rule. The APA recognizes some limited exceptions to these procedural requirements, but they are seldom invoked. If the required procedures are violated, the resulting rule may be invalid. The impetus for rulemaking may come from various sources, including Congress, the agency itself, or private parties who may petition an agency to begin a rulemaking (or repeal a rule). For instance, environmental groups have petitioned for stricter pollution controls to combat global warming.

Notice of the Proposed Rulemaking   When a federal agency decides to create a new rule, the agency publishes a notice of the proposed rulemaking proceedings in the *Federal Register,* a daily publication of the executive branch that prints government orders, rules, and regulations. The notice states where and when the proceedings will be held, the agency's legal authority for making the rule (usually its enabling legislation), and the terms or subject matter of the proposed rule.

RULEMAKING
The actions undertaken by administrative agencies when formally adopting new regulations or amending old ones. Under the Administrative Procedure Act, rulemaking includes notifying the public of proposed rules or changes and receiving and considering the public's comments.

NOTICE-AND-COMMENT RULEMAKING
A procedure in agency rulemaking that requires (1) notice, (2) opportunity for comment, and (3) a published draft of the final rule.

---

5. 5 U.S.C. Section 551(4).

"In some respects, matters of procedure constitute the very essence of ordered liberty under the Constitution."

—WILEY B. RUTLEDGE, 1894–1949
(Associate justice of the United States
Supreme Court, 1943–1949)

Comment Period   Following the publication of the notice of the proposed rulemaking proceedings, the agency must allow ample time for persons to comment on the proposed rule. The purpose of this comment period is to give interested parties the opportunity to express their views on the proposed rule in an effort to influence agency policy. The comments may be in writing or, if a hearing is held, may be given orally. The agency need not respond to all comments, but it must respond to any significant comments that bear directly on the proposed rule. The agency responds by either modifying its final rule or explaining, in a statement accompanying the final rule, why it did not make any changes. In some circumstances, particularly when the procedure being used in a specific instance is less formal, an agency may accept comments after the comment period is closed. The agency should summarize these *ex parte* (private, off-the-record) comments for possible review.

The Final Rule   After the agency reviews the comments, it drafts the final rule and publishes it in the *Federal Register*. Such a final rule must contain a "concise general statement of . . . basis and purpose" that describes the reasoning behind the rule.[6] The final rule may change the terms of the proposed rule, in light of the public comments, but cannot change the proposal too radically, or a new proposal and a new opportunity for comment are required. The final rule is later compiled along with the rules and regulations of other federal administrative agencies in the *Code of Federal Regulations* (C.F.R.). Final rules have binding legal effect unless the courts later overturn them. For this reason, they are often referred to as legislative rules. *Legislative rules* are substantive in that they affect legal rights, whereas *interpretive rules* issued by agencies simply declare policy and do not affect legal rights or obligations (see the discussion of informal agency actions later in this chapter).

     The court in the following case considered whether to enforce rules that were issued outside of the rulemaking procedure.

---

6. 5 U.S.C. Section 555(c).

Case 19.2   Hemp Industries Association v. Drug Enforcement Administration

United States Court of Appeals, Ninth Circuit, 2004.
357 F.3d 1012.

BACKGROUND AND FACTS   The members of the Hemp Industries Association (HIA) import and distribute sterilized hemp seed and oil, as well as cake derived from hemp seed, and make and sell food and cosmetic products made from hemp seed and oil. These products contain only nonpsychoactive trace amounts of tetrahydrocannabinols (THC).[a] On October 9, 2001, the U.S. Drug Enforcement

Administration (DEA) published an interpretive rule declaring that "any product that contains any amount of THC is a Schedule I controlled substance."[b] On the same day, the DEA proposed two legislative rules. One rule—DEA-205F—amended the listing of THC in "Schedule I" to include natural, as well as synthetic, THC. The second rule—DEA-206F—exempted from control nonpsychoactive hemp products that contain trace amounts of THC not intended to enter the human body. On March 21, 2003, without following formal rulemaking procedures, the DEA declared that these rules were final. This effectively banned the possession and sale of the food products of the HIA's members. The HIA petitioned the U.S. Court of Appeals for the Ninth Circuit to review the rules, asserting that they could not be enforced.

---

a. A *nonpsychoactive substance* is one that does not affect a person's mind or behavior. Nonpsychoactive hemp is derived from industrial hemp plants grown in Canada and Europe, the flowers of which contain only a trace amount of the THC contained in marijuana varieties grown for psychoactive use.

b. A *controlled substance* is a drug whose availability is restricted by law.

IN THE WORDS OF THE COURT . . . *BETTY B. FLETCHER,* Circuit Judge.

* * * *

* * * Appellants * * * argue that DEA-205F is a scheduling action—placing nonpsychoactive hemp in Schedule I for the first time—that fails to follow the procedures for such actions required by the Controlled Substances Act ("CSA").

* * * *

Under 21 U.S.C. [Section] 811(a) [of the CSA]:

the Attorney General may by rule—
(1) add to * * * a schedule * * * any drug or other substance if he—
* * *
(B) makes with respect to such drug or other substance the findings prescribed by subsection (b) of Section 812 of this title * * * .

Rules of the Attorney General under this subsection shall be made on the record after opportunity for a hearing pursuant to the rulemaking procedures prescribed by [the Administrative Procedure Act (APA).]

* * * *Formal rulemaking requires hearings on the record, and [the APA] invites parties to submit proposed findings and oppose the stated bases of tentative agency decisions, and requires the agency to issue formal rulings on each finding, conclusion, or exception on the record.* We will not reproduce the entirety of the [APA] here; it suffices to say that the DEA did not and does not claim to have followed formal rulemaking procedures. [Emphasis added.]

In addition, the DEA did not comply with [Section] 811(a)(1)(B), because the findings required by [Section] 812(b) were not made. Section 812(b) states:

(b) Placement on schedules; findings required. * * * A drug or other substance may not be placed in any schedule unless the findings required for such schedule are made with respect to such drug or other substance.

* * * *

The DEA does not purport to have met the requirements for placement of nonpsychoactive hemp on Schedule I * * * . Instead, the DEA argues that naturally occurring THC in those parts of the hemp plant excluded from the definition of "marijuana" have always been included under the listing for "THC" * * * .

* * * *

Two CSA provisions are relevant to determining whether Appellants' hemp products were banned before [DEA-205F and DEA-206F]: the definition of THC and the definition of marijuana. Both are unambiguous * * * : Appellants' products do not contain the "synthetic" "substances or derivatives" that are covered by the definition of THC, and nonpsychoactive hemp is explicitly excluded from the definition of marijuana.

* * * *

Under 21 U.S.C. [Section] 802(16) [of the CSA]:

The term "marihuana" means all parts of the plant *Cannabis sativa L.* * * * . Such term does not include the mature stalks of such plant, fiber produced from such stalks, oil or cake made from the seeds of such plant, any other compound, manufacture, salt, derivative, mixture, or preparation of such mature stalks (except the resin extracted therefrom), fiber, oil, or cake, or the sterilized seed of such plant which is incapable of germination.

The nonpsychoactive hemp in Appellants' products is derived from the "mature stalks" or is "oil and cake made from the seeds" of the Cannabis plant, and therefore fits within the plainly stated exception to the CSA definition of marijuana.

* * * Congress knew what it was doing, and its intent to exclude nonpsychoactive hemp from regulation is entirely clear.

CASE 19.2—CONTINUED

CASE 19.2–CONTINUED

DECISION AND REMEDY   The U.S. Court of Appeals for the Ninth Circuit held that DEA-205F and DEA-206F "are inconsistent with the unambiguous meaning of the CSA definitions of marijuana and THC" and that the DEA did not follow the proper administrative procedures required to schedule a substance. The court issued an injunction against the enforcement of the rules with respect to nonpsychoactive hemp and products containing it.

WHAT IF THE FACTS WERE DIFFERENT?   Suppose that the statutory definitions of THC and marijuana covered naturally occurring THC and nonpsychoactive hemp. Would the result in this case have been different? Explain.

THE E-COMMERCE DIMENSION   How might the Internet expedite formal rulemaking procedures such as those required by the U.S. Court of Appeals for the Ninth Circuit in this case? Discuss.

Informal Agency Action

Rather than take the time to conduct notice-and-comment rulemaking, agencies have increasingly been using more informal methods of policymaking. These include issuing interpretive rules, which are specifically exempted from the APA's requirements. Such rules simply declare the agency's interpretation of its enabling statute's meaning, and they impose no direct and legally binding obligations on regulated parties. In addition, agencies issue various other materials, such as "guidance documents," that advise the public on the agencies' legal and policy positions.

Such informal actions are exempt from the APA's requirements because they do not establish legal rights—a party cannot be directly prosecuted for violating an interpretive rule or a guidance document. Nevertheless, an agency's informal action can be of practical importance because it warns regulated entities that the agency may engage in formal rulemaking if they fail to heed the positions taken informally by the agency.

JUDICIAL DEFERENCE TO AGENCY DECISIONS

When asked to review agency decisions, courts historically granted some deference (significant weight) to the agency's judgment, often citing the agency's great expertise in the subject area of the regulation. This deference seems especially appropriate when applied to an agency's analysis of factual questions, but should it also extend to an agency's interpretation of its own legal authority? In *Chevron U.S.A., Inc. v. Natural Resources Defense Council, Inc.,*[7] the United States Supreme Court held that it should, thereby creating a standard of broadened deference to agencies on questions of legal interpretation.

The Holding in the *Chevron* Case

At issue in the *Chevron* case was whether the courts should defer to an agency's interpretation of a statute giving it authority to act. The Environmental Protection Agency (EPA) had interpreted the phrase "stationary source" in the Clean Air Act as referring to an entire manufacturing plant, and not to each facility within a plant. The agency's interpretation enabled it to adopt the so-called bubble policy, which allowed companies to offset increases in emissions in part

---

7. 467 U.S. 837, 104 S.Ct. 2778, 81 L.Ed.2d 694 (1984).

of a plant with decreases elsewhere in the plant—an interpretation that reduced the pollution-control compliance costs faced by manufacturers. An environmental group challenged the legality of the EPA's interpretation.

The Supreme Court held that the courts should defer to an agency's interpretation of *law* as well as fact. The Court found that the agency's interpretation of the statute was reasonable and upheld the bubble policy. The Court's decision in the *Chevron* case created a new standard for courts to use when reviewing agency interpretations of law, which involves the following two questions:

1. Did Congress directly address the issue in dispute in the statute? If so, the statutory language prevails.
2. If the statute is silent or ambiguous, is the agency's interpretation "reasonable"? If it is, a court should uphold the agency's interpretation even if the court would have interpreted the law differently.

When Courts Will Give *Chevron* Deference to Agency Interpretation

The notion that courts should defer to agencies on matters of law was controversial. Under the holding of the *Chevron* case, when the meaning of a particular statute's language is unclear and an agency interprets it, the court must follow the agency's interpretation as long as it is reasonable. This led to considerable discussion and litigation to test the boundaries of the *Chevron* holding. For instance, are courts required to give deference to all agency interpretations or only to those interpretations that result from adjudication or formal rulemaking procedures? The United States Supreme Court has held that in order for agency interpretations to be assured of *Chevron* deference, they must meet the formal legal standards for notice-and-comment rulemaking.[8] Nevertheless, there are still gray areas, and many agency interpretations are challenged in court.

In the case that follows, an environmental organization brought an action challenging the U.S. Forest Service's decision to issue a special use permit to a business that conducts helicopter-skiing operations in two national forests. As you will read in Chapter 21, the National Environmental Policy Act requires federal agencies to prepare an environmental impact statement (EIS) that considers every significant aspect of the environmental impact of a proposed action. Although the Forest Service prepared an EIS before issuing the use permit to the helicopter-skiing operation, environmental groups claimed that the EIS did not sufficiently analyze increasing recreational pressures in the forests. The groups sought to have the court invalidate the permit.

---

8. *United States v. Mead Corp.*, 533 U.S. 218, 121 S.Ct. 2164, 150 L.Ed.2d 292 (2001).

Case 19.3 Citizens' Committee to Save Our Canyons v. Krueger

United States Court of Appeals, Tenth Circuit, 2008.
513 F.3d 1169.

BACKGROUND AND FACTS   Under the National Forest Management Act (NFMA), the U.S. Forest Service manages

national forests in accordance with forest plans periodically developed for each forest. The plans for two national forests—the Wasatch-Cache and Uinta forests—were initially adopted in 1985 and revised in 2003. The Forest Service interpreted the 1985 forest plans as requiring the forests to allow helicopter

CASE 19.3–CONTINUED

skiing, and the plans expressly recognized helicopter skiing as a legitimate use of the national forests. Wasatch Powderbird Guides (WPG) has continuously operated a guided helicopter-skiing business in the Wasatch-Cache and Uinta national forests since 1973. It operates under the authority of special use permits periodically issued by the Forest Service. Citizens' Committee to Save Our Canyons and Utah Environmental Congress (referred to collectively as SOC) are nonprofit

organizations made up of members who use the areas in which WPG operates for nonmotorized uses, such as backcountry skiing, snowshoeing, hiking, and camping. They claim that their recreational opportunities and experiences are diminished by WPG's operations and argue that the Forest Service failed to comply with relevant laws when issuing WPG's most recent permit. The district court upheld the Forest Service permit, and SOC appealed.

IN THE WORDS OF THE COURT . . . *TYMKOVICH*, Circuit Judge.

In this appeal we consider the United States Forest Service's decision to issue a special use permit to Wasatch Powderbird Guides (WPG) to conduct helicopter skiing operations in two national forests. Citizens' Committee to Save Our Canyons and Utah Environmental Congress argue the decision violated the National Forest Management Act and the National Environmental Policy Act.

Under the Administrative Procedure Act ("APA"), which governs judicial review of agency actions, * * * we set aside the agency's action * * * if it is "arbitrary, capricious, an abuse of discretion, or otherwise not in accordance with law." We will also set aside an agency action if the agency has failed to follow required procedures.

Our review is highly deferential [respectful of the agency's reasoning]. The duty of a court reviewing agency action under the "arbitrary or capricious" standard is to ascertain whether the agency examined the relevant data and articulated a rational connection between the facts found and the decision made. Furthermore, in reviewing the agency's explanation, the reviewing court must determine whether the agency considered all relevant factors and whether there has been a clear error of judgment. A presumption of validity attaches to the agency action and the burden of proof rests with the appellants who challenge such action. [Emphasis added.]

* * * *

NFMA requires the Forest Service to "develop, maintain, and, as appropriate, revise land and resource management plans for units of the National Forest System." All permits the Forest Service issues "for the use and occupancy of National Forest System lands shall be consistent with the land management plans."

* * * The EIS examined various options and concluded an acceptable balance between helicopter skiing and other uses could be reached by imposing certain restrictions on WPG's operations. These restrictions reflect no special consideration for WPG's economic viability beyond the goal of providing "a range of diverse, recreational opportunities" including helicopter skiing. The EIS thoroughly explains the Forest Service's approach, and the 2005 permit includes a number of reasonable restrictions on WPG with the goal of allowing both helicopter skiers and other backcountry users to enjoy the national forests. In the end, the Forest Service's permit reflected the "type and level" of heli-skiing it thought appropriately balanced the competing recreational uses in the forests.

Taking the interpretation of the forest plans represented by the EIS as a whole, the EIS and the ultimate permitting decision comply with the Forest Service's interpretation of its forest plans. The Forest Service properly considered how particular options would affect the range of recreational opportunities available in the forests and balanced interests in a way it believed promoted multiple forest uses.

* * * *

In sum, the Forest Service's EIS fully disclosed and considered the impact of its decision to issue a special use permit to WPG. *Our objective is not to "fly speck" the [EIS], but rather, to make a pragmatic judgment whether the [EIS]'s form, content and preparation foster both informed decision-making and informed public participation.* The NEPA process in this case, including extensive public comment, considered a variety of options and yielded a number of reasonable restrictions on WPG's operations designed to minimize conflict among forest users. This is all NEPA requires. [Emphasis added.]

DECISION AND REMEDY   The U.S. Court of Appeals for the Tenth Circuit affirmed the district court's decision that upheld the Forest Service permit allowing WPG to conduct helicopter-skiing operations in two national forests. The Forest Service's EIS properly considered all relevant factors and allowed for public comment. Because the Forest Service's interpretation of the NFMA and NEPA was reasonable, the court found that the permit complied with federal laws.

WHAT IF THE FACTS WERE DIFFERENT?   Suppose that the Forest Service had granted WPG a permit for its helicopter-skiing operations on national forest land without preparing an EIS or soliciting public comment. How might that have changed the court's ruling in this case?

THE ETHICAL DIMENSION   If it turned out that the helicopter-skiing operation had paid a substantial sum to the Forest Service official who prepared the EIS to influence the official's findings, would the court have been able to consider this fact and invalidate the permit? Why or why not?

ENFORCEMENT AND ADJUDICATION

Although rulemaking is the most prominent agency activity, enforcement of the rules is also critical. Often, an agency itself enforces its rules. It identifies alleged violators and pursues civil remedies against them in a proceeding held by the agency rather than in federal court, although the agency's determinations are reviewable in court.

Investigation

After final rules are issued, agencies conduct investigations to monitor compliance with those rules or the terms of the enabling statute. A typical agency investigation of this kind might begin when a citizen reports a possible violation to the agency. Many agency rules also require considerable compliance reporting from regulated entities, and such a report may trigger an enforcement investigation. For example, environmental regulators often require reporting of emissions, and the Occupational Safety and Health Administration requires companies to report any work-related deaths.

Inspections and Tests   Many agencies gather information through on-site inspections. Sometimes, inspecting an office, a factory, or some other business facility is the only way to obtain the evidence needed to prove a regulatory violation. At other times, an inspection or test is used in place of a formal hearing to show the need to correct or prevent an undesirable condition. Administrative inspections and tests cover a wide range of activities, including safety inspections of underground coal mines, safety tests of commercial equipment and automobiles, and environmental monitoring of factory emissions. An agency may also ask a firm or individual to submit certain documents or records to the agency for examination. For instance, the Federal Trade Commission often asks to inspect corporate records for compliance.

Normally, business firms comply with agency requests to inspect facilities or business records because it is in any firm's interest to maintain a good relationship with regulatory bodies. In some instances, however, such as when a firm thinks an agency's request is unreasonable and may be detrimental to the firm's interest, the firm may refuse to comply with the request. In such situations, an agency may resort to the use of a subpoena or a search warrant.

Subpoenas   There are two basic types of subpoenas. The subpoena *ad testificandum* ("to testify") is an ordinary subpoena. It is a writ, or order, compelling a witness to appear at an agency hearing. The subpoena *duces tecum*[9] ("bring it with you") compels an individual or organization to hand over books, papers, records, or documents to the agency. An administrative agency may use either type of subpoena to obtain testimony or documents.

There are limits on what an agency can demand. To determine whether an agency is abusing its discretion in its pursuit of information as part of an investigation, a court may consider such factors as the following:

1. *The purpose of the investigation.* An investigation must have a legitimate purpose. An improper purpose is, for example, harassment. An agency may not issue an administrative subpoena to inspect business records if the agency's motive is to harass or pressure the business into settling an unrelated matter.

2. *The relevancy of the information being sought.* Information is relevant if it reveals that the law is being violated or if it assures the agency that the law is not being violated.

3. *The specificity of the demand for testimony or documents.* A subpoena must, for example, adequately describe the material being sought.

4. *The burden of the demand on the party from whom the information is sought.* In responding to a request for information, a party must bear the costs of, for example, copying the documents that must be handed over, but a business is generally protected from revealing information such as trade secrets.

Search Warrants   The Fourth Amendment protects against unreasonable searches and seizures by requiring that in most instances a physical search for evidence must be conducted under the authority of a search warrant. An agency's search warrant is an order directing law enforcement officials to search a specific place for a specific item and present it to the agency. Although it was once thought that administrative inspections were exempt from the warrant requirement, the United States Supreme Court held in *Marshall v. Barlow's, Inc.,*[10] that the requirement does apply to the administrative process.

Agencies can conduct warrantless searches in several situations. Warrants are not required to conduct searches in highly regulated industries. Firms that sell firearms or liquor, for example, are automatically subject to inspections without warrants. Sometimes, a statute permits warrantless searches of certain types of hazardous operations, such as coal mines. Also, a warrantless inspection in an emergency situation is normally considered reasonable.

---

9. Pronounced *doo*-suhs *tee*-kum.
10. 436 U.S. 307, 98 S.Ct. 1816, 56 L.Ed.2d 305 (1978).

Adjudication

After conducting an investigation of a suspected rule violation, an agency may begin to take administrative action against an individual or organization. Most administrative actions are resolved through negotiated settlements at their initial stages, without the need for formal **adjudication** (the resolution of the dispute through a hearing conducted by the agency).

Negotiated Settlements   Depending on the agency, negotiations may take the form of a simple conversation or a series of informal conferences. Whatever form the negotiations take, their purpose is to rectify the problem to the agency's satisfaction and eliminate the need for additional proceedings.

Settlement is an appealing option to firms for two reasons: to avoid appearing uncooperative and to avoid the expense involved in formal adjudication proceedings and in possible later appeals. Settlement is also an attractive option for agencies. To conserve their own resources and avoid formal actions, administrative agencies devote a great deal of effort to giving advice and negotiating solutions to problems.

Formal Complaints   If a settlement cannot be reached, the agency may issue a formal complaint against the suspected violator. EXAMPLE #1 The Environmental Protection Agency (EPA) finds that Acme Manufacturing, Inc., is polluting groundwater in violation of federal pollution laws. The EPA issues a complaint against the violator in an effort to bring the plant into compliance with federal regulations.□ This complaint is a public document, and a press release may accompany it. The party charged in the complaint responds by filing an answer to the allegations. If the charged party and the agency cannot agree on a settlement, the case will be adjudicated.

Agency adjudication may involve a trial-like arbitration procedure before an *administrative law judge (ALJ)*. The Administrative Procedure Act (APA) requires that before the hearing takes place, the agency must issue a notice that includes the facts and law on which the complaint is based, the legal authority for the hearing, and its time and place. The administrative adjudication process is described below and illustrated graphically in Exhibit 19–5 on the following page.

The Role of the Administrative Law Judge   The ALJ presides over the hearing and has the power to administer oaths, take testimony, rule on questions of evidence, and make determinations of fact. Although technically the ALJ is not an independent judge and works for the agency prosecuting the case (in our example, the EPA), the law requires an ALJ to be an unbiased adjudicator (judge).

Certain safeguards prevent bias on the part of the ALJ and promote fairness in the proceedings. For example, the APA requires that the ALJ be separate from an agency's investigative and prosecutorial staff. The APA also prohibits *ex parte* (private) communications between the ALJ and any party to an agency proceeding, such as the EPA or the factory. Finally, provisions of the APA protect the ALJ from agency disciplinary actions unless the agency can show good cause for such an action.

Hearing Procedures   Hearing procedures vary widely from agency to agency. Administrative agencies generally exercise substantial discretion over the type of procedure that will be used. Frequently, disputes are resolved through

ADJUDICATION
The act of rendering a judicial decision. In an administrative process, the proceeding in which an administrative law judge hears and decides on issues that arise when an administrative agency charges a person or a firm with violating a law or regulation enforced by the agency.

EXHIBIT 19-5 THE PROCESS OF FORMAL ADMINISTRATIVE ADJUDICATION

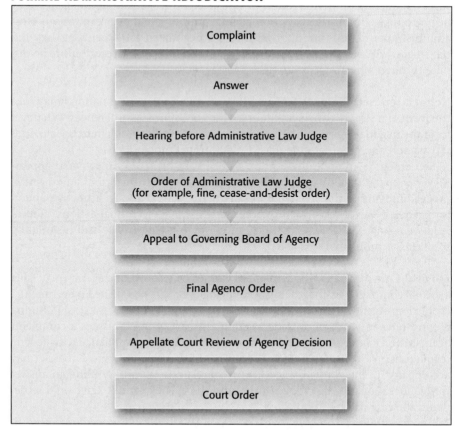

informal adjudication proceedings. **EXAMPLE #2** The Federal Trade Commission (FTC) charges Good Foods, Inc., with deceptive advertising. Representatives of Good Foods and of the FTC, their counsel, and the ALJ meet at a table in a conference room to resolve the dispute informally.□

A formal adjudicatory hearing, in contrast, resembles a trial in many respects. Prior to the hearing, the parties are permitted to undertake discovery—involving depositions, interrogatories, and requests for documents or other information, as described in Chapter 3—although the discovery process is not quite as extensive as it would be in a court proceeding. The hearing itself must comply with the procedural requirements of the APA and must also meet the constitutional standards of due process. During the hearing, the parties may give testimony, present other evidence, and cross-examine adverse witnesses. A significant difference between a trial and an administrative agency hearing, though, is that normally much more information, including hearsay (secondhand information), can be introduced as evidence during an administrative hearing. The burden of proof in an enforcement proceeding is placed on the agency.

Agency Orders　　Following a hearing, the ALJ renders an **initial order,** or decision, on the case. Either party can appeal the ALJ's decision to the board or commission

INITIAL ORDER
In the context of administrative law, an agency's disposition in a matter other than a rulemaking. An administrative law judge's initial order becomes final unless it is appealed.

that governs the agency. If the factory in the previous example is dissatisfied with the ALJ's decision, it can appeal the decision to the EPA. If the factory is dissatisfied with the commission's decision, it can appeal the decision to a federal court of appeals. If no party appeals the case, the ALJ's decision becomes the **final order** of the agency. The ALJ's decision also becomes final if a party appeals and the commission and the court decline to review the case. If a party appeals and the case is reviewed, the final order comes from the commission's decision or (if that decision is appealed to a federal appellate court) that of the court.

FINAL ORDER
The final decision of an administrative agency on an issue. If no appeal is taken, or if the case is not reviewed or considered anew by the agency commission, the administrative law judge's initial order becomes the final order of the agency.

LIMITATIONS ON AGENCY POWERS

Combining the functions normally divided among the three branches of government into an administrative agency concentrates considerable power in a single organization. Because of this concentration of authority, one of the major policy objectives of the government is to control the risks of arbitrariness and overreaching by administrative agencies without hindering the effective use of agency power to deal with particular problem areas, as Congress intends.

The judicial branch of the government exercises control over agency powers through the courts' review of agency actions. The executive and legislative branches also exercise control over agency authority.

Judicial Controls

The APA provides for judicial review of most agency decisions. As discussed above, if a charged party is dissatisfied with an agency's order, it can appeal the decision to a federal appeals court. Agency actions are not automatically subject to judicial review, however. Procedural doctrines such as exhaustion and ripeness may limit the opportunity of judicial review.

"Absolute discretion . . . is more destructive of freedom than any of man's other inventions."
—WILLIAM O. DOUGLAS, 1898–1980
(Associate justice of the United States Supreme Court, 1939–1975)

The Exhaustion Doctrine The *exhaustion doctrine* requires that a regulated party use all of its potential administrative remedies before going to court, even though the party might prefer to go straight to the independent federal courts, rather than going through the administrative adjudication process. Requiring the administrative process first allows the agency to evaluate the argument and enables a court to take advantage of the agency's own fact-finding capabilities before ruling. The exhaustion of administrative remedies is not required, though, if the party can demonstrate that those remedies are inadequate to address its challenge.

EXAMPLE #3 In the classic exhaustion case, a company was served with a complaint from the National Labor Relations Board (NLRB) alleging that it had engaged in unfair labor practices. The company argued that because it was not operating in interstate commerce, the NLRB had no jurisdiction. The United States Supreme Court rejected this argument and held that the company was required to first use administrative procedures to challenge the complaint.[11] □

The Ripeness Doctrine Under what is known as the *ripeness doctrine,* a court will not review an administrative agency's decision until the case is "ripe for

---

11. *Myers v. Bethlehem Shipbuilding Corp.,* 303 U.S. 41, 58 S.Ct. 459, 82 L.Ed. 638 (1938).

review." Generally, a case is ripe for review if the parties can demonstrate that they have met certain requirements. The party bringing the action must have *standing to sue* the agency (the party must have a direct stake in the outcome of the judicial proceeding), and there must be an *actual controversy* at issue. Recall from Chapter 3 that these are basic judicial requirements that must be met before any court will hear a case.

Standing requires that a plaintiff have an actual injury, that the injury be causally connected with the challenged action, and that the injury be one that can be successfully redressed by a judicial resolution of the case. The rationale for this doctrine is to prevent courts from entangling themselves in abstract disagreements over administrative policies. The doctrine also protects agencies from judicial interference until an administrative decision has been formalized and its effects are clear. The court can then evaluate both the appropriateness of an issue for judicial resolution and the hardship that the plaintiff will suffer if the court refuses to hear the case.

Executive Controls

The executive branch of government exercises control over agencies both through the president's power to appoint federal officers and through the president's veto power. The president may veto enabling legislation presented by Congress or congressional attempts to modify an existing agency's authority. In addition, the president has created a process whereby the Office of Information and Regulatory Affairs (OIRA) of the Office of Management and Budget reviews the cost-effectiveness of agency rules. The OIRA also reviews agencies' compliance with the Paperwork Reduction Act,[12] which requires agencies to minimize the paperwork burden on regulated entities. These reviews provide regulated entities with a pathway to challenge rules, through lobbying, even after the rules have been adopted. The reviews are not subject to the requirements of the Administrative Procedure Act.

Legislative Controls

Congress also exercises authority over agency powers. Through enabling legislation, Congress gives power to an agency. Of course, an agency cannot exceed the power that Congress delegates to it. Through subsequent legislation, Congress can take away that power or even abolish an agency altogether. Legislative authority is required to fund an agency, and enabling legislation usually sets certain time and monetary limits relating to the funding of particular programs. Congress can always revise these limits.

In addition to its power to create and fund agencies, Congress has the authority to investigate the implementation of its laws and the agencies that it has created. Individual legislators may also affect agency policy through their casework activities, which involve attempts to help their constituents deal with agencies.

Congress also has the power to "freeze" the enforcement of most federal regulations before the regulations take effect. Under the Small Business Regulatory Enforcement Fairness Act of 1996,[13] all federal agencies must submit final rules

---

12. Pub. L. No. 104-13, May 22, 1995, 109 Stat. 163, amending 44 U.S.C. Sections 3501 *et seq.*
13. 5 U.S.C. Sections 801–808.

to Congress before the rules become effective. If, within sixty days, Congress passes a joint resolution of disapproval concerning a rule, enforcement of the regulation is frozen while the rule is reviewed by congressional committees.

Other legislative checks on agency actions include the Administrative Procedure Act, discussed earlier in this chapter, and the laws discussed in the next section.

PUBLIC ACCOUNTABILITY

As a result of growing public concern over the powers exercised by administrative agencies, Congress passed several laws to make agencies more accountable through public scrutiny. We discuss here the most significant of these laws.

Freedom of Information Act

Enacted in 1966, the Freedom of Information Act (FOIA)[14] requires the federal government to disclose certain records to any person on request, even if no reason is given for the request. The FOIA exempts certain types of records. For other records, though, a request that complies with the FOIA procedures need only contain a reasonable description of the information sought. An agency's failure to comply with such a request can be challenged in a federal district court. The media, industry trade associations, public-interest groups, and even companies seeking information about competitors rely on these FOIA provisions to obtain information from government agencies.

Government in the Sunshine Act

Congress passed the Government in the Sunshine Act,[15] or open meeting law, in 1976. It requires that "every portion of every meeting of an agency" be open to "public observation." The act also requires procedures to ensure that the public is provided with adequate advance notice of the agency's scheduled meeting and agenda. Like the FOIA, the Sunshine Act contains certain exceptions. Closed meetings are permitted when (1) the subject of the meeting concerns accusing any person of a crime, (2) open meetings would frustrate implementation of future agency actions, or (3) the subject of the meeting involves matters relating to future litigation or rulemaking. Courts interpret these exceptions to allow open access whenever possible.

Regulatory Flexibility Act

Concern over the effects of regulation on the efficiency of businesses, particularly smaller ones, led Congress to pass the Regulatory Flexibility Act in 1980.[16] Under this act, whenever a new regulation will have a "significant impact upon a substantial number of small entities," the agency must conduct a regulatory flexibility analysis. The analysis must measure the cost that the rule would impose on small businesses and must consider less burdensome alternatives. The

"Law . . . is a human institution, created by human agents to serve human ends."

—HARLAN F. STONE, 1872–1946
(Chief Justice of the United States Supreme Court, 1941–1946)

---

14. 5 U.S.C. Section 552.
15. 5 U.S.C. Section 552b.
16. 5 U.S.C. Sections 601–612.

act also contains provisions to alert small businesses about forthcoming regulations. The act relieved small businesses of some record-keeping burdens, especially with regard to hazardous waste management.

Small Business Regulatory Enforcement Fairness Act

As mentioned above, the Small Business Regulatory Enforcement Fairness Act (SBREFA) of 1996 allows Congress to review new federal regulations for at least sixty days before they take effect. This period gives opponents of the rules time to present their arguments to Congress.

The SBREFA also authorizes the courts to enforce the Regulatory Flexibility Act. This helps to ensure that federal agencies, such as the Internal Revenue Service, consider ways to reduce the economic impact of new regulations on small businesses. Federal agencies are required to prepare guides that explain in plain English how small businesses can comply with federal regulations.

At the Small Business Administration, the SBREFA set up the National Enforcement Ombudsman to receive comments from small businesses about their dealings with federal agencies. Based on these comments, Regional Small Business Fairness Boards rate the agencies and publicize their findings.

Finally, the SBREFA allows small businesses to recover their expenses and legal fees from the government when an agency makes demands for fines or penalties that a court considers excessive.

STATE ADMINISTRATIVE AGENCIES

Although much of this chapter deals with federal administrative agencies, state agencies also play a significant role in regulating activities within the states. Many of the factors that encouraged the proliferation of federal agencies also fostered the growing presence of state agencies. Reasons for the growth of administrative agencies at all levels of government include the inability of Congress and state legislatures to oversee the actual implementation of their laws and the greater technical competence of the agencies.

Commonly, a state creates an agency as a parallel to a federal agency to provide similar services on a more localized basis. For instance, a state department of public welfare shoulders some of the same responsibilities at the state level as the Social Security Administration does at the federal level. A state pollution-control agency parallels the federal Environmental Protection Agency. Not all federal agencies have parallel state agencies, however. For instance, the Central Intelligence Agency has no parallel agency at the state level.

If the actions of parallel state and federal agencies conflict, the actions of the federal agency will prevail. **EXAMPLE #4** The Federal Aviation Administration (FAA) specifies the hours during which airplanes may land at and depart from airports. A California state agency issues inconsistent regulations governing the same activities. In a proceeding initiated by Interstate Distribution Corporation, an air transport company, to challenge the state rules, the FAA regulations would be held to prevail.□ The priority of federal law over conflicting state laws is based on the supremacy clause of the U.S. Constitution. This clause, which is found in Article VI of the Constitution, states that the Constitution and "the Laws of the United States which shall be made in Pursuance thereof . . . shall be the supreme Law of the Land."

Reviewing . . . Powers and Functions of Administrative Agencies

Assume that the Securities and Exchange Commission (SEC) has a rule under which it enforces statutory provisions prohibiting insider trading only when the insiders make monetary profits for themselves. Then the SEC makes a new rule, declaring that it has the statutory authority to bring an enforcement action against an individual even if she or he does not personally profit from the insider trading. In making the new rule, the SEC does not conduct a rulemaking proceeding but simply announces its new decision. A stockbrokerage firm objects and says that the new rule was unlawfully developed without opportunity for public comment. The brokerage firm challenges the rule in an action that ultimately is reviewed by a federal appellate court. Using the information presented in the chapter, answer the following questions.

1. Is the SEC an executive agency or an independent regulatory agency? Does it matter to the outcome of this dispute? Explain.

2. Suppose that the SEC asserts that it has always had the statutory authority to pursue persons for insider trading regardless of whether they personally profited from the transaction. This is the only argument the SEC makes to justify changing its enforcement rules. Would a court be likely to find that the SEC's action was arbitrary and capricious under the Administrative Procedure Act (APA)? Why or why not?

3. Would a court be likely to give *Chevron* deference to the SEC's interpretation of the law on insider trading? Why or why not?

4. Now assume that a court finds that the new rule is merely "interpretive." What effect would this determination have on whether the SEC had to follow the APA's rulemaking procedures?

Key Terms

adjudication 655
bureaucracy 644
delegation doctrine 643
enabling legislation 642

final order 657
initial order 656
legislative rule 643

notice-and-comment
    rulemaking 647
rulemaking 647

Chapter Summary

Agency Creation and Powers (See pages 642–644.)	1. Under the U.S. Constitution, Congress can delegate the implementation of its laws to government agencies. Congress can thus indirectly monitor an area in which it has passed laws without becoming bogged down in details relating to enforcement.
	2. Administrative agencies are created by enabling legislation, which usually specifies the name, composition, and powers of the agency.
	3. Administrative agencies exercise enforcement, rulemaking, and adjudicatory powers.
The Administrative Procedure Act (See pages 644–650.)	1. Agencies are authorized to create new regulations—their rulemaking function. This power is conferred on an agency in the enabling legislation.
	2. Agencies can create legislative rules, which are as important as formal acts of Congress.

CONTINUED

The Administrative Procedure Act— Continued

3. Notice-and-comment rulemaking is the most common rulemaking procedure. It involves the publication of the proposed regulation in the *Federal Register,* followed by a comment period to allow private parties to comment on the proposed rule.

Judicial Deference to Agency Decisions
(See pages 650–653.)

1. When reviewing agency decisions, courts typically grant deference (significant weight or consideration) to an agency's findings of fact and interpretations of law.

2. If Congress directly addressed the issue in dispute when enacting the statute, courts must follow the statutory language.

3. If the statute is silent or ambiguous, a court will uphold an agency's decision if the agency's interpretation of the statute was reasonable, even if the court would have interpreted the law differently. (This is known as *Chevron* deference.)

4. An agency must follow notice-and-comment rulemaking procedures before it is entitled to judicial deference in its interpretation of the law.

Enforcement and Adjudication
(See pages 653–657.)

1. Administrative agencies investigate the entities that they regulate, both during the rulemaking process to obtain data and after rules are issued to monitor compliance.

2. The most important investigative tools available to an agency are the following:

   a. Subpoenas—Orders that direct individuals to appear at a hearing or to hand over specified documents.

   b. Inspections and tests—Used to gather information and to correct or prevent undesirable conditions.

3. Limits on administrative investigations include the following:

   a. The investigation must be for a legitimate purpose.

   b. The information sought must be relevant, and the investigative demands must be specific and not unreasonably burdensome.

   c. The Fourth Amendment protects companies and individuals from unreasonable searches and seizures by requiring search warrants in most instances.

4. After a preliminary investigation, an agency may initiate an administrative action against an individual or organization by filing a complaint. Most such actions are resolved at this stage before they go through the formal adjudicatory process.

5. If there is no settlement, the case is presented to an administrative law judge (ALJ) in a proceeding similar to a trial.

6. After a case is concluded, the ALJ renders an initial order, which can be appealed by either party to the board or commission that governs the agency and ultimately to a federal appeals court. If no appeal is taken or the case is not reviewed, then the order becomes the final order of the agency. The charged party may be ordered to pay damages or to stop carrying on some specified activity.

Limitations on Agency Powers
(See pages 657–659.)

1. *Judicial controls*—Administrative agencies are subject to the judicial review of the courts. For example, a court may review whether an agency has exceeded the scope of its enabling legislation or has properly interpreted the laws.

2. *Executive controls*—The president can control agencies through appointments of federal officers and through vetoes of bills affecting agency powers.

3. *Legislative controls*—Congress can give power to an agency, take it away, increase or decrease the agency's funding, or abolish the agency. The Administrative Procedure Act of 1946 also limits agencies.

Public Accountability
(See pages 659–660.)

Congress has passed several laws to make agencies more accountable through public scrutiny. These laws include the Freedom of Information Act of 1966, the Government in the Sunshine Act of 1976, the Regulatory Flexibility Act of 1980, and the Small Business Regulatory Enforcement Fairness Act of 1996.

State Administrative Agencies
(See page 660.)

States create agencies that parallel federal agencies to provide similar services on a more localized basis. If the actions of parallel state and federal agencies conflict, the actions of the federal agency will prevail.

For Review

1. How are federal administrative agencies created?
2. What are the three basic functions of most administrative agencies?
3. What sequence of events must normally occur before an agency rule becomes law?
4. How do administrative agencies enforce their rules?
5. How do the three branches of government limit the power of administrative agencies?

Questions and Case Problems

19–1. Rulemaking and Adjudication Powers. For decades, the Federal Trade Commission (FTC) resolved fair trade and advertising disputes through individual adjudications. In the 1960s, the FTC began promulgating rules that defined fair and unfair trade practices. In cases involving violations of these rules, the due process rights of participants were more limited and did not include cross-examination. This was because, although anyone found violating a rule would receive a full adjudication, the legitimacy of the rule itself could not be challenged in the adjudication. Any party charged with violating a rule was almost certain to lose the adjudication. Affected parties complained to a court, arguing that their rights before the FTC were unduly limited by the new rules. What will the court examine to determine whether to uphold the new rules?

Question with Sample Answer

19–2. Assume that the Food and Drug Administration (FDA), using proper procedures, adopts a rule describing its future investigations. This new rule covers all future circumstances in which the FDA wants to regulate food additives. Under the new rule, the FDA is not to regulate food additives without giving food companies an opportunity to cross-examine witnesses. At a subsequent time, the FDA wants to regulate methylisocyanate, a food additive. The FDA undertakes an informal rulemaking procedure, without cross-examination, and regulates methylisocyanate. Producers protest, saying that the FDA promised them the opportunity for cross-examination. The FDA responds that the Administrative Procedure Act does not require such cross-examination and that it is free to withdraw the promise made in its new rule. If the

producers challenge the FDA in court, on what basis would the court rule in their favor?

For a sample answer to Question 19–2, go to Appendix I at the end of this text.

19–3. Arbitrary and Capricious Test. Lion Raisins, Inc., is a family-owned, family-operated business that grows raisins and markets them to private enterprises. In the 1990s, Lion also successfully bid on more than fifteen contracts awarded by the U.S. Department of Agriculture (USDA). In May 1999, a USDA investigation reported that Lion appeared to have falsified inspectors' signatures, given false moisture content, and changed the grade of raisins on three USDA raisin certificates issued between 1996 and 1998. Lion was subsequently awarded five more USDA contracts. In 2000, Lion was the low bidder on two new USDA contracts for school lunch programs. The USDA, however, awarded these contracts to other bidders and, on the basis of the May 1999 report, suspended Lion from participating in government contracts for one year. Lion filed a suit in the U.S. Court of Federal Claims against the USDA, seeking, in part, lost profits on the school lunch contracts on the ground that the USDA's suspension was arbitrary and capricious. What reasoning might the court employ to grant a summary judgment in Lion's favor? [*Lion Raisins, Inc. v. United States,* 51 Fed.Cl. 238 (2001)]

19–4. Investigation. Maureen Droge began working for United Air Lines, Inc. (UAL), as a flight attendant in 1990. In 1995, she was assigned to Paris, France, where she became pregnant. Because UAL does not allow its flight attendants to fly during their third trimester of pregnancy, Droge was placed on involuntary leave. She applied for temporary disability benefits through the

French social security system, but her request was denied because UAL does not contribute to the French system on behalf of its U.S.-based flight attendants. Droge filed a charge of discrimination with the U.S. Equal Employment Opportunity Commission (EEOC), alleging that UAL had discriminated against her and other Americans. The EEOC issued a subpoena, asking UAL to detail all benefits received by all UAL employees living outside the United States. UAL refused to provide the information, in part, on the grounds that it was irrelevant and compliance would be unduly burdensome. The EEOC filed a suit in a federal district court against UAL. Should the court enforce the subpoena? Why or why not? [*Equal Employment Opportunity Commission v. United Air Lines, Inc.,* 287 F.3d 643 (7th Cir. 2002)]

19–5. Judicial Controls. Under federal law, when accepting bids on a contract, an agency must hold "discussions" with all offerors. An agency may ask a single offeror for "clarification" of its proposal, however, without holding "discussions" with the others. Regulations define *clarifications* as "limited exchanges." In March 2001, the U.S. Air Force asked for bids on a contract. The winning contractor would examine, assess, and develop means of integrating national intelligence assets with the U.S. Department of Defense space systems, to enhance the capabilities of the Air Force's Space Warfare Center. Among the bidders were Information Technology and Applications Corp. (ITAC) and RS Information Systems, Inc. (RSIS). The Air Force asked the parties for more information on their subcontractors but did not allow them to change their proposals. Determining that there were weaknesses in ITAC's bid, the Air Force awarded the contract to RSIS. ITAC filed a suit in the U.S. Court of Federal Claims against the government, contending that the postproposal requests to RSIS, and its responses, were improper "discussions." Should the court rule in ITAC's favor? Why or why not? [*Information Technology & Applications Corp. v. United States,* 316 F.3d 1312 (Fed.Cir. 2003)].

19–6. Investigation. Riverdale Mills Corp. makes plastic-coated steel wire products in Northbridge, Massachusetts. Riverdale uses a water-based cleaning process that generates acidic and alkaline wastewater. To meet federal clean-water requirements, Riverdale has a system within its plant to treat the water. It then flows through a pipe that opens into a manhole-covered test pit outside the plant in full view of Riverdale's employees. Three hundred feet away, the pipe merges into the public sewer system. In October 1997, the U.S. Environmental Protection Agency (EPA) sent Justin Pimpare and Daniel Granz to inspect the plant. Without a search warrant and without Riverdale's express consent, the agents took samples from the test pit. Based on the samples, Riverdale and James Knott, the company's owner, were charged with criminal violations of the federal Clean Water Act. The defendants sued the EPA agents in a federal district court, alleging

violations of the Fourth Amendment. What right does the Fourth Amendment provide in this context? This right is based on a "reasonable expectation of privacy." Should the agents be held liable? Why or why not? [*Riverdale Mills Corp. v. Pimpare,* 392 F.3d 55 (1st Cir. 2004)]

19–7. Rulemaking. The Investment Company Act of 1940 prohibits a mutual fund from engaging in certain transactions in which there may be a conflict of interest between the manager of the fund and its shareholders. Under rules issued by the Securities and Exchange Commission (SEC), however, a fund that meets certain conditions may engage in an otherwise prohibited transaction. In June 2004, the SEC added two new conditions. A year later, the SEC reconsidered the new conditions in terms of the costs that they would impose on the funds. Within eight days, and without asking for public input, the SEC readopted the conditions. The Chamber of Commerce of the United States—which is both a mutual fund shareholder and an association with mutual fund managers among its members—asked the U.S. Court of Appeals for the Second Circuit to review the new rules. The Chamber charged, in part, that in readopting the rules, the SEC relied on materials not in the "rulemaking record" without providing an opportunity for public comment. The SEC countered that the information was otherwise "publicly available." In adopting a rule, should an agency consider information that is not part of the rulemaking record? Why or why not? [*Chamber of Commerce of the United States v. Securities and Exchange Commission,* 443 F.3d 890 (D.C.Cir. 2006)]

Case Problem with Sample Answer

19–8. A well-documented rise in global temperatures has coincided with a significant increase in the concentration of carbon dioxide in the atmosphere. Many scientists believe that the two trends are related, because when carbon dioxide is released into the atmosphere, it produces a greenhouse effect, trapping solar heat. Under the Clean Air Act (CAA) of 1963, the Environmental Protection Agency (EPA) is authorized to regulate "any" air pollutants "emitted into . . . the ambient air" that in its "judgment cause, or contribute to, air pollution." Calling global warming "the most pressing environmental challenge of our time," a group of private organizations asked the EPA to regulate carbon dioxide and other "greenhouse gas" emissions from new motor vehicles. The EPA refused, stating, among other things, that Congress last amended the CAA in 1990 without authorizing new, binding auto-emissions limits. The petitioners—nineteen states, including Massachusetts, and others—asked the U.S. Court of Appeals for the District of Columbia Circuit to review the EPA's denial. Did the EPA have the authority to regulate greenhouse gas emissions from new motor vehicles? If so, was its stated reason for refusing to do so consistent with that authority? Discuss. [*Massachusetts v. Environmental Protection Agency,* __ U.S. __, 127 S.Ct. 1438, 167 L.Ed.2d 248 (2007)]

After you have answered Problem 19–8, compare your answer with the sample answer given on the Web site that accompanies this text. Go to www.cengage.com/blaw/let, select "Chapter 19," and click on "Case Problem with Sample Answer."

A Question of Ethics

19–9. To ensure highway safety and protect driver health, Congress charged federal agencies with regulating the hours of service of commercial motor vehicle operators. Between 1940 and 2003, the regulations that applied to long-haul truck drivers were mostly unchanged. (Long-haul drivers are those who operate beyond a 150-mile radius of their base.) In 2003, the Federal Motor Carrier Safety Administration (FMCSA) revised the regulations significantly, increasing the number of daily and weekly hours that drivers could work. The agency had not considered the impact of the changes on the health of the drivers, however, and the revisions were overturned. The FMCSA then issued a notice that it would reconsider the revisions and opened them up for public comment. The agency analyzed the costs to the industry and the crash risks due to driver fatigue under different options and concluded that the safety benefits of not increasing

the hours did not outweigh the economic costs. In 2005, the agency issued a rule that was nearly identical to the 2003 version. Public Citizen, Inc., and others, including the Owner-Operator Independent Drivers Association, asked the U.S. Court of Appeals for the District of Columbia Circuit to review the 2005 rule as it applied to long-haul drivers. [*Owner-Operator Independent Drivers Association, Inc. v. Federal Motor Carrier Safety Administration,* 494 F.3d 188 (D.C.Cir. 2007)]

1. The agency's cost-benefit analysis included new methods that were not disclosed to the public in time for comments. Was this unethical? Should the agency have disclosed the new methodology sooner? Why or why not?
2. The agency created a graph to show the risk of a crash as a function of the time a driver spent on the job. The graph plotted the first twelve hours of a day individually, but the rest of the time was depicted with an aggregate figure at the seventeenth hour. This made the risk at those hours appear to be lower. Is it unethical for an agency to manipulate data? Explain.

Critical-Thinking Legal Question

19–10. Does Congress delegate too much power to federal administrative agencies? Do the courts defer too much to Congress in its grant of power to those agencies? What are the alternatives to the agencies that we encounter in every facet of our lives?

Interacting with the Internet

For updated links to resources available on the Web, as well as a variety of other materials, visit this text's Web site at

www.cengage.com/blaw/let

To view the text of the Administrative Procedure Act of 1946, go to

www.oalj.dol/.gov/libapa.htm

The Internet Law Library contains links to federal and state regulatory materials at

www.lawguru.com/ilawlib

PRACTICAL INTERNET EXERCISES

Go to this text's Web site at **www.cengage.com/blaw/let**, select "Chapter 19," and click on "Practical Internet Exercises." There you will find the following Internet research exercises that you can perform to learn more about the topics covered in this chapter.

Practical Internet Exercise 19–1: LEGAL PERSPECTIVE—The Freedom of Information Act
Practical Internet Exercise 19–2: MANAGEMENT PERSPECTIVE—Agency Inspections

BEFORE THE TEST

Go to this text's Web site at **www.cengage.com/blaw/let**, select "Chapter 19," and click on "Interactive Quizzes." You will find a number of interactive questions relating to this chapter.

Chapter 20

Consumer Protection

CHAPTER OBJECTIVES

After reading this chapter, you should be able to answer the following questions:

1. When will advertising be deemed deceptive?

2. What special rules apply to telephone solicitation?

3. What is Regulation Z, and to what type of transactions does it apply?

4. How does the Federal Food, Drug, and Cosmetic Act protect consumers?

5. What are the major federal statutes providing for consumer protection in credit transactions?

CONTENTS

- Advertising
- Labeling and Packaging
- Sales
- Health and Safety Protection
- Credit Protection

" Subject to specific constitutional limitations, when the legislature has spoken, the public interest has been declared in terms well nigh conclusive."

— WILLIAM O. DOUGLAS,
1898–1980 (Associate justice of the United States Supreme Court, 1939–1975)

The "public interest" referred to by Justice William O. Douglas in the chapter-opening quotation was evident during the 1960s and 1970s in what has come to be known as the consumer movement. Some have labeled the 1960s and 1970s "the age of the consumer" because so much legislation was passed in an attempt to protect consumers against purportedly unsafe products and unfair practices of sellers. Since the 1980s, the impetus driving the consumer movement has lessened, to a great extent because so many of its goals have been achieved. *Consumer law* consists of all of the statutes, administrative agency rules, and judicial decisions that serve to protect the interests of consumers.

In the first part of this chapter, we examine some of the sources and some of the major issues of consumer protection. Sources of consumer protection exist at all levels of government. At the federal level, a number of laws have been passed to define the duties of sellers and the rights of consumers. Exhibit 20–1 on the facing page shows selected areas of consumer law regulated by statutes. Federal administrative agencies, such as the Federal Trade Commission (FTC), also provide an important source of consumer protection. Nearly every agency and department of the federal government has an office of consumer affairs, and most states have one or more such offices, including the offices of state attorneys general, to assist consumers.

Because of the wide variation among state consumer protection laws, our primary focus here will be on federal legislation—specifically, on legislation governing deceptive advertising, telemarketing and electronic advertising, labeling and

EXHIBIT 20–1 SELECTED AREAS OF CONSUMER LAW REGULATED BY STATUTES

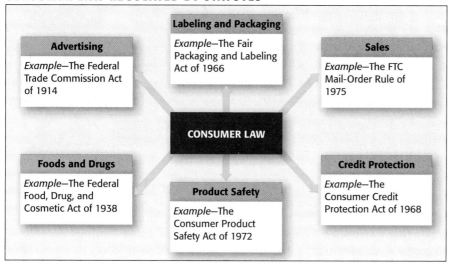

packaging, sales, health protection, product safety, and credit protection. Realize, though, that state laws often provide more sweeping and significant protections for the consumer than do federal laws.

ADVERTISING

One of the earliest—and still one of the most important—federal consumer protection laws is the Federal Trade Commission Act of 1914 (mentioned in Chapter 19). The act created the FTC to carry out the broadly stated goal of preventing unfair and deceptive trade practices, including deceptive advertising, within the meaning of Section 5 of the act. We look here at deceptive advertising and at laws regulating telemarketing and electronic advertising.

Deceptive Advertising

Generally, **deceptive advertising** occurs if a reasonable consumer would be misled by the advertising claim. Vague generalities and obvious exaggerations are permissible. These claims are known as *puffery*. Recall from the discussion of warranties in Chapter 11 that puffery consists of statements about a product that a reasonable person would not believe to be literally true. When a claim takes on the appearance of literal authenticity, however, it may create problems. Advertising that *appears* to be based on factual evidence but that in fact cannot be scientifically supported will be deemed deceptive. A classic example occurred in a 1944 case in which the claim that a skin cream would restore youthful qualities to aged skin was deemed deceptive.[1]

Some advertisements contain "half-truths," meaning that the presented information is true but incomplete and, therefore, leads consumers to a false conclusion. **EXAMPLE #1** The maker of Campbell's soups advertised that "most" Campbell's

DECEPTIVE ADVERTISING
Advertising that misleads consumers, either by making unjustified claims concerning a product's performance or by omitting a material fact concerning the product's composition or performance.

---

1. *Charles of the Ritz Distributors Corp. v. Federal Trade Commission*, 143 F.2d 676 (2d Cir. 1944).

These stuffed teddy bears were recalled because the plastic beads inside the toys could come out and create a choking hazard for young children. According to Exhibit 20–1 on the previous page, which area of consumer protection law governs such a recall? (Consumer Product Safety Commission/ Getty Images)

soups were low in fat and cholesterol and thus were helpful in fighting heart disease. What the ad did not say was that Campbell's soups were high in sodium and that high-sodium diets may increase the risk of heart disease. Hence, the FTC ruled that Campbell's claims were deceptive.▫ Advertising featuring an endorsement by a celebrity may be deemed deceptive if the celebrity does not actually use the product.

In the following case brought by the FTC, *Wired* magazine had already put the product in question on its list of top ten "snake-oil gadgets."

Case 20.1 **Federal Trade Commission v. QT, Inc.**

United States Court of Appeals, Seventh Circuit, 2008.
512 F.3d 858.
www.ca7.uscourts.gov[a]

BACKGROUND AND FACTS   QT, Inc., and various related companies heavily promoted the Q-Ray Ionized Bracelet on

a. Click on "Opinions" in the left-hand column. In the box for the case number, type "07" and "1662," and then click on "List Case." Follow the links to access the opinion. The U.S. Court of Appeals for the Seventh Circuit maintains this Web site.

television infomercials as well as on its Web site. In its promotions, the company made many claims about the pain-relief powers of these bracelets. The bracelets supposedly offered immediate and significant or complete pain relief and could cure chronic pain. At trial in the U.S. District Court for the Northern District of Illinois, the presiding judge labeled all such claims as fraudulent, forbade further promotional claims, and ordered the company to pay $16 million, plus interest, into a fund to be distributed to all customers. QT, Inc., appealed.

IN THE WORDS OF THE COURT . . . EASTERBROOK, Chief Judge.

* * * *

* * * According to the district court's findings, almost everything that defendants have said about the bracelet is false. Here are some highlights:

- Defendants promoted the bracelet as a miraculous cure for chronic pain, but it has no therapeutic effect.
- Defendants told consumers that claims of "immediate, significant or complete pain relief" had been "test-proven"; they hadn't.
  * * * *
- Defendants represented that the therapeutic effect wears off in a year or two, despite knowing that the bracelet's properties do not change. This assertion is designed to lead customers to buy new bracelets. Likewise the false statement that the bracelet has a "memory cycle specific to each individual wearer" so that only the bracelet's original wearer can experience pain relief is designed to increase sales by eliminating the second-hand market and "explaining" the otherwise-embarrassing fact that the buyer's friends and neighbors can't perceive any effect.

The magistrate judge [the judge presiding over the trial] did not commit a clear error, or abuse his discretion, in concluding that the defendants set out to bilk unsophisticated persons who found themselves in pain from arthritis and other chronic conditions.

Defendants maintain that the magistrate judge subjected their statements to an excessively rigorous standard of proof.

* * * *The Federal Trade Commission Act forbids false and misleading statements, and a statement that is plausible but has not been tested in the most reliable way cannot be condemned out of hand.* [Emphasis added.]

* * * For the Q-Ray Ionized Bracelet, * * * all statements about how the product works—Q-Rays, ionization, enhancing the flow of bio-energy, and the like—are blather. Defendants might as well have said: "Beneficent creatures from the 17th Dimension use this bracelet as a beacon to locate people who need pain relief, and whisk them off to their homeworld every night to provide help in ways unknown to our science."

* * * *Proof is what separates an effect new to science from a swindle.* Defendants themselves told customers that the bracelet's efficacy had been "test-proven"; * * * but defendants have no proof of the Q-Ray Ionized Bracelet's efficacy. The "tests" on which they relied were bunk. * * * What remain are testimonials, which are not a form of proof * * *. That's why the "testimonial" of someone who keeps elephants off the streets of a large city by snapping his fingers is the basis of a joke rather than proof of cause and effect. [Emphasis added.]

* * * *

Physicians know how to treat pain. Why pay $200 for a Q-Ray Ionized Bracelet when you can get relief from an aspirin tablet that costs 1¢?

DECISION AND REMEDY   The U.S. Court of Appeals for the Seventh Circuit affirmed the district court's decision. QT, Inc., was required to stop its deceptive advertising and to pay $16 million, plus interest, so that its customers could be reimbursed.

WHAT IF THE FACTS WERE DIFFERENT?   Assume that the defendant had actually conducted scientific studies, which had proved inconclusive. How might the judge have ruled in that situation?

THE ETHICAL DIMENSION   Most people have seen infomercials. Does the fact that QT, Inc., used infomercials to make fraudulent promotional claims mean that all products "pitched" on television are suspect? Why or why not?

Bait-and-Switch Advertising   The FTC has issued rules that govern specific advertising techniques. One of the most important rules is contained in the FTC's "Guides on Bait Advertising."[2] The rule is designed to prevent **bait-and-switch advertising**—that is, advertising a very low price for a particular item that will likely be unavailable to the consumer and then encouraging him or her to purchase a more expensive item. The low price is the "bait" to lure the consumer into the store. The salesperson is instructed to "switch" the consumer to a different, more expensive item. According to the FTC guidelines, bait-and-switch advertising occurs if the seller refuses to show the advertised item, fails to have reasonable quantities of it available, fails to promise to deliver the advertised item within a reasonable time, or discourages employees from selling the item.

BAIT-AND-SWITCH ADVERTISING
Advertising a product at a very attractive price (the "bait") and then, once the consumer is in the store, saying that the advertised product either is not available or is of poor quality. The customer is then urged to purchase ("switch" to) a more expensive item.

Online Deceptive Advertising   Deceptive advertising can occur in the online environment as well. For years, the FTC has actively monitored online advertising and has identified hundreds of Web sites that have made false or

2. 16 C.F.R. Section 288.

deceptive advertising claims. These claims have concerned products ranging from medical treatments for various diseases to exercise equipment and weight-loss aids.

The FTC has issued guidelines to help online businesses comply with existing laws prohibiting deceptive advertising.[3] These guidelines include three basic requirements. First, all ads—both online and offline—must be truthful and not misleading. Second, claims made in an ad must be substantiated; that is, advertisers must have evidence to back up their claims. Third, ads cannot be unfair, which the FTC defines as "likely to cause substantial consumer injury that consumers could not reasonably avoid and that is not outweighed by the benefit to consumers or competition."

The guidelines also call for "clear and conspicuous" disclosure of any qualifying or limiting information. The overall impression of the ad is important in meeting this requirement. The FTC suggests that advertisers should assume that consumers will not read an entire Web page. Therefore, to satisfy the "clear and conspicuous" requirement, advertisers should place the disclosure as close as possible to the claim being qualified or include the disclosure within the claim itself. If such placement is not feasible, the next-best location is on a section of the page to which a consumer can easily scroll. Generally, hyperlinks to a disclosure are recommended only for lengthy disclosures or for disclosures that must be repeated in a variety of locations on the Web page. If the disclosure is an integral part of a claim, however, it should be placed on the same page rather than hyperlinked.

FTC Actions against Deceptive Advertising   The FTC receives complaints from many sources, including competitors of alleged violators, consumers, consumer organizations, trade associations, Better Business Bureaus, government organizations, and state and local officials. If it receives numerous and widespread complaints about a problem, the FTC will investigate. If the FTC concludes that a given advertisement is unfair or deceptive, it sends a formal complaint to the alleged offender. The company may agree to settle the complaint without further proceedings; if not, the FTC can conduct a hearing before an administrative law judge (discussed in Chapter 1) in which the company can present its defense.

If the FTC succeeds in proving that an advertisement is unfair or deceptive, it usually issues a **cease-and-desist order** requiring the company to stop the challenged advertising. It might also require **counteradvertising,** in which the company advertises anew—in print, on the Internet, on radio, and on television—to inform the public about the earlier misinformation. The FTC sometimes initiates **multiple product orders,** which require a firm to cease and desist from false advertising in regard to more than one of its products, not just the product that was the subject of the action.

In some instances, the FTC may seek other remedies, such as restitution, when a company's deceptive act involves wrongful charges to consumers. EXAMPLE #2 Verity International, Ltd., billed phone-line subscribers who accessed certain online pornography sites at the rate for international calls to Madagascar. When consumers complained about the charges, Verity employees told them that the charges were valid and had to be paid, or the consumers would face further collection activity. A federal appellate court held that this representation of

CEASE-AND-DESIST ORDER
An administrative or judicial order prohibiting a person or business firm from conducting activities that an agency or court has deemed illegal.

COUNTERADVERTISING
New advertising that is undertaken pursuant to a Federal Trade Commission order for the purpose of correcting earlier false claims that were made about a product.

MULTIPLE PRODUCT ORDER
An administrative or judicial order that requires a firm to cease and desist from false advertising in regard to more than one of its products.

---

3. *Advertising and Marketing on the Internet: Rules of the Road,* September 2000. This guide is available at **www.ftc.gov/bcp/conline/pubs/buspubs/ruleroad.htm**.

"uncontestability" was deceptive and a violation of the FTC Act, and ordered Verity to pay nearly $18 million in restitution to consumers.[4]◻

Telemarketing and Electronic Advertising

The pervasive use of the telephone to market goods and services to homes and businesses led to the passage in 1991 of the Telephone Consumer Protection Act (TCPA).[5] The act prohibits telephone solicitation using an automatic telephone dialing system or a prerecorded voice. Most states also have laws regulating telephone solicitation. The TCPA also makes it illegal to transmit ads via fax without first obtaining the recipient's permission. (Similar issues have arisen with respect to junk e-mail, called *spam*—see Chapter 5.)

The act is enforced by the Federal Communications Commission (FCC) and also provides for a private right of action. The FCC imposes substantial fines ($11,000 each day) on companies that violate the junk fax provisions of the TCPA and has fined one company as much as $5.4 million for violations.[6] Consumers can recover any actual monetary loss resulting from a violation of the act or receive $500 in damages for each violation, whichever is greater. If a court finds that a defendant willfully or knowingly violated the act, the court has the discretion to treble (triple) the damages awarded. When many consumers file their complaints together as a class-action suit, the damages awarded can be large, as can the defendant's liability for attorneys' fees.

The Telemarketing and Consumer Fraud and Abuse Prevention Act of 1994[7] directed the FTC to establish rules governing telemarketing and to bring actions against fraudulent telemarketers. The FTC's Telemarketing Sales Rule of 1995[8] requires a telemarketer to identify the seller's name; describe the product being sold; and disclose all material facts related to the sale, including the total cost of the goods being sold, any restrictions on obtaining or using the goods, and whether a sale will be considered final and nonrefundable. The act makes it illegal for telemarketers to misrepresent information (including facts about their goods or services and earnings potential, for example). A telemarketer must also remove a consumer's name from its list of potential contacts if the consumer so requests. (For a discussion of how the Telemarketing Sales Rule applies to foreign telemarketers, see this chapter's *Beyond Our Borders* feature on page 673.) An amendment to the Telemarketing Sales Rule established the national Do Not Call Registry, which became effective in October 2003. Telemarketers must refrain from calling those consumers who have placed their names on the list.

> **REMEMBER**
> Changes in technology often require changes in the law.

Advertising is essential to business. Businesspersons who advertise via faxes, however, should know the applicable rules and be aware that the FCC aggressively enforces these rules. Ensure that all fax advertisements comply with the Telephone Consumer Protection Act and any state laws on faxes. Educate and train your employees about these laws. Do not send faxes without first obtaining the

---

4. *Federal Trade Commission v. Verity International, Ltd.,* 443 F.3d 48 (2006).
5. 47 U.S.C. Sections 227 *et seq.,* as modified by the Junk Fax Protection Act of 2005.
6. See *Missouri ex rel. Nixon v. American Blast Fax, Inc.,* 323 F.3d 649 (8th Cir. 2003); *cert.* denied, 540 U.S. 1104, 124 S.Ct. 1043, 157 L.Ed.2d 888 (2004).
7. 15 U.S.C. Sections 6101–6108.
8. 16 C.F.R. Sections 310.1–310.8.

recipient's permission, and develop effective opt-out procedures so that anyone who no longer wants to receive faxed advertisements can notify you. Make sure that your business respects these wishes. Keep reliable records of the faxes you send and maintain these records for at least four years. Do not purchase lists of fax numbers from outsiders. Avoiding consumer complaints about unwanted faxes and phone calls is the best way to avoid potentially significant liability. ◼

LABELING AND PACKAGING

A number of federal and state laws deal specifically with the information given on labels and packages. The rules are designed to ensure that labels provide accurate information about the product and to warn about possible dangers from its use or misuse. In general, labels must be accurate, and they must use words that are understood by the ordinary consumer. For example, a box of cereal cannot be labeled "giant" if that would exaggerate the amount of cereal contained in the box. In some instances, labels must specify the raw materials used in the product, such as the percentage of cotton, nylon, or other fibers used in a garment. In other instances, the products must carry a warning. Cigarette packages and advertising, for example, must include one of several warnings about the health hazards associated with smoking.[9]

Federal Statutes

Today's consumers are increasingly concerned about eating genetically modified crops and about the potential presence in foods of pesticides, hormones, and other harmful substances. Many consumers have thus switched to buying organic foods. How might an organic label be deceptive to consumers?
(Richard Anderson)

There are numerous federal laws regulating the labeling and packaging of products. These include the Wool Products Labeling Act of 1939,[10] the Fur Products Labeling Act of 1951,[11] the Flammable Fabrics Act of 1953,[12] and the Fair Packaging and Labeling Act of 1966.[13] The Comprehensive Smokeless Tobacco Health Education Act of 1986,[14] for example, requires that producers, packagers, and importers of smokeless tobacco include on the products' labels one of several warnings about the use of smokeless tobacco.

Food Labeling

Because the quality and safety of food are so important to consumers, several statutes deal specifically with food labeling. The Fair Packaging and Labeling Act requires that food product labels identify (1) the product; (2) the net quantity of the contents and, if the number of servings is stated, the size of the serving; (3) the manufacturer; and (4) the packager or distributor. The act includes additional requirements concerning descriptions on packages, savings claims, components of nonfood products, and standards for the partial filling of packages.

Food products must bear labels detailing the nutritional content, including how much fat the food contains and what kind of fat it is. The Nutrition Labeling and Education Act of 1990[15] requires standard nutrition facts (including fat content) on food labels; regulates the use of such

---

9. 15 U.S.C. Sections 1331 *et seq.*
10. 15 U.S.C. Section 68.
11. 15 U.S.C. Section 69.
12. 15 U.S.C. Section 1191.
13. 15 U.S.C. Sections 1451 *et seq.*
14. 15 U.S.C. Sections 4401–4408.
15. 21 U.S.C. Section 343.1.

One of the most difficult problems for the Federal Trade Commission (FTC) is protecting consumers from scams that originate outside the borders of the United States. This is one reason why prosecuting persons who send spam (junk e-mail–see Chapter 5) or perpetrate fraud in online sales (discussed later in this chapter) has proved to be so challenging. Those involved in the illegal operations frequently are located outside the United States, and the Internet gives them access to consumers across the globe.

The FTC has made some headway, though, in prosecuting telemarketers who violate the law from foreign locations under the Telemarketing Sales Rule (TSR). The TSR prohibits telemarketers from failing to disclose, in a clear and conspicuous manner, the total cost of, and the quantity of, any goods or services that are the subject of a sales offer. As discussed in the text, the rule also prohibits telemarketers from misrepresenting any material fact about the goods or services being offered. Significantly, the TSR applies even if the offer comes from a foreign firm, provided it is made to consumers in the United States.

An Advance-Fee Credit Card Scam That Originated in Canada

Oleg Oks and Aleksandr Oks, along with several other Canadian residents, started a number of sham business corporations in Ontario. Through these businesses, they placed unsolicited telephone calls to consumers throughout the United States. The telemarketers falsely offered to provide preapproved Visa or MasterCard credit cards to those consumers who agreed to permit defendants to debit their bank accounts electronically for an advance fee of $319. They represented the credit limit on these advance-fee cards as ranging from $1,000 to $10,000, with no annual fee and low interest rates.

Moreover, the telemarketers frequently promised additional items–such as a cellular telephone, satellite dish system, vacation package, or home security system–at no additional cost. *No consumer who paid the advanced fee received either a credit card or any of the complimentary gifts that were promised.*

Instead, consumers received "member benefits" packages that included items such as booklets on how to improve their creditworthiness or merchandise cards valid only for purchases from the catalogue provided. The Canadian telemarketers also started offering brand-name computers to consumers who agreed to have a fee debited from their bank accounts. No one received the promised computers, either.

The Canadian Government and the FTC Work Together to Prosecute the Illegal Telemarketing Operation

The FTC, working in conjunction with the U.S. Postal Inspection Service and various Canadian government and law enforcement agencies, conducted a lengthy investigation for several years. Ultimately, in 2007, Oleg and Aleksandr Oks pleaded guilty to criminal charges in Canada for deceptive advertising. They were sentenced to some jail time and probation and barred from telemarketing for ten years.[a]

The FTC filed a civil lawsuit against the Okses and other Canadian defendants in a federal court in Illinois for violating the FTC Act and the Telemarketing Sales Rule. The court found that the defendants had violated these laws and ordered them to pay nearly $5 million in damages.[b] A final judgment and permanent injunction were entered in the case in 2008.

FOR CRITICAL ANALYSIS Suppose that this scam had originated in a country that is not as friendly and cooperative with the United States as Canada is. In that situation, how would the FTC obtain sufficient evidence to prosecute the foreign telemarketers? Is the testimony of U.S. consumers regarding phone calls they receive sufficient proof? Why or why not?

a. Oleg was sentenced to a year in jail and two years of probation; Aleksandr received a six-month conditional sentence and twelve months of probation, as reported in a Federal Trade Commission press release, available at **www.ftc.gov/opa/2008/05/paclibert.shtm**.
b. *F.T.C. v. Oks*, ___ F.Supp.2d ___, (2007 WL 3307009 N.D.Ill. 2007). The order was entered by this same court on March 18, 2008.

terms as *fresh* and *low fat;* and authorizes certain health claims, subject to the federal Food and Drug Administration's approval. The FTC enforces these rules.

The U.S. Department of Agriculture (USDA) also plays a key role in regulating food safety, conducting inspections, and preventing foodborne illnesses. The USDA's Food Safety Inspection Service (FSIS), for instance, conducts inspections to ensure that the nation's commercial supply of meat, poultry, and egg products is safe to consume and correctly labeled and packaged.

SALES

A number of statutes protect consumers by requiring the disclosure of certain terms in sales transactions and providing rules governing home or door-to-door sales, mail-order transactions, referral sales, and unsolicited merchandise. The

REGULATION Z
A set of rules promulgated by the Federal Reserve Board of Governors to implement the provisions of the Truth-in-Lending Act.

"COOLING-OFF" LAWS
Laws that allow buyers a period of time, such as three days, in which to cancel door-to-door sales contracts.

Federal Reserve Board of Governors, for example, has issued **Regulation Z,** which governs credit provisions associated with sales contracts (discussed later in this chapter). Many states have also passed laws providing remedies to consumers in home sales. For example, a number of states have passed **"cooling-off" laws** that permit the buyers of goods sold door to door to cancel their contracts within a specified period of time, usually three to five business days after the sale. An FTC regulation also requires sellers to give consumers three days to cancel any door-to-door sale, and this rule applies in addition to any state law. Furthermore, states have provided a number of consumer protection measures, such as implied warranties, through the adoption of the Uniform Commercial Code.

Telephone and Mail-Order Sales

The FTC's Mail or Telephone Order Merchandise Rule of 1993, which amended the FTC's Mail-Order Rule of 1975,[16] provides specific protections for consumers who purchase goods over the phone or through the mails. The 1993 rule extended the 1975 rule to include sales in which orders are transmitted using computers, fax machines, or any similar means involving a telephone. Among other things, the rule requires mail-order merchants to ship orders within the time promised in their catalogues or advertisements, to notify consumers when orders cannot be shipped on time, and to issue a refund within a specified period of time when a consumer cancels an order.

In addition, under the Postal Reorganization Act of 1970[17] a consumer who receives *unsolicited* merchandise sent by U.S. mail can keep it, throw it away, or dispose of it in any manner that she or he sees fit. The recipient will not be obligated to the sender. **EXAMPLE #3** Serena receives a copy of the "cookbook of the month" from a company via the U.S. mail, even though she did not order the cookbook. She gives it to her friend, Vaya, who loves to cook. The following month, Serena receives a bill for $49.99 from the company that sent the cookbook. Under the 1970 act, because the cookbook was sent to her unsolicited through the U.S. mail, Serena is not obligated to pay the bill. □

Online Sales

Protecting consumers from fraudulent and deceptive sales practices conducted via the Internet has proved to be a challenging task. Nonetheless, the FTC and other federal agencies have brought a number of enforcement actions against those who perpetrate online fraud. Additionally, the laws mentioned in previous chapters, such as the federal statute prohibiting wire fraud (see Chapter 6), apply to online transactions.

Some states have amended their consumer protection statutes to cover Internet transactions as well. For example, the California legislature revised its Business and Professional Code to include transactions conducted over the Internet or by "any other electronic means of communication." Previously, that code covered only telephone, mail-order catalogue, radio, and television sales. Now any entity selling over the Internet in California must explicitly create an on-screen notice indicating its refund and return policies, its physical location, its legal name, and a number of other details. Various states are also setting up information sites to help consumers protect themselves.

---

16. 16 C.F.R. Sections 435.1–435.2.
17. 39 U.S.C. Section 3009.

HEALTH AND SAFETY PROTECTION

The laws discussed earlier regarding the labeling and packaging of products go a long way toward promoting consumer health and safety. There is a significant distinction, however, between regulating the information dispensed about a product and regulating the actual content of the product. The classic example is tobacco products. Producers of tobacco products are required to warn consumers about the hazards associated with the use of their products, but the sale of tobacco products has not been subjected to significant restrictions or banned outright despite the obvious dangers to health.[18] We now examine various laws that regulate the actual products made available to consumers.

Food and Drugs

The first federal legislation regulating food and drugs was enacted in 1906 as the Pure Food and Drugs Act.[19] That law, as amended in 1938, exists now as the Federal Food, Drug, and Cosmetic Act (FDCA).[20] The act protects consumers against adulterated and misbranded foods and drugs. In its present form, the act establishes food standards, specifies safe levels of potentially hazardous food additives, and sets classifications of food and food advertising. Most of these statutory requirements are monitored and enforced by the Food and Drug Administration (FDA).

The FDCA also charges the FDA with the responsibility of ensuring that drugs are safe before they are marketed to the public. Under an extensive set of procedures established by the FDA, drugs must be shown to be effective as well as safe, and the use of some food additives suspected of being carcinogenic is prohibited. A 1976 amendment to the FDCA[21] authorizes the FDA to regulate medical devices, such as pacemakers and other health devices and equipment, and to withdraw from the market any such device that is mislabeled.

The question in the following case was whether the U.S. Constitution provides terminally ill patients with a right of access to experimental drugs that have passed limited safety trials but have not been proved safe and effective.

---

18. We are ignoring recent civil litigation concerning the liability of tobacco product manufacturers for injuries that arise from the use of tobacco. See, for example, *Philip Morris USA v. Williams*, ___U.S. ___, 127 S.Ct. 1057, 166 L.Ed.2d 940 (2007).

19. 21 U.S.C. Sections 1–5, 7–15.

20. 21 U.S.C. Sections 301–393.

21. 21 U.S.C. Sections 352(o), 360(j), 360(k), and 360c–360k.

Case 20.2 Abigail Alliance for Better Access to Developmental Drugs v. von Eschenbach

United States Court of Appeals,
District of Columbia Circuit, 2007.
495 F.3d 695.

BACKGROUND AND FACTS The Food and Drug Administration (FDA) and Congress have created programs to provide terminally ill patients with access to promising experimental drugs before the completion of the clinical-testing process—which can be lengthy. The Abigail Alliance for Better Access to Developmental Drugs (Alliance), an organization of terminally ill patients and their supporters, asked the FDA to expand this access. The FDA responded that, among other things, "a reasonably precise estimate of response rate" and "enough experience to detect serious adverse effects" are "critical" in determining when experimental drugs should be made available. Accordingly, "it does not serve patients well to make drugs too widely available before there is a reasonable assessment of such risks to guide patient decisions, and experience in managing them."

CASE 20.2–CONTINUED

CASE 20.2–CONTINUED

Accepting Alliance's proposal "would upset the appropriate balance * * * by giving almost total weight to the goal of early availability and giving little recognition to the importance of marketing drugs with reasonable knowledge for patients and physicians of their likely clinical benefit and their toxicity." Alliance filed a suit in a federal district court against FDA commissioner Andrew von Eschenbach and others, arguing that the Constitution provides terminally ill patients with a fundamental right of access to experimental drugs. The court ruled in the defendants' favor. Alliance appealed to the U.S. Court of Appeals for the District of Columbia Circuit.

IN THE WORDS OF THE COURT . . . *GRIFFITH,* **Circuit Judge.**

* * * *

* * * [The due process clause of the Fifth Amendment to the Constitution] provides heightened protection against government interference with certain fundamental rights [by subjecting that interference to strict scrutiny] * * * .

* * * *

* * * *The Due Process Clause specially protects those fundamental rights * * * which are, objectively, deeply rooted in this Nation's history and tradition * * * .* [Emphasis added.]

* * * *

Drug regulation in the United States began with the Colonies and the States * * * . In the early history of our Nation, we observe not a tradition of protecting a right of access to drugs, but rather governments responding to the risks of new compounds as they become aware of and able to address those risks.

* * * *

The current regime of federal drug regulation began to take shape with the Food, Drug, and Cosmetic Act [FDCA] of 1938. The Act required that drug manufacturers provide proof that their products were safe before they could be marketed.

* * * Congress amended the FDCA in 1962 to explicitly require that the FDA only approve drugs deemed effective for public use. Thus, the Alliance argues that, prior to 1962, patients were free to make their own decisions whether a drug might be effective. * * * Alliance's argument ignores our Nation's history of drug safety regulation * * * . Nor can the Alliance override current FDA regulations simply by insisting that drugs which have completed [some] testing are safe enough for terminally ill patients. Current law bars public access to drugs undergoing clinical testing on safety grounds. *The fact that a drug * * * is safe for limited clinical testing in a controlled and closely monitored environment after detailed scrutiny of each trial participant does not mean that a drug is safe for use beyond supervised trials.* [Emphasis added.]

* * * *

* * * We conclude that the Alliance has not provided evidence of a right to procure and use experimental drugs that is deeply rooted in our Nation's history and traditions.

* * * *

Because the Alliance's claimed right is not fundamental, the Alliance's claim of a right of access to experimental drugs is subject only to rational basis scrutiny. *The rational basis test requires that the Alliance prove that the government's restrictions bear no rational relationship to a legitimate state interest.* [Emphasis added.]

* * * *

Applying the rational basis standard to the Alliance's complaint, we cannot say that the government's interest does not bear a rational relation to a legitimate state interest. * * * For the terminally ill, as for anyone else, a drug is unsafe if its potential for inflicting death or physical injury is not offset by the possibility of therapeutic benefit.

* * * Thus, we must conclude that * * * the Government has a rational basis for ensuring that there is a scientifically and medically acceptable level of knowledge about the risks and benefits of such a drug.

DECISION AND REMEDY   The U.S. Court of Appeals for the District of Columbia Circuit affirmed the lower court's decision, holding that terminally ill patients do not have a fundamental constitutional right of access to experimental drugs. Furthermore, "the FDA's policy of limiting access to investigational drugs is rationally related to the legitimate state interest of protecting patients, including the terminally ill, from potentially unsafe drugs with unknown therapeutic effects."

THE GLOBAL DIMENSION   Should the court have ruled that as long as a drug has been approved for use in any country, terminally ill patients in the United States should be given access to it? Explain.

THE LEGAL ENVIRONMENT DIMENSION   In light of the analysis in this case, what option is left to those who believe that terminally ill patients—not the government—should make the decision about whether to accept the risk associated with experimental drugs?

Consumer Product Safety

In 1972, Congress enacted the Consumer Product Safety Act,[22] which created the first comprehensive scheme of regulation over matters concerning consumer safety. The act also established the Consumer Product Safety Commission (CPSC) and gave it far-reaching authority over consumer safety.

The CPSC's Authority   The CPSC conducts research on the safety of individual products and maintains a clearinghouse on the risks associated with various products. The Consumer Product Safety Act authorizes the CPSC to set standards for consumer products and to ban the manufacture and sale of any product that the commission deems to be potentially hazardous to consumers. The CPSC also has authority to remove from the market any products it believes to be imminently hazardous and to require manufacturers to report on any products already sold or intended for sale if the products have proved to be hazardous. Additionally, the CPSC administers other product-safety legislation, including the Child Protection and Toy Safety Act of 1969[23] and the Federal Hazardous Substances Act of 1960.[24]

The CPSC's authority is sufficiently broad to allow it to ban any product that the commission believes poses merely an "unreasonable risk" to the consumer. Products banned by the CPSC have included various types of fireworks, cribs, and toys, as well as many products containing asbestos, lead, or vinyl chloride.

Notification Requirements   The Consumer Product Safety Act imposes notification requirements on distributors of consumer products. Distributors must immediately notify the CPSC when they receive information that a product "contains a defect which . . . creates a substantial risk to the public" or "an unreasonable risk of serious injury or death."

EXAMPLE #4 Aroma Housewares Company had been distributing a particular model of juicer for just over a year when it began receiving letters from customers. They complained that during operation the juicer had suddenly

---

22. 15 U.S.C. Sections 2051–2083.
23. 15 U.S.C. Section 1262(e).
24. 15 U.S.C. Sections 1261–1273.

exploded, sending pieces of glass and razor-sharp metal across the room. The company received twenty-three letters from angry consumers about the exploding juicer but waited more than six months before notifying the CPSC that the product posed a significant risk to the public. In a case filed by the federal government, the court held that when a company first receives information regarding a threat, the company is required to report the problem within twenty-four hours to the CPSC. The court also found that even if the company had to investigate the allegations, it should not have taken more than ten days to verify the information and report the problem. The court therefore held that the company had violated the law and ordered it to pay damages.[25] □

CREDIT PROTECTION

Because of the extensive use of credit by U.S. consumers, credit protection is one of the most important aspects of consumer protection legislation. A key statute regulating the credit and credit-card industries is the Truth-in-Lending Act (TILA), the name commonly given to Title 1 of the Consumer Credit Protection Act (CCPA),[26] which was passed by Congress in 1968.

Truth in Lending

The TILA is basically a *disclosure law*. It is administered by the Federal Reserve Board and requires sellers and lenders to disclose credit terms or loan terms so that individuals can shop around for the best financing arrangements. TILA requirements apply only to persons who, in the ordinary course of business, lend funds, sell on credit, or arrange for the extension of credit. Thus, sales or loans made between two consumers do not come under the protection of the act. Additionally, this law protects only debtors who are *natural* persons (as opposed to the artificial "person" of a corporation); it does not extend to other legal entities.

The disclosure requirements are found in Regulation Z, which was promulgated by the Federal Reserve Board. If the contracting parties are subject to the TILA, the requirements of Regulation Z apply to any transaction involving an installment sales contract that calls for payment to be made in more than four installments. Transactions subject to Regulation Z typically include installment loans, retail and installment sales, car loans, home-improvement loans, and certain real estate loans if the amount of financing is less than $25,000.

Under the provisions of the TILA, all of the terms of a credit instrument must be clearly and conspicuously disclosed. The TILA provides for contract rescission (cancellation) if a creditor fails to follow *exactly* the procedures required by the act.[27]

Equal Credit Opportunity In 1974, Congress enacted, as an amendment to the TILA, the Equal Credit Opportunity Act (ECOA).[28] The ECOA prohibits the denial of credit solely on the basis of race, religion, national origin, color, gender, marital status, or age. The act also prohibits credit discrimination on the

---

25. *United States v. Miram Enterprises, Inc.,* 185 F.Supp.2d 1148 (S.D.Ca. 2002).
26. 15 U.S.C. Sections 1601–1693r. The act was amended in 1980 by the Truth-in-Lending Simplification and Reform Act.
27. Note, though, that amendments to the TILA enacted in 1995 prevent borrowers from rescinding loans because of minor clerical errors in closing documents [15 U.S.C. Sections 1605, 1631, 1635, 1640, and 1641].
28. 15 U.S.C. Section 1643.

basis of whether an individual receives certain forms of income, such as public-assistance benefits.

Under the ECOA, a creditor may not require the signature of an applicant's spouse, or a cosigner, on a credit instrument if the applicant qualifies under the creditor's standards of creditworthiness for the amount requested. **EXAMPLE #5** Tonja, an African American, applied for financing with a used-car dealer. The dealer reviewed Tonja's credit report and, without submitting the application to the lender, decided that she would not qualify. Instead of informing Tonja that she did not qualify, the dealer told her that she needed a cosigner on the loan to purchase the car. According to a federal appellate court in 2004, the dealership qualified as a creditor in this situation because it unilaterally denied credit. Thus, the dealer could be held liable under the ECOA.[29] □

Credit-Card Rules The TILA also contains provisions regarding credit cards. One provision limits the liability of a cardholder to $50 per card for unauthorized charges made before the creditor is notified that the card has been lost. Another provision prohibits a credit-card company from billing a consumer for any unauthorized charges if the credit card was improperly issued by the company. **EXAMPLE #6** Ian receives an unsolicited credit card in the mail. The card is later stolen and used by the thief to make purchases. In this situation, Ian will not be liable for the unauthorized charges. □

Other provisions of the act set out specific procedures for both the credit-card company and its cardholders to use in settling disputes related to credit-card purchases. These procedures may be used if, for example, a cardholder thinks that an error has occurred in billing or wishes to withhold payment for a faulty product purchased by credit card.

Consumer Leases The Consumer Leasing Act (CLA) of 1988[30] amended the TILA to provide protection for consumers who lease automobiles and other goods. The CLA applies to those who lease or arrange to lease consumer goods in the ordinary course of their business. The act applies only if the goods are priced at $25,000 or less and if the lease term exceeds four months. The CLA and its implementing regulation, *Regulation M*,[31] require lessors to disclose in writing (or by electronic record) all of the material terms of the lease.

Fair Credit Reporting

In 1970, to protect consumers against inaccurate credit reporting, Congress enacted the Fair Credit Reporting Act (FCRA).[32] The act provides that consumer credit reporting agencies may issue credit reports to users only for specified purposes, including extending credit, issuing insurance policies, complying with a court order, and responding to a consumer's request for a copy of her or his own credit report. The act further provides that any time a consumer is denied credit or insurance on the basis of the consumer's credit report, or is charged more than others ordinarily would be for credit or insurance, the consumer must be notified of that fact and of the name and address of the credit reporting agency that issued the credit report.

---

29. *Treadway v. Gateway Chevrolet Oldsmobile, Inc.*, 362 F.3d 971 (7th Cir. 2004).

30. 15 U.S.C. Sections 1667–1667e.

31. 12 C.F.R. Part 213.

32. 15 U.S.C. Sections 1681 *et seq.*

The FCRA gives consumers a right to request the source of any information being given out by a credit agency, as well as the identity of anyone who has received an agency's report. Consumers are also permitted to have access to the information contained about them in a credit reporting agency's files. If a consumer discovers that the agency's files contain inaccurate information about his or her credit standing, the agency, on the consumer's written request, must investigate the matter and delete any unverifiable or erroneous information within a reasonable period of time. The agency's investigation should include contacting the creditor whose information the consumer disputes and should involve a systematic examination of its records.

The FCRA allows an award of punitive damages for a "willful" violation, such as when a lender fails to keep proper records of a consumer loan and incorrectly makes adverse credit reports about a consumer.[33] Under the FCRA, if an insurance company raises a customer's rates because of a credit score, the insurance company is required to notify the individual. In 2007, the United States Supreme Court held that even the failure to notify *new* customers that they are paying higher insurance rates as a result of their credit scores is an adverse action that can be considered a willful violation of the FCRA.[34]

Fair and Accurate Credit Transactions Act

In an effort to combat rampant identity theft (discussed in Chapter 6), Congress passed the Fair and Accurate Credit Transactions (FACT) Act of 2003.[35] The act established a national fraud alert system so that consumers who suspect that they have been or may be victimized by identity theft can place an alert in their credit files. The FACT Act also requires the major credit reporting agencies to provide consumers with free copies of their credit reports every twelve months. Another provision requires account numbers on credit-card receipts to be truncated (shortened) so that merchants, employees, and others who have access to the receipts cannot obtain a consumer's name and full credit-card number. The act also mandates that financial institutions work with the Federal Trade Commission to identify "red flag" indicators of identity theft and to develop rules for disposing of sensitive credit information.

The FACT Act also gives consumers who have been victimized by identity theft some assistance in rebuilding their credit reputations. For example, credit reporting agencies must stop reporting allegedly fraudulent account information once the consumer establishes that identify theft has occurred. Business owners and creditors are required to provide a consumer with copies of any records that can help the consumer prove that a particular account or transaction is fraudulent (records showing that an account was created by a fraudulent signature, for example). In addition, to help prevent the spread of erroneous credit information, the act allows consumers to report the accounts affected by identity theft directly to the creditors.

Fair Debt-Collection Practices

In 1977, Congress enacted the Fair Debt Collection Practices Act (FDCPA)[36] in an attempt to curb what were perceived to be abuses by collection agencies. The act applies only to specialized debt-collection agencies that regularly attempt to collect

---

33. See, for example, 469 F.Supp.2d 343 (E.D.Va. 2007).
34. *Safeco Insurance Co. of America v. Burr,* ___ U.S. ___, 127 S.Ct. 2201, 167 L.Ed.2d 1045 (2007).
35. 15 U.S.C. Section 1681; 20 U.S.C. Sections 9701–9708.
36. 15 U.S.C. Section 1692.

debts on behalf of someone else, usually for a percentage of the amount owed. Creditors attempting to collect debts are not covered by the act unless, by misrepresenting themselves, they cause the debtors to believe that they are collection agencies. In addition, attorneys who regularly try to obtain payment of consumer debts through legal proceedings do meet the FDCPA's definition of "debt collector."

Requirements under the Act The act explicitly prohibits a collection agency from using any of the following tactics:

1. Contacting the debtor at the debtor's place of employment if the debtor's employer objects.
2. Contacting the debtor during inconvenient or unusual times (for example, calling the debtor at three o'clock in the morning) or at any time if an attorney is representing the debtor.
3. Contacting third parties other than the debtor's parents, spouse, or financial adviser about payment of a debt unless a court authorizes such action.
4. Using harassment or intimidation (for example, using abusive language or threatening violence) or employing false and misleading information (for example, posing as a police officer).
5. Communicating with the debtor at any time after receiving notice that the debtor is refusing to pay the debt, except to advise the debtor of further action to be taken by the collection agency.

The FDCPA also requires a collection agency to include a **validation notice** when it initially contacts a debtor for payment of a debt or within five days of that initial contact. The notice must state that the debtor has thirty days in which to dispute the debt and to request a written verification of the debt from the collection agency. The debtor's request for debt validation must be in writing.

The following case involved the prohibition against contacting a third party other than the debtor's parents, spouse, or financial adviser about the payment of a debt. A consumer alleged that a debt-collection company violated Colorado's fair debt collection statute when it hired a third party—an automated mailing service—to send her the required validation notice. Although the case was brought under Colorado's fair debt collection statute, the state statute parallels the relevant portions of the FDCPA, and both prohibit communications between a debt collector and third parties.

VALIDATION NOTICE
An initial notice to a debtor from a collection agency, required by federal law, informing the debtor that he or she has thirty days to challenge the debt and request verification.

Case 20.3 Flood v. Mercantile Adjustment Bureau, LLC

Supreme Court of Colorado, 2008.
176 P.3d 769.
www.courts.state.co.us/supct/supctopinion.htm[a]

BACKGROUND AND FACTS In January 2000, Elizabeth Flood purchased a used automobile, which she subsequently financed through Citi Financial Transouth. Shortly thereafter, she discovered that the car had been damaged. When she returned it to the dealership, the dealer refused to give her a refund. Instead, he provided Flood with a replacement vehicle. Several months later, the replacement vehicle exhibited electrical

problems and finally broke down. Flood unsuccessfully attempted to rescind the sale. Flood then lost her job and missed several payments. Transouth repossessed her car and sold it for less than the amount owed. Transouth transferred Flood's delinquent account to Mercantile Adjustment Bureau (MAB). In 2004, MAB caused a written debt-collection communication to be sent to Flood. MAB electronically transmitted the necessary information to a mailing service company, Unimail, which then used a mechanized process to print the letter, stuff the envelope, and mail the communication. Flood filed a suit against MAB for, among other claims, impermissibly communicating with a third party

a. Click on "Colorado Supreme Court Case Announcements by Date," then click on "01/22/08" in the 2008 Case Announcements.

CASE 20.3–CONTINUED

in violation of a section of Colorado's Fair Debt Collection Practices Act, which is modeled after the federal Fair Debt Collection Practices Act of 1977. At trial, MAB prevailed. Flood appealed to the Supreme Court of Colorado.

IN THE WORDS OF THE COURT . . . HOBBS, Justice.

* * * *

[Two previous courts] ruled that the debt collection communication that Mercantile Adjustment Bureau, LLC ("MAB") sent to Elizabeth Flood complied with the notice provisions of section 12-14-109 [of Colorado's Fair Debt Collection Practices Act], and that MAB did not violate section 12-14-105(2) [of that act] when it utilized an automated mailing service to print and mail the communication.

* * * *

* * * Flood * * * alleged that MAB impermissibly communicated with a third party, in violation of section 12-14-105(2), by outsourcing the printing and mailing of its collection communications to Unimail [a mailing service company].

* * * *

In the case before us, the relevant provisions of the Colorado statute parallel the federal statute. Because the Colorado statute is patterned on the federal statute, we look to federal case law for persuasive guidance bearing on the construction of our state's law.

* * * *

Flood * * * argues that MAB violated the [Colorado statute] by using an automated mailing service to prepare and mail its debt collection communications. With certain exceptions, [the statute] prohibits communications between a debt collector and third parties. Our analysis * * * leads us to conclude that the [Colorado legislature] did not intend for section 12-14-105(2) [of the Colorado act] to prohibit a debt collector from using an automated mailing service. The federal statute contains a nearly identical provision. *The purpose of [this federal provision] is to "protect a consumer's reputation and privacy, as well as to prevent loss of jobs resulting from a debt collector's communication with a consumer's employer concerning the collection of a debt."* [Emphasis added.]

The record here shows that MAB utilized an entirely automated printing and mailing service. The county court found that MAB electronically transmitted the information included in its collection communications to Unimail. Unimail then printed the collection communications, which were mechanically stuffed into envelopes. The county court concluded that the use of such a highly automated procedure did not violate section 12-14-105(2) because it did not threaten the consumer with the risk of being coerced or embarrassed into paying a debt because the debt collector contacted an employer, family member, friend, or other third party.

We agree with the holding of the county court. The use of an automated mailing service, such as Unimail, by a debt collector is a *de minimus* [trivial] communication with a third party that cannot reasonably be perceived as a threat to the consumer's privacy or reputation.

Accordingly, we hold that MAB's use of Unimail to automatically print and mail its debt collection communications did not violate section 12-14-105(2). Thus, we affirm that part of the district court's judgment upholding the county court's judgment on this issue.

DECISION AND REMEDY   The Supreme Court of Colorado held that Mercantile Adjustment Bureau did not violate Colorado's statute prohibiting communications with a third party about an outstanding debt. The state supreme court affirmed the lower court's opinion on this issue, but reversed the decision on other grounds (the letter sent contained contradictory language and failed to effectively convey the required notices regarding the debtor's rights).

WHAT IF THE FACTS WERE DIFFERENT? Assume that Unimail had spot-checkers who read randomly selected letters to debtors prior to mailing to make sure that they were accurate. Would the court still have ruled in favor of Mercantile Adjustment Bureau? Why or why not?

THE LEGAL ENVIRONMENT DIMENSION Why might this ruling actually benefit debtors in the long run?

Enforcement of the Act The enforcement of the FDCPA is primarily the responsibility of the Federal Trade Commission. The act provides that a debt collector who fails to comply with the act is liable for actual damages, plus additional damages not to exceed $1,000 and attorneys' fees.

Reviewing . . . Consumer Protection

Leota Sage saw a local motorcycle dealer's newspaper advertisement for a MetroRider EZ electric scooter for $1,699. When she went to the dealership, however, she learned that the EZ model had been sold out. The salesperson told Sage that he still had the higher-end MetroRider FX model in stock for $2,199 and would offer her one for $1,999. Sage was disappointed but decided to purchase the FX model. When Sage said that she wished to purchase the scooter on credit, she was directed to the dealer's credit department. As she filled out the credit forms, the clerk told Sage, who is an African American, that she would need a cosigner to obtain a loan. Sage could not understand why she would need a cosigner and asked to speak to the store manager. The manager apologized, told her that the clerk was mistaken, and said that he would "speak to" the clerk about that. The manager completed Sage's credit application, and Sage then rode the scooter home. Seven months later, Sage received a letter from the manufacturer informing her that a flaw had been discovered in the scooter's braking system and that the model had been recalled. Using the information presented in the chapter, answer the following questions.

1. Had the dealer engaged in deceptive advertising? Why or why not?

2. Suppose that Sage had ordered the scooter through the dealer's Web site but the dealer had been unable to deliver it by the date promised. What would the FTC have required the merchant to do in that situation?

3. Assuming that the clerk required a cosigner based on Sage's race or gender, what act prohibits such credit discrimination?

4. What organization has the authority to ban the sale of scooters based on safety concerns?

Key Terms

bait-and-switch
   advertising 669
cease-and-desist order 670
cooling-off laws 674

counteradvertising 670
deceptive advertising 667
multiple product order 670

Regulation Z 674
validation notice 681

Chapter Summary

Deceptive Advertising
(See pages 667–671.)

1. *Definition of deceptive advertising*—Generally, an advertising claim will be deemed deceptive if it would mislead a reasonable consumer.

2. *Bait-and-switch advertising*—Advertising a lower-priced product (the "bait") when the intention is not to sell the advertised product but to lure consumers into the store and convince them to buy a higher-priced product (the "switch") is prohibited by the FTC.

3. *Online deceptive advertising*—The FTC has issued guidelines to help online businesses comply with existing laws prohibiting deceptive advertising. The guidelines do not set forth new rules but rather describe how existing laws apply to online advertising.

4. *FTC actions against deceptive advertising*—Include cease-and-desist orders (requiring the advertiser to stop the challenged advertising) and counteradvertising (requiring the advertiser to advertise to correct the earlier misinformation).

Telemarketing and Electronic Advertising
(See pages 671–672.)

The Telephone Consumer Protection Act of 1991 prohibits telephone solicitation using an automatic telephone dialing system or a prerecorded voice. It also prohibits transmitting advertising materials via fax without first obtaining the recipient's permission to do so.

Labeling and Packaging
(See pages 672–673.)

Manufacturers must comply with the labeling or packaging requirements for their specific products. In general, all labels must be accurate and not misleading.

Sales
(See pages 673–674.)

1. *Telephone and mail-order sales*—Federal and state laws govern certain practices of sellers that solicit over the telephone or through the mails. These laws prohibit the use of the mails to defraud individuals. The warranty and other provisions of the Uniform Commercial Code, as adopted by the states, also protect consumers against deceptive sales practices.

2. *Online sales*—Both state and federal laws protect consumers to some extent against fraudulent and deceptive online sales practices.

Health and Safety Protection
(See pages 675–678.)

1. *Food and drugs*—The Federal Food, Drug, and Cosmetic Act of 1938, as amended, protects consumers against adulterated and misbranded foods and drugs. The act establishes food standards, specifies safe levels of potentially hazardous food additives, and sets classifications of food and food advertising.

2. *Consumer product safety*—The Consumer Product Safety Act of 1972 seeks to protect consumers from risk of injury from hazardous products. The Consumer Product Safety Commission has the power to remove products that are deemed imminently hazardous from the market and to ban the manufacture and sale of hazardous products.

Credit Protection
(See pages 678–683.)

1. *Consumer Credit Protection Act, Title I (Truth-in-Lending Act, or TILA)*—A disclosure law that requires sellers and lenders to disclose credit terms or loan terms in certain transactions, including retail and installment sales and loans, car loans, home-improvement loans, and certain real estate loans. Additionally, the TILA provides for the following:

   a. **Equal credit opportunity**—Creditors are prohibited from discriminating on the basis of race, religion, marital status, gender, national origin, color, or age.

   b. **Credit-card protection**—Liability of cardholders for unauthorized charges is limited to $50, providing notice requirements are met; consumers are not liable for unauthorized charges made on unsolicited credit cards. The act also sets out procedures to be used in settling disputes between credit-card companies and their cardholders.

   c. **Consumer leases**—Consumers who lease automobiles and other goods priced at $25,000 or less are protected if the lease term exceeds four months.

2. *Fair Credit Reporting Act*—Entitles consumers to request verification of the accuracy of a credit report and to have unverified or false information removed from their files.

Credit Protection— Continued	**3.** *Fair and Accurate Credit Transactions Act*—Attempts to combat identity theft by establishing a national fraud alert system. Requires account numbers to be truncated and credit-reporting agencies to provide one free credit report a year to consumers. Assists victims of identity theft in rebuilding their credit.
	4. *Fair Debt Collection Practices Act*—Prohibits debt collectors from using unfair debt-collection practices, such as contacting the debtor at his or her place of employment if the employer objects, contacting the debtor at unreasonable times, or contacting third parties about the debt.

For Review

1. When will advertising be deemed deceptive?
2. What special rules apply to telephone solicitation?
3. What is Regulation Z, and to what type of transactions does it apply?
4. How does the Federal Food, Drug, and Cosmetic Act protect consumers?
5. What are the major federal statutes providing for consumer protection in credit transactions?

Questions and Case Problems

20–1. Unsolicited Merchandise. Andrew, a resident of California, received an advertising circular in the U.S. mail announcing a new line of regional cookbooks distributed by the Every-Kind Cookbook Co. Andrew didn't want any books and threw the circular away. Two days later, Andrew received in the mail an introductory cookbook entitled *Lower Mongolian Regional Cookbook,* as announced in the circular, on a "trial basis" from Every-Kind. Andrew did not go to the trouble to return the cookbook. Every-Kind demanded payment of $20.95 for the *Lower Mongolian Regional Cookbook.* Discuss whether Andrew can be required to pay for the book.

20–2. Credit Protection. Maria Ochoa receives two new credit cards on May 1. She solicited one of them from Midtown Department Store, and the other was sent unsolicited by High-Flying Airlines. During the month of May, Ochoa makes numerous credit-card purchases from Midtown Department Store, but she does not use the High-Flying Airlines card. On May 31, a burglar breaks into Ochoa's home and steals both credit cards. Ochoa notifies the Midtown Department Store of the theft on June 2, but she fails to notify High-Flying Airlines. Using the Midtown credit card, the burglar makes a $500 purchase on June 1 and a $200 purchase on June 3. The burglar then charges a vacation flight on the High-Flying Airlines card for $1,000 on June 5. Ochoa receives the bills for these charges and refuses to pay them. Discuss Ochoa's liability in these situations.

Question with Sample Answer

20–3. On June 28, a salesperson for Renowned Books called on the Gonchars at their home. After a very persuasive sales pitch by the agent, the Gonchars agreed in writing to purchase a twenty-volume set of historical encyclopedias from Renowned Books for a total of $299. A down payment of $35 was required, with the remainder of the cost to be paid in monthly payments over a one-year period. Two days later, the Gonchars, having second thoughts, contacted the book company and stated that they had decided to rescind the contract. Renowned Books said this would be impossible. Has Renowned Books violated any consumer law by not allowing the Gonchars to rescind their contract? Explain.

For a sample answer to Question 20–3, go to Appendix I at the end of this text.

20–4. Fair Credit Reporting Act. Source One Associates, Inc., is based in Poughquag, New York. Peter Easton, Source One's president, is responsible for its daily operations. Between 1995 and 1997, Source One received requests from persons in Massachusetts seeking financial information about individuals and businesses. To obtain this information, Easton first obtained the targeted individuals' credit reports through Equifax Consumer Information Services by claiming that the reports would be used only in connection with credit transactions involving the consumers. From the reports, Easton identified financial institutions at which the targeted individuals held accounts. He then called the institutions to learn the account balances by impersonating either officers of the institutions or the account holders. The information was then provided to Source One's customers for a fee. Easton did not know why the customers wanted the information. The state ("commonwealth") of Massachusetts filed a suit in a Massachusetts state court against Source One and Easton, alleging, among other things, violations of the Fair Credit Reporting Act (FCRA). Did the defendants violate the FCRA? Explain. [*Commonwealth v. Source One Associates, Inc.*, 436 Mass. 118, 763 N.E.2d 42 (2002)]

20–5. Deceptive Advertising. "Set Up & Ready to Make Money in Minutes Guaranteed!" the ads claimed. "The Internet Treasure Chest (ITC) will give you everything you need to start your own exciting Internet business including your own worldwide Web site all for the unbelievable price of only $59.95." The ITC "contains virtually everything you need to quickly and easily get your very own worldwide Internet business up, running, stocked with products, able to accept credit cards and ready to take orders almost immediately." What ITC's marketers—Damien Zamora and end70 Corp.—did not disclose were the significant additional costs required to operate the business: domain name registration fees, monthly Internet access and hosting charges, monthly fees to access the ITC product warehouse, and other "upgrades." The Federal Trade Commission filed a suit in a federal district court against end70 and Zamora, seeking an injunction and other relief. Are the defendants' claims "deceptive advertising"? If so, what might the court order the defendants to do to correct any misrepresentations? [*Federal Trade Commission v. end70 Corp.*, __ F.Supp.2d __ (N.D.Tex. 2003)]

Case Problem with Sample Answer

20–6. One of the products sold by McDonald's Corp. is the Happy Meal®, which consists of a McDonald's food entree, a small order of french fries, a small drink, and a toy. In the early 1990s, McDonald's began to aim its Happy Meal marketing at children aged one to three. In 1995, McDonald's began making nutritional information for its food products available in documents known as "McDonald's Nutrition Facts." Each document lists each food item that the restaurant serves and provides a nutritional breakdown, but the Happy Meal is not included. Marc Cohen filed a suit in an Illinois state court against McDonald's, alleging, among other things, that the defendant had violated a state law prohibiting consumer fraud and deceptive business practices by failing to adhere to the National Labeling and Education Act (NLEA) of 1990. The NLEA sets out different requirements for products specifically intended for children under the

age of four—generally, the products cannot declare the percent of daily value of nutritional components. Would this requirement be readily understood by a consumer who is not familiar with nutritional standards? Why or why not? Should a state court impose such regulations? Explain. [*Cohen v. McDonald's Corp.*, 347 Ill.App.3d 627, 808 N.E.2d 1, 283 Ill.Dec. 451 (1 Dist. 2004)]

After you have answered Problem 20–6, compare your answer with the sample answer given on the Web site that accompanies this text. Go to www.cengage.com/blaw/let, select "Chapter 20," and click on "Case Problem with Sample Answer."

20–7. Debt Collection. 55th Management Corp. in New York City owns residential property that it leases to various tenants. In June 2000, claiming that one of the tenants, Leslie Goldman, owed more than $13,000 in back rent, 55th retained Jeffrey Cohen, an attorney, to initiate nonpayment proceedings. Cohen filed a petition in a New York state court against Goldman, seeking recovery of the unpaid rent and at least $3,000 in attorneys' fees. After receiving notice of the petition, Goldman filed a suit in a federal district court against Cohen. Goldman contended that the notice of the petition constituted an initial contact that, under the Fair Debt Collection Practices Act (FDCPA), required a validation notice. Because Cohen did not give Goldman a validation notice at the time, or within five days, of the notice of the petition, Goldman argued that Cohen was in violation of the FDCPA. Should the filing of a suit in a state court be considered "communication," requiring a debt collector to provide a validation notice under the FDCPA? Why or why not? [*Goldman v. Cohen*, 445 F.3d 152 (2d Cir. 2006)]

A Question of Ethics

20–8. After graduating from law school— and serving time in prison for attempting to collect debts by posing as an FBI agent— Barry Sussman theorized that if a debt-collection business collected only debts that it owned as a result of buying checks written on accounts with insufficient funds (NSF checks), it would not be subject to the Federal Debt Collection Practices Act (FDCPA). Sussman formed Check Investors, Inc., to act on his theory. Check Investors bought more than 2.2 million NSF checks, with an estimated face value of about $348 million, for pennies on the dollar. Check Investors added a fee of $125 or $130 to the face amount of each check (which exceeds the legal limit in most states) and aggressively pursued its drawer to collect. The firm's employees were told to accuse drawers of being criminals and to threaten them with arrest and prosecution. The threats were false. Check Investors never took steps to initiate a prosecution. The employees contacted the drawers' family members and used "saturation phoning"—phoning a drawer numerous times in a short period. They used abusive language, referring to drawers as "deadbeats," "retards," "thieves," and "idiots." Between January 2000 and January 2003, Check Investors netted more than $10.2 million from its efforts. [*Federal Trade Commission v. Check Investors, Inc.*, 502 F.3d 159 (3d Cir. 2007)]

1. The Federal Trade Commission filed a suit in a federal district court against Check Investors and others, alleging, in part, violations of the FDCPA. Was Check Investors a "debt collector," collecting "debts," within the meaning of the FDCPA? If so, did its methods violate the FDCPA? Were its practices unethical? What might Check Investors argue in its defense? Discuss.
2. Are "deadbeats" the primary beneficiaries of laws such as the FDCPA? If not, how would you characterize debtors who default on their obligations?

Critical-Thinking Legal Question

20–9. Many states have enacted laws that go even further than federal law to protect the interests of consumers. These laws vary tremendously from state to state. Generally, is having different laws fair to sellers who may be prohibited from engaging in a practice in one state that is legal in another? How might these different laws affect a business? Is it fair that residents of one state have more protection than residents of another? Or should all consumer protection laws be federally legislated?

Video Question

20–10. Go to this text's Web site at **www.cengage.com/blaw/let** and select "Chapter 20." Click on "Video Questions" and view the video titled *Advertising Communication Law: Bait and Switch*. Then answer the following questions.

1. Is the auto dealership's advertisement for the truck in the video deceptive? Why or why not?
2. Is the advertisement for the truck an offer to which the dealership is bound? Does it matter if Betty detrimentally relied on the advertisement?
3. Is Tony committed to buying Betty's trade-in truck for $3,000 because that is what he told her over the phone?

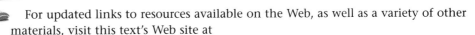

Interacting with the Internet

For updated links to resources available on the Web, as well as a variety of other materials, visit this text's Web site at

www.cengage.com/blaw/let

For a government-sponsored Web site containing reports on consumer issues, go to

www.consumer.gov

The Federal Trade Commission (FTC) offers extensive information on consumer protection laws, consumer problems, enforcement issues, and other topics relevant to consumer law at its Web site. Go to

www.ftc.gov

and click on "Consumer Protection."

PRACTICAL INTERNET EXERCISES

Go to this text's Web site at **www.cengage.com/blaw/let**, select "Chapter 20," and click on "Practical Internet Exercises." There you will find the following Internet research exercises that you can perform to learn more about the topics covered in this chapter.

Practical Internet Exercise 20–1: LEGAL PERSPECTIVE—**The Food and Drug Administration**
Practical Internet Exercise 20–2: SOCIAL PERSPECTIVE—**Nuisance Law**

BEFORE THE TEST

Go to this text's Web site at **www.cengage.com/blaw/let**, select "Chapter 20," and click on "Interactive Quizzes." You will find a number of interactive questions relating to this chapter.

Chapter 21

Protecting the Environment

CHAPTER OBJECTIVES

After reading this chapter, you should be able to answer the following questions:

1. Under what common law theories can polluters be held liable?
2. What is an environmental impact statement, and who must file one?
3. What does the Environmental Protection Agency do?
4. What major federal statutes regulate air and water pollution?
5. What is Superfund? To what categories of persons does liability under Superfund extend?

CONTENTS

> " *Man, however much he may like to pretend the contrary, is part of nature.* "
>
> — RACHEL CARSON,
> 1907–1964 (American writer and conservationist)

Concerns over the degradation of the environment have increased over time in response to the environmental effects of population growth, urbanization, and industrialization. Environmental protection is not without a price, however. For many businesses, the costs of complying with environmental regulations are high, and for some they may seem too high. A constant tension exists between the desirability of increasing profits and productivity and the need to protect the environment.

To a great extent, environmental law consists of statutes passed by federal, state, or local governments and regulations issued by administrative agencies. Before examining statutory and regulatory environmental laws, however, we look at the remedies available under the common law against environmental pollution.

COMMON LAW ACTIONS

Common law remedies against environmental pollution originated centuries ago in England. Those responsible for operations that created dirt, smoke, noxious odors, noise, or toxic substances were sometimes held liable under common law theories of nuisance or negligence. Today, injured individuals continue to rely on the common law to obtain damages and injunctions against business polluters.

Nuisance

NUISANCE
A common law doctrine under which persons may be held liable for using their property in a manner that unreasonably interferes with others' rights to use or enjoy their own property.

Under the common law doctrine of **nuisance,** persons may be held liable if they use their property in a manner that unreasonably interferes with others' rights to use or enjoy their own property. In these situations, the courts commonly balance the equities between the harm caused by the pollution and the costs of stopping it.

Courts have often denied injunctive relief on the ground that the hardships that would be imposed on the polluter and on the community are relatively greater than the hardships suffered by the plaintiff. EXAMPLE #1 A factory that causes neighboring landowners to suffer from smoke, soot, and vibrations may be left in operation if it is the core of a local economy. The injured parties may be awarded only monetary damages, which may include compensation for the decrease in the value of their property caused by the factory's operation.□

A property owner may be given relief from pollution if he or she can identify a distinct harm separate from that affecting the general public. This harm is referred to as a "private" nuisance. Under the common law, individuals were denied standing (access to the courts—see Chapter 3) unless they suffered a harm distinct from the harm suffered by the public at large. Some states still require this. EXAMPLE #2 A group of individuals who made their living by commercial fishing in a major river in New York sued for damages and to obtain an injunction against a company that was polluting the river. The court found that the plaintiffs had standing because they were particularly harmed by the pollution in the river.[1]□ A public authority (such as a state's attorney general), though, can sue to abate a "public" nuisance.

Negligence and Strict Liability

An injured party may sue a business polluter in tort under negligence and strict liability theories (discussed in Chapters 5 and 12). The basis for a negligence action is the business's alleged failure to use reasonable care toward the party whose injury was foreseeable and, of course, caused by the lack of reasonable care. For example, employees might sue an employer whose failure to use proper pollution controls contaminated the air and caused the employees to suffer respiratory illnesses. A developing area of tort law involves **toxic torts**—civil wrongs arising from exposure to a toxic substance, such as asbestos, radiation, or hazardous waste.

TOXIC TORT
A civil wrong arising from exposure to a toxic substance, such as asbestos, radiation, or hazardous waste.

Businesses that engage in ultrahazardous activities—such as the transportation of radioactive materials—are strictly liable for any injuries the activities cause. In a strict liability action, the injured party does not need to prove that the business failed to exercise reasonable care.

FEDERAL, STATE, AND LOCAL REGULATION

As mentioned, all levels of government in the United States regulate some aspect of the environment. In this section, we look at some of the ways in which the federal, state, and local governments control business activities and land use in the interests of environmental preservation and protection.

Federal Regulation

Congress has enacted a number of statutes to control the impact of human activities on the environment. Some of these laws have been passed to improve the quality of air and water. Some of them specifically regulate toxic chemicals, including pesticides, herbicides, and hazardous wastes. Exhibit 21–1 lists and

---

1. *Leo v. General Electric Co.*, 538 N.Y.S.2d 844, 145 A.D.2d 291 (1989).

EXHIBIT 21-1 MAJOR FEDERAL ENVIRONMENTAL STATUTES

POPULAR NAME	PURPOSE	STATUTE REFERENCE
Rivers and Harbors Appropriations Act (1899)	To prohibit ships and manufacturers from discharging and depositing refuse in navigable waterways.	33 U.S.C. Sections 401–418.
Federal Insecticide, Fungicide, and Rodenticide Act (1947)	To control the use of pesticides and herbicides.	7 U.S.C. Sections 136–136y.
Federal Water Pollution Control Act (1948)	To eliminate the discharge of pollutants from major sources into navigable waters.	33 U.S.C. Sections 1251–1387.
Clean Air Act (1963, 1970)	To control air pollution from mobile and stationary sources.	42 U.S.C. Sections 7401–7671q.
National Environmental Policy Act (1969)	To limit environmental harm from federal government activities.	42 U.S.C. Sections 4321–4370d.
Ocean Dumping Act (1972)	To prohibit the dumping of radiological, chemical, and biological warfare agents and high-level radioactive waste into the ocean.	16 U.S.C. Sections 1401–1445.
Endangered Species Act (1973)	To protect species that are threatened with extinction.	16 U.S.C. Sections 1531–1544.
Safe Drinking Water Act (1974)	To regulate pollutants in public drinking water systems.	42 U.S.C. Sections 300f–300j-25.
Resource Conservation and Recovery Act (1976)	To establish standards for hazardous waste disposal.	42 U.S.C. Sections 6901–6986.
Toxic Substances Control Act (1976)	To regulate toxic chemicals and chemical compounds.	15 U.S.C. Sections 2601–2692.
Comprehensive Environmental Response, Compensation, and Liability Act (1980)	To regulate the clean-up of hazardous waste–disposal sites.	42 U.S.C. Sections 9601–9675.
Oil Pollution Act (1990)	To establish liability for the clean-up of navigable waters after oil-spill disasters.	33 U.S.C. Sections 2701–2761.
Small Business Liability Relief and Brownfields Revitalization Act (2002)	To allow developers who comply with state voluntary clean-up programs to avoid federal liability for the properties that they decontaminate and develop.	42 U.S.C. Section 9628.

summarizes the major federal environmental statutes, most of which are discussed in this chapter.

Environmental Regulatory Agencies Much of the body of federal law governing business activities consists of the regulations issued and enforced by administrative agencies. The primary agency regulating environmental law is, of course, the Environmental Protection Agency (EPA), which was created in 1970 to coordinate federal environmental responsibilities. Other federal agencies with authority to regulate specific environmental matters include the Department of the Interior, the Department of Defense, the Department of Labor, the Food and Drug Administration, and the Nuclear Regulatory Commission. These regulatory agencies—and all other agencies of the federal government—must take environmental factors into consideration when making significant decisions.

Most federal environmental laws provide that private parties can sue to enforce environmental regulations if government agencies fail to do so—or if agencies go too far in their enforcement actions. Typically, a threshold hurdle in such suits is meeting the requirements for standing to sue.

State and local regulatory agencies also play a significant role in implementing federal environmental legislation. Typically, the federal government relies on state and local governments to enforce federal environmental statutes and regulations such as those regulating air quality.

Environmental Impact Statements   The National Environmental Policy Act (NEPA) of 1969[2] requires that an **environmental impact statement (EIS)** be prepared for every major federal action that significantly affects the quality of the environment. An EIS must analyze (1) the impact on the environment that the action will have, (2) any adverse effects on the environment and alternative actions that might be taken, and (3) irreversible effects the action might generate.

An action qualifies as "major" if it involves a substantial commitment of resources (monetary or otherwise). An action is "federal" if a federal agency has the power to control it. Construction by a private developer of a ski resort on federal land, for example, may require an EIS. Building or operating a nuclear plant, which requires a federal permit, would require an EIS, as would constructing a dam as part of a federal project. If an agency decides that an EIS is unnecessary, it must issue a statement supporting this conclusion. EISs have become instruments for private individuals, consumer interest groups, businesses, and others to challenge federal agency actions on the basis that the actions improperly threaten the environment.

> **ENVIRONMENTAL IMPACT STATEMENT (EIS)**
> A statement required by the National Environmental Policy Act for any major federal action that will significantly affect the quality of the environment. The statement must analyze the action's impact on the environment and explore alternative actions that might be taken.

State and Local Regulation

Many states regulate the degree to which the environment may be polluted. Thus, for example, even when state zoning laws permit a business's proposed development, the proposal may have to be altered to lessen the development's impact on the environment. State laws may restrict a business's discharge of chemicals into the air or water or regulate its disposal of toxic wastes. States may also regulate the disposal or recycling of other wastes, including glass, metal, and plastic containers and paper. Additionally, states may restrict the emissions from motor vehicles.

City, county, and other local governments control some aspects of the environment. For instance, local zoning laws control some land use. These laws may be designed to inhibit or regulate the growth of cities and suburbs or to protect the natural environment. In the interest of safeguarding the environment, such laws may prohibit certain land uses. An issue subject to ongoing debate is whether landowners should be compensated when restrictions are placed on the use of their property.

Other aspects of the environment may be subject to local regulation for other reasons. Methods of waste and garbage removal and disposal, for example, can have a substantial impact on a community. The appearance of buildings and other structures, including advertising signs and billboards, may affect traffic safety, property values, or local aesthetics. Noise generated by a business or its customers may be annoying, disruptive, or damaging to neighbors. The location

---

2. 42 U.S.C. Sections 4321–4370d.

and condition of parks, streets, and other publicly used land subject to local control affect the environment and can also affect business.

AIR POLLUTION

Federal involvement with air pollution goes back to the 1950s, when Congress authorized funds for air-pollution research. In 1963, the federal government passed the Clean Air Act,[3] which focused on multistate air pollution and provided assistance to the states. Various amendments, particularly in 1970, 1977, and 1990, have strengthened the government's authority to regulate the quality of air. These laws provide the basis for issuing regulations to control pollution coming primarily from mobile sources (such as automobiles) and stationary sources (such as electric utilities and industrial plants).

Mobile Sources

Automobiles and other vehicles are referred to as mobile sources of pollution. The EPA has issued regulations specifying standards for mobile sources of pollution, as well as for service stations. The agency periodically updates these standards in light of new developments and data.

Motor Vehicles Regulations governing air pollution from automobiles and other mobile sources specify pollution standards and establish time schedules for meeting the standards. EXAMPLE #3 Under the 1990 amendments to the Clean Air Act, automobile manufacturers were required to cut new automobiles' exhaust emissions of nitrogen oxide by 60 percent and of other pollutants by 35 percent by 1998. Regulations that became effective beginning with 2004 model cars called for nitrogen oxide tailpipe emissions to be cut by nearly 10 percent by 2007. For the first time, sport utility vehicles (SUVs) and light trucks were required to meet the same standards as automobiles. The amendments also required service stations to sell gasoline with a higher oxygen content in certain cities and to sell even cleaner-burning gasoline in the most polluted urban areas.□

When individuals or groups oppose regulations, they often file lawsuits in an attempt to *prevent* an agency from taking some regulatory action. As mentioned earlier, however, private parties also sometimes file lawsuits in an effort to *compel* an agency to take action in an area in which it has failed to act. A group of private organizations and several states took such an action when they sued to require the EPA to take global warming into account when adopting rules regulating carbon dioxide emissions. For a discussion of the United States Supreme Court's decision in this case, see this chapter's *Insight into Ethics* feature.

Updating Pollution-Control Standards The EPA attempts to update pollution-control standards when new scientific information becomes available. EXAMPLE #4 Studies conducted in the 1990s showed that very small particles of soot (2.5 microns, or about one-thirtieth the width of a human hair) might affect health as significantly as larger particles. Based on this evidence, in 1997 the EPA issued new particulate standards for motor vehicle exhaust systems and other sources of pollution. The EPA also instituted a more rigorous standard for ozone (the basic ingredient of smog), which is formed when sunlight combines with pollutants from cars and other sources.□

---

3. 42 U.S.C. Sections 7401 *et seq.*

The EPA's particulate standards and ozone standard were challenged in court by a number of business groups that claimed that the EPA had exceeded its authority under the Clean Air Act by issuing the stricter rules. Additionally, the groups claimed that the EPA had to take economic costs into account when developing new regulations. In 2001, however, the United States Supreme Court upheld the EPA's authority under the Clean Air Act to issue the standards. The Court also held that the EPA did not have to take economic costs into account when creating new rules.[4]

In 2006, the EPA again reevaluated its particulate standards and found that more than two hundred counties were not meeting the standards set in 1997. The EPA issued new regulations for daily (twenty-four-hour) exposure to particles of soot but did not change the annual particulate standards.[5]

An area in an office building undergoing the removal of asbestos, a hazardous air pollutant.
(Aaron Suggs/Creative Commons)

Stationary Sources

The Clean Air Act authorizes the EPA to establish air-quality standards for stationary sources (such as manufacturing plants) but recognizes that the primary responsibility for preventing and controlling air pollution rests with state and local governments. The standards are aimed at controlling hazardous air pollutants—that is, those likely to cause death or serious irreversible or incapacitating illness such as cancer or neurological or reproductive damage.

Insight into Ethics

Should the Supreme Court force the EPA to take the threat of global warming into account when drafting regulations?

For years, environmental groups have urged Congress to take action to curb emissions of so-called greenhouse gases, including carbon dioxide. They argue that these gases build up in the atmosphere and create a "greenhouse effect" that supposedly leads to global warming. These groups wanted Congress to mandate that the Environmental Protection Agency (EPA) consider global warming effects when instituting regulations—particularly with respect to carbon dioxide emissions from automobiles.

When Congress failed to act on global warming, environmental groups went directly to the EPA and asked the agency to regulate greenhouse gases, including carbon dioxide emissions from motor vehicles. The EPA refused, however, taking the position that the Clean Air Act did not authorize it to address global climate change or to regulate carbon dioxide emissions. As a result, the environmental groups and several states brought a lawsuit to force the EPA to act.

The Supreme Court Recognized the Threat of Global Warming

The United States Supreme Court's 2007 opinion in the case of *Massachusetts v. Environmental Protection Agency*[6] ultimately may become a landmark decision supporting plaintiffs and environmentalists. At issue was not only whether the EPA has the

---

4. *Whitman v. American Trucking Associations,* 531 U.S. 457, 121 S.Ct. 903, 149 L.Ed.2d 1 (2001).
5. 40 C.F.R. Part 50.
6. ___ U.S. ___, 127 S.Ct. 1438, 167 L.Ed.2d 248 (2007).

authority to regulate carbon dioxide under the Clean Air Act but also whether the plaintiffs had *standing* to bring their case at all. Recall from the discussion earlier in this chapter that to have standing, a plaintiff ordinarily must have suffered a particular harm that is distinct from that experienced by the public at large.

The EPA argued that because global warming has widespread effects on everyone, an individual plaintiff could not show the distinct harm that standing requires. Massachusetts claimed to have standing because its coastline, including lands owned by the state, faced an imminent threat from rising sea levels caused by global warming. The Supreme Court agreed and declared that "the harm associated with climate changes is serious and well recognized," including "severe and irreversible changes to natural ecosystems" and "a precipitate rise in sea levels." The fact that these effects are widely shared does not minimize their impact on Massachusetts, according to the majority of the Court. Hence, Massachusetts had standing to bring a lawsuit.

The Interpretation of the Clean Air Act

The Court also held that the Clean Air Act gives the EPA the authority to regulate carbon dioxide. The agency had contended that the language of the statute did not include carbon dioxide. The Court found that the act defines an air pollutant as "any physical, chemical . . . substance which is emitted into or otherwise enters the ambient air"—a definition that includes all airborne compounds. Thus, the statute's mandate that the EPA should regulate "any air pollutant" from cars that might "endanger public health or welfare" provides authority to regulate carbon dioxide. Indeed, the Court's interpretation of the Clean Air Act means that the EPA must take global warming into account and issue regulations on carbon dioxide emissions.

Controversy Continues

The Court's interpretation of the Clean Air Act has been controversial. Critics question whether it is proper for the Court to force agency regulation. When Congress last amended the Clean Air Act in 1990, major studies on global warming had already been conducted. Nevertheless, Congress did not include amendments that would have forced the EPA to set carbon dioxide emission standards. In his dissenting opinion, Justice Scalia also criticized the majority's broad definition of "pollutant" to include carbon dioxide, which is a by-product of human respiration.

Although environmental groups hailed the *Massachusetts* decision, others were highly critical. Some claim that the Court's ruling on standing will open the door to other plaintiffs and interest groups that would like to force Congress to legislate or agencies to regulate in certain areas. At least two federal courts have declined to extend the ruling to other subjects.[7]

Listing of Regulated Hazardous Air Pollutants   When Congress amended the Clean Air Act in 1970, it required the EPA to list all regulated hazardous air pollutants (HAPs) on a prioritized schedule. The EPA listed only eight substances for the next eighteen years. In 1990, Congress again amended the act and required the EPA to list more substances as HAPs. In all, 189 substances, including asbestos, benzene, beryllium, cadmium, and vinyl chloride, have been classified as hazardous. They are emitted from stationary sources by a variety of business activities, including smelting (melting ore to produce metal), dry cleaning, house painting, and commercial baking.

---

7. See *United States v. Genendo Pharmaceutical, N.V.,* 485 F.3d 958 (7th Cir. 2007); and *American Civil Liberties Union v. National Security Agency,* 493 F.3d 644 (6th Cir. 2007).

Mercury is one of the listed hazardous substances. The EPA attempted nonetheless to remove mercury from its list of designated HAPs emitted from electric utility steam-generating units. In the following case, New Jersey and others challenged this delisting.

Case 21.1 State of New Jersey v. Environmental Protection Agency

United States Court of Appeals for the District of Columbia Circuit, 2008.
517 F.3d 574.
www.cadc.uscourts.gov/bin/opinions/allopinions.asp[a]

BACKGROUND AND FACTS The Environmental Protection Agency (EPA) published a rule—the Delisting Rule—that had

a. This is the opinions page of the Court of Appeals for the District of Columbia. Select "February" and "2008" from the drop-down menus for "Month" and "Year" and click on "Go!" Scroll down to the listing for case number "05-1097a" and click on the link to access the opinion.

the effect of removing from its regulation the emissions of mercury from steam-generating electricity plants that used coal or oil as their energy sources. This Delisting Rule ran counter to the EPA's own conclusions at the end of 2000 that it was "appropriate and necessary" to regulate mercury emissions. At that time, it placed mercury on its list of hazardous air pollutants (HAPs) to be monitored at electricity-generating sites. New Jersey and fourteen additional states, plus various state agencies, challenged the EPA's action.

IN THE WORDS OF THE COURT . . . *ROGERS,* **Circuit Judge.**

* * * *

First, Congress required EPA to regulate more than one hundred specific HAPs, including mercury and nickel compounds. Further, EPA was required to list and to regulate, on a prioritized schedule, "all categories and subcategories of major sources and areas sources" that emit one or more HAPs. *In seeking to ensure that regulation of HAPs reflects the "maximum reduction in emissions which can be achieved by application of [the] best available control technology," Congress imposed specific, strict pollution control requirements on both new and existing sources of HAPs.* [Emphasis added.]

Second, Congress restricted the opportunities for EPA and others to intervene in the regulation of HAP sources. For HAPs that result in health effects other than cancer, as is true of mercury, Congress directed that the Administrator "may delete any source category" from the section 112(c)(1) list only after determining that "emissions from no source in the category or subcategory concerned . . . exceed a level which is adequate to protect public health with an ample margin of safety and no adverse environmental effect will result from emissions from any source."

* * * *

EPA maintains that it possesses authority to remove EGUs [electrical generating units] from * * * [the] list under the "fundamental principle of administrative law that an agency has inherent authority to reverse an earlier administrative determination or ruling where an agency has a principled basis for doing so."

EPA states in its brief that it has previously removed sources listed * * * without satisfying the requirements of [the statute]. But previous statutory violations cannot excuse the one now before the court. "We do not see how merely applying an unreasonable statutory interpretation for several years can transform it into a reasonable interpretation."

DECISION AND REMEDY The U.S. Court of Appeals for the District of Columbia Circuit ruled in favor of New Jersey and the other plaintiffs. The EPA was required to rescind its delisting of mercury.

CASE 21.1–CONTINUED

CASE 21.1–CONTINUED **WHAT IF THE FACTS WERE DIFFERENT?**   Suppose that the EPA had carried out scientific tests that showed mercury was relatively harmless as a by-product of electricity generation. How might this have affected the court's ruling?

THE GLOBAL DIMENSION   Because air pollution knows no borders, how did this ruling affect our neighboring countries?

Air Pollution Control Standards   The EPA sets primary and secondary levels of ambient standards—that is, the maximum levels of certain pollutants—and the states formulate plans to achieve those standards. Different standards apply depending on whether the sources of pollution are located in clean areas or polluted areas and whether they are existing sources or major new sources of pollution. Major new sources include existing sources in which a change in a method of operation increases emissions. Performance standards for major sources require the use of the *maximum achievable control technology,* or MACT, to reduce emissions. The EPA issues guidelines as to what equipment meets this standard.[8]

Violations of the Clean Air Act   For violations of emission limits under the Clean Air Act, the EPA can assess civil penalties of up to $25,000 per day. Additional fines of up to $5,000 per day can be assessed for other violations, such as failing to maintain the required records. To penalize those who find it more cost-effective to violate the act than to comply with it, the EPA is authorized to obtain a penalty equal to the violator's economic benefits from noncompliance. Persons who provide information about violators may be paid up to $10,000. Private individuals can also sue violators.

Those who knowingly violate the act may be subject to criminal penalties, including fines of up to $1 million and imprisonment for up to two years (for false statements or failures to report violations). Corporate officers are among those who may be subject to these penalties.

WATER POLLUTION

Water pollution stems mostly from industrial, municipal, and agricultural sources. Pollutants entering streams, lakes, and oceans include organic wastes, heated water, sediments from soil runoff, nutrients (including fertilizers and human and animal wastes), and toxic chemicals and other hazardous substances. We look here at laws and regulations governing water pollution.

Federal regulations governing the pollution of water can be traced back to the Rivers and Harbors Appropriations Act of 1899.[9] These regulations prohibited ships and manufacturers from discharging or depositing refuse in navigable waterways without a permit. In 1948, Congress passed the Federal Water Pollution Control Act (FWPCA),[10] but its regulatory system and enforcement powers seemed to be inadequate.

---

8. The EPA has also issued rules to regulate hazardous air pollutants emitted by landfills. 40 C.F.R. Sections 60.750–759.

9. 33 U.S.C. Sections 401–418.

10. 33 U.S.C. Sections 1251–1387.

The Clean Water Act

In 1972, amendments to the FWPCA—known as the Clean Water Act—established the following goals: (1) make waters safe for swimming, (2) protect fish and wildlife, and (3) eliminate the discharge of pollutants into the water. The amendments set specific time schedules, which were extended by amendment in 1977 and by the Water Quality Act of 1987.[11] Under these schedules, the EPA limits the discharge of various types of pollutants based on the technology available for controlling them. The 1972 act also requires municipal and industrial polluters to apply for permits before discharging wastes into navigable waters.

Under the act, violators are subject to a variety of civil and criminal penalties. Depending on the violation, civil penalties range from $10,000 per day to $25,000 per day, but not more than $25,000 per violation. Criminal penalties, which apply only if a violation was intentional, range from a fine of $2,500 per day and imprisonment for up to one year to a fine of $1 million and fifteen years' imprisonment. Injunctive relief and damages can also be imposed. The polluting party can be required to clean up the pollution or pay for the cost of doing so.

Before a company can obtain a federal license to "discharge" into navigable waters, the affected state must certify that water-protection laws will not be violated. Can a river routed through a hydropower dam "discharge" into itself for purposes of the Clean Water Act, thus requiring the dam's owner to obtain state approval? That was the question in the following case.

---

11. This act amended 33 U.S.C. Section 1251.

Case 21.2   S. D. Warren Co. v. Maine Board of Environmental Protection

Supreme Court of the United States, 2006.
547 U.S. 370, 126 S.Ct. 1843, 164 L.Ed.2d 625.
www.findlaw.com/casecode/supreme.html[a]

BACKGROUND AND FACTS   S. D. Warren Company generates electricity for a paper mill by operating hydropower dams on the Presumpscot River, which runs for twenty-five miles through southern Maine. Each dam creates a pond, from which water funnels into a canal, through turbines, and back to the riverbed. Operating the dams requires a license from the Federal Energy Regulatory Commission (FERC). Under the Clean Water Act, a license for an activity that causes a "discharge" into navigable waters requires the state in which the discharge occurs to certify that the discharge will not violate water-quality standards. To renew the licenses for the dams in 1999, Warren applied for certification from the Maine Department of Environmental Protection. The agency told Warren to maintain a minimum stream flow in the river and to allow passage for migratory fish and eels. Warren appealed to the state Board of Environmental Protection, which upheld the requirements. FERC licensed the dams subject to the conditions. Warren filed a suit in a Maine state court against the state agency, arguing that the dams do not result in discharges. The court ruled in the agency's favor. Warren appealed to the Supreme Judicial Court of Maine, the state's highest court, which affirmed the lower court's ruling. Warren then appealed to the United States Supreme Court.

a. In the "Browse" section, click on "2006 Decisions." When that page opens, scroll to the name of the case and click on it to read the opinion.

IN THE WORDS OF THE COURT . . . Justice SOUTER delivered the opinion of the Court.

*   *   *   *

   The dispute turns on the meaning of the word "discharge," the key to the state certification requirement under [the Clean Water Act]. *   *   * *Since it is neither defined in the statute nor a term of art, we are left to construe it in accordance with its ordinary or natural meaning.* [Emphasis added.]

CASE 21.2–CONTINUED

CASE 21.2–CONTINUED

When it applies to water, "discharge" commonly means a "flowing or issuing out," [according to] Webster's New International Dictionary * * * *, and this ordinary sense has consistently been the meaning intended when this Court has used the term in prior water cases.* [Emphasis added.]

* * * *

* * * This Court has not been alone, for the Environmental Protection Agency (EPA) and FERC have each regularly read "discharge" as having its plain meaning and thus covering releases from hydroelectric dams. Warren is, of course, entirely correct in cautioning us that because neither the EPA nor FERC [Federal Energy Regulatory Commission] has formally settled the definition, or even set out agency reasoning, these expressions of agency understanding do not command deference from this Court. But even so, the administrative usage of "discharge" in this way confirms our understanding of the everyday sense of the term.

* * * *

Congress passed the Clean Water Act to "restore and maintain the chemical, physical, and biological integrity of the Nation's waters," the "national goal" being to achieve "water quality which provides for the protection and propagation of fish, shellfish, and wildlife and provides for recreation in and on the water." To do this, the Act does not stop at controlling the "addition of pollutants," but deals with "pollution" generally, which Congress defined to mean "the man-made or man-induced alteration of the chemical, physical, biological, and radiological integrity of water."

The alteration of water quality as thus defined is a risk inherent in limiting river flow and releasing water through turbines. Warren itself admits that its dams "can cause changes in the movement, flow, and circulation of a river * * * caus[ing] a river to absorb less oxygen and to be less passable by boaters and fish." And several [other parties who submitted briefs in this case] alert us to the chemical modification caused by the dams, with "immediate impact on aquatic organisms, which of course rely on dissolved oxygen in water to breathe." Then there are the findings of the Maine Department of Environmental Protection that led to this appeal:

> The record in this case demonstrates that Warren's dams have caused long stretches of the natural river bed to be essentially dry and thus unavailable as habitat for indigenous populations of fish and other aquatic organisms; that the dams have blocked the passage of eels and sea-run fish to their natural spawning and nursery waters; that the dams have eliminated the opportunity for fishing in long stretches of river, and that the dams have prevented recreational access to and use of the river.

Changes in the river like these fall within a State's legitimate legislative business, and the Clean Water Act provides for a system that respects the States' concerns. [Emphasis added.]

State certifications under [the Clean Water Act] are essential in the scheme to preserve state authority to address the broad range of pollution * * * .

Reading [the Clean Water Act] to give "discharge" its common and ordinary meaning preserves the state authority apparently intended.

DECISION AND REMEDY   The United States Supreme Court affirmed the decision of the Maine Supreme Judicial Court. Under the Clean Water Act, an activity that may result in a "discharge" into navigable waters under a federal license requires state approval. Water flowing through a hydropower dam operated under a federal license constitutes such a "discharge."

WHAT IF THE FACTS WERE DIFFERENT?   Would the result in this case have been different if the water flowing through the turbines of Warren's dams improved in quality before returning to the river? Why or why not?

THE GLOBAL DIMENSION   Should the Court have ruled differently if the discharge had been released into international or foreign waters rather than into the waters of the United States? Explain.

Standards for Equipment

Regulations, for the most part, specify that the *best available control technology,* or BACT, be installed. The EPA issues guidelines as to what equipment meets this standard; essentially, the guidelines require the most effective pollution-control equipment available. New sources must install BACT equipment before beginning operations. Existing sources are subject to timetables for the installation of BACT equipment and must immediately install equipment that utilizes the *best practical control technology,* or BPCT. The EPA also issues guidelines as to what equipment meets this standard.

Wetlands

The Clean Water Act prohibits the filling or dredging of **wetlands** unless a permit is obtained from the Army Corps of Engineers. The EPA defines *wetlands* as "those areas that are inundated or saturated by surface or ground water at a frequency and duration sufficient to support, and that under normal circumstances do support, a prevalence of vegetation typically adapted for life in saturated soil conditions." In recent years, the EPA's broad interpretation of what constitutes a wetland subject to the regulatory authority of the federal government has generated substantial controversy.

EXAMPLE #5 One of the most controversial regulations was the "migratory-bird rule" issued by the Army Corps of Engineers. Under this rule, any bodies of water that could affect interstate commerce, including seasonal ponds or waters "used or suitable for use by migratory birds" that fly over state borders, were "navigable waters" subject to federal regulation as wetlands under the Clean Water Act. The rule was challenged in a case brought by a group of communities that wanted to build a landfill in a tract of land northwest of Chicago. The Army Corps of Engineers refused to grant a permit for the landfill on the ground that the shallow ponds formed a habitat for migratory birds. Ultimately, the United States Supreme Court held that the Army Corps of Engineers had exceeded its authority under the Clean Water Act. The Court stated that it was not prepared to hold that isolated and seasonal ponds, puddles, and "prairie potholes" become "navigable waters of the United States" simply because they serve as a habitat for migratory birds.[12] □

The United States Supreme Court revisited the issue of wetlands in 2006, again scaling back the reach of the Clean Water Act. Two disputes had arisen as to whether certain properties in Michigan could be developed by the owners or were protected as wetlands, and the Court consolidated the cases on appeal. One involved property deemed to be wetlands because it was near an unnamed ditch that flowed into the Sutherland-Oemig Drain, which ultimately connected to Lake St. Clair. The other involved acres of marshy land, some of which was adjacent to a creek that flowed into a river, which flowed into yet another river, eventually reaching Saginaw Bay. Although the lower courts had concluded that both properties were wetlands under the Clean Water Act, the Supreme Court reversed these decisions. The Court held that the act covers "only those wetlands with a continuous surface connection to bodies that are waters of the United States in their own right." The Court further held that navigable waters under the act include only relatively permanent, standing or flowing bodies of water— not intermittent or temporary flows of water.[13]

WETLANDS
Water-saturated areas of land that are designated by a government agency (such as the Army Corps of Engineers or the Environmental Protection Agency) as protected areas that support wildlife. Such areas cannot be filled in or dredged by private parties without a permit.

"Among the treasures of our land is water—fast becoming our most valuable, most prized, most critical resource."
—DWIGHT D. EISENHOWER,
1890–1969
(Thirty-fourth president of the United States, 1953–1961)

---

12. *Solid Waste Agency of Northern Cook County v. U.S. Army Corps of Engineers,* 531 U.S. 159, 121 S.Ct. 675, 148 L.Ed.2d 576 (2001).
13. *Rapanos v. United States,* 547 U.S. 715, 126 S.Ct. 2208, 165 L.Ed.2d 159 (2006).

Drinking Water

Another statute governing water pollution is the Safe Drinking Water Act of 1974.[14] This act requires the EPA to set maximum levels for pollutants in public water systems. Public water system operators must come as close as possible to meeting the EPA's standards by using the best available technology that is economically and technologically feasible. The EPA is particularly concerned about contamination from underground sources. Pesticides and wastes leaked from landfills or disposed of in underground injection wells are among the more than two hundred pollutants known to exist in groundwater used for drinking in at least thirty-four states. Many of these substances are associated with cancer and may cause damage to the central nervous system, liver, and kidneys.

The act was amended in 1996 to give the EPA more flexibility in setting regulatory standards. These amendments also imposed additional requirements on suppliers of drinking water. Each supplier must send to every household it supplies with water an annual statement describing the source of its water, the level of any contaminants contained in the water, and any possible health concerns associated with the contaminants.

Ocean Dumping

The Marine Protection, Research, and Sanctuaries Act of 1972[15] (popularly known as the Ocean Dumping Act), as amended in 1983, regulates the transportation and dumping of material into ocean waters. It prohibits entirely the ocean dumping of radiological, chemical, and biological warfare agents and high-level radioactive waste. The act also establishes a permit program for transporting and dumping other materials, and designates certain areas as marine sanctuaries. Each violation of any provision in the Ocean Dumping Act may result in a civil penalty of up to $50,000. A knowing violation is a criminal offense that may result in a $50,000 fine, imprisonment for not more than a year, or both. The court may also grant an injunction to prevent an imminent or continuing violation of the Ocean Dumping Act.

Clean-up efforts in Alaska's Prince William Sound following the Exxon Valdez *oil spill. How did this disaster change the law regarding oil spills? Who can be held responsible for clean-up costs?*
(Exxon Valdez Oil Spill Trustee Council/National Oceanic & Atmospheric Adminstration)

Oil Pollution

In response to the worst oil spill in North American history—more than 10 million gallons of oil that leaked into Alaska's Prince William Sound from the *Exxon Valdez* supertanker—Congress passed the Oil Pollution Act of 1990.[16] Under this act, any onshore or offshore oil facility, oil shipper, vessel owner, or vessel operator that discharges oil into navigable waters or onto an adjoining shore can be liable for clean-up costs, as well as damages.

Under the act, damage to natural resources, private property, and the local economy, including the increased cost of providing public services, is compensable. The penalties range from $2 million to $350 million, depend-

---

14. 42 U.S.C. Sections 300f to 300j-25.
15. 16 U.S.C. Sections 1401–1445.
16. 33 U.S.C. Sections 2701–2761.

ing on the size of the vessel and on whether the oil spill came from a vessel or an offshore facility. The party held responsible for the clean-up costs can bring a civil suit for contribution from other potentially liable parties. The act also decreed that by the year 2011, oil tankers using U.S. ports must be double hulled to limit the severity of accidental spills.

TOXIC CHEMICALS

Originally, most environmental clean-up efforts were directed toward reducing smog and making water safe for fishing and swimming. Today, the control of toxic chemicals used in agriculture and in industry has become increasingly important.

Pesticides and Herbicides

The Federal Insecticide, Fungicide, and Rodenticide Act (FIFRA) of 1947 regulates pesticides and herbicides.[17] Under FIFRA, pesticides and herbicides must be (1) registered before they can be sold, (2) certified and used only for approved applications, and (3) used in limited quantities when applied to food crops. The EPA can cancel or suspend registration of substances that are identified as harmful and may also inspect factories where the chemicals are made. Under 1996 amendments to FIFRA, the risk to people of developing cancer from any kind of exposure to the substance, including eating food that contains pesticide residues, must be no more than one in a million.[18]

It is a violation of FIFRA to sell a pesticide or herbicide that is either unregistered or has had its registration canceled or suspended. It is also a violation to sell a pesticide or herbicide with a false or misleading label or to destroy or deface any labeling required under the act. Penalties for commercial dealers include imprisonment for up to one year and a fine of no more than $25,000. Farmers and other private users of pesticides or herbicides who violate the act are subject to a $1,000 fine and incarceration for up to thirty days.

Can a state regulate the sale and use of federally registered pesticides? Tort suits against pesticide manufacturers were common long before the enactment of FIFRA in 1947 and continued to be a feature of the legal landscape at the time of FIFRA's amendments. Until the following case, however, the United States Supreme Court had never considered whether that statute preempts claims arising under state law.

> *"All property in this country is held under the implied obligation that the owner's use of it shall not be injurious to the community."*
> —JOHN HARLAN, 1899–1971
> (Associate justice of the United States Supreme Court, 1955–1971)

17. 7 U.S.C. Sections 135–136y.
18. 21 U.S.C. Section 346a.

Case 21.3 | **Bates v. Dow Agrosciences, LLC**

Supreme Court of the United States, 2005.
544 U.S. 431, 125 S.Ct. 1788, 161 L.Ed.2d 687.
www.findlaw.com/casecode/supreme.html[a]

BACKGROUND AND FACTS The Environmental Protection Agency (EPA) conditionally registered Strongarm, a new weed-killing pesticide, on March 8, 2000.[b] Dow Agrosciences, LLC, immediately sold Strongarm to Texas peanut farmers, who normally plant their crops around May 1. The label stated, "Use of Strongarm is recommended in all areas where peanuts are grown." When the farmers applied Strongarm to their fields, the pesticide damaged their crops while failing to

a. In the "Browse" section, click on "2005." In the result, click on the name of the case to access the opinion.

b. Strongarm might more commonly be called an herbicide, but FIFRA classifies it as a pesticide.

CASE 21.3–CONTINUED

CASE 21.3–CONTINUED

control the growth of weeds. After unsuccessfully attempting to negotiate with Dow, the farmers announced their intent to sue Strongarm's maker for violations of Texas state law. Dow filed a suit in a federal district court against the peanut farmers, asserting that FIFRA preempted their claims. The court issued a summary judgment in Dow's favor. The farmers appealed to the U.S. Court of Appeals for the Fifth Circuit, which affirmed the lower court's judgment. The farmers appealed to the United States Supreme Court.

IN THE WORDS OF THE COURT . . . Justice *STEVENS* delivered the opinion of the Court.

* * * *

Under FIFRA * * * , a pesticide is misbranded if its label contains a statement that is false or misleading in any particular, including a false or misleading statement concerning the efficacy of the pesticide. *A pesticide is also misbranded if its label does not contain adequate instructions for use, or if its label omits necessary warnings or cautionary statements.* [Emphasis added.]

* * * *

* * * [Section] 136v provides:

(a) * * * A State may regulate the sale or use of any federally registered pesticide or device in the State, but only if and to the extent [that] the regulation does not permit any sale or use prohibited by [FIFRA].

(b) * * * Such State shall not impose or continue in effect any requirements for labeling or packaging in addition to or different from those required under [FIFRA].

* * * *

* * * *Nothing in the text of FIFRA would prevent a State from making the violation of a federal labeling or packaging requirement a state offense,* thereby imposing its own sanctions on pesticide manufacturers who violate federal law. The imposition of state sanctions for violating state rules that merely duplicate federal requirements is equally consistent with the text of [Section] 136v. [Emphasis added.]

* * * *

* * * For a particular state rule to be preempted, it must satisfy two conditions. First, it must be a requirement "for labeling or packaging"; rules governing the design of a product, for example, are not preempted. Second, it must impose a labeling or packaging requirement that is "in addition to or different from those required under [FIFRA]." A state regulation requiring the word "poison" to appear in red letters, for instance, would not be preempted if an EPA regulation imposed the same requirement.

* * * Rules that require manufacturers to design reasonably safe products, to use due care in conducting appropriate testing of their products, to market products free of manufacturing defects, and to honor their express warranties or other contractual commitments plainly do not qualify as requirements for "labeling or packaging." None of these common-law rules requires that manufacturers label or package their products in any particular way. Thus, petitioners' claims for defective design, defective manufacture, negligent testing, and breach of express warranty are not preempted.

* * * *

Dow * * * argues that [this] "parallel requirements" reading of [Section] 136v(b) would "give juries in 50 States the authority to give content to FIFRA's misbranding prohibition, establishing a crazy-quilt of anti-misbranding requirements * * * ." Conspicuously absent from the submissions by Dow * * * is any plausible alternative interpretation of "in addition to or different from" that would give that phrase meaning. Instead, they appear to favor reading those words out of the statute * * * . This amputated version of [Section] 136v(b) would no doubt have clearly and succinctly commanded the preemption of *all* state requirements concerning labeling. *That Congress added the remainder of the provision is evidence of its intent to draw a distinction between state labeling requirements that are preempted and those that are not.* [Emphasis added.]

* * * *

In sum, under our interpretation, [Section] 136v(b) * * * preempts competing state labeling standards—imagine 50 different labeling regimes prescribing the color, font size, and wording of warnings—that would create significant inefficiencies for manufacturers. The provision also preempts any statutory or common-law rule that would impose a labeling requirement that diverges from those set out in FIFRA * * * . *It does not, however, preempt any state rules that are fully consistent with federal requirements.* [Emphasis added.]

DECISION AND REMEDY   The United States Supreme Court vacated the lower court's judgment. A state can regulate the sale and use of federally registered pesticides to the extent that it does not permit anything that FIFRA prohibits, but a state cannot impose any requirements for labeling or packaging in addition to or different from those that FIFRA requires. The Court remanded the case, however, for further proceedings subject to this standard, concerning certain state law claims "on which we have not received sufficient briefing."

WHAT IF THE FACTS WERE DIFFERENT?   Suppose that FIFRA required Strongarm's label to include the word *CAUTION*, and the Texas peanut farmers filed their claims under a state regulation that required the label to use the word *DANGER*. Would the result have been different?

THE LEGAL ENVIRONMENT DIMENSION   According to the Court's interpretation, what is required for a state regulation or rule to be preempted under FIFRA? Why is this significant?

Toxic Substances

The first comprehensive law covering toxic substances was the Toxic Substances Control Act of 1976.[19] The act was passed to regulate chemicals and chemical compounds that are known to be toxic—such as asbestos and polychlorinated biphenyls, popularly known as PCBs—and to institute investigation of any possible harmful effects from new chemical compounds. The regulations authorize the EPA to require that manufacturers, processors, and other organizations planning to use chemicals first determine their effects on human health and the environment. The EPA can regulate substances that potentially pose an imminent hazard or an unreasonable risk of injury to health or the environment. The EPA may require special labeling, limit the use of a substance, set production quotas, or prohibit the use of a substance altogether.

A hazardous waste disposal team cleans up toxic chemicals that spilled from a semitrailer onto a public highway.
(Courtesy of Minnesota Pollution Control Agency)

HAZARDOUS WASTE DISPOSAL

Some industrial, agricultural, and household wastes pose more serious threats than others. If not properly disposed of, these toxic chemicals may present a substantial danger to human health and the environment. If released into the environment, they may contaminate public drinking water resources.

19. 15 U.S.C. Sections 2601–2692.

Resource Conservation and Recovery Act

In 1976, Congress passed the Resource Conservation and Recovery Act (RCRA)[20] in reaction to the growing concern over the effects of hazardous waste materials on the environment. The RCRA required the EPA to determine which forms of solid waste should be considered hazardous and to establish regulations to monitor and control hazardous waste disposal. The act also requires all producers of hazardous waste materials to label and package properly any hazardous waste to be transported. The RCRA was amended in 1984 and 1986 to decrease the use of land containment in the disposal of hazardous waste and to require smaller generators of hazardous waste to comply with the act.

Under the RCRA, a company may be assessed a civil penalty of up to $25,000 for each violation.[21] Penalties are based on the seriousness of the violation, the probability of harm, and the extent to which the violation deviates from RCRA requirements. Criminal penalties include fines of up to $50,000 for each day of violation, imprisonment for up to two years (in most instances), or both.[22] Criminal fines and the period of imprisonment can be doubled for certain repeat offenders.

Superfund

POTENTIALLY RESPONSIBLE PARTY (PRP)
A party liable for the costs of cleaning up a hazardous waste disposal site under the Comprehensive Environmental Response, Compensation, and Liability Act (CERCLA). Any person who generated the hazardous waste, transported it, owned or operated the waste site at the time of disposal, or owns or operates the site at the present time may be responsible for some or all of the clean-up costs.

In 1980, Congress passed the Comprehensive Environmental Response, Compensation, and Liability Act (CERCLA),[23] commonly known as Superfund, to regulate the clean-up of leaking hazardous waste disposal sites. A special federal fund was created for that purpose. Because of its impact on the business community, the act is presented as this chapter's *Landmark in the Legal Environment* feature.

Superfund provides that when a release or a threatened release of hazardous chemicals from a site occurs, the EPA can clean up the site and recover the cost of the clean-up from the following persons: (1) the person who generated the wastes disposed of at the site, (2) the person who transported the wastes to the site, (3) the person who owned or operated the site at the time of the disposal, or (4) the current owner or operator. A person falling within one of these categories is referred to as a **potentially responsible party (PRP).**

Liability under Superfund is usually joint and several—that is, a person who generated *only a fraction of the hazardous waste* disposed of at the site may nevertheless be liable for *all* of the clean-up costs. CERCLA authorizes a party who has incurred clean-up costs to bring a "contribution action" against any other person who is liable or potentially liable for a percentage of the costs.

Preventing Legal Disputes

Purchasers of property can be held liable under Superfund for the cost of cleaning up hazardous wastes dumped by previous owners. It is therefore important to research the property that you are interested in buying to find out whether the property has been contaminated by hazardous wastes. Realize that it is up to you as the purchaser to raise environmental issues before signing any agreements—sellers,

---

20. 42 U.S.C. Sections 6901 *et seq.*
21. 42 U.S.C. Section 6928(a).
22. 42 U.S.C. Section 6928(d).
23. 42 U.S.C. Sections 9601–9675.

The origins of the Comprehensive Environmental Response, Compensation, and Liability Act (CERCLA) of 1980, commonly referred to as Superfund, can be traced to drafts that the Environmental Protection Agency (EPA) started to circulate in 1978.

Dump Sites Characterized as "Ticking Time Bombs"

EPA officials emphasized the necessity of new legislation by pointing to what they characterized as "ticking time bombs"—dump sites around the country that were ready to explode and injure the public with toxic fumes. The popular press was also running prominent stories about hazardous waste dump sites at the time. The New York Love Canal disaster first made headlines in 1978 when residents in the area complained about health problems, contaminated sludge oozing into their basements, and chemical "volcanoes" erupting in their yards. These problems were the result of approximately 21,000 tons of chemicals that Hooker Chemical had dumped into the canal from 1942 to 1953. By the middle of May 1980, the Love Canal situation was making the national news virtually every day, and it remained in the headlines for a month.

CERCLA—Its Purpose and Primary Elements

The basic purpose of CERCLA, which was amended in 1986, is to regulate the clean-up of leaking hazardous waste disposal sites. The act has four primary elements:

- It established an information-gathering and analysis system that enables the government to identify chemical dump sites and determine the appropriate action.

- It authorized the EPA to respond to hazardous substance emergencies and to arrange for the clean-up of a leaking site directly if the persons responsible for the problem fail to clean up the site.

- It created a Hazardous Substance Response Trust Fund (Superfund) to pay for the clean-up of hazardous sites using funds obtained through taxes on certain businesses.

- It allowed the government to recover the cost of clean-up from persons who were (even remotely) responsible for hazardous substance releases.

APPLICATION TO TODAY'S LEGAL ENVIRONMENT

The provisions of CERCLA profoundly affect today's businesses. Virtually any business decision relating to the purchase and sale of property, for example, requires an analysis of previous activities on the property to determine whether they resulted in contamination. Additionally, to avoid violating CERCLA, owners and managers of manufacturing plants must be extremely careful in arranging for the removal and disposal of any hazardous waste materials. Unless Congress significantly changes CERCLA and the way that it is implemented, businesses will continue to face potentially extensive liability for violations under this act.

RELEVANT WEB SITES

To locate information on the Web concerning Superfund, go to this text's Web site at **www.cengage.com/blaw/let**, select "Chapter 21," and click on "URLs for Landmarks."

---

title insurance companies, and real estate brokers will rarely pursue such matters. Although current property owners who pay clean-up costs can sue previous owners for a contribution to those costs, litigation is expensive and its outcome uncertain. Clearly, a more prudent course is to investigate the history of use of the land before buying it. When feasible, hire a private environmental site inspector to determine, at a minimum, whether the land has any obvious signs of contamination. Purchasers who perform good faith environmental inspections on property generally also receive lighter penalties and fines in the event that a violation later surfaces. ■

Reviewing . . .   **Protecting the Environment**

In the late 1980s, residents of Lake Caliopa, Minnesota, began noticing an unusually high number of lung ailments among their population. A group of concerned local citizens pooled their resources and commissioned a study of the frequency of these health conditions per capita compared with national averages. The study concluded that the frequency of asthma, bronchitis, and emphysema in Lake Caliopa was four to seven times the population nationwide. During the study period, citizens began expressing concerns about the large volume of smog emitted by the Cotton Design apparel manufacturing plant on the outskirts of town. The plant had opened its production facility two miles east of town beside the Tawakoni River in 1997 and employed seventy full-time workers by 2008. Just downstream on the Tawakoni River, the city of Lake Caliopa operated a public waterworks facility, which supplied all city residents with water.

In August 2008, the Minnesota Pollution Control Agency required Cotton Design to install new equipment to control air and water pollution. In May 2009, thirty citizens brought a class-action lawsuit in a Minnesota state court against Cotton Design for various respiratory ailments allegedly caused or compounded by smog from Cotton Design's factory. Using the information presented in the chapter, answer the following questions.

1. Under the common law, what would each plaintiff be required to identify in order to be given relief by the court?

2. Are air-quality regulations typically overseen by federal, state, or local governments?

3. What standard for limiting emissions into the air does Cotton Design's pollution-control equipment have to meet?

4. What information must the city send to every household that the city supplies with water?

Key Terms

environmental impact
   statement (EIS) 691
nuisance 688

potentially responsible
   party (PRP) 704

toxic tort 689
wetlands 699

Chapter Summary

Common Law Actions (See pages 688–689.)	1. *Nuisance*–A common law doctrine under which people may bring actions against pollution-causing activities. An action is permissible only if an individual suffers a harm separate and distinct from that of the general public.
	2. *Negligence and strict liability*–Parties may recover damages for injuries sustained as a result of a firm's pollution-causing activities if it can be demonstrated that the harm was a foreseeable result of the firm's failure to exercise reasonable care (negligence); businesses engaging in ultrahazardous activities are liable for whatever injuries the activities cause, regardless of whether the firms exercise reasonable care.
Federal, State, and Local Regulation (See pages 689–692.)	Activities affecting the environment are controlled at the local and state levels through regulations relating to land use, the disposal and recycling of garbage and waste, and pollution-causing activities in general. Federal regulation involves the following:
	1. *Environmental protection agencies*–The most well known of the agencies regulating environmental law is the federal Environmental Protection Agency (EPA), which was created in 1970 to coordinate federal environmental programs. The EPA administers most federal environmental policies and statutes.
	2. *Assessing environmental impact*–The National Environmental Policy Act of 1969 imposes environmental responsibilities on all federal agencies and requires the preparation of an environmental impact statement (EIS) for every major federal action. An EIS must analyze the action's impact on the environment, its adverse effects and possible alternatives, and its irreversible effects on environmental quality.
Air Pollution (See pages 692–696.)	1. *Mobile sources*–Automobiles and other vehicles are mobile sources of air pollution, and the EPA establishes pollution-control standards and time schedules for meeting these standards.

Air Pollution—Continued

2. *Stationary sources*—The Clean Air Act requires the EPA to list on a prioritized schedule all regulated hazardous air pollutants that are emitted from stationary sources. These include substances such as asbestos, mercury, and vinyl chloride that are known to cause damage to humans. Major sources of air pollution are required to use the *maximum achievable control technology* to reduce emissions.

Water Pollution
(See pages 696–701.)

1. *Clean Water Act*—This 1972 act amended an earlier federal law by setting specific time schedules to improve water quality. The act also requires cities and businesses to obtain a permit before discharging waste into navigable waters. Regulations specify that the *best available control technology* be installed in all new sources of water pollution, whereas existing sources must use the *best practical control technology.* The EPA issues guidelines as to what equipment meets these standards.

2. *Wetlands*—Certain water-saturated areas are designated wetlands and protected from dredging or filling without a permit. This is intended to provide natural habitat to support wildlife, such as migratory birds.

3. *Drinking water*—Federal law sets maximum levels for pollutants in public water systems and requires public systems to use the best available technology to prevent contamination from underground sources. Each supplier of public water must send to every household it supplies with water an annual statement describing the water's source, the level of any contaminants, and any possible health concerns associated with these contaminants.

4. *Ocean dumping*—Federal law prohibits the dumping of radiological, chemical, and biological warfare agents and high-level radioactive waste into the ocean.

5. *Oil pollution*—Federal law provides that any offshore or onshore oil facility, oil shipper, vessel owner, or vessel operator that discharges oil into navigable waters or onto a shoreline is liable for clean-up costs and damages.

Toxic Chemicals
(See pages 701–703.)

The federal government regulates the pesticides and herbicides that can be used in agriculture, as well as the use and transportation of chemical compounds known to be toxic.

Hazardous Waste Disposal
(See pages 703–705.)

Federal laws regulate the disposal of certain types of industrial, agricultural, and household wastes that present serious dangers to human health and the environment. These hazardous wastes must be properly labeled and packaged before they can be transported. Moreover, under the Superfund, when a hazardous substance is released into the environment, the EPA can clean up the site and recover the costs from a broad array of potentially responsible parties.

For Review

1. Under what common law theories can polluters be held liable?
2. What is an environmental impact statement, and who must file one?
3. What does the Environmental Protection Agency do?
4. What major federal statutes regulate air and water pollution?
5. What is Superfund? To what categories of persons does liability under Superfund extend?

Questions and Case Problems

21–1. Clean Air Act. Some scientific research indicates that there is no safe level of exposure to a cancer-causing agent. In theory, even one molecule of such a substance has the potential for causing cancer. Section 112 of the Clean Air Act requires that all cancer-causing substances be regulated to ensure a margin of safety. Some environmental groups have argued that all emissions of such substances must be eliminated if a margin of safety is to be reached. Such a total elimination would likely shut down many major U.S. industries. Should the Environmental Protection Agency totally eliminate all emissions of cancer-causing chemicals? Discuss.

Question with Sample Answer

21–2. Fruitade, Inc., is a processor of a soft drink called Freshen Up. Fruitade uses returnable bottles, which it cleans with a special acid to allow for further beverage processing. The acid is diluted with water and then allowed to pass into a navigable stream. Fruitade crushes its broken bottles and throws the crushed glass into the stream. Discuss fully any environmental laws that Fruitade has violated.

For a sample answer to Question 21–2, go to Appendix I at the end of this text.

21–3. Common Law Actions. Moonbay is a home-building corporation that primarily develops retirement communities. Farmtex owns a number of feedlots in Sunny Valley. Moonbay purchased 20,000 acres of farm-land in the same area and began building and selling homes on this acreage. In the meantime, Farmtex continued to expand its feedlot business, and eventually only 500 feet separated the two operations. Because of the odor and flies from the feedlots, Moonbay found it difficult to sell the homes in its development. Moonbay wants to enjoin Farmtex from operating its feedlots in the vicinity of the retirement home development. Under what common law theory would Moonbay file this action? Has Farmtex violated any federal environmental laws? Discuss.

21–4. Environmental Impact Statement. Greers Ferry Lake is in Arkansas, and its shoreline is under the management of the U.S. Army Corps of Engineers, which is part of the U.S. Department of Defense (DOD). The Corps's 2000 Shoreline Management Plan (SMP) rezoned numerous areas along the lake, authorized the Corps to issue permits for the construction of new boat docks in the rezoned areas, increased by 300 percent the area around habitable structures that could be cleared of vegetation, and instituted a Wildlife Enhancement Permit to allow limited modifications of the shoreline. In relation to the SMP's adoption, the Corps issued a Finding of No Significant Impact, which declared that no environmental impact statement (EIS) was necessary. The Corps issued thirty-two boat dock construction permits under the SMP before Save Greers Ferry Lake, Inc., filed a suit in a federal district court against the DOD, asking the court to, among other things, stop the Corps from acting under the SMP and

order it to prepare an EIS. What are the requirements for an EIS? Is an EIS needed in this case? Explain. [*Save Greers Ferry Lake, Inc. v. Department of Defense,* 255 F.3d 498 (8th Cir. 2001)]

21–5. CERCLA. Beginning in 1926, Marietta Dyestuffs Co. operated an industrial facility in Marietta, Ohio, to make dyes and other chemicals. In 1944, Dyestuffs became part of American Home Products Corp. (AHP), which sold the Marietta facility to American Cyanamid Co. in 1946. In 1950, AHP sold the rest of the Dyestuffs assets and all of its stock to Goodrich Co., which immediately liquidated the acquired corporation. Goodrich continued to operate the dissolved corporation's business, however. Cyanamid continued to make chemicals at the Marietta facility, and in 1993, it created Cytec Industries, Inc., which expressly assumed all environmental liabilities associated with Cyanamid's ownership and operation of the facility. Cytec spent nearly $25 million on clean-up costs and filed a suit in a federal district court against Goodrich to recover, under CERCLA, a portion of the costs attributable to the clean-up of hazardous wastes that may have been discarded at the site between 1926 and 1946. Cytec filed a motion for summary judgment in its favor. Should the court grant Cytec's motion? Explain. [*Cytec Industries, Inc. v. B. F. Goodrich Co.,* 196 F.Supp.2d 644 (S.D. Ohio 2002)]

Case Problem with Sample Answer

21–6. William Gurley was the president and majority stockholder in Gurley Refining Co. (GRC). GRC bought used oil, treated it, and sold it. The refining process created a by-product residue of oily waste. GRC disposed of this waste by dumping it at, among other locations, a landfill in West Memphis, Arkansas. In February 1992, after detecting hazardous chemicals at the site, the Environmental Protection Agency (EPA) asked Gurley about his assets, the generators of the material disposed of at the landfill, site operations, and the structure of GRC. Gurley refused to respond, except to suggest that the EPA ask GRC. In October, the EPA placed the site on its clean-up list and again asked Gurley for information. When he still refused to respond, the EPA filed a suit in a federal district court against him, asking the court to impose a civil penalty. In February 1999, Gurley finally answered the EPA's questions. Under CERCLA, a court may impose a civil penalty "not to exceed $25,000 for each day of noncompliance against any person who unreasonably fails to comply" with an information request. Should the court assess a penalty in this case? Why or why not? [*United States v. Gurley,* 384 F.3d 316 (6th Cir. 2004)]

After you have answered Problem 21–6, compare your answer with the sample answer given on the Web site that accompanies this text. Go to www.cengage.com/blaw/let, select "Chapter 21," and click on "Case Problem with Sample Answer."

21–7. Clean Water Act. The Anacostia River, which flows through Washington, D.C., is one of the ten most polluted rivers in the country. For bodies of water such as the Anacostia, the Clean Water Act (CWA) requires states (which, under the CWA, include the District of Columbia) to set a "total maximum daily load" (TMDL) for pollutants. A TMDL is to be set "at a level necessary to implement the applicable water-quality standards with seasonal variations." The Anacostia contains biochemical pollutants that consume oxygen, putting the river's aquatic life at risk for suffocation. In addition, the river is murky, stunting the growth of plants that rely on sunlight and impairing recreational use. The Environmental Protection Agency (EPA) approved one TMDL limiting the annual discharge of oxygen-depleting pollutants and a second limiting the seasonal discharge of pollutants contributing to turbidity. Neither TMDL limited daily discharges. Friends of the Earth, Inc. (FoE), asked a federal district court to review the TMDLs. What is FoE's best argument in this dispute? What is the EPA's likely response? What should the court rule, and why? [*Friends of Earth, Inc. v. Environmental Protection Agency,* 446 F.3d 140 (D.C.Cir. 2006)]

21–8. Environmental Impact Statement. The fourth largest crop in the United States is alfalfa, of which 5 percent is exported to Japan. RoundUp Ready alfalfa is genetically engineered to resist glyphosate, the active ingredient in the herbicide RoundUp. The U.S. Department of Agriculture (USDA) regulates genetically engineered agricultural products through the Animal and Plant Health Inspection Service (APHIS). APHIS concluded that RoundUp Ready alfalfa does not have any harmful health effects on humans or livestock and deregulated it. Geertson Seed Farms and others filed a suit in a federal district court against Mike Johanns (the secretary of the USDA) and others, asserting that APHIS's decision required the preparation of an environmental impact statement (EIS). The plaintiffs argued, among other things, that the introduction of RoundUp Ready alfalfa might significantly decrease the availability of, or even eliminate, all nongenetically engineered varieties. The plaintiffs were concerned that the RoundUp Ready alfalfa might contaminate standard alfalfa because alfalfa is pollinated by bees, which can travel as far as two miles from a pollen source. If contamination occurred, farmers would not be able to market "contaminated" varieties as "organic," which would affect the sales of "organic" livestock and exports to Japan, which does not allow the import of glyphosate-resistant alfalfa. Should an EIS be prepared in this case? Why or why not? [*Geertson Seed Farms v. Johanns,* __ F.Supp.2d __ (N.D.Cal. 2007)]

A Question of Ethics

21–9. In the Clean Air Act, Congress allowed California, which has particular problems with clean air, to adopt its own standard for emissions from cars and trucks, subject to the approval of the Environmental Protection Agency (EPA) according to certain criteria. Congress also allowed other states to adopt California's standard after the EPA's approval. In 2004, in an effort to address global warming, the California Air Resources Board amended the state's standard to attain "the maximum feasible and cost-effective reduction of GHG [greenhouse gas] emissions from motor vehicles." The regulation, which applies to new passenger vehicles and light-duty trucks for 2009 and later, imposes stricter limits on emissions of carbon dioxide through 2016. While EPA approval was pending, Vermont and other states adopted similar standards. Green Mountain Chrysler Plymouth Dodge Jeep and other auto dealers, automakers, and associations of automakers filed a suit in a federal district court against George Crombie (secretary of the Vermont Agency of Natural Resources) and others, seeking relief from the state regulations. [*Green Mountain Chrysler Plymouth Dodge Jeep v. Crombie,* 508 F.Supp.2d 295 (D.Vt. 2007)]

1. Under the Environmental Policy and Conservation Act (EPCA) of 1975, the National Highway Traffic Safety Administration sets fuel economy standards for new cars. The plaintiffs argued, among other things, that the EPCA, which prohibits states from adopting separate fuel economy standards, preempts Vermont's GHG regulation. Do the GHG rules equate to the fuel economy standards? Discuss.

2. Do Vermont's rules tread on the efforts of the federal government to address global warming internationally? Who should regulate GHG emissions? The federal government? The state governments? Both? Neither? Why?

3. The plaintiffs claimed that they would go bankrupt if they were forced to adhere to the state's GHG standards. Should they be granted relief on this basis? Does history support their claim? Explain.

Critical-Thinking Economic Question

21–10. It has been estimated that for every dollar spent cleaning up hazardous waste sites, administrative agencies spend seven dollars in overhead. Can you think of any way to trim the administrative costs associated with the clean-up of contaminated sites?

Interacting with the Internet

For updated links to resources available on the Web, as well as a variety of other materials, visit this text's Web site at

www.cengage.com/blaw/let

For information on the EPA's standards, guidelines, and regulations, go to the EPA's Web site at

www.epa.gov

To learn about the RCRA's "buy-recycled" requirements and other steps that the federal government has taken toward "greening the environment," go to

www.epa.gov/cpg

The Law Library of the Indiana University School of Law provides numerous links to online environmental law sources. Go to

www.law.indiana.edu/lawlibrary/index.shtml

PRACTICAL INTERNET EXERCISES

Go to this text's Web site at **www.cengage.com/blaw/let**, select "Chapter 21," and click on "Practical Internet Exercises." There you will find the following Internet research exercises that you can perform to learn more about the topics covered in this chapter.

Practical Internet Exercise 21–1: LEGAL PERSPECTIVE—**Nuisance Law**
Practical Internet Exercise 21–2: MANAGEMENT PERSPECTIVE—**Complying with Environmental Regulations**
Practical Internet Exercise 21–3: ETHICAL PERSPECTIVE—**Environmental Justice**

BEFORE THE TEST

Go to this text's Web site at **www.cengage.com/blaw/let**, select "Chapter 21," and click on "Interactive Quizzes." You will find a number of interactive questions relating to this chapter.

Chapter 22

Land-Use Control and Real Property

CHAPTER OBJECTIVES

After reading this chapter, you should be able to answer the following questions:

1. What are the different types of ownership interests in real property?

2. How can ownership interests in real property be transferred?

3. What is a leasehold estate, and how does it arise?

4. What are the respective duties of the landlord and tenant concerning the use and maintenance of leased property?

5. What limitations may be imposed on the rights of property owners?

CONTENTS

- The Nature of Real Property
- Ownership of Real Property
- Transfer of Ownership
- Leasehold Estates
- Landlord-Tenant Relationships
- Land-Use Control

" The right of property is the most sacred of all the rights of citizenship. "

— JEAN-JACQUES ROUSSEAU,
1712–1778 (French writer and philosopher)

From earliest times, property has provided a means for survival. Primitive peoples lived off the fruits of the land, eating the vegetation and wildlife. Later, as the wildlife was domesticated and the vegetation cultivated, property provided pasturage and farmland. In the twelfth and thirteenth centuries, the power of feudal lords was determined by the amount of land that they held; the more land they held, the more powerful they were. After the age of feudalism passed, property continued to be an indicator of family wealth and social position. In the Western world, the protection of an individual's right to his or her property has become, in the words of Jean-Jacques Rousseau in the chapter-opening quotation, one of the "most sacred of all the rights of citizenship."

Real property (sometimes called *realty* or *real estate*) means the land and everything permanently attached to the land. Everything else is **personal property** (or *personalty*). In this chapter, we first examine the nature of real property. We then look at the various ways in which real property can be owned and at how ownership rights in real property are transferred from one person to another. We also include a discussion of leased property and landlord-tenant relationships. Although real property includes more than land, it is generally referred to simply as "land." Hence, the dominion over land ownership and use that we discuss in the concluding pages of this chapter is commonly referred to as *land-use control.*

REAL PROPERTY
Land and everything attached to it, such as vegetation and buildings.

PERSONAL PROPERTY
Property that is movable; any property that is not real property.

THE NATURE OF REAL PROPERTY

Real property consists of land and the buildings, plants, and trees that it contains. Real property also includes subsurface and air rights, as well as personal property that has become permanently attached to real property. Whereas personal property is movable, real property—also called *real estate* or *realty*—is immovable.

Land

Land includes the soil on the surface of the earth and the natural products or artificial structures that are attached to it. It further includes all the waters contained on or under the earth's surface and the airspace above it. In other words, absent a contrary statute or case law, a landowner has the right to everything existing permanently below the surface of his or her property to the center of the earth and above it to the sky (subject to certain qualifications).

Airspace and Subsurface Rights

The owner of real property has rights to the airspace above the land, as well as to the soil and minerals underneath it. Limitations on either airspace rights or subsurface rights normally have to be indicated on the document that transfers title at the time of purchase. When no such limitations, or *encumbrances,* are noted, a purchaser can normally expect to have an unlimited right to possession of the property.

Airspace Rights   Early cases involving airspace rights dealt with such matters as whether a telephone wire could be run across a person's property when the wire did not touch any of the property and whether a bullet shot over a person's land constituted trespass. Today, disputes concerning airspace rights may involve the right of commercial and private planes to fly over property and the right of individuals and governments to seed clouds and produce rain artificially. Flights over private land normally do not violate property rights unless the flights are so low and so frequent that they directly interfere with the owner's enjoyment and use of the land. Leaning walls or buildings and projecting eave spouts or roofs may also violate the airspace rights of an adjoining property owner.

"The meek shall inherit the earth, but not the mineral rights."
—J. PAUL GETTY, 1892–1976
(American entrepreneur and industrialist)

Subsurface Rights   In many states, land ownership may be separated, in that the surface of a piece of land and the subsurface may have different owners. Subsurface rights can be extremely valuable, as these rights include the ownership of minerals, oil, and natural gas. Subsurface rights would be of little value, however, if the owner could not use the surface to exercise those rights. Hence, a subsurface owner will have a right (called a *profit,* to be discussed later in this chapter) to go onto the surface of the land to, for example, discover and mine minerals.

When the ownership is separated into surface and subsurface rights, each owner can pass title to what she or he owns without the consent of the other owner. Of course, conflicts can arise between a surface owner's use and the subsurface owner's need to extract minerals, oil, or natural gas. One party's interest may become subservient (secondary) to the other party's interest either by statute or case law. At common law and generally today, if the owners of the subsurface rights excavate (dig), they are absolutely liable if their excavation causes the surface to collapse. Depending on the circumstances, the excavators may also be liable for any damage to structures on the land. Many states have statutes that extend excavators' liability to include damage to structures on the property. Typically, these statutes provide precise requirements for excavations of various depths.

Plant Life and Vegetation

Plant life, both natural and cultivated, is also considered to be real property. In many instances, the natural vegetation, such as trees, adds greatly to the value of the realty. When a parcel of land is sold and the land has growing crops on it, the sale includes the crops, unless otherwise specified in the sales contract. When crops are sold by themselves, however, they are considered to be personal property or goods. Consequently, the sale of crops is a sale of goods, and therefore it is governed by the Uniform Commercial Code (see Chapter 11) rather than by real property law.

Fixtures

Certain personal property can become so closely associated with the real property to which it is attached that the law views it as real property. Such property is known as a **fixture**—a thing *affixed* to realty, meaning it is attached to it by roots; embedded in it; permanently situated on it; or permanently attached by means of cement, plaster, bolts, nails, or screws. The fixture can be physically attached to real property, be attached to another fixture, or even be without any actual physical attachment to the land (such as a statue). As long as the owner intends the property to be a fixture, normally it will be a fixture.

FIXTURE
A thing that was once personal property but has become attached to real property in such a way that it takes on the characteristics of real property and becomes part of that real property.

Fixtures are included in the sale of land if the sales contract does not provide otherwise. The sale of a house includes the land and the house and the garage on the land, as well as the cabinets, plumbing, and windows. Because these are permanently affixed to the property, they are considered to be a part of it. Unless otherwise agreed, however, the curtains and throw rugs are not included. Items such as drapes and window-unit air conditioners are difficult to classify. Thus, a contract for the sale of a house or commercial realty should indicate which items of this sort are included in the sale to avoid disputes.

EXAMPLE #1 A farm had an eight-tower center-pivot irrigation system, bolted to a cement slab and connected to an underground well. The bank held a mortgage note on the farm secured by "all buildings, improvements, and fixtures." The farm's owners had also used the property as security for other loans, but the contracts for those loans did not specifically mention fixtures or the irrigation system. Later, when the farmers were unable to repay their debts and filed for bankruptcy, a dispute arose between the bank and another creditor over the irrigation system. Ultimately, a court held that the irrigation system was a fixture because it was firmly attached to the land and integral to the operation of the farm. Therefore, the bank's security interest had priority over that of the other creditor.[1] □

Preventing Legal Disputes

One way to avoid certain disputes over real property is to make sure that any contract specifically lists which fixtures the parties intend to be included in a sale or transfer or subjected to a security interest. Without such a list, the parties may have very different ideas as to what is being transferred with the real property (or included as collateral for a loan). In the end, it is much simpler and less expensive to itemize fixtures in a contract than to engage in litigation. ■

OWNERSHIP OF REAL PROPERTY

Ownership of property is an abstract concept that cannot exist independently of the legal system. No one can actually possess or *hold* a piece of land, the air above it, the earth below it, and all the water contained on it. One can only possess

---

1. *In re Sand & Sage Farm & Ranch, Inc.*, 266 Bankr. 507 (D.Kans. 2001).

"Few . . . men own their property. The property owns them."

—ROBERT G. INGERSOLL, 1833–1899
(American politician and lecturer)

rights in real property. Numerous rights are involved in real property ownership, which is why property ownership is often viewed as a bundle of rights. These rights include the right to possess the property and the right to dispose of the property—by sale, gift, rental, and lease, for example. Traditionally, ownership interests in real property were referred to as *estates in land,* which include fee simple estates, life estates, and leasehold estates. We examine these estates in land, forms of concurrent ownership, and certain other interests in real property that is owned by others in the following subsections.

Ownership in Fee Simple

FEE SIMPLE ABSOLUTE
An ownership interest in land in which the owner has the greatest possible aggregation of rights, privileges, and power. Ownership in fee simple absolute is limited absolutely to a person and his or her heirs.

A person who holds the entire bundle of rights is said to be the owner in **fee simple absolute.** In a fee simple absolute, the owner has the greatest aggregation of rights, privileges, and power possible. The owner can give the property away or dispose of the property by *deed* (the instrument used to transfer property, as discussed later in this chapter) or by a will. When there is no will, the fee simple passes to the owner's legal heirs on her or his death. A fee simple absolute is potentially infinite in duration and is assigned forever to a person and her or his heirs without limitation or condition.[2] The owner has the right of *exclusive* possession and use of the property.

The rights that accompany a fee simple absolute include the right to use the land for whatever purpose the owner sees fit. Of course, other laws, including applicable zoning, noise, and environmental laws, may limit the owner's ability to use the property in certain ways.

In the following case, the court had to decide whether the noise—rock and roll music, conversation, and clacking pool balls—coming from a local bar (called a "saloon" during the days of cowboys in the United States) unreasonably interfered with a neighboring property owner's rights.

---

2. Note that in *fee simple defeasible,* ownership in fee simple will automatically terminate if a stated event occurs, such as when property is conveyed (transferred) to a school board only as long as it is used for school purposes.

Case 22.1 **Biglane v. Under the Hill Corp.**

Mississippi Supreme Court, 2007.
949 So.2d 9.
www.mssc.state.ms.us[a]

BACKGROUND AND FACTS In 1967, Nancy and James Biglane bought and refurbished a building at 27 Silver Street in Natchez, Mississippi, and opened the lower portion as a gift shop. In 1973, Andre Farish and Paul O'Malley bought the building next door, at 25 Silver Street, and opened the Natchez Under the Hill Saloon (the Saloon). Later, the Biglanes converted

the upper floors of their building into an apartment and moved in. Despite installing insulated walls and windows, locating the bedroom on the side of the building away from the Saloon, and placing the air-conditioning unit on the side nearest the Saloon, the Biglanes had a problem: the noise of the Saloon kept them wide awake at night. During the summer, the Saloon, which had no air-conditioning, opened its windows and doors, and live music echoed up and down the street. The Biglanes asked the Saloon to turn the music down, and the Saloon did so: thicker windows were installed, the loudest band was replaced, and the other bands were asked to keep their output below a certain level of decibels. Still dissatisfied, the Biglanes filed a suit in a Mississippi state court against the Saloon. The court enjoined the defendant from opening doors or windows when music was playing and ordered it to prevent its patrons from loitering in the street. Both parties appealed to the Mississippi Supreme Court.

---

a. In the center of the page, click on the "Search this site" link. On the next page, click on "Plain English." When that page opens, in the "Enter the ISYS Plain English query:" box, type "2005-CA-01751-SCT" and click on "Search." In the result, click on the first item in the list that includes that number to access the opinion. The Mississippi Supreme Court maintains this Web site.

IN THE WORDS OF THE COURT . . . *DIAZ*, Justice, for the Court.

* * * *

An entity is subject to liability * * * *when its conduct is a legal cause of an invasion of another's interest in the private use and enjoyment of land and that invasion is* * * * *intentional and unreasonable* * * * . [Emphasis added.]

* * * [The trial court] found ample evidence that the Biglanes frequently could not use or enjoy their property—significantly, that Mrs. Biglane often slept away from the apartment on weekends to avoid the noise and that she could not have her grandchildren over on the weekends because of the noise. The audiologist [one who diagnoses hearing problems] who testified for the Biglanes concluded that the noise levels were excessive and unreasonable * * * .

* * * *

* * * The trial court weighed the fact that the Biglanes knew or should have known that there was going to be some sort of noise associated with living within five feet of a * * * saloon which provides live music on the weekends.

* * * *

* * * *A reasonable use of one's property cannot be construed to include those uses which produce obnoxious noises, which in turn result in a material injury to owners of property in the vicinity, causing them to suffer substantial annoyance, inconvenience, and discomfort.* [Emphasis added.]

Accordingly, even a lawful business—which the Under the Hill Saloon certainly is—may * * * [not interfere] with its neighbors' enjoyment of their property. We recognize that each * * * case must be decided upon its own peculiar facts, taking into consideration the location and the surrounding circumstances. Ultimately, it is not necessary that other property owners should be driven from their dwellings, because it is enough that the enjoyment of life and property is rendered materially uncomfortable and annoying.

* * * *

In the case at hand, the trial court exercised its power to permit continued operation of the Saloon while setting conditions to its future operation. Namely, it found that the Saloon could not operate its business with its doors and windows opened during any time that amplified music is being played inside the saloon. The * * * court found that such a limitation is reasonable in that it should help contain the noise within the saloon, and should discourage the bar patrons from congregating or loitering in the streets outside of the saloon.

From a review of the record it is clear that the * * * court balanced the interests between the Biglanes and the Saloon in a quest for an equitable remedy that allowed the couple to enjoy their private apartment while protecting a popular business and tourist attraction from over-regulation.

DECISION AND REMEDY The Mississippi Supreme Court affirmed the lower court's injunction. The Saloon unreasonably interfered with the Biglanes' rights. "One landowner may not use his land so as to unreasonably annoy, inconvenience, or harm others."

THE ETHICAL DIMENSION At one point in their dispute, the Biglanes blocked off two parking lots that served the Saloon. Was this an unreasonable interference with the Saloon's rights? Explain.

THE LEGAL ENVIRONMENT DIMENSION Could repulsive odors emanating from a neighbor's property constitute unreasonable interference with a property owner's rights? Why or why not?

Life Estates

A **life estate** is an estate that lasts for the life of some specified individual. A **conveyance,** or transfer of real property, "to A for his life" creates a life estate.[3] In a life estate, the life tenant has fewer rights of ownership than the holder of a fee simple, because the rights necessarily cease to exist on the life tenant's death.

The life tenant has the right to use the land, provided that he or she commits no *waste* (injury to the land). In other words, the life tenant cannot injure the land in a manner that would adversely affect its value. The life tenant can use the land to harvest crops or, if mines and oil wells are already on the land, can extract minerals and oil from it, but the life tenant cannot exploit the land by creating new wells or mines. The life tenant is entitled to any rents or royalties generated by the realty and has other rights, such as the right to mortgage or lease the life estate. These cannot extend beyond the life of the tenant, however. In addition, with few exceptions, the owner of a life estate has an exclusive right to possession during his or her life.

Along with these rights, the life tenant also has some duties—to keep the property in repair and to pay property taxes. In short, the owner of the life estate has the same rights as a fee simple owner except that he or she must maintain the value of the property during his or her tenancy, less the decrease in value resulting from the normal use of the property allowed by the life tenancy.

Concurrent Ownership

Persons who share ownership rights simultaneously in particular property (including real property and personal property) are said to be concurrent owners. There are two principal types of **concurrent ownership:** *tenancy in common* and *joint tenancy.* Concurrent ownership rights can also be held as community property in some states, although this type of concurrent ownership is less common.

Tenancy in Common   The term **tenancy in common** refers to a form of co-ownership in which each of two or more persons owns an undivided interest in the property. The interest is undivided because each tenant has rights in the whole property. On the death of a tenant in common, that tenant's interest in the property passes to her or his heirs.

EXAMPLE #2 Four friends purchase a condominium unit in Hawaii together as tenants in common. This means that each of them has an ownership interest (one-fourth) in the whole. If one of the four owners, Trey, dies a year after the purchase, his ownership interest passes to his heirs (his wife and children, for example) rather than to the other tenants in common.■

Unless the co-tenants have agreed otherwise, a tenant in common can transfer her or his interest in the property to another without the consent of the remaining co-owners. Generally, it is presumed that a co-tenancy is a tenancy in common unless there is a clear intention to establish a joint tenancy (discussed next).

Joint Tenancy   In a **joint tenancy,** each of two or more persons owns an undivided interest in the property, but a deceased joint tenant's interest passes to the

---

3. A less common type of life estate is created by the conveyance "to A for the life of B." This is known as an *estate pur autre vie,* or an estate for the duration of the life of another.

surviving joint tenant or tenants. The right of a surviving joint tenant to inherit a deceased joint tenant's ownership interest—referred to as a *right of survivorship*—distinguishes a joint tenancy from a tenancy in common. EXAMPLE #3 Jerrold and Eva are married and purchase a house as joint tenants. The title to the house clearly expresses the intent to create a joint tenancy because it says "to Jerrold and Eva as joint tenants with right of survivorship." Jerrold has three children from a prior marriage. If Jerrold dies, his interest in the house automatically passes to Eva rather than to his children from the prior marriage. □

Although a joint tenant can transfer her or his rights by sale or gift to another without the consent of the other joint tenants, doing so terminates the joint tenancy. In such a situation, the person who purchases the property or receives it as a gift becomes a tenant in common, not a joint tenant. EXAMPLE #4 Three brothers—Brody, Saul, and Jacob—own a parcel as joint tenants. Brody is experiencing financial difficulties and sells his interest in the property to Beth. The sale terminates the joint tenancy, and now Beth, Saul, and Jacob hold the property as tenants in common. □

A joint tenant's interest can also be *levied against* (seized by court order) to satisfy the tenant's judgment creditors. If this occurs, the joint tenancy terminates, and the remaining owners hold the property as tenants in common. (Judgment creditors can also seize the interests of tenants in a tenancy in common.)

Community Property   Only a limited number of states[4] allow property to be owned by a married couple as **community property.** If property is held as community property, each spouse technically owns an undivided one-half interest in the property. This type of ownership applies to most property acquired by the husband or the wife during the course of the marriage. It generally does not apply to property acquired prior to the marriage or to property acquired by gift or inheritance during the marriage. After a divorce, community property is divided equally in some states and according to the discretion of the court in other states.

Nonpossessory Interests

In contrast to the types of property interests just described, some interests in land do not include any rights to possess the property. These interests are thus known as **nonpossessory interests.** Three forms of nonpossessory interests are easements, profits, and licenses.

An **easement** is the right of a person to make limited use of another person's real property without taking anything from the property. An easement, for example, can be the right to travel over another's property. In contrast, a **profit**[5] is the right to go onto land owned by another and take away some part of the land itself or some product of the land. EXAMPLE #5 Akmed is the owner of Sandy View. Akmed gives Carmen the right to go there and remove all the sand and gravel that she needs for her cement business. Carmen has a profit. □

In the context of real property, a **license** is the revocable right of a person to come onto another person's land. It is a personal privilege that arises from the

COMMUNITY PROPERTY
A form of concurrent ownership of property in which each spouse in a marriage technically owns an undivided one-half interest in property acquired during the marriage. This form of joint ownership occurs in only ten states and Puerto Rico.

NONPOSSESSORY INTEREST
In the context of real property, an interest in land that does not include any right to possess the property.

EASEMENT
A nonpossessory right to use another's property in a manner established by either express or implied agreement.

PROFIT
In real property law, the right to enter onto and remove things from the property of another (for example, the right to enter onto a person's land and remove sand and gravel from it).

LICENSE
In the context of real property, a revocable right or privilege of a person to come onto another person's land.

4. These states include Alaska, Arizona, California, Idaho, Louisiana, Nevada, New Mexico, Texas, Washington, and Wisconsin. Puerto Rico allows property to be owned as community property as well.
5. The term *profit*, as used here, does not refer to the "profits" made by a business firm. Rather, it means a gain or an advantage.

consent of the owner of the land and that can be revoked by the owner. A ticket to attend a movie at a theater is an example of a license. **EXAMPLE #6** A Broadway theater owner issues to Carla a ticket to see a play. If Carla is refused entry into the theater because she is improperly dressed, she has no right to force her way into the theater. The ticket is only a revocable license, not a conveyance of an interest in property.□

In essence, a license grants a person the authority to enter the land of another and perform a specified act or series of acts without obtaining any permanent interest in the land. What happens when a person with a license exceeds the authority granted and undertakes an action that is not permitted? That was the central issue in the following case.

Case 22.2   **Roman Catholic Church of Our Lady of Sorrows v. Prince Realty Management, LLC**

New York Supreme Court,
Appellate Division, Second Department, 2008.
47 A.D.3d 909, 850 N.Y.S.2d 569.

BACKGROUND AND FACTS   The Roman Catholic Church of Our Lady of Sorrows (the Church) and Prince Realty Management, LLC (Prince), own adjoining property in Queens County, New York. On August 19, 2005, the parties entered into an agreement by which the Church granted Prince a three-month license to use a three-foot strip of its property immediately adjacent to Prince's property. The license specifically authorized Prince to remove an existing chainlink fence on the licensed strip and to "put up plywood panels surrounding the construction site, including the [licensed strip]." The license also required that Prince restore the boundary line between the properties with a new brick fence. The purpose of the license was to allow Prince to erect a temporary plywood fence in order to protect Prince's property during the construction of a new building. During the term of the license, Prince installed structures consisting of steel piles and beams on the licensed property. The Church objected to the installation of these structures and repeatedly demanded that they be removed. The Church commenced an action to recover damages for breach of the license and for trespass. The trial court concluded that the Church had made a *prima facie* case showing that structures had been placed on its property by the defendant in violation of the license and that Prince had failed to dispute the plaintiff's claim that it had violated the agreement. Prince appealed.

IN THE WORDS OF THE COURT . . . *SKELOS*, J.P. [Justice Presiding]

*   *   *   *

The [trial court] properly granted the plaintiff summary judgment on its causes of action alleging breach of the license and trespass. *"A license, within the context of real property law, grants the licensee a revocable non-assignable privilege to do one or more acts upon the land of the licensor, without granting possession of any interest therein. A license is the authority to do a particular act or series of acts upon another's land, which would amount to a trespass without such permission."* Here, the evidentiary [related to the evidence] proof submitted by the plaintiff *   *   * established that the license granted the defendant a privilege to use a three-foot strip of its land for specified purposes, primarily consisting of the temporary erection of wooden fencing to protect the defendant's property during construction of a building, the removal of an existing chain link fence, and the installation of a new brick fence upon completion of the license. The plaintiff also submitted uncontroverted evidence that the defendant installed structures consisting of steel piles and beams on the licensed strip of property. Contrary to the defendant's contention, the license did not permit it to install structures of this nature on the plaintiff's property. Moreover, in opposition to the establishment of a *prima facie* case for summary judgment, the defendant offered no proof that the installation of these structures was reasonably related to its licensed use of the property. [Emphasis added.]

In addition, since the plaintiff established as a matter of law that the defendant violated the license by installing unauthorized structures on its property, the plaintiff also established as a matter of law that the defendant's installation of these structures constituted a trespass regardless of whether they were subsequently removed.

DECISION AND REMEDY   The New York appellate court held that the license did not permit the adjoining property owner (Prince) to install structures consisting of steel piles and beams on the licensed strip of property.

THE ETHICAL DIMENSION   The Church requested that the steel piles and beams be removed. The defendant resisted, but eventually did remove them. Was it still appropriate for the Church to file this lawsuit? Explain your answer.

THE LEGAL ENVIRONMENT DIMENSION   The Church sued for damages. What would be an appropriate calculation of those damages?

TRANSFER OF OWNERSHIP

Ownership of real property can pass from one person to another in a number of ways. Commonly, ownership interests in land are transferred by sale—the terms of the transfer are specified in a real estate sales contract. Often, real estate brokers or agents who are licensed by the state assist the buyers and sellers during sales transactions. (For a discussion of some issues involving online advertising by real estate professionals, see this chapter's *Online Developments* feature on the next page.) When real property is sold or transferred as a gift, title to the property is conveyed by means of a **deed**—the instrument of conveyance (transfer) of real property. We look here at voluntary transfers of real property and then consider some other ways in which ownership rights in real property can be transferred.

DEED
A document by which title to property (usually real property) is passed.

Listing Agreements

In a typical real estate transaction, the seller employs a real estate agent to find a buyer for the property by entering into a listing agreement with the agent. The listing agreement specifies the duration of the listing with that real estate agent, the terms under which the seller will sell the property, and the amount of commission the seller will pay. There are different types of listing agreements. If the contract gives the agent an exclusive right to sell the property, then it is an *exclusive agreement,* and only that real estate agent is authorized to sell the property for a specified period of time. In contrast, an *open listing* is nonexclusive; the seller agrees to pay a commission to the real estate agent who brings in a buyer. Thus, agents with other real estate firms may attempt to find a buyer and share in the commission with the listing agent.

Although many sales of real estate involve listing agreements, it is not necessary for a property owner to list the property with a real estate agent. Many owners offer their properties for sale directly without an agent. The ability to advertise real properties for sale via the Internet has made it easier for an owner to find a buyer without using an agent. Because an agent is not essential, listing agreements are not shown in Exhibit 22–1, which summarizes the steps involved in any sale of real property. (See page 721.)

The Internet has transformed the real estate business, just as it has transformed other industries. Today's real estate professionals market properties—and themselves—online. Given that the Internet knows no physical borders, what happens when an online advertisement reaches people outside the state in which the real estate professional is licensed? Is this illegal? Can the agent be sued for fraud if the ad contains misrepresentations?

State Licensing Statutes and Advertising

Every state requires any person (other than the owner) who sells or offers to sell real property in that state to obtain a license. To be licensed, a person normally must pass a state examination and pay a fee and then must take a minimum number of continuing education courses periodically (every year or two) to maintain the license. Usually, a person must also be licensed to list real property for sale or to negotiate the purchase, sale, lease, or exchange of real property or a business opportunity involving real property.[a] Often, a state agency, such as a real estate commission, is in charge of granting licenses and enforcing the laws and regulations governing real estate professionals.

State laws can differ on the exact activities that require a real estate license, though. Consider, for example, the problems faced by Stroman Realty, Inc., a licensed Realtor® in Texas. (The term *Realtor* is "a registered collective membership mark that identifies a real estate professional who is a member of the National Association of Realtors.") Stroman's business focused on reselling time shares (which allow the owner to use the property for a specified interval of time per year) on the secondary market. The company used a computerized service to match potential buyers with properties and maintained a Web site where buyers could view available times shares. Stroman advertised its time-share resale services both in print and via the Internet and frequently engaged in transactions involving parties in multiple states.

After a complaint from an Illinois resident, the Illinois agency in charge of enforcing licensing requirements sent Stroman a cease-and-desist letter. The agency stated that Stroman had engaged in a number of activities in Illinois that required a real estate license and ordered the company to stop these activities. Stroman filed a lawsuit asking a federal district court to stay (suspend) the administrative action, arguing that Illinois licensing law was unconstitutional and violated the dormant commerce clause (see Chapter 4). The federal court, however, refused to exercise jurisdiction on the constitutionality issue and dismissed Stroman's complaint. The court noted that the regulation of the real estate profession is clearly an important state interest and that Illinois was merely enforcing its licensing act when it took action against Stroman.[b]

Actions for Misrepresentations (Fraud)

Suppose that a real estate agent, either inadvertently or intentionally, makes a misstatement online about some important aspect of real property that is for sale. Someone, relying on the statements, responds to the ad and eventually contracts to buy the property, only to discover later that the ad misrepresented it. What remedies does the buyer have? In this situation, the buyer can complain to the state authority that granted the agent's license, and the state may even revoke the license. If the buyer wants to obtain damages or cancel the contract, however, he or she will have to sue the agent for fraud (see Chapters 5 and 11). At this point, jurisdictional problems may arise.

If the real estate agent and the buyer are located in different states and the Internet ad was the agent's only contact with the buyer's state, the buyer may have to travel to the agent's state to file the suit. Courts have reached different conclusions on the type of Internet advertising that permits a court to have jurisdiction over an out-of-state advertiser. In addition, courts may sometimes refuse to exercise jurisdiction over an out-of-state defendant even if they could do so (as the court did in the case just discussed involving Stroman Realty). Thus, people who are deceived when buying real property based on information in an online ad and who wish to sue the perpetrator of the fraud may be in a precarious position.

FOR CRITICAL ANALYSIS Do you think that the federal government should regulate the advertising of real property on the Internet to protect consumers from potential fraud? If so, what kind of regulations would be appropriate, and how might they be enforced?

---

a. See, for example, California Business and Professions Code Section 10131 and 26 Vermont Statutes Annotated Sections 2211-2212.

b. *Stroman Realty, Inc. v. Grillo,* 438 F.Supp.2d 929 (N.D.Ill. 2006); see also *Quilles v. Benden,* 2007 WL 1099477 (N.D.Ill. 2007).

Real Estate Sales Contracts

The sale of real estate is in some ways similar to the sale of goods because it involves a transfer of ownership, often with specific warranties. In a sale of real estate, however, certain formalities are observed that are not required in a sale of goods. The sale of real estate is a complicated transaction. Usually, after substantial negotiation between the parties (offers, counteroffers, responses), the parties enter into a detailed contract setting forth their agreement. A contract for a sale of land includes such terms as the purchase price, the type of deed the buyer will receive, the condition of the premises, and any items that will be included.

Unless the buyer pays cash for the property, the buyer must obtain financing through a mortgage loan. (As discussed in Chapter 13, a *mortgage* is a loan made by an individual or institution, such as a banking institution or trust company, for which the property is given as security.) Real estate sales contracts are often made contingent on the buyer obtaining financing at or below a specified rate of interest. The contract may also be contingent on the buyer selling other real property, the seller obtaining a survey and title insurance, and the property passing one or more inspections. Normally, the buyer is responsible for having the premises inspected for physical or mechanical defects and for insect infestation.

EXHIBIT 22-1 STEPS INVOLVED IN THE SALE OF REAL ESTATE

BUYER'S PURCHASE OFFER
Buyer offers to purchase Seller's property. The offer may be conditioned on Buyer's ability to obtain financing, on satisfactory inspections of the premises, on title examination, and the like. Included with the offer is earnest money, which will be placed in an escrow account.

SELLER'S RESPONSE
If Seller accepts Buyer's offer, then a contract is formed. Seller could also reject the offer or make a counteroffer that modifies Buyer's terms. Buyer may accept or reject Seller's counteroffer or make a counteroffer that modifies Seller's terms.

PURCHASE AND SALE AGREEMENT
Once an offer or a counteroffer is accepted, a purchase and sale agreement is formed.

TITLE EXAMINATION AND INSURANCE
Title examiner investigates and verifies Seller's rights in the property and discloses any claims or interests held by others. Buyer (and/or Seller) may purchase title insurance to protect against a defect in title.

FINANCING
Buyer may seek a mortgage loan to finance the purchase. Buyer agrees to grant lender an interest in the property as security for Buyer's indebtedness.

INSPECTION
Buyer has the property inspected for any physical problems, such as major structural or mechanical defects and insect infestation.

ESCROW
Buyer's purchase funds (including earnest money) are held in an escrow account by an escrow agent (such as a title company or a bank). This agent holds the deed transferring title received from Seller and any funds received from Buyer until all conditions of the sale have been met.

CLOSING
The escrow agent transfers the deed to Buyer and the proceeds of the sale to Seller. The proceeds are the purchase price less any amount already paid by Buyer and any closing costs to be paid by Seller. Included in the closing costs are fees charged for services performed by the lender, escrow agent, and title examiner. The purchase and sale of the property are complete.

CLOSING

The final step in the sale of real estate; also called *settlement* or *closing escrow.* The escrow agent coordinates the closing with the recording of deeds, the obtaining of title insurance, and other closing activities. A number of costs must be paid, in cash, at the time of closing, and they can range from several hundred to thousands of dollars, depending on the amount of the mortgage loan and other conditions of the sale.

ESCROW ACCOUNT

An account, generally held in the name of the depositor and the escrow agent, containing funds to be paid to a third person on fulfillment of the escrow condition.

Closing Date and Escrow   The contract usually fixes a date for performance, or **closing,** which is frequently four to twelve weeks after the contract is signed. On this day, the seller conveys the property to the buyer by delivering the deed to the buyer in exchange for payment of the purchase price. Deposits toward the purchase price normally are held in a special account, called an **escrow account,** until all of the conditions of sale have been met. Once the closing takes place, the funds remaining in the escrow account (after payments have been made to the escrow agency, title insurance company, and any lien holders) are transferred to the seller. The *escrow agent,* which may be a title company, bank, or special escrow company, acts as a neutral party in the sales transaction and facilitates the sale by allowing the buyer and seller to close the transaction without having to exchange documents and funds.

Implied Warranties in the Sale of New Homes   Most states recognize a warranty—the *implied warranty of habitability* (to be discussed later in this chapter in the context of leases)—in the sale of new homes. The seller of a new house warrants that it will be fit for human habitation even if the deed or contract of sale does not include such a warranty.

Essentially, the seller is warranting that the house is in reasonable working order and is of reasonably sound construction. Thus, under this warranty, the seller of a new home is in effect a guarantor of its fitness. In some states, the warranty protects not only the first purchaser but any subsequent purchaser as well.

Seller's Duty to Disclose Hidden Defects   In most jurisdictions, courts impose on sellers a duty to disclose any known defect that materially affects the value of the property and that the buyer could not reasonably discover. Failure to disclose such a material defect gives the buyer a right to *rescind* (cancel) the contract and to sue for damages based on fraud or misrepresentation.

A dispute may arise over whether the seller knew of the defect before the sale, and there is normally a limit to the time within which the buyer can bring a suit against the seller based on the defect. For instance, in Louisiana, where the following case was decided, the prescribed limit for a suit against a seller who knew, or can be presumed to have known, of the defect is one year from the day that the buyer discovered it. If the seller did not know of the defect, the limit is one year from the date of the sale.

Case 22.3 **Whitehead v. Humphrey**

Court of Appeal of Louisiana, Second Circuit, 2007.
954 So.2d 859.

BACKGROUND AND FACTS   Matthew Humphrey paid $44,000 for a home in Webster Parish, Louisiana, in the fall of 2003 and partially renovated it. Among other things, he replaced rotten wood underneath a bedroom window, leveled the porch, painted the interior, replaced sheetrock, tore out a wall, replaced a window, dug up eighty feet of field line for the septic system, and pumped out the septic tank. In February

2004, Terry and Tabitha Whitehead bought the house for $67,000. A few months after they moved in, problems began to develop with the air-conditioning unit, the fireplace, and the plumbing in the bathrooms. In May 2005, they discovered rotten wood behind the tile in the bathroom and around the front porch. In October, the Whiteheads filed a suit in a Louisiana state court against Humphrey, seeking to rescind the sale. The court awarded the plaintiffs the cost of repairing the fireplace ($1,675) and replacing some of the bad wood ($7,695). The Whiteheads appealed to a state intermediate appellate court.

IN THE WORDS OF THE COURT . . . *CARAWAY*, J. [Judge]

*   *   *   *

Terry Whitehead testified that when they were looking at the house to buy, the yard was a mess because all of the field lines for the sewer system had been dug up. However, he did not realize at that time that the septic tank was located under the driveway. As part of her pre-inspection of the house, Tabitha Whitehead testified that she flushed both of the toilets and they both worked.

The Whiteheads' initial problem concerned the master bathroom and began three or four months after they moved into the house. When the water backed up in the main bathroom in the spring of 2004, Tabitha called Roto-Rooter to correct the flow. It was then that she learned the septic tank was located under the driveway. This meant that the traffic across the driveway could cause problems with the tank and lines.

In May 2005 *   *   * the Whiteheads *   *   * began using the rear bathroom and experienced the same backing-up problem. At that time, the Whiteheads consulted Cook's Plumbing which provided the Whiteheads with an estimate totaling $12,000 which included relocation of the septic system and correction of other problems.

This evidence reveals that prior to the sale, the vendor and vendee were alerted to an issue regarding the sewer system. Corrective actions were taken, and no problems concerning the flushing of the toilets and flowage through the underground system prevented the Whiteheads from completing their purchase. *From this evidence, the ruling of the trial court *   *   * can be upheld from the view that neither side understood that a latent defect remained unresolved.* [Emphasis added.]

*   *   *   *

Accordingly, we find no manifest error in the trial court's factual determination that the Whiteheads discovered that the sewer system remained a problem with their residence in the spring of 2004, and therefore their failure to have filed suit within one year of that discovery caused [the limitations period] to run against that claim.

On the other hand, the trial court expressly found that Humphrey had knowledge of the rotten boards or sills underneath the house which were improperly repaired by Humphrey prior to the sale. *   *   * The evidence showed that the Whiteheads first discovered this problem in May 2005, five months prior to [their law]suit.

*   *   *   *

The trial court's judgment refused to rescind the sale and awarded a reduction in price based upon the cost of repairs of the defects in the fireplace and the wooden sills. From our review of the nature of these two defects, we find that the court properly used its discretion in rejecting rescission, and appellants' assignment of error seeking rescission and return of the sale price is without merit.

DECISION AND REMEDY   The state intermediate appellate court affirmed the lower court's conclusions regarding the defects in the Whiteheads' home. Rescission was not warranted for the sewer problems because the Whiteheads waited too long after their discovery to file a claim against Humphrey. The other defects "could be repaired with relative ease" and the "costs of those repairs were a small fraction of the sale price."

THE ETHICAL DIMENSION   Should the court have rescinded the sale despite the running of the limitations period on the Whiteheads' sewer claim? Why or why not?

THE LEGAL ENVIRONMENTAL DIMENSION   In Louisiana, a seller who knows of a defect and does not inform a buyer can be liable for the buyer's attorneys' fees in a suit based on that defect. Did Humphrey qualify as such a "bad faith" seller in this case? Explain.

Deeds

Possession and title to land are passed from person to person by means of a *deed*—the instrument of conveyance of real property. A deed is a writing signed by an owner of real property by which title to it is transferred to another.[6] Deeds must meet certain requirements, but unlike a contract, a deed does not have to be supported by legally sufficient consideration. Gifts of real property are common, and they require deeds even though there is no consideration for the gift. To be valid, a deed must include the following:

1. The names of the *grantor* (the giver or seller) and the *grantee* (the donee or buyer).
2. Words evidencing the intent to convey (for example, "I hereby bargain, sell, grant, or give"). No specific words are necessary, and if the deed does *not* specify the type of ownership being transferred, it presumptively transfers ownership in fee simple absolute.
3. A legally sufficient description of the land. The description must include enough detail to distinguish the property being conveyed from every other parcel of land. The property can be identified by reference to an official survey or recorded plat map, or each boundary can be described by *metes and bounds*. **Metes and bounds** is a system of measuring boundary lines by the distance between two points, often using physical features of the local geography (for example, "beginning at the southwesterly intersection of Court and Main Streets, then west 40 feet to the fence, then south 100 feet, then northeast approximately 120 feet back to the beginning").
4. The grantor's (and usually his or her spouse's) signature.
5. Delivery of the deed.

METES AND BOUNDS

A system of measuring boundary lines by the distance between two points, often using physical features of the local geography, such as roads, intersections, rivers, or bridges. The legal descriptions of real property contained in deeds often are phrased in terms of metes and bounds.

Warranty Deeds   Different types of deeds provide different degrees of protection against defects of title. A **warranty deed** makes the greatest number of warranties and thus provides the greatest protection for the buyer, or grantee. In most states, special language is required to create a general warranty deed; normally, the deed must include a written promise to protect the buyer against all claims of ownership of the property. Warranty deeds commonly include a number of *covenants,* or promises, that the grantor makes to the grantee.

A *covenant of seisin*[7] and a *covenant of the right to convey* warrant that the seller has title to the estate that the deed describes and the power to convey the estate, respectively. The covenant of seisin specifically assures the buyer that the seller has the purported quantity and quality of property. A *covenant against encumbrances* is a covenant that the property being sold or conveyed is not subject to any outstanding rights or interests that will diminish the value of the land, except as explicitly stated. Examples of common encumbrances include mortgages, liens, profits, easements, and private deed restrictions on the use of the land.

A *covenant of quiet enjoyment* guarantees that the buyer will not be disturbed in his or her possession of the land by the seller or any third persons. **EXAMPLE #7** Julio sells a two-acre lot and office building by warranty deed. Subsequently, a

WARRANTY DEED

A deed in which the seller assures (warrants to) the buyer that the grantor has title to the property conveyed in the deed, that there are no encumbrances on the property other than what the seller has represented, and that the buyer will enjoy quiet possession of the property; a deed that provides the greatest amount of protection for the grantee.

---

6. Note that in some states when a person purchases real property, the bank or lender receives a *trust deed* on the property until the homeowner pays off the mortgage. Despite its name, a trust deed is not used to transfer property. Instead, it is similar to a mortgage in that the lender holds the property as security for a loan.

7. Pronounced *see*-zuhn.

third person shows better title than Julio had and proceeds to evict the buyer. Here, the covenant of quiet enjoyment has been breached, and the buyer can sue to recover the purchase price of the land plus any other damages incurred as a result of the eviction.□

Quitclaim Deeds A **quitclaim deed** offers the least amount of protection against defects in the title. Basically, a quitclaim deed conveys to the buyer whatever interest the seller had; so, if the seller had no interest, then the buyer receives no interest. Quitclaim deeds are often used when the seller is uncertain as to the extent of his or her rights in the property.

A quitclaim deed can and often does serve as a release of the grantor's interest in a particular parcel of property. **EXAMPLE #8** After ten years of marriage, Sandi and Jim are getting a divorce. During the marriage, Sandi purchased a parcel of waterfront property next to her grandparents' home in Louisiana. Jim helped make some improvements to the property, but he is not sure what ownership interests, if any, he has in the property because Sandi used her own funds (acquired before the marriage) to purchase the lot. Jim agrees to quitclaim the property to Sandi as part of the divorce settlement, releasing any interest he might have in that piece of property.□

Recording Statutes

Every jurisdiction has **recording statutes,** which allow deeds to be recorded. Recording a deed gives notice to the public that a certain person is now the owner of a particular parcel of real estate. Thus, prospective buyers can check the public records to see whether there have been earlier transactions creating interests or rights in specific parcels of real property. Placing everyone on notice as to the identity of the true owner is intended to prevent the previous owners from fraudulently conveying the land to other purchasers. Deeds are recorded in the county in which the property is located. Many state statutes require that the grantor sign the deed in the presence of two witnesses before it can be recorded.

Will or Inheritance

Property that is transferred on an owner's death is passed either by will or by state inheritance laws. If the owner of land dies with a will, the land passes in accordance with the terms of the will. If the owner dies without a will, state inheritance statutes prescribe how and to whom the property will pass.

Adverse Possession

A person who wrongfully possesses (by occupying or using) the real property of another may eventually acquire title to it through **adverse possession.** Adverse possession is a means of obtaining title to land without delivery of a deed and without the consent of—or payment to—the true owner. Thus, adverse possession is a method of involuntarily transferring title to the property from the true owner to the adverse possessor.

Essentially, when one person possesses the real property of another for a certain statutory period of time (three to thirty years, with ten years being most common), that person acquires title to the land. For property to be held adversely, four elements must be satisfied:

QUITCLAIM DEED
A deed intended to pass any title, interest, or claim that the seller may have in the property but not warranting that such title is valid. A quitclaim deed offers the least amount of protection against defects in the title.

RECORDING STATUTE
A statute that allows deeds, mortgages, and other real property transactions to be recorded so as to provide notice to future purchasers or creditors of an existing claim on the property.

ADVERSE POSSESSION
The acquisition of title to real property by occupying it openly, without the consent of the owner, for a period of time specified by a state statute. The occupation must be actual, open, notorious, exclusive, and in opposition to all others, including the owner.

1. Possession must be *actual and exclusive;* that is, the possessor must take sole physical occupancy of the property.
2. The possession must be *open, visible, and notorious,* not secret or clandestine. The possessor must occupy the land for all the world to see.
3. Possession must be *continuous and peaceable for the required period of time.* This requirement means that the possessor must not be interrupted in the occupancy by the true owner or by the courts.
4. Possession must be *hostile and adverse.* In other words, the possessor must claim the property as against the whole world. He or she cannot be living on the property with the permission of the owner.

There are a number of public-policy reasons for the adverse possession doctrine. These include society's interest in resolving boundary disputes, in determining title when title to property is in question, and in ensuring that real property remains in the stream of commerce. More fundamentally, policies behind the doctrine include punishing owners who do not take action when they see adverse possession and rewarding possessors for putting land to productive use.

LEASEHOLD ESTATES

Often, real property is used by those who do not own it. A **lease** is a contract by which the owner of real property (the landlord, or lessor) grants to a person (the tenant, or lessee) an exclusive right to use and possess the property, usually for a specified period of time, in return for rent or some other form of payment. Property in the possession of a tenant is referred to as a **leasehold estate.**

The respective rights and duties of the landlord and tenant that arise under a lease agreement will be discussed shortly. Here we look at the types of leasehold estates, or tenancies, that can be created when real property is leased.

Fixed-Term Tenancy, or Tenancy for Years

A **fixed-term tenancy,** also called a *tenancy for years,* is created by an express contract by which property is leased for a specified period of time, such as a day, a month, a year, or a period of years. Signing a one-year lease to occupy an apartment, for instance, creates a fixed-term tenancy. Note that the term need not be specified by date and can be conditioned on the occurrence of an event, such as leasing a cabin for the summer or an apartment during Mardi Gras. At the end of the period specified in the lease, the lease ends (without notice), and possession of the apartment returns to the lessor. If the tenant dies during the period of the lease, the lease interest passes to the tenant's heirs as personal property. Often, leases include renewal or extension provisions.

Periodic Tenancy

A **periodic tenancy** is created by a lease that does not specify how long it is to last but does specify that rent is to be paid at certain intervals. This type of tenancy is automatically renewed for another rental period unless properly terminated. **EXAMPLE #9** Kayla enters a lease with Capital Properties. The lease states, "Rent is due on the tenth day of every month." This provision creates a periodic tenancy from month to month.◻ This type of tenancy can also extend from week to week or from year to year.

Under the common law, to terminate a periodic tenancy, the landlord or tenant must give at least one period's notice to the other party. If the tenancy extends from month to month, for example, one month's notice must be given prior to the last month's rent payment. State statutes may require a different period for notice of termination in a periodic tenancy, however.

Tenancy at Will

When a leasehold interest is created in which either party can terminate the tenancy without notice, it is called a **tenancy at will.** This type of tenancy can arise if a landlord rents certain property to a tenant "for as long as both agree" or allows a person to live on the premises without paying rent. Tenancy at will is rare in today's world because most state statutes require a landlord to provide some period of notice to terminate a tenancy (as previously noted). States may also require a landowner to have sufficient cause (reason) to end a residential tenancy. Certain events, such as the death of either party or the voluntary commission of waste by the tenant, automatically terminate a tenancy at will.

TENANCY AT WILL
A type of tenancy under which either party can terminate the tenancy without notice; usually arises when a tenant who has been under a tenancy for years retains possession, with the landlord's consent, after the tenancy for years has terminated.

LANDLORD-TENANT RELATIONSHIPS

In the past several decades, landlord-tenant relationships have become much more complex, as has the law governing them. Generally, the law has come to apply contract doctrines, such as those relating to implied warranties and unconscionability, to the landlord-tenant relationship. Increasingly, landlord-tenant relationships have become subject to specific state and local statutes and ordinances as well. In 1972, in an effort to create more uniformity in the law governing landlord-tenant relationships, the National Conference of Commissioners on Uniform State Laws issued the Uniform Residential Landlord and Tenant Act (URLTA). Twenty-one states have adopted variations of the URLTA.

A landlord-tenant relationship is established by a lease contract. A lease contract may be oral or written. In most states, statutes mandate that leases be in writing for some tenancies (such as those exceeding one year). Generally, to ensure the validity of a lease agreement, it should be in writing and do the following:

NOTE
Sound business practice dictates that a lease for commercial property should be written carefully and should clearly define the parties' rights and obligations.

1. Express an intent to establish the relationship.
2. Provide for the transfer of the property's possession to the tenant at the beginning of the term.
3. Provide that the property owner is entitled to retake possession at the end of the term.
4. Describe the property—for example, give its street address.
5. Indicate the length of the term, the amount of the rent, and how and when it is to be paid.

Illegality

State or local law often dictates permissible lease terms. For example, a state law or city ordinance might prohibit gambling houses. Thus, if a landlord and tenant intend that the leased premises be used only to house an illegal betting operation, their lease is unenforceable.

A property owner cannot legally discriminate against prospective tenants on the basis of race, color, national origin, religion, gender, or disability. In addition, a tenant cannot legally promise to do something counter to laws prohibiting discrimination. A commercial tenant, for example, cannot legally promise to do business only with members of a particular race.

Preventing Legal Disputes

Because of the many laws pertaining to lease terms and prohibiting discriminatory treatment, as a businessperson you would be wise to exercise caution when renting property to others. Find out what the laws are in your state, and investigate the background of prospective tenants. Hire an attorney to draft a lease agreement that complies with state laws rather than using a preprinted lease form, which may contain provisions not allowed in your state. Also, make sure that you understand what it takes to evict a tenant who does not pay rent in your state. Do not tell prospective renters more than they need to know about the selection process, why one prospective renter was selected over another, or to whom the property was ultimately leased. Never reveal any bias on your part against persons with children, disabilities, or other characteristics, or against persons of another race. Mistakes in this area can be costly in terms of legal fees and lost rent.■

Rights and Duties

The rights and duties of landlords and tenants generally pertain to four broad areas of concern—the possession, use, maintenance, and, of course, rent of leased property.

Possession   A landlord is obligated to give a tenant possession of the property that the tenant has agreed to lease. Many states follow the "English" rule, which requires the landlord to provide actual *physical possession* to the tenant (making sure that the previous tenant has vacated). Other states follow the "American" rule, which requires the landlord to transfer only the *legal right to possession* (thus, the new tenant is responsible for removing a previous tenant). After obtaining possession, the tenant retains the property exclusively until the lease expires, unless the lease states otherwise.

The covenant of quiet enjoyment mentioned previously also applies to leased premises. Under this covenant, the landlord promises that during the lease term, neither the landlord nor anyone having a superior title to the property will disturb the tenant's use and enjoyment of the property. This covenant forms the essence of the landlord-tenant relationship, and if it is breached, the tenant can terminate the lease and sue for damages.

If the landlord deprives the tenant of possession of the leased property or interferes with the tenant's use or enjoyment of it, an **eviction** occurs. An eviction occurs, for instance, when the landlord changes the lock and refuses to give the tenant a new key. A **constructive eviction** occurs when the landlord wrongfully performs or fails to perform any of the duties the lease requires, thereby making the tenant's further use and enjoyment of the property exceedingly difficult or impossible. Examples of constructive eviction include a landlord's failure to provide heat in the winter, light, or other essential utilities.

Use and Maintenance of the Premises   If the parties do not limit by agreement the uses to which the property may be put, the tenant may make any use of it, as long as the use is legal and reasonably relates to the purpose for which

EVICTION
A landlord's act of depriving a tenant of possession of the leased premises.

CONSTRUCTIVE EVICTION
A form of eviction that occurs when a landlord fails to perform adequately any of the undertakings (such as providing heat in the winter) required by the lease, thereby making the tenant's further use and enjoyment of the property exceedingly difficult or impossible.

the property is adapted or ordinarily used and does not injure the landlord's interest.

The tenant is responsible for any damage to the premises that he or she causes, intentionally or negligently, and may be held liable for the cost of returning the property to the physical condition it was in at the lease's inception. Also, the tenant is not entitled to create a *nuisance* by substantially interfering with others' quiet enjoyment of their property rights (the tort of nuisance was discussed in Chapter 21). Unless the parties have agreed otherwise, the tenant is not responsible for ordinary wear and tear and the property's consequent depreciation in value.

In some jurisdictions, landlords of residential property are required by statute to maintain the premises in good repair. Landlords must also comply with any applicable state statutes and city ordinances regarding maintenance and repair of buildings.

Implied Warranty of Habitability   The **implied warranty of habitability** requires a landlord who leases residential property to furnish premises that are in a habitable condition—that is, a condition that is safe and suitable for people to live in. Also, the landlord must make repairs to maintain the premises in that condition for the lease's duration. Some state legislatures have enacted this warranty into law. In other jurisdictions, courts have based the warranty on the existence of a landlord's statutory duty to keep leased premises in good repair, or they have simply applied it as a matter of public policy. Generally, this warranty applies to major, or *substantial,* physical defects that the landlord knows or should know about and has had a reasonable time to repair—for example, a large hole in the roof.

Rent   *Rent* is the tenant's payment to the landlord for the tenant's occupancy or use of the landlord's real property. Usually, the tenant must pay the rent even if she or he refuses to occupy the property or moves out, as long as the refusal or the move is unjustified and the lease is in force. Under the common law, if the leased premises were destroyed by fire or flood, the tenant still had to pay rent. Today, however, most states' statutes provide that if an apartment building burns down, tenants are not required to continue to pay rent.

In some situations, such as when a landlord breaches the implied warranty of habitability, a tenant may be allowed to withhold rent as a remedy. When rent withholding is authorized under a statute, the tenant must usually deposit the amount withheld into an *escrow account* and pay the landlord once the premises are made habitable.

Transferring Rights to Leased Property

Either the landlord or the tenant may wish to transfer her or his rights to the leased property during the term of the lease. If complete title to the leased property is transferred, the tenant becomes the tenant of the new owner. The new owner may collect subsequent rent but must abide by the terms of the existing lease agreement.

The tenant's transfer of his or her entire interest in the leased property to a third person is an *assignment of the lease.* Many leases require that the assignment have the landlord's written consent. An assignment that lacks consent can be avoided (nullified) by the landlord. State statutes may specify that the landlord may not unreasonably withhold such consent, though. Also, a landlord who knowingly accepts rent from the assignee may be held to have waived the consent requirement. When an assignment is valid, the assignee acquires all of the

IMPLIED WARRANTY OF HABITABILITY
An implied promise by a landlord that rented residential premises are fit for human habitation—that is, in a condition that is safe and suitable for people to live in. A similar implied promise is made by sellers of new homes in most states.

NOTE
Options that may be available to a tenant on a landlord's breach of the implied warranty of habitability include repairing the defect and deducting the amount from the rent, canceling the lease, and suing for damages.

tenant's rights under the lease. But an assignment does not release the assigning tenant from the obligation to pay rent should the assignee default.

The tenant's transfer of all or part of the premises for a period shorter than the lease term is a **sublease.** The same restrictions that apply to an assignment of the tenant's interest in leased property apply to a sublease. If the landlord's consent is required, a sublease without such permission is ineffective. Also, a sublease does not release the tenant from her or his obligations under the lease any more than an assignment does.

LAND-USE CONTROL

Property owners—even those who possess the entire bundle of rights set out earlier in this chapter—cannot do whatever they wish with their property. The rights of every property owner are subject to certain conditions and limitations.

There are three sources of land-use control. First, the law of torts (see Chapter 5) places on the owners of land obligations to protect the interests of individuals who come on the land and the interests of the owners of nearby land. Second, landowners may agree with others to restrict or limit the use of their property. Such agreements may "run with the land" when ownership is transferred to others. Thus, one who acquires real property with actual or *constructive* (imputed by law) notice of a restriction may be bound by an earlier, voluntary agreement to which he or she was not a party.

Third, controls are imposed by the government. Land use is subject to regulation by the state within whose political boundaries the land is located. Most states authorize control over land use through various planning boards and zoning authorities at a city or county level. The federal government does not engage in land-use control under normal circumstances, except with respect to federally owned land.[8] The federal government does influence state and local regulation, however, through the allocation of federal funds. Stipulations on land use may be a condition to the states' receiving such funds.

Sources of Public Control

The states' power to control the use of land through legislation is derived from their *police power* and the doctrine of *eminent domain*. Under their police power, state governments enact legislation that promotes the health, safety, and welfare of their citizens. This legislation includes land-use controls. The power of **eminent domain** is the government's authority to take private property for public use or purpose without the owner's consent. Typically, this is accomplished through a judicial proceeding to obtain title to the land.

Police Power

As an exercise of its police power,[9] a state can regulate the use of land within its jurisdiction. A few states control land use at the state level. Hawaii, for instance, employs a statewide land-use classification scheme. Some states have a land-permit

SUBLEASE
A lease executed by the lessee of real estate to a third person, conveying the same interest that the lessee enjoys but for a shorter term than that held by the lessee.

EMINENT DOMAIN
The power of a government to take land for public use from private citizens for just compensation.

---

8. Federal (and state) laws concerning environmental matters such as air and water quality, the protection of endangered species, and the preservation of natural wetlands are also a source of land-use control. Some of these laws were discussed in Chapter 21.
9. As pointed out in Chapter 4, the police power of a state encompasses the right to regulate private activities to protect or promote the public order, health, safety, morals, and general welfare.

process that operates in conjunction with local control. Florida, for example, uses such a scheme in certain areas of "critical environmental concern" to permit or prohibit development on the basis of available roads, sewers, and so on. Vermont also utilizes a statewide land-permit program.

Usually, however, a state authorizes its city or county governments to regulate the use of land within their local jurisdictions. A state confers this power through *enabling legislation.* Enabling legislation normally requires local governments to devise *general plans* before imposing other land-use controls. Enabling acts also typically authorize local bodies to enact *zoning laws* to regulate the use of land and the types of, and specifications for, structures. Local planning boards may regulate the development of subdivisions, in which private developers subdivide tracts of land and construct commercial or residential units for resale to others. Local governments may also enact growth-management ordinances to control development in their jurisdictions.

Government Plans   Most states require that land-use laws follow a local government's general plan. A **general plan** is a comprehensive, long-term scheme dealing with the physical development, and in some cases redevelopment, of a city or community. It addresses such concerns as types of housing, protection of natural resources, provision of public facilities and transportation, and other issues related to land use. A plan indicates the direction of growth in a community and the contributions that private developers must make toward providing public facilities, such as roads. If a proposed use is not authorized by the general plan, the plan may be amended to permit the use. (A plan may also be amended to preclude a proposed use.)

Even when a proposed use complies with a general plan, it may not be allowed. Most jurisdictions have requirements in addition to those in the general plan. These requirements are then included in *specific plans*—also called special, area, or community plans. Specific plans typically pertain to only a portion of a jurisdiction's area. For example, a specific plan may concern a downtown area subject to redevelopment efforts, an area with special environmental concerns, or an area with increased public transportation needs arising from population growth.

Zoning Laws   In addition to complying with a general plan and any specific plans, a particular land use must comply with zoning laws. The term **zoning** refers to the division of an area into districts to which specific land-use regulations apply. A typical zoning law consists of a zoning map and a zoning ordinance. The zoning map indicates the characteristics of each parcel of land within an area and divides that area into districts. The zoning ordinance specifies the restrictions on land use within those districts.

Zoning ordinances generally include two types of restrictions. One type pertains to the kind of land use—such as commercial versus residential—to which property within a particular district may be put. The second type dictates the engineering features and architectural design of structures built within that district.

Use Restrictions   Districts are typically zoned for residential, commercial, industrial, or agricultural use. Each district may be further subdivided for degree or intensity of use. **EXAMPLE #10** A residential district may be subdivided to permit a certain number of apartment buildings and a specific number of units in each building. Commercial and industrial districts are often zoned to permit

GENERAL PLAN
A comprehensive plan that local jurisdictions are often required by state law to devise and implement as a precursor to specific land-use regulations.

ZONING
The division of a city by legislative regulation into districts and the application in each district of regulations having to do with structural and architectural designs of buildings and prescribing the use to which buildings within designated districts may be put.

heavy or *light* activity. Heavy activity might include the operation of large factories. Light activity might encompass the operation of professional office buildings or small retail shops.□ Zoning that specifies the use to which property may be put is referred to as **use zoning.**

Structural Restrictions   Restrictions known as *bulk regulations* cover such details as minimum floor-space requirements and minimum lot-size restrictions. **EXAMPLE #11** A particular district's minimum floor-space requirements might specify that a one-story building contain a minimum of 1,240 square feet of floor space. Minimum lot-size restrictions might mandate that each single-family dwelling be built on a lot that is at least one acre in size.□ Referred to collectively as **bulk zoning,** these regulations also dictate *setback* (the distance between a building and a street, sidewalk, or other boundary) and the height of buildings, with different requirements for buildings in different areas.

Restrictions related to structure may also be concerned with such matters as architectural control, the overall appearance of a community, and the preservation of historic buildings. An ordinance may require that all proposed construction be approved by a design review board composed of local architects. A community may restrict the size and placement of outdoor advertising, such as billboards and business signs. A property owner may be prohibited from tearing down or remodeling a historic landmark or building. In challenges against these types of restrictions, the courts have generally upheld the regulations.

Variances   A **zoning variance** allows property to be used or structures to be built in some way that varies from the restrictions of a zoning ordinance. **EXAMPLE #12** A variance may exempt property from a use restriction to allow, for example, a bakery shop in a residential area. Or a variance may exempt a building from a height restriction so that, for example, a two-story house can be built in a district in which houses are otherwise limited to one floor.□ Some jurisdictions do not permit variances from use restrictions.

Variances may also exempt property from "area restrictions." In contrast to a "use" provision, an "area" restriction regulates the area, height, density, setback, or sideline attributes of a building or other development on a piece of property.

Variances are normally granted by local adjustment boards. In general, a property owner must meet three criteria to obtain a variance:

1. The owner must find it impossible to realize a reasonable return on the land as currently zoned.
2. The adverse effect of the zoning ordinance must be particular to the party seeking the variance and not have a similar effect on other owners in the same zone.
3. Granting the variance must not substantially alter the essential character of the zoned area.

The most important of these criteria is whether the variance would substantially alter the character of the area. Courts are more lenient about the other requirements when reviewing decisions of adjustment boards.

Subdivision Regulations   When subdividing a parcel of land into smaller plots, a private developer must comply not only with local zoning ordinances but also with local subdivision regulations. Subdivision regulations are different from zoning ordinances, although they may be administered by the same local agencies that oversee the zoning process. In the design of a subdivision, the local

USE ZONING
Zoning classifications based on the uses to which the land may be put.

BULK ZONING
Zoning regulations that restrict the amount of structural coverage on a particular parcel of land.

ZONING VARIANCE
The granting of permission by a municipality or other public board to a landowner to use his or her property in a way that does not strictly conform with the zoning regulations so as to avoid causing the landowner undue hardship.

authorities may demand, for example, the allocation of space for a public park or school or may require a developer to construct streets to accommodate a specific level of traffic.

Growth-Management Ordinances   To prevent population growth from moving ahead of the community's ability to provide necessary public services, local authorities may enact a growth-management ordinance to limit, for example, the number of residential building permits. A property owner may thus be precluded from constructing a residential building on his or her property even if the area is zoned for the use and the proposed structure complies with all other requirements. A growth-management ordinance may prohibit the issuance of residential building permits for a specific period of time, until the occurrence of a specific event (such as a decline in the total number of residents in the community), or on the basis of the availability of necessary public services (such as the capacity for drainage in the area or the proximity of hospitals and police stations).

Limitations on the Exercise of Police Power   The government's exercise of its police power to regulate the use of land is limited in at least three ways. Two of these limitations arise under the Fourteenth Amendment to the Constitution. The third limitation arises under the Fifth Amendment and requires that, under certain circumstances, the government must compensate an owner who is deprived of the use of his or her property.

Due Process and Equal Protection   A government cannot regulate the use of land in a way that violates either the due process clause or the equal protection clause of the Fourteenth Amendment. A government may be deemed to violate the due process clause if it acts arbitrarily or unreasonably. Thus, there must be a *rational basis* for classifications that are imposed on property. Any classification that is reasonably related to the health or general welfare of the public is deemed to have a rational basis.

Hiking on a beach at Olympic National Park in Washington. If this had once been private property, why would the government have been prohibited from taking it for public use without paying the owner?
(National Park Service Photo)

Under the equal protection clause, land-use controls cannot be discriminatory. A zoning ordinance is discriminatory if it affects one parcel of land in a way in which it does not affect surrounding parcels and if there is no rational basis for the difference. For example, classifying a single parcel in a way that does not accord with a general plan is discriminatory. Similarly, a zoning ordinance cannot be racially discriminatory. EXAMPLE #13 A community may not zone itself to exclude all low-income housing if the intention is to exclude minorities. □

Just Compensation   Under the Fifth Amendment, private property may not be taken for a public purpose without the payment of just compensation.[10] If government restrictions on a

_____
10. Although the Fifth Amendment pertains to actions taken by the federal government, the Fourteenth Amendment has been interpreted as extending this limitation to state actions.

"[A] strong public desire to improve the public condition is not enough to warrant achieving the desire by a shorter cut than . . . paying for the change."

—OLIVER WENDELL HOLMES, JR.,
1841–1935
(Associate justice of the United States Supreme Court, 1902–1932)

landowner's property rights are overly burdensome, the regulation may be deemed a taking. A *taking* occurs when a regulation denies an owner the ability to use his or her property for any reasonable income-producing or private purpose for which it is suited. This requires the government to pay the owner.

EXAMPLE #14 Suppose that Perez purchases a large tract of land with the intent to subdivide and develop it into residential properties. At the time of the purchase, there are no zoning laws restricting use of the land. After Perez has taken significant steps to develop the property, the county attempts to zone the tract for use as "public parkland only." If this prohibits Perez from developing any of the land, normally it will be deemed a taking. If the county does not fairly compensate Perez, the regulation will be held unconstitutional and void.□

A government regulation will generally be deemed a taking when it requires an owner to suffer a permanent physical invasion of the property and when it completely deprives an owner of all economically beneficial use. The United States Supreme Court has also identified several factors that it considers particularly significant in determining takings cases. These factors include the economic impact on the plaintiff and the extent the regulation interferes with distinct investment-backed expectations.[11]

Eminent Domain

As already noted, governments have an inherent power to take property for public use or purpose without the consent of the owner. This is the power of eminent domain, and it is very important in the public control of land use.

Every property owner holds his or her interest in land subject to a superior interest. Just as in medieval England the king was the ultimate landowner, so in the United States the government retains an ultimate ownership right in all land. This right, known as eminent domain, is sometimes referred to as the *condemnation power* of the government to take land for public use. It gives to the government a right to acquire possession of real property in the manner directed by the Constitution and the laws of the state whenever the public interest requires it. Property may not be taken for private benefit, but only for public use.

EXAMPLE #15 When a new public highway is to be built, the government must decide where to build it and how much land to condemn. After the government determines that a particular parcel of land is necessary for public use, it brings a judicial proceeding to obtain title to the land.□

Under the Fifth Amendment, although the government may take land for public use, it must pay fair and just compensation for it. Thus, in the previous highway example, after the proceeding to obtain title to the land, there is a second proceeding in which the court determines the *fair value* of the land. Fair value is usually approximately equal to market value.

In 2005, the United States Supreme Court ruled that the power of eminent domain can be used to further economic development.[12] Since that decision, a number of state legislatures have passed laws limiting the power of the government to use eminent domain, particularly for urban redevelopment projects that benefit private developers.

---

11. See *Lingle v. Chevron U.S.A. Inc.*, 544 U.S. 528, 125 S.Ct. 2074, 161 L.Ed.2d 876 (2005); and *Penn Central Transportation Co. v. New York City*, 438 U.S. 104, 124, 98 S.Ct. 2646, 57 L.Ed.2d 631 (1978).
12. *Kelo v. City of New London, Connecticut*, 545 U.S. 469, 125 S.Ct. 2655, 162 L.Ed.2d 439 (2005).

Reviewing . . . Land-Use Control and Real Property

Vern Shoepke purchased a two-story home on a one-acre lot in the town of Roche, Maine, from Walter and Eliza Bruster. The warranty deed that effected the transfer did not specify what covenants would be included in the conveyance. The property was adjacent to a public park that included a popular Frisbee golf course. (Frisbee golf is a sport similar to golf but using Frisbees.) Wayakichi Creek ran along the north end of the park and along Shoepke's property as part of a two-mile public trail system. The deed allowed Roche citizens the right to walk across a five-foot-wide section of the lot beside Wayakichi Creek. Teenagers regularly threw Frisbee golf discs from the walking path behind Shoepke's property over his yard to the adjacent park. Shoepke habitually shouted and cursed at the teenagers, demanding that they not throw objects over his yard. Two months after moving into his Roche home, Shoepke signed a lease agreement with Lauren Slater under which Slater agreed to rent the second floor for $645 per month for nine months. (The lease did not specify that Shoepke's consent would be required to sublease the second floor.) After three months of tenancy, Slater sublet the second floor to a local artist, Javier Indalecio. Over the remaining six months, Indalecio's use of oil paints damaged the carpeting in Shoepke's home. Using the information presented in the chapter, answer the following questions.

1. What is the term for the right of Roche citizens to walk across Shoepke's land on the trail?

2. In the warranty deed effecting the transfer of the property from the Brusters to Shoepke, what covenants would be inferred by most courts?

3. Can Shoepke hold Slater financially responsible for the carpeting damaged by Indalecio?

Key Terms

Chapter Summary

| The Nature of Real Property (See pages 711–713.) | Real property (also called real estate or realty) is immovable. It includes land, subsurface and air rights, plant life and vegetation, and fixtures. |

CONTINUED

**Ownership of
Real Property**
(See pages 713–719.)

1. *Fee simple absolute*–The most complete form of ownership.

2. *Life estate*–An estate that lasts for the life of a specified individual; ownership rights in a life estate necessarily cease to exist on the life tenant's death.

3. *Concurrent ownership*–Persons who share ownership rights simultaneously in a particular piece of property are said to be *concurrent* owners. The two main types of concurrent ownership are *tenancy in common* and *joint tenancy.*

   a. In a *tenancy in common,* each tenant owns an undivided interest in the property, and on one tenant's death, that tenant's property interest passes to his or her heirs.

   b. In a *joint tenancy,* each tenant owns an undivided interest in the property, and on the death of a joint tenant, that tenant's property interest transfers to the remaining tenant(s), not to the heirs of the deceased. This "right of survivorship" is what distinguishes a joint tenancy from all other forms of ownership.

   c. In a limited number of states, property that is owned by a husband and wife may be held as *community property* in which each spouse technically owns an undivided one-half interest.

4. *Nonpossessory interest*–An interest that involves the right to use real property but not to possess it. Easements, profits, and licenses are nonpossessory interests.

Transfer of Ownership
(See pages 719–726.)

1. *By deed*–When real property is sold or transferred as a gift, title to the property is conveyed by means of a deed. A deed must meet specific legal requirements. A *warranty deed* warrants the most extensive protection against defects of title. A *quitclaim deed* conveys to the grantee whatever interest the grantor had; it warrants less than any other deed. A deed may be recorded in the manner prescribed by *recording statutes* in the appropriate jurisdiction to give third parties notice of the owner's interest.

2. *By will or inheritance*–If the owner dies after having made a valid will, the land passes as specified in the will. If the owner dies without having made a will, the heirs inherit according to state inheritance statutes.

3. *By adverse possession*–When a person possesses the property of another for a statutory period of time (three to thirty years, with ten years being the most common), that person acquires title to the property, provided the possession is actual and exclusive, open and visible, continuous and peaceable, and hostile and adverse (without the permission of the owner).

Leasehold Estates
(See pages 726–727.)

A leasehold estate is an interest in real property that is held only for a limited period of time, as specified in the lease agreement. Types of tenancies relating to leased property include the following:

1. *Fixed-term tenancy, or tenancy for years*–Tenancy for a period of time stated by express contract.

2. *Periodic tenancy*–Tenancy for a period determined by the frequency of rent payments; automatically renewed unless proper notice is given.

3. *Tenancy at will*–Tenancy for as long as both parties agree; no notice of termination is required.

**Landlord-Tenant
Relationships**
(See pages 727–730.)

1. *Lease agreement*–The landlord-tenant relationship is created by a lease agreement. State or local laws may dictate whether the lease must be in writing and what lease terms are permissible.

2. *Rights and duties*–The rights and duties that arise under a lease agreement generally pertain to the following areas:

   a. Possession–The tenant has an exclusive right to possess the leased premises, which must be available to the tenant at the agreed-on time. Under the covenant of quiet

Landlord-Tenant Relationships— Continued	enjoyment, the landlord promises that during the lease term neither the landlord nor anyone having superior title to the property will disturb the tenant's use and enjoyment of the property.
	b. Use and maintenance of the premises—The tenant normally can make any legal use of the property but is responsible for any damage that he or she causes. The landlord must comply with laws that set specific standards for the maintenance of real property.
	c. The implied warranty of habitability—A landlord is required to furnish and maintain residential premises in a habitable condition (that is, in a condition safe and suitable for human life).
	d. Rent—The tenant must pay the rent as long as the lease is in force, unless the tenant justifiably refuses to occupy the property or withholds the rent because of the landlord's failure to maintain the premises properly.
	3. *Transferring rights to leased property*—
	a. If the landlord transfers complete title to the leased property, the tenant becomes the tenant of the new owner. The new owner may then collect the rent but must abide by the existing lease.
	b. Generally, tenants may assign their rights (but not their duties) under a lease contract to a third person. Tenants may also sublease leased property to a third person, but the original tenant is not relieved of any obligations to the landlord under the lease. In either case, the landlord's consent may be required.
Land-Use Control— Private Control (See page 730.)	1. *The law of torts*—Owners are obligated to protect the interests of those who come on the land and those who own nearby land.
	2. *Private agreements*—Owners may agree with others to limit the use of their property.
Land-Use Control— Government Police Power (See pages 730–734.)	1. Government plans—Most states require that local land-use laws follow a general plan.
	2. *Zoning laws*—Laws that divide an area into districts to which specific land-use regulations apply. Districts may be zoned for residential, commercial, industrial, or agricultural use. Within all districts, there may be minimum lot-size requirements, structural restrictions, and other bulk zoning regulations. A variance allows for the use of property in ways that vary from the restrictions.
	3. *Subdivision regulations*—Laws directing the dedication of specific plots of land to specific uses within a subdivision.
	4. *Growth-management ordinances*—Limits on, for example, the number of residential building permits.
	5. *Limits on the police power:*
	a. Due process and equal protection—Land-use controls cannot be arbitrary, unreasonable, or discriminatory.
	b. Just compensation—Private property taken for a public purpose requires payment of just compensation. "Taking" for a public purpose includes enacting overly burdensome regulations.
Land-Use Control— Eminent Domain (See page 734.)	1. *Condemnation power*—Governments have the inherent power to take property for public use without the consent of the owner.
	2. *Limits on the power of eminent domain*—Private property taken for a public purpose requires payment of just compensation.

For Review

1. What are the different types of ownership interests in real property?

2. How can ownership interests in real property be transferred?

3. What is a leasehold estate, and how does it arise?

4. What are the respective duties of the landlord and tenant concerning the use and maintenance of leased property?

5. What limitations may be imposed on the rights of property owners?

Questions and Case Problems

22–1. Tenant's Rights and Responsibilities. You are a student in college and plan to attend classes for nine months. You sign a twelve-month lease for an apartment. Discuss fully each of the following situations.

1. You have a summer job in another town and wish to assign the balance of your lease (three months) to a fellow student who will be attending summer school. Can you do so?

2. You are graduating in May. The lease will have three months remaining. Can you terminate the lease without liability by giving a thirty-day notice to the landlord?

Question with Sample Answer

22–2. The county intends to rezone an area from industrial use to residential use. Land within the affected area is largely undeveloped, but nonetheless it is expected that the proposed action will reduce the market value of the affected land by as much as 50 percent. Will the landowners be successful in suing to have the action declared a taking of their property, entitling them to just compensation?

For a sample answer to Question 22–2, go to Appendix I at the end of this text.

22–3. Property Ownership. Lorenz was a wanderer twenty-two years ago. At that time, he decided to settle down on an unoccupied, three-acre parcel of land that he did not own. People in the area indicated to him that they had no idea who owned the property. Lorenz built a house on the land, got married, and raised three children while living there. He fenced in the land, placed a gate with a sign above it that read "Lorenz's Homestead," and had trespassers removed. Lorenz is now confronted by Joe Reese, who has a deed in his name as owner of the property. Reese, claiming ownership of the land, orders Lorenz and his family off the property. Discuss who has the better "title" to the property.

22–4. Easements. In 1988, Gary Dubin began leasing property from Robert Chesebrough at 26011 Bouquet Canyon Road in Los Angeles County, California, to operate Alert Auto, a vehicle repair shop. There was a narrow driveway on one side of the premises, but blocking the widest means of access were crash posts on the adjacent unoccupied property, which Chesebrough also owned. The lease did not mention a means of access, but Dubin's primary customers were to be large trucks and motor homes, which could reach Alert Auto only over the wide driveway. Chesebrough had the posts removed. After his death, the Robert Newhall Chesebrough Trust became the owner of both properties, which Wespac Management Group, Inc., managed. In 2000, Wespac reinstalled the posts. Dubin filed a suit in a California state court against the trust and others, alleging that he had an easement, which the posts were obstructing, and sought damages and an injunction. The defendants denied the existence of any easement. Does Dubin have an easement? If so, how was it created? Explain. [*Dubin v. Robert Newhall Chesebrough Trust,* 96 Cal.App.4th 465, 116 Cal.Rptr.2d 872 (2 Dist. 2002)]

22–5. Commercial Lease Terms. Metropolitan Life Insurance Co. leased space in its Trail Plaza Shopping Center in Florida to Winn-Dixie Stores, Inc., to operate a supermarket. Under the lease, the landlord agreed not to permit "any [other] property located within the shopping center to be used for or occupied by any business dealing in or which shall keep in stock or sell for off-premises consumption any staple or fancy groceries" in more than "500 square feet of sales area." In 1999, Metropolitan leased 22,000 square feet of space in Trail Plaza to 99 Cent Stuff-Trail Plaza, LLC, under a lease that prohibited it from selling "groceries" in more than 500 square feet of "sales area." Shortly after 99 Cent Stuff opened, it began selling food and other products, including soap, matches, and paper napkins. Alleging that these sales violated the parties' leases, Winn-Dixie filed a suit in a Florida state court against 99 Cent Stuff and others. The defendants argued in part that the groceries provision covered only food and the 500-square-foot restriction included only shelf space, not store aisles. How should these lease terms be interpreted? Should the court grant an injunction in Winn-Dixie's favor? Explain. [*Winn-Dixie Stores, Inc. v. 99 Cent Stuff-Trail Plaza, LLC*, 811 So.2d 719 (Fla.App. 3 Dist. 2002)]

22–6. Easements. The Wallens family owned a cabin on Lummi Island in the state of Washington. A driveway ran from the cabin across their property to South Nugent Road. In 1952, Floyd Massey bought the adjacent lot and built a cabin. To gain access to his property, he used a bulldozer to extend the driveway without the Wallenses' permission but also without their objection. In 1975, the Wallenses sold their property to Wright Fish Co. Massey continued to use and maintain the driveway without permission or objection. In 1984, Massey sold his property to Robert Drake. Drake and his employees continued to use and maintain the driveway without permission or objection, although Drake knew it was located largely on Wright's property. In 1997, Wright sold its lot to Robert Smersh. The next year, Smersh told Drake to stop using the driveway. Drake filed a suit in a Washington state court against Smersh, claiming an easement by prescription (which is created by meeting the same requirements as adverse possession). Does Drake's use of the driveway meet all of the requirements? What should the court rule? Explain. [*Drake v. Smersh*, 122 Wash.App. 147, 89 P.3d 726 (Div. 1 2004)]

Case Problem with Sample Answer

22–7. The Hope Partnership for Education, a religious organization, proposed to build a private independent middle school in a blighted neighborhood in Philadelphia, Pennsylvania. In 2002, the Hope Partnership asked the Redevelopment Authority of the City of Philadelphia to acquire specific land for the project and sell it to the Hope Partnership for a nominal price. The land included a house at 1839 North Eighth Street owned by Mary Smith, whose daughter Veronica lived there with her family. The Authority offered Smith $12,000 for the house and initiated a taking of the property. Smith filed a suit in a Pennsylvania state court against the Authority, admitting that the house was a "substandard structure in a blighted area," but arguing that the taking was unconstitutional because its beneficiary was private. The Authority asserted that only the public purpose of the taking should be considered, not the status of the property's developer. On what basis can a government entity use the power of eminent domain to take property? What are the limits to this power? How should the court rule? Why? [*Redevelopment Authority of City of Philadelphia v. New Eastwick Corp.*, 588 Pa. 789, 906 A.2d 1197 (2006)]

After you have answered Problem 22–7, compare your answer with the sample answer given on the Web site that accompanies this text. Go to www.cengage.com/blaw/let, select "Chapter 22," and click on "Case Problem with Sample Answer."

22–8. Ownership in Fee Simple. Thomas and Teresa Cline built a house on a 76-acre parcel of real estate next to Roy Berg's home and property in Augusta County, Virginia. The homes were about 1,800 feet apart but in view of each other. After several disagreements between the parties, Berg equipped an 11-foot tripod with motion sensors and floodlights that intermittently illuminated the Clines' home. Berg also installed surveillance cameras that tracked some of the movement on the Clines' property. The cameras transmitted on an open frequency, which could be received by any television within range. The Clines asked Berg to turn off, or at least redirect, the lights. When he refused, they erected a fence for 200 feet along the parties' common property line. The 32-foot-high fence consisted of 20 utility poles spaced 10 feet apart with plastic wrap stretched between the poles. This effectively blocked the lights and cameras. Berg filed a suit against the Clines in a Virginia state court, complaining that the fence interfered unreasonably with his use and enjoyment of his property. He asked the court to order the Clines to take the fence down. What are the limits on an owner's use of property? How should the court rule in this case? Why? [*Cline v. Berg*, 273 Va. 142, 639 S.E.2d 231 (2007)]

A Question of Ethics

22–9. In 1999, Stephen and Linda Kailin bought the Monona Center, a mall in Madison, Wisconsin, from Perry Armstrong for $760,000. The contract provided, "Seller represents to Buyer that as of the date of acceptance Seller had no notice or knowledge of conditions affecting the Property or transaction" other than certain items disclosed at the time of the offer. Armstrong told the Kailins of the Center's eight tenants, their lease expiration dates, and the monthly and annual rent due under each lease. One of the lessees, Ring's All American Karate, occupied about a third of the Center's space under a five-year lease. Because of Ring's financial difficulties, Armstrong had agreed to reduce its rent for nine months in 1997. By the time of the sale to the Kailins, Ring owed $13,910 in unpaid rent, but Armstrong did not tell the Kailins, who did not ask. Ring continued to fail to pay rent and finally vacated the Center. The Kailins filed a suit in a Wisconsin state court against Armstrong and others, alleging, among other things, misrepresentation. [*Kailin v. Armstrong*, 2002 WI App 70, 252 Wis.2d 676, 643 N.W.2d 132 (2002)]

1. Did Armstrong have a duty to disclose Ring's delinquency and default to the Kailins? Does the failure of a tenant to pay rent constitute a defect that affects the value of the property? Why or why not?
2. Could the Kailins reasonably have discovered Ring's delinquency in rent payments? Explain.

Critical-Thinking Legal Question

22–10. Garza Construction Co. erects a silo (a grain storage facility) on Reeve's ranch. Garza also lends Reeve the money to pay for the silo under an agreement providing that the silo is not to become part of the land until Reeve completes the loan payments. Before the silo is paid for, Metropolitan State Bank, the mortgage holder on Reeve's land, forecloses on the property. Metropolitan contends that the silo is a fixture to the realty and that the bank is therefore entitled to the proceeds from its sale. Garza argues that the silo is personal property and that the proceeds should therefore go to Garza. Is the silo a fixture? Why or why not?

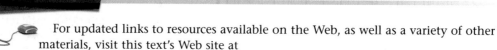

Interacting with the Internet

For updated links to resources available on the Web, as well as a variety of other materials, visit this text's Web site at

www.cengage.com/blaw/let

Information on the buying and financing of homes, as well as the full text of the Real Estate Settlement Procedures Act, is online at

www.hud.gov/buying

For information on condemnation procedures and rules under one state's (California's) law, go to

www.eminentdomainlaw.net/propertyguide.html

PRACTICAL INTERNET EXERCISES

Go to this text's Web site at **www.cengage.com/blaw/let**, select "Chapter 22," and click on "Practical Internet Exercises." There you will find the following Internet research exercises that you can perform to learn more about the topics covered in this chapter.

Practical Internet Exercise 22–1: LEGAL PERSPECTIVE—**Eminent Domain**
Practical Internet Exercise 22–2: MANAGEMENT PERSPECTIVE—**How to Challenge a Condemnation of Property**
Practical Internet Exercise 22–3: SOCIAL PERSPECTIVE—**The Rights of Tenants**

BEFORE THE TEST

Go to **www.cengage.com/blaw/let**, the Web site that accompanies this text. Select "Chapter 22" and click on "Interactive Quizzes." You will find a number of interactive questions relating to this chapter.

Chapter 23
Antitrust Law and Promoting Competition

CHAPTER OBJECTIVES

After reading this chapter, you should be able to answer the following questions:

1. What is a monopoly? What is market power? How do these concepts relate to each other?

2. What type of activity is prohibited by Section 1 of the Sherman Act? What type of activity is prohibited by Section 2 of the Sherman Act?

3. What are the four major provisions of the Clayton Act, and what types of activities do these provisions prohibit?

4. What agencies of the federal government enforce the federal antitrust laws?

5. What are four activities that are exempt from the antitrust laws?

CONTENTS

- The Sherman Antitrust Act

- Section 1 of the Sherman Act

- Section 2 of the Sherman Act

- The Clayton Act

- Enforcement and Exemptions

- U.S. Antitrust Laws in the Global Context

" Free competition is worth more to society than it costs."

— OLIVER WENDELL HOLMES, JR.,
1841–1935 (Associate justice of the United States Supreme Court, 1902–1932)

Today's antitrust laws are the direct descendants of common law actions intended to limit *restraints on trade* (agreements between firms that have the effect of reducing competition in the marketplace). Such actions date to the fifteenth century in England. In the United States, concern over monopolistic practices arose following the Civil War with the growth of large corporate enterprises and their attempts to reduce competition. To thwart competition, they legally tied themselves together in business trusts. A *business trust* is a form of business organization in which trustees hold title to property for the benefit of others. The most powerful of these trusts, the Standard Oil trust, is examined in this chapter's *Landmark in the Legal Environment* feature on page 743.

Many states tried to curb such monopolistic behavior by enacting statutes outlawing the use of trusts. That is why all the laws regulating economic competition today are referred to as **antitrust laws.** At the national level, Congress passed the Sherman Antitrust Act in 1890.[1] In 1914, Congress passed the Clayton Act[2] and the Federal Trade Commission Act[3] to further curb anticompetitive or unfair business practices. Congress later amended the 1914 acts to broaden and strengthen their coverage.

This chapter examines these major antitrust statutes, focusing particularly on the Sherman Act and the Clayton Act, as amended, and the types of activities they prohibit. Remember in reading this chapter that the basis of antitrust legislation is

ANTITRUST LAW
Laws protecting commerce from unlawful restraints.

---

1. 15 U.S.C. Sections 1–7.
2. 15 U.S.C. Sections 12–27.
3. 15 U.S.C. Sections 41–58.

the desire to foster competition. Antitrust legislation was initially created—and continues to be enforced—because of our belief that competition leads to lower prices, generates more product information, and results in a more equitable distribution of wealth between consumers and producers. As Oliver Wendell Holmes, Jr., indicated in the chapter-opening quotation, free competition is worth more to our society than the cost we pay for it. The cost includes government regulation of business behavior.

THE SHERMAN ANTITRUST ACT

In 1890, Congress passed "An Act to Protect Trade and Commerce against Unlawful Restraints and Monopolies"—commonly known as the Sherman Antitrust Act or, more simply, as the Sherman Act. The Sherman Act was and remains one of the government's most powerful weapons in the effort to maintain a competitive economy, as noted in this chapter's *Landmark in the Legal Environment* feature.

Major Provisions of the Sherman Act

Sections 1 and 2 contain the main provisions of the Sherman Act:

1. Every contract, combination in the form of trust or otherwise, or conspiracy, in restraint of trade or commerce among the several States, or with foreign nations, is hereby declared to be illegal [and is a felony punishable by a fine and/or imprisonment].
2. Every person who shall monopolize, or attempt to monopolize, or combine or conspire with any other person or persons, to monopolize any part of the trade or commerce among the several States, or with foreign nations, shall be deemed guilty of a felony [and is similarly punishable].

Differences between Section 1 and Section 2

These two sections of the Sherman Act are quite different. Violation of Section 1 requires two or more persons, as a person cannot contract or combine or conspire alone. Thus, the essence of the illegal activity is *the act of joining together.* Section 2, though, can apply either to one person or to two or more persons because it refers to "[e]very person." Thus, unilateral conduct can result in a violation of Section 2.

The cases brought to court under Section 1 of the Sherman Act differ from those brought under Section 2. Section 1 cases are often concerned with finding an agreement (written or oral) that leads to a restraint of trade. Section 2 cases deal with the structure of a monopoly that already exists in the marketplace. The term **monopoly** generally is used to describe a market in which there is a single seller or a very limited number of sellers. Whereas Section 1 focuses on agreements that are restrictive—that is, agreements that have a wrongful purpose—Section 2 looks at the so-called misuse of **monopoly power** in the marketplace.

Monopoly power exists when a firm has an extremely great amount of **market power**—the power to affect the market price of its product. Both Section 1 and Section 2 seek to curtail market practices that result in undesired monopoly pric-

MONOPOLY
A term generally used to describe a market in which there is a single seller or a very limited number of sellers.

MONOPOLY POWER
The ability of a monopoly to dictate what takes place in a given market.

MARKET POWER
The power of a firm to control the market price of its product. A monopoly has the greatest degree of market power.

The author of the Sherman Antitrust Act of 1890, Senator John Sherman, was the brother of the famed Civil War general William Tecumseh Sherman and a recognized financial authority. Sherman had been concerned for years about what he saw as diminishing competition within U.S. industry and the emergence of monopolies, such as the Standard Oil trust.

The Standard Oil Trust

By 1890, the Standard Oil trust had become the foremost petroleum refining and marketing combination in the United States. Streamlined, integrated, and centrally and efficiently controlled, Standard Oil maintained a monopoly over the industry that could not be disputed. The trust controlled 90 percent of the U.S. market for refined petroleum products, and small manufacturers were incapable of competing with such an industrial leviathan.

The increasing consolidation occurring in U.S. industry, and particularly the Standard Oil trust, came to the attention of the public in March 1881. Henry Demarest Lloyd, a young journalist from Chicago, published an article in the *Atlantic Monthly* entitled "The Story of a Great Monopoly." The article discussed the success of the Standard Oil Company and clearly demonstrated that the petroleum industry in the United States was dominated by one firm—Standard Oil. Lloyd's article, which was so popular that the issue was reprinted six times, marked the beginning of the U.S. public's growing awareness of, and concern over, the rise of monopolies.

The Passage of the Sherman Antitrust Act

The common law regarding trade regulation was not always consistent. Certainly, it was not very familiar to the members of Congress. The public concern over large business integrations and trusts was familiar, however. In 1888, in 1889, and again in 1890, Senator Sherman introduced in Congress bills designed to destroy the large combinations of capital that, he felt, were creating a lack of balance within the nation's economy. Sherman told Congress that the Sherman Act "does not announce a new principle of law, but applies old and well-recognized principles of the common law."[a] In 1890, the Fifty-First Congress enacted the bill into law.

In this chapter, we look closely at the major provisions of this act. Generally, the act prohibits business combinations and conspiracies that restrain trade and commerce, as well as certain monopolistic practices.

APPLICATION TO TODAY'S LEGAL ENVIRONMENT

The Sherman Antitrust Act remains very relevant to today's world. The widely publicized monopolization case brought against Microsoft Corporation in 2001 by the U.S. Department of Justice and a number of state attorneys general is just one example of the relevance of the Sherman Act to modern business developments and practices.[b]

RELEVANT WEB SITES

To locate information on the Web concerning the Sherman Antitrust Act, go to this text's Web site at **www.cengage.com/blaw/let**, select "Chapter 23," and click on "URLs for Landmarks."

a. 21 *Congressional Record* 2456 (1890).
b. *United States v. Microsoft Corp.,* 253 F.3d 34 (D.C.Cir. 2001). This case is also discussed in Example #8.

ing and output behavior. For a case to be brought under Section 2, however, the "threshold" or "necessary" amount of monopoly power must already exist. We will return to a discussion of these two sections of the Sherman Act after we look at the act's jurisdictional requirements.

Jurisdictional Requirements

The Sherman Act applies only to restraints that have a substantial impact on interstate commerce. The Sherman Act also extends to U.S. nationals abroad who are engaged in activities that have an effect on U.S. foreign commerce (as discussed later in this chapter). State laws regulate local restraints on competition.

Courts have generally held that any activity that substantially affects interstate commerce falls within the scope of the Sherman Act. As discussed in Chapter 4, courts have construed the meaning of *interstate commerce* broadly, bringing even local activities within the regulatory power of the national government.

One of Standard Oil's refineries in Richmond, California, around 1900. (Library of Congress)

SECTION 1 OF THE SHERMAN ACT

The underlying assumption of Section 1 of the Sherman Act is that society's welfare is harmed if rival firms are permitted to join in an agreement that consolidates their market power or otherwise restrains competition. The types of trade restraints that Section 1 of the Sherman Act prohibits generally fall into two broad categories: *horizontal restraints* and *vertical restraints,* both of which are discussed shortly. First, though, we look at the rules that the courts may apply when assessing the anticompetitive impact of alleged restraints on trade.

Per Se Violations versus the Rule of Reason

PER SE VIOLATION
A type of anticompetitive agreement that is considered to be so injurious to the public that there is no need to determine whether it actually injures market competition. Rather, it is in itself (*per se*) a violation of the Sherman Act.

RULE OF REASON
A test by which a court balances the positive effects (such as economic efficiency) of an agreement against its potentially anticompetitive effects. In antitrust litigation, many practices are analyzed under the rule of reason.

Some restraints are so blatantly and substantially anticompetitive that they are deemed **per se violations**—illegal *per se* (on their face, or inherently)—under Section 1. Other agreements, however, even though they result in enhanced market power, do not *unreasonably* restrain trade. Using what is called the **rule of reason,** the courts analyze anticompetitive agreements that allegedly violate Section 1 of the Sherman Act to determine whether they may, in fact, constitute reasonable restraints on trade.

The need for a rule-of-reason analysis of some agreements in restraint of trade is obvious—if the rule of reason had not been developed, virtually any business agreement could conceivably be held to violate the Sherman Act. Justice Louis Brandeis effectively phrased this sentiment in *Chicago Board of Trade v. United States,* a case decided in 1918:

> Every agreement concerning trade, every regulation of trade, restrains. To bind, to restrain, is of their very essence. The true test of legality is whether the restraint imposed is such as merely regulates and perhaps thereby promotes competition or whether it is such as may suppress or even destroy competition.[4]

When analyzing an alleged Section 1 violation under the rule of reason, a court will consider several factors. These factors include the purpose of the agreement, the parties' power to implement the agreement to achieve that purpose, and the effect or potential effect of the agreement on competition. A court might also consider whether the parties could have relied on less restrictive means to achieve their purpose.

Horizontal Restraints

HORIZONTAL RESTRAINT
Any agreement that in some way restrains competition between rival firms competing in the same market.

The term **horizontal restraint** is encountered frequently in antitrust law. A horizontal restraint is any agreement that in some way restrains competition between rival firms competing in the same market. In the following subsections, we look at several types of horizontal restraints.

---

4. 246 U.S. 231, 38 S.Ct. 242, 62 L.Ed. 683 (1918).

Price Fixing

Any **price-fixing agreement**—an agreement among competitors to fix prices—constitutes a *per se* violation of Section 1. Perhaps the definitive case regarding price-fixing agreements is still the 1940 case of *United States v. Socony-Vacuum Oil Co.*[5] In that case, a group of independent oil producers in Texas and Louisiana were caught between falling demand due to the Great Depression of the 1930s and increasing supply from newly discovered oil fields in the region. In response to these conditions, a group of major refining companies agreed to buy "distress" gasoline (excess supplies) from the independents so as to dispose of it in an "orderly manner." Although there was no explicit agreement as to price, it was clear that the purpose of the agreement was to limit the supply of gasoline on the market and thereby raise prices.

There may have been good business reasons for the agreement. Nonetheless, the United States Supreme Court recognized the dangerous effects that such an agreement could have on open and free competition. The Court held that the reasonableness of a price-fixing agreement is never a defense; any agreement that restricts output or artificially fixes price is a *per se* violation of Section 1. The rationale of the *per se* rule was best stated in what is now the most famous portion of the Court's opinion—footnote 59. In that footnote, Justice William O. Douglas compared a freely functioning price system to a body's central nervous system, condemning price-fixing agreements as threats to "the central nervous system of the economy."

EXAMPLE #1 The manufacturer of the prescription drug Cardizem CD, which can help prevent heart attacks, was about to lose its patent on the drug. Another company developed a generic version in anticipation of the patent expiring. After the two firms became involved in litigation over the patent, the first company agreed to pay the second company $40 million per year not to market the generic version until their dispute was resolved. This agreement was held to be a *per se* violation of the Sherman Act because it restrained competition between rival firms and delayed the entry of generic versions of Cardizem into the market.[6] □

Group Boycotts

A **group boycott,** or concerted refusal to deal, is an agreement by two or more buyers or sellers to boycott (refuse to deal with) a particular person or firm. Traditionally, the courts have considered group boycotts to constitute *per se* violations of Section 1 of the Sherman Act because they involve concerted action. This is particularly true if the group possesses market power and the boycott is intended to restrict or exclude a competitor. To prove a violation of Section 1, the plaintiff must demonstrate that the boycott or joint refusal to deal was undertaken with the intention of eliminating competition or preventing entry into a given market. If anticompetitive intent is lacking, however, the court may be inclined to weigh the potential benefits of the group's efforts against the harm inflicted by the boycott.[7] Although most boycotts are illegal, a few, such as group boycotts against a supplier for political reasons, may be protected under the First Amendment right to freedom of expression.

Horizontal Market Division

It is a *per se* violation of Section 1 of the Sherman Act for competitors to divide up territories or customers. **EXAMPLE #2** Manufacturers A, B, and C compete against each other in the states of Kansas,

PRICE-FIXING AGREEMENT
An agreement between competitors to fix the prices of products or services at a certain level.

GROUP BOYCOTT
The refusal by a group of competitors to deal with a particular person or firm; prohibited by the Sherman Act.

---

5. 310 U.S. 150, 60 S.Ct. 811, 84 L.Ed. 1129 (1940).

6. *In re Cardizem CD Antitrust Litigation,* 332 F.3d 896 (6th Cir. 2003).

7. See, for example, *NYNEX Corp. v. Discon, Inc.,* 525 U.S. 128, 119 S.Ct. 493, 142 L.Ed.2d 510 (1998).

Nebraska, and Iowa. By agreement, A sells products only in Kansas, B sells only in Nebraska, and C sells only in Iowa. This concerted action not only reduces marketing costs but also allows all three (assuming there is no other competition) to raise the price of the goods sold in their respective states. The same violation would take place if A, B, and C simply agreed that A would sell only to institutional purchasers (such as school districts, universities, state agencies and departments, and cities) in all three states, B only to wholesalers, and C only to retailers.▫

Trade Associations   Businesses in the same general industry or profession frequently organize trade associations to pursue common interests. The joint activities of the trade association may include exchanges of information, representation of the members' business interests before governmental bodies, advertising campaigns, and the setting of regulatory standards to govern the industry or profession.

Generally, the rule of reason is applied to many of these horizontal actions. If a court finds that a trade association practice or agreement that restrains trade is sufficiently beneficial both to the association and to the public, it may deem the restraint reasonable. **EXAMPLE #3** Lumber producers might be concerned about whether they are cutting more trees than expected future demand warrants, given the cutting levels of rival firms. The market for lumber might be widely dispersed over the whole nation, making it especially difficult for small firms to gauge overall demand in the market. Lumber firms might thus decide to form a trade association that could amass data on the output and price levels of its members in various markets. The association would benefit lumber firms by reducing the costs of projecting market demand. Such knowledge could also benefit society by making the lumber market function more smoothly, dampening cycles of oversupply and undersupply of lumber output.▫ Even if it did not make the industry function more smoothly, such knowledge would be unlikely to harm competition in the industry unless the industry was *concentrated*.

A **concentrated industry** is one in which either a single firm or a small number of firms control a large percentage of market sales. In concentrated industries, trade associations can be, and have been, used as a means to facilitate anticompetitive actions, such as fixing prices or allocating markets. When trade association agreements have substantially anticompetitive effects, a court will consider them to be in violation of Section 1 of the Sherman Act. For a discussion of how federal regulators are looking into alleged anticompetitive practices involving the Web-based multiple listing services of trade associations in the real estate industry, see this chapter's *Online Developments* feature. (For other potential problems with online advertising of real property, see the feature in Chapter 22 on page 720.)

Vertical Restraints

A **vertical restraint** of trade results from an agreement between firms at different levels in the manufacturing and distribution process. In contrast to horizontal relationships, which occur at the same level of operation, vertical relationships encompass the entire chain of production. The chain of production normally includes the purchase of inventory, basic manufacturing, distribution to wholesalers, and eventual sale of a product at the retail level. For some products, these distinct phases may be carried out by different firms. In other instances, a single

CONCENTRATED INDUSTRY
An industry in which a large percentage of market sales is controlled by either a single firm or a small number of firms.

VERTICAL RESTRAINT
Any restraint on trade created by agreements between firms at different levels in the manufacturing and distribution process.

Like almost every other product, homes are now being sold via the Internet on hundreds of thousands of Web sites. The most extensive listings of homes for sale, though, are found on the multiple listing services (MLS) sites that are available for every locality in the United States. An MLS site is developed through a cooperative agreement by real estate brokers in a particular market area to pool information about the properties they have for sale. Today, the majority of residential real estate sales involve the use of multiple listing services. Although MLS sites offer convenience by combining listings from many brokers, the sites have also raised antitrust concerns by restricting how certain brokers may use the sites. The Federal Trade Commission (FTC) and the U.S. Department of Justice have brought antitrust actions against both local real estate associations and the National Association of Realtors®, a national trade association for real estate brokers and agents, for attempting to restrict the use of MLS databases.

Boards of Realtors® Have Attempted to Limit Listings on Their Web Sites

In a given market area, the MLS listings are put together by the members of a local real estate association, typically called a Board of Realtors®, for the members' exclusive use. In many areas, Boards of Realtors have attempted to restrict the homes that can be listed on the official MLS Web site. In particular, the boards have tried to prevent discount brokers from listings the homes they have for sale.

The FTC's Bureau of Competition filed a complaint for violation of antitrust laws against the Board of Realtors in Austin, Texas, which had a rule prohibiting discount brokers from listing on its MLS site. After several months of negotiations, the FTC prevented the Austin board from adopting and enforcing "any rule that treats different types of real estate listing agreements differently." The FTC is now pursuing similar negotiations in other cities including Cleveland, Columbus, Detroit, and Indianapolis.

The NAR Tries to Restrict Virtual Brokers

The National Association of Realtors (NAR) represents more than 1 million individual member brokers and their affiliated agents and sales associates. Its policies govern the conduct of its members throughout the United States. In the 1990s, many members of the NAR began to create password-protected Web sites through which prospective home buyers could search the MLS database. The password would be given only to potential buyers who had registered as customers of the broker. The brokers who worked through these virtual office Web sites, or VOWs, came to be known as VOW-operating brokers. Because they had no need of physical offices, their

operating expenses were lower than those of traditional brokers. Soon both Cendant and RE/MAX, the largest and second-largest U.S. real estate franchisors, respectively, expressed concern that VOW-operating brokers would put downward pressure on brokers' commissions.

In response, the NAR developed a new policy for Web listings. The policy included an opt-out provision "that forbade any broker participating in a multiple listing service from conveying a listing to his or her customers via the Internet without the permission of the listing broker." In other words, a traditional broker could prevent her or his listings in the MLS database from being displayed on the Web site of a VOW-operating broker.

The U.S. Department of Justice Enters the Fray

The Antitrust Division of the U.S. Department of Justice, however, contended that the opt-out policy was anticompetitive and harmful to consumers. When the Justice Department indicated that it would bring an antitrust action against the NAR, the association modified its policy and eliminated the selective opt-out provision aimed specifically at VOW-operating brokers. Nevertheless, the revised policy still allowed brokers to prevent their listings from being displayed on any competitor's Web site. Thus, under the new policy, traditional brokers could still prevent VOW-operating brokers from providing the same MLS information via the Internet that traditional brokers could provide in person. The policy also permitted MLS sites to lower the quality of the data feed they provide brokers, thereby restraining brokers from using Internet-based features to enhance the services they offer customers.

In response, the Justice Department filed a suit in federal district court against the NAR, asserting that the association's policies had violated Section 1 of the Sherman Act by preventing real estate brokers from offering better services as well as lower costs to online consumers. The department contends that the NAR's policies constitute a "contract, combination, and conspiracy between NAR and its members which unreasonably restrains competition in brokerage service markets throughout the United States to the detriment of American consumers." In 2006, finding that the Justice Department had shown sufficient evidence of anticompetitive effects to allow the suit to go forward, the court denied the NAR's motion to dismiss the case.[a]

FOR CRITICAL ANALYSIS Why couldn't discount brokers simply create their own Web sites to list the houses they have for sale?

a. *United States v. National Association of Realtors,* 2006 WL 3434263 (N.D.Ill. 2006).

VERTICALLY INTEGRATED FIRM
A firm that carries out two or more functional phases (manufacture, distribution, and retailing, for example) of the chain of production.

firm carries out two or more of the separate functional phases. Such enterprises are considered to be **vertically integrated firms.**

Even though firms operating at different functional levels are not in direct competition with one another, they are in competition with other firms. Thus, agreements between firms standing in a vertical relationship may affect competition. Some vertical restraints are *per se* violations of Section 1; others are judged under the rule of reason.

Territorial or Customer Restrictions   In arranging for the distribution of its products, a manufacturing firm often wishes to insulate dealers from direct competition with other dealers selling the product. To this end, it may institute territorial restrictions or attempt to prohibit wholesalers or retailers from reselling the product to certain classes of buyers, such as competing retailers.

A firm may have legitimate reasons for imposing such territorial or customer restrictions. **EXAMPLE #4** A computer manufacturer may wish to prevent a dealer from cutting costs and undercutting rivals by selling computers without promotion or customer service, while relying on nearby dealers to provide these services. In this situation, the cost-cutting dealer reaps the benefits (sales of the product) paid for by other dealers who undertake promotion and arrange for customer service. By not providing customer service, the cost-cutting dealer may also harm the manufacturer's reputation.□

Territorial and customer restrictions are judged under the rule of reason. In *United States v. Arnold, Schwinn & Co.,*[8] a case decided in 1967, a bicycle manufacturer, Schwinn, was assigning specific territories to its wholesale distributors and authorizing certain retail dealers only if they agreed to advertise Schwinn bikes and give them the same prominence as other brands. The United States Supreme Court held that these vertical territorial and customer restrictions were *per se* violations of Section 1 of the Sherman Act. Ten years later, however, in *Continental T.V., Inc. v. GTE Sylvania, Inc.,*[9] a case involving similar restrictions imposed on retailers by a television manufacturer, the Supreme Court overturned the *Schwinn* decision. In the *Continental* decision, the Court held that such vertical restrictions should be judged under the rule of reason, and this rule is still applied in most vertical restraint cases. The *Continental* decision marked a definite shift from rigid characterization of these kinds of vertical restraints to a more flexible, economic analysis of the restraints under the rule of reason.

**RESALE PRICE
MAINTENANCE AGREEMENT**
An agreement between a manufacturer and a retailer in which the manufacturer specifies what the retail prices of its products must be.

Resale Price Maintenance Agreements   An agreement between a manufacturer and a distributor or retailer in which the manufacturer specifies what the retail prices of its products must be is referred to as a **resale price maintenance agreement.** Such agreements were once considered to be *per se* violations of Section 1 of the Sherman Act, but in 1997 the United States Supreme Court ruled that *maximum* resale price maintenance agreements should be judged under the rule of reason.[10] In these agreements, the manufacturer sets a maximum price that retailers and distributors can charge for its products.

The question before the Court in the following case was whether *minimum* resale price maintenance agreements should be treated as *per se* unlawful.

---

8. 388 U.S. 365, 87 S.Ct. 1856, 18 L.Ed.2d 1249 (1967).
9. 433 U.S. 36, 97 S.Ct. 2549, 53 L.Ed.2d 568 (1977).
10. *State Oil Co. v. Khan,* 522 U.S. 3, 118 S.Ct. 275, 139 L.Ed.2d 199 (1997).

Case 23.1 Leegin Creative Leather Producs, Inc. v. PSKS, Inc.

Supreme Court of the United States, 2007.
__ U.S. __, 127 S.Ct. 2705, 168 L.Ed.2d 623.
supct.law.cornell.edu/supct/index.html[a]

BACKGROUND AND FACTS   Leegin Creative Leather Products, Inc., designs, manufactures, and distributes leather goods and accessories. One of its brand names is Brighton. Kay's Kloset, owned by PSKS, Inc., started purchasing Brighton

a. In the "Archive of Decisions" section, in the "By party" subsection, click on "1990-present." In the result, in the "2006–2007" row, click on "1st party." On the next page, scroll to the name of the case and click on it. On the next page, click on the appropriate link to access the opinion.

goods from Leegin in 1995. Leegin required resellers of Brighton goods to charge customers a minimum price. This minimum price formed part of a resale price maintenance program that Leegin had instituted. When Leegin discovered that Kay's Kloset had been discounting Brighton products by 20 percent, Leegin stopped selling Brighton products to the store. PSKS sued Leegin in federal court, claiming that Leegin had violated antitrust law by imposing minimum prices. The U.S. District Court for the Eastern District of Texas entered a judgment against Leegin in the amount of almost $4 million. The U.S. Court of Appeals for the Fifth Circuit affirmed, and Leegin appealed to the United States Supreme Court.

IN THE WORDS OF THE COURT . . . Justice *KENNEDY* delivered the opinion of the Court.

* * * *

The rule of reason is the accepted standard for testing whether a practice restrains trade in violation of [Section] 1 [of the Sherman Act].

* * * *

Resort to per se *rules is confined to restraints* * * * *that would always or almost always tend to restrict competition and decrease output. To justify a per se prohibition a restraint must have manifestly anticompetitive effects, and lack* * * * *any redeeming virtue.* [Emphasis added.]

As a consequence, the *per se* rule is appropriate only after courts have had considerable experience with the type of restraint at issue, and only if courts can predict with confidence that it would be invalidated in all or almost all instances under the rule of reason.

* * * *

The reasoning of the Court's more recent jurisprudence has rejected the rationales on which [the application of the *per se* rule to minimum resale price maintenance agreements] was based. * * * [These rationales were] based on formalistic legal doctrine rather than demonstrable economic effect.

* * * Furthermore [the Court] treated vertical agreements a manufacturer makes with its distributors as analogous to a horizontal combination among competing distributors. * * * Our recent cases formulate antitrust principles in accordance with the appreciated differences in economic effect between vertical and horizontal agreements * * * .

* * * *

The justifications for vertical price restraints are similar to those for other vertical restraints. *Minimum resale price maintenance can stimulate interbrand competition* * * * *by reducing intrabrand competition* * * * . The promotion of interbrand competition is important because the primary purpose of the antitrust laws is to protect this type of competition. * * * *Resale price maintenance also has the potential to give consumers more options so that they can choose among low-price, low-service brands; high-price, high-service brands; and brands that fall in between.* [Emphasis added.]

* * * *

While vertical agreements setting minimum resale prices can have procompetitive justifications, they may have anticompetitive effects in other cases; and unlawful price fixing, designed solely to obtain monopoly profits, is an ever present temptation.

* * * *

Notwithstanding the risks of unlawful conduct, it cannot be stated with any degree of confidence that resale price maintenance always or almost always tends to restrict competition and decrease output. Vertical agreements establishing minimum resale

CASE 23.1–CONTINUED

CASE 23.1–CONTINUED

prices can have either procompetitive or anticompetitive effects, depending upon the circumstances in which they are formed. * * * As the [*per se*] rule would proscribe a significant amount of procompetitive conduct, these agreements appear ill suited for *per se* condemnation.

DECISION AND REMEDY   The United States Supreme Court reversed the judgment of the appellate court and remanded the case for further proceedings consistent with its opinion. The Court pointed out that a *per se* rule should be confined to restraints of trade that "would always or almost always tend to restrict competition and decrease output." The Court did not believe that a *per se* rule should apply to minimum resale price agreements because these agreements can stimulate interbrand competition and thus may have a procompetitive effect.

THE LEGAL ENVIRONMENT DIMENSION   Should the Court have applied the doctrine of *stare decisis* to hold that minimum resale price maintenance agreements are still subject to the *per se* rule? Why or why not?

THE GLOBAL DIMENSION   If a product or line of products is in competition with products provided by major foreign companies, is there more or less chance that resale price maintenance would lessen competition and restrict output? Explain.

SECTION 2 OF THE SHERMAN ACT

Section 1 of the Sherman Act proscribes certain concerted, or joint, activities that restrain trade. In contrast, Section 2 condemns "every person who shall monopolize, or attempt to monopolize." Thus, two distinct types of behavior are subject to sanction under Section 2: *monopolization* and *attempts to monopolize*. One tactic that may be involved in either offense is **predatory pricing.** Predatory pricing involves an attempt by one firm to drive its competitors from the market by selling its product at prices substantially *below* the normal costs of production. Once the competitors are eliminated, the firm will attempt to recapture its losses and go on to earn higher profits by driving prices up far above their competitive levels.

PREDATORY PRICING
The pricing of a product below cost with the intent to drive competitors out of the market.

Monopolization

MONOPOLIZATION
The possession of monopoly power in the relevant market and the willful acquisition or maintenance of that power, as distinguished from growth or development as a consequence of a superior product, business acumen, or historic accident.

The United States Supreme Court has defined the offense of **monopolization** as involving the following two elements: "(1) the possession of monopoly power in the relevant market and (2) the willful acquisition or maintenance of [that] power as distinguished from growth or development as a consequence of a superior product, business acumen, or historic accident."[11] A violation of Section 2 requires that both these elements—monopoly power and an intent to monopolize—be established.

Monopoly Power   The Sherman Act does not define *monopoly*. In economic parlance, monopoly refers to control of a single market by a single entity. It is well established in antitrust law, however, that a firm may be deemed a monopolist even though it is not the sole seller in a market. Additionally, size alone does not determine whether a firm is a monopoly. **EXAMPLE #5** A "mom and pop" grocery located in the isolated town of Happy Camp, California, is a monopolist if it is the only grocery serving that particular market. Size in relation to the market is

---

11. *United States v. Grinnell Corp.*, 384 U.S. 563, 86 S.Ct. 1698, 16 L.Ed.2d 778 (1966).

what matters because monopoly involves the power to affect prices and output.□

Monopoly power may be proved by direct evidence that the firm used its power to control prices and restrict output.[12] Usually, however, there is not enough evidence to show that the firm was intentionally controlling prices, so the plaintiff has to offer indirect, or circumstantial, evidence of monopoly power. To prove monopoly power indirectly, the plaintiff must show that the firm has a dominant share of the relevant market and that there are significant barriers for new competitors entering that market.

Relevant Market   Before a court can determine whether a firm has a dominant market share, it must define the relevant market. The relevant market consists of two elements: (1) a relevant product market and (2) a relevant geographic market.

Relevant Product Market   The relevant product market includes all products that, although produced by different firms, have identical attributes, such as sugar. It also includes products that are reasonably interchangeable for the purpose for which they are produced. Products will be considered reasonably interchangeable if consumers treat them as acceptable substitutes.[13]

What should the relevant product market include? This is often the key issue in monopolization cases because the way the market is defined may determine whether a firm has monopoly power. **EXAMPLE #6** In 2007, the Federal Trade Commission (FTC) filed a Section 2 claim against Whole Foods Market, Inc., which owns a nationwide chain of natural and organic food stores. The FTC was seeking to prevent Whole Foods from merging with Wild Oats Markets, Inc., its main competitor in nationwide high-end organic food supermarkets.

The FTC argued that the relevant product market consisted of only "premium natural and organic supermarkets (PNOS)" rather than all supermarkets. By defining the product market narrowly, the degree of a firm's market power is enhanced. A federal district court ruled against the FTC, finding that the relevant product market was not just PNOS but all supermarkets and allowing the merger to go forward. In 2008, however, a federal appellate court reversed and remanded that decision and ruled that an injunction should have been granted to the FTC to prevent the merger.[14]□

Deciding whether a relevant market existed in which competitors had market power was the main issue in the following case.

---

12. See, for example, *Broadcom Corp. v. Qualcomm, Inc.*, 501 F.3d 297 (3d Cir. 2007).
13. See, for example, *HDC Medical, Inc. v. Minntech Corp.*, 474 F.3d 543 (8th Cir. 2007).
14. *FTC v. Whole Foods Market, Inc.*, 533 F.3d 869 (D.C. Cir. 2008).

Case 23.2   **Newcal Industries, Inc. v. Ikon Office Solutions**

United States Court of Appeals, Ninth Circuit, 2008.
513 F.3d 1038.
www.ca9.uscourts.gov[a]

BACKGROUND AND FACTS   Newcal Industries and Ikon Office Solutions (IKON) compete in the brand-name copier equipment-leasing market for commercial customers and in

a. Click on "Opinions" and then "Opinions by Date" and then "2008." Go to "January" and find the decisions issued on "01/23/08." Click on the case name to access the opinion.

the provision of service. When a lease approaches its term, these companies compete for the lease of upgraded copier equipment. When a service contract approaches its term, these companies also compete to buy out the service contract in order to provide another one. Newcal alleged that IKON "tricked" its customers by amending its lease agreements and service contracts without disclosing that such amendments would lengthen the terms of the original agreements. The purpose of these contract extensions was to shield IKON

CASE 23.2–CONTINUED

customers from competition in the aftermarkets for upgraded copier equipment and service agreements. When IKON succeeded in extending the terms of the original contract, it was able to raise that contract's value. Consequently, Newcal and other competitors had to pay higher prices to buy out such contracts in the aftermarkets for upgraded equipment and services. Newcal brought claims under the Sherman Act, alleging antitrust violations. The district court held that Newcal had failed to allege a legally recognizable "relevant market" under the Sherman Act. Newcal appealed.

IN THE WORDS OF THE COURT . . . *THOMAS*, Circuit Judge.

*   *   *   *

First and foremost, *the relevant market must be a product market. The consumers do not define the boundaries of the market; the products or producers do. Second, the market must encompass the product at issue as well as all economic substitutes for the product.* As the Supreme Court has instructed, "The outer boundaries of a product market are determined by the reasonable interchangeability of use *   *   * between the product itself and substitutes for it." As such, the relevant market must include "the group or groups of sellers or producers who have actual or potential ability to deprive each other of significant levels of business." [Emphasis added.]

*   *   * Although the general market must include all economic substitutes, it is legally permissible to premise antitrust allegations on a submarket. That is, an antitrust claim may, under certain circumstances, allege restraints of trade within or monopolization of a small part of the general market of substitutable products. *In order to establish the existence of a legally cognizable submarket, the plaintiff must be able to show (but need not necessarily establish in the complaint) that the alleged submarket is economically distinct from the general product market.* In [another case], the Supreme Court listed several "practical indicia" [indicators] of an economically distinct submarket: "industry or public recognition of the submarket as a separate economic entity, the product's peculiar characteristics and uses, unique production facilities, distinct customers, distinct prices, sensitivity to price changes, and specialized vendors." [Emphasis added.]

*   *   *   *

*   *   * First, the law permits an antitrust claimant to restrict the relevant market to a single brand of the product at issue. Second, the law prohibits an antitrust claimant from resting on market *power* that arises solely from contractual rights that consumers knowingly and voluntarily gave to the defendant. Third, in determining whether the defendant's market power falls in the *   *   * category of contractually-created market power or in the *   *   * category of economic market power, the law permits an inquiry into whether a consumer's selection of a particular brand in the competitive market is the functional equivalent of a contractual commitment, giving that brand an agreed-upon right to monopolize its consumers in an aftermarket. The law permits an inquiry into whether consumers entered into such "contracts" knowing that they were agreeing to such a commitment.

*   *   *   *

The relevance of this point to the legal viability of Newcal's market definition may not be intuitively obvious, but it is nevertheless significant. *   *   * IKON has a contractually-created monopoly over services provided under *original* IKON contracts. That contractually-created monopoly *   *   * then gives IKON a unique *relationship* with those consumers, and the contractual *relationship* gives IKON a unique position in the wholly derivative aftermarket for replacement equipment and lease-end services. The allegation here is that IKON is *   *   * exploiting its unique position—its unique contractual relationship—to gain monopoly power in a derivative aftermarket in which its power is not contractually mandated.

*   *   *   *

*   *   * This case is not a case in which the alleged market power flows from contractual exclusivity. IKON is not simply enforcing a contractual provision that gives it the exclusive right to provide replacement equipment and lease-end services. Rather, it is leveraging a special relationship with its contracting partners to restrain trade in a wholly derivative aftermarket. We therefore reverse the district court's holding that * * * Newcal's complaint is legally invalid.

That holding, however, does not quite end the matter. In considering the legal validity of Newcal's alleged market, we must also determine whether IKON customers constitute a cognizable subset of the aftermarket, such that they qualify as a submarket * * *. That is, we have thus far concluded only that there is no *per se* rule against recognizing contractually-created submarkets and that such submarkets are potentially viable when the market at issue is a wholly derivative aftermarket. * * * A submarket * * * must bear the "practical indicia" of an independent economic entity in order to qualify as a cognizable submarket * * *. In this case, Newcal's complaint sufficiently alleges that IKON customers constitute a submarket according to all of those practical indicia.

DECISION AND REMEDY   The U.S. Court of Appeals for the Ninth Circuit reversed and remanded the district court's decision. The court concluded that there existed a legally recognizable relevant market.

WHAT IF THE FACTS WERE DIFFERENT?   Assume that IKON's contracts allowed its customers to "opt out" if they gave a sixty-day notice. Would the judge have ruled differently? Why or why not?

THE ETHICAL DIMENSION   Would there ever be any circumstances that could justify IKON's practice of amending customers' contracts without letting them know that the result was an extension of those original lease contracts? Explain your answer.

Relevant Geographical Market   The second component of the relevant market is the geographical boundaries of the market. For products that are sold nationwide, the geographical boundaries encompass the entire United States. If transportation costs are significant or if a producer and its competitors sell in only a limited area—one in which customers have no access to other sources of the product—then the geographical market is limited to that area. In this sense, a national firm may compete in several distinct areas, having monopoly power in one but not others. Generally, the geographical market is that section of the country within which a firm can increase its price a bit without attracting new sellers or without losing many customers to alternative suppliers outside that area.

The advent of e-commerce and the Internet is likely to change dramatically the notion of the size and limits of a geographical market. It may become difficult to perceive any geographical market as local, except for such products as concrete. **EXAMPLE #7** Clear Channel Communications, Inc., owns numerous radio stations and promotes and books concert tours. Malinda Heerwagen, who had attended various rock concerts in Chicago, Illinois, filed a lawsuit against Clear Channel alleging violations of Section 2. Heerwagen claimed that the company had used anticompetitive practices to acquire and maintain monopoly power in a national ticket market for live rock concerts, causing audiences to pay inflated prices for the tickets. Heerwagen argued that because Clear Channel sold tickets nationwide, the geographic market was the entire United States. The court, however, ruled that even though Clear Channel sold tickets nationally, the relevant market for concert tickets was local. The court reasoned that "[a] purchaser of a concert ticket is hardly likely to look outside of her own area, even if the price for tickets has increased inside her region and decreased for the same tour in other places."[15] □

---

15. *Heerwagen v. Clear Channel Communications,* 435 F.3d 219 (2d Cir. 2006).

The Intent Requirement   Monopoly power, in and of itself, does not constitute the offense of monopolization under Section 2 of the Sherman Act. The offense also requires an *intent* to monopolize. A dominant market share may be the result of good business judgment or the development of a superior product. It may simply be the result of historical accident. In these situations, the acquisition of monopoly power is not an antitrust violation.

If, however, a firm possesses market power as a result of carrying out some purposeful act to acquire or maintain that power through anticompetitive means, then it is in violation of Section 2. In most monopolization cases, intent may be inferred from evidence that the firm had monopoly power and engaged in anticompetitive behavior.

EXAMPLE #8   When Navigator, the first popular graphical Internet browser, used Java technology that was able to run on a variety of platforms, Microsoft Corporation perceived a threat to its dominance in the operating-system market. Microsoft developed a competing browser, Internet Explorer, and then began to require computer makers that wanted to install Windows to install Explorer and exclude Navigator. Microsoft also included codes in Windows that would cripple the operating system if Explorer was deleted and paid Internet service providers to distribute Explorer and exclude Navigator. Because of this pattern of exclusionary conduct, a court found that Microsoft was guilty of monopolization. The court reasoned that Microsoft's pattern of conduct could be rational only if the firm knew that it possessed monopoly power.[16]□

Preventing Legal Disputes

Because exclusionary conduct can have legitimate efficiency-enhancing effects, it can be difficult to determine when conduct will be viewed as anticompetitive and a violation of Section 2 of the Sherman Act. Thus, a business that possesses monopoly power must be careful that its actions cannot be inferred to be evidence of intent to monopolize. Even if your business does not have a dominant market share, you would be wise to take precautions. Make sure that you can articulate clear, legitimate reasons for your conduct and contracts and that you do not provide any direct evidence (damaging e-mails, for example) of an intent to exclude competitors. A court will be less likely to infer the intent to monopolize if the specific conduct was aimed at increasing output and lowering per-unit costs, improving product quality, or protecting a patented technology or innovation. Exclusionary conduct and agreements that have no redeeming qualities are much more likely to be deemed illegal. ■

Unilateral Refusals to Deal   As discussed previously, joint refusals to deal, called *group boycotts,* are subject to close scrutiny under Section 1 of the Sherman Act. A single manufacturer acting unilaterally, though, normally is free to deal, or not to deal, with whomever it wishes.

Nevertheless, in some instances, a unilateral refusal to deal will violate antitrust laws. These instances involve offenses proscribed under Section 2 of the Sherman Act and occur only if (1) the firm refusing to deal has—or is likely to acquire—monopoly power and (2) the refusal is likely to have an anticompetitive effect on a particular market.   **EXAMPLE #9**   The owner of three of the four

---

16. *United States v. Microsoft Corp.*, 253 F.3d 34 (D.C.Cir. 2001). Microsoft has faced numerous antitrust claims and has settled a number of lawsuits in which it was accused of antitrust violations and anticompetitive tactics.

major downhill ski areas in Aspen, Colorado, refused to continue participating in a jointly offered six-day "all Aspen" lift ticket. The Supreme Court ruled that the owner's refusal to cooperate with its smaller competitor was a violation of Section 2 of the Sherman Act. Because the company owned three-fourths of the local ski areas, it had monopoly power, and thus its unilateral refusal had an anticompetitive effect on the market.[17] □

Attempts to Monopolize

Section 2 also prohibits **attempted monopolization** of a market. Any action challenged as an attempt to monopolize must have been specifically intended to exclude competitors and garner monopoly power. In addition, the attempt must have had a "dangerous" probability of success—only *serious* threats of monopolization are condemned as violations. The probability cannot be dangerous unless the alleged offender possesses some degree of market power.[18]

> **ATTEMPTED MONOPOLIZATION**
> Any actions by a firm to eliminate competition and gain monopoly power.

As mentioned earlier, predatory pricing is a form of anticompetitive conduct that is commonly used by firms that are attempting to monopolize. In 2007, the United States Supreme Court ruled that *predatory bidding,* which is similar but involves the exercise of market power on the buying, or input, side, should be analyzed under the same standards as predatory pricing.[19] In predatory bidding, a firm deliberately bids up the prices of inputs to prevent its competitors from obtaining sufficient supplies to manufacture their products. To succeed in a predatory pricing (or predatory bidding) claim, a plaintiff must prove that the alleged predator has a "dangerous probability of recouping its investment in below-cost pricing" because low prices alone often stimulate competition. (Note that predatory pricing may also lead to claims of price discrimination, to be discussed shortly.)

THE CLAYTON ACT

In 1914, Congress attempted to strengthen federal antitrust laws by enacting the Clayton Act. The Clayton Act was aimed at specific anticompetitive or monopolistic practices that the Sherman Act did not cover. The substantive provisions of the act deal with four distinct forms of business behavior, which are declared illegal but not criminal. With regard to each of the four provisions, the act's prohibitions are qualified by the general condition that the behavior is illegal only if it substantially tends to lessen competition or create monopoly power. The major offenses under the Clayton Act are set out in Sections 2, 3, 7, and 8 of the act.

Section 2—Price Discrimination

Section 2 of the Clayton Act prohibits **price discrimination,** which occurs when a seller charges different prices to competing buyers for identical goods or services. Congress strengthened this section by amending it with the passage of the

> **PRICE DISCRIMINATION**
> Setting prices in such a way that two competing buyers pay two different prices for an identical product or service.

---

17. *Aspen Skiing Co. v. Aspen Highlands Skiing Corp.,* 472 U.S. 585, 105 S.Ct. 2847, 86 L.Ed.2d 467 (1985). See also *America Channel, LLC v. Time Warner Cable, Inc.,* 2007 WL 142173 (D.Minn. 2007); and *Z-Tel Communications, Inc. v. SBC Communications, Inc.,* 331 F.Supp.2d 513 (E.D.Tex. 2004).
18. See, for example, *Nobody in Particular Presents, Inc. v. Clear Channel Communications, Inc.,* 311 F.Supp.2d 1048 (D.Colo. 2004); and *City of Moundridge, KS v. Exxon Mobil Corp.,* 471 F.Supp.2d 20 (D.D.C. 2007).
19. *Weyerhaeuser Co. v. Ross-Simmons Hardwood Lumber Co., Inc.,* ___ U.S. ___, 127 S.Ct. 1069, 166 L.Ed.2d 911 (2007).

Suppose that the owner of this gas station agrees to buy gas only from Shell Oil Company. Does this agreement necessarily violate the Clayton Act? Why or why not? ("Iotae/Aaron"/Creative Commons)

Robinson-Patman Act in 1936. As amended, Section 2 prohibits direct and indirect price discrimination that cannot be justified by differences in production costs, transportation costs, or cost differences due to other reasons. In short, a seller is prohibited from reducing a price to one buyer below the price charged to that buyer's competitor.

Required Elements   To violate Section 2, the seller must be engaged in interstate commerce, the goods must be of like grade and quality, and goods must have been sold to two or more purchasers. In addition, the effect of the price discrimination must be to substantially lessen competition, to tend to create a monopoly, or to otherwise injure competition. Without proof of an actual injury resulting from the price discrimination, the plaintiff cannot recover damages.

Note that price discrimination claims can arise from discounts, offsets, rebates, or allowances given to one buyer over another. Moreover, giving favorable credit terms, delivery, or freight charges to only some buyers can also lead to allegations of price discrimination. For instance, offering goods to different customers at the same price but including free delivery for certain buyers may violate Section 2 in some circumstances.

Defenses   There are several statutory defenses to liability for price discrimination.

1. *Cost justification.* If the seller can justify the price reduction by demonstrating that a particular buyer's purchases saved the seller costs in producing and selling the goods, the seller will not be liable for price discrimination.

2. *Meeting the price of competition.* If the seller charged the lower price in a good faith attempt to meet an equally low price of a competitor, the seller will not be liable for price discrimination. **EXAMPLE #10** Water Craft was a retail dealership of Mercury Marine outboard motors in Baton Rouge, Louisiana. Mercury Marine also sold its motors to other dealers in the Baton Rouge area. When Water Craft discovered that Mercury was selling its outboard motors at a substantial discount to Water Craft's largest competitor, it filed a price discrimination lawsuit against Mercury. In this situation, the court held that Mercury Marine had shown that the discounts given to Water Craft's competitor were made in good faith to meet the low price charged by another manufacturer of marine motors.[20] □

3. *Changing market conditions.* A seller may lower its price on an item in response to changing conditions affecting the market for or the marketability of the goods concerned. Sellers are allowed to readjust their prices to meet the realities of the market without liability for price discrimination. Thus, if an advance in technology makes a particular product less marketable than it was previously, a seller can lower the product's price.

Section 3—Exclusionary Practices

Under Section 3 of the Clayton Act, sellers or lessors cannot sell or lease goods "on the condition, agreement or understanding that the . . . purchaser or lessee thereof shall not use or deal in the goods . . . of a competitor or competi-

---

20. *Water Craft Management, LLC v. Mercury Marine*, 457 F.3d 484 (5th Cir. 2006).

tors of the seller." In effect, this section prohibits two types of vertical agreements involving exclusionary practices—exclusive-dealing contracts and tying arrangements.

Exclusive-Dealing Contracts   A contract under which a seller forbids a buyer to purchase products from the seller's competitors is called an **exclusive-dealing contract.** A seller is prohibited from making an exclusive-dealing contract under Section 3 if the effect of the contract is "to substantially lessen competition or tend to create a monopoly."

EXAMPLE #11 In *Standard Oil Co. of California v. United States,*[21] a leading case decided by the United States Supreme Court in 1949, the then-largest gasoline seller in the nation made exclusive-dealing contracts with independent stations in seven western states. The contracts involved 16 percent of all retail outlets, with sales amounting to approximately 7 percent of all retail sales in that market. The Court noted that the market was substantially concentrated because the seven largest gasoline suppliers all used exclusive-dealing contracts with their independent retailers and together controlled 65 percent of the market. Looking at market conditions after the arrangements were instituted, the Court found that market shares were extremely stable and that entry into the market was apparently restricted. Thus, the Court held that Section 3 of the Clayton Act had been violated because competition was "foreclosed in a substantial share" of the relevant market. □

Note that since the Supreme Court's 1949 decision in the *Standard Oil* case, a number of subsequent decisions have called the holding in this case into doubt.[22] Today, it is clear that to violate antitrust law, an exclusive-dealing agreement (or tying arrangement, discussed next) must qualitatively and substantially harm competition. To prevail, a plaintiff must present affirmative evidence that the performance of the agreement will foreclose competition and harm consumers.

Tying Arrangements   When a seller conditions the sale of a product (the tying product) on the buyer's agreement to purchase another product (the tied product) produced or distributed by the same seller, a **tying arrangement,** or *tie-in sales agreement,* results. The legality of a tie-in agreement depends on many factors, particularly the purpose of the agreement and its likely effect on competition in the relevant markets (the market for the tying product and the market for the tied product).

EXAMPLE #12 In 1936, the United States Supreme Court held that International Business Machines and Remington Rand had violated Section 3 of the Clayton Act by requiring the purchase of their own machine cards (the tied product) as a condition for leasing their tabulation machines (the tying product). Because only these two firms sold completely automated tabulation machines, the Court concluded that each possessed market power sufficient to "substantially lessen competition" through the tying arrangements.[23] □

Section 3 of the Clayton Act has been held to apply only to commodities, not to services. Tying arrangements, however, can also be considered agreements

EXCLUSIVE-DEALING CONTRACT
An agreement under which a seller forbids a buyer to purchase products from the seller's competitors.

TYING ARRANGEMENT
An agreement between a buyer and a seller in which the buyer of a specific product or service becomes obligated to purchase additional products or services from the seller.

21. 337 U.S. 293, 69 S.Ct. 1051, 93 L.Ed. 1371 (1949).
22. See, for example, *Illinois Tool Works, Inc. v. Independent Ink, Inc.,* 547 U.S. 28, 126 S.Ct. 1281, 164 L.Ed.2d 26 (2006); and *Stop & Shop Supermarket Co. v. Blue Cross & Blue Shield of Rhode Island,* 373 F.3d 57 (1st Cir. 2004).
23. *International Business Machines Corp. v. United States,* 298 U.S. 131, 56 S.Ct. 701, 80 L.Ed. 1085 (1936).

that restrain trade in violation of Section 1 of the Sherman Act. Thus, cases involving tying arrangements of services have been brought under Section 1 of the Sherman Act. Although earlier cases condemned tying arrangements as illegal *per se,* courts now evaluate tying agreements under the rule of reason.

Section 7–Mergers

Under Section 7 of the Clayton Act, a person or business organization cannot hold stock and/or assets in another entity "where the effect . . . may be to substantially lessen competition." Section 7 is the statutory authority for preventing mergers or acquisitions that could result in monopoly power or a substantial lessening of competition in the marketplace. Section 7 applies to horizontal mergers and vertical mergers, both of which we discuss in the following subsections.

A crucial consideration in most merger cases is the **market concentration** of a product or business. Determining market concentration involves allocating percentage market shares among the various companies in the relevant market. When a small number of companies control a large share of the market, the market is concentrated. For example, if the four largest grocery stores in Chicago accounted for 80 percent of all retail food sales, the market clearly would be concentrated in those four firms. Competition, however, is not necessarily diminished solely as a result of market concentration, and other factors will be considered in determining whether a merger will violate Section 7. One factor of particular importance in evaluating the effects of a merger is whether the merger will make it more difficult for potential competitors to enter the relevant market.

Horizontal Mergers   Mergers between firms that compete with each other in the same market are called **horizontal mergers.** If a horizontal merger creates an entity with anything other than a small-percentage market share, the merger will be presumed illegal. When analyzing the legality of a horizontal merger, the courts consider three other factors: the overall concentration of the relevant product market, the relevant market's history of tending toward concentration, and whether the apparent design of the merger is to establish market power or to restrict competition.

The Federal Trade Commission (FTC) and the U.S. Department of Justice (DOJ) have established guidelines indicating which mergers will be challenged. Under the guidelines, the first factor to be considered is the degree of concentration in the relevant market. In determining market concentration, the FTC and the DOJ employ what is known as the *Herfindahl-Hirschman index (HHI)*. The HHI is computed by summing the squares of the percentage market shares of the firms in the relevant market. For example, if there are four firms with shares of 30 percent, 30 percent, 20 percent, and 20 percent, respectively, then the HHI equals 2,600 (900 + 900 + 400 + 400 = 2,600). If the premerger HHI is less than 1,000, then the market is unconcentrated, and the merger is unlikely to be challenged. If the premerger HHI is between 1,000 and 1,800, the industry is moderately concentrated, and the merger will be challenged only if it increases the HHI by 100 points or more.[24] If the HHI is greater than 1,800, the market is highly concentrated. In a highly concentrated market, a merger that produces an

---

MARKET CONCENTRATION
The degree to which a small number of firms control a large percentage share of a relevant market; determined by calculating the percentages held by the largest firms in that market.

HORIZONTAL MERGER
A merger between two firms that are competing in the same marketplace.

---

24. Compute the change in the index by doubling the product of the merging firms' premerger market shares. For example, a merger between a firm with a 5 percent share and one with a 6 percent share will increase the HHI by 2 × (5 × 6) = 60.

increase in the HHI of between 50 and 100 points raises significant competitive concerns. Mergers that produce an increase in the HHI of more than 100 points in a highly concentrated market are deemed likely to enhance market power. HHI figures were a factor in the following case.

Case 23.3 Chicago Bridge & Iron Co, v. Federal Trade Commission

United States Court of Appeals, Fifth Circuit, 2008.
___ F.3d ___.
www.ca5.uscourts.gov[a]

BACKGROUND AND FACTS Chicago Bridge & Iron Company, and its U.S. subsidiary of the same name, is a company that designs, engineers, and constructs industrial storage tanks for liquefied natural gas (LNG), liquefied petroleum gas (LPG), and liquid atmospheric gases, such as nitrogen, oxygen, and argon (LIN/LOX), as well as thermal vacuum chambers (TVCs) for testing aerospace satellites. In

a. On the left, click on "Opinions Page" and then in "Search for opinions where:" type "Chicago Bridge" in the "Title contains text:" box. Then click on the docket number listed.

these four separate markets, Chicago Bridge and another company, Pitt-Des Moines, Inc., have been the dominant firms. In 2001, Chicago Bridge acquired all of Pitt-Des Moines's assets for $84 million. The Federal Trade Commission (FTC) charged that Chicago Bridge's acquisition violated Section 7 of the Clayton Act and Section 5 of the Federal Trade Commission Act. An administrative law judge concurred, finding that the acquisition resulted in an undue increase in Chicago Bridge's market power that would not be constrained by timely entry of new competitors. At issue was the use of the Herfindahl-Hirschman index (HHI). The FTC calculated the HHI over a several-year period rather than on an annualized basis. Chicago Bridge appealed to the U.S. Court of Appeals for the Fifth Circuit.

IN THE WORDS OF THE COURT . . . DENNIS, Circuit Judge.

* * * *

The HHIs are just one element in the Government's strong *prima facie* case. Market concentration figures should be examined in the context of the entire *prima facie* case. Here, the *prima facie* case establishes without dispute that the two dominant, and often only, players in these four domestic markets are merging. This indisputable fact "bolster[s]" the Government's market concentration figures. Where the post-merger HHI exceeds 1,800, and the merger produces an increase in the HHI of more than 100 points, the merger guidelines create a presumption of adverse competitive consequences. The increases in HHIs in this case are extremely high. HHI increases of 2,635 for the LIN/LOX tank market, 3,911 for the LPG tank market, 4,956 for the LNG tank market, and 4,999 for the TVC tank market are predicted post-merger. An HHI of 10,000 denotes a complete monopoly. Post-acquisition HHIs for the four markets are: 5,845 for LIN/LOX, 8,380 for LPG, and 10,000 for the LNG and TVC markets.

* * * The Commission agrees with the ALJ [administrative law judge] that the use of HHIs based solely on sales from the 1996–2001 period is unreliable, and therefore extended the sales-data time period to an 11-year period, 1990–2001. When sales data are sporadic, a longer historical perspective may be necessary. * * * The Commission adequately explained why it chose an extended period: (1) the extended period provided more data points, which averages out the year-to-year fluctuations and "chance outcomes" and (2) [Chicago Bridge] presents no evidence that a structural change affected the market, and thus the same market conditions persist in the 1996–2001 time-period as the 11-year period, except the 11-year period has additional data points.

* * * *

In addition to its challenge of the selection of the time period, [Chicago Bridge] also argues that the "sporadic" nature of the sales data undermines all evidence of market power. * * * We agree that reliance on very limited data, such as two data points, may undermine an entire *prima facie* case. However, we find this to be a very limited exception * * * because the academic literature has not accepted any broad conclusion that small markets are all *per se* problematic.

* * * *

CASE 23.3–CONTINUED

CASE 23.3—CONTINUED

We find that the record contains substantial evidence to support the Commission's finding that the HHIs are not completely irrelevant in three of the four markets. Instead of ignoring HHIs, we agree with the Commission that they should be viewed with caution and within the larger picture of long-term trends and market structure. Long-term trends in the market and the Government's other evidence favor what the HHIs also indicate: the proposed merger will substantially lessen competition.

DECISION AND REMEDY   The U.S. Court of Appeals for the Fifth Circuit affirmed the Federal Trade Commission's decision that Chicago Bridge divest itself of its former competitor, Pitt-Des Moines.

THE GLOBAL DIMENSION   Assume that just prior to Chicago Bridge's acquisition of its only U.S. competitor, a multinational company based in Indonesia announced that it intended to enter all four of the markets mentioned in this case. How might this announcement affect the reasoning behind this case, if at all?

THE LEGAL ENVIRONMENT DIMENSION   What are some of the problems with attempting to measure industry concentration?

VERTICAL MERGER
The acquisition by a company at one level in a marketing chain of a company at a higher or lower level in the chain (such as a company merging with one of its suppliers or retailers).

Vertical Mergers   A **vertical merger** occurs when a company at one stage of production acquires a company at a higher or lower stage of production. An example of a vertical merger is a company merging with one of its suppliers or retailers. In the past, courts focused almost exclusively on "foreclosure" in assessing vertical mergers. Foreclosure occurs because competitors of the merging firms lose opportunities to sell or buy products from the merging firms.

Today, whether a vertical merger will be deemed illegal generally depends on several factors, such as whether the merger would produce a firm controlling an undue percentage share of the relevant market. The courts also analyze whether the merger would result in a significant increase in the concentration of firms in that market, the barriers to entry into the market, and the apparent intent of the merging parties.[25] Mergers that do not prevent competitors of either merging firm from competing in a segment of the market will not be condemned as "foreclosing" competition and are legal.

Section 8—Interlocking Directorates

Section 8 of the Clayton Act deals with *interlocking directorates*—that is, the practice of having individuals serve as directors on the boards of two or more competing companies simultaneously. Specifically, no person may be a director in two or more competing corporations at the same time if either of the corporations has capital, surplus, or undivided profits aggregating more than $25,319,000 or competitive sales of $2,531,900 or more. The Federal Trade Commission (FTC) adjusts the threshold amounts each year. (The amounts given here are those announced by the FTC in 2008.)

ENFORCEMENT AND EXEMPTIONS

CONTRAST
Section 5 of the Federal Trade Commission Act is broader than the other antitrust laws. It covers virtually all anticompetitive behavior, including conduct that does not violate either the Sherman Act or the Clayton Act.

The federal agencies that enforce the federal antitrust laws are the U.S. Department of Justice (DOJ) and the Federal Trade Commission (FTC). The FTC was established by the Federal Trade Commission Act of 1914. Section 5 of that

---

25. *United States v. Dairy Farmers of America, Inc.,* 426 F.3d 850 (6th Cir. 2005); *United States v. Philadelphia National Bank,* 374 U.S. 321, 83 S.Ct. 1715, 10 L.Ed.2d 915 (1963).

act condemns all forms of anticompetitive behavior that are not covered under other federal antitrust laws.

Only the DOJ can prosecute violations of the Sherman Act, which can be either criminal or civil offenses. Either the DOJ or the FTC can enforce the Clayton Act, but violations of that statute are not crimes and can be pursued only through civil proceedings. The DOJ or the FTC can ask the courts to impose various remedies, including **divestiture** (making a company give up one or more of its operating functions) and dissolution. A meatpacking firm, for example, might be forced to divest itself of control or ownership of butcher shops.

The FTC has the sole authority to enforce violations of Section 5 of the Federal Trade Commission Act. FTC actions are effected through administrative orders, but if a firm violates an FTC order, the FTC can seek court sanctions for the violation.

DIVESTITURE
The act of selling one or more of a company's divisions or parts, such as a subsidiary or plant; often mandated by the courts in merger or monopolization cases.

Private Actions

A private party who has been injured as a result of a violation of the Sherman Act or the Clayton Act can sue for damages and attorneys' fees. In some instances, private parties may also seek injunctive relief to prevent antitrust violations. The courts have determined that the ability to sue depends on the directness of the injury suffered by the would-be plaintiff. Thus, a person wishing to sue under the Sherman Act must prove (1) that the antitrust violation either caused or was a substantial factor in causing the injury that was suffered and (2) that the unlawful actions of the accused party affected business activities of the plaintiff that were protected by the antitrust laws.

Treble Damages

In recent years, more than 90 percent of all antitrust actions have been brought by private plaintiffs. One reason for this is that successful plaintiffs may recover **treble damages**—three times the damages that they have suffered as a result of the violation. Such recoveries by private plaintiffs for antitrust violations have been rationalized as encouraging people to act as "private attorneys general" who will vigorously pursue antitrust violators on their own initiative. In a situation involving a price-fixing agreement, normally each competitor is jointly and severally liable for the total amount of any damages, including treble damages if they are imposed.

TREBLE DAMAGES
Damages that, by statute, are three times the amount that the fact finder determines is owed.

Exemptions from Antitrust Laws

There are many legislative and constitutional limitations on antitrust enforcement. Most are statutory and judicially created exemptions that apply in such areas as labor, insurance, and foreign trade. These exemptions are listed in Exhibit 23–1 on page 762. One of the most significant of these exemptions covers joint efforts by businesspersons to obtain legislative, judicial, or executive action.

U.S. ANTITRUST LAWS IN THE GLOBAL CONTEXT

U.S. antitrust laws have a broad application. Not only may persons in foreign nations be subject to their provisions, but the laws may also be applied to protect foreign consumers and competitors from violations committed by U.S. business firms. Consequently, *foreign persons,* a term that by definition includes

EXHIBIT 23–1   EXEMPTIONS TO ANTITRUST ENFORCEMENT

EXEMPTION	SOURCE AND SCOPE
Labor	Clayton Act—Permits unions to organize and bargain without violating antitrust laws and specifies that strikes and other labor activities do not normally violate any federal law.
Agricultural associations	Clayton Act and Capper-Volstead Act of 1992—Allow agricultural cooperatives to set prices.
Fisheries	Fisheries Cooperative Marketing Act of 1976—Allows the fishing industry to set prices.
Insurance companies	McCarran-Ferguson Act of 1945—Exempts the insurance business in states in which the industry is regulated.
Exporters	Webb-Pomerene Act of 1918—Allows U.S. exporters to engage in cooperative activity to compete with similar foreign associations. Export Trading Company Act of 1982—Permits the U.S. Department of Justice to exempt certain exporters.
Professional baseball	The United States Supreme Court has held that professional baseball is exempt because it is not "interstate commerce."[a]
Oil marketing	Interstate Oil Compact of 1935—Allows states to set quotas on oil to be marketed in interstate commerce.
Defense activities	Defense Production Act of 1950—Allows the president to approve, and thereby exempt, certain activities to further the military defense of the United States.
Small businesses' cooperative research	Small Business Administration Act of 1958—Allows small firms to undertake cooperative research.
State actions	The United States Supreme Court has held that actions by a state are exempt if the state clearly articulates and actively supervises the policy behind its action.[b]
Regulated industries	Industries (such as airlines) are exempt when a federal administrative agency (such as the Federal Aviation Administration) has primary regulatory authority.
Businesspersons' joint efforts to seek government action	Cooperative efforts by businesspersons to obtain legislative, judicial, or executive action are exempt unless it is clear that an effort is "objectively baseless" and is an attempt to make anticompetitive use of government processes.[c]

a. *Federal Baseball Club of Baltimore, Inc. v. National League of Professional Baseball Clubs,* 259 U.S. 200, 42 S.Ct. 465, 66 L.Ed. 898 (1922). A federal district court has held that this exemption applies only to the game's reserve system. (Under the reserve system, teams hold players' contracts for the players' entire careers. The reserve system generally is being replaced by the free agency system.) See *Piazza v. Major League Baseball,* 831 F.Supp. 420 (E.D.Pa. 1993).
b. See *Parker v. Brown,* 317 U.S. 341, 63 S.Ct. 307, 87 L.Ed. 315 (1943).
c. *Eastern Railroad Presidents Conference v. Noerr Motor Freight, Inc.,* 365 U.S. 127, 81 S.Ct. 523, 5 L.Ed.2d 464 (1961); and *United Mine Workers of America v. Pennington,* 381 U.S. 657, 89 S.Ct. 1585, 14 L.Ed.2d 626 (1965).

foreign governments, may sue under U.S. antitrust laws in U.S. courts. (For a discussion of how antitrust lawsuits in the United Kingdom are beginning to resemble those in the United States, see this chapter's *Beyond Our Borders* feature.)

The Extraterritorial Application of U.S. Antitrust Laws

Section 1 of the Sherman Act provides for the extraterritorial effect of the U.S. antitrust laws. The United States is a major proponent of free competition in the global economy, and thus any conspiracy that has a *substantial effect* on U.S. commerce is within the reach of the Sherman Act. The violation may even occur outside the United States, and foreign governments as well as persons can be sued for violation of U.S. antitrust laws. Before U.S. courts will exercise jurisdiction and apply antitrust laws, it must be shown that the alleged violation had a substantial effect on U.S. commerce. U.S. jurisdiction is automatically invoked, however, when a *per se* violation occurs.

If a domestic firm, for example, joins a foreign cartel to control the production, price, or distribution of goods, and this cartel has a *substantial effect* on U.S. commerce, a *per se* violation may exist. Hence, both the domestic firm and the foreign cartel could be sued for violation of the U.S. antitrust laws. Likewise, if a foreign firm doing business in the United States enters into a price-fixing or other anticompetitive agreement to control a portion of U.S. markets, a *per se* violation may exist.

The Application of Foreign Antitrust Laws

Many other nations also have laws that promote competition and prohibit trade restraints. For example, Japanese antitrust laws forbid unfair trade practices, monopolization, and restrictions that unreasonably restrain trade. Several nations in Southeast Asia, including Indonesia, Malaysia, and Vietnam, have enacted statutes protecting competition. Argentina, Brazil, Chile, Peru, and several other Latin American countries have adopted modern antitrust laws as well. Most of the antitrust laws apply extraterritorially, as U.S. antitrust laws do. This means that a U.S. company may be subject to another nation's antitrust laws if the company's conduct has a substantial effect on that nation's commerce.

Several U.S. corporations have faced antitrust actions in the European Union (EU), which has laws that are stricter, at least with respect to fines, than those of the United States. The EU blocked a bid by General Electric Company to acquire Honeywell International, Inc., in 2001. The EU entered into its own antitrust

Shown here is the European Union's chief competition enforcer, Neelie Kroes. In a speech at an American Bar Association conference in 2007, she threatened to consider harsher remedies in future antitrust cases. She was specifically calling into question Microsoft Corporation's unwillingness to cooperate fully with her commission's request that Microsoft license some of its proprietary software to rivals. Why does a U.S. corporation have to worry about a foreign regulatory commission? (Photo Courtesy of the European Commissioner for Competition)

settlement with Microsoft Corporation, with remedies (including fines of $613 million as of 2008) that went beyond those imposed in the United States. The EU has also threatened additional fines for Microsoft's alleged failure to comply with requirements that it offer Windows without its private Media Player video and music applications.

Reviewing . . . Antitrust Law and Promoting Competition

The Internet Corporation for Assigned Names and Numbers (ICANN) is a nonprofit entity that organizes Internet domain names. It is governed by a board of directors elected by various groups with commercial interests in the Internet. One of ICANN's functions is to authorize an entity to serve as a registrar for certain "top level domains" (TLDs). ICANN entered into an agreement with VeriSign to provide registry services for the ".com" TLD in accordance with ICANN's specifications. VeriSign complained that ICANN was restricting the services that it could make available as a registrar and was blocking new services, imposing unnecessary conditions on those services, and setting prices at which the services were offered. VeriSign claimed that ICANN's control of the registry services for domain names violated Section 1 of the Sherman Act. Using the information presented in the chapter, answer the following questions.

1. Should ICANN's actions be judged under the rule of reason or deemed *per se* violations of Section 1 of the Sherman Act?

2. Should ICANN's actions be viewed as horizontal or vertical restraints of trade?

3. Does it matter that ICANN's leadership is chosen by groups with a commercial interest in the Internet?

4. If the dispute is judged under the rule of reason, what might be ICANN's defense for having a standardized set of registry services that must be used?

Key Terms

antitrust law 741	market concentration 758	resale price maintenance
attempted	market power 742	agreement 748
monopolization 755	monopolization 750	rule of reason 744
concentrated industry 746	monopoly 742	treble damages 761
divestiture 761	monopoly power 742	tying arrangement 757
exclusive-dealing	*per se* violation 744	vertical merger 760
contract 757	predatory pricing 750	vertical restraint 746
group boycott 745	price discrimination 755	vertically integrated
horizontal merger 758	price-fixing agreement 745	firm 748
horizontal restraint 744		

Chapter Summary

The Sherman Antitrust Act (1890)
(See pages 742–755.)

1. *Major provisions–*

   a. Section 1–Prohibits contracts, combinations, and conspiracies in restraint of trade.

     (1) Horizontal restraints subject to Section 1 include price-fixing agreements, group boycotts (joint refusals to deal), horizontal market divisions, and trade association agreements.

The Sherman Antitrust Act (1890)—Continued

    (2) Vertical restraints subject to Section 1 include territorial or customer restrictions, resale price maintenance agreements, and refusals to deal.

   b. Section 2—Prohibits monopolies and attempts to monopolize.

2. *Jurisdictional requirements*—The Sherman Act applies only to activities that have a significant impact on interstate commerce.

3. *Interpretive rules*—

   a. *Per se* rule—Applied to restraints on trade that are so inherently anticompetitive that they cannot be justified and are deemed illegal as a matter of law.

   b. Rule of reason—Applied when an anticompetitive agreement may be justified by legitimate benefits. Under the rule of reason, the lawfulness of a trade restraint will be determined by the purpose and effects of the restraint.

The Clayton Act (1914)
(See pages 755–760.)

The major provisions are as follows:

1. *Section 2*—As amended in 1936 by the Robinson-Patman Act, prohibits price discrimination that substantially lessens competition and prohibits a seller engaged in interstate commerce from selling to two or more buyers goods of similar grade and quality at different prices when the result is a substantial lessening of competition or the creation of a competitive injury.

2. *Section 3*—Prohibits exclusionary practices, such as exclusive-dealing contracts and tying arrangements, when the effect may be to substantially lessen competition.

3. *Section 7*—Prohibits mergers when the effect may be to substantially lessen competition or to tend to create a monopoly.

   a. Horizontal merger—The acquisition by merger or consolidation of a competing firm engaged in the same relevant market. Will be presumed unlawful if the entity created by the merger will have anything other than a small-percentage market share.

   b. Vertical merger—The acquisition by a seller of one of its buyers or vice versa. Will be unlawful if the merger prevents competitors of either merging firm from competing in a segment of the market that otherwise would be open to them, resulting in a substantial lessening of competition.

4. *Section 8*—Prohibits interlocking directorates.

Enforcement and Exemptions
(See pages 760–761.)

1. *Enforcement*—Federal agencies that enforce antitrust laws are the Department of Justice and the Federal Trade Commission, which was established by the Federal Trade Commission Act of 1914. Private parties who have been injured as a result of violations of the Sherman Act or Clayton Act may also bring civil suits. In recent years, many private parties have filed such suits largely because, if successful, they may be awarded treble damages and attorneys' fees.

2. *Exemptions*—Exemptions from antitrust laws apply in the following areas:

   a. Labor unions.

   b. Agricultural associations and fisheries.

   c. Insurance companies, when state regulation exists.

   d. Export trading companies.

   e. Professional baseball.

   f. Oil marketing.

   g. Cooperative research and production.

   h. Joint efforts by businesspersons to obtain legislative or executive action.

   i. Other activities, including certain national defense activities, state actions, and activities of certain regulated industries.

CONTINUED

U.S. Antitrust Laws in the Global Context
(See pages 000–000.)

1. *Application of U.S. laws*–U.S. antitrust laws are broad and can be applied in foreign nations to protect foreign consumers and competitors. Foreign governments and persons can also bring actions under U.S. antitrust laws. Section 1 of the Sherman Act applies to any conspiracy that has a substantial effect on U.S. commerce.

2. *Application of foreign laws*–Many other nations also have laws that promote competition and prohibit trade restraints and some are more restrictive than U.S. laws. These foreign antitrust laws are increasingly being applied to U.S. firms.

For Review

1. What is a monopoly? What is market power? How do these concepts relate to each other?
2. What type of activity is prohibited by Section 1 of the Sherman Act? What type of activity is prohibited by Section 2 of the Sherman Act?
3. What are the four major provisions of the Clayton Act, and what types of activities do these provisions prohibit?
4. What agencies of the federal government enforce the federal antitrust laws?
5. What are four activities that are exempt from the antitrust laws?

Questions and Case Problems

23–1. Sherman Act. An agreement that is blatantly and substantially anticompetitive is deemed a *per se* violation of Section 1 of the Sherman Act. Under what rule is an agreement analyzed if it appears to be anticompetitive but is not a *per se* violation? In making this analysis, what factors will a court consider?

Question with Sample Answer

23–2. Allitron, Inc., and Donovan, Ltd., are interstate competitors selling similar appliances, principally in the states of Illinois, Indiana, Kentucky, and Ohio. Allitron and Donovan agree that Allitron will no longer sell in Indiana and Ohio and that Donovan will no longer sell in Illinois and Kentucky. Have Allitron and Donovan violated any antitrust laws? If so, which law? Explain.

For a sample answer to Question 23–2, go to Appendix I at the end of this text.

23–3. Monopolization. Moist snuff is a smokeless tobacco product sold in small round cans from racks, which include point-of-sale (POS) ads. POS ads are critical because tobacco advertising is restricted and the number of people who use smokeless tobacco products is relatively small. In the moist-snuff market in the United States, there are only four competitors, including U.S. Tobacco Co. and its affiliates (USTC) and Conwood Co. In 1990, USTC, which held 87 percent of the market,

began to convince major retailers, including Wal-Mart Stores, Inc., to use USTC's "exclusive racks" to display its products and those of all other snuff makers. USTC agents would then destroy competitors' racks. USTC also began to provide retailers with false sales data to convince them to maintain its poor-selling items and drop competitors' less expensive products. Conwood's Wal-Mart market share fell from 12 percent to 6.5 percent. In stores in which USTC did not have rack exclusivity, however, Conwood's market share increased to 25 percent. Conwood filed a suit in a federal district court against USTC, alleging, in part, that USTC used its monopoly power to exclude competitors from the moist-snuff market. Should the court rule in Conwood's favor? What is USTC's best defense? Discuss. [*Conwood Co., L.P. v. U.S. Tobacco Co.*, 290 F.3d 768 (6th Cir. 2002)]

23–4. Restraint of Trade. Visa U.S.A., Inc., MasterCard International, Inc., American Express (Amex), and Discover are the four major credit- and charge-card networks in the United States. Visa and MasterCard are joint ventures, owned by the thousands of banks that are their members. The banks issue the cards, clear transactions, and collect fees from the merchants that accept the cards. In contrast, Amex and Discover themselves issue cards to customers, process transactions, and collect fees. Since 1995, Amex has asked banks to issue its cards. No bank has been willing to do so, however, because it would have to stop issuing Visa and MasterCard cards under those networks' rules barring member banks from issuing cards on rival networks. The U.S. Department of Justice filed a suit in a federal district court against Visa and MasterCard, alleging, among other things, that the rules were illegal restraints of trade under the Sherman Act. Do the rules harm competition? If so, how? What relief might the court order to stop any anticompetitiveness? [*United States v. Visa U.S.A., Inc.*, 344 F.3d 229 (2d Cir. 2003)]

23–5. Sherman Act. Dentsply International, Inc., is one of a dozen manufacturers of artificial teeth for dentures and other restorative devices. Dentsply sells its teeth to twenty-three dealers in dental products. The dealers supply the teeth to dental laboratories, which fabricate dentures for sale to dentists. There are hundreds of dealers that compete with one another on the basis of price and service. Some manufacturers sell directly to the laboratories. There are also thousands of laboratories that compete with one another on the basis of price and service. Because of advances in dental medicine, however, artificial-tooth manufacturing has low growth potential, and Dentsply dominates the industry. Dentsply's market share is greater than 75 percent and is about fifteen times larger than that of its closest competitor. Dentsply prohibits its dealers from marketing competitors' teeth unless they were selling the teeth before 1993. The federal government filed a suit in a federal district court against Dentsply, alleging, in part, a violation of Section 2 of the Sherman Act. What must the government show to succeed in its suit? Are those elements present in this case? What should the court rule? Explain. [*United States v. Dentsply International, Inc.*, 399 F.3d 181 (3d Cir. 2005)]

23–6. Price Fixing. Texaco Inc. and Shell Oil Co. are competitors in the national and international oil and gasoline markets. They refine crude oil into gasoline and sell it to service station owners and others. Between 1998 and 2002, Texaco and Shell engaged in a joint venture, Equilon Enterprises, to consolidate their operations in the western United States and a separate venture, Motiva Enterprises, for the same purpose in the eastern United States. This ended their competition in the domestic refining and marketing of gasoline. As part of the ventures, Texaco and Shell agreed to pool their resources and share the risks and profits of their joint activities. The Federal Trade Commission and several states approved the formation of these entities without restricting the pricing of their gasoline, which the ventures began to sell at a single price under the original Texaco and Shell brand names. Fouad Dagher and other station owners filed a suit in a federal district court against Texaco and Shell, alleging that the defendants were engaged in illegal price fixing. Do the circumstances in this case fit the definition of a price-fixing agreement? Explain. [*Texaco Inc. v. Dagher*, 547 U.S. 1, 126 S.Ct. 1276, 164 L.Ed.2d 1 (2006)]

23–7. In 1999, residents of the city of Madison, Wisconsin, became concerned that overconsumption of liquor seemed to be increasing near the campus of the University of Wisconsin–Madison (UW), leading to more frequent use of detoxification facilities and calls for police services in the campus area. Under pressure from UW, which shared these concerns, the city initiated a new policy, imposing conditions on area taverns to discourage price reduction "specials" believed to encourage high-volume and dangerous drinking. In 2002, the city began to draft an ordinance to ban all drink specials. Tavern owners responded by announcing that they had "voluntarily" agreed to discontinue drink specials on Friday and Saturday nights after 8 P.M. The city put its ordinance on hold. UW student Nic Eichenseer and others filed a suit in a Wisconsin state court against the Madison–Dane County Tavern League, Inc. (an association of local tavern owners), and others, alleging violations of antitrust law. On what might the plaintiffs base a claim for relief? Are the defendants in this case exempt from the antitrust laws? What should the court rule? Why? [*Eichenseer v. Madison–Dane County Tavern League, Inc.*, 2006 WI App 226, 725 N.W.2d 274 (2006)]

After you have answered Problem 23–7, compare your answer with the sample answer given on the Web site that accompanies this text. Go to www.cengage.com/blaw/let, **select "Chapter 23," and click on "Case Problem with Sample Answer."**

23–8. Price Discrimination. The customers of Sodexho, Inc., and Feesers, Inc., are institutional food service facilities such as school, hospital, and nursing home cafeterias. Feesers is a distributor that buys unprepared food from suppliers for resale to customers who run their own cafeterias. Sodexho is a food service management company that buys unprepared food from suppliers, prepares the food, and sells the meals to the facilities, which it also operates, under contracts with its clients. Sodexho uses a distributor, such as Sysco Corp., to buy the food from a supplier, such as Michael Foods, Inc. Sysco pays Michael's list price and sells the food to Sodexho at a lower price—which Sodexho has negotiated with Michael—plus an agreed mark-up. Sysco invoices Michael for the difference. Sodexho resells the food to its facilities at its cost, plus a "procurement fee." In sum, Michael charges Sysco less for food resold to Sodexho than it charges Feesers for the same products, and thus Sodexho's customers pay less than Feesers's customers for these products. Feesers filed a suit in a federal district court against Michael and others, alleging price discrimination. To establish its claim, what does Feesers have to show? What might be the most difficult element to prove? How should the court rule? Why? [*Feesers, Inc. v. Michael Foods, Inc.*, 498 F.3d 206 (3d Cir. 2007)]

A Question of Ethics

23–9. In the 1990s, DuCoa, L.P., made choline chloride, a B-complex vitamin essential for the growth and development of animals. The U.S. market for choline chloride was divided into thirds among DuCoa, Bioproducts, Inc., and Chinook Group Ltd. To stabilize the market and keep the price of the vitamin higher than it would otherwise be, the companies agreed to fix the price and allocate market share by deciding which of them would offer the lowest price to each customer. At times, however, the companies disregarded the agreement. During an increase in competitive activity in August 1997, Daniel Rose became president of DuCoa. The next month, a subordinate advised him of the conspiracy. By February 1998, Rose had begun to implement a strategy to persuade DuCoa's competitors to rejoin the conspiracy. By April, the three companies had reallocated their market shares and increased their prices. In June, the U.S. Department of Justice began to investigate allegations of price fixing in the vitamin market. Ultimately, a federal district court convicted Rose of conspiracy to violate Section 1 of the Sherman Act. [*United States v. Rose*, 449 F.3d 627 (5th Cir. 2006)]

1. The court "enhanced" Rose's sentence to thirty months' imprisonment, one year of supervised release, and a $20,000 fine based, among other things, on his role as "a manager or supervisor" in the conspiracy. Rose appealed this enhancement to the U.S. Court of Appeals for the Fifth Circuit. Was it fair to increase Rose's sentence on this ground? Why or why not?
2. Was Rose's participation in the conspiracy unethical? If so, how might Rose have behaved ethically instead? If not, could any of the participants' conduct be considered unethical? Explain.

Critical-Thinking Legal Question

23–10. Critics of antitrust law claim that in the long run, competitive market forces will eliminate private monopolies unless they are fostered by government regulation. Can you think of any examples of monopolies that continue to be fostered by government in the United States?

Interacting with the Internet

For updated links to resources available on the Web, as well as a variety of other materials, visit this text's Web site at

www.cengage.com/blaw/let

The Federal Trade Commission offers an abundance of information on antitrust law, including a handbook titled *Promoting Competition, Protecting Consumers: A Plain English Guide to Antitrust Laws,* which is available at

www.ftc.gov/bc/compguide/index.htm

The *Tech Law Journal* presents "news, records, and analysis of legislation, litigation, and regulation affecting the computer and Internet industry" in the area of antitrust law at

www.techlawjournal.com/atr/default.htm

To see the American Bar Association's Web page on antitrust law, go to

www.abanet.org/antitrust

PRACTICAL INTERNET EXERCISES

Go to this text's Web site at **www.cengage.com/blaw/let**, select "Chapter 23," and click on "Practical Internet Exercises." There you will find the following Internet research exercises that you can perform to learn more about the topics covered in this chapter.

Practical Internet Exercise 23–1: Legal Perspective—The Standard Oil Trust
Practical Internet Exercise 23–2: Management Perspective—Avoiding Antitrust Problems

BEFORE THE TEST

Go to **www.cengage.com/blaw/let**, the Web site that accompanies this text. Select "Chapter 23" and click on "Interactive Quizzes." You will find a number of interactive questions relating to this chapter.

Chapter 24

Investor Protection and Corporate Governance

CHAPTER OBJECTIVES

After reading this chapter, you should be able to answer the following questions:

1. What is meant by the term *securities*?

2. What are the two major statutes regulating the securities industry? When was the Securities and Exchange Commission created, and what are its major purposes and functions?

3. What is insider trading? Why is it prohibited?

4. What are some of the features of state securities laws?

5. What certification requirements does the Sarbanes-Oxley Act impose on corporate executives?

CONTENTS

- Securities Act of 1933

- Securities Exchange Act of 1934

- State Securities Laws

- Corporate Governance

- Online Securities Fraud

" It shall be unlawful for any person in the offer or sale of any security . . . to engage in any transaction, practice, or course of business which operates or would operate as a fraud or deceit upon the purchaser. "

— SECURITIES ACT OF 1933, SECTION 17

After the stock market crash of 1929, many members of Congress argued in favor of regulating securities markets. Basically, legislation for such regulation was enacted to provide investors with more information to help them make buying and selling decisions about **securities**—generally defined as any documents or records evidencing corporate ownership (stock) or debts (bonds)—and to prohibit deceptive, unfair, and manipulative practices. Today, the sale and transfer of securities are heavily regulated by federal and state statutes and by government agencies.

This chapter discusses the nature of federal securities regulation and its effect on the legal environment of business. We first examine the major traditional laws governing securities offerings and trading. We then discuss corporate governance and the Sarbanes-Oxley Act of 2002,[1] which affects certain types of securities transactions. Finally, we look at the problem of online securities fraud. Before we begin, though, the important role played by the Securities and Exchange Commission (SEC) in the regulation of federal securities laws requires some attention. We examine the origin and functions of the SEC in this chapter's *Landmark in the Legal Environment* feature on page 772.

SECURITY
Generally, a stock certificate, bond, note, debenture, warrant, or other document or record evidencing an ownership interest in a corporation or a promise to repay a corporation's debt.

SECURITIES ACT OF 1933

The Securities Act of 1933[2] governs initial sales of stock by businesses. The act was designed to prohibit various forms of fraud and to stabilize the securities industry by requiring that all essential information concerning the issuance of securities be

---

1. 15 U.S.C. Sections 7201 *et seq.*
2. 15 U.S.C. Sections 77–77aa.

During the stock market crash of 1929, hordes of investors crowded Wall Street to find out the latest news. How did this crash affect the future stock market? (National Archives)

INVESTMENT CONTRACT

In securities law, a transaction in which a person invests in a common enterprise with the reasonable expectation that profits will be derived primarily from the efforts of others.

made available to the investing public. Basically, the purpose of this act is to require disclosure. The 1933 act provides that all securities transactions must be registered with the SEC or be exempt from registration requirements.

What Is a Security?

Section 2(1) of the Securities Act of 1933 contains a broad definition of securities, which generally include the following:[3]

1. Instruments and interests commonly known as securities, such as preferred and common stocks, treasury stocks, bonds, debentures, and stock warrants.
2. Any interests commonly known as securities, such as stock options, puts, calls, and other types of privilege on a security or on the right to purchase a security or a group of securities in a national security exchange.
3. Notes, instruments, or other evidence of indebtedness, including certificates of interest in a profit-sharing agreement and certificates of deposit.
4. Any fractional undivided interest in oil, gas, or other mineral rights.
5. Investment contracts, which include interests in limited partnerships and other investment schemes.

In interpreting the act, the United States Supreme Court has held that an **investment contract** is any transaction in which a person (1) invests (2) in a common enterprise (3) reasonably expecting profits (4) derived *primarily* or *substantially* from others' managerial or entrepreneurial efforts. Known as the *Howey* test, this definition continues to guide the determination of what types of contracts can be considered securities.[4]

For our purposes, it is convenient to think of securities in their most common form—stocks and bonds issued by corporations. Bear in mind, though, that securities can take many forms, including interests in whiskey, cosmetics, worms, beavers, boats, vacuum cleaners, muskrats, and cemetery lots. Almost any stake in the ownership or debt of a company can be considered a security. Investment contracts in condominiums, franchises, limited partnerships in real estate, oil or gas or other mineral rights, and farm animals accompanied by care agreements have qualified as securities.

EXAMPLE #1 Alpha Telcom sold, installed, and maintained pay-phone systems. As part of its pay-phone program, Alpha guaranteed buyers a 14 percent return on the amount of their purchase. Alpha was operating at a net loss, however, and continually borrowed funds to pay investors the fixed rate of return it had promised. Eventually, the company filed for bankruptcy, and the SEC brought an action alleging that Alpha had violated the Securities Act of 1933. In this situation, a federal court concluded that the pay-phone program was a security because it involved an investment contract.[5] □

---

3. 15 U.S.C. Section 77b(1). Amendments in 1982 added stock options.
4. *SEC v. W. J. Howey Co.,* 328 U.S. 293, 66 S.Ct. 1100, 90 L.Ed. 1244 (1946).
5. *SEC v. Alpha Telcom, Inc.,* 187 F.Supp.2d 1250 (2002). See also *SEC v. Edwards,* 540 U.S. 389, 124 S.Ct. 892, 157 L.Ed.2d 813 (2004), in which the United States Supreme Court held that an investment scheme offering contractual entitlement to a fixed rate of return can be an investment contract and therefore can be considered a security under federal law.

Businesspersons should be aware that securities are not limited to stocks and bonds but can encompass a wide variety of interests. The analysis hinges on the nature of the transaction rather than the instrument or substance involved. Because Congress enacted securities laws to regulate investments, in whatever form and by whatever name they are called, virtually any type of security that might be sold as an investment can be subject to securities laws. When in doubt about whether an investment transaction involves securities, businesspersons should always seek the advice of an attorney who specializes in this area.

Registration Statement

Section 5 of the Securities Act of 1933 broadly provides that unless a security qualifies for an exemption, that security must be *registered* before it is offered to the public. Issuing corporations must file a *registration statement* with the SEC and must provide all investors with a *prospectus*. A **prospectus** is a written disclosure document that describes the security being sold, the financial operations of the issuing corporation, and the investment or risk attaching to the security. The 1933 act requires the issuer to deliver a prospectus to investors, and issuers use this document as a selling tool. The issuer has the option of delivering the prospectus electronically via the Internet.[6] In principle, the registration statement and the prospectus supply sufficient information to enable unsophisticated investors to evaluate the financial risk involved.

PROSPECTUS
A written document, required by securities laws, that describes the security being sold, the financial operations of the issuing corporation, and the investment or risk attaching to the security. It is designed to provide sufficient information to enable investors to evaluate the risk involved in purchasing the security.

Contents of the Registration Statement The registration statement must be written in plain English and fully describe the following:

1. The securities being offered for sale, including their relationship to the registrant's other capital securities.
2. The corporation's properties and business (including a financial statement certified by an independent public accounting firm).
3. The management of the corporation, including managerial compensation, stock options, pensions, and other benefits. Any interests of directors or officers in any material transactions with the corporation must be disclosed.
4. How the corporation intends to use the proceeds of the sale.
5. Any pending lawsuits or special risk factors.

DON'T FORGET
The purpose of the Securities Act of 1933 is disclosure—the SEC does not consider whether a security is worth the investment price.

All companies, both domestic and foreign, must file their registration statements electronically so that they can be posted on the SEC's electronic database, which is called EDGAR (Electronic Data Gathering, Analysis, and Retrieval). The EDGAR database includes material on initial public offerings (IPOs), proxy statements, corporations' annual reports, registration statements, and other documents that have been filed with the SEC. Investors can access the database via the Internet to obtain information that can be used to make investment decisions. (See the *Interacting with the Internet* section at the end of this chapter for the URL to access the EDGAR database.)

Registration Process The registration statement does not become effective until after it has been reviewed and approved by the SEC. The 1933 act restricts

---

6. Basically, an electronic prospectus must meet the same requirements as a printed prospectus. The SEC has special rules that address situations in which the graphics, images, or audio files in a printed prospectus cannot be reproduced in an electronic form. 17 C.F.R. Section 232.304.

In 1931, the U.S. Senate passed a resolution calling for an extensive investigation of securities trading. The investigation led, ultimately, to the passage by Congress of the Securities Act of 1933, which is also known as the truth-in-securities bill. In the following year, Congress passed the Securities Exchange Act. This 1934 act created the Securities and Exchange Commission (SEC).

Major Responsibilities of the SEC

The SEC was created as an independent regulatory agency with the function of administering the 1933 and 1934 acts. Its basic functions are as follows:

1. Interprets federal securities laws and investigates securities law violations.
2. Issues new rules and amends existing rules.
3. Oversees the inspection of securities firms, brokers, investment advisers, and ratings agencies.
4. Oversees private regulatory organizations in the securities, accounting, and auditing fields.
5. Coordinates U.S. securities regulation with federal, state, and foreign authorities.

The SEC's Expanding Regulatory Powers

Since its creation, the SEC's regulatory functions have gradually been increased by legislation granting it authority in different areas. For example, to further curb securities fraud, the Securities Enforcement Remedies and Penny Stock Reform Act of 1990[a] amended existing securities laws to allow SEC administrative law judges to hear cases involving many more types of alleged securities law violations; the SEC's enforcement options were also greatly expanded. In addition, the act provides that courts can prevent persons who have engaged in securities fraud from serving as officers and directors of publicly held corporations. The Securities Acts Amendments of 1990 authorized the SEC to seek sanctions against those who violate foreign securities laws.[b]

The National Securities Markets Improvement Act of 1996 expanded the power of the SEC to exempt persons, securities, and transactions from the requirements of the securities laws.[c] (This part of the act is also known as the Capital Markets Efficiency Act.) The act also limited the authority of the states to regulate certain securities transactions and particular investment advisory firms.[d] The Sarbanes-Oxley Act of 2002,[e] which you will read about later in this chapter, further expanded the authority of the SEC by directing the agency to issue new rules relating to corporate disclosure requirements and by creating an oversight board to regulate public accounting firms.

a. 15 U.S.C. Section 77g.
b. 15 U.S.C. Section 78a.
c. 15 U.S.C. Sections 77z-3, 78mm.
d. 15 U.S.C. Section 80b-3a.
e. 15 U.S.C. Sections 7201 *et seq.*

Shown here is the New York Stock Exchange. It is only one of the many markets in which securities are publicly traded. Indeed, in today's global context, New York is no longer the "king" of financial markets. In any event, security trading in the United States is heavily regulated. Does this regulation mean that investors face less risk?
(Luis Villa del Campo/Creative Commons)

APPLICATION TO TODAY'S LEGAL ENVIRONMENT

Congress and the SEC have been attempting to streamline the regulatory process generally. One goal is to make it more efficient and more relevant to today's securities trading practices. To this end, the SEC has embraced modern technology and communications methods, especially the Internet, more completely than many other federal agencies have. Another goal is to establish more oversight over securities transactions and accounting practices. Additionally, as the number and types of online securities frauds increase, the SEC is trying to keep pace by expanding its online fraud division.

RELEVANT WEB SITES

To locate information on the Web concerning the SEC, go to this text's Web site at **www.cengage.com/blaw/let**, select "Chapter 24," and click on "URLs for Landmarks."

the types of activities that an issuer can engage in at each stage in the registration process. If an issuer violates the restrictions discussed here, investors can rescind their contracts to purchase the securities. During the *prefiling period* (before the registration statement is filed), the issuer cannot either sell or offer to sell the securities. No advertising of an upcoming securities offering is allowed during the prefiling period.

Waiting Period   Once the registration statement has been filed, a waiting period of at least twenty days begins during which the SEC reviews the registration statement for completeness. Typically, the SEC staff members who review the registration statement ask the registrant to make numerous changes and additions, which can extend the length of the waiting period.[7]

During the waiting period, the securities can be offered for sale but cannot be sold by the issuing corporation. Only certain types of offers are allowed. All issuers can distribute a *preliminary prospectus,* called a **red herring prospectus.**[8] A red herring prospectus contains most of the information that will be included in the final prospectus but often does not include a price. General advertising is permitted, such as a **tombstone ad,** so named because historically the format resembled a tombstone. Such ads simply tell the investor where and how to obtain a prospectus.[9]

In 2005, the SEC, in recognition of modern communications technologies, reformed its rules to authorize the use of a *free-writing prospectus* during this period.[10] A **free-writing prospectus** is any type of written, electronic, or graphic offer that describes the issuer or its securities and includes a legend indicating that the investor can obtain the prospectus at the SEC's Web site. The issuer normally must file the free-writing prospectus with the SEC no later than the first date it is used. Certain inexperienced issuers are required to file a *preliminary prospectus* prior to the filing of a free-writing prospectus.

Posteffective Period   Once the SEC has reviewed and approved the registration statement and the twenty-day period has elapsed, the registration is effective. The issuer can now offer and sell the securities without restrictions. If the company issued a preliminary prospectus to investors, it must provide those investors with a final prospectus either prior to or at the time they purchase the securities. The issuer can require investors to download the final prospectus from a Web site, but it must notify investors of the Internet address at which they can access the prospectus.

RED HERRING PROSPECTUS
A preliminary prospectus that can be distributed to potential investors after the registration statement (for a securities offering) has been filed with the Securities and Exchange Commission. The name derives from the red legend printed across the prospectus stating that the registration has been filed but has not become effective.

TOMBSTONE AD
An advertisement, historically in a format resembling a tombstone, of a securities offering. The ad tells potential investors where and how they can obtain a prospectus.

FREE-WRITING PROSPECTUS
Any type of written, electronic, or graphic offer that describes the issuing corporation or its securities and includes a legend indicating that the investor can obtain the prospectus at the SEC's Web site.

---

7. It is common for the SEC to require a registrant to provide additional information more than once. Only after the registration statement has gone through several rounds of changes does the SEC give its approval. In these circumstances, because the process may have taken months to complete, registrants frequently request an acceleration of the twenty-day waiting period. If the SEC grants the request, registration can become effective without the issuer having to wait the full twenty days after the last round of changes.

8. The name *red herring* comes from the legend printed in red across the prospectus stating that the registration has been filed but has not become effective.

9. During the waiting period, the SEC also allows *road shows,* in which a corporate executive travels around speaking to institutional investors and securities analysts, as well as electronic road shows, which are viewed via real-time communications methods, such as Webcasting.

10. See SEC Rules 164 and 433. Note also that companies that qualify as "well-known seasoned issuers" under the SEC's rules (large corporations with stock valued at $700 million or more in the hands of the public) can even use a free-writing prospectus during the prefiling period.

EXAMPLE #2 Delphia, Inc., wants to make a public offering of its common stock. The firm files a registration statement and a prospectus with the SEC. On the same day, the company can make *offers* to sell the stock and start using a free-writing prospectus, but it cannot actually sell any of its stock. Delphia and its attorneys continue to work with the SEC and provide additional information to it for nearly six months. When the SEC finally indicates that it has all the necessary information for the registration statement to be approved, Delphia can request an acceleration of the twenty-day waiting period. Only *after* the SEC declares the registration to be effective and the waiting period has elapsed or been accelerated can Delphia sell the first shares in the issue.□

Exempt Securities

A number of specific securities are exempt from the registration requirements of the Securities Act of 1933. These securities—which can also generally be resold without being registered—include the following:[11]

1. Government-issued securities.
2. Bank and financial institution securities, which are regulated by banking authorities.
3. Short-term notes and drafts (negotiable instruments that have a maturity date that does not exceed nine months).
4. Securities of nonprofit, educational, and charitable organizations.
5. Securities issued by common carriers (railroads and trucking companies).
6. Any insurance, endowment, or annuity contract issued by a state-regulated insurance company.
7. Securities issued in a corporate reorganization in which one security is exchanged for another or in a bankruptcy proceeding.
8. Securities issued in stock dividends and stock splits.

Exhibit 24–1 summarizes the securities and transactions (discussed next) that are exempt from the registration requirements under the Securities Act of 1933 and SEC regulations.

Exempt Transactions

In addition to the exempt securities listed in the previous subsection, certain *transactions* are exempt from registration requirements. These transaction exemptions are very broad and can enable an issuer to avoid the high cost and complicated procedures associated with registration. Because the coverage of the exemptions overlaps somewhat, an offering may qualify for more than one. Therefore, many sales occur without registration.

BE AWARE
The issuer of an exempt security does not have to disclose the same information that other issuers do.

Regulation A Offerings   Securities issued by an issuer that has offered less than $5 million in securities during any twelve-month period are exempt from registration. Under Regulation A,[12] the issuer must file with the SEC a notice of the issue and an offering circular, which must also be provided to investors before the sale. This process is much simpler and less expensive than the procedures associated with full registration. Companies are allowed to "test the

---

11. 15 U.S.C. Section 77c.
12. 17 C.F.R. Sections 230.251–230.263.

EXHIBIT 24–1 EXEMPTIONS UNDER THE 1933 SECURITIES ACT

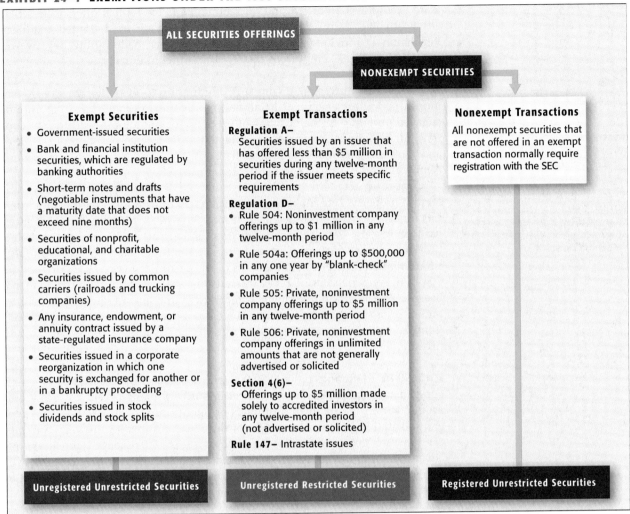

ALL SECURITIES OFFERINGS

NONEXEMPT SECURITIES

Exempt Securities

- Government-issued securities
- Bank and financial institution securities, which are regulated by banking authorities
- Short-term notes and drafts (negotiable instruments that have a maturity date that does not exceed nine months)
- Securities of nonprofit, educational, and charitable organizations
- Securities issued by common carriers (railroads and trucking companies)
- Any insurance, endowment, or annuity contract issued by a state-regulated insurance company
- Securities issued in a corporate reorganization in which one security is exchanged for another or in a bankruptcy proceeding
- Securities issued in stock dividends and stock splits

Unregistered Unrestricted Securities

Exempt Transactions

Regulation A–
Securities issued by an issuer that has offered less than $5 million in securities during any twelve-month period if the issuer meets specific requirements

Regulation D–
- Rule 504: Noninvestment company offerings up to $1 million in any twelve-month period
- Rule 504a: Offerings up to $500,000 in any one year by "blank-check" companies
- Rule 505: Private, noninvestment company offerings up to $5 million in any twelve-month period
- Rule 506: Private, noninvestment company offerings in unlimited amounts that are not generally advertised or solicited

Section 4(6)–
Offerings up to $5 million made solely to accredited investors in any twelve-month period (not advertised or solicited)

Rule 147– Intrastate issues

Unregistered Restricted Securities

Nonexempt Transactions

All nonexempt securities that are not offered in an exempt transaction normally require registration with the SEC

Registered Unrestricted Securities

waters" for potential interest before preparing the offering circular. To *test the waters* means to determine potential interest without actually selling any securities or requiring any commitment on the part of those who express interest. Small-business issuers (companies with annual revenues of less than $25 million) can also use an integrated registration and reporting system that uses simpler forms than the full registration system.

Some companies have sold their securities via the Internet using Regulation A. **EXAMPLE #3** In 1996, the Spring Street Brewing Company became the first company to sell securities via an online initial public offering (IPO). Spring Street raised about $1.6 million—without having to pay any commissions to brokers or underwriters.☐ Such online IPOs are particularly attractive to small companies and start-up ventures that may find it difficult to raise capital from institutional investors or through underwriters. By making the offering online under Regulation A, the company can avoid both commissions and the costly and time-consuming filings required for a traditional IPO under federal and state law.

Small Offerings—Regulation D   The SEC's Regulation D contains four separate exemptions from registration requirements for limited offers (offers that either involve a small dollar amount or are made in a limited manner). Regulation D provides that any of these offerings made during any twelve-month period are exempt from the registration requirements.

Rule 504   Noninvestment company offerings up to $1 million in any twelve-month period are exempt.[13] Noninvestment companies are firms that are not engaged primarily in the business of investing or trading in securities. (In contrast, an **investment company** is a firm that buys a large portfolio of securities and professionally manages it on behalf of many smaller shareholders/owners. A **mutual fund** is a type of investment company.)

> **EXAMPLE #4** Zeta Enterprises, L.P., is a limited partnership that develops commercial property. Zeta intends to offer $600,000 of its limited partnership interests for sale between June 1 and next May 31. The buyers will become limited partners in Zeta. Because an interest in a limited partnership meets the definition of a security (discussed earlier in this chapter), its sale is subject to the registration and prospectus requirements of the Securities Act of 1933. Under Rule 504, however, the sales of Zeta's interests are exempt from these requirements because Zeta is a noninvestment company making an offering of less than $1 million in a twelve-month period. Therefore, Zeta can sell its interests without filing a registration statement with the SEC or issuing a prospectus to any investor. □

Rule 504a   Offerings up to $500,000 in any one year by so-called blank-check companies—companies with no specific business plans except to locate and acquire currently unknown businesses or opportunities—are exempt if no general solicitation or advertising is used; the SEC is notified of the sales; and precautions are taken against nonexempt, unregistered resales.[14] The limits on advertising and unregistered resales do not apply if the offering is made solely in states that provide for registration and disclosure and the securities are sold in compliance with those provisions.[15]

Rule 505   Private, noninvestment company offerings up to $5 million in any twelve-month period are exempt, regardless of the number of **accredited investors** (banks, insurance companies, investment companies, the issuer's executive officers and directors, and persons whose income or net worth exceeds certain limits), so long as there are no more than thirty-five unaccredited investors; no general solicitation or advertising is used; the SEC is notified of the sales; and precautions are taken against nonexempt, unregistered resales. If the sale involves *any* unaccredited investors, *all* investors must be given material infor-

---

INVESTMENT COMPANY
A company that acts on behalf of many smaller shareholders/owners by buying a large portfolio of securities and professionally managing that portfolio.

MUTUAL FUND
A specific type of investment company that continually buys or sells to investors shares of ownership in a portfolio.

ACCREDITED INVESTORS
In the context of securities offerings, "sophisticated" investors, such as banks, insurance companies, investment companies, the issuer's executive officers and directors, and persons whose income or net worth exceeds certain limits.

---

13. 17 C.F.R. Section 230.504. Rule 504 is the exemption used by most small businesses, but that could change under new SEC Rule 1001. This rule permits, under certain circumstances, "testing the waters" for offerings of up to $5 million per transaction. These offerings can be made only to "qualified purchasers" (knowledgeable, sophisticated investors), though.

14. Precautions to be taken against nonexempt, unregistered resales include asking the investor whether he or she is buying the securities for others; before the sale, disclosing to each purchaser in writing that the securities are unregistered and thus cannot be resold, except in an exempt transaction, without first being registered; and indicating on the certificates that the securities are unregistered and restricted.

15. 17 C.F.R. Section 230.504a.

mation about the offering company, its business, and the securities before the sale. Unlike Rule 506 (discussed next), Rule 505 does not require that the issuer believe each unaccredited investor "has such knowledge and experience in financial and business matters that he [or she] is capable of evaluating the merits and the risks of the prospective investment."[16]

Rule 506 Private, noninvestment company offerings in unlimited amounts that are not generally solicited or advertised are exempt if the SEC is notified of the sales and precautions are taken against nonexempt, unregistered resales. As with Rule 505, there may be no more than thirty-five unaccredited investors, but there are no limits on the number of accredited investors. If there are *any* unaccredited investors, the issuer must provide *all* purchasers with material information about itself, its business, and the securities before the sale.[17] In contrast to Rule 505, the issuer must believe that each unaccredited investor has sufficient knowledge or experience in financial matters to be capable of evaluating the investment's merits and risks.

This exemption is perhaps most important to firms that want to raise funds through the sale of securities without registering them. It is often referred to as the *private placement* exemption because it exempts "transactions not involving any public offering."[18] This provision applies to private offerings to a limited number of persons who are sufficiently sophisticated and able to assume the risk of the investment (and who thus have no need for federal registration protection). It also applies to private offerings to similarly situated institutional investors.

EXAMPLE #5 Citco Corporation needs to raise capital to expand its operations. Citco decides to make a private $10 million offering of its common stock directly to two hundred accredited investors and a group of thirty highly sophisticated, but unaccredited, investors. Citco provides all of these investors with a prospectus and material information about the firm, including its most recent financial statements. As long as Citco notifies the SEC of the sale, this offering will likely qualify as an exempt transaction under Rule 506. The offering is nonpublic and not generally advertised. There are fewer than thirty-five unaccredited investors, and each of them possesses sufficient knowledge and experience to evaluate the risks involved. The issuer has provided all purchasers with the material information. Thus, Citco will *not* be required to comply with the registration requirements of the Securities Act of 1933. □

Small Offerings—Section 4(6) Under Section 4(6) of the Securities Act of 1933, an offer made *solely* to accredited investors is exempt if its amount is not more than $5 million. Any number of accredited investors may participate, but no unaccredited investors may do so. No general solicitation or advertising may be used; the SEC must be notified of all sales; and precautions must be taken against nonexempt, unregistered resales. Precautions are necessary because these are *restricted* securities and may be resold only by registration or in an exempt transaction. (The securities purchased and sold by most people who deal in stock are called, in contrast, *unrestricted* securities.)

> **KEEP IN MIND**
> An investor can be "sophisticated" by virtue of his or her education and experience or by investing through a knowledgeable, experienced representative.

---

16. 17 C.F.R. Section 230.505.
17. 17 C.F.R. Section 230.506.
18. 15 U.S.C. Section 77d(2).

Intrastate Offerings—Rule 147   Also exempt are intrastate transactions involving purely local offerings.[19] This exemption applies to most offerings that are restricted to residents of the state in which the issuing company is organized and doing business. For nine months after the last sale, virtually no resales may be made to nonresidents, and precautions must be taken against this possibility. These offerings remain subject to applicable laws in the state of issue.

Resales   Most securities can be resold without registration (although some resales may be subject to restrictions, as discussed above in connection with specific exemptions). The Securities Act of 1933 provides exemptions for resales by most persons other than issuers or underwriters. The average investor who sells shares of stock does not have to file a registration statement with the SEC. Resales of restricted securities acquired under Rule 504a, Rule 505, Rule 506, or Section 4(6), however, trigger the registration requirements unless the party selling them complies with Rule 144 or Rule 144A. These rules are sometimes referred to as "safe harbors."

Rule 144   Rule 144 exempts restricted securities from registration on resale if there is adequate current public information about the issuer, the person selling the securities has owned them for at least one year, they are sold in certain limited amounts in unsolicited brokers' transactions, and the SEC is given notice of the resale.[20] "Adequate current public information" refers to the reports that certain companies are required to file under the Securities Exchange Act of 1934. A person who has owned the securities for at least one year is subject to none of these requirements, unless the person is an affiliate. An *affiliate* is one who controls, is controlled by, or is in common control with the issuer.

Rule 144A   Securities that at the time of issue are not of the same class as securities listed on a national securities exchange or quoted in a U.S. automated interdealer quotation system may be resold under Rule 144A.[21] They may be sold only to a qualified institutional buyer (an institution, such as an insurance company or a bank that owns and invests at least $100 million in securities). The seller must take reasonable steps to ensure that the buyer knows that the seller is relying on the exemption under Rule 144A. A sample restricted stock certificate is shown in Exhibit 24–2.

CONTRAST
Securities do not have to be held for one year to be exempt from registration on a resale under Rule 144A, as they do under Rule 144.

Violations of the 1933 Act

It is a violation of the Securities Act of 1933 to intentionally defraud investors by misrepresenting or omitting facts in a registration statement or prospectus. Liability is also imposed on those who are negligent for not discovering the fraud. Selling securities before the effective date of the registration statement or under an exemption for which the securities do not qualify results in liability.

Criminal violations are prosecuted by the U.S. Department of Justice. Violators may be fined up to $10,000, imprisoned for up to five years, or both. The SEC is authorized to seek civil sanctions against those who willfully violate the 1933 act. It can request an injunction to prevent further sales of the securi-

---

19. 15 U.S.C. Section 77c(a)(11); 17 C.F.R. Section 230.147.
20. 17 C.F.R. Section 230.144.
21. 17 C.F.R. Section 230.144A.

EXHIBIT 24-2 A SAMPLE RESTRICTED STOCK CERTIFICATE

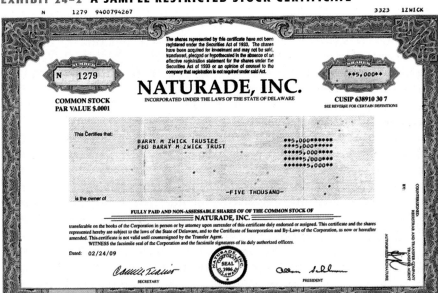

ties involved or ask the court to grant other relief, such as an order to a violator to refund profits. Parties who purchase securities and suffer harm as a result of false or omitted statements may also bring suits in a federal court to recover their losses and other damages.

There are three basic defenses to violations of the 1933 act. A defendant can avoid liability by proving that (1) the statement or omission was not material, (2) the plaintiff knew about the misrepresentation at the time of purchasing the stock, or (3) the defendant exercised *due diligence* in preparing the registration and reasonably believed at the time that the statements were true.

SECURITIES EXCHANGE ACT OF 1934

The Securities Exchange Act of 1934 provides for the regulation and registration of securities exchanges, brokers, dealers, and national securities associations, such as the National Association of Securities Dealers (NASD). Unlike the 1933 act, which is a one-time disclosure law, the 1934 act provides for continuous periodic disclosures by publicly held corporations to enable the SEC to regulate subsequent trading.

The Securities Exchange Act of 1934 applies to companies that have assets in excess of $10 million and five hundred or more shareholders. These corporations are referred to as Section 12 companies because they are required to register their securities under Section 12 of the 1934 act. Section 12 companies are required to file reports with the SEC annually and quarterly, and sometimes even monthly if specified events occur (such as a merger).

The act also authorizes the SEC to engage in market surveillance to deter undesirable market practices, such as fraud, market manipulation (attempts at illegally influencing stock prices), and misrepresentation. In addition, the act provides for the SEC's regulation of proxy solicitations for voting (discussed in Chapter 15).

Section 10(b), SEC Rule 10b-5, and Insider Trading

Section 10(b) is one of the most important sections of the Securities Exchange Act of 1934. This section proscribes the use of any manipulative or deceptive device in violation of SEC rules and regulations. Among the rules that the SEC has promulgated pursuant to the 1934 act is **SEC Rule 10b-5,** which prohibits the commission of fraud in connection with the purchase or sale of any security.

SEC RULE 10b-5
A rule of the Securities and Exchange Commission that makes it unlawful, in connection with the purchase or sale of any security, to make any untrue statement of a material fact or to omit a material fact if such omission causes the statement to be misleading.

Applicability of SEC Rule 10b-5   SEC Rule 10b-5 applies in virtually all cases concerning the trading of securities, whether on organized exchanges, in over-the-counter markets, or in private transactions. The rule covers, among other things, notes, bonds, agreements to form a corporation, and joint-venture agreements. Generally, it covers just about any form of security. It is immaterial whether a firm has securities registered under the 1933 act for the 1934 act to apply.

SEC Rule 10b-5 is applicable only when the requisites of federal jurisdiction—such as the use of stock exchange facilities, U.S. mail, or any means of interstate commerce—are present. Nevertheless, virtually every commercial transaction involves interstate contacts. In addition, the states have corporate securities laws, many of which include provisions similar to SEC Rule 10b-5.

INSIDER TRADING
The purchase or sale of securities on the basis of information that has not been made available to the public.

Insider Trading   One of the major goals of Section 10(b) and SEC Rule 10b-5 is to prevent so-called **insider trading,** which occurs when persons buy or sell securities on the basis of information that is not available to the public. Corporate directors, officers, and majority shareholders, for instance, often have advance inside information that can affect the future market value of the corporate stock. Obviously, if they act on this information, their positions give them a trading advantage over the general public and other shareholders. The 1934 Securities Exchange Act defines inside information and extends liability to those who take advantage of such information in their personal transactions when they know that the information is unavailable to those with whom they are dealing. Section 10(b) of the 1934 act and SEC Rule 10b-5 apply to anyone who has access to or receives information of a nonpublic nature on which trading is based—not just to corporate "insiders."

Evidence in an insider trading case against the former chief executive officer of Qwest Communications is delivered to a Denver courthouse. Why is insider trading deemed illegal? (AP Photo/Ed Andrieski)

Disclosure under SEC Rule 10b-5   Any material omission or misrepresentation of material facts in connection with the purchase or sale of a security may violate not only the Securities Act of 1933 but also the antifraud provisions of Section 10(b) of the 1934 act and SEC Rule 10b-5. The key to liability (which can be civil or criminal) under Section 10(b) and SEC Rule 10b-5 is whether the insider's information is *material.*

The following are some examples of material facts calling for disclosure under SEC Rule 10b-5:

1. Fraudulent trading in the company stock by a broker-dealer.
2. A dividend change (whether up or down).
3. A contract for the sale of corporate assets.
4. A new discovery, a new process, or a new product.

5. A significant change in the firm's financial condition.

6. Potential litigation against the company.

Note that any one of these facts, by itself, is not *automatically* considered a material fact. Rather, it will be regarded as a material fact if it is significant enough to affect an investor's decision as to whether to purchase or sell the company's securities. **EXAMPLE #6** Tron Corporation is the defendant in a class-action product liability lawsuit. Tron's attorney, Paula Frasier, believes it likely that the company will ultimately be held liable for damages, resulting in a considerable loss to the company. She advises Tron's directors, officers, and accountants that the company will probably be required to pay damages as a result of the suit. If Tron wants to make a stock offering before the end of the trial, it must disclose this potential liability and the financial consequences to the firm. These facts are significant enough to affect an investor's decision as to whether to purchase Tron's stock. □

The following is one of the landmark cases interpreting SEC Rule 10b-5. The SEC sued Texas Gulf Sulphur Company for issuing a misleading press release. The release underestimated the magnitude and value of a mineral discovery. The SEC also sued several of Texas Gulf Sulphur's directors, officers, and employees under SEC Rule 10b-5 for purchasing large amounts of the corporate stock prior to the announcement of the corporation's rich ore discovery.

Case 24.1   SEC v. Texas Gulf Sulphur Co.

United States Court of Appeals, Second Circuit, 1968.
401 F.2d 833.

BACKGROUND AND FACTS   Texas Gulf Sulphur Company (TGS) conducted aerial geophysical surveys over more than 15,000 square miles of eastern Canada. The operations indicated concentrations of commercially exploitable minerals. At one site near Timmins, Ontario, TGS drilled a hole that appeared to yield a core with an exceedingly high mineral content. TGS kept secret the results of the core sample. Officers and employees of the company made substantial purchases of TGS's stock or accepted stock options (rights to purchase stock) after learning of the ore discovery, even though further drilling was necessary to establish whether there was enough ore to be mined commercially. Several months later, TGS announced that the strike was expected to yield at least 25 million tons of ore. Subsequently, the price of TGS stock rose substantially. The Securities and Exchange Commission (SEC) brought a suit against the officers and employees of TGS for violating SEC Rule 10b-5. The officers and employees argued that the information on which they had traded had not been material at the time of their trades because the mine had not then been commercially proved. The trial court held that most of the defendants had not violated SEC Rule 10b-5, and the SEC appealed.

IN THE WORDS OF THE COURT . . . WATERMAN, Circuit Judge.

* * * *

* * * Whether facts are material within Rule 10b-5 when the facts relate to a particular event and are undisclosed by those persons who are knowledgeable thereof *will depend at any given time upon a balancing of both the indicated probability that the event will occur and the anticipated magnitude of the event in light of the totality of the company activity.* Here, * * * knowledge of the possibility, which surely was more than marginal, of the existence of a mine of the vast magnitude indicated by the remarkably rich drill core located rather close to the surface (suggesting mineability by the less expensive openpit method) within the confines of a large anomaly (suggesting an extensive region of mineralization) might well have affected the price of TGS stock

CASE 24.1—CONTINUED

CASE 24.1–CONTINUED

and would certainly have been an important fact to a reasonable, if speculative, investor in deciding whether he should buy, sell, or hold. [Emphasis added.]

* * * *

* * * A major factor in determining whether the * * * discovery was a material fact is the importance attached to the drilling results by those who knew about it. * * * The timing by those who knew of it of their stock purchases * * *—purchases in some cases by individuals who had never before purchased * * * TGS stock—virtually compels the inference that the insiders were influenced by the drilling results.

DECISION AND REMEDY   The appellate court ruled in favor of the SEC. All of the trading by insiders who knew of the mineral find before its true extent had been publicly announced violated SEC Rule 10b-5.

IMPACT OF THIS CASE ON TODAY'S LEGAL ENVIRONMENT   This landmark case affirmed the principle that the test of whether information is "material," for SEC Rule 10b-5 purposes, is whether it would affect the judgment of reasonable investors. The corporate insiders' purchases of stock and stock options indicated that they were influenced by the drilling results and that the information about the drilling results was material. The courts continue to cite this case when applying SEC Rule 10b-5 to cases of alleged insider trading.

WHAT IF THE FACTS WERE DIFFERENT?   Suppose that further drilling revealed that there was not enough ore at this site for it to be mined commercially. Would the defendants still have been liable for violating SEC Rule 10b-5? Why or why not?

RELEVANT WEB SITES   To locate information on the Web concerning the *SEC v. Texas Gulf Suphur Co.* decision, go to this text's Web site at **www.cengage.com/blaw/let**, select "Chapter 24," and click on "URLs for Landmarks."

The Private Securities Litigation Reform Act of 1995   One of the unintended effects of SEC Rule 10b-5 was to deter the disclosure of some material information, such as financial forecasts. To understand why, consider an example. **EXAMPLE #7** AQT Company announces that its projected earnings in a certain time period will be X amount. It turns out that the forecast is wrong. The earnings are in fact much lower, and the price of AQT's stock is affected—negatively. The shareholders then bring a class-action suit against the company, alleging that the directors violated SEC Rule 10b-5 by disclosing misleading financial information.▫

In an attempt to rectify this problem and promote disclosure, Congress passed the Private Securities Litigation Reform Act of 1995. Among other things, the act provides a "safe harbor" for publicly held companies that make forward-looking statements, such as financial forecasts. Those who make such statements are protected against liability for securities fraud as long as the statements are accompanied by "meaningful cautionary statements identifying important factors that could cause actual results to differ materially from those in the forward-looking statement."[22]

After the 1995 act was passed, a number of securities class-action suits were filed in state courts to skirt the requirements of the act. In response to this problem, Congress passed the Securities Litigation Uniform Standards Act of 1998 (SLUSA).[23] The act placed stringent limits on the ability of plaintiffs to bring

---

22. 15 U.S.C. Sections 77z-2, 78u-5.
23. Pub. L. No. 105-353. This act amended many sections of Title 15 of the *United States Code*.

class-action suits in state courts against firms whose securities are traded on national stock exchanges. The SLUSA not only prevents purchasers and sellers of securities from bringing class-action fraud claims under state securities laws, but also prevents investors who allege fraud from suing under state law.[24]

Outsiders and SEC Rule 10b-5   The traditional insider-trading case involves true insiders—corporate officers, directors, and majority shareholders who have access to (and trade on) inside information. Increasingly, liability under Section 10(b) of the 1934 act and SEC Rule 10b-5 is being extended to include certain "outsiders"—persons who trade on inside information acquired indirectly. Two theories have been developed under which outsiders may be held liable for insider trading: the *tipper/tippee theory* and the *misappropriation theory* (to be discussed shortly).

In the following case, the plaintiffs attempted to assert a third theory of liability—scheme liability—in a case argued before the United States Supreme Court. Can Section 10(b) and SEC Rule 10b-5 apply to outsiders—suppliers and customers—who seemingly "aid and abet" a scheme to "cook the books" in order to show inflated sales revenue figures for a publicly traded company?

---

24. See, *Merrill Lynch, Pierce, Fenner & Smith, Inc. v. Dabit,* 547 U.S. 71, 126 S.Ct. 1503, 164 L.Ed.2d 179 (2006).

Case 24.2 Stoneridge Investment Partners, LLC v. Scientific-Atlanta, Inc.

Supreme Court of the United States, 2008.
___ U.S. ___, 128 S.Ct. 761, 169 L.Ed.2d 627.
www.supremecourtus.gov/opinions/opinions.html[a]

BACKGROUND AND FACTS   In 2000, the cable operator Charter Communications wanted to keep its stock price high by satisfying stock analysts' expectations about its revenue growth. When it became apparent that revenues were not growing as projected, management at Charter devised an

accounting scheme that would artificially inflate its reported revenues. The scheme involved Charter's digital cable converter (set top) box suppliers, Scientific-Atlanta and Motorola. They agreed to overcharge Charter for the cable boxes in exchange for additional advertising on Charter's cable network. A group of investors, represented in this case by Stoneridge Investment Partners, sued Scientific-Atlanta and Motorola, alleging violation of Section 10(b) of the Securities Exchange Act of 1934 and of SEC Rule 10b-5. At trial, the district court dismissed the case. On appeal, the U.S. Court of Appeals for the Eighth Circuit upheld this ruling. Stoneridge then appealed to the United States Supreme Court.

a. Click on "Opinions" and go to 2008 to find this case, which was decided on 1/15/08. Click on the case name to access the opinion.

IN THE WORDS OF THE COURT . . . Justice *KENNEDY* delivered the opinion of the Court.

*   *   *   *

*   *   * Charter, a cable operator, engaged in a variety of fraudulent practices so its quarterly reports would meet Wall Street expectations for cable subscriber growth and operating cash flow. The fraud included misclassification of its customer base; delayed reporting of terminated customers; improper capitalization of costs that should have been shown as expenses; and manipulation of the company's billing cutoff dates to inflate reported revenues. In late 2000, Charter executives realized that, despite these efforts, the company would miss projected operating cash flow numbers by $15 to $20 million. To help meet the shortfall, Charter decided to alter its existing arrangements with respondents, Scientific-Atlanta and Motorola.

Respondents supplied Charter with the digital cable converter (set top) boxes that Charter furnished to its customers. Charter arranged to overpay respondents $20 for

CASE 24.2—CONTINUED

CASE 24.2–CONTINUED

each set top box it purchased until the end of the year, with the understanding that respondents would return the overpayment by purchasing advertising from Charter.

 *   *   *   *

Respondents had no role in preparing or disseminating Charter's financial statements. And their own financial statements booked the transactions as a wash, under generally accepted accounting principles. It is alleged [that] respondents knew or were in reckless disregard of Charter's intention to use the transactions to inflate its revenues and knew [that] the resulting financial statements issued by Charter would be relied upon by research analysts and investors.

 *   *   *   *

 *   *   * *In a typical Section 10(b) private action, a plaintiff must prove (1) a material misrepresentation or omission by the defendant; (2) scienter [guilty knowledge]; (3) a connection between the misrepresentation or omission and the purchase or sale of a security; (4) reliance upon the misrepresentation or omission; (5) economic loss; and (6) loss causation.* [In a previous Supreme Court case], the Court determined that Section 10(b) liability did not extend to aiders and abettors. [Emphasis added.]

 *   *   *   *

Reliance by the plaintiff upon the defendant's deceptive acts is an essential element of the Section 10(b) private cause of action. It ensures that, for liability to arise, the "requisite causal connection between a defendant's misrepresentation and a plaintiff's injury" exists as a predicate for liability. [Emphasis added.]

 *   *   * Respondents had no duty to disclose; and their deceptive acts were not communicated to the public. No member of the investing public had knowledge, either actual or presumed, of respondents' deceptive acts during the relevant times. Petitioner [Stoneridge], as a result, cannot show reliance upon any of respondents' actions except in an indirect chain that we find too remote for liability.

 *   *   *   *

 *   *   * In all events, we conclude respondents' deceptive acts, which were not disclosed to the investing public, are too remote to satisfy the requirement of reliance. It was Charter, not respondents, that misled its auditor and filed fraudulent financial statements; nothing respondents did made it necessary or inevitable for Charter to record the transactions as it did.

 *   *   * Were the implied cause of action to be extended to the practices described here, however, there would be a risk that the federal power would be used to invite litigation beyond the immediate sphere of securities litigation and in areas already governed by functioning and effective state-law guarantees.

 *   *   *   *

 *   *   * Extensive discovery and the potential for uncertainty and disruption in a lawsuit allow plaintiffs with weak claims to extort settlements from innocent companies. Adoption of petitioner's approach would expose a new class of defendants to these risks. *   *   * Contracting parties might find it necessary to protect against these threats, raising the costs of doing business. Overseas firms with no other exposure to our securities laws could be deterred from doing business here. This, in turn, may raise the cost of being a publicly traded company under our law and shift securities offerings away from domestic capital markets.

 *   *   *   *

The judgment of the Court of Appeals is affirmed, and the case is remanded for further proceedings consistent with this opinion.

DECISION AND REMEDY   The United States Supreme Court affirmed the federal appellate court's decision. The private right of action in Section 10(b) cannot be applied in this situation because Charter Communications' investors did not rely on Scientific-Atlanta's and Motorola's statements or representations.

THE ETHICAL DIMENSION   As suppliers to Charter, Scientific-Atlanta and Motorola simply engaged in an accounting fiction that, as the Court pointed out, appeared on their books as a "wash." Hence, these two companies conformed to generally accepted accounting rules. Nonetheless, was their behavior ethical? Why or why not?

THE GLOBAL DIMENSION   The Court noted that if it had ruled in favor of the investors bringing the suit, there would be negative effects on foreign companies doing business within the United States. Explain the logic behind this line of reasoning.

Tipper/Tippee Theory   Anyone who acquires inside information as a result of a corporate insider's breach of his or her fiduciary duty can be liable under SEC Rule 10b-5. This liability extends to **tippees** (those who receive "tips" from insiders) and even remote tippees (tippees of tippees).

The key to liability under this theory is that the inside information must be obtained as a result of someone's breach of a fiduciary duty to the corporation whose shares are involved in the trading. The tippee is liable under this theory only if (1) there is a breach of a duty not to disclose inside information, (2) the disclosure is in exchange for personal benefit, and (3) the tippee knows (or should know) of this breach and benefits from it.[25]

TIPPEE
A person who receives inside information.

Misappropriation Theory   Liability for insider trading may also be established under the misappropriation theory. This theory holds that an individual who wrongfully obtains (misappropriates) inside information and trades on it for her or his personal gain should be held liable because, in essence, she or he stole information rightfully belonging to another.

The misappropriation theory has been controversial because it significantly extends the reach of SEC Rule 10b-5 to outsiders who ordinarily would not be deemed fiduciaries of the corporations in whose stock they trade. **EXAMPLE #8** In one landmark case, James O'Hagan was a partner at the law firm of Dorsey & Whitney. A large corporation hired the firm to assist in a takeover of the Pillsbury Company. O'Hagan bought shares of Pillsbury stock. After the tender offer was announced, the stock price increased by more than 35 percent, and O'Hagan sold his shares for a profit of more than $4 million. The SEC prosecuted O'Hagan for securities fraud in violation of Rule 10b-5 under the misappropriation theory. Ultimately, the United States Supreme Court upheld O'Hagan's conviction under the misappropriation theory because he secretly converted the client-corporation's inside information for personal gain.[26] □

Insider Reporting and Trading—Section 16(b)

Section 16(b) of the 1934 act provides for the recapture by the corporation of all profits realized by certain insiders on any purchase and sale or sale and purchase of the corporation's stock within any six-month period. It is irrelevant whether the insider actually uses inside information; *all such **short-swing profits** must be returned to the corporation.* In this context, *insiders* means officers, directors, and large stockholders of Section 12 corporations (those owning 10 percent of the class of equity securities registered under Section 12 of the 1934 act).[27] To

---

25. See, for example, *Chiarella v. United States,* 445 U.S. 222, 100 S.Ct. 1108, 63 L.Ed.2d 348 (1980); and *Dirks v. SEC,* 463 U.S. 646, 103 S.Ct. 3255, 77 L.Ed.2d 911 (1983).
26. *United States v. O'Hagan,* 521 U.S. 642, 117 S.Ct. 2199, 138 L.Ed.2d 724 (1997).
27. 15 U.S.C. Section 78l. Note that Section 403 of the Sarbanes-Oxley Act of 2002 shortened the reporting deadlines specified in Section 16(b).

A proxy statement. Who regulates the content of proxy statements, and how? (Courtesy of Prudential Financial)

discourage such insiders from using nonpublic information about their companies to their personal benefit in the stock market, they must file reports with the SEC concerning their ownership and trading of the corporation's securities.

Section 16(b) applies not only to stock but also to warrants, options, and securities convertible into stock. In addition, the courts have fashioned complex rules for determining profits. Note that the SEC exempts a number of transactions under Rule 16b-3.[28] For all of these reasons, corporate insiders are wise to seek specialized counsel prior to trading in the corporation's stock. Exhibit 24–3 compares the effects of SEC Rule 10b-5 and Section 16(b).

Proxy Statements

Section 14(a) of the Securities Exchange Act of 1934 regulates the solicitation of proxies from shareholders of Section 12 companies. The SEC regulates the content of proxy statements. As discussed in Chapter 15, a proxy statement is sent to shareholders when corporate officials are requesting authority to vote on behalf of the shareholders in a particular election on specified issues. Whoever solicits a proxy must fully and accurately disclose in the proxy statement all of the facts that are pertinent to the matter on which the shareholders are to vote. In 2007, the SEC issued new rules allowing companies to post their proxy materials on Web sites rather than mailing the materials to shareholders (see this chapter's *Online Developments* feature for a discussion of these rules). SEC Rule 14a-9 is similar to the antifraud provisions of SEC Rule 10b-5. Remedies for violations are extensive; they range from injunctions that prevent a vote from being taken to monetary damages.

28. 17 C.F.R. Section 240.16b-3.

EXHIBIT 24-3 COMPARISON OF COVERAGE, APPLICATION, AND LIABILITY UNDER SEC RULE 10b-5 AND SECTION 16(b)

AREA OF COMPARISON	SEC RULE 10b–5	SECTION 16(b)
What is the subject matter of the transaction?	Any security (does not have to be registered).	Any security (does not have to be registered).
What transactions are covered?	Purchase or sale.	Short-swing purchase and sale or short-swing sale and purchase.
Who is subject to liability?	Virtually anyone with inside information under a duty to disclose—including officers, directors, controlling shareholders, and tippees.	Officers, directors, and certain 10 percent shareholders.
Is omission or misrepresentation necessary for liability?	Yes.	No.
Are there any exempt transactions?	No.	Yes, there are a number of exemptions.
Who may bring an action?	A person transacting with an insider, the SEC, or a purchaser or seller damaged by a wrongful act.	A corporation or a shareholder by derivative action.

Violations of the 1934 Act

As mentioned earlier, violations of Section 10(b) of the Securities Exchange Act of 1934 and SEC Rule 10b-5, including insider trading, may be subject to criminal or civil liability. For either criminal or civil sanctions to be imposed, however, *scienter* must exist—that is, the violator must have had an intent to defraud or knowledge of her or his misconduct (see Chapter 6). *Scienter* can be proved by showing that the defendant made false statements or wrongfully failed to disclose material facts.

Violations of Section 16(b) include the sale by insiders of stock acquired less than six months before the sale (or less than six months after the sale if selling short). These violations are subject to civil sanctions. Liability under Section 16(b) is strict liability. Thus, liability is imposed regardless of whether *scienter* or negligence existed.

Criminal Penalties   For violations of Section 10(b) and Rule 10b-5, an individual may be fined up to $5 million, imprisoned for up to twenty years, or both. A partnership or a corporation may be fined up to $25 million. Under Section 807 of the Sarbanes-Oxley Act of 2002, for a *willful* violation of the 1934 act the violator may, in addition to being subject to a fine, be imprisoned for up to twenty-five years. In a criminal prosecution under the securities laws, a jury is not allowed to speculate about whether a defendant acted willfully—the prosecution must prove beyond a reasonable doubt that the defendant knew he or she was acting wrongfully.[29]

In criminal prosecutions under Sections 10(b) and 14(a), the standard for assessing the materiality of a defendant's false statements to shareholders is the perspective of the reasonable investor. The issue in the following case was whether that standard also applies to statements in documents filed with the SEC.

---

29. See, for example, *United States v. Stewart,* 305 F.Supp.2d 368 (S.D.N.Y. 2004), a case involving Martha Stewart, founder of a well-known media and homemaking empire, who was later convicted on other charges.

Case 24.3 **United States v. Berger**

United States Court of Appeals, Ninth Circuit, 2007.
473 F.3d 1000.

BACKGROUND AND FACTS   Craig Consumer Electronics, Inc., bought car stereos, compact music centers, and small personal stereos from its offices in Hong Kong and sold the goods from its offices in California to retail stores. Richard Berger was Craig's president, chief executive officer, and board chairman. In 1994, Craig entered into a $50 million loan agreement with BT Commercial Corporation and other lenders. Under the agreement, Craig could borrow up to 85 percent of the value of its accounts receivable (the amount owed to it by retail stores) and up to 65 percent of the value of its inventory. Each business day, Craig provided the lenders with a "Borrowing Certificate" to report the amount of its accounts receivables and inventory. By early 1995, Craig lacked sufficient receivables and inventory to borrow funds for its operations. To hide these facts, Berger and others falsified the information in the certificates. They also hid Craig's true financial condition in reports filed with the Securities and Exchange Commission (SEC). In 1997, owing the banks more than $8.4 million, Craig filed for bankruptcy. Berger and others were convicted in a federal district court of, among other things, criminal violations of the Securities Exchange Act of 1934 for the false statements in the reports filed with the SEC. Berger was sentenced to six months in prison, fined $1.25 million, and ordered to pay the banks $3.14 million in restitution. Berger appealed to the U.S. Court of Appeals for the Ninth Circuit.

CASE 24.3—CONTINUED

IN THE WORDS OF THE COURT . . . *PREGERSON*, Circuit Judge.

*   *   *   *

*   *   * The indictment alleged that Berger made material omissions in mandatory filings with the SEC, in violation of Section 13(a) *   *   * and Section 32(a) of the 1934 Act. Section 13(a) is a mandatory filing provision, that requires certain companies to file with the SEC "information and documents *   *   * to keep reasonably current the information *   *   * in *   *   * a registration statement" as well as "annual reports *   *   * and *   *   * quarterly reports." *Section 32(a) provides criminal penalties for "any person who willfully and knowingly makes *   *   * any statement in any *   *   * report or document required to be filed *   *   * which statement was false or misleading with respect to any material fact *   *   * ."* [Emphasis added.]

Berger contends that when applying Section 32(a), courts should assess materiality from the perspective of the SEC [and asserts that in this case there was insufficient evidence that the falsehoods were material to the SEC].

*   *   * Berger contends that the SEC, as a regulatory body, makes decisions based on the information contained in a company's mandatory filings. Thus, Berger argues that the materiality of false statements made to the SEC *   *   * must also be assessed not from the reasonable investor's perspective, but from the SEC's perspective, in the context of its own regulatory decisions.

We disagree with Berger. The purpose of the 1934 Act was to benefit and protect investors, with proper agency decision making as a secondary concern.

Applying the "reasonable investor" materiality standard to Section 32(a) is consistent with the goals of the SEC. *   *   * The agency itself commences actions on filings it considers materially misleading to investors. In addition to being a regulatory body, the SEC acts as a repository of information intended to be disseminated to and used by the public. The mandatory filings at issue in this case, for example, were meant for investors' use. *   *   * *It is clear that the reporting requirements under the 1934 Act are intended to protect investors, and that materiality should be assessed from the reasonable investor's perspective.* [Emphasis added.]

*   *   *   *

Finally, Berger argues that "materiality must be assessed in the context of a decision." He points to Sections 10(b) and 14(a) for comparison. In the Section 10(b) context, courts assess materiality by examining a fact's potential to influence an investor's particular decision—the decision to buy or sell a security. Similarly, in Section 14(a), the false statement must have a tendency to influence a decision—how an investor will vote. Section 32(a), however, only criminalizes the filing of false information and does not expressly implicate any specific type of investment decision.

We disagree. In Sections 10(b) and 14(a), *   *   * the decision to buy or sell shares and the decision to vote a particular way *   *   * are enumerated as elements of the statutes. The language of Section 32(a) is distinct; it criminalizes the mere filing of a material false statement without requiring that the statement affect a particular investment decision. It thus appears that Congress intended Section 32(a) to act as a catch-all provision to punish those who file a false statement, whether or not the filing can be shown to affect a specific investment decision, as long as the false statement could affect a reasonable investor.

DECISION AND REMEDY   The U.S. Court of Appeals for the Ninth Circuit held that the materiality of false statements in reports filed with the SEC "must be assessed from the perspective of the reasonable investor" and affirmed Berger's conviction and the restitution order. The court vacated the prison term and fine, however, on the ground that certain factors were omitted or mistakenly applied, and remanded the case for reconsideration of the sentence.

THE ETHICAL DIMENSION   Assuming that Craig's default on the loan was inevitable, what did Berger do that was unethical? Explain.

THE GLOBAL DIMENSION   Considering that Craig bought goods overseas to sell in the United States, how much blame should the court have attributed to global electronics markets for the banks' losses?

Civil Sanctions   The SEC can also bring suit in a federal district court against anyone violating or aiding in a violation of the 1934 act or SEC rules by purchasing or selling a security while in the possession of material nonpublic information. The violation must occur on or through the facilities of a national securities exchange or from or through a broker or dealer. The court may assess as a penalty as much as triple the profits gained or the loss avoided by the guilty party. Profit or loss is defined as "the difference between the purchase or sale price of the security and the value of that security as measured by the trading price of the security at a reasonable period of time after public dissemination of the nonpublic information."[30]

The Insider Trading and Securities Fraud Enforcement Act of 1988 enlarged the class of persons who may be subject to civil liability for insider-trading violations. This act also gave the SEC authority to award **bounty payments** (rewards given by government officials for acts beneficial to the state) to persons providing information leading to the prosecution of insider-trading violations.[31]

Private parties may also sue violators of Section 10(b) and Rule 10b-5, but normally cannot bring an action against those who "aid and abet" under these rules. A private party may obtain rescission (cancellation) of a contract to buy securities or damages to the extent of the violator's illegal profits. Those found liable have a right to seek contribution from those who share responsibility for the violations, including accountants, attorneys, and corporations. For violations of Section 16(b), a corporation can bring an action to recover the short-swing profits.

BOUNTY PAYMENT
A reward (payment) given to a person or persons who perform a certain service, such as informing legal authorities of illegal actions.

STATE SECURITIES LAWS

Today, all states have their own corporate securities laws, or "blue sky laws," that regulate the offer and sale of securities within individual state borders. (The phrase *blue sky laws* dates to a 1917 decision by the United States Supreme Court in which the Court declared that the purpose of such laws was to prevent "speculative schemes which have no more basis than so many feet of 'blue sky.'")[32] Article 8 of the Uniform Commercial Code, which has been adopted by all of the states, also imposes various requirements relating to the purchase and sale of securities.

BE AWARE
Federal securities laws do not take priority over state securities laws.

Requirements under State Securities Laws

Despite some differences in philosophy, all state blue sky laws have certain features in common. Typically, state laws have disclosure requirements and antifraud provisions, many of which are patterned after Section 10(b) of the

---

30. The Insider Trading Sanctions Act of 1984, 15 U.S.C. Section 78u(d)(2)(A) and (C).
31. 15 U.S.C. Section 78u-1.
32. *Hall v. Geiger-Jones Co.*, 242 U.S. 539, 37 S.Ct. 217, 61 L.Ed. 480 (1917).

Securities Exchange Act of 1934 and SEC Rule 10b-5. State laws also provide for the registration or qualification of securities offered or issued for sale within the state and impose disclosure requirements. Unless an exemption from registration is applicable, issuers must register or qualify their stock with the appropriate state official, often called a *corporations commissioner.* Additionally, most state securities laws regulate securities brokers and dealers.

Concurrent Regulation

State securities laws apply mainly to intrastate transactions. Since the adoption of the 1933 and 1934 federal securities acts, the state and federal governments have regulated securities concurrently. Issuers must comply with both federal and state securities laws, and exemptions from federal law are not exemptions from state laws.

The dual federal and state system has not always worked well, particularly during the early 1990s, when the securities markets underwent considerable expansion. In response, Congress passed the National Securities Markets Improvement Act of 1996, which eliminated some of the duplicate regulations and gave the SEC exclusive power to regulate most national securities activities. The National Conference of Commissioners on Uniform State Laws then substantially revised the Uniform Securities Act and recommended it to the states for adoption in 2002. Unlike the previous version of this law, the new act is designed to coordinate state and federal securities regulation and enforcement efforts. Thirteen states have already adopted the Uniform Securities Act, and several other states are considering adoption.[33]

CORPORATE GOVERNANCE

CORPORATE GOVERNANCE
A set of policies or procedures affecting the way a corporation is directed or controlled.

Corporate governance can be narrowly defined as the relationship between a corporation and its shareholders. The Organization for Economic Cooperation and Development (OECD) provides a broader definition:

> Corporate governance is the system by which business corporations are directed and controlled. The corporate governance structure specifies the distribution of rights and responsibilities among different participants in the corporation, such as the board of directors, managers, shareholders, and other stakeholders, and spells out the rules and procedures for making decisions on corporate affairs.[34]

Although this definition has no legal value, it does set the tone for the ways in which modern corporations should be governed. In other words, effective corporate governance requires more than compliance with laws and regulations. The definition and focus of corporate governance principles vary around the world. For a discussion of corporate governance in other nations, see this chapter's *Beyond Our Borders* feature on the following page.

---

33. At the time this book went to press, the Uniform Securities Act had been adopted in Georgia, Hawaii, Idaho, Indiana, Iowa, Kansas, Maine, Minnesota, Missouri, Oklahoma, South Carolina, South Dakota, and Vermont, as well as in the U.S. Virgin Islands. Adoption legislation was pending in the District of Columbia, Michigan, Washington State, and Wisconsin. You can find current information on state adoptions at **www.nccusl.org**.

34. *Governance in the 21st Century: Future Studies* (OECD, 2001).

Corporate governance has become an issue of concern not only for U.S. corporations, but also for corporate entities around the world. With the globalization of business, a corporation's bad acts (or lack of control systems) can have far-reaching consequences. Different models of corporate governance exist, often depending on the degree of capitalism in the particular nation. In the United States, corporate governance tends to give priority to shareholders' interests. This approach encourages significant innovation and cost and quality competition. In contrast, the coordinated model of governance that prevails in continental Europe and Japan considers the interests of so-called stakeholders—employees, managers, suppliers, customers, and the community—to be a priority. The coordinated model still encourages innovation and cost and quality competition, but not to the same extent as the U.S. model.

FOR CRITICAL ANALYSIS   Why does the presence of a capitalist system affect a nation's perspective on corporate governance?

The Need for Effective Corporate Governance

The need for effective corporate governance arises in large corporations because corporate ownership (by shareholders) is separated from corporate control (by officers and managers). In the real world, officers and managers are tempted to advance their own interests, even when such interests conflict with those of the shareholders. The collapse of Enron Corporation and other well-publicized scandals in the corporate world in the early 2000s provide a clear illustration of the reasons for concern about managerial opportunism.

Attempts at Aligning the Interests of Officers with Those of Shareholders

Some corporations have sought to align the financial interests of their officers with those of the company's shareholders by providing the officers with **stock options,** which enable them to purchase shares of the corporation's stock at a set price. When the market price rises above that level, the officers can sell their shares for a profit. Because a stock's market price generally increases as the corporation prospers, the options give the officers a financial stake in the corporation's well-being and supposedly encourage them to work hard for the benefit of the shareholders.

STOCK OPTIONS
An agreement that grants the owner the option to buy a given number of shares of stock, usually within a set time period.

Options have turned out to be an imperfect device for providing effective governance, however. Executives in some companies have been tempted to "cook" the companies' books in order to keep share prices higher so that they could sell their stock for a profit. Executives in other corporations have experienced no losses when share prices dropped; instead, their options were "repriced" so that they did not suffer from the share price decline and could still profit from future increases above the lowered share price. Thus, although stock options theoretically can motivate officers to protect shareholder interests, stock option plans have often become a way for officers to take advantage of shareholders.

With stock options generally failing to work as planned and numerous headline-making scandals occurring within major corporations, there has been an outcry for more "outside" directors (those with no formal employment affiliation with the company). The theory is that independent directors will more closely monitor the actions of corporate officers. Hence, today we see more boards with outside directors. Note, though, that outside directors may not be truly independent of corporate officers; they may be friends or business associates of the leading officers. A study of board appointments found that the best way to increase one's probability of appointment was to "suck up" to the chief executive officer.[35]

Corporate Governance and Corporate Law

Effective corporate governance standards are designed to address problems (such as those briefly discussed above) and to motivate officers to make decisions to promote the financial interests of the company's shareholders. Generally, corporate governance entails corporate decision-making structures that monitor employees (particularly officers) to ensure that they are acting for the benefit of the shareholders. Thus, corporate governance involves, at a minimum:

1. The audited reporting of the corporation's financial progress, so that managers can be evaluated.
2. Legal protections for shareholders, so that violators of the law, who attempt to take advantage of shareholders, can be punished for misbehavior and victims can recover damages for any associated losses.

The Practical Significance of Effective Corporate Governance
Effective corporate governance may have considerable practical significance. A study by researchers at Harvard University and the Wharton School of Business found that firms providing greater shareholder rights had higher profits, higher sales growth, higher firm value, and other economic advantages.[36] Better corporate governance in the form of greater accountability to investors may therefore offer the opportunity to increase corporations' value.

Governance and Corporation Law   Corporate governance is the essential purpose of corporation law in the United States. These statutes set up the legal framework for corporate governance. Under the corporate law of Delaware, where most major companies incorporate, all corporations must have in place certain structures of corporate governance. The key structure of corporate law is, of course, the board of directors. Directors make the most important decisions about the future of the corporation and monitor the actions of corporate officers. Directors are elected by shareholders to look out for their best interests.

The Board of Directors   Some argue that shareholder democracy is key to improving corporate governance. If shareholders could vote on major corporate decisions, shareholders could presumably have more control over the corporation. Essential to shareholder democracy is the concept of electing the board of directors, usually at the corporation's annual meeting. Under corporate law, a corporation must have a board of directors elected by the shareholders. Virtually anyone can become a director, though some organizations, such as the New York Stock Exchange, require certain standards of service for directors of their listed corporations.

Directors have the responsibility of ensuring that officers are operating wisely and in the exclusive interest of shareholders. Directors receive reports from the officers and give them managerial directions. The board in theory controls the compensation of officers (presumably tied to performance). The reality, though, is

---

35. Jennifer Reingold, "Suck Up and Move Fast," *Fast Company*, January 2005, p. 34.
36. Paul A. Gompers, Joy L. Ishii, and Andrew Metrick, "Corporate Governance and Equity Prices," *Quarterly Journal of Economics*, Vol. 118 (2003), p. 107.

that corporate directors devote a relatively small amount of time to monitoring officers.

Ideally, shareholders would monitor the directors' supervision of officers. As one leading board monitor commented, "Boards of directors are like subatomic particles—they behave differently when they are observed." Consequently, monitoring directors, and holding them responsible for corporate failings, can induce the directors to do a better job of monitoring officers and ensuring that the company is being managed in the interest of shareholders. Although the directors can be sued for failing to do their jobs effectively, directors are rarely held personally liable.

Importance of the Audit Committee   One crucial board committee is known as the *audit committee*. The audit committee oversees the corporation's accounting and financial reporting processes, including both internal and outside auditors. Unless the committee members have sufficient expertise and are willing to spend the time to carefully examine the corporation's bookkeeping methods, however, the audit committee may be ineffective.

The audit committee also oversees the corporation's "internal controls." These are the measures taken to ensure that reported results are accurate; they are carried out largely by the company's internal auditing staff. As an example, these controls help to determine whether a corporation's debts are collectible. If the debts are not collectible, it is up to the audit committee to make sure that the corporation's financial officers do not simply pretend that payment will eventually be made.

The Role of the Compensation Committee   Another important committee of the board of directors is the *compensation committee*. This committee monitors and determines the compensation to be paid to the company's officers. As part of this process, it is responsible for assessing the officers' performance and for designing a compensation system that will better align the officers' interests with those of shareholders.

The Sarbanes-Oxley Act of 2002

As discussed in Chapter 2, in 2002, following a series of corporate scandals, Congress passed the Sarbanes-Oxley Act. The act separately addresses certain issues relating to corporate governance. Generally, the act attempts to increase corporate accountability by imposing strict disclosure requirements and harsh penalties for violations of securities laws. Among other things, the act requires chief corporate executives to take responsibility for the accuracy of financial statements and reports that are filed with the SEC. Chief executive officers and chief financial officers must personally certify that the statements and reports are accurate and complete.

The chairman of the Securities and Exchange Commission (SEC), Christopher Cox, uses a prop when testifying before Congress about the complexity of the Sarbanes-Oxley Act. Notice that the "for Dummies" book is quite thick. Why would the SEC chairman want Congress to simplify an act that his agency must enforce?
(AP Photo/Lawrence Jackson)

EXHIBIT 24-4   SOME KEY PROVISIONS OF THE
SARBANES-OXLEY ACT OF 2002 RELATING TO CORPORATE ACCOUNTABILITY

Certification Requirements—Under Section 906 of the Sarbanes-Oxley Act, the chief executive officers (CEOs) and chief financial officers (CFOs) of most major companies listed on public stock exchanges must certify financial statements that are filed with the SEC. For virtually all filed financial reports, CEOs and CFOs have to certify that such reports "fully comply" with SEC requirements and that all of the information reported "fairly represents in all material respects, the financial conditions and results of operations of the issuer."

Under Section 302 of the act, for each quarterly and annual filing with the SEC, CEOs and CFOs of reporting companies are required to certify that a signing officer reviewed the report and that it contains no untrue statements of material fact. Also, the signing officer or officers must certify that they have established an internal control system to identify all material information and that any deficiencies in the system were disclosed to the auditors.

Loans to Directors and Officers—Section 402 prohibits any reporting company, as well as any private company that is filing an initial public offering, from making personal loans to directors and executive officers (with a few limited exceptions, such as for certain consumer and housing loans).

Protection for Whistleblowers—Section 806 protects "whistleblowers"—employees who report ("blow the whistle" on) securities violations by their employers—from being fired or in any way discriminated against by their employers.

Blackout Periods—Section 306 prohibits certain types of securities transactions during "blackout periods"—periods during which the issuer's ability to purchase, sell, or otherwise transfer funds in individual account plans (such as pension funds) is suspended.

Enhanced Penalties for—

- *Violations of Section 906 Certification Requirements*—A CEO or CFO who certifies a financial report or statement filed with the SEC knowing that the report or statement does not fulfill all of the requirements of Section 906 will be subject to criminal penalties of up to $1 million in fines, ten years in prison, or both. *Willful* violators of the certification requirements may be subject to $5 million in fines, twenty years in prison, or both.

- *Violations of the Securities Exchange Act of 1934*—Penalties for securities fraud under the 1934 act were also increased (as discussed earlier in this chapter). Individual violators may be fined up to $5 million, imprisoned for up to twenty years, or both. Willful violators may be imprisoned for up to twenty-five years in addition to being fined.

- *Destruction or Alteration of Documents*—Anyone who alters, destroys, or conceals documents or otherwise obstructs any official proceeding will be subject to fines, imprisonment for up to twenty years, or both.

- *Other Forms of White-Collar Crime*—The act stiffened the penalties for certain criminal violations, such as federal mail and wire fraud, and ordered the U.S. Sentencing Commission to revise the sentencing guidelines for white-collar crimes (see Chapter 6).

Statute of Limitations for Securities Fraud—Section 804 provides that a private right of action for securities fraud may be brought no later than two years after the discovery of the violation or five years after the violation, whichever is earlier.

Additionally, the new rules require that certain financial and stock-transaction reports must be filed with the SEC earlier than was required under the previous rules. The act also mandates SEC oversight over a new entity, called the Public Company Accounting Oversight Board, which regulates and oversees public accounting firms. Other provisions of the act created new private civil actions and expanded the SEC's remedies in administrative and civil actions.

Because of the importance of this act for corporate leaders and for those dealing with securities transactions, we present excerpts and explanatory comments in Appendix H. We also highlight some of its key provisions relating to corporate accountability in Exhibit 24–4.

More Internal Controls and Accountability   The Sarbanes-Oxley Act includes some traditional securities law provisions but also introduces direct *federal* corporate governance requirements for public companies (companies whose shares are traded in the public securities markets). The law addresses many of the corporate governance procedures just discussed and creates new requirements in an attempt to make the system work more effectively. The requirements deal with independent monitoring of company officers by both the board of directors and auditors.

Sections 302 and 404 of Sarbanes-Oxley require high-level managers (the most senior officers) to establish and maintain an effective system of internal controls. Moreover, senior management must reassess the system's effectiveness on an annual basis. Some companies already had strong and effective internal control systems in place before the passage of the act, but others had to take expensive steps to bring their internal controls up to the new federal standard. These include "disclosure controls and procedures" to ensure that company financial reports are accurate and timely. Assessment must involve documenting financial results and accounting policies before reporting the results. By 2009, hundreds of companies had reported that they had identified and corrected shortcomings in their internal control systems.

Certification and Monitoring Requirements Section 906 requires that chief executive officers (CEOs) and chief financial officers (CFOs) certify that the information in the corporate financial statements "fairly represents in all material respects, the financial conditions and results of operations of the issuer." These corporate officers are subject to both civil and criminal penalties for violation of this section. This requirement makes officers directly accountable for the accuracy of their financial reporting and avoids any "ignorance defense" if shortcomings are later discovered.

Another requirement is to improve directors' monitoring of officers' activities. All members of the corporate audit committee for public companies must be outside directors. The New York Stock Exchange has a similar rule that also extends to the board's compensation committee. The audit committee must have a written charter that sets out its duties and provides for performance appraisal. At least one "financial expert" must serve on the audit committee, which must hold executive meetings without company officers being present. The audit committee must establish procedures for "whistleblowers" to report violations. In addition to reviewing the internal controls, the committee also monitors the actions of the outside auditor.

ONLINE SECURITIES FRAUD

A major problem facing the SEC today is how to enforce the antifraud provisions of the securities laws in the online environment. In 1999, in the first cases involving illegal online securities offerings, the SEC filed suit against three individuals for illegally offering securities on an Internet auction site.[37] In essence, all three indicated that their companies would go public soon and attempted to sell unregistered securities via the Web auction site. All of these actions were in violation of Sections 5, 17(a)(1), and 17(a)(3) of the 1933 Securities Act. Since then, the SEC has brought a variety of Internet-related fraud cases, including cases involving investment scams and the manipulation of stock prices in Internet chat rooms. The SEC regularly issues interpretive releases to explain

---

37. *In re Davis,* SEC Administrative File No. 3-10080 (October 20, 1999); *In re Haas,* SEC Administrative File No. 3-10081 (October 20, 1999); *In re Sitaras,* SEC Administrative File No. 3-10082 (October 20, 1999).

how securities laws apply in the online environment and revises its rules to address new issues that arise in the Internet context.

Investment Scams

An ongoing problem is how to curb online investment scams. One fraudulent investment scheme involved twenty thousand investors, who lost, in all, more than $3 million. Some cases have involved false claims about the earnings potential of home business programs, such as the claim that one could "earn $4,000 or more each month." Others have concerned claims of "guaranteed credit repair."

Using Chat Rooms to Manipulate Stock Prices

"Pumping and dumping" occurs when a person who has purchased a particular stock heavily promotes ("pumps up") that stock—thereby creating a great demand for it and driving up its price—and then sells ("dumps") it. The practice of pumping up a stock and then dumping it is quite old. In the online world, however, the process can occur much more quickly and efficiently.

EXAMPLE #9 A notorious example in this area involved Jonathan Lebed, a fifteen-year-old from New Jersey, who became the first minor ever charged with securities fraud by the SEC. The SEC charged that Lebed bought thinly traded stocks. After purchasing a stock, he would flood stock-related chat rooms, particularly at Yahoo's finance boards, with messages touting the stock's virtues. He used numerous false names so that no one would know that a single person was posting the messages. He would say that the stock was the most "undervalued stock in history" and that its price would jump by 1,000 percent "very soon." When other investors would then buy the stock, the price would go up quickly, and Lebed would sell out. The SEC forced the teenager to repay almost $300,000 in gains plus interest but allowed him to keep about $500,000 of the profits he made by trading small-company stocks that he also touted on the Internet.□

The SEC has been bringing an increasing number of cases against those who manipulate stock prices in this way. Many of these online investment scams are perpetrated through mass e-mails (spam), online newsletters, and chat rooms.

Hacking into Online Stock Accounts

The last few years have seen the emergence of a new form of "pumping and dumping" stock involving hackers who break into existing online stock accounts and make unauthorized transfers. Millions of people now buy and sell investments through online brokerage companies such as E*Trade and Ameritrade. Sophisticated hackers have learned to use online investing to their advantage.

By installing keystroke-monitoring software on computer terminals in public places, such as hotels, libraries, and airports, hackers can gain access to online account information. All they have to do is wait for a person to access an online trading account and then monitor the next several dozen keystrokes to determine the customer's account number and password. Once they have the log-in information, they can access the customer's account and liquidate her or his existing stock holdings. The hackers then use the customer's funds to purchase thinly traded, microcap securities, also known as penny stocks. The goal is to boost the price of a stock that the hacker has already purchased at a lower price. Then, when the stock price goes up, the hacker sells all the stock and wires the funds to either an offshore account or a dummy corporation, making it difficult for the SEC to trace the transactions and prosecute the offender.

EXAMPLE #10 Aleksey Kamardin, a twenty-one-year-old Florida student, purchased 55,000 shares of stock in Fuego Entertainment using an E*Trade account in his own name. Kamardin then hacked into other customers' accounts at E*Trade, Ameritrade, Schwab, and other brokerage companies, and used their funds to purchase a total of 458,000 shares of Fuego stock. When the stock price rose from $.88 per share to $1.28 per share, Kamardin sold all of his shares of Fuego, making a profit of $9,164.28 in about three hours. Kamardin did this with other thinly traded stocks as well, allegedly making $82,960 in about five weeks, and prompting the SEC to file charges against him. In July 2007, the SEC obtained a judgment against Kamardin, and he was ordered to repay the $82,960 in profits, plus $5,085 in interest, in addition to $130,000 in civil penalties.[38]□

So far, the brokerage companies have been covering their customers' losses from this new wave of frauds, but the potential for loss is substantial. E*Trade and Ameritrade have also increased security measures and are changing their software to prevent further intrusions into customers' online stock accounts.

---

38. You can read the SEC's complaint against Kamardin by going to the SEC's Web site at **www.sec.gov**, clicking on the 2007 link to litigation releases, and selecting "LR-19981."

Reviewing . . . **Investor Protection and Corporate Governance**

Dale Emerson served as the chief financial officer for Reliant Electric Company, a distributor of electricity serving portions of Montana and North Dakota. Reliant was in the final stages of planning a takeover of Dakota Gasworks, Inc., a natural gas distributor that operated solely within North Dakota. Emerson went on a weekend fishing trip with his uncle, Ernest Wallace. Emerson mentioned to Wallace that he had been putting in a lot of extra hours at the office planning a takeover of Dakota Gasworks. On returning from the fishing trip, Wallace met with a broker from Chambers Investments and purchased $20,000 of Reliant stock. Three weeks later, Reliant made a tender offer to Dakota Gasworks stockholders and purchased 57 percent of Dakota Gasworks stock. Over the next two weeks, the price of Reliant stock rose 72 percent before leveling out. Wallace then sold his Reliant stock for a gross profit of $14,400. Using the information presented in the chapter, answer the following questions.

1. Would registration with the SEC be required for Dakota Gasworks securities? Why or why not?

2. Did Emerson violate Section 10(b) of the Securities Exchange Act of 1934 and SEC Rule 10b-5? Why or why not?

3. What theory or theories might a court use to hold Wallace liable for insider trading?

4. Under the Sarbanes-Oxley Act of 2002, who would be required to certify the accuracy of financial statements filed with the SEC?

Key Terms

accredited investors 776	investment contract 770	short-swing profits 785
bounty payment 789	mutual fund 776	stock options 792
corporate governance 790	prospectus 771	tippee 785
free-writing prospectus 773	red herring prospectus 773	tombstone ad 773
insider trading 780	SEC Rule 10b-5 780	
investment company 776	security 769	

Chapter Summary

Securities Act of 1933 (See pages 769–779)	Prohibits fraud and stabilizes the securities industry by requiring disclosure of all essential information relating to the issuance of securities to the investing public.

1. *Registration requirements*–Securities, unless exempt, must be registered with the SEC before being offered to the public. The *registration statement* must include detailed financial information about the issuing corporation; the intended use of the proceeds of the securities being issued; and certain disclosures, such as interests of directors or officers and pending lawsuits.

2. *Prospectus*–The issuer must provide investors with a *prospectus* that describes the security being sold, the issuing corporation, and the risk attaching to the security.

3. *Exemptions*–The SEC has exempted certain offerings from the requirements of the Securities Act of 1933. Exemptions may be determined on the basis of the size of the issue, whether the offering is private or public, and whether advertising is involved. Exemptions are summarized in Exhibit 24–1 on page 775.

Securities Exchange Act of 1934 (See pages 779–789.)	Provides for the regulation and registration of securities exchanges, brokers, dealers, and national securities associations (such as the NASD). Maintains a continuous disclosure system for all corporations with securities on the securities exchanges and for those companies that have assets in excess of $10 million and five hundred or more shareholders (Section 12 companies).

1. *SEC Rule 10b-5 [under Section 10(b) of the 1934 act]*–

   a. Applies in virtually all cases concerning the trading of securities–a firm's securities do not have to be registered under the 1933 act for the 1934 act to apply.

   b. Applies only when the requisites of federal jurisdiction (such as use of the mails, stock exchange facilities, or any facility of interstate commerce) are present.

   c. Applies to insider trading by corporate officers, directors, majority shareholders, and any persons receiving inside information (information not available to the investing public) who base their trading on this information.

   d. Liability for violations can be civil or criminal.

   e. May be violated by failing to disclose "material facts" that must be disclosed under this rule.

   f. Liability may be based on the tipper/tippee or the misappropriation theory.

2. *Insider trading [under Section 16(b) of the 1934 act]*–To prevent corporate officers and directors from taking advantage of inside information, the 1934 act requires officers, directors, and shareholders owning 10 percent or more of the issued stock of a corporation to turn over to the corporation all short-term profits (called *short-swing profits*) realized from the purchase and sale or sale and purchase of corporate stock within any six-month period.

3. *Proxies [under Section 14(a) of the 1934 act]*–The SEC regulates the content of proxy statements sent to shareholders by corporate managers of Section 12 companies who are requesting authority to vote on behalf of the shareholders in a particular election on specified issues. Section 14(a) is essentially a disclosure law, with provisions similar to the antifraud provisions of SEC Rule 10b-5.

State Securities Laws (See pages 789–790.)	All states have corporate securities laws (*blue sky laws*) that regulate the offer and sale of securities within state borders; these laws are designed to prevent "speculative schemes which have no more basis than so many feet of 'blue sky.' " States regulate securities concurrently with the federal government. The Uniform Securities Act of 2002, which has been

State Securities Laws—Continued	adopted by thirteen states and is being considered by several others, is designed to promote coordination and reduce duplication between state and federal securities regulation.
Corporate Governance (See pages 790–795.)	1. *Definition*—Corporate governance is the system by which business corporations are governed, including policies and procedures for making decisions on corporate affairs.
	2. *The need for effective corporate governance*—Corporate governance is necessary in large corporations because corporate ownership (by the shareholders) is separated from corporate control (by officers and managers). This separation of corporate ownership and control can often result in conflicting interests. Corporate governance standards address such issues.
	3. *Sarbanes-Oxley Act of 2002*—This act attempts to increase corporate accountability by imposing strict disclosure requirements and harsh penalties for violations of securities laws.
Online Securities Fraud (See pages 795–797.)	A major problem facing the SEC today is how to enforce the antifraud provisions of the securities laws in the online environment. Internet-related forms of securities fraud include investment scams and the manipulation of stock prices in online chat rooms.

For Review

1. What is meant by the term *securities?*
2. What are the two major statutes regulating the securities industry? When was the Securities and Exchange Commission created, and what are its major purposes and functions?
3. What is insider trading? Why is it prohibited?
4. What are some of the features of state securities laws?
5. What certification requirements does the Sarbanes-Oxley Act impose on corporate executives?

Questions and Case Problems

24–1. Registration Requirements. Langley Brothers, Inc., a corporation incorporated and doing business in Kansas, decides to sell common stock worth $1 million to the public. The stock will be sold only within the state of Kansas. Joseph Langley, the chairman of the board, says the offering need not be registered with the Securities and Exchange Commission. His brother, Harry, disagrees. Who is right? Explain.

Question with Sample Answer

24–2. Huron Corp. has 300,000 common shares outstanding. The owners of these outstanding shares live in several different states. Huron has decided to split the 300,000 shares two for one. Will Huron Corp. have to file a registration statement and prospectus on the 300,000 new shares to be issued as a result of the split? Explain.

For a sample answer to Question 24–2, go to Appendix I at the end of this text.

24–3. Violations of the 1934 Act. 2TheMart.com, Inc., was conceived in January 1999 to launch an auction Web site to compete with eBay, Inc. On January 19, 2TheMart announced that its Web site was in its "final development" stages and was expected to be active by the end of July as a "preeminent" auction site. The company also said that it had "retained the services of leading Web site design and architecture consultants to design and construct" the site. Based on the announcement, investors rushed to buy 2TheMart's stock, causing a rapid increase in the price. On February 3, 2TheMart entered into an agreement with IBM to take preliminary steps to plan the site. Three weeks later, 2TheMart again announced that the site was "currently in final development." On June 1, 2TheMart signed a contract with IBM to design, build, and test the site, with a target delivery date of October 8. When 2TheMart's site did not debut as announced, Mary Harrington and others who had bought the stock filed a suit in a federal district court against the firm's officers, alleging violations of the Securities Exchange Act of 1934. The defendants responded, in part, that any alleged misrepresentations were not material and asked the court to dismiss the suit. How should the court rule, and why? [*In re 2TheMart.com, Inc. Securities Litigation,* 114 F.Supp.2d 955 (C.D.Ca. 2000)]

24–4. Insider Reporting and Trading. Ronald Bleakney, an officer at Natural Microsystems Corp. (NMC), a Section 12 corporation, directed NMC sales in North America, South America, and Europe. In November 1998, Bleakney sold more than 7,500 shares of NMC stock. The following March, Bleakney resigned from the firm, and the next month, he bought more than 20,000 shares of its stock. NMC provided some guidance to employees concerning the rules of insider trading, but with regard to Bleakney's transactions, the corporation said nothing about potential liability. Richard Morales, an NMC shareholder, filed a suit against NMC and Bleakney to compel recovery, under Section 16(b) of the Securities Exchange Act of 1934, of Bleakney's profits from the sale and purchase of his shares. (When Morales died, his executor Deborah Donoghue became the plaintiff.) Bleakney argued that he should not be liable because he relied on NMC's advice. Should the court order Bleakney to disgorge his profits? Explain. [*Donoghue v. Natural Microsystems Corp.,* 198 F.Supp.2d 487 (S.D.N.Y. 2002)]

24–5. SEC Rule 10b-5. Scott Ginsburg was chief executive officer (CEO) of Evergreen Media Corp., which owned and operated radio stations. In 1996, Evergreen became interested in acquiring EZ Communications, Inc., which also owned radio stations. To initiate negotiations, Ginsburg met with EZ's CEO, Alan Box, on Friday, July 12. Two days later, Scott phoned his brother Mark, who, on Monday, bought 3,800 shares of EZ stock. Mark discussed the deal with their father, Jordan, who bought 20,000 EZ shares on Thursday. On July 25, the day before the EZ bid was due, Scott phoned his parents' home, and Mark bought another 3,200 EZ shares. The same routine was followed over the next few days, with Scott periodically phoning Mark or Jordan, both of whom continued to buy EZ shares. Evergreen's bid was refused, but on August 5, EZ announced its merger with another company. The price of EZ stock rose 30 percent, increasing the value of Mark and Jordan's shares by $664,024 and $412,875, respectively. The Securities and Exchange Commission (SEC) filed a civil suit in a federal district court against Scott. What was the most likely allegation? What is required to impose sanctions for this offense? Should the court hold Scott liable? Why or why not? [*SEC v. Ginsburg,* 362 F.3d 1292 (11th Cir. 2004)]

Case Problem with Sample Answer

24–6. In 1997, WTS Transnational, Inc., required financing to develop a prototype of an unpatented fingerprint-verification system. At the time, WTS had no revenue, $655,000 in liabilities, and only $10,000 in assets. Thomas Cavanagh and Frank Nicolois, who operated an investment banking company called U.S. Milestone (USM), arranged the financing using Curbstone Acquisition Corp. Curbstone had no assets but had registered approximately 3.5 million shares of stock with the Securities and Exchange Commission (SEC). Under the terms of the deal, Curbstone acquired WTS, and the resulting entity was named Electro-Optical Systems Corp. (EOSC). New EOSC shares were issued to all of the WTS shareholders. Only Cavanagh and others affiliated with USM could sell EOSC stock to the public, however. Over the next few months, these individuals issued false press releases, made small deceptive purchases of EOSC shares at high prices, distributed hundreds of thousands of shares to friends and relatives, and sold their own shares at inflated prices through third party companies they owned. When the SEC began to investigate, the share price fell to its actual value, and innocent investors lost over $15 million. Were any securities laws violated in this case? If so, what might be an appropriate remedy? [*SEC v. Cavanagh,* 445 F.3d 105 (2d Cir. 2006)]

After you have answered Problem 24–6, compare your answer with the sample answer given on the Web site that accompanies this text. Go to www.cengage.com/blaw/let, select "Chapter 24," and click on "Case Problem with Sample Answer."

24–7. Securities Trading. Between 1994 and 1998, Richard Svoboda, a credit officer for NationsBank N.A., in Dallas, Texas, evaluated and approved his employer's extensions of credit to clients. These responsibilities gave Svoboda access to nonpublic information about the clients' earnings, performance, acquisitions, and business plans in confidential memos, e-mail, credit applications, and other sources. Svoboda devised a scheme with Michael Robles, an independent accountant, to use this information to trade securities. Pursuant to their scheme, Robles traded in the securities of more than twenty different companies and profited by more than $1 million. Svoboda also executed trades for his own profit of more than $200,000, despite their agreement that Robles would do all of the trading. Aware that their scheme violated NationsBank's policy, they attempted to conduct their trades to avoid suspicion. When NationsBank questioned Svoboda about his actions, he lied, refused to cooperate, and was fired. Did Svoboda or Robles commit any crimes? Are they subject to civil liability? If so, who could file a suit and on what ground? What are the possible sanctions? What might be a defense? How should a court rule? Discuss. [*SEC v. Svoboda,* 409 F.Supp.2d 331 (S.D.N.Y. 2006)]

A Question of Ethics

24–8. Melvin Lyttle told John Montana and Paul Knight about a "Trading Program" that purportedly would buy and sell securities in deals that were fully insured, as well as monitored and controlled by the Federal Reserve Bank. Without checking the details or even verifying whether the Program existed, Montana and Knight, with Lyttle's help, began to sell interests in the Program to investors. For a minimum investment of $1 million, the investors were promised extraordinary rates of return—from 10 percent to as much as 100 percent per week—without risk. They were told, among other things, that the Program would "utilize banks that can ensure full bank integrity of The Transaction whose undertaking[s] are in complete harmony with international banking rules and protocol and who [sic] guarantee maximum security of a Funder's Capital Placement Amount." Nothing was required but the investors' funds and their silence—the Program was to be kept secret. Over a four-month period in 1999, Montana raised approximately $23 million from twenty-two investors. The promised gains did not accrue, however. Instead, Montana, Lyttle, and Knight depleted investors' funds in high-risk trades or spent the funds on themselves. [*SEC v. Montana*, 464 F.Supp.2d 772 (S.D.Ind. 2006)]

1. The Securities and Exchange Commission (SEC) filed a suit in a federal district court against Montana and the others, seeking an injunction, civil penalties, and disgorgement with interest. The SEC alleged, among other things, violations of Section 10(b) of the Securities Exchange Act of 1934 and SEC Rule 10b-5. What is required to establish a violation of these laws? Describe how and why the facts in this case meet, or fail to meet, these requirements.

2. It is often remarked, "There's a sucker born every minute!" Does that phrase describe the Program's investors? Ultimately, about half of the investors recouped the amount they invested. Should the others be considered at least partly responsible for their own losses? Why or why not?

Critical-Thinking Ethical Question

24–9. Do you think that the tipper/tippee and misappropriation theories extend liability under SEC Rule 10b-5 too far? Why or why not?

Video Question

24–10. Go to this text's Web site at **www.cengage.com/blaw/let** and select "Chapter 24." Click on "Video Questions" and view the video titled *Mergers and Acquisitions*. Then answer the following questions.

1. Analyze whether the purchase of Onyx Advertising is a material fact that the Quigley Company had a duty to disclose under SEC Rule 10b-5.

2. Does it matter whether Quigley personally knew about or authorized the company spokesperson's statements? Why or why not?

3. Would Onyx Advertising be able to maintain a suit against the Quigley Company for violation of SEC Rule 10b-5? Why or why not?

4. Who else might be able to bring a suit against the Quigley Company for insider trading under SEC Rule 10b-5?

For updated links to resources available on the Web, as well as a variety of other materials, visit this text's Web site at

www.cengage.com/blaw/let

To access the SEC's EDGAR database, go to

www.sec.gov/edgar.shtml

The Center for Corporate Law at the University of Cincinnati College of Law examines many of the laws discussed in this chapter, including the Securities Act of 1933 and the Securities Exchange Act of 1934. Go to

www.law.uc.edu/CCL

PRACTICAL INTERNET EXERCISES

Go to this text's Web site at **www.cengage.com/blaw/let**, select "Chapter 24," and click on "Practical Internet Exercises." There you will find the following Internet research exercises that you can perform to learn more about the topics covered in this chapter.

Practical Internet Exercise 24–1: LEGAL PERSPECTIVE—**Electronic Delivery**
Practical Internet Exercise 24–2: MANAGEMENT PERSPECTIVE—**The SEC's Role**

BEFORE THE TEST

Go to this text's Web site at **www.cengage.com/blaw/let**, select "Chapter 24," and click on "Interactive Quizzes." You will find a number of interactive questions relating to this chapter.

Unit Four — Cumulative Business Hypothetical

Falwell Motors, Inc., is a large corporation that manufactures automobile batteries.

1. The Federal Trade Commission (FTC) learns that one of the retail stores that sells Falwell's batteries engages in deceptive advertising practices. What actions can the FTC take against the retailer?

2. For years, Falwell has shipped the toxic waste created by its manufacturing process to a waste-disposal site in the next county. The waste site has become contaminated by leakage from toxic waste containers delivered to the site by other manufacturers. Can Falwell be held liable for clean-up costs, even though its containers were not the ones that leaked? If so, what is the extent of its liability?

3. Falwell faces stiff competition from Alchem, Inc., another battery manufacturer. To acquire control over Alchem, Falwell makes a tender offer to Alchem's shareholders. If Falwell succeeds in its attempt and Alchem is merged into Falwell, will the merger violate any antitrust laws? Suppose the merger falls through. The vice president of Falwell's battery division and the president of Alchem agree to divide up the market between them, so they will not have to compete for customers. Is this agreement legal? Explain.

4. One of Falwell's employees learns that Falwell is contemplating a takeover of a rival. The employee tells her husband about the possibility. The husband calls their broker, who purchases shares in the target corporation for the employee and her husband, as well as for himself. Has the employee violated any securities law? Has her husband? Has the broker? Explain.

How to Brief Cases and Analyze Case Problems

HOW TO BRIEF CASES

To fully understand the law with respect to business, you need to be able to read and understand court decisions. To make this task easier, you can use a method of case analysis that is called *briefing*. There is a fairly standard procedure that you can follow when you "brief" any court case. You must first read the case opinion carefully. When you feel you understand the case, you can prepare a brief of it.

Although the format of the brief may vary, typically it will present the essentials of the case under headings such as those listed below.

1. Citation. Give the full citation for the case, including the name of the case, the date it was decided, and the court that decided it.

2. Facts. Briefly indicate (a) the reasons for the lawsuit; (b) the identity and arguments of the plaintiff(s) and defendant(s), respectively; and (c) the lower court's decision—if appropriate.

3. Issue. Concisely phrase, in the form of a question, the essential issue before the court. (If more than one issue is involved, you may have two—or even more—questions here.)

4. Decision. Indicate here—with a "yes" or "no," if possible—the court's answer to the question (or questions) in the Issue section above.

5. Reason. Summarize as briefly as possible the reasons given by the court for its decision (or decisions) and the case or statutory law relied on by the court in arriving at its decision.

AN EXAMPLE OF A BRIEFED SAMPLE COURT CASE

As an example of the format used in briefing cases, we present here a briefed version of the sample court case that was presented in Exhibit 1A–3 on page 33.

BERGER v. CITY OF SEATTLE
United States Court of Appeals,
Ninth Circuit, 2008.
512 F.3d 582.

FACTS The Seattle Center is an entertainment "zone" in downtown Seattle, Washington, that attracts nearly ten million tourists each year. The center encompasses theaters, arenas, museums, exhibition halls, conference rooms, outdoor stadiums, and restaurants, and features street performers. Under the authority of the city, the center's director issued rules in 2002 to address safety concerns and other matters. Among other things, street performers were required to obtain permits and wear badges. After members of the public filed numerous complaints of threatening behavior by street performer and balloon artist Michael Berger, Seattle Center staff cited Berger for several rules violations. He filed a suit in a federal district court against the city and others, alleging, in part, that the rules violated his free speech rights under the First Amendment to the U.S. Constitution. The court issued a judgment in the plaintiff's favor. The city appealed to the U.S. Court of Appeals for the Ninth Circuit.

ISSUE Did the rules issued by the Seattle Center under the city's authority meet the requirements for valid restrictions on speech under the First Amendment?

DECISION Yes. The U.S. Court of Appeals for the Ninth Circuit reversed the decision of the lower court and remanded the case for further proceedings. "Such content neutral and narrowly tailored rules * * * must be upheld."

REASON The court concluded first that the rules requiring permits and badges were "content neutral." Time, place, and manner restrictions do not violate the First Amendment if they burden all expression equally and do not allow officials to treat different messages differently. In this case, the rules met this test and thus did not discriminate based on content. The court also concluded that the rules were "narrowly tailored" to "promote a substantial government interest that would be achieved less effectively" otherwise. With the rules, the city was trying to "reduce territorial disputes among performers, deter patron harassment, and facilitate the identification and apprehension of offending performers." This was pursuant to the valid governmental objective of protecting the safety and convenience of the other performers and the public generally. The public's complaints about Berger and others showed that unregulated street performances posed a threat to these interests. The court was "satisfied that the city's permit scheme was designed to further valid governmental objectives."

REVIEW OF SAMPLE COURT CASE

Here, we provide a review of the briefed version to indicate the kind of information that is contained in each section.

CITATION The name of the case is *Berger v. City of Seattle*. Berger is the plaintiff; the City of Seattle is the defendant. The U.S. Court of Appeals for the Ninth Circuit decided this case in 2008. The citation states that this case can be found in volume 512 of the *Federal Reporter, Third Series*, on page 582.

FACTS The *Facts* section identifies the plaintiff and the defendant, describes the events leading up to this suit, the allegations made by the plaintiff in the initial suit, and (because this case is an appellate court decision) the lower court's ruling and the party appealing. The party appealing's argument on appeal is also sometimes included here.

ISSUE   The *Issue* section presents the central issue (or issues) decided by the court. In this case, the U.S. Court of Appeals for the Ninth Circuit considered whether certain rules imposed on street performers by local government authorities satisfied the requirements for valid restrictions on speech under the First Amendment to the U.S. Constitution.

DECISION   The *Decision* section includes the court's decision on the issues before it. The decision reflects the opinion of the judge or justice hearing the case. Decisions by appellate courts are frequently phrased in reference to the lower court's decision. In other words, the appellate court may "affirm" the lower court's ruling or "reverse" it. Here, the court determined that Seattle's rules were "content neutral" and "narrowly tailored" to "promote a substantial government interest that would otherwise be achieved less effectively." The court found in favor of the city and reversed the lower court's ruling in the plaintiff's (Berger's) favor.

REASON   The *Reason* section includes references to the relevant laws and legal principles that the court applied in coming to its conclusion in the case. The relevant law in the *Berger* case included the requirements under the First Amendment for evaluating the purpose and effect of government regulation with respect to expression. This section also explains the court's application of the law to the facts in this case.

ANALYZING CASE PROBLEMS

In addition to learning how to brief cases, students of business law and the legal environment also find it helpful to know how to analyze case problems. Part of the study of business law and the legal environment usually involves analyzing case problems, such as those included in this text at the end of each chapter.

For each case problem in this book, we provide the relevant background and facts of the lawsuit and the issue before the court. When you are assigned one of these problems, your job will be to determine how the court should decide the issue, and why. In other words, you will need to engage in legal analysis and reasoning. Here, we offer some suggestions on how to make this task less daunting. We begin by presenting a sample problem:

> While Janet Lawson, a famous pianist, was shopping in Quality Market, she slipped and fell on a wet floor in one of the aisles. The floor had recently been mopped by one of the store's employees, but there were no signs warning customers that the floor in that area was wet. As a result of the fall, Lawson injured her right arm and was unable to perform piano concerts for the next six months. Had she been able to perform the scheduled concerts, she would have earned approximately $60,000 over that period of time. Lawson sued Quality Market for this amount, plus another $10,000 in medical expenses. She claimed that the store's failure to warn customers of the wet floor constituted negligence and therefore the market was liable for her injuries. Will the court agree with Lawson? Discuss.

UNDERSTAND THE FACTS

This may sound obvious, but before you can analyze or apply the relevant law to a specific set of facts, you must clearly understand those facts. In other words, you should read through the case problem carefully—more than once, if necessary—to make sure you understand the identity of the plaintiff(s) and defendant(s) in the case and the progression of events that led to the lawsuit.

In the sample case problem just given, the identity of the parties is fairly obvious. Janet Lawson is the one bringing the suit; therefore, she is the plaintiff. Quality Market, against whom she is bringing the suit, is the defendant. Some of the case problems you may work on have multiple plaintiffs or defendants. Often, it is helpful to use abbreviations for the parties. To indicate a reference to a plaintiff, for example, the *pi* symbol—π—is often used, and a defendant is denoted by a *delta*—Δ—a triangle.

The events leading to the lawsuit are also fairly straightforward. Lawson slipped and fell on a wet floor, and she contends that Quality Market should be liable for her injuries because it was negligent in not posting a sign warning customers of the wet floor.

When you are working on case problems, realize that the facts should be accepted as they are given. For example, in our sample problem, it should be accepted that the floor was wet and that there was no sign. In other words, avoid making conjectures, such as "Maybe the floor wasn't too wet," or "Maybe an employee was getting a sign to put up," or "Maybe someone stole the sign." Questioning the facts as they are presented only adds confusion to your analysis.

LEGAL ANALYSIS AND REASONING

Once you understand the facts given in the case problem, you can begin to analyze the case. The *IRAC method* is a helpful tool to use in the legal analysis and reasoning process. IRAC is an acronym for **I**ssue, **R**ule, **A**pplication, **C**onclusion. Applying this method to our sample problem would involve the following steps:

1. First, you need to decide what legal **issue** is involved in the case. In our sample case, the basic issue is whether Quality Market's failure to warn customers of the wet floor constituted negligence. As discussed in Chapter 5, negligence is a *tort*—a civil wrong. In a tort lawsuit, the plaintiff seeks to be compensated for another's wrongful act. A defendant will be deemed negligent if he or she breached a duty of care owed to the plaintiff and the breach of that duty caused the plaintiff to suffer harm.

2. Once you have identified the issue, the next step is to determine what **rule of law** applies to the issue. To make this determination, you will want to review carefully the text of the chapter in which the relevant rule of law for the problem appears. Our sample case problem involves the tort of negligence, which is covered in Chapter 5. The applicable rule of law is the tort law principle that business owners owe a duty to exercise reasonable care to protect their customers ("business invitees"). Reasonable care, in this context, includes either removing—or warning customers of—*foreseeable* risks about which the owner *knew* or *should have known*. Business owners need not warn customers of "open and obvious" risks, however. If a business owner breaches this duty of care (fails to exercise the appropriate degree of care toward customers), and the breach of duty causes a customer to be injured, the business owner will be liable to the customer for the customer's injuries.

3. The next—and usually the most difficult—step in analyzing case problems is the **application** of the relevant rule of law to the specific facts of the case you are studying. In our sample problem, applying the tort law principle just discussed presents few difficulties. An employee of the store had mopped the floor in the aisle where Lawson slipped and fell, but no sign was present indicating that the floor was wet. That a customer might fall on a wet floor is clearly a foreseeable risk. Therefore, the failure to warn customers about the wet floor was a breach of the duty of care owed by the business owner to the store's customers.

4. Once you have completed Step 3 in the IRAC method, you should be ready to draw your **conclusion.** In our sample problem, Quality Market is liable to Lawson for her injuries, because the market's breach of its duty of care caused Lawson's injuries.

The fact patterns in the case problems presented in this text are not always as simple as those presented in our sample problem. Often, for example, a case has more than one plaintiff or defendant. A case may also involve more than one issue and have more than one applicable rule of law. Furthermore, in some case problems the facts may indicate that the general rule of law should not apply. For example, suppose that a store employee advised Lawson not to walk on the floor in the aisle because it was wet, but Lawson decided to walk on it anyway. This fact could alter the outcome of the case because the store could then raise the defense of *assumption of risk* (see Chapter 12). Nonetheless, a careful review of the chapter should always provide you with the knowledge you need to analyze the problem thoroughly and arrive at accurate conclusions.

The Constitution of the United States

PREAMBLE

We the People of the United States, in Order to form a more perfect Union, establish Justice, insure domestic Tranquility, provide for the common defence, promote the general Welfare, and secure the Blessings of Liberty to ourselves and our Posterity, do ordain and establish this Constitution for the United States of America.

ARTICLE I

Section 1. All legislative Powers herein granted shall be vested in a Congress of the United States, which shall consist of a Senate and House of Representatives.

Section 2. The House of Representatives shall be composed of Members chosen every second Year by the People of the several States, and the Electors in each State shall have the Qualifications requisite for Electors of the most numerous Branch of the State Legislature.

No Person shall be a Representative who shall not have attained to the Age of twenty five Years, and been seven Years a Citizen of the United States, and who shall not, when elected, be an Inhabitant of that State in which he shall be chosen.

Representatives and direct Taxes shall be apportioned among the several States which may be included within this Union, according to their respective Numbers, which shall be determined by adding to the whole Number of free Persons, including those bound to Service for a Term of Years, and excluding Indians not taxed, three fifths of all other Persons. The actual Enumeration shall be made within three Years after the first Meeting of the Congress of the United States, and within every subsequent Term of ten Years, in such Manner as they shall by Law direct. The Number of Representatives shall not exceed one for every thirty Thousand, but each State shall have at Least one Representative; and until such enumeration shall be made, the State of New Hampshire shall be entitled to chuse three, Massachusetts eight, Rhode Island and Providence Plantations one, Connecticut five, New York six, New Jersey four, Pennsylvania eight, Delaware one, Maryland six, Virginia ten, North Carolina five, South Carolina five, and Georgia three.

When vacancies happen in the Representation from any State, the Executive Authority thereof shall issue Writs of Election to fill such Vacancies.

The House of Representatives shall chuse their Speaker and other Officers; and shall have the sole Power of Impeachment.

Section 3. The Senate of the United States shall be composed of two Senators from each State, chosen by the Legislature thereof, for six Years; and each Senator shall have one Vote.

Immediately after they shall be assembled in Consequence of the first Election, they shall be divided as equally as may be into three Classes. The Seats of the Senators of the first Class shall be vacated at the Expiration of the second Year, of the second Class at the Expiration of the fourth Year, and of the third Class at the Expiration of the sixth Year, so that one third may be chosen every second Year; and if Vacancies happen by Resignation, or otherwise, during the Recess of the Legislature of any State, the Executive thereof may make temporary Appointments until the next Meeting of the Legislature, which shall then fill such Vacancies.

No Person shall be a Senator who shall not have attained to the Age of thirty Years, and been nine Years a Citizen of the United States, and who shall not, when elected, be an Inhabitant of that State for which he shall be chosen.

The Vice President of the United States shall be President of the Senate, but shall have no Vote, unless they be equally divided.

The Senate shall chuse their other Officers, and also a President pro tempore, in the Absence of the Vice President, or when he shall exercise the Office of President of the United States.

The Senate shall have the sole Power to try all Impeachments. When sitting for that Purpose, they shall be on Oath or Affirmation. When the President of the United States is tried, the Chief Justice shall preside: And no Person shall be convicted without the Concurrence of two thirds of the Members present.

Judgment in Cases of Impeachment shall not extend further than to removal from Office, and disqualification to hold and enjoy any Office of honor, Trust, or Profit under the United States: but the Party convicted shall nevertheless be liable and subject to Indictment, Trial, Judgment, and Punishment, according to Law.

Section 4. The Times, Places and Manner of holding Elections for Senators and Representatives, shall be prescribed in each State by the Legislature thereof; but the Congress may at any time by Law make or alter such Regulations, except as to the Places of chusing Senators.

The Congress shall assemble at least once in every Year, and such Meeting shall be on the first Monday in December, unless they shall by Law appoint a different Day.

Section 5. Each House shall be the Judge of the Elections, Returns, and Qualifications of its own Members, and a Majority of each shall constitute a Quorum to do Business; but a smaller Number may adjourn from day to day, and may be authorized to compel the Attendance of absent Members, in such Manner, and under such Penalties as each House may provide.

Each House may determine the Rules of its Proceedings, punish its Members for disorderly Behavior, and, with the Concurrence of two thirds, expel a Member.

Each House shall keep a Journal of its Proceedings, and from time to time publish the same, excepting such Parts as may in their Judgment require Secrecy; and the Yeas and Nays of the Members of either House on any question shall, at the Desire of one fifth of those Present, be entered on the Journal.

Neither House, during the Session of Congress, shall, without the Consent of the other, adjourn for more than three days, nor to any other Place than that in which the two Houses shall be sitting.

Section 6. The Senators and Representatives shall receive a Compensation for their Services, to be ascertained by Law, and paid out of the Treasury of the United States. They shall in all Cases, except Treason, Felony and Breach of the Peace, be privileged from Arrest during their Attendance at the Session of their respective Houses, and in going to and returning from the same; and for any Speech or Debate in either House, they shall not be questioned in any other Place.

No Senator or Representative shall, during the Time for which he was elected, be appointed to any civil Office under the Authority of the United States, which shall have been created, or the Emoluments whereof shall have been increased during such time; and no Person holding any Office under the United States, shall be a Member of either House during his Continuance in Office.

Section 7. All Bills for raising Revenue shall originate in the House of Representatives; but the Senate may propose or concur with Amendments as on other Bills.

Every Bill which shall have passed the House of Representatives and the Senate, shall, before it become a Law, be presented to the President of the United States; If he approve he shall sign it, but if not he shall return it, with his Objections to the House in which it shall have originated, who shall enter the Objections at large on their Journal, and proceed to reconsider it. If after such Reconsideration two thirds of that House shall agree to pass the Bill, it shall be sent together with the Objections, to the other House, by which it shall likewise be reconsidered, and if approved by two thirds of that House, it shall become a Law. But in all such Cases the Votes of both Houses shall be determined by Yeas and Nays, and the Names of the Persons voting for and against the Bill shall be entered on the Journal of each House respectively. If any Bill shall not be returned by the President within ten Days (Sundays excepted) after it shall have been presented to him, the Same shall be a Law, in like Manner as if he had signed it, unless the Congress by their Adjournment prevent its Return in which Case it shall not be a Law.

Every Order, Resolution, or Vote, to which the Concurrence of the Senate and House of Representatives may be necessary (except on a question of Adjournment) shall be presented to the President of the United States; and before the Same shall take Effect, shall be approved by him, or being disapproved by him, shall be repassed by two thirds of the Senate and House of Representatives, according to the Rules and Limitations prescribed in the Case of a Bill.

Section 8. The Congress shall have Power To lay and collect Taxes, Duties, Imposts and Excises, to pay the Debts and provide for the common Defence and general Welfare of the United States; but all Duties, Imposts and Excises shall be uniform throughout the United States;

To borrow Money on the credit of the United States;

To regulate Commerce with foreign Nations, and among the several States, and with the Indian Tribes;

To establish an uniform Rule of Naturalization, and uniform Laws on the subject of Bankruptcies throughout the United States;

To coin Money, regulate the Value thereof, and of foreign Coin, and fix the Standard of Weights and Measures;

To provide for the Punishment of counterfeiting the Securities and current Coin of the United States;

To establish Post Offices and post Roads;

To promote the Progress of Science and useful Arts, by securing for limited Times to Authors and Inventors the exclusive Right to their respective Writings and Discoveries;

To constitute Tribunals inferior to the supreme Court;

To define and punish Piracies and Felonies committed on the high Seas, and Offenses against the Law of Nations;

To declare War, grant Letters of Marque and Reprisal, and make Rules concerning Captures on Land and Water;

To raise and support Armies, but no Appropriation of Money to that Use shall be for a longer Term than two Years;

To provide and maintain a Navy;

To make Rules for the Government and Regulation of the land and naval Forces;

To provide for calling forth the Militia to execute the Laws of the Union, suppress Insurrections and repel Invasions;

To provide for organizing, arming, and disciplining, the Militia, and for governing such Part of them as may be employed in the Service of the United States, reserving to the States respectively, the Appointment of the Officers, and the Authority of training the Militia according to the discipline prescribed by Congress;

To exercise exclusive Legislation in all Cases whatsoever, over such District (not exceeding ten Miles square) as may, by Cession of particular States, and the Acceptance of Congress, become the Seat of the Government of the United States, and to exercise like Authority over all Places purchased by the Consent of the Legislature of the State in which the Same shall be, for the Erection of Forts, Magazines, Arsenals, dock-Yards, and other needful Buildings;—And

To make all Laws which shall be necessary and proper for carrying into Execution the foregoing Powers, and all other Powers vested by this Constitution in the Government of the United States, or in any Department or Officer thereof.

Section 9. The Migration or Importation of such Persons as any of the States now existing shall think proper to admit, shall not be prohibited by the Congress prior to the Year one thousand eight hundred and eight, but a Tax or duty may be imposed on such Importation, not exceeding ten dollars for each Person.

The privilege of the Writ of Habeas Corpus shall not be suspended, unless when in Cases of Rebellion or Invasion the public Safety may require it.

No Bill of Attainder or ex post facto Law shall be passed.

No Capitation, or other direct, Tax shall be laid, unless in Proportion to the Census or Enumeration herein before directed to be taken.

No Tax or Duty shall be laid on Articles exported from any State.

No Preference shall be given by any Regulation of Commerce or Revenue to the Ports of one State over those of another: nor shall Vessels bound to, or from, one State be obliged to enter, clear, or pay Duties in another.

No Money shall be drawn from the Treasury, but in Consequence of Appropriations made by Law; and a regular Statement and Account of the Receipts and Expenditures of all public Money shall be published from time to time.

No Title of Nobility shall be granted by the United States: And no Person holding any Office of Profit or Trust under them, shall, without the Consent of the Congress, accept of any present, Emolument, Office, or Title, of any kind whatever, from any King, Prince, or foreign State.

Section 10.   No State shall enter into any Treaty, Alliance, or Confederation; grant Letters of Marque and Reprisal; coin Money; emit Bills of Credit; make any Thing but gold and silver Coin a Tender in Payment of Debts; pass any Bill of Attainder, ex post facto Law, or Law impairing the Obligation of Contracts, or grant any Title of Nobility.

No State shall, without the Consent of the Congress, lay any Imposts or Duties on Imports or Exports, except what may be absolutely necessary for executing its inspection Laws: and the net Produce of all Duties and Imposts, laid by any State on Imports or Exports, shall be for the Use of the Treasury of the United States; and all such Laws shall be subject to the Revision and Controul of the Congress.

No State shall, without the Consent of Congress, lay any Duty of Tonnage, keep Troops, or Ships of War in time of Peace, enter into any Agreement or Compact with another State, or with a foreign Power, or engage in War, unless actually invaded, or in such imminent Danger as will not admit of delay.

ARTICLE II

Section 1.   The executive Power shall be vested in a President of the United States of America. He shall hold his Office during the Term of four Years, and, together with the Vice President, chosen for the same Term, be elected, as follows:

Each State shall appoint, in such Manner as the Legislature thereof may direct, a Number of Electors, equal to the whole Number of Senators and Representatives to which the State may be entitled in the Congress; but no Senator or Representative, or Person holding an Office of Trust or Profit under the United States, shall be appointed an Elector.

The Electors shall meet in their respective States, and vote by Ballot for two Persons, of whom one at least shall not be an Inhabitant of the same State with themselves. And they shall make a List of all the Persons voted for, and of the Number of Votes for each; which List they shall sign and certify, and transmit sealed to the Seat of the Government of the United States, directed to the President of the Senate. The President of the Senate shall, in the Presence of the Senate and House of Representatives, open all the Certificates, and the Votes shall then be counted. The Person having the greatest Number of Votes shall be the President, if such Number be a Majority of the whole Number of Electors appointed; and if there be more than one who have such Majority, and have an equal Number of Votes, then the House of Representatives shall immediately chuse by Ballot one of them for President; and if no Person have a Majority, then from the five highest on the List the said House shall in like Manner chuse the President. But in chusing the President, the Votes shall be taken by States, the Representation from each State having one Vote; A quorum for this Purpose shall consist of a Member or Members from two thirds of the States, and a Majority of all the States shall be necessary to a Choice. In every Case, after the Choice of the President, the Person having the greater Number of Votes of the Electors shall be the Vice President. But if there should remain two or more who have equal Votes, the Senate shall chuse from them by Ballot the Vice President.

The Congress may determine the Time of chusing the Electors, and the Day on which they shall give their Votes; which Day shall be the same throughout the United States.

No person except a natural born Citizen, or a Citizen of the United States, at the time of the Adoption of this Constitution, shall be eligible to the Office of President; neither shall any Person be eligible to that Office who shall not have attained to the Age of thirty five Years, and been fourteen Years a Resident within the United States.

In Case of the Removal of the President from Office, or of his Death, Resignation or Inability to discharge the Powers and Duties of the said Office, the same shall devolve on the Vice President, and the Congress may by Law provide for the Case of Removal, Death, Resignation or Inability, both of the President and Vice President, declaring what Officer shall then act as President, and such Officer shall act accordingly, until the Disability be removed, or a President shall be elected.

The President shall, at stated Times, receive for his Services, a Compensation, which shall neither be increased nor diminished during the Period for which he shall have been elected, and he shall not receive within that Period any other Emolument from the United States, or any of them.

Before he enter on the Execution of his Office, he shall take the following Oath or Affirmation: "I do solemnly swear (or affirm) that I will faithfully execute the Office of President of the United States, and will to the best of my Ability, preserve, protect and defend the Constitution of the United States."

Section 2.   The President shall be Commander in Chief of the Army and Navy of the United States, and of the Militia of the several States, when called into the actual Service of the United States; he may require the Opinion, in writing, of the principal Officer in each of the executive Departments, upon any Subject relating to the Duties of their respective Offices, and he shall have Power to grant Reprieves and Pardons for Offenses against the United States, except in Cases of Impeachment.

He shall have Power, by and with the Advice and Consent of the Senate to make Treaties, provided two thirds of the Senators present concur; and he shall nominate, and by and with the Advice and Consent of the Senate, shall appoint Ambassadors, other public Ministers and Consuls, Judges of the supreme Court, and all other Officers of the United States, whose Appointments are not herein otherwise provided for, and which shall be established by Law; but the Congress may by Law vest the Appointment of such inferior Officers, as they think proper, in the President alone, in the Courts of Law, or in the Heads of Departments.

The President shall have Power to fill up all Vacancies that may happen during the Recess of the Senate, by granting Commissions which shall expire at the End of their next Session.

Section 3.   He shall from time to time give to the Congress Information of the State of the Union, and recommend to their Consideration such Measures as he shall judge necessary and expedient; he may, on extraordinary Occasions, convene both Houses, or either of them, and in Case of Disagreement between them, with Respect to the Time of Adjournment, he may adjourn them to such Time as he shall think proper; he shall receive Ambassadors and other public Ministers; he shall take Care that the Laws be faithfully executed, and shall Commission all the Officers of the United States.

Section 4. The President, Vice President and all civil Officers of the United States, shall be removed from Office on Impeachment for, and Conviction of, Treason, Bribery, or other high Crimes and Misdemeanors.

ARTICLE III

Section 1. The judicial Power of the United States, shall be vested in one supreme Court, and in such inferior Courts as the Congress may from time to time ordain and establish. The Judges, both of the supreme and inferior Courts, shall hold their Offices during good Behaviour, and shall, at stated Times, receive for their Services a Compensation, which shall not be diminished during their Continuance in Office.

Section 2. The judicial Power shall extend to all Cases, in Law and Equity, arising under this Constitution, the Laws of the United States, and Treaties made, or which shall be made, under their Authority;—to all Cases affecting Ambassadors, other public Ministers and Consuls;—to all Cases of admiralty and maritime Jurisdiction;—to Controversies to which the United States shall be a Party;—to Controversies between two or more States;—between a State and Citizens of another State;—between Citizens of different States;—between Citizens of the same State claiming Lands under Grants of different States, and between a State, or the Citizens thereof, and foreign States, Citizens or Subjects.

In all Cases affecting Ambassadors, other public Ministers and Consuls, and those in which a State shall be a Party, the supreme Court shall have original Jurisdiction. In all the other Cases before mentioned, the supreme Court shall have appellate Jurisdiction, both as to Law and Fact, with such Exceptions, and under such Regulations as the Congress shall make.

The Trial of all Crimes, except in Cases of Impeachment, shall be by Jury; and such Trial shall be held in the State where the said Crimes shall have been committed; but when not committed within any State, the Trial shall be at such Place or Places as the Congress may by Law have directed.

Section 3. Treason against the United States, shall consist only in levying War against them, or, in adhering to their Enemies, giving them Aid and Comfort. No Person shall be convicted of Treason unless on the Testimony of two Witnesses to the same overt Act, or on Confession in open Court.

The Congress shall have Power to declare the Punishment of Treason, but no Attainder of Treason shall work Corruption of Blood, or Forfeiture except during the Life of the Person attainted.

ARTICLE IV

Section 1. Full Faith and Credit shall be given in each State to the public Acts, Records, and judicial Proceedings of every other State. And the Congress may by general Laws prescribe the Manner in which such Acts, Records and Proceedings shall be proved, and the Effect thereof.

Section 2. The Citizens of each State shall be entitled to all Privileges and Immunities of Citizens in the several States.

A Person charged in any State with Treason, Felony, or other Crime, who shall flee from Justice, and be found in another State, shall on Demand of the executive Authority of the State from which he fled, be delivered up, to be removed to the State having Jurisdiction of the Crime.

No Person held to Service or Labour in one State, under the Laws thereof, escaping into another, shall, in Consequence of any Law or Regulation therein, be discharged from such Service or Labour, but shall be delivered up on Claim of the Party to whom such Service or Labour may be due.

Section 3. New States may be admitted by the Congress into this Union; but no new State shall be formed or erected within the Jurisdiction of any other State; nor any State be formed by the Junction of two or more States, or Parts of States, without the Consent of the Legislatures of the States concerned as well as of the Congress.

The Congress shall have Power to dispose of and make all needful Rules and Regulations respecting the Territory or other Property belonging to the United States; and nothing in this Constitution shall be so construed as to Prejudice any Claims of the United States, or of any particular State.

Section 4. The United States shall guarantee to every State in this Union a Republican Form of Government, and shall protect each of them against Invasion; and on Application of the Legislature, or of the Executive (when the Legislature cannot be convened) against domestic Violence.

ARTICLE V

The Congress, whenever two thirds of both Houses shall deem it necessary, shall propose Amendments to this Constitution, or, on the Application of the Legislatures of two thirds of the several States, shall call a Convention for proposing Amendments, which, in either Case, shall be valid to all Intents and Purposes, as part of this Constitution, when ratified by the Legislatures of three fourths of the several States, or by Conventions in three fourths thereof, as the one or the other Mode of Ratification may be proposed by the Congress; Provided that no Amendment which may be made prior to the Year One thousand eight hundred and eight shall in any Manner affect the first and fourth Clauses in the Ninth Section of the first Article; and that no State, without its Consent, shall be deprived of its equal Suffrage in the Senate.

ARTICLE VI

All Debts contracted and Engagements entered into, before the Adoption of this Constitution shall be as valid against the United States under this Constitution, as under the Confederation.

This Constitution, and the Laws of the United States which shall be made in Pursuance thereof; and all Treaties made, or which shall be made, under the Authority of the United States, shall be the supreme Law of the Land; and the Judges in every State shall be bound thereby, any Thing in the Constitution or Laws of any State to the Contrary notwithstanding.

The Senators and Representatives before mentioned, and the Members of the several State Legislatures, and all executive and judicial Officers, both of the United States and of the several States, shall be bound by Oath or Affirmation, to support this Constitution; but no religious Test shall ever be required as a Qualification to any Office or public Trust under the United States.

ARTICLE VII

The Ratification of the Conventions of nine States shall be sufficient for the Establishment of this Constitution between the States so ratifying the Same.

AMENDMENT I [1791]

Congress shall make no law respecting an establishment of religion, or prohibiting the free exercise thereof; or abridging the freedom of speech, or of the press; or the right of the people peaceably to assembly, and to petition the Government for a redress of grievances.

AMENDMENT II [1791]

A well regulated Militia, being necessary to the security of a free State, the right of the people to keep and bear Arms, shall not be infringed.

AMENDMENT III [1791]

No Soldier shall, in time of peace be quartered in any house, without the consent of the Owner, nor in time of war, but in a manner to be prescribed by law.

AMENDMENT IV [1791]

The right of the people to be secure in their persons, houses, papers, and effects, against unreasonable searches and seizures, shall not be violated, and no Warrants shall issue, but upon probable cause, supported by Oath or affirmation, and particularly describing the place to be searched, and the persons or things to be seized.

AMENDMENT V [1791]

No person shall be held to answer for a capital, or otherwise infamous crime, unless on a presentment or indictment of a Grand Jury, except in cases arising in the land or naval forces, or in the Militia, when in actual service in time of War or public danger; nor shall any person be subject for the same offence to be twice put in jeopardy of life or limb; nor shall be compelled in any criminal case to be a witness against himself, nor be deprived of life, liberty, or property, without due process of law; nor shall private property be taken for public use, without just compensation.

AMENDMENT VI [1791]

In all criminal prosecutions, the accused shall enjoy the right to a speedy and public trial, by an impartial jury of the State and district wherein the crime shall have been committed, which district shall have been previously ascertained by law, and to be informed of the nature and cause of the accusation; to be confronted with the witnesses against him; to have compulsory process for obtaining witnesses in his favor, and to have the Assistance of Counsel for his defence.

AMENDMENT VII [1791]

In Suits at common law, where the value in controversy shall exceed twenty dollars, the right of trial by jury shall be preserved, and no fact tried by jury, shall be otherwise re-examined in any Court of the United States, than according to the rules of the common law.

AMENDMENT VIII [1791]

Excessive bail shall not be required, nor excessive fines imposed, nor cruel and unusual punishments inflicted.

AMENDMENT IX [1791]

The enumeration in the Constitution, of certain rights, shall not be construed to deny or disparage others retained by the people.

AMENDMENT X [1791]

The powers not delegated to the United States by the Constitution, nor prohibited by it to the States, are reserved to the States respectively, or to the people.

AMENDMENT XI [1798]

The Judicial power of the United States shall not be construed to extend to any suit in law or equity, commenced or prosecuted against one of the United States by Citizens of another State, or by Citizens or Subjects of any Foreign State.

AMENDMENT XII [1804]

The Electors shall meet in their respective states, and vote by ballot for President and Vice-President, one of whom, at least, shall not be an inhabitant of the same state with themselves; they shall name in their ballots the person voted for as President, and in distinct ballots the person voted for as Vice-President, and they shall make distinct lists of all persons voted for as President, and of all persons voted for as Vice-President, and of the number of votes for each, which lists they shall sign and certify, and transmit sealed to the seat of the government of the United States, directed to the President of the Senate;—The President of the Senate shall, in the presence of the Senate and House of Representatives, open all the certificates and the votes shall then be counted;—The person having the greatest number of votes for President, shall be the President, if such number be a majority of the whole number of Electors appointed; and if no person have such majority, then from the persons having the highest numbers not exceeding three on the list of those voted for as President, the House of Representatives shall choose immediately, by ballot, the President. But in choosing the President, the votes shall be taken by states, the representation from each state having one vote; a quorum for this purpose shall consist of a member or members from two-thirds of the states, and a majority of all states shall be necessary to a choice. And if the House of Representatives shall not choose a President whenever the right of choice shall devolve upon them, before the fourth day of March next following, then the Vice-President shall act as President, as in the case of the death or other constitutional disability of the President.—The person having the greatest number of votes as Vice-President, shall be the Vice-President, if such number be a majority of the whole number of Electors appointed, and if no person have a majority, then from the two highest numbers on the list, the Senate shall choose the Vice-President; a quorum for the purpose shall consist of two-thirds of the whole number of Senators, and a majority of the whole number shall be necessary to a choice. But no person constitutionally ineligible to the office of President shall be eligible to that of Vice-President of the United States.

AMENDMENT XIII [1865]

Section 1. Neither slavery nor involuntary servitude, except as a punishment for crime whereof the party shall have been duly convicted, shall exist within the United States, or any place subject to their jurisdiction.

Section 2. Congress shall have power to enforce this article by appropriate legislation.

AMENDMENT XIV [1868]

Section 1. All persons born or naturalized in the United States, and subject to the jurisdiction thereof, are citizens of the

United States and of the State wherein they reside. No State shall make or enforce any law which shall abridge the privileges or immunities of citizens of the United States; nor shall any State deprive any person of life, liberty, or property, without due process of law; nor deny to any person within its jurisdiction the equal protection of the laws.

Section 2. Representatives shall be apportioned among the several States according to their respective numbers, counting the whole number of persons in each State, excluding Indians not taxed. But when the right to vote at any election for the choice of electors for President and Vice President of the United States, Representatives in Congress, the Executive and Judicial officers of a State, or the members of the Legislature thereof, is denied to any of the male inhabitants of such State, being twenty-one years of age, and citizens of the United States, or in any way abridged, except for participation in rebellion, or other crime, the basis of representation therein shall be reduced in the proportion which the number of such male citizens shall bear to the whole number of male citizens twenty-one years of age in such State.

Section 3. No person shall be a Senator or Representative in Congress, or elector of President and Vice President, or hold any office, civil or military, under the United States, or under any State, who having previously taken an oath, as a member of Congress, or as an officer of the United States, or as a member of any State legislature, or as an executive or judicial officer of any State, to support the Constitution of the United States, shall have engaged in insurrection or rebellion against the same, or given aid or comfort to the enemies thereof. But Congress may by a vote of two-thirds of each House, remove such disability.

Section 4. The validity of the public debt of the United States, authorized by law, including debts incurred for payment of pensions and bounties for services in suppressing insurrection or rebellion, shall not be questioned. But neither the United States nor any State shall assume or pay any debt or obligation incurred in aid of insurrection or rebellion against the United States, or any claim for the loss or emancipation of any slave; but all such debts, obligations and claims shall be held illegal and void.

Section 5. The Congress shall have power to enforce, by appropriate legislation, the provisions of this article.

AMENDMENT XV [1870]

Section 1. The right of citizens of the United States to vote shall not be denied or abridged by the United States or by any State on account of race, color, or previous condition of servitude.

Section 2. The Congress shall have power to enforce this article by appropriate legislation.

AMENDMENT XVI [1913]

The Congress shall have power to lay and collect taxes on incomes, from whatever source derived, without apportionment among the several States, and without regard to any census or enumeration.

AMENDMENT XVII [1913]

Section 1. The Senate of the United States shall be composed of two Senators from each State, elected by the people thereof, for six years; and each Senator shall have one vote. The electors in each State shall have the qualifications requisite for electors of the most numerous branch of the State legislatures.

Section 2. When vacancies happen in the representation of any State in the Senate, the executive authority of such State shall issue writs of election to fill such vacancies: Provided, That the legislature of any State may empower the executive thereof to make temporary appointments until the people fill the vacancies by election as the legislature may direct.

Section 3. This amendment shall not be so construed as to affect the election or term of any Senator chosen before it becomes valid as part of the Constitution.

AMENDMENT XVIII [1919]

Section 1. After one year from the ratification of this article the manufacture, sale, or transportation of intoxicating liquors within, the importation thereof into, or the exportation thereof from the United States and all territory subject to the jurisdiction thereof for beverage purposes is hereby prohibited.

Section 2. The Congress and the several States shall have concurrent power to enforce this article by appropriate legislation.

Section 3. This article shall be inoperative unless it shall have been ratified as an amendment to the Constitution by the legislatures of the several States, as provided in the Constitution, within seven years from the date of the submission hereof to the States by the Congress.

AMENDMENT XIX [1920]

Section 1. The right of citizens of the United States to vote shall not be denied or abridged by the United States or by any State on account of sex.

Section 2. Congress shall have power to enforce this article by appropriate legislation.

AMENDMENT XX [1933]

Section 1. The terms of the President and Vice President shall end at noon on the 20th day of January, and the terms of Senators and Representatives at noon on the 3d day of January, of the years in which such terms would have ended if this article had not been ratified; and the terms of their successors shall then begin.

Section 2. The Congress shall assemble at least once in every year, and such meeting shall begin at noon on the 3d day of January, unless they shall by law appoint a different day.

Section 3. If, at the time fixed for the beginning of the term of the President, the President elect shall have died, the Vice President elect shall become President. If the President shall not have been chosen before the time fixed for the beginning of his term, or if the President elect shall have failed to qualify, then the Vice President elect shall act as President until a President shall have qualified; and the Congress may by law provide for the case wherein neither a President elect nor a Vice President elect shall have qualified, declaring who shall then act as President, or the manner in which one who is to act shall be selected, and such person shall act accordingly until a President or Vice President shall have qualified.

Section 4. The Congress may by law provide for the case of the death of any of the persons from whom the House of Representatives may choose a President whenever the right of choice shall have devolved upon them, and for the case of the death of any of the persons from whom the Senate may choose a Vice President whenever the right of choice shall have devolved upon them.

Section 5.   Sections 1 and 2 shall take effect on the 15th day of October following the ratification of this article.

Section 6.   This article shall be inoperative unless it shall have been ratified as an amendment to the Constitution by the legislatures of three-fourths of the several States within seven years from the date of its submission.

Amendment XXI [1933]

Section 1.   The eighteenth article of amendment to the Constitution of the United States is hereby repealed.

Section 2.   The transportation or importation into any State, Territory, or possession of the United States for delivery or use therein of intoxicating liquors, in violation of the laws thereof, is hereby prohibited.

Section 3.   This article shall be inoperative unless it shall have been ratified as an amendment to the Constitution by conventions in the several States, as provided in the Constitution, within seven years from the date of the submission hereof to the States by the Congress.

Amendment XXII [1951]

Section 1.   No person shall be elected to the office of the President more than twice, and no person who has held the office of President, or acted as President, for more than two years of a term to which some other person was elected President shall be elected to the office of President more than once. But this Article shall not apply to any person holding the office of President when this Article was proposed by the Congress, and shall not prevent any person who may be holding the office of President, or acting as President, during the term within which this Article becomes operative from holding the office of President or acting as President during the remainder of such term.

Section 2.   This article shall be inoperative unless it shall have been ratified as an amendment to the Constitution by the legislatures of three-fourths of the several States within seven years from the date of its submission to the States by the Congress.

Amendment XXIII [1961]

Section 1.   The District constituting the seat of Government of the United States shall appoint in such manner as the Congress may direct:

A number of electors of President and Vice President equal to the whole number of Senators and Representatives in Congress to which the District would be entitled if it were a State, but in no event more than the least populous state; they shall be in addition to those appointed by the states, but they shall be considered, for the purposes of the election of President and Vice President, to be electors appointed by a state; and they shall meet in the District and perform such duties as provided by the twelfth article of amendment.

Section 2.   The Congress shall have power to enforce this article by appropriate legislation.

Amendment XXIV [1964]

Section 1.   The right of citizens of the United States to vote in any primary or other election for President or Vice President, for electors for President or Vice President, or for Senator or Representative in Congress, shall not be denied or abridged by the United States, or any State by reason of failure to pay any poll tax or other tax.

Section 2.   The Congress shall have power to enforce this article by appropriate legislation.

Amendment XXV [1967]

Section 1.   In case of the removal of the President from office or of his death or resignation, the Vice President shall become President.

Section 2.   Whenever there is a vacancy in the office of the Vice President, the President shall nominate a Vice President who shall take office upon confirmation by a majority vote of both Houses of Congress.

Section 3.   Whenever the President transmits to the President pro tempore of the Senate and the Speaker of the House of Representatives his written declaration that he is unable to discharge the powers and duties of his office, and until he transmits to them a written declaration to the contrary, such powers and duties shall be discharged by the Vice President as Acting President.

Section 4.   Whenever the Vice President and a majority of either the principal officers of the executive departments or of such other body as Congress may by law provide, transmit to the President pro tempore of the Senate and the Speaker of the House of Representatives their written declaration that the President is unable to discharge the powers and duties of his office, the Vice President shall immediately assume the powers and duties of the office as Acting President.

Thereafter, when the President transmits to the President pro tempore of the Senate and the Speaker of the House of Representatives his written declaration that no inability exists, he shall resume the powers and duties of his office unless the Vice President and a majority of either the principal officers of the executive department or of such other body as Congress may by law provide, transmit within four days to the President pro tempore of the Senate and the Speaker of the House of Representatives their written declaration that the President is unable to discharge the powers and duties of his office. Thereupon Congress shall decide the issue, assembling within forty-eight hours for that purpose if not in session. If the Congress, within twenty-one days after receipt of the latter written declaration, or, if Congress is not in session, within twenty-one days after Congress is required to assemble, determines by two-thirds vote of both Houses that the President is unable to discharge the powers and duties of his office, the Vice President shall continue to discharge the same as Acting President; otherwise, the President shall resume the powers and duties of his office.

Amendment XXVI [1971]

Section 1.   The right of citizens of the United States, who are eighteen years of age or older, to vote shall not be denied or abridged by the United States or by any State on account of age.

Section 2.   The Congress shall have power to enforce this article by appropriate legislation.

Amendment XXVII [1992]

No law, varying the compensation for the services of the Senators and Representatives, shall take effect, until an election of Representatives shall have intervened.

Article 2 of the Uniform Commercial Code (Excerpts)

ARTICLE 2
SALES

Part 1 Short Title, General Construction and Subject Matter

§ 2-101. Short Title.

This Article shall be known and may be cited as Uniform Commercial Code—Sales.

§ 2-102. Scope; Certain Security and Other Transactions Excluded From This Article.

Unless the context otherwise requires, this Article applies to transactions in goods; it does not apply to any transaction which although in the form of an unconditional contract to sell or present sale is intended to operate only as a security transaction nor does this Article impair or repeal any statute regulating sales to consumers, farmers or other specified classes of buyers.

§ 2-103. Definitions and Index of Definitions.

(1) In this Article unless the context otherwise requires

(a) "Buyer" means a person who buys or contracts to buy goods.

(b) "Good faith" in the case of a merchant means honesty in fact and the observance of reasonable commercial standards of fair dealing in the trade.

(c) "Receipt" of goods means taking physical possession of them.

(d) "Seller" means a person who sells or contracts to sell goods.

(2) Other definitions applying to this Article or to specified Parts thereof, and the sections in which they appear are:

"Acceptance". Section 2-606.
"Banker's credit". Section 2-325.
"Between merchants". Section 2-104.
"Cancellation". Section 2-106(4).
"Commercial unit". Section 2-105.
"Confirmed credit". Section 2-325.
"Conforming to contract". Section 2-106.
"Contract for sale". Section 2-106.
"Cover". Section 2-712.
"Entrusting". Section 2-403.
"Financing agency". Section 2-104.
"Future goods". Section 2-105.
"Goods". Section 2-105.
"Identification". Section 2-501.
"Installment contract". Section 2-612.
"Letter of Credit". Section 2-325.

"Lot". Section 2-105.
"Merchant". Section 2-104.
"Overseas". Section 2-323.
"Person in position of seller". Section 2-707.
"Present sale". Section 2-106.
"Sale". Section 2-106.
"Sale on approval". Section 2-326.
"Sale or return". Section 2-326.
"Termination". Section 2-106.

(3) The following definitions in other Articles apply to this Article:

"Check". Section 3-104.
"Consignee". Section 7-102.
"Consignor". Section 7-102.
"Consumer goods". Section 9-109.
"Dishonor". Section 3-507.
"Draft". Section 3-104.

(4) In addition Article 1 contains general definitions and principles of construction and interpretation applicable throughout this Article.

As amended in 1994 and 1999.

§ 2-104. Definitions: "Merchant"; "Between Merchants"; "Financing Agency".

(1) "Merchant" means a person who deals in goods of the kind or otherwise by his occupation holds himself out as having knowledge or skill peculiar to the practices or goods involved in the transaction or to whom such knowledge or skill may be attributed by his employment of an agent or broker or other intermediary who by his occupation holds himself out as having such knowledge or skill.

(2) "Financing agency" means a bank, finance company or other person who in the ordinary course of business makes advances against goods or documents of title or who by arrangement with either the seller or the buyer intervenes in ordinary course to make or collect payment due or claimed under the contract for sale, as by purchasing or paying the seller's draft or making advances against it or by merely taking it for collection whether or not documents of title accompany the draft. "Financing agency" includes also a bank or other person who similarly intervenes between persons who are in the position of seller and buyer in respect to the goods (Section 2-707).

(3) "Between merchants" means in any transaction with respect to which both parties are chargeable with the knowledge or skill of merchants.

§ 2-105. Definitions: Transferability; "Goods"; "Future" Goods; "Lot"; "Commercial Unit".

(1) "Goods" means all things (including specially manufactured goods) which are movable at the time of identification to the contract for sale other than the money in which the price is to be paid, investment securities (Article 8) and things in action. "Goods" also includes the unborn young of animals

and growing crops and other identified things attached to realty as described in the section on goods to be severed from realty (Section 2–107).

(2) Goods must be both existing and identified before any interest in them can pass. Goods which are not both existing and identified are "future" goods. A purported present sale of future goods or of any interest therein operates as a contract to sell.

(3) There may be a sale of a part interest in existing identified goods.

(4) An undivided share in an identified bulk of fungible goods is sufficiently identified to be sold although the quantity of the bulk is not determined. Any agreed proportion of such a bulk or any quantity thereof agreed upon by number, weight or other measure may to the extent of the seller's interest in the bulk be sold to the buyer who then becomes an owner in common.

(5) "Lot" means a parcel or a single article which is the subject matter of a separate sale or delivery, whether or not it is sufficient to perform the contract.

(6) "Commercial unit" means such a unit of goods as by commercial usage is a single whole for purposes of sale and division of which materially impairs its character or value on the market or in use. A commercial unit may be a single article (as a machine) or a set of articles (as a suite of furniture or an assortment of sizes) or a quantity (as a bale, gross, or carload) or any other unit treated in use or in the relevant market as a single whole.

§ 2–106. Definitions: "Contract"; "Agreement"; "Contract for Sale"; "Sale"; "Present Sale"; "Conforming" to Contract; "Termination"; "Cancellation".

(1) In this Article unless the context otherwise requires "contract" and "agreement" are limited to those relating to the present or future sale of goods. "Contract for sale" includes both a present sale of goods and a contract to sell goods at a future time. A "sale" consists in the passing of title from the seller to the buyer for a price (Section 2–401). A "present sale" means a sale which is accomplished by the making of the contract.

(2) Goods or conduct including any part of a performance are "conforming" or conform to the contract when they are in accordance with the obligations under the contract.

(3) "Termination" occurs when either party pursuant to a power created by agreement or law puts an end to the contract otherwise than for its breach. On "termination" all obligations which are still executory on both sides are discharged but any right based on prior breach or performance survives.

(4) "Cancellation" occurs when either party puts an end to the contract for breach by the other and its effect is the same as that of "termination" except that the cancelling party also retains any remedy for breach of the whole contract or any unperformed balance.

§ 2–107. Goods to Be Severed From Realty: Recording.

(1) A contract for the sale of minerals or the like (including oil and gas) or a structure or its materials to be removed from realty is a contract for the sale of goods within this Article if they are to be severed by the seller but until severance a purported present sale thereof which is not effective as a transfer of an interest in land is effective only as a contract to sell.

(2) A contract for the sale apart from the land of growing crops or other things attached to realty and capable of severance

without material harm thereto but not described in subsection (1) or of timber to be cut is a contract for the sale of goods within this Article whether the subject matter is to be severed by the buyer or by the seller even though it forms part of the realty at the time of contracting, and the parties can by identification effect a present sale before severance.

(3) The provisions of this section are subject to any third party rights provided by the law relating to realty records, and the contract for sale may be executed and recorded as a document transferring an interest in land and shall then constitute notice to third parties of the buyer's rights under the contract for sale.

As amended in 1972.

Part 2 Form, Formation and Readjustment of Contract

§ 2–201. Formal Requirements; Statute of Frauds.

(1) Except as otherwise provided in this section a contract for the sale of goods for the price of $500 or more is not enforceable by way of action or defense unless there is some writing sufficient to indicate that a contract for sale has been made between the parties and signed by the party against whom enforcement is sought or by his authorized agent or broker. A writing is not insufficient because it omits or incorrectly states a term agreed upon but the contract is not enforceable under this paragraph beyond the quantity of goods shown in such writing.

(2) Between merchants if within a reasonable time a writing in confirmation of the contract and sufficient against the sender is received and the party receiving it has reason to know its contents, its satisfies the requirements of subsection (1) against such party unless written notice of objection to its contents is given within ten days after it is received.

(3) A contract which does not satisfy the requirements of subsection (1) but which is valid in other respects is enforceable

(a) if the goods are to be specially manufactured for the buyer and are not suitable for sale to others in the ordinary course of the seller's business and the seller, before notice of repudiation is received and under circumstances which reasonably indicate that the goods are for the buyer, has made either a substantial beginning of their manufacture or commitments for their procurement; or

(b) if the party against whom enforcement is sought admits in his pleading, testimony or otherwise in court that a contract for sale was made, but the contract is not enforceable under this provision beyond the quantity of goods admitted; or

(c) with respect to goods for which payment has been made and accepted or which have been received and accepted (Sec. 2–606).

§ 2–202. Final Written Expression: Parol or Extrinsic Evidence.

Terms with respect to which the confirmatory memoranda of the parties agree or which are otherwise set forth in a writing intended by the parties as a final expression of their agreement with respect to such terms as are included therein may not be contradicted by evidence of any prior agreement or of a contemporaneous oral agreement but may be explained or supplemented

(a) by course of dealing or usage of trade (Section 1–205) or by course of performance (Section 2–208); and

(b) by evidence of consistent additional terms unless the court finds the writing to have been intended also as a complete and exclusive statement of the terms of the agreement.

§ 2–203. Seals Inoperative.

The affixing of a seal to a writing evidencing a contract for sale or an offer to buy or sell goods does not constitute the writing a sealed instrument and the law with respect to sealed instruments does not apply to such a contract or offer.

§ 2–204. Formation in General.

(1) A contract for sale of goods may be made in any manner sufficient to show agreement, including conduct by both parties which recognizes the existence of such a contract.

(2) An agreement sufficient to constitute a contract for sale may be found even though the moment of its making is undetermined.

(3) Even though one or more terms are left open a contract for sale does not fail for indefiniteness if the parties have intended to make a contract and there is a reasonably certain basis for giving an appropriate remedy.

§ 2–205. Firm Offers.

An offer by a merchant to buy or sell goods in a signed writing which by its terms gives assurance that it will be held open is not revocable, for lack of consideration, during the time stated or if no time is stated for a reasonable time, but in no event may such period of irrevocability exceed three months; but any such term of assurance on a form supplied by the offeree must be separately signed by the offeror.

§ 2–206. Offer and Acceptance in Formation of Contract.

(1) Unless other unambiguously indicated by the language or circumstances

(a) an offer to make a contract shall be construed as inviting acceptance in any manner and by any medium reasonable in the circumstances;

(b) an order or other offer to buy goods for prompt or current shipment shall be construed as inviting acceptance either by a prompt promise to ship or by the prompt or current shipment of conforming or nonconforming goods, but such a shipment of non-conforming goods does not constitute an acceptance if the seller seasonably notifies the buyer that the shipment is offered only as an accommodation to the buyer.

(2) Where the beginning of a requested performance is a reasonable mode of acceptance an offeror who is not notified of acceptance within a reasonable time may treat the offer as having lapsed before acceptance.

§ 2–207. Additional Terms in Acceptance or Confirmation.

(1) A definite and seasonable expression of acceptance or a written confirmation which is sent within a reasonable time operates as an acceptance even though it states terms additional to or different from those offered or agreed upon, unless acceptance is expressly made conditional on assent to the additional or different terms.

(2) The additional terms are to be construed as proposals for addition to the contract. Between merchants such terms become part of the contract unless:

(a) the offer expressly limits acceptance to the terms of the offer;

(b) they materially alter it; or

(c) notification of objection to them has already been given or is given within a reasonable time after notice of them is received.

(3) Conduct by both parties which recognizes the existence of a contract is sufficient to establish a contract for sale although the writings of the parties do not otherwise establish a contract. In such case the terms of the particular contract consist of those terms on which the writings of the parties agree, together with any supplementary terms incorporated under any other provisions of this Act.

§ 2–208. Course of Performance or Practical Construction.

(1) Where the contract for sale involves repeated occasions for performance by either party with knowledge of the nature of the performance and opportunity for objection to it by the other, any course of performance accepted or acquiesced in without objection shall be relevant to determine the meaning of the agreement.

(2) The express terms of the agreement and any such course of performance, as well as any course of dealing and usage of trade, shall be construed whenever reasonable as consistent with each other; but when such construction is unreasonable, express terms shall control course of performance and course of performance shall control both course of dealing and usage of trade (Section 1–205).

(3) Subject to the provisions of the next section on modification and waiver, such course of performance shall be relevant to show a waiver or modification of any term inconsistent with such course of performance.

§ 2–209. Modification, Rescission and Waiver.

(1) An agreement modifying a contract within this Article needs no consideration to be binding.

(2) A signed agreement which excludes modification or rescission except by a signed writing cannot be otherwise modified or rescinded, but except as between merchants such a requirement on a form supplied by the merchant must be separately signed by the other party.

(3) The requirements of the statute of frauds section of this Article (Section 2–201) must be satisfied if the contract as modified is within its provisions.

(4) Although an attempt at modification or rescission does not satisfy the requirements of subsection (2) or (3) it can operate as a waiver.

(5) A party who has made a waiver affecting an executory portion of the contract may retract the waiver by reasonable notification received by the other party that strict performance will be required of any term waived, unless the retraction would be unjust in view of a material change of position in reliance on the waiver.

§ 2–210. Delegation of Performance; Assignment of Rights.

(1) A party may perform his duty through a delegate unless otherwise agreed or unless the other party has a substantial interest in having his original promisor perform or control the

acts required by the contract. No delegation of performance relieves the party delegating of any duty to perform or any liability for breach.

(2) Except as otherwise provided in Section 9–406, unless otherwise agreed, all rights of either seller or buyer can be assigned except where the assignment would materially change the duty of the other party, or increase materially the burden or risk imposed on him by his contract, or impair materially his chance of obtaining return performance. A right to damages for breach of the whole contract or a right arising out of the assignor's due performance of his entire obligation can be assigned despite agreement otherwise.

(3) The creation, attachment, perfection, or enforcement of a security interest in the seller's interest under a contract is not a transfer that materially changes the duty of or increases materially the burden or risk imposed on the buyer or impairs materially the buyer's chance of obtaining return performance within the purview of subsection (2) unless, and then only to the extent that, enforcement actually results in a delegation of material performance of the seller. Even in that event, the creation, attachment, perfection, and enforcement of the security interest remain effective, but (i) the seller is liable to the buyer for damages caused by the delegation to the extent that the damages could not reasonably by prevented by the buyer, and (ii) a court having jurisdiction may grant other appropriate relief, including cancellation of the contract for sale or an injunction against enforcement of the security interest or consummation of the enforcement.

(4) Unless the circumstances indicate the contrary a prohibition of assignment of "the contract" is to be construed as barring only the delegation to the assignee of the assignor's performance.

(5) An assignment of "the contract" or of "all my rights under the contract" or an assignment in similar general terms is an assignment of rights and unless the language or the circumstances (as in an assignment for security) indicate the contrary, it is a delegation of performance of the duties of the assignor and its acceptance by the assignee constitutes a promise by him to perform those duties. This promise is enforceable by either the assignor or the other party to the original contract.

(6) The other party may treat any assignment which delegates performance as creating reasonable grounds for insecurity and may without prejudice to his rights against the assignor demand assurances from the assignee (Section 2–609).

As amended in 1999.

Part 3 General Obligation and Construction of Contract

§ 2–301. General Obligations of Parties.

The obligation of the seller is to transfer and deliver and that of the buyer is to accept and pay in accordance with the contract.

§ 2–302. Unconscionable Contract or Clause.

(1) If the court as a matter of law finds the contract or any clause of the contract to have been unconscionable at the time it was made the court may refuse to enforce the contract, or it may enforce the remainder of the contract without the unconscionable clause, or it may so limit the application of any unconscionable clause as to avoid any unconscionable result.

(2) When it is claimed or appears to the court that the contract or any clause thereof may be unconscionable the parties shall be afforded a reasonable opportunity to present evidence as to its commercial setting, purpose and effect to aid the court in making the determination.

§ 2–303. Allocations or Division of Risks.

Where this Article allocates a risk or a burden as between the parties "unless otherwise agreed", the agreement may not only shift the allocation but may also divide the risk or burden.

§ 2–304. Price Payable in Money, Goods, Realty, or Otherwise.

(1) The price can be made payable in money or otherwise. If it is payable in whole or in part in goods each party is a seller of the goods which he is to transfer.

(2) Even though all or part of the price is payable in an interest in realty the transfer of the goods and the seller's obligations with reference to them are subject to this Article, but not the transfer of the interest in realty or the transferor's obligations in connection therewith.

§ 2–305. Open Price Term.

(1) The parties if they so intend can conclude a contract for sale even though the price is not settled. In such a case the price is a reasonable price at the time for delivery if

   (a) nothing is said as to price; or

   (b) the price is left to be agreed by the parties and they fail to agree; or

   (c) the price is to be fixed in terms of some agreed market or other standard as set or recorded by a third person or agency and it is not so set or recorded.

(2) A price to be fixed by the seller or by the buyer means a price for him to fix in good faith.

(3) When a price left to be fixed otherwise than by agreement of the parties fails to be fixed through fault of one party the other may at his option treat the contract as cancelled or himself fix a reasonable price.

(4) Where, however, the parties intend not to be bound unless the price be fixed or agreed and it is not fixed or agreed there is no contract. In such a case the buyer must return any goods already received or if unable so to do must pay their reasonable value at the time of delivery and the seller must return any portion of the price paid on account.

§ 2–306. Output, Requirements and Exclusive Dealings.

(1) A term which measures the quantity by the output of the seller or the requirements of the buyer means such actual output or requirements as may occur in good faith, except that no quantity unreasonably disproportionate to any stated estimate or in the absence of a stated estimate to any normal or otherwise comparable prior output or requirements may be tendered or demanded.

(2) A lawful agreement by either the seller or the buyer for exclusive dealing in the kind of goods concerned imposes unless otherwise agreed an obligation by the seller to use best efforts to supply the goods and by the buyer to use best efforts to promote their sale.

§ 2–307. Delivery in Single Lot or Several Lots.

Unless otherwise agreed all goods called for by a contract for sale must be tendered in a single delivery and payment is due only on such tender but where the circumstances give either party the right to make or demand delivery in lots the price if it can be apportioned may be demanded for each lot.

§ 2–308. Absence of Specified Place for Delivery.

Unless otherwise agreed

(a) the place for delivery of goods is the seller's place of business or if he has none his residence; but

(b) in a contract for sale of identified goods which to the knowledge of the parties at the time of contracting are in some other place, that place is the place for their delivery; and

(c) documents of title may be delivered through customary banking channels.

§ 2–309. Absence of Specific Time Provisions; Notice of Termination.

(1) The time for shipment or delivery or any other action under a contract if not provided in this Article or agreed upon shall be a reasonable time.

(2) Where the contract provides for successive performances but is indefinite in duration it is valid for a reasonable time but unless otherwise agreed may be terminated at any time by either party.

(3) Termination of a contract by one party except on the happening of an agreed event requires that reasonable notification be received by the other party and an agreement dispensing with notification is invalid if its operation would be unconscionable.

§ 2–310. Open Time for Payment or Running of Credit; Authority to Ship Under Reservation.

Unless otherwise agreed

(a) payment is due at the time and place at which the buyer is to receive the goods even though the place of shipment is the place of delivery; and

(b) if the seller is authorized to send the goods he may ship them under reservation, and may tender the documents of title, but the buyer may inspect the goods after their arrival before payment is due unless such inspection is inconsistent with the terms of the contract (Section 2–513); and

(c) if delivery is authorized and made by way of documents of title otherwise than by subsection (b) then payment is due at the time and place at which the buyer is to receive the documents regardless of where the goods are to be received; and

(d) where the seller is required or authorized to ship the goods on credit the credit period runs from the time of shipment but post-dating the invoice or delaying its dispatch will correspondingly delay the starting of the credit period.

§ 2–311. Options and Cooperation Respecting Performance.

(1) An agreement for sale which is otherwise sufficiently definite (subsection (3) of Section 2–204) to be a contract is not made invalid by the fact that it leaves particulars of performance to be specified by one of the parties. Any such specification must be made in good faith and within limits set by commercial reasonableness.

(2) Unless otherwise agreed specifications relating to assortment of the goods are at the buyer's option and except as otherwise provided in subsections (1)(c) and (3) of Section 2–319

specifications or arrangements relating to shipment are at the seller's option.

(3) Where such specification would materially affect the other party's performance but is not seasonably made or where one party's cooperation is necessary to the agreed performance of the other but is not seasonably forthcoming, the other party in addition to all other remedies

(a) is excused for any resulting delay in his own performance; and

(b) may also either proceed to perform in any reasonable manner or after the time for a material part of his own performance treat the failure to specify or to cooperate as a breach by failure to deliver or accept the goods.

§ 2–312. Warranty of Title and Against Infringement; Buyer's Obligation Against Infringement.

(1) Subject to subsection (2) there is in a contract for sale a warranty by the seller that

(a) the title conveyed shall be good, and its transfer rightful; and

(b) the goods shall be delivered free from any security interest or other lien or encumbrance of which the buyer at the time of contracting has no knowledge.

(2) A warranty under subsection (1) will be excluded or modified only by specific language or by circumstances which give the buyer reason to know that the person selling does not claim title in himself or that he is purporting to sell only such right or title as he or a third person may have.

(3) Unless otherwise agreed a seller who is a merchant regularly dealing in goods of the kind warrants that the goods shall be delivered free of the rightful claim of any third person by way of infringement or the like but a buyer who furnishes specifications to the seller must hold the seller harmless against any such claim which arises out of compliance with the specifications.

§ 2–313. Express Warranties by Affirmation, Promise, Description, Sample.

(1) Express warranties by the seller are created as follows:

(a) Any affirmation of fact or promise made by the seller to the buyer which relates to the goods and becomes part of the basis of the bargain creates an express warranty that the goods shall conform to the affirmation or promise.

(b) Any description of the goods which is made part of the basis of the bargain creates an express warranty that the goods shall conform to the description.

(c) Any sample or model which is made part of the basis of the bargain creates an express warranty that the whole of the goods shall conform to the sample or model.

(2) It is not necessary to the creation of an express warranty that the seller use formal words such as "warrant" or "guarantee" or that he have a specific intention to make a warranty, but an affirmation merely of the value of the goods or a statement purporting to be merely the seller's opinion or commendation of the goods does not create a warranty.

§ 2–314. Implied Warranty: Merchantability; Usage of Trade.

(1) Unless excluded or modified (Section 2–316), a warranty that the goods shall be merchantable is implied in a contract for their sale if the seller is a merchant with respect to goods of that

kind. Under this section the serving for value of food or drink to be consumed either on the premises or elsewhere is a sale.

(2) Goods to be merchantable must be at least such as

(a) pass without objection in the trade under the contract description; and

(b) in the case of fungible goods, are of fair average quality within the description; and

(c) are fit for the ordinary purposes for which such goods are used; and

(d) run, within the variations permitted by the agreement, of even kind, quality and quantity within each unit and among all units involved; and

(e) are adequately contained, packaged, and labeled as the agreement may require; and

(f) conform to the promises or affirmations of fact made on the container or label if any.

(3) Unless excluded or modified (Section 2–316) other implied warranties may arise from course of dealing or usage of trade.

§ 2–315. Implied Warranty: Fitness for Particular Purpose.

Where the seller at the time of contracting has reason to know any particular purpose for which the goods are required and that the buyer is relying on the seller's skill or judgment to select or furnish suitable goods, there is unless excluded or modified under the next section an implied warranty that the goods shall be fit for such purpose.

§ 2–316. Exclusion or Modification of Warranties.

(1) Words or conduct relevant to the creation of an express warranty and words or conduct tending to negate or limit warranty shall be construed wherever reasonable as consistent with each other; but subject to the provisions of this Article on parol or extrinsic evidence (Section 2–202) negation or limitation is inoperative to the extent that such construction is unreasonable.

(2) Subject to subsection (3), to exclude or modify the implied warranty of merchantability or any part of it the language must mention merchantability and in case of a writing must be conspicuous, and to exclude or modify any implied warranty of fitness the exclusion must be by a writing and conspicuous. Language to exclude all implied warranties of fitness is sufficient if it states, for example, that "There are no warranties which extend beyond the description on the face hereof."

(3) Notwithstanding subsection (2)

(a) unless the circumstances indicate otherwise, all implied warranties are excluded by expressions like "as is", "with all faults" or other language which in common understanding calls the buyer's attention to the exclusion of warranties and makes plain that there is no implied warranty; and

(b) when the buyer before entering into the contract has examined the goods or the sample or model as fully as he desired or has refused to examine the goods there is no implied warranty with regard to defects which an examination ought in the circumstances to have revealed to him; and

(c) an implied warranty can also be excluded or modified by course of dealing or course of performance or usage of trade.

(4) Remedies for breach of warranty can be limited in accordance with the provisions of this Article on liquidation or limitation of damages and on contractual modification of remedy (Sections 2–718 and 2–719).

§ 2–317. Cumulation and Conflict of Warranties Express or Implied.

Warranties whether express or implied shall be construed as consistent with each other and as cumulative, but if such construction is unreasonable the intention of the parties shall determine which warranty is dominant. In ascertaining that intention the following rules apply:

(a) Exact or technical specifications displace an inconsistent sample or model or general language of description.

(b) A sample from an existing bulk displaces inconsistent general language of description.

(c) Express warranties displace inconsistent implied warranties other than an implied warranty of fitness for a particular purpose.

§ 2–318. Third Party Beneficiaries of Warranties Express or Implied.

Note: If this Act is introduced in the Congress of the United States this section should be omitted. (States to select one alternative.)

Alternative A

A seller's warranty whether express or implied extends to any natural person who is in the family or household of his buyer or who is a guest in his home if it is reasonable to expect that such person may use, consume or be affected by the goods and who is injured in person by breach of the warranty. A seller may not exclude or limit the operation of this section.

Alternative B

A seller's warranty whether express or implied extends to any natural person who may reasonably be expected to use, consume or be affected by the goods and who is injured in person by breach of the warranty. A seller may not exclude or limit the operation of this section.

Alternative C

A seller's warranty whether express or implied extends to any person who may reasonably be expected to use, consume or be affected by the goods and who is injured by breach of the warranty. A seller may not exclude or limit the operation of this section with respect to injury to the person of an individual to whom the warranty extends.

As amended 1966.

§ 2–319. F.O.B. and F.A.S. Terms.

(1) Unless otherwise agreed the term F.O.B. (which means "free on board") at a named place, even though used only in connection with the stated price, is a delivery term under which

(a) when the term is F.O.B. the place of shipment, the seller must at that place ship the goods in the manner provided in this Article (Section 2–504) and bear the expense and risk of putting them into the possession of the carrier; or

(b) when the term is F.O.B. the place of destination, the seller must at his own expense and risk transport the goods to that place and there tender delivery of them in the manner provided in this Article (Section 2–503);

(c) when under either (a) or (b) the term is also F.O.B. vessel, car or other vehicle, the seller must in addition at his own expense and risk load the goods on board. If the term is F.O.B. vessel the buyer must name the vessel and in an appropriate case the seller must comply with the provisions of this Article on the form of bill of lading (Section 2–323).

(2) Unless otherwise agreed the term F.A.S. vessel (which means "free alongside") at a named port, even though used only in connection with the stated price, is a delivery term under which the seller must

(a) at his own expense and risk deliver the goods alongside the vessel in the manner usual in that port or on a dock designated and provided by the buyer; and

(b) obtain and tender a receipt for the goods in exchange for which the carrier is under a duty to issue a bill of lading.

(3) Unless otherwise agreed in any case falling within subsection (1)(a) or (c) or subsection (2) the buyer must seasonably give any needed instructions for making delivery, including when the term is F.A.S. or F.O.B. the loading berth of the vessel and in an appropriate case its name and sailing date. The seller may treat the failure of needed instructions as a failure of cooperation under this Article (Section 2–311). He may also at his option move the goods in any reasonable manner preparatory to delivery or shipment.

(4) Under the term F.O.B. vessel or F.A.S. unless otherwise agreed the buyer must make payment against tender of the required documents and the seller may not tender nor the buyer demand delivery of the goods in substitution for the documents.

§ 2–320. C.I.F. and C. & F. Terms.

(1) The term C.I.F. means that the price includes in a lump sum the cost of the goods and the insurance and freight to the named destination. The term C. & F. or C.F. means that the price so includes cost and freight to the named destination.

(2) Unless otherwise agreed and even though used only in connection with the stated price and destination, the term C.I.F. destination or its equivalent requires the seller at his own expense and risk to

(a) put the goods into the possession of a carrier at the port for shipment and obtain a negotiable bill or bills of lading covering the entire transportation to the named destination; and

(b) load the goods and obtain a receipt from the carrier (which may be contained in the bill of lading) showing that the freight has been paid or provided for; and

(c) obtain a policy or certificate of insurance, including any war risk insurance, of a kind and on terms then current at the port of shipment in the usual amount, in the currency of the contract, shown to cover the same goods covered by the bill of lading and providing for payment of loss to the order of the buyer or for the account of whom it may concern; but the seller may add to the price the amount of the premium for any such war risk insurance; and

(d) prepare an invoice of the goods and procure any other documents required to effect shipment or to comply with the contract; and

(e) forward and tender with commercial promptness all the documents in due form and with any indorsement necessary to perfect the buyer's rights.

(3) Unless otherwise agreed the term C. & F. or its equivalent has the same effect and imposes upon the seller the same obligations and risks as a C.I.F. term except the obligation as to insurance.

(4) Under the term C.I.F. or C. & F. unless otherwise agreed the buyer must make payment against tender of the required documents and the seller may not tender nor the buyer demand delivery of the goods in substitution for the documents.

§ 2–321. C.I.F. or C. & F.: "Net Landed Weights"; "Payment on Arrival"; Warranty of Condition on Arrival.

Under a contract containing a term C.I.F. or C. & F.

(1) Where the price is based on or is to be adjusted according to "net landed weights", "delivered weights", "out turn" quantity or quality or the like, unless otherwise agreed the seller must reasonably estimate the price. The payment due on tender of the documents called for by the contract is the amount so estimated, but after final adjustment of the price a settlement must be made with commercial promptness.

(2) An agreement described in subsection (1) or any warranty of quality or condition of the goods on arrival places upon the seller the risk of ordinary deterioration, shrinkage and the like in transportation but has no effect on the place or time of identification to the contract for sale or delivery or on the passing of the risk of loss.

(3) Unless otherwise agreed where the contract provides for payment on or after arrival of the goods the seller must before payment allow such preliminary inspection as is feasible; but if the goods are lost delivery of the documents and payment are due when the goods should have arrived.

§ 2–322. Delivery "Ex-Ship".

(1) Unless otherwise agreed a term for delivery of goods "ex-ship" (which means from the carrying vessel) or in equivalent language is not restricted to a particular ship and requires delivery from a ship which has reached a place at the named port of destination where goods of the kind are usually discharged.

(2) Under such a term unless otherwise agreed

(a) the seller must discharge all liens arising out of the carriage and furnish the buyer with a direction which puts the carrier under a duty to deliver the goods; and

(b) the risk of loss does not pass to the buyer until the goods leave the ship's tackle or are otherwise properly unloaded.

§ 2–323. Form of Bill of Lading Required in Overseas Shipment; "Overseas".

(1) Where the contract contemplates overseas shipment and contains a term C.I.F. or C. & F. or F.O.B. vessel, the seller unless otherwise agreed must obtain a negotiable bill of lading stating that the goods have been loaded on board or, in the case of a term C.I.F. or C. & F., received for shipment.

(2) Where in a case within subsection (1) a bill of lading has been issued in a set of parts, unless otherwise agreed if the documents are not to be sent from abroad the buyer may demand tender of the full set; otherwise only one part of the bill of lading need be tendered. Even if the agreement expressly requires a full set

(a) due tender of a single part is acceptable within the provisions of this Article on cure of improper delivery (subsection (1) of Section 2–508); and

(b) even though the full set is demanded, if the documents are sent from abroad the person tendering an incomplete set may nevertheless require payment upon furnishing an indemnity which the buyer in good faith deems adequate.

(3) A shipment by water or by air or a contract contemplating such shipment is "overseas" insofar as by usage of trade or agreement it is subject to the commercial, financing or shipping practices characteristic of international deep water commerce.

§ 2–324. "No Arrival, No Sale" Term.

Under a term "no arrival, no sale" or terms of like meaning, unless otherwise agreed,

(a) the seller must properly ship conforming goods and if they arrive by any means he must tender them on arrival but he assumes no obligation that the goods will arrive unless he has caused the non-arrival; and

(b) where without fault of the seller the goods are in part lost or have so deteriorated as no longer to conform to the contract or arrive after the contract time, the buyer may proceed as if there had been casualty to identified goods (Section 2–613).

§ 2–325. "Letter of Credit" Term; "Confirmed Credit".

(1) Failure of the buyer seasonably to furnish an agreed letter of credit is a breach of the contract for sale.

(2) The delivery to seller of a proper letter of credit suspends the buyer's obligation to pay. If the letter of credit is dishonored, the seller may on seasonable notification to the buyer require payment directly from him.

(3) Unless otherwise agreed the term "letter of credit" or "banker's credit" in a contract for sale means an irrevocable credit issued by a financing agency of good repute and, where the shipment is overseas, of good international repute. The term "confirmed credit" means that the credit must also carry the direct obligation of such an agency which does business in the seller's financial market.

§ 2–326. Sale on Approval and Sale or Return; Rights of Creditors.

(1) Unless otherwise agreed, if delivered goods may be returned by the buyer even though they conform to the contract, the transaction is

(a) a "sale on approval" if the goods are delivered primarily for use, and

(b) a "sale or return" if the goods are delivered primarily for resale.

(2) Goods held on approval are not subject to the claims of the buyer's creditors until acceptance; goods held on sale or return are subject to such claims while in the buyer's possession.

(3) Any "or return" term of a contract for sale is to be treated as a separate contract for sale within the statute of frauds section of this Article (Section 2–201) and as contradicting the sale aspect of the contract within the provisions of this Article or on parol or extrinsic evidence (Section 2–202).

As amended in 1999.

§ 2–327. Special Incidents of Sale on Approval and Sale or Return.

(1) Under a sale on approval unless otherwise agreed

(a) although the goods are identified to the contract the risk of loss and the title do not pass to the buyer until acceptance; and

(b) use of the goods consistent with the purpose of trial is not acceptance but failure seasonably to notify the seller of election to return the goods is acceptance, and if the goods conform to the contract acceptance of any part is acceptance of the whole; and

(c) after due notification of election to return, the return is at the seller's risk and expense but a merchant buyer must follow any reasonable instructions.

(2) Under a sale or return unless otherwise agreed

(a) the option to return extends to the whole or any commercial unit of the goods while in substantially their original condition, but must be exercised seasonably; and

(b) the return is at the buyer's risk and expense.

§ 2–328. Sale by Auction.

(1) In a sale by auction if goods are put up in lots each lot is the subject of a separate sale.

(2) A sale by auction is complete when the auctioneer so announces by the fall of the hammer or in other customary manner. Where a bid is made while the hammer is falling in acceptance of a prior bid the auctioneer may in his discretion reopen the bidding or declare the goods sold under the bid on which the hammer was falling.

(3) Such a sale is with reserve unless the goods are in explicit terms put up without reserve. In an auction with reserve the auctioneer may withdraw the goods at any time until he announces completion of the sale. In an auction without reserve, after the auctioneer calls for bids on an article or lot, that article or lot cannot be withdrawn unless no bid is made within a reasonable time. In either case a bidder may retract his bid until the auctioneer's announcement of completion of the sale, but a bidder's retraction does not revive any previous bid.

(4) If the auctioneer knowingly receives a bid on the seller's behalf or the seller makes or procures such as bid, and notice has not been given that liberty for such bidding is reserved, the buyer may at his option avoid the sale or take the goods at the price of the last good faith bid prior to the completion of the sale. This subsection shall not apply to any bid at a forced sale.

Part 4 Title, Creditors and Good Faith Purchasers

§ 2–401. Passing of Title; Reservation for Security; Limited Application of This Section.

Each provision of this Article with regard to the rights, obligations and remedies of the seller, the buyer, purchasers or other third parties applies irrespective of title to the goods except where the provision refers to such title. Insofar as situations are not covered by the other provisions of this Article and matters concerning title became material the following rules apply:

(1) Title to goods cannot pass under a contract for sale prior to their identification to the contract (Section 2–501), and unless otherwise explicitly agreed the buyer acquires by their identification a special property as limited by this Act. Any retention or reservation by the seller of the title (property) in goods shipped or delivered to the buyer is limited in effect to a reservation of a security interest. Subject to these provisions and to the provisions of the Article on Secured Transactions (Article 9), title to

goods passes from the seller to the buyer in any manner and on any conditions explicitly agreed on by the parties.

(2) Unless otherwise explicitly agreed title passes to the buyer at the time and place at which the seller completes his performance with reference to the physical delivery of the goods, despite any reservation of a security interest and even though a document of title is to be delivered at a different time or place; and in particular and despite any reservation of a security interest by the bill of lading

   (a) if the contract requires or authorizes the seller to send the goods to the buyer but does not require him to deliver them at destination, title passes to the buyer at the time and place of shipment; but

   (b) if the contract requires delivery at destination, title passes on tender there.

(3) Unless otherwise explicitly agreed where delivery is to be made without moving the goods,

   (a) if the seller is to deliver a document of title, title passes at the time when and the place where he delivers such documents; or

   (b) if the goods are at the time of contracting already identified and no documents are to be delivered, title passes at the time and place of contracting.

(4) A rejection or other refusal by the buyer to receive or retain the goods, whether or not justified, or a justified revocation of acceptance revests title to the goods in the seller. Such revesting occurs by operation of law and is not a "sale".

§ 2–402. Rights of Seller's Creditors Against Sold Goods.

(1) Except as provided in subsections (2) and (3), rights of unsecured creditors of the seller with respect to goods which have been identified to a contract for sale are subject to the buyer's rights to recover the goods under this Article (Sections 2–502 and 2–716).

(2) A creditor of the seller may treat a sale or an identification of goods to a contract for sale as void if as against him a retention of possession by the seller is fraudulent under any rule of law of the state where the goods are situated, except that retention of possession in good faith and current course of trade by a merchant-seller for a commercially reasonable time after a sale or identification is not fraudulent.

(3) Nothing in this Article shall be deemed to impair the rights of creditors of the seller

   (a) under the provisions of the Article on Secured Transactions (Article 9), or

   (b) where identification to the contract or delivery is made not in current course of trade but in satisfaction of or as security for a pre-existing claim for money, security or the like and is made under circumstances which under any rule of law of the state where the goods are situated would apart from this Article constitute the transaction a fraudulent transfer or voidable preference.

§ 2–403. Power to Transfer; Good Faith Purchase of Goods; "Entrusting".

(1) A purchaser of goods acquires all title which his transferor had or had power to transfer except that a purchaser of a limited interest acquires rights only to the extent of the interest purchased. A person with voidable title has power to transfer a good title to a good faith purchaser for value. When goods have been delivered under a transaction of purchase the purchaser has such power even though

   (a) the transferor was deceived as to the identity of the purchaser, or

   (b) the delivery was in exchange for a check which is later dishonored, or

   (c) it was agreed that the transaction was to be a "cash sale", or

   (d) the delivery was procured through fraud punishable as larcenous under the criminal law.

(2) Any entrusting of possession of goods to a merchant who deals in goods of that kind gives him power to transfer all rights of the entruster to a buyer in ordinary course of business.

(3) "Entrusting" includes any delivery and any acquiescence in retention of possession regardless of any condition expressed between the parties to the delivery or acquiescence and regardless of whether the procurement of the entrusting or the possessor's disposition of the goods have been such as to be larcenous under the criminal law.

(4) The rights of other purchasers of goods and of lien creditors are governed by the Articles on Secured Transactions (Article 9), Bulk Transfers (Article 6) and Documents of Title (Article 7).

As amended in 1988.

Part 5 Performance

§ 2–501. Insurable Interest in Goods; Manner of Identification of Goods.

(1) The buyer obtains a special property and an insurable interest in goods by identification of existing goods as goods to which the contract refers even though the goods so identified are non-conforming and he has an option to return or reject them. Such identification can be made at any time and in any manner explicitly agreed to by the parties. In the absence of explicit agreement identification occurs

   (a) when the contract is made if it is for the sale of goods already existing and identified;

   (b) if the contract is for the sale of future goods other than those described in paragraph (c), when goods are shipped, marked or otherwise designated by the seller as goods to which the contract refers;

   (c) when the crops are planted or otherwise become growing crops or the young are conceived if the contract is for the sale of unborn young to be born within twelve months after contracting or for the sale of crops to be harvested within twelve months or the next normal harvest season after contracting whichever is longer.

(2) The seller retains an insurable interest in goods so long as title to or any security interest in the goods remains in him and where the identification is by the seller alone he may until default or insolvency or notification to the buyer that the identification is final substitute other goods for those identified.

(3) Nothing in this section impairs any insurable interest recognized under any other statute or rule of law.

§ 2–502. Buyer's Right to Goods on Seller's Insolvency.

(1) Subject to subsections (2) and (3) and even though the goods have not been shipped a buyer who has paid a part or all

of the price of goods in which he has a special property under the provisions of the immediately preceding section may on making and keeping good a tender of any unpaid portion of their price recover them from the seller if:

(a) in the case of goods bought for personal, family, or household purposes, the seller repudiates or fails to deliver as required by the contract; or

(b) in all cases, the seller becomes insolvent within ten days after receipt of the first installment on their price.

(2) The buyer's right to recover the goods under subsection (1)(a) vests upon acquisition of a special property, even if the seller had not then repudiated or failed to deliver.

(3) If the identification creating his special property has been made by the buyer he acquires the right to recover the goods only if they conform to the contract for sale.

As amended in 1999.

§ 2–503. Manner of Seller's Tender of Delivery.

(1) Tender of delivery requires that the seller put and hold conforming goods at the buyer's disposition and give the buyer any notification reasonably necessary to enable him to take delivery. The manner, time and place for tender are determined by the agreement and this Article, and in particular

(a) tender must be at a reasonable hour, and if it is of goods they must be kept available for the period reasonably necessary to enable the buyer to take possession; but

(b) unless otherwise agreed the buyer must furnish facilities reasonably suited to the receipt of the goods.

(2) Where the case is within the next section respecting shipment tender requires that the seller comply with its provisions.

(3) Where the seller is required to deliver at a particular destination tender requires that he comply with subsection (1) and also in any appropriate case tender documents as described in subsections (4) and (5) of this section.

(4) Where goods are in the possession of a bailee and are to be delivered without being moved

(a) tender requires that the seller either tender a negotiable document of title covering such goods or procure acknowledgment by the bailee of the buyer's right to possession of the goods; but

(b) tender to the buyer of a non-negotiable document of title or of a written direction to the bailee to deliver is sufficient tender unless the buyer seasonably objects, and receipt by the bailee of notification of the buyer's rights fixes those rights as against the bailee and all third persons; but risk of loss of the goods and of any failure by the bailee to honor the non-negotiable document of title or to obey the direction remains on the seller until the buyer has had a reasonable time to present the document or direction, and a refusal by the bailee to honor the document or to obey the direction defeats the tender.

(5) Where the contract requires the seller to deliver documents

(a) he must tender all such documents in correct form, except as provided in this Article with respect to bills of lading in a set (subsection (2) of Section 2–323); and

(b) tender through customary banking channels is sufficient and dishonor of a draft accompanying the documents constitutes non-acceptance or rejection.

§ 2–504. Shipment by Seller.

Where the seller is required or authorized to send the goods to the buyer and the contract does not require him to deliver them at a particular destination, then unless otherwise agreed he must

(a) put the goods in the possession of such a carrier and make such a contract for their transportation as may be reasonable having regard to the nature of the goods and other circumstances of the case; and

(b) obtain and promptly deliver or tender in due form any document necessary to enable the buyer to obtain possession of the goods or otherwise required by the agreement or by usage of trade; and

(c) promptly notify the buyer of the shipment.

Failure to notify the buyer under paragraph (c) or to make a proper contract under paragraph (a) is a ground for rejection only if material delay or loss ensues.

§ 2–505. Seller's Shipment under Reservation.

(1) Where the seller has identified goods to the contract by or before shipment:

(a) his procurement of a negotiable bill of lading to his own order or otherwise reserves in him a security interest in the goods. His procurement of the bill to the order of a financing agency or of the buyer indicates in addition only the seller's expectation of transferring that interest to the person named.

(b) a non-negotiable bill of lading to himself or his nominee reserves possession of the goods as security but except in a case of conditional delivery (subsection (2) of Section 2–507) a non-negotiable bill of lading naming the buyer as consignee reserves no security interest even though the seller retains possession of the bill of lading.

(2) When shipment by the seller with reservation of a security interest is in violation of the contract for sale it constitutes an improper contract for transportation within the preceding section but impairs neither the rights given to the buyer by shipment and identification of the goods to the contract nor the seller's powers as a holder of a negotiable document.

§ 2–506. Rights of Financing Agency.

(1) A financing agency by paying or purchasing for value a draft which relates to a shipment of goods acquires to the extent of the payment or purchase and in addition to its own rights under the draft and any document of title securing it any rights of the shipper in the goods including the right to stop delivery and the shipper's right to have the draft honored by the buyer.

(2) The right to reimbursement of a financing agency which has in good faith honored or purchased the draft under commitment to or authority from the buyer is not impaired by subsequent discovery of defects with reference to any relevant document which was apparently regular on its face.

§ 2–507. Effect of Seller's Tender; Delivery on Condition.

(1) Tender of delivery is a condition to the buyer's duty to accept the goods and, unless otherwise agreed, to his duty to pay for them. Tender entitles the seller to acceptance of the goods and to payment according to the contract.

(2) Where payment is due and demanded on the delivery to the buyer of goods or documents of title, his right as against the seller to retain or dispose of them is conditional upon his making the payment due.

§ 2–508. Cure by Seller of Improper Tender or Delivery; Replacement.

(1) Where any tender or delivery by the seller is rejected because non-conforming and the time for performance has not yet expired, the seller may seasonably notify the buyer of his intention to cure and may then within the contract time make a conforming delivery.

(2) Where the buyer rejects a non-conforming tender which the seller had reasonable grounds to believe would be acceptable with or without money allowance the seller may if he seasonably notifies the buyer have a further reasonable time to substitute a conforming tender.

§ 2–509. Risk of Loss in the Absence of Breach.

(1) Where the contract requires or authorizes the seller to ship the goods by carrier

(a) if it does not require him to deliver them at a particular destination, the risk of loss passes to the buyer when the goods are duly delivered to the carrier even though the shipment is under reservation (Section 2–505); but

(b) if it does require him to deliver them at a particular destination and the goods are there duly tendered while in the possession of the carrier, the risk of loss passes to the buyer when the goods are there duly so tendered as to enable the buyer to take delivery.

(2) Where the goods are held by a bailee to be delivered without being moved, the risk of loss passes to the buyer

(a) on his receipt of a negotiable document of title covering the goods; or

(b) on acknowledgment by the bailee of the buyer's right to possession of the goods; or

(c) after his receipt of a non-negotiable document of title or other written direction to deliver, as provided in subsection (4)(b) of Section 2–503.

(3) In any case not within subsection (1) or (2), the risk of loss passes to the buyer on his receipt of the goods if the seller is a merchant; otherwise the risk passes to the buyer on tender of delivery.

(4) The provisions of this section are subject to contrary agreement of the parties and to the provisions of this Article on sale on approval (Section 2–327) and on effect of breach on risk of loss (Section 2–510).

§ 2–510. Effect of Breach on Risk of Loss.

(1) Where a tender or delivery of goods so fails to conform to the contract as to give a right of rejection the risk of their loss remains on the seller until cure or acceptance.

(2) Where the buyer rightfully revokes acceptance he may to the extent of any deficiency in his effective insurance coverage treat the risk of loss as having rested on the seller from the beginning.

(3) Where the buyer as to conforming goods already identified to the contract for sale repudiates or is otherwise in breach before risk of their loss has passed to him, the seller may to the extent of any deficiency in his effective insurance coverage treat the risk of loss as resting on the buyer for a commercially reasonable time.

§ 2–511. Tender of Payment by Buyer; Payment by Check.

(1) Unless otherwise agreed tender of payment is a condition to the seller's duty to tender and complete any delivery.

(2) Tender of payment is sufficient when made by any means or in any manner current in the ordinary course of business unless the seller demands payment in legal tender and gives any extension of time reasonably necessary to procure it.

(3) Subject to the provisions of this Act on the effect of an instrument on an obligation (Section 3–310), payment by check is conditional and is defeated as between the parties by dishonor of the check on due presentment.

As amended in 1994.

§ 2–512. Payment by Buyer Before Inspection.

(1) Where the contract requires payment before inspection non-conformity of the goods does not excuse the buyer from so making payment unless

(a) the non-conformity appears without inspection; or

(b) despite tender of the required documents the circumstances would justify injunction against honor under this Act (Section 5–109(b)).

(2) Payment pursuant to subsection (1) does not constitute an acceptance of goods or impair the buyer's right to inspect or any of his remedies.

As amended in 1995.

§ 2–513. Buyer's Right to Inspection of Goods.

(1) Unless otherwise agreed and subject to subsection (3), where goods are tendered or delivered or identified to the contract for sale, the buyer has a right before payment or acceptance to inspect them at any reasonable place and time and in any reasonable manner. When the seller is required or authorized to send the goods to the buyer, the inspection may be after their arrival.

(2) Expenses of inspection must be borne by the buyer but may be recovered from the seller if the goods do not conform and are rejected.

(3) Unless otherwise agreed and subject to the provisions of this Article on C.I.F. contracts (subsection (3) of Section 2–321), the buyer is not entitled to inspect the goods before payment of the price when the contract provides

(a) for delivery "C.O.D." or on other like terms; or

(b) for payment against documents of title, except where such payment is due only after the goods are to become available for inspection.

(4) A place or method of inspection fixed by the parties is presumed to be exclusive but unless otherwise expressly agreed it does not postpone identification or shift the place for delivery or for passing the risk of loss. If compliance becomes impossible, inspection shall be as provided in this section unless the place or method fixed was clearly intended as an indispensable condition failure of which avoids the contract.

§ 2–514. When Documents Deliverable on Acceptance; When on Payment.

Unless otherwise agreed documents against which a draft is drawn are to be delivered to the drawee on acceptance of the draft if it is payable more than three days after presentment; otherwise, only on payment.

§ 2–515. Preserving Evidence of Goods in Dispute.

In furtherance of the adjustment of any claim or dispute

(a) either party on reasonable notification to the other and for the purpose of ascertaining the facts and preserving evidence has the right to inspect, test and sample the goods including such of them as may be in the possession or control of the other; and

(b) the parties may agree to a third party inspection or survey to determine the conformity or condition of the goods and may agree that the findings shall be binding upon them in any subsequent litigation or adjustment.

Part 6 Breach, Repudiation and Excuse

§ 2–601. Buyer's Rights on Improper Delivery.

Subject to the provisions of this Article on breach in installment contracts (Section 2–612) and unless otherwise agreed under the sections on contractual limitations of remedy (Sections 2–718 and 2–719), if the goods or the tender of delivery fail in any respect to conform to the contract, the buyer may

(a) reject the whole; or

(b) accept the whole; or

(c) accept any commercial unit or units and reject the rest.

§ 2–602. Manner and Effect of Rightful Rejection.

(1) Rejection of goods must be within a reasonable time after their delivery or tender. It is ineffective unless the buyer seasonably notifies the seller.

(2) Subject to the provisions of the two following sections on rejected goods (Sections 2–603 and 2–604),

(a) after rejection any exercise of ownership by the buyer with respect to any commercial unit is wrongful as against the seller; and

(b) if the buyer has before rejection taken physical possession of goods in which he does not have a security interest under the provisions of this Article (subsection (3) of Section 2–711), he is under a duty after rejection to hold them with reasonable care at the seller's disposition for a time sufficient to permit the seller to remove them; but

(c) the buyer has no further obligations with regard to goods rightfully rejected.

(3) The seller's rights with respect to goods wrongfully rejected are governed by the provisions of this Article on Seller's remedies in general (Section 2–703).

§ 2–603. Merchant Buyer's Duties as to Rightfully Rejected Goods.

(1) Subject to any security interest in the buyer (subsection (3) of Section 2–711), when the seller has no agent or place of business at the market of rejection a merchant buyer is under a duty after rejection of goods in his possession or control to follow any reasonable instructions received from the seller with respect to the goods and in the absence of such instructions to make reasonable efforts to sell them for the seller's account if they are perishable or threaten to decline in value speedily. Instructions are not reasonable if on demand indemnity for expenses is not forthcoming.

(2) When the buyer sells goods under subsection (1), he is entitled to reimbursement from the seller or out of the proceeds for reasonable expenses of caring for and selling them, and if the expenses include no selling commission then to such commission as is usual in the trade or if there is none to a reasonable sum not exceeding ten per cent on the gross proceeds.

(3) In complying with this section the buyer is held only to good faith and good faith conduct hereunder is neither acceptance nor conversion nor the basis of an action for damages.

§ 2–604. Buyer's Options as to Salvage of Rightfully Rejected Goods.

Subject to the provisions of the immediately preceding section on perishables if the seller gives no instructions within a reasonable time after notification of rejection the buyer may store the rejected goods for the seller's account or reship them to him or resell them for the seller's account with reimbursement as provided in the preceding section. Such action is not acceptance or conversion.

§ 2–605. Waiver of Buyer's Objections by Failure to Particularize.

(1) The buyer's failure to state in connection with rejection a particular defect which is ascertainable by reasonable inspection precludes him from relying on the unstated defect to justify rejection or to establish breach

(a) where the seller could have cured it if stated seasonably; or

(b) between merchants when the seller has after rejection made a request in writing for a full and final written statement of all defects on which the buyer proposes to rely.

(2) Payment against documents made without reservation of rights precludes recovery of the payment for defects apparent on the face of the documents.

§ 2–606. What Constitutes Acceptance of Goods.

(1) Acceptance of goods occurs when the buyer

(a) after a reasonable opportunity to inspect the goods signifies to the seller that the goods are conforming or that he will take or retain them in spite of their nonconformity; or

(b) fails to make an effective rejection (subsection (1) of Section 2–602), but such acceptance does not occur until the buyer has had a reasonable opportunity to inspect them; or

(c) does any act inconsistent with the seller's ownership; but if such act is wrongful as against the seller it is an acceptance only if ratified by him.

(2) Acceptance of a part of any commercial unit is acceptance of that entire unit.

§ 2–607. Effect of Acceptance; Notice of Breach; Burden of Establishing Breach After Acceptance; Notice of Claim or Litigation to Person Answerable Over.

(1) The buyer must pay at the contract rate for any goods accepted.

(2) Acceptance of goods by the buyer precludes rejection of the goods accepted and if made with knowledge of a non-conformity cannot be revoked because of it unless the acceptance was on the reasonable assumption that the non-conformity would be sea-

sonably cured but acceptance does not of itself impair any other remedy provided by this Article for non-conformity.

(3) Where a tender has been accepted

(a) the buyer must within a reasonable time after he discovers or should have discovered any breach notify the seller of breach or be barred from any remedy; and

(b) if the claim is one for infringement or the like (subsection (3) of Section 2–312) and the buyer is sued as a result of such a breach he must so notify the seller within a reasonable time after he receives notice of the litigation or be barred from any remedy over for liability established by the litigation.

(4) The burden is on the buyer to establish any breach with respect to the goods accepted.

(5) Where the buyer is sued for breach of a warranty or other obligation for which his seller is answerable over

(a) he may give his seller written notice of the litigation. If the notice states that the seller may come in and defend and that if the seller does not do so he will be bound in any action against him by his buyer by any determination of fact common to the two litigations, then unless the seller after seasonable receipt of the notice does come in and defend he is so bound.

(b) if the claim is one for infringement or the like (subsection (3) of Section 2–312) the original seller may demand in writing that his buyer turn over to him control of the litigation including settlement or else be barred from any remedy over and if he also agrees to bear all expense and to satisfy any adverse judgment, then unless the buyer after seasonable receipt of the demand does turn over control the buyer is so barred.

(6) The provisions of subsections (3), (4) and (5) apply to any obligation of a buyer to hold the seller harmless against infringement or the like (subsection (3) of Section 2–312).

§ 2–608. Revocation of Acceptance in Whole or in Part.

(1) The buyer may revoke his acceptance of a lot or commercial unit whose non-conformity substantially impairs its value to him if he has accepted it

(a) on the reasonable assumption that its nonconformity would be cured and it has not been seasonably cured; or

(b) without discovery of such non-conformity if his acceptance was reasonably induced either by the difficulty of discovery before acceptance or by the seller's assurances.

(2) Revocation of acceptance must occur within a reasonable time after the buyer discovers or should have discovered the ground for it and before any substantial change in condition of the goods which is not caused by their own defects. It is not effective until the buyer notifies the seller of it.

(3) A buyer who so revokes has the same rights and duties with regard to the goods involved as if he had rejected them.

§ 2–609. Right to Adequate Assurance of Performance.

(1) A contract for sale imposes an obligation on each party that the other's expectation of receiving due performance will not be impaired. When reasonable grounds for insecurity arise with respect to the performance of either party the other may in writing demand adequate assurance of due performance and until he receives such assurance may if commercially reasonable suspend any performance for which he has not already received the agreed return.

(2) Between merchants the reasonableness of grounds for insecurity and the adequacy of any assurance offered shall be determined according to commercial standards.

(3) Acceptance of any improper delivery or payment does not prejudice the party's right to demand adequate assurance of future performance.

(4) After receipt of a justified demand failure to provide within a reasonable time not exceeding thirty days such assurance of due performance as is adequate under the circumstances of the particular case is a repudiation of the contract.

§ 2–610. Anticipatory Repudiation.

When either party repudiates the contract with respect to a performance not yet due the loss of which will substantially impair the value of the contract to the other, the aggrieved party may

(a) for a commercially reasonable time await performance by the repudiating party; or

(b) resort to any remedy for breach (Section 2–703 or Section 2–711), even though he has notified the repudiating party that he would await the latter's performance and has urged retraction; and

(c) in either case suspend his own performance or proceed in accordance with the provisions of this Article on the seller's right to identify goods to the contract notwithstanding breach or to salvage unfinished goods (Section 2–704).

§ 2–611. Retraction of Anticipatory Repudiation.

(1) Until the repudiating party's next performance is due he can retract his repudiation unless the aggrieved party has since the repudiation cancelled or materially changed his position or otherwise indicated that he considers the repudiation final.

(2) Retraction may be by any method which clearly indicates to the aggrieved party that the repudiating party intends to perform, but must include any assurance justifiably demanded under the provisions of this Article (Section 2–609).

(3) Retraction reinstates the repudiating party's rights under the contract with due excuse and allowance to the aggrieved party for any delay occasioned by the repudiation.

§ 2–612. "Installment Contract"; Breach.

(1) An "installment contract" is one which requires or authorizes the delivery of goods in separate lots to be separately accepted, even though the contract contains a clause "each delivery is a separate contract" or its equivalent.

(2) The buyer may reject any installment which is non-conforming if the non-conformity substantially impairs the value of that installment and cannot be cured or if the non-conformity is a defect in the required documents; but if the non-conformity does not fall within subsection (3) and the seller gives adequate assurance of its cure the buyer must accept that installment.

(3) Whenever non-conformity or default with respect to one or more installments substantially impairs the value of the whole contract there is a breach of the whole. But the aggrieved party reinstates the contract if he accepts a non-conforming

installment without seasonably notifying of cancellation or if he brings an action with respect only to past installments or demands performance as to future installments.

§ 2–613. Casualty to Identified Goods.

Where the contract requires for its performance goods identified when the contract is made, and the goods suffer casualty without fault of either party before the risk of loss passes to the buyer, or in a proper case under a "no arrival, no sale" term (Section 2–324) then

(a) if the loss is total the contract is avoided; and

(b) if the loss is partial or the goods have so deteriorated as no longer to conform to the contract the buyer may nevertheless demand inspection and at his option either treat the contract as voided or accept the goods with due allowance from the contract price for the deterioration or the deficiency in quantity but without further right against the seller.

§ 2–614. Substituted Performance.

(1) Where without fault of either party the agreed berthing, loading, or unloading facilities fail or an agreed type of carrier becomes unavailable or the agreed manner of delivery otherwise becomes commercially impracticable but a commercially reasonable substitute is available, such substitute performance must be tendered and accepted.

(2) If the agreed means or manner of payment fails because of domestic or foreign governmental regulation, the seller may withhold or stop delivery unless the buyer provides a means or manner of payment which is commercially a substantial equivalent. If delivery has already been taken, payment by the means or in the manner provided by the regulation discharges the buyer's obligation unless the regulation is discriminatory, oppressive or predatory.

§ 2–615. Excuse by Failure of Presupposed Conditions.

Except so far as a seller may have assumed a greater obligation and subject to the preceding section on substituted performance:

(a) Delay in delivery or non-delivery in whole or in part by a seller who complies with paragraphs (b) and (c) is not a breach of his duty under a contract for sale if performance as agreed has been made impracticable by the occurrence of a contingency the nonoccurrence of which was a basic assumption on which the contract was made or by compliance in good faith with any applicable foreign or domestic governmental regulation or order whether or not it later proves to be invalid.

(b) Where the causes mentioned in paragraph (a) affect only a part of the seller's capacity to perform, he must allocate production and deliveries among his customers but may at his option include regular customers not then under contract as well as his own requirements for further manufacture. He may so allocate in any manner which is fair and reasonable.

(c) The seller must notify the buyer seasonably that there will be delay or non-delivery and, when allocation is required under paragraph (b), of the estimated quota thus made available for the buyer.

§ 2–616. Procedure on Notice Claiming Excuse.

(1) Where the buyer receives notification of a material or indefinite delay or an allocation justified under the preceding section he may by written notification to the seller as to any delivery concerned, and where the prospective deficiency substantially impairs the value of the whole contract under the provisions of this Article relating to breach of installment contracts (Section 2–612), then also as to the whole,

(a) terminate and thereby discharge any unexecuted portion of the contract; or

(b) modify the contract by agreeing to take his available quota in substitution.

(2) If after receipt of such notification from the seller the buyer fails so to modify the contract within a reasonable time not exceeding thirty days the contract lapses with respect to any deliveries affected.

(3) The provisions of this section may not be negated by agreement except in so far as the seller has assumed a greater obligation under the preceding section.

Part 7 Remedies

§ 2–701. Remedies for Breach of Collateral Contracts Not Impaired.

Remedies for breach of any obligation or promise collateral or ancillary to a contract for sale are not impaired by the provisions of this Article.

§ 2–702. Seller's Remedies on Discovery of Buyer's Insolvency.

(1) Where the seller discovers the buyer to be insolvent he may refuse delivery except for cash including payment for all goods theretofore delivered under the contract, and stop delivery under this Article (Section 2–705).

(2) Where the seller discovers that the buyer has received goods on credit while insolvent he may reclaim the goods upon demand made within ten days after the receipt, but if misrepresentation of solvency has been made to the particular seller in writing within three months before delivery the ten day limitation does not apply. Except as provided in this subsection the seller may not base a right to reclaim goods on the buyer's fraudulent or innocent misrepresentation of solvency or of intent to pay.

(3) The seller's right to reclaim under subsection (2) is subject to the rights of a buyer in ordinary course or other good faith purchaser under this Article (Section 2–403). Successful reclamation of goods excludes all other remedies with respect to them.

§ 2–703. Seller's Remedies in General.

Where the buyer wrongfully rejects or revokes acceptance of goods or fails to make a payment due on or before delivery or repudiates with respect to a part or the whole, then with respect to any goods directly affected and, if the breach is of the whole contract (Section 2–612), then also with respect to the whole undelivered balance, the aggrieved seller may

(a) withhold delivery of such goods;

(b) stop delivery by any bailee as hereafter provided (Section 2–705);

(c) proceed under the next section respecting goods still unidentified to the contract;

(d) resell and recover damages as hereafter provided (Section 2–706);

(e) recover damages for non-acceptance (Section 2–708) or in a proper case the price (Section 2–709);

(f) cancel.

§ 2–704. Seller's Right to Identify Goods to the Contract Notwithstanding Breach or to Salvage Unfinished Goods.

(1) An aggrieved seller under the preceding section may

(a) identify to the contract conforming goods not already identified if at the time he learned of the breach they are in his possession or control;

(b) treat as the subject of resale goods which have demonstrably been intended for the particular contract even though those goods are unfinished.

(2) Where the goods are unfinished an aggrieved seller may in the exercise of reasonable commercial judgment for the purposes of avoiding loss and of effective realization either complete the manufacture and wholly identify the goods to the contract or cease manufacture and resell for scrap or salvage value or proceed in any other reasonable manner.

§ 2–705. Seller's Stoppage of Delivery in Transit or Otherwise.

(1) The seller may stop delivery of goods in the possession of a carrier or other bailee when he discovers the buyer to be insolvent (Section 2–702) and may stop delivery of carload, truckload, planeload or larger shipments of express or freight when the buyer repudiates or fails to make a payment due before delivery or if for any other reason the seller has a right to withhold or reclaim the goods.

(2) As against such buyer the seller may stop delivery until

(a) receipt of the goods by the buyer; or

(b) acknowledgment to the buyer by any bailee of the goods except a carrier that the bailee holds the goods for the buyer; or

(c) such acknowledgment to the buyer by a carrier by reshipment or as warehouseman; or

(d) negotiation to the buyer of any negotiable document of title covering the goods.

(3) (a) To stop delivery the seller must so notify as to enable the bailee by reasonable diligence to prevent delivery of the goods.

(b) After such notification the bailee must hold and deliver the goods according to the directions of the seller but the seller is liable to the bailee for any ensuing charges or damages.

(c) If a negotiable document of title has been issued for goods the bailee is not obliged to obey a notification to stop until surrender of the document.

(d) A carrier who has issued a non-negotiable bill of lading is not obliged to obey a notification to stop received from a person other than the consignor.

§ 2–706. Seller's Resale Including Contract for Resale.

(1) Under the conditions stated in Section 2–703 on seller's remedies, the seller may resell the goods concerned or the undelivered balance thereof. Where the resale is made in good faith and in a commercially reasonable manner the seller may recover the difference between the resale price and the contract price together with any incidental damages allowed under the provisions of this Article (Section 2–710), but less expenses saved in consequence of the buyer's breach.

(2) Except as otherwise provided in subsection (3) or unless otherwise agreed resale may be at public or private sale including sale by way of one or more contracts to sell or of identification to an existing contract of the seller. Sale may be as a unit or in parcels and at any time and place and on any terms but every aspect of the sale including the method, manner, time, place and terms must be commercially reasonable. The resale must be reasonably identified as referring to the broken contract, but it is not necessary that the goods be in existence or that any or all of them have been identified to the contract before the breach.

(3) Where the resale is at private sale the seller must give the buyer reasonable notification of his intention to resell.

(4) Where the resale is at public sale

(a) only identified goods can be sold except where there is a recognized market for a public sale of futures in goods of the kind; and

(b) it must be made at a usual place or market for public sale if one is reasonably available and except in the case of goods which are perishable or threaten to decline in value speedily the seller must give the buyer reasonable notice of the time and place of the resale; and

(c) if the goods are not to be within the view of those attending the sale the notification of sale must state the place where the goods are located and provide for their reasonable inspection by prospective bidders; and

(d) the seller may buy.

(5) A purchaser who buys in good faith at a resale takes the goods free of any rights of the original buyer even though the seller fails to comply with one or more of the requirements of this section.

(6) The seller is not accountable to the buyer for any profit made on any resale. A person in the position of a seller (Section 2–707) or a buyer who has rightfully rejected or justifiably revoked acceptance must account for any excess over the amount of his security interest, as hereinafter defined (subsection (3) of Section 2–711).

§ 2–707. "Person in the Position of a Seller".

(1) A "person in the position of a seller" includes as against a principal an agent who has paid or become responsible for the price of goods on behalf of his principal or anyone who otherwise holds a security interest or other right in goods similar to that of a seller.

(2) A person in the position of a seller may as provided in this Article withhold or stop delivery (Section 2–705) and resell (Section 2–706) and recover incidental damages (Section 2–710).

§ 2–708. Seller's Damages for Non-Acceptance or Repudiation.

(1) Subject to subsection (2) and to the provisions of this Article with respect to proof of market price (Section 2–723), the measure of damages for non-acceptance or repudiation by the buyer is the difference between the market price at the time and place for tender and the unpaid contract price together with any incidental damages provided in this Article (Section 2–710), but less expenses saved in consequence of the buyer's breach.

(2) If the measure of damages provided in subsection (1) is inadequate to put the seller in as good a position as performance would have done then the measure of damages is the profit (including reasonable overhead) which the seller would have made from full performance by the buyer, together with

any incidental damages provided in this Article (Section 2–710), due allowance for costs reasonably incurred and due credit for payments or proceeds of resale.

§ 2–709. Action for the Price.

(1) When the buyer fails to pay the price as it becomes due the seller may recover, together with any incidental damages under the next section, the price

    (a) of goods accepted or of conforming goods lost or damaged within a commercially reasonable time after risk of their loss has passed to the buyer; and

    (b) of goods identified to the contract if the seller is unable after reasonable effort to resell them at a reasonable price or the circumstances reasonably indicate that such effort will be unavailing.

(2) Where the seller sues for the price he must hold for the buyer any goods which have been identified to the contract and are still in his control except that if resale becomes possible he may resell them at any time prior to the collection of the judgment. The net proceeds of any such resale must be credited to the buyer and payment of the judgment entitles him to any goods not resold.

(3) After the buyer has wrongfully rejected or revoked acceptance of the goods or has failed to make a payment due or has repudiated (Section 2–610), a seller who is held not entitled to the price under this section shall nevertheless be awarded damages for non-acceptance under the preceding section.

§ 2–710. Seller's Incidental Damages.

Incidental damages to an aggrieved seller include any commercially reasonable charges, expenses or commissions incurred in stopping delivery, in the transportation, care and custody of goods after the buyer's breach, in connection with return or resale of the goods or otherwise resulting from the breach.

§ 2–711. Buyer's Remedies in General; Buyer's Security Interest in Rejected Goods.

(1) Where the seller fails to make delivery or repudiates or the buyer rightfully rejects or justifiably revokes acceptance then with respect to any goods involved, and with respect to the whole if the breach goes to the whole contract (Section 2–612), the buyer may cancel and whether or not he has done so may in addition to recovering so much of the price as has been paid

    (a) "cover" and have damages under the next section as to all the goods affected whether or not they have been identified to the contract; or

    (b) recover damages for non-delivery as provided in this Article (Section 2–713).

(2) Where the seller fails to deliver or repudiates the buyer may also

    (a) if the goods have been identified recover them as provided in this Article (Section 2–502); or

    (b) in a proper case obtain specific performance or replevy the goods as provided in this Article (Section 2–716).

(3) On rightful rejection or justifiable revocation of acceptance a buyer has a security interest in goods in his possession or control for any payments made on their price and any expenses reasonably incurred in their inspection, receipt, transportation, care and custody and may hold such goods and resell them in like manner as an aggrieved seller (Section 2–706).

§ 2–712. "Cover"; Buyer's Procurement of Substitute Goods.

(1) After a breach within the preceding section the buyer may "cover" by making in good faith and without unreasonable delay any reasonable purchase of or contract to purchase goods in substitution for those due from the seller.

(2) The buyer may recover from the seller as damages the difference between the cost of cover and the contract price together with any incidental or consequential damages as hereinafter defined (Section 2–715), but less expenses saved in consequence of the seller's breach.

(3) Failure of the buyer to effect cover within this section does not bar him from any other remedy.

§ 2–713. Buyer's Damages for Non-Delivery or Repudiation.

(1) Subject to the provisions of this Article with respect to proof of market price (Section 2–723), the measure of damages for non-delivery or repudiation by the seller is the difference between the market price at the time when the buyer learned of the breach and the contract price together with any incidental and consequential damages provided in this Article (Section 2–715), but less expenses saved in consequence of the seller's breach.

(2) Market price is to be determined as of the place for tender or, in cases of rejection after arrival or revocation of acceptance, as of the place of arrival.

§ 2–714. Buyer's Damages for Breach in Regard to Accepted Goods.

(1) Where the buyer has accepted goods and given notification (subsection (3) of Section 2–607) he may recover as damages for any non-conformity of tender the loss resulting in the ordinary course of events from the seller's breach as determined in any manner which is reasonable.

(2) The measure of damages for breach of warranty is the difference at the time and place of acceptance between the value of the goods accepted and the value they would have had if they had been as warranted, unless special circumstances show proximate damages of a different amount.

(3) In a proper case any incidental and consequential damages under the next section may also be recovered.

§ 2–715. Buyer's Incidental and Consequential Damages.

(1) Incidental damages resulting from the seller's breach include expenses reasonably incurred in inspection, receipt, transportation and care and custody of goods rightfully rejected, any commercially reasonable charges, expenses or commissions in connection with effecting cover and any other reasonable expense incident to the delay or other breach.

(2) Consequential damages resulting from the seller's breach include

    (a) any loss resulting from general or particular requirements and needs of which the seller at the time of contracting had reason to know and which could not reasonably be prevented by cover or otherwise; and

    (b) injury to person or property proximately resulting from any breach of warranty.

§ 2–716. Buyer's Right to Specific Performance or Replevin.

(1) Specific performance may be decreed where the goods are unique or in other proper circumstances.

(2) The decree for specific performance may include such terms and conditions as to payment of the price, damages, or other relief as the court may deem just.

(3) The buyer has a right of replevin for goods identified to the contract if after reasonable effort he is unable to effect cover for such goods or the circumstances reasonably indicate that such effort will be unavailing or if the goods have been shipped under reservation and satisfaction of the security interest in them has been made or tendered. In the case of goods bought for personal, family, or household purposes, the buyer's right of replevin vests upon acquisition of a special property, even if the seller had not then repudiated or failed to deliver.

As amended in 1999.

§ 2–717. Deduction of Damages From the Price.

The buyer on notifying the seller of his intention to do so may deduct all or any part of the damages resulting from any breach of the contract from any part of the price still due under the same contract.

§ 2–718. Liquidation or Limitation of Damages; Deposits.

(1) Damages for breach by either party may be liquidated in the agreement but only at an amount which is reasonable in the light of the anticipated or actual harm caused by the breach, the difficulties of proof of loss, and the inconvenience or nonfeasibility of otherwise obtaining an adequate remedy. A term fixing unreasonably large liquidated damages is void as a penalty.

(2) Where the seller justifiably withholds delivery of goods because of the buyer's breach, the buyer is entitled to restitution of any amount by which the sum of his payments exceeds

(a) the amount to which the seller is entitled by virtue of terms liquidating the seller's damages in accordance with subsection (1), or

(b) in the absence of such terms, twenty per cent of the value of the total performance for which the buyer is obligated under the contract or $500, whichever is smaller.

(3) The buyer's right to restitution under subsection (2) is subject to offset to the extent that the seller establishes

(a) a right to recover damages under the provisions of this Article other than subsection (1), and

(b) the amount or value of any benefits received by the buyer directly or indirectly by reason of the contract.

(4) Where a seller has received payment in goods their reasonable value or the proceeds of their resale shall be treated as payments for the purposes of subsection (2); but if the seller has notice of the buyer's breach before reselling goods received in part performance, his resale is subject to the conditions laid down in this Article on resale by an aggrieved seller (Section 2–706).

§ 2–719. Contractual Modification or Limitation of Remedy.

(1) Subject to the provisions of subsections (2) and (3) of this section and of the preceding section on liquidation and limitation of damages,

(a) the agreement may provide for remedies in addition to or in substitution for those provided in this Article and may limit or alter the measure of damages recoverable under this Article, as by limiting the buyer's remedies to return of the goods and repayment of the price or to repair and replacement of nonconforming goods or parts; and

(b) resort to a remedy as provided is optional unless the remedy is expressly agreed to be exclusive, in which case it is the sole remedy.

(2) Where circumstances cause an exclusive or limited remedy to fail of its essential purpose, remedy may be had as provided in this Act.

(3) Consequential damages may be limited or excluded unless the limitation or exclusion is unconscionable. Limitation of consequential damages for injury to the person in the case of consumer goods is prima facie unconscionable but limitation of damages where the loss is commercial is not.

§ 2–720. Effect of "Cancellation" or "Rescission" on Claims for Antecedent Breach.

Unless the contrary intention clearly appears, expressions of "cancellation" or "rescission" of the contract or the like shall not be construed as a renunciation or discharge of any claim in damages for an antecedent breach.

§ 2–721. Remedies for Fraud.

Remedies for material misrepresentation or fraud include all remedies available under this Article for non-fraudulent breach. Neither rescission or a claim for rescission of the contract for sale nor rejection or return of the goods shall bar or be deemed inconsistent with a claim for damages or other remedy.

§ 2–722. Who Can Sue Third Parties for Injury to Goods.

Where a third party so deals with goods which have been identified to a contract for sale as to cause actionable injury to a party to that contract

(a) a right of action against the third party is in either party to the contract for sale who has title to or a security interest or a special property or an insurable interest in the goods; and if the goods have been destroyed or converted a right of action is also in the party who either bore the risk of loss under the contract for sale or has since the injury assumed that risk as against the other;

(b) if at the time of the injury the party plaintiff did not bear the risk of loss as against the other party to the contract for sale and there is no arrangement between them for disposition of the recovery, his suit or settlement is, subject to his own interest, as a fiduciary for the other party to the contract;

(c) either party may with the consent of the other sue for the benefit of whom it may concern.

§ 2–723. Proof of Market Price: Time and Place.

(1) If an action based on anticipatory repudiation comes to trial before the time for performance with respect to some or all of the goods, any damages based on market price (Section 2–708 or Section 2–713) shall be determined according to the price of such goods prevailing at the time when the aggrieved party learned of the repudiation.

(2) If evidence of a price prevailing at the times or places described in this Article is not readily available the price

prevailing within any reasonable time before or after the time described or at any other place which in commercial judgment or under usage of trade would serve as a reasonable substitute for the one described may be used, making any proper allowance for the cost of transporting the goods to or from such other place.

(3) Evidence of a relevant price prevailing at a time or place other than the one described in this Article offered by one party is not admissible unless and until he has given the other party such notice as the court finds sufficient to prevent unfair surprise.

§ 2–724. Admissibility of Market Quotations.

Whenever the prevailing price or value of any goods regularly bought and sold in any established commodity market is in issue, reports in official publications or trade journals or in newspapers or periodicals of general circulation published as the reports of such market shall be admissible in evidence. The circumstances of the preparation of such a report may be shown to affect its weight but not its admissibility.

§ 2–725. Statute of Limitations in Contracts for Sale.

(1) An action for breach of any contract for sale must be commenced within four years after the cause of action has accrued. By the original agreement the parties may reduce the period of limitation to not less than one year but may not extend it.

(2) A cause of action accrues when the breach occurs, regardless of the aggrieved party's lack of knowledge of the breach. A breach of warranty occurs when tender of delivery is made, except that where a warranty explicitly extends to future performance of the goods and discovery of the breach must await the time of such performance the cause of action accrues when the breach is or should have been discovered.

(3) Where an action commenced within the time limited by subsection (1) is so terminated as to leave available a remedy by another action for the same breach such other action may be commenced after the expiration of the time limited and within six months after the termination of the first action unless the termination resulted from voluntary discontinuance or from dismissal for failure or neglect to prosecute.

(4) This section does not alter the law on tolling of the statute of limitations nor does it apply to causes of action which have accrued before this Act becomes effective.

ARTICLE 2A
LEASES

Part 1 General Provisions

§ 2A–101. Short Title.

This Article shall be known and may be cited as the Uniform Commercial Code—Leases.

§ 2A–102. Scope.

This Article applies to any transaction, regardless of form, that creates a lease.

§ 2A–103. Definitions and Index of Definitions.

(1) In this Article unless the context otherwise requires:

(a) "Buyer in ordinary course of business" means a person who in good faith and without knowledge that the sale to him [or her] is in violation of the ownership rights or security interest or leasehold interest of a third party in the goods buys in ordinary course from a person in the business of selling goods of that kind but does not include a pawnbroker. "Buying" may be for cash or by exchange of other property or on secured or unsecured credit and includes receiving goods or documents of title under a preexisting contract for sale but does not include a transfer in bulk or as security for or in total or partial satisfaction of a money debt.

(b) "Cancellation" occurs when either party puts an end to the lease contract for default by the other party.

(c) "Commercial unit" means such a unit of goods as by commercial usage is a single whole for purposes of lease and division of which materially impairs its character or value on the market or in use. A commercial unit may be a single article, as a machine, or a set of articles, as a suite of furniture or a line of machinery, or a quantity, as a gross or carload, or any other unit treated in use or in the relevant market as a single whole.

(d) "Conforming" goods or performance under a lease contract means goods or performance that are in accordance with the obligations under the lease contract.

(e) "Consumer lease" means a lease that a lessor regularly engaged in the business of leasing or selling makes to a lessee who is an individual and who takes under the lease primarily for a personal, family, or household purpose [, if the total payments to be made under the lease contract, excluding payments for options to renew or buy, do not exceed $_____].

(f) "Fault" means wrongful act, omission, breach, or default.

(g) "Finance lease" means a lease with respect to which:

(i) the lessor does not select, manufacture or supply the goods;

(ii) the lessor acquires the goods or the right to possession and use of the goods in connection with the lease; and

(iii) one of the following occurs:

(A) the lessee receives a copy of the contract by which the lessor acquired the goods or the right to possession and use of the goods before signing the lease contract;

(B) the lessee's approval of the contract by which the lessor acquired the goods or the right to possession and use of the goods is a condition to effectiveness of the lease contract;

(C) the lessee, before signing the lease contract, receives an accurate and complete statement designating the promises and warranties, and any disclaimers of warranties, limitations or modifications of remedies, or liquidated damages, including those of a third party, such as the manufacturer of the goods, provided to the lessor by the person supplying the goods in connection with or as part of the contract by which the lessor acquired the goods or the right to possession and use of the goods; or

(D) if the lease is not a consumer lease, the lessor, before the lessee signs the lease contract, informs the lessee in writing (a) of the identity of the person supplying the goods to the lessor, unless the lessee has selected that person and directed the lessor to acquire the goods or the right to possession and use of the goods from that person, (b) that the lessee is entitled under this Article to any promises and warranties, including those of any third party, provided to the lessor by the person supplying the goods in connection with or as part of the contract by which the lessor acquired the goods or the right to possession and use of the goods, and (c) that the lessee may communicate with the person supplying the goods to the lessor and receive an accurate and complete statement of those promises and warranties, including any disclaimers and limitations of them or of remedies.

(h) "Goods" means all things that are movable at the time of identification to the lease contract, or are fixtures (Section 2A–309), but the term does not include money, documents, instruments, accounts, chattel paper, general intangibles, or minerals or the like, including oil and gas, before extraction. The term also includes the unborn young of animals.

(i) "Installment lease contract" means a lease contract that authorizes or requires the delivery of goods in separate lots to be separately accepted, even though the lease contract contains a clause "each delivery is a separate lease" or its equivalent.

(j) "Lease" means a transfer of the right to possession and use of goods for a term in return for consideration, but a sale, including a sale on approval or a sale or return, or retention or creation of a security interest is not a lease. Unless the context clearly indicates otherwise, the term includes a sublease.

(k) "Lease agreement" means the bargain, with respect to the lease, of the lessor and the lessee in fact as found in their language or by implication from other circumstances including course of dealing or usage of trade or course of performance as provided in this Article. Unless the context clearly indicates otherwise, the term includes a sublease agreement.

(l) "Lease contract" means the total legal obligation that results from the lease agreement as affected by this Article and any other applicable rules of law. Unless the context clearly indicates otherwise, the term includes a sublease contract.

(m) "Leasehold interest" means the interest of the lessor or the lessee under a lease contract.

(n) "Lessee" means a person who acquires the right to possession and use of goods under a lease. Unless the context clearly indicates otherwise, the term includes a sublessee.

(o) "Lessee in ordinary course of business" means a person who in good faith and without knowledge that the lease to him [or her] is in violation of the ownership rights or security interest or leasehold interest of a third party in the goods, leases in ordinary course from a person in the business of selling or leasing goods of that kind but does not include a pawnbroker. "Leasing" may be for cash or by exchange of other property or on secured or unsecured credit and includes receiving goods or documents of title under a pre-existing lease contract but does not include a transfer in bulk or as security for or in total or partial satisfaction of a money debt.

(p) "Lessor" means a person who transfers the right to possession and use of goods under a lease. Unless the context clearly indicates otherwise, the term includes a sublessor.

(q) "Lessor's residual interest" means the lessor's interest in the goods after expiration, termination, or cancellation of the lease contract.

(r) "Lien" means a charge against or interest in goods to secure payment of a debt or performance of an obligation, but the term does not include a security interest.

(s) "Lot" means a parcel or a single article that is the subject matter of a separate lease or delivery, whether or not it is sufficient to perform the lease contract.

(t) "Merchant lessee" means a lessee that is a merchant with respect to goods of the kind subject to the lease.

(u) "Present value" means the amount as of a date certain of one or more sums payable in the future, discounted to the date certain. The discount is determined by the interest rate specified by the parties if the rate was not manifestly unreasonable at the time the transaction was entered into; otherwise, the discount is determined by a commercially reasonable rate that takes into account the facts and circumstances of each case at the time the transaction was entered into.

(v) "Purchase" includes taking by sale, lease, mortgage, security interest, pledge, gift, or any other voluntary transaction creating an interest in goods.

(w) "Sublease" means a lease of goods the right to possession and use of which was acquired by the lessor as a lessee under an existing lease.

(x) "Supplier" means a person from whom a lessor buys or leases goods to be leased under a finance lease.

(y) "Supply contract" means a contract under which a lessor buys or leases goods to be leased.

(z) "Termination" occurs when either party pursuant to a power created by agreement or law puts an end to the lease contract otherwise than for default.

(2) Other definitions applying to this Article and the sections in which they appear are:

"Accessions". Section 2A–310(1).

"Construction mortgage". Section 2A–309(1)(d).

"Encumbrance". Section 2A–309(1)(e).

"Fixtures". Section 2A–309(1)(a).

"Fixture filing". Section 2A–309(1)(b).

"Purchase money lease". Section 2A–309(1)(c).

(3) The following definitions in other Articles apply to this Article:

"Accounts". Section 9–106.

"Between merchants". Section 2–104(3).

"Buyer". Section 2–103(1)(a).

"Chattel paper". Section 9–105(1)(b).

"Consumer goods". Section 9–109(1).

"Document". Section 9–105(1)(f).

"Entrusting". Section 2–403(3).

"General intangibles". Section 9–106.

"Good faith". Section 2–103(1)(b).

"Instrument". Section 9–105(1)(i).

"Merchant". Section 2–104(1).

"Mortgage". Section 9–105(1)(j).

"Pursuant to commitment". Section 9–105(1)(k).

"Receipt". Section 2–103(1)(c).

"Sale". Section 2–106(1).

"Sale on approval". Section 2–326.

"Sale or return". Section 2–326.

"Seller". Section 2–103(1)(d).

(4) In addition Article 1 contains general definitions and principles of construction and interpretation applicable throughout this Article.

As amended in 1990 and 1999.

§ 2A–104. Leases Subject to Other Law.

(1) A lease, although subject to this Article, is also subject to any applicable:

(a) certificate of title statute of this State: (list any certificate of title statutes covering automobiles, trailers, mobile homes, boats, farm tractors, and the like);

(b) certificate of title statute of another jurisdiction (Section 2A–105); or

(c) consumer protection statute of this State, or final consumer protection decision of a court of this State existing on the effective date of this Article.

(2) In case of conflict between this Article, other than Sections 2A–105, 2A–304(3), and 2A–305(3), and a statute or decision referred to in subsection (1), the statute or decision controls.

(3) Failure to comply with an applicable law has only the effect specified therein.

As amended in 1990.

§ 2A–105. Territorial Application of Article to Goods Covered by Certificate of Title.

Subject to the provisions of Sections 2A–304(3) and 2A–305(3), with respect to goods covered by a certificate of title issued under a statute of this State or of another jurisdiction, compliance and the effect of compliance or noncompliance with a certificate of title statute are governed by the law (including the conflict of laws rules) of the jurisdiction issuing the certificate until the earlier of (a) surrender of the certificate, or (b) four months after the goods are removed from that jurisdiction and thereafter until a new certificate of title is issued by another jurisdiction.

§ 2A–106. Limitation on Power of Parties to Consumer Lease to Choose Applicable Law and Judicial Forum.

(1) If the law chosen by the parties to a consumer lease is that of a jurisdiction other than a jurisdiction in which the lessee resides at the time the lease agreement becomes enforceable or within 30 days thereafter or in which the goods are to be used, the choice is not enforceable.

(2) If the judicial forum chosen by the parties to a consumer lease is a forum that would not otherwise have jurisdiction over the lessee, the choice is not enforceable.

§ 2A–107. Waiver or Renunciation of Claim or Right After Default.

Any claim or right arising out of an alleged default or breach of warranty may be discharged in whole or in part without consideration by a written waiver or renunciation signed and delivered by the aggrieved party.

§ 2A–108. Unconscionability.

(1) If the court as a matter of law finds a lease contract or any clause of a lease contract to have been unconscionable at the time it was made the court may refuse to enforce the lease contract, or it may enforce the remainder of the lease contract without the unconscionable clause, or it may so limit the application of any unconscionable clause as to avoid any unconscionable result.

(2) With respect to a consumer lease, if the court as a matter of law finds that a lease contract or any clause of a lease contract has been induced by unconscionable conduct or that unconscionable conduct has occurred in the collection of a claim arising from a lease contract, the court may grant appropriate relief.

(3) Before making a finding of unconscionability under subsection (1) or (2), the court, on its own motion or that of a party, shall afford the parties a reasonable opportunity to present evidence as to the setting, purpose, and effect of the lease contract or clause thereof, or of the conduct.

(4) In an action in which the lessee claims unconscionability with respect to a consumer lease:

(a) If the court finds unconscionability under subsection (1) or (2), the court shall award reasonable attorney's fees to the lessee.

(b) If the court does not find unconscionability and the lessee claiming unconscionability has brought or maintained an action he [or she] knew to be groundless, the court shall award reasonable attorney's fees to the party against whom the claim is made.

(c) In determining attorney's fees, the amount of the recovery on behalf of the claimant under subsections (1) and (2) is not controlling.

§ 2A–109. Option to Accelerate at Will.

(1) A term providing that one party or his [or her] successor in interest may accelerate payment or performance or require collateral or additional collateral "at will" or "when he [or she] deems himself [or herself] insecure" or in words of similar import must be construed to mean that he [or she] has power to do so only if he [or she] in good faith believes that the prospect of payment or performance is impaired.

(2) With respect to a consumer lease, the burden of establishing good faith under subsection (1) is on the party who exercised the power; otherwise the burden of establishing lack of good faith is on the party against whom the power has been exercised.

Part 2 Formation and Construction of Lease Contract

§ 2A–201. Statute of Frauds.

(1) A lease contract is not enforceable by way of action or defense unless:

(a) the total payments to be made under the lease contract, excluding payments for options to renew or buy, are less than $1,000; or

(b) there is a writing, signed by the party against whom enforcement is sought or by that party's authorized agent, sufficient to indicate that a lease contract has been made between the parties and to describe the goods leased and the lease term.

(2) Any description of leased goods or of the lease term is sufficient and satisfies subsection (1)(b), whether or not it is specific, if it reasonably identifies what is described.

(3) A writing is not insufficient because it omits or incorrectly states a term agreed upon, but the lease contract is not enforceable under subsection (1)(b) beyond the lease term and the quantity of goods shown in the writing.

(4) A lease contract that does not satisfy the requirements of subsection (1), but which is valid in other respects, is enforceable:

(a) if the goods are to be specially manufactured or obtained for the lessee and are not suitable for lease or sale to others in the ordinary course of the lessor's business, and the lessor, before notice of repudiation is received and under circumstances that reasonably indicate that the goods are for the lessee, has made either a substantial beginning of their manufacture or commitments for their procurement;

(b) if the party against whom enforcement is sought admits in that party's pleading, testimony or otherwise in court that a lease contract was made, but the lease contract is not enforceable under this provision beyond the quantity of goods admitted; or

(c) with respect to goods that have been received and accepted by the lessee.

(5) The lease term under a lease contract referred to in subsection (4) is:

(a) if there is a writing signed by the party against whom enforcement is sought or by that party's authorized agent specifying the lease term, the term so specified;

(b) if the party against whom enforcement is sought admits in that party's pleading, testimony, or otherwise in court a lease term, the term so admitted; or

(c) a reasonable lease term.

§ 2A–202. Final Written Expression: Parol or Extrinsic Evidence.

Terms with respect to which the confirmatory memoranda of the parties agree or which are otherwise set forth in a writing intended by the parties as a final expression of their agreement with respect to such terms as are included therein may not be contradicted by evidence of any prior agreement or of a contemporaneous oral agreement but may be explained or supplemented:

(a) by course of dealing or usage of trade or by course of performance; and

(b) by evidence of consistent additional terms unless the court finds the writing to have been intended also as a complete and exclusive statement of the terms of the agreement.

§ 2A–203. Seals Inoperative.

The affixing of a seal to a writing evidencing a lease contract or an offer to enter into a lease contract does not render the writing a sealed instrument and the law with respect to sealed instruments does not apply to the lease contract or offer.

§ 2A–204. Formation in General.

(1) A lease contract may be made in any manner sufficient to show agreement, including conduct by both parties which recognizes the existence of a lease contract.

(2) An agreement sufficient to constitute a lease contract may be found although the moment of its making is undetermined.

(3) Although one or more terms are left open, a lease contract does not fail for indefiniteness if the parties have intended to make a lease contract and there is a reasonably certain basis for giving an appropriate remedy.

§ 2A–205. Firm Offers.

An offer by a merchant to lease goods to or from another person in a signed writing that by its terms gives assurance it will be held open is not revocable, for lack of consideration, during the time stated or, if no time is stated, for a reasonable time, but in no event may the period of irrevocability exceed 3 months. Any such term of assurance on a form supplied by the offeree must be separately signed by the offeror.

§ 2A–206. Offer and Acceptance in Formation of Lease Contract.

(1) Unless otherwise unambiguously indicated by the language or circumstances, an offer to make a lease contract must be construed as inviting acceptance in any manner and by any medium reasonable in the circumstances.

(2) If the beginning of a requested performance is a reasonable mode of acceptance, an offeror who is not notified of acceptance within a reasonable time may treat the offer as having lapsed before acceptance.

§ 2A–207. Course of Performance or Practical Construction.

(1) If a lease contract involves repeated occasions for performance by either party with knowledge of the nature of the performance and opportunity for objection to it by the other, any course of performance accepted or acquiesced in without objection is relevant to determine the meaning of the lease agreement.

(2) The express terms of a lease agreement and any course of performance, as well as any course of dealing and usage of trade, must be construed whenever reasonable as consistent with each other; but if that construction is unreasonable, express terms control course of performance, course of performance controls both course of dealing and usage of trade, and course of dealing controls usage of trade.

(3) Subject to the provisions of Section 2A–208 on modification and waiver, course of performance is relevant to show a waiver or modification of any term inconsistent with the course of performance.

§ 2A–208. Modification, Rescission and Waiver.

(1) An agreement modifying a lease contract needs no consideration to be binding.

(2) A signed lease agreement that excludes modification or rescission except by a signed writing may not be otherwise

modified or rescinded, but, except as between merchants, such a requirement on a form supplied by a merchant must be separately signed by the other party.

(3) Although an attempt at modification or rescission does not satisfy the requirements of subsection (2), it may operate as a waiver.

(4) A party who has made a waiver affecting an executory portion of a lease contract may retract the waiver by reasonable notification received by the other party that strict performance will be required of any term waived, unless the retraction would be unjust in view of a material change of position in reliance on the waiver.

§ 2A–209. Lessee under Finance Lease as Beneficiary of Supply Contract.

(1) The benefit of the supplier's promises to the lessor under the supply contract and of all warranties, whether express or implied, including those of any third party provided in connection with or as part of the supply contract, extends to the lessee to the extent of the lessee's leasehold interest under a finance lease related to the supply contract, but is subject to the terms warranty and of the supply contract and all defenses or claims arising therefrom.

(2) The extension of the benefit of supplier's promises and of warranties to the lessee (Section 2A–209(1)) does not: (i) modify the rights and obligations of the parties to the supply contract, whether arising therefrom or otherwise, or (ii) impose any duty or liability under the supply contract on the lessee.

(3) Any modification or rescission of the supply contract by the supplier and the lessor is effective between the supplier and the lessee unless, before the modification or rescission, the supplier has received notice that the lessee has entered into a finance lease related to the supply contract. If the modification or rescission is effective between the supplier and the lessee, the lessor is deemed to have assumed, in addition to the obligations of the lessor to the lessee under the lease contract, promises of the supplier to the lessor and warranties that were so modified or rescinded as they existed and were available to the lessee before modification or rescission.

(4) In addition to the extension of the benefit of the supplier's promises and of warranties to the lessee under subsection (1), the lessee retains all rights that the lessee may have against the supplier which arise from an agreement between the lessee and the supplier or under other law.

As amended in 1990.

§ 2A–210. Express Warranties.

(1) Express warranties by the lessor are created as follows:

(a) Any affirmation of fact or promise made by the lessor to the lessee which relates to the goods and becomes part of the basis of the bargain creates an express warranty that the goods will conform to the affirmation or promise.

(b) Any description of the goods which is made part of the basis of the bargain creates an express warranty that the goods will conform to the description.

(c) Any sample or model that is made part of the basis of the bargain creates an express warranty that the whole of the goods will conform to the sample or model.

(2) It is not necessary to the creation of an express warranty that the lessor use formal words, such as "warrant" or "guarantee," or that the lessor have a specific intention to make a warranty, but an affirmation merely of the value of the goods or a statement purporting to be merely the lessor's opinion or commendation of the goods does not create a warranty.

§ 2A–211. Warranties Against Interference and Against Infringement; Lessee's Obligation Against Infringement.

(1) There is in a lease contract a warranty that for the lease term no person holds a claim to or interest in the goods that arose from an act or omission of the lessor, other than a claim by way of infringement or the like, which will interfere with the lessee's enjoyment of its leasehold interest.

(2) Except in a finance lease there is in a lease contract by a lessor who is a merchant regularly dealing in goods of the kind a warranty that the goods are delivered free of the rightful claim of any person by way of infringement or the like.

(3) A lessee who furnishes specifications to a lessor or a supplier shall hold the lessor and the supplier harmless against any claim by way of infringement or the like that arises out of compliance with the specifications.

§ 2A–212. Implied Warranty of Merchantability.

(1) Except in a finance lease, a warranty that the goods will be merchantable is implied in a lease contract if the lessor is a merchant with respect to goods of that kind.

(2) Goods to be merchantable must be at least such as

(a) pass without objection in the trade under the description in the lease agreement;

(b) in the case of fungible goods, are of fair average quality within the description;

(c) are fit for the ordinary purposes for which goods of that type are used;

(d) run, within the variation permitted by the lease agreement, of even kind, quality, and quantity within each unit and among all units involved;

(e) are adequately contained, packaged, and labeled as the lease agreement may require; and

(f) conform to any promises or affirmations of fact made on the container or label.

(3) Other implied warranties may arise from course of dealing or usage of trade.

§ 2A–213. Implied Warranty of Fitness for Particular Purpose.

Except in a finance of lease, if the lessor at the time the lease contract is made has reason to know of any particular purpose for which the goods are required and that the lessee is relying on the lessor's skill or judgment to select or furnish suitable goods, there is in the lease contract an implied warranty that the goods will be fit for that purpose.

§ 2A–214. Exclusion or Modification of Warranties.

(1) Words or conduct relevant to the creation of an express warranty and words or conduct tending to negate or limit a warranty must be construed wherever reasonable as consistent with each other; but, subject to the provisions of Section 2A–202 on parol or extrinsic evidence, negation or limitation is inoperative to the extent that the construction is unreasonable.

(2) Subject to subsection (3), to exclude or modify the implied warranty of merchantability or any part of it the language must

mention "merchantability", be by a writing, and be conspicuous. Subject to subsection (3), to exclude or modify any implied warranty of fitness the exclusion must be by a writing and be conspicuous. Language to exclude all implied warranties of fitness is sufficient if it is in writing, is conspicuous and states, for example, "There is no warranty that the goods will be fit for a particular purpose".

(3) Notwithstanding subsection (2), but subject to subsection (4),

(a) unless the circumstances indicate otherwise, all implied warranties are excluded by expressions like "as is" or "with all faults" or by other language that in common understanding calls the lessee's attention to the exclusion of warranties and makes plain that there is no implied warranty, if in writing and conspicuous;

(b) if the lessee before entering into the lease contract has examined the goods or the sample or model as fully as desired or has refused to examine the goods, there is no implied warranty with regard to defects that an examination ought in the circumstances to have revealed; and

(c) an implied warranty may also be excluded or modified by course of dealing, course of performance, or usage of trade.

(4) To exclude or modify a warranty against interference or against infringement (Section 2A–211) or any part of it, the language must be specific, be by a writing, and be conspicuous, unless the circumstances, including course of performance, course of dealing, or usage of trade, give the lessee reason to know that the goods are being leased subject to a claim or interest of any person.

§ 2A–215. Cumulation and Conflict of Warranties Express or Implied.

Warranties, whether express or implied, must be construed as consistent with each other and as cumulative, but if that construction is unreasonable, the intention of the parties determines which warranty is dominant. In ascertaining that intention the following rules apply:

(a) Exact or technical specifications displace an inconsistent sample or model or general language of description.

(b) A sample from an existing bulk displaces inconsistent general language of description.

(c) Express warranties displace inconsistent implied warranties other than an implied warranty of fitness for a particular purpose.

§ 2A–216. Third-Party Beneficiaries of Express and Implied Warranties.

Alternative A

A warranty to or for the benefit of a lessee under this Article, whether express or implied, extends to any natural person who is in the family or household of the lessee or who is a guest in the lessee's home if it is reasonable to expect that such person may use, consume, or be affected by the goods and who is injured in person by breach of the warranty. This section does not displace principles of law and equity that extend a warranty to or for the benefit of a lessee to other persons. The operation of this section may not be excluded, modified, or limited, but an exclusion, modification, or limitation of the warranty, including any with respect to rights and remedies, effective against the lessee is also effective against any beneficiary designated under this section.

Alternative B

A warranty to or for the benefit of a lessee under this Article, whether express or implied, extends to any natural person who may reasonably be expected to use, consume, or be affected by the goods and who is injured in person by breach of the warranty. This section does not displace principles of law and equity that extend a warranty to or for the benefit of a lessee to other persons. The operation of this section may not be excluded, modified, or limited, but an exclusion, modification, or limitation of the warranty, including any with respect to rights and remedies, effective against the lessee is also effective against the beneficiary designated under this section.

Alternative C

A warranty to or for the benefit of a lessee under this Article, whether express or implied, extends to any person who may reasonably be expected to use, consume, or be affected by the goods and who is injured by breach of the warranty. The operation of this section may not be excluded, modified, or limited with respect to injury to the person of an individual to whom the warranty extends, but an exclusion, modification, or limitation of the warranty, including any with respect to rights and remedies, effective against the lessee is also effective against the beneficiary designated under this section.

§ 2A–217. Identification.

Identification of goods as goods to which a lease contract refers may be made at any time and in any manner explicitly agreed to by the parties. In the absence of explicit agreement, identification occurs:

(a) when the lease contract is made if the lease contract is for a lease of goods that are existing and identified;

(b) when the goods are shipped, marked, or otherwise designated by the lessor as goods to which the lease contract refers, if the lease contract is for a lease of goods that are not existing and identified; or

(c) when the young are conceived, if the lease contract is for a lease of unborn young of animals.

§ 2A–218. Insurance and Proceeds.

(1) A lessee obtains an insurable interest when existing goods are identified to the lease contract even though the goods identified are nonconforming and the lessee has an option to reject them.

(2) If a lessee has an insurable interest only by reason of the lessor's identification of the goods, the lessor, until default or insolvency or notification to the lessee that identification is final, may substitute other goods for those identified.

(3) Notwithstanding a lessee's insurable interest under subsections (1) and (2), the lessor retains an insurable interest until an option to buy has been exercised by the lessee and risk of loss has passed to the lessee.

(4) Nothing in this section impairs any insurable interest recognized under any other statute or rule of law.

(5) The parties by agreement may determine that one or more parties have an obligation to obtain and pay for insurance covering the goods and by agreement may determine the beneficiary of the proceeds of the insurance.

§ 2A–219. Risk of Loss.

(1) Except in the case of a finance lease, risk of loss is retained by the lessor and does not pass to the lessee. In the case of a finance lease, risk of loss passes to the lessee.

(2) Subject to the provisions of this Article on the effect of default on risk of loss (Section 2A–220), if risk of loss is to pass to the lessee and the time of passage is not stated, the following rules apply:

(a) If the lease contract requires or authorizes the goods to be shipped by carrier

(i) and it does not require delivery at a particular destination, the risk of loss passes to the lessee when the goods are duly delivered to the carrier; but

(ii) if it does require delivery at a particular destination and the goods are there duly tendered while in the possession of the carrier, the risk of loss passes to the lessee when the goods are there duly so tendered as to enable the lessee to take delivery.

(b) If the goods are held by a bailee to be delivered without being moved, the risk of loss passes to the lessee on acknowledgment by the bailee of the lessee's right to possession of the goods.

(c) In any case not within subsection (a) or (b), the risk of loss passes to the lessee on the lessee's receipt of the goods if the lessor, or, in the case of a finance lease, the supplier, is a merchant; otherwise the risk passes to the lessee on tender of delivery.

§ 2A–220. Effect of Default on Risk of Loss.

(1) Where risk of loss is to pass to the lessee and the time of passage is not stated:

(a) If a tender or delivery of goods so fails to conform to the lease contract as to give a right of rejection, the risk of their loss remains with the lessor, or, in the case of a finance lease, the supplier, until cure or acceptance.

(b) If the lessee rightfully revokes acceptance, he [or she], to the extent of any deficiency in his [or her] effective insurance coverage, may treat the risk of loss as having remained with the lessor from the beginning.

(2) Whether or not risk of loss is to pass to the lessee, if the lessee as to conforming goods already identified to a lease contract repudiates or is otherwise in default under the lease contract, the lessor, or, in the case of a finance lease, the supplier, to the extent of any deficiency in his [or her] effective insurance coverage may treat the risk of loss as resting on the lessee for a commercially reasonable time.

§ 2A–221. Casualty to Identified Goods.

If a lease contract requires goods identified when the lease contract is made, and the goods suffer casualty without fault of the lessee, the lessor or the supplier before delivery, or the goods suffer casualty before risk of loss passes to the lessee pursuant to the lease agreement or Section 2A–219, then:

(a) if the loss is total, the lease contract is avoided; and

(b) if the loss is partial or the goods have so deteriorated as to no longer conform to the lease contract, the lessee may nevertheless demand inspection and at his [or her] option either treat the lease contract as avoided or, except in a finance lease that is not a consumer lease, accept the goods with due allowance from the rent payable for the balance of the lease term for the deterioration or the deficiency in quantity but without further right against the lessor.

Part 3 Effect of Lease Contract
§ 2A–301. Enforceability of Lease Contract.

Except as otherwise provided in this Article, a lease contract is effective and enforceable according to its terms between the parties, against purchasers of the goods and against creditors of the parties.

§ 2A–302. Title to and Possession of Goods.

Except as otherwise provided in this Article, each provision of this Article applies whether the lessor or a third party has title to the goods, and whether the lessor, the lessee, or a third party has possession of the goods, notwithstanding any statute or rule of law that possession or the absence of possession is fraudulent.

§ 2A–303. Alienability of Party's Interest Under Lease Contract or of Lessor's Residual Interest in Goods; Delegation of Performance; Transfer of Rights.

(1) As used in this section, "creation of a security interest" includes the sale of a lease contract that is subject to Article 9, Secured Transactions, by reason of Section 9–109(a)(3).

(2) Except as provided in subsections (3) and Section 9–407, a provision in a lease agreement which (i) prohibits the voluntary or involuntary transfer, including a transfer by sale, sublease, creation or enforcement of a security interest, or attachment, levy, or other judicial process, of an interest of a party under the lease contract or of the lessor's residual interest in the goods, or (ii) makes such a transfer an event of default, gives rise to the rights and remedies provided in subsection (4), but a transfer that is prohibited or is an event of default under the lease agreement is otherwise effective.

(3) A provision in a lease agreement which (i) prohibits a transfer of a right to damages for default with respect to the whole lease contract or of a right to payment arising out of the transferor's due performance of the transferor's entire obligation, or (ii) makes such a transfer an event of default, is not enforceable, and such a transfer is not a transfer that materially impairs the prospect of obtaining return performance by, materially changes the duty of, or materially increases the burden or risk imposed on, the other party to the lease contract within the purview of subsection (4).

(4) Subject to subsection (3) and Section 9–407:

(a) if a transfer is made which is made an event of default under a lease agreement, the party to the lease contract not making the transfer, unless that party waives the default or otherwise agrees, has the rights and remedies described in Section 2A–501(2);

(b) if paragraph (a) is not applicable and if a transfer is made that (i) is prohibited under a lease agreement or (ii) materially impairs the prospect of obtaining return performance by, materially changes the duty of, or materially increases the burden or risk imposed on, the other party to the lease contract, unless the party not making the transfer agrees at any time to the transfer in the lease contract or otherwise, then, except as limited by contract, (i) the transferor is liable to the party not making the transfer for damages caused by the transfer to the extent that the damages could not reasonably be prevented by the party not making the transfer and (ii) a court having jurisdiction may grant other appropriate relief, including cancellation of the lease contract or an injunction against the transfer.

(5) A transfer of "the lease" or of "all my rights under the lease", or a transfer in similar general terms, is a transfer of rights and, unless the language or the circumstances, as in a transfer for security, indicate the contrary, the transfer is a delegation of duties by the transferor to the transferee. Acceptance by the transferee constitutes a promise by the transferee to perform those duties. The promise is enforceable by either the transferor or the other party to the lease contract.

(6) Unless otherwise agreed by the lessor and the lessee, a delegation of performance does not relieve the transferor as against the other party of any duty to perform or of any liability for default.

(7) In a consumer lease, to prohibit the transfer of an interest of a party under the lease contract or to make a transfer an event of default, the language must be specific, by a writing, and conspicuous.

As amended in 1990 and 1999.

§ 2A–304. Subsequent Lease of Goods by Lessor.

(1) Subject to Section 2A–303, a subsequent lessee from a lessor of goods under an existing lease contract obtains, to the extent of the leasehold interest transferred, the leasehold interest in the goods that the lessor had or had power to transfer, and except as provided in subsection (2) and Section 2A–527(4), takes subject to the existing lease contract. A lessor with voidable title has power to transfer a good leasehold interest to a good faith subsequent lessee for value, but only to the extent set forth in the preceding sentence. If goods have been delivered under a transaction of purchase the lessor has that power even though:

(a) the lessor's transferor was deceived as to the identity of the lessor;

(b) the delivery was in exchange for a check which is later dishonored;

(c) it was agreed that the transaction was to be a "cash sale"; or

(d) the delivery was procured through fraud punishable as larcenous under the criminal law.

(2) A subsequent lessee in the ordinary course of business from a lessor who is a merchant dealing in goods of that kind to whom the goods were entrusted by the existing lessee of that lessor before the interest of the subsequent lessee became enforceable against that lessor obtains, to the extent of the leasehold interest transferred, all of that lessor's and the existing lessee's rights to the goods, and takes free of the existing lease contract.

(3) A subsequent lessee from the lessor of goods that are subject to an existing lease contract and are covered by a certificate of title issued under a statute of this State or of another jurisdiction takes no greater rights than those provided both by this section and by the certificate of title statute.

As amended in 1990.

§ 2A–305. Sale or Sublease of Goods by Lessee.

(1) Subject to the provisions of Section 2A–303, a buyer or sublessee from the lessee of goods under an existing lease contract obtains, to the extent of the interest transferred, the leasehold interest in the goods that the lessee had or had power to transfer, and except as provided in subsection (2) and Section 2A–511(4), takes subject to the existing lease contract. A lessee with a voidable leasehold interest has power to transfer a good leasehold interest to a good faith buyer for value or a good faith sublessee for value, but only to the extent set forth in the preceding sentence. When goods have been delivered under a transaction of lease the lessee has that power even though:

(a) the lessor was deceived as to the identity of the lessee;

(b) the delivery was in exchange for a check which is later dishonored; or

(c) the delivery was procured through fraud punishable as larcenous under the criminal law.

(2) A buyer in the ordinary course of business or a sublessee in the ordinary course of business from a lessee who is a merchant dealing in goods of that kind to whom the goods were entrusted by the lessor obtains, to the extent of the interest transferred, all of the lessor's and lessee's rights to the goods, and takes free of the existing lease contract.

(3) A buyer or sublessee from the lessee of goods that are subject to an existing lease contract and are covered by a certificate of title issued under a statute of this State or of another jurisdiction takes no greater rights than those provided both by this section and by the certificate of title statute.

§ 2A–306. Priority of Certain Liens Arising by Operation of Law.

If a person in the ordinary course of his [or her] business furnishes services or materials with respect to goods subject to a lease contract, a lien upon those goods in the possession of that person given by statute or rule of law for those materials or services takes priority over any interest of the lessor or lessee under the lease contract or this Article unless the lien is created by statute and the statute provides otherwise or unless the lien is created by rule of law and the rule of law provides otherwise.

§ 2A–307. Priority of Liens Arising by Attachment or Levy on, Security Interests in, and Other Claims to Goods.

(1) Except as otherwise provided in Section 2A–306, a creditor of a lessee takes subject to the lease contract.

(2) Except as otherwise provided in subsection (3) and in Sections 2A–306 and 2A–308, a creditor of a lessor takes subject to the lease contract unless the creditor holds a lien that attached to the goods before the lease contract became enforceable.

(3) Except as otherwise provided in Sections 9–317, 9–321, and 9–323, a lessee takes a leasehold interest subject to a security interest held by a creditor of the lessor.

As amended in 1990 and 1999.

§ 2A–308. Special Rights of Creditors.

(1) A creditor of a lessor in possession of goods subject to a lease contract may treat the lease contract as void if as against the creditor retention of possession by the lessor is fraudulent under any statute or rule of law, but retention of possession in good faith and current course of trade by the lessor for a commercially reasonable time after the lease contract becomes enforceable is not fraudulent.

(2) Nothing in this Article impairs the rights of creditors of a lessor if the lease contract (a) becomes enforceable, not in current

course of trade but in satisfaction of or as security for a pre-existing claim for money, security, or the like, and (b) is made under circumstances which under any statute or rule of law apart from this Article would constitute the transaction a fraudulent transfer or voidable preference.

(3) A creditor of a seller may treat a sale or an identification of goods to a contract for sale as void if as against the creditor retention of possession by the seller is fraudulent under any statute or rule of law, but retention of possession of the goods pursuant to a lease contract entered into by the seller as lessee and the buyer as lessor in connection with the sale or identification of the goods is not fraudulent if the buyer bought for value and in good faith.

§ 2A–309. Lessor's and Lessee's Rights When Goods Become Fixtures.

(1) In this section:

(a) goods are "fixtures" when they become so related to particular real estate that an interest in them arises under real estate law;

(b) a "fixture filing" is the filing, in the office where a mortgage on the real estate would be filed or recorded, of a financing statement covering goods that are or are to become fixtures and conforming to the requirements of Section 9–502(a) and (b);

(c) a lease is a "purchase money lease" unless the lessee has possession or use of the goods or the right to possession or use of the goods before the lease agreement is enforceable;

(d) a mortgage is a "construction mortgage" to the extent it secures an obligation incurred for the construction of an improvement on land including the acquisition cost of the land, if the recorded writing so indicates; and

(e) "encumbrance" includes real estate mortgages and other liens on real estate and all other rights in real estate that are not ownership interests.

(2) Under this Article a lease may be of goods that are fixtures or may continue in goods that become fixtures, but no lease exists under this Article of ordinary building materials incorporated into an improvement on land.

(3) This Article does not prevent creation of a lease of fixtures pursuant to real estate law.

(4) The perfected interest of a lessor of fixtures has priority over a conflicting interest of an encumbrancer or owner of the real estate if:

(a) the lease is a purchase money lease, the conflicting interest of the encumbrancer or owner arises before the goods become fixtures, the interest of the lessor is perfected by a fixture filing before the goods become fixtures or within ten days thereafter, and the lessee has an interest of record in the real estate or is in possession of the real estate; or

(b) the interest of the lessor is perfected by a fixture filing before the interest of the encumbrancer or owner is of record, the lessor's interest has priority over any conflicting interest of a predecessor in title of the encumbrancer or owner, and the lessee has an interest of record in the real estate or is in possession of the real estate.

(5) The interest of a lessor of fixtures, whether or not perfected, has priority over the conflicting interest of an encumbrancer or owner of the real estate if:

(a) the fixtures are readily removable factory or office machines, readily removable equipment that is not primarily used or leased for use in the operation of the real estate, or readily removable replacements of domestic appliances that are goods subject to a consumer lease, and before the goods become fixtures the lease contract is enforceable; or

(b) the conflicting interest is a lien on the real estate obtained by legal or equitable proceedings after the lease contract is enforceable; or

(c) the encumbrancer or owner has consented in writing to the lease or has disclaimed an interest in the goods as fixtures; or

(d) the lessee has a right to remove the goods as against the encumbrancer or owner. If the lessee's right to remove terminates, the priority of the interest of the lessor continues for a reasonable time.

(6) Notwithstanding paragraph (4)(a) but otherwise subject to subsections (4) and (5), the interest of a lessor of fixtures, including the lessor's residual interest, is subordinate to the conflicting interest of an encumbrancer of the real estate under a construction mortgage recorded before the goods become fixtures if the goods become fixtures before the completion of the construction. To the extent given to refinance a construction mortgage, the conflicting interest of an encumbrancer of the real estate under a mortgage has this priority to the same extent as the encumbrancer of the real estate under the construction mortgage.

(7) In cases not within the preceding subsections, priority between the interest of a lessor of fixtures, including the lessor's residual interest, and the conflicting interest of an encumbrancer or owner of the real estate who is not the lessee is determined by the priority rules governing conflicting interests in real estate.

(8) If the interest of a lessor of fixtures, including the lessor's residual interest, has priority over all conflicting interests of all owners and encumbrancers of the real estate, the lessor or the lessee may (i) on default, expiration, termination, or cancellation of the lease agreement but subject to the agreement and this Article, or (ii) if necessary to enforce other rights and remedies of the lessor or lessee under this Article, remove the goods from the real estate, free and clear of all conflicting interests of all owners and encumbrancers of the real estate, but the lessor or lessee must reimburse any encumbrancer or owner of the real estate who is not the lessee and who has not otherwise agreed for the cost of repair of any physical injury, but not for any diminution in value of the real estate caused by the absence of the goods removed or by any necessity of replacing them. A person entitled to reimbursement may refuse permission to remove until the party seeking removal gives adequate security for the performance of this obligation.

(9) Even though the lease agreement does not create a security interest, the interest of a lessor of fixtures, including the lessor's residual interest, is perfected by filing a financing statement as a fixture filing for leased goods that are or are to become fixtures in accordance with the relevant provisions of the Article on Secured Transactions (Article 9).

As amended in 1990 and 1999.

§ 2A–310. Lessor's and Lessee's Rights When Goods Become Accessions.

(1) Goods are "accessions" when they are installed in or affixed to other goods.

(2) The interest of a lessor or a lessee under a lease contract entered into before the goods became accessions is superior to all interests in the whole except as stated in subsection (4).

(3) The interest of a lessor or a lessee under a lease contract entered into at the time or after the goods became accessions is superior to all subsequently acquired interests in the whole except as stated in subsection (4) but is subordinate to interests in the whole existing at the time the lease contract was made unless the holders of such interests in the whole have in writing consented to the lease or disclaimed an interest in the goods as part of the whole.

(4) The interest of a lessor or a lessee under a lease contract described in subsection (2) or (3) is subordinate to the interest of

(a) a buyer in the ordinary course of business or a lessee in the ordinary course of business of any interest in the whole acquired after the goods became accessions; or

(b) a creditor with a security interest in the whole perfected before the lease contract was made to the extent that the creditor makes subsequent advances without knowledge of the lease contract.

(5) When under subsections (2) or (3) and (4) a lessor or a lessee of accessions holds an interest that is superior to all interests in the whole, the lessor or the lessee may (a) on default, expiration, termination, or cancellation of the lease contract by the other party but subject to the provisions of the lease contract and this Article, or (b) if necessary to enforce his [or her] other rights and remedies under this Article, remove the goods from the whole, free and clear of all interests in the whole, but he [or she] must reimburse any holder of an interest in the whole who is not the lessee and who has not otherwise agreed for the cost of repair of any physical injury but not for any diminution in value of the whole caused by the absence of the goods removed or by any necessity for replacing them. A person entitled to reimbursement may refuse permission to remove until the party seeking removal gives adequate security for the performance of this obligation.

§ 2A–311. Priority Subject to Subordination.

Nothing in this Article prevents subordination by agreement by any person entitled to priority.

As added in 1990.

Part 4 Performance of Lease Contract: Repudiated, Substituted and Excused

§ 2A–401. Insecurity: Adequate Assurance of Performance.

(1) A lease contract imposes an obligation on each party that the other's expectation of receiving due performance will not be impaired.

(2) If reasonable grounds for insecurity arise with respect to the performance of either party, the insecure party may demand in writing adequate assurance of due performance. Until the insecure party receives that assurance, if commercially reasonable the insecure party may suspend any performance for which he [or she] has not already received the agreed return.

(3) A repudiation of the lease contract occurs if assurance of due performance adequate under the circumstances of the particular case is not provided to the insecure party within a reasonable time, not to exceed 30 days after receipt of a demand by the other party.

(4) Between merchants, the reasonableness of grounds for insecurity and the adequacy of any assurance offered must be determined according to commercial standards.

(5) Acceptance of any nonconforming delivery or payment does not prejudice the aggrieved party's right to demand adequate assurance of future performance.

§ 2A–402. Anticipatory Repudiation.

If either party repudiates a lease contract with respect to a performance not yet due under the lease contract, the loss of which performance will substantially impair the value of the lease contract to the other, the aggrieved party may:

(a) for a commercially reasonable time, await retraction of repudiation and performance by the repudiating party;

(b) make demand pursuant to Section 2A–401 and await assurance of future performance adequate under the circumstances of the particular case; or

(c) resort to any right or remedy upon default under the lease contract or this Article, even though the aggrieved party has notified the repudiating party that the aggrieved party would await the repudiating party's performance and assurance and has urged retraction. In addition, whether or not the aggrieved party is pursuing one of the foregoing remedies, the aggrieved party may suspend performance or, if the aggrieved party is the lessor, proceed in accordance with the provisions of this Article on the lessor's right to identify goods to the lease contract notwithstanding default or to salvage unfinished goods (Section 2A–524).

§ 2A–403. Retraction of Anticipatory Repudiation.

(1) Until the repudiating party's next performance is due, the repudiating party can retract the repudiation unless, since the repudiation, the aggrieved party has cancelled the lease contract or materially changed the aggrieved party's position or otherwise indicated that the aggrieved party considers the repudiation final.

(2) Retraction may be by any method that clearly indicates to the aggrieved party that the repudiating party intends to perform under the lease contract and includes any assurance demanded under Section 2A–401.

(3) Retraction reinstates a repudiating party's rights under a lease contract with due excuse and allowance to the aggrieved party for any delay occasioned by the repudiation.

§ 2A–404. Substituted Performance.

(1) If without fault of the lessee, the lessor and the supplier, the agreed berthing, loading, or unloading facilities fail or the agreed type of carrier becomes unavailable or the agreed manner of delivery otherwise becomes commercially impracticable, but a commercially reasonable substitute is available, the substitute performance must be tendered and accepted.

(2) If the agreed means or manner of payment fails because of domestic or foreign governmental regulation:

(a) the lessor may withhold or stop delivery or cause the supplier to withhold or stop delivery unless the lessee provides a means or manner of payment that is commercially a substantial equivalent; and

(b) if delivery has already been taken, payment by the means or in the manner provided by the regulation discharges the lessee's obligation unless the regulation is discriminatory, oppressive, or predatory.

§ 2A–405. Excused Performance.

Subject to Section 2A–404 on substituted performance, the following rules apply:

(a) Delay in delivery or nondelivery in whole or in part by a lessor or a supplier who complies with paragraphs (b) and (c) is not a default under the lease contract if performance as agreed has been made impracticable by the occurrence of a contingency the nonoccurrence of which was a basic assumption on which the lease contract was made or by compliance in good faith with any applicable foreign or domestic governmental regulation or order, whether or not the regulation or order later proves to be invalid.

(b) If the causes mentioned in paragraph (a) affect only part of the lessor's or the supplier's capacity to perform, he [or she] shall allocate production and deliveries among his [or her] customers but at his [or her] option may include regular customers not then under contract for sale or lease as well as his [or her] own requirements for further manufacture. He [or she] may so allocate in any manner that is fair and reasonable.

(c) The lessor seasonably shall notify the lessee and in the case of a finance lease the supplier seasonably shall notify the lessor and the lessee, if known, that there will be delay or nondelivery and, if allocation is required under paragraph (b), of the estimated quota thus made available for the lessee.

§ 2A–406. Procedure on Excused Performance.

(1) If the lessee receives notification of a material or indefinite delay or an allocation justified under Section 2A–405, the lessee may by written notification to the lessor as to any goods involved, and with respect to all of the goods if under an installment lease contract the value of the whole lease contract is substantially impaired (Section 2A–510):

(a) terminate the lease contract (Section 2A–505(2)); or

(b) except in a finance lease that is not a consumer lease, modify the lease contract by accepting the available quota in substitution, with due allowance from the rent payable for the balance of the lease term for the deficiency but without further right against the lessor.

(2) If, after receipt of a notification from the lessor under Section 2A–405, the lessee fails so to modify the lease agreement within a reasonable time not exceeding 30 days, the lease contract lapses with respect to any deliveries affected.

§ 2A–407. Irrevocable Promises: Finance Leases.

(1) In the case of a finance lease that is not a consumer lease the lessee's promises under the lease contract become irrevocable and independent upon the lessee's acceptance of the goods.

(2) A promise that has become irrevocable and independent under subsection (1):

(a) is effective and enforceable between the parties, and by or against third parties including assignees of the parties, and

(b) is not subject to cancellation, termination, modification, repudiation, excuse, or substitution without the consent of the party to whom the promise runs.

(3) This section does not affect the validity under any other law of a covenant in any lease contract making the lessee's promises irrevocable and independent upon the lessee's acceptance of the goods.

As amended in 1990.

Part 5 Default

A. In General

§ 2A–501. Default: Procedure.

(1) Whether the lessor or the lessee is in default under a lease contract is determined by the lease agreement and this Article.

(2) If the lessor or the lessee is in default under the lease contract, the party seeking enforcement has rights and remedies as provided in this Article and, except as limited by this Article, as provided in the lease agreement.

(3) If the lessor or the lessee is in default under the lease contract, the party seeking enforcement may reduce the party's claim to judgment, or otherwise enforce the lease contract by self-help or any available judicial procedure or nonjudicial procedure, including administrative proceeding, arbitration, or the like, in accordance with this Article.

(4) Except as otherwise provided in Section 1–106(1) or this Article or the lease agreement, the rights and remedies referred to in subsections (2) and (3) are cumulative.

(5) If the lease agreement covers both real property and goods, the party seeking enforcement may proceed under this Part as to the goods, or under other applicable law as to both the real property and the goods in accordance with that party's rights and remedies in respect of the real property, in which case this Part does not apply.

As amended in 1990.

§ 2A–502. Notice After Default.

Except as otherwise provided in this Article or the lease agreement, the lessor or lessee in default under the lease contract is not entitled to notice of default or notice of enforcement from the other party to the lease agreement.

§ 2A–503. Modification or Impairment of Rights and Remedies.

(1) Except as otherwise provided in this Article, the lease agreement may include rights and remedies for default in addition to or in substitution for those provided in this Article and may limit or alter the measure of damages recoverable under this Article.

(2) Resort to a remedy provided under this Article or in the lease agreement is optional unless the remedy is expressly agreed to be exclusive. If circumstances cause an exclusive or limited remedy to fail of its essential purpose, or provision for an exclusive remedy is unconscionable, remedy may be had as provided in this Article.

(3) Consequential damages may be liquidated under Section 2A–504, or may otherwise be limited, altered, or excluded unless the limitation, alteration, or exclusion is unconscionable. Limitation, alteration, or exclusion of consequential damages for injury to the person in the case of consumer goods is prima facie unconscionable but limitation, alteration, or exclusion of damages where the loss is commercial is not prima facie unconscionable.

(4) Rights and remedies on default by the lessor or the lessee with respect to any obligation or promise collateral or ancillary to the lease contract are not impaired by this Article.

As amended in 1990.

§ 2A–504. Liquidation of Damages.

(1) Damages payable by either party for default, or any other act or omission, including indemnity for loss or diminution of

anticipated tax benefits or loss or damage to lessor's residual interest, may be liquidated in the lease agreement but only at an amount or by a formula that is reasonable in light of the then anticipated harm caused by the default or other act or omission.

(2) If the lease agreement provides for liquidation of damages, and such provision does not comply with subsection (1), or such provision is an exclusive or limited remedy that circumstances cause to fail of its essential purpose, remedy may be had as provided in this Article.

(3) If the lessor justifiably withholds or stops delivery of goods because of the lessee's default or insolvency (Section 2A–525 or 2A–526), the lessee is entitled to restitution of any amount by which the sum of his [or her] payments exceeds:

(a) the amount to which the lessor is entitled by virtue of terms liquidating the lessor's damages in accordance with subsection (1); or

(b) in the absence of those terms, 20 percent of the then present value of the total rent the lessee was obligated to pay for the balance of the lease term, or, in the case of a consumer lease, the lesser of such amount or $500.

(4) A lessee's right to restitution under subsection (3) is subject to offset to the extent the lessor establishes:

(a) a right to recover damages under the provisions of this Article other than subsection (1); and

(b) the amount or value of any benefits received by the lessee directly or indirectly by reason of the lease contract.

§ 2A–505. Cancellation and Termination and Effect of Cancellation, Termination, Rescission, or Fraud on Rights and Remedies.

(1) On cancellation of the lease contract, all obligations that are still executory on both sides are discharged, but any right based on prior default or performance survives, and the cancelling party also retains any remedy for default of the whole lease contract or any unperformed balance.

(2) On termination of the lease contract, all obligations that are still executory on both sides are discharged but any right based on prior default or performance survives.

(3) Unless the contrary intention clearly appears, expressions of "cancellation," "rescission," or the like of the lease contract may not be construed as a renunciation or discharge of any claim in damages for an antecedent default.

(4) Rights and remedies for material misrepresentation or fraud include all rights and remedies available under this Article for default.

(5) Neither rescission nor a claim for rescission of the lease contract nor rejection or return of the goods may bar or be deemed inconsistent with a claim for damages or other right or remedy.

§ 2A–506. Statute of Limitations.

(1) An action for default under a lease contract, including breach of warranty or indemnity, must be commenced within 4 years after the cause of action accrued. By the original lease contract the parties may reduce the period of limitation to not less than one year.

(2) A cause of action for default accrues when the act or omission on which the default or breach of warranty is based is or should have been discovered by the aggrieved party, or when the default occurs, whichever is later. A cause of action for indemnity accrues when the act or omission on which the claim for indemnity is based is or should have been discovered by the indemnified party, whichever is later.

(3) If an action commenced within the time limited by subsection (1) is so terminated as to leave available a remedy by another action for the same default or breach of warranty or indemnity, the other action may be commenced after the expiration of the time limited and within 6 months after the termination of the first action unless the termination resulted from voluntary discontinuance or from dismissal for failure or neglect to prosecute.

(4) This section does not alter the law on tolling of the statute of limitations nor does it apply to causes of action that have accrued before this Article becomes effective.

§ 2A–507. Proof of Market Rent: Time and Place.

(1) Damages based on market rent (Section 2A–519 or 2A–528) are determined according to the rent for the use of the goods concerned for a lease term identical to the remaining lease term of the original lease agreement and prevailing at the times specified in Sections 2A–519 and 2A–528.

(2) If evidence of rent for the use of the goods concerned for a lease term identical to the remaining lease term of the original lease agreement and prevailing at the times or places described in this Article is not readily available, the rent prevailing within any reasonable time before or after the time described or at any other place or for a different lease term which in commercial judgment or under usage of trade would serve as a reasonable substitute for the one described may be used, making any proper allowance for the difference, including the cost of transporting the goods to or from the other place.

(3) Evidence of a relevant rent prevailing at a time or place or for a lease term other than the one described in this Article offered by one party is not admissible unless and until he [or she] has given the other party notice the court finds sufficient to prevent unfair surprise.

(4) If the prevailing rent or value of any goods regularly leased in any established market is in issue, reports in official publications or trade journals or in newspapers or periodicals of general circulation published as the reports of that market are admissible in evidence. The circumstances of the preparation of the report may be shown to affect its weight but not its admissibility.

As amended in 1990.

B. Default by Lessor
§ 2A–508. Lessee's Remedies.

(1) If a lessor fails to deliver the goods in conformity to the lease contract (Section 2A–509) or repudiates the lease contract (Section 2A–402), or a lessee rightfully rejects the goods (Section 2A–509) or justifiably revokes acceptance of the goods (Section 2A–517), then with respect to any goods involved, and with respect to all of the goods if under an installment lease contract the value of the whole lease contract is substantially impaired (Section 2A–510), the lessor is in default under the lease contract and the lessee may:

(a) cancel the lease contract (Section 2A–505(1));

(b) recover so much of the rent and security as has been paid and is just under the circumstances;

(c) cover and recover damages as to all goods affected whether or not they have been identified to the lease contract (Sections 2A–518 and 2A–520), or recover damages for nondelivery (Sections 2A–519 and 2A–520);

(d) exercise any other rights or pursue any other remedies provided in the lease contract.

(2) If a lessor fails to deliver the goods in conformity to the lease contract or repudiates the lease contract, the lessee may also:

(a) if the goods have been identified, recover them (Section 2A–522); or

(b) in a proper case, obtain specific performance or replevy the goods (Section 2A–521).

(3) If a lessor is otherwise in default under a lease contract, the lessee may exercise the rights and pursue the remedies provided in the lease contract, which may include a right to cancel the lease, and in Section 2A–519(3).

(4) If a lessor has breached a warranty, whether express or implied, the lessee may recover damages (Section 2A–519(4)).

(5) On rightful rejection or justifiable revocation of acceptance, a lessee has a security interest in goods in the lessee's possession or control for any rent and security that has been paid and any expenses reasonably incurred in their inspection, receipt, transportation, and care and custody and may hold those goods and dispose of them in good faith and in a commercially reasonable manner, subject to Section 2A–527(5).

(6) Subject to the provisions of Section 2A–407, a lessee, on notifying the lessor of the lessee's intention to do so, may deduct all or any part of the damages resulting from any default under the lease contract from any part of the rent still due under the same lease contract.

As amended in 1990.

§ 2A–509. Lessee's Rights on Improper Delivery; Rightful Rejection.

(1) Subject to the provisions of Section 2A–510 on default in installment lease contracts, if the goods or the tender or delivery fail in any respect to conform to the lease contract, the lessee may reject or accept the goods or accept any commercial unit or units and reject the rest of the goods.

(2) Rejection of goods is ineffective unless it is within a reasonable time after tender or delivery of the goods and the lessee seasonably notifies the lessor.

§ 2A–510. Installment Lease Contracts: Rejection and Default.

(1) Under an installment lease contract a lessee may reject any delivery that is nonconforming if the nonconformity substantially impairs the value of that delivery and cannot be cured or the nonconformity is a defect in the required documents; but if the nonconformity does not fall within subsection (2) and the lessor or the supplier gives adequate assurance of its cure, the lessee must accept that delivery.

(2) Whenever nonconformity or default with respect to one or more deliveries substantially impairs the value of the installment lease contract as a whole there is a default with respect to the whole. But, the aggrieved party reinstates the installment lease contract as a whole if the aggrieved party accepts a nonconforming delivery without seasonably notifying of cancellation or brings an action with respect only to past deliveries or demands performance as to future deliveries.

§ 2A–511. Merchant Lessee's Duties as to Rightfully Rejected Goods.

(1) Subject to any security interest of a lessee (Section 2A–508(5)), if a lessor or a supplier has no agent or place of business at the market of rejection, a merchant lessee, after rejection of goods in his [or her] possession or control, shall follow any reasonable instructions received from the lessor or the supplier with respect to the goods. In the absence of those instructions, a merchant lessee shall make reasonable efforts to sell, lease, or otherwise dispose of the goods for the lessor's account if they threaten to decline in value speedily. Instructions are not reasonable if on demand indemnity for expenses is not forthcoming.

(2) If a merchant lessee (subsection (1)) or any other lessee (Section 2A–512) disposes of goods, he [or she] is entitled to reimbursement either from the lessor or the supplier or out of the proceeds for reasonable expenses of caring for and disposing of the goods and, if the expenses include no disposition commission, to such commission as is usual in the trade, or if there is none, to a reasonable sum not exceeding 10 percent of the gross proceeds.

(3) In complying with this section or Section 2A–512, the lessee is held only to good faith. Good faith conduct hereunder is neither acceptance or conversion nor the basis of an action for damages.

(4) A purchaser who purchases in good faith from a lessee pursuant to this section or Section 2A–512 takes the goods free of any rights of the lessor and the supplier even though the lessee fails to comply with one or more of the requirements of this Article.

§ 2A–512. Lessee's Duties as to Rightfully Rejected Goods.

(1) Except as otherwise provided with respect to goods that threaten to decline in value speedily (Section 2A–511) and subject to any security interest of a lessee (Section 2A–508(5)):

(a) the lessee, after rejection of goods in the lessee's possession, shall hold them with reasonable care at the lessor's or the supplier's disposition for a reasonable time after the lessee's seasonable notification of rejection;

(b) if the lessor or the supplier gives no instructions within a reasonable time after notification of rejection, the lessee may store the rejected goods for the lessor's or the supplier's account or ship them to the lessor or the supplier or dispose of them for the lessor's or the supplier's account with reimbursement in the manner provided in Section 2A–511; but

(c) the lessee has no further obligations with regard to goods rightfully rejected.

(2) Action by the lessee pursuant to subsection (1) is not acceptance or conversion.

§ 2A–513. Cure by Lessor of Improper Tender or Delivery; Replacement.

(1) If any tender or delivery by the lessor or the supplier is rejected because nonconforming and the time for performance has not yet expired, the lessor or the supplier may seasonably notify the lessee of the lessor's or the supplier's intention to cure and may then make a conforming delivery within the time provided in the lease contract.

(2) If the lessee rejects a nonconforming tender that the lessor or the supplier had reasonable grounds to believe would be

acceptable with or without money allowance, the lessor or the supplier may have a further reasonable time to substitute a conforming tender if he [or she] seasonably notifies the lessee.

§ 2A–514. Waiver of Lessee's Objections.

(1) In rejecting goods, a lessee's failure to state a particular defect that is ascertainable by reasonable inspection precludes the lessee from relying on the defect to justify rejection or to establish default:

(a) if, stated seasonably, the lessor or the supplier could have cured it (Section 2A–513); or

(b) between merchants if the lessor or the supplier after rejection has made a request in writing for a full and final written statement of all defects on which the lessee proposes to rely.

(2) A lessee's failure to reserve rights when paying rent or other consideration against documents precludes recovery of the payment for defects apparent on the face of the documents.

§ 2A–515. Acceptance of Goods.

(1) Acceptance of goods occurs after the lessee has had a reasonable opportunity to inspect the goods and

(a) the lessee signifies or acts with respect to the goods in a manner that signifies to the lessor or the supplier that the goods are conforming or that the lessee will take or retain them in spite of their nonconformity; or

(b) the lessee fails to make an effective rejection of the goods (Section 2A–509(2)).

(2) Acceptance of a part of any commercial unit is acceptance of that entire unit.

§ 2A–516. Effect of Acceptance of Goods; Notice of Default; Burden of Establishing Default after Acceptance; Notice of Claim or Litigation to Person Answerable Over.

(1) A lessee must pay rent for any goods accepted in accordance with the lease contract, with due allowance for goods rightfully rejected or not delivered.

(2) A lessee's acceptance of goods precludes rejection of the goods accepted. In the case of a finance lease, if made with knowledge of a nonconformity, acceptance cannot be revoked because of it. In any other case, if made with knowledge of a nonconformity, acceptance cannot be revoked because of it unless the acceptance was on the reasonable assumption that the nonconformity would be seasonably cured. Acceptance does not of itself impair any other remedy provided by this Article or the lease agreement for nonconformity.

(3) If a tender has been accepted:

(a) within a reasonable time after the lessee discovers or should have discovered any default, the lessee shall notify the lessor and the supplier, if any, or be barred from any remedy against the party notified;

(b) except in the case of a consumer lease, within a reasonable time after the lessee receives notice of litigation for infringement or the like (Section 2A–211) the lessee shall notify the lessor or be barred from any remedy over for liability established by the litigation; and

(c) the burden is on the lessee to establish any default.

(4) If a lessee is sued for breach of a warranty or other obligation for which a lessor or a supplier is answerable over the following apply:

(a) The lessee may give the lessor or the supplier, or both, written notice of the litigation. If the notice states that the person notified may come in and defend and that if the person notified does not do so that person will be bound in any action against that person by the lessee by any determination of fact common to the two litigations, then unless the person notified after seasonable receipt of the notice does come in and defend that person is so bound.

(b) The lessor or the supplier may demand in writing that the lessee turn over control of the litigation including settlement if the claim is one for infringement or the like (Section 2A–211) or else be barred from any remedy over. If the demand states that the lessor or the supplier agrees to bear all expense and to satisfy any adverse judgment, then unless the lessee after seasonable receipt of the demand does turn over control the lessee is so barred.

(5) Subsections (3) and (4) apply to any obligation of a lessee to hold the lessor or the supplier harmless against infringement or the like (Section 2A–211).

As amended in 1990.

§ 2A–517. Revocation of Acceptance of Goods.

(1) A lessee may revoke acceptance of a lot or commercial unit whose nonconformity substantially impairs its value to the lessee if the lessee has accepted it:

(a) except in the case of a finance lease, on the reasonable assumption that its nonconformity would be cured and it has not been seasonably cured; or

(b) without discovery of the nonconformity if the lessee's acceptance was reasonably induced either by the lessor's assurances or, except in the case of a finance lease, by the difficulty of discovery before acceptance.

(2) Except in the case of a finance lease that is not a consumer lease, a lessee may revoke acceptance of a lot or commercial unit if the lessor defaults under the lease contract and the default substantially impairs the value of that lot or commercial unit to the lessee.

(3) If the lease agreement so provides, the lessee may revoke acceptance of a lot or commercial unit because of other defaults by the lessor.

(4) Revocation of acceptance must occur within a reasonable time after the lessee discovers or should have discovered the ground for it and before any substantial change in condition of the goods which is not caused by the nonconformity. Revocation is not effective until the lessee notifies the lessor.

(5) A lessee who so revokes has the same rights and duties with regard to the goods involved as if the lessee had rejected them.

As amended in 1990.

§ 2A–518. Cover; Substitute Goods.

(1) After a default by a lessor under the lease contract of the type described in Section 2A–508(1), or, if agreed, after other default by the lessor, the lessee may cover by making any purchase or lease of or contract to purchase or lease goods in substitution for those due from the lessor.

(2) Except as otherwise provided with respect to damages liquidated in the lease agreement (Section 2A–504) or otherwise determined pursuant to agreement of the parties (Sections 1–102(3) and 2A–503), if a lessee's cover is by lease agreement substantially similar to the original lease agreement and the

new lease agreement is made in good faith and in a commercially reasonable manner, the lessee may recover from the lessor as damages (i) the present value, as of the date of the commencement of the term of the new lease agreement, of the rent under the new lease agreement applicable to that period of the new lease term which is comparable to the then remaining term of the original lease agreement minus the present value as of the same date of the total rent for the then remaining lease term of the original lease agreement, and (ii) any incidental or consequential damages, less expenses saved in consequence of the lessor's default.

(3) If a lessee's cover is by lease agreement that for any reason does not qualify for treatment under subsection (2), or is by purchase or otherwise, the lessee may recover from the lessor as if the lessee had elected not to cover and Section 2A–519 governs. As amended in 1990.

§ 2A–519. Lessee's Damages for Non-Delivery, Repudiation, Default, and Breach of Warranty in Regard to Accepted Goods.

(1) Except as otherwise provided with respect to damages liquidated in the lease agreement (Section 2A–504) or otherwise determined pursuant to agreement of the parties (Sections 1–102(3) and 2A–503), if a lessee elects not to cover or a lessee elects to cover and the cover is by lease agreement that for any reason does not qualify for treatment under Section 2A–518(2), or is by purchase or otherwise, the measure of damages for non-delivery or repudiation by the lessor or for rejection or revocation of acceptance by the lessee is the present value, as of the date of the default, of the then market rent minus the present value as of the same date of the original rent, computed for the remaining lease term of the original lease agreement, together with incidental and consequential damages, less expenses saved in consequence of the lessor's default.

(2) Market rent is to be determined as of the place for tender or, in cases of rejection after arrival or revocation of acceptance, as of the place of arrival.

(3) Except as otherwise agreed, if the lessee has accepted goods and given notification (Section 2A–516(3)), the measure of damages for non-conforming tender or delivery or other default by a lessor is the loss resulting in the ordinary course of events from the lessor's default as determined in any manner that is reasonable together with incidental and consequential damages, less expenses saved in consequence of the lessor's default.

(4) Except as otherwise agreed, the measure of damages for breach of warranty is the present value at the time and place of acceptance of the difference between the value of the use of the goods accepted and the value if they had been as warranted for the lease term, unless special circumstances show proximate damages of a different amount, together with incidental and consequential damages, less expenses saved in consequence of the lessor's default or breach of warranty. As amended in 1990.

§ 2A–520. Lessee's Incidental and Consequential Damages.

(1) Incidental damages resulting from a lessor's default include expenses reasonably incurred in inspection, receipt, transportation, and care and custody of goods rightfully rejected or goods the acceptance of which is justifiably revoked, any commer-

cially reasonable charges, expenses or commissions in connection with effecting cover, and any other reasonable expense incident to the default.

(2) Consequential damages resulting from a lessor's default include:

(a) any loss resulting from general or particular requirements and needs of which the lessor at the time of contracting had reason to know and which could not reasonably be prevented by cover or otherwise; and

(b) injury to person or property proximately resulting from any breach of warranty.

§ 2A–521. Lessee's Right to Specific Performance or Replevin.

(1) Specific performance may be decreed if the goods are unique or in other proper circumstances.

(2) A decree for specific performance may include any terms and conditions as to payment of the rent, damages, or other relief that the court deems just.

(3) A lessee has a right of replevin, detinue, sequestration, claim and delivery, or the like for goods identified to the lease contract if after reasonable effort the lessee is unable to effect cover for those goods or the circumstances reasonably indicate that the effort will be unavailing.

§ 2A–522. Lessee's Right to Goods on Lessor's Insolvency.

(1) Subject to subsection (2) and even though the goods have not been shipped, a lessee who has paid a part or all of the rent and security for goods identified to a lease contract (Section 2A–217) on making and keeping good a tender of any unpaid portion of the rent and security due under the lease contract may recover the goods identified from the lessor if the lessor becomes insolvent within 10 days after receipt of the first installment of rent and security.

(2) A lessee acquires the right to recover goods identified to a lease contract only if they conform to the lease contract.

C. Default by Lessee

§ 2A–523. Lessor's Remedies.

(1) If a lessee wrongfully rejects or revokes acceptance of goods or fails to make a payment when due or repudiates with respect to a part or the whole, then, with respect to any goods involved, and with respect to all of the goods if under an installment lease contract the value of the whole lease contract is substantially impaired (Section 2A–510), the lessee is in default under the lease contract and the lessor may:

(a) cancel the lease contract (Section 2A–505(1));

(b) proceed respecting goods not identified to the lease contract (Section 2A–524);

(c) withhold delivery of the goods and take possession of goods previously delivered (Section 2A–525);

(d) stop delivery of the goods by any bailee (Section 2A–526);

(e) dispose of the goods and recover damages (Section 2A–527), or retain the goods and recover damages (Section 2A–528), or in a proper case recover rent (Section 2A–529)

(f) exercise any other rights or pursue any other remedies provided in the lease contract.

(2) If a lessor does not fully exercise a right or obtain a remedy to which the lessor is entitled under subsection (1), the lessor

may recover the loss resulting in the ordinary course of events from the lessee's default as determined in any reasonable manner, together with incidental damages, less expenses saved in consequence of the lessee's default.

(3) If a lessee is otherwise in default under a lease contract, the lessor may exercise the rights and pursue the remedies provided in the lease contract, which may include a right to cancel the lease. In addition, unless otherwise provided in the lease contract:

(a) if the default substantially impairs the value of the lease contract to the lessor, the lessor may exercise the rights and pursue the remedies provided in subsections (1) or (2); or

(b) if the default does not substantially impair the value of the lease contract to the lessor, the lessor may recover as provided in subsection (2).

As amended in 1990.

§ 2A–524. Lessor's Right to Identify Goods to Lease Contract.

(1) After default by the lessee under the lease contract of the type described in Section 2A–523(1) or 2A–523(3)(a) or, if agreed, after other default by the lessee, the lessor may:

(a) identify to the lease contract conforming goods not already identified if at the time the lessor learned of the default they were in the lessor's or the supplier's possession or control; and

(b) dispose of goods (Section 2A–527(1)) that demonstrably have been intended for the particular lease contract even though those goods are unfinished.

(2) If the goods are unfinished, in the exercise of reasonable commercial judgment for the purposes of avoiding loss and of effective realization, an aggrieved lessor or the supplier may either complete manufacture and wholly identify the goods to the lease contract or cease manufacture and lease, sell, or otherwise dispose of the goods for scrap or salvage value or proceed in any other reasonable manner.

As amended in 1990.

§ 2A–525. Lessor's Right to Possession of Goods.

(1) If a lessor discovers the lessee to be insolvent, the lessor may refuse to deliver the goods.

(2) After a default by the lessee under the lease contract of the type described in Section 2A–523(1) or 2A–523(3)(a) or, if agreed, after other default by the lessee, the lessor has the right to take possession of the goods. If the lease contract so provides, the lessor may require the lessee to assemble the goods and make them available to the lessor at a place to be designated by the lessor which is reasonably convenient to both parties. Without removal, the lessor may render unusable any goods employed in trade or business, and may dispose of goods on the lessee's premises (Section 2A–527).

(3) The lessor may proceed under subsection (2) without judicial process if that can be done without breach of the peace or the lessor may proceed by action.

As amended in 1990.

§ 2A–526. Lessor's Stoppage of Delivery in Transit or Otherwise.

(1) A lessor may stop delivery of goods in the possession of a carrier or other bailee if the lessor discovers the lessee to be insolvent and may stop delivery of carload, truckload, planeload, or larger shipments of express or freight if the lessee repudiates or fails to make a payment due before delivery, whether for rent, security or otherwise under the lease contract, or for any other reason the lessor has a right to withhold or take possession of the goods.

(2) In pursuing its remedies under subsection (1), the lessor may stop delivery until

(a) receipt of the goods by the lessee;

(b) acknowledgment to the lessee by any bailee of the goods, except a carrier, that the bailee holds the goods for the lessee; or

(c) such an acknowledgment to the lessee by a carrier via reshipment or as warehouseman.

(3) (a) To stop delivery, a lessor shall so notify as to enable the bailee by reasonable diligence to prevent delivery of the goods.

(b) After notification, the bailee shall hold and deliver the goods according to the directions of the lessor, but the lessor is liable to the bailee for any ensuing charges or damages.

(c) A carrier who has issued a nonnegotiable bill of lading is not obliged to obey a notification to stop received from a person other than the consignor.

§ 2A–527. Lessor's Rights to Dispose of Goods.

(1) After a default by a lessee under the lease contract of the type described in Section 2A–523(1) or 2A–523(3)(a) or after the lessor refuses to deliver or takes possession of goods (Section 2A–525 or 2A–526), or, if agreed, after other default by a lessee, the lessor may dispose of the goods concerned or the undelivered balance thereof by lease, sale, or otherwise.

(2) Except as otherwise provided with respect to damages liquidated in the lease agreement (Section 2A–504) or otherwise determined pursuant to agreement of the parties (Sections 1–102(3) and 2A–503), if the disposition is by lease agreement substantially similar to the original lease agreement and the new lease agreement is made in good faith and in a commercially reasonable manner, the lessor may recover from the lessee as damages (i) accrued and unpaid rent as of the date of the commencement of the term of the new lease agreement, (ii) the present value, as of the same date, of the total rent for the then remaining lease term of the original lease agreement minus the present value, as of the same date, of the rent under the new lease agreement applicable to that period of the new lease term which is comparable to the then remaining term of the original lease agreement, and (iii) any incidental damages allowed under Section 2A–530, less expenses saved in consequence of the lessee's default.

(3) If the lessor's disposition is by lease agreement that for any reason does not qualify for treatment under subsection (2), or is by sale or otherwise, the lessor may recover from the lessee as if the lessor had elected not to dispose of the goods and Section 2A–528 governs.

(4) A subsequent buyer or lessee who buys or leases from the lessor in good faith for value as a result of a disposition under this section takes the goods free of the original lease contract and any rights of the original lessee even though the lessor fails to comply with one or more of the requirements of this Article.

(5) The lessor is not accountable to the lessee for any profit made on any disposition. A lessee who has rightfully rejected or justifiably revoked acceptance shall account to the lessor for any excess over the amount of the lessee's security interest (Section 2A–508(5)).

As amended in 1990.

§ 2A–528. Lessor's Damages for Non-acceptance, Failure to Pay, Repudiation, or Other Default.

(1) Except as otherwise provided with respect to damages liquidated in the lease agreement (Section 2A–504) or otherwise determined pursuant to agreement of the parties (Section 1–102(3) and 2A–503), if a lessor elects to retain the goods or a lessor elects to dispose of the goods and the disposition is by lease agreement that for any reason does not qualify for treatment under Section 2A–527(2), or is by sale or otherwise, the lessor may recover from the lessee as damages for a default of the type described in Section 2A–523(1) or 2A–523(3)(a), or if agreed, for other default of the lessee, (i) accrued and unpaid rent as of the date of the default if the lessee has never taken possession of the goods, or, if the lessee has taken possession of the goods, as of the date the lessor repossesses the goods or an earlier date on which the lessee makes a tender of the goods to the lessor, (ii) the present value as of the date determined under clause (i) of the total rent for the then remaining lease term of the original lease agreement minus the present value as of the same date of the market rent as the place where the goods are located computed for the same lease term, and (iii) any incidental damages allowed under Section 2A–530, less expenses saved in consequence of the lessee's default.

(2) If the measure of damages provided in subsection (1) is inadequate to put a lessor in as good a position as performance would have, the measure of damages is the present value of the profit, including reasonable overhead, the lessor would have made from full performance by the lessee, together with any incidental damages allowed under Section 2A–530, due allowance for costs reasonably incurred and due credit for payments or proceeds of disposition.

As amended in 1990.

§ 2A–529. Lessor's Action for the Rent.

(1) After default by the lessee under the lease contract of the type described in Section 2A–523(1) or 2A–523(3)(a) or, if agreed, after other default by the lessee, if the lessor complies with subsection (2), the lessor may recover from the lessee as damages:

(a) for goods accepted by the lessee and not repossessed by or tendered to the lessor, and for conforming goods lost or damaged within a commercially reasonable time after risk of loss passes to the lessee (Section 2A–219), (i) accrued and unpaid rent as of the date of entry of judgment in favor of the lessor (ii) the present value as of the same date of the rent for the then remaining lease term of the lease agreement, and (iii) any incidental damages allowed under Section 2A–530, less expenses saved in consequence of the lessee's default; and

(b) for goods identified to the lease contract if the lessor is unable after reasonable effort to dispose of them at a reasonable price or the circumstances reasonably indicate that effort will be unavailing, (i) accrued and unpaid rent as of the date of entry of judgment in favor of the lessor, (ii) the present value as of the same date of the rent for the then remaining lease term of the lease agreement, and (iii) any incidental damages allowed under Section 2A–530, less expenses saved in consequence of the lessee's default.

(2) Except as provided in subsection (3), the lessor shall hold for the lessee for the remaining lease term of the lease agreement any goods that have been identified to the lease contract and are in the lessor's control.

(3) The lessor may dispose of the goods at any time before collection of the judgment for damages obtained pursuant to subsection (1). If the disposition is before the end of the remaining lease term of the lease agreement, the lessor's recovery against the lessee for damages is governed by Section 2A–527 or Section 2A–528, and the lessor will cause an appropriate credit to be provided against a judgment for damages to the extent that the amount of the judgment exceeds the recovery available pursuant to Section 2A–527 or 2A–528.

(4) Payment of the judgment for damages obtained pursuant to subsection (1) entitles the lessee to the use and possession of the goods not then disposed of for the remaining lease term of and in accordance with the lease agreement.

(5) After default by the lessee under the lease contract of the type described in Section 2A–523(1) or Section 2A–523(3)(a) or, if agreed, after other default by the lessee, a lessor who is held not entitled to rent under this section must nevertheless be awarded damages for non-acceptance under Sections 2A–527 and 2A–528.

As amended in 1990.

§ 2A–530. Lessor's Incidental Damages.

Incidental damages to an aggrieved lessor include any commercially reasonable charges, expenses, or commissions incurred in stopping delivery, in the transportation, care and custody of goods after the lessee's default, in connection with return or disposition of the goods, or otherwise resulting from the default.

§ 2A–531. Standing to Sue Third Parties for Injury to Goods.

(1) If a third party so deals with goods that have been identified to a lease contract as to cause actionable injury to a party to the lease contract (a) the lessor has a right of action against the third party, and (b) the lessee also has a right of action against the third party if the lessee:

(i) has a security interest in the goods;

(ii) has an insurable interest in the goods; or

(iii) bears the risk of loss under the lease contract or has since the injury assumed that risk as against the lessor and the goods have been converted or destroyed.

(2) If at the time of the injury the party plaintiff did not bear the risk of loss as against the other party to the lease contract and there is no arrangement between them for disposition of the recovery, his [or her] suit or settlement, subject to his [or her] own interest, is as a fiduciary for the other party to the lease contract.

(3) Either party with the consent of the other may sue for the benefit of whom it may concern.

§ 2A–532. Lessor's Rights to Residual Interest.

In addition to any other recovery permitted by this Article or other law, the lessor may recover from the lessee an amount that will fully compensate the lessor for any loss of or damage to the lessor's residual interest in the goods caused by the default of the lessee.

As added in 1990.

The Administrative Procedure Act of 1946 (Excerpts)

Note: You can access the full text of the Administrative Procedure Act online by going to **uscode.house.gov/search/criteria.shtml**. In the "Title" box, type "5," and in the "Section" box, type a relevant section number (such as "551"). Click on "Search," and in the list of "documents found," click on the citation to access the text of the statute. The Office of the Law Revision Council of the U.S. House of Representatives maintains this Web site.

Section 551. Definitions

For the purpose of this subchapter—

* * * *

(4) "rule" means the whole or a part of an agency statement of general or particular applicability and future effect designed to implement, interpret, or prescribe law or policy or describing the organization, procedure, or practice requirements of an agency and includes the approval or prescription for the future of rates, wages, corporate or financial structures or reorganizations thereof, prices, facilities, appliances, services or allowances therefor or of valuations, costs, or accounting, or practices bearing on any of the foregoing[.]

* * * *

Section 552. Public Information; Agency Rules, Opinions, Orders, Records, and Proceedings

(a) Each agency shall make available to the public information as follows:

(1) Each agency shall separately state and currently publish in the Federal Register for the guidance of the public—

(A) descriptions of its central and field organization and the established places at which, the employees * * * from whom, and the methods whereby, the public may obtain information, make submittals or requests, or obtain decisions;

* * * *

(C) rules of procedure, descriptions of forms available or the places at which forms may be obtained, and instructions as to the scope and contents of all papers, reports, or examinations;

(D) substantive rules of general applicability adopted as authorized by law, and statements of general policy or interpretations of general applicability formulated and adopted by the agency[.] * * *

* * * *

Section 552b. Open Meetings

* * * *

(j) Each agency subject to the requirements of this section shall annually report to Congress regarding its compliance with such requirements, including a tabulation of the total number of agency meetings open to the public, the total number of meetings closed to the public, the reasons for closing such meetings, and a description of any litigation brought against the agency under this section, including any costs assessed against the agency in such litigation * * *.

* * * *

Section 553. Rule Making

* * * *

(b) General notice of proposed rule making shall be published in the Federal Register, unless persons subject thereto are named and either personally served or otherwise have actual notice thereof in accordance with law. * * *

(c) After notice required by this section, the agency shall give interested persons an opportunity to participate in the rule making through submission of written data, views, or arguments with or without opportunity for oral presentation. * * *

* * * *

Section 554. Adjudications

* * * *

(b) Persons entitled to notice of an agency hearing shall be timely informed of—

(1) the time, place, and nature of the hearing;

(2) the legal authority and jurisdiction under which the hearing is to be held; and

(3) the matters of fact and law asserted.

* * * *

(c) The agency shall give all interested parties opportunity for—

(1) the submission and consideration of facts, arguments, offers of settlement, or proposals of adjustment when time, the nature of the proceeding, and the public interest permit; and

(2) to the extent that the parties are unable so to determine a controversy by consent, hearing and decision on notice * * *.

* * * *

Section 555. Ancillary Matters

* * * *

(c) Process, requirement of a report, inspection, or other investigative act or demand may not be issued, made, or enforced except as authorized by law. A person compelled to submit data or evidence is entitled to retain or, on payment of lawfully prescribed costs, procure a copy or transcript thereof, except that in a nonpublic investigatory proceeding the witness may for good cause be limited to inspection of the official transcript of his testimony.

* * * *

(e) Prompt notice shall be given of the denial in whole or in part of a written application, petition, or other request of an interested person made in connection with any agency proceeding. * * *

Section 556. Hearings; Presiding Employees; Powers and Duties; Burden of Proof; Evidence; Record as Basis of Decision

* * * *

(b) There shall preside at the taking of evidence—

(1) the agency;

(2) one or more members of the body which comprises the agency; or

(3) one or more administrative law judges * * *.

* * * *

(c) Subject to published rules of the agency and within its powers, employees presiding at hearings may—

(1) administer oaths and affirmations;

(2) issue subpoenas authorized by law;

(3) rule on offers of proof and receive relevant evidence;

(4) take depositions or have depositions taken when the ends of justice would be served;

(5) regulate the course of the hearing;

(6) hold conferences for the settlement or simplification of the issues by consent of the parties or by the use of alternative means of dispute resolution as provided in subchapter IV of this chapter;

(7) inform the parties as to the availability of one or more alternative means of dispute resolution, and encourage use of such methods;

* * * *

(9) dispose of procedural requests or similar matters;

(10) make or recommend decisions in accordance with * * * this title; and

(11) take other action authorized by agency rule consistent with this subchapter.

* * * *

Section 702. Right of Review

A person suffering legal wrong because of agency action * * * is entitled to judicial review thereof. An action in a court of the United States seeking relief other than money damages and stating a claim that an agency or an officer or employee thereof acted or failed to act in an official capacity or under color of legal authority shall not be dismissed nor relief therein be denied on the ground that it is against the United States or that the United States is an indispensable party. The United States may be named as a defendant in any such action, and a judgment or decree may be entered against the United States: Provided, [t]hat any mandatory or injunctive decree shall specify the [f]ederal officer or officers (by name or by title), and their successors in office, personally responsible for compliance. * * *

* * * *

Section 704. Actions Reviewable

Agency action made reviewable by statute and final agency action for which there is no other adequate remedy in a court are subject to judicial review. A preliminary, procedural, or intermediate agency action or ruling not directly reviewable is subject to review on the review of the final agency action.

The Uniform Partnership Act (Excerpts)

(The Uniform Partnership Act was amended in 1997 to provide limited liability for partners in a limited liability partnership. Over half the states, including District of Columbia, Puerto Rico, and the U.S. Virgin Islands, have adopted this latest version of the UPA.)

ARTICLE 1
GENERAL PROVISIONS

SECTION 101. Definitions In this [Act]:

* * * *

(6) "Partnership" means an association of two or more persons to carry on as co-owners a business for profit formed under Section 202, predecessor law, or comparable law of another jurisdiction.

(7) "Partnership agreement" means the agreement, whether written, oral, or implied, among the partners concerning the partnership, including amendments to the partnership agreement.

(8) "Partnership at will" means a partnership in which the partners have not agreed to remain partners until the expiration of a definite term or the completion of a particular undertaking.

(9) "Partnership interest" or "partner's interest in the partnership" means all of a partner's interests in the partnership, including the partner's transferable interest and all management and other rights.

(10) "Person" means an individual, corporation, business trust, estate, trust, partnership, association, joint venture, government, governmental subdivision, agency, or instrumentality, or any other legal or commercial entity.

* * * *

SECTION 103. Effect of Partnership Agreement; Nonwaivable Provisions.

(a) Except as otherwise provided in subsection (b), relations among the partners and between the partners and the partnership are governed by the partnership agreement. To the extent the partnership agreement does not otherwise provide, this [Act] governs relations among the partners and between the partners and the partnership.

(b) The partnership agreement may not:

(1) vary the rights and duties under Section 105 except to eliminate the duty to provide copies of statements to all of the partners;

(2) unreasonably restrict the right of access to books and records under Section 403(b);

(3) eliminate the duty of loyalty under Section 404(b) or 603(b)(3), but:

(i) the partnership agreement may identify specific types or categories of activities that do not violate the duty of loyalty, if not manifestly unreasonable; or

(ii) all of the partners or a number or percentage specified in the partnership agreement may authorize or ratify, after full disclosure of all material facts, a specific act or transaction that otherwise would violate the duty of loyalty;

(4) unreasonably reduce the duty of care under Section 404(c) or 603(b)(3);

(5) eliminate the obligation of good faith and fair dealing under Section 404(d), but the partnership agreement may prescribe the standards by which the performance of the obligation is to be measured, if the standards are not manifestly unreasonable;

(6) vary the power to dissociate as a partner under Section 602(a), except to require the notice under Section 601(1) to be in writing;

(7) vary the right of a court to expel a partner in the events specified in Section 601(5);

* * * *

SECTION 105. Execution, Filing, and Recording of Statements.

(a) A statement may be filed in the office of [the Secretary of State]. A certified copy of a statement that is filed in an office in another State may be filed in the office of [the Secretary of State]. Either filing has the effect provided in this [Act] with respect to partnership property located in or transactions that occur in this State.

(b) A certified copy of a statement that has been filed in the office of the [Secretary of State] and recorded in the office for recording transfers of real property has the effect provided for recorded statements in this [Act]. A recorded statement that is not a certified copy of a statement filed in the office of the [Secretary of State] does not have the effect provided for recorded statements in this [Act].

* * * *

SECTION 106. Governing Law.

(a) Except as otherwise provided in subsection (b), the law of the jurisdiction in which a partnership has its chief executive office governs relations among the partners and between the partners and the partnership.

(b) The law of this State governs relations among the partners and between the partners and the partnership and the liability of partners for an obligation of a limited liability partnership.

* * * *

ARTICLE 2
NATURE OF PARTNERSHIP

SECTION 201. Partnership as Entity.

(a) A partnership is an entity distinct from its partners.

(b) A limited liability partnership continues to be the same entity that existed before the filing of a statement of qualification under Section 1001.

SECTION 202. Formation of Partnership.

*   *   *   *

(c) In determining whether a partnership is formed, the following rules apply:

(1) Joint tenancy, tenancy in common, tenancy by the entireties, joint property, common property, or part ownership does not by itself establish a partnership, even if the co-owners share profits made by the use of the property.

(2) The sharing of gross returns does not by itself establish a partnership, even if the persons sharing them have a joint or common right or interest in property from which the returns are derived.

(3) A person who receives a share of the profits of a business is presumed to be a partner in the business, unless the profits were received in payment:

(i) of a debt by installments or otherwise;

(ii) for services as an independent contractor or of wages or other compensation to an employee;

(iii) of rent;

(iv) of an annuity or other retirement or health benefit to a beneficiary, representative, or designee of a deceased or retired partner;

(v) of interest or other charge on a loan, even if the amount of payment varies with the profits of the business, including a direct or indirect present or future ownership of the collateral, or rights to income, proceeds, or increase in value derived from the collateral; or

(vi) for the sale of the goodwill of a business or other property by installments or otherwise.

SECTION 203. Partnership Property.

Property acquired by a partnership is property of the partnership and not of the partners individually.

SECTION 204. When Property is Partnership Property.

*   *   *   *

(d) Property acquired in the name of one or more of the partners, without an indication in the instrument transferring title to the property of the person's capacity as a partner or of the existence of a partnership and without use of partnership assets, is presumed to be separate property, even if used for partnership purposes.

ARTICLE 3
RELATIONS OF PARTNERS TO PERSONS DEALING WITH PARTNERSHIP

SECTION 301. Partner Agent of Partnership.

Subject to the effect of a statement of partnership authority under Section 303:

(1) Each partner is an agent of the partnership for the purpose of its business. An act of a partner, including the execution of an instrument in the partnership name, for apparently carrying on in the ordinary course the partnership business or business of the kind carried on by the partnership binds the partnership, unless the partner had no authority to act for the partnership in the particular matter and the person with whom the partner was dealing knew or had received a notification that the partner lacked authority.

(2) An act of a partner which is not apparently for carrying on in the ordinary course the partnership business or business of the kind carried on by the partnership binds the partnership only if the act was authorized by the other partners.

*   *   *   *

SECTION 303. Statement of Partnership Authority.

(a) A partnership may file a statement of partnership authority, which:

(1) must include:

(i) the name of the partnership;

(ii) the street address of its chief executive office and of one office in this State, if there is one;

(iii) the names and mailing addresses of all of the partners or of an agent appointed and maintained by the partnership for the purpose of subsection (b); and

(iv) the names of the partners authorized to execute an instrument transferring real property held in the name of the partnership; and

(2) may state the authority, or limitations on the authority, of some or all of the partners to enter into other transactions on behalf of the partnership and any other matter.

*   *   *   *

(d) Except as otherwise provided in subsection (g), a filed statement of partnership authority supplements the authority of a partner to enter into transactions on behalf of the partnership as follows:

(1) Except for transfers of real property, a grant of authority contained in a filed statement of partnership authority is conclusive in favor of a person who gives value without knowledge to the contrary, so long as and to the extent that a limitation on that authority is not then contained in another filed statement. A filed cancellation of a limitation on authority revives the previous grant of authority.

(2) A grant of authority to transfer real property held in the name of the partnership contained in a certified copy of a filed statement of partnership authority recorded in the office for recording transfers of that real property is conclusive in favor of a person who gives value without knowledge to the contrary, so long as and to the extent that a certified copy of a filed statement containing a limitation on that authority is not then of record in the office for recording transfers of that real property. The recording in the office for recording transfers of that real property of a certified copy of a filed cancellation of a limitation on authority revives the previous grant of authority.

(e) A person not a partner is deemed to know of a limitation on the authority of a partner to transfer real property held in the name of the partnership if a certified copy of the filed statement containing the limitation on authority is of record in the office for recording transfers of that real property.

(f) Except as otherwise provided in subsections (d) and (e) and Sections 704 and 805, a person not a partner is not deemed to know of a limitation on the authority of a partner merely because the limitation is contained in a filed statement.

* * * *

SECTION 305. Partnership Liable for Partner's Actionable Conduct.

(a) A partnership is liable for loss or injury caused to a person, or for a penalty incurred, as a result of a wrongful act or omission, or other actionable conduct, of a partner acting in the ordinary course of business of the partnership or with authority of the partnership.

(b) If, in the course of the partnership's business or while acting with authority of the partnership, a partner receives or causes the partnership to receive money or property of a person not a partner, and the money or property is misapplied by a partner, the partnership is liable for the loss.

SECTION 306. Partner's Liability.

(a) Except as otherwise provided in subsections (b) and (c), all partners are liable jointly and severally for all obligations of the partnership unless otherwise agreed by the claimant or provided by law.

(b) A person admitted as a partner into an existing partnership is not personally liable for any partnership obligation incurred before the person's admission as a partner.

(c) An obligation of a partnership incurred while the partnership is a limited liability partnership, whether arising in contract, tort, or otherwise, is solely the obligation of the partnership. A partner is not personally liable, directly or indirectly, by way of contribution or otherwise, for such an obligation solely by reason of being or so acting as a partner. This subsection applies notwithstanding anything inconsistent in the partnership agreement that existed immediately before the vote required to become a limited liability partnership under Section 1001(b).

SECTION 307. Actions by and Against Partnership and Partners.

(a) A partnership may sue and be sued in the name of the partnership.

* * * *

(d) A judgment creditor of a partner may not levy execution against the assets of the partner to satisfy a judgment based on a claim against the partnership unless the partner is personally liable for the claim under Section 306 and:

(1) a judgment based on the same claim has been obtained against the partnership and a writ of execution on the judgment has been returned unsatisfied in whole or in part;

(2) the partnership is a debtor in bankruptcy;

(3) the partner has agreed that the creditor need not exhaust partnership assets;

(4) a court grants permission to the judgment creditor to levy execution against the assets of a partner based on a finding that partnership assets subject to execution are clearly insufficient to satisfy the judgment, that exhaustion of partnership assets is excessively burdensome, or that the grant of permission is an appropriate exercise of the court's equitable powers; or

(5) liability is imposed on the partner by law or contract independent of the existence of the partnership.

(e) This section applies to any partnership liability or obligation resulting from a representation by a partner or purported partner under Section 308.

SECTION 308. Liability of Purported Partner.

(a) If a person, by words or conduct, purports to be a partner, or consents to being represented by another as a partner, in a partnership or with one or more persons not partners, the purported partner is liable to a person to whom the representation is made, if that person, relying on the representation, enters into a transaction with the actual or purported partnership. If the representation, either by the purported partner or by a person with the purported partner's consent, is made in a public manner, the purported partner is liable to a person who relies upon the purported partnership even if the purported partner is not aware of being held out as a partner to the claimant. If partnership liability results, the purported partner is liable with respect to that liability as if the purported partner were a partner. If no partnership liability results, the purported partner is liable with respect to that liability jointly and severally with any other person consenting to the representation.

(b) If a person is thus represented to be a partner in an existing partnership, or with one or more persons not partners, the purported partner is an agent of persons consenting to the representation to bind them to the same extent and in the same manner as if the purported partner were a partner, with respect to persons who enter into transactions in reliance upon the representation. If all of the partners of the existing partnership consent to the representation, a partnership act or obligation results. If fewer than all of the partners of the existing partnership consent to the representation, the person acting and the partners consenting to the representation are jointly and severally liable.

* * * *

ARTICLE 4
RELATIONS OF PARTNERS TO EACH OTHER AND TO PARTNERSHIP

SECTION 401. Partner's Rights and Duties.

* * * *

(b) Each partner is entitled to an equal share of the partnership profits and is chargeable with a share of the partnership losses in proportion to the partner's share of the profits.

* * * *

(f) Each partner has equal rights in the management and conduct of the partnership business.

(g) A partner may use or possess partnership property only on behalf of the partnership.

(h) A partner is not entitled to remuneration for services performed for the partnership, except for reasonable compensation for services rendered in winding up the business of the partnership.

(i) A person may become a partner only with the consent of all of the partners.

(j) A difference arising as to a matter in the ordinary course of business of a partnership may be decided by a majority of the partners. An act outside the ordinary course of business of a partnership and an amendment to the partnership agreement may be undertaken only with the consent of all of the partners.

* * * *

SECTION 403. Partner's Rights and Duties with Respect to Information.

(a) A partnership shall keep its books and records, if any, at its chief executive office.

(b) A partnership shall provide partners and their agents and attorneys access to its books and records. It shall provide former partners and their agents and attorneys access to books and records pertaining to the period during which they were partners. The right of access provides the opportunity to inspect and copy books and records during ordinary business hours. A partnership may impose a reasonable charge, covering the costs of labor and material, for copies of documents furnished.

* * * *

SECTION 404. General Standards of Partner's Conduct.

(a) The only fiduciary duties a partner owes to the partnership and the other partners are the duty of loyalty and the duty of care set forth in subsections (b) and (c).

(b) A partner's duty of loyalty to the partnership and the other partners is limited to the following:

(1) to account to the partnership and hold as trustee for it any property, profit, or benefit derived by the partner in the conduct and winding up of the partnership business or derived from a use by the partner of partnership property, including the appropriation of a partnership opportunity;

(2) to refrain from dealing with the partnership in the conduct or winding up of the partnership business as or on behalf of a party having an interest adverse to the partnership; and

(3) to refrain from competing with the partnership in the conduct of the partnership business before the dissolution of the partnership.

(c) A partner's duty of care to the partnership and the other partners in the conduct and winding up of the partnership business is limited to refraining from engaging in grossly negligent or reckless conduct, intentional misconduct, or a knowing violation of law.

(d) A partner shall discharge the duties to the partnership and the other partners under this [Act] or under the partnership agreement and exercise any rights consistently with the obligation of good faith and fair dealing.

(e) A partner does not violate a duty or obligation under this [Act] or under the partnership agreement merely because the partner's conduct furthers the partner's own interest.

* * * *

SECTION 405. Actions by Partnership and Partners.

(a) A partnership may maintain an action against a partner for a breach of the partnership agreement, or for the violation of a duty to the partnership, causing harm to the partnership.

(b) A partner may maintain an action against the partnership or another partner for legal or equitable relief, with or without an accounting as to partnership business, to:

(1) enforce the partner's rights under the partnership agreement;

(2) enforce the partner's rights under this [Act], including:

(i) the partner's rights under Sections 401, 403, or 404;

(ii) the partner's right on dissociation to have the partner's interest in the partnership purchased pursuant to Section 701 or enforce any other right under [Article] 6 or 7; or

(iii) the partner's right to compel a dissolution and winding up of the partnership business under or enforce any other right under [Article] 8; or

(3) enforce the rights and otherwise protect the interests of the partner, including rights and interests arising independently of the partnership relationship.

* * * *

ARTICLE 5
TRANSFEREES AND CREDITORS OF PARTNER

SECTION 501. Partner Not Co-Owner of Partnership Property.

A partner is not a co-owner of partnership property and has no interest in partnership property which can be transferred, either voluntarily or involuntarily.

SECTION 502. Partner's Transferable Interest in Partnership.

The only transferable interest of a partner in the partnership is the partner's share of the profits and losses of the partnership and the partner's right to receive distributions. The interest is personal property.

SECTION 503. Transfer of Partner's Transferable Interest.

(a) A transfer, in whole or in part, of a partner's transferable interest in the partnership:

(1) is permissible;

(2) does not by itself cause the partner's dissociation or a dissolution and winding up of the partnership business; and

(3) does not, as against the other partners or the partnership, entitle the transferee, during the continuance of the partnership, to participate in the management or conduct of the partnership business, to require access to information concerning partnership transactions, or to inspect or copy the partnership books or records.

* * * *

SECTION 504. Partner's Transferable Interest Subject to Charging Order.

(a) On application by a judgment creditor of a partner or of a partner's transferee, a court having jurisdiction may charge the transferable interest of the judgment debtor to satisfy the judgment. The court may appoint a receiver of the share of the distributions due or to become due to the judgment debtor in respect of the partnership and make all other orders, directions, accounts, and inquiries the judgment debtor might have made or which the circumstances of the case may require.

* * * *

ARTICLE 6
PARTNER'S DISSOCIATION

SECTION 601. Events Causing Partner's Dissociation.

A partner is dissociated from a partnership upon the occurrence of any of the following events:

(1) the partnership's having notice of the partner's express will to withdraw as a partner or on a later date specified by the partner;

(2) an event agreed to in the partnership agreement as causing the partner's dissociation;

(3) the partner's expulsion pursuant to the partnership agreement;

(4) the partner's expulsion by the unanimous vote of the other partners if:

(i) it is unlawful to carry on the partnership business with that partner;

(ii) there has been a transfer of all or substantially all of that partner's transferable interest in the partnership, other than a transfer for security purposes, or a court order charging the partner's interest, which has not been foreclosed;

(iii) within 90 days after the partnership notifies a corporate partner that it will be expelled because it has filed a certificate of dissolution or the equivalent, its charter has been revoked, or its right to conduct business has been suspended by the jurisdiction of its incorporation, there is no revocation of the certificate of dissolution or no reinstatement of its charter or its right to conduct business; or

(iv) a partnership that is a partner has been dissolved and its business is being wound up;

(5) on application by the partnership or another partner, the partner's expulsion by judicial determination because:

(i) the partner engaged in wrongful conduct that adversely and materially affected the partnership business;

(ii) the partner willfully or persistently committed a material breach of the partnership agreement or of a duty owed to the partnership or the other partners under Section 404; or

(iii) the partner engaged in conduct relating to the partnership business which makes it not reasonably practicable to carry on the business in partnership with the partner;

(6) the partner's:

(i) becoming a debtor in bankruptcy;

(ii) executing an assignment for the benefit of creditors;

(iii) seeking, consenting to, or acquiescing in the appointment of a trustee, receiver, or liquidator of that partner or of all or substantially all of that partner's property; or

(iv) failing, within 90 days after the appointment, to have vacated or stayed the appointment of a trustee, receiver, or liquidator of the partner or of all or substantially all of the partner's property obtained without the partner's consent or acquiescence, or failing within 90 days after the expiration of a stay to have the appointment vacated;

(7) in the case of a partner who is an individual:

(i) the partner's death;

(ii) the appointment of a guardian or general conservator for the partner; or

(iii) a judicial determination that the partner has otherwise become incapable of performing the partner's duties under the partnership agreement;

* * * *

SECTION 602. Partner's Power to Dissociate; Wrongful Dissociation.

(a) A partner has the power to dissociate at any time, rightfully or wrongfully, by express will pursuant to Section 601(1).

(b) A partner's dissociation is wrongful only if:

(1) it is in breach of an express provision of the partnership agreement; or

(2) in the case of a partnership for a definite term or particular undertaking, before the expiration of the term or the completion of the undertaking:

(i) the partner withdraws by express will, unless the withdrawal follows within 90 days after another partner's dissociation by death or otherwise under Section 601(6) through (10) or wrongful dissociation under this subsection;

(ii) the partner is expelled by judicial determination under Section 601(5);

(iii) the partner is dissociated by becoming a debtor in bankruptcy; or

(iv) in the case of a partner who is not an individual, trust other than a business trust, or estate, the partner is expelled or otherwise dissociated because it willfully dissolved or terminated.

(c) A partner who wrongfully dissociates is liable to the partnership and to the other partners for damages caused by the dissociation. The liability is in addition to any other obligation of the partner to the partnership or to the other partners.

SECTION 603. Effect of Partner's Dissociation.

(a) If a partner's dissociation results in a dissolution and winding up of the partnership business, [Article] 8 applies; otherwise, [Article] 7 applies.

(b) Upon a partner's dissociation:

(1) the partner's right to participate in the management and conduct of the partnership business terminates, except as otherwise provided in Section 803;

(2) the partner's duty of loyalty under Section 404(b)(3) terminates; and

(3) the partner's duty of loyalty under Section 404(b)(1) and (2) and duty of care under Section 404(c) continue only with regard to matters arising and events occurring before the partner's dissociation, unless the partner participates in winding up the partnership's business pursuant to Section 803.

ARTICLE 7
PARTNER'S DISSOCIATION WHEN BUSINESS NOT WOUND UP

SECTION 701. Purchase of Dissociated Partner's Interest.

(a) If a partner is dissociated from a partnership without resulting in a dissolution and winding up of the partnership business under Section 801, the partnership shall cause the dissociated partner's interest in the partnership to be purchased for a buyout price determined pursuant to subsection (b).

(b) The buyout price of a dissociated partner's interest is the amount that would have been distributable to the dissociating partner under Section 807(b) if, on the date of dissociation, the assets of the partnership were sold at a price equal to the greater of the liquidation value or the value based on a sale of the entire business as a going concern without the dissociated partner and the partnership were wound up as of that date. Interest must be paid from the date of dissociation to the date of payment.

(c) Damages for wrongful dissociation under Section 602(b), and all other amounts owing, whether or not presently due, from the dissociated partner to the partnership, must be offset against the buyout price. Interest must be paid from the date the amount owed becomes due to the date of payment.

* * * *

SECTION 702. Dissociated Partner's Power to Bind and Liability to Partnership.

(a) For two years after a partner dissociates without resulting in a dissolution and winding up of the partnership business, the partnership, including a surviving partnership under [Article] 9, is bound by an act of the dissociated partner which would have bound the partnership under Section 301 before dissociation only if at the time of entering into the transaction the other party:

(1) reasonably believed that the dissociated partner was then a partner;

(2) did not have notice of the partner's dissociation; and

(3) is not deemed to have had knowledge under Section 303(e) or notice under Section 704(c).

(b) A dissociated partner is liable to the partnership for any damage caused to the partnership arising from an obligation incurred by the dissociated partner after dissociation for which the partnership is liable under subsection (a).

SECTION 703. Dissociated Partner's Liability to Other Persons.

(a) A partner's dissociation does not of itself discharge the partner's liability for a partnership obligation incurred before dissociation. A dissociated partner is not liable for a partnership obligation incurred after dissociation, except as otherwise provided in subsection (b).

(b) A partner who dissociates without resulting in a dissolution and winding up of the partnership business is liable as a partner to the other party in a transaction entered into by the partnership, or a surviving partnership under [Article] 9, within two years after the partner's dissociation, only if the partner is liable for the obligation under Section 306 and at the time of entering into the transaction the other party:

(1) reasonably believed that the dissociated partner was then a partner;

(2) did not have notice of the partner's dissociation; and

(3) is not deemed to have had knowledge under Section 303(e) or notice under Section 704(c).

* * * *

SECTION 704. Statement of Dissociation.

(a) A dissociated partner or the partnership may file a statement of dissociation stating the name of the partnership and that the partner is dissociated from the partnership.

(b) A statement of dissociation is a limitation on the authority of a dissociated partner for the purposes of Section 303(d) and (e).

(c) For the purposes of Sections 702(a)(3) and 703(b)(3), a person not a partner is deemed to have notice of the dissociation 90 days after the statement of dissociation is filed.

* * * *

ARTICLE 8
WINDING UP PARTNERSHIP BUSINESS

SECTION 801. Events Causing Dissolution and Winding Up of Partnership Business.

A partnership is dissolved, and its business must be wound up, only upon the occurrence of any of the following events:

(1) in a partnership at will, the partnership's having notice from a partner, other than a partner who is dissociated under Section 601(2) through (10), of that partner's express will to withdraw as a partner, or on a later date specified by the partner;

(2) in a partnership for a definite term or particular undertaking:

(i) within 90 days after a partner's dissociation by death or otherwise under Section 601(6) through (10) or wrongful dissociation under Section 602(b), the express will of at least half of the remaining partners to wind up the partnership business, for which purpose a partner's rightful dissociation pursuant to Section 602(b)(2)(i) constitutes the expression of that partner's will to wind up the partnership business;

(ii) the express will of all of the partners to wind up the partnership business; or

(iii) the expiration of the term or the completion of the undertaking;

(3) an event agreed to in the partnership agreement resulting in the winding up of the partnership business;

(4) an event that makes it unlawful for all or substantially all of the business of the partnership to be continued, but a cure of illegality within 90 days after notice to the partnership of the event is effective retroactively to the date of the event for purposes of this section;

(5) on application by a partner, a judicial determination that:

(i) the economic purpose of the partnership is likely to be unreasonably frustrated;

(ii) another partner has engaged in conduct relating to the partnership business which makes it not reasonably practicable to carry on the business in partnership with that partner; or

(iii) it is not otherwise reasonably practicable to carry on the partnership business in conformity with the partnership agreement; or

* * * *

SECTION 802. Partnership Continues after Dissolution.

(a) Subject to subsection (b), a partnership continues after dissolution only for the purpose of winding up its business. The partnership is terminated when the winding up of its business is completed.

(b) At any time after the dissolution of a partnership and before the winding up of its business is completed, all of the partners, including any dissociating partner other than a wrongfully dissociating partner, may waive the right to have the partnership's business wound up and the partnership terminated. In that event:

(1) the partnership resumes carrying on its business as if dissolution had never occurred, and any liability incurred by the partnership or a partner after the dissolution and before the waiver is determined as if dissolution had never occurred; and

(2) the rights of a third party accruing under Section 804(1) or arising out of conduct in reliance on the dissolution before the third party knew or received a notification of the waiver may not be adversely affected.

SECTION 803. Right to Wind Up Partnership.

(a) After dissolution, a partner who has not wrongfully dissociated may participate in winding up the partnership's business, but on application of any partner, partner's legal representative, or transferee, the [designate the appropriate court], for good cause shown, may order judicial supervision of the winding up.

(b) The legal representative of the last surviving partner may wind up a partnership's business.

(c) A person winding up a partnership's business may preserve the partnership business or property as a going concern for a reasonable time, prosecute and defend actions and proceedings, whether civil, criminal, or administrative, settle and close the partnership's business, dispose of and transfer the partnership's property, discharge the partnership's liabilities, distribute the assets of the partnership pursuant to Section 807, settle disputes by mediation or arbitration, and perform other necessary acts.

SECTION 804. Partner's Power to Bind Partnership After Dissolution.

Subject to Section 805, a partnership is bound by a partner's act after dissolution that:

(1) is appropriate for winding up the partnership business; or

(2) would have bound the partnership under Section 301 before dissolution, if the other party to the transaction did not have notice of the dissolution.

SECTION 805. Statement of Dissolution.

(a) After dissolution, a partner who has not wrongfully dissociated may file a statement of dissolution stating the name of the partnership and that the partnership has dissolved and is winding up its business.

(b) A statement of dissolution cancels a filed statement of partnership authority for the purposes of Section 303(d) and is a limitation on authority for the purposes of Section 303(e).

(c) For the purposes of Sections 301 and 804, a person not a partner is deemed to have notice of the dissolution and the limitation on the partners' authority as a result of the statement of dissolution 90 days after it is filed.

* * * *

SECTION 807. Settlement of Accounts and Contributions among Partners.

(a) In winding up a partnership's business, the assets of the partnership, including the contributions of the partners required by this section, must be applied to discharge its obligations to creditors, including, to the extent permitted by law, partners who are creditors. Any surplus must be applied to pay in cash the net amount distributable to partners in accordance with their right to distributions under subsection (b).

(b) Each partner is entitled to a settlement of all partnership accounts upon winding up the partnership business. In settling accounts among the partners, profits and losses that result from the liquidation of the partnership assets must be credited and charged to the partners' accounts. The partnership shall make a distribution to a partner in an amount equal to any excess of the credits over the charges in the partner's account. A partner shall contribute to the partnership an amount equal to any excess of the charges over the credits in the partner's account but excluding from the calculation charges attributable to an obligation for which the partner is not personally liable under Section 306.

* * * *

(d) After the settlement of accounts, each partner shall contribute, in the proportion in which the partner shares partnership losses, the amount necessary to satisfy partnership obligations that were not known at the time of the settlement and for which the partner is personally liable under Section 306.

* * * *

ARTICLE 10
LIMITED LIABILITY PARTNERSHIP

SECTION 1001. Statement of Qualification.

(a) A partnership may become a limited liability partnership pursuant to this section.

(b) The terms and conditions on which a partnership becomes a limited liability partnership must be approved by the vote necessary to amend the partnership agreement except, in the case of a partnership agreement that expressly considers obligations to contribute to the partnership, the vote necessary to amend those provisions.

(c) After the approval required by subsection (b), a partnership may become a limited liability partnership by filing a statement of qualification. The statement must contain:

(1) the name of the partnership;

(2) the street address of the partnership's chief executive office and, if different, the street address of an office in this State, if any;

(3) if the partnership does not have an office in this State, the name and street address of the partnership's agent for service of process;

(4) a statement that the partnership elects to be a limited liability partnership; and

(5) a deferred effective date, if any.

* * * *

SECTION 1002. Name.

The name of a limited liability partnership must end with "Registered Limited Liability Partnership", "Limited Liability Partnership", "R.L.L.P.", "L.L.P.", "RLLP," or "LLP".

SECTION 1003. Annual Report.

(a) A limited liability partnership, and a foreign limited liability partnership authorized to transact business in this State, shall file an annual report in the office of the [Secretary of State] which contains:

(1) the name of the limited liability partnership and the State or other jurisdiction under whose laws the foreign limited liability partnership is formed;

(2) the street address of the partnership's chief executive office and, if different, the street address of an office of the partnership in this State, if any; and

(3) if the partnership does not have an office in this State, the name and street address of the partnership's current agent for service of process.

(b) An annual report must be filed between [January 1 and April 1] of each year following the calendar year in which a partnership files a statement of qualification or a foreign partnership becomes authorized to transact business in this State.

* * * *

ARTICLE 11
FOREIGN LIMITED LIABILITY PARTNERSHIP

SECTION 1101. Law Governing Foreign Limited Liability Partnership.

(a) The law under which a foreign limited liability partnership is formed governs relations among the partners and between the partners and the partnership and the liability of partners for obligations of the partnership.

* * * *

SECTION 1102. Statement of Foreign Qualification.

(a) Before transacting business in this State, a foreign limited liability partnership must file a statement of foreign qualification. The statement must contain:

(1) the name of the foreign limited liability partnership which satisfies the requirements of the State or other juris-

diction under whose law it is formed and ends with "Registered Limited Liability Partnership", "Limited Liability Partnership", "R.L.L.P.", "L.L.P.", "RLLP," or "LLP";

(2) the street address of the partnership's chief executive office and, if different, the street address of an office of the partnership in this State, if any;

(3) if there is no office of the partnership in this State, the name and street address of the partnership's agent for service of process; and

(4) a deferred effective date, if any.

* * * *

SECTION 1104. Activities Not Constituting Transacting Business.

(a) Activities of a foreign limited liability partnership which do not constitute transacting business for the purpose of this [article] include:

(1) maintaining, defending, or settling an action or proceeding;

(2) holding meetings of its partners or carrying on any other activity concerning its internal affairs;

(3) maintaining bank accounts;

(4) maintaining offices or agencies for the transfer, exchange, and registration of the partnership's own securities or maintaining trustees or depositories with respect to those securities;

(5) selling through independent contractors;

(6) soliciting or obtaining orders, whether by mail or through employees or agents or otherwise, if the orders require acceptance outside this State before they become contracts;

(7) creating or acquiring indebtedness, with or without a mortgage, or other security interest in property;

(8) collecting debts or foreclosing mortgages or other security interests in property securing the debts, and holding, protecting, and maintaining property so acquired;

(9) conducting an isolated transaction that is completed within 30 days and is not one in the course of similar transactions; and

(10) transacting business in interstate commerce.

(b) For purposes of this [article], the ownership in this State of income-producing real property or tangible personal property, other than property excluded under subsection (a), constitutes transacting business in this State.

* * * *

The Revised Uniform Limited Partnership Act (Excerpts)

ARTICLE 1
GENERAL PROVISIONS

Section 101. Definitions.

As used in this [Act], unless the context otherwise requires:

(1) "Certificate of limited partnership" means the certificate referred to in Section 201, and the certificate as amended or restated.

(2) "Contribution" means any cash, property, services rendered, or a promissory note or other binding obligation to contribute cash or property or to perform services, which a partner contributes to a limited partnership in his capacity as a partner.

(3) "Event of withdrawal of a general partner" means an event that causes a person to cease to be a general partner as provided in Section 402.

(4) "Foreign limited partnership" means a partnership formed under the laws of any state other than this State and having as partners one or more general partners and one or more limited partners.

(5) "General partner" means a person who has been admitted to a limited partnership as a general partner in accordance with the partnership agreement and named in the certificate of limited partnership as a general partner.

(6) "Limited partner" means a person who has been admitted to a limited partnership as a limited partner in accordance with the partnership agreement.

(7) "Limited partnership" and "domestic limited partnership" mean a partnership formed by two or more persons under the laws of this State and having one or more general partners and one or more limited partners.

(8) "Partner" means a limited or general partner.

(9) "Partnership agreement" means any valid agreement, written or oral, of the partners as to the affairs of a limited partnership and the conduct of its business.

(10) "Partnership interest" means a partner's share of the profits and losses of a limited partnership and the right to receive distributions of partnership assets.

(11) "Person" means a natural person, partnership, limited partnership (domestic or foreign), trust, estate, association, or corporation.

(12) "State" means a state, territory, or possession of the United States, the District of Columbia, or the Commonwealth of Puerto Rico.

Section 102. Name.

The name of each limited partnership as set forth in its certificate of limited partnership:

(1) shall contain without abbreviation the words "limited partnership";

(2) may not contain the name of a limited partner unless (i) it is also the name of a general partner or the corporate name of a corporate general partner, or (ii) the business of the limited partnership had been carried on under that name before the admission of that limited partner;

(3) may not be the same as, or deceptively similar to, the name of any corporation or limited partnership organized under the laws of this State or licensed or registered as a foreign corporation or limited partnership in this State; and

(4) may not contain the following words [here insert prohibited words].

Section 103. Reservation of Name.

(a) The exclusive right to the use of a name may be reserved by:

(1) any person intending to organize a limited partnership under this [Act] and to adopt that name;

(2) any domestic limited partnership or any foreign limited partnership registered in this State which, in either case, intends to adopt that name;

(3) any foreign limited partnership intending to register in this State and adopt that name; and

(4) any person intending to organize a foreign limited partnership and intending to have it register in this State and adopt that name.

(b) The reservation shall be made by filing with the Secretary of State an application, executed by the applicant, to reserve a specified name. If the Secretary of State finds that the name is available for use by a domestic or foreign limited partnership, he [or she] shall reserve the name for the exclusive use of the applicant for a period of 120 days. Once having so reserved a name, the same applicant may not again reserve the same name until more than 60 days after the expiration of the last 120-day period for which that applicant reserved that name. The right to the exclusive use of a reserved name may be transferred to any other person by filing in the office of the Secretary of State a notice of the transfer, executed by the applicant for whom the name was reserved and specifying the name and address of the transferee.

Section 104. Specified Office and Agent.

Each limited partnership shall continuously maintain in this State:

(1) an office, which may but need not be a place of its business in this State, at which shall be kept the records required by Section 105 to be maintained; and

(2) an agent for service of process on the limited partnership, which agent must be an individual resident of this State, a domestic corporation, or a foreign corporation authorized to do business in this State.

Section 105. Records to Be Kept.

(a) Each limited partnership shall keep at the office referred to in Section 104(1) the following:

(1) a current list of the full name and last known business address of each partner, separately identifying the general

partners (in alphabetical order) and the limited partners (in alphabetical order);

(2) a copy of the certificate of limited partnership and all certificates of amendment thereto, together with executed copies of any powers of attorney pursuant to which any certificate has been executed;

(3) copies of the limited partnership's federal, state and local income tax returns and reports, if any, for the three most recent years;

(4) copies of any then effective written partnership agreements and of any financial statements of the limited partnership for the three most recent years; and

(5) unless contained in a written partnership agreement, a writing setting out:

(i) the amount of cash and a description and statement of the agreed value of the other property or services contributed by each partner and which each partner has agreed to contribute;

(ii) the times at which or events on the happening of which any additional contributions agreed to be made by each partner are to be made;

(iii) any right of a partner to receive, or of a general partner to make, distributions to a partner which include a return of all or any part of the partner's contribution; and

(iv) any events upon the happening of which the limited partnership is to be dissolved and its affairs wound up.

(b) Records kept under this section are subject to inspection and copying at the reasonable request and at the expense of any partner during ordinary business hours.

Section 106. Nature of Business.

A limited partnership may carry on any business that a partnership without limited partners may carry on except [here designate prohibited activities].

Section 107. Business Transactions of Partners with Partnership.

Except as provided in the partnership agreement, a partner may lend money to and transact other business with the limited partnership and, subject to other applicable law, has the same rights and obligations with respect thereto as a person who is not a partner.

ARTICLE 2
FORMATION; CERTIFICATE
OF LIMITED PARTNERSHIP

Section 201. Certificate of Limited Partnership.

(a) In order to form a limited partnership, a certificate of limited partnership must be executed and filed in the office of the Secretary of State. The certificate shall set forth:

(1) the name of the limited partnership;

(2) the address of the office and the name and address of the agent for service of process required to be maintained by Section 104;

(3) the name and the business address of each general partner;

(4) the latest date upon which the limited partnership is to dissolve; and

(5) any other matters the general partners determine to include therein.

(b) A limited partnership is formed at the time of the filing of the certificate of limited partnership in the office of the Secretary of State or at any later time specified in the certificate of limited partnership if, in either case, there has been substantial compliance with the requirements of this section.

Section 202. Amendment to Certificate.

(a) A certificate of limited partnership is amended by filing a certificate of amendment thereto in the office of the Secretary of State. The certificate shall set forth:

(1) the name of the limited partnership;

(2) the date of filing the certificate; and

(3) the amendment to the certificate.

(b) Within 30 days after the happening of any of the following events, an amendment to a certificate of limited partnership reflecting the occurrence of the event or events shall be filed:

(1) the admission of a new general partner;

(2) the withdrawal of a general partner; or

(3) the continuation of the business under Section 801 after an event of withdrawal of a general partner.

(c) A general partner who becomes aware that any statement in a certificate of limited partnership was false when made or that any arrangements or other facts described have changed, making the certificate inaccurate in any respect, shall promptly amend the certificate.

(d) A certificate of limited partnership may be amended at any time for any other proper purpose the general partners determine.

(e) No person has any liability because an amendment to a certificate of limited partnership has not been filed to reflect the occurrence of any event referred to in subsection (b) of this section if the amendment is filed within the 30-day period specified in subsection (b).

(f) A restated certificate of limited partnership may be executed and filed in the same manner as a certificate of amendment.

Section 203. Cancellation of Certificate.

A certificate of limited partnership shall be cancelled upon the dissolution and the commencement of winding up of the partnership or at any other time there are no limited partners. A certificate of cancellation shall be filed in the office of the Secretary of State and set forth:

(1) the name of the limited partnership;

(2) the date of filing of its certificate of limited partnership;

(3) the reason for filing the certificate of cancellation;

(4) the effective date (which shall be a date certain) of cancellation if it is not to be effective upon the filing of the certificate; and

(5) any other information the general partners filing the certificate determine.

Section 204. Execution of Certificates.

(a) Each certificate required by this Article to be filed in the office of the Secretary of State shall be executed in the following manner:

(1) an original certificate of limited partnership must be signed by all general partners;

(2) a certificate of amendment must be signed by at least one general partner and by each other general partner designated in the certificate as a new general partner; and

(3) a certificate of cancellation must be signed by all general partners.

(b) Any person may sign a certificate by an attorney-in-fact, but a power of attorney to sign a certificate relating to the admission of a general partner must specifically describe the admission.

(c) The execution of a certificate by a general partner constitutes an affirmation under the penalties of perjury that the facts stated therein are true.

Section 205. Execution by Judicial Act.

If a person required by Section 204 to execute any certificate fails or refuses to do so, any other person who is adversely affected by the failure or refusal may petition the [designate the appropriate court] to direct the execution of the certificate. If the court finds that it is proper for the certificate to be executed and that any person so designated has failed or refused to execute the certificate, it shall order the Secretary of State to record an appropriate certificate.

Section 206. Filing in Office of Secretary of State.

(a) Two signed copies of the certificate of limited partnership and of any certificates of amendment or cancellation (or of any judicial decree of amendment or cancellation) shall be delivered to the Secretary of State. A person who executes a certificate as an agent or fiduciary need not exhibit evidence of his [or her] authority as a prerequisite to filing. Unless the Secretary of State finds that any certificate does not conform to law, upon receipt of all filing fees required by law he [or she] shall:

(1) endorse on each duplicate original the word "Filed" and the day, month, and year of the filing thereof;

(2) file one duplicate original in his [or her] office; and

(3) return the other duplicate original to the person who filed it or his [or her] representative.

(b) Upon the filing of a certificate of amendment (or judicial decree of amendment) in the office of the Secretary of State, the certificate of limited partnership shall be amended as set forth therein, and upon the effective date of a certificate of cancellation (or a judicial decree thereof), the certificate of limited partnership is cancelled.

Section 207. Liability for False Statement in Certificate.

If any certificate of limited partnership or certificate of amendment or cancellation contains a false statement, one who suffers loss by reliance on the statement may recover damages for the loss from:

(1) any person who executes the certificate, or causes another to execute it on his behalf, and knew, and any general partner who knew or should have known, the statement to be false at the time the certificate was executed; and

(2) any general partner who thereafter knows or should have known that any arrangement or other fact described in the certificate has changed, making the statement inaccurate in any respect within a sufficient time before the statement was relied upon reasonably to have enabled that general partner to cancel or amend the certificate, or to file a petition for its cancellation or amendment under Section 205.

Section 208. Scope of Notice.

The fact that a certificate of limited partnership is on file in the office of the Secretary of State is notice that the partnership is a limited partnership and the persons designated therein as general partners are general partners, but it is not notice of any other fact.

Section 209. Delivery of Certificates to Limited Partners.

Upon the return by the Secretary of State pursuant to Section 206 of a certificate marked "Filed," the general partners shall promptly deliver or mail a copy of the certificate of limited partnership and each certificate of amendment or cancellation to each limited partner unless the partnership agreement provides otherwise.

ARTICLE 3
LIMITED PARTNERS

Section 301. Admission of Additional Limited Partners.

(a) A person becomes a limited partner on the later of:

(1) the date the original certificate of limited partnership is filed; or

(2) the date stated in the records of the limited partnership as the date that person becomes a limited partner.

(b) After the filing of a limited partnership's original certificate of limited partnership, a person may be admitted as an additional limited partner:

(1) in the case of a person acquiring a partnership interest directly from the limited partnership, upon compliance with the partnership agreement or, if the partnership agreement does not so provide, upon the written consent of all partners; and

(2) in the case of an assignee of a partnership interest of a partner who has the power, as provided in Section 704, to grant the assignee the right to become a limited partner, upon the exercise of that power and compliance with any conditions limiting the grant or exercise of the power.

Section 302. Voting.

Subject to Section 303, the partnership agreement may grant to all or a specified group of the limited partners the right to vote (on a per capita or other basis) upon any matter.

Section 303. Liability to Third Parties.

(a) Except as provided in subsection (d), a limited partner is not liable for the obligations of a limited partnership unless he [or she] is also a general partner or, in addition to the exercise of his [or her] rights and powers as a limited partner, he [or she] participates in the control of the business. However, if the limited partner participates in the control of the business, he [or she] is liable only to persons who transact business with the limited partnership reasonably believing, based upon the limited partner's conduct, that the limited partner is a general partner.

(b) A limited partner does not participate in the control of the business within the meaning of subsection (a) solely by doing one or more of the following:

(1) being a contractor for or an agent or employee of the limited partnership or of a general partner or being an officer, director, or shareholder of a general partner that is a corporation;

(2) consulting with and advising a general partner with respect to the business of the limited partnership;

(3) acting as surety for the limited partnership or guaranteeing or assuming one or more specific obligations of the limited partnership;

(4) taking any action required or permitted by law to bring or pursue a derivative action in the right of the limited partnership;

(5) requesting or attending a meeting of partners;

(6) proposing, approving, or disapproving, by voting or otherwise, one or more of the following matters:

(i) the dissolution and winding up of the limited partnership;

(ii) the sale, exchange, lease, mortgage, pledge, or other transfer of all or substantially all of the assets of the limited partnership;

(iii) the incurrence of indebtedness by the limited partnership other than in the ordinary course of its business;

(iv) a change in the nature of the business;

(v) the admission or removal of a general partner;

(vi) the admission or removal of a limited partner;

(vii) a transaction involving an actual or potential conflict of interest between a general partner and the limited partnership or the limited partners;

(viii) an amendment to the partnership agreement or certificate of limited partnership; or

(ix) matters related to the business of the limited partnership not otherwise enumerated in this subsection (b), which the partnership agreement states in writing may be subject to the approval or disapproval of limited partners;

(7) winding up the limited partnership pursuant to Section 803; or

(8) exercising any right or power permitted to limited partners under this [Act] and not specifically enumerated in this subsection (b).

(c) The enumeration in subsection (b) does not mean that the possession or exercise of any other powers by a limited partner constitutes participation by him [or her] in the business of the limited partnership.

(d) A limited partner who knowingly permits his [or her] name to be used in the name of the limited partnership, except under circumstances permitted by Section 102(2), is liable to creditors who extend credit to the limited partnership without actual knowledge that the limited partner is not a general partner.

Section 304. Person Erroneously Believing Himself [or Herself] Limited Partner.

(a) Except as provided in subsection (b), a person who makes a contribution to a business enterprise and erroneously but in good faith believes that he [or she] has become a limited partner in the enterprise is not a general partner in the enterprise and is not bound by its obligations by reason of making the contribution, receiving distributions from the enterprise, or exercising any rights of a limited partner, if, on ascertaining the mistake, he [or she]:

(1) causes an appropriate certificate of limited partnership or a certificate of amendment to be executed and filed; or

(2) withdraws from future equity participation in the enterprise by executing and filing in the office of the Secretary of State a certificate declaring withdrawal under this section.

(b) A person who makes a contribution of the kind described in subsection (a) is liable as a general partner to any third party who transacts business with the enterprise (i) before the person withdraws and an appropriate certificate is filed to show withdrawal, or (ii) before an appropriate certificate is filed to show that he [or she] is not a general partner, but in either case only if the third party actually believed in good faith that the person was a general partner at the time of the transaction.

Section 305. Information.

Each limited partner has the right to:

(1) inspect and copy any of the partnership records required to be maintained by Section 105; and

(2) obtain from the general partners from time to time upon reasonable demand (i) true and full information regarding the state of the business and financial condition of the limited partnership, (ii) promptly after becoming available, a copy of the limited partnership's federal, state, and local income tax returns for each year, and (iii) other information regarding the affairs of the limited partnership as is just and reasonable.

ARTICLE 4
GENERAL PARTNERS

Section 401. Admission of Additional General Partners.

After the filing of a limited partnership's original certificate of limited partnership, additional general partners may be admitted as provided in writing in the partnership agreement or, if the partnership agreement does not provide in writing for the admission of additional general partners, with the written consent of all partners.

Section 402. Events of Withdrawal.

Except as approved by the specific written consent of all partners at the time, a person ceases to be a general partner of a limited partnership upon the happening of any of the following events:

(1) the general partner withdraws from the limited partnership as provided in Section 602;

(2) the general partner ceases to be a member of the limited partnership as provided in Section 702;

(3) the general partner is removed as a general partner in accordance with the partnership agreement;

(4) unless otherwise provided in writing in the partnership agreement, the general partner: (i) makes an assignment for the benefit of creditors; (ii) files a voluntary petition in bank-

ruptcy; (iii) is adjudicated a bankrupt or insolvent; (iv) files a petition or answer seeking for himself [or herself] any reorganization, arrangement, composition, readjustment, liquidation, dissolution, or similar relief under any statute, law, or regulation; (v) files an answer or other pleading admitting or failing to contest the material allegations of a petition filed against him [or her] in any proceeding of this nature; or (vi) seeks, consents to, or acquiesces in the appointment of a trustee, receiver, or liquidator of the general partner or of all or any substantial part of his [or her] properties;

(5) unless otherwise provided in writing in the partnership agreement, [120] days after the commencement of any proceeding against the general partner seeking reorganization, arrangement, composition, readjustment, liquidation, dissolution, or similar relief under any statute, law, or regulation, the proceeding has not been dismissed, or if within [90] days after the appointment without his [or her] consent or acquiescence of a trustee, receiver, or liquidator of the general partner or of all or any substantial part of his [or her] properties, the appointment is not vacated or stayed or within [90] days after the expiration of any such stay, the appointment is not vacated;

(6) in the case of a general partner who is a natural person,

    (i) his [or her] death; or

    (ii) the entry of an order by a court of competent jurisdiction adjudicating him [or her] incompetent to manage his [or her] person or his [or her] estate;

(7) in the case of a general partner who is acting as a general partner by virtue of being a trustee of a trust, the termination of the trust (but not merely the substitution of a new trustee);

(8) in the case of a general partner that is a separate partnership, the dissolution and commencement of winding up of the separate partnership;

(9) in the case of a general partner that is a corporation, the filing of a certificate of dissolution, or its equivalent, for the corporation or the revocation of its charter; or

(10) in the case of an estate, the distribution by the fiduciary of the estate's entire interest in the partnership.

Section 403. General Powers and Liabilities.

(a) Except as provided in this [Act] or in the partnership agreement, a general partner of a limited partnership has the rights and powers and is subject to the restrictions of a partner in a partnership without limited partners.

(b) Except as provided in this [Act], a general partner of a limited partnership has the liabilities of a partner in a partnership without limited partners to persons other than the partnership and the other partners. Except as provided in this [Act] or in the partnership agreement, a general partner of a limited partnership has the liabilities of a partner in a partnership without limited partners to the partnership and to the other partners.

Section 404. Contributions by General Partner.

A general partner of a limited partnership may make contributions to the partnership and share in the profits and losses of, and in distributions from, the limited partnership as a general partner. A general partner also may make contributions to and share in profits, losses, and distributions as a limited partner. A person who is both a general partner and a limited partner has the rights and powers, and is subject to the restrictions and liabilities, of a general partner and, except as provided in the part-

nership agreement, also has the powers, and is subject to the restrictions, of a limited partner to the extent of his [or her] participation in the partnership as a limited partner.

Section 405. Voting.

The partnership agreement may grant to all or certain identified general partners the right to vote (on a per capita or any other basis), separately or with all or any class of the limited partners, on any matter.

ARTICLE 5
FINANCE

Section 501. Form of Contribution.

The contribution of a partner may be in cash, property, or services rendered, or a promissory note or other obligation to contribute cash or property or to perform services.

Section 502. Liability for Contribution.

(a) A promise by a limited partner to contribute to the limited partnership is not enforceable unless set out in a writing signed by the limited partner.

(b) Except as provided in the partnership agreement, a partner is obligated to the limited partnership to perform any enforceable promise to contribute cash or property or to perform services, even if he [or she] is unable to perform because of death, disability, or any other reason. If a partner does not make the required contribution of property or services, he [or she] is obligated at the option of the limited partnership to contribute cash equal to that portion of the value, as stated in the partnership records required to be kept pursuant to Section 105, of the stated contribution which has not been made.

(c) Unless otherwise provided in the partnership agreement, the obligation of a partner to make a contribution or return money or other property paid or distributed in violation of this [Act] may be compromised only by consent of all partners. Notwithstanding the compromise, a creditor of a limited partnership who extends credit, or, otherwise acts in reliance on that obligation after the partner signs a writing which reflects the obligation and before the amendment or cancellation thereof to reflect the compromise may enforce the original obligation.

Section 503. Sharing of Profits and Losses.

The profits and losses of a limited partnership shall be allocated among the partners, and among classes of partners, in the manner provided in writing in the partnership agreement. If the partnership agreement does not so provide in writing, profits and losses shall be allocated on the basis of the value, as stated in the partnership records required to be kept pursuant to Section 105, of the contributions made by each partner to the extent they have been received by the partnership and have not been returned.

Section 504. Sharing of Distributions.

Distributions of cash or other assets of a limited partnership shall be allocated among the partners and among classes of partners in the manner provided in writing in the partnership agreement. If the partnership agreement does not so provide in writing, distributions shall be made on the basis of the value, as stated in the partnership records required to be kept pursuant to Section 105, of the contributions made by each partner to the extent they have been received by the partnership and have not been returned.

ARTICLE 6
DISTRIBUTIONS AND WITHDRAWAL

Section 601. Interim Distributions.

Except as provided in this Article, a partner is entitled to receive distributions from a limited partnership before his [or her] withdrawal from the limited partnership and before the dissolution and winding up thereof to the extent and at the times or upon the happening of the events specified in the partnership agreement.

Section 602. Withdrawal of General Partner.

A general partner may withdraw from a limited partnership at any time by giving written notice to the other partners, but if the withdrawal violates the partnership agreement, the limited partnership may recover from the withdrawing general partner damages for breach of the partnership agreement and offset the damages against the amount otherwise distributable to him [or her].

Section 603. Withdrawal of Limited Partner.

A limited partner may withdraw from a limited partnership at the time or upon the happening of events specified in writing in the partnership agreement. If the agreement does not specify in writing the time or the events upon the happening of which a limited partner may withdraw or a definite time for the dissolution and winding up of the limited partnership, a limited partner may withdraw upon not less than six months' prior written notice to each general partner at his [or her] address on the books of the limited partnership at its office in this State.

Section 604. Distribution Upon Withdrawal.

Except as provided in this Article, upon withdrawal any withdrawing partner is entitled to receive any distribution to which he [or she] is entitled under the partnership agreement and, if not otherwise provided in the agreement, he [or she] is entitled to receive, within a reasonable time after withdrawal, the fair value of his [or her] interest in the limited partnership as of the date of withdrawal based upon his [or her] right to share in distributions from the limited partnership.

Section 605. Distribution in Kind.

Except as provided in writing in the partnership agreement, a partner, regardless of the nature of his [or her] contribution, has no right to demand and receive any distribution from a limited partnership in any form other than cash. Except as provided in writing in the partnership agreement, a partner may not be compelled to accept a distribution of any asset in kind from a limited partnership to the extent that the percentage of the asset distributed to him [or her] exceeds a percentage of that asset which is equal to the percentage in which he [or she] shares in distributions from the limited partnership.

Section 606. Right to Distribution.

At the time a partner becomes entitled to receive a distribution, he [or she] has the status of, and is entitled to all remedies available to, a creditor of the limited partnership with respect to the distribution.

Section 607. Limitations on Distribution.

A partner may not receive a distribution from a limited partnership to the extent that, after giving effect to the distribution, all liabilities of the limited partnership, other than liabilities to partners on account of their partnership interests, exceed the fair value of the partnership assets.

Section 608. Liability Upon Return of Contribution.

(a) If a partner has received the return of any part of his [or her] contribution without violation of the partnership agreement or this [Act], he [or she] is liable to the limited partnership for a period of one year thereafter for the amount of the returned contribution, but only to the extent necessary to discharge the limited partnership's liabilities to creditors who extended credit to the limited partnership during the period the contribution was held by the partnership.

(b) If a partner has received the return of any part of his [or her] contribution in violation of the partnership agreement or this [Act], he [or she] is liable to the limited partnership for a period of six years thereafter for the amount of the contribution wrongfully returned.

(c) A partner receives a return of his [or her] contribution to the extent that a distribution to him [or her] reduces his [or her] share of the fair value of the net assets of the limited partnership below the value, as set forth in the partnership records required to be kept pursuant to Section 105, of his [or her] contribution which has not been distributed to him [or her].

ARTICLE 7
ASSIGNMENT OF PARTNERHSIP INTERESTS

Section 701. Nature of Partnership Interest.

A partnership interest is personal property.

Section 702. Assignment of Partnership Interest.

Except as provided in the partnership agreement, a partnership interest is assignable in whole or in part. An assignment of a partnership interest does not dissolve a limited partnership or entitle the assignee to become or to exercise any rights of a partner. An assignment entitles the assignee to receive, to the extent assigned, only the distribution to which the assignor would be entitled. Except as provided in the partnership agreement, a partner ceases to be a partner upon assignment of all his [or her] partnership interest.

Section 703. Rights of Creditor.

On application to a court of competent jurisdiction by any judgment creditor of a partner, the court may charge the partnership interest of the partner with payment of the unsatisfied amount of the judgment with interest. To the extent so charged, the judgment creditor has only the rights of an assignee of the partnership interest. This [Act] does not deprive any partner of the benefit of any exemption laws applicable to his [or her] partnership interest.

Section 704. Right of Assignee to Become Limited Partner.

(a) An assignee of a partnership interest, including an assignee of a general partner, may become a limited partner if and to the extent that (i) the assignor gives the assignee that right in accordance with authority described in the partnership agreement, or (ii) all other partners consent.

(b) An assignee who has become a limited partner has, to the extent assigned, the rights and powers, and is subject to the restrictions and liabilities, of a limited partner under the partnership agreement and this [Act]. An assignee who becomes a limited partner also is liable for the obligations of his [or her] assignor to make and return contributions as provided in Articles 5 and 6. However, the assignee is not obligated for liabilities unknown to the assignee at the time he [or she] became a limited partner.

(c) If an assignee of a partnership interest becomes a limited partner, the assignor is not released from his [or her] liability to the limited partnership under Sections 207 and 502.

Section 705. Power of Estate of Deceased or Incompetent Partner.

If a partner who is an individual dies or a court of competent jurisdiction adjudges him [or her] to be incompetent to manage his [or her] person or his [or her] property, the partner's executor, administrator, guardian, conservator, or other legal representative may exercise all of the partner's rights for the purpose of settling his [or her] estate or administering his [or her] property, including any power the partner had to give an assignee the right to become a limited partner. If a partner is a corporation, trust, or other entity and is dissolved or terminated, the powers of that partner may be exercised by its legal representative or successor.

ARTICLE 8
DISSOLUTION

Section 801. Nonjudicial Dissolution.

A limited partnership is dissolved and its affairs shall be wound up upon the happening of the first to occur of the following:

(1) at the time specified in the certificate of limited partnership;

(2) upon the happening of events specified in writing in the partnership agreement;

(3) written consent of all partners;

(4) an event of withdrawal of a general partner unless at the time there is at least one other general partner and the written provisions of the partnership agreement permit the business of the limited partnership to be carried on by the remaining general partner and that partner does so, but the limited partnership is not dissolved and is not required to be wound up by reason of any event of withdrawal if, within 90 days after the withdrawal, all partners agree in writing to continue the business of the limited partnership and to the appointment of one or more additional general partners if necessary or desired; or

(5) entry of a decree of judicial dissolution under Section 802.

Section 802. Judicial Dissolution.

On application by or for a partner the [designate the appropriate court] court may decree dissolution of a limited partnership whenever it is not reasonably practicable to carry on the business in conformity with the partnership agreement.

Section 803. Winding Up.

Except as provided in the partnership agreement, the general partners who have not wrongfully dissolved a limited partnership or, if none, the limited partners, may wind up the limited partnership's affairs; but the [designate the appropriate court]

court may wind up the limited partnership's affairs upon application of any partner, his [or her] legal representative, or assignee.

Section 804. Distribution of Assets.

Upon the winding up of a limited partnership, the assets shall be distributed as follows:

(1) to creditors, including partners who are creditors, to the extent permitted by law, in satisfaction of liabilities of the limited partnership other than liabilities for distributions to partners under Section 601 or 604;

(2) except as provided in the partnership agreement, to partners and former partners in satisfaction of liabilities for distributions under Section 601 or 604; and

(3) except as provided in the partnership agreement, to partners first for the return of their contributions and secondly respecting their partnership interests, in the proportions in which the partners share in distributions.

ARTICLE 9
FOREIGN LIMITED PARTNERSHIPS

Section 901. Law Governing.

Subject to the Constitution of this State, (i) the laws of the state under which a foreign limited partnership is organized govern its organization and internal affairs and the liability of its limited partners, and (ii) a foreign limited partnership may not be denied registration by reason of any difference between those laws and the laws of this State.

Section 902. Registration.

Before transacting business in this State, a foreign limited partnership shall register with the Secretary of State. In order to register, a foreign limited partnership shall submit to the Secretary of State, in duplicate, an application for registration as a foreign limited partnership, signed and sworn to by a general partner and setting forth:

(1) the name of the foreign limited partnership and, if different, the name under which it proposes to register and transact business in this State;

(2) the State and date of its formation;

(3) the name and address of any agent for service of process on the foreign limited partnership whom the foreign limited partnership elects to appoint; the agent must be an individual resident of this State, a domestic corporation, or a foreign corporation having a place of business in, and authorized to do business in, this State;

(4) a statement that the Secretary of State is appointed the agent of the foreign limited partnership for service of process if no agent has been appointed under paragraph (3) or, if appointed, the agent's authority has been revoked or if the agent cannot be found or served with the exercise of reasonable diligence;

(5) the address of the office required to be maintained in the state of its organization by the laws of that state or, if not so required, of the principal office of the foreign limited partnership;

(6) the name and business address of each general partner; and

(7) the address of the office at which is kept a list of the names and addresses of the limited partners and their capital contributions, together with an undertaking by the foreign limited

partnership to keep those records until the foreign limited partnership's registration in this State is cancelled or withdrawn.

Section 903. Issuance of Registration.

(a) If the Secretary of State finds that an application for registration conforms to law and all requisite fees have been paid, he [or she] shall:

(1) endorse on the application the word "Filed", and the month, day, and year of the filing thereof;

(2) file in his [or her] office a duplicate original of the application; and

(3) issue a certificate of registration to transact business in this State.

(b) The certificate of registration, together with a duplicate original of the application, shall be returned to the person who filed the application or his [or her] representative.

Section 904. Name.

A foreign limited partnership may register with the Secretary of State under any name, whether or not it is the name under which it is registered in its state of organization, that includes without abbreviation the words "limited partnership" and that could be registered by a domestic limited partnership.

Section 905. Changes and Amendments.

If any statement in the application for registration of a foreign limited partnership was false when made or any arrangements or other facts described have changed, making the application inaccurate in any respect, the foreign limited partnership shall promptly file in the office of the Secretary of State a certificate, signed and sworn to by a general partner, correcting such statement.

Section 906. Cancellation of Registration.

A foreign limited partnership may cancel its registration by filing with the Secretary of State a certificate of cancellation signed and sworn to by a general partner. A cancellation does not terminate the authority of the Secretary of State to accept service of process on the foreign limited partnership with respect to [claims for relief] [causes of action] arising out of the transactions of business in this State.

Section 907. Transaction of Business Without Registration.

(a) A foreign limited partnership transacting business in this State may not maintain any action, suit, or proceeding in any court of this State until it has registered in this State.

(b) The failure of a foreign limited partnership to register in this State does not impair the validity of any contract or act of the foreign limited partnership or prevent the foreign limited partnership from defending any action, suit, or proceeding in any court of this State.

(c) A limited partner of a foreign limited partnership is not liable as a general partner of the foreign limited partnership solely by reason of having transacted business in this State without registration.

(d) A foreign limited partnership, by transacting business in this State without registration, appoints the Secretary of State as its agent for service of process with respect to [claims for relief] [causes of action] arising out of the transaction of business in this State.

Section 908. Action by [Appropriate Official].

The [designate the appropriate official] may bring an action to restrain a foreign limited partnership from transacting business in this State in violation of this Article.

ARTICLE 10
DERIVATIVE ACTIONS

Section 1001. Right of Action.

A limited partner may bring an action in the right of a limited partnership to recover a judgment in its favor if general partners with authority to do so have refused to bring the action or if an effort to cause those general partners to bring the action is not likely to succeed.

Section 1002. Proper Plaintiff.

In a derivative action, the plaintiff must be a partner at the time of bringing the action and (i) must have been a partner at the time of the transaction of which he [or she] complains or (ii) his [or her] status as a partner must have devolved upon him by operation of law or pursuant to the terms of the partnership agreement from a person who was a partner at the time of the transaction.

Section 1003. Pleading.

In a derivative action, the complaint shall set forth with particularity the effort of the plaintiff to secure initiation of the action by a general partner or the reasons for not making the effort.

Section 1004. Expenses.

If a derivative action is successful, in whole or in part, or if anything is received by the plaintiff as a result of a judgment, compromise, or settlement of an action or claim, the court may award the plaintiff reasonable expenses, including reasonable attorney's fees, and shall direct him [or her] to remit to the limited partnership the remainder of those proceeds received by him [or her].

ARTICLE 11
MISCELLANEOUS

Section 1101. Construction and Application.

This [Act] shall be so applied and construed to effectuate its general purpose to make uniform the law with respect to the subject of this [Act] among states enacting it.

Section 1102. Short Title.

This [Act] may be cited as the Uniform Limited Partnership Act.

Section 1103. Severability.

If any provision of this [Act] or its application to any person or circumstance is held invalid, the invalidity does not affect other provisions or applications of the [Act] which can be given effect without the invalid provision or application, and to this end the provisions of this [Act] are severable.

Section 1104. Effective Date, Extended Effective Date, and Repeal.

Except as set forth below, the effective date of this [Act] is _____ and the following acts [list existing limited partnership acts] are hereby repealed:

(1) The existing provisions for execution and filing of certificates of limited partnerships and amendments thereunder and cancellations thereof continue in effect until [specify time required to create central filing system], the extended effective date, and Sections 102, 103, 104, 105, 201, 202, 203, 204 and 206 are not effective until the extended effective date.

(2) Section 402, specifying the conditions under which a general partner ceases to be a member of a limited partnership, is not effective until the extended effective date, and the applicable provisions of existing law continue to govern until the extended effective date.

(3) Sections 501, 502 and 608 apply only to contributions and distributions made after the effective date of this [Act].

(4) Section 704 applies only to assignments made after the effective date of this [Act].

(5) Article 9, dealing with registration of foreign limited partnerships, is not effective until the extended effective date.

(6) Unless otherwise agreed by the partners, the applicable provisions of existing law governing allocation of profits and losses (rather than the provisions of Section 503), distributions to a withdrawing partner (rather than the provisions of Section 604), and distributions of assets upon the winding up of a limited partnership (rather than the provisions of Section 804) govern limited partnerships formed before the effective date of this [Act].

Section 1105. Rules for Cases Not Provided For in This [Act].

In any case not provided for in this [Act] the provisions of the Uniform Partnership Act govern.

Section 1106. Savings Clause.

The repeal of any statutory provision by this [Act] does not impair, or otherwise affect, the organization or the continued existence of a limited partnership existing at the effective date of this [Act], nor does the repeal of any existing statutory provision by this [Act] impair any contract or affect any right accrued before the effective date of this [Act].

The Revised Model Business Corporation Act (Excerpts)

CHAPTER 2.
INCORPORATION

§ 2.01 Incorporators

One or more persons may act as the incorporator or incorporators of a corporation by delivering articles of incorporation to the secretary of state for filing.

§ 2.02 Articles of Incorporation

(a) The articles of incorporation must set forth:

(1) a corporate name * * * ;

(2) the number of shares the corporation is authorized to issue;

(3) the street address of the corporation's initial registered office and the name of its initial registered agent at that office; and

(4) the name and address of each incorporator.

(b) The articles of incorporation may set forth:

(1) the names and addresses of the individuals who are to serve as the initial directors;

(2) provisions not inconsistent with law regarding:

(i) the purpose or purposes for which the corporation is organized;

(ii) managing the business and regulating the affairs of the corporation;

(iii) defining, limiting, and regulating the powers of the corporation, its board of directors, and shareholders;

(iv) a par value for authorized shares or classes of shares;

(v) the imposition of personal liability on shareholders for the debts of the corporation to a specified extent and upon specified conditions;

(3) any provision that under this Act is required or permitted to be set forth in the bylaws; and

(4) a provision eliminating or limiting the liability of a director to the corporation or its shareholders for money damages for any action taken, or any failure to take any action, as a director, except liability for (A) the amount of a financial benefit received by a director to which he is not entitled; (B) an intentional infliction of harm on the corporation or the shareholders; (C) [unlawful distributions]; or (D) an intentional violation of criminal law.

(c) The articles of incorporation need not set forth any of the corporate powers enumerated in this Act.

§ 2.03 Incorporation

(a) Unless a delayed effective date is specified, the corporate existence begins when the articles of incorporation are filed.

(b) The secretary of state's filing of the articles of incorporation is conclusive proof that the incorporators satisfied all conditions precedent to incorporation except in a proceeding by the state to cancel or revoke the incorporation or involuntarily dissolve the corporation.

§ 2.04 Liability for Preincorporation Transactions

All persons purporting to act as or on behalf of a corporation, knowing there was no incorporation under this Act, are jointly and severally liable for all liabilities created while so acting.

§ 2.05 Organization of Corporation

(a) After incorporation:

(1) if initial directors are named in the articles of incorporation, the initial directors shall hold an organizational meeting, at the call of a majority of the directors, to complete the organization of the corporation by appointing officers, adopting bylaws, and carrying on any other business brought before the meeting;

(2) if initial directors are not named in the articles, the incorporator or incorporators shall hold an organizational meeting at the call of a majority of the incorporators:

(i) to elect directors and complete the organization of the corporation; or

(ii) to elect a board of directors who shall complete the organization of the corporation.

(b) Action required or permitted by this Act to be taken by incorporators at an organizational meeting may be taken without a meeting if the action taken is evidenced by one or more written consents describing the action taken and signed by each incorporator.

(c) An organizational meeting may be held in or out of this state.

* * * *

CHAPTER 3.
PURPOSES AND POWERS

§ 3.01 Purposes

(a) Every corporation incorporated under this Act has the purpose of engaging in any lawful business unless a more limited purpose is set forth in the articles of incorporation.

(b) A corporation engaging in a business that is subject to regulation under another statute of this state may incorporate under this Act only if permitted by, and subject to all limitations of, the other statute.

§ 3.02 General Powers

Unless its articles of incorporation provide otherwise, every corporation has perpetual duration and succession in its corporate name and has the same powers as an individual to do all things necessary or convenient to carry out its business and affairs, including without limitation power:

(1) to sue and be sued, complain and defend in its corporate name;

(2) to have a corporate seal, which may be altered at will, and to use it, or a facsimile of it, by impressing or affixing it or in any other manner reproducing it;

(3) to make and amend bylaws, not inconsistent with its articles of incorporation or with the laws of this state, for managing the business and regulating the affairs of the corporation;

(4) to purchase, receive, lease, or otherwise acquire, and own, hold, improve, use, and otherwise deal with, real or personal property, or any legal or equitable interest in property, wherever located;

(5) to sell, convey, mortgage, pledge, lease, exchange, and otherwise dispose of all or any part of its property;

(6) to purchase, receive, subscribe for, or otherwise acquire; own, hold, vote, use, sell, mortgage, lend, pledge, or otherwise dispose of; and deal in and with shares or other interests in, or obligations of, any other entity;

(7) to make contracts and guarantees, incur liabilities, borrow money, issue its notes, bonds, and other obligations (which may be convertible into or include the option to purchase other securities of the corporation), and secure any of its obligations by mortgage or pledge of any of its property, franchises, or income;

(8) to lend money, invest and reinvest its funds, and receive and hold real and personal property as security for repayment;

(9) to be a promoter, partner, member, associate, or manager of any partnership, joint venture, trust, or other entity;

(10) to conduct its business, locate offices, and exercise the powers granted by this Act within or without this state;

(11) to elect directors and appoint officers, employees, and agents of the corporation, define their duties, fix their compensation, and lend them money and credit;

(12) to pay pensions and establish pension plans, pension trusts, profit sharing plans, share bonus plans, share option plans, and benefit or incentive plans for any or all of its current or former directors, officers, employees, and agents;

(13) to make donations for the public welfare or for charitable, scientific, or educational purposes;

(14) to transact any lawful business that will aid governmental policy;

(15) to make payments or donations, or do any other act, not inconsistent with law, that furthers the business and affairs of the corporation.

* * * *

CHAPTER 5.
OFFICE AND AGENT

§ 5.01 Registered Office and Registered Agent

Each corporation must continuously maintain in this state:

(1) a registered office that may be the same as any of its places of business; and

(2) a registered agent, who may be:

(i) an individual who resides in this state and whose business office is identical with the registered office;

(ii) a domestic corporation or not-for-profit domestic corporation whose business office is identical with the registered office; or

(iii) a foreign corporation or not-for-profit foreign corporation authorized to transact business in this state whose business office is identical with the registered office.

* * * *

§ 5.04 Service on Corporation

(a) A corporation's registered agent is the corporation's agent for service of process, notice, or demand required or permitted by law to be served on the corporation.

(b) If a corporation has no registered agent, or the agent cannot with reasonable diligence be served, the corporation may be served by registered or certified mail, return receipt requested, addressed to the secretary of the corporation at its principal office. Service is perfected under this subsection at the earliest of:

(1) the date the corporation receives the mail;

(2) the date shown on the return receipt, if signed on behalf of the corporation; or

(3) five days after its deposit in the United States Mail, if mailed postpaid and correctly addressed.

(c) This section does not prescribe the only means, or necessarily the required means, of serving a corporation.

CHAPTER 6.
SHARES AND DISTRIBUTIONS

* * * *

Subchapter B. Issuance of Shares
* * * *

§ 6.21 Issuance of Shares

(a) The powers granted in this section to the board of directors may be reserved to the shareholders by the articles of incorporation.

(b) The board of directors may authorize shares to be issued for consideration consisting of any tangible or intangible property or benefit to the corporation, including cash, promissory notes, services performed, contracts for services to be performed, or other securities of the corporation.

(c) Before the corporation issues shares, the board of directors must determine that the consideration received or to be received for shares to be issued is adequate. That determination by the board of directors is conclusive insofar as the adequacy of consideration for the issuance of shares relates to whether the shares are validly issued, fully paid, and nonassessable.

(d) When the corporation receives the consideration for which the board of directors authorized the issuance of shares, the shares issued therefor are fully paid and nonassessable.

(e) The corporation may place in escrow shares issued for a contract for future services or benefits or a promissory note, or make other arrangements to restrict the transfer of the shares, and may credit distributions in respect of the shares against their purchase price, until the services are performed, the note is paid, or the benefits received. If the services are not performed, the note is not paid, or the benefits are not received, the shares escrowed or restricted and the distributions credited may be cancelled in whole or part.

* * * *

§ 6.27 Restriction on Transfer or Registration of Shares and Other Securities

(a) The articles of incorporation, bylaws, an agreement among shareholders, or an agreement between shareholders and the corporation may impose restrictions on the transfer or registration of transfer of shares of the corporation. A restriction does not affect shares issued before the restriction was adopted unless the holders of the shares are parties to the restriction agreement or voted in favor of the restriction.

(b) A restriction on the transfer or registration of transfer of shares is valid and enforceable against the holder or a transferee of the holder if the restriction is authorized by this section and its existence is noted conspicuously on the front or back of the certificate or is contained in the information statement [sent to the shareholder]. Unless so noted, a restriction is not enforceable against a person without knowledge of the restriction.

(c) A restriction on the transfer or registration of transfer of shares is authorized:

(1) to maintain the corporation's status when it is dependent on the number or identity of its shareholders;

(2) to preserve exemptions under federal or state securities law;

(3) for any other reasonable purpose.

(d) A restriction on the transfer or registration of transfer of shares may:

(1) obligate the shareholder first to offer the corporation or other persons (separately, consecutively, or simultaneously) an opportunity to acquire the restricted shares;

(2) obligate the corporate or other persons (separately, consecutively, or simultaneously) to acquire the restricted shares;

(3) require the corporation, the holders of any class of its shares, or another person to approve the transfer of the restricted shares, if the requirement is not manifestly unreasonable;

(4) prohibit the transfer of the restricted shares to designated persons or classes of persons, if the prohibition is not manifestly unreasonable.

(e) For purposes of this section, "shares" includes a security convertible into or carrying a right to subscribe for or acquire shares.

* * * *

CHAPTER 7.
SHAREHOLDERS
Subchapter A. Meetings
§ 7.01 Annual Meeting

(a) A corporation shall hold annually at a time stated in or fixed in accordance with the bylaws a meeting of shareholders.

(b) Annual shareholders' meetings may be held in or out of this state at the place stated in or fixed in accordance with the bylaws. If no place is stated in or fixed in accordance with the bylaws, annual meetings shall be held at the corporation's principal office.

(c) The failure to hold an annual meeting at the time stated in or fixed in accordance with a corporation's bylaws does not affect the validity of any corporate action.

* * * *

§ 7.05 Notice of Meeting

(a) A corporation shall notify shareholders of the date, time, and place of each annual and special shareholders' meeting no fewer than 10 nor more than 60 days before the meeting date. Unless this Act or the articles of incorporation require otherwise, the corporation is required to give notice only to shareholders entitled to vote at the meeting.

(b) Unless this Act or the articles of incorporation require otherwise, notice of an annual meeting need not include a description of the purpose or purposes for which the meeting is called.

(c) Notice of a special meeting must include a description of the purpose or purposes for which the meeting is called.

(d) If not otherwise fixed * * *, the record date for determining shareholders entitled to notice of and to vote at an annual or special shareholders' meeting is the day before the first notice is delivered to shareholders.

(e) Unless the bylaws require otherwise, if an annual or special shareholders' meeting is adjourned to a different date, time, or place, notice need not be given of the new date, time, or place if the new date, time, or place is announced at the meeting before adjournment. * * *

* * * *

§ 7.07 Record Date

(a) The bylaws may fix or provide the manner of fixing the record date for one or more voting groups in order to determine the shareholders entitled to notice of a shareholders' meeting, to demand a special meeting, to vote, or to take any other action. If the bylaws do not fix or provide for fixing a record date, the board of directors of the corporation may fix a future date as the record date.

(b) A record date fixed under this section may not be more than 70 days before the meeting or action requiring a determination of shareholders.

(c) A determination of shareholders entitled to notice of or to vote at a shareholders' meeting is effective for any adjournment of the meeting unless the board of directors fixes a new record date, which it must do if the meeting is adjourned to a date more than 120 days after the date fixed for the original meeting.

(d) If a court orders a meeting adjourned to a date more than 120 days after the date fixed for the original meeting, it may provide that the original record date continues in effect or it may fix a new record date.

Subchapter B. Voting
§ 7.20 Shareholders' List for Meeting

(a) After fixing a record date for a meeting, a corporation shall prepare an alphabetical list of the names of all its shareholders who are entitled to notice of a shareholders' meeting. The list must be arranged by voting group (and within each voting group by class or series of shares) and show the address of and number of shares held by each shareholder.

(b) The shareholders' list must be available for inspection by any shareholder, beginning two business days after notice of the meeting is given for which the list was prepared and continuing through the meeting, at the corporation's principal office or at a place identified in the meeting notice in the city where the meeting will be held. A shareholder, his agent, or attorney is entitled on written demand to inspect and, subject to the requirements of section 16.02(c), to copy the list, during regular business hours and at his expense, during the period it is available for inspection.

(c) The corporation shall make the shareholders' list available at the meeting, and any shareholder, his agent, or attorney is entitled to inspect the list at any time during the meeting or any adjournment.

(d) If the corporation refuses to allow a shareholder, his agent, or attorney to inspect the shareholders' list before or at the meeting (or copy the list as permitted by subsection (b)), the [name or describe] court of the county where a corporation's principal office (or, if none in this state, its registered office) is located, on application of the shareholder, may summarily order the inspection or copying at the corporation's expense and may postpone the meeting for which the list was prepared until the inspection or copying is complete.

(e) Refusal or failure to prepare or make available the shareholders' list does not affect the validity of action taken at the meeting.

* * * *

§ 7.22 Proxies

(a) A shareholder may vote his shares in person or by proxy.

(b) A shareholder may appoint a proxy to vote or otherwise act for him by signing an appointment form, either personally or by his attorney-in-fact.

(c) An appointment of a proxy is effective when received by the secretary or other officer or agent authorized to tabulate votes. An appointment is valid for 11 months unless a longer period is expressly provided in the appointment form.

* * * *

§ 7.28 Voting for Directors; Cumulative Voting

(a) Unless otherwise provided in the articles of incorporation, directors are elected by a plurality of the votes cast by the shares entitled to vote in the election at a meeting at which a quorum is present.

(b) Shareholders do not have a right to cumulate their votes for directors unless the articles of incorporation so provide.

(c) A statement included in the articles of incorporation that "[all] [a designated voting group of] shareholders are entitled to cumulate their votes for directors" (or words of similar import) means that the shareholders designated are entitled to multiply the number of votes they are entitled to cast by the number of directors for whom they are entitled to vote and cast the product for a single candidate or distribute the product among two or more candidates.

(d) Shares otherwise entitled to vote cumulatively may not be voted cumulatively at a particular meeting unless:

(1) the meeting notice or proxy statement accompanying the notice states conspicuously that cumulative voting is authorized; or

(2) a shareholder who has the right to cumulate his votes gives notice to the corporation not less than 48 hours before the time set for the meeting of his intent to cumulate his votes during the meeting, and if one shareholder gives this notice all other shareholders in the same voting group participating in the election are entitled to cumulate their votes without giving further notice.

* * * *

Subchapter D. Derivative Proceedings

* * * *

§ 7.41 Standing

A shareholder may not commence or maintain a derivative proceeding unless the shareholder:

(1) was a shareholder of the corporation at the time of the act or omission complained of or became a shareholder through transfer by operation of law from one who was a shareholder at that time; and

(2) fairly and adequately represents the interests of the corporation in enforcing the right of the corporation.

§ 7.42 Demand

No shareholder may commence a derivative proceeding until:

(1) a written demand has been made upon the corporation to take suitable action; and

(2) 90 days have expired from the date the demand was made unless the shareholder has earlier been notified that the demand has been rejected by the corporation or unless irreparable injury to the corporation would result by waiting for the expiration of the 90 day period.

* * * *

CHAPTER 8.
DIRECTORS AND OFFICERS
Subchapter A. Board of Directors

* * * *

§ 8.02 Qualifications of Directors

The articles of incorporation or bylaws may prescribe qualifications for directors. A director need not be a resident of this state or a shareholder of the corporation unless the articles of incorporation or bylaws so prescribe.

§ 8.03 Number and Election of Directors

(a) A board of directors must consist of one or more individuals, with the number specified in or fixed in accordance with the articles of incorporation or bylaws.

(b) If a board of directors has power to fix or change the number of directors, the board may increase or decrease by 30 percent or less the number of directors last approved by the shareholders, but only the shareholders may increase or decrease by more than 30 percent the number of directors last approved by the shareholders.

(c) The articles of incorporation or bylaws may establish a variable range for the size of the board of directors by fixing a minimum and maximum number of directors. If a variable range is established, the number of directors may be fixed or changed from time to time, within the minimum and maximum, by the shareholders or the board of directors. After shares are issued, only the shareholders may change the range for the size of the board or change from a fixed to a variable-range size board or vice versa.

(d) Directors are elected at the first annual shareholders' meeting and at each annual meeting thereafter unless their terms are staggered under section 8.06.

*   *   *   *

§ 8.08 Removal of Directors by Shareholders

(a) The shareholders may remove one or more directors with or without cause unless the articles of incorporation provide that directors may be removed only for cause.

(b) If a director is elected by a voting group of shareholders, only the shareholders of that voting group may participate in the vote to remove him.

(c) If cumulative voting is authorized, a director may not be removed if the number of votes sufficient to elect him under cumulative voting is voted against his removal. If cumulative voting is not authorized, a director may be removed only if the number of votes cast to remove him exceeds the number of votes cast not to remove him.

(d) A director may be removed by the shareholders only at a meeting called for the purpose of removing him and the meeting notice must state that the purpose, or one of the purposes, of the meeting is removal of the director.

*   *   *   *

Subchapter B. Meetings and Action of the Board

§ 8.20 Meetings

(a) The board of directors may hold regular or special meetings in or out of this state.

(b) Unless the articles of incorporation or bylaws provide otherwise, the board of directors may permit any or all directors to participate in a regular or special meeting by, or conduct the meeting through the use of, any means of communication by which all directors participating may simultaneously hear each other during the meeting. A director participating in a meeting by this means is deemed to be present in person at the meeting.

*   *   *   *

§ 8.22 Notice of Meeting

(a) Unless the articles of incorporation or bylaws provide otherwise, regular meetings of the board of directors may be held without notice of the date, time, place, or purpose of the meeting.

(b) Unless the articles of incorporation or bylaws provide for a longer or shorter period, special meetings of the board of directors must be preceded by at least two days' notice of the date, time, and place of the meeting. The notice need not describe the purpose of the special meeting unless required by the articles of incorporation or bylaws.

*   *   *   *

§ 8.24 Quorum and Voting

(a) Unless the articles of incorporation or bylaws require a greater number, a quorum of a board of directors consists of:

(1) a majority of the fixed number of directors if the corporation has a fixed board size; or

(2) a majority of the number of directors prescribed, or if no number is prescribed the number in office immediately before the meeting begins, if the corporation has a variable-range size board.

(b) The articles of incorporation or bylaws may authorize a quorum of a board of directors to consist of no fewer than one-third of the fixed or prescribed number of directors determined under subsection (a).

(c) If a quorum is present when a vote is taken, the affirmative vote of a majority of directors present is the act of the board of directors unless the articles of incorporation or bylaws require the vote of a greater number of directors.

(d) A director who is present at a meeting of the board of directors or a committee of the board of directors when corporate action is taken is deemed to have assented to the action taken unless: (1) he objects at the beginning of the meeting (or promptly upon his arrival) to holding it or transacting business at the meeting; (2) his dissent or abstention from the action taken is entered in the minutes of the meeting; or (3) he delivers written notice of his dissent or abstention to the presiding officer of the meeting before its adjournment or to the corporation immediately after adjournment of the meeting. The right of dissent or abstention is not available to a director who votes in favor of the action taken.

*   *   *   *

Subchapter C. Standards of Conduct

§ 8.30 General Standards for Directors

(a) A director shall discharge his duties as a director, including his duties as a member of a committee:

(1) in good faith;

(2) with the care an ordinarily prudent person in a like position would exercise under similar circumstances; and

(3) in a manner he reasonably believes to be in the best interests of the corporation.

(b) In discharging his duties a director is entitled to rely on information, opinions, reports, or statements, including financial statements and other financial data, if prepared or presented by:

(1) one or more officers or employees of the corporation whom the director reasonably believes to be reliable and competent in the matters presented;

(2) legal counsel, public accountants, or other persons as to matters the director reasonably believes are within the person's professional or expert competence; or

(3) a committee of the board of directors of which he is not a member if the director reasonably believes the committee merits confidence.

(c) A director is not acting in good faith if he has knowledge concerning the matter in question that makes reliance otherwise permitted by subsection (b) unwarranted.

(d) A director is not liable for any action taken as a director, or any failure to take any action, if he performed the duties of his office in compliance with this section.

*   *   *   *

Subchapter D. Officers

*   *   *   *

§ 8.41 Duties of Officers

Each officer has the authority and shall perform the duties set forth in the bylaws or, to the extent consistent with the bylaws, the duties prescribed by the board of directors or by direction of an officer authorized by the board of directors to prescribe the duties of other officers.

§ 8.42 Standards of Conduct for Officers

(a) An officer with discretionary authority shall discharge his duties under that authority:

(1) in good faith;

(2) with the care an ordinarily prudent person in a like position would exercise under similar circumstances; and

(3) in a manner he reasonably believes to be in the best interests of the corporation.

(b) In discharging his duties an officer is entitled to rely on information, opinions, reports, or statements, including financial statements and other financial data, if prepared or presented by:

(1) one or more officers or employees of the corporation whom the officer reasonably believes to be reliable and competent in the matters presented; or

(2) legal counsel, public accountants, or other persons as to matters the officer reasonably believes are within the person's professional or expert competence.

(c) An officer is not acting in good faith if he has knowledge concerning the matter in question that makes reliance otherwise permitted by subsection (b) unwarranted.

(d) An officer is not liable for any action taken as an officer, or any failure to take any action, if he performed the duties of his office in compliance with this section.

* * * *

CHAPTER 11.
MERGER AND SHARE EXCHANGE

§ 11.01 Merger

(a) One or more corporations may merge into another corporation if the board of directors of each corporation adopts and its shareholders (if required * * *) approve a plan of merger.

(b) The plan of merger must set forth:

(1) the name of each corporation planning to merge and the name of the surviving corporation into which each other corporation plans to merge;

(2) the terms and conditions of the merger; and

(3) the manner and basis of converting the shares of each corporation into shares, obligations, or other securities of the surviving or any other corporation or into cash or other property in whole or part.

(c) The plan of merger may set forth:

(1) amendments to the articles of incorporation of the surviving corporation; and

(2) other provisions relating to the merger.

* * * *

§ 11.04 Merger of Subsidiary

(a) A parent corporation owning at least 90 percent of the outstanding shares of each class of a subsidiary corporation may merge the subsidiary into itself without approval of the shareholders of the parent or subsidiary.

(b) The board of directors of the parent shall adopt a plan of merger that sets forth:

(1) the names of the parent and subsidiary; and

(2) the manner and basis of converting the shares of the subsidiary into shares, obligations, or other securities of the parent or any other corporation or into cash or other property in whole or part.

(c) The parent shall mail a copy or summary of the plan of merger to each shareholder of the subsidiary who does not waive the mailing requirement in writing.

(d) The parent may not deliver articles of merger to the secretary of state for filing until at least 30 days after the date it mailed a copy of the plan of merger to each shareholder of the subsidiary who did not waive the mailing requirement.

(e) Articles of merger under this section may not contain amendments to the articles of incorporation of the parent corporation (except for amendments enumerated in section 10.02).

* * * *

§ 11.06 Effect of Merger or Share Exchange

(a) When a merger takes effect:

(1) every other corporation party to the merger merges into the surviving corporation and the separate existence of every corporation except the surviving corporation ceases;

(2) the title to all real estate and other property owned by each corporation party to the merger is vested in the surviving corporation without reversion or impairment;

(3) the surviving corporation has all liabilities of each corporation party to the merger;

(4) a proceeding pending against any corporation party to the merger may be continued as if the merger did not occur or the surviving corporation may be substituted in the proceeding for the corporation whose existence ceased;

(5) the articles of incorporation of the surviving corporation are amended to the extent provided in the plan of merger; and

(6) the shares of each corporation party to the merger that are to be converted into shares, obligations, or other securities of the surviving or any other corporation or into cash or other property are converted and the former holders of the shares are entitled only to the rights provided in the articles of merger or to their rights under chapter 13.

(b) When a share exchange takes effect, the shares of each acquired corporation are exchanged as provided in the plan, and the former holders of the shares are entitled only to the exchange rights provided in the articles of share exchange or to their rights under chapter 13.

* * * *

CHAPTER 13.
DISSENTERS' RIGHTS

Subchapter A. Right to Dissent and Obtain Payment for Shares

* * * *

§ 13.02 Right to Dissent

(a) A shareholder is entitled to dissent from, and obtain payment of the fair value of his shares in the event of, any of the following corporate actions:

(1) consummation of a plan of merger to which the corporation is a party (i) if shareholder approval is required for the merger by [statute] or the articles of incorporation and the shareholder is entitled to vote on the merger or (ii) if the corporation is a subsidiary that is merged with its parent under section 11.04;

(2) consummation of a plan of share exchange to which the corporation is a party as the corporation whose shares will be acquired, if the shareholder is entitled to vote on the plan;

(3) consummation of a sale or exchange of all, or substantially all, of the property of the corporation other than in the usual and regular course of business, if the shareholder is entitled to vote on the sale or exchange, including a sale in dissolution, but not including a sale pursuant to court order or a sale for cash pursuant to a plan by which all or substantially all of the net proceeds of the sale will be distributed to the shareholders within one year after the date of sale;

(4) an amendment of the articles of incorporation that materially and adversely affects rights in respect of a dissenter's shares because it:

(i) alters or abolishes a preferential right of the shares;

(ii) creates, alters, or abolishes a right in respect of redemption, including a provision respecting a sinking fund for the redemption or repurchase, of the shares;

(iii) alters or abolishes a preemptive right of the holder of the shares to acquire shares or other securities;

(iv) excludes or limits the right of the shares to vote on any matter, or to cumulate votes, other than a limitation by dilution through issuance of shares or other securities with similar voting rights; or

(v) reduces the number of shares owned by the shareholder to a fraction of a share if the fractional share so created is to be acquired for cash * * * ; or

(5) any corporate action taken pursuant to a shareholder vote to the extent the articles of incorporation, bylaws, or a resolution of the board of directors provides that voting or nonvoting shareholders are entitled to dissent and obtain payment for their shares.

(b) A shareholder entitled to dissent and obtain payment for his shares under this chapter may not challenge the corporate action creating his entitlement unless the action is unlawful or fraudulent with respect to the shareholder or the corporation.

* * * *

Subchapter B. Procedure for Exercise of Dissenters' Rights

* * * *

§ 13.21 Notice of Intent to Demand Payment

(a) If proposed corporate action creating dissenters' rights under section 13.02 is submitted to a vote at a shareholders' meeting, a shareholder who wishes to assert dissenters' rights (1) must deliver to the corporation before the vote is taken written notice of his intent to demand payment for his shares if the proposed action is effectuated and (2) must not vote his shares in favor of the proposed action.

(b) A shareholder who does not satisfy the requirements of subsection (a) is not entitled to payment for his shares under this chapter.

* * * *

§ 13.25 Payment

(a) * * * [A]s soon as the proposed corporate action is taken, or upon receipt of a payment demand, the corporation shall pay each dissenter * * * the amount the corporation estimates to be the fair value of his shares, plus accrued interest.

* * * *

§ 13.28 Procedure If Shareholder Dissatisfied with Payment or Offer

(a) A dissenter may notify the corporation in writing of his own estimate of the fair value of his shares and amount of interest due, and demand payment of his estimate (less any payment under section 13.25) * * * if:

(1) the dissenter believes that the amount paid under section 13.25 * * * is less than the fair value of his shares or that the interest due is incorrectly calculated;

(2) the corporation fails to make payment under section 13.25 within 60 days after the date set for demanding payment; or

(3) the corporation, having failed to take the proposed action, does not return the deposited certificates or release the transfer restrictions imposed on uncertificated shares within 60 days after the date set for demanding payment.

(b) A dissenter waives his right to demand payment under this section unless he notifies the corporation of his demand in writing under subsection (a) within 30 days after the corporation made or offered payment for his shares.

* * * *

CHAPTER 14.
DISSOLUTION
Subchapter A. Voluntary Dissolution

* * * *

§ 14.02 Dissolution by Board of Directors and Shareholders

(a) A corporation's board of directors may propose dissolution for submission to the shareholders.

(b) For a proposal to dissolve to be adopted:

(1) the board of directors must recommend dissolution to the shareholders unless the board of directors determines that because of conflict of interest or other special circumstances it should make no recommendation and communicates the basis for its determination to the shareholders; and

(2) the shareholders entitled to vote must approve the proposal to dissolve as provided in subsection (e).

(c) The board of directors may condition its submission of the proposal for dissolution on any basis.

(d) The corporation shall notify each shareholder, whether or not entitled to vote, of the proposed shareholders' meeting in accordance with section 7.05. The notice must also state that the purpose, or one of the purposes, of the meeting is to consider dissolving the corporation.

(e) Unless the articles of incorporation or the board of directors (acting pursuant to subsection (c)) require a greater vote or a vote by voting groups, the proposal to dissolve to be adopted must be approved by a majority of all the votes entitled to be cast on that proposal.

* * * *

§ 14.05 Effect of Dissolution

(a) A dissolved corporation continues its corporate existence but may not carry on any business except that appropriate to wind up and liquidate its business and affairs, including:

(1) collecting its assets;

(2) disposing of its properties that will not be distributed in kind to its shareholders;

(3) discharging or making provision for discharging its liabilities;

(4) distributing its remaining property among its shareholders according to their interests; and

(5) doing every other act necessary to wind up and liquidate its business and affairs.

(b) Dissolution of a corporation does not:

(1) transfer title to the corporation's property;

(2) prevent transfer of its shares or securities, although the authorization to dissolve may provide for closing the corporation's share transfer records;

(3) subject its directors or officers to standards of conduct different from those prescribed in chapter 8;

(4) change quorum or voting requirements for its board of directors or shareholders; change provisions for selection, resignation, or removal of its directors or officers or both; or change provisions for amending its bylaws;

(5) prevent commencement of a proceeding by or against the corporation in its corporate name;

(6) abate or suspend a proceeding pending by or against the corporation on the effective date of dissolution; or

(7) terminate the authority of the registered agent of the corporation.

* * * *

Subchapter C. Judicial Dissolution

§ 14.30 Grounds for Judicial Dissolution

The [name or describe court or courts] may dissolve a corporation:

(1) in a proceeding by the attorney general if it is established that:

(i) the corporation obtained its articles of incorporation through fraud; or

(ii) the corporation has continued to exceed or abuse the authority conferred upon it by law;

(2) in a proceeding by a shareholder if it is established that:

(i) the directors are deadlocked in the management of the corporate affairs, the shareholders are unable to break the deadlock, and irreparable injury to the corporation is threatened or being suffered, or the business and affairs of the corporation can no longer be conducted to the advantage of the shareholders generally, because of the deadlock;

(ii) the directors or those in control of the corporation have acted, are acting, or will act in a manner that is illegal, oppressive, or fraudulent;

(iii) the shareholders are deadlocked in voting power and have failed, for a period that includes at least two consecutive annual meeting dates, to elect successors to directors whose terms have expired; or

(iv) the corporate assets are being misapplied or wasted;

(3) in a proceeding by a creditor if it is established that:

(i) the creditor's claim has been reduced to judgment, the execution on the judgment returned unsatisfied, and the corporation is insolvent; or

(ii) the corporation has admitted in writing that the creditor's claim is due and owing and the corporation is insolvent; or

(4) in a proceeding by the corporation to have its voluntary dissolution continued under court supervision.

* * * *

CHAPTER 16.
RECORDS AND REPORTS

Subchapter A. Records

§ 16.01 Corporate Records

(a) A corporation shall keep as permanent records minutes of all meetings of its shareholders and board of directors, a record of all actions taken by the shareholders or board of directors without a meeting, and a record of all actions taken by a committee of the board of directors in place of the board of directors on behalf of the corporation.

(b) A corporation shall maintain appropriate accounting records.

(c) A corporation or its agent shall maintain a record of its shareholders, in a form that permits preparation of a list of the names and addresses of all shareholders, in alphabetical order by class of shares showing the number and class of shares held by each.

(d) A corporation shall maintain its records in written form or in another form capable of conversion into written form within a reasonable time.

(e) A corporation shall keep a copy of the following records at its principal office:

(1) its articles or restated articles of incorporation and all amendments to them currently in effect;

(2) its bylaws or restated bylaws and all amendments to them currently in effect;

(3) resolutions adopted by its board of directors creating one or more classes or series of shares, and fixing their relative rights, preferences, and limitations, if shares issued pursuant to those resolutions are outstanding;

(4) the minutes of all shareholders' meetings, and records of all action taken by shareholders without a meeting, for the past three years;

(5) all written communications to shareholders generally within the past three years, including the financial statements furnished for the past three years * * *;

(6) a list of the names and business addresses of its current directors and officers; and

(7) its most recent annual report delivered to the secretary of state * * *.

§ 16.02 Inspection of Records by Shareholders

(a) Subject to section 16.03(c), a shareholder of a corporation is entitled to inspect and copy, during regular business hours at the corporation's principal office, any of the records of the corporation described in section 16.01(e) if he gives the corporation written notice of his demand at least five business days before the date on which he wishes to inspect and copy.

(b) A shareholder of a corporation is entitled to inspect and copy, during regular business hours at a reasonable location specified by the corporation, any of the following records of the corporation if the shareholder meets the requirements of subsection (c) and gives the corporation written notice of his demand at least five business days before the date on which he wishes to inspect and copy:

(1) excerpts from minutes of any meeting of the board of directors, records of any action of a committee of the board of directors while acting in place of the board of directors on behalf of the corporation, minutes of any meeting of the shareholders, and records of action taken by the shareholders or board of directors without a meeting, to the extent not subject to inspection under section 16.02(a);

(2) accounting records of the corporation; and

(3) the record of shareholders.

(c) A shareholder may inspect and copy the records identified in subsection (b) only if:

(1) his demand is made in good faith and for a proper purpose;

(2) he describes with reasonable particularity his purpose and the records he desires to inspect; and

(3) the records are directly connected with his purpose.

(d) The right of inspection granted by this section may not be abolished or limited by a corporation's articles of incorporation or bylaws.

(e) This section does not affect:

(1) the right of a shareholder to inspect records under section 7.20 or, if the shareholder is in litigation with the corporation, to the same extent as any other litigant;

(2) the power of a court, independently of this Act, to compel the production of corporate records for examination.

(f) For purposes of this section, "shareholder" includes a beneficial owner whose shares are held in a voting trust or by a nominee on his behalf.

The Sarbanes-Oxley Act of 2002 (Excerpts and Explanatory Comments)

Note: The author's explanatory comments appear in italics following the excerpt from each section.

SECTION 302

Corporate responsibility for financial reports[1]

(a) Regulations required

The Commission shall, by rule, require, for each company filing periodic reports under section 13(a) or 15(d) of the Securities Exchange Act of 1934 (15 U.S.C. 78m, 78o(d)), that the principal executive officer or officers and the principal financial officer or officers, or persons performing similar functions, certify in each annual or quarterly report filed or submitted under either such section of such Act that—

(1) the signing officer has reviewed the report;

(2) based on the officer's knowledge, the report does not contain any untrue statement of a material fact or omit to state a material fact necessary in order to make the statements made, in light of the circumstances under which such statements were made, not misleading;

(3) based on such officer's knowledge, the financial statements, and other financial information included in the report, fairly present in all material respects the financial condition and results of operations of the issuer as of, and for, the periods presented in the report;

(4) the signing officers—

(A) are responsible for establishing and maintaining internal controls;

(B) have designed such internal controls to ensure that material information relating to the issuer and its consolidated subsidiaries is made known to such officers by others within those entities, particularly during the period in which the periodic reports are being prepared;

(C) have evaluated the effectiveness of the issuer's internal controls as of a date within 90 days prior to the report; and

(D) have presented in the report their conclusions about the effectiveness of their internal controls based on their evaluation as of that date;

(5) the signing officers have disclosed to the issuer's auditors and the audit committee of the board of directors (or persons fulfilling the equivalent function)—

(A) all significant deficiencies in the design or operation of internal controls which could adversely affect the issuer's ability to record, process, summarize, and report financial data and have identified for the issuer's auditors any material weaknesses in internal controls; and

(B) any fraud, whether or not material, that involves management or other employees who have a significant role in the issuer's internal controls; and

(6) the signing officers have indicated in the report whether or not there were significant changes in internal controls or in other factors that could significantly affect internal controls subsequent to the date of their evaluation, including any corrective actions with regard to significant deficiencies and material weaknesses.

(b) Foreign reincorporations have no effect

Nothing in this section shall be interpreted or applied in any way to allow any issuer to lessen the legal force of the statement required under this section, by an issuer having reincorporated or having engaged in any other transaction that resulted in the transfer of the corporate domicile or offices of the issuer from inside the United States to outside of the United States.

(c) Deadline

The rules required by subsection (a) of this section shall be effective not later than 30 days after July 30, 2002.

EXPLANATORY COMMENTS: *Section 302 requires the chief executive officer (CEO) and chief financial officer (CFO) of each public company to certify that they have reviewed the company's quarterly and annual reports to be filed with the Securities and Exchange Commission (SEC). The CEO and CFO must certify that, based on their knowledge, the reports do not contain any untrue statement of a material fact or any half-truth that would make the report misleading, and that the information contained in the reports fairly presents the company's financial condition.*

In addition, this section also requires the CEO and CFO to certify that they have created and designed an internal control system for their company and have recently evaluated that system to ensure that it is effectively providing them with relevant and accurate financial information. If the signing officers have found any significant deficiencies or weaknesses in the company's system or have discovered any evidence of fraud, they must have reported the situation, and any corrective actions they have taken, to the auditors and the audit committee.

SECTION 306

Insider trades during pension fund blackout periods[2]

(a) Prohibition of insider trading during pension fund blackout periods

(1) In general

Except to the extent otherwise provided by rule of the Commission pursuant to paragraph (3), it shall be unlawful for any director or executive officer of an issuer of any

---

1. This section of the Sarbanes-Oxley Act is codified at 15 U.S.C. Section 7241.

2. Codified at 15 U.S.C. Section 7244.

equity security (other than an exempted security), directly or indirectly, to purchase, sell, or otherwise acquire or transfer any equity security of the issuer (other than an exempted security) during any blackout period with respect to such equity security if such director or officer acquires such equity security in connection with his or her service or employment as a director or executive officer.

(2) Remedy

   (A) In general

   Any profit realized by a director or executive officer referred to in paragraph (1) from any purchase, sale, or other acquisition or transfer in violation of this subsection shall inure to and be recoverable by the issuer, irrespective of any intention on the part of such director or executive officer in entering into the transaction.

   (B) Actions to recover profits

   An action to recover profits in accordance with this subsection may be instituted at law or in equity in any court of competent jurisdiction by the issuer, or by the owner of any security of the issuer in the name and in behalf of the issuer if the issuer fails or refuses to bring such action within 60 days after the date of request, or fails diligently to prosecute the action thereafter, except that no such suit shall be brought more than 2 years after the date on which such profit was realized.

(3) Rulemaking authorized

The Commission shall, in consultation with the Secretary of Labor, issue rules to clarify the application of this subsection and to prevent evasion thereof. Such rules shall provide for the application of the requirements of paragraph (1) with respect to entities treated as a single employer with respect to an issuer under section 414(b), (c), (m), or (o) of Title 26 to the extent necessary to clarify the application of such requirements and to prevent evasion thereof. Such rules may also provide for appropriate exceptions from the requirements of this subsection, including exceptions for purchases pursuant to an automatic dividend reinvestment program or purchases or sales made pursuant to an advance election.

(4) Blackout period

For purposes of this subsection, the term "blackout period", with respect to the equity securities of any issuer—

   (A) means any period of more than 3 consecutive business days during which the ability of not fewer than 50 percent of the participants or beneficiaries under all individual account plans maintained by the issuer to purchase, sell, or otherwise acquire or transfer an interest in any equity of such issuer held in such an individual account plan is temporarily suspended by the issuer or by a fiduciary of the plan; and

   (B) does not include, under regulations which shall be prescribed by the Commission—

      (i) a regularly scheduled period in which the participants and beneficiaries may not purchase, sell, or otherwise acquire or transfer an interest in any equity of such issuer, if such period is—

         (I) incorporated into the individual account plan; and

         (II) timely disclosed to employees before becoming participants under the individual account plan or as a subsequent amendment to the plan; or

      (ii) any suspension described in subparagraph (A) that is imposed solely in connection with persons becoming participants or beneficiaries, or ceasing to be participants or beneficiaries, in an individual account plan by reason of a corporate merger, acquisition, divestiture, or similar transaction involving the plan or plan sponsor.

(5) Individual account plan

For purposes of this subsection, the term "individual account plan" has the meaning provided in section 1002(34) of Title 29, except that such term shall not include a one-participant retirement plan (within the meaning of section 1021(i)(8)(B) of Title 29).

(6) Notice to directors, executive officers, and the Commission

In any case in which a director or executive officer is subject to the requirements of this subsection in connection with a blackout period (as defined in paragraph (4)) with respect to any equity securities, the issuer of such equity securities shall timely notify such director or officer and the Securities and Exchange Commission of such blackout period.

* * * * *

EXPLANATORY COMMENTS: *Corporate pension funds typically prohibit employees from trading shares of the corporation during periods when the pension fund is undergoing significant change. Prior to 2002, however, these blackout periods did not affect the corporation's executives, who frequently received shares of the corporate stock as part of their compensation. During the collapse of Enron, for example, its pension plan was scheduled to change administrators at a time when Enron's stock price was falling. Enron's employees therefore could not sell their shares while the price was dropping, but its executives could and did sell their stock, consequently avoiding some of the losses. Section 306 was Congress's solution to the basic unfairness of this situation. This section of the act required the SEC to issue rules that prohibit any director or executive officer from trading during pension fund blackout periods. (The SEC later issued these rules, entitled Regulation Blackout Trading Restriction, or Reg BTR.) Section 306 also provided shareholders with a right to file a shareholder's derivative suit against officers and directors who have profited from trading during these blackout periods (provided that the corporation has failed to bring a suit). The officer or director can be forced to return to the corporation any profits received, regardless of whether the director or officer acted with bad intent.*

SECTION 402
Periodical and other reports[3]
* * * *

(i) Accuracy of financial reports

Each financial report that contains financial statements, and that is required to be prepared in accordance with (or reconciled to) generally accepted accounting principles under this chapter and filed with the Commission shall reflect all material correcting adjustments that have been identified by a regis-

---

3. This section of the Sarbanes-Oxley Act amended some of the provisions of the 1934 Securities Exchange Act and added the paragraphs reproduced here at 15 U.S.C. Section 78m.

tered public accounting firm in accordance with generally accepted accounting principles and the rules and regulations of the Commission.

(j) Off-balance sheet transactions

Not later than 180 days after July 30, 2002, the Commission shall issue final rules providing that each annual and quarterly financial report required to be filed with the Commission shall disclose all material off-balance sheet transactions, arrangements, obligations (including contingent obligations), and other relationships of the issuer with unconsolidated entities or other persons, that may have a material current or future effect on financial condition, changes in financial condition, results of operations, liquidity, capital expenditures, capital resources, or significant components of revenues or expenses.

(k) Prohibition on personal loans to executives

(1) In general

It shall be unlawful for any issuer (as defined in section 7201 of this title), directly or indirectly, including through any subsidiary, to extend or maintain credit, to arrange for the extension of credit, or to renew an extension of credit, in the form of a personal loan to or for any director or executive officer (or equivalent thereof) of that issuer. An extension of credit maintained by the issuer on July 30, 2002, shall not be subject to the provisions of this subsection, provided that there is no material modification to any term of any such extension of credit or any renewal of any such extension of credit on or after July 30, 2002.

(2) Limitation

Paragraph (1) does not preclude any home improvement and manufactured home loans (as that term is defined in section 1464 of Title 12), consumer credit (as defined in section 1602 of this title), or any extension of credit under an open end credit plan (as defined in section 1602 of this title), or a charge card (as defined in section 1637(c)(4)(e) of this title), or any extension of credit by a broker or dealer registered under section 78o of this title to an employee of that broker or dealer to buy, trade, or carry securities, that is permitted under rules or regulations of the Board of Governors of the Federal Reserve System pursuant to section 78g of this title (other than an extension of credit that would be used to purchase the stock of that issuer), that is—

(A) made or provided in the ordinary course of the consumer credit business of such issuer;

(B) of a type that is generally made available by such issuer to the public; and

(C) made by such issuer on market terms, or terms that are no more favorable than those offered by the issuer to the general public for such extensions of credit.

(3) Rule of construction for certain loans

Paragraph (1) does not apply to any loan made or maintained by an insured depository institution (as defined in section 1813 of Title 12), if the loan is subject to the insider lending restrictions of section 375b of Title 12.

(l) Real time issuer disclosures

Each issuer reporting under subsection (a) of this section or section 78o(d) of this title shall disclose to the public on a rapid and current basis such additional information concerning material changes in the financial condition or operations of the issuer, in plain English, which may include trend and qualitative information and graphic presentations, as the Commission determines, by rule, is necessary or useful for the protection of investors and in the public interest.

EXPLANATORY COMMENTS: *Corporate executives during the Enron era typically received extremely large salaries, significant bonuses, and abundant stock options, even when the companies for which they worked were suffering. Executives were also routinely given personal loans from corporate funds, many of which were never paid back. The average large company during that period loaned almost $1 million a year to top executives, and some companies, including Tyco International and Adelphia Communications Corporation, loaned hundreds of millions of dollars to their executives every year. Section 402 amended the 1934 Securities Exchange Act to prohibit public companies from making personal loans to executive officers and directors. There are a few exceptions to this prohibition, such as home-improvement loans made in the ordinary course of business. Note also that while loans are forbidden, outright gifts are not. A corporation is free to give gifts to its executives, including cash, provided that these gifts are disclosed on its financial reports. The idea is that corporate directors will be deterred from making substantial gifts to their executives by the disclosure requirement—particularly if the corporation's financial condition is questionable—because making such gifts could be perceived as abusing their authority.*

SECTION 403

Directors, officers, and principal stockholders[4]

(a) Disclosures required

(1) Directors, officers, and principal stockholders required to file

Every person who is directly or indirectly the beneficial owner of more than 10 percent of any class of any equity security (other than an exempted security) which is registered pursuant to section 78l of this title, or who is a director or an officer of the issuer of such security, shall file the statements required by this subsection with the Commission (and, if such security is registered on a national securities exchange, also with the exchange).

(2) Time of filing

The statements required by this subsection shall be filed—

(A) at the time of the registration of such security on a national securities exchange or by the effective date of a registration statement filed pursuant to section 78l(g) of this title;

(B) within 10 days after he or she becomes such beneficial owner, director, or officer;

(C) if there has been a change in such ownership, or if such person shall have purchased or sold a security-based swap agreement (as defined in section 206(b) of the Gramm-Leach-Bliley Act (15 U.S.C. 78c note)) involving such equity security, before the end of the second business day following the day on which the subject transaction has been executed, or at such other

---

4. This section of the Sarbanes-Oxley Act amended the disclosure provisions of the 1934 Securities Exchange Act, at 15 U.S.C. Section 78p.

time as the Commission shall establish, by rule, in any case in which the Commission determines that such 2-day period is not feasible.

(3) Contents of statements

A statement filed—

(A) under subparagraph (A) or (B) of paragraph (2) shall contain a statement of the amount of all equity securities of such issuer of which the filing person is the beneficial owner; and

(B) under subparagraph (C) of such paragraph shall indicate ownership by the filing person at the date of filing, any such changes in such ownership, and such purchases and sales of the security-based swap agreements as have occurred since the most recent such filing under such subparagraph.

(4) Electronic filing and availability

Beginning not later than 1 year after July 30, 2002—

(A) a statement filed under subparagraph (C) of paragraph (2) shall be filed electronically;

(B) the Commission shall provide each such statement on a publicly accessible Internet site not later than the end of the business day following that filing; and

(C) the issuer (if the issuer maintains a corporate website) shall provide that statement on that corporate website, not later than the end of the business day following that filing.

* * * *

EXPLANATORY COMMENTS: *This section dramatically shortens the time period provided in the Securities Exchange Act of 1934 for disclosing transactions by insiders. The prior law stated that most transactions had to be reported within ten days of the beginning of the following month, although certain transactions did not have to be reported until the following fiscal year (within the first forty-five days). Because some of the insider trading that occurred during the Enron fiasco did not have to be disclosed (and was therefore not discovered) until long after the transactions, Congress added this section to reduce the time period for making disclosures. Under Section 403, most transactions by insiders must be electronically filed with the SEC within two business days. Also, any company that maintains a Web site must post these SEC filings on its site by the end of the next business day. Congress enacted this section in the belief that if insiders are required to file reports of their transactions promptly with the SEC, companies will do more to police themselves and prevent insider trading.*

SECTION 404

Management assessment of internal controls[5]

(a) Rules required

The Commission shall prescribe rules requiring each annual report required by section 78m(a) or 78o(d) of this title to contain an internal control report, which shall—

(1) state the responsibility of management for establishing and maintaining an adequate internal control structure and procedures for financial reporting; and

(2) contain an assessment, as of the end of the most recent fiscal year of the issuer, of the effectiveness of the internal control structure and procedures of the issuer for financial reporting.

(b) Internal control evaluation and reporting

With respect to the internal control assessment required by subsection (a) of this section, each registered public accounting firm that prepares or issues the audit report for the issuer shall attest to, and report on, the assessment made by the management of the issuer. An attestation made under this subsection shall be made in accordance with standards for attestation engagements issued or adopted by the Board. Any such attestation shall not be the subject of a separate engagement.

EXPLANATORY COMMENTS: *This section was enacted to prevent corporate executives from claiming they were ignorant of significant errors in their companies' financial reports. For instance, several CEOs testified before Congress that they simply had no idea that the corporations' financial statements were off by billions of dollars. Congress therefore passed Section 404, which requires each annual report to contain a description and assessment of the company's internal control structure and financial reporting procedures. The section also requires that an audit be conducted of the internal control assessment, as well as the financial statements contained in the report. This section goes hand in hand with Section 302 (which, as discussed previously, requires various certifications attesting to the accuracy of the information in financial reports).*

Section 404 has been one of the more controversial and expensive provisions in the Sarbanes-Oxley Act because it requires companies to assess their own internal financial controls to make sure that their financial statements are reliable and accurate. A corporation might need to set up a disclosure committee and a coordinator, establish codes of conduct for accounting and financial personnel, create documentation procedures, provide training, and outline the individuals who are responsible for performing each of the procedures. Companies that were already well managed have not experienced substantial difficulty complying with this section. Other companies, however, have spent millions of dollars setting up, documenting, and evaluating their internal financial control systems. Although initially creating the internal financial control system is a onetime-only expense, the costs of maintaining and evaluating it are ongoing. Some corporations that spent considerable sums complying with Section 404 have been able to offset these costs by discovering and correcting inefficiencies or frauds within their systems. Nevertheless, it is unlikely that any corporation will find compliance with this section to be inexpensive.

SECTION 802 (A)

Destruction, alteration, or falsification of records in Federal investigations and bankruptcy[6]

Whoever knowingly alters, destroys, mutilates, conceals, covers up, falsifies, or makes a false entry in any record, document, or tangible object with the intent to impede, obstruct, or influence the investigation or proper administration of any matter within the jurisdiction of any department or agency of the United States or any case filed under title 11, or in relation to

---

5. Codified at 15 U.S.C. Section 7262.

6. Codified at 15 U.S.C. Section 1519.

or contemplation of any such matter or case, shall be fined under this title, imprisoned not more than 20 years, or both.

Destruction of corporate audit records[7]

(a) (1) Any accountant who conducts an audit of an issuer of securities to which section 10A(a) of the Securities Exchange Act of 1934 (15 U.S.C. 78j-1(a)) applies, shall maintain all audit or review workpapers for a period of 5 years from the end of the fiscal period in which the audit or review was concluded.

(2) The Securities and Exchange Commission shall promulgate, within 180 days, after adequate notice and an opportunity for comment, such rules and regulations, as are reasonably necessary, relating to the retention of relevant records such as workpapers, documents that form the basis of an audit or review, memoranda, correspondence, communications, other documents, and records (including electronic records) which are created, sent, or received in connection with an audit or review and contain conclusions, opinions, analyses, or financial data relating to such an audit or review, which is conducted by any accountant who conducts an audit of an issuer of securities to which section 10A(a) of the Securities Exchange Act of 1934 (15 U.S.C. 78j-1(a)) applies. The Commission may, from time to time, amend or supplement the rules and regulations that it is required to promulgate under this section, after adequate notice and an opportunity for comment, in order to ensure that such rules and regulations adequately comport with the purposes of this section.

(b) Whoever knowingly and willfully violates subsection (a)(1), or any rule or regulation promulgated by the Securities and Exchange Commission under subsection (a)(2), shall be fined under this title, imprisoned not more than 10 years, or both.

(c) Nothing in this section shall be deemed to diminish or relieve any person of any other duty or obligation imposed by Federal or State law or regulation to maintain, or refrain from destroying, any document.

EXPLANATORY COMMENTS: *Section 802(a) enacted two new statutes that punish those who alter or destroy documents. The first statute is not specifically limited to securities fraud cases. It provides that anyone who alters, destroys, or falsifies records in federal investigations or bankruptcy may be criminally prosecuted and sentenced to a fine or to up to twenty years in prison, or both. The second statute requires auditors of public companies to keep all audit or review working papers for five years but expressly allows the SEC to amend or supplement these requirements as it sees fit. The SEC has, in fact, amended this section by issuing a rule that requires auditors who audit reporting companies to retain working papers for seven years from the conclusion of the review. Section 802(a) further provides that anyone who knowingly and willfully violates this statute is subject to criminal prosecution and can be sentenced to a fine, imprisoned for up to ten years, or both if convicted.*

This portion of the Sarbanes-Oxley Act implicitly recognizes that persons who are under investigation often are tempted to respond by destroying or falsifying documents that might prove their complicity in wrongdoing. The severity of the punishment should provide a strong incentive for these individuals to resist the temptation.

SECTION 804

Time limitations on the commencement of civil actions arising under Acts of Congress[8]

(a) Except as otherwise provided by law, a civil action arising under an Act of Congress enacted after the date of the enactment of this section may not be commenced later than 4 years after the cause of action accrues.

(b) Notwithstanding subsection (a), a private right of action that involves a claim of fraud, deceit, manipulation, or contrivance in contravention of a regulatory requirement concerning the securities laws, as defined in section 3(a)(47) of the Securities Exchange Act of 1934 (15 U.S.C. 78c(a)(47)), may be brought not later than the earlier of—

(1) 2 years after the discovery of the facts constituting the violation; or

(2) 5 years after such violation.

EXPLANATORY COMMENTS: *Prior to the enactment of this section, Section 10(b) of the Securities Exchange Act of 1934 had no express statute of limitations. The courts generally required plaintiffs to have filed suit within one year from the date that they should (using due diligence) have discovered that a fraud had been committed but no later than three years after the fraud occurred. Section 804 extends this period by specifying that plaintiffs must file a lawsuit within two years after they discover (or should have discovered) a fraud but no later than five years after the fraud's occurrence. This provision has prevented the courts from dismissing numerous securities fraud lawsuits.*

SECTION 806

Civil action to protect against retaliation in fraud cases[9]

(a) Whistleblower protection for employees of publicly traded companies.—

No company with a class of securities registered under section 12 of the Securities Exchange Act of 1934 (15 U.S.C. 78l), or that is required to file reports under section 15(d) of the Securities Exchange Act of 1934 (15 U.S.C. 78o(d)), or any officer, employee, contractor, subcontractor, or agent of such company, may discharge, demote, suspend, threaten, harass, or in any other manner discriminate against an employee in the terms and conditions of employment because of any lawful act done by the employee—

(1) to provide information, cause information to be provided, or otherwise assist in an investigation regarding any conduct which the employee reasonably believes constitutes a violation of section 1341, 1343, 1344, or 1348, any rule or regulation of the Securities and Exchange Commission, or any provision of Federal law relating to fraud against shareholders, when the information or assistance is provided to or the investigation is conducted by—

(A) a Federal regulatory or law enforcement agency;

(B) any Member of Congress or any committee of Congress; or

---

7. Codified at 15 U.S.C. Section 1520.

8. Codified at 28 U.S.C. Section 1658.

9. Codified at 18 U.S.C. Section 1514A.

(C) a person with supervisory authority over the employee (or such other person working for the employer who has the authority to investigate, discover, or terminate misconduct); or

(2) to file, cause to be filed, testify, participate in, or otherwise assist in a proceeding filed or about to be filed (with any knowledge of the employer) relating to an alleged violation of section 1341, 1343, 1344, or 1348, any rule or regulation of the Securities and Exchange Commission, or any provision of Federal law relating to fraud against shareholders.

(b) Enforcement action.—

(1) In general.—A person who alleges discharge or other discrimination by any person in violation of subsection (a) may seek relief under subsection (c), by—

(A) filing a complaint with the Secretary of Labor; or

(B) if the Secretary has not issued a final decision within 180 days of the filing of the complaint and there is no showing that such delay is due to the bad faith of the claimant, bringing an action at law or equity for de novo review in the appropriate district court of the United States, which shall have jurisdiction over such an action without regard to the amount in controversy.

(2) Procedure.—

(A) In general.—An action under paragraph (1)(A) shall be governed under the rules and procedures set forth in section 42121(b) of title 49, United States Code.

(B) Exception.—Notification made under section 42121(b)(1) of title 49, United States Code, shall be made to the person named in the complaint and to the employer.

(C) Burdens of proof.—An action brought under paragraph (1)(B) shall be governed by the legal burdens of proof set forth in section 42121(b) of title 49, United States Code.

(D) Statute of limitations.—An action under paragraph (1) shall be commenced not later than 90 days after the date on which the violation occurs.

(c) Remedies.—

(1) In general.—An employee prevailing in any action under subsection (b)(1) shall be entitled to all relief necessary to make the employee whole.

(2) Compensatory damages.—Relief for any action under paragraph (1) shall include—

(A) reinstatement with the same seniority status that the employee would have had, but for the discrimination;

(B) the amount of back pay, with interest; and

(C) compensation for any special damages sustained as a result of the discrimination, including litigation costs, expert witness fees, and reasonable attorney fees.

(d) Rights retained by employee.—Nothing in this section shall be deemed to diminish the rights, privileges, or remedies of any employee under any Federal or State law, or under any collective bargaining agreement.

EXPLANATORY COMMENTS: *Section 806 is one of several provisions that were included in the Sarbanes-Oxley Act to encourage and protect whistleblowers—that is, employees who report their employer's alleged violations of securities law to the authorities. This section applies to employees, agents, and independent contractors who work for publicly traded companies or testify about such a company during an investigation. It sets up an administrative procedure at the Department of Labor for individuals who claim that their employer retaliated against them (fired or demoted them, for example) for blowing the whistle on the employer's wrongful conduct. It also allows the award of civil damages—including back pay, reinstatement, special damages, attorneys' fees, and court costs—to employees who prove that they suffered retaliation. Since this provision was enacted, whistleblowers have filed numerous complaints with the Department of Labor under this section.*

SECTION 807
Securities fraud[10]

Whoever knowingly executes, or attempts to execute, a scheme or artifice—

(1) to defraud any person in connection with any security of an issuer with a class of securities registered under section 12 of the Securities Exchange Act of 1934 (15 U.S.C. 78l) or that is required to file reports under section 15(d) of the Securities Exchange Act of 1934 (15 U.S.C. 78o(d)); or

(2) to obtain, by means of false or fraudulent pretenses, representations, or promises, any money or property in connection with the purchase or sale of any security of an issuer with a class of securities registered under section 12 of the Securities Exchange Act of 1934 (15 U.S.C. 78l) or that is required to file reports under section 15(d) of the Securities Exchange Act of 1934 (15 U.S.C. 78o(d)); shall be fined under this title, or imprisoned not more than 25 years, or both.

EXPLANATORY COMMENTS: *Section 807 adds a new provision to the federal criminal code that addresses securities fraud. Prior to 2002, federal securities law had already made it a crime—under Section 10(b) of the Securities Exchange Act of 1934 and SEC Rule 10b-5, both of which are discussed in Chapter 21—to intentionally defraud someone in connection with a purchase or sale of securities, but the offense was not listed in the federal criminal code. Also, paragraph 2 of Section 807 goes beyond what is prohibited under securities law by making it a crime to obtain by means of false or fraudulent pretenses any money or property from the purchase or sale of securities. This new provision allows violators to be punished by up to twenty-five years in prison, a fine, or both.*

SECTION 906
Failure of corporate officers to certify financial reports[11]

(a) Certification of periodic financial reports.—Each periodic report containing financial statements filed by an issuer with

---

10. Codified at 18 U.S.C. Section 1348.
11. Codified at 18 U.S.C. Section 1350.

7–2A. QUESTION WITH SAMPLE ANSWER

Each system has its advantages and its disadvantages. In a common law system, the courts independently develop the rules governing certain areas of law, such as torts and contracts. This judge-made law exists in addition to the laws passed by a legislature. Judges must follow precedential decisions in their jurisdictions, but courts may modify or even overturn precedents when deemed necessary. Also, if there is no case law to guide a court, the court may create a new rule of law. In a civil law system, the only official source of law is a statutory code. Courts are required to interpret the code and apply the rules to individual cases, but courts may not depart from the code. In theory, the law code will set forth all the principles needed for the legal system. Common law and civil law systems are not wholly distinct. For example, the United States has a common law system, but crimes are defined by statute as in civil law systems. Civil law systems may allow considerable room for judges to develop law: law codes cannot be so precise as to address every contested issue, so the judiciary must interpret the codes. There are also significant differences among common law countries. The judges of different common law nations have produced differing common law principles. The roles of judges and lawyers under the different systems should be taken into account. Among other factors that should be considered in establishing a business law system and in deciding what regulations to impose are the goals that the system and its regulations are intended to achieve and the expectations of those to whom both will apply, including foreign and domestic investors.

8–2A. QUESTION WITH SAMPLE ANSWER

1. This is the most likely example of copyright infringement. Generally, determining whether the reproduction of copyrighted material constitutes copyright infringement is done on a case-by-case basis under the "fair use" doctrine, as expressed in Section 107 of the Copyright Act. Determining factors include the "purpose and character" of a use, such as whether it is "of a commercial nature"; "the amount and substantiality of the portion used in relation to the copyrighted work as a whole"; and "the effect of the use on the potential market" for the copied work. In this question, the DVD store owner is copying copyright-protected works in their entirety for commercial purposes, thereby affecting the market for the works.
2. Taping a television program "for purposes such as * * * teaching * * * is not an infringement of copyright" under Section 107 of the Copyright Act.

9–2A. QUESTION WITH SAMPLE ANSWER

According to the question, Janine was apparently unconscious or otherwise unable to agree to a contract for the nursing services she received while she was in the hospital. As you read in the chapter, however, sometimes the law will create a fictional contract in order to prevent one party from unjustly receiving a benefit at the expense of another. This is known as a quasi contract and provides a basis for Nursing Services to recover the value of the services it provided while Janine was in the hospital. As for the at-home services that were provided to Janine, because Janine was aware that those services were being provided for her, Nursing Services can recover for those services under an implied-in-fact contract. Under this type of contract, the conduct of the parties creates and defines the terms. Janine's acceptance of the services constitutes her agreement to form a contract, and she will probably be required to pay Nursing Services in full.

10–2A. QUESTION WITH SAMPLE ANSWER

A novation exists when a new, valid contract expressly or impliedly discharges a prior contract by the substitution of a party. Accord and satisfaction exists when the parties agree that the original obligation can be discharged by a substituted performance. In this case, Fred's agreement with Iba to pay off Junior's debt for $1,100 (rather than the $1,000 owed) is definitely a valid contract. The terms of the contract substitute Fred as the debtor for Junior, and Junior is definitely discharged from further liability. This agreement is a novation.

11–2A. QUESTION WITH SAMPLE ANSWER

Anne has entered into an enforceable contract to subscribe to *E-Commerce Weekly*. In this problem, the offer to deliver, via e-mail, the newsletter was presented by the offeror with a statement of how to accept—by clicking on the "SUBSCRIBE" button. Consideration was in the promise to deliver the newsletter and in the price that the subscriber agreed to pay. The offeree had an opportunity to read the terms of the subscription agreement before making the contract. Whether she actually read those terms does not matter.

12–2A. QUESTION WITH SAMPLE ANSWER

If Colt can prove that all due care was exercised in the manufacture of the pistol, Colt cannot be held liable in an action based on negligence. Under the theory of strict liability in tort, however, Colt can be held liable regardless of the degree of care exercised. The doctrine of strict liability states that a merchant-seller who sells a defective product that is unreasonably dangerous is liable for injuries caused by that product (even if all possible care in preparation and sale is exercised), provided that the product has not been substantially changed after the time of sale. Therefore, if Wayne can prove the pistol is defective, is unreasonably dangerous, and caused him injury, Colt as a merchant is strictly liable, because there is no evidence that the pistol has been altered since the date of its manufacture.

13–2A. QUESTION WITH SAMPLE ANSWER

A trustee is given avoidance powers by the Bankruptcy Code. One situation in which the trustee can avoid transfers of property or payments by a debtor to a creditor is when such transfer constitutes a *preference*. A preference is a transfer of property or payment that favors one creditor over another. For a preference to exist, the debtor must be insolvent and must have made payment for a preexisting debt within ninety days of the filing of the petition in bankruptcy. The Code provides that the debtor is *presumed* to be insolvent during this ninety-day period. If the payment is made to an insider (and in this case payment was made to a close relative), the preference period is extended to one year, but the presumption of insolvency still applies only to the ninety-day period. In this case, the trustee has an excellent chance of having both payments declared preferences. The payment to Cool Springs was within ninety days of the filing of the petition, and it is doubtful that Cool Springs could overcome the presumption that Peaslee was insolvent at the time the payment was made. The $5,000 payment was made to an insider, Peaslee's father, and any payment made to an insider within one year of the petition of bankruptcy is a preference—as long as the debtor was insolvent at the time of payment. The facts indicate that Peaslee probably was insolvent at the time he paid his father. If he was not, the payment is not a preference, and the trustee's avoidance of the transfer would be improper.

14–2A. QUESTION WITH SAMPLE ANSWER

1. A limited partner's interest is assignable. In fact, assignment allows the assignee to become a substituted limited partner with the consent of the remaining partners. The assignment, however, does not dissolve the limited partnership.
2. Bankruptcy of the limited partnership itself causes dissolution, but bankruptcy of one of the limited partners does not dissolve the partnership unless it causes the bankruptcy of the firm.
3. The retirement, death, or insanity of a general partner dissolves the partnership unless the business can be continued by the remaining general partners. Because Dorinda was the only general partner, her death dissolves the limited partnership.

15–2A. QUESTION WITH SAMPLE ANSWER

Directors are personally answerable to the corporation and the shareholders for breach of their duty to exercise reasonable care in conducting the affairs of the corporation. Reasonable care is defined as the degree of care that a reasonably prudent person would use in the conduct of personal business affairs. When directors delegate the running of corporate affairs to officers, the directors are expected to use reasonable care in the selection and supervision of such officers. Failure to do so will make the directors liable for negligence or mismanagement. A director who dissents from an action by the board is not personally liable for losses resulting from that action. Unless the dissent is entered into the board meeting minutes, however, the director is presumed to have assented. Therefore, the first issue in the case of AstroStar, Inc., is whether the board members failed to use reasonable care in the selection of the president. If so, and particularly if the board failed to provide a reasonable amount of supervision (and openly embezzled funds indicate that failure), the directors will be personally liable. This liability will include Eckhart unless she can prove that she dissented and that she tried to reasonably supervise the new president. Considering the facts in this case, it is questionable that Eckhart could prove this.

16–2A. QUESTION WITH SAMPLE ANSWER

Agency is usually a consensual relationship in that the principal and agent agree that the agent will have the authority to act for the principal, binding the principal to any contract with a third party. If no agency in fact exists, the purported agent's contracts with third parties are not binding on the principal. In this case, no agency by agreement was created. Brown may claim that an agency by estoppel was created; however, this argument will fail. Agency by estoppel is applicable only when a *principal* causes a third person to believe that another person is the principal's

agent. Then the third party's actions in dealing with the agent are in reliance on the principal's words or actions and the third party's reasonable belief that the agent has authority. This is said to estop the principal from claiming that, in fact, no agency existed. Acts and declarations of the *agent*, however, do not in and of themselves create an agency by estoppel, because such actions should not reasonably lead a third person to believe that the purported agent has authority. In this case, Wade's declarations and allegations alone led Brown to believe that Wade was an agent. Gett's actions were not involved. It is not reasonable to believe that someone is an agent solely because he or she is a friend of the principal. Therefore, Brown cannot hold Gett liable unless Gett ratifies Wade's contract—which is unlikely, as Wade has disappeared with the rare coin.

17–2A. QUESTION WITH SAMPLE ANSWER

The Occupational Safety and Health Act (OSHA) requires employers to provide safe working conditions for employees. The act prohibits employers from discharging or discriminating against any employee who refuses to work when the employee believes in good faith that he or she will risk death or great bodily harm by undertaking the employment activity. Denton and Carlo had sufficient reason to believe that the maintenance job required of them by their employer involved great risk, and therefore, under OSHA, their discharge was wrongful. Denton and Carlo can turn to the Occupational Safety and Health Administration, which is part of the U.S. Department of Labor, for assistance.

18–2A. QUESTION WITH SAMPLE ANSWER

Educational requirements can be legally imposed provided that the educational requirement is directly related to, and necessary for, performance of the job. The requirement of a high school diploma is not a direct, job-related requirement in this case. Chinawa obviously comes under the 1964 Civil Rights Act, Title VII, as amended, and the educational requirement under the circumstances is definitely discriminatory against minorities.

19–2A. QUESTION WITH SAMPLE ANSWER

The court will consider first whether the agency followed the procedures prescribed in the Administrative Procedure Act (APA). Ordinarily, courts will not require agencies to use procedures beyond those of the APA. Courts will, however, compel agencies to follow their own rules. If an agency has adopted a rule granting extra procedures, the agency must provide those extra procedures, at least until the rule is formally rescinded. Ultimately, in this case, the court will most likely rule for the food producers.

20–3A. QUESTION WITH SAMPLE ANSWER

Yes. A regulation of the Federal Trade Commission (FTC) under Section 5 of the Federal Trade Commission Act makes it a violation for door-to-door sellers to fail to give consumers three days to cancel any sale. In addition, a number of state statutes require this three-day "cooling off" period to protect consumers from unscrupulous door-to-door sellers. Because the Gonchars sought to rescind the contract within the three-day period, Renowned Books was obligated to agree to cancel the contract. Its failure to allow rescission was in violation of the FTC regulation and of most state statutes.

21–2A. QUESTION WITH SAMPLE ANSWER

Fruitade has violated a number of federal environmental laws if such actions are being taken without a permit. First, because the dumping is in a navigable waterway, the River and Harbor Act of 1886, as amended, has been violated. Second, the Clean Water Act of 1972, as amended, has been violated. This act is designed to make the waters safe for swimming, to protect fish and wildlife, and to eliminate discharge of pollutants into the water. Both the crushed glass and the acid violate this act. Third, the Toxic Substances Control Act of 1976 was passed to regulate chemicals that are known to be toxic and could have an effect on human health and the environment. The acid in the cleaning fluid or compound could come under this act.

22–2A. QUESTION WITH SAMPLE ANSWER

Because all land-use regulations necessarily limit the ways in which property may be used, a regulation by itself will not generally be considered a compensable taking. Compensation will be required only if the regulation itself is found to be overly burdensome and thus subject to the requirement that just compensation be paid. Rezoning the land from industrial use to commercial use—despite the expected reduction in its market value—would probably not be considered a compensable taking because it would not prevent the owner from using the land for a reasonable income-producing or private purpose.

23–2A. QUESTION WITH SAMPLE ANSWER

Yes. The major antitrust law being violated is the Sherman Act, Section 1. Allitron and Donovan are engaged in interstate commerce, and the agreement to divide marketing territories between them is a contract in restraint of trade. The U.S. Department of Justice could seek fines of up to $1 million for each corporation, and the officers or directors responsible could be imprisoned for up to three years. In addition, the U.S. Department of Justice could institute civil proceedings to restrain this conduct.

24–2A. QUESTION WITH SAMPLE ANSWER

No. Under federal securities law, a stock split is exempt from registration requirements. This is because no *sale* of stock is involved. The existing shares are merely being split, and no consideration is received by the corporation for the additional shares created.

A

acceptance A voluntary act by the offeree that shows assent, or agreement, to the terms of an offer; may consist of words or conduct.

accredited investors In the context of securities offerings, "sophisticated" investors, such as banks, insurance companies, investment companies, the issuer's executive officers and directors, and persons whose income or net worth exceeds certain limits.

act of state doctrine A doctrine providing that the judicial branch of one country will not examine the validity of public acts committed by a recognized foreign government within its own territory.

actionable Capable of serving as the basis of a lawsuit. An actionable claim can be pursued in a lawsuit or other court action.

actual malice The deliberate intent to cause harm, which exists when a person makes a statement either knowing that it is false or showing a reckless disregard for whether it is true. In a defamation suit, a statement made about a public figure normally must be made with actual malice for the plaintiff to recover damages.

actus reus A guilty (prohibited) act. The commission of a prohibited act is one of the two essential elements required for criminal liability, the other element being the intent to commit a crime.

adhesion contract A "standard-form" contract, such as that between a large retailer and a consumer, in which the dominant party dictates the terms.

adjudicate To render a judicial decision. In the administrative process, adjudication is the trial-like proceeding in which an administrative law judge hears and decides issues that arise when an administrative agency charges a person or a firm with violating a law or regulation enforced by the agency.

adjudication The act of rendering a judicial decision. In an administrative process, the proceeding in which an administrative law judge hears and decides on issues that arise when an administrative agency charges a person or a firm with violating a law or regulation enforced by the agency.

administrative agency A federal or state government agency established to perform a specific function. Administrative agencies are authorized by legislative acts to make and enforce rules in order to administer and enforce the acts.

administrative law The body of law created by administrative agencies (in the form of rules, regulations, orders, and decisions) in order to carry out their duties and responsibilities.

administrative law judge (ALJ) One who presides over an administrative agency hearing and has the power to administer oaths, take testimony, rule on questions of evidence, and make determinations of fact.

administrative process The procedure used by administrative agencies in the administration of law.

adverse possession The acquisition of title to real property by occupying it openly, without the consent of the owner, for a period of time specified by a state statute. The occupation must be actual, open, notorious, exclusive, and in opposition to all others, including the owner.

affirmative action Job-hiring policies that give special consideration to members of protected classes in an effort to overcome present effects of past discrimination.

agency A relationship between two parties in which one party (the agent) agrees to represent or act for the other (the principal).

agreement A meeting of two or more minds in regard to the terms of a contract, usually broken down into two events: an offer and an acceptance.

alien corporation A designation in the United States for a corporation formed in another country but doing business in the United States.

alternative dispute resolution (ADR) The resolution of disputes in ways other than those involved in the traditional judicial process. Negotiation, mediation, and arbitration are forms of ADR.

answer Procedurally, a defendant's response to the plaintiff's complaint.

anticipatory repudiation An assertion or action by a party indicating that he or she will not perform an obligation that the party is contractually obligated to perform at a future time.

antitrust law Laws protecting commerce from unlawful restraints.

apparent authority Authority that is only apparent, not real. In agency law, a person may be deemed to have had the power to act as an agent for another party if the other party's manifestations to a third party led the third party to believe that an agency existed when, in fact, it did not.

appropriation In tort law, the use by one person of another person's name, likeness, or other identifying characteristic without permission and for the benefit of the user.

arbitration The settling of a dispute by submitting it to a disinterested third party (other than a court), who renders a decision that is (most often) legally binding.

arbitration clause A clause in a contract that provides that, in the event of a dispute, the parties will submit the dispute to arbitration rather than litigate the dispute in court.

arson The intentional burning of a building owned by another. Some statutes have expanded this to include any real property regardless of ownership and the destruction of property by other means—for example, by explosion.

articles of incorporation The document filed with the appropriate governmental agency, usually the secretary of state, when a business is incorporated. State statutes usually prescribe what kind of information must be contained in the articles of incorporation.

articles of organization The document filed with a designated state official by which a limited liability company is formed.

articles of partnership A written agreement that sets forth each partner's rights and obligations with respect to the partnership.

artisan's lien A possessory lien given to a person who has made improvements and added value to another person's personal property as security for payment for services performed.

assault Any word or action intended to make another person fearful of immediate physical harm; a reasonably believable threat.

assignment The act of transferring to another all or part of one's rights arising under a contract.

assumption of risk A doctrine under which a plaintiff may not recover for injuries or damage suffered from risks he or she knew of and voluntarily assumed.

attachment In the context of judicial liens, a court-ordered seizure and taking into custody of property prior to the securing of a judgment for a past-due debt.

attempted monopolization Any actions by a firm to eliminate competition and gain monopoly power.

authorization card A card signed by an employee that gives a union permission to act on his or her behalf in negotiations with management.

automatic stay In bankruptcy proceedings, the suspension of virtually all litigation and other action by

creditors against the debtor or the debtor's property. The stay is effective the moment the debtor files a petition in bankruptcy.

award In litigation, the amount of monetary compensation awarded to a plaintiff in a civil lawsuit as damages. In the context of alternative dispute resolution, the decision rendered by an arbitrator.

B

backdating The practice of marking a document with a date that precedes the actual date. Persons who backdate stock options are picking a date when the stock was trading at a lower price than the date of the options grant.

bait-and-switch advertising Advertising a product at a very attractive price (the "bait") and then, once the consumer is in the store, saying that the advertised product either is not available or is of poor quality. The customer is then urged to purchase ("switch" to) a more expensive item.

bankruptcy court A federal court of limited jurisdiction that handles only bankruptcy proceedings, which are governed by federal bankruptcy law.

battery The unprivileged, intentional touching of another.

beyond a reasonable doubt The standard of proof used in criminal cases. If there is any reasonable doubt that a criminal defendant committed the crime with which she or he has been charged, then the verdict must be "not guilty."

bilateral contract A type of contract that arises when a promise is given in exchange for a return promise.

bill of rights The first ten amendments to the U.S. Constitution.

binding authority Any source of law that a court must follow when deciding a case. Binding authorities include constitutions, statutes, and regulations that govern the issue being decided, as well as court decisions that are controlling precedents within the jurisdiction.

bona fide occupational qualification (BFOQ) An identifiable characteristic reasonably necessary to the normal operation of a particular business. These characteristics can include gender, national origin, and religion, but not race.

bounty payment A reward (payment) given to a person or persons who perform a certain service, such as informing legal authorities of illegal actions.

breach The failure to perform a legal obligation.

breach of contract The failure, without legal excuse, of a promisor to perform the obligations of a contract.

brief A formal legal document prepared by a party's attorney (in answer to the appellant's brief) and submitted to an appellate court when a case is appealed. The appellant's brief outlines the facts and issues of the case, the judge's rulings or jury's findings that should be reversed or modified, the applicable law, and the arguments on the client's behalf.

browse-wrap terms Terms and conditions of use that are presented to an Internet user at the time certain products, such as software, are being downloaded but to which the user need not agree (by clicking "I agree," for example) before being able to install or use the product.

bulk zoning Zoning regulations that restrict the amount of structural coverage on a particular parcel of land.

bureaucracy The organizational structure, consisting of government bureaus and agencies, through which the government implements and enforces the laws.

burglary The act of unlawfully entering or breaking into a building with the intent to commit a felony. (Some state statutes expand this to include the intent to commit any crime.)

business ethics Ethics in a business context; a consensus as to what constitutes right or wrong behavior in the world of business and the application of moral principles to situations that arise in a business setting.

business invitee A person, such as a customer or a client, who is invited onto business premises by the owner of those premises for business purposes.

business judgment rule A rule that immunizes corporate management from liability for actions that result in corporate losses or damages if the actions are undertaken in good faith and are within both the power of the corporation and the authority of management to make.

business necessity A defense to allegations of employment discrimination in which the employer demonstrates that an employment practice that discriminates against members of a protected class is related to job performance.

business tort Wrongful interference with another's business rights.

buyout price The amount payable to a partner on his or her dissociation from a partnership, based on the amount distributable to that partner if the firm were wound up on that date, and offset by any damages for wrongful dissociation.

bylaws Internal rules of management adopted by a corporation or other organization.

C

case law The rules of law announced in court decisions. Case law includes the aggregate of reported cases that interpret judicial precedents, statutes, regulations, and constitutional provisions.

categorical imperative A concept developed by the philosopher Immanuel Kant as an ethical guideline for behavior. In deciding whether an action is right or wrong, or desirable or undesirable, a person should evaluate the action in terms of what would happen if everybody else in the same situation, or category, acted the same way.

causation in fact An act or omission without which an event would not have occurred.

cease-and-desist order An administrative or judicial order prohibiting a person or business firm from conducting activities that an agency or court has deemed illegal.

certificate of limited partnership The basic document filed with a designated state official by which a limited partnership is formed.

certification mark A mark used by one or more persons, other than the owner, to certify the region, materials, mode of manufacture, quality, or other characteristic of specific goods or services.

checks and balances The principle under which the powers of the national government are divided among three separate branches—the executive, legislative, and judicial branches—each of which exercises a check on the actions of the others.

choice-of-language clause A clause in a contract designating the official language by which the contract will be interpreted in the event of a future disagreement over the contract's terms.

choice-of-law clause A clause in a contract designating the law (such as the law of a particular state or nation) that will govern the contract.

citation A reference to a publication in which a legal authority—such as a statute or a court decision—or other source can be found.

civil law The branch of law dealing with the definition and enforcement of all private or public rights, as opposed to criminal matters.

civil law system A system of law derived from that of the Roman Empire and based on a code rather than case law; the predominant system of law in the nations of continental Europe and the nations that were once their colonies. In the United States, Louisiana, because of its historical ties to France, has in part a civil law system.

click-on agreement An agreement that arises when a buyer, engaging in a transaction on a computer, indicates his or her assent to be bound by the terms of an offer by clicking on a button that says, for example, "I agree"; sometimes referred to as a *click-on license* or a *click-wrap agreement.*

close corporation A corporation whose shareholders are limited to a small group of persons, often including only family members. In a close corporation, the shareholders' rights to transfer shares to others are usually restricted.

closed shop A firm that requires union membership as a condition of employment. The closed shop was made illegal by the Labor-Management Relations Act of 1947.

closing The final step in the sale of real estate; also called *settlement* or *closing escrow*. The escrow agent coordinates the closing with the recording of deeds, the obtaining of title insurance, and other closing activities. A number of costs must be paid, in cash, at the time of closing, and they can range from several hundred to thousands of dollars, depending on the amount of the mortgage loan and other conditions of the sale.

collective bargaining The process by which labor and management negotiate the terms and conditions of employment, including working hours and workplace conditions.

collective mark A mark used by members of a cooperative, association, union, or other organization to certify the region, materials, mode of manufacture, quality, or other characteristic of specific goods or services.

comity The principle by which one nation defers to and gives effect to the laws and judicial decrees of another nation. This recognition is based primarily on respect.

commerce clause The provision in Article I, Section 8, of the U.S. Constitution that gives Congress the power to regulate interstate commerce.

commercial impracticability A doctrine under which a court may excuse the parties from performing a contract when the performance becomes much more difficult or costly due to an event that the parties did not foresee or anticipate at the time the contract was made.

commingle To mix funds or goods together in one mass so that they no longer have separate identities. In corporate law, if personal and corporate interests are commingled to the extent that the corporation has no separate identity, a court may "pierce the corporate veil" and expose the shareholders to personal liability.

common law The body of law developed from custom or judicial decisions in English and U.S. courts, not attributable to a legislature.

community property A form of concurrent ownership of property in which each spouse in a marriage technically owns an undivided one-half interest in property acquired during the marriage. This form of joint ownership occurs in only ten states and Puerto Rico.

comparative negligence A rule in tort law that reduces the plaintiff's recovery in proportion to the plaintiff's degree of fault, rather than barring recovery completely; used in the majority of states.

compensatory damages A monetary award equivalent to the actual value of injuries or damage sustained by the aggrieved party.

complaint The pleading made by a plaintiff alleging wrongdoing on the part of the defendant; the document that, when filed with a court, initiates a lawsuit.

computer crime Any act that is directed against computers and computer parts, that uses computers as instruments of crime, or that involves computers and constitutes abuse.

concentrated industry An industry in which a large percentage of market sales is controlled by either a single firm or a small number of firms.

concurrent jurisdiction Jurisdiction that exists when two different courts have the power to hear a case. For example, some cases can be heard in a federal or a state court.

concurrent ownership Joint ownership.

condition A qualification, provision, or clause in a contractual agreement, the occurrence or nonoccurrence of which creates, suspends, or terminates the obligations of the contracting parties.

condition precedent In a contractual agreement, a condition that must be met before a party's promise becomes absolute.

confession of judgment The act or agreement of a debtor in permitting a judgment to be entered against him or her by a creditor, for an agreed sum, without the institution of legal proceedings.

confiscation A government's taking of a privately owned business or personal property without a proper public purpose or an award of just compensation.

conforming goods Goods that conform to contract specifications.

consent Voluntary agreement to a proposition or an act of another; a concurrence of wills.

consequential damages Special damages that compensate for a loss that does not directly or immediately result from the breach (for example, lost profits). For the plaintiff to collect consequential damages, they must have been reasonably foreseeable at the time the breach or injury occurred.

consideration Generally, the value given in return for a promise. The consideration must be something of legally sufficient value, and there must be a bargained-for exchange.

constitutional law The body of law derived from the U.S. Constitution and the constitutions of the various states.

constructive discharge A termination of employment brought about by making the employee's working conditions so intolerable that the employee reasonably feels compelled to leave.

constructive eviction A form of eviction that occurs when a landlord fails to perform adequately any of the undertakings (such as providing heat in the winter) required by the lease, thereby making the tenant's further use and enjoyment of the property exceedingly difficult or impossible.

consumer-debtor An individual whose debts are primarily consumer debts (debts for purchases made primarily for personal, family, or household use).

contract An agreement that can be enforced in court; formed by two or more competent parties who agree, for consideration, to perform or to refrain from performing some legal act now or in the future.

contributory negligence A rule in tort law that completely bars the plaintiff from recovering any damages if the damage suffered is partly the plaintiff's own fault; used in a minority of states.

conversion Wrongfully taking or retaining possession of an individual's personal property and placing it in the service of another.

conveyance The transfer of a title to land from one person to another by deed; a document (such as a deed) by which an interest in land is transferred from one person to another.

"cooling-off" laws Laws that allow buyers a period of time, such as three days, in which to cancel door-to-door sales contracts.

copyright The exclusive right of an author or originator of a literary or artistic production to publish, print, or sell that production for a statutory period of time. A copyright has the same monopolistic nature as a patent or trademark, but it differs in that it applies exclusively to works of art, literature, and other works of authorship (including computer programs).

corporate governance A set of policies or procedures affecting the way a corporation is directed or controlled.

corporate social responsibility The idea that corporations can and should act ethically and be accountable to society for their actions.

corporation A legal entity formed in compliance with statutory requirements that is distinct from its shareholder-owners.

correspondent bank A bank in which another bank has an account (and vice versa) for the purpose of facilitating fund transfers.

cost-benefit analysis A decision-making technique that involves weighing the costs of a given action against the benefits of that action.

co-surety A joint surety; a person who assumes liability jointly with another surety for the payment of an obligation.

counteradvertising New advertising that is undertaken pursuant to a Federal Trade Commission order for the purpose of correcting earlier false claims that were made about a product.

counterclaim A claim made by a defendant in a civil lawsuit against the plaintiff. In effect, the defendant is suing the plaintiff.

counteroffer An offeree's response to an offer in which the offeree rejects the original offer and at the same time makes a new offer.

covenant not to compete A contractual promise of one party to refrain from conducting business similar to that of another party for a certain period of time and within a specified geographic area. Courts commonly enforce such covenants if they are reasonable in terms of time and geographic area and are part of, or supplemental to, a contract for the sale of a business.

cover A buyer's or lessee's purchase on the open market of goods to substitute for those promised but never delivered by the seller. Under the UCC, if the cost of cover exceeds the cost of the contract goods, the buyer or lessee can recover the difference, plus incidental and consequential damages.

cram-down provision A provision of the Bankruptcy Code that allows a court to confirm a debtor's Chapter 11 reorganization plan even though only one class of creditors has accepted it. To exercise the court's right under this provision, the court must demonstrate that the plan does not discriminate unfairly against any creditors and is fair and equitable.

creditors' composition agreement An agreement formed between a debtor and his or her creditors in which the creditors agree to accept a lesser sum than that owed by the debtor in full satisfaction of the debt.

crime A wrong against society proclaimed in a statute and punishable by society through fines and/or imprisonment—or, in some cases, death.

criminal law Law that defines and governs actions that constitute crimes. Generally, criminal law has to do with wrongful actions committed against society for which society demands redress.

cure The right of a party who tenders nonconforming performance to correct that performance within the contract period [UCC 2–508(1)].

cyber crime A crime that occurs online, in the virtual community of the Internet, as opposed to the physical world.

cyber mark A trademark in cyberspace.

cyber tort A tort committed in cyberspace.

cyberlaw An informal term used to refer to all laws governing electronic communications and transactions, particularly those conducted via the Internet.

cybersquatting The act of registering a domain name that is the same as, or confusingly similar to, the trademark of another and then offering to sell that domain name back to the trademark owner.

cyberterrorist A hacker whose purpose is to exploit a target computer for a serious impact, such as corrupting a program to sabotage a business.

D

damages The monetary amount awarded by a court in a civil action to compensate a plaintiff for injury or loss.

debtor in possession (DIP) In Chapter 11 bankruptcy proceedings, a debtor who is allowed to continue in possession of the estate in property (the business) and to continue business operations.

deceptive advertising Advertising that misleads consumers, either by making unjustified claims concerning a product's performance or by omitting a material fact concerning the product's composition or performance.

deed A document by which title to property (usually real property) is passed.

defamation Anything published or publicly spoken that causes injury to another's good name, reputation, or character.

default The failure to observe a promise or to dischage an obligation. The term is commonly used to mean the failure to pay a debt when it is due.

default judgment A judgment entered by a court against a defendant who has failed to appear in court to answer or defend against the plaintiff's claim.

defendant One against whom a lawsuit is brought; the accused person in a criminal proceeding.

defense A reason offered and alleged by a defendant in an action or suit as to why the plaintiff should not recover or establish what she or he seeks.

delegation The transfer of a contractual duty to a third party. The party delegating the duty (the delegator) to the third party (the delegatee) is still obliged to perform on the contract should the delegatee fail to perform.

delegation doctrine A doctrine based on Article I, Section 8, of the U.S. Constitution, which has been construed to allow Congress to delegate some of its power to make and implement laws to administrative agencies.

deposition The testimony of a party to a lawsuit or a witness taken under oath before a trial.

discharge In bankruptcy proceedings, the extinction of the debtor's dischargeable debts, which relieves the debtor of the obligation to pay the debts; in contract law, discharge occurs when the parties have fully performed their contractual obligations or when events, conduct of the parties, or operation of law releases the parties from performance.

disclosed principal A principal whose identity is known to a third party at the time the agent makes a contract with the third party.

discovery A phase in the litigation process during which the opposing parties may obtain information from each other and from third parties prior to trial.

disparagement of property An economically injurious falsehood made about another's product or property; a general term for torts that are more specifically referred to as *slander of quality* or *slander of title*.

disparate-impact discrimination A form of employment discrimination that results from certain employer practices or procedures that, although not discriminatory on their face, have a discriminatory effect.

disparate-treatment discrimination A form of employment discrimination that results when an employer intentionally discriminates against employees who are members of protected classes.

dissociation The severance of the relationship between a partner and a partnership when the partner ceases to be associated with the carrying on of the partnership business.

dissolution The formal disbanding of a partnership or a corporation. It can take place by (1) acts of the partners or, in a corporation, acts of the shareholders and board of directors; (2) the subsequent illegality of the firm's business; (3) the expiration of a time period stated in a partnership agreement or a certificate of incorporation; or (4) judicial decree.

distributed network A network that can be used by persons located (distributed) around the country or the globe to share computer files.

distribution agreement A contract between a seller and a distributor of the seller's products setting out the terms and conditions of the distributorship.

diversity of citizenship Under Article III, Section 2, of the U.S. Constitution, a basis for federal district court jurisdiction over a lawsuit between (1) citizens of different states, (2) a foreign country and citizens of a state or of different states, or (3) citizens of a state and citizens or subjects of a foreign country. The amount in controversy must be more than $75,000 before a federal district court can take jurisdiction in such cases.

divestiture The act of selling one or more of a company's divisions or parts, such as a subsidiary or plant; often mandated by the courts in merger or monopolization cases.

dividend A distribution to corporate shareholders of corporate profits or income, disbursed in proportion to the number of shares held.

docket The list of cases entered on a court's calendar and thus scheduled to be heard by the court.

domain name The last part of an Internet address, such as "westlaw.com." The top level (the part of the name to the right of the period) indicates the type of entity that operates the site ("com" is an abbreviation for "commercial"). The second level (the part of the name to the left of the period) is chosen by the entity.

domestic corporation In a given state, a corporation that does business in, and is organized under the law of, that state.

double jeopardy A situation occurring when a person is tried twice for the same criminal offense; prohibited by the Fifth Amendment to the Constitution.

dram shop act A state statute that imposes liability on the owners of bars and taverns, as well as those who serve alcoholic drinks to the public, for injuries resulting from accidents caused by intoxicated persons when the sellers or servers of alcoholic drinks contributed to the intoxication.

due process clause The provisions in the Fifth and Fourteenth Amendments to the Constitution that guarantee that no person shall be deprived of life, liberty, or property without due process of law. Similar clauses are found in most state constitutions.

dumping The selling of goods in a foreign country at a price below the price charged for the same goods in the domestic market.

duress Unlawful pressure brought to bear on a person, causing the person to perform an act that she or he would not otherwise perform.

duty of care The duty of all persons, as established by tort law, to exercise a reasonable amount of care in their dealings with others. Failure to exercise due care, which is normally determined by the reasonable person standard, constitutes the tort of negligence.

E

e-agent A computer program that by electronic or other automated means can independently initiate an action or respond to electronic messages or data without review by an individual.

easement A nonpossessory right to use another's property in a manner established by either express or implied agreement.

e-contract A contract that is formed electronically.

e-evidence Evidence that consists of computer-generated or electronically recorded information, including e-mail, voice mail, spreadsheets, word-processing documents, and other data.

embezzlement The fraudulent appropriation of funds or other property by a person to whom the funds or property has been entrusted.

eminent domain The power of a government to take land for public use from private citizens for just compensation.

employment at will A common law doctrine under which either party may terminate an employment relationship at any time for any reason, unless a contract specifies otherwise.

employment discrimination Treating employees or job applicants unequally on the basis of race, color, national origin, religion, gender, age, or disability; prohibited by federal statutes.

enabling legislation Statutes enacted by Congress that authorize the creation of an administrative agency and specify the name, composition, and powers of the agency being created.

entrapment In criminal law, a defense in which the defendant claims that he or she was induced by a public official—usually an undercover agent or police officer—to commit a crime that he or she would otherwise not have committed.

entrepreneur One who initiates and assumes the financial risk of a new business enterprise and undertakes to provide or control its management.

environmental impact statement (EIS) A statement required by the National Environmental Policy Act for any major federal action that will significantly affect the quality of the environment. The statement must analyze the action's impact on the environment and explore alternative actions that might be taken.

equal dignity rule In most states, a rule stating that express authority given to an agent must be in writing if the contract to be made on behalf of the principal is required to be in writing.

equal protection clause The provision in the Fourteenth Amendment to the Constitution that guarantees that no state will "deny to any person within its jurisdiction the equal protection of the laws." This clause mandates that the state governments must treat similarly situated individuals in a similar manner.

equitable principles and maxims General propositions or principles of law that have to do with fairness (equity).

escrow account An account, generally held in the name of the depositor and the escrow agent, containing funds to be paid to a third person on fulfillment of the escrow condition.

e-signature Under the Uniform Electronic Transactions Act, any electronic sound, symbol, or process attached to electronically stored information and intended to function as a signature. This definition is intentionally broad in order to give legal effect to acts that people intend to be the equivalent of their written signatures.

establishment clause　The provision in the First Amendment to the Constitution that prohibits the government from establishing any state-sponsored religion or enacting any law that promotes religion or favors one religion over another.

estate in property　In bankruptcy proceedings, all of the debtor's interests in property currently held, wherever located, together with certain jointly owned property, property transferred in transactions voidable by the trustee, proceeds and profits from the property of the estate, and certain property interests to which the debtor becomes entitled within 180 days after filing for bankruptcy.

estop　To bar, impede, or preclude someone from doing something.

ethical reasoning　A reasoning process in which an individual links his or her moral convictions or ethical standards to the particular situation at hand.

ethics　Moral principles and values applied to social behavior.

eviction　A landlord's act of depriving a tenant of possession of the leased premises.

exclusionary rule　In criminal procedure, a rule under which any evidence that is obtained in violation of the accused's constitutional rights guaranteed by the Fourth, Fifth, and Sixth Amendments, as well as any evidence derived from illegally obtained evidence, will not be admissible in court.

exclusive distributorship　A distributorship in which the seller and the distributor of the seller's products agree that the distributor will distribute only the seller's products.

exclusive jurisdiction　Jurisdiction that exists when a case can be heard only in a particular court or type of court.

exclusive-dealing contract　An agreement under which a seller forbids a buyer to purchase products from the seller's competitors.

exculpatory clause　A provision that releases a contractual party from liability in the event of monetary or physical injury, no matter who is at fault.

executed contract　A contract that has been completely performed by both parties.

executive agency　An administrative agency within the executive branch of government. At the federal level, executive agencies are those within the cabinet departments.

executory contract　A contract that has not yet been fully performed.

export　To sell goods and services to buyers located in other countries.

express contract　A contract in which the terms of the agreement are stated in words, oral or written.

express warranty　A seller's or lessor's oral or written promise or affirmation of fact, ancillary to an underlying sales or lease agreement, as to the quality, description, or performance of the goods being sold or leased.

expropriation　The seizure by a government of a privately owned business or personal property for a proper public purpose and with just compensation.

F

family limited liability partnership (FLLP)　A type of limited liability partnership owned by family members or fiduciaries of family members.

federal form of government　A system of government in which the states form a union and the sovereign power is divided between the central government and the member states.

federal question　A question that pertains to the U.S. Constitution, acts of Congress, or treaties. A federal question provides a basis for federal jurisdiction.

fee simple absolute　An ownership interest in land in which the owner has the greatest possible aggregation of rights, privileges, and power. Ownership in fee simple absolute is limited absolutely to a person and his or her heirs.

felony　A crime—such as arson, murder, rape, or robbery—that carries the most severe sanctions, ranging from one year in a state or federal prison to the death penalty.

fiduciary　As a noun, a person having a duty created by his or her undertaking to act primarily for another's benefit in matters connected with the undertaking. As an adjective, a relationship founded on trust and confidence.

filtering software　A computer program that is designed to block access to certain Web sites based on their content. The software blocks the retrieval of a site whose URL or key words are on a list within the program.

final order　The final decision of an administrative agency on an issue. If no appeal is taken, or if the case is not reviewed or considered anew by the agency commission, the administrative law judge's initial order becomes the final order of the agency.

firm offer　An offer (by a merchant) that is irrevocable without consideration for a stated period of time or, if no definite period is stated, for a reasonable time (neither period to exceed three months). A firm offer by a merchant must be in writing and must be signed by the offeror.

fixed-term tenancy　A type of tenancy under which property is leased for a specified period of time, such as a month, a year, or a period of years.

fixture A thing that was once personal property but has become attached to real property in such a way that it takes on the characteristics of real property and becomes part of that real property.

***force majeure* clause** A provision in a contract stipulating that certain unforeseen events—such as war, political upheavals, or acts of God—will excuse a party from liability for nonperformance of contractual obligations.

foreign corporation In a given state, a corporation that does business in the state without being incorporated therein.

foreign exchange market A worldwide system in which foreign currencies are bought and sold.

forgery The fraudulent making or altering of any writing in a way that changes the legal rights and liabilities of another.

formal contract A contract that by law requires a specific form for its validity. Negotiable instruments and letters of credit are examples of formal contracts.

forum-selection clause A provision in a contract designating the court, jurisdiction, or tribunal that will decide any disputes arising under the contract.

franchise Any arrangement in which the owner of a trademark, trade name, or copyright licenses another to use that trademark, trade name, or copyright in the selling of goods or services.

franchisee One receiving a license to use another's (the franchisor's) trademark, trade name, or copyright in the sale of goods and services.

franchisor One licensing another (the franchisee) to use the owner's trademark, trade name, or copyright in the selling of goods or services.

fraudulent misrepresentation Any misrepresentation, either by misstatement or by omission of a material fact, knowingly made with the intention of deceiving another and on which a reasonable person would and does rely to his or her detriment.

free exercise clause The provision in the First Amendment to the Constitution that prohibits the government from interfering with people's religious practices or forms of worship.

free-writing prospectus Any type of written, electronic, or graphic offer that describes the issuing corporation or its securities and includes a legend indicating that the investor can obtain the prospectus at the SEC's Web site.

frustration of purpose A court-created doctrine under which a party to a contract will be relieved of his or her duty to perform when the objective purpose for performance no longer exists (due to reasons beyond that party's control).

G

garnishment A legal process used by a creditor to collect a debt by seizing property of the debtor (such as wages) that is being held by a third party (such as the debtor's employer).

general partner In a limited partnership, a partner who assumes responsibility for the management of the partnership and liability for all partnership debts.

general plan A comprehensive plan that local jurisdictions are often required by state law to devise and implement as a precursor to specific land-use regulations.

good samaritan statute A state statute stipulating that persons who provide emergency services to, or rescue, someone in peril cannot be sued for negligence, unless they act recklessly, thereby causing further harm.

grand jury A group of citizens called to decide, after hearing the state's evidence, whether a reasonable basis (probable cause) exists for believing that a crime has been committed and that a trial ought to be held.

group boycott The refusal by a group of competitors to deal with a particular person or firm; prohibited by the Sherman Act.

guarantor A person who agrees to satisfy the debt of another (the debtor) only after the principal debtor defaults. Thus, a guarantor's liability is secondary.

H

hacker A person who uses one computer to break into another. Professional computer programmers refer to such persons as "crackers."

historical school A school of legal thought that emphasizes the evolutionary process of law and looks to the past to discover what the principles of contemporary law should be.

holding company A company whose business activity is holding shares in another company.

homestead exemption A law permitting a debtor to retain the family home, either in its entirety or up to a specified dollar amount, free from the claims of unsecured creditors or trustees in bankruptcy.

horizontal merger A merger between two firms that are competing in the same marketplace.

horizontal restraint Any agreement that in some way restrains competition between rival firms competing in the same market.

hot-cargo agreement An agreement in which employers voluntarily agree with unions not to handle, use, or deal in other employers' goods that were not produced by union employees; a type of secondary boycott explicitly prohibited by the Labor-Management Reporting and Disclosure Act of 1959.

I

I-551 Alien Registration Receipt The I-551 Alien Registration Receipt, commonly known as a "green card," is proof that a foreign-born individual is lawfully admitted for permanent residency in the United States. Persons seeking employment can prove to prospective employers that they are legally within the U.S. by showing this receipt.

I-9 Verification All employers in the United States must verify the employment eligibility and identity of newly hired workers by completing an I-9 Employment Eligibility Verification form within three business days.

identity theft The act of stealing another's identifying information—such as a name, date of birth, or Social Security number—and using that information to access the victim's financial resources.

implied warranty A warranty that the law derives by inference from the nature of the transaction or the relative situations or circumstances of the parties.

implied warranty of fitness for a particular purpose A warranty that goods sold or leased are fit for a particular purpose. The warranty arises when any seller or lessor knows the particular purpose for which a buyer or lessee will use the goods and knows that the buyer or lessee is relying on the skill and judgment of the seller or lessor to select suitable goods.

implied warranty of habitability An implied promise by a landlord that rented residential premises are fit for human habitation—that is, in a condition that is safe and suitable for people to live in. A similar implied promise is made by sellers of new homes in most states.

implied warranty of merchantability A warranty that goods being sold or leased are reasonably fit for the ordinary purpose for which they are sold or leased, are properly packaged and labeled, and are of fair quality. The warranty automatically arises in every sale or lease of goods made by a merchant who deals in goods of the kind sold or leased.

implied-in-fact contract A contract formed in whole or in part from the conduct of the parties (as opposed to an express contract).

impossibility of performance A doctrine under which a party to a contract is relieved of his or her duty to perform when performance becomes objectively impossible or totally impracticable (through no fault of either party).

incidental beneficiary A third party who incidentally benefits from a contract but whose benefit was not the reason the contract was formed; an incidental beneficiary has no rights in a contract and cannot sue to have the contract enforced.

independent contractor One who works for, and receives payment from, an employer but whose working conditions and methods are not controlled by the employer. An independent contractor is not an employee but may be an agent.

independent regulatory agency An administrative agency that is not considered part of the government's executive branch and is not subject to the authority of the president. Independent agency officials cannot be removed without cause.

indictment A charge by a grand jury that a named person has committed a crime.

informal contract A contract that does not require a specified form or formality to be valid.

information A formal accusation or complaint (without an indictment) issued in certain types of actions (usually criminal actions involving lesser crimes) by a government prosecutor.

information return A tax return submitted by a partnership that only reports the income and losses earned by the business. The partnership as an entity does not pay taxes on the income received by the partnership. A partner's profit from the partnership (whether distributed or not) is taxed as individual income to the individual partner.

initial order In the context of administrative law, an agency's disposition in a matter other than a rulemaking. An administrative law judge's initial order becomes final unless it is appealed.

inside director A person on the board of directors who is also an officer of the corporation.

insider trading The purchase or sale of securities on the basis of *inside information* (information that has not been made available to the public).

insider trading The purchase or sale of securities on the basis of information that has not been made available to the public.

intellectual property Property resulting from intellectual, creative processes.

intended beneficiary A third party for whose benefit a contract is formed; an intended beneficiary can sue the promisor if such a contract is breached.

intentional tort A wrongful act knowingly committed.

international law The law that governs relations among nations. National laws, customs, treaties, and international conferences and organizations are generally considered to be the most important sources of international law.

international organization Any membership group that operates across national borders. These organizations can be governmental organizations, such as the United Nations, or nongovernmental organizations (NGOs), such as the Red Cross.

interrogatories A series of written questions for which written answers are prepared by a party to a lawsuit, usually with the assistance of the party's attorney, and then signed under oath.

investment company A company that acts on behalf of many smaller shareholders/owners by buying a large portfolio of securities and professionally managing that portfolio.

investment contract In securities law, a transaction in which a person invests in a common enterprise with the reasonable expectation that profits will be derived primarily from the efforts of others.

J

joint and several liability In partnership law, a plaintiff can file a lawsuit against all of the partners together (jointly) or one or more of the partners separately (severally, or individually). All partners in a partnership can be held liable regardless of whether the partner participated in, knew about, or ratified the conduct that gave rise to the lawsuit.

joint liability Shared liability. In partnership law, partners share liability for partnership obligations and debts. Thus, if a third party sues a partner on a partnership debt, the partner has the right to insist that the other partners be sued with him or her.

joint tenancy The joint ownership of property by two or more co-owners in which each co-owner owns an undivided portion of the property. On the death of one of the joint tenants, his or her interest automatically passes to the surviving joint tenant(s).

judicial review The process by which a court decides on the constitutionality of legislative enactments and actions of the executive branch.

jurisdiction The authority of a court to hear and decide a specific case.

jurisprudence The science or philosophy of law.

justiciable controversy A controversy that is not hypothetical or academic but real and substantial; a requirement that must be satisfied before a court will hear a case.

L

larceny The wrongful taking and carrying away of another person's personal property with the intent to permanently deprive the owner of the property. Some states classify larceny as either grand or petit, depending on the property's value.

law A body of enforceable rules governing relationships among individuals and between individuals and their society.

lease In real property law, a contract by which the owner of real property (the landlord, or lessor) grants to a person (the tenant, or lessee) an exclusive right to use and possess the property, usually for a specified period of time, in return for rent or some other form of payment; under the UCC, a transfer of the right to possess and use goods for a period in exchange for payment.

leasehold estate An estate in realty held by a tenant under a lease. In every leasehold estate, the tenant has a qualified right to possess and/or use the land.

legal positivism A school of legal thought centered on the assumption that there is no law higher than the laws created by a national government. Laws must be obeyed, even if they are unjust, to prevent anarchy.

legal realism A school of legal thought of the 1920s and 1930s that generally advocated a less abstract and more realistic approach to the law, an approach that takes into account customary practices and the circumstances in which transactions take place. This school left a lasting imprint on American jurisprudence.

legislative rule An administrative agency rule that carries the same weight as a congressionally enacted statute.

lessee In a lease of personal property, a person who acquires the right to possess and use another's goods for a period in exchange for paying rent.

lessor In a lease of personal property, a person who transfers his or her right to possess and use certain goods for a period to another in exchange for payment (rent).

letter of credit A written instrument, usually issued by a bank on behalf of a customer or other person, in which the issuer promises to honor drafts or other demands for payment by third persons in accordance with the terms of the instrument.

libel Defamation in writing or other form having the quality of permanence (such as a digital recording).

license In the context of intellectual property law, an agreement permitting the use of a trademark, copyright, patent, or trade secret for certain limited purposes; in the context of real property, a revocable right or privilege of a person to come on to another person's land.

lien An encumbrance on (claim against) property to satisfy a debt or protect a claim for the payment of a debt.

life estate An interest in land that exists only for the duration of the life of some person, usually the holder of the estate.

limited liability company (LLC) A hybrid form of business enterprise that offers the limited liability of the corporation but the tax advantages of a partnership.

limited liability limited partnership (LLLP) A type of limited liability partnership in which the liability of all of the partners, including general partners, is limited to the amount of their investments.

limited liability partnership (LLP) A hybrid form of business organization that is used mainly by professionals who normally do business in a partnership. Like a partnership, an LLP is a pass-through entity for tax purposes, but the personal liability of the partners is limited.

limited partner In a limited partnership, a partner who contributes capital to the partnership but has no right to participate in the management and operation of the business. The limited partner assumes no liability for partnership debts beyond the capital contributed.

limited partnership A partnership consisting of one or more general partners (who manage the business and are liable to the full extent of their personal assets for debts of the partnership) and one or more limited partners (who contribute only assets and are liable only up to the extent of their contributions).

liquidated damages An amount, stipulated in the contract, to be paid in the event of a default or breach of contract. The amount must be a reasonable estimate of the damages that would result from a breach in order for the court to enforce it as liquidated damages.

liquidation The sale of all of the nonexempt assets of a debtor and the distribution of the proceeds to the debtor's creditors. Chapter 7 of the Bankruptcy Code provides for liquidation bankruptcy proceedings.

litigation The process of resolving a dispute through the court system.

long arm statute A state statute that permits a state to obtain personal jurisdiction over nonresident defendants. A defendant must have certain "minimum contacts" with that state for the statute to apply.

M

mailbox rule A rule providing that an acceptance of an offer becomes effective on dispatch (on being placed in an official mailbox), if mail is expressly or impliedly an authorized means of communication of acceptance of the offer.

malpractice Professional misconduct or the lack of the requisite degree of skill as a professional. Negligence—the failure to exercise due care—on the part of a professional, such as a physician, is commonly referred to as malpractice.

market concentration The degree to which a small number of firms control a large percentage share of a relevant market; determined by calculating the percentages held by the largest firms in that market.

market power The power of a firm to control the market price of its product. A monopoly has the greatest degree of market power.

market-share liability Liability shared among all firms that manufactured and distributed a particular product during a certain period of time in proportion to the firms' respective shares of the market. Only some jurisdictions apply this theory and only when the true source of the harmful product is unidentifiable.

mechanic's lien A statutory lien on the real property of another, created to ensure payment for work performed and materials furnished in the repair or improvement of real property, such as a building.

mediation A method of settling disputes outside of court by using the services of a neutral third party, who acts as a communicating agent between the parties and assists them in negotiating a settlement.

member A person who has an ownership interest in a limited liability company.

mens rea Mental state, or intent. A wrongful mental state is as necessary as a wrongful act to establish criminal liability. What constitutes a mental state varies according to the wrongful action. Thus, for murder, the *mens rea* is the intent to take a life.

merchant A person engaged in the purchase and sale of goods. Under the UCC, a person who deals in goods of the kind involved in the sales contract, or who holds himself or herself out as having skill and knowledge peculiar to the practices or goods involved in the transaction, or who employs a merchant as an intermediary. For definitions, see UCC 2–104.

meta tag A key word in a document that can serve as an index reference to the document. On the Web, search engines return results based, in part, on the tags in Web documents.

metes and bounds A system of measuring boundary lines by the distance between two points, often using physical features of the local geography, such as roads, intersections, rivers, or bridges. The legal descriptions of real property contained in deeds often are phrased in terms of metes and bounds.

minimum wage The lowest wage, either by government regulation or union contract, that an employer may pay an hourly worker.

mirror image rule A common law rule that requires that the terms of the offeree's acceptance adhere exactly to the terms of the offeror's offer for a valid contract to be formed.

misdemeanor A lesser crime than a felony, punishable by a fine or incarceration in jail for up to one year.

mitigation of damages A rule requiring a plaintiff to do whatever is reasonable to minimize the damages caused by the defendant.

money laundering Falsely reporting income that has been obtained through criminal activity as income obtained through a legitimate business enterprise—in effect, "laundering" the "dirty money."

monopolization The possession of monopoly power in the relevant market and the willful acquisition or maintenance of that power, as distinguished from growth or development as a consequence of a superior product, business acumen, or historic accident.

monopoly A term generally used to describe a market in which there is a single seller or a very limited number of sellers.

monopoly power The ability of a monopoly to dictate what takes place in a given market.

moral minimum The minimum degree of ethical behavior expected of a business firm, which is usually defined as compliance with the law.

mortgage A written instrument giving a creditor an interest in (lien on) the debtor's real property as security for payment of a debt.

mortgagee Under a mortgage agreement, the creditor who takes a security interest in the debtor's property.

mortgagor Under a mortgage agreement, the debtor who gives the creditor a security interest in the debtor's property in return for a mortgage loan.

motion for a directed verdict In a jury trial, a motion for the judge to take the decision out of the hands of the jury and to direct a verdict for the party who filed the motion on the ground that the other party has not produced sufficient evidence to support her or his claim.

motion for a new trial A motion asserting that the trial was so fundamentally flawed (because of error, newly discovered evidence, prejudice, or another reason) that a new trial is necessary to prevent a miscarriage of justice.

motion for judgment *n.o.v.* A motion requesting the court to grant judgment in favor of the party making the motion on the ground that the jury's verdict against him or her was unreasonable and erroneous.

motion for judgment on the pleadings A motion by either party to a lawsuit at the close of the pleadings requesting the court to decide the issue solely on the pleadings without proceeding to trial. The motion will be granted only if no facts are in dispute.

motion for summary judgment A motion requesting the court to enter a judgment without proceeding to trial. The motion can be based on evidence outside the pleadings and will be granted only if no facts are in dispute.

motion to dismiss A pleading in which a defendant asserts that the plaintiff's claim fails to state a cause of action (that is, has no basis in law) or that there are other grounds on which a suit should be dismissed. Although the defendant normally is the party requesting a dismissal, either the plaintiff or the court can also make a motion to dismiss the case.

multiple product order An administrative or judicial order that requires a firm to cease and desist from false advertising in regard to more than one of its products.

mutual fund A specific type of investment company that continually buys or sells to investors shares of ownership in a portfolio.

mutual rescission An agreement between the parties to cancel their contract, releasing the parties from further obligations under the contract. The object of the agreement is to restore the parties to the positions they would have occupied had no contract ever been formed.

N

national law Laws that pertain to a particular nation (as opposed to international law).

natural law The belief that government and the legal system should reflect universal moral and ethical principles that are inherent in human nature. The natural law school is the oldest and one of the most significant schools of legal thought.

negligence The failure to exercise the standard of care that a reasonable person would exercise in similar circumstances.

negligence *per se* An action or failure to act in violation of a statutory requirement.

negotiation A process in which parties attempt to settle their dispute informally, with or without attorneys to represent them.

nonpossessory interest In the context of real property, an interest in land that does not include any right to possess the property.

normal trade relations (NTR) status A status granted in an international treaty by a provision stating that the citizens of the contracting nations may enjoy the privileges accorded by either party to citizens of its NTR nations. Generally, this status is designed to establish equality of international treatment.

notary public A public official authorized to attest to the authenticity of signatures.

notice-and-comment rulemaking A procedure in agency rulemaking that requires (1) notice, (2) opportunity for comment, and (3) a published draft of the final rule.

novation The substitution, by agreement, of a new contract for an old one, with the rights under the old one being terminated. Typically, novation involves the substitution of a new party for one of the original parties to the contract.

nuisance A common law doctrine under which persons may be held liable for using their property in a manner that unreasonably interferes with others' rights to use or enjoy their own property.

O

objective theory of contracts A theory under which the intent to form a contract will be judged by outward, objective facts (what the party said when entering into the contract, how the party acted or appeared, and the circumstances surrounding the transaction) as interpreted by a reasonable person, rather than by the party's own secret, subjective intentions.

offer A promise or commitment to do or refrain from doing some specified act in the future.

offeree A person to whom an offer is made.

offeror A person who makes an offer.

online dispute resolution (ODR) The resolution of disputes with the assistance of organizations that offer dispute-resolution services via the Internet.

operating agreement In a limited liability company, an agreement in which the members set forth the details of how the business will be managed and operated. State statutes typically give the members wide latitude in deciding for themselves the rules that will govern their organization.

order for relief A court's grant of assistance to a complainant. In bankruptcy proceedings, the order relieves the debtor of the immediate obligation to pay the debts listed in the bankruptcy petition.

ordinance A regulation enacted by a city or county legislative body to govern matters not covered by state or federal law.

outside director A person on the board of directors who does not hold a management position in the corporation.

P

partially disclosed principal A principal whose identity is unknown by a third party, but the third party knows that the agent is or may be acting for a principal at the time the agent and the third party form a contract.

partnership An agreement by two or more persons to carry on, as co-owners, a business for profit.

pass-through entity A business entity that has no tax liability. The entity's income is passed through to the owners, and the owners pay taxes on the income.

patent A government grant that gives an inventor the exclusive right or privilege to make, use, or sell his or her invention for a limited time period.

peer-to-peer (p2p) networking The sharing of resources (such as files, hard drives, and processing styles) among multiple computers without necessarily requiring a central network server.

penalty An amount, stipulated in the contract, to be paid in the event of a default or breach of contract. When the amount is not a reasonable measure of damages, the court will not enforce it but will limit recovery to actual damages.

per se violation A type of anticompetitive agreement that is considered to be so injurious to the public that there is no need to determine whether it actually

injures market competition. Rather, it is in itself (*per se*) a violation of the Sherman Act.

perfect tender rule A rule under which a seller or lessor is required to deliver goods that conform perfectly to the requirements of the contract. A tender of nonconforming goods automatically constitutes a breach of contract.

performance In contract law, the fulfillment of one's duties arising under a contract with another; the normal way of discharging one's contractual obligations.

periodic tenancy A lease interest in land for an indefinite period involving payment of rent at fixed intervals, such as week to week, month to month, or year to year.

personal property Property that is movable; any property that is not real property.

persuasive authority Any legal authority or source of law that a court may look to for guidance but on which it need not rely in making its decision. Persuasive authorities include cases from other jurisdictions and secondary sources of law.

petition in bankruptcy The document that is filed with a bankruptcy court to initiate bankruptcy proceedings. The official forms required for a petition in bankruptcy must be completed accurately, sworn to under oath, and signed by the debtor.

petty offense In criminal law, the least serious kind of criminal offense, such as a traffic or building-code violation.

pierce the corporate veil An action in which a court disregards the corporate entity and holds the shareholders personally liable for corporate debts and obligations.

plaintiff One who initiates a lawsuit.

plea bargaining The process by which a criminal defendant and the prosecutor in a criminal case work out a mutually satisfactory disposition of the case, subject to court approval; usually involves the defendant's pleading guilty to a lesser offense in return for a lighter sentence.

pleadings Statements made by the plaintiff and the defendant in a lawsuit that detail the facts, charges, and defenses involved in the litigation. The complaint and answer are part of the pleadings.

police powers Powers possessed by the states as part of their inherent sovereignty. These powers may be exercised to protect or promote the public order, health, safety, morals, and general welfare.

positive law The body of conventional, or written, law of a particular society at a particular point in time.

potentially responsible party (PRP) A party liable for the costs of cleaning up a hazardous waste disposal site under the Comprehensive Environmental Response, Compensation, and Liability Act (CERCLA). Any person who generated the hazardous waste, transported it, owned or operated the waste site at the time of disposal, or owns or operates the site at the present time may be responsible for some or all of the clean-up costs.

power of attorney A written document, which is usually notarized, authorizing another to act as one's agent; can be special (permitting the agent to do specified acts only) or general (permitting the agent to transact all business for the principal).

precedent A court decision that furnishes an example or authority for deciding subsequent cases involving identical or similar facts.

predatory behavior Business behavior that is undertaken with the intention of unlawfully driving competitors out of the market.

predatory pricing The pricing of a product below cost with the intent to drive competitors out of the market.

preemption A doctrine under which certain federal laws preempt, or take precedence over, conflicting state or local laws.

preemptive rights Rights held by shareholders that entitle them to purchase newly issued shares of a corporation's stock, equal in percentage to shares already held, before the stock is offered to any outside buyers. Preemptive rights enable shareholders to maintain their proportionate ownership and voice in the corporation.

preference In bankruptcy proceedings, property transfers or payments made by the debtor that favor (give preference to) one creditor over others. The bankruptcy trustee is allowed to recover payments made both voluntarily and involuntarily to one creditor in preference over another.

preferred creditor In the context of bankruptcy, a creditor who has received a preferential transfer from a debtor.

price discrimination Setting prices in such a way that two competing buyers pay two different prices for an identical product or service.

price-fixing agreement An agreement between competitors to fix the prices of products or services at a certain level.

prima facie case A case in which the plaintiff has produced sufficient evidence of his or her claim that the case can go to a jury; a case in which the evidence compels a decision for the plaintiff if the defendant produces no affirmative defense or evidence to disprove the plaintiff's assertion. (*Prima facie* means "on initial examination of consideration"; it also means "legally sufficient.")

primary source of law A document that establishes the law on a particular issue, such as a constitution, a statute, an administrative rule, or a court decision.

principle of rights The principle that human beings have certain fundamental rights (to life, freedom, and the pursuit of happiness, for example). Those who adhere to this "rights theory" believe that a key factor in determining whether a business decision is ethical is how that decision affects the rights of various groups. These groups include the firm's owners, its employees, the consumers of its products or services, its suppliers, the community in which it does business, and society as a whole.

privilege A legal right, exemption, or immunity granted to a person or a class of persons. In the context of defamation, an absolute privilege immunizes the person making the statements from a lawsuit, regardless of whether the statements were malicious.

probable cause Reasonable grounds for believing that a person should be arrested or searched.

probate court A state court of limited jurisdiction that conducts proceedings relating to the settlement of a deceased person's estate.

procedural law Law that establishes the methods of enforcing the rights established by substantive law.

product liability The legal liability of manufacturers, sellers, and lessors of goods to consumers, users, and bystanders for injuries or damages that are caused by the goods.

profit In real property law, the right to enter onto and remove things from the property of another (for example, the right to enter onto a person's land and remove sand and gravel from it).

promise An assertion that something either will or will not happen in the future.

promisee A person to whom a promise is made.

promisor A person who makes a promise.

promissory estoppel A doctrine that applies when a promisor makes a clear and definite promise on which the promisee justifiably relies; such a promise is binding if justice will be better served by the enforcement of the promise.

prospectus A written document, required by securities laws, that describes the security being sold, the financial operations of the issuing corporation, and the investment or risk attaching to the security. It is designed to provide sufficient information to enable investors to evaluate the risk involved in purchasing the security.

protected class A group of persons protected by specific laws because of the group's defining characteristics. Under laws prohibiting employment discrimination, these characteristics include race, color, religion, national origin, gender, age, and disability.

proximate cause Legal cause; exists when the connection between an act and an injury is strong enough to justify imposing liability.

proxy In corporation law, a written agreement between a stockholder and another under which the stockholder authorizes the other to vote the stockholder's shares in a certain manner.

puffery A salesperson's exaggerated claims concerning the quality of property offered for sale. Such claims involve opinions rather than facts and are not considered to be legally binding promises or warranties.

punitive damages Monetary damages that may be awarded to a plaintiff to punish the defendant and deter future similar conduct.

Q

quasi contract A fictional contract imposed on parties by a court in the interests of fairness and justice; usually imposed to avoid the unjust enrichment of one party at the expense of another.

question of fact In a lawsuit, an issue that involves only disputed facts, and not what the law is on a given point. Questions of fact are decided by the jury in a jury trial (by the judge if there is no jury).

question of law In a lawsuit, an issue involving the application or interpretation of a law. Only a judge, not a jury, can rule on questions of law.

quitclaim deed A deed intended to pass any title, interest, or claim that the seller may have in the property but not warranting that such title is valid. A quitclaim deed offers the least amount of protection against defects in the title.

quorum The number of members of a decision-making body that must be present before business may be transacted.

quota A set limit on the amount of goods that can be imported.

R

ratification The act of accepting and giving legal force to an obligation that previously was not enforceable.

reaffirmation agreement An agreement between a debtor and a creditor in which the debtor voluntarily agrees to pay, or reaffirm, a debt dischargeable in bankruptcy. To be enforceable, the agreement must be made before the debtor is granted a discharge.

real property Land and everything attached to it, such as vegetation and buildings.

reasonable person standard The standard of behavior expected of a hypothetical "reasonable person"; the standard against which negligence is measured and that must be observed to avoid liability for negligence.

recording statute A statute that allows deeds, mortgages, and other real property transactions to be recorded so as to provide notice to future purchasers or creditors of an existing claim on the property.

red herring prospectus A preliminary prospectus that can be distributed to potential investors after the registration statement (for a securities offering) has been filed with the Securities and Exchange Commission. The name derives from the red legend printed across the prospectus stating that the registration has been filed but has not become effective.

reformation A court-ordered correction of a written contract so that it reflects the true intentions of the parties.

regulation Z A set of rules promulgated by the Federal Reserve Board of Governors to implement the provisions of the Truth-in-Lending Act.

remedy The relief given to an innocent party to enforce a right or compensate for the violation of a right.

reply Procedurally, a plaintiff's response to a defendant's answer.

res ipsa loquitur A doctrine under which negligence may be inferred simply because an event occurred, if it is the type of event that would not occur in the absence of negligence. Literally, the term means "the facts speak for themselves."

resale price maintenance agreement An agreement between a manufacturer and a retailer in which the manufacturer specifies what the retail prices of its products must be.

respondeat superior Latin for "let the master respond." A doctrine under which a principal or an employer is held liable for the wrongful acts committed by agents or employees while acting within the course and scope of their agency or employment.

restitution An equitable remedy under which a person is restored to his or her original position prior to loss or injury, or placed in the position he or she would have been in had the breach not occurred.

retained earnings The portion of a corporation's profits that has not been paid out as dividends to shareholders.

revocation In contract law, the withdrawal of an offer by an offeror; unless the offer is irrevocable, it can be revoked at any time prior to acceptance without liability.

right of contribution The right of a co-surety who pays more than her or his proportionate share on a debtor's default to recover the excess paid from other co-sureties.

right of first refusal The right to purchase personal or real property—such as corporate shares or real estate—before the property is offered for sale to others.

right of reimbursement The legal right of a person to be restored, repaid, or indemnified for costs, expenses, or losses incurred or expended on behalf of another.

right of subrogation The right of a person to stand in the place of (be substituted for) another, giving the substituted party the same legal rights that the original party had.

right-to-work law A state law providing that employees may not be required to join a union as a condition of retaining employment.

robbery The act of forcefully and unlawfully taking cash, personal property, or any other article of value from another. Force or intimidation is usually necessary for an act of theft to be considered robbery.

rule of four A rule of the United States Supreme Court under which the Court will not issue a writ of *certiorari* unless at least four justices approve of the decision to issue the writ.

rule of reason A test by which a court balances the positive effects (such as economic efficiency) of an agreement against its potentially anticompetitive effects. In antitrust litigation, many practices are analyzed under the rule of reason.

rulemaking The actions undertaken by administrative agencies when formally adopting new regulations or amending old ones. Under the Administrative Procedure Act, rulemaking includes notifying the public of proposed rules or changes and receiving and considering the public's comments.

S

S corporation A close business corporation that has met certain requirements set out in the Internal Revenue Code and thus qualifies for special income tax treatment. Essentially, an S corporation is taxed the same as a partnership, but its owners enjoy the privilege of limited liability.

sale The passing of title to property from the seller to the buyer for a price.

sales contract A contract for the sale of goods under which the ownership of goods is transferred from a seller to a buyer for a price.

scienter Knowledge on the part of the misrepresenting party that material facts have been falsely represented or omitted with an intent to deceive.

search warrant An order granted by a public authority, such as a judge, that authorizes law enforcement personnel to search particular premises or property.

SEC rule 10b-5 A rule of the Securities and Exchange Commission that makes it unlawful, in connection with the purchase or sale of any security, to make any untrue statement of a material fact or to omit a material fact if such omission causes the statement to be misleading.

secondary boycott A union's refusal to work for, purchase from, or handle the products of a secondary employer, with whom the union has no dispute, in order to force that employer to stop doing business with the primary employer, with whom the union has a labor dispute.

secondary source of law A publication that summarizes or interprets the law, such as a legal encyclopedia, a legal treatise, or an article in a law review.

security Generally, a stock certificate, bond, note, debenture, warrant, or other document or record evidencing an ownership interest in a corporation or a promise to repay a corporation's debt.

self-defense The legally recognized privilege to protect oneself or one's property against injury by another. The privilege of self-defense usually applies only to acts that are reasonably necessary to protect oneself, one's property, or another person.

self-incrimination The giving of testimony that may subject the testifier to criminal prosecution. The Fifth Amendment to the Constitution protects against self-incrimination by providing that no person "shall be compelled in any criminal case to be a witness against himself."

seniority system In regard to employment relationships, a system in which those who have worked longest for the employer are first in line for promotions, salary increases, and other benefits. They are also the last to be laid off if the workforce must be reduced.

service mark A mark used in the sale or the advertising of services to distinguish the services of one person or company from those of others. Titles, character names, and other distinctive features of radio and television programs may be registered as service marks.

sexual harassment In the employment context, demands for sexual favors in return for job promotions or other benefits, or language or conduct that is so sexually offensive that it creates a hostile working environment.

shareholder's derivative suit A suit brought by a shareholder to enforce a corporate cause of action against a third person.

slander Defamation in oral form.

slander of quality (trade libel) The publication of false information about another's product, alleging that it is not what its seller claims.

slander of title The publication of a statement that denies or casts doubt on another's legal ownership of any property, causing financial loss to that property's owner.

small claims court A special court in which parties may litigate small claims (such as $5,000 or less).

Attorneys are not required in small claims courts and, in some states, are not allowed to represent the parties.

sociological school A school of legal thought that views the law as a tool for promoting justice in society.

sole proprietorship The simplest form of business organization, in which the owner is the business. The owner reports business income on his or her personal income tax return and is legally responsible for all debts and obligations incurred by the business.

sovereign immunity A doctrine that immunizes foreign nations from the jurisdiction of U.S. courts when certain conditions are satisfied.

spam Bulk, unsolicited ("junk") e-mail.

specific performance An equitable remedy requiring exactly the performance that was specified in a contract; usually granted only when money damages would be an inadequate remedy and the subject matter of the contract is unique (for example, real property).

standing to sue The requirement that an individual must have a sufficient stake in a controversy before he or she can bring a lawsuit. The plaintiff must demonstrate that he or she has been either injured or threatened with injury.

stare decisis A common law doctrine under which judges are obligated to follow the precedents established in prior decisions.

statute of frauds A state statute under which certain types of contracts must be in writing to be enforceable.

statute of limitations A federal or state statute setting the maximum time period during which a certain action can be brought or certain rights enforced.

statute of repose Basically, a statute of limitations that is not dependent on the happening of a cause of action. Statutes of repose generally begin to run at an earlier date and run for a longer period of time than statutes of limitations.

statutory law The body of law enacted by legislative bodies (as opposed to constitutional law, administrative law, or case law).

stock certificate A certificate issued by a corporation evidencing the ownership of a specified number of shares in the corporation.

stock options An agreement that grants the owner the option to buy a given number of shares of stock, usually within a set time period.

stock warrant A certificate that grants the owner the option to buy a given number of shares of stock, usually within a set time period.

strict liability Liability regardless of fault. Strict liability may be imposed in cases involving abnormally dangerous activities, dangerous animals, or defective products.

strike An action undertaken by unionized workers when collective bargaining fails. The workers leave their jobs, refuse to work, and (typically) picket the employer's workplace.

sublease A lease executed by the lessee of real estate to a third person, conveying the same interest that the lessee enjoys but for a shorter term than that held by the lessee.

substantive law Law that defines, describes, regulates, and creates legal rights and obligations.

summary jury trial (SJT) A method of settling disputes, used in many federal courts, in which a trial is held, but the jury's verdict is not binding. The verdict acts only as a guide to both sides in reaching an agreement during the mandatory negotiations that immediately follow the summary jury trial.

summons A document informing a defendant that a legal action has been commenced against him or her and that the defendant must appear in court on a certain date to answer the plaintiff's complaint. The document is delivered by a sheriff or any other person so authorized.

supremacy clause The clause in Article VI of the Constitution that provides that the Constitution, laws, and treaties of the United States are "the supreme Law of the Land." Under this clause, state and local laws that directly conflict with federal law will be rendered invalid.

surety A person, such as a cosigner on a note, who agrees to be primarily responsible for the debt of another.

suretyship An express contract in which a third party to a debtor-creditor relationship (the surety) promises to be primarily responsible for the debtor's obligation.

symbolic speech Nonverbal expressions of beliefs. Symbolic speech, which includes gestures, movements, and articles of clothing, is given substantial protection by the courts.

T

tangible employment action A significant change in employment status, such as a change brought about by firing or failing to promote an employee; reassigning the employee to a position with significantly different responsibilities; or effecting a significant change in employment benefits.

tangible property Property that has physical existence and can be distinguished by the senses of touch, sight, and so on. A car is tangible property; a patent right is intangible property.

tariff A tax on imported goods.

tenancy at will A type of tenancy under which either party can terminate the tenancy without notice;

usually arises when a tenant who has been under a tenancy for years retains possession, with the landlord's consent, after the tenancy for years has terminated.

tenancy in common Co-ownership of property in which each party owns an undivided interest that passes to her or his heirs at death.

tender An unconditional offer to perform an obligation by a person who is ready, willing, and able to do so.

tender of delivery Under the Uniform Commercial Code, a seller's or lessor's act of placing conforming goods at the disposal of the buyer or lessee and giving the buyer or lessee whatever notification is reasonably necessary to enable the buyer or lessee to take delivery.

third party beneficiary One for whose benefit a promise is made in a contract but who is not a party to the contract.

tippee A person who receives inside information.

tombstone ad An advertisement, historically in a format resembling a tombstone, of a securities offering. The ad tells potential investors where and how they can obtain a prospectus.

tort A civil wrong not arising from a breach of contract; a breach of a legal duty that proximately causes harm or injury to another.

tortfeasor One who commits a tort.

toxic tort A civil wrong arising from exposure to a toxic substance, such as asbestos, radiation, or hazardous waste.

trade dress The image and overall appearance of a product—for example, the distinctive decor, menu, layout, and style of service of a particular restaurant. Basically, trade dress is subject to the same protection as trademarks.

trade name A term that is used to indicate part or all of a business's name and that is directly related to the business's reputation and goodwill. Trade names are protected under the common law (and under trademark law, if the name is the same as that of the firm's trademarked product).

trade secret Information or a process that gives a business an advantage over competitors that do not know the information or process.

trademark A distinctive mark, motto, device, or emblem that a manufacturer stamps, prints, or otherwise affixes to the goods it produces so that they may be identified on the market and their origins made known. Once a trademark is established (under the common law or through registration), the owner is entitled to its exclusive use.

treaty In international law, a formal written agreement negotiated between two nations or among several nations. In the United States, all treaties must be approved by the Senate.

treble damages Damages that, by statute, are three times the amount that the fact finder determines is owed.

trespass to land The entry onto, above, or below the surface of land owned by another without the owner's permission or legal authorization.

trespass to personal property The unlawful taking or harming of another's personal property; interference with another's right to the exclusive possession of his or her personal property.

tying arrangement An agreement between a buyer and a seller in which the buyer of a specific product or service becomes obligated to purchase additional products or services from the seller.

U

U.S. trustee A government official who performs certain administrative tasks that a bankruptcy judge would otherwise have to perform.

ultra vires A Latin term meaning "beyond the power." In corporate law, it refers to acts of a corporation that are beyond its express and implied powers to undertake.

unconscionable A term used to describe a contract or clause that is void on the basis of public policy because one party, as a result of disproportionate bargaining power, is forced to accept terms that are unfairly burdensome and that unfairly benefit the dominant party.

undisclosed principal A principal whose identity is unknown by a third person, and the third person has no knowledge that the agent is acting for a principal at the time the agent and the third person form a contract.

unenforceable contract A valid contract rendered unenforceable by some statute or law.

uniform law A model law created by the National Conference of Commissioners on Uniform State Laws and/or the American Law Institute for the states to consider adopting. If a state adopts the law, it becomes statutory law in that state. Each state has the option of adopting or rejecting all or part of a uniform law.

unilateral contract A contract that results when an offer can be accepted only by the offeree's performance.

union shop A firm that requires all workers, once employed, to become union members within a specified period of time as a condition of their continued employment.

unreasonably dangerous product In product liability law, a product that is defective to the point of threatening a consumer's health and safety. A product will be considered unreasonably dangerous if it is dangerous beyond the expectation of the ordinary consumer or if a less dangerous alternative was economically feasible for the manufacturer, but the manufacturer failed to produce it.

use zoning Zoning classifications based on the uses to which the land may be put.

utilitarianism An approach to ethical reasoning that evaluates behavior in light of the consequences of that behavior for those who will be affected by it, rather than on the basis of any absolute ethical or moral values. In utilitarian reasoning, a "good" decision is one that results in the greatest good for the greatest number of people affected by the decision.

V

valid contract A contract that results when the elements necessary for contract formation (agreement, consideration, contractual capacity, and legal purpose) are present.

validation notice An initial notice to a debtor from a collection agency, required by federal law, informing the debtor that he or she has thirty days to challenge the debt and request verification.

venue The geographic district in which a legal action is tried and from which the jury is selected.

vertical merger The acquisition by a company at one level in a marketing chain of a company at a higher or lower level in the chain (such as a company merging with one of its suppliers or retailers).

vertical restraint Any restraint on trade created by agreements between firms at different levels in the manufacturing and distribution process.

vertically integrated firm A firm that carries out two or more functional phases (manufacture, distribution, and retailing, for example) of the chain of production.

vesting The creation of an absolute or unconditional right or power.

vicarious liability Legal responsibility placed on one person for the acts of another; indirect liability imposed on a supervisory party (such as an employer) for the actions of a subordinate (such as an employee) because of the relationship between the two parties.

void contract A contract having no legal force or binding effect.

voidable contract A contract that may be legally avoided (canceled, or annulled) at the option of one or both of the parties.

voir dire Old French phrase meaning "to speak the truth." In legal language, the phrase refers to the process in which the attorneys question prospective jurors to learn about their backgrounds, attitudes, biases, and other characteristics that may affect their ability to serve as impartial jurors.

voluntary consent Knowledge of, and genuine assent to, the terms of a contract. If a contract is formed as a result of a mistake, misrepresentation, undue influence, or duress, voluntary consent is lacking, and the contract will be voidable.

voting trust An agreement (trust contract) under which legal title to shares of corporate stock is transferred to a trustee who is authorized by the shareholders to vote the shares on their behalf.

W

warranty deed A deed in which the seller assures (warrants to) the buyer that the grantor has title to the property conveyed in the deed; that there are no encumbrances on the property other than what the seller has represented, and that the buyer will enjoy quiet possession of the property; a deed that provides the greatest amount of protection for the grantee.

watered stock Shares of stock issued by a corporation for which the corporation receives, as payment, less than the stated value of the shares.

wetlands Water-saturated areas of land that are designated by a government agency (such as the Army Corps of Engineers or the Environmental Protection Agency) as protected areas that support wildlife. Such areas cannot be filled in or dredged by private parties without a permit.

whistleblowing An employee's disclosure to government authorities, upper-level managers, or the press that the employer is engaged in unsafe or illegal activities.

white-collar crime Nonviolent crime committed by individuals or corporations to obtain a personal or business advantage.

winding up The second of two stages in the termination of a partnership or corporation. Once the firm is dissolved, it continues to exist legally until the process of winding up all business affairs (collecting and distributing the firm's assets) is complete.

workers' compensation laws State statutes establishing an administrative procedure for compensating workers for injuries that arise out of—or in the course of—their employment, regardless of fault.

workout An out-of-court agreement between a debtor and creditors in which the parties work out a payment plan or schedule under which the debtor's debts can be discharged.

writ of attachment A court's order, issued prior to a trial to collect a debt, directing the sheriff or other public officer to seize nonexempt property of the debtor. If the creditor prevails at trial, the seized property can be sold to satisfy the judgment.

writ of *certiorari* A writ from a higher court asking the lower court for the record of a case.

writ of execution A court's order, issued after a judgment has been entered against a debtor, directing the sheriff to seize (levy) and sell any of the debtor's nonexempt real or personal property. The proceeds of the sale are used to pay off the judgment, accrued interest, and costs of the sale; any surplus is paid to the debtor.

wrongful discharge An employer's termination of an employee's employment in violation of the law.

Z

zoning The division of a city by legislative regulation into districts and the application in each district of regulations having to do with structural and architectural designs of buildings and prescribing the use to which buildings within designated districts may be put.

zoning variance The granting of permission by a municipality or other public board to a landowner to use his or her property in a way that does not strictly conform with the zoning regulations so as to avoid causing the landowner undue hardship.

Table of Cases

Index